MW01013938

UNIVERSITY CASEBOOK SERIES®

INTERNATIONAL CRIMINAL LAW AND ITS ENFORCEMENT

CASES AND MATERIALS

FOURTH EDITION

BETH VAN SCHAACK
Visiting Professor of Law,
Stanford Law School

RONALD C. SLYE
Professor of Law,
Seattle University School of Law

444 Cedar Street, Suite 700
St. Paul, MN 55101
1-877-888-1330

Printed in the United States of America

ISBN: 978-1-64242-760-8

To Miles, Brooke & Charlie

PREFACE TO THE FOURTH EDITION

This text presents a comprehensive introduction to the law, theory, institutions, and practice of international criminal law (ICL). It provides a solid grounding in the historical development of international criminal law and related institutions alongside contemporary developments in the field that will be of interest to students focused on public international law, criminal law, and human rights. Students undertaking this course of study will emerge ready to practice international criminal law, with an enriched understanding of domestic criminal law principles and a firm comprehension of the structure and sources of public international law. They will also enjoy a stronger theoretical and comparative understanding of penal processes and the formation of international law more generally. The text also considers questions of policy—how should members of the international community address the commission of grave international crimes being committed around the world and what role do prosecutions play in the prevention of atrocities?

This is primarily a book of substantive international criminal law. After a brief introduction to place international criminal law in the context of international and criminal law generally, Part II presents a discussion of the international, domestic, and hybrid institutions adjudicating international criminal law. Part III covers the crimes within the jurisdiction of the International Criminal Court (war crimes, crimes against humanity, genocide, and aggression). Subsequent chapters in this part also address the crimes of torture and terrorism, because they are closely related to the core international crimes and are similarly prosecuted under expansive principles of extraterritorial jurisdiction. The final chapter in this part provides an opportunity to synthesize the material from the previous chapters by focusing the question of what crime to charge an accused and issues arising therefrom. The text does not cover other transnational crimes—such as money laundering, trafficking in people and narcotics, and international arms dealing—that are primarily (but not exclusively) defined by domestic law and prosecuted before domestic tribunals. Part IV is concerned with principles of individual responsibility essential to international criminal law, including theories of responsibility (superior responsibility and complicity, for example), the inchoate crimes (conspiracy and incitement), defenses, sentencing, and reparations.

Although the text does not offer a comprehensive treatment of international criminal procedure, it does include materials (notes, questions, and some cases) on selected procedural issues that present unique challenges in international criminal law, such as cumulative charging and sentencing. In this way, the book will complement the study of comparative law or comparative criminal procedure by highlighting the way in which international and quasi-international criminal tribunals are addressing common procedural problems, meshing different legal traditions, and—in many respects—creating *sui generis* procedures appropriate for international criminal law. This text thus enables the course to serve as an introduction to international legal reasoning and legal process.

Because of the centrality of the post-World War II period to this field, many of the chapters begin with a backward glance. Although we have reluctantly removed some of the more extensive excerpts from this era, we have preserved many of these historical materials. We think it is important for students to understand the history of the development of ICL. The rulings at Nuremberg, and to a lesser extent Tokyo, remain iconic benchmarks in the development of ICL, and almost every international and domestic court that has addressed an issue of international criminal law has cited to the post-World War II jurisprudence. This reliance on the Nuremberg and Tokyo proceedings was not surprising during the early days of the *ad hoc* tribunals, as those post-World War II tribunals provided the only applicable international jurisprudence on many of the issues confronting more modern tribunals. Today, even with the rich caselaw of the *ad hoc* tribunals, international and domestic courts continue to refer to the touchstone of ICL for precedential authority.

The chapters then undertake an elemental analysis of international crimes as they have developed and evolved in international law and focus on the challenges of interpreting and applying these norms in a criminal prosecution. The book cross references the jurisprudence of the various international tribunals and scrutinizes the text of and deliberations surrounding the Statute of the International Criminal Court (ICC) with an emphasis on understanding the prosecution's burden, available defenses, and sources of proof. The book also occasionally presents relevant domestic cases (both civil and criminal) in an effort to identify an emerging global "common law" of international criminal law.

While the first three editions drew heavily on the jurisprudence of the *ad hoc* International Criminal Tribunals for the former Yugoslavia and Rwanda, we have incorporated into this new edition some of the more recent materials from the ICC. The Court now has 122 members, although the rate of ratification has slowed considerably and two states (Burundi and the Philippines) have withdrawn from the Rome Statute. Since this book was first published, the ICC went from a nascent court with little jurisprudence, to a more established institution. It has ten situation countries under investigation: Uganda, the Democratic Republic of Congo, Darfur (Sudan), Kenya, Central African Republic (two open investigations), Libya, Mali, Côte d'Ivoire, Georgia, and Burundi. A number of additional situations are the subject of preliminary examinations, which is the process by which the Prosecution decides whether to open a full investigation: Afghanistan, Colombia, Guinea, Iraq/the United Kingdom, Nigeria, Palestine, The Philippines, Bangladesh/Myanmar, Ukraine, and Venezuela. The fact that the Court is officially "out of Africa" has dissipated much of the resistance within some elements of the African Union. The Court is in pre-trial, trial, and appellate proceedings with defendants hailing from many of these situation countries, although a number of high-profile fugitives remain at large, including the deposed former President of Sudan, Omar al-Bashir, the subject of two outstanding arrest warrants. At the same time, the Court has experienced significant set-backs, particularly in terms of faltering or withheld state cooperation; has generated jurisprudence that has stoked significant controversy within the academic and diplomatic communities; and is increasingly perceived as an inefficient and ineffective institution despite some important points of progress. As you will no doubt see in the materials we have provided, the ICC is charting its own course rather than adopting the precedents of the *ad hoc* tribunals.

We have made some notable substantive additions and changes to this edition of the book. First, we have updated the material on universal jurisdiction. The atrocities underway in Syria have contributed to a revival of the principle of universal jurisdiction, especially in Europe, as domestic courts step up in the face of entrenched impunity at the multilateral level. Second, we have revived the chapter on Hybrid Courts, which had been deleted from the prior edition of the book. The hybrid tribunal model is experiencing a renaissance, with new institutions being established for Kosovo and the Central African Republic and being contemplated elsewhere, including in South Sudan. Third, the crises in Syria, Yemen, and Burma/Myanmar feature more prominently, even though there has been little in the way of accountability for the war crimes and crimes against humanity underway there. Fourth, we have added excerpts from some of the more recent ICC decisions, including those related to superior responsibility, head of state immunity, reparations, and sexual violence. We have, for example, replaced the Pinochet decision from the House of Lords with the Al Bashir opinion from the ICC on head of state immunity. Fifth, we have removed some of the materials on the "global war on terror" in order to make room for some of the more significant developments in international criminal law at the international level. For example, we have removed the *Hamdan* decision and many of the notes associated with that case. The remaining chapters have also been updated to feature further developments in the law.

Reflecting the enormous growth of material concerning the enforcement of international humanitarian law, we have devoted two chapters to those materials. The first, the Legal Regulation of Armed Conflict, addresses the interface between international humanitarian law and international criminal law. It thus discusses the classification of conflicts (armed conflict versus unrest, and international versus non-international armed conflicts) and the nexus with the armed conflict required for an act to be subject to international criminal law. The next chapter, War Crimes, delves into the specific substantive crimes arising from armed conflicts that are subject to prosecution at the international level.

We should note that this course will necessarily engage with difficult content related to human rights abuses, including sexual and gender-based violence (SGBV). Students—and professors—may find some of the reading to be emotionally and intellectually challenging. It is important to be aware of these reactions and engage in self-care as needed.

The book contains a rich array of Notes & Questions at the end of each major substantive section. Like all Notes & Questions, these are meant to elaborate upon the issues presented in the principal case(s), but also suggest areas of class discussion, further study, and research for students looking for paper topics. Many of the Notes & Questions highlight areas of the law that remain fluid and open for debate. They also provide more detail on the context in which the principal case emerged in order to provide a window into the way in which international criminal law operates. We have sometimes reproduced larger portions of the major opinions than is customary in a casebook in order to provide context to the decision, as well as to familiarize the student with the structure and methodology of international opinions. We hope that this will assist our readers in translating case-reading and analytical skills they developed from studying domestic U.S. cases into the international arena. Finally, each major chapter and many of the major sections end with a problem or two that can be used for writing assignments, small group work, or in-class discussion.

A few words of house-keeping:

- We have used three asterisks (* * *) to indicate text that we have omitted from the primary excerpts. By contrast, where the original texts reproduce edited material, an ellipsis (alone, in parentheticals, or in brackets) will generally appear.

- We have fixed obvious typographical errors and misspellings in the principal cases without notation. We have, however, usually maintained the European spelling of words where employed in original sources (such as defence counsel, organisation, wilful, etc.).

- We have removed most case citations. To the extent that we have retained the footnotes or endnotes of the principal cases, these are presented in their original numbering. Where we have added a footnote, we have designated it with an asterisk (*). When Latin maxims or obscure terms of art are employed, we have provided a translation or explanation in brackets.

- We no longer provide URLs for online materials on the assumption that these materials can easily be found with any search engine.

- Most of the cases we excerpt are written in enumerated paragraphs. We have endeavored to retain the original enumeration. Many headings and sub-headings within the cases have been removed.

Where they have been retained, we have generally omitted the outline designations (I, A, (i), etc.).

- Many of the translations provided are informal ones undertaken by us or one of our research assistants. Where there is a published English translation of a case, we have at times edited the translation for ease of comprehension with reference to the original source.

- We use the terms "state," "nation," and "country" interchangeably to mean a nation state, rather than a U.S. state.

International criminal law is now an established subset of public international law whose content is being actively litigated in domestic and international fora. Although many of the issues that had long been the subject of scholarly speculation are now part of a burgeoning jurisprudence, important areas of law remain unsettled. Accordingly, this casebook cannot promise a complete treatment of this now established field. Instead, we have endeavored to revel a bit in the open questions in our Notes, Questions, and Problems. International criminal law remains a dynamic area of law, which is what makes this course such a joy and such a challenge to teach. We, of course, welcome suggestions for improving and updating this volume going forward.

BETH VAN SCHAACK
STANFORD, CALIFORNIA

RONALD C. SLYE
SEATTLE, WASHINGTON

July 31, 2019

ACKNOWLEDGMENTS

Many people contributed to this text. We would like to pay special tribute to our reviewers who provided excellent feedback on this and previous drafts of this casebook and others who gave us various forms of assistance and advice throughout the project, including Garth Abraham, Roland Adjovi, Diane Marie Amann, Almudena Bernabeu, Ted Biagini, June Carbone, Linda Carter, Rhonda Copelon, Omar Dajani, Shahram Dana, Meg DeGuzman, Matt Eisenbrandt, Megan Fairlie, Glenda Fick, Ryan Goodman, Kevin Jon Heller, Derek Jinks, Karen Keck, Linda Keller, Jonathan Klaaren, Harold Hongju Koh, Steve Kostas, Susan Lamb, Mike McVicker, Bénédict De Moerloose, Justin Mohammed, Neelam Noorani, R. John Pritchard, Jaya Ramji-Nogales, Rod Rastan, Francisco Rivera, Andreas Schüller, Stephen I. Vladeck, and Alex Whiting.

Many law student research assistants contributed to this effort. For this edition, we are especially grateful to Tara Ohrtman and Julia Neusner from Stanford Law School and Justin Loveland from Seattle University School of Law who performed the herculean task of updating the index. We also wish to acknowledge the many law students in our courses on International Criminal Law, International Human Rights, and Transitional Justice whose lively and stimulating comments enhanced the materials and problems in this text. We would also like to thank the faculty and students of the University of the Witwatersrand School of Law, and those U.S. and African students who participated in Seattle University's summer program in South Africa, who helped us to incorporate African perspectives on international criminal law.

The authors received considerable support from their home institutions for this project. In particular, we would like to thank our respective deans: M. Elizabeth Magill and Jenny S. Martinez (Stanford) and Annette Clark (Seattle). We are also indebted to the international law librarians at our home institutions for their tireless searching for obscure international and foreign sources: Robert Menanteaux (Seattle) and Sergio Stone (Stanford). For their excellent editorial assistance, we are indebted to Junsen Ohno and Nora Santos at Seattle.

We would also like to acknowledge the support and patience of Ryan Pfeiffer of Foundation Press, especially during the "last mile" of manuscript preparation, and the helpful comments from members of the Press's Editorial Board. Heidi Postlewait of the Office of Information and Communications Technology has our gratitude for permission to reproduce some of the maps in the book.

Finally, we would like to thank the following authors and publishers for granting us permission to reprint copyrighted material:

Miriam J. Aukerman, *Extraordinary Evil, Ordinary Crime: A Framework for Understanding Transitional Justice*, 15 HARV. HUM. RTS. J. 39 (2002).

Jonathan A. Bush, *"The Supreme . . . Crime" and its Origins: The Lost Legislative History of the Crime of Aggressive War,* 102 COLUM. L. REV. 2324 (2002).

Laurel E. Fletcher, *From Indifference to Engagement: Bystanders and International Criminal Justice*, 26 MICH. J. INT'L L. 1013 (2005).

John Langbein, *The Legal History of Torture*, in TORTURE: A COLLECTION, at 93 (Sanford Levinson ed., 2004).

Noah B. Novogrodsky, *Speaking To Africa: The Early Success Of The Special Court For Sierra Leone*, 5 SANTA CLARA J. INT'L L. 194 (2006).

RESTATEMENT (3RD) FOREIGN RELATIONS LAW OF THE UNITED STATES, copyright 1987 by the American Law Institute. Reprinted with permission. All rights reserved.

RESTATEMENT (4TH) FOREIGN RELATIONS LAW OF THE UNITED STATES, copyright 2017 by the American Law Institute. Reprinted with permission. All rights reserved.

Nico Schrijver, THE USE OF FORCE UNDER THE U.N. CHARTER: RESTRICTIONS AND LOOPHOLES (2003).

Scott L. Silliman, *On Military Commissions*, 37 Case W. Res. J. Int'l L. 529 (2005).

Ivan Simonovic, *Attitudes and Types of Reaction Toward Past War Crimes and Human Rights Abuses*, 29 YALE J. INT'L L. 343 (2004).

International Military Tribunal (Nuremberg), Judgment And Sentences October 1, 1946, *reprinted in* 41 AM. J. INT'L. L. 172 (Jan. 1947), reproduced with permission from © The American Society of International Law.

Trial of General Tomoyuki Yamashita, United States Military Commission, Manila, 8th October–7th December, 1945, *available in* IV LAW REPORTS OF TRIALS OF WAR CRIMINALS 1 (1948) (William S. Hein & Co. Buffalo NY 1997).

SUMMARY OF CONTENTS

PART IV. INDIVIDUAL CRIMINAL RESPONSIBILITY FOR INTERNATIONAL CRIMES

TABLE OF CONTENTS

TABLE OF CASES

The principal cases are in bold type.

LIST OF MAPS

We have provided maps for many of the countries in which the cases included in the text have arisen. We have placed these maps in an Appendix at the conclusion of the book since they are useful at multiple points throughout the text.

UNIVERSITY CASEBOOK SERIES®

INTERNATIONAL CRIMINAL LAW AND ITS ENFORCEMENT

CASES AND MATERIALS

FOURTH EDITION

PART I

INTRODUCTION

> The privilege of opening the first trial in history for crimes against the peace of the world imposes a grave responsibility. The wrongs which we seek to condemn and punish have been so calculated, so malignant, and so devastating, that civilization cannot tolerate their being ignored, because it cannot survive their being repeated. That four great nations, flushed with victory and stung with injury, stay the hand of vengeance and voluntarily submit their captive enemies to the judgment of the law is one of the most significant tributes that Power has ever paid to Reason.
>
> —Justice Robert H. Jackson, Chief Prosecutor, International Military Tribunal at Nuremberg

The prosecutions at Nuremberg and Tokyo after World War II were the first attempt to articulate a global vision of international criminal justice. Robert Jackson's oft-cited opening statement at Nuremberg illustrates the felt need to develop such a system at the end of one of the worst wars of human history. The magnitude of the threat facing the world compelled efforts to combat it, not as traditionally had been done with raw power, but with reason, courts, and justice. The development of that vision—including its theory, laws, and institutions—gave rise to the field of international criminal law, which is the subject of this casebook.

International criminal law imposes criminal responsibility on individuals for certain violations of public international law. The legal norms within international criminal law share several characteristics. First, offenses against this body of law are criminalized at the international level, although they may also find expression in domestic penal codes. Second, these violations give rise to individual *criminal* liability. At the same time, they may also engender state and individual *civil* (tort) responsibility such that violations may generate parallel proceedings against different classes of defendant/respondent under different theories of liability. In this way, international criminal law encompasses parts of both international humanitarian law (also called the "law of war") and international human rights law, but transcends both. Third, international criminal law violations are prosecuted before international penal tribunals, such as the *ad hoc* war crimes tribunals created by the United Nations and the permanent International Criminal Court (ICC), and hybrid institutions that mix international and domestic elements. At the same time, these violations are increasingly prosecuted before domestic courts under various jurisdictional principles, many of which accord domestic courts an expansive extraterritorial reach. Indeed, and fourth, international criminal law violations may trigger state obligations to prosecute offenders under treaty law and, some would argue, customary international law. Much of modern international criminal law finds expression in treaties and the burgeoning jurisprudence of the modern war crimes tribunals. The field also borrows heavily from basic principles of domestic criminal law, at times sampling from, blending, and reconciling the civil law and common law penal traditions.

The field of international criminal law has a disparate and ancient lineage in international prohibitions against piracy, the slave trade, and war crimes. Most international criminal law, however, dates from the World War II period and the proceedings before the Nuremberg and Tokyo Tribunals and contemporaneous occupation courts convened by the victorious Allies. This postwar period heralded a wave of optimism about the power of law and judicial institutions to restrain collective violence and protect the vulnerable. Just as the ink was drying on the judgments against the major World War II defendants, however, the Cold War set in, paralyzing efforts to put permanent international criminal law institutions in place. As a result, for many years, the development of international criminal law was largely relegated to obscure United Nations drafting committees, a smattering of domestic proceedings in transitional societies, and the writings of a few dogged academics.

The thawing of the Cold War, and the re-appearance of genocide in Europe, sparked a renaissance in international criminal law. Developments since 1994—including the establishment of multiple international and hybrid criminal tribunals with jurisdiction over the worst international crimes and the activation of the principle of universal jurisdiction—attest that the Nuremberg legacy of holding individuals criminally accountable for international law violations is not mere history. The enforcement of international criminal law has once again emerged as a central, and expected, feature of transitional justice in the wake of war and repression. The field is no longer in a fledgling state; rather, it is sufficiently developed at this time to constitute a separate and discrete discipline.

As a result of postwar institutional and political developments, international criminal law is now adjudicated in a number of different domestic, regional, and international fora, and this book draws from, and recounts, the work of a broad range of such institutions. Most importantly, referenced sources include the jurisprudence of the various international and hybrid criminal tribunals (dedicated to the conflicts and violence in the former Yugoslavia, Rwanda, Sierra Leone, Timor-Leste, Kosovo, Lebanon, Iraq, and Cambodia), the International Court of Justice, treaty bodies (such as the Human Rights Committee), regional human rights institutions (such as the European Court of Human

Rights), formal domestic courts, alternative or traditional courts (such as the *gacaca* proceedings in Rwanda), and transitional justice institutions (such as truth commissions and lustration panels). In addition, domestic and international cases assigning civil (as opposed to criminal) liability are a relevant source of jurisprudence to the extent that they are predicated upon tort analogs of international crimes and forms of responsibility (such as complicity and superior responsibility). Even a quick scan of the citations of the cases presented herein reveals that these international and domestic institutions are engaged in an iterative process of vertical and horizontal cross-fertilization with respect to the norms, principles, and processes of international criminal law.

The original *ad hoc* tribunals have fully implemented their completion strategies and the International Criminal Court has assumed its position as the flagship international criminal tribunal. And yet, the ICC faces mounting challenges. These include the loss of some states' support, in part due to the Court's perceived "targeting" of African defendants and powerful heads of state; a lack of consistent state cooperation and compliance with the ICC Statute, court orders, and Security Council referral resolutions; and the activation of the still-controversial crime of aggression. Detractors, and even supporters, argue that the Court lacks effectiveness and/or efficiency, which has given rise to a reform movement within the Assembly of States Parties (ASP). In addition, the potential role of the Court in ongoing conflicts—such as Syria, Myanmar, and Yemen—remains controversial, particularly given heightened animosity toward the Court among the three non-party permanent members of the Security Council. Indeed, the situation in Syria (for which there are few prospects for accountability at the time of publication) is often singled out as a test of the global system of international criminal justice. Nevertheless, many of the perceived weaknesses of the Court are not endemic to the institution itself; rather, they are the result of the ASP (and the United Nations in general) not authorizing sufficient resources for, providing adequate support to, or cooperating effectively with the institution. The perceived limitations of the Court have inspired new thinking about the benefits of hybrid institutions for situations such as the Central African Republic and South Sudan.

For its part, the Court continues to go about its work. It has completed several trials with mixed results and has other defendants in pre-trial, trial, and appellate proceedings. In short, the Court is now fully operational with all the imperfections and complications faced by any criminal tribunal, and then some. As you complete this course, keep these challenges in mind and consider the way in which the international community can and should respond as the Court commences its third decade of work. Consider also the extent to which the international community should continue to utilize *ad hoc* tribunals, hybrid institutions, and other justice mechanisms to deliver international justice for the worst crimes known to humankind.

CHAPTER 1

WHAT IS INTERNATIONAL CRIMINAL LAW?

I. INTRODUCTION

This introductory chapter situates international criminal law within the fields of transitional justice and domestic criminal law. It begins with a brief overview of the field of transitional justice and identifies criminal prosecutions as one of many options available to states experiencing or emerging out of mass violence and armed conflict. It then juxtaposes international criminal law with the traditional philosophical underpinnings of the criminal law. This return to first principles should stimulate your thinking about the way in which international criminal law institutions and processes are similar to, and diverge from, other transitional justice options and domestic criminal law.

II. TRANSITIONAL JUSTICE MECHANISMS

As a system of criminal law, international criminal law assumes that the prosecution of individuals accused of transgressions furthers desirable substantive norms and societal outcomes. However, in situations in which international criminal law is applicable—during or following armed conflict, repression, and mass violence—there are a multitude of other ways a state or the international community can respond. The various options available to address such situations marks the field of transitional justice. A full discussion of transitional justice is beyond the scope of this text; however, it may be useful at this point to consider what alternatives to criminal prosecutions are available to address the commission of international crimes. In practice, many of these alternatives are employed alongside criminal prosecutions. Consider the following excerpt:

Ivan Šimonović, Attitudes and Types of Reaction Toward Past War Crimes and Human Rights Abuses, 29 YALE J. INT'L L. 343 (2004)

The importance of a reliable justice system and the rule of law is universally accepted. Nonetheless, controversy still surrounds the extent to which seeking justice for past war crimes and grave human rights abuses represents a precondition for—or an impediment to—the overall stability of post-conflict and transitional societies. Human rights advocates tend to regard the implementation of judicial norms and institutions as an omnipotent cure against war crimes and human rights abuses; diplomats and other peacemakers are far more skeptical, sometimes regarding justice as mere window-dressing or, worse, as a direct impediment to peace. Actual experience does not provide straightforward answers. Different societies have taken different paths to confront post-conflict and transition challenges—and have met with both success and shortcomings. Moreover "simple" transitions from a repressive regime to democracy (such as in Argentina, Chile, or El Salvador) should be distinguished from transitions following patterns of atrocity that had racial, religious, or ethnic underpinnings (such as in South Africa, Rwanda, Guatemala, or Bosnia and Herzegovina). This variety, however, should not discourage the international community from trying to identify possible patterns; to the contrary, richness of experience, if systemized, can illustrate more clearly the current state of international justice and, possibly, where it is going. * * *

II. Attitudes Toward Past War Crimes and Human Rights Abuses

The analysis begins with attitudes. * * * Of course, the most interesting are the prevailing attitudes—the ones that are supported by the dominant political forces within the post-conflict or transitional society itself. Four basic attitudes correspond to the different possible combinations of responses to the choices just described—to forget or to establish truth; to punish or to pardon:

(1) "Willful ignorance"—to forget and to pardon;

(2) "Historical record"—to establish the truth, but to pardon;

(3) "Pragmatic retribution"—to forget, but still punish; and

(4) "No peace without justice"—to establish the truth and to punish the perpetrators. * * *

Each of the attitudes can be traced back to certain identifiable motives, as illustrated by some historical examples. The desire for "willful ignorance" derives from a perception that past experience is so controversial, divisive, and painful as to merit being forgotten—being cast into oblivion. This may also be the opportunistic position taken by a politically important group seeking to hide its responsibility for past events. In either case, this attitude reflects an attempt to cut off the divisive past in a single instant, looking only to the future. A typical moral justification for such an attitude is the idea that any solution that prevents human suffering and can bring about an immediate peace is a good one. * * *

By contrast, the search to establish the "historical record" is motivated by the belief that, in spite of the desire to facilitate reconciliation by pardoning the perpetrators of abuse, knowing and recording the events that have taken place is essential to avoid their repetition. Some also contend that revealing the truth provides symbolic satisfaction to the victims. This attitude may be honestly held and well-intentioned, but it may also represent a compromise between former abusers and their victims, who settle for the limited satisfaction of truth, rather than receive actual redress through punishment. * * *

"Pragmatic retribution" is motivated by the will to get rid of the abusers fast, but without raising controversial issues from the past. From this perspective, pragmatism is more important than justice. It is considered essential to eliminate the perpetrators of abuses from political life by either taking administrative measures to exclude them or by punishing them for crimes that are not directly tied to war crimes and abuses, and, therefore, not politically divisive. * * *

Finally, those who take the "no peace without justice" approach are motivated by the belief that only legal proceedings against the perpetrators of war crimes and human rights abuses can: (1) provide the truth and punishment necessary to satisfy the victims; (2) prevent individual retaliation for past injustices; and (3) prevent history from repeating itself. Victims and human rights nongovernmental organizations (NGOs) typically adopt this position, but it can also become the dominant attitude of a post-conflict society, or even of the international community in particular situations. * * *

Interpreting the attitudes of different post-conflict and transition societies is an inexact science that requires the identification of various indicators. Reactions, however, usually take some kind of legal form and can be more easily identified. A typology of four basic forms of reaction toward past war crimes and human rights abuses corresponds to the set of societal choices identified above—to forget or establish the truth; to pardon or punish the guilty:

(1) Amnesty—to forget and to pardon;

(2) Truth commissions—to establish the truth, but to pardon;

(3) Lustration or substitute criminal charges—to forget and to punish;

(4) Individual or collective criminal justice proceedings—to establish the truth and to punish.

Amnesty reflects the highest level of commitment to the "willful ignorance" response. It can be a blanket amnesty—anonymous, *en masse*, with no conditions and no questions asked. Alternatively, a conditional or individual amnesty can be established, covering the majority of crimes in exchange for cooperation in establishing full truth about the past. * * *

Truth commissions reflect a high level of commitment to establishing the truth, but also a willingness to pardon the offenders. Establishing a reliable historical record can be important because past abuses can be systematically hidden (as in the case of disappeared persons in Latin America), or because different sides to the conflict may offer competing and conflicting versions of the "truth" about past events. In any case, truth commissions offer at least the possibility of symbolic satisfaction for the victims and can help mitigate the risks of future conflict.

Lustration [the removal or barring of individuals from government or private posts] or the use of substitute criminal charges [such as corruption charges] reflects the desire to simultaneously avoid the risks related to establishing the truth [and] to punish the perpetrators in some way. * * * [T]hrough the process of lustration [individuals may be] excluded from active political life and prohibited from participating in public administration (especially positions with the military or police). * * *

Substitute criminal charges impose a higher degree of punishment than lustration; they not only place restrictions on participation in public life or administration, but they also involve actual imprisonment of the convicted person. Lustration requires some legal determination of the scope of persons affected and the extent of consequences for those individuals; legal institutions are designated to perform the process. Substitute criminal charges do not require any changes to the legal system; existing rules and institutions are used to punish and remove the accused individuals from public life.

Finally, reaction can take the form of any number of complex proceedings based on the pursuit of individual or collective responsibility. These trial-based proceedings combine a strong demand for establishing the truth with a desire to mete out either collective or individual punishment against the perpetrators. Proceedings focused on collective responsibility represent a form of reaction targeting a collective body considered responsible for the abuse of victims who are entitled to compensation. * * * Collective responsibility can be regulated through various legal institutions, but its basis is the awarding of compensation.

Proceedings focused on individual criminal responsibility represent a form of reaction oriented toward both establishing the truth and punishing the individual criminal perpetrators. Responsibility can be established through national proceedings; through courts in third countries that exercise universal jurisdiction; through proceedings before *ad hoc* tribunals, such as those for the former Yugoslavia and for Rwanda; through hybrid tribunals involving a mix of national and international judges and prosecutors, such as those in Sierra Leone, East Timor, and Kosovo; or before the International Criminal Court (ICC). The laws regulating individual criminal responsibility are contained in national criminal codes, international criminal law, and the statutes of *ad hoc* tribunals or the ICC.

Each of the four basic attitudes to past war crimes and human rights abuses described [above] corresponds to a certain form of reaction * * *:

(1) "Willful ignorance" corresponds to amnesty;

(2) "Historical record" corresponds to truth commissions;

(3) "Pragmatic retribution" corresponds to lustration or substitute criminal charges; and

(4) "No peace without justice" corresponds to proceedings based on individual or collective responsibility.

These relationships between attitudes and their corresponding types of reaction can also be presented graphically [see Figure 4, p. 9].

If the attitude toward past war crimes and human rights abuses is "willful ignorance," then the suitable form of reaction is amnesty. A willingness to forget and to pardon is reflected in amnesty's grant of immunity from prosecution. The past is buried, for better or worse, and perpetrators of at least some crimes and human rights abuses get a legal waiver from prosecution. Amnesty can increase stability by eliminating the uncertainty surrounding the potential prosecutions—or their potential misuse. Its shortcoming is the potential frustration of the victims—possibly providing the motivation to seek individual revenge. Furthermore, crimes or abuses might reoccur because they were neither symbolically condemned nor individually or collectively punished.

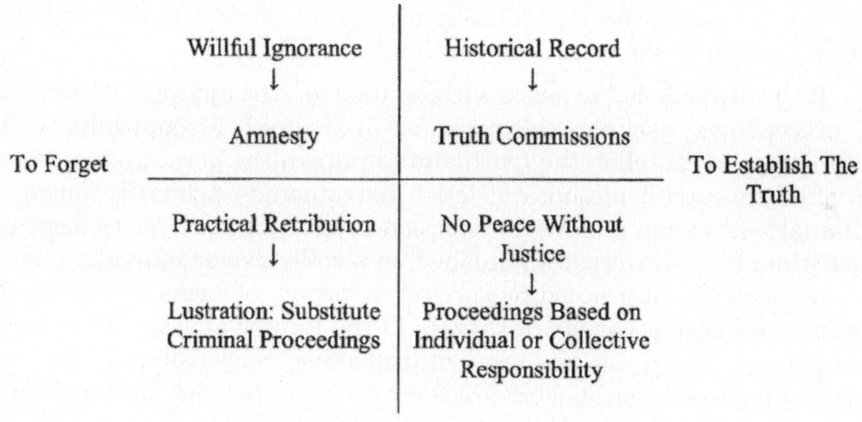

Figure 4. Attitudes and Types of Reaction Toward Past War Crimes and Human Rights Abuses

If the attitude is "historical record," truth commissions represent a suitable form of reaction. This instrument enables the establishment of the truth—often with far reaching political impact—but without punishing the perpetrators (or at least certain categories of the perpetrators), thus meeting the two goals of those who prioritize the historical record. The benefits provided by truth commissions include the opportunity to face the past, to identify both the victims and the perpetrators, and, in this way, to provide some level of protection against similar events in the future. Victims receive some level of symbolic satisfaction, but without pushing perpetrators too hard and risking the reemergence of conflict. The shortcoming of this approach is that victims who know the truth—but who are also aware that the perpetrators have not been punished—might be motivated to seek individual revenge.

If the attitude is "pragmatic retribution," then the suitable type of reaction is lustration or substitute criminal proceedings. The willingness to eliminate the perpetrators from political life is reflected in their exclusion from participation in certain sectors of public life—or in the imposition of individual punishment through criminal proceedings for some measure of their crimes, which also removes them from the political scene (at least temporarily). These proceedings, however, avoid rehashing certain controversies from the past. Instead, war criminals and human rights abusers are treated as mere common criminals (which, quite often, they also are). This approach serves to rid society of the most dangerous people without risking widespread social or political instability. The difficulty is that war crimes or abuses may reoccur because they were never properly confronted and condemned in the first instance. Substitute criminal proceedings, however, can be a good way to prepare the society psychologically for future prosecutions of more serious and politically sensitive crimes; when it has been established that a former leader has been engaged in corruption or murder, it is easier to accept that he or she was a war criminal as well.

If the attitude is "no peace without justice," the appropriate reaction is proceedings seeking collective or individual responsibility. The willingness to establish the truth and to punish the perpetrators can be satisfied through a plethora of legal instruments—primarily courts or tribunals—that can provide satisfaction to the victims. Society faces the past when perpetrators are punished on a collective or individual basis. Of course, different proceedings provide a variety of forms of relief to the victims and pose a variety of threats to the former abusers. In general, proceedings based on theories of collective responsibility are less threatening to former abusers precisely because they are not targeted at any single individual, and because findings of criminal responsibility give rise to obligations that are most clearly financial, not moral. On the other hand, financial compensation likely fails to vindicate the victims' claims as completely as individual prosecutions and punishment might (although the degree of victim satisfaction could depend on the nature of the abuses committed or the circumstances of the particular victim). Proceedings based on individual responsibility provide that benefit, and the resultant catharsis can help the victims forgive past suffering. Major drawbacks include the possibility that proceedings against the accused individuals can take a long period of time (in some cases years), that they might be misused against political enemies, and that if people who maintain considerable influence are pushed into a corner, they will fight until the bitter end. * * *

Understanding attitudes and types of reaction toward past war crimes and human rights abuses as basic choices—between whether to forget the past or to establish the truth, between whether to pardon or punish the perpetrators—allows us to identify trends which are helpful in creating an abstract systematization of practical experiences. Increases in the number of proceedings based on individual or collective responsibility provide empirical evidence of the increasing importance attached to the establishment of truth and to the punishment of the perpetrators.

Although there seems to be a shift in attitude toward the establishment of truth and punishment, there is no set of reaction types toward past war crimes and human rights abuses, however, that can be generally regarded as optimal. Approaches to past war crimes and human rights abuses should be holistic, taking into account various social, legal, political, and moral dimensions, and the most suitable reaction should take into account questions of appropriate timing and other specific circumstances. Differentiation of various types of reaction, knowledge of their strengths and weaknesses, and flexibility in combining them makes such fine-tuning easier. Practical experience is being generated all over the world, and it is important to learn from that experience.

Flexibility in combining various types of reaction can ensure that the response chosen is prompt and pragmatic, and that justice is finally satisfied. At least the gravest crimes must be met with criminal proceedings (*certus an*, *incertus quando*). Amnesties, for example, are more and more often reduced to cover only minor crimes, sometimes conditioning amnesty on cooperation with truth commissions. Besides establishing the historical record, truth commissions can help to gather evidence for criminal proceedings. Lustration or substitute criminal charges can help to remove criminals and abusers from public life quickly, which does not preclude their criminal prosecution for war crimes and human rights abuses when the conditions are ready. Proceedings based on collective responsibility can sometimes provide for the fast compensation of the victims, while individual criminal prosecutions of abusers cannot proceed until the criminals are apprehended and the evidentiary cases well-developed.

Considering the impact of globalization, and especially the development of the international protection of human rights, international support for confronting past injustice in post-conflict and transitional societies is increasing. Although international involvement in dealing with past war crimes and abuses is important to guarantee justice for all, it remains crucial for wounded societies to strengthen their own national justice systems in order to ensure sustainable peace and the rule of law.

NOTES & QUESTIONS

1. Confronting the Past

It is now accepted wisdom that nations must confront the legacy of past violence if they are to move forward successfully towards peace. The United Nations addresses this imperative through the Office of the High Commissioner for Human Rights (OHCHR); the Special Rapporteur on the Promotion of Truth, Justice, Reparation and Guarantees of Non-Recurrence; the office of the U.N. Secretary-General; Sustainable Development Goal #16 on access of justice; and the U.N. Development Program. Human rights treaty bodies are increasingly recognizing a right to truth and justice. Non-governmental agencies (such as the International Center for Transitional Justice) devote themselves to the study and promotion of transitional justice. How should nations choose between these multiple transitional justice options? How might these various institutions reinforce or impede each other? For a discussion, *see* Mark Osiel, *Choosing Among Alternative Responses to Mass Atrocity: Between the Individual and the Collectivity*, ETHICS & INTERNATIONAL AFFAIRS (Sept. 2015). As discussed more fully in Chapter 17 on Defenses Under International Criminal Law, amnesty laws are disfavored under international law. Might there be a time when "willful ignorance" can effectuate a positive transition? Is it possible that a society could function with such a "collective amnesia"?

2. Spain

Spain is often cited as an example of a state that engaged in no meaningful transitional justice process and yet put a repressive past behind it with some success. The fascist Francisco Franco, *el generalísimo*, rose to power in 1936 in the midst of the Spanish civil war. During World War II, he was supportive of the Axis side, but managed to largely stay out of the War; he declared total neutrality by 1943 when the tide was turning against Germany. Throughout his reign, his focus was more internal, overseeing a repressive apparatus that some historians say was responsible for up to 80,000 executions and thousands of other deaths through forced labor. Because he was not involved in acts of international aggression, the Allies largely left him alone after World War II, although Spain was for a time quite marginalized in Europe. Franco died in 1975, opening the way for a transition to democracy.

Only recently has Spanish society beginning to revisit the events of the Franco years with an eye toward demanding some sort of accountability for abuses. Indeed, this effort has become inter-generational, with the children and grandchildren of victims pushing for transitional justice responses in the face of impunity, the "pact of forgetting" (*pacto del olvido*), and gaps in the evidentiary record and their own personal histories. To date, there have been symbolic gestures, such as the removal of the last statutes of Franco, as well as some payment of reparations and exhumations of mass graves to locate the disappeared, but no prosecutions or other more retributive processes have taken place. Judge Baltasar Garzón, who became famous for initiating the cases against Chilean Augusto Pinochet and other Latin American defendants in Spain, also launched investigations into Franco-era crimes; he attempted to get around the 1977 general amnesty by arguing that it did not govern cases of disappearances since no body had been found. Judge Garzón was prosecuted in Spain for "malfeasance" for his efforts, but was acquitted. Garzón has since challenged the lawfulness of the suit against him before the European Court of Human Rights. In the meantime, the U.N. Committee on Enforced Disappearances recommended that Spain uncover the fate of Franco's victims, and authorities in Argentina initiated investigations into cases of murder and disappearances in Spain under the doctrine of universal jurisdiction. In October 2018, a Spanish court rejected letters rogatory from the Argentinean court requesting assistance in accessing documents and witnesses related to the Argentinean investigation. Does the Spanish example suggest that states need not investigate and provide redress for past violations to achieve peace and democracy after repression?

3. Simple v. Complex Transitions

Šimonović, the former U.N. Assistant Secretary-General for Human Rights and Special Adviser to the Secretary-General on the Responsibility to Protect, makes a distinction between "simple" transitions from a repressive regime to democracy and more complex ones involving "racial, religious, or ethnic underpinnings." Is this distinction meaningful? Why might one type of transition be more difficult than another? Which attitudes and reactions might be prevalent in a "simple" versus a more "complex" transition? For a discussion on the unique challenges faced by multi-ethnic states, *see* Elena A. Baylis, *Beyond Rights: Legal Process and Ethnic Conflicts,* 25 MICH. J. INT'L L. 529 (2004); Anna Morawiec Mansfield, *Ethnic But Equal: The Quest for a New Democratic Order in Bosnia and Herzegovina*, 103 COLUM. L. REV. 2052 (2003). Might certain transitional justice mechanisms actually deepen an ethnic or religious divide during or after a period of transition? Consider, for example, the cases of Iraq or Bangladesh, which are taken up in subsequent chapters.

4. Truth Commissions

The phenomenon of the truth commission emerged initially as a response to mass violence in countries (mostly in Latin America) where prosecutions were precluded by the operation of an amnesty law, the lack of political will, a still-entrenched military, or other obstacles. Truth commissions provide an alternative form of justice by establishing a historical record of abuses, including the institutional and systemic conditions that made such abuses possible; providing a safe space for victims (and at times perpetrators) to bear witness; investigating certain exemplary "window cases" that reflect the nature of the mass violence; investigating the fate of the disappeared; creating an environment more ripe for reconciliation and forgiveness than adversarial trials; issuing or recommending reparations; and proposing institutional reforms to prevent the recurrence of past violence.

Truth commissions come in many forms and reflect different origins. Some truth commissions, such as the commission established in El Salvador, identify individual perpetrators ("name names"); others have been limited to considering causes, patterns, and consequences of violence. Commissions are often presided over by respected public figures. In addition to trained lawyers or judges, commissioners often come from a wide variety of other professional backgrounds. Past commissioners have included prominent religious figures, individuals trained in medicine and other healing professions, diplomats, and specialists in conflict resolution. Some truth commissions are established with the involvement of the international community or within the United Nations; others emerge domestically. In South Africa, the Truth and Reconciliation Commission (TRC) was empowered to issue conditional amnesties to individuals implicated in domestic and international crimes, so long as the perpetrator revealed the full truth of his or her crimes and such crimes were politically-motivated. On the South African innovation, *see* Charles Villa-Vicencio & Wilhelm Verwoerd, LOOKING BACK REACHING FORWARD: REFLECTIONS ON THE TRUTH AND RECONCILIATION COMMISSION OF SOUTH AFRICA (2000). Various truth commissions are discussed in detail in Priscilla B. Hayner, UNSPEAKABLE TRUTHS: TRANSITIONAL JUSTICE AND THE CHALLENGE OF TRUTH COMMISSIONS (2nd ed. 2011). Is a truth commission the best that can be hoped for—a "consolation prize"—by individuals seeking greater accountability? Or is it a principled means of providing justice and moving forward? Whereas truth commissions originally emerged as a "second best" option where prosecutions were deemed politically impossible or inexpedient, they since have become a complementary feature in several transitional contexts, such as Sierra Leone and Timor-Leste, because many believe that they offer societal benefits that cannot be achieved by criminal prosecutions alone.

5. Kenya

In 2003, shortly after the return of multi-party democracy, the Kenyan Government established a task force, chaired by Makau Mutua, a Kenyan national who was Dean of the Law School at the University of Buffalo, to recommend whether Kenya should establish a truth commission. (See the Appendix for a map of Kenya.) The task force traveled throughout the country consulting extensively with the people of Kenya and concluded in 2004 that such a commission should be established. Despite this recommendation, no commission was established. In 2007, Kenyans went to the polls. The election was marred with irregularities that were later documented by numerous commissions of inquiry. The lead opposition candidate, Raila Odinga, was at one point ahead by over a million votes, only to have that lead evaporate in less than twenty-four hours. In the face of vote-rigging claims against all candidates, the incumbent Mwai Kibaki quickly claimed victory and was sworn in during a hastily organized late-night ceremony as allegations of fraud and vote-rigging began to circulate. The country erupted into violence in January and February of 2008, resulting in the death of over 1,100 people, and the displacement of over 300,000. While the violence was in part politically motivated, there was also a strong ethnic element, with majority ethnic groups in one area killing and expelling members of different ethnic groups.

The former U.N. Secretary General, Dr. Kofi Annan, mediated a peace agreement among the competing factions, resulting in a series of reform initiatives. These reforms, collectively referred to as Agenda Four (referencing their place in the agreement mediated by Dr. Annan), included the creation of the following four commissions:

1) a commission to examine the conduct of the election and to recommend electoral reforms;
2) a commission to investigate the election-related violence, including identifying those responsible;
3) a commission to draft a new Constitution; and
4) a Truth, Justice & Reconciliation Commission to examine the historical roots of the recent violence.

All four commissions have completed their work; the Constitutional commission has produced a draft constitution that was adopted in August, 2010; and the Truth, Justice & Reconciliation Commission submitted its report and recommendations in May 2013.

As a result of the work of the commission tasked with investigating the post-election violence (colloquially referred to as the "Waki Commission," after its chair, Judge Philip Waki of the Kenya Court of Appeal), and the failure of the Kenyan Government to implement the recommendation of the Waki Commission to establish a special tribunal to prosecute individuals responsible for the post-election violence, the Prosecutor of the International Criminal Court used his *proprio motu* powers for the first time to request authority from a Pre-Trial Chamber to initiate an investigation into allegations of crimes against humanity and war crimes in Kenya. This request was granted in March 2010 and investigations and six indictments ensued. The initial indictments were divided into two cases each involving three individuals representing the two competing political factions from the 2007 elections. Four of the six indictments were later withdrawn by the Prosecutor, in part because a number of witnesses recanted their testimony against the individual suspects amidst allegations of rampant witness tampering. This included the indictment of Uhuru Kenyatta, who joined forces with his earlier political opponent and fellow indictee, William Ruto, to be elected President and Deputy President, respectively. Opposition to the ICC emerged as a major theme in their electoral campaign, leading some commentators to label them the "Coalition of the Accused." The charges in the two remaining cases, against Deputy President William Ruto and the radio announcer Joshua arap Sang, were vacated by a two-to-one vote of the Trial Chamber without prejudice with respect to possible future proceedings. Meanwhile, although the Kenyan judiciary established an International Crimes Division to prosecute individuals responsible for the 2007–2008 violence, as of August 2019 very few such prosecutions have been initiated. (For a brief summary of the Kenyan situation before the ICC, see *infra* Chapter 5.)

Kenya is thus the most recent example of a state employing multiple approaches to addressing international crimes, ranging from international and domestic prosecutions, numerous commissions of inquiry, and a truth commission. Significantly, the truth commission was called a Truth, Justice & Reconciliation Commission, thus breaking with the more common practice of focusing only on truth and reconciliation and responding to criticism that the South African commission ignored the justice imperative. The truth commission had both domestic and international elements, consisting of six Kenyan Commissioners and three international Commissioners. The Kenyan Commissioners were chosen by the Parliament and President; the international Commissioners were chosen by the Panel of Eminent African Personalities, consisting of Kofi Annan, Graça Machel, and Benjamin Mkapa. (One author of this casebook, Prof. Slye, was the only non-African Commissioner). The Kenyan truth commission was marred by controversy during much of its life as its Chairman was linked to three human rights violations within the commission's mandate, including a massacre committed by the Kenyan security forces that resulted in about 1,000 deaths and thousands of rapes. Notwithstanding this challenge, the commission collected over 40,000 statements from individual Kenyans, which is the largest number of any statements collected by a truth commission. The end of its process was further impaired by interference from the President's office to remove references in its Report to the illegal and irregular acquisition of land by the founding President, Jomo Kenyatta, whose son is the current President. The three international Commissioners dissented from those changes, and in their dissent included the original unaltered paragraphs. For more on the TJRC, *see* Ronald C. Slye, THE KENYAN TJRC: AN OUTSIDER'S VIEW FROM THE INSIDE (2018). Given the many Kenyan initiatives, do you think the ICC should have intervened? If so, what should its relationship be with these domestic processes?

6. A Truth Commission for US Torture?

The language of truth and reconciliation became part of the public discourse in the United States following revelations that detainees in the wars in Afghanistan and Iraq had been mistreated by U.S. personnel and the Obama Administration's release of the "torture memos" written by the Office of Legal Counsel of the U.S. Justice Department. Mirroring the debate found in other countries confronting past violations, some in the United States called for criminal prosecutions of responsible individuals up the chain of command; others argued that we should put the past behind us and focus on preventing violations in the future. Senator Patrick Leahy (D-VT) introduced legislation to establish a truth commission, but President Obama and the majority in Congress opposed the proposal. In 2009, the Senate Intelligence Committee under the leadership of Dianne Feinstein (D-CA) announced that it would review the CIA's detention and interrogation program. The Committee approved a 6000-page report based on classified data that apparently contains "startling details" about the CIA program. Although a 525-page executive summary and key findings were released, the full report has yet to be declassified.

In the absence of a public government initiative, the non-governmental Constitution Project convened a bipartisan Task Force on Detainee Treatment that concluded in a 600-page report released in 2013 that the nation's highest officials bear responsibility for the fact that the United States engaged in the practice of torture—as that crime is authoritatively defined under international law—in Iraq, Afghanistan, and Guantánamo Bay, Cuba. To date, there have been only a handful of prosecutions for the most egregious of cases of mistreatment and murder. In connection with the United States' Fourth Periodic Report under the International Covenant on Civil and Political Rights, the U.N. Human Rights Committee in 2014 criticized this "meager record." In 2016, Donald Trump was elected President on a platform that included a pledge to increase the population of the detention facilities at Guantánamo Bay and to reinstate the use of waterboarding and other forms of torture. What are the pros and cons of the United States prosecuting former and current government officials alleged to have committed or authorized torture and other forms of mistreatment of those in U.S. custody? Would you recommend such prosecutions, a truth commission, or some other form of inquiry into such past violations? The Office of the Prosecutor of the ICC attempted to open an investigation into the situation in Afghanistan, but was not given approval to do so by the Pre-Trial Chamber as was required. This opinion is excerpted in Chapter 5 on the ICC.

7. *Gacaca* Courts

The *ad hoc* international tribunal for Rwanda indicted dozens of high level defendants in the Rwandan genocide, and other states (including Canada, France, Germany, and Belgium) have brought cases against a number of individuals pursuant to universal jurisdiction. Rwanda was thus faced with the prospect of prosecuting thousands of lower-level perpetrators. With an estimated 130,000 accused in prisons throughout the country, however, any such goal became impossible to achieve. Indeed, five years after the genocide, only 6,000 cases had been tried. At that rate, it would have taken over a century to resolve all of the outstanding cases. Therefore, the government revived a traditional dispute resolution mechanism called *gacaca* (pronounced "ga-cha-cha"), which literally means "justice from the grass." According to the National Service of Gacaca Jurisdictions, the objectives of the *gacaca* courts were to:

1) reveal the truth about what happened,
2) speed up genocide trials,
3) eradicate the culture of impunity,
4) reconcile the Rwandans and reinforce their unity, and
5) prove that the Rwandan society has the capacity to settle its own problems through a system of justice based on Rwandan custom.

Defendants in *gacaca* courts stood before members of the community without counsel. Anyone from the community could speak either for or against the accused. To support the revelation of the truth, and to further reconciliation, those defendants who confessed to their crimes in front of the community and apologized had their sentences reduced. Those who refused to confess, plead guilty, repent, or ask for forgiveness but were nevertheless found guilty could be sentenced to life imprisonment. Those accused of planning or organizing the genocide, and government, military, or religious leaders who committed or encouraged others to commit crimes against humanity or genocide, were not subject to the *gacaca* process, but were to be handled by either ordinary civilian or military courts. The *gacaca* process wound down in 2012. For more on *gacaca* courts, *see* Maya Sosnov, *The Adjudication of Genocide: Gacaca and the Road to Reconciliation in Rwanda*, 36 DENV. J. INT'L L. & POL'Y 125 (2008).

Does the *gacaca* process adhere to Rwanda's human rights obligations as contained in the International Covenant on Civil and Political Rights and other treaties? Given the post-genocidal exigencies and the limited legal resources available, should Rwanda be entitled to a "margin of appreciation" with respect to these obligations? How useful might the *gacaca* mechanism be outside of the Rwandan context? In addition to the due process deficits of *gacaca*, the process also fell sway to corruption. As you study the International Criminal Court in this course, consider to what extent such alternative justice mechanisms satisfy the requirements of complementarity. *See* Linda M. Keller, *Achieving Peace With Justice: The International Criminal Court and Ugandan Alternative Justice Mechanisms*, 23 CONN. J. INT'L L. 209 (2008).

8. Lustration

Lustration ("purification," from the Latin *lustrare*, meaning "to shed light" or "to purify") describes the practice of removing members of the prior regime and barring them from holding positions of trust and authority in the new regime. For example, a lustration law might remove a member of the security police from his position and bar him from public service. Lustrations occurred in Germany after World War II through various de-Nazification programs, in Eastern Europe after the fall of communism and totalitarianism in the 1990s, with the blunt de-Baathification initiated by the U.S. administration in Iraq, and elsewhere. Lustration provides a less punitive means of neutralizing supporters of a prior regime. The burden of proof for removing an individual is usually less than that involved in criminal proceedings.

Lustration laws have been attacked on human rights grounds as violating the right to work, privacy, assembly, expression, judicial review, and non-discrimination. Legal challenges to lustration laws have generally failed, however. *See, e.g.*, Judgment, Case of Sidabras and Diautas v. Lithuania, Applications nos. 55480/00 and 59330/00 (ECHR 27 July 2004) (finding by the European Court of Human Rights that the challenged lustration measures pursued legitimate aims of protecting national security and public order but were overbroad in application by preventing employment within certain spheres of the private sector); Constitutional Court Decision on the Screening Law, Ref. No. Pl. US1/92 (Czech and Slovak Republic 1992) (upholding the constitutionality of the Czech lustration law, but limiting its scope). For a comparison of varied lustration laws, *see* Roman David, *Lustration Laws in Action: The Motives and Evaluation of Lustration Policy in Czech Republic and Poland (1989–2001)*, 28 LAW & SOC. INQUIRY 387 (2003); Mark Gibney, *Decommunization: Human Rights Lessons from the Past and Present, and Prospects for the Future*, 23 DENV. J. INT'L L. & POL'Y 87 (1994); Herman Schwartz, *Lustration in Eastern Europe*, 1 PARKER SCHOOL J. E. EUROP. L. 141 (1994).

III. THE PURPOSES OF THE CRIMINAL LAW

International criminal law is at base a system of criminal law. Thus, it may be useful here to provide a brief review of the foundational philosophies of criminal law. The excerpt below discusses the goals of criminal justice and the variety of theoretical frameworks that justify prosecution and punishment, including desert/retribution/vengeance, deterrence, rehabilitation, restorative justice, expressivism, and social solidarity. As you proceed through this casebook, consider to what extent international criminal law either reflects domestic criminal law precepts or diverges from them in terms of its operation, objectives, and susceptibility to extra-legal imperatives.

Miriam J. Aukerman, Extraordinary Evil, Ordinary Crime: A Framework for Understanding Transitional Justice, 15 HARV. HUM. RTS. J. 39 (2002)

A. Desert/Retribution/Vengeance

Desert theory is premised on the relationship between punishment and culpability. "Retributivism is a very straightforward theory of punishment," writes penologist Michael Moore. "We are justified in punishing because and only because offenders deserve it." Unlike other theories of criminal justice, "just deserts" is thus explicitly backward-looking. For a pure retributivist, there is a Kantian categorical imperative to punish, whether or not punishment will prevent future crime. While desert theory is distinctive in its concern for the past rather than the future, it is like most other approaches to criminal justice in its focus on the offender. Victims may receive satisfaction from the knowledge that the perpetrator is punished. But because crime is an offense against society as a whole, it is society, and not the victim, that determines the perpetrator's guilt and the appropriate level of punishment. Moreover, decisions about the seriousness of the offense are based on the offender's moral culpability, not on the degree of harm suffered by the victim.

Three basic questions usually arise in considering approaches to punishment: who should be punished, how much should they be punished, and why should they be punished? The real debate in desert theory concerns the third question: why punish? The tension among desert theorists—like the skepticism of critics of retribution—is grounded in a deep discomfort with vengeance. Revenge, some fear, will lead to a downward spiral of violence and recrimination. * * *

Desert theorists have responded to the "vengeance problem" in several ways. Some have sought to prove that retribution and vengeance are not the same thing, or that retribution can be justified without reliance on the concept of revenge. Other theorists, notably Susan Jacoby, have sought to rehabilitate the concept of revenge itself. Jacoby argues that we should recognize that criminal justice is based on revenge and stop pretending that "justice and vengeance have nothing, perish the uncivilized thought, to do with each other." Law serves to channel vengeance, thereby both discouraging less controlled forms of victims' justice, such as vigilantism, and restoring the moral and social equilibrium that was violently disturbed by the offender. * * *

The problem with such intuition-based arguments for retribution is that not everyone shares the desire to punish. * * * As [Carlos] Nino argues, retributivism "presupposes that it is sometimes appropriate to redress one evil with another evil. However, when I add the evil of the crime to the evil of the punishment . . . my moral arithmetic leads me consistently [to] believe that we have 'two evils' rather than 'one good.' "

B. Deterrence

The term "deterrence" is often used interchangeably with "prevention." In fact, deterrence is only one way to prevent crime. Under deterrence theory, potential offenders may still be *capable* of committing crimes (since they are not incapacitated) and may still *desire* to commit crimes (since they are not rehabilitated). But despite their capacity and desire, potential offenders are inhibited by the "intimidation or terror of the law." There are two main types of deterrence: individual deterrence and general deterrence. Individual deterrence seeks to prevent future crime by setting sentences that are strict enough to ensure that a particular offender will not reoffend. General deterrence, on the other hand, attempts to prevent crime by "inducing other citizens who might be tempted to commit crime to desist out of fear of the penalty." Notably, deterrence theory does not allow, much less require, the punishment of all who are guilty. Moreover, general deterrence does not even require punishment of all those who might be deterrable as individuals. If exemplary punishments adequately prevent future crime, they are sufficient.

Deterrence occurs, writes Nigel Walker, when people refrain from certain actions because they fear the possible consequences of those actions. In other words, the potential benefit of committing crime is outweighed by the risk of sanctions. Deterrence thus assumes that, were it not for the possibility of adverse consequences, people would engage in crime. "A person is not deterred," writes Walker, "if he refrains because he is not tempted, or is tempted but restrained by his code of manners or morals." Deterrence also assumes that the potential offender will undertake a two-part calculation, assessing both the gravity of the consequences and the likelihood of getting caught. This calculation is based not on the objective severity of sanctions or the real risk of apprehension, but on the potential offender's subjective assessment of these factors. Thus, the effectiveness of any deterrent depends on the potential offender's perception of possible sanctions, and on her assessment of her ability to evade law enforcement. The actual severity or certainty of punishment is less important than its perceived severity or certainty.

While the logic of deterrence is intuitively appealing, the available empirical evidence regarding the effectiveness of deterrence in domestic criminal justice systems is inconclusive. There are several possible reasons for this. First, it is difficult to prove that threats of legal sanctions, rather than other motivations, have prevented people from offending. "Marginal deterrence," the amount by which deterrence increases or decreases based on changes in the severity of sanctions, is particularly difficult to demonstrate. The problem is not in showing that deterrence can occur when punishment is certain, swift, and severe, but in determining when and to what extent it occurs under real-world conditions, under which punishment is never certain, rarely swift, and only sometimes severe. Second, effectiveness depends on context. The risk of detection and punishment must not be so low as to be readily discounted, and the penalty must be adequately publicized. Moreover, the offender and the crime must be deterrable; that is, they must be rational. Heightened enforcement and increased sanctions may reduce crimes that reflect rational choices, but they are unlikely to have an impact on irrational offenders. Deterrence, then, only works in relation to some crimes and some offenders.

C. Rehabilitation

Rehabilitation seeks to prevent the future commission of crime by curing previous offenders of their criminal tendencies. Thus, the success of rehabilitation is measured by recidivism rates, rather than by changes in the aggregate incidence of crime. There are two possible reasons for wanting to "cure" the offender. First, one might argue that society will be safer once the offender is rehabilitated and is no longer committing crimes. Second, one could believe that offenders should be given the opportunity to have productive lives for their own sake. Rehabilitation de-emphasizes the link between the gravity of the crime and the severity of the sentence. Appropriate rehabilitative sentences reflect the measures necessary to reintegrate a particular offender into the community. Once an offender has been rehabilitated, further punishment is unnecessary. Strict proportionality is not required; among offenders who commit the same crime, some will take longer than others to rehabilitate.

The primary objection raised by critics of rehabilitation is that it simply does not work. Even researchers who favor rehabilitation believe that treatment programs are effective only with certain types of offenders. Other critics argue that rehabilitation denigrates human dignity. Still others attack the allegedly benevolent purpose of rehabilitation, since rehabilitative regimes may in fact inflict a greater deprivation of liberty on their subjects than avowedly punitive programs.

D. Restorative Justice

Two major paradigms fall within the rubric of restorative justice. The first focuses on compensating victims and views crime as a harm that criminal justice should seek to undo. Under this view, the purpose of punishment is to repair injuries to victims, and thus the goal of criminal justice is for the offender to provide restitution to the victim. The second paradigm envisions crime as conflict and criminal justice as a form of conflict resolution. The basic assumptions of this approach are:

(1) Crime is primarily a conflict among individuals resulting in injuries to victims, communities and the offenders themselves; only secondarily is it law-breaking.

(2) The overarching aim of the criminal justice process should be to reconcile parties while repairing the injuries caused by crime.

(3) The criminal justice process should facilitate active participation by victims, offenders and their communities. It should not be dominated by the government to the exclusion of others.

Under this view, the goal of criminal justice is the reconciliation of the offender, victim, and community.

These two paradigms, compensation and conflict resolution, are often linked. An apology without restitution may mean little; if a friend apologizes for taking a pen but does not return it, her statement is worthless. "Apologies set the record straight; restitution sets out to make a new record," explains theologian Donald Shriver. Yet conflict resolution cannot rest on compensation alone, particularly since it is often impossible to restore to the victim what she has lost or repair the harm that she has suffered. While a stolen pen can be replaced, a murdered child cannot.

Restorative justice differs from retribution, deterrence and rehabilitation in its focus on the victim. Restorative justice raises questions about the identities of the parties to the conflict. In other words, it asks whose interests are relevant to the case. In the West, crimes are defined as offenses against the state; in this way, as Nils Christie argues, the state has stolen conflicts from victims, communities and offenders. "Virtually every facet of the criminal justice system works to reduce victims, offenders and communities to passive participants," notes Daniel Van Ness. Restorative justice aims to return conflicts to the parties to the conflict. Yet the idea that crimes are offenses against society at large should not be ignored, for offenders harm not only specific victims but also entire societies. Thus, restorative justice must consider the interests of both the individual victim and the wider community.

Theoretically, the compensatory paradigm of restorative justice is somewhat disconnected from culpability, since the degree of harm caused may not reflect the blameworthiness of the offender. Proportionality in this context is based on the amount of harm inflicted on the victim, not the maliciousness of the offender's intent. The conflict resolution paradigm, on the other hand, is more likely adequately to address culpability; a victim will be angrier at someone who hits her intentionally than at someone who does so accidentally, and will require more of the offender in order to resolve the conflict.

E. Communication/Condemnation/Social Solidarity

For Emile Durkheim, punishment is a form of moral communication used to express condemnation and strengthen social solidarity. Durkheim argues that the "true function [of punishment] is to maintain social cohesion intact." Crimes, according to Durkheim, are acts that violate a society's fundamental moral code of sacred norms, thereby weakening those norms. Punishment plays a critical role in preventing the collapse of the moral order by limiting the "demoralizing" effects of crime. Punishment also functions as a collective response that demonstrates and reaffirms the real force of the common moral order. By punishing, a society expresses its shared moral outrage, strengthening and reinforcing the norms of social life. Punitive rituals, by articulating shared sentiments, help to reflect and sustain a society's moral values, thereby strengthening the bonds of community. For Durkheim, sanctioning offenders is a way to communicate the continuing validity of the law, a "language" which "expresses the feeling inspired by the disapproved behaviour." Thus the two central premises of the "Durkheimian school" of thought are that punishment communicates social condemnation, and that it therefore plays a role in reaffirming, or even creating, social identity and/or social solidarity.

In examining the Durkheimian school, three points are worth noting. First, to argue that punishment is a form of communication sheds no light on the message being conveyed. Different forms of punishment communicate different messages and produce different forms of social solidarity. Moreover, because other approaches to criminal justice rely on the communication of particular messages, like those of deterrence or moral reformation, the communicative paradigm is intertwined with, though conceptually distinct from, the theories discussed above.

Second, in describing the impact of punishment on the construction of social identity, Durkheimian theorists focus on why a society punishes, not why a society *says* it punishes. After all, in adopting purpose provisions for penal codes, legislatures do not express a desire to shore up the social order, but rather use the language of retribution, deterrence, rehabilitation, or restorative justice. Moreover, descriptions of the consequences of punishment for social control or identity do not explain why one *should* punish. David Garland may well be right that punishment is sometimes used to express and construct the dominant moral order. But the idea that ruling elites employ punishment as a way to establish the legitimacy of their social vision is not an affirmative reason to punish.

Third, if punishment is imposed in order to express societal reprobation, then condemnation, not punitive treatment, is the central goal. Under this view, while a prisoner-of-war camp may be harsher than a prison, such incarceration does not constitute "punishment," since it is not an expression of social condemnation. If one punishes in order to communicate moral values, it matters less that offenders pay for their misdeeds, than it does that society finds a way of adequately expressing its disapproval. Prosecuting and sanctioning offenders is an important way of communicating reprobation, but it is not the only one. If one justifies punishment as a means of communication, one must explain why punitive sanctions are the most appropriate form of censure.

NOTES & QUESTIONS

1. Criminal Trials

Societies in transition often aim to achieve truth, justice, reconciliation, stability, and peace. Are criminal trials too "blunt" an instrument for such purposes? Might criminal trials actually hinder the attainment of some of these goals? The issues raised here are often simplified into a question of peace versus justice. Can a peaceful society be sustained without justice or is justice essential for a true transition from a history of violence? Are there ways to sequence responses to mass violence that allow for an immediate response, but postpone traditional justice mechanisms? As you proceed through this casebook, consider the way in which the cases presented might impact a society emerging from repression or war. Is the particular prosecution likely to encourage or hinder reconciliation and peace?

2. Duty to Prosecute

Some scholars have argued that international law no longer offers states the choice as to whether to prosecute serious international criminal law violations. Consider this argument:

> [T]he central importance of the rule of law in civilized societies requires, within defined but principled limits, prosecution of especially atrocious crimes. [I]nternational law itself helps assure the survival of fragile democracies when its clear pronouncement removes certain atrocious crimes from the provincial realm of a country's internal politics and thereby places those crimes squarely within the scope of universal concern and the conscience of all civilized people.
>
> [R]ecently developed principles of international law, both customary and conventional, already impose significant obligations in this regard. * * * [T]hree comprehensive human rights treaties that do not explicitly require States Parties to prosecute violations nonetheless impose a general duty to investigate allegations of torture, extra-legal killings, and forced disappearances, and, subject to evidentiary and other legitimate constraints, to prosecute those who are responsible. A state's complete failure to punish repeated or notorious instances of these offenses violates its obligations under customary international law.
>
> These duties represent a departure from the traditional approach of international human rights law. While it has long been recognized that international law requires states to respect and

> ensure human rights, that same law has generally allowed governments to determine how their obligations will be fulfilled. But the measures used to secure human rights are no longer subject to the broad discretion of governments when it comes to a core set of fundamental rights that merit special protection. When torture, disappearances, and illegal killings occur, governments must make good-faith efforts to bring the wrongdoers to justice. * * * [T]he treaty and customary obligations to punish atrocious crimes are consistent with a limited program of prosecutions, but would be breached by wholesale impunity. Prosecutions of those most responsible for designing and implementing a past system of state violence or for the most notorious violations would best comport with common standards of justice.

Diane F. Orentlicher, *Settling Accounts: The Duty to Prosecute Human Rights Violations of a Prior Regime*, 100 YALE L.J. 2537, 2540–1 (1991).

The late Carlos Nino, an Argentine legal philosopher, provided a response to Orentlicher's argument using the case of Argentina, where some limited prosecutions occurred after the collapse of the military regime in 1983 until pressure from the military led to the establishment of a series of laws curtailing prosecutions (including an amnesty law and a "full stop" law putting an end date on prosecutions). He argued:

> [Orentlicher's] theoretical discussion does not sufficiently account for the varied and often quite difficult realities successor governments must face. Orentlicher concentrates on questions of morals and law, and infers some conclusions about [a] duty selectively to prosecute past violations of human rights. But the problem of inferring those conclusions is not so much related to moral or legal normative premises, but to factual ones which also condition the conclusions. I believe that Orentlicher leaves aside some relevant circumstances that successor governments may confront and that are crucial in deciding whether to prosecute human rights violations. * * *
>
> Beginning with the moral dimension, the extent of the duty of a government selectively to prosecute past human rights abuses depends, of course, on the theory that underlies the justification of punishment. Only the theory of mandatory retribution—the view that every crime should be meted out by a proportional punishment, whatever the consequences of the policy—has implications different from the rest. In other places, I have described the irrationality and moral difficulty of this view of punishment. Though it is true that many people approach the issue of human rights violations with a strong retributive impulse, almost all who think momentarily about the issue are not prepared to defend a policy of punishing those abuses once it becomes clear that such a policy would probably provoke, by a causal chain, similar or even worse abuses. One might be a retributivist of the permissive variety, holding that a past wrong makes the criminal lose his immunity from punishment, but whether the state is

morally obligated to punish him depends on the consequences of that punishment. * * *

Of course there are valuable consequences of punishment, for instance, to deter similar deeds by demonstrating that no group is above the law, or to consolidate a democracy which presupposes respect for the rule of law. But prosecutions may have some limit and must be counterbalanced with the aim of preserving the democratic system. This last caveat is all the more sensible once we realize that the preservation of the democratic system is a prerequisite of those very prosecutions and the loss of it is a necessary antecedent to massive violation of human rights. Mandatory retribution, which values punishment above all else, raises the issue of whether equality before the law is infringed when the need to protect valuable institutions, like democracy, leads to a selection of the agents who will be prosecuted for human rights abuses. The position that there is such an infringement of the requirement of equality presupposes mandatory retribution as the correct view of punishment. * * *

As a last preliminary matter, there remains some reference to the premises related to law, in this case to international law. * * * Ultimately, a necessary criterion for the validity of any norm of positive law, including positive international law, is the willingness of the governing institutions, in this case states and international bodies, to enforce it. Orentlicher has not shown sufficiently that this is the case with the norm which supposedly establishes the duty of successor governments to selectively prosecute past violations of human rights. Orentlicher's arguments are stronger if we interpret them as stating propositions about how international law should be reformed or developed rather than about what already exists.

Carlos S. Nino, *The Duty to Punish Past Abuses of Human Rights Put Into Context: The Case of Argentina*, 100 YALE L.J. 2619, 2619–22 (1991). For more on Argentina's transition, *see* Carlos S. Nino, RADICAL EVIL ON TRIAL (1996). Does a failure to prosecute create a culture of impunity that enables violations to continue, or can nations "draw a thick line" after a repressive past and launch a democratic future without prosecutions? How might a transitional society suffer without criminal trials? How might such a society suffer with them? Do you agree with Nino's more consequentialist approach to criminal punishment? In other words, do you think it is justified for a country to forego prosecutions if they may lead to resistance from, for example, the military in a way that might threaten a transition to democracy?

3. Deterrence

Will criminal justice deter international crimes or are such crimes immune from deterrence effects? Consider the following:

The focus of punishment should be the prevention of such deliberately induced aberrant contexts, within which habitually

> lawful social relations degenerate into unrestrained violence. * * * Where leaders engage in some form of rational cost-benefit calculation, the threat of punishment can increase the costs of a policy that is criminal under international law. Leaders may be desperate, erratic, or even psychotic, but incitement to ethnic violence is usually aimed at the acquisition and sustained exercise of power. * * * Momentary glory and political ascendancy, to be followed by downfall and humiliation, are considerably less attractive than long-term political viability. Furthermore, in an integrated world community, international legitimacy is a valuable asset for aspiring statesmen, no matter how remote their fiefdoms may be. Even an isolated Somali or Afghan warlord cannot entirely disregard the relation between international acceptance and long-term survival. The stigmatization associated with indictment, as much as apprehension and prosecution, may significantly threaten the attainment of sustained political power.

Payam Akhavan, *Beyond Impunity: Can International Criminal Justice Prevent Future Atrocities?*, 95 AM. J. INT'L. L. 7, 11–13 (2001). In Akhavan's view, international criminal prosecutions can stigmatize ethnic cleansing and similar acts, and thus contribute to bringing about a culture of "habitual lawfulness," such that persecutions and atrocities do not present themselves as real alternatives to peaceful multiethnic coexistence. *Id.* at 12. Akhavan argues that "it is not necessary . . . to punish a large number of perpetrators in order to achieve deterrence." Instead, "[t]he punishment of particular individuals—whether star villains such as Karadžić or Mladić or ordinary perpetrators such as Tadić and Erdemović—becomes an instrument through which respect for the rule of law is instilled into the popular consciousness." Payam Akhavan, *Justice in the Hague, Peace in the Former Yugoslavia?*, 20 HUM. RTS. Q. 737, 746, 748 (1999).

Consider the following counterpoint:

> Actual experience with efforts at deterrence is not encouraging. During the course of World War II, the Allies made the prosecution of German and Japanese leaders a major war aim. Beginning in 1941, the United States and the United Kingdom issued a series of highly publicized warnings that violations of the laws of war would be punished, and that superior orders would not be accepted as a defense. * * * Similarly, in the former Yugoslavia, the Security Council and various individual states repeatedly warned combatants that those committing atrocities would eventually be prosecuted. But, as Professor Theodor Meron has observed, "there is no empirical evidence of effective deterrence in either case." * * * Even if we assume that those committing atrocities engage in rational cost-benefit calculations (weighing the risk of prosecution against the personal and political gain of continued participation in ethnic cleansing and similar acts), most probably view the risk of prosecution as slight. * * * For most offenders, especially low-ranking offenders, the risk of prosecution

> must appear to be almost the equivalent of losing the war crimes prosecution lottery. * * *
>
> Even if successful, the contribution of such mass prosecutions to deterrence is uncertain at best. Members of the Hutu community [in Rwanda] may well view such prosecutions as illegitimate, a case of "victor's justice." If so, prosecutions may do more to fuel inter-ethnic tensions than to promote national reconciliation, and a shift in the political fortunes of the ethnic communities in Rwanda might lead to a catastrophic renewal of hostilities. * * * [T]he vast majority of combatants in Bosnia were probably more or less representative of the civilian population of the communities from which they came. They understood in general terms the limits imposed on warfare by international humanitarian law. They accepted the legitimacy of such norms, and they believed that such norms should generally be followed. But at the same time, most did not view their own actions—even when they involved attacks on civilians—to be wrongful.

David Wippman, *Atrocities, Deterrence, and the Limits of International Justice*, 23 FORDHAM INT'L L. J. 473, 474, 476–7, 483, 477 (1999). Professor and Judge Meron elsewhere has written: "Instead of despairing over the prospects of deterrence, the international community should enhance the probability of punishment by encouraging prosecutions before national courts, especially of third states, by making *ad hoc* Tribunals effective and by establishing a vigorous, standing international criminal court." Theodor Meron, *From Nuremberg to the Hague*, 149 MIL. L. REV. 107, 110–11 (1995).

For a critical response and a discussion of the potential of the ICC to exert a deterrent effect, *see* James F. Alexander, *The International Criminal Court and the Prevention of Atrocities: Predicting the Court's Impact*, 54 VILLANOVA L. REV. 1 (2009). Alexander identifies five ways that the ICC might contribute to deterrence:

1) By exerting a general deterrent effect on potential perpetrators (which depends on the certainty and severity of punishment and the "rationality" of relevant actors);
2) By inspiring domestic courts to investigate and prosecute offenders pursuant to the principle of complementarity;
3) By incapacitating or sidelining the accused;
4) By displacing "self-help" efforts to achieve justice, individualizing collective guilt, and developing a reliable historical record; and
5) By serving as a tool for global moral education.

For more on the general theory of deterrence, *see* Johannes Andenæs, *The General Preventive Effects of Punishment*, 114 U. PA. L. REV. 949 (1966).

Political scientists Hyeran Jo and Beth Simmons present empirical evidence of a deterrent effect of various types of ICC action in (1) governments that depend on aid relationships and (2) rebel groups with secessionist or governance goals. They posit that the ICC exerts a moderating effect through both prosecutorial deterrence (where the threat of legal retribution changes actors' behavioral calculi) and social deterrence (where support for accountability signals potential social costs to would-be perpetrators). These effects are stronger in countries with established governmental or non-governmental human rights institutions. *See* Hyeran Jo & Beth A. Simmons, *Can the International Criminal Court Deter Atrocity*?, 70 INT'L ORG. 443 (2016).

4. Deterrence in Practice: The Sudan

In 2005, the U.N. Security Council referred the situation in Darfur since 2002 to the ICC with Resolution 1593. In 2009, the ICC indicted President Omar Al Bashir of the Sudan and several other government officials, including Ahmad Muhammad Harun, who was Minister of Humanitarian Affairs until he was appointed Governor of South and then North Kordofan state. In response, President Al Bashir mobilized African and Arab leaders on his behalf and expelled a number of aid groups from the Sudan. Meanwhile, clashes between government troops and rebels flared up in South Kordofan, one of the so-called "Two Areas" wracked by violence in southern Sudan since 2011. A video of Harun suggests that he ordered Sudanese troops to take no prisoners. At the same time, civilians in Darfur were again under attack by government forces, notwithstanding the presence of a joint United Nations-African Union peacekeeping mission there (UNAMID). Indicted Sudanese rebel leaders have turned themselves in to the ICC in order to contest the charges against them; by contrast, all indicted government officials remain the subject of warrants for their arrest. Until recently, President Al Bashir continued to travel internationally, including to ICC member states, some of whom claimed he enjoyed immunity (discussed in Chapter 17 on Defenses) although his freedom of movement had been significantly constrained.

Months of street protests against Al Bashir and the deteriorating economic conditions produced by his autocratic rule culminated in a military coup on April 11, 2019. Al Bashir is currently being detained in the Sudan by the transitional military council (TMC) that is currently in power. Calls to hand him over to the ICC for prosecution have gone unheeded, and he is currently facing corruption charges in the Sudan. Shortly after taking power, the TMC brutally suppressed peaceful protesters calling for justice and a return to civilian rule. Some estimate that as many as 200 people have been killed in protest-related violence. As of July 2019 members of the opposition and the TMC have negotiated a power-sharing deal that promise elections and the return to civilian rule within three years. Harun has been arrested on corruption charges. Given the current circumstances, do the Sudanese cases better support the argument of Akhavan or Wippman? Can the ICC possibly exert a deterrent impact in the absence of a police force or concerted international movement to arrest fugitives? Why might Sudan be willing to pursue a corruption case against Harun but not charge him with international crimes?

5. Creating an Historical Record

Are criminal trials good mechanisms for creating or preserving an historical record? Or, should such tasks be assigned to truth commissions, non-judicial commissions of inquiry, or academics? Consider this view:

> The issues before a court, no matter how broad their potential impact on society, are framed in a microcosm: the resolution of a dispute between one party and another. For it is only in concrete, specific factual situations that a court issues its rulings on the law. * * * Both lawyers and historians are trained in the investigation and analysis of facts. Within this commonality, however, significant differences emerge. Because of evidentiary limitations, attorneys focus on primary sources—eyewitnesses and contemporaneous documents. While historians use these sources, they are comfortable examining secondary sources as well. Historians can debate facts for years, in books, reviews, articles and conferences, while lawyers have a specific time period, usually quite short, within which to gather their factual evidence. Lawyers, as noted, approach facts as zealous advocates for the point of view that would be in their client's best interest. Historians, on the other hand, aspire to a more objective approach, although whether or not they achieve it is open to question. Most importantly, the legal process is characterized by a judge or jury whose function is to resolve the factual debate. In a legal case, the judge or jury "finds" the facts based on what is presented by the parties. This becomes the official version of the facts, at least as far as the judicial system is concerned. There is no comparable process to resolve historical debate.

Stephen Whinston, *Can Lawyers Be Good Historians?: A Critical Examination of the Siemens Slave-Labor Cases*, 20 BERK. J. INT'L L. 160, 161–162 (2002) (discussing slave labor and other WWII civil cases brought in U.S. courts).

6. Preventing Atrocities

In 2011, U.S. President Obama issued U.S. Presidential Study Directive 10 (PSD-10), which declared that "Preventing mass atrocities and genocide is a core national security interest and a core moral responsibility of the United States" and ordered the creation of an inter-agency Atrocities Prevention Board (APB). This Directive reflects the fact that while past administrations have committed to the system of international justice and to the prosecution of perpetrators of international crimes, not enough has been done to prevent atrocities from happening in the first place. The APB was charged with coordinating a whole-of-government approach to preventing and mitigating mass atrocities and genocide. It met on a monthly basis to identify and address specific atrocity threats and to oversee institutional changes that are designed to make the U.S. government more nimble and effective. These include the creation of a National Intelligence Estimate on the risk of mass atrocities around the world based on early warning factors and known trigger events (such as elections or natural disasters). The Department of the Treasury was tasked with better utilizing its existing sanctioning tools to block the flow of money to abusive regimes and perpetrators of mass atrocities, and to develop new sanctions authorities that can target groups and individuals fomenting violence. The Department of Defense integrated the prevention of atrocities into its doctrine and planning. The Department of State undertook multilateral, regional, and bilateral efforts with a particular focus on the African Union and Latin America, where governments are building regional networks around the atrocity prevention imperative.

Finally, the PSD-10 report recommended that the United States increase assistance to justice mechanisms domestically and internationally to ensure that the international and hybrid tribunals had the personnel, resources, and evidence they need to discharge their mandates. The PSD-10 report also mandated that the United States help build domestic prosecutorial capacity at home and abroad in keeping with the principle of complementarity. President Trump has retained the APB, but it is less active. As you review the U.S. penal law discussed in this text, consider areas of reform that would be consistent with the PSD-10 report. Why might it be easier for the international community to respond to atrocities after they have occurred than to work towards prevention?

7. For Further Reading

On the issue of transitional justice, *see* Priscilla Hayner, UNSPEAKABLE TRUTHS: TRANSITIONAL JUSTICE AND THE CHALLENGE OF TRUTH COMMISSIONS (2nd ed. 2011); M. Cherif Bassiouni, THE CHICAGO PRINCIPLES ON POST-CONFLICT JUSTICE (2007); TRUTH V. JUSTICE: THE MORALITY OF TRUTH COMMISSIONS (Robert I. Rotberg and Dennis Thompson eds., 2000); FEMINIST PERSPECTIVES ON TRANSITIONAL JUSTICE (Martha Albertson Fineman and Estelle Zinsstag eds., 2013); ASSESSING THE IMPACT OF TRANSITIONAL JUSTICE: CHALLENGES FOR EMPIRICAL RESEARCH 115, 122 (Hugo Van Der Merwe et al. eds., 2009); Mark Drumbl, ATROCITY, PUNISHMENT, AND INTERNATIONAL LAW (2007); Martha Minow, BETWEEN VENGEANCE AND FORGIVENESS: FACING HISTORY AFTER GENOCIDE AND MASS VIOLENCE (1998); ACCOUNTABILITY FOR ATROCITIES: NATIONAL AND INTERNATIONAL RESPONSES (Jane E. Stromseth ed., 2003); Ruti Teitel, TRANSITIONAL JUSTICE (2000). More generally see issues of the specialty journal, THE INTERNATIONAL JOURNAL OF TRANSITIONAL JUSTICE, published by Oxford University Press, and the reports published by the International Center for Transitional Justice, which can be found on their website. On the objectives of the criminal law, *see* Larry Alexander, *The Philosophy of Criminal Law, in* THE OXFORD HANDBOOK OF JURISPRUDENCE AND PHILOSOPHY OF LAW 815 (Jules Coleman & Scott Shapiro eds., 2002); Henry M. Hart, Jr., *The Aims of the Criminal Law*, 23 LAW & CONTEMPORARY PROBLEMS 401 (1958).

PROBLEM

Imagine that you are a senior legal adviser to the U.S. Department of War (which eventually became the Department of Defense) in 1945. Various

German units around Europe began capitulating in April of that year. Following the German military's unconditional surrender on May 7, the Allies are holding millions of German prisoners in so-called *Rheinwiesenlager* ("Rhine meadow camps"), which are often over-crowded and lacking in essential services. Thousands more soldiers are surrendering around Europe, including almost a million German soldiers from the Eastern Front. Detainees have been designated "Disarmed Enemy Forces" rather than "Prisoners of War," because the Allies fear that they cannot adhere to the provisions of the 1929 Geneva Convention governing POWs.

Among those surrendering are Hermann Göring and other high-ranking Nazi leaders, although Hitler and Goebbels have committed suicide. Other Nazi leaders, such as Admiral Karl Dönitz—whom Hitler, in his last will and testament, designated as his successor—have been arrested or captured. Many other SS and Nazi officers are trying to escape through "ratlines" across Spain and elsewhere. The Allies have also discovered and liberated dozens of concentration and extermination (or death) camps around Europe; others (including Treblinka) were destroyed by the Germans as the war began to turn against the Axis powers. Millions of people have been displaced around the continent; some were deported, others fled oncoming troops.

With the signing of the Declaration Regarding the Defeat of Germany and the Assumption of Supreme Authority by the Allied Powers on June 5, the Allies have assumed full governing authority (including at the state and local level) within Germany. They created the Allied Control Council to manage the occupation and this joint authority. The Japanese surrender will not occur until August 1945, and the Allies will face similar challenges in the Pacific theater.

The Secretary of War has asked you to outline a postwar plan for addressing the range of crimes and atrocities committed during World War II. What options exist? How will you deal with the German military and civilian leadership versus the rank and file? What about the various Nazi organizations, such as the SS (*Schutzstaffel*) paramilitary organization and the Gestapo secret police? How will you address the rehabilitation of victims? What precedents can you draw upon for inspiration? What legal framework should govern any post-war program of justice and accountability?

PART II

JURISDICTION

This part introduces the rules governing jurisdiction over international crimes, as well as the various institutions before which principles of international criminal law may be applied or interpreted. This material highlights the variety of international, hybrid, regional, and domestic institutions that currently interpret international criminal law, and thus the bodies of jurisprudence to which a litigant or judge may look for ascertaining the applicable substantive law.

Jurisdiction is most usefully divided into three dimensions: prescriptive, adjudicative, and enforcement. Jurisdiction to prescribe relates to the power of a state to enact substantive laws (generally by its legislature, but also by administrative agencies) to regulate criminal conduct. Many states have enacted statutes that penalize international crimes, regardless of where such crimes are committed. Jurisdiction to adjudicate relates to the authority of a state to subject persons accused of the commission of crimes—regardless of whether those crimes are defined by national or international law—to its judicial processes. In the realm of international criminal law, some states will allow for the investigation and/or prosecution of international crimes to commence even when the suspected perpetrator has no links to the forum. Jurisdiction to enforce concerns a state's power to compel a person to comply with its law and to appear for a judicial process.

International criminal law implicates all three species of jurisdiction. For example, many states incorporate the international prohibition against torture into their domestic law, and empower their courts to prosecute perpetrators who are present in the territory (see *infra* Chapter 11 on Torture). Although the extent to which a state exercises each form of jurisdiction with respect to extraterritorial conduct is often a function of municipal law, international law may place some limits on the exercise of domestic forms of jurisdiction. The impact of these international law rules on the exercise of jurisdiction by a particular state is often a function of the authority accorded international law in general in the domestic legal system. For example, the rules of public international law generally prohibit states from exercising their enforcement jurisdiction within the territory of another state without permission. That said, there are certain exceptions for situations of hot pursuit, and some states have engaged in "snatch and grab" operations without significant sanction.

International and quasi-international tribunals apply a mixture of international and domestic law according to applicable rules set forth in their constitutive statutes. The establishment of the various international and quasi-international criminal tribunals has also occasioned the development of nascent rules allocating jurisdictional authority as between international and domestic tribunals. Some international tribunals assert primacy over any concurrent domestic prosecution, while others are subordinate to domestic assertions of adjudicative jurisdiction. Thus, the International Criminal Tribunal for the Former Yugoslavia (ICTY) and the International Criminal Tribunal for Rwanda (ICTR) claimed primacy over domestic courts by virtue of their creation pursuant to Chapter VII of the UN Charter. The ICC, by contrast, will generally defer to domestic prosecutions under the doctrine of complementarity. (See Rome Statute Art. 17, and the discussion *infra* in Chapter 2 on International Jurisdiction.) The enforcement jurisdiction of international and quasi-international tribunals depends not only on their origins, but also on the amount of political support they enjoy among relevant states and the level of cooperation they receive.

Most prosecutions of international criminal law occur in domestic courts. In fact the International Criminal Court's (ICC) complementarity provisions are designed to ensure that this continues to be the case. In contrast to the vertical allocation of jurisdiction between international and domestic authorities, the horizontal allocation of jurisdiction between states remains subject to diplomatic negotiation rather than firm international rules or norms. Although public international law contains some rules allocating legal authority among states, clear standards or procedures to resolve simultaneous assertions of jurisdiction where jurisdiction is concurrent between multiple domestic fora are lacking. For example, a transaction or incident may involve parties hailing from different states, produce effects in different states, or injure parties affiliated with different states. Under such circumstances, questions may arise about which states are empowered to regulate the transnational conduct in question and which state's assertion of adjudicative jurisdiction should be given primacy. With the increase in claims to extraterritorial jurisdiction over international crimes, states and other interested parties have begun grappling with identifying principles—such as subsidiarity, exhaustion of local remedies, and *forum non conveniens*—to help guide this inquiry. The extent to which international law has developed rules for prioritizing certain jurisdictional bases over others is the subject of Chapter 3 on Domestic Jurisdiction.

Finally, hybrid courts occupy a middle ground between international and domestic institutions. They are meant to address some of the weaknesses of purely international and purely national courts. With their roots in the place where the crimes occurred, hybrid tribunals tend not to suffer from the remoteness of international tribunals. They are thus generally more accessible to victims, witnesses, and others, and at least in theory have more legitimacy than a purely international court. At the same time they avoid some of the weaknesses of purely domestic courts, such as capture by local interests, lack of capacity (particularly found in societies emerging out of mass atrocity), and lack of international legitimacy. While we, along with others, thought that hybrid tribunals were declining in importance, a recent resurgence of hybrid tribunals—including those now in operation and in the planning stages—underscores the continuing importance of this type of institution, which we introduce in Chapter 4.

This part starts with a chapter on International Jurisdiction that highlights challenges to the exercise of international jurisdiction between the World War II era and the creation of the ICTY in 1993. It then discusses the post-Cold War evolution of international criminal law institution building with the creation of the *ad hoc* criminal tribunals. The next chapter on Domestic Jurisdiction presents several instances in which domestic courts have asserted forms of extraterritorial jurisdiction over international crimes. We then turn to Hybrid Tribunals and highlight some of the advantages and tensions of this unique approach to international criminal justice. Finally, we conclude with the creation and operation of the ICC, the preeminent international institution devoted to the adjudication and interpretation of international criminal law.

CHAPTER 2

INTERNATIONAL JURISDICTION

I. INTRODUCTION

While every indication is that domestic courts will continue to play the primary role in prosecuting international crimes (particularly with the adoption by the ICC's architects of complementarity rather than primacy with respect to domestic jurisdiction), the last three decades have seen a marked shift towards the use of international and hybrid institutions. Since the international criminal law renaissance in the mid-1990s, multiple international and quasi-international tribunals with jurisdiction to prosecute international crimes have been established. While the oldest of those institutions was created almost three decades ago, criminal prosecutions before international tribunals date back at least 500 years. The trial that many point to as the earliest example of an international criminal tribunal is the prosecution of Peter van Hagenbach in 1474 in Breisach, Germany, by a panel of twenty-seven judges from the Holy Roman Empire. Not all agree that the forum in Breisach qualifies as an international tribunal. Georg Schwarzenberger in his classic treatise on international law argues that the Breisach trial involved "quasi-international law," as it took place within the Holy Roman Empire but at a time when the Empire's constituent parts were beginning to secede. Thus, while the prosecution of Hagenbach occurred under the authority of a supreme sovereign (and thus looks like a purely domestic matter), the growing pressures for secession within the Empire made relations among its constituent parts more international than domestic. *See* Georg Schwarzenberger, INTERNATIONAL LAW AS APPLIED BY INTERNATIONAL COURTS: THE LAW OF ARMED CONFLICT (Vol. 2) 462–466 (1968). By modern standards, the Breisach trial presents a troubling precedent as the first international criminal tribunal, because the defendant in that case was reportedly subjected to torture during the investigative phase of the trial. *Id.* at 464.

There are multiple ways that international criminal tribunals have been created in the modern era: for example, by victorious allied powers (Nuremberg and Tokyo); by the U.N. Security Council (International criminal Tribunals for the former Yugoslavia (ICTY) and Rwanda (ICTR)); and by treaty (ICC). The Nuremberg and Tokyo Tribunals are the precursors to the modern international criminal tribunals. Yet, those ancestral tribunals are significantly different in their provenance from the tribunals established in the last two decades. Following upon the establishment of the ICTY and ICTR to address violations of international criminal law that occurred in Yugoslavia and Rwanda, hybrid tribunals have emerged primarily in response to violations elsewhere (e.g., Cambodia, Sierra Leone, Lebanon, Central African

Republic, and Kosovo). Hybrid tribunals have been created primarily by international agreements between the United Nations and the host state. (A nascent tribunal for Kosovo involves the European Union). Up until the creation of the ICC, all of these international and hybrid tribunals have been *ad hoc*. In other words, these pre-ICC tribunals have all been established with a mandate limited in one of three ways: first, to a particular geographical area; second, and in most cases, to a particular period of time; and third, and in some cases, to a particular class of individuals and crimes. Furthermore, these were never expected to be permanent and, indeed, many have been shuttered. The *ad hoc* nature of the earlier courts raised questions about their legitimacy and cost effectiveness. But where can, or should, such claims of illegitimacy be adjudicated? We take up that question below in the context of the post-World War II tribunals and the ICTY.

II. THE WORLD WAR II INTERNATIONAL MILITARY TRIBUNALS

World War II proved to be a watershed in the development of international criminal law. This fertile period heralded the development of two international tribunals for adjudicating claims of international criminal law violations. The International Military Tribunal for the Trial of German Major War Criminals (the IMT or Nuremberg Tribunal) and the International Military Tribunal for the Far East (the IMTFE or Tokyo Tribunal) were established to prosecute high level German and Japanese military and civilian authorities for crimes committed in the context of World War II. At the same time, the codification of the major international crimes began in this post-war period. As you will see throughout this book, the precedents established at this foundational stage retain relevance today.

Both the Nuremberg and Tokyo Tribunals were established with the involvement of the four victorious allied powers: France, the Soviet Union, the United Kingdom, and the United States. The Nuremberg Tribunal was established pursuant to the London Agreement of August 8, 1945. The Tokyo Tribunal emerged from a military order of the U.S. government, although with the acquiescence of the other allied powers. It is notable that neither of these tribunals enjoyed the "consent" of the vanquished state or its polity except insofar as the victors, as occupiers, held German and Japanese sovereignty "in trust" following the war. The British, French, and Soviets were more inclined to punish, and in some cases execute, the defeated officials without legal process. Pressure from the United States resulted in the adoption of a legal procedure to adjudge German and Japanese officials accused of violations of international law. While the Nuremberg and Tokyo trials were not the first instance of the use of law to hold defeated enemies accountable, they are the most prominent examples.

Twenty-four Nazi leaders were indicted before the IMT. One was too ill to stand trial (Gustav Krupp von Boheln); one committed suicide (Robert Ley); and one was tried and convicted to death *in absentia* (Martin Bormann). The other twenty-one were tried before the Tribunal. Three of those were acquitted (Hjalmar Schacht, Franz von Papen, and Hans Fritzsche); seven were sentenced to prison terms ranging from ten years to life (Rudolf Hess, Walter Funk, Karl Dönitz, Erich Raeder, Baldur von Schirach, Albert Speer, and Constantin von Neurath). The other eleven were sentenced to death (Hermann Göring, Joachim von Ribbentrop, Wilhelm Keitel, Ernest Kaltenbrunner, Alfred Rosenberg, Hans Frank, Wilhelm Frick, Julius Streicher, Fritz Saukel, Alfred Jodl, and Arthur Seyss-Inquart). These defendants were all executed except Goering, who committed suicide hours before he was scheduled to be executed. It has been suggested that he accomplished this with the help of a young American guard who, perhaps unwittingly, smuggled a cyanide pill into Goering's cell.

The Chief of Counsel for the United States before the International Military Tribunal at Nuremberg was Justice Robert H. Jackson. Justice Jackson took a one-year leave from his position as Associate Justice of the U.S. Supreme Court to participate in the first truly international prosecution of individuals responsible for war crimes, crimes against humanity, and crimes against peace (what we today call the crime of aggression). In his opening address to the Nuremberg Tribunal, Justice Jackson directly addressed the novelty of creating an international criminal tribunal to prosecute the leaders of a defeated nation. In so doing, he also anticipated criticisms of the post-World War II tribunals, echoes of which are still heard today in connection with efforts to support accountability for violations of international criminal law.

Robert H. Jackson, Chief of Counsel for the United States, Nuremberg Germany, November 21, 1945

May it please Your Honors:

The privilege of opening the first trial in history for crimes against the peace of the world imposes a grave responsibility. The wrongs which we seek to condemn and punish have been so calculated, so malignant, and so devastating, that civilization cannot tolerate their being ignored, because it cannot survive their being repeated. That four great nations, flushed with victory and stung with injury stay the hand of vengeance and voluntarily submit their captive enemies to the judgment of the law is one of the most significant tributes that Power has ever paid to Reason.

This Tribunal, while it is novel and experimental, is not the product of abstract speculations nor is it created to vindicate legalistic theories. This inquest represents the practical effort of four of the most mighty of nations, with the support of 17 more, to utilize international law to meet the greatest menace of our times-aggressive war. The common sense of mankind demands that law shall not stop with the punishment of petty crimes by little people. It must also reach men who possess themselves of great power and make deliberate and concerted use of it to set in motion evils which leave no home in the world untouched. It is a cause of that magnitude that the United Nations will lay before Your Honors. * * *

In justice to the nations and the men associated in this prosecution, I must remind you of certain difficulties which may leave their mark on this case. Never before in legal history has an effort been made to bring within the scope of a single litigation the developments of a decade, covering a whole continent, and involving a score of nations, countless individuals, and innumerable events. Despite the magnitude of the task, the world has demanded immediate action. This demand has had to be met, though perhaps at the cost of finished craftsmanship. To my country, established courts, following familiar procedures, applying well-thumbed precedents, and dealing with the legal consequences of local and limited events seldom commence a trial within a year of the event in litigation. Yet less than 8 months ago today the courtroom in which you sit was an enemy fortress in the hands of German SS troops. Less than 8 months ago nearly all our witnesses and documents were in enemy hands. The law had not been codified, no procedures had been established, no tribunal was in existence, no usable courthouse stood here, none of the hundreds of tons of official German documents had been examined, no prosecuting staff had been assembled, nearly all of the present defendants were at large, and the four prosecuting powers had not yet joined in common cause to try them. I should be the last to deny that the case may well suffer from incomplete researches and quite likely will not be the example of professional work which any of the prosecuting nations would normally wish to sponsor. It is, however, a completely adequate case to the judgment we shall ask you to render, and its full development we shall be obliged to leave to historians.

Before I discuss particulars of evidence, some general considerations which may affect the credit of this trial in the eyes of the world should be candidly faced. There is a dramatic disparity between the circumstances of the accusers and of the accused that might discredit our work if we should falter, in even minor matters, in being fair and temperate.

Unfortunately, the nature of these crimes is such that both prosecution and judgment must be by victor nations over vanquished foes. The worldwide scope of the aggressions carried out by these men has left but few real neutrals. Either the victors must judge the vanquished or we must leave the defeated to judge themselves. After the First World War, we learned the futility of the latter course. The former high station of these defendants, the notoriety of their acts, and the adaptability of their conduct to provoke retaliation make it hard to distinguish between the demand for a just and measured retribution, and the unthinking cry for vengeance which arises from the anguish of war.

It is our task, so far as humanly possible, to draw the line between the two. We must never forget that the record on which we judge these defendants today is the record on which history will judge us tomorrow. To pass these defendants a poisoned chalice is to put it to our own lips as well. We must summon such detachment and intellectual integrity to our task that this Trial will commend itself to posterity as fulfilling humanity's aspirations to do justice.

At the very outset, let us dispose of the contention that to put these men to trial is to do them an injustice entitling them to some special consideration. These defendants may be hard pressed but they are not ill-used. * * * If these men are the first war leaders of a defeated nation to be prosecuted in the name of the law, they are also the first to be given a chance to plead for their lives in the name of the law. Realistically, the Charter of this Tribunal, which gives them a hearing, is also the source of their only hope. It may be that these men of troubled conscience, whose only wish is that the world forget them, do not regard a trial as a favor. But they do have a fair opportunity to defend themselves—a favor which these men, when in power, rarely extended to their fellow countrymen. Despite the fact that public opinion already condemns their acts, we agree that here they must be given a presumption of innocence, and we accept the burden of proving criminal acts and the responsibility of these defendants for their commission. * * *

We would also make clear that we have no purpose to incriminate the whole German people. We know that the Nazi Party was not put in power by a majority of the German vote. We know it came to power by an evil alliance between the most extreme of the Nazi revolutionists, the most unrestrained of the German reactionaries, and the most aggressive of the German militarists. If the German populace had willingly accepted the Nazi program, no Storm-troopers would have been needed in the early days of the Party and there would have been no need for concentration camps or the Gestapo, both of which institutions were inaugurated as soon as the Nazis gained control of the German State. Only after these lawless innovations proved successful at home were they taken abroad.

The German people should know by now that the people of the United States hold them in no fear, and in no hate. * * * The case as presented by the United States will be concerned with the brains and authority back of all the crimes. These defendants were men of a station and rank which does not soil its own hands with blood. They were men who knew how to use lesser folk as tools. We want to reach the planners and designers, the inciters and leaders without whose evil architecture the world would not have been for so long scourged with the violence and lawlessness, and wracked with the agonies and convulsions, of this terrible war. * * *

The end of the war and capture of these prisoners presented the victorious Allies with the question whether there is any legal responsibility on high-ranking men for acts which I have described. Must such wrongs either be ignored or redressed in hot blood? Is there no standard in the law for a deliberate and reasoned judgment on such conduct?

The Charter of this Tribunal evidences a faith that the law is not only to govern the conduct of little men, but that even rulers are, as Lord Chief Justice Coke put it to King James, " 'under God and the law.' " The United States believed that the law long has afforded standards by which a juridical hearing could be conducted to make sure that we punish only the right men and for the right reasons. Following the instructions of the late President Roosevelt and the decision of the Yalta conference President Truman directed representatives of the United States to formulate a proposed International Agreement, which was submitted during the San Francisco Conference to Foreign Ministers of the United Kingdom, the Soviet Union, and the Provisional Government of France. With many modifications, that proposal has become the Charter of this Tribunal.

But the Agreement which sets up the standards by which these prisoners are to be judged does not express the views of the signatory nations alone. Other nations with diverse but highly respected systems of jurisprudence also have signified adherence to it. These are Belgium, The Netherlands, Denmark, Norway, Czechoslovakia, Luxembourg, Poland, Greece, Yugoslavia, Ethiopia, Australia, Haiti, Honduras, Panama, New Zealand, Venezuela, and India. You judge, therefore, under an organic act which represents the wisdom, the sense of justice, and the will of 21 governments, representing an overwhelming majority of all civilized people. * * *

While this declaration of the law by the Charter is final, it may be contended that the prisoners on trial are entitled to have it applied to their conduct only most charitably if at all. It may be said that this is new law, not authoritatively declared at the time they did the acts it condemns, and that this declaration of the law has taken them by surprise.

I cannot, of course, deny that these men are surprised that this is the law; they really are surprised that there is any such thing as law. These defendants did not rely on any law at all. Their program ignored and defied all law. That this is so will appear from many acts and statements, of which I cite but a few.

In the Führer's speech to all military commanders on November 23, 1939 he reminded them that at the moment Germany had a pact with Russia, but declared: "Agreements are to be kept only as long as they serve a certain purpose." Later in the same speech he announced: "A violation of the neutrality of Holland and Belgium will be of no importance." A top-secret document, entitled "Warfare as a Problem of Organization," dispatched by the Chief of the High Command to all commanders on April 19, 1938, declared that "the normal rules of war towards neutrals may be considered to apply on the basis whether operation of rules will create greater advantages or disadvantages for the belligerents." And from the files of the German Navy Staff, we have a "Memorandum on Intensified Naval War," dated October 15, 1939, which begins by stating a desire to comply with International Law. "However," it continues, "if decisive successes are expected from any measure considered as a war necessity, it must be carried through even if it is not in agreement with international law." International law, natural law, German law, any law at all was to these men simply a propaganda device to be invoked when it helped and to be ignored when it would condemn what they wanted to do. That men may be protected in relying upon the law at the time they act is the reason we find laws of retrospective operations unjust. But these men cannot bring themselves within the reason of the rule which in some systems of jurisprudence prohibits *ex post facto* laws. They cannot show that they ever relied upon international law in any state or paid it the slightest regard. * * *

But if it be thought that the Charter, whose declarations concededly bind us all, does contain new law I still do not shrink from demanding its strict application by this Tribunal. The rule of law in the world, flouted by the lawlessness incited by these defendants, had to be restored at the cost to my country of over a million casualties, not to mention those of other nations. I cannot subscribe to the perverted reasoning that society may advance and strengthen the rule of law by the expenditure of morally innocent lives but that progress in the law may never be made at the price of morally guilty lives.

It is true of course, that we have no judicial precedent for the Charter. But international law is more than a scholarly collection of abstract and immutable principles. It is an outgrowth of treaties and agreements between nations and of accepted customs. Yet every custom has its origin in some single act, and every agreement has to be initiated by the action of some state. Unless we are prepared to abandon every principle of growth for international law, we cannot deny that our own day has the right to institute customs and to conclude agreements that will themselves become sources of a newer and strengthened international law. International law is not capable of development by the normal processes of legislation, for there is no continuing international legislative authority. Innovations and revisions in international law are brought about by the action of governments such as those I have cited, designed to meet a change in circumstances. It grows, as did the common law, through decisions reached from time to time in adapting settled principles to new situations. The fact is that when the law evolves by the case method, as did the common law and as international law must do if it is to advance at all, it advances at the expense of those who wrongly guessed the law and learned too late their error. The law, so far as international law can be decreed, had been clearly pronounced when these acts took place. Hence, I am not disturbed by the lack of judicial precedent for the inquiry it is proposed to conduct. * * *

The real complaining party at your bar is Civilization. * * * Civilization asks whether law is so laggard as to be utterly helpless to deal with crimes of this magnitude by criminals of this order of importance. It does not expect that you can make war impossible. It does expect that your juridical action will put the forces of international law, its precepts, its prohibitions and, most of all, its sanctions, on the side of peace, so that men and women of good will, in all countries, may have " 'leave to live by no man's leave, underneath the law'."

NOTES & QUESTIONS

1. The Defendants

Justice Jackson argues that the military tribunal provides an unprecedented benefit to the defendants—the opportunity to defend themselves and justify their actions. Previous armed conflicts often ended with the summary execution of the leaders of the defeated nation. At most, such individuals might have been subject to a show trial, but often there was not even an attempt to pretend that their execution was part of a legal, rather than political, process. How persuasive do you find Justice Jackson's argument that the defendants here are in fact better off than their historical predecessors?

2. The Purpose of Prosecutions

What is the purpose of holding a trial of vanquished leaders? Is it to provide an opportunity for the defendants to justify their actions? Is it to provide a justification for the victorious nations to convict and execute those who wronged them? Can you think of other purposes that may be served by subjecting the vanquished to legal process?

3. The Tokyo Tribunal

While both the German and Japanese defendants challenged the jurisdiction of the respective tribunals, the opinion that is most cited for the controversy surrounding the novel creation of an international criminal tribunal is the dissent filed by Judge R.B. Pal of India before the Far East Tribunal. The judges of the Tribunal had originally agreed that they would issue a single opinion; however, Judge Pal joined the Tribunal later and reserved the right to file a dissenting opinion. In fact, he had apparently prepared to dissent even before the trial had taken place and used his opinion to portray Japan as a liberator of Asia from Western domination and challenge the legitimacy of the whole project. *See* Arnold C. Brackman, THE OTHER NUREMBERG: THE UNTOLD STORY OF THE TOKYO WAR CRIMES TRIALS 71 (1987).

The United States of America v. Akaki, Sadao et al., International Military Tribunal for the Far East, Dissentient Judgment of Justice R.B. Pal (IMTFE)

Reprinted in R. John Pritchard, ed., THE TOKYO MAJOR WAR CRIMES TRIAL: THE RECORDS OF THE INTERNATIONAL MILITARY TRIBUNAL FOR THE FAR EAST, Vol. 105.

[Justice Pal begins his dissent by setting forth the substantive legal issue facing the Tribunal: whether aggressive war was a crime under international law at the time of the acts committed by the Japanese defendants.]

I must dispose of some preliminary matters concerning ourselves. The accused at the earliest possible opportunity expressed their apprehension of injustice in the hands of the Tribunal as at present constituted. The apprehension is that the members of the Tribunal being representatives of the nations which defeated Japan and which are accusers in this action, the accused cannot expect a fair and impartial trial at their hands and consequently the Tribunal as constituted should not proceed with this trial. * * *

[H]ere is an international tribunal for the trial of the present accused. The judges are here no doubt from the different victor nations, but they are here in their personal capacities. * * * The defense took several other objections to the trial; of these the substantial ones may be subdivided under two heads:

Those relating strictly to the jurisdiction of the Tribunal.

Those which, while assuming the jurisdiction of the Tribunal, call on the Tribunal to discharge the accused of the charges contained in several counts on the ground that they do not disclose any offence at all. * * *

The first substantial objection relating to the jurisdiction of the Tribunal is that the crimes triable by this tribunal must be limited to those committed in or in connection with the war which ended in the surrender on 2 September 1945. In my judgment this objection must be sustained. It is preposterous to think that defeat in a war should subject the defeated nation and its nationals to trial for all the delinquencies of their entire existence. There is nothing in the Potsdam Declaration and in the Instrument of Surrender which would entitle the Supreme Commander or the Allied Powers to proceed against the persons who might have committed crimes in or in connection with any other war. * * *

In my opinion, therefore, crimes alleged to have been committed in or in connection with any conflict, hostility, incident or war not forming part of the war which ended in the surrender of the 2nd September, 1945 are outside the jurisdiction of the Tribunal. * * *

I may now take up the material questions of law involved in the case as specified above. These were also raised by the defense in their preliminary objections. The questions are:

(1) Whether a war of the alleged character is [a] crime in international law.

(2) Whether individual members of a State commit a crime in international law by preparing, etc. for such a war.

[Justice Pal then discussed the Prosecutor's argument that the law to be applied against the defendants is to be found in the language of the Charter establishing the Tribunal.]

But whatever be the prosecution view, in my opinion, the criminality or otherwise of the acts alleged must be determined with reference to the rules of international law existing at the date of the commission of the alleged acts. In my opinion, the Charter cannot and has not defined any such crime and has not, in any way, limited our authority and jurisdiction to apply the rules of international law as may be found by us to the facts alleged in this case. * * *

Unconditional surrender implies a complete defeat and an admission of such complete defeat. It imports complete surrender to the might and mercy of the victor. What the vanquished gets, he gets, not by a stipulation, but by the grace of the victor; it does not matter that some indication of the policy to be followed is graciously indicated by the victor even before the formal surrender. Of course, by saying this, I do not mean to say that the defeated party has no protection whatsoever from the whims of the victor's might. International law and usage purport to define the rights and duties of the victor in such a case. However impotent such law may be to afford any real protection, it at least does not legally place the vanquished at the absolute mercy of the victor. * * *

All that I need to point out here is that so far as the terms of the demand of surrender and of the ultimate surrender go there is nothing in them to vest any absolute sovereignty in respect of Japan or of the Japanese people either in the victor nations or in the Supreme Commander. Further there is nothing in them which either expressly or by necessary implication would authorize the victor nations or the Supreme Commander to legislate for Japan and for the Japanese or in respect of war crimes. * * *

Article 5 of the Charter, it is said, defines the different categories of crimes. The article in its plain terms purports only to provide for "jurisdiction over persons and offenses." In so doing the Charter says: "the following acts . . . are crimes coming within the jurisdiction of the Tribunal. . . ." The intention, in my opinion, is not to enact that these acts do constitute crimes but that the crimes, if any, in respect to these acts, would be triable by the Tribunal. Whether or not these acts constitute any crime is left open for determination by the Tribunal with reference to the appropriate law. In my opinion, this is the only possible view that we can take of these provisions of the Charter. The Potsdam Declaration and the Instrument of Surrender certainly did not contemplate that the Allied Powers would have authority to give whatever character they might choose to past acts and then meet such acts with such justice as they might, in the future, determine. It is impossible to read into these instruments any such authority and I cannot for a moment imagine that the Allied Powers would assume such a grave power in violation of the solemn declarations made in them, and perhaps in disregard of international law and usage. I do not see any reason why we should make such an uncharitable assumption against the Allied Powers or against the Supreme Commander when such reading of the Charter is not the only possible reading. * * *

The clear intention is that we are to be "a judicial tribunal" and not "a manifestation of power." The intention is that we are to act as a court of law and act under international law. We are to find out, by the application of the appropriate rules of international law, whether the acts constitute any crime under the already existing law, *dehors* ["outside"] the Declaration, the Agreement or, the Charter. Even if the Charter, the Agreement or the Declaration schedules them as crimes, it would only be the decision of the relevant authorities that they are crimes under the already existing law. But the Tribunal must come to its own decision. It was never intended to bind the Tribunal by the decision of these bodies, for otherwise the Tribunal will not be a "judicial tribunal" but a mere tool for the manifestation of power.

The so called trial held according to the definition of crime now given by the victors obliterates the centuries of civilization which stretch between us and the summary slaying of the defeated in a war. A trial with law thus prescribed will only be a sham employment of legal process for the satisfaction of a thirst for revenge. It does not correspond to any idea of justice. Such a trial may justly create the feeling that the setting up of a tribunal like the present is much more a political than a legal affair, an essentially political objective having thus been cloaked by a juridical appearance. Formalized vengeance can bring only an ephemeral satisfaction, with every probability of ultimate regret; but vindication of law through genuine legal process alone may contribute substantially to the re-establishment of order and decency in international relations.

But that is not the only consideration which influences me to the view I am taking of the Charter in this respect. The contrary view would make the Charter *ultra vires*. * * *

The Allied Powers have nowhere given the slightest indication of their intention to assume any power which does not belong to them in law. It is therefore pertinent to inquire what is the extent of the lawful authority of a victor over the vanquished in international relations. * * * When Lord Wright says that the victors have accurately defined the crime in accordance with the existing international law, he overlooks the fact that if it is not open to the Tribunal to examine this definition with reference to the existing law, it becomes a definition now given by the victor, though it may happen to be a correct definition. In my opinion, such a power is opposed to the principles of international law and it will be a dangerous usurpation of power by the victor, unwarranted by any principle of justice. * * *

Under international law, as it now stands, a victor nation or a union of victor nations would have the authority to establish a tribunal for the trial of war criminals, but no authority to legislate and promulgate a new law of war crimes. When such a nation or group of nations proceeds to promulgate a Charter for the purpose of the trial of war criminals, it does so only under the authority of international law and not in exercise of any sovereign authority. I believe, even in relation to the defeated nationals or to the occupied territory a victor nation is not a sovereign authority. * * *

Prisoners of war, so long as they remain so, are under the protection of international law. No national state, neither the victor nor the vanquished, can make any *ex post facto* law affecting their liability for past acts, particularly when they are placed on trial before an international tribunal. Their own state might try and punish them in its own national court, either already existing or created specially for the purpose; and, even if we assume that for this purpose, it might create some *ex post facto* law binding on such national tribunal, it does not follow that it would have been competent to create law for the application by an international tribunal. So long as the prisoners are placed on trial before an international tribunal, it does not matter whether as prisoners of war, by the victor state, or, as its citizens, by the vanquished state, neither state can legislate so as to give any *ex post facto* law to be applied by that international tribunal in order to determine their crime. Such states might have an option in the matter of setting up the tribunal: they might create a national tribunal for the trial. We are not concerned with what they might or might not have done in defining the law in such a case. But as soon as they set up an international tribunal, they cannot create any law defining the crime for such tribunal. * * *

In my judgment therefore, it is beyond the competence of any victor nation to go beyond the rules of international law as they exist, give new definitions of crimes and then punish the prisoners for having committed offense according to this new definition. This is really not a norm in abhorrence of the retroactivity of law: it is something more substantial. To allow any nation to do that will be to allow usurpation of power which international law denies that nation.

Keeping all this in view my reading of the Charter is that it does not purport to define war crimes; it simply enacts what matters will come up for trial before the Tribunal, leaving it to the Tribunal to decide, with reference to the international law, what offense, if any, has been committed by the persons placed on trial. * * *

I believe the Tribunal, established by the Charter, is not set up in a field unoccupied by any law. If there is such a thing as international law, the field where the Tribunal is being established is already occupied by that law and that law will operate at least until its operation is validly ousted by any authority. Even the Charter itself derives its authority from this international law. In my opinion it cannot override the authority of this law and the Tribunal is quite competent, under the authority of this international law, to question the validity or otherwise of the provisions of the Charter. At any rate unless and until the Charter expressly or by necessary implication overrides the application of international law, that law shall continue to apply and a Tribunal validly established by a Charter under the authority of such international law will be quite competent to investigate the question whether any provision of the Charter is or is not *ultra vires*. * * *

As I have pointed out above, a victor nation is, under the international law, competent to set up a Tribunal for the trial of war criminals, but such a conqueror is not competent to legislate on international law. A tribunal set up by such a nation will certainly be a valid body. But if the nation in question purports also to legislate beyond its competency under the recognized rules of [the] international system, that legislation may be *ultra vires* and I do not see what can debar the Tribunal from examining this question if called upon to apply this legislated norm. It makes no difference in this respect that the same document which sets up the Tribunal also purports to legislate. This fact would not obligate the Tribunal:

To uphold the authority of its promulgator in every other respect.

To uphold every provision of the document promulgating the Tribunal.

To construe the Charter in any particular manner.

After careful consideration of the question I come to the conclusion that the Charter has not defined the crime in question; that it was not within the competence of its author to define any crime; that even if any crime would have been defined by the Charter that definition would have been *ultra vires* and would not have been binding on us, that it is within our competence to question its authority in this respect and that the law applicable to this case is the international law to be found by us.

NOTES & QUESTIONS

1. The Origins of the WWII Tribunals

The Charters of the Nuremberg and Tokyo Tribunals derived from the London Agreement of August 8, 1945, among the four Allied powers. The London Agreement included the Charter for the Nuremberg Tribunal. While the Nuremberg Charter was the product of a joint declaration by the four victorious powers in World War II, and thus was created through a multilateral process, the Charter of the Tokyo Tribunal was created through a special proclamation issued by the Supreme Allied Commander of the Far East, U.S. General Douglas MacArthur. The Tokyo Charter was similar to the Nuremberg Charter; however, there were some significant differences. For one, the United States, through General MacArthur, exercised far more control and influence over the Tokyo trials than it did at Nuremberg.

While the prosecutions at Nuremberg were pursued by a multinational team that shared equal power and responsibility, the Tokyo prosecutions were led by a single Chief of Counsel from the United States chosen by MacArthur with Associate Counsel from the Allies. In addition, all of the decisions of the Tokyo Tribunal were subject to review by MacArthur, although he never exercised this power; there was no provision for review of any of the Nuremberg decisions. In addition, each of the accused at Tokyo had an American defense counsel in addition to one or more Japanese defense counsel. Most treatments of the post-World War II trials focus on the Nuremberg Tribunal, and make a passing reference to the Tokyo trials at most. This is in part due to the fact that the Tokyo materials were for many years much less accessible to researchers and scholars than those of the Nuremberg trials. The full judgment, for example, was only first published in 1977. The earliest publication of Pal's dissent was in 1953 by Sanyal & Co. of Calcutta, India—a publishing house that no longer exists. It has been theorized that the dissent was not published until Japan accepted the outcome of the Tokyo proceedings by way of the 1952 Treaty of San Francisco, the peace treaty between the United States and Japan.

2. The Tokyo Charter

Excerpts from the Charter for the Tokyo Tribunal follow:

Section I

Constitution of Tribunal

Article 1. Tribunal Established. The International Military Tribunal for the Far East [IMTFE] is hereby established for the just and prompt trial and punishment of the major war criminals in the Far East. The permanent seat of the Tribunal is in Tokyo.

Article 2. Members. The Tribunal shall consist of not less than six nor more than eleven Members, appointed by the Supreme Commander for the Allied Powers from the names submitted by the Signatories to the Instrument of Surrender, India, and the Commonwealth of the Philippines.

Section II

Jurisdiction and General Provisions

Article 5. Jurisdiction Over Persons and Offenses. The Tribunal shall have the power to try and punish Far Eastern war criminals who as individuals or as members of organizations are charged with offenses which include Crimes against Peace. The following acts, or any of them, are crimes coming within the jurisdiction of the Tribunal for which there shall be individual responsibility:

(a) Crimes against Peace: Namely, the planning, preparation, initiation or waging of a declared or undeclared war of aggression, or a war in violation of international law, treaties, agreements or assurances, or participation in a common plan or conspiracy for the accomplishment of any of the foregoing;

(b) Conventional War Crimes: Namely, violations of the laws or customs of war;

(c) Crimes against Humanity: Namely, murder, extermination, enslavement, deportation, and other inhumane acts committed before or during the war, or persecution on political or racial grounds in execution of or in connection with any crime within the jurisdiction of the Tribunal, whether or not in violation of the domestic law of the country where perpetrated. Leaders, organizers, instigators and accomplices participating in the formulation or execution of a common plan or conspiracy to commit any of the foregoing crimes are responsible for all acts performed by any person in execution of such plan.

Article 6. Responsibility of Accused. Neither the official position, at any time, of an accused, nor the fact that an accused acted pursuant to order of his government or of a superior shall, of itself, be sufficient to free such accused from responsibility for any crime with which he is charged, but such circumstances may be considered in mitigation of punishment if the Tribunal determines that justice so requires.

3. The Tokyo Tribunal

At the time of Japan's surrender, the Japanese Cabinet launched war crimes trials of Japanese defendants, perhaps thinking that the principle of double jeopardy would prevent subsequent trials by the Allies. Eight accused were tried according to this plan, but all were subsequently re-tried by the Tokyo Tribunal. *See* Howard S. Levie, TERRORISM IN WAR, THE LAW OF WAR CRIMES 141 (1993). The Allies divided potential suspects into three classes based on Article 5 of the Tokyo Charter: Class A (accused of planning and launching an aggressive war), Class B (accused of conventional war crimes), and Class C (accused of crimes against humanity).

The Class A defendants at Tokyo comprised four former premiers: Kiichirō Hiranuma, Kōki Hirota, Kuniaki Koiso, Hideki Tōjō; three former foreign ministers: Matsuoka Yōsuke, Mamoru Shigemitsu, Shigenori Tōgō; four former war ministers: Sadao Araki, Shunroku Hata, Seishirō Itagaki, Jirō Minami; two former navy ministers: Nagano Osami, Shigetarō Shimada; six former generals: Kenji Doihara, Heitarō Kimura, Iwane Matsui, Akira Mutō, Kenryō Satō, Yoshijirō Umezu; two former ambassadors: Hiroshi Ōshima, Toshio Shiratori; three former economic and financial leaders: Naoki Hoshino, Okinori Kaya, Teiichi Suzuki; one imperial adviser: Kōichi Kido; one theorist: Shūmei Ōkawa; one admiral: Takasumi Oka; and one colonel: Kiichirō Hashimoto. Unlike in Germany, no industrialists were prosecuted. Over 5,000 Class B and C defendants (none of whom was a civilian) were prosecuted in domestic courts around the region by the Allies, including the United States, the Netherlands, France, China, and Australia.

The majority opinion in *U.S. v. Araki* is over 1,200 pages long, and it took over a week to deliver orally. Pal's dissent, which the Allies originally barred from publication, is over half as long. The majority opinion, authored by Judge Webb of Australia, resulted in the sentencing of seven defendants to death by hanging, sixteen to life imprisonment, one to twenty years' imprisonment, and one to seven years' imprisonment. Five separate opinions critical of the majority opinion were ultimately issued, although Pal's was the only one that dissented from the entire majority opinion and argued for a complete acquittal. In the Nuremberg proceedings, only the Soviet judge dissented on the grounds that certain sentences were too lenient and certain acquittals were not merited. For more on the background of the Tokyo Tribunal, and particularly Pal's dissent, *see* Elizabeth S. Kopelman, *Ideology and International Law: The Dissent of the Indian Justice at the Tokyo War Crimes Trial*, 23 N.Y.U. J. INT'L L. & POL. 373 (1991). Professor Kopelman notes that the Tokyo Tribunal heard testimony from 419 witnesses, accepted affidavits from an additional 779, admitted 4,336 exhibits, produced a transcript of 48,412 pages, used 417 days in court, consumed over 100 tons of paper, and cost the U.S. government over US $9,000,000.

Emperor Hirohito and members of his family were not indicted or called as witnesses by the Tokyo Tribunal, notwithstanding that the emperor was viewed by many as the architect of Japanese imperialism and Prince Yasuhiko Asaka (the emperor's uncle by marriage) was implicated in the so-called "Rape of Nanking." There is speculation that General MacArthur thought the occupation would proceed more smoothly with the emperor in place, albeit with a renunciation of any claims to divinity. The President of the Tribunal (Judge Webb) and the French judge (Judge Bernard) objected in their dissents to the exclusion of the emperor and, as late as 1950, the Soviets advocated for the creation of a special court to try the emperor and other officials who had escaped indictment. By the 1950s, most of the living Tokyo defendants sentenced to terms of imprisonment had been paroled. Two defendants returned to high government positions in Japan.

4. Justice Radhabinod Pal

Consider this portrait:

> Part of the fascination of Pal's Dissent is that it is not easy to place him politically. He seems at times almost schizophrenic, with some of his comments suggesting a conservative positivist and others suggesting a radical "Third World" perspective. Described by Tōjō's American defense attorney as "the only deep student of international law on the bench," Pal had been legal adviser to the British India Government from 1927 until his appointment to the High Court of Calcutta in 1941. He was a member of the International Law Association, an ex-Vice-Chancellor of Calcutta University, and an Advocate before the Supreme Court of India who had published two series of lectures dealing with Indian legal history. After the Trial he served as a member, and subsequently as Chairman (in 1958 and 1962), of the United Nations International Law Commission and published a series of lectures entitled *Crimes in International Relations*, in which he elaborated

> on many of the themes raised in his *Dissentient Judgment*. He also co-edited a series of publications entitled "Contributions to the Progressive Development of International Law" (with B.V.A. Röling, the Dutch judge at Tokyo) and was appointed National Professor of Jurisprudence by the Government of India in 1959. In 1962 Sweden nominated him for a seat on the World Court. He died in 1967 at the age of 81.

Kopelman, *supra*, at 378–9 (citations omitted). Another commentator has described Justice Pal's opinion as infused with "Indian independence politics" (India received independence in 1947). Jonathan A. Bush, *"The Supreme . . . Crime" and its Origins: The Lost Legislative History of the Crime of Aggressive War*, 102 COLUM. L. REV. 2324, 2375–6 (2002). Do you agree? The Japanese later paid homage to Justice Pal in Tokyo's Yasukuni Shrine, where many Japanese war heroes are interred, including (controversially) some individuals convicted by the Tokyo Tribunal. Visits by Japanese leaders to the shrine continue to cause controversy.

5. Critiques of the Tribunals

Some scholars have criticized both the Nuremberg and Tokyo Tribunals as an exercise of one-sided victor's justice, and thus as an illegitimate exercise of power by the Allies over their defeated enemies. Others argue that such prosecutions derive much of their legitimacy from the fact that they are initiated by victors to an armed conflict. Does Pal accept the proposition that a victorious party to an armed conflict can prosecute members of a defeated enemy? What constraints would Pal place on such prosecutions? For a cogent critique, *see* Richard H. Minear, VICTORS' JUSTICE: THE TOKYO WAR CRIMES TRIAL (1971). If the Tokyo and Nuremberg Tribunals are an illegitimate exercise of "victors' justice," what, if anything, should the Allies have done in order to hold German and Japanese officials accountable for their crimes? For an early, and still nuanced, discussion of this and other related issues, *see* Herbert Wechsler, *The Issues of the Nuremberg Trial*, 62 POL. SCI. Q. 11 (1947).

6. Occupation Trials

The vast majority of prosecutions related to crimes during World War II did not occur before the two international tribunals, but were conducted by domestic tribunals around the world or by the separate victorious powers in their respective zones of occupation. These latter trials were authorized in Germany under Allied Control Council Law No. 10. While the substantive provisions of Control Council Law No. 10 were similar to the Nuremberg Charter, there were significant differences. See *infra* Chapter 10 on Crimes Against Humanity. Similar military tribunals were established in Asia, and resulted in the conviction and execution of far more people than the international tribunals. Recent scholarship has begun to focus on some of these lesser-known military tribunals. In Hong Kong, for example, war crimes trials were held by both Australia and the United Kingdom. *See, e.g.*, Suzannah Linton, *Rediscovering the War Crimes Trials in Hong Kong, 1946–1948*, 13 MELBOURNE J. INT'L L. 284 (2012); HONG KONG'S WAR CRIMES TRIALS (Suzannah Linton ed., 2013).

7. Further Reading

For a firsthand description of the Nuremberg trial by one of the U.S. prosecutors, *see* Telford Taylor, THE ANATOMY OF THE NUREMBERG TRIALS: A PERSONAL MEMOIR (1992). For interesting analysis of the Nuremberg trials by U.S. and Soviet scholars, *see* THE NUREMBERG TRIAL AND INTERNATIONAL LAW (George Ginsburgs & V. N. Kudriavtsev eds., 1990). For a fulsome discussion of the trials under Control Council Law No. 10, *see* Kevin Jon Heller, THE NUREMBERG MILITARY TRIBUNALS AND THE ORIGINS OF INTERNATIONAL CRIMINAL LAW (2011).

III. THE MODERN *AD HOC* INTERNATIONAL TRIBUNALS

The next great experiment with international jurisdiction occurred with the establishment of an *ad hoc* International Tribunal for the Prosecution of Persons Responsible for Serious Violations of International Humanitarian Law Committed in the Territory of the Former Yugoslavia since 1991 (ICTY). At the close of World War II, which had unleashed ethnic tensions between Croat (exemplified by the *Ustaše*) and Serbian (exemplified by the *Četniks*) nationalist groups, the former resistance hero Josip Broz ("Tito") successfully unified the Federal Republic of Yugoslavia under the banner of national unity and, eventually, market socialism. This federation—composed of six republics (Slovenia, Croatia, Bosnia-Herzegovina, Serbia, Montenegro and Macedonia) and two autonomous units (Vojvodina and Kosovo) located in the Socialist Republic of Serbia—lasted until Tito's death and the collapse of the Soviet Union. These events ushered in a revival of ethnic nationalism and sectarian tension in the late 1980s. In 1991, Slovenia, Croatia, and Macedonia declared their independence from the federation; Bosnia-Herzegovina followed suit a year later. The Serb-dominated Yugoslav National Army (JNA) was mobilized in 1991 in an attempt to prevent the dissolution of the country.

Full-scale wars emerged in which Serbian militias supported the JNA's incursions in the newly independent states. Serbian-dominated regions in Croatia and Bosnia also declared their independence and took up arms against their former compatriots along ethnic lines. The war in Bosnia proceeded along two fronts, as both the rump Yugoslavia and the newly independent Croatia sought to annex Bosnian territory inhabited by individuals of Serbian and Croatian descent. The war that unfolded was extremely violent, generating images of concentration camps reminiscent of the Nazi death camps, mass rape, and descriptions of atrocities that gave rise to the neologism "ethnic cleansing." After several short-lived ceasefires, a lasting—if initially fragile—peace finally arrived with the signing of the Dayton Peace Accords in December 1995 by the presidents of Bosnia-Herzegovina (Alija Izetbegović), Croatia (Franjo Tudjman), and Serbia (Slobodan Milošević).

In the midst of the war, the United Nations Security Council addressed the conflict in Yugoslavia in seriatim resolutions. In

Resolution 780 adopted on October 6, 1992, the Security Council directed the Secretary General, at the time the Egyptian diplomat Boutros Boutros-Ghali, to establish a Commission of Experts to document violations of international law. As this investigation was ongoing, governmental, intergovernmental, and nongovernmental calls emerged for the creation of an *ad hoc* international tribunal in the Nuremberg tradition to assign individual responsibility for the documented abuses. The interim report of the Commission of Experts (document S/25274) echoed these recommendations. In Resolution 808 adopted February 22, 1993, the Security Council unanimously decided "that an international tribunal shall be established for the prosecution of persons responsible for serious violations of international humanitarian law committed in the territory of the former Yugoslavia since 1991." The Council further directed the Secretary General to prepare specific proposals for such a tribunal. In his subsequent report, Boutros-Ghali presented a tribunal blueprint and appended a draft statute setting forth existing international humanitarian and criminal law. *See* Report of the Secretary-General Pursuant to Paragraph 2 of Security Council Resolution 808, U.N. SCOR, U.N. Doc. S/25704 (1993). Invoking its Chapter VII powers, the Security Council unanimously adopted the draft statute in Resolution 827 on May 25, 1993. S.C. Res. 827, U.N. Doc. S/RES/827 (May 25, 1993). The ICTY was thus established.

Against the backdrop of these geo-political forces, Duško Tadić became the first defendant in the Tribunal's custody. Tadić was a Serbian café owner in the *opština* ("municipality") of Prijedor in Bosnia. Although his patrons were multi-ethnic, Tadić joined the Serbian Democratic Party (SDS), whose founder and first President was Radovan Karadžić, later prosecuted and convicted by the ICTY. Serb forces eventually staged a bloodless takeover of the *opština*. The region was significant to the cause of a greater Serbia as the municipality formed part of the land corridor linking Serb-dominated areas in the Croatian Krajina with Serbia and Montenegro to the east and south. In the summer of 1992, Serb forces confined more than 3000 Bosnian Muslim and Bosnian Croat citizens in the administrative center of an iron ore mine at Omarska. Abuses of detainees were rampant.

Tadić came to the Tribunal in 1995 by way of a deferral motion by the prosecution pursuant to Rule 9(iii) of the ICTY's Rules of Procedure and Evidence submitted to Germany, where Tadić had been detained on genocide and war crimes charges under German law. Rule 9(iii) allowed the Tribunal to make a request for deferral where a national court investigation "is closely related to, or otherwise involves, significant factual or legal questions which may have implications for investigations or prosecutions before the Tribunal." He was charged with war crimes and crimes against humanity. The defense unsuccessfully sought the dismissal of the charges against Tadić on the grounds that because the German proceedings had substantially commenced, a new trial before the international tribunal would violate the accused's double jeopardy rights (or the principle of *ne bis in idem* ("not again about the same") as it is known in international criminal law). *See Prosecutor v. Tadić*, Case No. IT–94–I, Brief Of The Defense Providing Additional Information And Documents In Respect Of Proceedings Under German Law (Oct. 30, 1995).

Tadić immediately challenged the legality of creating an international tribunal through the Security Council rather than through a multilateral treaty or some other mechanism. The Trial Chamber concluded that it did not have the authority to adjudicate a challenge to its own legitimacy, and thus dismissed Tadić's claim that the Tribunal was not lawfully created. *Prosecutor v. Tadić*, Case No. IT–94–I–1, Decision on Defence Motion on Jurisdiction (August 10, 1995). In its first opinion, the Appellate Chamber (the court of last resort) agreed with the Trial Chamber's dismissal of the jurisdictional challenge, but asserted that it and the Trial Chamber did have the ability to adjudicate the legality of its own creation. *Prosecutor v. Tadić*, Case No. IT–94–I–1, Decision on Defence Motion for Interlocutory Appeal on Jurisdiction (Oct. 2, 1995). The following excerpts concern the Appeals Chamber's analysis of the legal authority of the Security Council to create an *ad hoc* international criminal tribunal. This opinion is also significant for the assertion that such a court has the inherent authority to determine its own legitimacy ("*compétence de la compétence*" or "*kompetenz-kompetenz*"), and thus to determine whether in fact the Security Council acted *ultra vires* ("beyond its powers"). (See the Appendix for a map of Yugoslavia.)

Prosecutor v. Duško Tadić a/k/a "Dule," Case No. IT–94–1–AR72, Decision on the Defence Motion for Interlocutory Appeal on Jurisdiction (Oct. 2, 1995)

The Judgement Under Appeal

1. The Appeals Chamber of the International Tribunal for the Prosecution of Persons Responsible for Serious Violations of International Humanitarian Law Committed in the Territory of Former Yugoslavia since 1991 (hereinafter "International Tribunal") is seized of an appeal lodged by Appellant the Defence against a judgement rendered by the Trial Chamber II on 10 August 1995. By that judgement, Appellant's motion challenging the jurisdiction of the International Tribunal was denied.

2. Before the Trial Chamber, Appellant had launched a three-pronged attack:

a) illegal foundation of the International Tribunal;

b) wrongful primacy of the International Tribunal over national courts;

c) lack of jurisdiction *ratione materiae* ["by reason of the subject matter," i.e. subject matter jurisdiction].

The judgement under appeal denied the relief sought by Appellant; * * * Appellant now alleges error of law on the part of the Trial Chamber. * * *

Unlawful Establishment of the International Tribunal

9. The first ground of appeal attacks the validity of the establishment of the International Tribunal.

10. In discussing the Defence plea to the jurisdiction of the International Tribunal on grounds of invalidity of its establishment by the Security Council, the Trial Chamber declared:

> There are clearly enough matters of jurisdiction which are open to determination by the International Tribunal, questions of time, place and nature of an offence charged. These are properly described as jurisdictional, whereas the validity of the creation of the International Tribunal is not truly a matter of jurisdiction but rather the lawfulness of its creation [. . .] (Decision at Trial [on the Interlocutory Appeal], at para. 4).

There is a *petitio principii* [circularity] underlying this affirmation and it fails to explain the criteria by which the Trial Chamber disqualifies the plea of invalidity of the establishment of the International Tribunal as a plea to jurisdiction. What is more important, that proposition implies a narrow concept of jurisdiction reduced to pleas based on the limits of its scope in time and space and as to persons and subject-matter (*ratione temporis, loci, personae and materiae*). But jurisdiction is not merely an ambit or sphere (better described in this case as "competence"); it is basically—as is visible from the Latin origin of the word itself, *jurisdiction*—a legal power, hence necessarily a legitimate power, "to state the law" (*dire le droit*) within this ambit, in an authoritative and final manner. * * * The same concept is found even in current dictionary definitions:

> [Jurisdiction] is the power of a court to decide a matter in controversy and presupposes the existence of a duly constituted court with control over the subject matter and the parties. Black's Law Dictionary, 712 (6th ed. 1990) (citing Pinner v. Pinner, 33 N.C.App. 204, 234 S.E.2d 633).

11. A narrow concept of jurisdiction may, perhaps, be warranted in a national context but not in international law. International law, because it lacks a centralized structure, does not provide for an integrated judicial system operating an orderly division of labour among a number of tribunals, where certain aspects or components of jurisdiction as a power could be centralized or vested in one of them but not the others. In international law, every tribunal is a self-contained

system (unless otherwise provided). This is incompatible with a narrow concept of jurisdiction, which presupposes a certain division of labour. Of course, the constitutive instrument of an international tribunal can limit some of its jurisdictional powers, but only to the extent to which such limitation does not jeopardize its "judicial character," as shall be discussed later on. Such limitations cannot, however, be presumed and, in any case, they cannot be deduced from the concept of jurisdiction itself.

12. In sum, if the International Tribunal were not validly constituted, it would lack the legitimate power to decide in time or space or over any person or subject-matter. The plea based on the invalidity of constitution of the International Tribunal goes to the very essence of jurisdiction as a power to exercise the judicial function within any ambit. It is more radical than, in the sense that it goes beyond and subsumes, all the other pleas concerning the scope of jurisdiction. This issue is a preliminary to and conditions all other aspects of jurisdiction.

Admissibility of Plea Based on the Invalidity of the Establishment of the International Tribunal

13. Before the Trial Chamber, the Prosecutor maintained that:

> (1) the International Tribunal lacks authority to review its establishment by the Security Council (Prosecutor Trial Brief, at 10–12); and that in any case
>
> (2) the question whether the Security Council in establishing the International Tribunal complied with the United Nations Charter raises "political questions" which are "non-justiciable" (id. at 12–14).

The Trial Chamber approved this line of argument. This position comprises two arguments: one relating to the power of the International Tribunal to consider such a plea; and another relating to the classification of the subject-matter of the plea as a "political question" and, as such, "non-justiciable," i.e., regardless of whether or not it falls within its jurisdiction.

14. In its decision, the Trial Chamber declares:

> [I]t is one thing for the Security Council to have taken every care to ensure that a structure appropriate to the conduct of fair trials has been created; it is an entirely different thing in any way to infer from that careful structuring that it was intended that the International Tribunal be empowered to question the legality of the law which established it. The competence of the International Tribunal is precise and narrowly defined; as described in Article 1 of its Statute, it is to prosecute persons responsible for serious violations of international humanitarian law, subject to spatial and temporal limits, and to do so in accordance with the Statute. That is the full extent of the competence of the International Tribunal. (Decision at Trial, at para. 8).

Both the first and the last sentences of this quotation need qualification. The first sentence assumes a subjective stance, considering that jurisdiction can be determined exclusively by reference to or inference from the intention of the Security Council, thus totally ignoring any residual powers which may derive from the requirements of the "judicial function" itself. That is also the qualification that needs to be added to the last sentence.

Indeed, the jurisdiction of the International Tribunal, which is defined in the middle sentence and described in the last sentence as "the full extent of the competence of the International Tribunal," is not, in fact, so. It is what is termed in international law "original" or "primary" and sometimes "substantive" jurisdiction. But it does not include the "incidental" or "inherent" jurisdiction which derives automatically from the exercise of the judicial function.

15. To assume that the jurisdiction of the International Tribunal is absolutely limited to what the Security Council "intended" to entrust it with, is to envisage the International Tribunal exclusively as a "subsidiary organ" of the Security Council (see United Nations Charter, Arts. 7(2) & 29),* a "creation" totally fashioned to the smallest detail by its "creator" and remaining totally in its power and at its mercy. But the Security Council not only decided to establish a subsidiary organ (the only legal means available to it for setting up such a body), it also clearly intended to establish a special kind of "subsidiary organ": a tribunal.

16. In treating a similar case in its advisory opinion on the *Effect of the United Nationals Administrative Tribunal*, the International Court of Justice declared

> "[T]he view has been put forward that the Administrative Tribunal is a subsidiary, subordinate, or secondary organ, and that, accordingly, the Tribunal's judgments cannot bind the General Assembly which established it. [. . .] The question cannot be determined on the basis of the description of the relationship between the General Assembly and the Tribunal, that is, by considering whether the Tribunal is to be regarded as a subsidiary, a subordinate, or a secondary organ, or on the basis of the fact that it was established by the General Assembly. It depends on the intention of the General Assembly in establishing the Tribunal and on the nature of the functions conferred upon it by its Statute. An examination of the language of the Statute of the Administrative Tribunal has shown that the General Assembly intended to establish a judicial body." (*Effect of Awards of Compensation Made by the United Nations*

* Eds.: Article 7(2) of the Charter provides that any of the six major bodies of the United Nations (the General Assembly, the Security Council, the Economic and Social Council, the Trusteeship Council, the International Court of Justice, and the Secretariat) may create such subsidiary bodies "as may be found necessary." Article 29 reiterates that the Security Council may establish subsidiary bodies "as it deems necessary for the performance of its functions," i.e., the maintenance of international peace and security.

Administrative Tribunal, 1954 I.C.J. Reports 47, at 60–1 (Advisory Opinion of 13 July)). * * *

18. This power [of a court to determine its own competence], known as the principle of "*Kompetenz-Kompetenz*" in German or "*la compétence de la compétence*" in French, is part, and indeed a major part, of the incidental or inherent jurisdiction of any judicial or arbitral tribunal, consisting of its "jurisdiction to determine its own jurisdiction." It is a necessary component in the exercise of the judicial function and does not need to be expressly provided for in the constitutive documents of those tribunals, although this is often done (see, e.g., Statute of the International Court of Justice, Art. 36, para. 6 ["In the event of a dispute as to whether the Court has jurisdiction, the matter shall be settled by the decision of the Court"]). But in the words of the International Court of Justice:

> [T]his principle, which is accepted by the general international law in the matter of arbitration, assumes particular force when the international tribunal is no longer an arbitral tribunal [. . .] but is an institution which has been pre-established by an international instrument defining its jurisdiction and regulating its operation. (*Nottebohm Case (Liech. v. Guat.)*, 1953 I.C.J. Reports 7, 119 (21 March)).

This is not merely a power in the hands of the tribunal. In international law, where there is no integrated judicial system and where every judicial or arbitral organ needs a specific constitutive instrument defining its jurisdiction, "the first obligation of the Court—as of any other judicial body—is to ascertain its own competence." (Judge Cordova, dissenting opinion, *Advisory Opinion on Judgments of the Administrative Tribunal of the I.L.O. Upon Complaints Made Against the U.N.E.S.C.O.*, 1956 I.C.J. Reports, 77, 163 (Advisory Opinion of 23 October)(Cordova, J., dissenting)).

19. It is true that this power can be limited by an express provision in the arbitration agreement or in the constitutive instruments of standing tribunals, though the latter possibility is controversial, particularly where the limitation risks undermining the judicial character or the independence of the Tribunal. But it is absolutely clear that such a limitation, to the extent to which it is admissible, cannot be inferred without an express provision allowing the waiver or the shrinking of such a well-entrenched principle of general international law. As no such limitative text appears in the Statute of the International Tribunal, the International Tribunal can and indeed has to exercise its "*compétence de la compétence*" and examine the jurisdictional plea of the Defence, in order to ascertain its jurisdiction to hear the case on the merits.

20. It has been argued by the Prosecutor, and held by the Trial Chamber that:

> [T]his International Tribunal is not a constitutional court set up to scrutinise the actions of organs of the United Nations. It is, on the contrary, a criminal tribunal with clearly defined powers, involving a quite specific and limited criminal jurisdiction. If it is to confine its adjudications to those specific limits, it will have no authority to investigate the legality of its creation by the Security Council. (Decision at Trial, at para. 5; *see also* paras. 7, 8, 9, 17, 24, *passim).*

There is no question, of course, of the International Tribunal acting as a constitutional tribunal, reviewing the acts of the other organs of the United Nations, particularly those of the Security Council, its own "creator." It was not established for that purpose, as is clear from the definition of the ambit of its "primary" or "substantive" jurisdiction in Articles 1 to 5 of its Statute. But this is beside the point. The question before the Appeals Chamber is whether the International Tribunal, in exercising this "incidental" jurisdiction, can examine the legality of its establishment by the Security Council, solely for the purpose of ascertaining its own "primary" jurisdiction over the case before it.

21. The Trial Chamber has sought support for its position in some *dicta* of the International Court of Justice (ICJ) or its individual Judges, (*see* Decision at Trial, at paras. 10–13), to the effect that:

> Undoubtedly, the [ICJ] does not possess powers of judicial review or appeal in respect of decisions taken by the United Nations organs concerned. (*Legal Consequences for States of the Continued Presence of South Africa in Namibia (South-West Africa) Notwithstanding Security Council Resolution 276* (1970), 1971 I.C.J. Reports 16, at para. 89 (Advisory Opinion of 21 June) (hereinafter *Namibia Advisory Opinion*)).

All these *dicta*, however, address the hypothesis of the Court exercising such judicial review as a matter of "primary" jurisdiction. They do not address at all the hypothesis of examination of the legality of the decisions of other organs as a matter of "incidental" jurisdiction, in order to ascertain and be able to exercise its "primary" jurisdiction over the matter before it. Indeed, in the *Namibia Advisory Opinion*, immediately after the *dictum* reproduced above and quoted by the Trial Chamber (concerning its "primary" jurisdiction), the International Court of Justice proceeded to exercise the very same "incidental" jurisdiction discussed here:

> [T]he question of the validity or conformity with the Charter of General Assembly resolution 2145 (XXI) or of related Security Council resolutions does not form the subject of the request for advisory opinion. However, in the exercise of its judicial function and since objections have been advanced the Court, in the course of its reasoning, will consider these objections before determining any legal consequences arising from those resolutions. (Id. at para. 89). * * *

22. In conclusion, the Appeals Chamber finds that the International Tribunal has jurisdiction to examine the plea against its jurisdiction based on the invalidity of its establishment by the Security Council.

Is the Question at Issue Political and as Such Non-Justiciable?

[The Court rejected the assertion that the case presented a political question, concluding that the political nature of a dispute will not result in non-justiciability so long as the case turns on the resolution of a legal question.]

The Issue of Constitutionality

26. Many arguments have been put forward by Appellant in support of the contention that the establishment of the International Tribunal is invalid under the Charter of the United Nations or that it was not duly established by law. * * *

27. * * * These arguments raise a series of constitutional issues which all turn on the limits of the power of the Security Council under Chapter VII of the Charter of the United Nations and determining what action or measures can be taken under this Chapter, particularly the establishment of an international criminal tribunal. Put in the interrogative, they can be formulated as follows:

> 1. Was there really a threat to the peace justifying the invocation of Chapter VII as a legal basis for the establishment of the International Tribunal?
>
> 2. Assuming such a threat existed, was the Security Council authorized, with a view to restoring or maintaining peace, to take any measures at its own discretion, or was it bound to choose among those expressly provided for in Articles 41 and 42 (and possibly Article 40 as well)?
>
> 3. In the latter case, how can the establishment of an international criminal tribunal be justified, as it does not figure among the ones mentioned in those Articles, and is of a different nature?

The Power of the Security Council to Invoke Chapter VII

28. Article 39 opens Chapter VII of the Charter of the United Nations and determines the conditions of application of this Chapter. It provides:

> The Security Council shall determine the existence of any threat to the peace, breach of the peace, or act of aggression and shall make recommendations, or decide what measures shall be taken in accordance with Articles 41 and 42, to maintain or restore international peace and security. (United Nations Charter, 26 June 1945, Art. 39).

It is clear from this text that the Security Council plays a pivotal role and exercises a very wide discretion under this Article. But this does not mean that its powers are unlimited. The Security Council is an organ of an international organization, established by a treaty which serves as a constitutional framework for that organization. The Security Council is thus subjected to certain constitutional limitations, however broad its powers under the [Charter] may be. Those powers cannot, in any case, go beyond the limits of the jurisdiction of the Organization at large, not to mention other specific limitations or those which may derive from the internal division of power within the Organization. In any case, neither the text nor the spirit of the Charter conceives of the Security Council as *legibus solutus* (unbound by law). * * *

29. What is the extent of the powers of the Security Council under Article 39 and the limits thereon, if any? The Security Council plays the central role in the application of both parts of the Article. It is the Security Council that makes the determination that there exists one of the situations justifying the use of the "exceptional powers" of Chapter VII. And it is also the Security Council that chooses the reaction to such a situation: it either makes recommendations (i.e., opts not to use the exceptional powers but to continue to operate under Chapter VI) or decides to use the exceptional powers by ordering measures to be taken in accordance with Articles 41 and 42 with a view to maintaining or restoring international peace and security. The situations justifying resort to the powers provided for in Chapter VII are a "threat to the peace," a "breach of the peace" or an "act of aggression." While the "act of aggression" is more amenable to a legal determination, the "threat to the peace" is more of a political concept. But the determination that there exists such a threat is not a totally unfettered discretion, as it has to remain, at the very least, within the limits of the Purposes and Principles of the Charter.

30. It is not necessary for the purposes of the present decision to examine any further the question of the limits of the discretion of the Security Council in determining the existence of a "threat to the peace." . . . [A]n armed conflict (or a series of armed conflicts) has been taking place in the territory of the former Yugoslavia since long before the decision of the Security Council to establish this International Tribunal. If it is considered an international armed conflict, there is no doubt that it falls within the literal sense of the words "breach of the peace" (between the parties or, at the very least, would be a "threat to the peace" of others). But even if it were considered merely as an "internal armed conflict," it would still constitute a "threat to the peace" according to the settled practice of the Security Council and the common understanding of the United Nations membership in general. Indeed, the practice of the Security Council is rich with cases of civil war or internal strife which it classified as a "threat to the peace" and dealt with under Chapter VII, with the encouragement or even at the behest of the General Assembly, such as the Congo crisis at the beginning of the 1960s and, more recently, Liberia and Somalia. It can thus be said that there is a common

understanding, manifested by the "subsequent practice" of the membership of the United Nations at large, that the "threat to the peace" of Article 39 may include, as one of its species, internal armed conflicts.

* * *

The Range of Measures Envisaged Under Chapter VII

31. Once the Security Council determines that a particular situation poses a threat to the peace or that there exists a breach of the peace or an act of aggression, it enjoys a wide margin of discretion in choosing the course of action: as noted above (see para. 29) it can either continue, in spite of its determination, to act via recommendations, i.e., as if it were still within Chapter VI ("Pacific Settlement of Disputes") or it can exercise its exceptional powers under Chapter VII. In the words of Article 39, it would then "decide what measures shall be taken in accordance with Articles 41 and 42, to maintain or restore international peace and security."

A question arises in this respect as to whether the choice of the Security Council is limited to the measures provided for in Articles 41 and 42 of the Charter (as the language of Article 39 suggests), or whether it has even larger discretion in the form of general powers to maintain and restore international peace and security under Chapter VII at large. In the latter case, one of course does not have to locate every measure decided by the Security Council under Chapter VII within the confines of Articles 41 and 42, or possibly Article 40. In any case, under both interpretations, the Security Council has a broad discretion in deciding on the course of action and evaluating the appropriateness of the measures to be taken. The language of Article 39 is quite clear as to the channeling of the very broad and exceptional powers of the Security Council under Chapter VII through Articles 41 and 42. These two Articles leave to the Security Council such a wide choice as not to warrant searching, on functional or other grounds, for even wider and more general powers than those already expressly provided for in the Charter. These powers are coercive *vis-à-vis* the culprit State or entity. But they are also mandatory *vis-à-vis* the other Member States, [which] are under an obligation to cooperate with the Organization (Article 2, paragraph 5, Articles 25, 48) and with one another (Articles 49), in the implementation of the action or measures decided by the Security Council.

The Establishment of the International Tribunal as a Measure Under Chapter VII

32. As with the determination of the existence of a threat to the peace, a breach of the peace or an act of aggression, the Security Council has a very wide margin of discretion under Article 39 to choose the appropriate course of action and to evaluate the suitability of the measures chosen, as well as their potential contribution to the restoration or maintenance of peace. But here again, this discretion is not unfettered; moreover, it is limited to the measures provided for in Articles 41 and 42. Indeed, in the case at hand, this last point serves as

a basis for the Appellant's contention of invalidity of the establishment of the International Tribunal.

In its resolution 827, the Security Council considers that "in the particular circumstances of the former Yugoslavia," the establishment of the International Tribunal "would contribute to the restoration and maintenance of peace" and indicates that, in establishing it, the Security Council was acting under Chapter VII (S.C. Res. 827, U.N. Doc. S/RES/827 (1993)). However, it did not specify a particular Article as a basis for this action.

Appellant has attacked the legality of this decision at different stages before the Trial Chamber as well as before this Chamber on at least three grounds:

a) that the establishment of such a tribunal was never contemplated by the framers of the Charter as one of the measures to be taken under Chapter VII; as witnessed by the fact that it figures nowhere in the provisions of that Chapter, and more particularly in Articles 41 and 42 which detail these measures;

b) that the Security Council is constitutionally or inherently incapable of creating a judicial organ, as it is conceived in the Charter as an executive organ, hence not possessed of judicial powers which can be exercised through a subsidiary organ;

c) that the establishment of the International Tribunal has neither promoted, nor was capable of promoting, international peace, as demonstrated by the current situation in the former Yugoslavia.

What Article of Chapter VII Serves as a Basis for the Establishment of a Tribunal?

33. The establishment of an international criminal tribunal is not expressly mentioned among the enforcement measures provided for in Chapter VII, and more particularly in Articles 41 and 42. Obviously, the establishment of the International Tribunal is not a measure under Article 42, as these are measures of a military nature, implying the use of armed force. Nor can it be considered a "provisional measure" under Article 40. These measures, as their denomination indicates, are intended to act as a "holding operation," producing a "stand-still" or a "cooling-off" effect, "without prejudice to the rights, claims or position of the parties concerned." (United Nations Charter, Art. 40). They are akin to emergency police action rather than to the activity of a judicial organ dispensing justice according to law. Moreover, not being enforcement action, according to the language of Article 40 itself ("before making the recommendations or deciding upon the measures provided for in Article 39"), such provisional measures are subject to the Charter limitation of Article 2, paragraph 7, and the question of their mandatory or

recommendatory character is subject to great controversy; all of which renders inappropriate the classification of the International Tribunal under these measures.

34. *Prima facie*, the International Tribunal matches perfectly the description in Article 41 of "measures not involving the use of force." Appellant, however, has argued before both the Trial Chamber and this Appeals Chamber, that:

> * * * [I]t is clear that the establishment of a war crimes tribunal was not intended. The examples mentioned in this article focus upon economic and political measures and do not in any way suggest judicial measures.

It has also been argued that the measures contemplated under Article 41 are all measures to be undertaken by Member States, which is not the case with the establishment of the International Tribunal.

35. The first argument does not stand by its own language. Article 41 reads as follows:

> The Security Council may decide what measures not involving the use of armed force are to be employed to give effect to its decisions, and it may call upon the Members of the United Nations to apply such measures. These may include complete or partial interruption of economic relations and of rail, sea, air, postal, telegraphic, radio, and other means of communication, and the severance of diplomatic relations. (United Nations Charter, Art. 41).

It is evident that the measures set out in Article 41 are merely illustrative examples which obviously do not exclude other measures. All the Article requires is that they do not involve "the use of force." It is a negative definition.

That the examples do not suggest judicial measures goes some way towards the other argument that the Article does not contemplate institutional measures implemented directly by the United Nations through one of its organs but, as the given examples suggest, only action by Member States, such as economic sanctions (though possibly coordinated through an organ of the Organization). However, as mentioned above, nothing in the Article suggests the limitation of the measures to those implemented by States. The Article only prescribes what these measures cannot be. Beyond that it does not say or suggest what they have to be. * * *

36. Logically, if the Organization can undertake measures which have to be implemented through the intermediary of its Members, it can *a fortiori* undertake measures which it can implement directly via its organs, if it happens to have the resources to do so. It is only for want of such resources that the United Nations has to act through its Members. But it is of the essence of "collective measures" that they are collectively undertaken. Action by Member States on behalf of the Organization is

but a poor substitute *faute de mieux* ["for want of something better"], or a "second best" for want of the first. This is also the pattern of Article 42 on measures involving the use of armed force. In sum, the establishment of the International Tribunal falls squarely within the powers of the Security Council under Article 41.

Can the Security Council Establish a Subsidiary Organ with Judicial Powers?

37. The argument that the Security Council, not being endowed with judicial powers, cannot establish a subsidiary organ possessed of such powers is untenable: it results from a fundamental misunderstanding of the constitutional set-up of the Charter. Plainly, the Security Council is not a judicial organ and is not provided with judicial powers (though it may incidentally perform certain quasi-judicial activities such as effecting determinations or findings). The principal function of the Security Council is the maintenance of international peace and security, in the discharge of which the Security Council exercises both decision-making and executive powers.

38. The establishment of the International Tribunal by the Security Council does not signify, however, that the Security Council has delegated to it some of its own functions or the exercise of some of its own powers. Nor does it mean, in reverse, that the Security Council was usurping for itself part of a judicial function which does not belong to it but to other organs of the United Nations according to the Charter. The Security Council has resorted to the establishment of a judicial organ in the form of an international criminal tribunal as an instrument for the exercise of its own principal function of maintenance of peace and security, i.e., as a measure contributing to the restoration and maintenance of peace in the former Yugoslavia.

The General Assembly did not need to have military and police functions and powers in order to be able to establish the United Nations Emergency Force in the Middle East ("UNEF") in 1956. Nor did the General Assembly have to be a judicial organ possessed of judicial functions and powers in order to be able to establish UNAT. In its advisory opinion in the *Effect of Awards* [case], the International Court of Justice, in addressing practically the same objection, declared:

> [T]he Charter does not confer judicial functions on the General Assembly. [. . .] By establishing the Administrative Tribunal, the General Assembly was not delegating the performance of its own functions: it was exercising a power which it had under the Charter to regulate staff relations. (Effect of Awards, at 61).

Was the Establishment of the International Tribunal An Appropriate Measure?

39. The third argument is directed against the discretionary power of the Security Council in evaluating the appropriateness of the chosen measure and its effectiveness in achieving its objective, the restoration

of peace. Article 39 leaves the choice of means and their evaluation to the Security Council, which enjoys wide discretionary powers in this regard; and it could not have been otherwise, as such a choice involves political evaluation of highly complex and dynamic situations. It would be a total misconception of what are the criteria of legality and validity in law to test the legality of such measures *ex post facto* by their success or failure to achieve their ends (in the present case, the restoration of peace in the former Yugoslavia, in quest of which the establishment of the International Tribunal is but one of many measures adopted by the Security Council).

40. For the aforementioned reasons, the Appeals Chamber considers that the International Tribunal has been lawfully established as a measure under Chapter VII of the Charter. * * *

NOTES & QUESTIONS

1. Alternatives to Chapter VII Resolution

The ICTY was established by a Security Council resolution under Chapter VII of the U.N. Charter. How else could the international community have established an *ad hoc* war crimes tribunal? What commends the route taken? Might other routes have been preferable? Why? Could, for example, the General Assembly establish a tribunal given its role within the U.N. system? Could a regional body, such as the League of Arab States or the African Union, establish a criminal tribunal. Note that the African Union has adopted a Protocol to the instrument establishing the main human rights body, the African Court of Human & People's Rights, that would add a criminal chamber. It has yet to garner the necessary signatures to enter into force. *See* Protocol on Amendments to the Protocol on the Statute of the African Court of Justice & Human Rights, Assembly/AU/Dec.529(XXIII) (2014) (the "Malabo Protocol"). Could a concerned group of states establish a tribunal on their own for Syria by way of an international agreement within the tradition of the Nuremberg Tribunal? Revisit this question below when you have studied the International Criminal Court, which was established by treaty, and the hybrid tribunals, which were established in a variety of ways, but generally all with the consent of the territorial/nationality state.

2. Primacy over Domestic Courts

Like the two World War II *ad hoc* tribunals, the ICTY was established with primacy over national courts. In other words, if both the ICTY and a domestic court asserted the right to prosecute a particular defendant over which they both had jurisdiction, the ICTY's assertion of jurisdiction would prevail over that of the national court. *See* Article 9 of the ICTY Statute:

> Article 9
>
> Concurrent jurisdiction
>
> 1. The International Tribunal and national courts shall have concurrent jurisdiction to prosecute persons for serious violations

of international humanitarian law committed in the territory of the former Yugoslavia since 1 January 1991.

2. The International Tribunal shall have primacy over national courts. At any stage of the procedure, the International Tribunal may formally request national courts to defer to the competence of the International Tribunal in accordance with the present Statute and the Rules of Procedure and Evidence of the International Tribunal.

Rules 8 and 9 of the ICTY's Rules of Procedure and Evidence (RPE) set forth the procedure for requesting such a deferral. Tadić challenged the primacy of the ICTY as an infringement on the sovereignty of Germany, where he had been arrested and was facing prosecution under German law for crimes committed in the former Yugoslavia. Why would an assertion of jurisdiction by the ICTY violate the sovereignty of Germany? Does Tadić have standing to raise a defense based upon a breach of a right held by Germany? The ICTR similarly enjoyed primacy over domestic prosecutions.

3. The Political Question Doctrine in International Criminal Law

The Trial Chamber accepted the Prosecution's position that the issue of the Tribunal's creation was a "political question" not amenable to judicial consideration. This ruling was overturned on appeal. Consider whether international law recognizes (or should recognize) the political question doctrine. How would a litigant go about arguing that such a doctrine should be recognized under international law given the structure of the international legal system? Might there be aspects of the establishment of the Tribunal that are in fact political questions, as the Tribunal seems to concede in para. 39? In United States law, the political question doctrine is rooted in both the text and the tripartite structure of the Constitution as well as in prudential concerns about judicial competency. The U.S. Supreme Court articulated the elements of the doctrine in *Baker v. Carr,* 369 U.S. 186, 217 (1962). A litigant must establish one of the following factors in order to prevail on the defense:

- a textually demonstrable constitutional commitment of the issue to a coordinate political department;
- a lack of judicially discoverable and manageable standards for resolving it;
- the impossibility of deciding without an initial policy determination of a kind clearly for nonjudicial discretion;
- the impossibility of a court's undertaking independent resolution without expressing lack of respect due to coordinate branches of government;
- an unusual need for unquestioning adherence to a political decision already made; or
- the potentiality of embarrassment from multifarious pronouncements by various departments on one question.

In United States jurisprudence, non-justiciability is most often invoked in cases affecting U.S. foreign relations, although *Baker v. Carr* makes clear that "it is error to suppose that every case or controversy which touches foreign relations lies beyond judicial cognizance." *Id.* at 211. Nonetheless, several international law tort cases brought in U.S. federal courts have been dismissed on the grounds that they raised non-justiciable political questions. For example, in *Iwanowa v. Ford Motor Co.*, 67 F. Supp. 2d 424 (D.N.J. 1999), the district court found a claim by an individual forced to work for a German Ford subsidiary during World War II to be non-justiciable on four of the six *Baker* factors. Specifically, the court found a constitutional commitment to the executive branch with respect to war reparations, and that enabling the litigation to go forward would demonstrate a lack of respect for the political branches and could generate multifarious pronouncements by various branches of government because of an existing treaty with Germany dealing with war reparations. Finally, the court found that the existence of potentially thousands of 50-year-old claims resulted in a lack of judicially manageable standards. *Id.* at 485–89.

4. *Compétence de la Compétence*

The Appeals Chamber declares that it has the power to determine its own competence. What is the source of the ICTY's authority to do so? Suppose the Security Council in Resolution 827 establishing the ICTY explicitly stated that the Tribunal did not have the authority to question its own creation. Would Tadić's challenge then be allowed? Instead of restricting the authority of the Tribunal, suppose the Security Council stated that no defendant could challenge the legality of the creation of the Tribunal. Would that change your analysis? Would either limitation on the ICTY's powers be "lawful" within the reasoning of the Tribunal? What would have been the effect if the Tribunal had ruled here that it in fact was improperly established?

5. Judicial Review of Security Council Resolutions

In refusing to question its own creation, the Trial Chamber had ruled:

> [T]his International Tribunal is not a constitutional court set up to scrutinise the actions of organs of the United Nations. It is, on the contrary, a criminal tribunal with clearly defined powers, involving a quite specific and limited criminal jurisdiction. If it is to confine its adjudications to those specific limits, it will have no authority to investigate the legality of its creation by the Security Council.

Prosecutor v. Tadić, Case No. IT–94–1–T, Decision on the Defense Motion on Jurisdiction, para. 5 (Aug. 10, 1995). In the instant opinion, the Appeals Chamber reasons that the Tribunal is empowered to consider the legality of its own creation. This opinion has been described as the *Marbury v. Madison*, 5 U.S. 137 (1803), of international criminal law. In that case, the United States Supreme Court established that the federal courts have the power of judicial review over acts of coequal branches of government. Does the ICTY in fact engage in a form of judicial review here, even though it eschews any notion that it is a "constitutional court" in para. 20? Is it, nonetheless, still acting in a constitutional capacity? The International Court of Justice (ICJ) has denied that it exercises the power of judicial review. *See Legal Consequences for States of the Continued Presence of South Africa in*

Namibia (South-West Africa) Notwithstanding Security Council Resolution 276 (1970), 1971 I.C.J. Reports 16, at para. 89 (Advisory Opinion of 21 June). For a discussion of the propriety of ICJ judicial review over Security Council action, *see* José E. Alvarez, *Judging the Security Council*, 90 AM. J. INT'L L. 1 (1996). Might the ICTY have greater powers than the ICJ in this capacity? Why?

6. Chapter VII and Internal Armed Conflicts

In the instant opinion, the Appeals Chamber quickly dismisses the contention that internal armed conflicts do not trigger the Security Council's Chapter VII powers to address breaches to international peace and security with reference to "settled practice" and a "common understanding." How might an internal armed conflict threaten international peace and security? How would an intervention by the Council in a civil war be reconciled with the fundamental principle of non-intervention in internal affairs set forth in Article 2(4) of the U.N. Charter: "All Members shall refrain in their international relations from the threat or use of force against the territorial integrity or political independence of any state, or in any other manner inconsistent with the Purposes of the United Nations."

7. Article 41 Powers of the Security Council

The ICTY determines that it was within the Security Council's power to create a judicial organ, notwithstanding that Article 41 does not list judicial institutions or functions as available non-military measures. At the time the Charter was drafted, the Nuremburg and Tokyo Tribunals were also being established. If the Charter's drafters had meant for the Security Council to be empowered to create courts, would they not have listed something to this effect in Article 41? Is the ICTY's interpretation of that Article in keeping with the *ejusdem generis* ("of the same kind") principle of statutory interpretation, which dictates that where a statute includes a list of specific classes of persons or things and then refers to them in general terms, the general statements only apply to the same kind of persons or things specifically listed?

8. "Established by Law"

A number of human rights instruments set forth the right to have a criminal charge determined by a tribunal that has been "established by law" (*see, e.g.*, Article 14(1) of the International Covenant on Civil and Political Rights (ICCPR)). Tadić thus invoked human rights law to challenge whether the ICTY had been "established by law" given its *ad hoc* nature. What does it mean when human rights instruments require that an accused be tried only by a tribunal "established by law"? The Tribunal agreed that "an international criminal court could [not] be set up at the mere whim of a group of governments. Such a court ought to be rooted in the rule of law and offer all guarantees embodied in the relevant international instruments. Then the court may be said to be 'established by law.' " *Id.* at para. 42. On this point, the Tribunal explored several interpretations of this requirement as follows:

> 43. * * * [T]here are three possible interpretations of the term "established by law." First, as Appellant argues, "established by law" could mean established by a legislature. Appellant claims that

> the International Tribunal is the product of a "mere executive order" and not of a "decision making process under democratic control, necessary to create a judicial organisation in a democratic society." Therefore Appellant maintains that the International Tribunal [has] not been "established by law." * * *

The Tribunal ruled that the fact that it was not set up by a legislature was of no moment:

> It is clear that the legislative, executive and judicial division of powers which is largely followed in most municipal systems does not apply to the international setting nor, more specifically, to the setting of an international organization such as the United Nations. Among the principal organs of the United Nations the divisions between judicial, executive and legislative functions are not clear cut. * * * There is * * * no legislature, in the technical sense of the term, in the United Nations system and, more generally, no Parliament in the world community. * * * Consequently the separation of powers element of the requirement that a tribunal be "established by law" finds no application in an international law setting. The aforementioned principle can only impose an obligation on States concerning the functioning of their own national systems. * * *

Id. at para. 43. A second possible interpretation would provide:

> 44. * * * that the words "established by law" refer to establishment of international courts by a body which, though not a Parliament, has a limited power to take binding decisions. In our view, one such body is the Security Council when, acting under Chapter VII of the United Nations Charter, it makes decisions binding by virtue of Article 25 of the Charter. * * * Appellant takes the position that, given the differences between the United Nations system and national division of powers, discussed above, the conclusion must be that the United Nations system is not capable of creating the International Tribunal unless there is an amendment to the United Nations Charter. We disagree. It does not follow from the fact that the United Nations has no legislature that the Security Council is not empowered to set up this International Tribunal if it is acting pursuant to an authority found within its constitution, the United Nations Charter. * * * In addition, the establishment of the International Tribunal has been repeatedly approved and endorsed by the "representative" organ of the United Nations, the General Assembly: this body not only participated in its setting up, by electing the Judges and approving the budget, but also expressed its satisfaction with, and encouragement of the activities of the International Tribunal in various resolutions.

The third possible interpretation is that the Tribunal's establishment must be in accordance with the rule of law. "This appears to be the most sensible and most likely meaning of the term in the context of international law. For a tribunal such as this one to be established according to the rule of law, it must be established in accordance with the proper international standards; it must provide all the guarantees of fairness, justice and even-handedness, in full conformity with internationally recognized human rights instruments." *Id.* at para. 45.

> 45. * * * While the Human Rights Committee has not determined that "extraordinary" tribunals or "special" courts are incompatible with the requirement that tribunals be established by law, it has taken the position that the provision is intended to ensure that any court, be it "extraordinary" or not, should genuinely afford the accused the full guarantees of fair trial set out in Article 14 of the International Covenant on Civil and Political Rights. (See General Comment on Article 14, H.R. Comm. 43rd Sess., Supp. No. 40, at para. 4, U.N. Doc. A/43/40 (1988)). * * * The practice of the Human Rights Committee with respect to State reporting obligations indicates its tendency to scrutinise closely "special" or "extraordinary" criminal courts in order to ascertain whether they ensure compliance with the fair trial requirements of Article 14.

Is the Tribunal's reconciliation of the requirement that tribunals be "established by law" and the *ad hoc* nature of the ICTY convincing? Would these human rights concerns be lessened if the Tribunal were established by treaty, as a subsidiary body of the General Assembly, as a hybrid body by treaty with the impacted state, or as extraordinary chambers within the courts of the former Yugoslavia? The opinion references the Human Rights Committee. That body of human rights experts considers state compliance with the ICCPR. It has no criminal jurisdiction.

9. Other Options?

In this opinion, the Appeals Chamber determines that it was within the Security Council's competence to establish a criminal tribunal in the exercise of its Chapter VII powers. Assuming the legality of the Security Council's action, is the establishment of a court of law an appropriate response to restore peace and security in an ongoing war with international dimensions? How was the court to accomplish this function? What other measures was the Security Council empowered to undertake under the Charter? Might these have been more effective responses? Recall that the massacre at Srebrenica, in which upwards of 8,000 Muslim men and boys were killed, occurred after the establishment of the Tribunal. Does this indicate that the Tribunal was a failure at restoring peace and security? How would you demonstrate that a tribunal exerted a deterrent effect or, to the contrary, simply exacerbated the conflict or emboldened militants who felt they had nothing to lose? Is there a role for the ICTY to consider these questions as it undertakes its work? Is there anything in its constitutive documents that suggests otherwise? Have the ICC proceedings exerted a deterrent effect in ICC situation countries? How would such an effect be measured?

10. Judge Pal on *Tadić*

How might Judge Pal have ruled in the *Tadić* case? Near the end of his dissent before the Tokyo Tribunal, Judge Pal refers to the power found in Chapter VII of the newly-enacted U.N. Charter:

> Chapter VII of that Charter provides for "action with respect to threats to the peace, breaches of the peace, and acts of aggression." The provisions of this chapter do not contemplate any steps against individuals. It may safely be asserted that the coercive actions envisaged by Chapter VII would not be invoked individually against those who might be responsible for the functioning of the offending collective entity.

In contrast, Hans Kelsen, writing in 1950, concluded that the Security Council had the authority to create a judicial tribunal, so long as the tribunal so created was independent. *See* Hans Kelsen, THE LAW OF THE UNITED NATIONS: A CRITICAL ANALYSIS OF ITS FUNDAMENTAL PROBLEMS 477 (1950).

11. A New Victor's Justice?

The ICTY indicted individuals from all the various ethnic groups in the former Yugoslavia. Nonetheless, over the years, various leaders charged the Tribunal with unfairly focusing on their affinity group. The dynamics at the ICTR were quite different. Rwanda happened to have a rotating seat on the Security Council at the time the Council passed Resolution 955 establishing the ICTR. Rwanda had originally pushed for the establishment of an *ad hoc* tribunal along the lines of the Yugoslav Tribunal with a confined temporal jurisdiction. It ultimately cast the sole negative vote on Resolution 955 establishing the ICTR, however, in part because the Tribunal would not apply the death penalty, did not have jurisdiction over attacks against Tutsi individuals committed prior to the 1994 genocide (deemed "pilot projects for extermination" by the Rwandan Ambassador to the U.N.), but did have jurisdiction for all of 1994, even post-genocide.

The ICTR only prosecuted Hutu defendants accused of committing genocide and crimes against humanity against Tutsi victims. This is notwithstanding the fact that the Rwandan Patriotic Front (RPF), the Tutsi-led rebel force that finally ended the genocide, has been accused of committing revenge killings and other atrocities, just not on the scale of the Tutsi genocide. This conduct fell within the temporal jurisdiction of the ICTR, which encompassed all of 1994 against the wishes of Rwanda at the time the Tribunal was under construction. When Carla del Ponte of Switzerland, the then-ICTR prosecutor, indicated an intention to investigate RPF members, Rwanda withheld cooperation with the ICTR, which included bans on witness travel. The Security Council eventually replaced the Prosecutor and del Ponte's replacement dropped the issue. *See generally* Lars Waldorf, *"A Mere Pretense of Justice": Complementarity, Sham Trials, and Victor's Justice at the Rwanda Tribunal*, 33 FORDHAM INT'L L. J. 1221 (2011).

IV. COMPLETION STRATEGY

With prompting from the U.N. Security Council, both *ad hoc* tribunals submitted proposed "Completion Strategies" to wind down their work. The Completion Strategy raised a pressing question with respect to international jurisdiction: which cases are most appropriately heard at the international level, and which cases are more appropriately heard at the domestic level? As you will see below, this is one of the fundamental issues raised by the ICC Statute.

The winding down of the *ad hoc* tribunals was accomplished by concluding trials of the highest-ranking military, political, and civilian leaders, and referring cases involving lower-ranking defendants to national courts. Under the plan ratified by the Security Council in Resolutions 1503 and 1534, the Tribunals were to complete investigations by the end of 2004, all trial activities at first instance by the end of 2008, and all of their work in 2010. These deadlines slipped badly. The achievement of the Completion Strategies in the proposed timeframe was hindered by the inability to apprehend key defendants, including former Republika Srpska President Radovan Karadžić (who was finally captured in 2008), Bosnian Serb military leader Ratko Mladić (who was apprehended in 2011), and Rwandan *financier* Felicien Kabuga, a major contributor to extremist Hutu political parties and militias who remains at large along with seven other ICTR indictees. Are such deadlines likely to increase or decrease cooperation in the region? For more on the Completion Strategies, *see* Daryl Mundis, *The Judicial Effects of the "Completion Strategies" on the Ad Hoc International Criminal Tribunals*, 99 AM. J. INT'L. L. 142 (2005). (Mundis is now the Registrar of the Special Tribunal for Lebanon).

To facilitate the Completion Strategy, the ICTY judges amended Rule 28 to provide guidance in determining whether cases should be referred or retained by the *ad hoc* tribunals. (The judges of the *ad hoc* tribunals are empowered to amend their own Rules of Procedure and Evidence (RPE)). The amendment was implemented without input from the Office of the Prosecutor. Rule 28 provides:

> On receipt of an indictment for review from the Prosecutor, the Registrar shall consult with the President. The President shall refer the matter to the Bureau [composed of the President, the Vice-President and the Presiding Judges of the Trial Chambers] which shall determine whether the indictment, *prima facie*, concentrates on one or more of the most senior leaders suspected of being most responsible for crimes within the jurisdiction of the Tribunal. If the Bureau determines that the indictment meets this standard, the President shall designate one of the permanent Trial Chamber Judges for the review under Rule 47. If the Bureau determines that the indictment does not meet this standard, the President shall return the indictment to the Registrar to communicate this finding to the Prosecutor.

In civil law countries, judges—so called *juges d'instruction* (or investigating magistrates)—participate in decisions about whom to indict in advance without executive oversight. The trial on the merits then proceeds in front of a different judge. This judicial function at the indictment phase is unknown in the common law system, which serves as a closer model for the *ad hoc* tribunals. Indeed, Article 16(2) of the

ICTY Statute provides that the prosecutor "shall not seek or receive instructions from any Government or from any other source." The judges of the ICTR refused to adopt a version of Rule 28 on the ground that it interfered with prosecutorial discretion and independence.

The judges of both tribunals also amended Rule 11*bis** to enable the national court referrals. The ICTY version of the Rule states:

> (A) After an indictment has been confirmed and prior to the commencement of trial, irrespective of whether or not the accused is in the custody of the Tribunal, the President may appoint a bench of three Permanent Judges selected from the Trial Chambers (hereinafter referred to as the "Referral Bench"), which solely and exclusively shall determine whether the case should be referred to the authorities of a State:
>
> (i) in whose territory the crime was committed; or
>
> (ii) in which the accused was arrested; or
>
> (iii) having jurisdiction and being willing and adequately prepared to accept such a case,
>
> so that those authorities should forthwith refer the case to the appropriate court for trial within that State.
>
> (B) The Referral Bench may order such referral *proprio motu* or at the request of the Prosecutor, after having given to the Prosecutor and, where applicable, the accused, the opportunity to be heard and after being satisfied that the accused will receive a fair trial and that the death penalty will not be imposed or carried out.
>
> (C) In determining whether to refer the case in accordance with paragraph (A), the Referral Bench shall, in accordance with Security Council Resolution 1534 (2004), consider the gravity of the crimes charged and the level of responsibility of the accused.

The ICTR version of subsection (C) directs the Trial Chamber to satisfy itself that the "accused will receive a fair trial in the courts of the State concerned and that the death penalty will not be imposed or carried out."

The rule is silent as to whether the accused can request a referral. It is unclear if this possibility was contemplated. There is no "legislative history" for the Tribunals' RPEs because the judges adopt the rules in private plenary sessions. While the ICTY had little trouble referring low-level cases to the courts of the former Yugoslavia (*see, e.g.*, the charges against Gojko Janković), the ICTR initially refused to refer cases to Rwanda. For example, the Prosecutor sought the transfer of the case against Yussuf Munyakazi—a businessman and leader of a Hutu militia indicted by the ICTR for genocide and crimes against humanity—to Rwanda pursuant to Rule 11*bis*. In 2008, the Appeals Chamber affirmed

* Rules designated as *bis*, *ter*, *quater*, etc. are amendments inserted within rules that are already consecutively numbered. They come from the Latin—i.e. *bis* is second, *ter is* third, etc.

a Trial Chamber decision to deny the transfer on the grounds that the implementation of life imprisonment in Rwanda in certain cases amounted to a life sentence spent in total isolation, and that Rwanda could not guarantee the safety of witnesses. The Appeals Chamber did note, however, that Rwanda had reformed many of the other legal impediments to transfer by, for example, abolishing the death penalty and improving judicial independence. *See Prosecutor v. Munyakazi*, Case No. ICTR–97–36–R11*bis*, Decision on the Prosecution's Appeal Against Decision on Referral Under Rule 11*bis*, paras. 26–31 (Oct. 8, 2008). Ironically, during this same period Rwanda accepted convicted defendants from the Special Court for Sierra Leone (SCSL) into its prisons.

Fears with respect to the Rwandan judicial system were not limited to those suspects whose cases are subject to referral. Individuals acquitted by the ICTR also fear persecution upon their return to Rwanda. Many of the acquitted live in an ICTR "safe house" in Arusha, Tanzania, although Italy accepted Father Hormisdas Nsengimana. *See, e.g., Prosecutor v. Ntagerura*, Case No. ICTR–99–46–A28 (May 15, 2008) (deciding that a "request note" by the Tribunal to Canada was sufficient to obligate that country to grant Ntagerura asylum). *See generally*, Kevin Jon Heller, *What Happens to the Acquitted?*, 21 LEIDEN J. INT'L L. 663 (2008).

The ICTR finally succeeded in referring a case to Rwanda pursuant to Rule 11*bis* in June 2011. The case against pastor Jean Bosco Uwinkindi, who was found in Uganda and was the subject for a reward for his arrest funded by the United States, involved claims of genocide and extermination as a crime against humanity. In the decision authorizing the transfer, the Chamber noted that some of the concerns raised with respect to earlier requests for transfer—in particular the availability of witnesses and their protection—have been adequately addressed. In addition, the Chamber formally requested that the African Commission on Human and People's Rights, a regional human rights body, be appointed to oversee the trial and present any issues it observes to the President of the ICTR. *See Prosecutor v. Jean Uwinkindi*, Case No. ICTR–2001–75–R11*bis*, Decision on Prosecutor's Request for Referral to the Republic of Rwanda (June 28, 2011). Uwinkindi's domestic trial began in 2014 and he was given a life sentence. A year prior to this transfer, the ICTR referred over fifty case files to Rwanda concerning suspects who had been investigated but not yet indicted.

To date, Rwanda has been the only country in Africa willing to accept cases from the ICTR. In Europe, France and the Netherlands have expressed a willingness to accept ICTR referrals. No cases have been referred successfully to the Netherlands, as Dutch law does not currently allow such referrals. In fact, the prosecution of Michel Bagaragaza was to be held in the Netherlands, but failed for lack of jurisdiction. Bagaragaza languished in pre-trial detention during the attempt to transfer his case, and subsequently entered a confidential plea agreement with the prosecution in June 2008, making him the ninth defendant to plead guilty to genocide in Rwanda. France has accepted two cases from the ICTR: Wenceslas Munyeshyaka, a priest in charge of a parish in which many Rwandans who sought refuge were murdered, and who is alleged to have participated directly in killings and rapes; and Laurent Bucyibaruta, the governor of Gikongoro province during the genocide who is alleged to have used his position to direct and incite the genocide. France's tardiness in moving forward with these cases led to a complaint being filed against it before the European Court of Human Rights. The French investigation against Munyeshyaka yielded no charges; Bucyibaruta was charged with genocide and crimes against humanity.

In 2010, the Security Council with Resolution 1966 established the Mechanism for International Criminal Tribunals (MICT) to manage the continuing "jurisdiction, rights and obligations and essential functions" of the ICTY and ICTR upon their closure. The ICTR branch commenced its work in July 2012; the ICTY branch, a year later. (The SCSL has its own skeletal residual mechanism co-located in the Hague). The work of the *ad hoc* tribunals is gradually being assumed by this new institution, which is now called the International Residual Mechanism for Criminal Tribunals ("IRMCT"). Relevant residual functions include fugitive tracking; witness protection issues; appeals, reviews of judgments, and retrials; contempt charges; the enforcement of sentences and requests for parole; and the tribunals' legacy and archives. As a hybridity feature, the IRMCT is also monitoring cases referred to national jurisdictions and responding to requests for assistance from national authorities that are pursuing their own criminal or immigration cases against Rwandan and Yugoslav defendants found in their midst, a task that is proving to be more pressing than had originally been anticipated. Another top priority remains securing the arrest of the eight ICTR indictees who remain at large. Once apprehended, the three most senior fugitives will have their cases tried by the IRMCT; the other files have been referred to national courts. One, Protais Mpirinya is rumored to be in Zimbabwe. A roster of judges and other experts staff the MICT.

NOTES & QUESTIONS

1. Rule 11*bis*

As noted above, Rule 11*bis* governs referrals to national courts, but is silent with respect to whether an accused may request such a referral. Should the Tribunals permit a defendant to request a referral? Does the Rule contemplate referrals outside of the region? Might these be preferable to trials proceeding in national courts in the affected region? Studies of war crimes prosecutions in the states of the former Yugoslavia show discrepancies in outcomes based upon the ethnicity of the defendant. *See, e.g.*, Organization for Security and Cooperation in Europe (OSCE), *Public*

Opinion Survey on Attitudes Towards the ICTY and Domestic War Crimes Trials (2009). Should a state that originally transferred a defendant to the ICTY have a "right of first refusal" to prosecute that individual? Should the state of nationality? Would the ICTY or ICTR be able to provide investigative or analytical support to national courts lacking in expertise in international criminal law or military analysis? How can the *ad hoc* tribunals ensure from afar that the rights of the accused are respected in these national proceedings? Do they in fact have such a duty?

2. Rights of the Accused Under the Completion Strategy

Might the implementation of the Completion Strategy harm the rights of the accused? In an interlocutory appeal in the *Milošević* case, Judge David Hunt (Australia) critiqued what he viewed as the tendency of the Appeals Chamber to

> reverse or ignore its previously carefully considered interpretations of the law or of the procedural rules, with a consequential destruction of the rights of the accused enshrined in the tribunal's Statute and in customary international law.... The only reasonable explanation for these decisions appears to be a desire to assist the prosecution to bring the Completion Strategy to a speedy conclusion. The tribunal will not be judged by the number of convictions which it enters or by the speed with which it concludes the Completion Strategy which the Security Council has endorsed, but by the fairness of its trials. The Majority Appeals Chamber Decision and others in which the Completion Strategy has been given priority over the rights of the accused will leave a spreading stain on this Tribunal's reputation.

Prosecutor v. Milošević, Case No. IT–02–54–AR73.4, Dissenting Opinion of Judge Hunt on Admissibility of Evidence In Chief in the Form of Written Statement, paras. 20–22 (Oct. 21, 2003). The majority opinion does not mention the Completion Strategy, but does discuss policy considerations, including the "economic management of criminal trials before the tribunal."

3. Further Reading

For further reading on the legacies of the *ad hoc* tribunals, *see* Diane Orentlicher, SOME KIND OF JUSTICE: THE ICTY'S IMPACT IN BOSNIA & SERBIA (2018); Sara Kendall & Sarah Nouwen, *Speaking of Legacy: Toward an Ethos of Modesty at the International Criminal Tribunal for Rwanda*, 110 AM. J. INT'L L. 212 (2016); Lana Ljuboja, *Justice in an Uncooperative World: ICTY and ICTR Foreshadow ICC Ineffectiveness*, 32 HOUSTON J. INT'L L. 767 (2010); Lilian A. Barria & Stephen D. Roper, *How Effective are International Criminal Tribunals? An Analysis of the ICTY and the ICTR*, 9 INT'L J. HUM. RTS. 349 (2005); ASSESSING THE LEGACY OF THE ICTY (Richard H. Steinberg ed., 2011); Bert Swart et al., THE LEGACY OF THE INTERNATIONAL CRIMINAL TRIBUNAL FOR THE FORMER YUGOSLAVIA (2011).

CHAPTER 3

DOMESTIC JURISDICTION

I. INTRODUCTION

Historically, what we would today call international criminal law was primarily adjudicated before domestic courts. While we are witnessing a shift to the international level for the prosecution of some cases, there is no question that domestic courts will continue to play an important role in defining, prosecuting, and enforcing international criminal law. This decentralization is attributable to a confluence of factors on the international scene, including the limited jurisdiction and resources of the International Criminal Court, the understandable reluctance of the international community to create new standalone justice institutions, the centrality of the concept of complementarity to the ICC Statute, obligations contained in many international crimes treaties to either prosecute those who breach treaty rules or to extradite them elsewhere for trial, and the increased capacity of domestic legal systems to address the commission of international crimes. The ability of domestic courts to adjudicate international crimes depends, of course, on the existence of the proper legal framework with respect to both jurisdiction and substantive law. This chapter focuses on the former. We address the latter through later chapters devoted to specific crimes.

The classical view of domestic jurisdiction under international law is based upon a robust defense of national sovereignty and the close to unrestricted power of a state to regulate activities of its nationals or criminal conduct undertaken within, or directed toward, its territory. Beyond this basic approach, two competing positions emerged under international law—one based upon a presumption of permission, the other on a presumption of prohibition. The first asserted that states could only act internationally if there was a clear rule permitting such action. The second position affirmed that states could engage in any activity internationally so long as there was no clear rule prohibiting such activity. The case of the *S.S. Lotus,* 1927 P.C.I.J. (ser. A) No. 10 (Sept. 7), provided an opportunity for the Permanent Court of International Justice (PCIJ)—the judicial branch of the League of Nations and the precursor to the International Court of Justice (ICJ)—to address these two competing theories of state sovereignty and international law.

The *Lotus Case* involved the assertion of jurisdiction by Turkey over a French national involved in a maritime accident that resulted in the death of, and injury to, Turkish nationals. France espoused the first position, arguing that no rule of international law specifically allowed the Turkish courts to assert jurisdiction over a matter solely because it involved Turkish victims. Turkey asserted the second position, arguing that there was no rule prohibiting its assertion of jurisdiction. The PCIJ ruled in favor of the Turkish exercise of criminal jurisdiction, thus articulating a broad principle that states were free to act internationally except in the face of a clear rule of prohibition. It reasoned as follows:

> International law governs relations between independent States. The rules of law binding upon States therefore emanate from their own free will as expressed in conventions or by usages generally accepted as expressing principles of law and established in order to regulate the relations between these co-existing independent communities or with a view to the achievement of common aims. Restrictions upon the independence of States cannot therefore be presumed. * * * Far from laying down a general prohibition to the effect that States may not extend the application of their laws and the jurisdiction of their courts to persons, property and acts outside their territory, [international law] leaves them in this respect a wide measure of discretion which is only limited in certain cases by prohibitive rules; as regards other cases, every State remains free to adopt the principles which it regards as best and most suitable. * * * [A]ll that can be required of a State is that it should not overstep the limits which international law places upon its jurisdiction; within these limits, its title to exercise jurisdiction rests in its sovereignty.
>
> It follows from the foregoing that the contention of the French Government to the effect that Turkey must in each case be able to cite a rule of international law authorizing her to exercise jurisdiction, is opposed to the generally accepted international law. * * * [I]n practice, [the French argument] would therefore in many cases result in paralyzing the action of the courts, owing to the impossibility of citing a universally accepted rule on which to support the exercise of their jurisdiction. * * *Consequently, Turkey, by instituting, in virtue of the discretion which international law leaves to every sovereign State, the criminal proceedings in question, has not, in the absence of such principles, acted in a manner contrary to the principles of international law within the meaning of the special agreement.

Although the *Lotus Case* was about the exercise of domestic jurisdiction, it has been cited for the broader principle that states retain residual freedom to act in situations in which international law does not prescribe a contrary rule. Some commentators have rejected this far-reaching interpretation. See, on this point, Judge Shahabuddeen's dissenting opinion in the *Legality of the Threat or Use of Nuclear Weapons Advisory Opinion*, I.C.J. Reports 1996, pp. 394–396, arguing that, at least in the case of nuclear weapons that threaten to "bring civilization to an end and annihilate mankind," the applicability of the principle established in the *Lotus Case* is limited given the enormous development of international law since that case was decided.

International law today provides five broad justifications for a state to assert domestic jurisdiction: territoriality, effects, nationality, protection, and universality. When a state criminalizes and seeks to prosecute certain undesirable conduct committed within its territory, it is asserting territorial jurisdiction. Certain extraterritorial spaces may be treated as national territory. This includes the territorial sea, airspace, flagship vessels, diplomatic posts, the contiguous high seas, etc. As we shall see, this prosecutorial authority even extends to crimes committed on ships flying flags of convenience that have no tangible connection to the territorial state other than the act of registration. This rather peculiar scenario was operative in the abortive Comoros preliminary examination before the ICC, which concerned an attempt to breach Israel's blockade of the Gaza Strip in 2010. There, the Union of the Comoros attempted to invoke ICC jurisdiction over events that took place on the flag ships of several ICC member states; the Prosecutor declined to move forward, largely on gravity grounds, although the PTC has twice asked for reconsideration. *See* Office of the Prosecutor (OTP), Situation on Registered Vessels of Comoros, Greece, and Cambodia, Article 53(1) Report, ¶¶ 24, 137–148 (Nov. 6, 2014). The Prosecutor appealed the second decision, but the Appeals Chamber ruled that the OTP must reconsider by December 2019, although it did confirm that the "ultimate decision" was hers to make. *See* Situation on Registered Vessels of Comoros, the Hellenic Republic & the Kingdom of Cambodia, Case No. ICC–01/13 OA 2, Judgment on the Appeal of the Prosecutor against Pre-Trial Chamber I's 'Decision on the "Application for Judicial Review by the Government of the Union of the Comoros" ' (Sept. 2, 2019).

The territorial principle also contains two expansive sub-principles. First, under the "subjective territorial principle," a state may assert jurisdiction over criminal acts commenced within the state, even if they are ultimately consummated abroad. Several treaties addressed to transnational crimes—such as the 1929 International Convention for the Suppression of Counterfeiting Currency, 112 L.N.T.S. 371, and the 1936 Convention for the Suppression of the Illicit Traffic in Dangerous Drugs, 198 L.N.T.S. 299—exemplify this approach. Second, and inversely, under the "objective territorial principle" a state may assert jurisdiction over acts committed abroad that are consummated within the territory of the prosecuting state. A variation of this latter principle—applied most often in the antitrust, securities, and narcotics contexts—allows a state to regulate acts that cause effects within the state, or are intended to do so, even if the act that creates the effects is committed outside the state. This principle is tangentially at play in the ICC's consideration of harm to the Rohingya Muslim minority in Myanmar/Burma, who find themselves seeking refuge in the territory of Bangladesh, an ICC state party. There, a Pre-Trial Chamber of the ICC ruled that the Office of the Prosecutor can proceed with a preliminary examination of crimes initiated within Myanmar/Burma, such as deportation, persecution, and other inhumane acts, but which have effects in the territory of Bangladesh. *See* Pre-Trial Chamber I, Decision on the "Prosecution's Request for a Ruling on Jurisdiction under Article 19(3) of the Statute," Case No. ICC–RoC46(3)–01/18 (Sept. 6, 2018).

Pursuant to the nationality principle, a state may also apply its criminal law to its nationals, who may be either perpetrators or victims of criminal acts. This "nationality principle" thus comes in two forms: the "active personality principle" permits jurisdiction when the *offender* is a national or resident of the state prescribing or prosecuting undesirable conduct. The "passive personality principle" permits jurisdiction where the *victim* is a national or resident of the prosecuting state.

The active personality principle is common and uncontroversial. By way of example, in the United States, the Military Extraterritorial Jurisdiction Act of 2000 ("MEJA"), 18 U.S.C. § 3261, allows for the prosecution of certain felonies committed by individuals employed by or accompanying the U.S. armed forces abroad. In addition, this principle is increasingly invoked with respect to the crime of sex trafficking as in 18 U.S.C. § 2423, which states:

> (b) *Travel with intent to engage in illicit sexual conduct.* A person who travels in interstate commerce or travels into the United States, or a United States citizen or alien admitted for permanent residence in the United States who travels in foreign commerce, for the purpose of engaging in any illicit sexual conduct with another person shall be fined under this title or imprisoned not more than 30 years, or both.
>
> (c) *Engaging in illicit sexual conduct in foreign places.* Any United States citizen or alien admitted for permanent residence who travels in foreign commerce, and engages in any illicit sexual conduct with another person shall be fined under this title or imprisoned not more than 30 years, or both.

The United Kingdom has a similar statute (see Sect. 72 of the Sex Offenders Act of 2003 (c.42)) that allows prosecution of a U.K. subject or resident for sexual offenses committed outside of the territory of the U.K., so long as the activity was also an offense in the territory in which the activity took place and was an offense under U.K. law as well. An important Dutch case applied this principle to complicity in war crimes committed in Iraq by a Dutch citizen. *Public Prosecutor v. Frans Cornelis Adrianus van Anraat*, Rechtbank-Gravenhage [Rb], The Hague, 13 December 2005, RvdW 09/751003-04 s4.1, *aff'd*, Gerechtshof-Gravenhage [Hof], The Hague, 9 May 2007, RvdW 2200050906-2 (Netherlands).

In contrast, the exercise of passive personality jurisdiction is more rare, and more contested. The United States, for example, originally rejected the passive personality principle in the 1887 *Cutting Case*, in which the United States successfully protested Mexico's effort to prosecute a U.S. national for allegedly libeling a Mexican national in the United States. Notwithstanding this history, the principle is becoming less controversial as states increasingly promulgate terrorism treaties and adopt terrorism legislation to protect their nationals from acts of terrorism abroad. *See, e.g.*, 18 U.S.C. § 2332 (criminalizing the killing of a U.S. national abroad). The Restatement (Fourth) of Foreign Relations Law (hereinafter "Restatement (Fourth)") notes that the passive personality principle

> is more controversial than territorial or active-personality jurisdiction. However, states increasingly have exercised passive-personality jurisdiction, particularly with respect to criminal offenses where a state's nationals are targeted by reason of their nationality. These include terrorist offenses and attacks on a state's diplomatic representatives or other officials. The use of passive-personality jurisdiction with respect to these crimes has met little opposition. It is less clear whether passive-personality jurisdiction is generally accepted more broadly.

RESTATEMENT (FOURTH) OF THE FOREIGN RELATIONS LAW OF THE UNITED STATES § 411, reporters' note 1 (Am. Law Inst. 2018).* The French take a particularly expansive approach to passive personality jurisdiction. The Code Pénal, Art. 113-7 states:

> French criminal law is applicable to any felony, as well as to any misdemeanor punishable by imprisonment, committed by a French or foreign national outside the territory of the French Republic, where the victim is a French national at the time of the offense.

While it is generally understood that this article is to be invoked only with respect to cases involving national security, this limitation is not apparent from the article itself. Compare this statute to the position taken by France in the *Lotus Case*. For a general discussion of the passive personality principle, *see* Geoffrey R. Watson, *The Passive Personality Principle*, 28 TEX. INT'L L.J. 1 (1993).

Conduct that threatens interests that are vital to the state may also be criminalized pursuant to the protective principle of jurisdiction. Statutes embodying this basis of jurisdiction generally target extraterritorial offenses directed against the security of the state or threatening the integrity of governmental functions. Such statutes are those criminalizing espionage, counterfeiting, falsification of official documents, perjury before consular officials, and conspiracy to violate the

---

* The Restatement is a product of the American Law Institute (ALI), a private membership organization based in the United States dedicated to the clarification and simplification of the law. Foreign relations law in the United States includes aspects of public international law as well as that federal law of relevance to the United States' international relations. While the Restatement has only persuasive authority, both domestic and international authorities widely and approvingly cite it as some of the materials in this casebook demonstrate.

immigration or customs laws. In *Joyce v. DPP*, (1946) A.C. 347 (U.K.), the defendant (a U.S. citizen carrying a fraudulently-obtained British passport) was charged with treason for providing aid and comfort to the enemy in the form of propaganda broadcasts in Germany in the World War II era. In *Kawakita v. United States*, 343 U.S. 717 (1952), the defendant was prosecuted for treason for torturing Allied prisoners of war who were being forced to work in a Japanese factory. Likewise, Israel invoked the protective principle (among other jurisdictional grounds) to justify its abduction and prosecution of Adolf Eichmann, even though the state of Israel did not exist at the time Eichmann acted. *Attorney-General of the Government of Israel v Eichmann,* 36 I.L.R. 277 [1962] (Isr.).

Finally, the universality principle allows all states to define and prosecute perpetrators of certain violations of international law (*delicta juris gentium*) regardless of the nationality of the perpetrator, the nationality of the victim, or the place of commission. Universal jurisdiction in its purest form allows for assertions of jurisdiction absent any connections to the prosecuting forum (and potentially even *in absentia* if allowed by the relevant system). Many states have, however, rendered their universal jurisdiction statutes more conditional, by requiring the presence of the accused in the forum or other relevant connections. Such limitations are not required by international law, although they may reflect domestic policy considerations or domestic law precepts. Universal jurisdiction is the subject of Section III below.

While the classical view of domestic jurisdiction centered on well-defined categories of jurisdiction, many exercises of jurisdiction manifest numerous bases of jurisdiction, especially when multiple victims or perpetrators, or transnational conduct, are involved. The Third Restatement took a less categorical approach, directing the decision-maker to weigh a number of factors to determine appropriate assertions of jurisdiction. The Fourth Restatement abandons any claim that customary international law requires the factor-based approach, but still acknowledges that assertions of jurisdiction should be reasonable. As you read through the relevant excerpts from both Restatements, ask yourself what are the benefits and limitations of each approach. Which do you prefer, and why?

The American Law Institute, RESTATEMENT (FOURTH) OF FOREIGN RELATIONS

§ 401. Categories of Jurisdiction

The foreign relations law of the United States divides jurisdiction into three categories:

(a) jurisdiction to prescribe, i.e., the authority of a state to make law applicable to persons, property, or conduct;

(b) jurisdiction to adjudicate, i.e., the authority of a state to apply law to persons or things, in particular through the processes of its courts or administrative tribunals; and

(c) jurisdiction to enforce, i.e., the authority of a state to exercise its power to compel compliance with law.

§ 402. United States Practice with Respect to Jurisdiction to Prescribe

(1) Subject to the constitutional limits set forth in § 403*, the United States exercises jurisdiction to prescribe law with respect to:

(a) persons, property, and conduct within its territory;

(b) conduct that has a substantial effect within its territory;

(c) the conduct, interests, status, and relations of its nationals and residents outside its territory;

(d) certain conduct outside its territory that harms its nationals;

(e) certain conduct outside its territory by persons not its nationals or residents that is directed against the security of the United States or against a limited class of other fundamental U.S. interests; and

(f) certain offenses of universal concern, such as piracy, slavery, forced labor, trafficking in persons, recruitment of child soldiers, torture, extrajudicial killing, genocide, and certain acts of terrorism, even if no specific connection exists between the United States and the persons or conduct being regulated.

(2) In exercising jurisdiction to prescribe, the United States takes account of the legitimate interests of other nations as a matter of prescriptive comity.

§ 405. Reasonableness in Interpretation

As a matter of prescriptive comity, courts in the United States may interpret federal statutory provisions to include other limitations on their applicability.

§ 406. Interpretation Consistent with International Law

Where fairly possible, courts in the United States construe federal statutes to avoid conflict with international law governing jurisdiction to prescribe. If a federal statute cannot be so construed, the federal statute is controlling as a matter of federal law.

---

* Eds.: § 403 states that any exercise of prescriptive jurisdiction may not exceed any limits imposed by the U.S. Constitution.

§ 407. Customary International Law Governing Jurisdiction to Prescribe

Customary international law permits exercises of prescriptive jurisdiction if there is a genuine connection between the subject of the regulation and the state seeking to regulate. The genuine connection usually rests on a specific connection between the state and the subject being regulated, such as territory, effects, active personality, passive personality, or protection. In the case of universal jurisdiction, the genuine connection rests on the universal concern of states in suppressing certain offenses.

The American Law Institute, RESTATEMENT (THIRD) OF FOREIGN RELATIONS

§ 403. Limitations on Jurisdiction to Prescribe

(1) Even when one of the bases for jurisdiction under § 402 is present [outlining the territorial, nationality, and protective principles], a state may not exercise jurisdiction to prescribe law with respect to a person or activity having connections with another state when the exercise of such jurisdiction is unreasonable.

(2) Whether exercise of jurisdiction over a person or activity is unreasonable is determined by evaluating all relevant factors, including, where appropriate:

(a) the link of the activity to the territory of the regulating state, *i.e.*, the extent to which the activity takes place within the territory, or has substantial, direct, and foreseeable effect upon or in the territory;

(b) the connections, such as nationality, residence, or economic activity, between the regulating state and the person principally responsible for the activity to be regulated, or between that state and those whom the regulation is designed to protect;

(c) the character of the activity to be regulated, the importance of regulation to the regulating state, the extent to which other states regulate such activities, and the degree to which the desirability of such regulation is generally accepted;

(d) the existence of justified expectations that might be protected or hurt by the regulation;

(e) the importance of the regulation to the international political, legal, or economic system;

(f) the extent to which the regulation is consistent with the traditions of the international system;

(g) the extent to which another state may have an interest in regulating the activity; and

(h) the likelihood of conflict with regulation by another state.

(3) When it would not be unreasonable for each of two states to exercise jurisdiction over a person or activity, but the prescriptions by the two states are in conflict, each state has an obligation to evaluate its own as well as the other state's interest in exercising jurisdiction, in light of all the relevant factors, Subsection (2); a state should defer to the other state if that state's interest is clearly greater.

§ 421. Jurisdiction to Adjudicate

(1) A state may exercise jurisdiction through its courts to adjudicate with respect to a person or thing if the relationship of the state to the person or thing is such as to make the exercise of jurisdiction reasonable.

(2) In general, a state's exercise of jurisdiction to adjudicate with respect to a person or thing is reasonable if, at the time jurisdiction is asserted:

(a) the person or thing is present in the territory of the state, other than transitorily;

(b) the person, if a natural person, is domiciled in the state;

(c) the person, if a natural person, is resident in the state;

(d) the person, if a natural person, is a national of the state;

(e) the person, if a corporation or comparable juridical person, is organized pursuant to the law of the state;

(f) a ship, aircraft or other vehicle to which the adjudication relates is registered under the laws of the state;

(g) the person, whether natural or juridical, has consented to the exercise of jurisdiction;

(h) the person, whether natural or juridical, regularly carries on business in the state;

(i) the person, whether natural or juridical, had carried on activity in the state, but only in respect of such activity;

(j) the person, whether natural or juridical, has carried on outside the state an activity having a substantial, direct, and foreseeable effect within the state, but only in respect of such activity; or

(k) the thing that is the subject of adjudication is owned, possessed, or used in the state, but only in respect of a claim reasonably connected with that thing.

In light of the different bases for asserting jurisdiction discussed above, consider which jurisdictional principles are at work in the case that follows. (Note that all references are to the Third Restatement).

United States v. Ali Mohamed Ali, Also Known as Ahmed Ali Adan, Also Known as Ismail Ali

718 F.3d 929 (D.C.Cir. 2013).

■ BROWN, CIRCUIT JUDGE: Ali Mohamed Ali, a Somali national, helped negotiate the ransom of a merchant vessel and its crew after they were captured by marauders in the Gulf of Aden. Though he claims merely to have defused a tense situation, the government believes he was in cahoots with these brigands from the very start. * * * The government says Ali is a pirate; he protests that he is not. Though a trial will determine whether he is in fact a pirate, the question before us is whether the government's allegations are legally sufficient. And the answer to that question is complicated by a factor the district court deemed critical: Ali's alleged involvement was limited to acts he committed on land and in territorial waters—not upon the high seas. Thus, the district court restricted the charge of aiding and abetting piracy to his conduct on the high seas and dismissed the charge of conspiracy to commit piracy. Eventually, the district court also dismissed the hostage taking charges, concluding that prosecuting him for his acts abroad would violate his right to due process. On appeal, we affirm dismissal of the charge of conspiracy to commit piracy. We reverse, however, the district court's dismissal of the hostage taking charges, as well as its decision to limit the aiding and abetting piracy charge.

I. Background

A. *Modern Piracy*

Mention "pirates" to most Americans and you are more likely to evoke Johnny Depp's droll depiction of Captain Jack Sparrow than concern about the international scourge of piracy that long ago led most civilized states to declare such marauders the enemy of all mankind. In unstable parts of the world, piracy is serious business, and these troubled waters have seen a resurgence in pirate attacks, both successful and attempted. Pirate attacks have become increasingly daring, as well as commonplace, with pirates targeting large commercial vessels in transit, hijacking these ships, and ransoming the crews. These predatory activities have proven especially lucrative in the Gulf of Aden (situated between the Arabian Peninsula and the Horn of Africa and bounded by a long stretch of Somalia's coast), where pirates can exploit a key trade route undeterred by Somalia's unstable government.

B. *Ali's Offense and Prosecution*

Ali * * * [allegedly] plotted the capture of the *CEC Future*, a Danish-owned merchant ship that flew a Bahamian flag and carried cargo owned by a U.S. corporation. On November 7, 2008, while the *CEC Future* was traveling in the Gulf of Aden on the "high seas"—*i.e.*, outside any nation's territorial waters—Ali's compatriots launched their attack. Wielding AK-47s and a rocket-propelled grenade, the raiders fired warning shots, boarded the ship, and seized the crew. They then forced crewmembers at gunpoint to reroute the ship to Point Ras Binna, off the coast of Somalia, where, on November 9, Ali came aboard and assumed the role of interpreter. The ship traveled that same day to Eyl, a Somali port, and remained at anchor there until it was ransomed the following January.

Except for a brief period of "minutes" during which the *CEC Future* entered the high seas, the ship traversed exclusively territorial waters while Ali was aboard. Ali promptly began negotiating with the owners of the *CEC Future*, starting with an initial demand of $7 million for the release of the ship, its crew, and its cargo. Discussions continued into January 2009, when Ali and the *CEC Future*'s owners agreed to a $1.7 million ransom. As payment for his assistance, Ali also demanded $100,000 (a figure he later reduced to $75,000) be placed in a personal bank account. On January 14, the pirates received the agreed-upon $1.7 million, and two days later Ali and his cohorts left the ship. Ali's share amounted to $16,500—one percent of the total ransom less expenses. He later received his separate $75,000 payment via wire transfer to the account he had previously specified.

As it happens, "pirate hostage negotiator" is not the only line on Ali's resume. In June 2010, he was appointed Director General of the Ministry of Education for the Republic of Somaliland, a self-proclaimed sovereign state within Somalia. When he received an email in March 2011 inviting him to attend an education conference in Raleigh, North Carolina, he agreed. Little did he know it was all an elaborate ruse. For some time, federal prosecutors had been busy building a case against Ali, charging him via criminal complaint and later obtaining a formal indictment. When Ali landed at Dulles International Airport on April 20, 2011, to attend the sham conference, he was promptly arrested.

A grand jury issued a four-count superseding indictment against Ali, charging him first with conspiracy to commit piracy under the law of nations, in violation of 18 U.S.C. § 371, which makes it a crime for "two or more persons" to "conspire . . . to commit any offense against the United States." Invoking aiding and abetting liability under 18 U.S.C. § 2, Count Two charged Ali with committing piracy under the law of nations, in violation of 18 U.S.C. § 1651, which provides, "Whoever, on the high seas, commits the crime of piracy as defined by the law of nations, and is afterwards brought into or found in the United States, shall be imprisoned for life." Counts Three and Four analogously charged Ali with conspiracy to commit hostage taking and aiding and abetting hostage taking, in violation of 18 U.S.C. §§ 1203 and 2. The hostage taking statute prescribes criminal penalties for

> whoever, whether inside or outside the United States, seizes or detains and threatens to kill, to injure, or to continue to detain another person in order to compel a third person or a governmental organization to do or abstain from doing any act as an explicit or implicit condition for the release of the person detained, or attempts or conspires to do so. * * *

The government now challenges the district court's dismissal of Counts One, Three, and Four, as well as limitation of Count Two. We have jurisdiction over this interlocutory appeal because the government challenges an "order of a district court dismissing an indictment . . . as to any one or more counts." 18 U.S.C. § 3731.

II. The Piracy Charges

In most cases, the criminal law of the United States does not reach crimes committed by foreign nationals in foreign locations against foreign interests. Two judicial presumptions promote this outcome. The first is the presumption against the extraterritorial effect of statutes: "When a statute gives no clear indication of an extraterritorial application, it has none." *Morrison v. Nat'l Austl. Bank Ltd.*, 130 S. Ct. 2869, 2878 (2010). The second is the judicial presumption that "an act of Congress ought never to be construed to violate the law of nations if any other possible construction remains," *Murray v. Schooner Charming Betsy*, 6 U.S. (2 Cranch) 64, 118 (1804)—the so-called *Charming Betsy* canon. Because international law itself limits a state's authority to apply its laws beyond its borders, *see* RESTATEMENT (THIRD) OF FOREIGN RELATIONS LAW §§ 402–03, *Charming Betsy* operates alongside the presumption against extraterritorial effect to check the exercise of U.S. criminal jurisdiction. Neither presumption imposes a substantive limit on Congress's legislative authority, but they do constrain judicial inquiry into a statute's scope.

Piracy, however, is no ordinary offense. The federal piracy statute clearly applies extraterritorially to "[w]hoever, on the high seas, commits the crime of piracy as defined by the law of nations," even though that person is only "afterwards brought into or found in the United States." 18 U.S.C. § 1651. Likewise, through the principle of universal jurisdiction, international law permits states to "define and prescribe punishment for certain offenses recognized by the community of nations as of universal concern." RESTATEMENT, *supra*, at § 404; *see United States v. Yunis*, 924 F.2d 1086, 1091 (D.C. Cir. 1991). And of all such universal crimes, piracy is the oldest and most widely acknowledged. "Because he commits hostilities upon the subjects and property of any or all nations, without any regard to right or duty, or any pretence of public authority," the pirate is "*hostis humani generis*," *United States v. Brig Malek Adhel*, 43 U.S. (2 How.) 210, 232 (1844)—in other words, "an enemy of the human race," *United States v. Smith*, 18 (5 Wheat.) U.S. 153, 161 (1820). Thus, "all nations [may punish] all persons, whether natives or foreigners, who have committed this offence against any persons whatsoever, with whom they are in amity." *Id.* at 162. Universal jurisdiction is not some idiosyncratic domestic invention but a creature of international law. Unlike the average criminal, a pirate may easily find himself before an American court despite committing his offense on the other side of the globe. Ali's situation is a bit more complicated, though. His indictment contains no straightforward charge of piracy.

Rather, the government accuses him of two inchoate offenses relating to piracy: conspiracy to commit piracy and aiding and abetting piracy.

On their face, both ancillary statutes apply generally and without exception: § 2 to "*[w]hoever* . . . aids, abets, counsels, commands, induces or procures" the commission of "an offense against the United States," 18 U.S.C. § 2(a) (emphasis added), and § 371 to persons who "do any act to effect the object of the conspiracy" to "commit *any* offense against the United States," 18 U.S.C. § 371 (emphasis added). But so powerful is the presumption against extraterritorial effect that even such generic language is insufficient rebuttal. That leaves both statutes ambiguous as to their application abroad, requiring us to resort to interpretive canons to guide our analysis. Given this ambiguity in the extraterritorial scope of the two ancillary statutes, we consider whether applying them to Ali's actions is consistent with international law. * * * Ultimately, Ali's assault on his conspiracy charge prevails for the same reason the attack on the aiding and abetting charge fails.

A. *Aiding and Abetting Piracy*

We begin with Ali's charge of aiding and abetting piracy. Aiding and abetting is a theory of criminal liability, not a separate offense—one that allows a defendant who "aids, abets, counsels, commands, induces or procures" commission of a crime to be punished as a principal, 18 U.S.C. § 2(a). "All that is necessary is to show some affirmative participation which at least encourages the principal offender to commit the offense, with all its elements, as proscribed by the statute." *United States v. Raper*, 676 F.2d 841, 850 (D.C. Cir. 1982). From Ali's perspective, it is not enough that acts of piracy were committed on the high seas and that he aided and abetted them. Rather, he believes any acts of aiding and abetting he committed must themselves have occurred in extraterritorial waters and not merely supported the capture of the *CEC Future* on the high seas.

Ali's argument involves two distinct (though closely related) inquiries. First, does the *Charming Betsy* canon pose any obstacle to prosecuting Ali for aiding and abetting piracy? For we assume, absent contrary indication, Congress intends its enactments to comport with international law. Second, is the presumption against extraterritoriality applicable to acts of aiding and abetting piracy not committed on the high seas?

1. Piracy and the *Charming Betsy* Canon

Section 1651 criminalizes "the crime of piracy as defined by the law of nations." Correspondence between the domestic and international definitions is essential to exercising universal jurisdiction. Otherwise, invocation of the magic word "piracy" would confer universal jurisdiction on a nation and vest its actions with the authority of international law. As a domestic matter, doing so may be perfectly legal. But because *Charming Betsy* counsels against interpreting federal statutes to contravene international law, we must satisfy ourselves that prosecuting Ali for aiding and abetting piracy would be consistent with the law of nations.

Though § 1651's invocation of universal jurisdiction may comport with international law, that does not tell us whether § 2's broad aider and abettor liability covers conduct neither within U.S. territory nor on the high seas. Resolving that difficult question requires examining precisely what conduct constitutes piracy under the law of nations. Luckily, defining piracy is a fairly straightforward exercise. Despite not being a signatory, the United States has recognized, via United Nations Security Council resolution, that the U.N. Convention on the Law of the Sea ("UNCLOS") "sets out the legal framework applicable to combating piracy and armed robbery at sea." S.C. Res. 2020, U.N. Doc. S/Res/2020, at 2 (Nov. 22, 2011). According to UNCLOS:

> Piracy consists of any of the following acts:
>
> (a) any illegal acts of violence or detention, or any act of depredation, committed for private ends by the crew or the passengers of a private ship . . . and directed:
>
> > (i) on the high seas, against another ship . . . or against persons or property on board such ship . . . ;
> >
> > (ii) against a ship, . . . persons or property in a place outside the jurisdiction of any State;
>
> (b) any act of voluntary participation in the operation of a ship . . . with knowledge of facts making it a pirate ship . . . ;
>
> (c) any act of inciting or of intentionally facilitating an act described in subparagraph (a) or (b).

UNCLOS, art. 101, Dec. 10, 1982, 1833 U.N.T.S. 397, 436. By including "intentionally facilitating" a piratical act within its definition of piracy, article 101(c) puts to rest any worry that American notions of aider and abettor liability might fail to respect the international understanding of piracy. One question remains: does international law require facilitative acts take place on the high seas?

Explicit geographical limits—"on the high seas" and "outside the jurisdiction of any state"—govern piratical acts under article 101(a)(i) and (ii). Such language is absent, however, in article 101(c), strongly suggesting a facilitative act need not occur on the high seas so long as its predicate offense has. So far, so good; *Charming Betsy* poses no problems.

Ali endeavors nonetheless to impute a "high seas" requirement to article 101(c) by pointing to UNCLOS article 86, which states, "The provisions of this Part apply to all parts of the sea that are not included in the exclusive economic zone, in the territorial sea or in the internal waters of a State, or in the archipelagic waters of an archipelagic State." 1833 U.N.T.S. at 432. Though, at first glance, the language at issue appears generally applicable, there are several problems with Ali's theory that article 86 imposes a strict high seas requirement on all provisions in Part VII. For one thing, Ali's reading would result in numerous redundancies throughout UNCLOS where, as in article 101(a)(i), the term "high seas" is already used, and interpretations resulting in textual surplusage are typically disfavored. Similarly, many of the provisions to which article 86 applies explicitly concern conduct outside the high seas. *See, e.g.*, UNCLOS, art. 92(1), 1833 U.N.T.S. at 433 ("A ship may not change its flag during a voyage or while in a port of call. . . ."); *id.* art. 100, 1833 U.N.T.S. at 436 ("All States shall cooperate to the fullest possible extent in the repression of piracy on the high seas or in any other place outside the jurisdiction of any State."). Ali's expansive interpretation of article 86 is simply not plausible. * * *

Thwarted by article 101's text, Ali contends that even if facilitative acts count as piracy, a nation's universal jurisdiction over piracy offenses is limited to high seas conduct. In support of this claim, Ali invokes UNCLOS article 105, which reads,

> On the high seas, or in any other place outside the jurisdiction of any State, every State may seize a pirate ship or aircraft, or a ship or aircraft taken by piracy and under the control of pirates and arrest the persons and seize the property on board. The courts of the State which carried out the seizure may decide upon the penalties to be imposed. . . .

1833 U.N.T.S. at 437. Ali understands article 105's preface to govern the actual enforcement of antipiracy law—and, by extension, to restrict universal jurisdiction to the high seas—even if the definition of piracy is more expansive. In fact, Ali gets it backward. Rather than curtailing the categories of persons who may be prosecuted as pirates, the provision's reference to the high seas highlights the broad authority of nations to apprehend pirates even in international waters. His reading also proves too much, leaving nations incapable of prosecuting even those undisputed pirates they discover within their own borders—a far cry from "universal" jurisdiction. Article 105 is therefore no indication international law limits the liability of aiders and abettors to their conduct on the high seas. * * * Because international law permits prosecuting acts of aiding and abetting piracy committed while not on the high seas, the *Charming Betsy* canon is no constraint on the scope of Count Two.

2. Piracy and the Presumption Against Extraterritorial Effect

Ali next attempts to achieve through the presumption against extraterritoriality what he cannot with *Charming Betsy*. Generally, the extraterritorial reach of an ancillary offense like aiding and abetting or conspiracy is coterminous with that of the underlying criminal statute. And when the underlying criminal statute's extraterritorial reach is unquestionable, the presumption is rebutted with equal force for aiding and abetting. *See United States v. Hill*, 279 F.3d 731, 739 (9th Cir. 2002) ("[A]iding and abetting[ ] and conspiracy . . . have been deemed to confer extraterritorial jurisdiction to the same extent as the offenses that underlie them."); *see also Yunis*, 924 F.2d at 1091 (analyzing underlying offenses under extraterritoriality canon but conducting no separate analysis with respect to conspiracy conviction). Ali admits the piracy statute must have some extraterritorial reach—after all, its very terms cover conduct outside U.S. territory—but denies that the extraterritorial scope extends to any conduct that was not itself perpetrated on the high seas. * * *

Ali claims the government seeks to use aider and abettor liability to expand the extraterritorial scope of the piracy statute beyond conduct on the high seas. Because § 1651 expressly targets crimes committed on the high seas, he believes Congress intended its extraterritorial effect—and, by extension, that of the aiding and abetting statute—to extend to international waters and no further. * * * [E]xtending aider and abettor liability to those who facilitate such conduct furthers the goal of deterring piracy on the high seas—even when the facilitator stays close to shore. * * * Section 1651's high seas language refers to the very feature of piracy that makes it such a threat: that it exists outside the reach of any territorial authority, rendering it both notoriously difficult to police and inimical to international commerce. As UNCLOS § 101(c) recognizes, it is self-defeating to prosecute those pirates desperate enough to do the dirty work but immunize the planners, organizers, and negotiators who remain ashore. * * * By defining piracy in terms of the law of nations, § 1651 incorporated this extraterritorial application of the international law of piracy and indicates Congress's intent to subject extraterritorial acts like Ali's to prosecution. * * * That is not to say § 1651's high seas requirement plays no role in prosecuting Ali for aiding and abetting piracy, for the government must prove *someone* committed piratical acts while on the high seas. That is an element the government must prove at trial, but not one it must show Ali perpetrated personally.

B. Conspiracy to Commit Piracy

Though the aiding and abetting statute reaches Ali's conduct, his conspiracy charge is another matter. In many respects conspiracy and aiding and abetting are alike, which would suggest the government's ability to charge Ali with one implies the ability to charge him with both. While conspiracy is a "separate and distinct" offense in the United States, *Pinkerton v. United States*, 328 U.S. 640, 643 (1946), it is also a theory of liability like aiding and abetting; "[a]s long as a substantive offense was done in furtherance of the conspiracy, and was reasonably foreseeable as a necessary or natural consequence of the unlawful agreement, then a conspirator will be held vicariously liable for the offense committed by his or her co-conspirators." *United States v. Moore*, 651 F.3d 30, 80 (D.C. Cir. 2011) (per curiam).

Yet a crucial difference separates the two theories of liability. Because § 371, like § 2, fails to offer concrete evidence of its application abroad, we turn, pursuant to the *Charming Betsy* canon, to international law to help us resolve this ambiguity of meaning. Whereas UNCLOS, by including facilitative acts within article 101's definition of piracy, endorses aider and abettor liability for pirates, the convention is silent on conspiratorial liability. International law provides for limited instances in which nations may prosecute the crimes of foreign nationals committed abroad, and, in invoking universal jurisdiction here, the government predicates its prosecution of Ali on one of those theories. And although neither side disputes the applicability of universal jurisdiction to piracy as defined by the law of nations, UNCLOS's plain language does not include *conspiracy* to commit piracy. The government offers us no reason to believe otherwise, and at any rate, we are mindful that "imposing liability on the basis of a violation of 'international law' or the 'law of nations' or the 'law of war' generally must be based on norms *firmly* grounded in international law." *Hamdan v. United States*, 696 F.3d 1238, 1250 n.10 (D.C. Cir. 2012) (emphasis added). International law does not permit the government's abortive use of universal jurisdiction to charge Ali with conspiracy. Thus, the *Charming Betsy* doctrine, which was no impediment to Ali's aider and abettor liability, cautions against his prosecution for conspiracy.

The government hopes nonetheless to salvage its argument through appeal to § 371's text. Though courts construe statutes, when possible, to accord with international law, Congress has full license to enact laws that supersede it. * * * Homing in on the phrase "any offense against the United States" in § 371, the government contends Congress intended the statute to apply to all federal criminal statutes, even when the result conflicts with international law. Yet, as we explained above, if we are to interpret § 371 as supplanting international law, we need stronger evidence than this. * * * Under international law, prosecuting Ali for conspiracy to commit piracy would require the United States to have universal jurisdiction over his offense. And such jurisdiction would only exist if the underlying charge actually falls within UNCLOS's definition of piracy. Because conspiracy, unlike aiding and abetting, is not part of that definition, and because § 371 falls short of expressly rejecting international law, *Charming Betsy* precludes Ali's prosecution for conspiracy to commit piracy. The district court properly dismissed Count One.

III. The Hostage Taking Charges

The linguistic impediments that trouble Counts One and Two do not beset the charges for hostage taking under 18 U.S.C. § 1203. The statute's extraterritorial scope is as clear as can be, prescribing punishments against "whoever, whether inside or outside the United States, seizes or detains and threatens to kill, to injure, or to continue to detain another person in order to compel a third person or a governmental organization to do or abstain from doing any act." 18 U.S.C. § 1203(a). We also need not worry about *Charming Betsy*'s implications, as § 1203 unambiguously criminalizes Ali's conduct.

Section 1203 likely reflects international law anyway, as it fulfills U.S. treaty obligations under the widely supported International Convention Against the Taking of Hostages, Dec. 17, 1979, 18 I.L.M. 1456, 1316 U.N.T.S. 205. Nor, as in the case of the federal piracy statute, is there any uncertainty as to the availability of conspiratorial liability, since the statute applies equally to any person who "attempts or conspires to" commit hostage taking. 18 U.S.C. § 1203(a).

Faced with this reality, Ali has adopted a different strategy when it comes to Counts Three and Four, swapping his statutory arguments for constitutional ones. He relies on the principle embraced by many courts that the Fifth Amendment's guarantee of due process may impose limits on a criminal law's extraterritorial application even when interpretive canons do not. Though this Circuit has yet to speak definitively, several other circuits have reasoned that before a federal criminal statute is given extraterritorial effect, due process requires "a sufficient nexus between the defendant and the United States, so that such application would not be arbitrary or fundamentally unfair." *United States v. Davis*, 905 F.2d 245, 248–49 (9th Cir. 1990).[6] Others have approached the due process issue in more cautious terms. Likewise, the principle is not without its scholarly critics. We need not decide, however, whether the Constitution limits the extraterritorial exercise of federal criminal jurisdiction. Either way, Ali's prosecution under § 1203 safely satisfies the requirements erected by the Fifth Amendment.[7]

A. *Due Process and Extraterritorial Conduct*

In support of his due process argument, Ali cites a panoply of cases concerning personal jurisdiction in the context of civil suits. It is true courts have periodically borrowed the language of personal jurisdiction in discussing the due process constraints on extraterritoriality. But Ali's flawed analogies do not establish actual standards for judicial inquiry; the law of personal jurisdiction is simply inapposite. To the extent the nexus requirement serves as a proxy for due process, it addresses the broader concern of ensuring that "a United States court will assert jurisdiction only over a defendant who should reasonably anticipate being haled into court in this country." *United States v. Klimavicius-Viloria*, 144 F.3d 1249, 1257 (9th Cir. 1998). What appears to be the animating principle governing the due process limits of extraterritorial

---

[6] Some courts have suggested grouping these decisions into two categories: those that "look for real effects or consequences accruing in the United States before they find [a] nexus" and those that "require only that extraterritorial prosecution be neither arbitrary nor fundamentally unfair, and are not concerned with whether a sufficient nexus exists." United States v. Campbell, 798 F. Supp. 2d 293, 306–07 (D.D.C. 2011). The distinction may be illusory, with the "nexus" inquiry serving more as a proxy for whether a particular prosecution is unfair. See id. at 307. For present purposes, that question is purely academic, as Ali does not tether his argument to a particular version of the due process argument.

[7] Ali has not cited—and we have not found—any case in which extraterritorial application of a federal criminal statute was actually deemed a due process violation. Although that does not mean such a result is beyond the realm of possibility, it does suggest Ali's burden is a heavy one, for he traverses uncharted territory.

jurisdiction is the idea that "no man shall be held criminally responsible for conduct which he could not reasonably understand to be proscribed." *Bouie v. City of Columbia*, 378 U.S. 347, 351 (1964) (internal quotation marks omitted). The "ultimate question" is whether "application of the statute to the defendant [would] be arbitrary or fundamentally unfair." *United States v. Juda*, 46 F.3d 961, 967 (9th Cir. 1995).

United States v. Shi, 525 F.3d 709 (9th Cir. 2008), is most on point. *Shi* dealt with a due process challenge to the defendant's prosecution under 18 U.S.C. § 2280, which implements the Convention for the Suppression of Unlawful Acts Against the Safety of Maritime Navigation, Mar. 10, 1988, 27 I.L.M. 672, 1678 U.N.T.S. 222. *See* 525 F.3d at 717–24. Because "the Maritime Safety Convention . . . expressly provides foreign offenders with notice that their conduct will be prosecuted by any state signatory," due process required no specific nexus between the defendant and the United States. In other words, the treaty at issue in *Shi* did what the International Convention Against the Taking of Hostages does here: provide global notice that certain generally condemned acts are subject to prosecution. We agree with the Ninth Circuit that the Due Process Clause demands no more. * * * [I]t is the "universal condemnation of the offender's conduct," not some theory of universal jurisdiction, that drove the Ninth Circuit's reasoning. * * * By that standard, hostage taking is also an offense whose proscription "is a result of universal condemnation of those activities and general interest in cooperating to suppress them, as reflected in widely-accepted international agreements and resolutions of international organizations." RESTATEMENT, *supra*, at § 404 cmt. a. * * *

Ali also complains that though China was a signatory to the relevant international agreement in *Shi*, Somalia is not a party to the International Convention Against the Taking of Hostages, meaning his home nation has not consented to U.S. criminal jurisdiction over its hostage-taking nationals. True, as a matter of *international* law, this case may not be so obvious as those in which "the flag nation has consented to the application of United States law to the defendants." *United States v. Angulo-Hernández*, 565 F.3d 2, 11 (1st Cir. 2009). But Ali mistakes the due process inquiry for the customary international law of jurisdiction. "Whatever merit [these] claims may have as a matter of international law, they cannot prevail before this court. . . . Our duty is to enforce the Constitution, laws, and treaties of the United States, not to conform the law of the land to norms of customary international law." *Yunis*, 924 F.2d at 1091. Whatever due process requires here, the Hostage Taking Convention suffices by "expressly provid[ing] foreign offenders with notice that their conduct will be prosecuted by any state signatory." *Shi*, 525 F.3d at 723. *That* is what *Shi* said. It did not hold that due process depends on the participation of the *defendant's* nation in the agreement. * * *

IV. CONCLUSION

We affirm the district court's dismissal of Count One. We reverse the district court's narrowing of the scope of Count Two to acts Ali performed while on the high seas and reverse dismissal of Counts Three and Four.

NOTES & QUESTIONS

1. Case Outcome

Ali, who spent most of his adult life in the United States, was tried in a district court on the charges that survived the above appellate challenge. The jury found him not guilty of piracy; they deadlocked on the hostage-taking charges. Can you imagine why a jury might reach this outcome? Prosecutors initially planned a retrial, but eventually dropped all charges in February 2014 (in part due to double jeopardy concerns).

2. The Holding

Is the D.C. Circuit's reasoning on facilitation and the process of treaty interpretation persuasive or should the court have found a "high seas" requirement for this form of responsibility? Should the court have allowed the conspiracy to commit piracy charge to stand? On what basis did the court determine that there was no due process violation when the defendant was being prosecuted for acts with virtually no U.S. nexus? Ali's precise role in the *CEC Future* attack was contested, although it is undisputed that he helped to negotiate the ransom demand. Should this be enough to render him an accomplice to the prior act of piracy? If so, are insurance companies that engage in such negotiations on behalf of their insured also facilitating piracy?

In *United States v. Shibin*, 722 F.3d 233 (4th Cir. 2013), the Fourth Circuit reached largely the same conclusions in a case presenting strikingly similar facts (the defendant acted as negotiator and translator following an act of piracy). In upholding the charges against Shibin, the Fourth Circuit also cited U.N. Security Council resolutions (e.g., Resolution 1976 of April 11, 2011, and Resolution 2020 of November 22, 2011) encouraging states to investigate and prosecute those who finance, plan, organize, and unlawfully profit from pirate attacks, on the theory that most pirate "kingpins" are not located on the high seas. The court also ruled that the exercise of jurisdiction did not depend on international law or the principle of universal jurisdiction; rather, Congress has the authority to enforce its laws beyond the territorial boundaries of the United States by virtue of the Define and Punish Clause (U.S. Const. art. I, § 8, cl. 10), or the Necessary and Proper Clause (U.S. Const. art. I, § 8, cl. 18) with respect to the obligation to implement the underlying treaties. In other words, U.S. law was deemed to provide a separate and complete basis of jurisdiction over the crimes in question.

3. *United States v. Yunis*

The principal case cites *United States v. Yunis*, 924 F.2d 1086 (D.C. Cir. 1991). Fawaz Yunis, a Lebanese national, was the first suspected terrorist arrested overseas by U.S. law enforcement officials and convicted in the United States for an attack against U.S. citizens on foreign soil. The United

States Federal Bureau of Investigations (FBI) engaged a yacht, a naval munitions ship, an aircraft carrier, and a twin-engine aircraft as part of "Operation Goldenrod" to lure and then apprehend Yunis in the Mediterranean Sea on a bogus drug deal. Yunis was sentenced to serve thirty years for his offenses, which reflects mitigation for the fact that he allowed two hostages with medical conditions to disembark. The United States deported him in 2005 to Lebanon after he had served nearly 16 years in federal prison.

A case involving the first World Trade Center bombing and a conspiracy to bomb U.S. airliners addressed many of the same issues involved with the exercise of extraterritorial jurisdiction. *See U.S. v. Yousef*, 327 F.3d 56 (2d Cir. 2003). In that case, the Second Circuit Court of Appeals concluded that "the indefinite category of 'terrorism' is not subject to universal jurisdiction." Do the new terrorism treaties call this conclusion into question?

4. The Hostage Taking Act

The Hostage Taking Act, 18 U.S.C. §§ 1203, provides that:

> **(b) (1)** It is not an offense under this section if the conduct required for the offense occurred outside the United States unless—
>
> **(A)** the offender or the person seized or detained is a national of the United States;
>
> **(B)** the offender is found in the United States; or
>
> **(C)** the governmental organization sought to be compelled is the Government of the United States.
>
> **(2)** It is not an offense under this section if the conduct required for the offense occurred inside the United States, each alleged offender and each person seized or detained are nationals of the United States, and each alleged offender is found in the United States, unless the governmental organization sought to be compelled is the Government of the United States.

The U.S. Congress enacted the Hostage Taking Act in response to the United States' ratification of the International Convention Against the Taking of Hostages, 1316 U.N.T.S. 205. That treaty, in turn, was a response by the U.N. General Assembly to a rash of hostage-taking incidents in the 1970s. The Convention was opened for signature on December 18, 1979, and entered into force on June 3, 1983. It contains the following provisions of relevance to the principal case:

> **Article 1**
>
> 1. Any person who seizes or detains and threatens to kill, to injure or to continue to detain another person (hereinafter referred to as the "hostage") in order to compel a third party, namely, a State, an international intergovernmental organization, a natural or juridical person, or a group of persons, to do or abstain from doing any act as an explicit or implicit condition for the release of the hostage commits the offence of taking of hostages ("hostage-taking") within the meaning of this Convention.

2. Any person who:
   a. attempts to commit an act of hostage-taking, or
   b. participates as an accomplice of anyone who commits or attempts to commit an act of hostage-taking likewise commits an offence for the purposes of this Convention.

Article 5

1. Each State Party shall take such measures as may be necessary to establish its jurisdiction over any of the offences set forth in article 1 which are committed:
   a. in its territory or on board a ship or aircraft registered in that State;
   b. by any of its nationals or, if that State considers it appropriate, by those stateless persons who have their habitual residence in its territory;
   c. in order to compel that State to do or abstain from doing any act; or
   d. with respect to a hostage who is a national of that State, if that State considers it appropriate.
2. Each State Party shall likewise take such measures as may be necessary to establish its jurisdiction over the offences set forth in article 1 in cases where the alleged offender is present in its territory and it does not extradite him to any of the States mentioned in paragraph 1 of this article.
3. This Convention does not exclude any criminal jurisdiction exercised in accordance with internal law.

What theories of jurisdiction are reflected in the treaty and in the United States' implementing legislation? Has the United States accurately implemented the treaty's jurisdictional provisions? Why would the treaty and legislation allow for the prosecution of someone whose only connection to the prosecuting state is the fact that the perpetrator is in that state's custody? What state interests are advanced by such a prosecution? Returning to the main case, was Ali "found" in the United States?

5. Passive Personality Jurisdiction

The passive personality principle of jurisdiction allows states to exercise jurisdiction over crimes committed against their nationals. *Yunis* involved both universal and passive personality jurisdiction because there happened to be two U.S. citizens on board—Thomas Landry Slade, a professor at the American University in Beirut, and his son. Yunis unsuccessfully argued that the exercise of jurisdiction based upon the passive personality principle was not appropriate when United States citizens were not specifically targeted (indeed, he claimed he did not know that there happened to be two U.S. citizens on board). Do you agree? In other words, does it matter if the perpetrators of an act of terrorism or other international crime were indifferent to whether U.S. citizens were on board the aircraft? At least one federal court has found that asserting jurisdiction in the United States based upon passive personality does not require that the offender intend to target U.S. citizens. *Biton v Palestinian Interim Self-Government Authority,* 510 F.Supp. 2d 144, 146 (D.D.C. 2007) ("[T]his Court has exercised extraterritorial jurisdiction in state-sponsored terrorism cases, based in part on the passive personality principle, even though the victims were not targeted because of their U.S. citizenship."). In *Yunis*, the airline in question was not registered in the United States, did not depart from the United States, was not bound for the United States, did not even fly over the United States, and was seized to pressure the Arab League to expel all Palestinians from Lebanon because they were considered a security threat. What U.S. interests are at stake? In a bizarre twist of fate, the two Americans who happened to be on board the flight Yunis hijacked were hijacked again by a grenade-wielding Palestinian as they tried to fly home.

6. Jurisdictional Defenses

Somalia is not a party to the International Convention Against the Taking of Hostages. With respect to Yunis, Jordan (the territory within which the original hijacking occurred) acceded to the International Convention Against the Taking of Hostages on February 19, 1986, prior to the assertion of jurisdiction, but Lebanon (of which Yunis was a national) did not accede to that treaty until December 4, 1997. (A state accedes to a treaty when it ratifies it after the treaty has entered into force). Does it matter that Jordan but not Lebanon was a party to the Hostages Convention at the time the suit was brought? Is it significant that in both *Yunis* and *Ali*, neither state was a party when the underlying events happened?

By ratifying a treaty authorizing, or mandating, the use of expansive jurisdictional bases, do states waive in advance any jurisdictional defenses that may be raised by nationals being prosecuted thereunder? In *United States v. Emmanuel*, 611 F.3d 783, 809 (11th Cir. 2010), the court determined that it was of no moment that the prosecuted acts of torture were committed before the territorial state ratified the Torture Convention. In that case, however, the defendant—the son of Charles Taylor of Liberia—was a U.S. citizen deemed subject to validly enacted U.S. laws.

7. *Male Captus Bene Detentus*

Ali, Yunis, and Shibin all unsuccessfully argued that the United States had no personal jurisdiction over them. Ali was lured to the United States under false pretenses; Yunis was seized on the high seas, also following a ruse; and Shibin was arrested by Somalian forces and turned over to the FBI (there is no extradition treaty between the United States and Somalia).

For many states, the way in which an accused is brought before their courts is irrelevant (the principle of *male captus, bene detentus*—wrongly captured, properly detained); others will refuse jurisdiction where an individual was apprehended in violation of international law or international obligations. The United States applies the *male captus* principle, which it calls the *Ker-Frisbee* doctrine from its jurisprudential origins. *See U.S. v. Alvarez-Machain,* 504 U.S. 655 (1992). A notable exception to *Ker-Frisbee* was articulated in *United States v. Toscanino*, 500 F.2d 267 (2d Cir. 1974), which held that jurisdiction should be barred where cruel or outrageous treatment in violation of the due process clause was used. In addition to potentially infringing the rights of defendants, such operations also implicate public international law and protections afforded to state sovereignty.

A memorandum by the Department of Justice's Office of Legal Counsel on the legality of arrest operations in violation of international law states that 18 U.S.C. § 3052 grants the FBI broad investigative and apprehension authority when crimes against the United States are at issue, including permission to undertake an extraterritorial capture without the cooperation or consent of the custodial state, even if such actions would be in violation of customary international law, unexecuted treaty obligations (such as Article 2(4) of the U.N. Charter), or a valid extradition treaty. *See* 13 U.S. Op. Off. Legal Counsel 163 (1989). A recent example of such a "snatch and grab" operation involved Anu Anas Al-Liby, who was captured in Tripoli, Libya, in October 2013 by U.S. Special Forces, the CIA, and the FBI. He was later taken aboard a Navy ship and subsequently transferred to federal custody to face charges alleging his involvement in the 1998 embassy bombings in Kenya and Tanzania. He died of liver disease before his trial. A simultaneous operation in Somalia failed to capture an alleged mastermind of the 2013 Westgate shopping mall attack in Nairobi, Kenya. (Ahmed Godane, who claimed responsibility for the Westgate attack, was killed in September 2014 in a U.S. drone strike in Somalia.)

By contrast, in the British Commonwealth, the principle of *male captus, bene detentus* no longer holds sway. The first case to break with the traditional approach was *R. v. Hartley,* [1978] 2 N.Z.L.R. 199 (C.A.). The accused was arrested in Australia and forcibly placed on a plane to New Zealand in disregard of the extradition treaty between the two countries. The court found that the accused was the victim of an illegal detention, and that this abuse of his right to due process gave the court the authority to stay the proceedings. This precedent was applied subsequently in Australia (*Levinge v. Director of Custodial Services and others*, (1987) 9 N.S.W.L.R. 546), South Africa (*State v. Ebrahim*, [1991] 2 S.A. 553 (S. Afr. App. Div.)), Canada (*R. v. Jewitt*, [1985] 2 S.C.R. 128; *O'Connor v. The Queen*, [1995] 4 S.C.R. 411), and the U.K. (*R. v. Horseferry Road Magistrates' Court, Ex parte Bennett,* [1993] 3 All E.R. 138 (H.L.)). In *Bennett,* the court noted that "the judiciary accept [sic] a responsibility for the maintenance of the rule of law that embraces a willingness to oversee executive action and to refuse to countenance behavior that threatens either basic human rights or the rule of law." *Id.* at 61–62.

So far, international tribunals have largely applied the *male captus, bene detentus* principle. The ICTY Appeals Chamber held that the apprehension of an accused in a manner that violates a state's sovereignty in cases involving "universally condemned offences" does not negate the Tribunal's jurisdiction. In the same decision, the Appeals Chamber noted in *dicta* that an apprehension or detention that includes serious violations of certain human rights (such as torture or cruel, inhuman, or degrading treatment) could divest the Tribunal of jurisdiction. *See Prosecutor v. Dragan Nikolić,* Case No. IT–94–2–AR73, Decision On Interlocutory Appeal Concerning Legality of Arrest (June 5, 2003).

The International Criminal Tribunal for Rwanda (ICTR) also held in *dicta* that it could decline—as a matter of discretion—to exercise its jurisdiction in cases "where to exercise that jurisdiction in light of serious and egregious violations of the accused's right would prove detrimental to the court's integrity." *Prosecutor v. Barayagwiza*, Case No. ICTR–97–19, Decision on the Extremely Urgent Motion by the Defence for Orders to Review and/or Nullify the Arrest and Provisional Detention of the Suspect, para. 74 (Nov. 3, 1999). The ICTR further noted, "In a situation where an accused is very seriously mistreated, maybe even subjected to inhuman, cruel or degrading treatment, or torture, before being handed over to the Tribunal, this may constitute a legal impediment to the exercise of jurisdiction over such an accused." *Id.* at para. 114.

The ICC touched on the issue in a challenge to the jurisdiction of the Court by Thomas Lubanga Dyilo. Lubanga argued that his arrest and detention by authorities in the Democratic Republic of the Congo were illegal, and thus he could not receive a fair trial before the ICC. In denying Lubanga's claim, both the Pre-Trial Chamber and the Appeals Chamber noted in *dicta* that it should not assert jurisdiction over a suspect whose fundamental rights were breached in such a way as to make a fair trial impossible. Such violations would involve serious harm to bodily integrity rights, such as torture, and not challenges to the procedure by which a suspect was detained and transported to the court. *Prosecutor v. Thomas Lubanga Dyilo*, Case No. ICC–01/04–01/06 (OA4), Judgment on the Appeal of Mr. Thomas Lubanga Dyilo against the Decision on the Defence Challenge to the Jurisdiction of the Court pursuant to article 19(2)(a) of the Statute of 3 October 2006 (Dec. 14, 2006).

8. Reasonableness

Excluding universal jurisdiction, the Restatement (Third) subjected the exercise of other forms of prescriptive and adjudicative jurisdiction to a reasonableness test. Reference to comity and the requirement of a genuine connection between the state seeking to regulate and the subject of the regulation in the Restatement (Fourth) suggests a similar reasonableness requirement, though with much less specificity than that provided in the Restatement (Third). Is such a test likely to be helpful in resolving conflicts where states have concurrent jurisdiction? Is the greater specificity of such a test found in the Restatement (Third) to be preferred over the more general references in the Restatement (Fourth)? Should the reasonableness of an exercise of jurisdiction be determined on the basis of reciprocity? In other words, should the reasonableness of a particular exercise of jurisdiction be premised at all upon whether other implicated (or protesting) states would exercise their jurisdiction in the same circumstances and to the same extent? Alternatively, should reasonableness be seen as an expression of comity: "the recognition which one nation allows within its territory to the legislative, executive, or judicial acts of another nation, having due regard both to international duty and convenience" that is borne of "neither a matter of absolute obligation, on the one hand, nor of mere courtesy and good will, upon the other." *Hilton v. Guyot*, 159 U.S. 113, 163–64 (1895). The Restatement (Fourth) appears to adopt this latter approach. For a discussion of the various rationales for limiting national jurisdiction, see the majority and dissenting opinions of the United States Supreme Court in *Hartford Fire Insurance Co. v. California*, 509 U.S. 764 (1993), which addressed the extraterritorial application of U.S. antitrust law.

The Restatement (Third) did not subject the exercise of universal jurisdiction to a reasonableness limitation. The Restatement (Fourth) provides that U.S. courts should take into account the legitimate interests of other nations as a matter of comity for all bases of jurisdiction, including universality. Which approach is better? Should a state's prescriptive or adjudicative jurisdiction be broader with respect to universal crimes than with respect to ordinary domestic crimes? Should the principle of comity influence the assertion of jurisdiction over universal crimes, or are such crimes so egregious or unique that assertions of jurisdiction over them should be assessed independently of the interests of other nations?

9. *Aut Dedere Aut Judicare*

The Hostages Treaty—like many multilateral treaties defining international crimes—contains in Article 5(2) the principle of *aut dedere aut judicare* ("either extradite or adjudicate") (also occasionally referred to as *aut dedere aut prosequi* ("either extradite or prosecute")), which requires parties to the treaty to either investigate/prosecute or to extradite offenders found within their territory. The principle bespeaks increasing recognition that states are bound to act, either through prosecution or through extradition, to ensure that individuals who perpetrate international crimes are brought to justice. This provision appears in a number of multilateral treaties proscribing international and transnational crimes. Given that many of these treaties are well-subscribed to, can it be said that the obligation to prosecute or extradite individuals accused of committing international crimes is now one of customary international law? In other words, is there a general duty to prosecute international crimes, or to extradite offenders, where defendants are within a state's reach? Should there be? What developments in international law would it take to reach the conclusion that states were bound by general international law to either extradite or prosecute? The International Law Commission is studying the *aut dedere aut judicare* principle.

II. UNIVERSAL JURISDICTION

As discussed in *Ali*, universal jurisdiction refers to the authority of *any* state to assert jurisdiction over an unlawful act, regardless of the nationality of the perpetrator or victim, and regardless of where the act took place. Universal jurisdiction developed in response to the crimes of piracy and later the slave trade, in part because these crimes had no fixed geographic location and transcended national boundaries. Both crimes remain subject to universal jurisdiction. *See, e.g.*, Article 19, Geneva Convention on the High Seas of 29 April 1958 ("On the high seas, or in any other place outside the jurisdiction of any State, every State may seize a pirate ship or aircraft . . . and arrest the persons and seize the property on board. The courts of the State which carried out the seizure may decide upon the penalties to be imposed."). Universal jurisdiction today is justified more on the basis of the severity of the crime, the shared interest in not offering safe haven to abusers, and the undesirable consequences of impunity. Under these theories, states exercising universal jurisdiction are agents of the international community enforcing obligations that are universally accepted. The individual state interests in prosecution are thus less salient than they are with respect to prosecutions according to the territorial, nationality, or protective principles.

Universal jurisdiction is not without its detractors and has been the subject of suit before the International Court of Justice (ICJ). The first suit involved Belgium's expansive universal jurisdiction law, enacted on June 16, 1993, to cover war crimes and then amended on February 10, 1999, to cover acts of genocide and crimes against humanity. *See* The Act of 16 June 1993 Concerning the Punishment of Grave Breaches of the Geneva Conventions of 12 August 1949 and their Additional Protocols I and II of 18 June 1977 (Official Journal of 05.08.1993, at 17751–17755); The Law of 10 February 1999 Concerning the Punishment of Serious Violations of International Humanitarian Law, reprinted at 38 I.L.M. 918 (1999). The law as originally drafted and first amended provided for universal jurisdiction within Belgium for war crimes, crimes against humanity, and genocide—even *in absentia*. It also allowed private parties with no connections to Belgium to initiate criminal suits, and withheld immunity defenses even for sitting heads of state.

The first case to result in a conviction under the 1993 version of the law involved the Rwandan genocide and the so-called "Butare Four"—factory director Alphonse Higaniro; former professor at Butare University Vincent Ntezimana; and Benedictine nuns Sister Gertrude (Consolata Mukangango) and Sister Kizito (Julienne Mukabutera). A jury convicted the four of war crimes in June 2001 for their participation in the killing of Tutsi individuals in their home country of Rwanda and sentenced them to between 12 and 20 years' imprisonment. The defendants had fled to Belgium after the genocide in Rwanda, and no extradition treaty was in place between the two countries. *See* Luc Reydams, *Belgium's First Application of Universal Jurisdiction: The Butare Four Case*, 1 J. INT'L CRIM. JUST. 428 (2003).

On April 11, 2000, the Brussels Tribunal of the First Instance issued an international arrest warrant pursuant to Belgium's universal jurisdiction statute against Abdulaye Yerodia Ndombasi, then the foreign minister of the Democratic Republic of the Congo (DRC) in the government of President Laurent-Désiré Kabila. Authorities accused Yerodia—who allegedly incited hatred against the Tutsi population of the DRC prior to becoming Foreign Minister—of crimes against humanity and war crimes. The court's investigation was based on victim and witness testimony, some of them Belgian nationals. The arrest warrant was distributed to other states through INTERPOL, the International Criminal Police Organization.

In response, the DRC instituted proceedings against Belgium before the ICJ seeking the annulment of the arrest warrant and claiming "moral injury." The DRC originally challenged the Belgian legislation directly, arguing that Belgium lacked authority under international law to issue the arrest warrant. Later, the DRC narrowed its case to the claim that Yerodia was entitled to diplomatic immunity by virtue of his position as Foreign Minister. Invoking the *non ultra petita* rule ("not more than asked"), which dictates that an adjudicative body should not pronounce upon more than it has been asked to decide, the full Court ultimately ruled only on this latter ground. It held that the issuance of an arrest warrant against an incumbent foreign minister, regardless of the nature of the charges against him, violated that official's right to enjoy immunity from criminal jurisdiction and ordered that Belgium cancel the warrant in question. This aspect of the Court's ruling is discussed *infra* in Chapter 17 on Defenses Under International Criminal Law. At the time the Court ruled, the immunity issue was no longer relevant because Yerodia had stepped down as Foreign Minister and thus was no longer entitled to the applicable immunity; however, the Court proceeded to judgment on the grounds that a legal dispute properly existed on the date the case was referred.

Several judges insisted that the jurisdictional question of Belgium's competence to issue the arrest warrant was foundational, and indeed antecedent, to the immunities question. One set of judges reasoned in a Joint and Separate Opinion that, "if there is no jurisdiction *en principe*, then the question of an immunity from a jurisdiction which would otherwise exist simply does not arise." And so, several judges took it upon themselves to consider the lawfulness of universal jurisdiction under international law, even though the parties had relinquished their arguments on this point. One of these separate opinions is below—a joint and separate opinion by the judges hailing from the United Kingdom, the Netherlands, and the United States. Separate opinions from the French president of the Court and a dissenting opinion from the *ad hoc* Belgian judge are reproduced in the Notes. (See the Appendix for a map of the DRC.)

Arrest Warrant of 11 April 2000 (Democratic Republic of the Congo v. Belgium)

2002 I.C.J. Reports 3 (Feb. 14).
Joint Sep. Op. Higgins, Kooijmans & Buergenthal.

6. As Mr. Yerodia was a non-national of Belgium and the alleged offences described in the arrest warrant occurred outside of the territory over which Belgium has jurisdiction, the victims being non-Belgians, the arrest warrant was necessarily predicated on universal jurisdiction.

Indeed, both it and the enabling legislation of 1993 and 1999 expressly say so. Moreover, Mr. Yerodia himself was outside of Belgium at the time the warrant was issued. * * *

19. We therefore turn to the question whether States are entitled to exercise jurisdiction over persons having no connection with the forum State when the accused is not present in the State's territory. The necessary point of departure must be the sources of international law identified in Article 38, paragraph 1(c), of the Statute of the Court, together with obligations imposed upon all United Nations Members by Security Council resolutions, or by such General Assembly resolutions as meet the criteria enunciated by the Court in the case concerning *Legality of the Threat or Use of Nuclear Weapons*, Advisory Opinion (I.C.J. Reports 1996, p. 226, para. 70).*

20. Our analysis may begin with national legislation, to see if it evidences a State practice. Save for the Belgian legislation of 10 February 1999, national legislation, whether in fulfillment of international treaty obligations to make certain international crimes offences also in national law, or otherwise, does not suggest a universal jurisdiction over these offences. Various examples typify the more qualified practice. The Australian War Crimes Act of 1945, as amended in 1988, provides for the prosecution in Australia of crimes committed between 1 September 1939 and 8 May 1945 by persons who were Australian citizens or residents at the times of being charged with the offences (ss. 9 and 11). The United Kingdom War Crimes Act of 1991 enables proceedings to be brought for murder, manslaughter or culpable homicide, committed between 1 September 1935 and 5 June 1945, in a place that was part of Germany or under German occupation, and in circumstances where the accused was at the time, or has become, a British citizen or resident of the United Kingdom. The statutory jurisdiction provided for by France, Germany and (in even broader terms) the Netherlands, refer for their jurisdictional basis to the jurisdictional provisions in those international treaties to which the legislation was intended to give effect. It should be noted, however, that the German Government on 16 January 2002 has submitted a legislative proposal to the German Parliament, section 1 of which provides:

> This Code governs all the punishable acts listed herein violating public international law, [and] in the case of felonies listed herein [this Code governs] even if the act was committed abroad and does not show any link to [Germany].

The Criminal Code of Canada 1985 allows the execution of jurisdiction when at the time of the act or omission the accused was a Canadian

* Eds.: The cited paragraph states that in some cases a General Assembly resolution may have "normative value." To determine if a General Assembly resolution has such a normative value, the Court states "it is necessary to look at its content and the conditions of its adoption; it is also necessary to see whether an *opinio juris* exists as to its normative character. Or a series of resolutions may show the gradual evolution of the *opinio juris* required for the establishment of a new rule."

citizen or "employed by Canada in a civilian or military capacity;" or the "victim is a Canadian citizen or a citizen of a State that is allied with Canada in an armed conflict," or when "at the time of the act or omission Canada could, in conformity with international law, exercise jurisdiction over the person on the basis of the person's presence in Canada" (Art. 7).

21. All of these illustrate the trend to provide for the trial and punishment under international law of certain crimes that have been committed extraterritorially. But none of them, nor the many others that have been studied by the Court, represent a classical assertion of a universal jurisdiction over particular offences committed elsewhere by persons having no relationship or connection with the forum State.

22. The case law under these provisions has largely been cautious so far as reliance on universal jurisdiction is concerned. In the *Pinochet* case in the English courts, the jurisdictional basis was clearly treaty based, with the double criminality rule required for extradition being met by English legislation in September 1988, after which date torture committed abroad was a crime in the United Kingdom as it already was in Spain. In Australia the Federal Court referred to a group of crimes over which international law granted universal jurisdiction, even though national enabling legislation would also be needed (*Nulyarimma*, 1999: genocide). The High Court confirmed the authority of the legislature to confer jurisdiction on the courts to exercise a universal jurisdiction over war crimes (*Polyukovich*, 1991). In Austria (whose Penal Code emphasizes the double-criminality requirement), the Supreme Court found that it had jurisdiction over persons charged with genocide, given that there was not a functioning legal system in the State where the crimes had been committed nor a functioning international criminal tribunal at that point in time (*Cvjetkovic*, 1994). In France it has been held by a *juge d'instruction* that the Genocide Convention does not provide for universal jurisdiction (*in re Javor*, reversed in the *Cour d'Appel* on other grounds. The *Cour de Cassation* ruling equally does not suggest universal jurisdiction). The *Munyeshyaka* finding by the *Cour d'Appel* (1998) relies for a finding—at first sight inconsistent—upon cross-reference into the Statute of the International Tribunal for Rwanda as the jurisdictional basis. In the *Qaddafi* case the *Cour d'Appel* relied on passive personality and not on universal jurisdiction (in the *Cour de Cassation* it was immunity that assumed central importance).

23. In the *Bouterse* case the Amsterdam Court of Appeal concluded that torture was a crime against humanity, and as such an "extraterritorial jurisdiction" could be exercised over a non-national. However, in the *Hoge Raad*, the Dutch Supreme Court attached conditions to this exercise of extraterritorial jurisdiction (nationality, or presence within the Netherlands at the moment of arrest) on the basis of national legislation.

24. By contrast, a universal jurisdiction has been asserted by the Bavarian Higher Regional Court in respect of a prosecution for genocide

(the accused in this case being arrested in Germany). And the case law of the United States has been somewhat more ready to invoke "universal jurisdiction," though considerations of passive personality have also been of key importance (*Yunis*, 1988; *Bin Laden*, 2000).

25. An even more ambiguous answer is to be derived from a study of the provisions of certain important treaties of the last 30 years, and the obligations imposed by the parties themselves. * * *

27. Article VI of the Convention on the Prevention and Punishment of the Crime of Genocide, 9 December 1948, provides:

> Persons charged with genocide or any of the other acts enumerated in Article III shall be tried by a competent tribunal of the State in the territory of which the act was committed, or by such international penal tribunal as may have jurisdiction with respect to those Contracting Parties which shall have accepted its jurisdiction.

This is an obligation to assert territorial jurisdiction, though the *travaux préparatoires* do reveal an understanding that this obligation was not intended to affect the right of a State to exercise criminal jurisdiction on its own nationals for acts committed outside the State (A/C 6/SR, 134; p. 5). Article VI also provides a potential grant of non-territorial competence to a possible future international tribunal—even this not being automatic under the Genocide Convention but being restricted to those Contracting Parties which would accept its jurisdiction. In recent years it has been suggested in the literature that Article VI does not prevent a State from exercising universal jurisdiction in a genocide case. (And see, more generally, Restatement (Third) of the Foreign Relations Law of the United States (1987), § 404.)

28. Article 49 of the First Geneva Convention, Article 50 of the Second Geneva Convention, Article 129 of the Third Geneva Convention and Article 146 of the Fourth Geneva Convention, all of 12 August 1949, provide:

> Each High Contracting Party shall be under the obligation to search for persons alleged to have committed, or to have ordered to be committed, * * * grave breaches, and shall bring such persons, regardless of their nationality, before its own courts. It may also, if it prefers, and in accordance with the provisions of its own legislation, hand such persons over for trial to another High Contracting Party concerned, provided such High Contracting Party has made out a prima facie case.

29. Article 85, paragraph 1, of the First Additional Protocol to the 1949 Geneva Convention incorporates this provision by reference.

30. The stated purpose of the provision was that the offences would not be left unpunished (the extradition provisions playing their role in this objective). It may immediately be noted that this is an early form of

the *aut dedere aut prosequi* [provisions] to be seen in later conventions. But the obligation to prosecute is primary, making it even stronger.

31. No territorial or nationality linkage is envisaged, suggesting a true universality principle* * *. But a different interpretation is given in the authoritative Pictet Commentary: Geneva Convention for the Amelioration of the Condition of the Wounded and Sick in Armed Forces in the Field (1952), which contends that this obligation was understood as being an obligation upon States parties to search for offenders who may be on their territory. Is it a true example of universality, if the obligation to search is restricted to [their] own territory? Does the obligation to search imply a permission to prosecute *in absentia*, if the search had no result?

32. As no case has touched upon this point, the jurisdictional matter remains to be judicially tested. In fact, there has been a remarkably modest corpus of national case law emanating from the jurisdictional possibilities provided in the Geneva Conventions or in Additional Protocol I. * * *

35. The Hague Convention for the Suppression of Unlawful Seizure of Aircraft, 16 December 1970, making preambular reference to the "urgent need" to make such acts

> "punishable as an offence and to provide for appropriate measures with respect to prosecution and extradition of offenders," provided in Article 4(1) for an obligation to take such measures as may be necessary to establish jurisdiction over these offences and other acts of violence against passengers or crew:
>
> (a) when the offence is committed on board an aircraft registered in that State;
>
> (b) when the aircraft on board which the offence is committed lands in its territory with the alleged offender still on board;
>
> (c) when the offence is committed on board an aircraft leased without crew to a lessee who has his principal place of business or, if the lessee has no such place of business, his permanent residence, in that State.

Article 4(2) provided for a comparable obligation to establish jurisdiction where the alleged offender was present in the territory and if he was not extradited pursuant to Article 8 by the territory. Thus here too was a treaty provision for *aut dedere aut prosequi*, of which the limb was in turn based on the principle of "primary universal repression." The jurisdictional bases provided for in Articles 4(1)(b) and 4(2), requiring no territorial connection beyond the landing of the aircraft or the presence of the accused, were adopted only after prolonged discussion. The *travaux préparatoires* show States for whom mere presence was an insufficient ground for jurisdiction beginning reluctantly to support this particular type of formula because of the gravity of the offence. Thus the representative of the United Kingdom stated that his country "would see great difficulty in assuming jurisdiction merely on the ground that an aircraft carrying a hijacker had landed in United Kingdom territory." * * *

38. The Convention against Torture, of 10 December 1984, establishes in Article 5 an obligation to establish jurisdiction

(a) When the offences are committed in any territory under its jurisdiction or on board a ship or aircraft registered in that State;

(b) When the alleged offender is a national of that State;

(c) When the victim is a national of that State if that State considers it appropriate.

If the person alleged to have committed the offence is found in the territory of a State party and is not extradited, submission of the case to the prosecuting authorities shall follow (Art. 7). Other grounds of criminal jurisdiction exercised in accordance with the relevant national law are not excluded (Art. 5, para. 3), making clear that Article 5, paragraphs 1 and 2, must not be interpreted *a contrario*. (See J. H. Burgers and H. Danelius, *The United Nations Convention against Torture*, 1988, p. 133.) * * *

41. The parties to these treaties agreed both to grounds of jurisdiction and as to the obligation to take the measures necessary to establish such jurisdiction. The specified grounds relied on links of nationality of the offender, or the ship or aircraft concerned, or of the victim. * * * These may properly be described as treaty-based broad extraterritorial jurisdiction. But in addition to these were the parallel provisions whereby a State party in whose jurisdiction the alleged perpetrator of such offences is found, shall prosecute him or extradite him. By the loose use of language the latter has come to be referred to as "universal jurisdiction," though this is really an obligatory territorial jurisdiction over persons, albeit in relation to acts committed elsewhere.

42. Whether this obligation (whether described as the duty to establish universal jurisdiction, or, more accurately, the jurisdiction to establish a territorial jurisdiction over persons for extraterritorial events) is an obligation only of treaty law, *inter partes* or, whether it is now, at least as regards the offences articulated in the treaties, an obligation of customary international law was pleaded by the Parties in this case but not addressed in any great detail. * * *

45. That there is no established practice in which States exercise universal jurisdiction, properly so called, is undeniable. As we have seen, virtually all national legislation envisages links of some sort to the forum State; and no case law exists in which pure universal jurisdiction has formed the basis of jurisdiction. This does not necessarily indicate, however, that such an exercise would be unlawful. In the first place,

national legislation reflects the circumstances in which a State provides in its own law the ability to exercise jurisdiction. But a State is not required to legislate up to the full scope of the jurisdiction allowed by international law. The war crimes legislation of Australia and the United Kingdom afford examples of countries making more confined choices for the exercise of jurisdiction. Further, many countries have no national legislation for the exercise of well recognized forms of extraterritorial jurisdiction, sometimes notwithstanding treaty obligations to enable themselves so to act. National legislation may be illuminating as to the issue of universal jurisdiction, but not conclusive as to its legality. Moreover, while none of the national case law to which we have referred happens to be based on the exercise of a universal jurisdiction properly so called, there is equally nothing in this case law which evidences an *opinio juris* on the illegality of such a jurisdiction. In short, national legislation and case law—that is, State practice—is neutral as to exercise of universal jurisdiction. * * *

47. The contemporary trends, reflecting international relations as they stand at the beginning of the new century, are striking. The movement is towards bases of jurisdiction other than territoriality. "Effects" or "impact" jurisdiction is embraced both by the United States and, with certain qualifications, by the European Union. Passive personality jurisdiction, for so long regarded as controversial, is now reflected not only in the legislation of various countries (the United States, Ch. 113A, 1986 Omnibus Diplomatic and Antiterrorism Act; France, Art. 689, Code of Criminal Procedure, 1975), and today meets with relatively little opposition, at least so far as a particular category of offences is concerned.

48. In civil matters we already see the beginnings of a very broad form of extraterritorial jurisdiction. Under the Alien Torts Claim Act, the United States, basing itself on a law of 1789, has asserted a jurisdiction both over human rights violations and over major violations of international law, perpetrated by non-nationals overseas. Such jurisdiction, with the possibility of ordering payment of damages, has been exercised with respect to torture committed in a variety of countries (Paraguay, Chile, Argentina, Guatemala), and with respect to other major human rights violations in yet other countries. While this unilateral exercise of the function of guardian of international values has been much commented on, it has not attracted the approbation of States generally.

49. Belgium—and also many writers on this subject—find support for the exercise of a universal criminal jurisdiction *in absentia* in the "Lotus" case. Although the case was clearly decided on the basis of jurisdiction over damage to a vessel of the Turkish navy and to Turkish nationals, it is the famous dictum of the Permanent Court which has attracted particular attention. * * * The Permanent Court acknowledged that consideration had to be given as to whether these principles would

apply equally in the field of criminal jurisdiction, or whether closer connections might there be required. The Court noted the importance of the territorial character of criminal law but also the fact that all or nearly all systems of law extend their action to offences committed outside the territory of the State which adopts them, and they do so in ways which vary from State to State. After examining the issue the Court finally concluded that for an exercise of extraterritorial criminal jurisdiction (other than within the territory of another State) it was equally necessary to "prove the existence of a principle of international law restricting the discretion of States as regards criminal legislation." * * *

51. That being said, the dictum represents the high water mark of laissez-faire in international relations, and an era that has been significantly overtaken by other tendencies. The underlying idea of universal jurisdiction properly so-called (as in the case of piracy, and possibly in the Geneva Conventions of 1949), as well as the *aut dedere aut prosequi* variation, is a common endeavour in the face of atrocities. The series of multilateral treaties with their special jurisdictional provisions reflect a determination by the international community that those engaged in war crimes, hijacking, hostage taking, torture should not go unpunished. Although crimes against humanity are not yet the object of a distinct convention, a comparable international indignation at such acts is not to be doubted. And those States and academic writers who claim the right to act unilaterally to assert a universal criminal jurisdiction over persons committing such acts, invoke the concept of acting as "agents for the international community." This vertical notion of the authority of action is significantly different from the horizontal system of international law envisaged in the "*Lotus*" case.

At the same time, the international consensus that the perpetrators of international crimes should not go unpunished is being advanced by a flexible strategy, in which newly-established international criminal tribunals, treaty obligations and national courts all have their part to play. We reject the suggestion that the battle against impunity is "made over" to international treaties and tribunals, with national courts having no competence in such matters. Great care has been taken when formulating the relevant treaty provisions not to exclude other grounds of jurisdiction that may be exercised on a voluntary basis. * * *

53. This brings us once more to the particular point that divides the Parties in this case: is it a precondition of the assertion of universal jurisdiction that the accused be within the territory?

54. Considerable confusion surrounds this topic, not helped by the fact that legislators, courts and writers alike frequently fail to specify the precise temporal moment at which any such requirement is said to be in play. Is the presence of the accused within the jurisdiction said to be required at the time the offence was committed? At the time the arrest warrant is issued? Or at the time of the trial itself? An examination of national legislation, cases and writings reveals a wide variety of temporal

linkages to the assertion of jurisdiction. This incoherent practice cannot be said to evidence a precondition to any exercise of universal criminal jurisdiction. The fact that in the past the only clear example of an agreed exercise of universal jurisdiction was in respect of piracy, outside of any territorial jurisdiction, is not determinative. The only prohibitive rule (repeated by the Permanent Court in the "*Lotus*" case) is that criminal jurisdiction should not be exercised, without permission, within the territory of another State. The Belgian arrest warrant envisaged the arrest of Mr. Yerodia in Belgium, or the possibility of his arrest in third States at the discretion of the States concerned. This would in principle seem to violate no existing prohibiting rule of international law. * * *

56. Some jurisdictions provide for trial *in absentia*; others do not. If it is said that a person must be within the jurisdiction at the time of the trial itself, that may be a prudent guarantee for the right of fair trial but has little to do with bases of jurisdiction recognized under international law.

57. On what basis is it claimed, alternatively, that an arrest warrant may not be issued for non-nationals in respect of offences occurring outside the jurisdiction? The textual provisions themselves of the 1949 Geneva Convention and the First Additional Protocol give no support to this view. The great treaties on aerial offences, hijacking, narcotics and torture are built around the concept of *aut dedere aut prosequi*. Definitionally, this envisages presence on the territory. There cannot be an obligation to extradite someone you choose not to try unless that person is within your reach. National legislation, enacted to give effect to these treaties, quite naturally also may make mention of the necessity of the presence of the accused. These sensible realities are critical for the obligatory exercise of *aut dedere aut prosequi* jurisdiction, but cannot be interpreted *a contrario* so as to exclude a voluntary exercise of a universal jurisdiction.

58. If the underlying purpose of designating certain acts as international crimes is to authorize a wide jurisdiction to be asserted over persons committing them, there is no rule of international law (and certainly not the *aut dedere* principle) which makes illegal co-operative overt acts designed to secure their presence within a State wishing to exercise jurisdiction.

59. If, as we believe to be the case, a State may choose to exercise a universal criminal jurisdiction *in absentia*, it must also ensure that certain safeguards are in place. They are absolutely essential to prevent abuse and to ensure that the rejection of impunity does not jeopardize stable relations between States. No exercise of criminal jurisdiction may occur which fails to respect the inviolability or infringes the immunities of the person concerned. We return below to certain aspects of this facet, but will say at this juncture that commencing an investigation on the basis of which an arrest warrant may later be issued does not of itself violate those principles. The function served by the international law of

immunities does not require that States fail to keep themselves informed. A State contemplating bringing criminal charges based on universal jurisdiction must first offer to the national State of the prospective accused person the opportunity itself to act upon the charges concerned. * * * Further, such charges may only be laid by a prosecutor or *juge d'instruction* who acts in full independence, without links to or control by the government of that State. Moreover, the desired equilibrium between the battle against impunity and the promotion of good inter-State relations will only be maintained if there are some special circumstances that do require the exercise of an international criminal jurisdiction and if this has been brought to the attention of the prosecutor or *juge d'instruction*. For example, persons related to the victims of the case will have requested the commencement of legal proceedings.

60. It is equally necessary that universal criminal jurisdiction be exercised only over those crimes regarded as the most heinous by the international community.

61. Piracy is the classical example. This jurisdiction was, of course, exercised on the high seas and not as an enforcement jurisdiction within the territory of a non-agreeing State. But this historical fact does not mean that universal jurisdiction only exists with regard to crimes committed on the high seas or in other places outside national territorial jurisdiction. Of decisive importance is that this jurisdiction was regarded as lawful because the international community regarded piracy as damaging to the interests of all. War crimes and crimes against humanity are no less harmful to the interests of all because they do not usually occur on the high seas. War crimes (already since 1949 perhaps a treaty-based provision for universal jurisdiction) may be added to the list. The specification of their content is largely based upon the 1949 Conventions and those parts of the 1977 Additional Protocols that reflect general international law. Recent years have also seen the phenomenon of an alignment of national jurisdictional legislation on war crimes, specifying those crimes under the statutes of the [International Criminal Tribunal for the former Yugoslavia (ICTY), International Criminal Tribunal for Rwanda] and the intended [International Criminal Court]. * * *

65. It would seem (without in any way pronouncing upon whether Mr. Yerodia did or did not perform the acts with which he is charged in the warrant) that the acts alleged do fall within the concept of "crimes against humanity" and would be within that small category in respect of which an exercise of universal jurisdiction is not precluded under international law.

NOTES & QUESTIONS

1. Additional ICJ Opinions

In his separate opinion, President Guillaume, the French judge, focused on the development of what he described as "compulsory, albeit subsidiary, universal jurisdiction" in treaties addressed to international and transnational crimes:

> Whenever the perpetrator of any of the offences covered by these conventions is found in the territory of a State, that State is under an obligation to arrest him, and then extradite or prosecute. It must have first conferred jurisdiction on its courts to try him if he is not extradited. Thus, universal punishment of the offences in question is assured, as the perpetrators are denied refuge in all States. By contrast, none of these texts [treaties containing *aut dedere aut judicare* provisions] has contemplated establishing jurisdiction over offences committed abroad by foreigners against foreigners when the perpetrator is not present in the territory of the State in question. Universal jurisdiction *in absentia* is unknown to international conventional law. * * * Hence, Belgium essentially seeks to justify its position by relying on the practice of States and their *opinio juris*. However, the national legislation and jurisprudence cited in the case file do not support the Belgian argument, * * * [I]nternational law knows only one true case of universal jurisdiction: piracy. Further, a number of international conventions provide for the establishment of subsidiary universal jurisdiction for purposes of the trial of certain offenders arrested on national territory and not extradited to a foreign country. Universal jurisdiction *in absentia* as applied in the present case is unknown to international law. * * *
>
> Having found that neither treaty law nor international customary law provide a State with the possibility of conferring universal jurisdiction on its courts where the author of the offence is not present on its territory, Belgium contends lastly that, even in the absence of any treaty or custom to this effect, it enjoyed total freedom of action. To this end it cites from the Judgment of the Permanent Court of International Justice in the *"Lotus"* case. * * * Hence, so Belgium claimed, in the absence of any prohibitive rule it was entitled to confer upon itself a universal jurisdiction *in absentia*. * * * The situation is different today, it seems to me—totally different. The adoption of the United Nations Charter proclaiming the sovereign equality of States, and the appearance on the international scene of new States, born of decolonization, have strengthened the territorial principle. * * * [A]t no time has it been envisaged that jurisdiction should be conferred upon the courts of every State in the world to prosecute such crimes, whoever their authors and victims and irrespective of the place where the offender is to be found. To do this would, moreover, risk creating total judicial chaos. It would also be to encourage the arbitrary for

> the benefit of the powerful, purportedly acting as agent for an ill-defined "international community." Contrary to what is advocated by certain publicists, such a development would represent not an advance in the law but a step backward.

Separate Opinion of President Guillaume, ¶¶ 9–16. Judge *ad hoc* Bula (Congo) as well as Judges Rezak (Brazil) and Ranjera (Madagascar) reached conclusions similar to that of President Guillaume.

The Belgian *ad hoc* Judge issued a dissent:

> There is no rule of *conventional international law* to the effect that universal jurisdiction *in absentia* is prohibited. The most important legal basis, in the case of universal jurisdiction for war crimes is Article 146 of the IVth Geneva Convention of 1949, which lays down the principle *aut dedere aut judicare*. A textual interpretation of this Article does not logically presuppose the presence of the offender, as the Congo tries to show. * * * There is no *customary international law* to this effect either. The Congo submits there is a State practice, evidencing an *opinio juris* asserting that universal jurisdiction, *per se*, requires the presence of the offender on the territory of the prosecuting State. Many national systems giving effect to the obligation *aut dedere aut judicare* and/or the Rome Statute for an International Criminal Court indeed require the presence of the offender. * * * However, there are also examples of national systems that do not require the presence of the offender on the territory of the prosecuting State. Governments and national courts in the same State may hold different opinions on the same question, which makes it even more difficult to identify the *opinio juris* in that State. And even where national law requires the presence of the offender, this is not necessarily the expression of an *opinio juris* to the effect that this is a requirement under international law.
>
> The "*Lotus*" case is not only an authority on jurisdiction, but also on the formation of customary international law as was set out above. A "negative practice" of States, consisting in their abstaining from instituting criminal proceedings, cannot, in itself, be seen as evidence of an *opinio juris*. Only if this abstinence was based on a conscious decision of the States in question can this practice generate customary international law. As in the case of immunities, such abstinence may be attributed to other factors than the existence of an *opinio juris*. There may be good political or practical reasons for a State not to assert jurisdiction in the absence of the offender. It may be politically inconvenient to have such a wide jurisdiction because it is not conducive to international relations and national public opinion may not approve of trials against foreigners for crimes committed abroad. * * * A practical consideration may be the difficulty in obtaining the evidence in trials of extraterritorial crimes. Another practical reason may be that States are afraid of overburdening their court system.

Dissenting Opinion Judge *ad hoc* Van Den Wyngaert, ¶¶ 43–56.

2. The Vitality of the Lotus Principle

The *Arrest Warrant* case was the first opportunity for an international court since *Lotus* to directly address issues of extraterritorial domestic jurisdiction. Was the DRC's original argument that the exercise of universal jurisdiction in this case violated the principle of sovereign equality of nations persuasive? Would the same argument hold true were Yerodia a private citizen? What remains of the *Lotus* principle according to the authors of the Joint and Separate Opinion? Has it indeed been "overtaken by other tendencies," as argued in the opinion (para. 51)? Or, does it undergird their ultimate conclusion? Did the *Lotus* prosecution implicate prescriptive or enforcement jurisdiction? What about the Belgian arrest warrant? What safeguards as advocated by the joint and separate opinion exist in order to ensure the lawful and orderly exercise of universal jurisdiction? Who bears the burden of proving a customary international law rule—the party that would contest jurisdiction or the party that would assert jurisdiction?

3. Types of Universal Jurisdiction

In the principal case, the joint opinion notes that the Belgian law was particularly expansive in that it allowed for the launch of an investigation and the issuance of an arrest warrant when the defendant was not on Belgian territory. In contrast, the joint opinion notes that other states have universal jurisdiction statutes that are more "qualified" in that they require the presence of the accused or the victim or impose other procedural hurdles. These include the provision of some form of centralized control over the commencement or continuation of suits by a high-level authority—such as the Attorney General, Minister of Justice, or Director of Public Prosecutions—or some showing that the act in question would have been criminal in the territorial state (akin to double criminality) or has not been prosecuted elsewhere (akin to double jeopardy). How helpful is a comparative approach to determining the legality of Belgium's particular legal framework? What do the international criminal law treaties cited by the opinions contribute to the judges' analysis? Many of the universal jurisdiction statutes cited in the above opinions have been amended or updated by states that have joined the ICC. How might this impact the Court's analysis? The Sixth (Legal) Committee of the General Assembly is studying the concept of universal jurisdiction and has invited states to share information about their legal frameworks with reference to the definition, reach, and application of the principle. The Secretary General has compiled these submissions in a series of reports that can be located online.

4. The Presence of the Defendant

Members of the ICJ in the *Arrest Warrant Case* split on the legality of exercises of universal jurisdiction without the defendant present on the prosecuting state's territory. Judge *ad hoc* Van den Wyngaert (Belgium) invoked the *Lotus* principle and argued that there was no rule in international law against the assertion of universal jurisdiction without the presence of the accused. By contrast, the President, Judge Guillaume (France), stated that the relevant treaties required the presence of the accused and established a form of "compulsory, albeit subsidiary, universal jurisdiction" (para. 7). Is the presence of the defendant a necessary precondition for the initiation, or completion, of a prosecution based on universal jurisdiction, or is it simply a practicality that facilitates the exercise of universal jurisdiction? In states that disallow *in absentia* proceedings, should *investigations* be allowed to proceed without the defendant present and even if the political branches are unlikely to pursue extradition requests? If extradition is not likely to be forthcoming, why might states nonetheless commence an investigation? Where the extradition of citizens is allowed (and in many states, it is not), under what circumstances are states likely to extradite their nationals in response to suits brought under the universal jurisdiction principle? For a discussion of universal jurisdiction and *in absentia* proceedings, *see* Mohamed M. El Zeidy, *Universal Jurisdiction* in Absentia*: Is it a Legal Valid Option for Repressing Heinous Crimes?*, 37 INT'L LAW. 835 (2003); Ryan Rabinovitch, *Universal Jurisdiction* in Absentia, 28 FORDHAM INT'L L. J. 500 (2005).

5. Extradition and Universal Jurisdiction

Spain obtained the first extradition on the basis of universal jurisdiction in the *Cavallo* case, in which the Mexican Supreme Court granted the Spanish request for the extradition of Argentine Ricardo Miguel Cavallo. Cavallo was involved in a clandestine detention center in the ESMA naval school during the dirty war era (1976–83) and was discovered in 2000 living in Mexico. Cavallo was detained by INTERPOL trying to flee the country on a plane bound for Argentina. In interpreting the relevant domestic and international law, including an extradition treaty between Mexico and Spain and a range of human rights treaties, a Mexican judge recommended that Cavallo be extradited to Spain, which had issued an international arrest warrant against him. The decision whether or not to extradite someone is a political one in Mexico, and the Ministry of Foreign Affairs decided that the extradition should proceed. Cavallo unsuccessfully initiated *amparo* proceedings (similar to the writ of *habeas corpus*) before the Supreme Court. At the time of his 2003 extradition, Cavallo could not be prosecuted in Argentina due to a pair of laws—called *Punto Final* (ley 23.492) and *Obediencia Debida* (ley 23.521)—which established a firm deadline on initiating new prosecutions and recognized the defense of superior orders, respectively. These laws were later repealed, and Spain eventually extradited Cavallo back to Argentina, with Mexico's consent, for prosecution. He was eventually convicted and sentenced to life imprisonment in 2011.

The United States later extradited ex-Colonel Inocente Orlando Montano to Spain to stand trial for the massacre of six Jesuit priests (five of whom were of Spanish nationality), their housekeeper, and her daughter in El Salvador during that country's dirty war. Montano entered the United States unlawfully, having failed to disclose that he was the Salvadoran Vice Minister of Defense & Public Safety. He was prosecuted in the United States for immigration fraud, served his sentence, and then was extradited to Spain. *Inocente Orlando Montano v. Neil Elks, et al.*, Order, No. 5:16-HC-2066-BO (Aug. 21, 2017).

6. *In Absentia* Proceedings

Many legal systems, particularly those of the civil law tradition, allow for *in absentia* trials, especially where the defendant flees the jurisdiction after proceedings have been initiated so long as a re-trial is available once custody is obtained over the accused. *See, e.g.*, Codice Di Procedura Penale [C.P.P] art. 420–quater (Italy). Italy, for example, initiated *in absentia* proceedings against one Air Force officer, Joseph Romano, and 22 U.S. Central Intelligence Agency agents in connection with the rendition of a terrorism suspect (Imam Hassan Mustafa Osama Nasr, a.k.a. Abu Omar) from Italy to Egypt where the suspect was allegedly tortured. *See generally* Francesco Messineo, *The* Abu Omar *Case in Italy: 'Extraordinary Renditions' and State Obligations to Criminalize and Prosecute Torture Under the U.N. Torture Convention*, 7 J. INT'L CRIM. JUST. 1023 (2009). The majority of the defendants were convicted, ordered to pay compensation, and may be subject to arrest pursuant to a European Arrest Warrant (EAW), which has replaced a system of extradition throughout the European Union. *See* Oreste Pollicino, *European Arrest Warrant and Constitutional Principles of the Member States,* 9 GERMAN L.J. 1313 (2008). Notably, this case does not involve universal jurisdiction but rather territorial jurisdiction.

Romano was eventually pardoned by the Italian President, probably on the grounds that his prosecution might have been in violation of the NATO Status of Forces Agreement (SOFA) in place between the United States and Italy—an agreement that allocates jurisdiction for members of the armed forces, but not CIA personnel. The highest-ranking American convicted, CIA base chief Robert Seldon Lady, was detained in Panama in July 2013 on the basis of an international arrest warrant obtained by Italy. He was later released. Although he has not served any jail time, a villa he owned in Italy—reportedly his planned retirement home—was seized to pay damages. Several Italian intelligence agents were also convicted in connection with the rendition, but these judgments were reversed by the court of cassation on the ground that they were premised on classified information. One of the CIA agents, Sabrina De Sousa, was due to be extradited from Portugal to serve her sentence in Italy when she was pardoned. The European Court of Human Rights ruled that Italy's involvement in the rendition violated its obligations under the European Convention of Human Rights. *Nasr & Ghali v. Italy*, App. No. 44883/09, Judgment (Feb. 23, 2016).

7. Human Rights Implications of *In Absentia* Proceedings

In absentia proceedings may under certain circumstances run afoul of states' human rights obligations, although many civil law systems allow them so long as certain procedural protections are in place. The International Covenant on Civil and Political Rights (ICCPR) contains a long list of procedural guarantees that all states parties must provide to individuals accused of crimes. Article 14(3)(d) provides that "the accused shall be entitled to be tried in his presence." In *Mbenge v. Zaire*, No. CCPR/C/18/D/16/1977, U.N. Doc. A/38/40 (1983), the U.N. Human Rights Committee—the expert body charged with evaluating states parties' compliance with the Covenant—held that the ICCPR allows for trials *in absentia* provided that certain due process requirements are met:

> [P]roceedings *in absentia* are in some circumstances (for instance, when the accused person, although informed of the proceedings sufficiently in advance, declines to exercise his right to be present) permissible in the interest of the proper administration of justice. Nevertheless, the effective exercise of the [due process] rights under article 14 presupposes that the necessary steps should be taken to inform the accused beforehand about the proceedings against him.

Id. at para. 14.1. *See also Maleki v. Italy*, Communication No. 699/1996, U.N. Doc. CCPR/C/66/D/699/1996 (1999) (trial *in absentia* violated the ICCPR's provisions on the right to be tried in one's presence, because the state "failed to show that the [defendant] was summoned in a timely manner and that he was informed of the proceedings against him"); *Colozza v. Italy*, 89 Eur. Ct. H.R. (ser. A) at para. 30 (1985), *reprinted in* 7 E.H.H.R. 516 (holding that "a person 'charged with a criminal offence' is entitled to take part in the hearing" and that the right to a fair trial guaranteed under the European Convention for the Protection of Human Rights and Fundamental Freedoms had been violated where the defendant was denied a re-trial when he appeared to contest his *in absentia* conviction). This jurisprudence was subsequently codified in the Committee's General Comment No. 32 of 2007. Of the modern international tribunals, only the Special Tribunal for Lebanon allows for *in absentia* proceedings, a feature discussed in Chapter 12 on Terrorism.

8. *Parties Civiles*

Congolese victims of the defendant initiated the *Yerodia* case in Belgium. Many civil law jurisdictions provide for some form of intervention by the injured party in criminal proceedings. *See generally* Jonathan Doak, *Victims' Rights in Criminal Trials: Prospects for Participation*, 32 J. L. & SOC'Y 294 (2005); Richard S. Frase, *Comparative Criminal Justice as a Guide to American Law Reform: How Do the French Do It, How Can We Find Out, and Why Should We Care?* 78 CAL. L. REV. 539 (1990). In such systems, injured parties can initiate criminal proceedings when a prosecutor fails to act. When victims constitute themselves as *parties civiles*, they may be empowered to act as a co-prosecutor and, as such, receives a number of procedural advantages, such as the right to employ the full investigatory facilities of the state, which would be unavailable in a strictly civil proceeding. Likewise, they are no longer considered witnesses and thus cannot be examined without being offered counsel. The procedure may allow *parties civiles* to file a criminal case directly with the investigating magistrate (*juge d'instruction*), who must determine if jurisdiction is proper, rather than through a prosecutor, who could decide not to pursue the action. A *partie civile* can then appeal the decision of the *juge d'instruction* and the court.

In asserting the role of *partie civile*, the victim can also often obtain relief, by way of reparation or restitution, within the context of a criminal trial. *See* Jean Larguier, *The Civil Action for Damages* in *French Criminal Procedure*, 39 TUL. L. REV. 687, 688–89 (1965). Once a civil judgment is issued, it can be executed wherever the defendant's assets are found under general principles governing the enforcement of foreign judgments or any operative enforcement treaty. Even common law courts that do not employ the *partie civile* mechanism may enforce the civil portion of these judgments on the basis of their procedures for the recognition and enforcement of foreign judgments. *See, e.g.*, *Raulin v. Fischer* [1911] 2 K.B. 93 (Eng.). Although this system has been well established in Europe, some states—including Belgium—have significantly curtailed its availability in cases involving extraterritorial jurisdiction. What commends such a system as compared with the common law tradition, which depends on a sharper distinction between criminal and civil proceedings and relegates the victim to the role of witness for the prosecution?

9. Amended Belgian Universal Jurisdiction Law

In addition to the *Yerodia* case, victim groups in Belgium initiated other cases against high-level and high-profile political figures such as Israeli Prime Minister Ariel Sharon (concerning his alleged involvement in the murder of civilians in the Sabra and Shatila refugee camps in Lebanon) and United States Generals Tommy Franks and Norman Schwarzkopf (for alleged war crimes committed in the first Gulf War). The effort prompted a swift diplomatic response from implicated states. The United States even went so far as to threaten to remove NATO's headquarters from Brussels. In response, Belgium amended its universal jurisdiction law in 2003 to require some substantial connection between Belgium and the criminal conduct in question, such as the presence of the defendant or the victim (for at least 3 years) in Belgium, unless a treaty that Belgium has signed requires otherwise. Under the current version of the law, victims can only initiate suits as *parties civiles* if the defendant is in Belgium. The decision of a prosecutor not to proceed with the case on prudential grounds (for example where she determines that a case should proceed elsewhere) cannot be appealed. Pending cases were "grandfathered" in and continue under the former version of the law.

Should victim groups and their advocates have refrained from initiating such obviously contentious suits against powerful world figures in order to lessen the risk of political backlash and legislative amendment? Should the lawyers have refused to pursue such cases under the rationale that they might risk the ability to bring future cases? Or was it the right of the clients and the obligation of their lawyers to use all legal means to prosecute their cases, regardless of the risk of a political or legislative backlash? *See generally* Steven Ratner, *Belgium's War Crimes Statute: A Postmortem*, 97 AM. J. INT'L L. 888 (2003). Spain's universal jurisdiction statute, which as discussed below is also quite expansive, has also come under attack from within and outside Spain and was eventually amended to limit its reach.

10. Crimes Subject to Universal Jurisdiction

The Second Restatement (1965) cited only piracy as subject to universal jurisdiction. The Third Restatement § 404 listed piracy, slavery, forced labor, trafficking in persons, recruitment of child soldiers, torture, extrajudicial killing, genocide, and "perhaps certain acts of terrorism" as crimes subject to universal jurisdiction in the United States. Why are crimes against humanity and war crimes not mentioned? In the Restatement commentary, the ALI noted that "the United States has not exercised universal jurisdiction to the full extent permitted by customary international law," noting that "customary international law recognizes universal jurisdiction with respect to crimes against humanity and war crimes." Restatement (Third) § 402, Reporters Note 10. The Fourth Restatement § 413 lists the following crimes as subject to universal jurisdiction as a matter of international law: genocide, crimes against humanity, war crimes, certain acts of terrorism (without the hedging), piracy, the slave trade, and torture. Why do you think the United States has legislated for universal jurisdiction beyond what the Restatement authors claim is allowed under international law (by including forced labor, trafficking in persons, recruitment of child soldiers, and extrajudicial killings)?

What changed in the period of time from 1965 to 2018 to justify the expansion of the list of universal jurisdiction crimes? Many states have codified international crimes and universal jurisdiction in connection with their ratification of the Statute of the International Criminal Court (ICC Statute). The Preamble to the ICC Statute states that "it is the duty of every State to exercise its criminal jurisdiction over those responsible for international crimes," although the treaty does not mandate the codification of universal jurisdiction *per se*.

Although international law may provide for universal jurisdiction over these crimes, most states require domestic enabling legislation that both criminalizes the activity and provides for universal jurisdiction before they will exercise such jurisdiction. *See, e.g., Nulyarimma v. Thompson* [1999] F.C.A. 1192, paras. 20–22 (holding that absent domestic legislation, Australian courts do not have jurisdiction over international crimes). In the United States, the notion that there were federal "common law crimes" was abandoned in 1812. *See United States v. Hudson and Goodwin*, 11 U.S. 32 (1812). United States courts may, however, take cognizance of international crimes as they are defined by international law. *See* 18 U.S.C. § 1651 (defining piracy with reference to international law); *United States v. Smith*, 18 U.S. 153, 160–161 (1820) (determining that the constitutional power "to define and punish felonies on the high seas and offenses against the law of nations" allows Congress to invoke international law by reference and that piracy was sufficiently defined under international law to be prosecutable). Several modern cases involving piracy off the horn of Africa required courts to determine and apply the modern international rules governing piracy. *See, e.g., United States v. Dire et al.*, 680 F.3d 446 (4th Cir. 2012).

11. Universal Jurisdiction Under the Genocide Convention

The Genocide Convention at Article VI provides that

> Persons charged with genocide or any of the other acts enumerated in article III [conspiracy, incitement, attempt, or complicity to commit genocide] shall be tried by a competent tribunal of the State in the territory of which the act was committed, or by such international penal tribunal as may have jurisdiction with respect

> to those Contracting Parties which shall have accepted its jurisdiction.

This provision was enacted after a protracted debate among states concerning whether universal jurisdiction should apply to the crime. Does the Genocide Convention preclude the use of universal jurisdiction for the crime of genocide? Israel invoked passive personality jurisdiction, protective jurisdiction, and universality to defend its prosecution of Adolf Eichmann for organizing the deportation of Jewish people and others to death camps. In *Attorney General of Israel v. Eichmann*, 36 I.L.R. 5 (D.C. Jm. 1961), aff'd, 36 I.L.R. 277, 304 (S.Ct. Isr. 1962), the Israeli Supreme Court upheld Israel's power to prosecute Eichmann pursuant to either principle:

> Article 6 imposes on the parties contractual obligations with future effect, that is to say, obligations which bind them to prosecute for crimes of genocide which may be committed within their territories in the future. This obligation, however, has nothing to do with the universal *power* vested in every State to prosecute for crimes of this type committed in the past—a power which is based on customary international law. * * * In regard to the crimes directed against the Jews, * * * additional support [is found] in the connecting link between the State of Israel and the Jewish people—including that between the State of Israel and the Jewish victims of the holocaust—and the National Home in Palestine. * * * If in our judgment we have concentrated on the international and universal character of the crimes of which the appellant has been convicted, one of the reasons for our so doing is that some of them were directed against non-Jewish groups (Poles, Slovenes, Czechs and gipsies [sic]).

The State of Israel was formed in 1948, three years after the conclusion of World War II and the Holocaust. Can Israel invoke the passive personality principle for acts committed against individuals who at the time were not citizens of Israel? Is genocide now subject to universal jurisdiction as a matter of customary international law? Should it be? Was it at the time of the *Eichmann* case (1960)? How would you make arguments in this regard based upon the elements of customary international law (state practice and *opinio juris*)? Is it relevant that no states objected strongly to the prosecution of Eichmann by Israel? Israel was one of the first states to implement the Nuremberg crimes into its domestic criminal code and empower its courts to exercise universal jurisdiction. *See* Nazis and Nazi Collaborators (Punishment) Law, 5710–1950, 4 LSI 154 (1949–50) (Isr.). A United States court saw no problem in extraditing an accused war criminal to Israel for prosecution under the universality principle. In *Demjanjuk v. Petrovsky*, 776 F.2d 571, 582–83 (6th Cir. 1985), an appeals court ruled:

> [T]he fact that the State of Israel was not in existence when Demjanjuk allegedly committed the offenses is no bar to Israel's exercising jurisdiction under the universality principle. When proceeding on that jurisdictional premise, neither the nationality of the accused or the victim(s), nor the location of the crime is significant. The underlying assumption is that the crimes are

offenses against the law of nations or against humanity and that the prosecuting nation is acting for all nations. This being so, Israel or any other nation, regardless of its status in 1942 or 1943, may undertake to vindicate the interest of all nations by seeking to punish the perpetrators of such crimes.

12. The Princeton Principles

In 2000, a group of scholars and jurists convened the Princeton Project on Universal Jurisdiction with sponsorship from the Woodrow Wilson School of Public and International Affairs and the International Commission of Jurists, among others. The group drafted a series of principles to guide the prosecution of international crimes in national courts under universal jurisdiction. The goal was to articulate a coherent rationale for universal jurisdiction and set forth criteria for determining when it is appropriate to assert such jurisdiction. The Principles adopt a cautionary tone, noting that the "imprudent or untimely exercise of universal jurisdiction could disrupt the quest for peace and national reconciliation in nations struggling to recover from violent conflict or political oppression." Principle 8 states:

> Where more than one state has or may assert jurisdiction over a person and where the state that has custody of the person has no basis for jurisdiction other than the principle of universality, that state or its judicial organs shall, in deciding whether to prosecute or extradite, base their decision on an aggregate balance of the following criteria:
>
> (a) multilateral or bilateral treaty obligations;
>
> (b) the place of commission of the crime;
>
> (c) the nationality connection of the alleged perpetrator to the requesting state;
>
> (d) the nationality connection of the victim to the requesting state;
>
> (e) any other connection between the requesting state and the alleged perpetrator, the crime, or the victim;
>
> (f) the likelihood, good faith, and effectiveness of the prosecution in the requesting state;
>
> (g) the fairness and impartiality of the proceedings in the requesting state;
>
> (h) convenience to the parties and witnesses, as well as the availability of evidence in the requesting state; and
>
> (i) the interests of justice.

The Princeton Principles identify the following crimes as subject to universal jurisdiction: piracy, slavery, war crimes, crimes against the peace (known today as the crime of aggression), crimes against humanity, genocide, and torture.

How useful are these factors in allocating jurisdiction? Should universal jurisdiction be exercised as a "last resort," such that states should defer prosecution to other states that may assert jurisdiction based on territoriality or nationality? Or does such a prioritization eviscerate the very concept of universal jurisdiction and ignore legitimate interests being exercised by the state invoking universal jurisdiction? Might a court without traditional ties to a case provide a more impartial or disinterested forum for prosecution? Might the gravity of the offense justify a prosecution with fewer links to the prosecuting state? Or are these concerns outweighed by the fear of states overreaching in the exercise of their jurisdictional powers? Or by the ability of victims to attend and participate in such a trial?

13. Universal Jurisdiction and Immunities

The Princeton Principles make no mention of the relationship between exercises of jurisdiction and immunities. The failure to make allowances for common law immunities led to the sole dissent by a notable participant in the Princeton project, Lord Nicolas Browne-Wilkinson, the senior law lord who wrote the lead opinion permitting General Augusto Pinochet's extradition to Spain. Browne-Wilkinson argued:

> If the law were to be so established, states antipathetic to Western powers would be likely to seize both active and retired officials and military personnel of such Western powers and stage a show trial for alleged international crimes. . . . It is naïve to think that, in such cases, the national state of the accused would stand by and watch the trial proceed: resort to force would be more probable. In any event the fear of such legal actions would inhibit the use of peacekeeping forces when it is otherwise desirable and also the free interchange of diplomatic personnel.

Return to this point when you review the materials on immunities in Chapter 17.

14. Universal Jurisdiction in Spain

Like Belgium, Spain also implemented a far-reaching jurisdictional statute allowing for assertions of universal jurisdiction. The original legislation is set forth below. Also as in Belgium, the law was significantly amended after several high profile cases were filed involving defendants from all over the world with little connection to Spain. The amendments made in 2009 and 2014 are discussed in a Note following the next principal case, which proceeded under the legislation set forth below.

Article 23 of the Ley Organica del Poder Judicial
("Organic Law of Judiciary Power")*

1. Under criminal law, Spanish jurisdiction will extend to proceedings for crimes and offences committed in Spanish territory or on board Spanish sailing vessels or aircraft, without affecting laws in international treaties to which Spain is party.

2. In addition, it will recognize the offences defined in Spanish Criminal law as crimes, even if they have been committed outside of Spanish national territory, when those who are criminally responsible are Spanish nationals or foreigners who have been granted Spanish nationality before

* Eds.: An organic law, or *loi organique*, is legislation that addresses the organization and operation of institutions created by the constitution, such as the parliament or the judiciary.

the time of the perpetration of the crime, and when [certain] requirements are met. . . .

3. Spain's jurisdiction will extend to crimes committed by Spanish nationals or foreigners outside of its national territory when they can be defined as falling within the definition of the following crimes under Spanish Criminal Law as:

a) treason against the peace and independence of the State

b) against the Crown, its consort, its heir or Regent

c) rebellion and sedition

d) falsification of the Royal signature or stamp, the State stamp, minister's signatures or public and official stamps

e) falsification of Spanish currency and its issuing

f) any other kind of falsification which directly prejudices the credit or interests of the State and the introduction or issuing of that which is falsified

g) attacks on authorities or Spanish civil servants

h) those perpetrated by Spanish civil servants residing abroad in the performance of their duties and crimes against Spanish public administration

i) those relating to exchange control

4. Spanish jurisdiction is equally competent to recognize crimes committed by Spanish nationals or foreigners outside of Spanish territory which can be defined, according to Spanish criminal law, as one of the following:

a) genocide

b) terrorism

c) piracy and the illegal hijacking of aircraft

d) falsification of foreign currency

e) crimes related to prostitution and the corruption of minors or invalids

f) illegal trafficking of toxic, psychotropic and narcotic drugs

g) crimes related to female genital mutilation, provided that those responsible are found in Spain

h) and any other which, according to international treaties and conventions, should be pursued in Spain.

Under the authority of the original Article 23.4, investigating judges in Spain first initiated, and ultimately consolidated, universal jurisdiction cases arising out of Chile and Argentina. The Argentine cases involved a far-flung investigation into approximately 100 suspects. In contrast, the Chilean cases centered around General Pinochet and his immediate subordinates. Spain issued international detention orders against several former military officials, such as Leopoldo Fortunato Galtieri, ex-head of the Second Corps of the Argentine Army, and Adolfo Scilingo, a former Captain in the

Argentine Navy. Spanish officials arrested Scilingo in Madrid while he was giving testimony in an investigation of other defendants. During his testimony, Scilingo admitted to participating in so-called "death flights" whereby prisoners from the Navy Mechanics' School (ESMA) were "disposed of" by being dumped in the ocean. But it was the dramatic case against General Augusto Pinochet in Spain that exemplified the modern concept of universal jurisdiction, primarily because the United Kingdom detained Pinochet in response to an international arrest warrant issued by Spain. The Pinochet proceedings are summarized in greater detail in Chapter 17 on Defenses Under International Criminal Law. For a discussion of the Spanish cases, *see* Naomi Roht-Arriaza, THE PINOCHET EFFECT: TRANSNATIONAL JUSTICE IN THE AGE OF HUMAN RIGHTS (2005).

Emboldened by the wave of optimism among adherents of universal jurisdiction following the arrest of General Pinochet, additional suits were filed in Spain under the authority of Article 23.4, excerpted above, involving Chinese, United States, Salvadoran, Congolese, Israeli, and Guatemalan defendants. For example, 1992 Nobel Peace Prize winner Rigoberta Menchú Tum and a group of Spanish and Guatemalan non-governmental and solidarity organizations—such as the Association Against Torture, *D'Amistiada Amb el Poble of Guatemala*, and the Association of the Center for Documentation and Solidarity of Latin America and Africa—initiated a suit in December 1999 against several Guatemalan government officials, including former head of state General Efraín Ríos Montt. The complaint charged the defendants with terrorism, genocide, and torture stemming from the civil war in which more than 200,000 people (mostly Mayan indigenous people, but some Spanish citizens and others as well) were killed or disappeared as detailed in the report of the U.N.-sponsored Commission on Historical Clarification (CEH) report, *Memory of Silence*.

The procedural history of this case is complex and inconstant:

- A Spanish court initially found jurisdiction over the alleged crimes. *See* Auto del Juzgado Central de Instruccion No. 1 con relación al Caso Guatemala por genocidio, Madrid March 27, 2000.
- On an appeal by the Public Prosecutor, who challenged jurisdiction, an *en banc* Criminal Chamber of the *Audiencia Nacional* (National Court) on December 13, 2000 ruled that the case could not go forward "at this moment," because the complainants had not adequately demonstrated a failure of local remedies and, as such, the case did not satisfy the subsidiarity principle as articulated by the Spanish courts in the Chilean and Argentine cases. *See Caso Guatemala* (Rigoberta Menchú Tum), Audiencia Nacional (sala penal) (December 13, 2000).
- The claimants appealed the dismissal of the case to the *Tribunal Supremo* (Supreme Court), which rejected jurisdiction with a slim majority on the grounds that principles of public international law required the Spanish courts to stay

their hands where the case could be prosecuted by the territorial state, the majority of the victims were not Spanish and the perpetrators were not present in Spain, and the Genocide Convention does not authorize universal jurisdiction. *See* Decision of the Supreme Court (Criminal Division) Concerning the Guatemala Genocide Case; Decision No. 327/2003; Appeal for an Annulment of Judgment No. 803/2001 (February 25, 2003).

- The victims then turned to the Constitutional Court, whose opinion follows, claiming that they had a constitutional right to a judgment based on law and the right of access to the courts.

Constitutional Court Judgment No. 237/2005 (Sept. 26, 2005)

The Second Chamber of the Constitutional Court * * * hereby pronounces * * *

I. Findings of Fact * * *

2. The appeal is based on the following facts summarized below with respect to the object of the petition for protection:

a) On December 2, 1999 Ms. Ribogerta Menchú Tum filed a crime report at the duty court of the National Court [Audiencia Nacional], detailing events which she described as possible crimes of genocide, torture, terrorism, murder and false imprisonment perpetrated in Guatemala between 1978 and 1986 by different persons who during that period held positions of civil and military authority. The events set forth in the report include the assault on the Spanish Embassy in Guatemala in 1980, in which 37 people died, as well as the death of several priests of Spanish and other nationalities, and family members of the complainant. She deemed the Spanish National Court to have jurisdiction to hear these matters pursuant to the provisions of Art. 23.4, paragraphs (a), (b) and (g) of the Organic Law of the Judiciary (hereinafter, "LOPJ"). * * *

II. Conclusions of Law * * *

3. * * * As underscored in the Findings of Fact, the nucleus of the controversy resides in the openly restrictive interpretation of both the National Court and the Supreme Court of the rule for attributing jurisdiction found in Art. 23.4 LOPJ, the consequence of which was to deny that Spanish courts have jurisdiction to hear cases based on events defined as genocide, terrorism and torture. Since the appeal was filed against both decisions (the National Court's Order of December 13, 2000 and the Supreme Court's judgment of February 25, 2003), and since their respective decisions were based on different arguments, they should be analyzed separately. * * *

[I]t should be underscored *a priori* with respect to both the National Court's order and the Supreme Court's judgment that in principle Art. 23.4 LOPJ gives a broad scope to the principle of universal justice, since the only express limitation that it introduces in that regard is *res judicata*, that is, that the accused may not have been acquitted, pardoned or convicted in a foreign country. In other words, from the perspective of a literal interpretation of the precept, as well as from the perspective of the *voluntas legislatoris* ["the will of the legislator"], it must be concluded that the Organic Law of the Judiciary provides absolute universal jurisdiction, that is, without being subject to restrictive criteria of correction or procedural requisites, and without any hierarchical order with respect to the rest of rules for attributing jurisdiction, since in contrast to other criteria, the criteria for determining universal justice is based on the particular nature of the crimes being prosecuted. * * *

4. As indicated earlier, the order of the National Court under appeal, based on previous decisions of that same court, invokes the Convention on Genocide, and particularly its Art. VI, and concludes by affirming the subsidiarity of Spanish jurisdiction with respect to territorial jurisdiction. * * * The National Court commenced with the idea that [Art. VI], which sets forth the obligation of states to prosecute criminal acts committed in their territories, certainly does not prohibit the remaining signatory parties from establishing extraterritorial criteria of jurisdiction for genocide. As it eloquently underscored, citing prior decisions, that limitation would be contrary "to the spirit of the Convention, which seeks a commitment on the part of the signatory parties, using their respective criminal laws, to prosecute genocide as an international crime and to prevent impunity with respect to such a serious offense." Nevertheless, the Court immediately concluded that Article VI of the Convention imposes the principle of subsidiarity with regard to the acts of jurisdictions other than those set forth therein.

Disregarding the fact that the decision under appeal does not state the reasons that led to this conclusion, but rather the relation of subsidiarity is inferred from the mere mention of the criterion of territoriality (or an international criminal court), we must commence by affirming that there are undoubtedly both procedural as well as political and criminal grounds for supporting the priority of the *locus delicti*, which is part of the classic heritage of international criminal law. Based on that fact, and to address the question that we left pending, it is true that from a theoretical perspective the subsidiarity principle should not be understood as an opposite or divergent rule that introduces the so-called concurrency principle, because when there are concurrent jurisdictions in order to avoid duplicating proceedings and violating the rule against double jeopardy, it is imperative to introduce a priority rule. Since (at least at the level of principles) all states are jointly committed to prosecuting these atrocious crimes that affect the international community, elementary procedural and political-criminal considerations must give priority to the jurisdiction in which the crime was committed. * * *

The National Court's order under appeal * * * defined the terms for applying the rule of subsidiarity: "the courts of one state should refrain from exercising jurisdiction over acts constituting genocide that are being tried in the courts of the country in which those acts occurred or in an international court." Interpreting that affirmation literally, the courts of a third country should only refrain from acting when proceedings have been commenced in the territorial jurisdiction or in an international court. Or, in any case, a reasonable modification of the subsidiarity rule would cause the extraterritorial jurisdiction to refrain from acting if the crimes will foreseeably be tried in the near future. But *sensu contrario*, to activate universal extraterritorial jurisdiction it should suffice for the complainant to provide serious and reasonable evidence of the failure to act of the courts, which would reflect either a lack of will or a lack of capacity to effectively repress those crimes. Nevertheless, the Order of 2003, making use of an extremely restrictive interpretation of the rule of subsidiarity, which the National Court itself had defined, takes this one step further and requires the complainants to fully prove the legal impossibility or the prolonged inactivity of the courts, to the point of demanding proof that the Guatemalan courts have effectively rejected the complaint * * *—an impossible task, a *probatio diabolica* ["devil's proof"]. In other respects, this defeats the purpose of universal jurisdiction set forth in Art. 23.4 LOPJ and in the Convention on Genocide, since it would precisely be the failure to act of the courts of the state in which the acts were committed, failing to respond to the complaint and thus, preventing the presentation of evidence demanded by the National Court, which would block the international jurisdiction of a third state, thus resulting in impunity for the genocide committed. In summary, this strict restriction of universal jurisdiction, in open contradiction of the hermeneutical [i.e., interpretive] *pro actione* rule [which disfavors interpretations that would limit the right to effective judicial protection], deserves the reproach of the Constitutional Court as a violation of Art. 24.1 [of the Spanish Constitution (*Constitución Española* ("CE")), which states "All persons have the right to the effective protection of the judges and courts in the exercise of their rights and legitimate interests, and in no case may there be a lack of defense."]. * * *

[T]he Supreme Court arrived at the conclusion that only when it is expressly authorized in treaty law can recourse to unilateral universal jurisdiction be considered legitimate and applicable by virtue of both Art. 96 [of the Spanish Constitution ("Validly concluded international treaties once officially published in Spain shall constitute part of the internal legal order")] and Art. 27 of the Vienna Convention on the Law of Treaties, according to which international treaties cannot be contravened in the internal law of each state.

It is an extremely strict interpretation that, moreover, is devoid of argumentative support to conclude that mentioning only some of the possible mechanisms for repressing genocide, and the Convention's subsequent silence with regard to international territorial jurisdiction is tantamount to prohibiting the signatory states to the Convention (which, paradoxically would exclude those which are not) from adopting in their laws other methods for repressing the crime and, thus, in fact from following the mandate in Art. I of the Convention. From the unilateral perspective of the states, and excepting the reference to international courts, what Art. VI of the Convention sets forth is the minimum obligation that commits the states to prosecute international law crimes within their territories. In such terms, that is, assuming that the Convention does not prohibit, but rather leaves the signatory states free to establish subsequent methods for prosecuting genocide * * *.

In effect, this lack of authorization that the Supreme Court perceives in the Convention on Genocide for a state to unilaterally assume international jurisdiction cannot be reconciled with the principle of universal repression and the obligation to prevent impunity with regard to that crime in international law which, as had been affirmed, presides in the spirit of the Convention and is a part of international customary law (and even *jus cogens*, as the best legal scholars have underscored). In that regard [the Supreme Court's opinion] is directly opposed and contradicts the very existence of a Convention on Genocide and its objectives and goals, that the signatory parties should agree to relinquish a mechanism for prosecuting that crime, especially when taking into account that the possibility of effectively exercising the priority criterion of jurisdiction (territory) is often limited by the circumstances of a specific case. It is likewise a contradiction of the Convention that being a party thereto implies limiting the possibilities for combating that crime, which other states that have not signed it would have at their disposal, since they would not be limited by this alleged and questionable prohibition.

6. Since the Supreme Court deems that the Convention on Genocide does not recognize universal jurisdiction, the Second Chamber of that High Court [*Tribunal Supremo*] maintained that assuming unilateral jurisdiction in our internal law should therefore be limited by other principles, based on the practices of international customary law. This culminated in a restriction of the scope of application of Art. 23.4 LOPJ, requiring in order for it to be deemed applicable certain "points of connection," such as, the alleged perpetrator must be present in Spanish territory, the victims must be Spanish nationals, or there must be another direct connection to national interests. * * * To support this argument that international custom restricts the scope of the principle of universal jurisdiction, the Supreme Court cited international case law or decisions from the courts of other states. * * * In that regard, we must first underscore that it is quite debatable that this is indeed the rule in international customary law, particularly in view of the fact that the

selection of case law presented by the Supreme Court in support of its thesis does not lead to that conclusion, but rather to the contrary. * * * As the dissenting [High Court] judges indicated, the German case law cited in the majority opinion do not represent the *status quaestionis* ["the status of the question"] in that country, since decisions of the German Constitutional Court rendered subsequent to the case law cited in the judgment under appeal support the principle of universal jurisdiction without requiring connections to national interests (citing, as an example, the Judgment of December 12, 2000, which ratified a conviction for genocide issued by German courts against Serbian citizens for crimes committed in Bosnia-Herzegovina against Bosnian victims). Concerning the judgment of the International Court of Justice in The Hague in the *Yerodia* [*Arrest Warrant*] *Case*, it cannot be used as a precedent to support the claimed restrictions on universal jurisdiction, since it contains no pronouncement as to universal jurisdiction with regard to genocide, but rather was limited to reviewing the question of whether international laws of personal immunity had been violated, as expressly requested by the Democratic Republic of the Congo in its complaint. * * *

[I]t is questionable that the judgment fails to mention that, contrary to what it implies, Spanish law is not the only national law that includes the principle of universal jurisdiction without limiting it to national interests, including the law of Belgium (Art. 7 of the Law of July, 16, 1993, amended by the Law of February 10, 1999, which extends universal jurisdiction to genocide), Denmark (Art. 8.6 of its Criminal Code), Sweden (Law on the Convention on Genocide of 1964), Italy (Art. 7.5 Criminal Code) or Germany, states which all include to a greater or lesser degree the repression of different crimes against the international community within the scope of their jurisdictions, without restrictions based on national connections. * * *

7. * * * Undoubtedly, the presence of the alleged perpetrator in Spanish territory is an unavoidable prerequisite for his trial and eventual conviction, given that trials *in absentia* do not exist in our legislation (with exceptions that are not relevant in this case). For that reason, judicial procedures such as extradition provide a fundamental means for effectively fulfilling the purpose of universal jurisdiction: the prosecution and punishment of crimes which, due to their specific characteristics, affect the international community as a whole. But this conclusion cannot convert this circumstance into a requisite *sine qua non* for exercising jurisdiction and commencing proceedings, especially when this would subject the access to universal jurisdiction to a far-reaching restriction that is not contemplated in our legislation and, moreover, contradicts the very foundation and objectives inherent in that institution.

8. In addition to the presence in Spanish territory of the alleged perpetrator, the judgment under appeal introduces two other points of connection: the principle of jurisdiction over criminal conduct committed

against one's citizens, rendering universal jurisdiction dependent on the victims being Spanish nationals, and the requirement of the connection of the crimes committed to other relevant Spanish interests, which is simply a generic reformulation of the so-called principle of interest or of defense. These restrictions once again appear to have been based on international custom, the judgment referring without further details to the fact that "a significant part of legal scholarship and some national courts" have tended to recognize the relevance of certain points of connection.

Thus we must affirm that this radically restrictive interpretation of the principle of universal jurisdiction set forth in Art. 23.4 LOPJ, which would be better described as a teleological reduction (since it surpasses the grammatical sense of the precept), exceeds the limits of what is constitutionally admissible from the perspective of the framework of the right to effective protection of the courts guaranteed in Art. 24.1 CE, to the extent that it implies a *contra legem* reduction based on corrective criteria that cannot even implicitly be considered as being present in the law and which, moreover is clearly contrary to the purpose on which the institution is inspired, altering the principle of universal jurisdiction to the point of its being unrecognizable as it is conceived in international law, and having the effect of reducing the scope of the application of the precept to the point of constituting a de facto repeal of Art. 23.4 LOPJ.

In effect, the right to the effective protection of the courts with respect to access to the courts has been weakened in the present case, because an interpretation in accordance with the *telos* ["purpose"] of the precept would satisfy the exercise of the fundamental right of access to the courts and would thus be fully compatible with the *pro actione* principle, and because, without any degree of forced interpretation the literal sense of the precept analyzed fulfills that purpose, therefore safeguarding the right guaranteed in Art. 24.1 CE. Thus, the forced and unfounded interpretation to which the Supreme Court has subjected this precept implies an illegitimate restriction of that fundamental right, since it violates the requirement that "the courts, when interpreting legally-established procedural requisites should consider the *ratio* ["rationale"] of the provision with a view to preventing mere formalisms or an unreasoned interpretation of procedural rules from precluding a decision on the merits, and thus contravening the requirements of the principle of proportionality," by constituting a "denial of access to the courts based on an excessively rigorous interpretation of the applicable provision."

9. Thus, this restriction based on the nationality of the victims adds a limitation that is not provided for by law and which, moreover, cannot be justified teleologically since, especially with respect to genocide, it contradicts the very nature of the crime and the shared objective that it be combated universally, which in this case is practically precluded from the onset. Pursuant to Art. 607 of the Criminal Code,

genocide is legally defined by the victims belonging to a national, ethnic, racial, or religious group, and because acts of genocide are purposely intended to annihilate those groups, specifically based on membership therein. In consequence, the Supreme Court's interpretation implies that the crime of genocide can only be relevant for Spanish courts when the victims are Spanish nationals and, moreover, when such acts are intended to destroy Spaniards as a group. The improbability of that scenario should suffice to demonstrate that this was not the objective of the legislature when establishing universal jurisdiction in Art. 23.4 LOPJ, and that this interpretation is incompatible with the objective of that institution. * * *

[T]he determining question is that making the jurisdiction to hear cases of international crimes such as genocide and terrorism subject to the concurrence of national interests in the terms set forth in the judgment is in no way compatible with the principle of universal jurisdiction. The international and cross-border repression sought through the principle of universal justice is based exclusively on the particular characteristics of the crimes covered thereby, whose harm (paradigmatically in the case of genocide) transcends the specific victims and affects the international community as a whole. Consequently, their repression and punishment constitute not only a commitment, but also a shared interest among all states, whose legitimacy in consequence does not depend on the ulterior individual interests of each of them. In that regard, the concept of universal jurisdiction in current international law is not based on points of connection founded on the individual interests of a state * * *.

In contrast to the foregoing, the Supreme Court's thesis on universal jurisdiction * * * practically constitutes a de facto repeal of Art. 23.4 LOPJ. Moreover, the extreme rigor with which the High Court applies its criteria reinforces the incompatibility of its pronouncements with the right to the effective protection of the courts with respect to access to the courts, since it requires that the connection to national interests be directly related to the crime that serves as a basis for attributing jurisdiction, expressly excluding interpretations that are less strict (and thus more in keeping with the *pro actione* principle), such as the connection of national interests linked to other crimes connected to main one, or more generically, the context surrounding those crimes.

10. The foregoing demonstrates that both the Order of the National Court of December 13, 2000 and the Supreme Court Judgment of February 25, 2003 violate the appellants' right to the effective protection of the courts as regards access to the courts, and thus their appeal should be allowed and, in consequence the aforementioned decisions annulled and the proceedings remanded to the National Court to be recommenced from the moment immediately prior to rendering the Order of the National Court annulled herein. * * *

NOTES & QUESTIONS

1. The Jurisprudence

The Constitutional Court's decision is largely grounded on principles of domestic constitutional law. Nonetheless, what might it contribute to the development of customary international law rules concerning the exercise of universal jurisdiction? What does it say about the law in this area if these four judicial bodies within a single legal system can reach such contrary results when presented with such a case? In early 2004, a socialist government was elected to power in Spain. Does this help to explain the difference between the Supreme Court and Constitutional Court decisions? *See generally* Naomi Roht-Arriaza, *Universal Jurisdiction—Spain—Extraterritorial Jurisdiction—Genocide 1948 Genocide Convention Construed—Crimes against Humanity—Guatemala*, 100 AM. J. INT'L L. 207 (2006); Hervé Ascensio, *The Spanish Constitutional Tribunal's Decision in* Guatemalan Generals: *Unconditional Universality is Back*, 4 J. INT'L CRIM. JUST. 586 (2006).

2. Standing of Complainants

As noted, the criminal case in Spain was brought by Rigoberta Menchú Tum and a number of Spanish and Guatemalan public interest organizations pursuant to the *acción popular* (*actio popularis* or "popular action"). The constitutions of Spain and Portugal, among other states, provide an open standing to sue, through "citizen enforcement," to challenge actions that violate the laws without the need to show any special legal interest (*see, e.g.*, Article 125 of the Spanish Constitution). What commends such a practice? How does it compare with standing principles operative in the United States and elsewhere? Is this a recipe for judicial chaos or a useful doctrine to advance collective claims in the absence of, or as an alternative to, a class action mechanism?

3. Subsidiarity

The Supreme Court of Spain had adopted a strict version of the principle of subsidiarity announced by the lower court. According to its interpretation, the Spanish courts were barred from hearing the case unless there was a direct legislative impediment to the case going forward in Guatemala; a policy of non-prosecution, inhospitable courts, or an inactive prosecutor would not suffice to allow Spanish courts to exercise universal jurisdiction. The Supreme Court was concerned that the lower court's version of subsidiarity would require the courts of one nation to sit in judgment on the strength and legitimacy of another nation's court. Is judging the legitimacy of another nation's court consistent with the concept of co-equal sovereign states? Is it better to have such determinations made by the judicial or political branches of a foreign government? Is such an inquiry less problematic for an international court, such as the International Criminal Court, exercising its complementarity jurisdiction? A case in Guatemala did, ultimately, go forward as discussed in Note 8 below.

4. Peruvian Cases

In a subsequent case against ex-President Alberto Fujimori and other high-ranking Peruvian officials, the Spanish Supreme Court backtracked slightly and subjected the exercise of universal jurisdiction to a "necessity of jurisdictional intervention" test. Judgment No. 712/2003 (Tribunal Supremo (Sala de lo Penal) May 20, 2003). According to this test, the Spanish courts must consider whether the territorial courts are exercising "effective jurisdiction." Despite its name, this "effective jurisdiction" test does not look at the efficacy of the actions of the territorial courts. Rather the effective jurisdiction test only asks whether the acts at issue are *in fact* the subject of a prosecution, without inquiring into the quality of the prosecution. Thus, assertions of *de facto* impunity as a result of weak or fraudulent prosecutions, or prosecutions that are proceeding slowly or not at all, are not relevant to this "effective jurisdiction" test.

Because Peruvian courts were initiating investigations, the Spanish cases did not proceed in the *Fujimori* case. In April 2009, a Peruvian court convicted Fujimori of crimes against humanity—the first time an elected head of state was convicted by a court in his country of origin of human rights violations. Is the "effective jurisdiction" test developed in the Peruvian cases a better approach to regulating the exercise of universal jurisdiction than the rule of reason developed by the Constitutional Court in the *Caso Guatemala* case above? Could courts exercising universal jurisdiction employ prudential doctrines of abstention, such as comity or *forum non conveniens*? According to the latter doctrine, courts may dismiss a suit where the balance of public and private factors suggest it should be heard in another nation's courts. *See Piper Aircraft Co. v. Reyno*, 454 U.S. 235 (1981). For a discussion of the *Fujimori* case, *see* Jo-Marie Burt, *Guilty as Charged: The Trial of Former Peruvian President Alberto Fujimori for Human Rights Violations*, 3 INT'L J. TRANS'L JUST. 384 (2009) (arguing that "it was the combined impact of international and domestic pressure in favor of an accountability agenda that opened the door to criminal prosecutions in Peru and the later adoption of an accountability agenda by state elites.").

5. Strategic Concerns

Recall that the Audiencia Nacional (the court below the Supreme Court) effectively reserved jurisdiction by declining to accept the case "at this moment," because the complainants had not demonstrated the failure of local remedies in Guatemala. This left open the possibility that the Audiencia might later accept jurisdiction if prosecutions were not forthcoming in Guatemala. Although they ultimately prevailed before the Constitutional Court, should the complainants as a strategic matter have appealed the decision of the Audiencia Nacional to the Spanish Supreme Court, widely believed to be a more conservative court? In retrospect, the appeal to the Supreme Court generated a more restrictive opinion than the one the plaintiffs had appealed, which had at least entertained the possibility that if a *de facto* impunity persisted, the Audiencia would reconsider whether the case would go forward. Should the complainants have better developed their case about the lack of legal redress in Guatemala rather than press their appeal? If you had been the complainants' lawyer, what course of action would you have recommended following the issuance of the Audiencia's ruling?

6. The Nexus Requirement

Was the Supreme Court acting reasonably in requiring some form of nexus between the forum state and the crime in order to proceed? In particular, was it appropriate to require this link with the primary charges in the suit (genocide against the Mayan population) and not just in ancillary counts (the assassination of Spaniards at the embassy)? Consider Principle 8 of the Princeton Principles. The Supreme Court reasoned that some such connection increases legitimacy and better respects the non-intervention principle set forth in Article 2(7) of the U.N. Charter. What sort of nexus would have satisfied the Court? The dissent argued that, even assuming this to be the right rule, there were enough connections between this suit and Spain to satisfy the majority's nexus requirement. Should it have been enough that Spanish victims were targeted because they were defending others from genocide?

7. The 2009 and 2014 Amendments

In 2009, Spain amended Article 23.4 of its legislation as follows:

> Spanish jurisdiction is equally competent to recognize crimes committed by Spanish nationals or foreigners outside of Spanish territory which can be defined, according to Spanish criminal law, as one of the following:
>
> a) genocide and crimes against humanity
>
> b) terrorism
>
> c) piracy and the illegal hijacking of aircraft
>
> d) crimes related to prostitution and the corruption of minors or invalids
>
> e) illegal trafficking of toxic, psychotropic and narcotic drugs
>
> f) illegal trafficking or clandestine immigration of persons, whether or not workers
>
> g) crimes related to female genital mutilation, provided that those responsible are found in Spain
>
> h) and any other which, according to international treaties and conventions, should be pursued in Spain.
>
> Notwithstanding whatever may be provided in the treaties and conventions ratified by Spain, the Spanish courts shall only have jurisdiction over the above crimes when it has been duly shown that the alleged perpetrators are present in Spain, that the victims are of Spanish nationality or that there is some demonstrated relevant link to Spanish interests and, in any case, that no other competent court or international Tribunal has begun proceedings that constitute an effective investigation and prosecution of these punishable acts. Any criminal process begun in Spain shall be conditionally dismissed when the record reflects the beginning of

criminal proceedings in another state or international tribunal with regard to the crimes described in the preceding paragraph.

In 2014, the law was amended again. This time, the statute limited jurisdiction with respect to several crimes (including genocide, crimes against humanity, war crimes, disappearances, trafficking, and terrorism) to offenses committed by or against Spanish nationals or individuals who habitually reside in Spain. The law also contains a complementarity provision, withholding jurisdiction where the crime is being prosecuted before an international tribunal or in the territorial or nationality state.

What are the primary changes to Article 23.4 in these two sets of amendments? Are they beneficial? What were the Spanish legislators likely trying to achieve in making such amendments? Should the Spanish Supreme Court feel vindicated by the amendments? Could *Caso Guatemala* be brought under the current legislation?

8. *Caso Guatemala*: Case Update

Following the Constitutional Court's ruling excerpted above, Spain issued an international arrest warrant for the defendants (one of whom, Montt, had announced his intention to run for office in Guatemala). At first, the Guatemalan courts ruled that the extraditions to Spain could go forward; later, the High Court reversed these decisions. In January 2008, a Spanish judge issued a ruling denouncing the lack of cooperation from the Guatemalan authorities. Groups of victims travelled to Madrid to give testimony; other victims gave testimony in Guatemala pursuant to letters rogatory and other processes of judicial cooperation. Over 250 massacres are discussed in the official complaint. *See generally* Naomi Roht-Arriaza, *Making The State Do Justice: Transnational Prosecutions And International Support For Criminal Investigations In Post-Armed Conflict Guatemala*, 9 CHI. J. INT'L L. 79 (2008); Paul "Woody" Scott, *The Guatemala Genocide Cases: Universal Jurisdiction And Its Limits*, 9 CHI.-KENT J. INT'L & COMP. L. 100 (2009).

Meanwhile, on January 26, 2012, Guatemalan Attorney General Claudia Paz y Paz indicted Montt for genocide and crimes against humanity—the first time a former head of state has been prosecuted for genocide in a national court—after he lost his parliamentary immunity. A United Nations-sponsored truth commission (the Commission for Historical Clarification (*Comisión para el Esclarecimiento Histórico*)) found that nearly half of all reported violations of human rights occurred in 1982 while Montt ruled Guatemala. The Montt trial opened in March 2013, and the defendant was convicted. However, the Constitutional Court annulled the decision on procedural grounds in May 2013 and ordered a partial retrial. The retrial began in January 2015. In October 2017, the Constitutional Court concluded that because Rios Montt suffered from dementia, special procedures should apply to his case, including holding the proceedings behind closed doors. Before the trial could conclude, Rios Montt died on April 1, 2018, at the age of 91. For more detail on the evidence presented at the trial, *see* www.riosmontt-trial.org. The tendency of trials abroad in foreign or international courts to inspire domestic proceedings has been termed the "Justice

Cascade." For a discussion, *see* Kathryn Sikkink, THE JUSTICE CASCADE: HOW HUMAN RIGHTS PROSECUTIONS ARE CHANGING WORLD POLITICS (2011).

9. The Empirics of Universal Jurisdiction Cases

In a seminal empirical study, Professor Máximo Langer catalogued over 1000 "cases" worldwide invoking the principle of universal jurisdiction. This total includes complaints filed by victims or victims' groups in jurisdictions (mainly civil law states) that do not necessarily ripen into a full-blown prosecution. Cases that have actually progressed beyond this preliminary stage to trigger the actions of the public authorities (by way of an indictment, formal investigation, or actual prosecution) are very rare; indeed, of Langer's 1050 complaints, only thirty two cases went to trial. Of those, about 80% of cases resulted in a conviction on at least some of the charges.

In terms of the origins of the cases that went to verdict, Belgium and Netherlands are in the lead. Belgium and Spain once had the most expansive universal jurisdiction statutes (since scaled back); they also claim the most failed cases—i.e., cases that were dismissed early on without reaching a verdict. As for the origin of defendants themselves, they tend to come from formerly repressive regimes or war-torn countries, e.g., Rwanda, the ex-Yugoslavia, Germany, Guatemala, the Democratic Republic of Congo. Indeed, of the thirty five cases that had gone to trial at the time Langer's paper was published, twenty-four involved defendants hailing from Yugoslavia, Rwanda, and Nazi Germany. Two of these trials proceeded *in absentia*. For the full study, *see* Maximo Langer, *The Diplomacy of Universal Jurisdiction: The Political Branches and the Transnational Prosecution of International Crimes*, 105 AM. J. INT'L L. 1 (2011). In a subsequent article Langer and a co-author trace the "quiet expansion" of universal jurisdiction occasioned by a host of factors, including the incorporation of Rome Statute crimes, the entrenched impunity in Syria and elsewhere, and the massive refugee flows to states with universal jurisdiction on their books. Maximo Langer & Mackenzie Eason, *The Quiet Expansion of Universal Jurisdiction*, 30 EUROP. J. INT'L L. ___ (forthcoming 2019); Maximo Langer, *Universal Jurisdiction is Not Disappearing: The Shift from 'Global Enforcer' to 'No Safe Haven' Universal Jurisdiction*, 13 J. INT'L CRIM. JUST. 245 (2015). At the time this book is going to press, a couple of dozen cases are still ongoing, most now in France.

10. Universal Jurisdiction and Neocolonialism

France, Spain, and Belgium have all invoked universal jurisdiction against defendants hailing from their former colonies. Some have argued that the assertion of universal jurisdiction by former colonial powers against individuals from their former colonies is a form of neocolonialism. Should former colonial states refrain from exercising universal jurisdiction under these circumstances? Recall that the many connections between Spain and Guatemala are all the result of the colonial history shared by those two countries. Although many universal jurisdiction cases are proceeding in Europe and involve defendants hailing from former colonies, there are exceptions such as the case of Hissène Habré, the former President of Chad, which is discussed in the next Note. In addition, a South African court has held that its police service must investigate international crimes (including those committed at ZANU PF rape camps) committed in neighboring Zimbabwe. *National Commissioner of the South African Police Service v. Southern African Human Rights Litigation Centre* [2013] ZASCA 168; [2014] 1 All SA 435 (SCA) (Nov. 27, 2013). Other cases are moving forward in Argentina involving alleged crimes committed in China and Spain during the latter's civil war.

11. Universal Jurisdiction in the United States

In contrast to some other states, there have been only a few universal jurisdiction cases in the United States despite the legal authority to launch such prosecutions. Pursuant to the Torture Convention, for example, the United States enacted a statute authorizing the exercise of universal jurisdiction by U.S. courts over torture committed extraterritorially. It states:

> Whoever outside the United States commits or attempts to commit torture shall be fined under this title or imprisoned not more than 20 years, or both, and if death results to any person from conduct prohibited by this subsection, shall be punished by death or imprisoned for any term of years or for life."

18 U.S.C. § 2340a (1994). The statute grants jurisdiction where the alleged offender is a national of the United States or where the alleged offender is present in the United States, regardless of the nationality of either victim or offender. The United States can also assert universal jurisdiction over the crime of genocide, 18 U.S.C. § 1091; the use and recruitment of child soldiers, 18 U.S.C. § 2442; a range of terrorism crimes, e.g., 18 U.S.C. § 2339B; the financing of terrorism, 18 U.S.C. § 2332d; piracy, 18 U.S.C. § 1651; and numerous trafficking and slavery crimes, 18 U.S.C. § 1596. By contrast, the United States can only prosecute war crimes when they are committed by, or against, a U.S. citizen per 18 U.S.C. § 2441. Why might this be the case?

Despite receiving credible information about the presence of human rights abusers within the United States for over a decade, the torture statute has only been invoked once, in a 2006 case brought against Chuckie Taylor (the son of the former Liberian President Charles Taylor, and also known as Roy M. Belfast, Jr. and Charles McArthur Emmanuel) for acts of torture while he was commander of the Anti-Terrorism Unit of Liberia. Taylor *fils* was convicted in October 2008 and sentenced to 97 years' imprisonment in January 2009. *See United States v. Emmanuel*, 611 F.3d 783 (11th Cir. 2010) (upholding the constitutionality of the torture statute and Taylor's conviction). A judge ordered Taylor to pay $22M to his victims. In preparation for his criminal trial, Taylor sought the discovery of information concerning the United States' counter-terrorism policies to aid in the preparation of his defense, including the then-classified "Torture Memos." The court ruled that it was only speculative that such materials would contain any exculpatory material. *United States v. Belfast*, 2007 WL 1879909, *4 (S.D. Fla. 2007). This decision was affirmed on appeal, with the 11th Circuit holding that "[t]he Torture Act contains a specific and unambiguous definition of torture that is derived from the definition provided in the [treaty]. The language of that statute—not an executive branch memorandum—is what controls the definition of the crime." *Emmanuel*, 611 F.3d at 823.

The United States has more frequently invoked the universal jurisdiction provisions of its terrorism and piracy statutes. In particular, a number of ongoing cases against members of al-Shabaab ("the youth")—a Somalia-based organization designated as a Foreign Terrorist Organization under § 219 of the Immigration and Nationality Act—charge material support to terrorism and have no U.S. nexus. In *U.S. v. Mohamed Ibrahim Ahmed et al.*, the defendant was charged under, *inter alia*, 18 U.S.C. § 2339D with conspiring to obtain, and actually obtaining, military-type training from al-Shabaab. He moved to dismiss these charges on the ground that the 5th Amendment prohibits the United States from asserting jurisdiction over him. The judge denied the motion, reasoning:

> Both the material support and the military-type training statutes explicitly grant extraterritorial jurisdiction, as follows: extraterritorial jurisdiction may be exercised when the 'offender is brought into . . . the United States.' There is no dispute that the defendant was involuntarily brought into the United States after the offense conduct. Indeed, the indictment alleges that the defendant 'will be first brought to and arrested' in the district. This alone is a sufficient statutory predicate for jurisdiction.

U.S. v. Mohamed Ibrahim Ahmed et al., 2011 U.S. Dist. LEXIS 123182, **4–5 (S.D.N.Y.). The defendant—an Eritrean national and permanent resident of Sweden who was arrested in Nigeria—later pled guilty and was sentenced to nine years in prison.

12. Immigration Remedies

Rather than resorting to criminal prosecutions with respect to individuals accused of committing international crimes found in its territory, the United States has primarily invoked immigration remedies. For example, Enos Kagaba, a Rwandan businessman, was arrested on December 14, 2001, at the Minneapolis-St. Paul International Airport as he attempted to enter the U.S. He was charged with fraud and attempting to enter the country under a false identity. After the Immigration and Customs Enforcement's Human Rights Violators and Public Safety Unit (HRVPSU) learned that he was subject to an international arrest warrant issued by Rwanda, he was deported pursuant to 8 U.S.C. § 1182(a)(3)(E) (rendering aliens participating in genocide ineligible for admission). This is the first removal order in the U.S. for an individual accused of genocide. Kagaba was convicted of genocide in Rwanda and is serving a life sentence. *See also* 8 U.S.C. § 1227 (a)(4)(D) (defining as deportable aliens individuals who "[p]articipated in Nazi persecution, genocide, or the commission of any act of torture or extrajudicial killing").

In another example, in 2013, and following a mistrial, Beatrice Munyenyezi was convicted of entering the United States and securing U.S. citizenship by lying about her role in the Rwandan genocide. Her husband and his mother were convicted of genocide and crimes against humanity by the ICTR. *See Prosecutor v. Nyiramasuhuko*, Case No. ICTR–98–42–T, Judgement and Sentence (June 24, 2011). Why would the United States not seek to prosecute these individuals under 18 U.S.C. § 1091? The Rwandan genocide occurred in 1993; universal jurisdiction was added to the U.S. genocide statute in 2007 with the Genocide Accountability Act of 2007, Pub. L. 110-151 (Dec. 21, 2007).

13. Universal Jurisdiction and Due Process

Defendants in universal jurisdiction cases in U.S. courts regularly assert that the 5th Amendment Due Process Clause is violated when there is no connection among the defendant, the victim, the criminal conduct, and the prosecuting state. In *United States v. Davis*, 905 F.2d 245, 248–49 (9th Cir. 1990), the United States Ninth Circuit Court of Appeals held that

> [i]n order to apply extraterritorially a federal criminal statute to a defendant consistently with due process, there must be a sufficient nexus between the defendant and the United States, so that such application would not be arbitrary or fundamentally unfair.

In that case, the court—drawing upon the objective territorial and protective principles of international law—concluded that a sufficient nexus existed to satisfy due process because the defendant had attempted to smuggle illicit contraband into the country. Charles "Chuckie" Taylor, Jr. raised a similar argument during his prosecution under the U.S. Torture Act, 18 U.S.C. § 2340 (see *supra*). Given that Taylor is a presumptive U.S. citizen (he was born in Boston), the court ruled that the nationality principle applied and satisfied any due process nexus requirement even for extraterritorial acts with no other connection to the United States. *United States v. Emmanuel*, 2007 WL 2002452, *45–47 (S.D. Fla. 2007). The court specifically reserved the question of whether Taylor's mere attempt to enter the United States would have been sufficient, thus leaving open the question of whether the United States can constitutionally exercise universal jurisdiction. *Id.* at *47–48 n.12.

14. For Further Reading

Amnesty International, Redress Trust, Human Rights Watch, the International Committee of the Red Cross, and TRIAL have all compiled universal jurisdiction statutes and case notes. In addition, *see generally* Wolfgang Kaleck, *From Pinochet To Rumsfeld: Universal Jurisdiction In Europe 1998–2008*, 30 MICH. J. INT'L L. 927 (2009). For a discussion of the history of universal jurisdiction, *see* Kenneth C. Randall, *Universal Jurisdiction Under International Law*, 66 TEX. L. REV. 785 (1988) and M. Cherif Bassiouni, *Universal Jurisdiction for International Crimes: Historical Perspectives and Contemporary Practice*, 42 VA. J. INT'L L. 81 (2001). For a discussion of policy implications of universal jurisdiction by an individual involved in the Princeton Process, *see* Diane F. Orentlicher, *Whose Justice? Reconciling Universal Jurisdiction with Democratic Principles*, 92 GEO. L. J. 1057 (2004).

III. COURTS MARTIAL AND MILITARY COMMISSIONS

Some international criminal law violations may also be adjudicated within national systems of military justice. The two most common such fora are courts martial and military commissions. Courts martial are military courts that prosecute members of the military subject to military law, including the law of war. Courts martial may also be employed to prosecute enemy prisoners of war for war crimes, individuals subject to martial law, or civilians within occupied territory. The 1949 Geneva Conventions require that prisoners of war on trial for war crimes be prosecuted under the same procedures and standards that would apply to the prosecuting army's own members. In the United States, trials by courts martial are governed by the Manual for Courts-Martial (MCM), prescribed by Executive Order, which contains the procedural and evidentiary rules for courts martial, as well as the Uniform Code of Military Justice (UCMJ). In 1951, the UCMJ replaced the Articles of War—first drafted in 1775 to govern the continental army. *See* 10 U.S.C. §§ 801–940 (1988). Congress enacted the UCMJ in part to increase the level of due process available in courts martial. The UCMJ also established a civilian court—the U.S. Court of Appeals for the Armed Forces—to oversee the entire military justice system. Its decisions are subject to *certiorari* review by the U.S. Supreme Court. A general court martial is convened for the most serious offenses and is presided over by a military judge possibly sitting on a panel with other members of the military.

Some of the military offenses within the UCMJ have domestic law analogs, whereas others are specific to the military (e.g., desertion (Article 85) or conduct unbecoming an officer (Article 133)). The UCMJ does not contain specific war crimes prohibitions; rather, a catch all "general article" (Article 134) of the UCMJ incorporates federal law governing non-capital offenses into the Uniform Code. The intentional mistreatment of an interned civilian by a U.S. soldier can thus be charged as assault under Article 128 of the UCMJ or as a war crime as set forth in 18 U.S.C. § 2441 (the federal War Crimes Act) incorporated by reference in Article 134 (although this latter option has never been used). The murder of a civilian, however, can only be charged within a courts martial as murder under Article 118, because the operative federal statute (18 U.S.C. § 2441) makes the killing of a protected person a capital offense. *See* Maj. Martin N. White, *Charging War Crimes: A Primer for the Practitioner*, 2006 ARMY LAW. 1. Should the UCMJ contain enumerated war crimes rather than invoking them by reference? *See* Maj. Mynda G. Ohman, *Integrating Title 18 War Crimes into Title 10: A Proposal to Amend the Uniform Code of Military Justice,* 57 AIR FORCE L. REV. 1 (2005).

Military commissions historically have been used for the prosecution of spies and saboteurs who do not constitute prisoners of war, or to dispense "battlefield justice" when courts martial or the regular courts are unavailable. Consider this short history of the use of military commissions by the United States:

> This country has a rich historical tradition of trying by military commission those accused of violations of the law of war when the civil courts are either not open or considered not suitable. One of the first was the trial of Major John Andre, Adjutant-General to the British Army, in 1780 on a charge that he had crossed the battle lines to meet with Benedict Arnold and had been captured in disguise and while using an assumed name. Many others were conducted during the Revolutionary War period, as well as during the Mexican and Civil Wars. Two of the most recent, and perhaps of greatest relevance to an analysis of the Guantánamo Bay commissions, were conducted during World War II. In the first [*Ex Parte Quirin*, 317 U.S. 1 (1942)], after the declaration of war between the United States and Germany, eight Nazi saboteurs disembarked from two German submarines at Amagansett Beach on Long Island and at Ponte Vedra Beach in Florida, respectively, and proceeded to bury their uniforms and don civilian attire. They thereafter set about to sabotage war industries and war facilities in this country, but were quickly captured and prosecuted by a military commission convened by President Roosevelt and held in Washington DC. All eight were convicted, and six of the eight were electrocuted only five days after being sentenced to death by the commission.
>
> The Supreme Court, in the context of reviewing the district court's denial of petitions for habeas corpus, issued a carefully limited ruling affirming the government's power to detain and try the saboteurs by military commission under the circumstances presented. In the second [*Johnson v. Eisentrager*, 339 U.S. 763 (1950)], after the surrender of Germany but before the surrender of Japan, twenty-one German nationals were convicted by a military commission sitting in China of violating the laws of war by collecting and furnishing to the Japanese armed forces intelligence concerning American forces and their movements. They were sentenced to prison terms and relocated to occupied Germany to serve them. The Supreme Court, again in the context of a district court denial of petitions for habeas corpus, held that enemy aliens, who at no relevant time and in no stage of their captivity had been within our territorial jurisdiction, had no constitutional right to access our courts. The Court also reiterated that a military commission is a lawful tribunal to adjudge enemy offenses against the laws of war.
>
> The military commissions which gave rise to both the *Quirin* and *Eisentrager* cases, as well as the one used to prosecute General Yamashita, the Commanding General of the

> Imperial Japanese Army in the Philippines [*In re Yamashita*, 327 U.S. 1 (1946)], were war courts, one of three types of military commissions. The other two types of commissions are martial law courts, such as those used during the Civil War in *Ex parte Milligan* [71 U.S. 2 (4 Wall.) (1866)] and in World War II in *Duncan v. Kahanamoku* [327 U.S. 304, 307 (1946)]; and occupation courts, such as the one used in *Madsen v. Kinsella* [343 U.S. 341, 343 (1952)] for the trial of an American dependent wife charged with murdering her husband in occupied Germany in violation of the German criminal code. The military commissions currently being used at Guantánamo Bay are of the first type, war courts.

Scott L. Silliman, *On Military Commissions*, 37 CASE W. RES. J. INT'L L. 529, 530–532 (2005). Although historically military commissions were not governed by statute, they were conducted largely according to the procedural rules then governing courts martial. The *Yamashita* opinion cited above is discussed in Chapter 14 on Superior Responsibility.

Adjudicative bodies charged with enforcing human rights norms have criticized the exercise of jurisdiction by military courts over civilians. In its 2007 General Comment No. 32 (building on General Comment No. 13 of 1984), the Human Rights Committee, which is charged with interpreting ICCPR, has noted that such courts

> may raise serious problems as far as the equitable, impartial and independent administration of justice is concerned. Therefore, it is important to take all necessary measures to ensure that such trials take place under conditions which genuinely afford the full guarantees stipulated in article 14. Trials of civilians by military or special courts should be exceptional, i.e. limited to cases where the State party can show that resorting to such trials is necessary and justified by objective and serious reasons, and where with regard to the specific class of individuals and offences at issue the regular civilian courts are unable to undertake the trials.

See also Incal v. Turkey (41/1997/825/1031), [1998] ECHR 48 (June 9, 1998) (invalidating trial of civilian by military tribunal). *See generally* Sangeeta Shah, *The Human Rights Committee and Military Trials of Civilians:* Madani v. Algeria, 8 HUM. RTS. L. REV. 139 (2008).

In reaction to the attacks against the United States on September 11, 2001, President George W. Bush issued an Executive Order mandating the prosecution through military commission of certain non-U.S. citizens determined either to be members of al Qaeda; or to have participated in international terrorism as a perpetrator, accomplice, etc.; or to have harbored any such individual. *See* President's Military Order of November 13, 2001, Detention, Treatment, and Trial of Certain Non-Citizens in the War Against Terrorism, 66 Fed. Reg. 57,833. The order envisioned military commissions operating without many of the due process guarantees now available in the courts martial process pursuant to the MCM, including public trials, rights of confrontation, and a right of appeal. The U.S. Secretary of Defense subsequently issued Military Commission Order No. 1, Procedures for Trials by Military Commissions on March 21, 2002. This Order added some procedural protections—such as the defendant's right to be informed of the charges against him, a presumption of innocence, a "beyond a reasonable doubt" standard for conviction, a right to counsel, a right to remain silent, etc.—but still drew significant criticism.

In *Hamdan v. Rumsfeld*, 548 U.S. 557 (2006), the Supreme Court invalidated the military commission scheme, declaring it to be a violation of the UCMJ and treaties to which the United States is a party. Congress responded by passing the Military Commission Act (MCA) (Pub. L. No. 109–366, 120 Stat. 2600 (Oct. 17, 2006)), which authorized the President to create the commissions and prosecute "[a]ny alien unlawful enemy combatant." *Id.* at § 948c. The MCA also removed the right of any detainee in U.S. custody to appeal their detention to the civilian courts through the writ of *habeas corpus*. In this regard, the MCA made retroactive the habeas-stripping provisions in the Detainee Treatment Act of 2005 (Pub. L. No. 109–148, §§ 1001–1006 (2005)). The MCA will be considered in greater depth in Chapter 7 on War Crimes. In *Boumediene v. Bush*, 553 U.S. 723 (2008), the Supreme Court ruled that detainees being held on Guantánamo had constitutional rights to *habeas corpus*. Following the issuance of this opinion, many detainees filed petitions for the writ of *habeas corpus* in the U.S. federal district courts. The majority of these cases resulted in a ruling that the individual detained should be released. To date, the military commissions have prosecuted only a handful of defendants; many other charges have resulted in acquittal, been withdrawn, or been dismissed. Although President Trump indicated an intention to send additional defendants to Guantánamo for trial, so far this has not come to pass and the military commissions continue to experience legal setbacks.

For further reading, *see* Kevin J. Barry, *Military Commissions: Trying American Justice*, 2003 ARMY LAW. 1; Melvin Heard, Lt. Robert P. Monahan, William Ryan, Esq., & E. Page Wilkins, *Military Commissions: A Legal and Appropriate Means of Trying Suspected Terrorists?*, 49 NAVAL L. REV. 71 (2002); Harold Hongju Koh, Agora: *Military Commissions: The Case Against Military Commissions*, 96 AM. J. INT'L L. 337 (2002); Maj. Timothy C. MacDonnell, *Military Commissions and Courts-Martial: A Brief Discussion of the Constitutional and Jurisdictional Distinctions Between the Two Courts*, 2002 ARMY LAW. 19; Daryl A. Mundis, Agora: *Military Commissions: The Use of Military Commissions to Prosecute Individuals Accused of Terrorist Acts*, 96 AM. J. INT'L L. 320 (2002). The Congressional Research Service has conducted an analysis on military commissions, Jennifer K.

Elsea, THE MILITARY COMMISSIONS ACT OF 2009: OVERVIEW AND LEGAL ISSUES (March 7, 2014).

CHAPTER 4

HYBRID JUSTICE INSTITUTIONS

I. INTRODUCTION

After the U.N. Security Council formed the two *ad hoc* tribunals in the mid-1990s, additional situations of mass violence erupted in places such as Sierra Leone and Timor-Leste. By then, however, a form of "tribunal fatigue" had set in within the Security Council, with China making it plain that it would not support a resolution establishing another *ad hoc* tribunal. As a result, attention shifted to the U.N. Secretariat to take the lead on developing judicial institutions to ensure some measure of accountability in the face of international crimes. A new model emerged that, it was hoped, would cloak the proceedings with legitimacy without requiring the construction of another international institution from scratch. These second-generation *ad hoc* tribunals have been described as "hybrid" or "mixed," because they possess qualities of both domestic and international courts. For example, they are usually situated within the target state; are staffed by international and domestic personnel (judges, prosecutors, investigators, defense counsel, and support staff) working in tandem; and apply a mixture of international and domestic law, including local criminal law and procedure. With the establishment of the ICC, it was largely assumed that there would be no more need for additional *ad hoc* institutions. This assumption proved premature as it became clear that the ICC—given resource, jurisdictional, and political constraints—would only be able to handle a fraction of the situations demanding justice around the globe. As such, justice entrepreneurs see an enduring need to create, enable, and support additional accountability mechanisms to respond to the commission of international crimes when the political will for an ICC referral is lacking, the ICC is inappropriate or foreclosed for whatever reason, or only a fraction of the abuses or perpetrators in question are before the ICC.

This chapter provides a brief overview of hybrid models of international justice along with select opinions that touch upon some of the promises and challenges inherent to hybridizing justice. To date, several varieties of mixed tribunals have emerged that can be plotted along a spectrum of hybridity. Some take the form of specialized chambers that are integrated into, or grafted onto, the national court system, as seen in the War Crimes Chamber of the State Court of Bosnia-Herzegovina; others are more in the nature of stand-alone institutions that are largely independent from the domestic court system, such as those established in Sierra Leone, Cambodia, Lebanon, and the Central

African Republic. Capacity-building has emerged as a key objective with these models. In the Bosnian special chamber, for example, certain key positions were originally reserved for foreign professionals; these foreign experts were gradually sunsetted out. Hybrid tribunals depend in varying degrees on the existence of a functioning national legal system that is capable of administering impartial justice. The Iraqi High Tribunal, which was largely a domestic court with international advisors, was plagued by due process deficits.

Hybrid tribunals may be established by treaty between the United Nations and the host state, such as the tribunals in Sierra Leone and Cambodia; by U.N. administrations exercising sovereignty in trust in an immediate post-conflict situation, as occurred in Kosovo and Timor-Leste; or by domestic legislation. Because these institutions have historically been created at the invitation of, or by agreement with, the host state, they are more consensual than the original *ad hoc* tribunals, which were, in essence, imposed on the states in question. Mixed tribunals are meant to address some of the shortfalls of *ad hoc* international tribunals, such as their high startup and maintenance expenses, their distance from the location where the events in question occurred, and their lack of "technology transfer" to help rebuild or strengthen national systems.

Below, we feature opinions from two hybrid tribunals: the Special Court for Sierra Leone (SCSL)—which is largely considered a success—and the Extraordinary Chambers in the Courts of Cambodia (ECCC)—which generated some important jurisprudence but has been plagued by controversy since its inception. (See the Appendix for a map of Sierra Leone and Cambodia.) As you read the excerpts and material below, reflect on whether and when hybrid tribunals are better placed than purely international tribunals or purely domestic courts to provide accountability for international crimes.

II. THE SPECIAL COURT FOR SIERRA LEONE

The international community sponsored the creation of a hybrid tribunal in Sierra Leone to respond to violations of international criminal law committed in connection with the country's brutal civil war as described below:

> Already desperately poor and badly misgoverned, Sierra Leone erupted in a full-fledged civil war in March 1991 when guerillas calling themselves the Revolutionary United Front (RUF) invaded the country from neighboring Liberia. RUF leader Foday Sankoh had met then-Liberian rebel commander Charles Taylor in Libya and the two leaders coordinated attacks, exchanged weapons and shared tactics that would redefine brutality in West Africa.

The ensuing war was characterized by grave human rights abuses committed by rebels and government-affiliated troops alike. Over a ten-year period, armed units in Sierra Leone kidnapped rural populations, extracted forced labor in diamond mines and created more than a million refugees. Before the war was over, the RUF and Government forces were joined in the conflict by the Armed Forces Revolutionary Council [AFRC—a group of army officers that eventually overthrew the elected government], mercenary armies—including the South African-headed firm "Executive Outcomes"—several regional and U.N. peacekeeping collections and a militia known as the Civilian Defence Forces (CDF). In all, more than 70,000 people were killed. Thousands more were abducted and forced into sexual slavery, unwanted marriages and domestic servitude. Countless children were killed in the fighting; many who survived were severely damaged by their experiences.

Desperate to quiet the conflict, the Government of Sierra Leone entered into a short-lived agreement with the warring factions in 1996 in Abidjan. The failure of that accord was followed by an agreement between the Government and the RUF signed in Lomé, Togo on July 7, 1999. That agreement sought to end the war and called for the creation of a truth and reconciliation commission to address past crimes. Significantly, the Lomé Accord provided a blanket amnesty for perpetrators of the atrocities committed in the course of the war.[12] Foday Sankoh[13] received an individual pardon in the Lomé Agreement as well as the position of Minister for Mining in the future government of Sierra Leone. International observers, represented by the United Nations, the Commonwealth, ECOWAS and the Organisation of African Unity endorsed the accord as "moral guarantors," although, the United Nations Secretary-General's Special Representative appended a reservation to his signature insisting that amnesty could not apply to crimes against humanity and war crimes.[15]

Almost immediately, the cease-fire recognized in the Lomé Accord fell apart and fighting resumed. The RUF and other groups attacked U.N. peacekeepers in Sierra Leone and in 2000, armed combatants took nearly 500 foreign troops hostage. In

---

[12] Peace Agreement between the Government of Sierra Leone and the Revolutionary United Front of Sierra Leone, art. IX, July 7, 1999 ("Lomé Accord"), available online at http://www.sierra-leone.org/lomeaccord.html.

[13] Foday Sankoh was a leader and founder of the Revolutionary United Front (RUF), which started the Sierra Leonean civil war in which between 50,000 and 200,000 people were killed. Sankoh was indicted on 17 counts for various war crimes, including crimes against humanity, rape, sexual slavery and extermination, but died in 2003 while awaiting trial at the Special Court. See BBC Obituary, 30 July, 2003, http://news.bbc.co.uk/2/hi/africa/3109521.stm.

[15] *Seventh Report of the Secretary-General on the United Nations Observer Mission in Sierra Leone*, Security Council, U.N. Doc. S/1999/836.

May 2000, British Special Forces, acting at the request of the Government of Sierra Leone, freed the hostages and arrested Foday Sankoh. Notwithstanding the domestic amnesty of the previous year, the Government of Sierra Leone then wrote to the U.N. Secretary-General requesting the establishment of an international tribunal to bring RUF leaders to trial.[18] Security Council Resolution 1315 recalled the reservation of the Special Representative at Lomé and authorized the Secretary-General to begin negotiations to establish a Special Court for Sierra Leone. On January 16, 2002, the United Nations and the Government of Sierra Leone entered into an agreement to establish the Special Court to prosecute "persons who bear the greatest responsibility for the commission of crimes against humanity, war crimes and other serious violations of international humanitarian law, as well as crimes under relevant Sierra Leonean law committed within the territory of Sierra Leone."[20]

Noah B. Novogrodsky, *Speaking to Africa: The Early Success of the Special Court for Sierra Leone*, 5 SANTA CLARA J. INT'L L. 194, 196–98 (2006).

In the case that follows, several defendants challenged the hybrid nature of the Special Court and its legality within the country's constitutional system. Morris Kallon was a commander of the RUF and the AFRC forces who allegedly ordered attacks on civilians, humanitarian workers, and peacekeepers; Sam Hinga Norman was the Minister of Internal Affairs and national coordinator of the Civilian Defense Forces (CDF), a pro-government militia comprised predominantly of traditional hunters known as *Kamajors;* and Brima Bazzy Kamara allegedly led several attacks on Freetown on behalf of joint RUF and AFRC forces. The case makes reference to Articles 122 and 125 of Chapter VII, concerning the Judiciary, of the 1991 Constitution of Sierra Leone. We reproduce those provisions here:

> 122. Jurisdiction of the Supreme Court: (1) The Supreme Court shall be the final court of appeal in and for Sierra Leone and shall have such appellate and other jurisdiction as may be conferred upon it by this Constitution or any other law. * * *
>
> 125. Supervisory Jurisdiction: The Supreme Court shall have supervisory jurisdiction over all other Courts in Sierra Leone and over any adjudicating authority; and in exercise of its supervisory jurisdiction shall have power to issue such

---

[18] Annex to Letter dated 9 August 2000 from the Permanent Representative of Sierra Leone to the United Nations addressed to the President of the Security Council, S/2000/786, 10 August 2000.

[20] Agreement Between the United Nations and the Government of Sierra Leone on the Establishment of a Special Court for Sierra Leone, Jan. 16, 2002, ¶ 1, *available at* https://ihl-databases.icrc.org/ihl/INTRO/605.

directions, orders or writs including writs of habeas corpus, orders of certiorari, mandamus and prohibition as it may consider appropriate for the purposes of enforcing or securing the enforcement of its supervisory powers.

Prosecutor v. Morris Kallon et al., Case No. SCSL–2004–15–AR72(E), Decision on Constitutionality and Lack of Jurisdiction (March 13, 2004)

In the Appeals Chamber

8. The submissions in support of the Accused Kallon's motion may be summarized as follows:

a) The Special Court was created by an Agreement dated 16 January 2002 ("the Special Court Agreement") between the United Nations ("U.N.") and the Government of Sierra Leone ("the Government") and the latter was duty bound to abide by and honour the Constitution. The Government failed to comply with the Constitution in the establishment of the Special Court and consequently the Special Court is unconstitutional and has no jurisdiction to prosecute persons before it since it has not been established by law.

b) While accepting that the Special Court Agreement 2002 (Ratification) Act 2002 ("the Ratification Act") asserts that the Special Court Agreement was, for the part of the Government, signed under the authority of the President pursuant to section 40(4) of the Constitution, the creation of the Special Court clearly amends the judicial framework and court structure in Sierra Leone. According to the provisions of section 108(4) of the Constitution such amendments cannot be made without a referendum of the people of Sierra Leone and no such referendum has been held.

c) The Government, in creating the Special Court, as a court sitting in Sierra Leone, presiding over crimes committed in Sierra Leone, by nationals of Sierra Leone, "with a view to potentially imprisoning persons convicted by the Special Court in Sierra Leone, acted unconstitutionally in bypassing the views and wishes of the people of Sierra Leone in relying on section 40(4) of the Constitution instead of section 108 of the Constitution in the creation of the Special Court." * * *

The Accused Hinga Norman's motion is almost identical to that for Kallon except for the following additional submissions:

a) The concurrent jurisdiction and primacy granted the Special Court under Article 8(1) and (2) of the Statute of the Special Court for Sierra Leone ("the Statute of the Court") contravene section 122 and section 125 of the Constitution.

b) In May 2000 when the Special Court Agreement was concluded the government controlled only one-third of Sierra Leone territory. It therefore lacked "effective control" and the habitual obedience of the majority of the population and was consequently not in a position to negotiate an agreement, thereby rendering the Special Court Agreement nugatory. * * *

15. [In the motion on behalf of Brima Bazzy Kamara,] the Defence submits that the Ratification Act is a Sierra Leonean Statute creating Sierra Leonean law and creating crimes of Sierra Leone. As such the Act must be interpreted pursuant to the Constitution. Any exercise of judicial power is invalid. Articles 2, 3 and 4 of the Statute of the Special Court create crimes unknown to Sierra Leonean domestic law prior to the passing of the Ratification Act. The Act therefore offends the Constitution insofar as it purports to create a liability for punishment prior to the passing of the Act. * * *

Jurisdiction of the Special Court

30. In resolving the first question [concerning whether the Special Court can determine the validity of its own creation], the Agreement between the U.N. and the Government of Sierra Leone which may be termed the primordial constitutive document, must necessarily be our starting point, together with the Statute of the Special Court.

31. Article I of the Special Court Agreement is captioned "Establishment of the Special Court" and it states:

> 1. There is hereby established a Special Court for Sierra Leone to prosecute persons who bear the greatest responsibility for serious violations of international humanitarian law and Sierra Leonean law committed in the territory of Sierra Leone since 30 December 1996.
>
> 2. The Special Court shall function in accordance with the Statute of the Special Court for Sierra Leone. The Statute is annexed to the Agreement and forms an integral part thereof.

32. The conduct of legal proceedings in the Special Court is governed by Article 14 of the Statute, which empowers the Special Court to apply the Rules of Procedure and Evidence of the ICTR, obtaining at the time of the establishment of the Special Court, the necessary changes to be made (Article 14(1)). Furthermore, the Special Court is mandated to amend the Rules or adopt additional Rules where the applicable Rules do not, or do not adequately, provide for a specific situation (Article 14(2)).

33. A perusal of the Rules reveals that the Appeals Chamber of the Special Court is clothed with the exclusive power to determine, as soon as practicable, issues relating to jurisdiction. In the words of Rule 72(E):

> Preliminary motions made in the Trial Chamber prior to the Prosecutor's opening statement which raise a serious issue

relating to jurisdiction shall be referred to the Appeals Chamber, where they will proceed to a determination as soon as practicable.

34. It is beyond argument, therefore, that the Appeals Chamber of the Special Court has the competence to determine whether or not the Special Court has jurisdiction to decide on the lawfulness and validity of its creation. * * *

Constitutionality of the Special Court

38. Many arguments and submissions hereinbefore referred to have been put forward by Defence Counsel in support of their contentions that the Special Court is unconstitutional, that the Government acted unconstitutionally in establishing it and that the Special Court is, therefore, an *ultra vires* and unconstitutional institution.

39. It is, therefore, necessary to examine the means by which the Special Court was established with a view to determining whether the appropriate procedures were followed and relevant legal requirements fulfilled.

40. The Report of the Secretary-General states that the Security Council by its Resolution 1315 (2000) of 14 August 2000, requested the Secretary-General to negotiate an agreement with the Sierra Leone Government to create an independent Special Court to prosecute persons who bear the greatest responsibility for the commission of crimes against humanity, war crimes and other serious violations of international humanitarian law, as well as crimes committed under relevant Sierra Leonean law committed within the territory of Sierra Leone. * * *

42. The Secretary-General's Report examines and analyses the nature and specificity of the Special Court emphasizing that, unlike the ICTY and ICTR which were established by resolution of the Security Council, the Special Court,

> is established by an agreement between the United Nations and the Government of Sierra Leone and is therefore *a treaty-based and sui generis court of mixed jurisdiction and composition.* Its implementation at the national level would require that the Special Court Agreement is incorporated in the national law of Sierra Leone in accordance with constitutional requirements. * * *

44. The Special Court Agreement was signed on 16 January 2002 by the duly authorized representatives of the U.N. and the Government, namely, Hans Correll, Assistant Secretary-General for Legal Affairs, and Soloman Berewa, Attorney-General and Minister of Justice, respectively. In article 21 it is provided that "the Agreement shall enter into force on the day after both Parties have notified each other in writing that the legal requirements for entry into force have been complied with."

45. The Ratification Act was enacted in March 2002. In its Memorandum of Objects and Reasons it is stated that the object of the Bill is to make provision for the ratification and implementation of the Agreement between the Government and the U.N. signed on 16 January 2002, for the establishment of the Special Court.

46. In the preamble to the Ratification Act it is also stated that the Special Court Agreement was signed under the authority of the President and that by the proviso to section 40(4) of the Constitution it is required to be ratified by an Act of Parliament.

47. Counsel for the Accused Hinga Norman, however, contends that the creation of the Special Court by the Government "in agreement with the United Nations by virtue of the Special Court Agreement (Ratification) Act 2000 in effect amends fundamental aspects of the Constitution of Sierra Leone for which no referendum was held." Counsel for the Accused Hinga Norman goes on to argue that the establishment of the Special Court clearly amends the judicial framework and Court structure in Sierra Leone and cites section 120(1) of the Constitution which states: "The Judicial power of Sierra Leone shall be vested in the Judiciary of which the Chief Justice shall be the head."

48. Those arguments and submission are erroneous, if not fallacious, for four main reasons.

49. First, the Special Court is *not* part of the Judiciary of Sierra Leone and this fact is explicitly stated in section 11(2) of the Ratification Act: "The Special Court shall not form part of the Judiciary of Sierra Leone."

50. Secondly, under Article 119(d) of the Special Court Agreement, unlike the Judiciary of Sierra Leone, the Special Court possesses the judicial capacity necessary to "(e)nter into agreements with States as may be necessary for the exercise of its functions and for the operation of the Special Court." This means in effect that the Special Court has the power to conclude treaties, which power the national courts do not have.

51. Thirdly, as a treaty-based organ the Special Court, "is not anchored in any existing system (i.e. United Nations administrative law or the national law of the State of the seat.)"

52. Fourthly "the Special Court for Sierra Leone is established *outside* the national court system." [Emphasis supplied.]

53. For these reasons and having regard to the provisions of section 40(4) of the Constitution, the argument that the creation of the Special Court in effect amends the Constitution and that consequently a referendum should have been held is without substance. The establishment of the Special Court under Article 1 of the Special Court Agreement fulfills the relevant constitutional requirements and the appropriate procedures were certainly followed. * * *

Does the Special Court Provide for Fair Trial Safeguards as Required for it to be Established by Law?

54. Having fulfilled the conditions as to its establishment, the next question to be considered is whether the Special Court provides the necessary and fundamental safeguards for a fair trial. This is the necessary criterion which will enable this Chamber to determine whether the Special Court has been "established by law."

55. As was stated earlier, the Special Court Agreement is an international agreement governed by international law. The Special Court is accordingly an international tribunal and it is a norm of international law that for it to be "established by law," its establishment must accord with the rule of law. This means that it must be established according to proper international criteria; it must have the mechanisms and facilities to dispense even-handed justice, providing at the same time all the guarantees of fairness and it must be in tune with international human rights instruments.

56. A perusal of the Statute of the Special Court and the Rules bears witness that the various criteria mentioned have been observed and that the Special Court has been established according to the rule of law.

57. For instance, Article 17 of the Statute, dealing with Rights of the Accused, provides:

1. All accused shall be equal before the Special Court.
2. The accused shall be entitled to a fair and public hearing, subject to measures ordered by the Special Court for the protection of victims and witnesses.
3. The accused shall be presumed innocent until proved guilty according to the provision of the present Statute.

58. The Statute then goes on to produce the fair trial guarantees to be found in Article 14 of the ICCPR.[64] Other fair trial guarantees are stipulated in Article 13 of the Statute. This states that the Judges shall be persons of high moral character, impartiality and integrity who shall be independent in the performance of their functions. Similar provisions can be found in the Rules, all aimed at ensuring equality of arms and a fair trial. The establishment of the Special Court, therefore, accords with the rule of law. * * *

Concurrent Jurisdiction and Primacy

63. We now turn to the question of concurrency and primacy and that of effective control raised, as separate issues, by Counsel for the accused Hinga Norman.

64. Article 8 of the Statute of the Special Court states:

---

[64] International Covenant on Civil and Political Rights, GA Res. 2200A(XXI), 21 U.N. GAOR Suppl. (No. 16) at 52, entered into force 23 March 1976.

> 1. The Special Court and the national courts of Sierra Leone shall have concurrent jurisdiction.
>
> 2. The Special Court shall have primacy over the national courts of Sierra Leone. At any stage of the procedure, the Special Court may formally request a national court to defer to its competence in accordance with the present Statute and the Rules of procedure and Evidence.

65. Counsel for the Accused Hinga Norman complains that Article 8 contravenes sections 122 and 125 of the Constitution. It is further submitted that the granting of concurrent jurisdiction and primacy to the Special Court of Sierra Leone is *ultra vires* the Constitution since the Special Court is not mentioned in Chapter VII of the Constitution which creates and grants supervisory role and primacy to the Supreme Court of Sierra Leone as the final Court of adjudication. It is contended that the Judicial Framework and Court Structure is thereby amended.

66. It is obvious that the Special Court could not have been mentioned in Chapter VII of the Constitution for the simple reason that the Special Court did not exist when the constitution was promulgated.

67. As we have already held, the Special Court is not part of the Judiciary of Sierra Leone. It is the product of a treaty agreement between the Government and the U.N. The Statute of the Court is annexed to the Special Court Agreement and forms an "integral part" of it. Concurrent jurisdiction with the Sierra Leone national courts and primacy over them emanate from that Agreement of which Article 8 of the Statute of the Court is a part. The Special Court Agreement has been ratified according to law thereby incorporating it into the Laws of Sierra Leone.

68. Although Article 8 may appear repugnant when viewed in light of sections 122 and 125 of the Constitution, it does not, in our judgement, amend the judicial framework or court structure of Sierra Leone because the Special Court is not part of the Sierra Leone Judiciary and is outside the structure of the national courts.

69. It is instructive to note that the Statutes of the ICTY and the ICTR have similar provisions. Each of those International Tribunals has concurrent jurisdiction with national courts to prosecute persons for serious violations of international humanitarian law and each has primacy over national courts. Each of those Tribunals, at any stage of the procedure may formally request national courts to defer to the competence of the Tribunal in accordance with their respective Statutes and Rules of procedure. While acknowledging that the ICTY and ICTR have Chapter VII powers of the U.N. Charter ensuring that there is an obligation on all U.N. members to co-operate, in the case of the Special Court, as the Agreement is between the U.N. and Sierra Leone, its primacy is limited to Sierra Leone alone, as also the obligation to co-operate with the Special Court.

70. Article 8 is intended to ensure that for offences other than those committed by "peacekeepers and related personnel," the Special Court will have primacy over the national courts of Sierra Leone. This is consistent with the Special Court's mandate to prosecute "those who bear the greatest responsibility for serious violations of international humanitarian law and Sierra Leonean law committed in the territory of Sierra Leone since 30 November 1996. . ."

71. In our judgement, Article 8 does not contravene the Constitution as alleged or at all particularly having regard to our finding that the Special Court is an international tribunal. * * *

83. For all the reasons given, I have come to the conclusion that each of these Preliminary Motions ought to be dismissed and they are hereby dismissed.

NOTES & QUESTIONS

1. Case Outcome

Sam Hinga Norman's trial began on June 3, 2004, and was concluded in September 2006. On January 17, 2007, Norman was flown to Dakar, Senegal for a medical procedure but died prior to the issuance of a verdict. The case was terminated. Mr. Norman had consistently claimed he was innocent throughout his trial; complained about the medical facilities available to him; and expressed concern for his safety. Pursuant to the Rules of Detention of the Special Court, an inquiry was initiated into the death of Mr. Norman, given that he died while in the custody of the Special Court. Appeals Chamber Judge Renate Winter from Austria conducted the inquiry. On July 16, 2007, Justice Winter submitted her report to the President of the Special Court concluding that Mr. Norman had been provided with proper care while in the Court's custody. Specifically, Justice Winter found that Mr. Norman had died of natural causes, and that a full autopsy found no indications of violence or evidence of poison within his body.

2. The Constitutionality of the Special Court

As discussed in the principal opinion, defendants attacked the constitutionality of the Special Court on the grounds that it altered the nation's judicial structure. Which of the defendants' arguments is the most compelling? Do you agree with the Appeals Chamber's rejection of the defendants' premise that the Court is a domestic court? In paragraph 71, the Special Court concludes that the Special Court Agreement does not violate the Sierra Leonean Constitution. Is the Special Court empowered to interpret the Constitution? Do you agree that states could create alternative court structures by treaty to prosecute their nationals? Could such a tribunal be created in the United States without amending Article III of the United States Constitution? The status of the Special Court as an international court was also crucial to the finding that the Court did not have to give effect to the amnesty law enacted domestically or to principles of head-of-state immunity advanced by ex-President Charles Taylor of Liberia, as will be discussed more fully in Chapter 17 on Defenses Under International Criminal Law.

3. International v. Domestic Court

Which features of the SCSL did the Special Court find most dispositive in reaching its determination that the tribunal is not a domestic court? How domestic does a hybrid court have to be to trigger domestic constitutional, statutory, or common law governing the judicial process, such as a jury trial right, immunities, or *ex post facto* protections? How international does it have to be to avoid these potential constraints? Take, for example, the Extraordinary African Chambers (EAC) established to prosecute former Chadian President Hissène Habré.

By way of background, a 1992 Truth Commission determined that the government of Hissène Habré of Chad was responsible for systematic torture and upwards of 40,000 political murders. *Le Crimes et Détournements de l'Ex-Président Habré et des Ses Complices, Rapport de la Commission d'Enquête du Ministère Tchadien de la Justice* (1993). After being toppled by the Libyan-backed Idriss Deby in 1990, Habré went into exile in Senegal. At that time, Chadian refugees—with assistance from a coalition of non-governmental organizations—brought a criminal claim against him in Senegalese courts, but the case was dismissed on appeal with affirmation by the *Cour de Cassation* (the court of last resort) on the ground that Senegal had not incorporated the Torture Convention into its domestic law so its courts lacked jurisdiction over the crime. An investigation against Habré commenced in Belgium under that state's universal jurisdiction law and an extradition request issued. Senegalese authorities arrested Habré on November 15, 2005 and arraigned him before a Dakar court, which ruled that Habré was entitled to immunity under international law based upon its reading of the *Yerodia* case, *supra*. Days later, the Senegalese government, as a result of intense pressure from western countries, re-arrested Habré and submitted the matter to the African Union ("AU"). At the time, the AU chair was Nigerian President Olusegun Obasanjo, who was himself under pressure to hand over former Liberian President Charles Taylor for trial at the Special Court for Sierra Leone on war crime charges.

The AU created a Committee of Eminent African Jurists to determine where Habré should be tried; many NGOs recommended extradition to Belgium if a trial could not be organized in Africa within one year. In its report, the Committee recommended that Senegal exercise jurisdiction over Habré, as he was present in Senegal, and adapt its legislation accordingly. The Committee found that Chad was obliged under the Torture Convention to provide juridical assistance to the Senegalese authorities, including facilitating access to victims and witnesses. It also recommended that an envisioned regional court, which would merge the African Court of Justice and the African Court of Human and People's Rights, should be granted criminal jurisdiction over the core international crimes. On January 31, 2007, the Senegalese National Assembly passed a number of laws allowing prosecution of genocide, crimes against humanity, war crimes, and torture even if committed outside Senegal and creating an express exception to the *ex post facto* prohibition where the

> acts or omissions [were] regarded as criminal offense according to the general principles of law recognized by the community of nations, whether or not they constituted a legal transgression in force at that time and in that place.

See Code Pénal du Sénégal, Article 431. The Constitution and Code of Criminal Procedure were similarly amended.

Notwithstanding the removal of these legal impediments, Senegal did not move forward with the case, arguing that it would be too costly. As a result, Belgium instituted proceedings against Senegal before the ICJ in February 2009 seeking to compel Senegal to either prosecute Habré or extradite him to Belgium in keeping with Senegal's obligations under the Convention Against Torture and Other Cruel, Inhuman and Degrading Treatment or Punishment and customary international law. The ICJ found that Senegal had breached its obligations under the Convention to conduct a preliminary inquiry and ultimately submit the case to its competent authorities for the purpose of prosecution (if it chose not to extradite him) for acts of torture committed after the treaty entered into force in 1987. In particular, it held at para. 58 that:

> The obligations of a State party to conduct a preliminary inquiry into the facts and to submit the case to its competent authorities for prosecution are triggered by the presence of the alleged offender in its territory, regardless of the nationality of the offender or the victims, or of the place where the alleged offences occurred. All the other States parties have a common interest in compliance with these obligations by the State in whose territory the alleged offender is present.

The Court found it had no jurisdiction over claims relating to alleged breaches of customary international law. *See Questions Relating to the Obligation to Prosecute or Extradite (Belgium v. Senegal)*, Judgment, 2012 I.C.J. Reports 422 (July 20).

While Belgium's case was before the ICJ, following a petition filed by Habré, the Court of Justice of the Economic Community of West African States (ECOWAS) ruled that Senegal's amendments to its Code Pénal might be contrary to the principle of non-retroactivity. *See Hissène Habré v. Republic of Senegal*, Judgment No. ECW/CCJ/JUD/06/10 (18 Nov. 2010). As such, it suggested that the trial should commence before an *ad hoc* tribunal of an international character. The African Union confirmed the mandate of Senegal to "try Hissène Habré on behalf of Africa" before such a tribunal. The African Union and Senegal ultimately entered into an agreement to create an *ad hoc* chamber within the Senegalese court structure applying Senegalese criminal procedure and substantive international criminal law and staffed by a judges from Senegal and two from elsewhere on the continent exercising what amounts to a form of internationalized universal jurisdiction. Habré was convicted of crimes against humanity and war crimes in 2016 and is serving what amounts to a life sentence, marking the first time an African head of state faced justice in the courts of another African state. The trial represented a form of "victims' justice;" for decades, victims' groups had pushed for Habré's prosecution and over 4,000 victims registered as civil parties. *See* Reed Brody, *Bringing a Dictator to Justice: The Case of Hissène Habré*, 113 J. INT'L CRIM. JUST. 209 (2015); Konstantinos D. Magliveras, *Fighting Impunity Unsuccessfully in Africa: A Critique of the African Union's Handling of the Hissène Habré Affair*, 22 AFR. J. INT'L & COMP. L. 420 (2014).

4. Personal Jurisdiction and Prosecutorial Discretion

The Statute of the Special Court for Sierra Leone contains a limitation on personal jurisdiction at Article 1, which directs the Special Court to prosecute "persons who bear the greatest responsibility for serious violations of international humanitarian law . . . , including those leaders who, in committing such crimes, have threatened the establishment of and implementation of the peace process in Sierra Leone." The SCSL Prosecutor indicted an equal number of individuals from all parties to the conflict. Should the Prosecution have focused its energies on members of the RUF, who reneged on the initial peace agreements, rather than members of the AFRC, who committed equally serious crimes but later integrated into the new government, or the CDF, who supported the constitutional order in the face of an insurrection? Norman, for example, was the Minister of Foreign Affairs for Sierra Leone when he was indicted. Many Sierra Leoneans view him as a national hero for coordinating the Civilian Defense Forces against the rebel forces.

5. The Sierra Leone Truth and Reconciliation Commission

The Sierra Leonean Parliament established a Truth and Reconciliation Commission (TRC) in advance of the Special Court as an element of the Lomé Peace Accord "to address impunity, break the cycle of violence, provide a forum for both the victims and the perpetrators of human rights violations to tell their story, [and] get a clear picture of the past in order to facilitate genuine healing and reconciliation." It was largely funded by international donors. Although a Commission of Experts was convened to address the issues of coordination and cooperation between the Special Court and TRC, no formal agreement was ever concluded. In the end, Chief Prosecutor David Crane (United States) announced that he would not use information obtained from the TRC before the Special Court.

The simultaneous work of criminal courts and truth commissions raises a number of questions about the potential for institutional coordination and conflict. For example: How should these institutions address conflicting findings of fact? Will criminal defendants be prejudiced or will public expectations be raised if truth commissions assign individual responsibility in advance of trials? Might truth commissions contaminate evidence? Might the existence of criminal prosecutions chill perpetrators who might be willing to participate in a truth commission? How might the sequencing of truth commissions after criminal trials, or a formal agreement between institutions, avoid these concerns? Truth commissions tend to be substantially cheaper than international trials. For a discussion of the challenges of concurrent transitional justice mechanisms, *see* Elizabeth M. Evenson, Note, *Truth and Justice in Sierra Leone: Coordination Between*

Commission and Court, 104 COLUM. L. REV. 730 (2004); William Schabas, *The Relationship Between Truth Commissions and International Courts: The Case of Sierra Leone*, 2003 HUM. RTS. Q. 1035.

6. Information Sharing

Three models of information sharing have been identified where criminal trials and truth commissions operate concurrently:

- The "fire wall" model disallows any information sharing from the commission to the court, or vice versa.
- The "free access" model ensures that all commission information, including confidential information, is available to the court, perhaps subject to subpoena.
- The "conditional sharing" model provides that some information is shared between the commission and the court subject to a particularized court order, a showing of need, and/or clear notice to truth commission participants of the possibility of disclosure. Sharing could also be restricted to exculpatory or inculpatory evidence, or decisive evidence of guilt or innocence, generated by the commission.

See Marieke Wierda, Priscilla Hayner & Paul Van Zyl, EXPLORING THE RELATIONSHIP BETWEEN THE SPECIAL COURT AND THE TRUTH AND RECONCILIATION COMMISSION OF SIERRA LEONE 8 (The International Center for Transitional Justice 2002).

What are the benefits and problems of each approach? Might a state's preference for one model over another change where only limited prosecutions of those most responsible are envisioned? Should a truth commission become, in effect, the investigative arm of the criminal tribunal? Is this realistic in a context like Sierra Leone, where the budget and investigative capacities of the Special Court vastly exceeded those of the TRC? Why might the Special Court's Chief Prosecutor have unilaterally adopted the firewall model? Was this a missed opportunity to benefit from the work of the Commission?

7. The Risk of Political Spectacles

The issue of coordination between the Sierra Leonean TRC and Special Court came to a head in 2003 when the TRC requested a public hearing to secure the testimony of defendant Norman to add to the historical record which, in the TRC's view, would not be complete without his testimony. Norman agreed to appear, against the advice of counsel, in order to "be heard by the people of Sierra Leone and be recorded for posterity" in light of a delay in his trial before the Special Court. *Prosecutor v. Hinga Norman*, Case No. SCSL–2003–08–PT, Decision on Appeal by the Truth and Reconciliation Commission for Sierra Leone and Chief Samuel Hinga Norman JP Against the Decision of His Lordship, Mr. Justice Bankole Thompson Delivered on 30 October 2003 to Deny the TRC's Request to Hold a Public Hearing with Chief Samuel Hinga Norman, para. 17 (Nov. 28, 2003). Norman's testimony was particularly coveted because he was considered a national hero by many for his role leading the CDF against the rebels. The President of the Special

Court, Justice Geoffrey Robertson (United Kingdom), acting in an administrative capacity, affirmed the decision of the Presiding Judge to prohibit Norman's public testimony before the Commission, reasoning that such a procedure:

> might appear as a spectacle. A man in custody awaiting trial on very serious charges is to be paraded, in the very court where that trial will shortly be held, before a Bishop rather than a presiding judge and permitted to broadcast live to the nation for a day or so uninterrupted. Thereafter for the following day or days, he will be examined by a barrister and then questioned from the bench by the Bishop and some five or six fellow Commissioners. In the immediate vicinity will be press, prosecutors and "victims." His counsel will be present and permitted to interject but there are no fixed procedures and no Rules of Evidence. The event will have the appearance of a trial, at least the appearance of a sort of trial familiar from centuries past, although the first day of uninterrupted testimony may resemble more a very long party political broadcast. It is not necessary to speculate on the consequences of this spectacle: there may be none. There may be those the Prosecution fears which could lead to intimidation of witnesses and the rally of dormant forces. There may be those that doubtless informed the original advice of his lawyers against testifying—namely fodder for the Prosecution, an adverse effect on public perceptions of his innocence and a consequent disheartening of potential defence witnesses. There will probably, I fear, be this consequence, namely intense anxiety amongst other indictees, especially from rival factions, and concerns over whether they should testify to the TRC as well, or in rebuttal. The spectacle of the TRC sitting in court may set up a public expectation that it will indeed pass judgement on indictees thus confronted and questioned, whose guilt or innocence it is the special duty of the Special Court to determine.

Id. at para. 30. As an alternative to a public hearing, Judge Robertson stated that Norman was entitled to provide written comments to the TRC as a function of his free speech rights. *Id.* at para. 41. The TRC did not seek such a statement, and none was provided. Did the decision by Judge Robertson undermine the truth commission process? How else might the testimony of Norman before the TRC have been effectuated without providing him with a platform to address the nation?

8. Right Against Self-Incrimination

Should a right against self-incrimination apply to testimony given before a truth commission? If such a rule is desirable, how would it be instituted in the constitutive documents of the relevant institutions? In the alternative, should an individual's participation in a truth commission process be considered a mitigating factor at sentencing by a criminal tribunal? South African legislation provided that self-incriminating statements before the Truth & Reconciliation Commission could not be used in the courts of South Africa. The same was true for statements made before the Kenyan Truth, Justice & Reconciliation Commission. Should such a rule apply to the courts of other nations that might exercise universal jurisdiction over perpetrators? An NGO study conducted in Freetown by the Post-Conflict Reintegration Initiative for Development and Empowerment (PRIDE) suggested that ex-combatants would be less likely to participate in the TRC process if evidence given could be used against them, although many participants indicated they would still provide such testimony.

9. Timor-Leste

Like in Sierra Leone, the Special Panels in East Timor (convened to prosecute post-referendum violence that largely destroyed the nascent country's infrastructure) operated alongside a truth commission, the so-called Commission for Reception, Truth and Reconciliation (CRTR). Here, however, this dual arrangement was by design. In addition to taking victim testimony, the CRTR had as its mandate the reintegration of former combatants. Accordingly, it provided for a process of rehabilitation and expressions of contrition whereby perpetrators could endeavor to reconcile with their communities through full confession and the completion of acts of penance. The CRTR's founding instrument, UNTAET Regulation 2001/10, outlined a "Community Reconciliation Process" (CRP), through which lower-level perpetrators could gain immunity from criminal and civil prosecution by submitting a statement to the Commission. Eligibility was determined on the basis of the nature of the crime, the total number of acts the applicant committed, and the applicant's role in the commission of the crime. Only crimes such as theft, minor assault, arson, killing of livestock, or destruction of crops were deemed appropriate for the CRP. Those individuals who committed a "serious criminal offence"—including crimes against humanity, torture, murder, or a sexual offence as defined by the Indonesian Criminal Code—were ineligible.

When testifying before the CRTR, the respondent's statement was to include a full description of relevant acts, an admission of responsibility for the acts, and a renunciation of the use of violence as a means to achieve political objectives. The Commission then referred the case to a panel of community representatives in the location in which the attacks occurred. The local panel convened a public hearing at which the applicant, victims, and other community members were permitted to speak. The panel questioned the applicant during the hearing before selecting an "act of reconciliation" for the applicant to perform. The panel and applicant then signed and registered a "Community Reconciliation Agreement." The district court had jurisdiction to reject the agreement if it determined that the required reconciliatory act was disproportionate to the crime. Non-performance resulted in the case being turned over to authorities for prosecution, possibly culminating in a prison term or fine. Is there any way for these reconciliation elements to be integrated into a criminal justice model, or are multiple institutions inevitable? For a brief discussion of the East Timorese approach to justice and reconciliation, *see* Carsten Stahn, *Accommodating Individual Criminal Responsibility and National Reconciliation: The UN Truth Commission for East Timor*, 95 AM. J. INT'L L. 952 (2001).

10. Child Soldiers

In the course of negotiations for the Special Court, the question of juvenile justice emerged as a point of contention. During the civil war, abuses were committed by child soldiers, many of whom were forcibly conscripted into the national and rebel forces. Some civil society groups in Sierra Leone demanded that child soldiers be held accountable for their crimes. Some international children's and human rights NGOs objected that prosecutions would impede efforts aimed at rehabilitation and reintegration and consume resources better deployed for the prosecution of the leaders ultimately responsible for the abuses. U.N. Secretary-General Kofi Annan originally proposed that a Juvenile Chamber of the Special Court be authorized to prosecute defendants as young as fifteen. The proposal made allowance for anonymous proceedings and the appointment of a *guardian ad litem*, if needed. The "disposition" of the case might have involved supervision, community service, foster care, education, or training in lieu of incarceration. *See Report of the Secretary-General on the Establishment of a Special Court for Sierra Leone*, U.N. Doc. S/2000/915 (Oct. 4, 2000). In the end, no special chamber was created. Instead, Article 7 of the Special Court's Statute provided:

> Article 7: Jurisdiction Over Persons of 15 Years of Age
>
> 1. The Special Court shall have no jurisdiction over any person who was under the age of 15 at the time of the alleged commission of the crime. Should any person who was at the time of the alleged commission of the crime between 15 and 18 years of age come before the Court, he or she shall be treated with dignity and a sense of worth, taking into account his or her young age and the desirability of promoting his or her rehabilitation, reintegration into and assumption of a constructive role in society, and in accordance with international human rights standards, in particular the rights of the child.
>
> 2. In the disposition of a case against a juvenile offender, the Special Court shall order any of the following: care guidance and supervision orders, community service orders, counseling, foster care, correctional, educational and vocational training programmes, approved schools and, as appropriate, any programmes of disarmament, demobilization and reintegration or programmes of child protection agencies.

Despite this statutory authority, the Prosecutor announced that he would not prosecute individuals younger than eighteen-years old as a matter of policy.

By way of comparison, Article 26 of the ICC Statute forbids the prosecution of individuals who were less than eighteen years old at the time of their alleged crimes. Nonetheless, Dominic Ongwen, a member of the Lord's Resistance Army, is being prosecuted for crimes committed in and around Uganda when he was an adult, including the abduction and enslavement of children as young as six years old. He was abducted when he was young (reports range from age 9 to 13), but remained with the organization and rose within its ranks. He ultimately surrendered to U.S. forces in the Central African Republic in 2015 and was transferred to The Hague. His trial is ongoing. Thousands of other former LRA soldiers have received amnesty in Uganda under the Amnesty Act of 2000. How should international criminal law reconcile the dual role of child soldiers as perpetrators and victims? Should international criminal law go the way of many domestic systems in treating juvenile offenders as adults? If prosecuted, should juvenile defendants be presumed to know the difference between a lawful and an unlawful order or a civilian and a combatant?

In addition to allowing for the prosecution of child soldiers, the SCSL Statute also allowed for the prosecution for war crimes of individuals involved in recruiting and employing child soldiers. The case upholding these charges will be presented in Chapter 17 on Defenses Under International Criminal Law. For the most current data on children affected by armed conflicts, see the work of the Secretary-General's Special Representative for Children and Armed Conflict: Report of the Secretary-General, Children and Armed Conflict, U.N. Doc. A/73/907–S/2019/509 (June 20, 2019). In the year prior to the issuance of the report, 13,600 children benefited from release and reintegration. Nonetheless, children continue to be recruited and used in armed conflicts, particularly in Somalia, Nigeria, Syria, Yemen, and the Democratic Republic of the Congo. Organizations such as Geneva Call work with non-state armed groups to execute deeds of commitment and action plans in which they pledge to end child recruitment and use in armed conflict. Contrary to the image of the quintessential child soldier abducted as a young boy, many child soldiers join voluntarily for a range of ideological and pragmatic reasons and about 40% of child soldiers worldwide are girls. *See* Mark Drumbl, REIMAGINING CHILD SOLDIERS IN INTERNATIONAL LAW & POLICY (2012).

11. Liability of Peacekeepers

During the conflict in Sierra Leone, members of ECOMOG, the military wing of the Economic Community of West African States, allegedly committed summary executions and other abuses in Sierra Leone. Article 1 of the Statute for the Special Court borrows the principle of complementarity from the ICC Statute and provides that peacekeepers are subject to the primary jurisdiction of their sending state and are subject to the Special Court's jurisdiction only if the sending state is unwilling or unable to prosecute. The sending states, however, are not party to the Special Court Agreement between Sierra Leone and the United Nations. Are they nonetheless under any obligation to cooperate with the Court? Although in the preamble to Resolution 1478 on the Situation in Liberia, the Security Council called upon all states to "cooperate fully" with the Special Court, this recommendation is not part of its "decision" under Chapter VII. No prosecutions of ECOMOG soldiers commenced before the Special Court. Would such prosecutions have detracted from the mission of the Special Court? Would it be preferable for the regular Sierra Leonean courts to prosecute peacekeepers? This might require a waiver by the sending state of any rights to exercise jurisdiction set forth in a Status of Forces Agreement (SOFA) or Status of Mission Agreement (SOMA) governing the provision of troops in the first instance. For more on the liability of peacekeepers, *see* Susan A. Notar, Current Event: *Peacekeepers as Perpetrators: Sexual Exploitation and Abuse of Women and Children in the Democratic Republic of the Congo*, 14 AM. U. J. GENDER SOC. POL'Y & L. 413 (2006).

12. Charles Taylor

The Statute of the Special Court is limited to crimes committed "in the territory of Sierra Leone" by Article 1(1). Nonetheless, the former President of Liberia, Charles Taylor, was convicted by the SCSL in connection with Taylor's provision of arms and other assistance to rebels in Sierra Leone in exchange for diamonds, even though there was no evidence he ever stepped foot in Sierra Leone. How would you argue the territorial jurisdiction question if you were an SCSL prosecutor or defense counsel? Is it enough that extraterritorial acts had an effect on the territory of Sierra Leone? In August 2003, Liberia filed suit against Sierra Leone in the International Court of Justice claiming that the Special Court had no authority to impose legal obligations on states that are not party to the U.N. Agreement and that Taylor is immune from prosecution as a Head of State. The claim was inadmissible because Sierra Leone is not a party to the ICJ.

Although the Special Court enjoyed primacy vis-à-vis the courts of Sierra Leone, as the creature of a treaty between the United Nations and Sierra Leone it has no primacy over other states. What should happen when an accused is abroad? At one point, the SCSL asked the Government of Ghana to detain Taylor while he was on a trip to that country in June 2003. The request went unheeded, and Taylor returned to Liberia. In August 2003, Nigeria granted him asylum, which lasted until Ellen Johnson-Sirleaf, the then-newly elected President of Liberia, requested his return to face charges before the SCSL. Nigerian officials arrested Taylor on the border with Cameroon and transported him to the SCSL. Out of fears that a trial in Freetown would be politically destabilizing, the SCSL prosecuted the case in The Hague using the facilities of the ICC. The ICTY and ICTR have been criticized for operating far from the events in question. Can the same critique be leveled against the SCSL in light of its decision to sit abroad? Taylor was convicted and granted what amounts to a life sentence.

III. THE EXTRAORDINARY CHAMBERS IN THE COURTS OF CAMBODIA

The Extraordinary Chambers in the Courts of Cambodia (ECCC) was one of the first hybrid institutions to be contemplated, although its creation took almost a decade. The Tribunal's temporal jurisdiction is historical: it is prosecuting only those most responsible for the international crimes committed by the Khmer Rouge in Cambodia between 1975 and 1979. Its personal jurisdiction is limited to senior leaders of the Khmer Rouge and those deemed "most responsible" for the regime's crimes. It has jurisdiction over the core international crimes as well as some Cambodian domestic crimes. (See the Appendix for a map of Cambodia.)

The Khmer Rouge, otherwise known as the Party of Democratic Kampuchea, seized power in Cambodia from the American-backed Lon Nol government on April 17, 1975. The Khmer Rouge encountered a nation destabilized by a still fresh civil war, frequent invasions by neighbors, periodic *coups d'état*, and a full-scale American incursion that had dropped over 250,000 tons of bombs in an effort to disrupt the Ho Chi Minh trail during the Vietnam War. Under the leadership of Pol Pot, the Khmer Rouge immediately dismantled Cambodian society and installed a brutally repressive state. This marked "year zero" in what turned out to be a four-year campaign to create a "New Cambodia." By the time a Vietnamese invasion opened the killing fields for the world to see, approximately two million people had perished.

The draconian measures instituted by the Khmer Rouge regime in the quest to remake Cambodian society included the liquidation of the Lon Nol army and members of the former regime; the extermination of the elite and educated; a complete evacuation of the urban centers; the incineration of books, libraries, banks, places of worship, and university facilities; the criminalization of the usage of foreign languages; the abolition of money, private property, markets, and salaries; the dissolution of families and the separation of children from their parents; the execution of ethnic minorities; the prohibition of religious practice and education; and the systematic hunt for real and imagined political opponents.

The first stage of the revolution witnessed the brutal and systematic execution of former military officers and their families. In all, state agents reportedly killed 100,000 to 200,000 people during this initial purge. Khmer Rouge cadre identified victims at check points or summoned them by announcements over loudspeakers that instructed people with administrative or military experience to identify themselves. After supplying elaborate "biographies" attesting to any number of treasonous and seditious activities, these individuals and their families were executed. The regime also eliminated others who were Western-educated or landowners.

A fundamental tenet of Khmer Rouge ideology was that all citizens had to be proper Khmers, as defined by the revolution. This purification required the extermination or forced assimilation of all non-Khmer ethnic groups, including ethnic Vietnamese, Chinese, Cham (Khmer Muslims), Thai, and rural indigenous communities. Eventually, the Khmer Rouge exhausted "the other" and turned upon itself. An alleged coup attempt in 1976 prompted full-scale purges aimed at all party leaders, local officials, military officers, and citizens supposedly associated with the political "opposition." Khmer Rouge cadres recruited a vast network of spies throughout society to identify dissidents and enemies of the state. Friends and family of the accused were instantly guilty by association, and children were encouraged to denounce their parents. The regime justified the intensified repression that followed on the ground that the revolution was at all times in jeopardy of sabotage by counterrevolutionary forces. It confined Khmer Rouge cadres accused of sedition, treachery, and collusion with Vietnam in detention centers where they were tortured to extract putative "confessions." Archives from Tuol Sleng Prison (a.k.a. S-21), the apex of the torture and extermination system, indicate that 20,000 people were "smashed to bits" within the prison.

The Khmer Rouge regime was finally halted when Vietnam—with assistance from former Khmer Rouge functionaries—invaded Cambodia on January 7, 1979, and installed the People's Republic of Kampuchea. Nonetheless, western anti-communism tinged with lingering United States animosity toward Vietnam led the United Nations—in a lamentable expression of *realpolitik*—to allow the Khmer Rouge government to retain its seat in the U.N. General Assembly as a "government-in-exile."

Almost two decades later, the co-Prime Ministers of Cambodia wrote to the U.N. Secretary-General requesting assistance with the establishment of an international tribunal to prosecute surviving members of the Khmer Rouge regime. Soon thereafter, however, the first Prime Minister, Hun Sen, staged a palace coup to vault himself into position as the sole Prime Minister; a few years later, Pol Pot, the symbolic head of the Khmer Rouge, died under mysterious circumstances; and several high ranking Khmer Rouge leaders defected from their jungle hideouts in northwestern Cambodia to the government accompanied by great fanfare. Under these circumstances, Hun Sen soured on the idea of creating an institution he could not control. Nonetheless, by then, the process had taken on a life of its own.

Meanwhile, the U.N. General Assembly requested the establishment of a Commission of Experts to examine the evidence and recommend a course of conduct to end impunity in Cambodia. In a 1999 report, the Commission recommended the establishment of another U.N.-based tribunal, under either Chapter VI or VII of the U.N. Charter, that would be based in Thailand or elsewhere outside of Cambodia. The Commission rejected a mixed tribunal, which had been proposed by the Cambodian government, because the Commission was concerned about the prevalence of corruption, the risk of political influence, the quality of the members of the local bar, and the ability of the local courts to meet international due process standards. *See* Report of the Group of Experts for Cambodia, established pursuant to G.A. Res. 52/135, U.N. GAOR, 53d Sess., Annex, 110, U.N. Doc. A/53/850, S/1999/231 (Mar. 16, 1999). The Security Council did not act on these recommendations, so the Secretary-General began negotiations with the government of Cambodia to establish the quasi-international tribunal that was favored by the government. Several contentious issues emerged immediately regarding institutional design (such as whether there would be a majority of international or domestic personnel and who would appoint key personnel) and the validity of a prior amnesty enacted for members of the Khmer Rouge. The Secretary-General's concern was that the government was attempting to create a judicial process that could be politically controlled rather than an independent and impartial tribunal meeting international standards. In 2001, the Cambodian Parliament passed legislation, the Law on the Establishment of Extraordinary Chambers in the Courts of Cambodia for the Prosecution of Crimes Committed During the Period of Democratic Kampuchea, which resolved these outstanding issues in favor of the government's position.

In the face of this *fait accompli* and continued intransigence on the part of the government, the Secretary-General withdrew from the negotiations in February 2002. For this, he drew significant fire from influential members of the General Assembly committed to seeing a tribunal in Cambodia, the U.N.'s own Special Representative for Human Rights in Cambodia, and the U.N. High Commissioner for Human Rights. Members of the NGO community split on this issue: some took the hard line against the risk of a flawed process, whereas others argued that the perfect should not be the enemy of the good. The impasse ended when the U.N. General Assembly by resolution (U.N. Doc. A/RES/57/228) requested that the Secretary-General continue the negotiations on the basis of the 2001 law. On the same day it passed this resolution, and apparently oblivious to this irony, the General Assembly passed another resolution (U.N. Doc. A/RES/57/225) expressing concern about "interference by the executive in the independence of the judiciary" in Cambodia. The General Assembly eventually approved the agreement between the United Nations and the Royal Government of Cambodia in 2003. The agreement entered into force on April 29, 2005.

In early 2006, the ECCC was formally established on the premises of the High Command Headquarters of the Royal Cambodian Armed Forces on the outskirts of Phnom Penh. By November 2009, the trial of one accused, Kaing Guek Eav (also known as "Duch"), had been completed (Case 001). Duch was convicted for his role directing the notorious torture center known as S-21, or Tuol Sleng, where approximately 14,000 men, women, and children were detained, interrogated, and tortured during the Khmer Rouge period. The vast majority of these victims were then taken to Choeung Ek (also known as "the killing fields") and summarily executed. (Tuol Sleng, a former girl's school, and Choeung Ek are now museums dedicated to memorializing the victims of the Khmer Rouge regime).

The trial of the other four suspects in custody commenced later (Case 002). Only the cases against Nuon Chea and Khieu Samphan went to judgment. Ieng Thirith—one of the few women to be prosecuted before an international or quasi-international tribunal—was declared unfit to stand trial and later passed away in 2015; her husband, Ieng Sary, died in 2013 mid-trial. Case 002 was bifurcated into two sets of charges. Case 002/01 dealt with the forced evacuation of Phnom Penh and a single execution site. The defendants were found guilty, a verdict largely confirmed on appeal. Case 002/02 added charges of genocide (against ethnic minorities), crimes against humanity (including forced marriage), and war crimes. This trial resulted in another guilty plea and life imprisonment.

Since its establishment, the ECCC has been plagued with allegations of corruption and political interference. At first, the corruption allegations were petty and bureaucratic in nature, focusing on nepotism in hiring and allegations that Cambodian staff had to provide kickbacks to government officials. Most of the defense counsel filed a request asking the judges to investigate the allegations of corruption, arguing that—if true—such corruption endangered their clients' right to a fair trial. The investigating judges dismissed the request less than two weeks after it was filed, reasoning *inter alia* that accepting the request would amount to an abuse of power as the facts alleged do not fall within the jurisdictional mandate of the ECCC.

Eventually, the corruption allegations began to touch upon the work of the tribunal itself when a dispute arose between the Cambodian and foreign Co-Prosecutors over whether to undertake additional investigations beyond the five individuals then already in custody (Cases 003 and 004). Under the agreement establishing the ECCC, such disputes between the two Co-Prosecutors are to be resolved by the Pre-Trial Chamber and a request by one of the Co-Prosecutors to investigate a suspect may proceed in the face of objection by the other Co-Prosecutor unless the Pre-Trial Chamber rules otherwise. Canadian jurist Robert Petit argued in his submissions that the only requirement to open an investigation was the determination that there were reasonable grounds for believing that additional crimes within the jurisdiction of the ECCC had been committed. By contrast, his Cambodian counterpart, Ms. Chea Leang, argued that extra-legal factors—such as the limited nature of the ECCC's mandate, the threat of instability, and resource constraints—counseled against any expansion of charges. The Cambodian Prime Minister, Hun Sen, publicly stated that he did not want the Court to investigate or charge additional persons, leading to the charges of political interference in the judicial process.

In August 2009, the Pre-Trial Chamber deadlocked over the request submitted by Petit, and thus investigations proceeded against five additional suspects. The Pre-Trial Chamber split along national lines: the two international judges voted in favor of the investigations and the three Cambodian judges voted against. Because decisions of the Court require a supermajority (i.e. at least one international judge must be in the majority), the investigation was allowed to proceed. Soon after the decision was announced, Petit abruptly resigned, citing personal reasons. His successors continued with the investigation, but the schism between the international and national personnel was never resolved. Indeed, in Cases 003 and 004, the Co-Investigating Judges issued competing

Closing Orders, ending their investigations, with respect to defendants Meas Muth and Yim Tith. True to form, the international judge called for charges to be filed, whereas the national judge reasoned that the defendants did not fall within the ECCC's personal jurisdiction because they were too junior.

Pre-trial detention has been the norm at the ECCC and has been the subject of much litigation. Duch, for example, had been detained for nine years before his trial, seven under the auspices of the Cambodian Military Court and two under the jurisdiction of the ECCC. In a ruling that could be used to challenge the prevalent use of pre-trial detention within the domestic Cambodian system, the ECCC found that Duch's detention prior to his trial violated his rights (because it exceeded the three-year limit under Cambodian law and the international right to a trial "within a reasonable period of time"), and ordered that he both receive credit for time served against any sentence that may be imposed, as well as additional credit to compensate him for the violation of his rights. Under the internal rules of the Court a suspect may be detained prior to trial for a year at a time, subject to two renewals, for a total of three years.

NOTES & QUESTIONS

1. Mixed Composition

The Security Council premised the proposed staffing of the two original *ad hoc* tribunals on the belief that the tribunals would be more impartial if they did not include nationals of the states involved in the underlying events in top positions. As such, nationals of the former Yugoslavia and Rwanda served mainly as defense counsel and translators. With the hybrid tribunals, nationals occupy key posts by design in order to enhance domestic involvement in the process and enable local capacity building. The proportion of international versus domestic staff is not consistent across hybrid tribunals.

In this regard, compare the composition of personnel in the ECCC with the SCSL. Most SCSL judges were foreign given that Sierra Leone used some of its slots to appoint foreign judges. With respect to the ECCC, all of the important roles incorporate joint international-domestic representation. And yet, there are no provisions for how work and decision-making are to be divided among the Co-Prosecutors, Co-Investigating Judges, or Co-Defense counsel. A disagreement between the Co-Prosecutors goes before a panel of judges; is this an appropriate arrangement? Are there adequate safeguards within the ECCC Statute to ensure that the Cambodian personnel—who might be more susceptible to political manipulation than their foreign counterparts—will remain impartial? Although the various panels within the ECCC contain a majority of Cambodian judges, as noted above, decisions require a supermajority vote. Any ruling by the ECCC Trial Chamber thus requires the affirmative vote of at least four out of five judges per Article 14 (new) of the ECCC Law.

Should the international community fund an institution in which national personnel dominate all court organs, as is the case with the ECCC? Or should the international community only fund institutions that have a significant number of national personnel? Does the institutional requirement of a supermajority (thus requiring the vote of at least one international judge), risk the resentment of the Cambodian judges, staff, and public? How should such an institution balance the objectivity provided by international personnel with the domestic legitimacy provided by local staff?

2. Sources of Criminal Procedure

In addition to a mixed staff, the ECCC drew upon the procedural law of Cambodia as well as procedural principles existing within international law. Although the ECCC Statute gives domestic Cambodian procedural law primacy over international procedural law, Cambodian procedural law is scant. For example, Article 125 of the *Kram* [code] on Criminal Procedure states that "evidence of a criminal offense may be produced by any means in order to convince the judge." Further review of Cambodia's criminal procedure reveals that virtually anything short of a coerced confession constitutes admissible evidence. This has led at least one commentator, human rights lawyer Scott Warden, to observe that Cambodia effectively has no rules of evidence. The ECCC Statute makes provisions for such circumstances. Several articles state that "guidance may be sought" at the international level (1) where Cambodian procedural rules "do not deal with a particular matter," (2) where "there is uncertainty regarding their interpretation or application," or (3) "if there is a question regarding their consistency with international standards" (Articles 20, 23, 33). In contrast, Article 15 of the ICTY Statute permits the judges to formulate the rules of procedure and evidence as they deem necessary for the fairness and efficiency of the proceedings. Do these guidance clauses in the ECCC Statute empower the ECCC judges to draft new rules in the way that the judges of the *ad hoc* tribunals may do? For further discussion of criminal procedure law in Cambodia, *see* Scott Worden, *An Anatomy of the Extraordinary Chambers*, *in* BRINGING THE KHMER ROUGE TO JUSTICE: PROSECUTING MASS VIOLENCE BEFORE THE CAMBODIAN COURTS 171 (Jaya Ramji & Beth Van Schaack eds., 2005). The procedures to be adopted by the ECCC emerged as a contentious issue in the early days of the institution, with the international and Cambodian judges lining up on opposite sides of virtually every debate.

3. Funding Justice

Unlike the two ad hoc tribunals created by the Security Council, the ECCC and many second-generation tribunals are dependent upon voluntary funding and contributions from the target state. With the ECCC, even the national component has depended upon contributions by donor states. The U.N. Secretary-General appointed Professor David Scheffer, former U.S. Ambassador-at-Large for War Crimes Issues, as his Special Expert on U.N. Assistance to the Khmer Rouge to help raise funds for the ECCC. When funding fell short, the U.N. General Assembly authorized subvention grants from U.N. assessments, although this remained controversial. The ECCC process was originally budgeted at $56.3 over three years, an amount considerably less than the annual budgets of the ICTY and ICTR (approximately $270 million each). These funds, however, were largely exhausted before the first charges were issued. The Special Court for Sierra Leone's operational budget was originally projected at $57 million for three years. It cost nearly double that by the end of 2006. What areas of the ECCC's work are likely to suffer on such a lean budget? In an impoverished nation like Cambodia, is funding the ECCC to try a handful of septuagenarians a good use of international donor funds?

4. Subject Matter Jurisdiction

In addition to the three core international crimes—genocide, crimes against humanity, and war crimes—the ECCC have jurisdiction over the crimes of homicide, torture, and religious persecution drawn from the 1956 Penal Code, which was never abrogated by the Khmer Rouge. This Code has been amended several times since its enactment, so the ECCC will be applying, in effect, "dead law." Why might these domestic crimes have been included within the subject matter jurisdiction of the ECCC? The Co-Prosecutors' July 18, 2007, Initial Submission had requested that Duch be indicted for the three core international crimes (war crimes, genocide, and crimes against humanity) as well as certain domestic crimes under the 1956 Penal Code, namely torture and homicide. The ECCC's Co-Investigating Judges originally indicted Duch on August 21, 2008, for war crimes (grave breaches of the 1949 Geneva Conventions) and crimes against humanity under principles of direct and accomplice liability. The Co-Investigating Judges justified indicting solely on the basis of international criminal law on the ground that the acts "must be accorded the highest available legal classification."

On August 21, 2008, the Co-Prosecutors appealed the Indictment (contained in the Co-Investigating Judges' "Closing Order" ending the initial investigation), arguing that Duch should also have been charged with the domestic crimes of murder and torture. The Co-Prosecutors did not appeal the rejection of the proposed genocide charges. In support of their appeal, the Co-Prosecutors argued that the Co-Investigating Judges have discretion with respect to findings of fact, but only limited discretion to determine the legal consequences of those facts. In addition, the Co-Prosecutors argued that the decision of the Co-Investigating Judges divests the Prosecution's ability to utilize cumulative charging—which is generally allowed where crimes contain different material elements—in situations in which it is unclear which crimes the evidence will ultimately prove and desirable to fully account for the totality of an accused's wrongdoing. The domestic charges were ultimately reinstated on appeal. As you study substantive international criminal law in the next Part, consider why the Co-Prosecutors insisted on cumulative charging. We take up cumulative charging later in 13.

5. Genocide

As noted above, the Co-Investigating Judges refused a prosecutorial suggestion to charge Duch with genocide. In December 2009, the Co-Investigating Judges indicted the remaining identified defendants with genocide. The charges relate to the targeting of the ethnic Cham and Vietnamese minorities, and not to the vast majority of the offences alleged against the former regime leaders, which are in the nature of auto-genocide involving Khmer victims. Given the small number of victims affected by the genocide charge, and the limited resources available to the ECCC, should the genocide charges have been brought? Or should the Court focus on the war crimes and crimes against humanity charges that affect the vast majority of Khmer Rouge victims, including the Cham and Vietnamese? For more on the question of genocide in Cambodia, see Chapter 9.

6. Amnesty and Pardon

In 1979, Vietnam staged a trial *in absentia* of Ieng Sary and Pol Pot before a People's Revolutionary Tribunal, which convicted the defendants of genocide, defined idiosyncratically as the:

> planned massacres of groups of innocent people, expulsion of inhabitants of cities and villages in order to concentrate them and force them to do hard labor in conditions leading to their physical and mental destruction; wiping out religion, destroying political, cultural and social structures and family and social relations.

See Decree Law No. 1: Establishment of the People's Revolutionary Tribunal at Phnom Penh to Try the Pol Pot-Ieng Sary Clique for the Crime of Genocide, *reproduced in* GENOCIDE IN CAMBODIA: DOCUMENTS FROM THE TRIAL OF POL POT AND IENG SARY 45 (Howard J. De Nike, John Quigley & Kenneth J. Robinson eds., 2000). King Norodom Sihanouk later pardoned Ieng Sary, and the legislature adopted an amnesty for individuals who had violated legislation outlawing the Khmer Rouge. Article 11 of the Agreement between the U.N. and the Government of Cambodia left the force and effect of such decrees for the ECCC to determine:

> 1. The Royal Government of Cambodia shall not request an amnesty or pardon for any persons who may be investigated for or convicted of crimes referred to in the present Agreement.
>
> 2. This provision is based upon a declaration by the Royal Government of Cambodia that until now, with regard to matters covered in the law, there has been only one case, dated 14 September 1996, when a pardon was granted to only one person with regard to a 1979 conviction on the charge of genocide. The United Nations and the Royal Government of Cambodia agree that the scope of this pardon is a matter to be decided by the Extraordinary Chambers.

The ECCC has ruled that the pardon and amnesty do not provide a bar to the prosecution of Ieng Sary. Excerpts from that opinion, and a similar opinion from the Sierra Leone tribunal, are discussed in greater detail in Chapter 17 on Defenses Under International Criminal Law.

7. Statutes of Limitation

The Khmer Rouge held power from 1975 to 1979 and then continued an insurgency from the northwestern provinces until 1993 when the United Nations brokered the Paris Peace Accords and staged multiparty elections. The Cambodian law establishing the Extraordinary Chambers announces that the international crimes over which the ECCC have jurisdiction have no statutes of limitation. In the 1956 Penal Code, felonies (designated as *crimes*) carried a ten-year statute of limitation as compared to misdemeanors (*délits*), which carried a five-year statute of limitation. Article 3 (new) of the ECCC law provided that:

> The Extraordinary Chambers shall have the power to bring to trial all Suspects who committed any of these crimes set forth in the 1956 Penal Code, and which were committed during the period from 17 April 1975 to 6 January 1979:
>
> - Homicide (Article 501, 503, 504, 505, 506, 507 and 508)
> - Torture (Article 500)
> - Religious Persecution (Articles 209 and 210)
>
> The statute of limitations set forth in the 1956 Penal Code shall be extended for an additional 30 years for the crimes enumerated above, which are within the jurisdiction of the Extraordinary Chambers.

Can such pronouncements eliminate a defense that would otherwise be available to defendants prosecuted before the ECCC? Not surprisingly, the Defense argued that Article 3 (new) of the ECCC law was invalid because it attempted to revive a right to prosecute domestic crimes after the limitation period had expired. The Co-Prosecutors argued that the statute of limitations tolled until 1993—when a new constitution was promulgated, internationally-monitored elections were held, the government was reconstituted, and the war officially came to a close per the Paris Peace Agreement—and, in any case, homicide and torture are universally criminalized, so the principle of legality could not be violated by their prosecution.

The ECCC ultimately dismissed the charges brought against Duch under the 1956 Penal Code but allowed that the international charges could go forward. In so ruling, it held that the statute of limitations tolled while the Khmer Rouge remained in power, but it failed to reach agreement as to whether the tolling continued until 1993. The three Cambodian judges would have ruled that the statute was tolled, thus allowing the charges to stand. By contrast, while the two international judges agreed that the national judicial capacity was incapacitated during the era of Khmer Rouge rule (1975–1979), it was only weakened thereafter; as a result, they would have ruled that the statute of limitations should not be suspended until 1993 and thus the charges should be dismissed. Because the Chamber was unable to garner the affirmative vote of at least four judges per the supermajority rule, the charges failed. *See* Co-Prosecutor v. Duch, Decision on the Defence Preliminary Objection Concerning the Statute of Limitations of Domestic Courts, Case File No. 001/18-07-2007/ECCC/TC (July 26, 2010).

8. Statutes of Limitation and the Ex Post Facto Prohibition

In 1968, states drafted a treaty to abolish statutes of limitation for war crimes and crimes against humanity. The operative section provides that no statutory limitation shall apply to war crimes, crimes against humanity, or genocide. *See* U.N. Convention on the Non-Applicability of Statutory

Limitations to War Crimes and Crimes Against Humanity, Nov. 26, 1968, 660 U.N.T.S. 195. The treaty entered into force in 1970, prior to the time the Khmer Rouge were in power, but has only attracted 52 state parties. A similarly treaty within the Council of Europe entered into force in 2003 with only four ratifications.

In the 1980s and 90s, France prosecuted several World War II defendants—including Paul Touvier and Maurice Papon—for crimes against humanity under domestic legislation. Both Touvier and Papon challenged their convictions before the European Court of Human Rights on the grounds that they ran afoul of Article 7 of the European Convention on Human Rights, which provides:

1. No one shall be held guilty of any criminal offence on account of any act or omission which did not constitute a criminal offence under national or international law at the time when it was committed. Nor shall a heavier penalty be imposed than the one that was applicable at the time the criminal offence was committed.
2. This article shall not prejudice the trial and punishment of any person for any act or omission which, at the time when it was committed, was criminal according the general principles of law recognized by civilized nations.

See also Article 15, ICCPR (same). In both cases, the ECHR ruled that the French law fell within the exception to retroactivity recognized in sub-section 2 above, as the Nuremberg Charter did not contain a period of prescription for its crimes.

Under U.S. law (*Stogner v. California*, 539 U.S. 607 (2003)), a law extending a criminal statute of limitations after the existing limitations period has expired violates the U.S. Constitution's *ex post facto* clause when it is applied to revive a previously time-barred prosecution. Such a statute, the Court reasoned, creates the kind of "manifestly unjust and oppressive" retroactive effects that the *ex post facto* clause seeks to avoid, because it essentially aggravates the penalties associated with a crime as compared to those in place when it was committed. A vigorous dissent from the Court's conservative wing in *Stogner* argued that the California statute should have been left standing because:

1. it did not criminalize previously innocent conduct,
2. the punishment was limited to what could be assigned at the time the offense was committed so there was no aggravation of the offense,
3. it did not alter the government's burden vis-à-vis the elements of the crime, and
4. any concern about stale evidence could be dealt with by the jury and the applicable burden of proof.

These treaties may suggest an international law basis for overcoming any defense of prescription by the Khmer Rouge defendants with respect to international crimes, but not domestic crimes. Do these treaties diminish the force of any arguments defendants might make about their right to repose? Is it relevant that Cambodia has not signed or ratified the U.N. treaty? That very few states have?

9. Genocide Justice Act

In 1991, the U.S. Congress passed the Genocide Justice Act (22 U.S.C. § 2256, Pub. L. 103–236, 108 Stat. 486 (1994)), which authorized the creation of a documentation center in Cambodia, later named the Documentation Center of Cambodia (DC-Cam) to "develop the United States proposal for the establishment of an international criminal tribunal for the prosecution of those accused of genocide in Cambodia." Why would accountability in Cambodia garner such attention from the U.S. Congress? DC-Cam staff now conduct outreach throughout the country about the work of the ECCC and are documenting the stories of survivors and former members of the Khmer Rouge. These interviews provide opportunities for Cambodians to participate as civil parties before the ECCC. This rolling work is the closest thing to a truth commission that Cambodia has ever had. Given that the ECCC only prosecuted a handful of Khmer Rouge members, should Cambodia stage a more formal truth commission to complement the work of the ECCC? *See* Jaya Ramji(-Nogales), *Reclaiming Cambodian History: The Case for a Truth Commission*, 24 FLETCHER FOR. WORLD AFF. 137 (2000).

10. Tortured Confessions

In response to a request by counsel for Ieng Thirith, the investigating judges postponed ruling on whether evidence from confessions elicited using torture may be used to support the truth of the statements in the confession, stating that

> it is not possible at this stage to affirm that no element of the truth can ever be found in the confessions [obtained by torture]. The reliability of the statements cannot be assessed until the end of the investigation, when the case file is deemed complete. At that point, as with all of the evidence in the case file, the reliability of the confessions will be assessed on a case-by-case basis, with the understanding that the Co-Investigating Judges will proceed with utmost caution given the nature of the evidence and the manner in which it was obtained.

Office of the Co-Investigating Judges, Order on Use of Statements which were or may have been Obtained by Torture, July 28, 2009 (public redacted version). In the same opinion, the Co-Investigating Judges ruled that evidence obtained from torture could be used for other than the truth of the substance of the confession, such as for evidence that a particular individual was detained or for evidence that torture was employed. Should evidence obtained by torture be judged on a "case-by-case" basis, or should there be a bright line prohibiting any use of such evidence to prove the truth of the matter confessed? *See generally* Michael Scharf, *Tainted Provenance: When, If Ever, Should Torture Evidence be Admissible?* 65 WASHINGTON & LEE L. REV. 129 (2008).

11. For Further Reading

Professor Mark Kersten and Kirsten Ainley have recently produced the DAKAR GUIDELINES ON THE ESTABLISHMENT OF HYBRID COURTS (2019) as part of the Hybrid Justice project (www.hybridjustice.com) following extensive collaboration among, and consultation with, academic and practitioner experts on hybrid justice. *See also* Laura A. Dickinson, *The Promise of Hybrid Courts*, 97 AM. J. INT'L L. 295 (2003); Laura A. Dickinson, *The Relationship between Hybrid Courts and International Courts: The Case of Kosovo*, 37 NEW ENG. L. REV. 1059 (2003); Beth Van Schaack, *The Building Blocks of Hybrid Justice*, 44 DENV. J. INT'L LAW & POL'Y 169 (2016); Etelle R. Higonnet, *Restructuring Hybrid Courts: Local Empowerment and National Criminal Justice Reform*, 23 ARIZ. J. INT'L & COMP. L. 347 (2006); Suzannah Linton, *Cambodia, East Timor and Sierra Leone: Experiments in International Justice*, 12 CRIM. L. FORUM 185 (2001); John D. Ciorciari & Anne Heindel, HYBRID JUSTICE: THE EXTRAORDINARY CHAMBERS IN THE COURTS OF CAMBODIA (2014); and Frédéric Mégret, *In Defense of Hybridity: Towards a Representational Theory of International Criminal Justice*, 38 CORNELL INT'L L. J. 725 (2005). For a critical perspective, arguing that hybrid tribunals often exhibit some of the problematic elements of both domestic and international courts, see Chandra Lekha Sriram, *Wrong-Sizing International Justice? The Hybrid Tribunal in Sierra Leone*, 29 FORDHAM INT'L L. J. 472 (2006).

IV. ONCE AND FUTURE HYBRID SYSTEMS

At the time this book goes to press, many of the original *ad hoc* international and hybrid tribunals have completed their work. A few more are under construction or in contemplation. We touch on a few developments here.

A. FORMER YUGOSLAVIA

Although the Security Council created the ICTY for the former Yugoslavia, there were concerns that certain elements of the violence in Kosovo would fall outside the ICTY's jurisdiction, including allegations of organ trafficking in neighboring Albania. (See the Appendix for a map of Yugoslavia.) After the war in Kosovo, the United Nations established a United Nations Interim Administration of Kosovo (UNMIK) to assume responsibility for governance and economic reconstruction of the region. In exercising its powers over the administration of the judiciary, UNMIK sprinkled international judges, prosecutors, and defense counsel throughout the criminal courts of Kosovo in order to remove the appearance of bias in inter-ethnic war crimes cases. These judges are subject to the same substantive and procedural law as their Kosovar colleagues, but the cases to which they are assigned are determined by UNMIK or by the international personnel themselves. This effort evolved into the creation of the Kosovo Specialist Chambers (KSC) and a Specialist Prosecutor's Office. Although technically part of the Kosovar judiciary, the KSC sit extraterritorially in The Hague for security reasons and to hinder political interference in their work. The KSC have jurisdiction over crimes committed or commenced in Kosovo, which will include crimes consummated in neighboring Albania.

B. TIMOR-LESTE

The Special Panels in Timor-Leste, convened to prosecute international crimes committed in the wake of that country's independence referendum, are now defunct. They are largely considered a failure of international justice because the vast majority of perpetrators resided in Indonesia and were thus effectively out of reach of the Special Panels. A scholarly evaluation of the Special Panels concluded that judgments were poorly written and reasoned, at times failing to identify the applicable elements of crimes, the operative theory of liability, or the facts establishing either. In addition, the report recorded breaches of the rights of the accused, in particular with respect to the equality of arms and the issuing of convictions for un-indicted conduct. *See* David Cohen, INDIFFERENCE AND ACCOUNTABILITY: THE UNITED NATIONS AND THE POLITICS OF INTERNATIONAL JUSTICE IN EAST TIMOR (2006). A handful of prosecutions took place within Indonesia before the so-called Ad Hoc Human Rights Court, although no one of much consequence was prosecuted. *See* Susannah Linton, *Unraveling the First Three Trials at Indonesia's Ad Hoc Court for Human Rights Violations in East Timor*, 17 LEIDEN J. INT'L L. 303 (2004).

C. LEBANON

The United Nations and Lebanon co-created the Special Tribunal for Lebanon (STL) in The Hague to address terrorist violence in Lebanon, prompted by the car-bomb assassination on February 14, 2005 of the former Lebanese Prime Minister, Rafiq Hariri and twenty-two others. (See the Appendix for a map of Lebanon.)

In terms of subject matter jurisdiction, the Lebanese government demanded that the applicable law be largely based on Lebanese domestic law. As such, the Tribunal can assert jurisdiction over

> (a) The provisions of the Lebanese Criminal Code relating to the prosecution and punishment of acts of terrorism, crimes and offences against life and personal integrity, illicit associations and failure to report crimes and offences, including the rules regarding the material elements of a crime, criminal participation and conspiracy; and
>
> (b) Articles 6 and 7 of the Lebanese law of 11 January 1958 on 'Increasing the penalties for sedition, civil war and interfaith struggle.'

The Tribunal's personal jurisdiction is broad, including all those responsible for perpetrating, organizing, and sponsoring the alleged crimes. We provide more background to the creation of the STL and discuss some of its jurisprudence in Chapter 12 on Terrorism.

D. IRAQI HIGH TRIBUNAL

On December 9, 2003, the Iraqi Governing Council voted to establish the Iraqi Special Tribunal (later called the Iraqi High Tribunal (IHT)) to try Iraqi defendants for genocide, war crimes, crimes against humanity, and stipulated violations of Iraqi law. The legal committee of the Governing Council drafted the Statute of the High Tribunal following significant consultation with experts in the Coalition Provisional Authority (CPA), NGOs, and Iraqi lawyers and judges who provided advice on Iraqi criminal law and procedure. The drafters of the Statute stated that they intended to comply with international standards of due process of law and to focus on the crimes committed under international law. At the same time, the drafters sought to take into account the apparent wishes of the Iraqi people, namely that this process be substantially an Iraqi process and that the death penalty be available.

The Tribunal exercised jurisdiction over crimes committed by Iraqi citizens from July 17, 1968 (the day the Ba'ath Party seized power) through May 1, 2003 (the day U.S. President Bush declared major hostilities over and the beginning of the occupation). The Iraqi High Tribunal was designed to try cases stemming from several distinct operations attributable to Saddam Hussein's regime, including the initial purge of individuals affiliated with the prior regime, the Anfal Campaign in the Kurdish regions, the Iran-Iraq war, the repression of the "Marsh Arabs," and the invasion of Kuwait. The Tribunal had trial chambers (each with five judges), an appeals chamber (nine members), investigative judges, and departments for prosecution and administration. The Tribunal followed the Iraqi civil law custom in which crimes are investigated by investigative judges rather than police officers.

A Tribunal investigative judge and former magistrate under the Ba'athist regime, Ra'id Juhi, first arraigned Saddam Hussein and eleven other defendants in July 2004 for the killing of 148 Shiites in Dujail, allegedly in retaliation for a failed assassination attempt against President Hussein. The trial that followed was marked with disruptions, allegations of government interference, and violence. Several Iraqi defense counsel, one judge, and several prospective judges have been assassinated. Hussein was found guilty and sentenced to death. An unsuccessful appeal followed, and Hussein was executed in December 2006. In the Dujail judgment, the IHT confirmed its legitimacy as follows:

> The High Iraqi Tribunal was established on a self-evident truth that countries have judicial authority over crimes that are part of international criminal law just as they have jurisdiction over the crimes published according to national legislation. And, the Iraqi government that undertook the management and power

> on May 20, 2006 has chosen to accept the decision of the government council to establish an Iraqi tribunal having judicial power to judge Iraqi citizens and non-Iraqis residing in Iraq and accused of committing war crimes, crimes against humanity, extermination or other crimes specified by virtue of the national Iraqi law. * * * As for the subsequent requests by the defense attorneys regarding the transfer of the trials outside of Iraq, there is a firm rule in law that crimes committed inside national territory should be tried in those lands. This is based on the necessity of re-affirming regional sovereignty. And within the context of international criminal law, the former president of the International Criminal Tribunal for Yugoslavia has expressed these principles, which are of important and practical characteristics: first, the state in which a crime is committed is generally the best place to find evidence, and second, the legal system that is known by the resident or citizen or accused is preferable because he understands it. * * * Therefore, the proceedings or any penalty resulting from this trial in the country affected by the crime shall have a psychological and administrative effect which may help society understand what happened in addition to understanding the response of others, and this may play a preventive role for future or probable crimes.

Al-Dujail Case, Case No. 1/9 First/2005, Judgment, pp. 31–33 (Nov. 5, 2006). (The above is an edited version of an unofficial translation provided by Case Western Reserve Law School).

At the time of Hussein's execution, the IHT had already begun proceedings with respect to the next incident, the 1987–88 anti-Kurd campaign in Al-Anfal headed by Ali Hasan al-Majid ("Chemical Ali"), a cousin of Saddam Hussein, and aimed at the "Arabization" of Kurdish regions. The Al-Anfal campaign involved the use of ground offensives, aerial bombing, the destruction of settlements, mass deportation, concentration camps, firing squads, and chemical warfare and produced 100,000 to 200,000 victims. Hussein and six other defendants were indicted for crimes against humanity and genocide. This case went forward with the remaining defendants and resulted in conviction, which was upheld on appeal.

E. CENTRAL AFRICAN REPUBLIC SPECIAL CRIMINAL COURT

The latest effort in this tradition is the Special Criminal Court ("SCC") for the Central African Republic (CAR). (See the Appendix for a map of CAR.) The SCC is the product of newly-passed legislation, which follows on the heels of a U.N. commission of inquiry recommendation, an August 2014 agreement between CAR and the United Nations that contemplates the establishment of the SCC, and a Special Investigation Cell formed by presidential decree to begin investigations. The legislation envisions a mixed bench composed of international and domestic judges in roughly equal numbers. The Prosecutor is a foreign national, but the Chief Justice hails from CAR. It is anticipated that the SCC will be in existence for five years, subject to renewal at the initiative of the government in consultation with the United Nations. This new hybrid entity is unique in that it was created after CAR self-referred the situation on its territory to the ICC in December 2004. The ICC Office of the Prosecutor has now opened two separate CAR investigations: one relating to violence surrounding the 2003 coup that deposed President Angé-Felix Patassé, and the other concerned with crimes committed since 2012 by the Séléka and their anti-Balaka foes. The SCC is meant to complement this work. Its temporal jurisdiction remains open-ended in light of ongoing abuses. Because the armed groups that will be the target of investigation and prosecution are still operating in parts of CAR, strong measures for witness protection and judicial security have been necessary. The role of the U.N. Multidimensional Integrated Stabilization Mission ("MINUSCA") in assisting the SCC is also unprecedented. UNSCR 2149 empowers MINUSCA to "support and work with the Transitional Authorities to arrest and bring to justice those responsible for war crimes and crimes against humanity in the country, including through cooperation with States of the region and the ICC" and to "adopt urgent temporary measures . . . to maintain basic law and order and fight impunity." MINUSCA forces have already arrested some atrocity crimes suspects and will be involved in assisting with SCC logistics and the nomination of international personnel.

PROBLEM

Syria's modern history has been marked by instability, violence, and repression, and the Assad family has been at the center of Syrian politics for much of it. After rising through the military ranks, President Bashar al-Assad's father, Hafez al-Assad launched a bloodless coup in 1970. Once in power, Assad *père* was ruthless about consolidating his authority, suppressing internal dissent, and using patronage politics and manipulations of the welfare state to maintain power. A series of uprisings prompted a brutal response, particularly in January and February 1982, when Hafez crushed a Sunni rebellion in Hama, leveling much of the Old City. It is estimated that the army slaughtered upwards of 10,000 civilians—likely many more, but the final death toll remains unknown and unknowable. These "events" (as they are called) have long stood as a warning to would-be dissidents. Hama was followed by decades of repression characterized by gross human rights violations, including arbitrary arrests and detentions, systemic torture, forced disappearances, and summary executions.

Meanwhile, Hafez's second son, Bashar al-Assad, pursued a medical degree in ophthalmology and then studied abroad in the United Kingdom. Upon his father's death, Assad was nominated to the Presidency by the Ba'ath Party. Once elected, his inaugural speech hinted he might be willing to change course when it came to political freedoms and civil rights. Early moves—such as measures aimed at economic liberalization, the release of political prisoners, and certain overtures to the West—suggested cautious reforms could replace his father's unbending authoritarianism. This period of time—dubbed the "Damascus spring"—inspired a flourishing of civic discourse and opposition activism within civil society. Nonetheless, renewed crackdowns on sources of dissent and the reversal of minor reforms suggested more continuity than change. "Like father, like son," as the saying goes.

Many thought that the Syrian police state would be immune to the Arab Spring. Indeed, Syrians had felt the warmth of spring in the recent past, but it had proven to be illusory. Nonetheless, following uprisings in Tunisia, Egypt, and Libya, the winds of revolution arrived in Syria in March 2011. Demonstrators took to the streets to demand the release of political prisoners, greater press freedoms, and the end of the decades-long state of emergency. Although the protests were largely peaceful, the army overreacted, particularly in Dara'a, by deploying troops and tanks and by opening fire on civilians. Nonetheless, the uprisings spread, consuming suburbs of Damascus, Dara'a, Hama, and Homs—the latter of which became the epicenter of the revolution. Violence by paramilitaries and pro-government militia, the dreaded *shabiha*, gave the government deniability for some of the worst atrocities.

The Syrian battle space became a crowded one. As the revolution unfurled, the Assad regime stood accused as the main culprit. With support from Gulf states, an armed opposition eventually formed from village defense forces and defectors. It has been accused of committing its own breaches of humanitarian law, including custodial abuses of government soldiers. The emergence of the Islamic State of Iraq and the Levant/Da'esh (ISIL) on the scene triangulated the violence and brought it to an even more alarming level of brutality. ISIL has served as a bridge between the wars in Syria and Iraq given the high degree of conflict spillover. Finally, the involvement of Western powers who are at once adversaries and allies—aligned with opposing sides in the internal armed conflict but also focused on a common foe in the form of ISIL—has complicated events on the ground and generated new risks to civilians.

All told, virtually every international crime that forms part of the international penal code has been committed in and around Syria. (For a survey, *see* Beth Van Schaack, *Mapping War Crimes in Syria*, 92 INT'L L. STUD. 282 (2016)). The Syrian people have witnessed and been subjected to deliberate, indiscriminate, and disproportionate attacks; the misuse of conventional, unconventional, and improvised weapon systems; industrial-grade custodial abuses in a vast network of formal and informal prisons; unrelenting siege warfare; the denial of humanitarian aid and what appears to be the deliberate use of starvation as a weapon of war; sexual violence, including the sexual enslavement of Yezidi women and girls trafficked from Iraq and the sexual torture of detained men and boys; and the intentional destruction of irreplaceable cultural property. Thousands of Syrians are missing, many of them victims of enforced disappearances. The longstanding taboo against the use of chemical weapons has been repeatedly flouted, and the sectarian nature of the violence has raised the specter of genocide against ethno-religious minorities. Violence in the region has contributed to the biggest exodus of refugees since World War II. Over half of Syria's pre-war population is displaced, with a fourth of the population seeking refuge outside of the country.

Imagine that the war is over and a political transition has installed a coalition Government of National Unity. You have been asked to present a blueprint for an *ad hoc* tribunal to prosecute individuals accused of the commission of international crimes. As you engage in this exercise of institutional design, consider the following elements:

1) Temporal jurisdiction
2) Territorial jurisdiction
3) Personal jurisdiction
4) Subject matter jurisdiction
5) Rules of procedure & evidence
6) The relationship between this institution and domestic Syrian courts
7) Structure (number and allocation of judges)
8) Openings for international expertise
9) The role, if any, of the League of Arab States
10) The role of victims in the proceedings
11) Sources of funding
12) Venue (i.e., where would the tribunal be based)
13) Lifespan

Consider also whether you would recommend that Syria ratify the Rome Statute of the International Criminal Court and issue a declaration under Article 12(3) accepting retroactive jurisdiction over the period of the war.

CHAPTER 5

THE INTERNATIONAL CRIMINAL COURT

I. INTRODUCTION

Although a permanent international criminal court was not formally established until 2002, the idea of such an institution has been under consideration for many years. Immediately after the formation of the United Nations, the drafters of the Convention on the Prevention and Punishment of the Crime of Genocide contemplated the establishment of a permanent international criminal court. *See* Convention on the Prevention and Punishment of the Crime of Genocide, Dec. 9, 1948, art. VI, 78 U.N.T.S. 277 (entered into force Jan. 12, 1951) (providing that individuals charged with committing genocide shall be tried "by a competent tribunal of the State in the territory of which the act was committed, *or by such international penal tribunal as may have jurisdiction*") (emphasis added). The International Law Commission (ILC)—established by the General Assembly in 1947 to promote the progressive development of international law and its codification—was commissioned to study "the desirability and possibility of establishing an international judicial organ for the trial of persons charged with genocide or other crimes." *See* Prevention and Punishment of the Crime of Genocide, G.A. Res. 260(III)(B), U.N. Doc. A/810 (1948). With the advent of the Cold War, work on the permanent international criminal court stalled, in part because delegates could not agree on a definition of the crime of "aggression" against the backdrop of United States and Soviet proxy wars throughout the developing world. In the late 1980s, a collection of Latin American and Caribbean states re-invigorated the project, primarily because they wanted an international mechanism to combat the transnational illicit drug trade.

With prompting from the General Assembly, the ILC again turned its attention to drafting a statute for a permanent international criminal court. Early drafts did not include definitions of crimes. Instead, reference was made to a Draft Code of Offenses Against the Peace and Security of Mankind, which the ILC was simultaneously drafting. Eventually, however, these efforts merged.

The ILC completed a draft statute in 1994 that formed the basis for intensified consideration by an *Ad Hoc* Committee on the Establishment of an International Criminal Court and then a Preparatory Committee on the Establishment of an International Criminal Court formed by the General Assembly. *See* G.A. Res. 49/53, U.N. GAOR, 49th Sess., U.N. Doc. A/RES/49/53 (Dec. 9, 1994) (establishing the *Ad Hoc* Committee);

G.A. Res. 50/46, U.N. GAOR, 50th Sess., U.N. Doc. A/RES/50/46 (Dec. 11, 1995) (establishing the Preparatory Committee). After convening six separate sessions, the Preparatory Committee produced a consolidated draft Statute that served as the basis for comprehensive negotiations at a Diplomatic Conference of Plenipotentiaries on the Establishment of an International Criminal Court held from June 15 to July 17, 1998, in Rome, Italy. (Plenipotentiaries are state agents invested with full powers to act on behalf of the state.) A final Statute was completed and adopted in July 1998 at a Diplomatic Conference in Rome, Italy. The final result was the Rome Statute of the International Criminal Court. Delegations from 120 states, over 30 observers, intergovernmental organizations, and hundreds of non-governmental organizations attended the Diplomatic Conference. (M. Cherif Bassiouni, THE LEGISLATIVE HISTORY OF THE INTERNATIONAL CRIMINAL COURT (2005), provides a useful description of the negotiating and drafting history of the Court.) In 2010, plenipotentiaries met again in Kampala, Uganda, for the first Review Conference of the ICC. The crime of aggression became prosecutable at the end of 2017 when the 30th state, Palestine, ratified the amendments defining the crime of aggression and creating a jurisdictional regime. See Chapter 8 on the Crime of Aggression.

II. THE ICC IN OPERATION

We set out below a summary of the procedures by which a situation and case are brought before the ICC and the Court's current docket. As you read it, review the relevant provisions of the ICC Statute.

Ronald C. Slye & Beth Van Schaack, The International Criminal Court in Action: Anatomy of a Case (2019)

How does a case come before the ICC? In this piece, we draw upon the ICC's Statute, regulations, Rules of Procedure and Evidence, and written policies, coupled with its current practice, to illustrate the life of an ICC case from initial referral to final conviction or acquittal.

First, a note about terminology. It is important to distinguish between *crimes* within the jurisdiction of the Court; *cases* prosecuted before the Court against particular individuals; and *situations* that are referred to the Court or are the subject of action by the Office of the Prosecution (OTP). The crimes within the jurisdiction of the Court (i.e. its subject matter jurisdiction) are war crimes, crimes against humanity, genocide, and aggression.[1] Each crime is defined in a separate article in the Rome Statute (*see* Articles 5–8*bis*). The elements of each crime are

---

[1] In addition, the Court has jurisdiction over offences against the administration of justice, such as giving false testimony before the Court (Art. 70). A handful of such cases have proceeded in connection with the Central African Republic and Kenya situations. Remarkably, Jeanne-Pierre Bemba was acquitted in his main case but convicted of witness tampering in his Article 70 case along with 4 co-accused.

further set out in the Elements of Crimes (*see* Article 9). Individuals who are suspected of having committed one of these crimes are prosecuted as part of a *case*. A case may involve just one person (e.g., Uhuru Kenyatta of Kenya) or more than one person (e.g., the case of William Ruto and Joshua arap Sang of Kenya). *Situation* refers to a group of crimes (or "crime base") within the Court's jurisdiction committed within a particular geographic and temporal context. Usually a situation encompasses a state (e.g., Mali, Uganda), but not always (e.g., Darfur, which is only one part of the state of the Sudan). The ICC brings cases against individuals accused of committing crimes as part of a situation that is referred to the Court or that is initiated under the Prosecutor's *proprio motu* powers.

Trigger Mechanisms

A situation comes before the Court through one of three trigger mechanisms: a State Party referral; a Security Council referral; or on the Prosecutor's own initiative through the exercise of her *proprio motu* powers (Article 13). Upon receiving a referral, or upon deciding to exercise her *proprio motu* powers, the Prosecutor notifies the President of the Court of the referral, or of her intent to initiate her own investigation into a situation, for the purpose of assigning the situation to a Pre-Trial Chamber (Regulation 45).

State Parties and the Prosecutor can only trigger proceedings with respect to crimes committed on either a State Party's territory or by a State Party's nationals (Article 12(2)). Non-party states can, however, indicate through an *ad hoc* declaration that they accept the jurisdiction of the ICC over particular crimes committed on their territory or by their nationals (Article 12(3)). Such states may then be the subject of a referral by a State Party or *proprio motu* action by the Prosecutor as well. The Security Council is not so limited; it can refer a situation to the Court involving crimes committed on the territory of non-party states or by the nationals of non-party states. Each trigger mechanism is discussed in more detail below.

State Referral. A state that is a party to the Rome Treaty may refer a situation to the Prosecutor in which one of the four crimes within the jurisdiction of the Court is believed to have been committed (Article 14) so long as the preconditions for jurisdiction are met (Article 12(2)). Four of the eleven situations currently in the investigative stage are the products of self-referrals, which is to say they are the products of a State Party referring a situation on its own territory to the Court (Uganda, Central African Republic (CAR) (two self-referrals), Democratic Republic of the Congo (DRC), and Mali). CAR is currently subject to two investigations. The first relates to an armed conflict in 2002–3, the second to crimes connected to the Séléka revolution in September 2012. The Union of the Comoros submitted a referral to the ICC in May 2013 concerning a 2010 Israeli raid on a humanitarian aid flotilla bound for the Gaza strip and consisting of ICC State-Party-flagged vessels

(Comoros, Cambodia, and Greece) (*see* Article 12(2)(a)). This is the first referral of a situation by a State Party involving alleged crimes committed on the territory of another State Party. A second occurred in September 2018, when a group of states (Argentina, Canada, Colombia, Chile, Paraguay, and Peru) referred the situation regarding the Bolivarian Republic of Venezuela since 2014 to the Court.

Security Council Referral. The Security Council may, pursuant to its powers under Chapter VII of the UN Charter, refer a matter to the Prosecutor (Article 13). Chapter VII of the United Nations Charter sets forth the Security Council's powers to address a threat to the peace, breach of the peace, or act of aggression.[2] The Security Council has referred two situations involving non-party states to the Court (Darfur and Libya). The Council has come under increasing pressure to refer the situation in Syria as well, although so far Russia and China have blocked the implementation of any coercive measures before the Council, including an effort led by Switzerland and France (and eventually supported by the United States) to refer the situation to the Court. It is not clear whether the Court has the authority to determine whether the Security Council is acting properly under its Chapter VII powers in making a referral. To date, neither the Prosecutor nor any of the other parties to a situation before the Court has challenged the authority of the Security Council to refer a particular situation to the Court. In response to the Security Council referral of the Libya situation, however, the Office of the Prosecutor has clarified that it does not have jurisdiction to determine the legality of the use of force or to evaluate the proper scope of NATO's mandate as some language in the referral might suggest.[3] (Recall from Chapter 2 on International Jurisdiction that the ICTY did evaluate whether the Security Council was acting properly under its Chapter VII authority when it created the tribunal.) However, in all situations, including those referred by the Security Council, the Prosecutor must satisfy herself that there is a reasonable basis for an investigation and comply with the other requirements in the Rome Statute for initiating an investigation, including the requirements of Article 53.

The Exercise of *Proprio Motu* Powers. The Prosecutor may on her own initiative request that the Court assert its jurisdiction over a situation. To do so, however, she must seek approval before a three-judge Pre-Trial Chamber (PTC) (Articles 15(3)–(5), 57). So far, the Prosecutor has used her *proprio motu* powers to bring four situations before the Court: Kenya, Côte d'Ivoire, Georgia, and Burundi.

---

[2] Article 39 of the U.N. Charter states: "The Security Council shall determine the existence of any threat to the peace, breach of the peace, or act of aggression and shall make recommendations, or decide what measures shall be taken in accordance with Articles 41 and 42, to maintain or restore international peace and security."

[3] *See* Third Report of the Prosecutor of the International Criminal Court to the UN Security Council pursuant to UNSCR 1970 (2011), para.54.

The Prosecutor can exercise her *proprio motu* powers on the basis of information that has come to her from any source, including individuals, groups, states, inter-governmental organizations (IGOs), and non-governmental organizations (NGOs) (Article 15(2)). The Prosecutor may also seek additional information from any reliable source and undertake a preliminary examination of any matter that, in the judgment of the Prosecutor, is "not manifestly outside the jurisdiction of the court."[4] Indeed, the Prosecutor has indicated that she believes she has a legal duty to seek to open an investigation into a situation if all the criteria established by the Statute are fulfilled. By the end of 2018, the Prosecutor had received over 13,000 communications from a variety of sources. Most such communications were clearly outside of the Court's jurisdiction and did not require any further analysis. As an example, in 2018 the Prosecutor received 673 communications pursuant to Article 15, out of which 443 were manifestly outside of the Court's jurisdiction. Twenty-eight required further analysis, 158 were linked to a situation already under analysis, and 44 were linked to an ongoing investigation or prosecution.[5]

If the Prosecutor, after evaluating the information submitted, concludes that there is a reasonable basis to proceed with an investigation into the situation, she will notify relevant states and determine whether they plan to refer the situation to the Court. If the Prosecutor determines that there is not a reasonable basis to proceed with an investigation, then she confidentially notifies the sender of the information. If the states concerned do not refer the situation to the Court, then the Prosecutor may submit a request to open an investigation to a Pre-Trial Chamber (Articles 15(3)–(5), 57). If the Pre-Trial Chamber concludes there is no reasonable basis to proceed with an investigation into the situation, the Prosecutor may later submit a similar request based upon new facts or evidence regarding the situation (Article 15(5)). If the Pre-Trial Chamber agrees that there is a reasonable basis to proceed with an investigation, the Prosecutor then moves to the investigations phase (Article 15(4)).

Deferral by the Security Council

Notwithstanding that a proceedings have been initiated before the Court, the U.N. Security Council retains the ability to defer action before the Court for a year on a renewable basis. Article 16 provides:

> No investigation or prosecution may be commenced or proceeded with under this Statute for a period of 12 months after the Security Council, in a resolution adopted under Chapter VII of the Charter of the United Nations, has requested the Court to that effect; that request may be renewed by the Council under the same conditions.

4 OTP, Policy Paper on Preliminary Examinations (November 2013), para. 2.

5 OTP, Report on Preliminary Examination Activities 2018 (December 5, 2018) para. 18.

Although there have been requests for the Council to exercise its deferral power in connection with the Libya and Kenya situations, so far, the Article 16 remains unutilized when it comes to live situations before the Court (although it has been invoked by the Council in other contexts).

Preliminary Examinations

Before initiating an investigation into particular cases involving particular crimes and defendants, the Prosecutor undertakes what is called a preliminary examination. While the term "preliminary examination" is used only in Article 15, the Prosecutor undertakes a similar process with respect to state and Security Council referrals. In all such cases the Prosecutor considers those factors listed under Article 53(1).[6] This occurs once a situation is successfully triggered before the Court (either by a referral or by the exercise of the Prosecutor's *proprio motu* powers). Depending on the outcome of the preliminary examination, the Prosecutor may (1) decline to initiate an investigation, (2) continue to assess relevant national proceedings, (3) continue to collect information, or (4) initiate an investigation, subject to judicial review in the event of a situation triggered by the Prosecutor's *proprio motu* powers. The Prosecutor must initiate a full-scale investigation, with an eye toward identifying responsible individuals, unless she believes there is no reasonable basis to proceed based upon the following factors set forth in Article 53(1)(a)–(c): jurisdiction, admissibility (which encompasses a consideration of complementarity and gravity), and the interests of justice. Although there are three main considerations, technically, a preliminary examination involves four phases as set forth below. It should be emphasized that this analysis is undertaken on the basis of very limited information that is publicly available, provided by outside parties, or located at the seat of the Court; the Prosecutor does not undertake anything in the way of a full-scale evidentiary investigation. Although she does not enjoy full investigative powers at this stage, she can seek additional information from states, U.N. organs, NGOs, and other parties concerned, as well as receive written or oral testimony at the seat of the Court (Article 15(2) and Rule 104(2)).

Phase 1: Filter. Phase 1 involves an initial assessment of information received by the Office, whether from states, individuals, or organizations. This information is analyzed and placed into one of four categories: (1) matters that are manifestly outside the jurisdiction of the Court; (2) matters that are already subject to a preliminary examination; (3) matters already subject to a formal investigation or prosecution; or (4) matters that do not fit any of the other three categories and thus require

[6] The Rules of Procedure and Evidence of the Court make clear that in determining whether there is reasonable basis to proceed with an investigation under the Prosecutor's *proprio motu* powers under Article 15, the Prosecutor is to consider the factors set out in Articles 53(1)(a)–(c). (Rule 48) In all its functions, the OTP is guided by three overarching principles: independence (Article 42), impartiality (derived from Article 21(3)), and objectivity. The last criterion requires the OTP to investigate both incriminating and exonerating circumstances (Article 54(1)).

further analysis. This last category of information may result in the initiation of a new preliminary examination and thus eventually new cases to be brought before the Court. Phase 1 is essentially a filter to eliminate potential cases that are manifestly outside the jurisdiction of the Court.

Phase 2: Jurisdiction (Articles 11–13). There are multiple types of jurisdiction that must be evaluated by the Prosecutor during the preliminary examination: temporal, subject matter, and nationality/territorial. The Prosecutor must determine that there is a reasonable basis to believe that all three of these jurisdictional requirements have been met to proceed to the investigations phase.

Temporal Jurisdiction. The ICC only has jurisdiction for acts that were committed after the Rome Treaty came into effect on July 1, 2002 (Article 11). Temporal jurisdiction may also depend on: when the Rome Treaty comes into effect for a particular state; in the case of a Security Council referral, any effective date included in the referral resolution; and in the case of an *ad hoc* declaration by a non-state party accepting jurisdiction under Article 12(3), the date specified in that declaration. A state can, in effect, back-date an acceptance of jurisdiction by way of an Article 12(3) declaration as happened with respect to Côte d'Ivoire. There has been some speculation that a State Party could also back-date the Court's jurisdiction by way of an Article 12(3) declaration, although this has never been tested.

Subject Matter Jurisdiction. The Prosecutor must establish a reasonable basis for believing that one of the four crimes within the jurisdiction of the Court has been committed. To do so, the Prosecutor must consider as a preliminary matter the *chapeau* or circumstantial elements (e.g., the existence of an armed conflict as a predicate for war crimes and whether an attack against a civilian population was widespread or systematic as a predicate for crimes against humanity); the nexus between the specific criminal acts alleged and these contextual elements; the *de facto* or *de jure* role of alleged perpetrators; and any required mental element (e.g., specific or general intent, the intent to destroy in whole or in part a protected class of people, or knowledge of the widespread or systematic attack against a civilian population). Because this is a threshold-setting exercise, attribution of responsibility to particular individuals may be impossible at this stage. For example, a preliminary examination into the situation in Venezuela was closed in 2006 because former Chief Prosecutor Luis Moreno Ocampo determined that the acts alleged did not rise to the level of crimes against humanity. It has since been reopened in connection with political unrest since April 2017.

Preconditions to Jurisdiction (Nationality/Territorial Jurisdiction). Absent a Security Council referral, the Prosecutor can only consider crimes that have been committed on the territory of a State Party or by the nationals of a State Party (Article 12). As indicated above, a non-party state can also lodge an *ad hoc* declaration with the Court indicating that it will accept the Court's jurisdiction in the event of a referral. For example, the cases involving crimes committed in Côte d'Ivoire originally came before the Court as a result of an *ad hoc* declaration by the state (submitted in 2003 and reaffirmed in 2010) followed by a *proprio motu* investigation by the Prosecutor; Côte d'Ivoire later ratified the Rome Statute in 2013. In April 2014, the Government of Ukraine lodged with the Court a declaration under Article 12(3) accepting jurisdiction over crimes that allegedly were committed on its territory from November 21, 2013 to February 22, 2014 in connection with the Maidan protests (this period of time would exclude events in connection with the Russian occupation of Crimea). It later submitted a second such declaration accepting jurisdiction from February 2014 onward. As of this writing the Prosecutor has undertaken a preliminary examination of the situation in Ukraine. As noted above, the date the Rome Treaty comes into force for such a state may also be relevant, as jurisdiction over acts committed in the territory of a state, or by the national of a state, may not exist prior to that state's ratification.

The Palestinian National Authority (PNA) submitted a declaration under Article 12(3) in 2009 with respect to acts committed on its territory since July 1, 2002. The then Prosecutor, Moreno Ocampo, determined that it was not for the Prosecutor to determine whether the PNA constituted a state for the purpose of the Rome Statute, and so the preliminary examination into the situation was closed in April 2012. In November 2012, the U.N. General Assembly granted Palestine the status of non-member observer state in the United Nations (G.A. Res. 67/19). Palestinian authorities then submitted a second Article 12(3) declaration, which was accepted, and ratified the treaty. In May 2018, it referred the situation in Palestine since June 2014 to the Court.

Lawyers representing members of the Freedom and Justice Party of Egypt (the party of the former President Morsi) submitted a declaration under Article 12(3) with respect to acts committed on the territory of Egypt after June 1, 2013. The Prosecutor concluded that the purported declaration submitted to the Registrar was not submitted by a person with the requisite authority to represent the State of Egypt and thus accept the jurisdiction of the Court on its behalf.

Phase 3: Admissibility (Article 17). Assuming jurisdiction exists, the Prosecutor then considers whether any cases that the situation might generate would be admissible. Admissibility is an inquiry that is separate and apart from the existence of jurisdiction. Admissibility involves two distinct inquiries: complementarity and gravity. The assessment of admissibility is made based upon the specific facts as they exist at the time of the evaluation, and thus admissibility may change over time. The admissibility analysis takes place at two distinct phases, with slightly different emphases. During the preliminary examination phase, there are no specific cases (i.e. specific individuals accused of committing specific acts within the jurisdiction of the Court). As a result, admissibility is assessed with respect to potential cases—i.e. the types of people and crimes likely to be the subject of future cases, taking into account the policy of focusing on those who bear the greatest responsibility for the most serious crimes. A separate admissibility analysis is later undertaken with respect to particular suspects and cases that emerge from the situation before the Court.

Complementarity. For complementarity, the Prosecutor must assess whether genuine investigations or prosecutions have been undertaken by a state with jurisdiction over the matter. As part of a preliminary examination, the Prosecutor will consider whether there are adequate domestic proceedings involving potential defendants (Article 53). If there are, then the Prosecutor will not move forward with an investigation but will continue to monitor the situation. This has been the OTP's posture with respect to the situation in Colombia, which has been the subject of a preliminary examination since 2004. The Prosecutor has determined that there is a reasonable basis to believe that war crimes and crimes against humanity have been committed by paramilitary groups and state forces. So far, however, the OTP has declined to go forward with an investigation because it has determined that there are some genuine national proceedings involving these alleged crimes, which militate against the ICC asserting its jurisdiction.

As mentioned above, a second complementarity analysis may occur once the Prosecutor has opened an investigation into a situation and has identified specific accused (see below). An accused person or a state that would also have jurisdiction over the case can initiate an admissibility challenge at this time, and the Court may, *sua sponte*, determine the admissibility of a case (Article 19). If admissibility is challenged in a particular case, the Court must determine whether the ICC suspects are the subject of domestic investigations or prosecutions for the same conduct that serves as the basis for the proposed charges before the ICC (Article 17). If there is no such state investigation or prosecution, then the requirements of complementarity have been met. If there is such an investigation or prosecution, then the Prosecutor will assess the genuineness of such an investigation or prosecution. The Prosecutor must consider three possibilities in evaluating the genuineness of an investigation or prosecution: (1) are the national proceedings undertaken with the intent to shield the individual from being held accountable for the same crimes at the ICC; (2) have the national proceedings been delayed in a manner that is inconsistent with an intent to bring the individual concerned to justice; and (3) are the proceedings not being conducted independently or impartially, or otherwise in a manner consistent with an intent to bring the individual to justice? (Art. 17(2))

Complementarity Factors. In a policy paper on preliminary examinations,[7] the Prosecutor identified the following factors to assess with respect to complementarity. Determining whether national proceedings have been undertaken with the intent to shield the individual, the OTP will consider whether domestic authorities have:

- Undertaken manifestly insufficient steps in the investigation or prosecution;
- Deviated from standard practices or procedures;
- Ignored evidence or given it insufficient weight;
- Intimidated victims, witnesses, or judicial personnel;
- Generated findings that are irreconcilable with evidence tendered;
- Demonstrated manifest inadequacies in charging and modes of liability in relation to the gravity of the alleged conduct and the purported role of the accused;
- Generated flawed judicial findings arising from mistaken identification, defective forensic examination, failures of disclosure, fabricated evidence, manipulated or coerced statements, and/or undue admission or non-admission of evidence;
- Allocated insufficient resources for the proceedings at hand as compared with overall capacities; and
- Refused to provide information or to cooperate with the ICC.

Whether there has been an unjustified delay involves a consideration of:

- The pace of investigative steps and proceedings;
- Whether the delay in the proceedings can be objectively justified in the circumstances; and
- Whether there is other evidence of a lack of intent to bring the person(s) concerned to justice.

The independence of national proceedings is evaluated according to:

- The alleged involvement of the state apparatus, including those departments responsible for law and order, in the commission of the alleged crimes;
- The constitutional role and powers vested in the different institutions of the criminal justice system;
- The extent to which appointment and dismissal of investigators, prosecutors, and judges affect due process in the case;

---

[7] OTP, "Policy Paper on Preliminary Examinations" (November 2013) ("OTP Policy Paper").

- The application of a regime of immunity and jurisdictional privileges for alleged perpetrators belonging to governmental institutions;
- Political interference in the investigation, prosecution, or trial;
- Parties' recourse to extra-judicial bodies; and
- Corruption of investigators, prosecutors and judges.

National proceedings will be considered partial or impartial based upon:

- Connections between the suspected perpetrators and competent authorities responsible for investigation, prosecution or adjudication of the crimes;
- Public statements, awards, sanctions, promotions or demotions, deployments, dismissals or reprisals in relation to investigative, prosecutorial or judicial personnel concerned; and
- The extent to which the rights of the accused are consistent with those provided in Article 67 of the Rome Statute and principles of due process recognized by international law as elaborated in relevant international instruments and customary international law.

The state's inability to undertake a genuine investigation or prosecution will depend upon:

- Whether, due to a total or substantial collapse or unavailability of its national judicial system, the state is
  - unable to collect the necessary evidence and testimony,
  - unable to obtain the accused, or
  - is otherwise unable to carry out its proceedings.

Finally, the Prosecutor may also look at the following factors in assessing complementarity:

- The ability of the competent authorities to exercise their judicial powers in the territory concerned;
- The absence of conditions of security for witnesses, investigators, prosecutors, and judges, or the lack of adequate protection systems;
- The absence of the required legislative framework to prosecute the same conduct or forms of responsibility;
- The lack of adequate resources for effective investigations and prosecutions; and
- Violations of the fundamental rights of the accused.

The domestic investigation or prosecution will usually be conducted by the state on whose territory the alleged crimes occurred or by the state of nationality of the accused. However, if any state that has jurisdiction over the alleged crime is genuinely investigating or prosecuting the matter, then the requirements of complementarity are not met and the case is inadmissible before the Court. (Presumably, a state exercising universal jurisdiction could also trigger complementarity, but this has never been tested and remains controversial).

Gravity. The second component of admissibility is *gravity*. At the preliminary examination phase, the situational gravity, including the gravity of potential cases, is at issue. Later the prosecutor determines which cases within the situation are sufficiently grave to bring before the Court. At either phase, the concept of gravity includes both quantitative and qualitative elements, including the scale, nature, manner of commission of the crimes, and their impact (Regulation 29(2)). To assess the scale of the crimes, the Prosecutor will look at:

> the number of direct and indirect victims, the extent of the damage caused by the crimes, in particular the bodily or psychological harm caused to the victims and their families, or their geographical or temporal spread (high intensity of the crimes over a brief period or low intensity of crimes over an extended period).[8]

The nature of the crimes refers to the specific elements of each offense (e.g. killings, torture, rapes). With respect to the manner of commission of the crimes, the Prosecutor looks to the

> means employed to execute the crime, the degree of participation and intent of the perpetrator (if discernible at this stage), the extent to which the crimes were systematic or result from a plan or organised policy or otherwise resulted from the abuse of power or official capacity, and elements of particular cruelty, including the vulnerability of the victims, any motives involving discrimination, or the use of rape and sexual violence as a means of destroying groups.[9]

Finally, to assess the impact of the crimes, the Prosecutor will look to "the sufferings endured by the victims and their increased vulnerability; the terror subsequently instilled, or the social, economic and environmental damage inflicted on the affected communities."[10]

A preliminary examination into the situation in Iraq was initially closed in part on the basis of a finding that while crimes within the jurisdiction of the Court may have been committed by ICC State Parties, the crimes alleged did not satisfy the element of gravity. Iraq is not a State Party to the ICC Statute and has not submitted an Article 12(3) *ad hoc* declaration accepting the jurisdiction of the Court; however, the United Kingdom, a State Party, had troops stationed in Iraq as part of

---

8 OTP Policy Paper, para. 62.

9 OTP Policy Paper, para. 64.

10 OTP Policy Paper, para. 65.

Operation Iraqi Freedom. The Prosecutor received Article 15 communications containing allegations that British troops had committed crimes within the jurisdiction of the Court or were accessories to crimes committed by nationals of non-party states. Former Prosecutor Moreno Ocampo determined in February 2006 that the available information did not indicate the commission of intentional attacks on civilians or that excessive force in relation to the military advantage to be gained was utilized. With respect to alleged custodial abuses, by contrast, the Prosecutor concluded that there was a reasonable basis to believe that crimes within the jurisdiction of the Court had been committed (namely, the wilful killing and inhuman treatment of 4–12 individuals). He determined, however, the required gravity threshold was not met, particularly as compared with other situations before the Court.

On January 10, 2014, the European Center for Constitutional and Human Rights and an organization called Public Interest Lawyers submitted a communication to the Prosecutor concerning alleged responsibility of officials of the United Kingdom with respect to war crimes involving systematic detainee abuse in Iraq from 2003 until 2008. Based upon an initial assessment of the information received, the Prosecutor concluded that this recent communication includes information that was not available to her Office at the time of the original decision in 2006, and has thus initiated a preliminary examination to determine whether there is a reasonable basis to proceed with an investigation. In the meantime, the lawyer associated with Public Interest Lawyers has been disbarred and the organization shuttered, in part based upon proof that it had falsified evidence about abuses by U.K. armed forces in Iraq.

Phase 4: Interests of Justice (Article 53(1)(c)). While the Prosecutor must show that there are reasonable grounds for believing that the requirements of complementarity and gravity are met, the "interests of justice" element is a countervailing consideration.[11] Such interests are considered only once the requirements of jurisdiction and admissibility are met. So far, no situation subject to a preliminary examination has been fully analyzed with respect to this element.

The Prosecutor will not move forward with an investigation if she concludes that there are substantial reasons for believing that the interests of justice would not be served by proceeding with such an investigation. In making this assessment, the Prosecutor takes into account the gravity of the crimes, as well as the views of victims and other relevant stakeholders, such as political, religious, and community leaders, states, and inter-governmental and non-governmental organizations.

[11] The OTP has a separate policy paper on this inquiry. *See* The Interests of Justice (September 2007).

The current Prosecutor has indicated that she will rarely decide not to proceed with an investigation based upon an evaluation of the interests of justice:

> In light of the mandate of the Office and the object and purpose of the Statute, there is a strong presumption that investigations and prosecutions will be in the interests of justice, and therefore a decision not to proceed on the grounds of the interests of justice would be highly exceptional.[12]

The OTP has indicated that this inquiry does not include matters affecting international peace and security, which (in its estimation) are within the province of the Security Council. The OTP has also emphasized that there are no other statutory criteria underlying the decision to undertake a full-scale investigation. Of relevance to criticism that the Court is "targeting" Africa, the OTP points to the following internal policy:

> Geo-political implications, or geographical balance between situations, are not relevant criteria for determining whether to open an investigation into a situation under the Statute.[13]

In its policy papers, the OTP has also made clear that it need not prosecute "all sides" in order to address perceptions of bias. Rather, the OTP is to focus on those most responsible for the most serious crimes.[14]

Summary of Preliminary Examinations and the Initiation of an Investigation

In sum, while conducting a preliminary examination, the Prosecutor first assesses the question of jurisdiction. If there are reasonable grounds for concluding that crimes within the jurisdiction of the Court have been committed, then the Prosecutor turns to the elements of complementarity and gravity. Once the Prosecutor has satisfied herself that there is a reasonable basis for believing that there is jurisdiction and that the situation is admissible, she will analyze the interests of justice. Assuming none of these factors counsels otherwise, the Prosecutor will undertake an investigation into a situation based on the information provided to her (which can come from states, individuals, groups or organizations)

If the preliminary examination arises out of a situation referred to the Prosecutor either by a state or the Security Council, and the Prosecutor decides not to proceed with an investigation because she has a reasonable basis for believing that the requirements of jurisdiction or admissibility have not been met, then either the state or the Security Council may request that the Pre-Trial Chamber review that decision. Upon completion of that review the Pre-Trial Chamber may request that

12 OTP Policy Paper, para. 71.

13 OTP Policy Paper, para. 29.

14 OTP Policy Paper, para. 66.

the Prosecutor reconsider her decision not to proceed (Article 53(3)(a)). The Comoros, for example, appealed the Prosecutor's decision to close—on grounds of insufficient gravity—the preliminary investigation into the 2010 flotilla raid. The PTC requested the Prosecutor to "reconsider" her previous decision. The Prosecutor reaffirmed her original decision. The PTC then ordered her to reconsider again. The Prosecutor then appealed this decision. A judgment from the Appeals Chamber is expected in September 2019.

At the moment, the Prosecutor is undertaking preliminary examinations in nine situations. These situations are being considered with respect to two phases of analysis:

> Phase 2 (subject matter jurisdiction): Bangladesh/Myanmar, Republic of the Philippines, Ukraine, and Venezuela.
>
> Phase 3 (admissibility): Colombia, Guinea, Iraq/U.K., Nigeria, and Palestine.

In six situations and based upon the above criteria, the decision was made not to proceed with an investigation with respect to the following situations: Gabon, Honduras, Comoros (on appeal), Republic of Korea, Iraq (since re-opened), and Venezuela (since re-opened). The Prosecutor occasionally informs States Parties and the public about the status of her preliminary examinations; these reports are posted on the OTP website in the interests of transparency. There are no strict timelines for completing the preliminary examination process; some situations have been under consideration for a decade given the nature of the inquiry, the complexity of the issues involved, and the scope and pace of national proceedings (as in Colombia).

Investigations & Case Development

Once the Prosecutor has completed the preliminary examination and decided to proceed with an investigation, she establishes a team of investigators with representation from each of the three divisions of the OTP: Jurisdiction, Complementarity and Cooperation (JCCD); Investigations; and Prosecution. The joint team then analyzes the information and evidence collected during the preliminary examination stage, develops additional evidence, and begins to formulate a case hypothesis.

In developing the case hypotheses, the team also aims to focus on crimes that are the most serious (including sexual- and gender-based violence and violence against children) and that best represent the scale and impact of the crimes arising from the situation (Article 54(1)(b); OTP Regulation 34(2)).

The Prosecutor may undertake investigations on the territory of a state with its approval. If a State Party does not cooperate with such a request, the Pre-Trial Chamber may authorize such on-site investigations but only if the state's failure to cooperate is due to the unavailability of any authority or any component of its judicial system competent to execute a request for cooperation. If a State Party otherwise fails to comply with a request to cooperate with the Court, the Court may make a finding to that effect and refer the matter to either the Assembly of State Parties (ASP) or, if the matter arose from a Security Council referral, to the Council.

Only States Parties are under treaty-based obligations to comply with the Court. Non-party states may be under similar obligations if imposed on them by the Security Council, e.g., in the referral resolution. In the two Security Council referrals to date, however, only the territorial states (Sudan and Libya) have been so ordered; other U.N. member states are merely "urged" to cooperate with the Court. To date, the Court has made several findings of non-cooperation, primarily with respect to the travel of President Omar Al-Bashir to a number of States Parties, including Malawi, Chad, Djibouti, South Africa, and Jordan. In their defense, these states argued that Al Bashir enjoyed head of state immunity, an argument recently rejected by the ICC Appeals Chamber (see Chapter 17). So far, however, the Security Council has not responded in any concrete way to effectuate its referrals—a source of sharp criticism.

Once the Prosecutor has undertaken sufficient investigations and found reasonable grounds to believe that an individual has committed a crime within the jurisdiction of the Court, the Prosecutor may request that the Pre-Trial Chamber issue a warrant of arrest or a summons to appear against such an individual (Article 58).

Admissibility Challenge

Once the Prosecutor has identified a defendant who will be charged in connection with crimes committed within a referred situation, a state or the accused can launch an admissibility challenge with respect to that individual (Article 19). The Court can also undertake an admissibility analysis on its own motion. In general, admissibility can only be challenged once, unless there are "exceptional circumstances" (Article 19(4)). If there is no domestic investigation or prosecution of the matter under consideration, then the requirements of complementarity have been met, the case is deemed admissible, and the proceedings before the Court continue. This is an "empirical" question based on inactivity at the domestic level at the time of the Court's consideration of admissibility.[15]

If there is a domestic investigation or prosecution, then the Prosecutor must establish whether these domestic proceedings encompass substantially the same individuals and conduct that is the subject of the Prosecutor's investigation. If the domestic proceedings do meet the same person/same conduct standard, then the Court will assess the genuineness of such an investigation or prosecution. The Prosecutor

[15] OTP Policy Paper, para. 47. The "reasons" for the inactivity—e.g., the lack of a legal framework, the existence of statutory bars such as amnesty or immunity laws; the focus on low-level direct perpetrators; or lack of political will—is of no moment in this analysis. *Id.* at para. 48.

must consider three possibilities in evaluating the genuineness of an investigation or prosecution: (1) the national proceedings are undertaken with the intent to shield the individual from being held accountable for the same crimes at the ICC; (2) the national proceedings have been delayed in a manner that is inconsistent with an intent to bring the individual concerned to justice; and (3) the proceedings are not being conducted independently or impartially, or otherwise in a manner consistent with an intent to bring the individual to justice (Article 17(2)).

Considerable debate remains on whether, and to what extent, the Court may consider due process protections during the admissibility inquiry. The admissibility provisions of the ICC Statute do not expressly mandate such considerations. In the Libya cases, however, the fact that neither defendant had ready access to their appointed or chosen defense counsel (in part due to security concerns) was considered evidence of the state's inability to proceed. The Prosecutor has indicated that she will assess due process concerns pursuant to Article 21(3) in light of internationally-recognized human rights standards.

Confirmation of Charges

Within a reasonable time after the appearance of a suspect before the Court—whether pursuant to arrest, summons, or voluntary surrender—the Pre-Trial Chamber holds a hearing to confirm the charges for which the Prosecutor has requested a trial (Article 61). Normally the accused will be present for the confirmation of charges hearing, but the Pre-Trial Chamber may proceed with a hearing without the presence of the accused if the suspect has waived his right to be present, or if the suspect has fled or cannot be found and all reasonable steps have been taken to locate him and inform him of the hearing Article 61(2).

To have each charge confirmed, the Prosecutor must establish that there are substantial grounds to believe that the suspect committed the crime (Article 61(5)). If the Pre-Trial Chamber concludes that there is sufficient evidence to establish substantial grounds to believe that the person committed the crime charged, then the charge is confirmed. If this evidentiary threshold is not met with respect to a charged crime, then the Pre-Trial Chamber may either decline to confirm that charge or adjourn the hearing and request the Prosecutor to either provide additional evidence or amend the charges if the evidence suggests a different crime within the jurisdiction of the Court has been committed. The confirmation of charges against ex-President Laurent Gbagbo, who was prosecuted in connection with the Côte d'Ivoire situation, was adjourned following a confirmation of charges hearing in February 2013. A Pre-Trial Chamber ruled in June 2013 that there was insufficient evidence to confirm the charges against Gbagbo. Accordingly, it ordered the Prosecutor to continue her investigation and provide additional evidence with respect to all charges. The Prosecutor unsuccessfully appealed this ruling, and an amended Document Containing the Charges

(DCC)—the equivalent of an indictment—was submitted in January 2014, and charges were confirmed against Gbagbo on June 12, 2014, after the Prosecutor submitted further requested information. In January 2019, the defendant and his co-accused, Blé Goudé, were acquitted on a no case to answer motion.

Trial

Upon the confirmation of the charges, the President constitutes a Trial Chamber for the case. The Court's Rules of Procedure and Evidence (RPE) should be consulted for a more detailed understanding of how the trial proceedings are conducted. We briefly mention here some of the more interesting provisions of the rules and procedures governing trials at the Court.

The trial will usually take place in The Hague, although the Court has considered hearing cases elsewhere in order to be closer to the site of victims, witnesses, and evidence.[16] To date, all sittings of the Court have occurred at The Hague, in part because the judges refused to convene *in situ*. Trials are normally held in public, but parts of the proceedings may be held *in camera* to protect victims or witnesses or to protect confidential or sensitive information that will be presented as evidence (Articles 64(7) and 68).

An accused may plead guilty to some or all of the charges. Even if the accused pleads guilty to all of the charges, the Trial Chamber may request the presentation of additional evidence or even order a full trial if the Trial Chamber is of the opinion that a trial would further the interests of justice, and in particular the interests of victims. If the Trial Chamber orders a full trial, then the admission of guilt shall have no effect and the case may be remitted to another Trial Chamber (Article 65(4)). The first guilty plea before the ICC came in 2016 in the Mali situation when Ahmad al-Faqi al-Mahdi, a member of the Al Qaida-linked Ansar Dine, pled guilty to the destruction of cultural property in Timbuktu.

Victims are independently represented throughout the trial and may also present their views and concerns during the proceedings if the Court concludes that the personal interests of the victims are affected. They may also ask the Court to put questions to witnesses related to their concerns. Such presentations are done in a way that is not inconsistent with the rights of the accused to a fair and impartial trial (Article 68(3)).

The Court—which is composed only of judges and does not utilize lay juries—has more expansive and permissive rules of evidence than

---

[16] Article 3(3); RPE 100. In the Kenya cases, the Court heard arguments about whether it should hold proceedings somewhere closer to Kenya, in part due to the fact that two of the accused are the President and Deputy President of Kenya. The Court ultimately decided to hear the cases in The Hague. The ASP later amended the RPE to provide for the excusal from presence at trial of a suspect who is "mandated to fulfill extraordinary public duties at the highest national level," notwithstanding that the ICC Statute requires their presence. RPE 134*quater*.

common law systems such as the United States. Thus, the Court may hear any evidence and evaluate its relevance, keeping in mind the effect the admission of such evidence may have on a fair trial for the accused (Article 69(4)). So, for example, while hearsay evidence is admissible, the judges have signaled that it will have less probative weight. Evidence that is obtained in violation of the Rome Statute or in violation of international human rights law shall not be admissible if the violation casts "substantial doubt" on the reliability of the evidence or if its admission would be "antithetical to and would seriously damage the integrity of the proceedings" (Article 69(7)).

The Chamber is prohibited from requiring corroboration to prove any crime, and in particular crimes of sexual violence (RPE 63(4)). The Rules of Procedure and Evidence set out further requirements for proving crimes of sexual violence, and in particular when, if at all, the words or actions of a victim may be used to infer consent (RPE 70–71). An elaborate procedure is also provided for dealing with evidence that a state asserts would, if revealed, harm its national security interests (Article 72).

The decision of the Trial Chamber shall be by a majority of the judges hearing the matter. If the accused is convicted, a separate hearing is held with respect to sentencing. The maximum sentence that can be imposed is life imprisonment when the crimes are of exceptional gravity, although as a general matter a sentence of a term of years cannot exceed thirty years (Article 77).

Appeals

Convictions, acquittals, and sentences may be appealed by the Prosecutor or a convicted person (Article 81). In addition, interlocutory appeals may be made against a decision regarding jurisdiction or admissibility, regarding the release of a person, or against decisions by the Pre-Trial Chamber involving investigations (Article 82). In addition, per Article 82(1)(d), an appeal may be available for an

> issue that would significantly affect the fair and expeditious conduct of the proceedings or the outcome of the trial, and for which, in the opinion of the Pre-Trial or Trial Chamber, an immediate resolution by the Appeals Chamber may materially advance the proceedings.

Normally, an appeal will not have suspensive effect (Article 82(3)).

The Trial Chamber may at any time during the trial change the legal characterization of the facts to, for example, characterize the pled facts as a crime against humanity instead of a war crime, or to change the mode of liability. (Regulations of the Court, Regulation 55). For example, in the prosecution of Germain Katanga, the Trial Chamber notified the parties at the end of the trial that it was likely to change Katanga's mode of liability to "common purpose" from the Prosecutor's original indictment of "indirect co-perpetration."[17] This was a particularly controversial decision given that it came at the end of the trial without allowing the Prosecutor or the defendants to make any arguments for or against this change. The final judgment did in fact recharacterize the mode of liability.[18]

Reparations

The Court may order that a convicted person pay specific reparations to victims—including restitution, compensation, and rehabilitation costs—or that such amounts should be paid out of the Trust Fund for Victims (Article 75). The Trust Fund for Victims is also already active in several ICC situation counties. For example, in the case involving Thomas Lubanga Dyilo arising out of the situation in the DRC, the Trial Chamber in 2017 set reparations at $10 million for 425 victims who had been, or would later be, identified. Lubanga and some victims appealed the amount and the methodology employed to reach that amount. In July 2019, the Appeals Chamber largely affirmed the reparations scheme.[19] Reparations have also been ordered against Al Mahdi, who pled guilty to the destruction of cultural property in the Mali situation.[20]

NOTES & QUESTIONS

1. Preconditions to the Exercise of Jurisdiction

Except in the situation of a Security Council referral, the Rome Statute requires that either the territorial state or the state of nationality of the accused be a member of the Court before an investigation may commence (Article 12). Why only these grounds? What other grounds might have been considered? Should the Court have allowed for jurisdiction over defendants hailing from any state, even non-parties? What about defendants on the territory of a State Party (the so-called custodial state)? Or the state of the nationality of the victims? Why might these grounds have been rejected by negotiating states?

2. Prosecutorial Discretion at the ICC

Under what circumstances can the Prosecutor decline to go forward with a prosecution that has been referred to it pursuant to one of the trigger

[17] *The Prosecutor v. Germain Katang and Mathieu Ngudjolo Chui*, Case No. ICC–01/04–01/07, Decision on the Implementation of Regulation 55 of the Regulations of the Court Severing the Charges Against the Accused Persons (November 21, 2012). Judge Van den Wyngaert dissented from this decision, and from that part of the eventual judgment that relied upon the recharacterization of the facts to change the mode of liability. In the *Lubanga* judgment, the Trial Chamber used Regulation 55 to recharacterize the facts to describe a non-international armed conflict rather than an international armed conflict. *The Prosecutor v. Thomas Lubanga Dyilo*, Case No. ICC–01/04–01/06, Judgment Pursuant to Article 74 of the Statute, para. 566 (March 14, 2012).

[18] *The Prosecutor v. Germain Katanga*, Judgment Pursuant to Article 74 of the Statute, Case No. ICC–01/04–01/07–2325–tENG (March 7, 2014).

[19] *The Prosecutor v. Thomas Lubanga Dyilo*, Judgment on the Appeals against Trial Chamber II's 'Decision Setting the Size of the Reparations Award for which Thomas Lubanga is Liable', Case No. ICC–01/04–01/06 A7 A8 (July 18, 2019).

[20] *The Prosecutor v. Ahmad Al Faqi Al Mahdi*, Reparations Order, Case No. ICC–01/12–10/15–236 (Aug. 17, 2017).

mechanisms set forth in Article 13? Consider, in particular, Article 53 of the ICC Statute. The referral of the situation in Uganda has triggered criticism from local NGOs and others who believe the referral undermined efforts at reaching a negotiated solution and ultimately peace in the region. How would such views come before the Prosecutor? Can and should the Prosecutor take such arguments into account in determining whether to proceed? Should the Prosecutor have declined to issue indictments in this case in light of these views? Why would the drafters of the ICC Statute give such powers to the Prosecution to reject cases referred to the Court? Do these powers exist even in the face of a Security Council Chapter VII referral? Should they?

3. *Proprio Motu* Powers

The United States, among other states, was opposed to the idea of a Prosecutor who could initiate an investigation *proprio motu*. Why would states oppose granting the Prosecutor such powers? Are there adequate safeguards in the Statute to cabin prosecutorial discretion? Out of the ten situations under investigation, four have been initiated by the Prosecutor (Kenya, Côte d'Ivoire, Georgia, and Burundi). It sought approval from the PTC to open an investigation in Afghanistan in connection with crimes committed by Afghan and foreign forces, but this was denied unanimously in April 2019 on the grounds that an investigation would not serve the interests of justice. That decision is reproduced below.

4. The Security Council and the ICC

The debate over the relationship between the Security Council and the ICC remained contentious throughout the drafting of the Rome Statute. An early draft of Article 16 (then designated as Article 23(3)) of the Rome Statute read:

> No prosecution may be commenced under this Statute arising from a situation which is being dealt with by the Security Council as a threat to or a breach of the peace or an act of aggression under Chapter VII of the Charter, unless the Security Council otherwise decides.

(Recall that pursuant to Article 27(3) of the U.N. Charter, decisions under Chapter VII "shall be made by an affirmative vote of nine members including the concurring votes of the permanent members."). The final formulation of Article 16 is the result of a proposal from Singapore (the so-called "Singapore Compromise") introduced during the August 1997 preparatory proceedings. Compare this earlier formulation to the text ultimately adopted at Article 16. How does the role of the Security Council vis-à-vis the ICC differ in the two formulations? Which grants greater powers to the Security Council? Should there be any role for the Security Council in the Court's work beyond serving as a trigger mechanism, or should the Court be entirely "de-politicized?" Does the inclusion of Article 16 increase the likelihood that states will "bargain" with the Security Council to ensure a deferral as Kenya did following the indictment of high-profile Kenyan figures, including individuals who eventually became President and Deputy President of the country?

Recall the earlier discussion about the ICTY's powers of judicial review over Security Council action. Is the ICC empowered to exercise "judicial review" in such circumstances to determine whether the Security Council is validly acting pursuant to Chapter VII? After threatening to veto peacekeeping operations, the United States twice secured Chapter VII Security Council resolutions (pursuant to Article 16 of the ICC Statute) requesting the ICC to defer for one-year investigation or prosecution of nationals of non-party states participating in United Nations operations. *See* S/RES/1422 (2002) and S/RES/1487 (2003). This resolution was not renewed in 2004 after allegations of abuse by U.S. service members in foreign detention centers emerged and provoked widespread international outrage. Should peacekeepers be immune from prosecution before the ICC? Would they be immune under Article 27? Might crimes by peacekeepers be an instance when the prosecutor should decline to prosecute pursuant to Article 53?

5. The African Union and the ICC

At one point, all of the current situations before the Court involved Africa (although a number of non-African situations were the subject of preliminary examinations). (See the Appendix for a map of Africa.) This led many critics, particularly in Africa, to accuse the Court of "targeting Africa." The African Union began to raise concerns about the ICC with the indictment of President Al Bashir of Sudan. This criticism accelerated with the opening of the Kenyan situation before the Court, particularly after two of the Kenyan suspects, Uhuru Kenyatta and William Ruto, declared their candidacy for President and Deputy President of Kenya respectively, and then were elected to those positions in March 2013. The African Union joined with the Government of Kenya in requesting that the Security Council invoke its powers under Article 16 of the Rome Statute to suspend the Kenyan cases. The African Union also requested that the Security Council suspend the case against President Al Bashir of Sudan. To date, the Security Council has declined to use its powers under Article 16 to suspend any case or situation before the Court.

Why do you think the African Union has raised concerns about the Kenyan and Sudanese cases and not other African cases? Do you think the Security Council should suspend cases involving sitting heads of state or other high government officials? If not, how do you respond to the argument of Kenya and the African Union that the cases interfered with the ability of the President and Deputy President of Kenya to fulfill their constitutional obligations? Is the fact that they were elected after their indictment by the ICC relevant? In the end, all the Kenya cases failed and the campaign against the Court within the African Union has faded somewhat.

6. For Further Reading

Several "legislative histories" for the ICC Statute exist, including THE INTERNATIONAL CRIMINAL COURT: THE MAKING OF THE ROME STATUTE—ISSUES, NEGOTIATIONS, RESULTS (Roy S. Lee ed., 1999); COMMENTARY ON THE ROME STATUTE OF THE INTERNATIONAL CRIMINAL COURT (Otto Triffterer & Kai Ambos eds., 3rd ed., 2016); THE LEGISLATIVE HISTORY OF THE

INTERNATIONAL CRIMINAL COURT: INTRODUCTION, ANALYSIS, AND INTEGRATED TEXT (M. Cherif Bassiouni ed., 2005).

III. THE UNITED STATES AND THE ICC

Should or will the United States join the ICC? Prior to the administration of President George W. Bush, the United States was an active proponent of international criminal justice and the establishment of a permanent international criminal court. Indeed, the United States signed (but did not ratify) the ICC Statute in the waning days of the Clinton administration and on the last day the treaty was open for signature (December 31, 2000, per Article 125 of the Statute), although President Clinton indicated that he did not recommend that his successor submit the treaty for ratification. The Bush administration, however, pursued a policy of "active opposition" to the Court, at least in its first term. In an unprecedented move, the Bush Administration "unsigned" the treaty in May 2002 in a terse letter to U.N. Secretary-General Kofi Annan from Ambassador John Bolton, then-Undersecretary of State for Arms Control and International Security and currently President Donald Trump's National Security Adviser. (Technically, this letter was a notification of the United States' intent not to ratify the treaty as opposed to a true "unsigning").

Bolton, who was later appointed as the United States Representative to the United Nations in a recess appointment, has been a staunch opponent of the Court even prior to assuming public office. In 1999, Bolton was invited to draft an imaginary "Presidential Speech" regarding the ICC for an edited volume. *See* John Bolton, *Speech Two: Reject and Oppose the International Criminal Court, in* TOWARD AN INTERNATIONAL CRIMINAL COURT? THREE OPTIONS PRESENTED AS PRESIDENTIAL SPEECHES 37 (Alton Frye ed., 1999). In 2018, after having been appointed National Security Adviser, he was able to deliver formal remarks, ostensibly outlining U.S. policy towards the Court under the Trump Administration. The latter speech drew heavily on themes he had first articulated in his fictitious speech. Compare this text to the 2012 speech that follows by then-State Department Legal Adviser Harold Hongju Koh.

John Bolton, Protecting American Constitutionalism & Sovereignty from International Threats, The Federalist Society (Washington D.C., Sept. 10, 2018)

After years of effort by self-styled "global governance" advocates, the ICC, a supranational tribunal that could supersede national sovereignties and directly prosecute individuals for alleged war crimes, was agreed to in 1998. For ICC proponents, this supranational, independent institution has always been critical to their efforts to overcome the perceived failures of nation-states, even those with strong constitutions, representative government, and the rule of law. In theory, the ICC holds perpetrators of the most egregious atrocities accountable for their crimes, provides justice to the victims, and deters future abuses. In practice, however, the Court has been ineffective, unaccountable, and indeed, outright dangerous. Moreover, the largely unspoken, but always central, aim of its most vigorous supporters was to constrain the United States. The objective was not limited to targeting individual U.S. service members, but rather America's senior political leadership, and its relentless determination to keep our country secure. * * *

Today, on the eve of September 11th, I want to deliver a clear and unambiguous message on behalf of the President of the United States. The United States will use any means necessary to protect our citizens and those of our allies from unjust prosecution by this illegitimate court. We will not cooperate with the ICC. We will provide no assistance to the ICC. We will not join the ICC. We will let the ICC die on its own. After all, for all intents and purposes, the ICC is already dead to us.

The United States bases this policy on five principal concerns about the Court, its purported authority, and its effectiveness. First, the International Criminal Court unacceptably threatens American sovereignty and U.S. national security interests. The Prosecutor in The Hague claims essentially unfettered discretion to investigate, charge, and prosecute individuals, regardless of whether their countries have acceded to the Rome Statute. The Court in no way derives these powers from any grant of consent by non-parties to the Rome Statute. Instead, the ICC is an unprecedented effort to vest power in a supranational body without the consent of either nation-states or the individuals over which it purports to exercise jurisdiction. It certainly has no consent whatsoever from the United States. As Americans, we fully understand that consent of the governed is a prerequisite to true legal legitimacy, and we reject such a flagrant violation of our national sovereignty. * * *

Second, the International Criminal Court claims jurisdiction over crimes that have disputed and ambiguous definitions, exacerbating the Court's unfettered powers. The definitions of crimes, especially crimes of aggression, are vague and subject to wide-ranging interpretation by the ICC. Had the ICC existed during the Second World War, America's enemies would no doubt be eager to find the United States and its allies culpable for war crimes for the bombing campaigns over Germany and Japan. The "crime of aggression" could become a pretext for politically motivated investigations. Was the mission of U.S. Navy SEALs that killed Osama Bin Laden in Pakistan a crime of aggression? What about the U.S. and coalition strikes in Syria to protect innocent children from chemical weapons? How about U.S. military exercises with allies and partners around the world? Or Israel's actions to defend itself on countless occasions? * * * And here we come directly to the unspoken but powerful agenda of the ICC's supporters: the hope that its essentially political nature, in defining crimes such as "aggression," will intimidate U.S. decision makers, and others in democratic societies. * * *

Third, the International Criminal Court fails in its fundamental objective to deter and punish atrocity crimes. Since its 2002 inception, the Court has spent over $1.5 billion dollars, while attaining only eight convictions. This dismal record is hardly a deterrent to dictators and despots determined to commit horrific atrocities. In fact, despite ongoing ICC investigations, atrocities continue to occur in the Democratic Republic of the Congo, Sudan, Libya, Syria, and many other nations. The hard men of history are not deterred by fantasies of international law such as the ICC. The idea that faraway bureaucrats and robed judges would strike fear into the hearts of the likes of Saddam Hussein, Hitler, Stalin, and Gadhafi is preposterous, even cruel. Time and again, history has proven that the only deterrent to evil and atrocity is what Franklin Roosevelt once called "the righteous might" of the United States and its allies—a power that, perversely, could be threatened by the ICC's vague definition of aggression crimes. Thus, we see, paradoxically, that the dangers of the International Criminal Court stem from both its potential strength and its manifest weakness.

Fourth, the International Criminal Court is superfluous, given that domestic U.S. judicial systems already hold American citizens to the highest legal and ethical standards. U.S. service members in the field must operate fully in accordance with the law of armed conflict. When violations of law do occur, the United States takes appropriate and swift action to hold perpetrators accountable. We are a democratic nation, with the most robust system of investigation, accountability, and transparency in the world. We believe in the rule of law, and we uphold it. We don't need the ICC to tell us our duty, or second-guess our decisions. ICC proponents argue that robust domestic judicial systems are fully consistent with the Court because of the so-called complementarity principle. * * * And yet, there is little precedent for the ICC to determine how to apply the complementarity principle. How is the ICC Prosecutor to judge when this principle has been met? Under what circumstances will the ICC be satisfied? How much sensitive documentation would the ever-toiling bureaucrats in The Hague demand from a sovereign government? And, who has the last word? If it's the ICC, the United States would manifestly be subordinated to the Court. * * *

Fifth, the International Criminal Court's authority has been sharply criticized and rejected by most of the world. Today, more than 70 nations, representing two-thirds of the world's population, and over 70% of the world's armed forces, are not members of the ICC. Several African nations have recently withdrawn or threatened to withdraw their membership, citing the disproportionate number of arrest warrants against Africans. To them, the ICC is just the latest European neocolonial enterprise to infringe upon their sovereign rights. Israel too has sharply criticized the ICC. While the Court welcomes the membership of the so-called "State of Palestine," it has threatened Israel—a liberal, democratic nation—with investigation into its actions to defend citizens from terrorist attacks in the West Bank and Gaza. There has also been a suggestion that the ICC will investigate Israeli construction of housing projects on the West Bank. * * * The United States supports a direct and robust peace process, and we will not allow the ICC, or any other organization, to constrain Israel's right to self-defense.

In sum, an international court so deeply divisive and so deeply flawed can have no legitimate claim to jurisdiction over the citizens of sovereign nations that have rejected its authority. * * * We take this position not because we oppose justice for victims of atrocities, but because we believe that perpetrators should face legitimate, effective, and accountable prosecution for their crimes, by sovereign national governments. * * * If the Court comes after us, Israel or other U.S. allies, we will not sit quietly. We will take the following steps, among others, in accordance with the American Servicemembers' Protection Act and our other legal authorities. We will negotiate even more binding, bilateral agreements to prohibit nations from surrendering U.S. persons to the ICC. And we will ensure that those we have already entered are honored by our counterpart governments. We will respond against the ICC and its personnel to the extent permitted by U.S. law. We will ban its judges and prosecutors from entering the United States. We will sanction their funds in the U.S. financial system, and we will prosecute them in the U.S. criminal system. We will do the same for any company or state that assists an ICC investigation of Americans. We will take note if any countries cooperate with ICC investigations of the United States and its allies, and we will remember that cooperation when setting U.S. foreign assistance, military assistance, and intelligence sharing levels. We will consider taking steps in the UN Security Council to constrain the Court's sweeping powers, including ensuring that the ICC does not exercise jurisdiction over Americans and the nationals of our allies that have not ratified the Rome Statute.

This Administration will fight back to protect American constitutionalism, our sovereignty, and our citizens. No committee of foreign nations will tell us how to govern ourselves and defend our freedom. We will stand up for the U.S. Constitution abroad, just as we do at home. And, as always, in every decision we make, we will put the interests of the American People FIRST.

Harold Hongju Koh, International Justice 5.0 (2012)

Delivered as the Justice Address 2012 at the Vera Institute of Justice, The Paley Center, in New York (Nov. 8, 2012) and as a keynote lecture at Leiden University, Campus The Hague (Nov. 16, 2012).

[O]ur relationship with the ICC has had ebbs and flows. But please do not misread our skepticism of certain institutions as hostility to the bedrock norms and values of international criminal justice. In fact, taking a stand for justice and the rule of law is part of our national character. Of course, many in our country still have fundamental concerns about the Rome Statute that have prevented us from becoming a party. This is hardly surprising, given concerns about the potential risks of politicized prosecutions, the United States' unique posture of having more troops and other personnel deployed overseas than any other nation, and that we are frequently called upon to help ensure global peace, justice and security. But if you ask Americans a concrete, practical question—should specific perpetrators of genocide, war crimes, or crimes against humanity be held accountable for their crimes in particular cases—the typical American answer to that question would be an unequivocal "yes."

Moreover, the United States has long recognized that international criminal justice, and accountability for those responsible for atrocities, is in our national security interests as well as in our humanitarian interests. Among other things, supporting global criminal justice serves U.S. national interests by promoting a culture of accountability that can help increase stability and thus decrease the need for far more costly military interventions in the future. We have much to gain from the effective functioning of the rule of law, and the architecture of international criminal justice can play an important part in that effort.

By early 2009, Secretary Hillary Rodham Clinton had made clear that "whether we work toward joining or not, we will end hostility toward the ICC, and look for opportunities to encourage effective ICC action in ways that promote U.S. interests by bringing war criminals to justice." And the United States has sought to make our approach to the ICC more congruent with our broader approach to international criminal justice. So, while the United States will always protect U.S. personnel, we are engaging with States Parties to the Rome Statute on issues of concern, and we have applied a pragmatic, case-by-case approach towards ICC issues. Let me review not only what we've said, but what we've done:

First, from the beginning of this administration we have dropped the hostile rhetoric. With almost 10 years' experience with the ICC under our belts, we had seen that the Court could play a key role in bringing perpetrators of the worst atrocities to justice and providing an important forum for advancing US interests.

Second, we have begun to engage with the Assembly of States Parties (ASP) and the Court. Our "smart power" view is that the way to advance U.S. interests is not to shut ourselves off to those with whom we disagree, but to engage and work for mutually beneficial improvements. Absenting ourselves from meetings of States Parties and discussions about aggression allowed States Parties to develop a definition of aggression without U.S. input, which greatly complicated our efforts when we did eventually engage on that topic in an effort to promote a more legally coherent outcome. We now regularly attend meetings of the

ASP as an "observer" and we participated constructively at the Review Conference in Kampala. We are closely monitoring the evolving jurisprudence of the Court. And we have also actively engaged with the Office of the Prosecutor and the Registry to consider specific ways that we can support specific prosecutions already underway in all of the situations currently before the Court, including through cooperation on witness protection issues, and we have responded positively to a number of requests.

Third, we have publicly urged cooperation and expressed support for the Court's work in *all* of the ongoing situations in which the Court has begun formal investigations or prosecutions, both in our diplomacy and in multilateral settings. To take just a few examples, last year, we supported the UN Security Council's referral of the situation in Libya to the ICC, our first affirmative vote for a referral, adopted even as atrocities were being perpetrated. This represented an historic milestone in the fight against impunity, and we have continued to support the Court's engagement there. President Obama has made strong statements about the importance of accountability and cooperation with the ICC's efforts in Kenya and Côte d'Ivoire. Secretary Clinton has made equally strong statements throughout her travels about the ICC's work to ensure justice for the victims of atrocities in these and other situations before the Court. Following the landmark *Lubanga* judgment, both the White House and State Department issued strong statements about the historic nature of the conviction and the message that it sends to those who engage in the brutal practice of conscripting and using children to participate actively in hostilities. The United States has also supported recent U.N. Security Council presidential statements urging cooperation with the Court and supporting regional efforts to arrest Joseph Kony, emphasizing the importance of Bosco Ntaganda's arrest in the DRC, and stressing the importance of accountability for abuses and violations on all sides in Côte d'Ivoire, while encouraging the Ivorian government to continue its cooperation with the ICC. * * *

Fourth, we continue to find it a serious cause for concern that nine individuals who are the subject of existing ICC arrest warrants have not yet been apprehended. For example, we have urged all States to refrain from providing political or financial support to the Sudanese suspects who remain at large, including by discouraging states from welcoming these individuals. In the U.N. Security Council, Ambassador Susan Rice and other senior diplomats have repeatedly called for Sudan to cooperate with the ICC and for states to oppose invitations, facilitation, or support for travel by those subject to existing arrest warrants.

Fifth, on a related front, we have noted that states can lend expertise and logistical assistance to apprehend current ICC fugitives. * * *

Everyone knows that the ICC is not the exact court we wanted, but it is the Court that exists, and we fully understand that the ICC has the potential in many cases to advance common goals in promoting accountability. Thus, the current policy toward the Court has been based less on an abstract debate about the value of the Court and more on a direct focus on the specific: *do the ICC's efforts in this context complement U.S. efforts to ensure that perpetrators of this particular atrocity be held accountable and advance U.S. interests and values?* If the answer to those questions is yes—and it nearly always has been—we've been able to view ICC prosecutions as part of the solution. This is part of our broader "smart power" approach: not to shut ourselves off to those with whom we disagree, but to engage and work for mutually beneficial improvements that advance U.S. interests, including our interest in justice and the rule of law.

Putting all of this together, as I made clear more than two years ago in a speech at New York University,

> What you quite explicitly do *not* see from this Administration is U.S. hostility towards the Court. You do not see what international lawyers might call a concerted effort to frustrate the object and purpose of the Rome Statute. That is explicitly not the policy of this administration. Because although the United States is not a party to the Rome Statute, we share with the States Parties a deep and abiding interest in seeing the Court successfully complete the important prosecutions it has already begun. * * *

[T]he key to winning greater international and U.S. support going forward will be for the ICC to focus on strengthening itself as a fair and legitimate criminal justice institution that acts with prudence in deciding which cases to pursue. Critical to the future success of the ICC, and the views of the United States and others in the international community of it, will be its attention to the four values: (1) building institutional legitimacy; (2) promoting a jurisprudence of legality, with detailed reasoning and steeped in precedent; (3) fostering a spirit of international cooperation; and (4) developing an institutional reputation for professionalism and fairness.

NOTES & QUESTIONS

1. "Unsigning" the Treaty

Does it matter whether the United States signs or "unsigns" the treaty? Why do you think the Bush Administration did not simply remain a signatory to the ICC treaty without submitting it for ratification? (For example, the United States signed the Genocide Convention in 1948 when it was first opened for signature, and President Harry S. Truman submitted the treaty for ratification in 1949. The necessary two-thirds vote was elusive, however, and it was not until 1986 that the Senate consented to ratification.) Might this approach have avoided the political fallout occasioned by "unsigning" the treaty? Even without ratification, did the United States owe certain obligations to the ICC based solely upon having signed the treaty in 2001? Consider Article 18 of the Vienna Convention on the Laws of Treaty:

Article 18: Obligation Not To Defeat The Object And Purpose Of A Treaty Prior To Its Entry Into Force

A State is obliged to refrain from acts which would defeat the object and purpose of a treaty when:

(a) it has signed the treaty or has exchanged instruments constituting the treaty subject to ratification, acceptance or approval, until it shall have made its intention clear not to become a party to the treaty; or

(b) it has expressed its consent to be bound by the treaty, pending the entry into force of the treaty and provided that such entry into force is not unduly delayed.

As indicated in the Koh excerpt, the relationship between the United States and the Court warmed during the second term of the Bush Administration and even more so under President Barack Obama. Why would the Obama Administration not withdraw the Bolton letter given the degree of apparent cooperation with the Court as indicated by the Koh speech? Is there an argument that the Koh speech excerpted above, delivered when he was Legal Adviser, actually annulled the Bolton letter?

2. Binding Third Parties

A major objection of the United States to the ICC Statute is that the treaty violates basic treaty principles because it "binds" non-state parties. For example, Article 34 of the Vienna Convention on the Law of Treaties states that "A treaty does not create either obligations or rights for a third State without its consent" (*pacta tertiis nec nocent nec prosunt*). How does the Rome Statute "bind" non-state parties in terms of creating obligations for such states? Are U.S. nationals already "bound" by the law of any foreign country in which they may commit a crime? Does the complementarity regime of the ICC Statute "bind" non-party states? Recall the principles of domestic jurisdiction in Chapter 3, and particularly the principle of universal jurisdiction contained in a number of international criminal law treaties. How, if at all, does the ICC Statute change the traditional state-based system of jurisdiction over crimes committed on foreign soil?

3. United States Fears

If the United States is not a party to the treaty, and is a permanent member of the Security Council able to control referrals from that body and propose deferrals under Article 16, what does it have to fear from the Court? Many U.S. allies in Europe and elsewhere are parties to the Court and their troops are working alongside U.S. military personnel in Afghanistan (which is a party to the ICC and has been the subject of a preliminary examination by the OTP since 2006), Iraq, and elsewhere. Does this suggest that the United States' fears are unjustified? Recall that the situation in Afghanistan, which joined the Court in 2003, is subject to a preliminary examination by the OTP. The U.S. has an Article 98 agreement with Afghanistan (see the full text of the agreement below); there is also a Status of Forces Agreement in place that makes U.S. personnel immune from criminal prosecution by Afghan authorities. Did the preliminary examination in Afghanistan justify U.S. fears toward the Court? *See* Brett D. Schaefer and Steven Groves, *The*

ICC Investigation in Afghanistan Vindicates U.S. Policy Toward the ICC (The Heritage Foundation, September 14, 2009); R. Chuck Mason, *Status of Forces Agreement (SOFA): What Is It, and How Has It Been Utilized?* (Congressional Research Service, March 15, 2012). Given the United States' evolving stance toward the Court, what will it take for the United States to join the Court? Should advocates push for this? Might the United States be better able to protect U.S. service members from politicized prosecutions by being a member of the Court, which would entitle it to nominate and vote on the Court's executive personnel (*see* Articles 36 and 42)?

Another objection of the United States to the ICC concerns alleged incompatibilities between the Rome Statute and the U.S. Constitution in terms of official immunities and procedural safeguards that would be available before U.S. courts. With respect to the due process concerns, the lack of a jury trial and the treaty's double jeopardy provisions (*see* Articles 20 and 81–84) emerge as the most salient concerns. The United States has also expressed concerns that State Parties or the Prosecutor will commence frivolous or vindictive suits against the United States and its nationals, especially given the United States' global visibility and worldwide troop commitments. Are there sufficient procedural safeguards in the Rome Statute to protect against such "malicious prosecutions?" Finally, opponents of the Court have also argued that ratification would contravene constitutional provisions dealing with the establishment of courts (namely, Article 1, Section 8 and Article III, Section 1 of the Constitution). Are any of these considerations a bar to U.S. ratification of the Court? Reconsider your responses to all these questions when you read the Pre-Trial Chamber's response to the Prosecutor's request to open an investigation into the Afghanistan situation.

4. "Article 98" Agreements

To protect itself and its nationals from the reach of the ICC, the United States undertook a series of diplomatic and legislative actions. One controversial move involved the pursuit of bilateral agreements in which State Parties pledged not to surrender each other's citizens to the ICC. (Human rights advocates called such agreements "Bilateral Immunity Agreements"). The United States argued that such agreements are authorized by Article 98(2) of the Rome Statute, which reads:

> Article 98(2) *Cooperation with respect to waiver of immunity and consent to surrender*
>
> The Court may not proceed with a request for surrender which would require the requested State to act inconsistently with its obligations under international agreements pursuant to which the consent of a sending State is required to surrender a person of that State to the Court, unless the Court can first obtain the cooperation of the sending State for the giving of consent for the surrender.

The 2002 agreement with Afghanistan, a Party to the ICC, is typical:

> Agreement between the Government of the Transitional Islamic State of Afghanistan and the Government of the United States of

America regarding the surrender of persons to the International Criminal Court

The Government of the Transitional Islamic State of Afghanistan and the Government of the United States, hereinafter "the Parties,"

Reaffirming the importance of bringing to justice those who commit genocide, crimes against humanity and war crimes.

Recalling that the Rome Statute of the International Criminal Court done at Rome on July 17, 1998 by the United Nations Diplomatic Conference of Plenipotentiaries on the Establishment of an International Criminal Court is intended to complement and not supplant national criminal jurisdiction.

Considering that the Parties have each expressed their intention to investigate and to prosecute where appropriate acts within the jurisdiction of the International Criminal Court alleged to have been committed by its officials, employees, military personnel or other nationals.

Bearing in mind Article 98 of the Rome Statute.

Hereby agree as follows:

1. For purposes of this agreement, "persons" are current or former Government officials, employees (including contractors), or military personnel or nationals of one Party.

2. Persons of one Party present in the territory of the other shall not, absent the expressed consent of the first party:

(a) be surrendered or transferred by any means to the International Criminal Court for any purpose, or

(b) be surrendered or transferred by any means to any other entity or third country, or expelled to a third country, for the purpose of surrender to or transfer to the International Criminal Court.

3. When the United States extradites, surrenders, or otherwise transfers a person of the other Party to a third country, the United States will not agree to the surrender or transfer of that person to the International Criminal Court by the third country, absent the expressed consent of the Government of Afghanistan.

4. When the Government of Afghanistan extradites, surrenders, or otherwise transfers a person of the United States of America to a third country, the Government of Afghanistan will not agree to the surrender or transfer of that person to the International Criminal Court by a third country, absent the expressed consent of the Government of the United States.

5. Each Party agrees, subject to its international legal obligations, not to knowingly facilitate, consent to or cooperate with efforts by any third party or country to effect the extradition,

surrender, or transfer of a person of the other Party to the International Criminal Court.

6. This Agreement shall enter into force upon an exchange of notes confirming that each Party has completed the necessary domestic legal requirements to bring the Agreement into force. It will remain in force until one year after the date on which one Party notifies the other of its intent to terminate this Agreement. The provisions of this Agreement shall continue to apply with respect to any act occurring, or any allegation arising, before the effective date of termination.

Pursuant to Article 98, the Bush Administration negotiated over 100 bilateral agreements, which are available on the Georgetown Law Center's website. Opponents of these agreements have reasoned that Article 98 was drafted to accommodate pre-existing agreements between states such as Status of Forces Agreements (SOFAs) or Status of Mission Agreements (SOMAs) that permit a state sending troops (the "sending state") into another state (the "receiving state") to retain jurisdiction over those personnel. Is the agreement with Afghanistan and others like it consistent with the terms of Article 98? Are such agreements consistent with the apparent intent of that Article or with the object and purpose of the Rome Statute? What weight should be given to such considerations (*see* Articles 31–32 of the Vienna Convention on interpreting treaties)? The United States has pursued such agreements with parties and non-parties to the Rome Statute alike. (The agreements with non-parties prohibit signatories from sending U.S. nationals to third party states that are members of the Court). Are such agreements consistent with obligations undertaken by parties to the Rome Statute? It appears that these all remain in effect. Should the Obama Administration have worked to dissolve them? How should the Court interpret these agreements? Are they binding on the Court as an institution?

5. American Servicemembers' Protection Act of 2002

In 2002, the United States Congress passed the American Servicemembers' Protection Act (ASPA), 22 U.S.C.A. §§ 7421–7432, which authorizes the use of military force to "liberate" any American or citizen of a U.S.-allied country being held by the Court. This so-called "Invade the Hague" statute also restricted U.S. participation in United Nations peacekeeping missions unless United States service members were granted immunity from prosecution and mandated the withholding of military aid from parties to the Rome Statute that did not enter into Article 98 agreements or otherwise qualify for a waiver. ASPA, § 2004, also limits U.S. involvement in the Court as follows:

> Notwithstanding section 1782 of title 28, United States Code, or any other provision of law, no United States Court, and no agency or entity of any State or local government, including any court, may cooperate with the International Criminal Court in response to a request for cooperation submitted by the International Criminal Court pursuant to the Rome Statute.

> Notwithstanding any other provision of law, no agency or entity of the United States Government or of any State or local government, including any court, may provide support to the International Criminal Court.
>
> Notwithstanding any other provision of law, no funds appropriated under any provision of law may be used for the purpose of assisting the investigation, arrest, detention, extradition, or prosecution of any United States citizen or permanent resident alien by the International Criminal Court.
>
> No agent of the International Criminal Court may conduct, in the United States or any territory subject to the jurisdiction of the United States, any investigative activity relating to a preliminary inquiry, investigation, prosecution, or other proceeding at the International Criminal Court.

How do such provisions protect American service members, the ostensible purpose of ASPA? Would such a statute have been lawful under the Vienna Convention had the U.S. not promulgated the Bolton letter? President Bush issued waivers to a number of ICC members that did not enter into Article 98 agreements, and Congress amended the statute in 2008 to eliminate the prohibitions on the provision of military aid to ICC parties—can you imagine why? The anti-cooperative provisions quoted above remain in place, however.

As ASPA was being finalized, Senator Christopher Dodd (D-CT) proposed an amendment, enacted at § 2015, that reads:

> Nothing in this title shall prohibit the United States from rendering assistance to international efforts to bring to justice Saddam Hussein, Slobodan Milosevic, Osama bin Laden, other members of Al Qaida, leaders of Islamic Jihad, and other foreign nationals accused of genocide, war crimes or crimes against humanity.

What forms of assistance does this provision allow, if any? For a discussion, see Julian Bava & Kiel Ireland, *The American Service-Members' Protection Act: Pathways to & Constraints on U.S. Cooperation with the International Criminal Court*, 12 EYES ON THE ICC 1 (2016–17). Senator Dodd's father, Senator Thomas J. Dodd, was Executive Trial Counsel at Nuremberg. In that capacity, he cross-examined a number of the Nuremberg defendants and led important inculpatory evidence. Dodd's experience is chronicled in LETTERS FROM NUREMBERG: MY FATHER'S NARRATIVE OF A QUEST FOR JUSTICE (2007).

6. Funding for the Court

Article 115 of the ICC Statute states that the expenses of the Court and the ASP are to be provided for by assessed contributions from States Parties. Notwithstanding an influx of new cases and proceedings before the Court, the ASP for some time authorized what amounted to a zero-growth budget. In 2009, when there were four situations under investigation, the budget was €101 million. In 2014, a modest budgetary increase was allowed to €112 million. In 2019, the Committee of Budget and Finance approved a budget of €148 million.

Article 115 also contemplates funding from the United Nations "subject to the approval of the General Assembly, in particular in relation to the expenses incurred due to referrals by the Security Council." Proceedings involving two situations (Darfur and Libya), with multiple defendants, owe their origins to Security Council referrals. Should the General Assembly authorize additional funds for the Court for these two situations pursuant to Article 115(2)? The two referral resolutions indicate that "none of the expenses incurred in connection with the referral, including expenses related to investigations or prosecutions in connection with that referral, shall be borne by the United Nations." *See, e.g.*, S.C. Res. 1593, ¶ 7, U.N. Doc. S/RES/1593 (Mar. 31, 2005). Can the Security Council dictate this when it is the General Assembly that manages the United Nations' budget? Why would Security Council members refuse additional funding to the Court in connection with their referrals?

In addition to ASPA, the U.S. Congress also enacted several prohibitions on funding the Court. One that remains in force is found in the Admiral James W. Nance and Meg Donovan Foreign Relations Authorization Act, Fiscal Years 2000 and 2001. In particular, Section 705(b) reads:

> (b) PROHIBITION—None of the funds authorized to be appropriated by this or any other Act may be obligated for use by, or for support of, the International Criminal Court unless the United States has become a party to the Court pursuant to a treaty made under Article II, section 2, clause 2 of the Constitution.

Unlike typical budgetary constraints, this prohibition has no sunset clause. Would this provision be implicated if U.S. assessments to the United Nations were to go indirectly toward the Court by operation of Article 115(b)? Could the United States provide funding to the Trust Fund for Victims, which is an institution that is separate from the ICC and the ASP altogether, although it was created by the Rome Statute?

7. Making Good on Its Threats

President Trump applauded the decision of the PTC to deny the Prosecutor's request to open an investigation in Afghanistan: "Since the creation of the ICC, the United States has consistently declined to join the court because of its broad, unaccountable prosecutorial powers; the threat it poses to American sovereignty; and other deficiencies that render it illegitimate. Any attempt to target American, Israeli, or allied personnel for prosecution will be met with a swift and vigorous response." After the Bolton speech, the United States made good on its threats and revoked the visa of Fatou Bensouda, the chief Prosecutor of the ICC—prior to the PTC ruling below. She has been able to visit the United States for her regular briefings of the Security Council but not for other purposes. The OTP responded with a statement:

> The Office of the Prosecutor has an independent and impartial mandate under the Rome Statute of the ICC. The Prosecutor and her Office will continue to undertake that statutory duty with utmost commitment and professionalism, without fear or favour.

8. For Further Reading

For additional information on the U.S. position vis-à-vis the ICC *see* Eric M. Meyer, *International Law: The Compatibility of the Rome Statute of the International Criminal Court with the U.S. Bilateral Immunity Agreements Included in the American Servicemembers' Protection Act*, 58 OKLA. L. REV. 97 (2005); Douglas E. Edlin, *The Anxiety of Sovereignty: Britain, the United States and the International Criminal Court*, 29 B.C. INT'L & COMP. L. REV. 1 (2006); Gerhard Hafner, *An Attempt to Explain the Position of the USA Towards the ICC*, 3 J. INT'L CRIM. JUST. 323 (2005); David Scheffer, *The Future U.S. Relationship with the International Criminal Court,* 17 PACE INT'L L. REV. 161 (2005); William A. Schabas, *United States Hostility to the International Criminal Court: It's All About the Security Council*, 15 EUR. J. INT'L L. 701 (2004); Diane Orentlicher, *Unilateral Multilateralism: United States Policy Toward the International Criminal Court*, 36 CORNELL INT'L L. J. 415 (2004). The American Society of International Law (ASIL) convened a high-level task force to consider U.S. policy toward the Court. Its report, entitled *U.S. Policy Toward the International Criminal Court: Furthering Positive Engagement* (2009), contains a number of recommendations. *See also* ASIL, *Beyond Kampala: Next Steps for U.S. Principled Engagement with the International Criminal Court* (2010).

IV. COMPLEMENTARITY & ADMISSIBILITY

In contrast to the *ad hoc* tribunals that preceded it, the ICC's jurisdiction is complementary with that of domestic courts as set forth in the Preamble (clause 10), Article 1, and Articles 17–19. Accordingly, the ICC is to complement pre-existing domestic criminal justice processes and assert jurisdiction only when those processes have failed or are inoperative. As you review the relevant provisions of the ICC Statute, consider how the principles of complementarity and gravity will be applied. How is the ICC to determine the willingness and ability of national courts to proceed or the gravity of the alleged crimes? What standards should the Court employ? Should the ICC's drafters have included more objective criteria for these concepts? When might a situation involving the commission of international crimes be considered insufficiently grave to sustain ICC jurisdiction?

The issue of complementarity is at the heart of the controversy between the U.S. and the Court. Below are excerpts from ICC decisions concerning admissibility in the context of the situations in Uganda, Kenya, Libya, and Afghanistan. The decisions in full touch on issues of procedure (when should a determination of admissibility be made and who can trigger such a determination?) and due process (what, if any, rights does an accused have with respect to admissibility determinations?). We focus here on part of the applicable substantive test for admissibility: what is the proper test for meeting the threshold of gravity, what type of domestic processes render a case inadmissible, and what other considerations emerge at the admissibility stage? As you read through these excerpts, ask yourself whether they strengthen or weaken arguments by Bolton and others that the Court violates state sovereignty or is otherwise a threat to U.S. interests.

The first excerpt involves the situation in the Democratic Republic of the Congo and was issued under seal. (See the Appendix for a map of the DRC.) The Prosecutor sought to indict Thomas Lubanga Dyilo and Bosco Ntaganda, former rebels active in the Union of Congolese Patriots (UPC) and the Patriotic Forces for the Liberation of Congo (FPLC). The Pre-Trial Chamber granted a warrant of arrest against Lubanga, who became the first defendant to go to trial before the ICC, but denied it for Ntaganda on the grounds of inadmissibility. In particular, the Pre-Trial Chamber ruled that Ntaganda was not a central figure in the decision-making processes of his group and lacked any authority over the development or implementation of important policies. This was notwithstanding that Ntaganda was in a command position over sector commanders and field officers. The Prosecutor appealed, which generated the first major decision concerning admissibility and the gravity requirement of Article 17. The Appeals Chamber first ruled that the Pre-Trial Chamber erroneously considered the admissibility of the case prior to the issuance of an arrest warrant. It reasoned that Article 58 governing arrest warrants sets forth an exhaustive set of substantive and procedural prerequisites for the issuance of a warrant that does not include an admissibility determination. In any case, it observed that allowing an *ex parte* admissibility determination prior to the issuance of an arrest warrant did not sufficiently protect the interests of the accused. The Chamber's opinion on the gravity determination is below.

Situation in the Democratic Republic of the Congo, Case No. ICC–01/04–168–US–Exp, Judgment on the Prosecutor's Appeal against the Decision of Pre-Trial Chamber I entitled "Decision on the Prosecutor's Application for Warrants of Arrest, Article 58" (July 13, 2006)

In the Appeals Chamber

The Interpretation of "Gravity" Under Article 17(1)(D) of the Statute

54. The Appeals Chamber will now turn to the Pre-Trial Chamber's interpretation of article 17(1)(d) of the Statute. * * * The Appeals Chamber is of the view that the Pre-Trial Chamber's interpretation of article 17(1)(d) of the Statute contains errors, which, if not addressed now, could lead to future cases being declared inadmissible on grounds that are incorrect. Given that these proceedings are currently *ex parte*, Prosecutor only, and in light of its findings above, the Appeals Chamber will not at this stage proceed to determine admissibility in this case in the absence of submissions from other participants.

55. Article 17(1) of the Statute reads: "[h]aving regard to paragraph 10 of the Preamble and article 1, the Court shall determine that a case is inadmissible where: . . . (d) the case is not sufficient gravity to justify further action by the Court."

56. In the impugned decision, the Pre-Trial Chamber interpreted this article and came to the conclusion that the gravity threshold provided for in article 17(1)(d) of the Statute was met: "[. . .] if the following three questions can be answered affirmatively:

i) Is the conduct which is the object of the case systematic or large-scale (due consideration should also be given to the social alarm caused to the international community by the relevant type of conduct)?

ii) Considering the position of the relevant person in the State entity, organisation or armed group to which he belongs, can it be considered that such person falls within the category of most senior leaders of the situation under investigation?; and

iii) Does the relevant person fall within the category of most senior leaders suspected of being most responsible, considering (1) the role played by the relevant person through acts or omissions when the State entities, organisations or armed groups to which he belongs commit systematic or large-scale crimes within the jurisdiction of the Court, and (2) the role played by such State entities, organisations or armed groups in the overall commission of crimes within the jurisdiction of the Court in the relevant situation?"

57. The Pre-Trial Chamber had reached this conclusion on the basis of a literal, contextual and teleological interpretation of article 17(1)(d) of the Statute, also taking into account what the Pre-Trial Chamber described as applicable principles and rules of international law. * * *

59. The first prong of the Pre-Trial Chamber's test for the gravity threshold—that the conduct must be systematic or large-scale—is the result of a contextual interpretation by the Pre-Trial Chamber of article 17(1)(d) of the Statute. The Pre-Trial Chamber opined that the selection of the crimes over which the Court had jurisdiction had been gravity-driven itself; only the most serious crimes fell under the jurisdiction of the Court. Hence, the Pre-Trial Chamber stated that in order for a case to reach the gravity threshold of article 17(1)(d) of the Statute, the "relevant conduct must present particular features which render it especially grave." The Pre-Trial Chamber went on to state that two features would have to be considered in this respect: First of all, whether the conduct was either systematic or large-scale, because "[i]f isolated instances of criminal activity were sufficient, there would be no need to establish an additional gravity threshold beyond the gravity-driven

selection of the crimes (which are defined by both contextual and specific elements) included within the material jurisdiction of the Court." Secondly, in the Pre-Trial Chamber's opinion "due consideration must be given to the social alarm such conduct may have caused in the international community." The Pre-Trial Chamber did not explain further why the social alarm caused would be taken into account.

60. The Pre-Trial Chamber derived the second and third prongs of its test for the gravity threshold through a teleological interpretation of article 17(1)(d) of the Statute. The Pre-Trial Chamber argued that the deterrent effect of the Court had to be maximized and that "any retributory effect of the activities of the Court must be subordinate to the higher purpose of prevention." The Pre-Trial Chamber went on to state that not only the relevant conduct but also three additional factors would have to be considered to determine whether a case meets the gravity threshold, namely whether the suspect is one of the most senior leaders, the role the suspect played when the State entities, organizations or armed groups to which the suspect belonged committed systematic or large-scale crimes within the jurisdiction of the Court, and, lastly, the role of the suspect's State entity, organization or armed group in the overall commission of crimes in the relevant situation. The Pre-Trial Chamber derived these three factors from its consideration that persons who meet this threshold "are the ones who can most effectively prevent or stop the commission of those crimes." The Pre-Trial Chamber opined that "only by concentrating on this type of individual can the deterrent effects of the activities of the Court be maximised because other senior leaders in similar circumstances will know that solely by doing what they can to prevent the systematic or large-scale commission of crimes within the jurisdiction of the Court can they be sure that they will not be prosecuted by the Court."

61. The Pre-Trial Chamber sought to support its interpretation of article 17(1)(d) of the Statute and its test for the gravity-threshold by reference to the procedural law and practice of the *ad hoc* international criminal tribunals of the United Nations, the International Criminal Tribunal for the Former Yugoslavia ("ICTY") and the International Criminal Tribunal for Rwanda ("ICTR"). Notably, the Pre-Trial Chamber referred to the terms of the United Nations Security Council resolution 1534 of 26 March 2004 and pointed to rule 28(A) of the ICTY Rules of Procedure and Evidence, which provides that indictments before the ICTY must concentrate on "the most senior leaders suspected for being most responsible for crimes under the jurisdiction of the Tribunal" and to rule 11 bis(C) of the ICTY Rules of Procedure and Evidence, which makes the level of responsibility of the suspect a consideration of the decision by the ICTY to refer a case to a national jurisdiction. Furthermore, the Pre-Trial Chamber pointed out that the indictments before the ICTY and ICTR regarding any of the most senior leaders included either systematic or large-scale criminal activities. * * *

63. In relation to the second prong of its test—most senior leader—the Pre-Trial Chamber considered in relation to the case against Mr. Bosco Ntaganda whether he had "*de jure* or *de facto* authority to negotiate, sign and implement ceasefires or peace agreements, or participate in negotiations relating to controlling access of MONUC [United Nations Organization Mission in the DRC] or other U.N. personnel to Bunia or other parts of the territory of Ituri in the hands of the UPC/FPLC during the second half of 2002 and in 2003." The Pre-Trial Chamber came to the conclusion that the "evidence and information provided to support the Prosecution's Application do not show reasonable grounds to believe that during the relevant period Mr. Ntaganda (1) was a core actor in the decision-making process of the UPC/FPLC's policies/practices; (2) had *de jure* or *de facto* autonomy to change such policies/practices; or (3) had *de jure* or *de facto* autonomy to prevent the implementation of such policies/practices."

64. As to the third prong of the Pre-Trial Chamber's test, the Pre-Trial Chamber appeared to consider that the following factors were considerations that, in principle, would argue against the case fulfilling the gravity requirement of article 17(1)(d) of the Statute: The FPLC was exclusively the military wing of the broader political movement called the UPC; Mr. Ntaganda did not hold any official role within the UPC; and the UPC/FPLC was merely a regional group operating only in the Ituri region.

65. The application of the test developed by the Pre-Trial Chamber led the Chamber to declare the case against Mr. Bosco Ntaganda inadmissible. * * *

68. The Appeals Chamber finds that the test developed by the Pre-Trial Chamber is incorrect. * * *

70. In requiring conduct that is either systematic or large-scale, the Pre-Trial Chamber introduces at the admissibility stage of proceedings criteria that effectively blur the distinction between the jurisdictional requirements for war crimes and crimes against humanity that were adopted when defining the crimes that fall within the jurisdiction of the Court. First, with respect to war crimes, the requirement of large-scale commission under the Statute is *alternative* to the requirement of commission as part of a policy. Second, the statutory requirement of either large-scale commission or part of a policy is not absolute but qualified by the expression "in particular." Third, the requirement of "systematic" commission of crimes is not contained in article 8 but only in article 7 on crimes against humanity.

71. The Prosecutor is correct in arguing that imposing a legal requirement of "large-scale or systematic" within article 17(1)(d) of the Statute would not only render inutile article 8(1) of the Statute contrary to the principles of interpretation but would further contradict the express intent of the drafters in rejecting any such fixed requirement

therein. Indeed, it would be inconsistent with article 8(1) of the Statute if a war crime that was not part of a plan or policy or part of a large-scale commission could not, under any circumstances, be brought before the International Criminal Court because of the gravity requirement of article 17(1)(d) of the Statute.

72. As to the "social alarm" caused to the international community by the relevant conduct, which, in the Pre-Trial Chamber's opinion, is a consideration for the first prong of the Pre-Trial Chamber's test, the Pre-Trial Chamber has not explained from where it derived this criterion. It is not mentioned in the Statute at all. As the Prosecutor has correctly pointed out in his document in support, the criterion of "social alarm" depends upon subjective and contingent reactions to crimes rather than upon their objective gravity. The crimes listed in articles 5 to 8 of the Statute have been carefully selected. As is apparent from the Preamble and articles 1 and 5 of the Statute, these crimes are considered the most serious crimes of international concern. The subjective criterion of social alarm therefore is not a consideration that is necessarily appropriate for the determination of the admissibility of a case pursuant to article 17(1)(d) of the Statute.

73. The second and third prongs of the test developed by the Pre-Trial Chamber are also based on a flawed interpretation of article 17(1)(d) of the Statute. The Pre-Trial Chamber stated that the deterrent effect would be greatest if the International Criminal Court only dealt with the highest ranking perpetrators. In this context, the Pre-Trial Chamber stated that persons at the top who play a major role "are the ones who can most effectively prevent or stop the commission of such crimes" and that "only by concentrating on this type of individual can the deterrent effects of the Court be maximized." This assertion is questionable: It may indeed have a deterrent effect if high-ranking leaders who are suspected of being responsible for having committed crimes within the jurisdiction of the Court are brought before the International Criminal Court. But that the deterrent effect is highest if all other categories of perpetrators *cannot* be brought before the Court is difficult to understand. It seems more logical to assume that the deterrent effect of the Court is highest if no category of perpetrators is *per se* excluded from potentially being brought before the Court.

74. The imposition of rigid standards primarily based on top seniority may result in neither retribution nor prevention being achieved. Also, the capacity of individuals to prevent crimes in the field should not be implicitly or inadvertently assimilated to the preventative role of the Court more generally. Whether prevention is interpreted as a long-term objective, i.e. the overall result of the Court's activities generally, or as a factor in a specific situation, the preventative role of the Court may depend on many factors, much broader than the capacity of an individual to prevent crimes.

75. The predictable exclusion of many perpetrators on the grounds proposed by the Pre-Trial Chamber could severely hamper the preventative, or deterrent, role of the Court which is a cornerstone of the creation of the International Criminal Court, by announcing that any perpetrators other than those at the very top are automatically excluded from the exercise of the jurisdiction of the Court.

76. The particular role of a person or, for that matter, an organization, may vary considerably depending on the circumstances of the case and should not be exclusively assessed or predetermined on excessively formalistic grounds.

77. Criteria considered by the Pre-Trial Chamber such as the national or regional scope of activities of a group or organization, the exclusively military character of a group, the capacity to negotiate agreements, the absence of an official position, the capacity to change or prevent a policy, are not necessarily directly related to the gravity as set out in article 17(1)(d). They ignore the highly variable constitutions and operations of different organizations and could encourage any future perpetrators to avoid criminal responsibility before the International Criminal Court simply by ensuring that they are not a visible part of the high-level decision-making process. Also, individuals who are not at the very top of an organization may still carry considerable influence and commit, or generate the widespread commission of, very serious crimes. In other words, predetermination of inadmissibility on the above grounds could easily lead to the automatic exclusion of perpetrators of most serious crimes in the future. * * *

82. For the reasons stated above, the Appeals Chamber finds that the three-pronged test that has been established by the Pre-Trial Chamber is flawed. The application of such a flawed test by the Pre-Trial Chamber to the circumstances of the case against Mr. Bosco Ntaganda was necessarily incorrect.

NOTES & QUESTIONS

1. Case Outcome

Upon reversing the finding of inadmissibility, the Appeals Chamber remanded the case to the Pre-Trial Chamber to determine whether, on the basis of Article 58(1) alone, an arrest warrant against Ntaganda should be issued. The Pre-Trial Chamber eventually unsealed a warrant against him, charging him alongside Lubanga with enlisting, conscripting, and using child soldiers in armed conflict. Lubanga was ultimately convicted. In April 2013, Ntaganda showed up at the U.S. embassy in Kigali, Rwanda, after his followers were routed by forces controlled by rival Sultani Makenga and were forced to flee across the border from DRC. Ntaganda thus found himself in Rwanda, a country that had once placed him in charge of its proxy forces when they integrated with the DRC armed forces (the FARDC) in 2009, supported his M23 mutiny against the FARDC in 2012, but then dropped him in favor of Makenga in early 2013. Ntaganda obviously decided that facing charges before the ICC was a safer bet than the fate that might befall him were he to remain on the run, go undercover in Rwanda, or linger embedded within forces of dubious loyalty. The fact that the United States had recently authorized the payment of a reward for information leading to his arrest under its War Crimes Rewards Program (WCRP), a development that had not yet been formally announced but had been made public in a well-read blog, may have played a role in his decision to turn himself in on his own terms, rather than on the terms of a reward-seeker. Ntaganda was recently convicted.

2. Gravity

In practice, what types of crimes will the Appeals Chamber's gravity framework exclude? What about a situation in which three international peacekeepers are killed in an internal armed conflict waged largely in compliance with humanitarian law? What about a situation in which a multilateral force engaged in humanitarian intervention bombed a bridge being traversed by a civilian train, killing hundreds, in an effort to neutralize a repressive regime's supply route? What about the depredations of a particularly sadistic, but relatively low-level, prison guard? Should these situations be considered sufficiently grave to merit ICC jurisdiction? Should the notion of gravity be wholly quantitative or is there a qualitative dimension to it? Should the Prosecutor approach the gravity determination in case selection differently than the Court in considering its own jurisdiction? For more on the concept of gravity, *see* Margaret M. DeGuzman, *Gravity and the Legitimacy of the International Criminal Court*, 32 FORDHAM INT'L L. J. 1400 (2009). DeGuzman argues that the concept of gravity is central to the Court's institutional legitimacy vis-à-vis key audiences (the public, states, victims). Do you agree?

If you were the ICC's Chief Prosecutor, how would you formulate a gravity policy? In a policy paper, the OTP signaled its approach as follows:

> Regulation 34(1) of the Regulations of the Office and the Prosecution's Strategic Plan direct the Office to conduct its investigations towards ensuring that charges are brought against those persons who appear to be the most responsible for the identified crimes. In order to perform an objective and open-ended investigation, the Office will first focus on the crime base in order to identify the organisations (including their structures) and individuals allegedly responsible for the commission of the crimes. That may entail the need to consider the investigation and prosecution of a limited number of mid- and high-level perpetrators in order to ultimately build the evidentiary foundations for case(s) against those most responsible. The Office may also decide to prosecute lower level-perpetrators where their conduct has been particularly grave or notorious.

OTP, Policy Paper on Case Selection & Prioritisation (Sept. 15, 2016).

3. Self-Referral and Complementarity

Why would Uganda, the DRC, Mali, and the CAR "self-refer" crimes in their midst to the ICC when, in most cases, states attempt to shield their internal matters from international scrutiny? Do such self-referrals satisfy the principle of complementarity? Are Uganda, the DRC, Mali, and the CAR "unwilling" or "unable" to prosecute offenders as required by Article 17 of the ICC Statute? This question is particularly acute with respect to Uganda, whose judicial system is fully functioning and largely competent. (Indeed, an International Crimes Division has been established although it has been underutilized). Should states be entitled to externalize the political or other costs of prosecuting offenders in their midst to the ICC? Some commentators have posited a duty upon states to prosecute international crimes that occur on their territories; do such self-referrals allow states to escape from these duties? Although the Ugandan government tried to focus the referral on abuses committed by the LRA, the Prosecutor made clear that states can only refer entire situations to the Court, such that abuses by government forces are not beyond scrutiny by the Court given that Article 13(a) contemplates the referral of "situations" rather than "parties" or particular defendants. As a practical matter, however, is the Prosecutor likely to focus on state actors in the context of a self-referral? So far, all the indictments arising out of the Ugandan referral involve LRA members. *See* Human Rights Watch, UPROOTED AND FORGOTTEN IMPUNITY AND HUMAN RIGHTS ABUSES IN NORTHERN UGANDA (Sept. 2005). For a fuller discussion of self-referrals and complementarity, *see* Payam Akhavan, *The Lord's Resistance Army Case: Uganda's Submission of the First State Referral to the International Criminal Court*, 99 AM. J. INT'L L. 403 (2005); Claus Kreß, *"Self-Referrals" and "Waivers of Complementarity": Some Considerations in Law and Policy*, 2 J. INT'L CRIM. JUST. 944 (2004).

4. The Test of Complementarity

Do Article 17(2) and (3) provide an exhaustive list of grounds for determining the inability or unwillingness of a national system to proceed? How much judicial activity should be necessary to provoke a deferral? Is it enough that the state has opened an investigation? Issued indictments? Is totally intent on proceeding, but is still in the investigative phase? The decision below touches upon these issues. By way of background, Pre-Trial Chamber II granted authority to the Prosecutor to commence a *proprio motu* investigation into post-election violence in Kenya. (See the Appendix for a map of Kenya.) Once two sets of high-profile political figures—including the future President and Deputy President of the country—were summoned to appear, Kenya launched a complementarity challenge. The Pre-Trial Chamber rejected the challenge and deemed the cases admissible. Kenya appealed; the defendants' filings all concurred with Kenya's position. The victims, represented by the Office of Public Counsel for the Victims (OPCV), joined the Prosecution in opposing the appeal.

The Prosecutor v. Ruto et al., Judgment on the Appeal of the Republic of Kenya against the Decision of Pre-Trial Chamber II of 30 May 2011 entitled 'Decision on the Application by the Government of Kenya Challenging the Admissibility of the Case Pursuant to Article 19(2)(b) of the Statute', Case No. ICC–01/09–01/11–307 OA (Aug. 30, 2011)

In the Appeals Chamber

27. The principal issue raised by Kenya under this ground of appeal is the interpretation of the words, "[t]he case is being investigated [. . .] by a State which has jurisdiction over it" in article 17 (1) (a) of the Statute. In particular, Kenya challenges the correctness of the Pre-Trial Chamber's finding that for a case to be inadmissible before the Court, a national jurisdiction must be investigating the same person and for the same conduct as in the case already before the Court."

28. In its Admissibility Challenge before the Pre-Trial Chamber, Kenya submitted that the Court had not yet authoritatively established the meaning of the word "case" in article 17 (1) of the Statute. Kenya submitted that * * * the Appeals Chamber had declined to rule on the findings of other Chambers of the Court that in order for a case to be inadmissible, "national proceedings must encompass both the conduct and the person that is the subject of the case before the ICC", the so-called 'same person/same conduct' test. In the view of Kenya, rather than the 'same person/same conduct' test, the test developed by the Pre-Trial Chamber in the Article 15 Decision should be applied to the Admissibility Challenge. According to that test, the national proceedings must "cover the same conduct in respect of persons at the same level in the hierarchy being investigated by the ICC." In Kenya's Reply of 16 May 2011, Kenya submitted furthermore that "any argument that there *must* be identity of *individuals* as well as of *subject matter* being investigated by a State and by the Prosecutor of the ICC is necessarily false as the State may simply not have evidence available to the Prosecutor of the ICC or may even be deprived of that evidence." Kenya also submitted that "there is simply no guarantee that an identical cohort of individuals will fall for investigation by the State seeking to exclude ICC admissibility as by the Prosecutor seeking to establish it." Kenya also recalled that it was required under article 19 (5) of the Statute to bring the admissibility challenge "at the earliest proper moment [. . .], an event 'triggered' by the issue of summonses against the six Kenyan nationals some few weeks beforehand." * * *

Determination by the Appeals Chamber

34. The Pre-Trial Chamber in the Impugned Decision applied the 'same person/same conduct' test in deciding whether the case was

admissible under article 17(1)(a) of the Statute. The Pre-Trial Chamber noted that in the Judgment in *Katanga*, the Appeals Chamber had declined to rule on the correctness or otherwise of the 'same conduct' component of the 'same person/same conduct' test, as this question was not decisive for the determination of that appeal [since Katanga was in fact under investigation within the DRC]. The Pre-Trial Chamber also stated that the Appeals Chamber had only declined to rule on the 'same conduct' component of the test, and that the Pre-Trial Chamber "can clearly infer that the Appeals Chamber ruled on part of the test, namely that a determination of the admissibility of a 'case' must at least encompass the 'same person.' " * * *

40. * * * Article 19 of the Statute relates to the admissibility of concrete cases. The cases are defined by the warrant of arrest or summons to appear issued under article 58, or the charges brought by the Prosecutor and confirmed by the Pre-Trial Chamber under article 61. Article 58 requires that for a warrant of arrest or a summons to appear to be issued, there must be reasonable grounds to believe that the person named therein has committed a crime within the jurisdiction of the Court. Similarly, under regulation 52 of the Regulations of the Court, the document containing the charges must identify the person against whom confirmation of the charges is sought and the allegations against him or her. Articles 17(1)(c) and 20(3) of the Statute state that the Court cannot try a person tried by a national court for the same conduct unless the requirements of article 20(3)(a) or (b) of the Statute [setting out the defense of double jeopardy] are met. Thus, the defining elements of a concrete case before the Court are the individual and the alleged conduct. It follows that for such a case to be inadmissible under article 17(1)(a) of the Statute, the national investigation must cover the same individual and substantially the same conduct as alleged in the proceedings before the Court.

41. The Admissibility Challenge that gave rise to the present appeal was brought under article 19(2)(b) of the Statute in relation to a case in which a summons to appear has been issued against specific suspects for specific conduct. Accordingly, as regards the present appeal, the 'case' in terms of article 17(1)(a) is the case as defined in the summons. This case is only inadmissible before the Court if the same suspects are being investigated by Kenya for substantially the same conduct. The words 'is being investigated', in this context, signify the taking of steps directed at ascertaining whether those suspects are responsible for that conduct, for instance by interviewing witnesses or suspects, collecting documentary evidence, or carrying out forensic analyses. The mere preparedness to take such steps or the investigation of other suspects is not sufficient. This is because unless investigative steps are actually taken in relation to the suspects who are the subject of the proceedings before the Court, it cannot be said that the same case is (currently) under investigation by the Court and by a national jurisdiction, and there is therefore no conflict

of jurisdictions. It should be underlined, however, that determining the existence of an investigation must be distinguished from assessing whether the State is "unwilling or unable genuinely to carry out the investigation or prosecution", which is the second question to consider when determining the admissibility of a case. For assessing whether the State is indeed investigating, the genuineness of the investigation is not at issue; what is at issue is whether there are investigative steps.

42. Kenya's submission that "it cannot be right that in all circumstances in every Situation and in every case that may come before the ICC the persons being investigated by the Prosecutor must be exactly the same as those being investigated by the State if the State is to retain jurisdiction" cannot be accepted. It disregards the fact that the proceedings have progressed and that specific suspects have been identified. At this stage of the proceedings, where summonses to appear have been issued, the question is no longer whether suspects at the same hierarchical level are being investigated by Kenya, but whether the same suspects are the subject of investigation by both jurisdictions for substantially the same conduct.

43. Kenya seeks to counter this conclusion by suggesting that a national jurisdiction may not always have the same evidence available as the Prosecutor and therefore may not be investigating the same suspects as the Court. This argument is not persuasive for two reasons. First, if a State does not investigate a given suspect because of lack of evidence, then there simply is no conflict of jurisdictions, and no reason why the case should be inadmissible before the Court. Second, what is relevant for the admissibility of a concrete case under articles 17(1)(a) and 19 of the Statute is not whether the same evidence in the Prosecutor's possession is available to a State, but whether the State is carrying out steps directed at ascertaining whether these suspects are responsible for substantially the same conduct as is the subject of the proceedings before the Court.

44. Kenya also argues that there should be a "leaway [sic] in the exercise of discretion in the application of the principle of complementarity" to allow domestic proceedings to progress. This argument has no merit because, as explained above, the purpose of the admissibility proceedings under article 19 of the Statute is to determine whether the case brought by the Prosecutor is inadmissible because of a jurisdictional conflict. Unless there is such a conflict, the case is admissible. The suggestion that there should be a presumption in favour of domestic jurisdictions does not contradict this conclusion. Although article 17(1)(a) to (c) of the Statute does indeed favour national jurisdictions, it does so only to the extent that there actually are, or have been, investigations and/or prosecutions at the national level. If the suspect or conduct have not been investigated by the national jurisdiction, there is no legal basis for the Court to find the case inadmissible. * * *

46. Similarly, the argument that once the summons to appear was issued, Kenya was constrained, under article 19(5) of the Statute, to bring the admissibility challenge "at the earliest opportunity" and therefore it could not be "expected to have prepared every aspect of its Admissibility Application in detail in advance of this date" is also misconceived. Article 19(5) of the Statute requires a State to challenge admissibility as soon as possible once it is in a position to actually assert a conflict of jurisdictions. The provision does not require a State to challenge admissibility just because the Court has issued a summons to appear.

47. Accordingly, the Appeals Chamber finds that given the specific stage that the proceedings had reached, the 'same person/same conduct' test applied by the Pre-Trial Chamber was the correct test. The Pre-Trial Chamber thus made no error of law.

[Kenya also argued that the PTC did not appropriately consider the evidence in the record, particularly the lists of suspects provided by the Attorney General, instructions disseminated to prosecutorial authorities to investigate cases, and a document indicating that Kenya was undertaking a "bottom up" strategy towards prosecutions. The Prosecutor argued that much of this "evidence" was actually proof that the suspects in question were no being investigated.]

56. Regarding an alleged error of fact, the Appeals Chamber has ruled in previous decisions that its review is corrective and not *de novo*. It will therefore not interfere unless it is shown that the Pre-Trial or Trial Chamber committed a clear error, namely: misappreciated the facts, took into account irrelevant facts or failed to take into account relevant facts. As to the "misappreciation of facts" the Appeals Chamber will not disturb a Pre-Trial or Trial Chamber's evaluation of the facts just because the Appeals Chamber might have come to a different conclusion. It will interfere only in the case where it cannot discern how the Chamber's conclusion could have reasonably been reached from the evidence before it. * * *

62. The Pre-Trial Chamber found [Kenya's] assertions in themselves insufficient to establish that an investigation was ongoing and required proof that Kenya was taking specific steps to investigate the three suspects. The Appeals Chamber cannot identify any error in this approach. As explained in paragraph 40 above, for a successful challenge of the admissibility of a case under articles 17(1)(a), first alternative, and 19 of the Statute, the same case as that before the Court must be under investigation by a State, i.e. the State must take steps directed at ascertaining whether the suspects are responsible for substantially the same conduct as that alleged in the proceedings before the Court. As Kenya also acknowledges, a State that challenges the admissibility of a case bears the burden of proof to show that the case is inadmissible. To discharge that burden, the State must provide the Court

with evidence of a sufficient degree of specificity and probative value that demonstrates that it is indeed investigating the case. * * *

70. In the circumstances, the Appeals Chamber can find no clear error in the Pre-Trial Chamber's assessment of the annexes that Kenya had submitted. Therefore, the Pre-Trial Chamber's finding that in relation to the three suspects Kenya has not established that it is carrying out an investigation cannot be faulted.

83. In addition, contrary to the submissions of Kenya, the Pre-Trial Chamber did not infer that investigations had to be completed before an admissibility challenge could be raised. As correctly pointed out by the Prosecutor, the Pre-Trial Chamber merely required that concrete progressive investigative steps be taken and demonstrated at the time when an admissibility challenge is raised.

84. Kenya's assertions that the Pre-Trial Chamber simply did not believe it even though there was no evidence contradicting Kenya's submissions, and that the Chamber adopted a hostile attitude and made erroneous findings on the basis of Kenya's legal submissions is equally unfounded. Nowhere in the Impugned Decision did the Pre-Trial Chamber find that Kenya was not to be trusted. The Pre-Trial Chamber rejected the Admissibility Challenge not because it did not trust Kenya or doubted its intentions, but rather because Kenya failed to discharge its burden to provide sufficient evidence to establish that it was investigating the three suspects. 85. In sum, no clear error in the Pre-Trial Chamber's treatment of Kenya's proposal to submit updated investigation reports can be identified. Nor can it be said that the Pre-Trial Chamber was biased against Kenya.

NOTES & QUESTIONS

1. Primacy v. Complementarity

Why would primacy be adopted for the *ad hoc* tribunals but not the ICC? What policies underlie the concept of complementarity? Given the jurisprudence above, how well do you think these policies have been furthered? According to one commentator (a legal adviser within the ICC OTP), one way of thinking about it is that "complementarity [is] the inverse of primacy as practised at the *ad hoc* Tribunals, designed to avoid flooding the permanent court with cases more appropriate for the national level." However, it is the ICC, and not national courts, that makes the ultimate decision as to admissibility, and states parties will be in breach of their treaty obligations if they fail to abide by a ruling on forum allocation by the ICC. *See* Rod Rastan, *What is 'Substantially the Same Conduct'?: Unpacking the ICC's 'First Limb' Complementarity Jurisprudence*, 15 J. INT'L CRIM. JUST. 1 (2017).

The principle of jurisdictional complementarity can be traced to negotiations surrounding the drafting of the Genocide Convention. That treaty at Article VI envisions a standing international criminal court with jurisdiction over the crime of genocide. This reference to an anticipated international court proved controversial during the treaty negotiations, with some states wanting the imagined court to have jurisdiction only if the state with territorial jurisdiction had failed to act. This position did not prevail, and the Genocide Convention now provides equal jurisdictional competency between the international court and the courts of the territorial state: "persons charged with genocide shall be tried by a competent tribunal of the State in the territory of which the act was committed, or by such international penal tribunal as may have jurisdiction with respect to those Contracting Parties which shall have accepted its jurisdiction." Genocide Convention, Art. VI.

2. Same Person/Conduct

In its submissions to the Court in connection with its admissibility challenge, Kenya argued that it was sufficient to show domestic activity in relation to the situation as a whole. *The Prosecutor v. Ruto et al.*, Case No. ICC–01/09–01/11–19, Application on Behalf of the Government of the Republic of Kenya Pursuant to Art. 19 of the ICC Statute, ¶ 32 (Mar. 31, 2011). The Pre-Trial Chamber, however, applied the same person/same conduct test. How should this test be applied? Does it require complete congruence with respect to the suspects involved, the incidents under consideration, the legal characterization of the facts, the mode or theory of liability? Is your answer influenced by the fact that complementarity is linked to the defense of *ne bis in idem*, or double jeopardy, as set forth in Article 20 of the Statute? The Appeals Chamber changes this formulation slightly in paras. 40–43. Is this slight change meaningful? On balance, is this test too narrow or burdensome, such that even genuinely willing and able states will lose admissibility challenges before the Court? For further discussion of complementarity and the Kenya cases, *see* Christine Bjork & Juanita Goebertus, *Complementarity in Action: The Role of Civil Society and the ICC in Rule of Law Strengthening in Kenya*, 14 YALE HUM. RTS. & DEV. L. J. 5 (2011); Kevin Jon Heller, *Radical Complementarity,* 14 J. INT'L CRIM. JUST. 637 (2016); and Ronald C. Slye, THE KENYAN TJRC: AN OUTSIDER'S VIEW FROM THE INSIDE, Ch. 6 (2018).

3. Complementarity and Due Process

Should the ICC be concerned about deferrals to national jurisdiction where a defendant might be exposed to a legal system whose due process standards fall short of what she might receive before the ICC or what international standards would require? Does a state's inability to provide this level of due process render a case admissible before the ICC pursuant to the Court's complementarity regime? What if a state's procedural rules and excessive prosecutorial zeal are likely to make it *easier* to convict an individual than would be the case before the ICC? Is such a state "unwilling" or "unable" to prosecute? Does the ICC Statute allow a defendant (as opposed to an implicated state) to challenge a determination of inadmissibility? For a discussion, *see* Kevin Jon Heller, *The Shadow Side of Complementarity: The Effect of Article 17 of the Rome Statute on National Due Process*, 17 CRIM. L. F. 255 (2006).

The admissibility challenges of Libya to the ICC prosecutions of Abdullah Al-Senussi and Saif Al-Islam Gaddafi directly implicate these issues. (See the Appendix for a map of Libya.) Saif Gaddafi was at the time of these decisions being held by a militia force in Zintan, a part of the country not controlled by the National Transitional Council (the then-central government). Libya argued before the Court that it was currently investigating Mr. Gaddafi for various acts constituting crimes against humanity. Gaddafi's defense counsel before the Court argued that his client could not receive a fair trial and would be tried *in absentia*, such that the case was admissible and the Court should not defer to a domestic Libyan prosecution.

Situation in Libya, Case No. ICC–01/11–01/11–344–Red, Decision on the Admissibility of the Case Against Saif Al-Islam Gaddafi (May 31, 2013)

In the Pre-Trial Chamber

25. Libya challenges the admissibility of the case on the basis that its national judicial system is actively investigating Mr. Gaddafi for his alleged criminal responsibility for multiple acts of murder and persecution, committed pursuant to or in furtherance of a state policy, amounting to crimes against humanity. * * *

52. The Chamber is guided by the jurisprudence of the Appeals Chamber that "a State that challenges the admissibility of a case bears the burden of proof to show that the case is inadmissible". The Chamber observes that the inadmissibility of the case is premised on both limbs of article 17(1)(a) of the Statute and the challenging State is required to substantiate all aspects of its allegations to the extent required by the concrete circumstances of the case. The principle of complementarity expresses a preference for national investigations and prosecutions but does not relieve a State, in general, from substantiating all requirements set forth by the law when seeking to successfully challenge the admissibility of a case.

53. [T]he Chamber notes that an evidentiary debate on the State's unwillingness or inability will be meaningful only when doubts arise with regard to the genuineness of the domestic investigations or prosecutions. Depending on the circumstances, the Chamber may seek additional evidence to satisfy itself that genuine investigations or prosecutions are being carried out. In the present case, based on the submissions made and the available evidence, the Chamber considered that the ability of Libya to investigate and prosecute required further analysis. As a consequence, the Chamber took the initiative of asking specific questions in this regard to Libya and the other parties and participants, both at the Admissibility Hearing held in October 2012 and in the Chamber's decision issued on 7 December 2012. The Chamber will determine, in light of its own assessment, whether it is satisfied that the State is

conducting genuine investigations or prosecutions on the basis of the submissions and the evidence received in response.

54. The Chamber notes that the Statute does not set out a standard of proof for the purposes of a determination on the admissibility of a case. Different standards of proof are explicitly set out in the Statute for distinct stages of the proceedings from the issuance of a warrant of arrest, to the confirmation of charges and the final trial judgment.[95] Those standards of proof, however, do not apply to the admissibility determination, which deals *inter alia* with the question as to whether domestic authorities are taking concrete and progressive steps to investigate or prosecute the same case that is before the Court. The Chamber is guided by the jurisprudence of the Appeals Chamber to the effect that the State "must provide the Court with evidence of a sufficient degree of specificity and probative value that demonstrates that it is indeed investigating the case". In the view of the Chamber, such evidence shall *demonstrate* that Libya is taking concrete and progressive steps towards ascertaining Mr. Gaddafi's responsibility.

55. In exemplifying the type of evidence that may be considered to demonstrate that an investigation is in progress, the Appeals Chamber has mentioned interviewing witnesses or suspects, collecting documentary evidence, or carrying out forensic analyses. Therefore, the Chamber has reminded Libya of the necessity to provide concrete, tangible and pertinent evidence that proper investigations are currently ongoing and has clarified that:

> [T]he concept of "evidence," within the context of admissibility proceedings, does not refer exclusively to evidence on the merits of the national case that may have been collected as part of the purported domestic investigation to prove the alleged crimes. In this context, "evidence" rather means all material capable of proving that an investigation is ongoing and that appropriate measures are being envisaged to carry out the proceedings.
>
> Accordingly, the Chamber is of the view that evidence for the purposes of substantiating the Admissibility Challenge may also include, depending on the circumstances, directions, orders and decisions issued by authorities in charge of the investigation as well as internal reports, updates, notifications or submissions contained in the file arising from the Libyan investigation of the case, to the extent that they demonstrate that Libyan authorities are taking concrete and progressive steps to ascertain whether Mr. Gaddafi is responsible for the conduct underlying the warrant of arrest issued by the Court.
>
> * * *

[95] *See* articles 53(1)(a), 58(1)(a), 61(7) and 66(3) of the Statute.

57. Article 17 of the Statute reads, in the relevant part:

> 1. Having regard to paragraph 10 of the Preamble and article 1, the Court shall determine that a case is inadmissible where: (a) The case is being investigated or prosecuted by a State which has jurisdiction over it, unless the State is unwilling or unable genuinely to carry out the investigation or prosecution.

58. The Chamber notes that the Appeals Chamber has stated that article 17(1)(a) of the Statute contemplates a two-step test, according to which the Chamber, in considering an admissibility challenge, shall address in turn two questions: (i) whether, at the time of the proceedings in respect of an admissibility challenge, there is an ongoing investigation or prosecution of the case at the national level; and, in case the answer to the first question is in the affirmative, (ii) whether the State is unwilling or unable genuinely to carry out such investigation or prosecution.

59. The specificities of the case together with considerations of fairness and expeditiousness have led the Chamber to address both aspects of the test throughout the proceedings and in this comprehensive decision.

60. The correct interpretation of the term "case" within the meaning of article 17(1)(a) of the Statute was discussed at length with the parties and participants in these proceedings. Mindful of the submissions, the Chamber's findings are set forth hereunder. Thereafter, the Chamber will examine the evidence presented in the case in order to determine whether the challenging party has demonstrated that it is investigating the same case.

61. The "case" within the meaning of article 17 of the Statute is characterised by two components: the person and the conduct. While it is uncontested that national investigations must cover the "same person", the "conduct" part of the test raises issues of interpretation and needs further clarification. * * *

74. In the Lubanga case, Pre-Trial Chamber I found for the first time that for a case to be inadmissible before the Court, national proceedings must "encompass both the person and the conduct which is the subject of the case before the Court." This test later became the settled jurisprudence of the Pre-Trial Chambers.

75. Pre-Trial Chambers have also indicated that a case encompasses "specific incidents during which one or more crimes within the jurisdiction of the Court seem to have been committed by one or more identified suspects", without clarifying, however, what would be encompassed by the notion of "incident".

76. The Appeals Chamber endorsed the Pre-Trial Chambers' approach with respect to the specific nature of the admissibility test when it found that "article 19 of the Statute relates to the admissibility of concrete cases" and that "the defining elements of a concrete case

before the Court are the individual and the alleged conduct". Thus, the validity of the "same person/same conduct" test has been confirmed by the Appeals Chamber. However, rather than referring to "incidents", the Appeals Chamber referred to the conduct "as alleged in the proceedings before the Court". In addition, the Appeals Chamber has stated that the investigation or prosecution must cover "substantially" the same conduct:

> [T]he defining elements of a concrete case before the Court are the individual and the alleged conduct. It follows that for such a case to be inadmissible under article 17(1)(a) of the Statute, the national investigation must cover the same individual and substantially the same conduct as alleged in the proceedings before the Court.

77. The Chamber considers that the determination of what is "substantially the same conduct as alleged in the proceedings before the Court" will vary according to the concrete facts and circumstances of the case and, therefore, requires a case-by-case analysis.

78. In the case at hand, the conduct allegedly under investigation by Libya must be compared to the conduct attributed to Mr. Gaddafi in the Warrant of Arrest issued against him by the Chamber, as well as in the Chamber's decision on the Prosecutor's application for the warrant of arrest.

79. In the Warrant of Arrest, the Chamber found reasonable grounds to believe that:

> Saif Al-Islam Gaddafi is criminally responsible as an indirect co-perpetrator, under article 25(3)(a) of the Statute, for the following crimes committed by Security Forces under his control in various localities of the Libyan territory, in particular in Benghazi, Misrata, Tripoli and other neighboring cities, from 15 February 2011 until at least 28 February 2011:
>
> > murder as a crime against humanity, within the meaning of article 7(1)(a) of the Statute; and
> >
> > persecution as a crime against humanity, within the meaning of article 7(1)(h) of the Statute.[130]

80. The Warrant of Arrest does not refer to specific instances of killings and acts of persecution, but rather refers to acts of such a nature resulting from Mr. Gaddafi's use of the Libyan Security Forces to target the civilian population which was demonstrating against Gaddafi's regime or those perceived to be dissidents to the regime.

81. Conversely, the Article 58 Decision includes a long, non-exhaustive list of alleged acts of murder and persecution committed

---

[130] Pre-Trial Chamber I, Warrant of Arrest for Saif Al-Islam Gaddafi, 27 June 2011, ICC–01/11–01/11–3; Pre-Trial Chamber I, Decision on the "Prosecutor's Application Pursuant to Article 58 as to Muammar Mohammed Abu Minyar Gaddafi, Saif Al-Islam Gaddafi and Abdullah Al-Senussi", 27 June 2011, ICC–01/11–01/11–1, P. 6.

against an identified category of people within certain temporal and geographical parameters, on the basis of which the Chamber was satisfied that throughout Libya—in particular in Tripoli, Misrata, Benghazi, Al-Bayda, Derna, Tobruk and Ajdabiya—killings and inhuman acts amounting to persecution on political grounds were committed by the Security Forces from 15 February 2011 until at least 28 February 2011 as part of an attack against the civilian demonstrators and/or perceived dissidents to Gaddafi's regime.

82. The Chamber notes that the events expressly mentioned in the Article 58 Decision do not represent unique manifestations of the form of criminality alleged against Mr. Gaddafi in the proceedings before the Court. They constitute rather samples of a course of conduct of the Security Forces, under Mr. Gaddafi's control, that allegedly carried out an attack committed across Libya from 15 February 2011 onwards against the civilians who were dissidents or perceived dissidents to Gaddafi's regime, which resulted in an unspecified number of killings and acts of persecution.

83. Therefore, in the circumstances of the case at hand and bearing in mind the purpose of the complementarity principle, the Chamber considers that it would not be appropriate to expect Libya's investigation to cover exactly the same acts of murder and persecution mentioned in the Article 58 Decision as constituting instances of Mr. Gaddafi's alleged course of conduct. Instead, the Chamber will assess, on the basis of the evidence provided by Libya, whether the alleged domestic investigation addresses the same conduct underlying the Warrant of Arrest and Article 58 Decision, namely that: Mr. Gaddafi used his control over relevant parts of the Libyan State apparatus and Security Forces to deter and quell, by any means, including by the use of lethal force, the demonstrations of civilians, which started in February 2011 against Muammar Gaddafi's regime; in particular, that Mr. Gaddafi activated the Security Forces under his control to kill and persecute hundreds of civilian demonstrators or alleged dissidents to Muammar Gaddafi's regime, across Libya, in particular in Benghazi, Misrata, Tripoli and other neighbouring cities, from 15 February 2011 to at least 28 February 2011. * * *

[The Chamber then proceeded to discuss its analysis of "(i) whether Libyan legislation sufficiently captures the same conduct for which the suspect is charged before this Court; and (ii) whether an investigation against Mr. Gaddafi for the same conduct as that alleged in the proceedings before the Court is ongoing at the domestic level." The Chamber concluded that although the crimes for which Libya said it would charge Gaddafi do not cover all aspects of the charges before the ICC, they "substantially capture" the activity that is the focus of the ICC arrest warrant, and thus prong (i) of the above test is met. On the second prong, however, the Chamber found that Libya had not sufficiently demonstrated that the scope of the domestic investigation covered the same case as set out in the Warrant of Arrest issued by the Court (para 135). Having established that the first limb of the admissibility test of article 17(1)(a) had not been met (i.e. that there was not an investigation at the domestic level that concerned the same conduct as the proposed international prosecution), the Chamber went on to address the second limb of the 17(1)(a) test, i.e. the willingness or ability of Libya to genuinely investigate and prosecute. Excerpts from that part of the Chamber's opinion follow.]

B. Findings of the Chamber in Relation to the Inability of Libya Genuinely to Carry Out the Investigation or Prosecution

199. Turning to the matter of whether Libya is able genuinely to investigate or prosecute the case against Saif Al-Islam Gaddafi, the Chamber recalls that according to article 17(3) of the Statute:

> In order to determine inability in a particular case, the Court shall consider whether, due to a total or substantial collapse or unavailability of its national judicial system, the State is unable to obtain the accused or the necessary evidence and testimony or otherwise is unable to carry out its proceedings.

200. The Chamber considers that the ability of a State genuinely to carry out an investigation or prosecution must be assessed in the context of the relevant national system and procedures. In other words, the Chamber must assess whether the Libyan authorities are capable of investigating or prosecuting Mr. Gaddafi in accordance with the substantive and procedural law applicable in Libya. * * *

203. The Chamber notes that Libya has confirmed that the trial of Mr. Gaddafi will be conducted in accordance with the general criminal procedure of Libya as the application of the "People's Court procedure" was declared unconstitutional by the Libyan Supreme Court on 23 December 2012.

Unavailability of the National System

204. Having considered the responses and evidence received, the Chamber takes note of the efforts deployed by Libya under extremely difficult circumstances to improve security conditions, rebuild institutions and restore the rule of law. In this regard, it takes note, in particular, of the Libyan submissions on specific measures of assistance received from national governments and regional and international organizations to enhance capacity, inter alia, with respect to transitional justice. The Chamber emphasises the relevance of specific submissions related to progress made, as well as those regarding the proposed strategy to improve the effectiveness and accountability of the police service, the security for the courts and participants in the proceedings, to reform the detention centres and to bring practices of torture to an end.

205. Without prejudice to these achievements, it is apparent from the submissions that multiple challenges remain and that Libya continues to face substantial difficulties in exercising its judicial powers

fully across the entire territory. Due to these difficulties, which are further explained below, the Chamber is of the view that its national system cannot yet be applied in full in areas or aspects relevant to the case, being thus "unavailable" within the terms of article 17(3) of the Statute. As a consequence, Libya is "unable to obtain the accused" and the necessary testimony and is also "otherwise unable to carry out [the] proceedings" in the case against Mr. Gaddafi in compliance with its national laws, in accordance with the same provision.

(i) Inability to Obtain the Accused

206. The Chamber notes that Libya has not yet been able to secure the transfer of Mr. Gaddafi from his place of detention under the custody of the Zintan militia into State authority. In response to a specific request for clarification from the Chamber, the Libyan representatives indicated that "[e]fforts to arrange Mr. Gaddafi's transfer to a detention facility in Tripoli where other Gaddafi-era officials are presently held are still ongoing." Libya subsequently reiterated that efforts to arrange Mr. Gaddafi's transfer to detention in Tripoli are ongoing and that it will shortly begin implementation of its recently devised proposal to train members of the Zintan brigade so that they may form part of the judicial police who will be responsible for guarding Mr. Gaddafi upon his transfer to Tripoli. It estimated that the transfer will take place "before the earliest possible estimated commencement date of the trial in May 2013" and that the national security proceedings in Zintan will also be transferred to the Tripoli court at this point if they proceed to trial.

207. The Chamber has no doubt that the central Government is deploying all efforts to obtain Mr. Gaddafi's transfer but, in spite of Libya's recent assurances, no concrete progress to this effect has been shown since the date of his apprehension on 19 November 2011. The Chamber is not persuaded that this problem may be resolved in the near future and no evidence has been produced in support of that contention.

208. The Chamber notes the submissions of Libya that in absentia trials are not permitted under Libyan law when the accused is present on Libyan territory and his location is known to the authorities. As a result, without the transfer of Mr. Gaddafi into the control of the central authorities, the trial cannot take place.

(ii) Inability to Obtain Testimony

209. The Chamber is also concerned about the lack of capacity to obtain the necessary testimony due to the inability of judicial and governmental authorities to ascertain control and provide adequate witness protection. The Chamber notes in this regard that it has been reported that conflict-related detainees including senior former regime members have not been protected from torture and mistreatment in detention facilities. Strong concerns have been raised at the highest levels of the Libyan Government by United Nations Support Mission in Libya about instances of torture and death from torture in detention

centres that had been brought to its attention. The Government has been urged to commence State inspections and assume full control over detention facilities as soon as possible.

210. Contrary to the suggestion of the Prosecutor, the Chamber is of the view that this lack of full control over certain detention facilities has a direct bearing on the investigation against Mr. Gaddafi. In this regard, it is noteworthy that in the 1 May 2012 Admissibility Challenge, Libya envisaged taking the statements of two witnesses for Mr. Gaddafi's case. In response to a subsequent request for clarification by the Chamber, the Libyan Government stated that it has not been possible for the Libyan prosecuting authorities to conduct interviews with these two individuals as they are presently being held in detention facilities which are not yet under the control of the Libyan Government.

211. The Chamber notes the various submissions received during the admissibility proceedings in regard to witness protection programs under Libyan law. Libya has indicated that the measures for witness protection applicable at pre-trial can be continued at trial as it is within the discretionary powers of the trial judge to receive evidence in whatever form he or she deems appropriate. However, further to its submission that trial judges have discretionary powers to order protective measures, Libya has presented no evidence about specific protection programs that may exist under domestic law. It is unclear, for instance, whether the domestic law provides for the immunity of statements made by witnesses at trial. In addition, it is unclear whether witnesses for the suspect may effectively benefit from such programs. As such, the Libyan Government has failed to substantiate its assertions that it envisages the implementation of protective measures for witnesses who agree to testify in the case against Mr. Gaddafi. Therefore, and in light of the circumstances, the Chamber is not persuaded by the assertion that the Libyan authorities currently have the capacity to ensure protective measures.

(iii) Otherwise Unable to Carry Out Its Proceedings: Appointment of Defence Counsel

212. The Libyan Government submits that the suspect has not exercised his right to appoint counsel as set out in article 106 of the Libyan Code of Criminal Procedure. The Defence cautions that significant practical impediments exist to securing any legal representation for Mr. Gaddafi in view of the security situation in Libya and the risk faced by lawyers who act for associates of the former regime.

213. The Chamber notes that this position was confirmed by the Libyan Government during the Admissibility Hearing. Indeed, attempts to secure legal representation for Mr. Gaddafi have seemingly failed. In response to a query from the Chamber as to the concrete steps that have been taken in order to secure independent legal representation for Mr. Gaddafi, Libya indicates that Libyan Ministry of Justice officials have engaged in continuing high-level contacts with the Libyan Law Society

and the Popular Lawyer's Office in order to find a suitably qualified lawyer. Later, Libya added that it is in the process of approaching the Bar Associations of Tunisia and Egypt in order to obtain suitably qualified and experienced counsel who will be permitted, together with a Libyan lawyer, to represent Mr. Gaddafi.

214. These submissions, however, fall short of substantiating whether and how the difficulties in securing a lawyer for the suspect may be overcome in the future. The Chamber notes that Libya has recently submitted that the interrogation of Mr. Gaddafi without the presence of his counsel is not a breach of Libyan law, as the presence of counsel during interrogations pursuant to article 106 of the Libyan Code of Criminal Procedure is only required where counsel has been appointed. However, the Chamber is concerned that this important difficulty appears to be an impediment to the progress of proceedings against Mr. Gaddafi. If this impediment is not removed, a trial cannot be conducted in accordance with the rights and protections of the Libyan national justice system, including those enshrined in articles 31 and 33 of its 2011 Constitutional Declaration.

215. In light of the above, although the authorities for the administration of justice may exist and function in Libya, a number of legal and factual issues result in the unavailability of the national judicial system for the purpose of the case against Mr. Gaddafi. As a consequence, Libya is, in the view of the Chamber, unable to secure the transfer of Mr. Gaddafi's custody from his place of detention under the Zintan militia into State authority and there is no concrete evidence that this problem may be resolved in the near future. Moreover, the Chamber is not persuaded that the Libyan authorities have the capacity to obtain the necessary testimony. Finally, the Chamber has noted a practical impediment to the progress of domestic proceedings against Mr. Gaddafi as Libya has not shown whether and how it will overcome the existing difficulties in securing a lawyer for the suspect.

NOTES & QUESTIONS

1. Case Update

The Libyan government filed an appeal against the above judgment, requesting its reversal and a finding that the case against Mr. Gaddafi was inadmissible. The Appeals Chamber upheld the finding of admissibility, concluding that the legal tests applied by the Pre-Trial Chamber and its application of those tests to the facts were proper. *Prosecutor v. Saif Al-Islam Gaddafi and Abdullah Al-Senussi,* Case No. ICC–01/11–01/11 OA 4, Judgment on the Appeal of Libya against the Decision of Pre-Trial Chamber I of 31 May 2013 entitled "Decision on the Admissibility of the case against Saif Al-Islam Gaddafi" (Redacted) (May 21, 2014). Judge Anita Ušacka (Latvia) dissented from the Appeal Chamber's opinion. In her dissent, Judge Ušacka recounted in detail the origins and development of the "same person/substantially the same conduct" test. Judge Ušacka argued that this test "disregards the principle of complementarity laid out in paragraph 10 of the Preamble and article 1 of the Statute." *Prosecutor v. Saif Al-Islam Gaddafi and Abdullah Al-Senussi,* Case No. ICC–01/11–01/11 OA 4, Dissenting Opinion of Judge Anita Ušacka, Judgment on the Appeal of Libya against the Decision of Pre-Trial Chamber I of 31 May 2013 entitled "Decision on the Admissibility of the case against Saif Al-Islam Gaddafi" (Redacted) para. 47 (May 21, 2014). She further reasoned:

> 51. * * * But, in my opinion, article 17 (1) (a) of the Statute, applied in accordance with the principle of complementarity, does not require domestic authorities to investigate "(substantially) the same" conduct as the conduct that forms the basis of the "case before the Court." This means that, contrary to how I understand the Impugned Decision, I do not think that the domestic investigation or prosecution needs to focus on largely or precisely the same acts or omissions that form the basis for the alleged crimes or on largely or precisely the same acts or omissions of the person(s) under investigation or prosecution to whom the crimes are allegedly attributed.
>
> 52. Establishing such a rigid requirement would oblige domestic authorities to investigate or prosecute exactly or nearly exactly the conduct that forms the basis for the "case before the Court" at the time of the admissibility proceedings, thereby being obliged to "copy" the case before the Court. Instead of complementing each other, the relationship between the Court and the State would be competitive, requiring the State to do its utmost to fulfil the requirements set by the Court.
>
> 53. Such an approach would strongly intrude upon the sovereignty of States and the discretion afforded to national prosecutorial authorities, with the consequence that the Court would become a "supervisory" authority, checking in detail not only the "scope" and content of any investigative and prosecutorial steps, but also scrutinising the State's substantive and procedural law and how it relates to the crimes in the Rome Statute.
>
> 54. This approach not only disregards the many differences in the legal frameworks and in the practice of criminal justice between domestic jurisdictions and the Court, but also between the various domestic jurisdictions. National cases can differ from the "case before the Court" in respect of evidence, such as available witnesses, victims, and the number and locations of incidents that are under investigation or prosecution.
>
> 55. Further, such an approach could potentially preclude a State from focusing its investigations on a wider scope of activities and could even have the perverse effect of encouraging that State to investigate only the narrower case selected by the Prosecutor. I view this as a harmful potential effect, particularly so in a situation such as Libya, where the actions of the Gaddafi regime in February 2011 (which is also the time period of the alleged crimes in the

Court's warrant of arrest) triggered the Security Council referral, but where the change of government many months later led to the initiation of a transitional justice process. In such a situation, it may be assumed that the interests of the people of Libya and of the victims of the former regime could be better and more directly addressed by Libyan investigations and prosecutions in a process of transitional justice. Weighing the interests at stake in conformity with the principle of complementarity, it could indeed be said that "[i]t seems plainly more important that Libyans have the experience of transitional justice than that the ICC works its mandate." * * *

58. As opposed to solely relying on the "same person/ (substantially) the same conduct" test, I would prefer that the Court, in comparing a case before the Court and a domestic case, be guided by a complementarity scheme that contains multiple criteria that are assessed by reference to the concrete circumstances of each specific case. In the case at hand, "conduct" is one of the essential elements in deciding whether the "case before the Court" is being investigated or prosecuted by domestic authorities. In my view, contrary to the opinion of my colleagues, "conduct" should be understood much more broadly than under the current test. While there should be a nexus between the conduct being investigated and prosecuted domestically and that before the Court, this "conduct" and any crimes investigated or prosecuted in relation thereto do not need to cover all of the same material and mental elements of the crimes before the Court and also does not need to include the same acts attributed to an individual under suspicion. In the case at hand, it may be argued that the goal of fighting impunity is also achieved, even if not exactly the same conduct as that before the Court is under investigation by Libya, but if the suspect's link to the use of the Security Forces in Libya and their consequences are the subject of the investigation of the Libyan authorities. Beyond that, the domestic investigations might even potentially focus on subsequent time periods, if the crimes allegedly committed through the use of Security Forces are considered by the domestic authorities to be graver than those on which the Court's investigations concentrate. * * *

63. To follow my suggested approach would most likely lead to the conclusion that Libya is investigating the same case against Mr. Gaddafi and would, depending on a finding in relation to the second limb of article 17(1)(a) of the Statute, make the case before the Court inadmissible.

Do you agree with Judge Ušacka? Does the "same person/substantially same conduct" test intrude upon a state's sovereignty? Judge Ušacka notes that Libya has embarked upon a process of transitional justice. Should more deference be given to states undertaking such processes in the aftermath of armed conflict or repression? If so, what provisions of the Statute, if any, allow such deference? *See* Payam Akhavan, *Complementarity Conundrums:*

The ICC Clock in Transitional Times, 14 J. INT'L CRIM. JUST. 1043 (2016) (discussing the extent to which the ICC should accommodate the time and resource constraints of national judicial systems in transitional situations).

2. International v. Domestic Crimes

If a state is prosecuting an ICC suspect for a domestic instead of an international crime, should such a case be found to be admissible? In other words, if a suspect is indicted for murder as a crime against humanity before the ICC, and a state is prosecuting the suspect for the same act as the common crime of murder, is the case admissible? In a part of the opinion not reproduced above, the Chamber made clear that such a case would be inadmissible. In other words, a domestic prosecution for an "ordinary crime," rather than as an international crime, will satisfy complementarity and result in the case being deemed inadmissible before the ICC. What difference does it make if a court prosecutes an individual for murder as opposed to murder as a crime against humanity? Do you think the Chamber is correct in saying that for the purposes of admissibility it should not matter? Kevin John Heller argues that "as long as a state is making a genuine effort to bring a suspect to justice, the ICC should find his or her case inadmissible regardless of the conduct the state investigates or the prosecutorial strategy the state pursues." Kevin Jon Heller, *Radical Complementarity,* 14 J. INT'L CRIM. JUST. 637 (2016).

3. Al-Senussi

In a companion opinion concerning the admissibility of the case of Abdullah Al-Senussi, Pre-Trial Chamber I found that case inadmissible. Like in the *Gaddafi* case, the Defense Counsel for Al-Senussi supported a finding of admissibility arguing, among other things, that "the administration of justice [of Libya] is manifestly biased against Mr. Al-Senussi and designed not to bring him to any genuine form of justice." *Prosecutor v. Saif Al-Islam Gaddafi and Abdullah Al-Senussi,* Case No. ICC–01/11–01/11, Decision on the Admissibility of the Case against Adbullah Al-Senussi, para. 181 (October 11, 2013). The Pre-Trial Chamber in *Al-Senussi* found (1) that there was an investigation by the Libyan authorities of Al-Senussi, and that concrete steps had been taken that allowed the Chamber to identify the scope and subject matter of such proceedings as demonstrated by witness statements and other evidence provided by Libya; and (2) that this investigation encompassed substantially the same conduct as the case before the Court. Al-Senussi's would-be lawyers argued that they had not yet had a chance to consult with their client, who was in government custody.

As with the *Gaddafi* opinion, the Appeals Chamber also upheld the decision of the Pre-Trial Chamber. *Prosecutor v. Saif Al-Islam Gaddafi and Abdullah Al-Senussi,* Case No. ICC–01/11–01/11 OA6, Judgment on the Appeal of Mr. Abdullah Al-Senussi against the Decision of Pre-Trial Chamber I of 11 October 2013 entitled "Decision on the Admissibility of the Case against Abdullah Al-Senussi" (July 24, 2014). Why do you think the same Pre-Trial Chamber came to a different conclusion in *Al-Senussi* a mere five months after issuing the *Gaddafi* opinion? Are the facts sufficiently distinguishable? For a discussion, *see* Michele Tedeschini, *Complementarity in Practice: the ICC's Inconsistent Approach in the Gaddafi and Al-Senussi Admissibility Decisions*, AMSTERDAM L. FOR. 76 (Summer 2015).

4. Amnesties and the ICC

Should the existence of an amnesty law in the territorial or nationality state affect the ICC's jurisdiction? In January 2000, Ugandan authorities enacted an amnesty law to push the peace process forward. The Act originally applied to anyone who had engaged in armed rebellion against the government. Although many NGOs and local officials endorsed the legislation, the U.N. High Commissioner on Human Rights critiqued the measure—at least with respect to leadership of the LRA—as promoting a culture of impunity. *See* U.N. High Commissioner for Human Rights, Report on the Mission Undertaken by Her Office, Pursuant to Commission Resolution 2000/60, to Assess the Situation on the Ground with Regard to the Abduction of Children from Northern Uganda, U.N. Doc. E/CN.4/2000/86 (2001). (The High Commissioner for Human Rights, a position created in 1994, has principal responsibility for U.N. human rights activities under the direction of the U.N. Secretary-General).

In any case, the amnesty policy failed to convince members of the LRA to lay down their arms, and the Ugandan government withdrew the amnesty offer to high-level LRA members upon referring the situation to the ICC. Accordingly, the Act only provided protection to low-and medium-level LRA members from prosecution, who were granted amnesty through a process administered by an Amnesty Commission. As of May 2012, over 27,000 people had taken advantage of the amnesty. While the offer of amnesty was allowed to lapse in May 2012, the offer was reinstated a year later, for an additional two years, after a broad coalition of civil society organizations in northern Uganda lobbied for its reinstatement. In June 2019, the Ugandan government adopted a National Transitional Justice Policy that reiterated that there would be no blanket amnesty, but that the government would encourage those amnestied to participate in "traditional justice processes for purposes of meaningful reintegration and reconciliation." The ICC Prosecutor has announced that she intends to focus her investigation on LRA leaders, and all of the indictments to date have been consistent with this approach. Will the application of Uganda's amnesty law impact the ICC's work at all? What if the Prosecutor decided she needed to indict lower level LRA members in order to lay a foundation to prosecute the LRA leaders? What deference, if any, should the ICC give to domestic amnesty laws? Could an amnesty meet the requirements of Article 17? Or should the presence of an amnesty be conclusive evidence of a state's unwillingness to investigate or prosecute? The legality and legal effects of amnesties will be considered in greater depth in Chapter 17 on Defenses Under International Criminal Law.

5. Universal Jurisdiction and the International Criminal Court

What is the difference between universal and international jurisdiction? Is one more palatable than the other? Is one a greater infringement on national sovereignty than another? As this chapter has discussed, the ICC is to declare inadmissible a case that is being investigated by a state "with jurisdiction over it," unless the state is unwilling or unable to carry out the investigation or prosecution. Should the ICC refrain from proceeding only when a state with a traditional connection to the crime (e.g., the territorial or nationality state) is exercising jurisdiction, or should it also stay its hand where states are exercising universal jurisdiction over a case? Might states invoke universal jurisdiction in an effort to impede the activity of the ICC?

6. Security Council Referrals and Complementarity

Are Security Council referrals subject to the complementarity regime? In other words, should the ICC decline to exercise jurisdiction even upon a Security Council referral where a state asserts its domestic jurisdiction over the situation or case? The OTP seems to think such referrals might be subject to complementarity. In response to the Security Council's Darfur referral, and in an effort to invoke complementarity, the Government of Sudan created several judicial and quasi-judicial mechanisms to consider the crimes committed in Darfur, including a Darfur Special Court, a Judicial Investigations Committee, and a National Commission of Inquiry. In considering the admissibility of the situation in Darfur, the then-Prosecutor reviewed the activities of these institutions to determine whether the Government of the Sudan was addressing the cases that the Prosecutor was likely to select for prosecution. The then-Prosecutor concluded that the Special Court to date had heard cases involving only ordinary crimes, as opposed to crimes within the jurisdiction of the ICC. He reasoned: "Based upon the current OTP assessments, it does not appear that the national authorities have investigated or prosecuted, or are investigating and prosecuting, cases that are or will be the focus of OTP attention such as to render those cases inadmissible before the ICC." *Third Report of the Prosecutor of the International Criminal Court to the U.N. Security Council Pursuant to UNSCR 1593 (2005),* Office of the Prosecutor (June 14, 2006).

7. The Afghanistan Situation

In October 2017, the Prosecutor sought approval from the Pre-Trial Chamber to open an investigation into the situation in Afghanistan, which joined the Court in 2003 and had been subject to a preliminary examination since 2006. (See the Appendix for a map of Afghanistan.) The Prosecutor indicated that she intended to investigate "alleged crimes committed on the territory of Afghanistan in the period since 1 May 2003 [when the Rome Statute entered into force for Afghanistan], as well as other alleged crimes that have a nexus to the armed conflict in Afghanistan and are sufficiently linked to the situation and were committed on the territory of other States Parties in the period since 1 July 2002," when the Court was founded. This formulation clearly covered acts by the Taliban, Afghan forces, coalition forces, and U.S. personnel (from both the Department of Defense and the Central Intelligence Agency); it could also have encompassed crimes committed in Europe as part of the United States' program of extraordinary rendition. That program had already been the subject of suit before the European Court of Human Rights. *See, e.g., Al-Nashiri v. Poland*, App. No. 28761/11, Judgment (July 24, 2014) (finding Poland failed to uphold its human rights obligations by allowing the secret detention, torture, and rendition of individuals suspected of terrorist acts on its territory). In order to proceed to a full investigation, the Prosecutor was required to seek approval from a Pre-Trial Chamber per Article 15. The opinion that issued follows.

Situation in the Islamic Republic of Afghanistan, Decision Pursuant to Article 15 of the Rome Statute on the Authorisation of an Investigation into the Situation in the Islamic Republic of Afghanistan, Case No. ICC–02/17–33 (Apr. 12, 2019)

In the Pre-Trial Chamber

39. The proceedings under article 15 are triggered by an entirely discretional request of the Prosecution. It is therefore its sole responsibility to identify and select specific incidents and conducts in the context of ongoing preliminary examinations, pursuant to the conditions set forth in article 53. The scope of the Chamber's scrutiny must remain confined to the incidents or category of incidents and, possibly, the groups of alleged offenders referred to by the Prosecution; at this stage it is not possible for the Pre-Trial Chamber to extend such scope by recommending further investigations, irrespective of the fact that these may emerge as appropriate on the basis of the materials under its scrutiny. The responsibility of the Pre-Trial Chamber is limited to determining whether, in light of the information made available by the Prosecution, the investigation should or should not be authorised, taking into account all the conditions set forth by the Statute including the interests of justice; in the event that the Pre-Trial Chamber determines that all relevant requirements are satisfied, the object and purpose of article 15 as a boundary to prosecutorial discretion require that the Pre-Trial Chamber also sets specific limits to the authorised investigation. * * *

59. Furthermore, as to the Agreement of 30 September 2014 between the United States and Afghanistan pursuant to article 98, requiring the consent of a sending State to surrender a national of that State to the Court, the Chamber concurs with the Prosecution that agreements entered into pursuant to article 98(2) of the Statute do not deprive the Court of its jurisdiction over persons covered by such agreements. Quite to the contrary, article 98(2) operates precisely in cases where the Court's jurisdiction is already established under articles 11 and 12 and provides for an exception to the obligation of States Parties to arrest and surrender individuals.

Determinations By The Chamber On Issues Of Admissibility

71. At this initial stage, the admissibility test calls for a twofold assessment: first, as to whether the relevant States are conducting or have conducted national proceedings in the same matter (complementarity); second, if the conclusion is in the negative, as to whether the gravity threshold is met (gravity). For the purpose of this

assessment, the Chamber must conduct a comparison between the potential cases that may arise out of the situation and the cases which have been or are being allegedly investigated or prosecuted by national authorities. This assessment is prognostic in nature and must be guided by the indicative lists of the most serious incidents and by the preliminary lists of persons or groups provided by the Prosecution. It is done without prejudice to determinations to be made at a later stage, where cases are actually brought before the Chamber and in light of any and all piece of relevant information which may become available. * * *

Complementarity

74. With reference to national proceedings in Afghanistan against the Taliban and other armed groups, the Prosecution asserts that the information available indicates that no national investigations or prosecutions have been conducted or are ongoing against those who appear most responsible for the crimes under the Court's jurisdiction allegedly committed by members of these groups; it also clarifies that those members of anti-government armed groups captured and detained in the context of the non-international armed conflict have principally been accused of crimes against the State under the 1976 Penal Code, the 1987 Penal Law on Crimes against Internal and External Security of the Democratic Republic of Afghanistan, and the 2008 Law on Combat against Terrorist Offences. Accordingly, the Prosecution concludes that the potential cases against members of the Taliban and other anti-governmental armed groups that could likely arise from an investigation would be currently admissible. The Prosecution also submits that the Afghan Parliament passed a general amnesty in 2007, which entered into force in 2009 and provides legal immunity to all belligerent parties, including those opposing the government, without temporal limitations or any exception for international crimes. * * *

76. With respect to alleged crimes committed by the Afghan Forces, the Prosecution submits that at the stage of the Request no national investigations had been conducted or were ongoing against those who appear most responsible for the alleged crimes; the Afghan authorities appear to have opened a very limited number of proceedings relating to the torture or cruel treatment of conflict-related detainees which only target low to mid-level officials, and not those who may bear the greatest responsibility. * * *

78. As regards the crimes allegedly committed by the US Forces and the CIA, the Prosecution states that available information indicates that no national investigations have been conducted against those who may be most responsible for the incidents set out in the Request and in Annexes 2C and 3C. More specifically, the Prosecutor submits that, whilst most of the information appears to be presented in 'clusters of statistics', where more concrete information is somehow available investigations and prosecutions appear to have focused exclusively on direct perpetrators and their immediate superiors. The Prosecutor also

refers to a number of internal oversight reports, indicating that the reporting and investigation of detainee abuse has been both insufficient and inadequate.

79. As regards the information about investigation efforts at the domestic level in the US made available by the Prosecution, the Chamber notes that the information does not show that criminal investigations or prosecutions have been conducted on the incidents referred to and relied upon by the Prosecution, also bearing in mind that national proceedings designed to result in non-judicial and administrative measures rather than criminal prosecutions do not result in inadmissibility under article 17. The Chamber, conclusively, finds that at this stage that the potential cases arising from the incidents presented by the Prosecution appear to be admissible.

Gravity

80. Article 17(1)(d) states that a case may be inadmissible if it 'is not of sufficient gravity to justify further action by the Court'. In proceedings under article 15, such an assessment is provisional in nature because it is conducted in abstract in a moment when investigations have not yet commenced. The Prosecution makes detailed submissions showing that all the crimes alleged in the Request in respect of various groups of perpetrators meet the threshold of sufficient gravity. * * *

84. With reference to the crimes allegedly committed by the Taliban and other anti-governmental armed groups, the Chamber specifically highlights the devastating and unfinished systemic consequences on the life of innocent people of the brutal violence inflicted upon civilians and other protected persons in Afghanistan for a prolonged period of time; the gruesome public display of violence aimed at instilling fear and inspiring subjugation in the population as well as the recurrent targeting of women, even very young, and vulnerable civilians.

85. In relation to the crimes allegedly committed by the Afghan National Security Forces, the US forces and CIA, the Chamber notes the gravity per se of the crime of torture, which is radically banned by international law, and the circumstance that the conducts have allegedly been committed by public officials in their functions.

86. Conclusively, the Chamber finds that the gravity threshold under article 17(1)(d) is met in respect of all the 'categories' of crimes for which the Prosecution requests authorisation to investigate.

Determinations By The Chamber On The Interests Of Justice

87. Having determined that both the jurisdiction and the admissibility requirements are satisfied, it remains for the Chamber to determine, in accordance with article 53(1)(c) of the Statute, whether, taking into account the gravity of the crime and the interests of victims, there are nonetheless substantial reasons to believe that an investigation would not serve the interests of justice. The Prosecution, consistently with the approach taken in previous cases, does not engage in detailed

submissions on the matter and simply states that it has not identified any reason which would make an investigation contrary to the interests of justice. As for the victims, 680 out of the 699 applications welcomed the prospect of an investigation aimed at bringing culprits to justice, preventing crime and establishing the truth. * * *

89. In the absence of a definition or other guidance in the statutory texts, the meaning of the interests of justice as a factor potentially precluding the exercise of the prosecutorial discretion must be found in the overarching objectives underlying the Statute: the effective prosecution of the most serious international crimes, the fight against impunity and the prevention of mass atrocities. All of these elements concur in suggesting that, at the very minimum, an investigation would only be in the interests of justice if prospectively it appears suitable to result in the effective investigation and subsequent prosecution of cases within a reasonable time frame.

90. The Chamber must therefore analyse whether, in light of the specific features of the situation in Afghanistan, it is likely, or at all possible, that authorising an investigation would result in favouring those objectives. An investigation can hardly be said to be in the interests of justice if the relevant circumstances are such as to make such investigation not feasible and inevitably doomed to failure. In making any investigation or prosecution only worth doing if and to the extent that it can be considered as genuinely instrumental to those objectives, the Statute reiterates the idea that the Court is not meant—or equipped—to address any and all scenarios where the most serious international crimes might have been committed; therefore, focusing on those scenarios where the prospects for successful and meaningful investigations are serious and substantive is key to its ultimate success.

91. The following factors appear to be particularly relevant: (i) the significant time elapsed between the alleged crimes and the Request; (ii) the scarce cooperation obtained by the Prosecutor throughout this time, even for the limited purposes of a preliminary examination, as such based on information rather than evidence; and (iii) the likelihood that both relevant evidence and potential relevant suspects might still be available and within reach of the Prosecution's investigative efforts and activities at this stage. * * *

93. First, most of the incidents referred to in the Request allegedly occurred between 2005 and 2015; most of them date back to the early part of that decade. During this period, by its own admission, the Prosecution was not in a position to meaningfully act for the purposes of preserving evidence, or for the protection of witnesses. The very availability of evidence for crimes dating back so long in time is also far from being likely. The Chamber notes that, during the eleven-year-long preliminary examination, no request was filed under article 57(3)(c) of the Statute and rule 47 of the Rules in order to preserve evidence.

94. Second, subsequent changes within the relevant political landscape both in Afghanistan and in key States (both parties and non-parties to the Statute), coupled with the complexity and volatility of the political climate still surrounding the Afghan scenario, make it extremely difficult to gauge the prospects of securing meaningful cooperation from relevant authorities for the future, whether in respect of investigations or of surrender of suspects; suffice it to say that nothing in the present conjuncture gives any reason to believe such cooperation can be taken for granted. Indeed, the Prosecution acknowledges the difficulties in securing albeit minimal cooperation from the relevant authorities as one of the reasons explaining the unusual duration of the preliminary examination. The Chamber has noted the Prosecution's submissions to the effect that even neutral, low-impact activities proved unfeasible. Accordingly, it seems reasonable to assume that these difficulties will prove even trickier in the context of an investigation proper.

95. Furthermore, the Chamber notes that, in light of the nature of the crimes and the context where they are alleged to have occurred, pursuing an investigation would inevitably require a significant amount of resources. In the foreseeable absence of additional resources for the coming years in the Court's budget, authorising the investigation would therefore result in the Prosecution having to reallocate its financial and human resources; in light of the limited amount of such resources, this will go to the detriment of other scenarios (be it preliminary examinations, investigations or cases) which appear to have more realistic prospects to lead to trials and thus effectively foster the interests of justice, possibly compromising their chances for success.

96. In summary, the Chamber believes that, notwithstanding the fact all the relevant requirements are met as regards both jurisdiction and admissibility, the current circumstances of the situation in Afghanistan are such as to make the prospects for a successful investigation and prosecution extremely limited. Accordingly, it is unlikely that pursuing an investigation would result in meeting the objectives listed by the victims favouring the investigation, or otherwise positively contributing to it. It is worth recalling that only victims of specific cases brought before the Court could ever have the opportunity of playing a meaningful role in as participants in the relevant proceedings; in the absence of any such cases, this meaningful role will never materialise in spite of the investigation having been authorised; victims' expectations will not go beyond little more than aspirations. This, far from honouring the victims' wishes and aspiration that justice be done, would result in creating frustration and possibly hostility vis-a-vis the Court and therefore negatively impact its very ability to pursue credibly the objectives it was created to serve.

For these reasons, the chamber hereby decides that an investigation into the situation in Afghanistan at this stage would not serve the interests of justice and, accordingly, rejects the request.

NOTES & QUESTIONS

1. The Interests of Justice

This is the first ICC opinion discussing "the interests of justice" prong of Article 53. Does Afghanistan present the type of situation that this provision was meant to address? Is that article even relevant to this inquiry? Compare the organs of the Court addressed in Articles 15 and 53. The Prosecutor can appeal or attempt to revisit this outcome. According to Article 15(d): "The refusal of the Pre-Trial Chamber to authorize the investigation shall not preclude the presentation of a subsequent request by the Prosecutor based on new facts or evidence regarding the same situation."

2. The Article 98 Agreement and SOFAs

How does the Court deal with the Article 98 agreement between the United States and Afghanistan? Are you convinced by the Court's approach? Does the fact that the United States and Afghanistan have also entered into a series of Status of Forces Agreements (SOFAs) impact the Court's jurisdiction at all? These agreements generally grant the United States exclusive jurisdiction over any armed forces deployed on Afghan territory. If so, does it matter whether the SOFA was executed before or after Afghanistan joined the Court? Is this an illustration of the old maxim *"nemo dat quod non habet"*—no one can give what they do not have? Upon entering into the SOFA with the United States, did Afghanistan relinquish its full jurisdiction over U.S. personnel or only its adjudicative and enforcement jurisdiction (leaving its prescriptive jurisdiction intact)—does this matter? Is the ICC's jurisdiction based upon an act of delegation by states or is there another basis grounded in international law, such as the fact that international crimes are subject to universal jurisdiction or perhaps some form of international jurisdiction, unmoored from any domestic jurisdictional competency? For a discussion, see Michael A. Newton, *How the International Criminal Court Threatens Treaty Norms*, 49 VAND. J. TRANSN'L L. 371 (2016); Rod Rastan, *The Jurisdictional Scope of Situations Before the International Criminal Court*, 23 CRIM. L. F. 1, 20 (2012).

3. Politicized Opinions?

One of the United States' core fears about the Court is that it would issue politicized opinions against the United States given the country's high profile role in international affairs and the controversial nature of some elements of its foreign policy. Commentators have argued that the PTC bowed to political pressure in refusing the Prosecutor's request to open an investigation. For example, Katherine Gallagher of the Center for Constitutional Rights—which submitted an Article 15 communication to the OTP on behalf of victims of the Afghanistan conflict, including two individuals still detained on Guantánamo—argued in an interview that the ruling is "dangerous" and "misguided":

> If what the Pre-Trial Chamber claims it wanted to do was bolster the credibility of the International Criminal Court and operate in the interests of justice, including the interests of victims, it went in the opposite direction. The only people who could be applauding this decision, frankly, are Donald Trump and John Bolton. * * *

> One can only conclude that this is the result of some serious political pressure by the United States, including not only on the court, but member states of the court. * * * It sends the message that bullying works. * * * [T]his says, "Obstruct, and you will be rewarded with impunity."

ICC Makes "Dangerous Decision" to Drop Probe into U.S. War Crimes in Afghanistan After U.S. Pressure, DEMOCRACY NOW! (April 17, 2019). Do you think the PTC succumbed to political pressure, or that the outcome is defensible on the merits, or both?

4. Withholding Cooperation

Recall that the American Servicemembers Protection Act (ASPA) prevents the United States from engaging in any cooperation with the Court except in the circumstances contained in the Dodd Amendment, i.e., in connection with a case against a foreign national accused of genocide, war crimes or crimes against humanity. How would the OTP investigate cases arising out of the Afghanistan situation without assistance from the United States? For its part, Afghanistan has indicated consistently that it would cooperate with the Court and that the imperative of justice must be balanced with efforts to promote stability. *See* Statement by H.E. Ambassador Mahmoud Saikal, Statements at the 16th Session of Assembly of States Parties to the Rome Statute of the ICC (Dec. 8, 2017).

PROBLEMS

1. Myanmar/Burma

Rakhine State is one of the poorest regions in Myanmar/Burma and has been subjected to years of neglect. (See the Appendix for a map of Myanmar/Burma.) Although Rohingya and ethnic Rakhine communities (themselves an oppressed group) have enjoyed periods of harmony, the country's history has been punctuated by inter-communal violence dating back to the independence era. According to many observers, the national and local governments have cultivated these hostilities, in part to deflect criticism from their neglect of the region and in part to consolidate their political power. In any case, the authorities have consistently failed to intervene to prevent further such sectarian violence or punish the perpetrators.

For many decades, the Rohingya minority has been subjected to discrimination, violations of their fundamental human rights, and acts of persecution, including strict and discriminatory restrictions on their freedom of movement (with implications for their ability to pursue their livelihoods and gain access to education, water, food, and sanitation), the free exercise of their religion, equal access to healthcare and education, and rights to marry and bear children. The latter include formal and informal restrictions on marriages and on the number of children a family may have. To be sure, these latter legal strictures are arbitrarily and inconsistently enforced and can often be circumvented through the payment of bribes to officials; nonetheless, they exist on the books, they were inspired by spurious concerns about over-population among the Rohingya, and they are disproportionately invoked against the Rohingya. A U.N. Fact Finding Mission (FFM) noted that the Rohingya are "portrayed as an existential threat that might 'swallow other races' with their 'incontrollable birth rates.' " Human Rights Council, Report of the Independent International Fact-Finding Mission on Myanmar, ¶ 25, U.N. Doc. A/HRC/39/64 (Aug. 24, 2018).

The Rohingya have experienced several rounds of ethnic cleansing in the past. The process of repatriating and resettling large groups of refugees has helped to lay the groundwork for demonstrably false accounts that the Rohingya are illegal migrants or "Bengalis" who hail from Bangladesh. These often-forcible repatriations have also facilitated the Rohingya's civic expungement. For example, largescale violence in 1978 spurred tens of thousands of Rohingya to flee Myanmar. When they returned, they had been stripped of many of their citizenship rights, or deleted from family household lists. The 1982 Citizenship Law (which does not acknowledge the Rohingya as an officially-recognized ethnic minority) and a program of "citizen verification" followed, whereby most Rohingya were denied Myanmar citizenship, disenfranchised, and effectively rendered stateless.

Against this backdrop of protracted and institutionalized discrimination, the Rohingya have increasingly been subjected to acts of physical intimidation and violence. Human rights groups have documented the cyclical and escalating commission of a full range of abuses, including extrajudicial killing, arbitrary detention, torture, disappearances, sexual violence, and forcible displacement and deportation. This conduct intensified in 2012 when clashes broke out between ethnic Rakhine and Rohingya civilians, ostensibly in response to the alleged rape of a young Rakhine woman. Although the government attempted to portray these pogroms as stemming from spontaneous sectarianism, there is evidence that the violence was at least partially state-sanctioned. Security forces reportedly helped to coordinate assaults and, with armed Rakhine civilians, jointly attacked Rohingya villages and civilians. In other places, the military and police promised to protect the Rohingya but then vanished when violence broke out or simply stood by while the carnage unfolded around them.

The government's involvement in these events has been justified under the guise of counter-terrorism. As the standard narrative recounts, the Arakan Rohingya Salvation Army (ARSA, formerly known as Harakah al-Yaqin) emerged in 2016. The group allegedly claimed responsibility for several attacks against police stations and border crossings in Rakhine State. The current crisis followed ARSA's most recent attack, which occurred on or about August 25, 2017, against several government outposts. In response to these events, the government ordered the military to conduct "clearance operations," ostensibly aimed at apprehending Rohingya militants. In reality, these operations resulted in the commission of further mass atrocities against civilians on an even more virulent scale. It should be noted that some accounts posit that the ARSA attack of August 2017 served as a mere pretext to escalate violence by a government that had a well-planned campaign teed up and was waiting for the right moment to unleash it. At a minimum, as the FFM found, "the 'Rohingya crisis', has been used by the military to reaffirm itself as the protector of a nation under threat, and further cement its political role." *Id.* at ¶ 14. In addition, some observers question whether ARSA offers a credible threat to the government or has any genuine indigenous support among the Rohingya.

The bloodshed starting in 2017 was of a different order of magnitude in terms of the obvious degree of advanced preparation and the ferocity of the violence. The evidence that these operations were preplanned and premeditated is compelling. For example, "[p]rotective fences around Rohingya houses were removed [and] knives and other sharp implements were confiscated," apparently to eliminate obstacles to the anticipated attacks and means of self-defense. *Id.* at ¶ 45. Witnesses also reported a buildup of governmental weaponry in advance of the August 2017 attacks. In any case, it is clear that authorities responded to ARSA's actions with disproportionate force, working with police and local civilians to unleash a ruthless campaign. These operations involved opening fire on civilians as well as conducting house-by-house raids and arson attacks that left men, women, and children dead, burned, or maimed. In some cases, military members reportedly came through first followed by Rakhine civilians with more rudimentary weapons.

In addition to this interpersonal violence, government-led operations resulted in massive internal displacements, forcible population transfers (some effectuated under the pretext of "protecting" people from violence), waves of refugee flows into Bangladesh, and the confinement of many Rohingya in wretched and effectively permanent internment camps or "ghettos" in Rakhine state. The FFM described this latter phenomenon as amounting to an "arbitrary deprivation of liberty." *Id.* at ¶ 29. Amnesty International described it as "apartheid." Amnesty International, "CAGED WITHOUT A ROOF": APARTHEID IN MYANMAR'S RAKHINE STATE. The armed and security forces, working with and through local actors, have razed entire villages, making it effectively impossible for Rohingya to return to their homes or to remain in Rakhine State. That arsonists specifically targeted Rohingya homes for destruction—while ethnic Rakhine structures were left untouched—has also been confirmed by satellite imagery. Such destruction occurred even after Myanmar claimed that "clearance operations" had been halted as well as in the immediate aftermath of Myanmar ratifying a refugee repatriation agreement with Bangladesh.

All told, over a million Rohingya have been forced out of, or have fled, Myanmar and are in refugee encampments, such as Cox's Bazar, in Bangladesh and elsewhere under circumstances in which it is clear that the intent is to expunge them permanently from Myanmar. This marked the fastest refugee outflow since the Rwandan genocide. *See* UN Office for the Coordination of Humanitarian Affairs (OCHA), *Rohingya Refugee Crisis*. To be sure, in 2012 and thereafter, thousands of Rohingya took flight without being forcibly deported *per se*. But, these people have seen massacres before and so when violence resumed in 2017, they fled for their lives *en masse*. The Myanmar government has begun to discuss repatriation, but the precise modalities of this process remain problematic given the degree of destruction in Rohingya neighborhoods in Rakhine State and the unwillingness of the

Rohingya to return without guarantees of citizenship rights. As a result, the process remains stalled.

Myanmar has not ratified the ICC Statute, but neighboring Bangladesh has. Does the ICC have jurisdiction over any of this violence? How would you make the jurisdictional case if you were the Prosecutor seeking to open an investigation *proprio motu*? Take a look at Articles 5–8 of the ICC Statute. What crimes would you charge? Reconsider these facts in particular when you review the chapter on genocide.

2. United States-Mexico Border*

On April 6, 2018, the Trump Administration directed federal prosecutors along the southwest border of the United States to implement a "Zero Tolerance Policy." Under the Zero Tolerance Policy, all improper entry offences into the United States from Mexico are to be referred for criminal prosecution.

In May 2018, the Department of Homeland Security determined that the Zero Tolerance Policy would apply to alien adults arriving illegally into the United States with minor children. As explained by the Department of Homeland Security's Office of Inspector General, "[b]ecause minor children cannot be held in criminal custody with an adult, alien adults who entered the United States illegally would have to be separated from any accompanying minor children when the adults were referred for criminal prosecution."** As a result, over 2,000 children who accompanied their parents to the U.S. border were separated from their parents. As further noted by the Inspector General, "a lack of a fully integrated Federal immigration information technology system made it difficult for DHS to reliably track separated parents and children." The Inspector General found that children who are too young to talk, referred to as "pre-verbal children," at the time of separation from their parents were not provided with "wrist bracelets or other means of identification, nor does the Border Patrol fingerprint or photograph most children during processing to ensure that they can be easily linked with the proper file."

Many of the families who have presented themselves at the U.S.-Mexico border claim that they have a well-founded fear of persecution if they are returned to their home country, and have come to the United States for the purpose of applying for asylum. Parents who have their children removed are either 1) placed in detention pending criminal prosecution; 2) placed in removal proceedings; or 3) summarily removed from the country by returning them to their home country, which is often El Salvador, Guatemala, or Honduras.

Does the ICC have jurisdiction over some or all of the acts committed by U.S. officials on the US-Mexico border? If you were the ICC Prosecutor how would you argue that the Pre Trial Chamber should give you authority to

---

* Note that we have slightly adjusted the facts as we understand them concerning events at the US-Mexico border in order to more clearly raise the issue of potential ICC involvement.

** Office of the Inspector General, Department of Homeland Security, Special Review—Initial Observations Regarding Family Separation Issues Under the Zero Tolerance Policy, OIG-18-84 (September 27, 2018).

open a *proprio motu* investigation into the border situation? Mexico ratified the ICC Statute in 2005 (becoming the 100th country to do so).

PART III

SUBSTANTIVE INTERNATIONAL CRIMINAL LAW

INTRODUCTION

Part III of this text corresponds to what many national penal codes call the "Special Part." It presents a discussion of the core international crimes: war crimes, crimes against the peace or aggression, crimes against humanity, and genocide. We also include torture and terrorism as stand-alone crimes because they are closely related to the core crimes and are the subject of active prosecution by states under extraterritorial forms of jurisdiction. In addition, torture constitutes a war crime and a crime against humanity, as do some acts of terrorism. This part thus focuses on crimes within the jurisdiction of the International Criminal Court (ICC) and other international, or quasi-international, tribunals. Excluded are other transnational crimes—such as money laundering, trafficking in people and narcotics, and international arms dealing—on the theory that such crimes are primarily (but not exclusively) defined by domestic law and prosecuted before domestic tribunals. Some of these transnational crimes were originally slated to be within the subject matter jurisdiction of the ICC. Indeed, Trinidad and Tobago first proposed re-opening discussions on a permanent international criminal court after years of Cold War quiescence because they wanted an international forum to prosecute transnational drug crimes. As negotiations for the ICC progressed, however, the focus moved from prosecuting these crimes to the core "atrocity" crimes.

The international crimes of genocide, torture, war crimes, and a host of terrorism crimes were made the subject of multilateral treaties. Although some of these treaties envision international enforcement mechanisms, most also assume that member states will incorporate the definitions of international crimes into their domestic penal codes. The treaty definitions of these crimes do not, however, always reflect the clarity that one would expect from a penal provision that must provide potential perpetrators with fair notice of prescribed conduct. Indeed, many definitions of international crimes, such as genocide, appear to have been drafted more as retrospective condemnations of past abuses rather than as comprehensive criminal codes for prospective enforcement. Other definitions of international crimes fail to clearly delineate the *actus reus* or *mens rea* of the crime—the key elements of domestic crimes. As one commentator has observed: "By and large, specialists in public international law have labored in acoustic isolation from their brethren working the vein of municipal criminal law." Mirjan Damaška, *The Shadow Side of Command Responsibility*, 49 AM. J. COMP. L. 455, 495 (2001).

By contrast, the international community has not drafted a standalone treaty dedicated to either crimes against humanity or aggression, although both crimes were central to post-World War II criminal proceedings and now can be prosecuted by the International Criminal Court. The International Law Commission is drafting a treaty on crimes against humanity (an initiative stimulated by Professor Leila Sadat, who is the Special Adviser on Crimes Against Humanity to the ICC OTP) that melds elements from the classic international criminal law treaties but also mutual legal assistance provisions drawn from transnational crimes treaties.

As you will see in the materials that follow, in the early days, international and domestic tribunals struggled to apply international criminal law definitions in the context of actual prosecutions. Courts today are demonstrating a greater facility for adjudicating highly technical aspects of this body of law. Indeed, since the last version of this textbook was published, it has become clear that the rate of innovation in substantive international criminal law (ICL) is slowing considerably. Like many incipient areas of law, the progress of ICL development since its renaissance in the 1990s proceeded in great leaps, with early cases addressing vast open areas of legal doctrine. In this process, the judges on the international criminal tribunals engaged in a full-scale—if unacknowledged—refashioning of ICL through their jurisprudence by updating and expanding historical treaties, even at the expense of fealty to negotiated compromises; by more precisely identifying the elements of international crimes, forms of responsibility, defenses, and other penal doctrines; and by adding content to customary international law concepts and vaguely-worded treaty provisions. Today's decisions, by contrast, are increasingly applying established law to novel facts. ICL has thus begun to exhibit features of a more mature body of law with modern innovations happening primarily at the outer edges of doctrine. In his seminal text, LAW'S EMPIRE (1986), the legal philosopher Ronald Dworkin has employed a tree metaphor to describe this process, whereby jurisprudence of the likes of *Prosecutor v. Tadic* and *Prosecutor v. Akayesu* (both excerpted herein) provided the trunk for modern ICL, whereas decisions in the more recent cases, perched on ever narrower branches, are making increasingly nuanced refinements to established doctrine. As in the domestic historical narrative—by which account legislative primacy eventually supplanted the common law crime—international crimes are increasingly finding expression in more positivistic sources of law, thus obviating the need for, and diminishing the discretion of, international judges to make law in the face of gaps or deficiencies. As a result, there has been less and less space for judges to build upon the ICL edifice, and the defense of *nullum crimen sine lege* ("no crime without law")—once ubiquitous in the early cases—has retreated in significance.

At this point, it may be useful to review some basic criminal law theory and terminology. A crime is defined in terms of its elements. Elements are thus the building blocks of a crime. The American Law Institute's Model Penal Code (MPC) defines "element of an offense" and "material element of an offense" as follows at § 1.13(9) and (10):

> (i) such conduct or (ii) such attendant circumstances or (iii) such a result of conduct as
>
> (a) is included in the description of the forbidden conduct in the definition of the offense; or
>
> (b) establishes the required kind of culpability; or
>
> (c) negatives an excuse or justification for such conduct; or
>
> (d) negatives a defense under the statute of limitations; or
>
> (e) establishes jurisdiction or venue;
>
> "Material element of an offense" means an element that does not relate exclusively to the statute of limitations, jurisdiction, venue, or to any other matter similarly unconnected with (i) the harm or evil, incident to conduct, sought to be prevented by the law defining the offense, or (ii) the existence of a justification or excuse for such conduct.

Elements may be thus addressed to physical conduct, a mental state, an attendant circumstance or context in which the crime occurred, or a result. Except in the rare circumstance of strict liability crimes (which do not require any mental state), a person is guilty of a criminal offense only where she performs a voluntary act (the *actus reus*) that causes harm with the appropriate mental state (the *mens rea*) under the appropriate conditions (circumstantial elements or attendant circumstances). In order to secure a conviction—and overcome the presumption of innocence—a prosecutor must present evidence that proves the existence of each element of the crime charged beyond a reasonable doubt.

The *actus reus* element ensures that involuntary movements and criminal thoughts alone are not punished: "A crime is committed only if the evil thinker becomes an evil doer." Charles E. Torcia, WHARTON'S CRIMINAL LAW § 25 (1978). Most crimes are defined in terms of prohibited conduct; in some cases, however, individuals may also be punished for omissions—the failure to act when there is a duty to act. Superior Responsibility, the subject of Chapter 14 in the next part, is a doctrine of omission. The inchoate crimes allow for punishment before the actor has committed any harm to individual or public interests. Conspiracy and incitement to commit genocide are two salient inchoate crimes within international criminal law. Some crimes are defined in terms of prescribed results. For example, the crime of murder requires a particular result: the death of the victim. Such result crimes (in contrast to purely conduct crimes) contain an implicit causation element encompassing notions of "but for" and proximate or legal causation. *See, e.g.*, § 2.03(1) of the Model Penal Code (MPC). Crimes may also be defined with reference to potential defenses. For example, murder in some jurisdictions is found where a defendant intentionally kills another without justification.

The requirement of *mens rea* is reflected in the old adage *actus non facit reum nisi mens sit rea* ("an act does not make one guilty unless the mind is guilty"). *Mens rea* translates literally to mean a "guilty mind." In modern parlance, the *mens rea* element of a crime still embodies a notion of moral blameworthiness, but relates more technically to the particular mental state provided by the definition of the offense. The U.S. Supreme Court has ruled that a *mens rea* requirement in criminal law is "universal and persistent in mature systems of law." *Morissette v. United States*, 342 U.S. 246, 250 (1952). Many common law offenses failed to state any *mens rea* element. It was only where they did that they were called "specific intent crimes." Today, a specific-intent crime is considered one in which the definition of the crime includes an intent to do some further act or achieve some further or more remote consequence beyond the conduct that constitutes the *actus reus* of the crime. Thus, common-law burglary, for example, requires a showing that the defendant engaged in a breaking and entry of the dwelling of another with the intent to commit a felony therein. Such crimes often involve two *mens rea* elements: general intent (associated with the conduct in question) and specific intent (*dolus specialis*). Genocide is a specific intent crime within international criminal law—it requires a showing of intentional harm to members of a protected group with the intent to destroy that group in whole or in part.

The standardization of mental states was a key feature of the MPC. Common law crimes display a colorful array of potential mental states, including such descriptors as: willfully, deliberately, with a depraved heart, maliciously, wantonly, with design, with intent, with knowledge. A comparable variety of forms appear in international criminal law. The MPC, which can provide a useful template for drafting penal definitions, consolidated this variety into four standard culpable mental states as follows:

§ 2.02. General Requirements of Culpability

(1) *Minimum Requirements of Culpability*. Except as provided in Section 2.05 [delineating a narrow category of strict liability crimes], a person is not guilty of an offense unless he acted purposely, knowingly, recklessly or negligently, as the law may require, with respect to each material element of the offense.

(2) *Kinds of Culpability Defined*.

(a) *Purposely*. A person acts purposely with respect to a material element of an offense when:

(i) if the element involves the nature of his conduct or a result thereof, it is his conscious object to engage in conduct of that nature or to cause such a result; and

(ii) if the element involves the attendant circumstances, he is aware of the existence of such circumstances or he believes or hopes that they exist.

(b) *Knowingly*. A person acts knowingly with respect to a material element of an offense when:

(i) if the element involves the nature of his conduct or the attendant circumstances, he is aware that his conduct is of that nature or that such circumstances exist; and

(ii) if the element involves a result of his conduct, he is aware that it is practically certain that his conduct will cause such a result.

(c) *Recklessly*. A person acts recklessly with respect to a material element of an offense when he consciously disregards a substantial and unjustifiable risk that the material element exists or will result from his conduct. The risk must be of such a nature and degree that, considering the nature and purpose of the actor's conduct and the circumstances known to him, its disregard involves a gross deviation from the standard of conduct that a law-abiding person would observe in the actor's situation.

(d) *Negligently*. A person acts negligently with respect to a material element of an offense when he should be aware of a substantial and unjustifiable risk that the material element exists or will result from his conduct. The risk must be of such a nature and degree that the actor's failure to perceive it, considering the nature and purpose of his conduct and the circumstances known to him, involves a gross deviation from the standard of care that a reasonable person would observe in the actor's situation. * * *

> (7) *Requirement of Knowledge Satisfied by Knowledge of High Probability.* When knowledge of the existence of a particular fact is an element of an offense, such knowledge is established if a person is aware of a high probability of its existence, unless he actually believes that it does not exist. * * *
>
> (9) *Culpability as to Illegality of Conduct.* Neither knowledge nor recklessness or negligence as to whether conduct constitutes an offense or as to the existence, meaning or application of the law determining the elements of an offense is an element of such offense, unless the definition of the offense or the Code so provides.

Under the MPC schema, each physical element of a crime (conduct, attendant circumstance, or result) can be associated with a different mental state (and the mental states are defined somewhat differently for each type of element). The MPC accordingly provides a series of interpretive rules that govern where the definitions of crimes are ambiguous or incomplete vis-à-vis the required mental state.

> (3) *Culpability Required Unless Otherwise Provided.* When the culpability sufficient to establish a material element of an offense is not prescribed by law, such element is established if a person acts purposely, knowingly or recklessly with respect thereto.
>
> (4) *Prescribed Culpability Requirement Applies to All Material Elements.* When the law defining an offense prescribes the kind of culpability that is sufficient for the commission of an offense, without distinguishing among the material elements thereof, such provision shall apply to all the material elements of the offense, unless a contrary purpose plainly appears.
>
> (5) *Substitutes for Negligence, Recklessness and Knowledge.* When the law provides that negligence suffices to establish an element of an offense, such element also is established if a person acts purposely, knowingly or recklessly. When recklessness suffices to establish an element, such element also is established if a person acts purposely or knowingly. When acting knowingly suffices to establish an element, such element also is established if a person acts purposely. * * *
>
> (8) *Requirement of Wilfulness Satisfied by Acting Knowingly.* A requirement that an offense be committed wilfully is satisfied if a person acts knowingly with respect to the material elements of the offense, unless a purpose to impose further requirements appears. * * *
>
> (10) *Culpability as Determinant of Grade of Offense.* When the grade or degree of an offense depends on whether the offense is committed purposely, knowingly, recklessly or negligently, its grade or degree shall be the lowest for which the determinative

kind of culpability is established with respect to any material element of the offense.

In point (4) above, the MPC provides a default rule of statutory interpretation with respect to *mens rea*: if a single *mens rea* term is provided, it should be interpreted to modify each of the other elements of the offense absent a plainly contrary purpose. In addition, note that the MPC dispenses with the notion of specific intent completely, although such crimes map nicely onto the purpose mental state.

Compare the MPC's formulation of *mens rea* standards with that of the ICC Statute, at Article 30:

> Article 30: Mental Element
>
> 1. Unless otherwise provided, a person shall be criminally responsible and liable for punishment for a crime within the jurisdiction of the Court only if the material elements are committed with intent and knowledge.
>
> 2. For the purposes of this article, a person has intent where:
>
>   (a) In relation to conduct, that person means to engage in the conduct;
>
>   (b) In relation to a consequence, that person means to cause that consequence or is aware that it will occur in the ordinary course of events.
>
> 3. For the purposes of this article, "knowledge" means awareness that a circumstance exists or a consequence will occur in the ordinary course of events. "Know" and "knowingly" shall be construed accordingly.

Attendant circumstances are those situational elements that concern facts unrelated to the defendant's conduct or mental state that must exist in order to establish the commission of a crime. For example, the crime of statutory rape requires that one participant in a sexual act be under the age of consent. In this way, the involvement of a minor is an attendant circumstance of the crime. In international crimes, the attendant circumstances elements usually appear in the *chapeau* ("hat") of the statutory provision—that portion of the definition that applies to all component acts constituting the criminal conduct. Attendant circumstances include the existence of an armed conflict (for war crimes) or a widespread or systematic attack (for crimes against humanity).

The ICC Statute contains a consensus definition for most international crimes, although these diverge from customary international law at times. The definition of genocide directly mirrors the operative treaty definition. Other definitions (such as crimes against humanity, some war crimes, and aggression) were the subject of intense debate among state delegates and other participants in the negotiations surrounding the treaty that formed the ICC. Indeed, the definition of aggression initially eluded consensus during the Rome Conference, as will be discussed in greater detail in Chapter 8, *infra*. In 2010, a consensus definition was promulgated, which was finally activated in 2017.

Prior to the finalization of the ICC Statute in Rome, the U.S. delegation proposed that more precise "Elements of Crimes" be subsequently drafted to govern the work of the Court. Ultimately, Article 9 contemplated such elements. Although the Elements of Crimes are not binding on the Court, they are to "assist the Court in the interpretation and application of" the ICC Statute's Special Part. Article 10 of the ICC Statute states that "nothing in this Part shall be interpreted as limiting or prejudicing in any way existing or developing rules of international law for purposes other than this Statute." This implies that international crimes exist in customary international law as well as in treaty law and that the terms of the ICC Statute should not affect the definition or evolution of international crimes under customary international law. As you review the cases in the chapters that follow, consider to what extent the ICC Statute and its Elements of Crimes reflect, and diverge from, the international criminal law jurisprudence emanating from other judicial bodies. Also, consider how realistic the Article 10 command is as a practical matter.

NOTES & QUESTIONS

1. The Model Penal Code

This text will occasionally refer to the provisions of the MPC in an effort to illustrate criminal law principles and encourage a comparison between domestic and international criminal law. The MPC is an effort of the American Law Institute (ALI) to modernize, standardize and—in some cases—reform the penal law in the United States on the basis of "contemporary reasoned judgment." The ALI is a non-governmental organization of judges, lawyers, and law professors in the United States that has drafted a series of "Restatements" on particular areas of law based upon a survey of governing rules. When the time came to consider the criminal law, the ALI opted for a model code because it determined that the criminal law was too fragmented to merit a Restatement. Pursuant to § 1.02, the Code's purposes are: (a) to forbid and prevent conduct that unjustifiably and inexcusably inflicts or threatens substantial harm to individual or public interests; (b) to subject to public control persons whose conduct indicates that they are disposed to commit crimes; (c) to safeguard conduct that is without fault from condemnation as criminal; (d) to give fair warning of the nature of the conduct declared to constitute an offense; and (e) to differentiate on reasonable grounds between serious and minor offenses. *See* Markus Dirk Dubber, AN INTRODUCTION TO THE MODEL PENAL CODE, § 3 (2015). The ALI adopted the MPC in 1962. It released official commentaries in the 1980s and most recently revisited the Code's sentencing and sexual assault provisions. The MPC structure mirrors that of a civil law code, containing a "General Part" that presents a set of general penal principles applicable to each of the specific offenses contained in the "Special Part" of the Code. The MPC thus covers general principles of liability, defenses, and justifications; the definitions of specific crimes; and principles of sanction and punishment.

The MPC is addressed primarily to the state legislatures, because most penal law in the United States is a function of state, rather than federal, law. Federal penal authority is limited to the prohibition and punishment of crimes that touch on uniquely federal interests. More than half of the states in the United States have amended their criminal codes to reflect aspects of the MPC; other states, such as New Jersey and Pennsylvania, have adopted the major provisions "to a substantial degree" according to the ALI. By contrast, the U.S. federal penal code has been impervious to the MPC's influence. As a point of trivia, the director of ALI and the MPC's chief reporter, Herbert Wechsler, also served as assistant attorney general for the United States in charge of the war division from 1944–1946. In that capacity, he helped develop the legal framework for the Nazi postwar trials and served as chief technical advisor to the U.S. judges sitting at Nuremberg. *See* Herbert Wechsler, *The Challenge of a Model Penal Code*, 65 HARV. L. REV. 1097 (1952); Herbert Weschler, *Codification of Criminal Law in the United States: The Model Penal Code*, 68 COLUM. L. REV. 1425 (1968).

2. The *Mens Rea* of International Crimes

Many international crimes are defined in terms of conduct performed "wilfully." For example, Article 8(1)(a) of the Rome Statute establishing the International Criminal Court provides for jurisdiction over the following grave breaches of the 1949 Geneva Conventions:

> (i) Wilful killing; * * *
>
> (iii) Wilfully causing great suffering, or serious injury to body or health; * * *
>
> (vi) Wilfully depriving a prisoner of war or other protected person of the rights of fair and regular trial;

Article 8(2)(b) also lists the following additional war crimes:

> (i) Intentionally directing attacks against the civilian population as such or against individual civilians not taking direct part in hostilities;
>
> (ii) Intentionally directing attacks against civilian objects, that is, objects which are not military objectives;
>
> (iii) Intentionally directing attacks against personnel, installations, material, units or vehicles involved in a humanitarian assistance or peacekeeping mission in accordance with the Charter of the United Nations, as long as they are entitled to the protection given to civilians or civilian objects under the international law of armed conflict;
>
> (iv) Intentionally launching an attack in the knowledge that such attack will cause incidental loss of life or injury to civilians or damage to civilian objects or widespread, long-term and severe damage to the natural environment which would be clearly excessive in relation to the concrete and direct overall military advantage anticipated; * * *

Compare these mental states with those elucidated in the MPC. Which mental state does "wilfully" implicate? How would a jurisdiction that has adopted the MPC resolve this question? How should the ICC? Consider the elements of Article 8(2)(a)(i), wilful killing, as contained in the Elements of Crimes:

1) The perpetrator killed one or more persons.
2) Such person or persons were protected under one or more of the Geneva Conventions of 1949.
3) The perpetrator was aware of the factual circumstances that established that protected status.
4) The conduct took place in the context of and was associated with an international armed conflict.
5) The perpetrator was aware of factual circumstances that established the existence of an armed conflict.

Does Article 30 of the ICC Statute assist with the resolution of the *mens rea* question set forth above? On the *mens rea* of international crimes generally, *see* Roger S. Clark, *The Mental Element in International Criminal Law: The Rome Statute of the International Criminal Court and the Elements of Offences*, 123 CRIM. L. FOR. 291 (2001); William A. Schabas, Mens Rea *and the International Criminal Tribunal for the Former Yugoslavia (ICTY)*, 37 NEW ENG. L. REV. 1015 (2002–3); Gerhard Werle, *Individual Criminal Responsibility in Article 25 ICC Statute*, 5 J. INT'L CRIM. JUST. 953 (2007); Johan Van der Vyver, *The International Criminal Court and the Concept of* Mens Rea *in International Criminal Law*, UNIV. MIAMI INT'L & COMP. L. REV. 57 (2004).

3. Knowingly

Sometimes knowledge of a material fact or attendant circumstance is a required element of an offense. An individual has knowledge if she is aware of the fact or believes it exists. Some jurisdictions may also permit a finding of knowledge for "willful blindness": when a person is aware of a high probability of the existence of a fact in question and deliberately fails to investigate in order to avoid confirmation of the fact. Cases have also found that a person has knowledge of a given fact when he has the means to obtain such knowledge, or when he has notice of other facts that would put him on inquiry as to the existence of that fact, or where he has information sufficient to generate a reasonable belief as to that fact, or when the circumstances are such that a reasonable person would believe that such a fact existed. Is a person who avoids taking steps to dispel or confirm suspicions as culpable as one who is actually aware of a fact? As you review the materials that follow, consider what formulation of "knowledge" is operative in international criminal law. The "knowledge" mental state is particularly important for the doctrine of superior responsibility, as you will see in Chapter 14.

4. Recklessness and Negligence

Does the MPC adequately distinguish between culpable negligence and recklessness? In most penal systems, criminal liability ends at recklessness, with some exceptions for negligence crimes such as criminal mischief or negligent homicide. A person behaves negligently when she deviates from the standard of care that a reasonable person would have observed in the actor's position. (Although negligence is defined as a *mens rea* state, it is in some respects the absence of a mental state given that the actor is unaware of the risk of harm). Should negligent behavior be criminally punished given that the individual has not purposefully behaved wrongly? Can negligent behavior be deterred where the negligent actor fails to accurately perceive the risks of her conduct? Is negligence truly a mental state where the perpetrator is by definition unaware of a risk? For culpable negligence, the prosecutor must ordinarily show gross negligence, i.e., more than the mere deviation of the standard of care that would constitute civil negligence. Why would the drafters of the ICC dispense with any notion of negligence or recklessness? *See* Jerome Hall, *Negligent Behavior Should be Excluded from Penal Liability*, 63 COLUM. L. REV. 632 (1963). Are there any international crimes that incorporate a negligence *mens rea*?

5. Motive

Motive is defined as the ulterior intention—the reason by which an intended act is committed. It is axiomatic that motive plays little part in the definitions of crimes or in the substantive criminal law. Thus, someone who intentionally kills another as an act of euthanasia still commits a punishable murder. Motive may, however, render an act non-criminal, for example where an individual kills another in self-defense. Motive takes on greater importance in issues of criminal procedure: it may influence prosecutorial discretion, jury nullification, and sentencing. Despite this doctrine, courts often confuse issues of intent and motive, especially with respect to specific intent crimes. Keep this in mind as you review the materials that follow. In addition, identify which international crimes—if any—contain a motive element.

6. Inchoate Crimes

Inchoate crimes are offenses that are punished before a criminal act has actually been committed but after the intent to commit the act has been formed. Many domestic laws recognize three distinct categories of inchoate crimes—the crimes of attempt, conspiracy, and incitement/ solicitation. At times, possession is also considered an inchoate crime. Criminal law developed the notion of an inchoate crime because of the need for law enforcement to be able to prevent crimes before they occur. Inchoate crimes in international criminal law will be taken up in the part of this text on Individual Criminal Responsibility.

CHAPTER 6

THE LEGAL REGULATION OF ARMED CONFLICT

I. INTRODUCTION

The next three chapters address the legal regulation of war and its effects. The law governing armed conflicts has historically been bifurcated between the *jus ad bellum* and the *jus in bello*. The former addresses the legality of going to war and historically took the form of theological, and then secular, "just war" theories; the latter concedes the *de facto* existence of war and seeks to regulate belligerent conduct within it. By the late nineteenth century, the right to wage war began to be viewed as an inherent attribute of state sovereignty. Diplomats, international lawyers, and scholars largely abandoned the effort to establish standards for determining when states had the right to go to war and turned their attention to developing the *jus in bello* to mitigate the effects of war.

In the immediate post-World War I period, however, the *jus ad bellum* experienced a resurgence in the form of efforts to establish the League of Nations—which was to be a forum to settle international disputes through peaceful means—and the promulgation of the 1928 Kellogg-Briand Pact, which sought to outlaw aggressive war. Although the League had some successes, neither of these efforts prevented World War II. That global conflict gave rise to the term "crimes against the peace"—one of the criminal charges leveled at German and Japanese defendants before the Nuremberg and Tokyo tribunals. The prevention of yet another world war was a primary aim of the United Nations, whose Charter is devoted to the collective response to threats to the peace, the repression of acts of aggression, and the peaceful resolution of disputes. Article 2(4) specifically prohibits threats or uses of force against the territorial integrity or political independence of any state.

The Charter, which is binding on U.N. member states, does not mention *crimes* against the peace, however. After its brief appearance in the Nuremberg and Tokyo Charters, the crime of launching a war of aggression all but disappeared from the pantheon of international criminal law (ICL) until the revival of the project to create a permanent International Criminal Court (ICC) and the resurrection of the crime of aggression. With the codification of a crime of aggression in amendments to the ICC Statute, the *jus ad bellum* and *jus in bello* have been reunited, although the full scope of the crime of aggression—the modern lexicon for crimes against the peace—has yet to be determined. The classical and modern crime of aggression—as part of the *jus ad bellum*—is the subject of Chapter 8. This chapter is devoted to the interface between international humanitarian law and international criminal law and determining the existence of an armed conflict—the predicate for a war crimes charge. Chapter 7 covers the penal aspects of the *jus in bello*.

II. THE INTERFACE OF INTERNATIONAL HUMANITARIAN LAW & INTERNATIONAL CRIMINAL LAW

International humanitarian law (IHL), also called "the law of armed conflict," describes those international rules governing the conduct of hostilities and punishable acts therein—in other words, the *jus in bello*. As long as groups of people, and later states, have waged war, there have been rules in place defining acceptable behavior in armed conflict. Indeed, "[t]he end of a great war frequently brings a revision of the laws of war in its wake." Allison Marston Danner, *When Courts Make Law: How the International Criminal Tribunals Recast the Laws of War,* 59 VAND. L. REV. 1, 1 (2006). Many of these rules are now contained in a web of bilateral and multilateral treaties, making international humanitarian law the most codified area of international criminal law. Indeed, the fundamental principles of IHL are now universally accepted by the states of the world, and the Geneva Conventions of 1949 are the first international treaties to achieve universal ratification. A rich body of customary international law has also developed to supplement this extensive treaty regime. The International Committee of the Red Cross (ICRC) has conducted a massive study of the customary international law applicable in times of armed conflict. Relevant treaties, state practice, jurisprudence, domestic and international law rules, and military manuals have all been compiled in a Customary International Humanitarian Law Database on the ICRC's website. *See also* Jean-Marie Henckaerts & Louise Doswald-Beck, CUSTOMARY INTERNATIONAL HUMANITARIAN LAW (2005). This legacy belies the claim by Cicero that *silent enim leges inter arma*—the laws are silent among those at war—although the enforcement of these rules remains sporadic.

The material that follows addresses first principles within the *jus in bello*, starting with the definition of armed conflict and what level of violence triggers the application of IHL. Next is the question of when an armed conflict is classified as international versus non-international and the implications of that distinction. The final section considers the nexus required to charge violent acts committed during an armed conflict as war crimes (as opposed to other international crimes or even ordinary domestic crimes).

A. WHEN DOES INTERNATIONAL HUMANITARIAN LAW APPLY: THE DEFINITION OF ARMED CONFLICT

International humanitarian law only applies in the context of an armed conflict (or in a situation of occupation). It is thus important as a preliminary matter to distinguish between those situations that qualify as armed conflicts, and thus trigger the *jus in bello* and the prohibitions against war crimes, and those that do not qualify as armed conflicts, and are thus primarily regulated by domestic law or other international rules. The next excerpted opinion concerns hostilities in the Republic of North Macedonia, which was for a time known as the Former Yugoslav Republic of Macedonia (FYROM),* which was waged from January to September 2001 between the state security forces (generally the police with support from the Macedonian army) and the Albanian National Liberation Army (NLA). The FYROM remained relatively peaceful following its declaration of independence from Yugoslavia in 1991. It became increasingly destabilized, however, during the 1998–99 war in Kosovo when thousands of Kosovar Albanian refugees flooded its borders. By 2000, Albanian insurgents (some indigenous to the region and some from Kosovo) began to press for independence from FYROM. Eventually, a NATO ceasefire monitoring force intervened and helped broker an accord (the Ohrid Framework Agreement) that gave greater autonomy to the Albanian minority in FYROM.

The case below—which was the only one before the ICTY involving crimes committed in the FYROM—came to the tribunal by virtue of a request made to the FYROM authorities to defer the matter to the ICTY. The ICTY Prosecutor charged the Minister of the Interior at the time, Ljube Boškoski, under the doctrine of superior responsibility for failing to prevent the crimes in question. She charged Boškoski's co-defendant, Johan Tarčulovski, with participating in a joint criminal enterprise to unlawfully attack civilians. In attempting to defeat the war crimes counts in the indictment, the defendants had earlier challenged the jurisdiction of the Tribunal on the ground that there was no armed conflict in FYROM in 2001 that would support charges of war crimes. The *Boškoski* Trial Chamber ruled that such a determination is a factual question to be addressed by the Trial Chamber at trial. *See Prosecutor v. Boškoski*, Case No. IT–04–82–AR72.1, Decision on Interlocutory Appeal on Jurisdiction (July 22, 2005). The Trial Chamber addressed this argument in its Judgment with reference to the test earlier developed in *Tadić* as set forth below. The map of the former Yugoslavia in the Map Appendix will help you identify the relevant regions within the former Yugoslavia. As you read the except below, which retains much of the original evidentiary analysis to give a flavor of the nature of this type of analysis, pay particular attention on the amount and types of evidence the Tribunal reviewed to reach the conclusions it did.

* FYROM originally agreed to retain the "former" in its moniker as a result of a dispute with Greece, which has a region called Macedonia. Greek officials were concerned that a country named Macedonia might stoke irredentist aspirations among Greece's Macedonian minority. In 2018, the conflict was resolved and the country was renamed the Republic of North Macedonia.

Prosecutor v. Boškoski & Tarčulovski, Case No. IT–04–82–T, Judgement (July 10, 2008)

In the Trial Chamber

173. The Accused are each charged with three counts of violations of the laws or customs of war pursuant to Article 3 of the Statute, namely one count of murder, one count of wanton destruction of cities, towns or villages not justified by military necessity, and one count of cruel treatment. There are several preliminary requirements which must be satisfied for the applicability of Article 3 of the Statute. In addition to being satisfied that the crimes charged fall under this provision, it must be established that there was an armed conflict, whether international or internal, at the time material to the Indictment and that the acts of the Accused are closely related to this armed conflict. * * *

175. The test for armed conflict was set out by the Appeals Chamber in the *Tadić* Jurisdiction Decision: "[a]n armed conflict exists whenever there is a resort to armed force between States or protracted armed violence between governmental authorities and organised armed groups or between such groups within a State." This test has been consistently applied in subsequent jurisprudence. Given the circumstances of that case, the Trial Chamber in *Tadić* interpreted this test in the case of internal armed conflict as consisting of two criteria, namely (i) the intensity of the conflict and (ii) the organisation of the parties to the conflict, as a way to distinguish an armed conflict "from banditry, unorganized and short-lived insurrections, or terrorist activities, which are not subject to international humanitarian law." This approach has been followed in subsequent judgements, although care is needed not to lose sight of the requirement for protracted armed violence in the case of an internal armed conflict, when assessing the intensity of the conflict. The criteria are closely related. They are factual matters which ought to be determined in light of the particular evidence available and on a case-by-case basis.

176. The Trial Chamber in *Tadić* noted that factors relevant to this determination are addressed in the Commentary to Common Article 3 of the Geneva Conventions.[709] These "convenient criteria" were identified

---

[709] ICRC Commentary to Geneva Convention I, pp. 49–50. These "convenient criteria" (which are in no way obligatory) are:

1. That the rebel party has an organized military force, an authority responsible for its acts, acting within a determinate territory and having the means of respecting and ensuring respect for the Convention.

2. The legal Government is obliged to use the regular military forces against insurgents organized as military and in possession of a part of the national territory.

3.

   a. The *de jure* Government has recognized the insurgents as belligerents; or
   b. That it has claimed for itself the rights of a belligerent; or
   c. That it has accorded the insurgents recognition as belligerents for the purpose only of the convention; or

by the drafters of Common Article 3 during negotiations of the Geneva Conventions in order to distinguish an armed conflict from lesser forms of violence, although these were rejected from the final text. While these criteria give some useful indications of armed conflict, they remain examples only. The drafters of the Commentary were of the view that Common Article 3 should be applied as widely as possible and could still be applicable in cases where "armed strife breaks out in a country, but does not fulfill any of the above conditions." * * *

177. Various indicative factors have been taken into account by Trial Chambers to assess the "intensity" of the conflict. These include the seriousness of attacks and whether there has been an increase in armed clashes, the spread of clashes over territory and over a period of time, any increase in the number of government forces and mobilisation and the distribution of weapons among both parties to the conflict, as well as whether the conflict has attracted the attention of the United Nations Security Council, and whether any resolutions on the matter have been passed. Trial Chambers have also taken into account in this respect the number of civilians forced to flee from the combat zones; the type of weapons used, in particular the use of heavy weapons, and other military equipment, such as tanks and other heavy vehicles; the blocking or besieging of towns and the heavy shelling of these towns; the extent of destruction and the number of casualties caused by shelling or fighting; the quantity of troops and units deployed; existence and change of front lines between the parties; the occupation of territory, and towns and villages; the deployment of government forces to the crisis area; the closure of roads; cease fire orders and agreements, and the attempt of representatives from international organizations to broker and enforce cease fire agreements.

178. At a more systemic level, an indicative factor of internal armed conflict is the way that organs of the State, such as the police and military, use force against armed groups. In such cases, it may be instructive to analyse the use of force by governmental authorities, in particular, how certain human rights are interpreted, such as the right to life and the right to be free from arbitrary detention, in order to appreciate if the situation is one of armed conflict. As is known, in situations falling short of armed conflict, the State has the right to use

---

d. That the dispute has been admitted to the agenda of the U.N. Security Council or the General Assembly as being a threat to the peace, breach of the peace or an act of aggression.

4.

a. The insurgents have an organisation that purports to have the characteristics of a State.

b. The insurgent civil authority exercises *de facto* authority over the persons within determinate territory.

c. The armed forces act under the direction of the organized civil authority and are prepared to observe the ordinary laws of war.

d. The insurgent civil authority agrees to be bound by the provisions of the Convention.

force to uphold law and order, including lethal force, but, where applicable, human rights law restricts such usage to what is no more than absolutely necessary and which is strictly proportionate to certain objectives.[735] . . . However, when a situation reaches the level of armed conflict, the question what constitutes an arbitrary deprivation of life is interpreted according to the standards of international humanitarian law, where a different proportionality test applies.[738] * * *

184. The Boškoski and Tarčulovski Defences have argued that since international law distinguishes between armed conflict and acts of "banditry, unorganized and short-lived insurrections, or terrorist activities, which are not subject to international humanitarian law," acts of a terrorist nature may not be taken into account in the determination of the existence of an armed conflict. The implication of this argument would seem to be that all terrorist acts should be excluded from the assessment of the intensity of violence in FYROM in 2001. Without prejudice to the question of the qualification of the acts of the NLA [Albanian National Liberation Army] as terrorist in nature, the Chamber considers that this interpretation is a misreading of the jurisprudence of the Tribunal, reviewed below.

185. The Trial Chamber in *Tadić* relied on the ICRC Commentary to the Geneva Conventions of 1949 to explain that the elements of intensity and organisation of the parties may be used solely for the purpose, as a minimum, to distinguish an armed conflict from lesser forms of violence such as "terrorist activities." The part of the Commentary relied upon noted that the Conventions' drafters did not intend the term "armed conflict" to apply "to any and every isolated event

---

[735] Under the European Convention on Human Rights, for example, such objectives are (a) self-defence (including defence of others), (b) in order to make a lawful arrest or to prevent the escape of a person lawfully detained, or (c) action lawfully taken for the purpose of quelling a riot or insurrection. Article 2, ECHR (1950). *See, e.g. McCann and Others v. United Kingdom*, ECtHR, App. No. 18984/91 (27 September 1995), paras. 148–149: "The text of Article 2 [of the Convention], read as a whole, demonstrates that paragraph 2 does not primarily define instances where it is permitted to kill an individual, but describes the situation where it is permitted to 'use force' which may result, as an unintended outcome, in the deprivation of life. The use of force, however, must be no more than 'absolutely necessary' for the achievement of one of the purposes set out in sub-paragraphs (a), (b) or (c) [. . .] In particular, the force used must be strictly proportionate achievement of the aims set out in sub-paragraphs 2 (a), (b) and (c) of Article 2."

[738] It is noted that even in cases involving armed conflict some courts have assessed the use of force with reference to the proportionality principle under human rights standards. For example, the Israeli Supreme Court has held that a civilian who is directly participating in hostilities cannot be killed if less harmful means can be employed, such as arrest, interrogation, and trial, "[t]hus, if a terrorist taking a direct part in hostilities can be arrested, interrogated and tried, those are the means which should be employed." *The Public Committee against Torture in Israel et al. v. The Government of Israel et al.*, Israel, Supreme Court, Judgment of 14 December 2006, HCJ 769/02, at para. 40. The European Court of Human Rights did not pronounce itself on the existence or qualification of an armed conflict in Chechnya, however, it observed in regards to the situation that, "[t]he presence of a very large group of armed fighters in Katyr-Yurt, and their active resistance to the law enforcement bodies [. . .] may have justified use of lethal force by the agents of the State, thus bringing the situation within paragraph 2 of Article 2." *Isayeva v. Russia*, ECtHR, App. No. 57950/00 (24 February 2005) para. 180. *See* also *Isayeva, Yusupova and Bazayeva v. Russia*, ECtHR, App. Nos. 57947–49/00 (24 February 2005) para. 178; *Güleç v. Turkey*, ECtHR, App. No. 21593/93 (27 July 1998) paras. 71–73.

involving the use of force and obliging the officers of the peace to have resort to their weapons." Rather, Common Article 3 was to apply to "conflicts which are in many respects similar to an international war, but take place within the confines of a single country," that is, where "armed forces" on either side are engaged in "hostilities." The essential point made by the Trial Chamber in *Tadić* is that isolated acts of violence, such as certain terrorist activities committed in peace time, would not be covered by Common Article 3. This conclusion reflected the Appeals Chamber's determination in *Tadić* that an armed conflict of a non-international character exists when there is "*protracted* violence between governmental authorities and organized groups or between such groups within a State." In applying this test, what matters is whether the acts are perpetrated in isolation or as part of a protracted campaign that entails the engagement of both parties in hostilities. It is immaterial whether the acts of violence perpetrated may or may not be characterised as terrorist in nature. This interpretation is consistent with the Appeals Chamber's observation in *Kordić*, that "[t]he requirement of *protracted* fighting is significant in excluding mere cases of civil unrest or *single* acts of terrorism."

186. The element of "protracted" armed violence in the definition of internal armed conflict has not received much explicit attention in the jurisprudence of the Tribunal.[758] It adds a temporal element to the definition of armed conflict. The Chamber is also conscious of Article 8(2)(d) of the Rome Statute of the International Criminal Court relating to serious violations of Common Article 3 which "applies to armed conflicts not of an international character and thus does not apply to situations of internal disturbances and tensions, such as riots, isolated and sporadic acts of violence or other acts of a similar nature."

187. The view that terrorist acts may be constitutive of protracted violence is also consistent with the logic of international humanitarian law, which prohibits "acts of terrorism" [in Article 33, of Geneva Convention IV] and "acts or threats of violence the primary purpose of which is to spread terror among the civilian population" [in Article 51(2) of Protocol I and Article 13(2) of Protocol II] in both international and non-international armed conflicts and to which individual criminal responsibility may attach. It would be nonsensical that international humanitarian law would prohibit such acts if these were not considered to fall within the rubric of armed conflict.

188. In addition, the Chamber notes that some national courts have not excluded acts of a terrorist nature when considering the evidence of

[758] While no Chamber has explicitly defined what is meant by the word "protracted," there is a significant pattern of Trial Chambers examining incidents of violence outside the temporal limits of an indictment to determine whether armed violence is "protracted," particularly when the period of indictment is less than one year. *See, e.g., Tadić* Trial Judgement, paras. 566–567 (finding that the intensity of fighting between various entities in Yugoslavia from 1991 rose to the level of an armed conflict with regard to an indictment period from May to December 1992) * * *.

armed conflict. The National Criminal Chamber of Peru found that the threshold of Common Article 3 had been met in respect of the situation related to acts committed by the Shining Path, such as murder of civilians, acts of sabotage against embassies and public and private enterprises' facilities, and armed ambushes against State forces and responses to these.[764] The Nigerian Supreme Court in 1972 rejected the defence of superior orders in respect of the deliberate killing of an unarmed person by non-uniformed members of the rebel forces known as the Biafran Army during the civil war, but did not discount this act as being part of the armed conflict.[765] The Supreme Court of the United States did not refrain from the determination that Common Article 3 applied to the armed conflict it identified between the United States and al Qaeda in spite of the "terrorist" acts perpetrated by al Qaeda or the U.S. Government's view that the latter was a terrorist organisation.[766]

189. The Supreme Court of Israel has also qualified the situation between Israel and "terrorist organizations" as an armed conflict in a number of judgements.[767] In a 2006 judgement, the Israeli Supreme Court recognised that a "continuous situation of armed conflict" existed between Israel and the various "Palestinian terrorist organizations" since the first *intifada* [uprising], due to the "constant, continual, and murderous wave of terrorist attacks" and the armed response to these. The Court observed that "in today's reality, a terrorist organization is likely to have considerable military capabilities. At times, they have military capabilities that exceed those of states. Confrontation with those dangers cannot be restricted within the state and its penal law." Furthermore, the U.N. Commission of Inquiry on Lebanon concluded that "the hostilities that took place from 12 July to 14 August [2006] constitute an international armed conflict," but noted "its *sui generis* nature in that active hostilities took place only between Israel and Hezbollah fighters."[771] In its report, the Commission stated that the fact that Israel considered Hezbollah to be a terrorist organisation and its fighters terrorists did not influence its qualification of the conflict.

190. These cases indicate that national courts and U.N. bodies have not discounted acts of a terrorist nature in their consideration of acts

---

[764] *Case of Abimael Guzmán Reinoso and others*, Peru, Expediente acumulado No. 560–03, Decision of 13 October 2006 (National Criminal Chamber), paras. 470–476.

[765] *Pius Nwaoga v. The State*, Nigeria, Supreme Court, 3 March 1972, All Nigeria Law Reports, Part 1, Vol. 1, p. 149; ILR vol. 52, 1979, p 494, at p 497. * * *

[766] *Hamdan v. Rumsfeld*, 548 U.S. 557 (2006).

[767] *Ajuri v. IDF Commander*, HCJ 7015/02; HCJ 7019/02, Israel, Supreme Court, Judgement of 3 September 2002, para. 1; *The Public Committee against Torture in Israel et al. v. The Government of Israel et al.*, Israel, Supreme Court, Judgment of 14 December 2006, HCJ 769/02, para. 16, also citing: *El Saka v. The State of Israel* (unpublished), HCJ 9255/00; *Kn'aan v. The Commander of IDF Forces in the Judea and Samaria Area* (unpublished), HCJ 2461/01; *Barake v. The Minister of Defence*, 56(2) PD, HCJ 9293/01; *Almandi v. The Minister of Defence*, 56(3) PD 30, HCJ 3451/02; *Ibrahim v. The Commander of IDF Forces in the West Bank* (unpublished), HCJ 8172/02; *Mara'abe v. The Prime Minister of Israel*, HJC 7957/04.

[771] Report of the Commission of Inquiry on Lebanon, pursuant to Human Rights Council Resolution S-2/1, UN Doc. A/HRC/3/2, 23 November 2006, paras. 8–9 and 57.

amounting to armed conflict. Nothing in the jurisprudence of the Tribunal suggests a different approach should be taken to the issue provided that terrorist acts amount to "protracted violence." In view of the above considerations, the Chamber considers that while isolated acts of terrorism may not reach the threshold of armed conflict, when there is protracted violence of this type, especially where they require the engagement of the armed forces in hostilities, such acts are relevant to assessing the level of intensity with regard to the existence of an armed conflict. * * *

193. In view of these considerations, the Chamber will apply the test laid down by the Appeals Chamber in the *Tadić* Jurisdiction Decision in its examination of the events in FYROM in 2001. It will treat the indicative factors identified above, together with the systemic consideration of the use of force by the State authorities, as providing useful practical guidance to an evaluation of the intensity criterion in the particular factual circumstances of this case.

194. The jurisprudence of the Tribunal has established that armed conflict of a non-international character may only arise when there is protracted violence between governmental authorities and *organised* armed groups or between such groups within a State. The required degree of organisation of such an armed group for the purpose of Common Article 3 has not been specifically defined in legal texts or in jurisprudence. Nevertheless, certain elements of this minimal level of organisation have been elaborated by the Tribunal's jurisprudence.

195. In *Tadić*, the Appeals Chamber distinguished between the situation of individuals acting on behalf of a State without specific instructions from that of individuals making up "*an organised and hierarchically structured group*, such as a military unit or, in case of war or civil strife, armed bands of irregulars or rebels." The Chamber observed that "an organised group [. . .] normally has a structure, a chain of command and a set of rules as well as the outward symbols of authority" and that its members do not act on their own but conform "to the standards prevailing in the group" and are "subject to the authority of the head of the group." Thus, for an armed group to be considered organised, it would need to have some hierarchical structure and its leadership requires the capacity to exert authority over its members. * * *

197. While the jurisprudence of the Tribunal requires an armed group to have "some degree of organisation," the warring parties do not necessarily need to be as organised as the armed forces of a State. Neither does the degree of organisation for an armed group to a conflict to which Common Article 3 applies need be at the level of organisation required for parties to Additional Protocol II armed conflicts, which must have responsible command, and exercise such control over a part of the territory as to enable them to carry out sustained and concerted military operations and to implement the Protocol. Additional Protocol II requires

a higher standard than Common Article 3 for establishment of an armed conflict. It follows that the degree of organisation required to engage in "protracted violence" is lower than the degree of organisation required to carry out "sustained and concerted military operations." In this respect, it is noted that during the drafting of Article 8(2)(f) of the Rome Statute of the International Criminal Court covering "other" serious violations of the laws and customs of war applicable in non-international armed conflicts, delegates rejected a proposal to introduce the threshold of applicability of Additional Protocol II to the section, and instead accepted a proposal to include in the *chapeau* the test of "protracted armed conflict," as derived from the Appeals Chamber's decision in *Tadić*. This indicates that the latter test was considered to be distinct from, and a lower threshold than, the test under Additional Protocol II. This difference in the required degree of organisation is logical in view of the more detailed rules of international humanitarian law that apply in Additional Protocol II conflicts, which mean that "there must be some degree of stability in the control of even a modest area of land for them to be capable of effectively applying the rules of the Protocol."[792] By contrast, Common Article 3 reflects basic humanitarian protections, and a party to an armed conflict only needs a minimal degree of organisation to ensure their application.

199. Trial Chambers have taken into account a number of factors when assessing the organization of an armed group. These fall into five broad groups. In the first group are those factors signaling the presence of a command structure, such as the establishment of a general staff or high command, which appoints and gives directions to commanders, disseminates internal regulations, organises the weapons supply, authorises military action, assigns tasks to individuals in the organisation, and issues political statements and communiqués, and which is informed by the operational units of all developments within the unit's area of responsibility. Also included in this group are factors such as the existence of internal regulations setting out the organisation and structure of the armed group; the assignment of an official spokesperson; the communication through communiqués reporting military actions and operations undertaken by the armed group; the existence of headquarters; internal regulations establishing ranks of servicemen and defining duties of commanders and deputy commanders of a unit, company, platoon or squad, creating a chain of military hierarchy between the various levels of commanders; and the dissemination of internal regulations to the soldiers and operational units.

200. Secondly, factors indicating that the group could carry out operations in an organized manner have been considered, such as the group's ability to determine a unified military strategy and to conduct

[792] ICRC Commentary on Additional Protocol II, p 1353. Thus, for instance, caring for the wounded and the sick, or detaining prisoners and treating them decently, as provided in Articles 4 (Fundamental guarantees) and 5 (Persons whose liberty has been restricted). * * *

large scale military operations; the capacity to control territory; whether there is territorial division into zones of responsibility in which the respective commanders are responsible for the establishment of Brigades and other units and appoint commanding officers for such units; the capacity of operational units to coordinate their actions; and the effective dissemination of written and oral orders and decisions.

201. In the third group are factors indicating a level of logistics have been taken into account, such as the ability to recruit new members; the providing of military training; the organized supply of military weapons; the supply and use of uniforms; and the existence of communications equipment for linking headquarters with units or between units.

202. In a fourth group, factors relevant to determining whether an armed group possessed a level of discipline and the ability to implement the basic obligations of Common Article 3 have been considered, such as the establishment of disciplinary rules and mechanisms; proper training; and the existence of internal regulations and whether these are effectively disseminated to members.

203. A fifth group includes those factors indicating that the armed group was able to speak with one voice, such as its capacity to act on behalf of its members in political negotiations with representatives of international organisations and foreign countries; and its ability to negotiate and conclude agreements such as cease fire or peace accords.

204. The Tarčulovski Defence submitted that the "terrorist" nature of the activities of the NLA and alleged violations of international humanitarian law militated against the NLA being considered as a party to an armed conflict because they showed that the "NLA did not have [the] authority to control the forces on the ground." The Chamber accepts that a high number of international humanitarian law violations by the members of an armed group may be indicative of poor discipline and a lack of hierarchical command in the group in some instances. It is noted that one national court has held that a pattern of violations of rules of international humanitarian law such as terrorist attacks indicates a lack of responsible command under Article 1 of Additional Protocol II, although the court nonetheless found that Common Article 3 applied.[829] However, the Chamber also recognises that some terrorist attacks actually involve a high level of planning and a coordinated command structure for their implementation. In other words, this question is a factual determination to be made on a case-by-case basis.

205. Where members of armed groups engage in acts that are prohibited under international humanitarian law, such as "acts of terrorism," "acts or threats the primary purpose of which is to spread fear in the civilian population," hostage-taking, the use of human shields,

[829] *Case of Abimael Guzmán Reinoso and others*, Expediente acumulado No 560–03, Peru, Judgment of the National Criminal Chamber (*Sala Pena Nacional*) of 13 October 2006; ILDC 670 (PE 2006), para. 470.

feigning protected status, attacking historic or religious monuments or buildings or using such objects in support of the military effort, or serious violations of Common Article 3, they are liable to prosecution and punishment. However, so long as the armed group possesses the organizational *ability* to comply with the obligations of international humanitarian law, even a pattern of such type of violations would not necessarily suggest that the party did not possess the level of organization required to be a party to an armed conflict. The Chamber cannot merely infer a lack of organization of the armed group by reason of the fact that international humanitarian law was frequently violated by its members. In assessing this factor the Chamber needs to examine how the attacks were planned and carried out—that is, for example, whether they were primarily the result of a military strategy ordered by those leading the group or whether they were perpetrated by members deciding to commit attacks of their own accord.

206. In view of the above analysis, the Chamber will apply the test laid down by the Appeals Chamber in the *Tadić* Jurisdiction Decision in its examination of the facts of the events in FYROM in 2001, using the indicative factors identified above as a practical guide to determining whether the criterion of organisation of the parties was met.

207. The Indictment alleges the existence of an armed conflict in FYROM between the FYROM Security Forces and the National Liberation Army (NLA), beginning in January 2001 and continuing through until late September 2001. The Chamber will discuss below whether the Prosecution has demonstrated that the acts of violence that occurred in FYROM in the material time reached the level of intensity required by the jurisprudence of the Tribunal and that the NLA possessed the characteristics of an organised armed group within the meaning of the *Tadić* test to establish the existence of an armed conflict.

(a) Intensity of the Conflict

208. While the existence of an armed conflict in the alleged period, or in any part of it, is disputed and is a most material allegation in this case, it is noted that the evidence concerning the events relied on as evidencing the intensity of the conflict is far from comprehensive, often incomplete, and in most cases, consists of or relies on media and other second-hand reports. Typically, it lacks detail relevant to a consideration of the allegation, such as the numbers of persons engaged in each event, its duration, types of weapons used, identity of the persons engaged or the unit (if any) to which they belonged; facts which are relevant to whether there were, indeed, violent acts by an organised group, *i.e.* the NLA, and not merely disorganised expressions of violence not associated with the NLA. * * *

211. A further problem with the evidence in relation to violent incidents of 2001 is that sources often refer to acts perpetrated by "terrorists," "armed Albanian groups," or "diversion terrorist groups" which may or may not be in reference to acts of the NLA. It has not been

possible for the Chamber in all cases to verify whether the act may be properly attributed to the NLA. The Chamber takes into account the fact that certain incidents or clashes may have involved other groups or individuals who for various reasons undertook acts of violence in order to disrupt the peace during this period. With these deficiencies in mind, the Chamber will examine in the evidence of the events in FYROM of 2001 in chronological order.

212. In January 2001, there is evidence of two attacks on police stations carried out by armed Albanian groups in Aračinovo and Tearce in the Tetovo region, respectively. Concerning the attack on Tearce police station, the use of grenades, and automatic weapons as well as a hand rocket-launcher or hand grenades was reported. It is suggested that the NLA had taken responsibility for this attack. The month of February saw an increase in FYROM military presence along the northern border with Kosovo. At least three incidents were reported in the border village of Tanuševci. There is evidence that an armed NLA group kidnapped a team of journalists, later releasing them unharmed. On the same day, an army border patrol came under attack from armed men wearing black camouflage gear and an exchange of fire ensued leaving several "members of the NLA" wounded. The fighting in the Tanuševci area is alleged to have occurred as a result of the NLA's attempt to control access to the Skopska Crna Gora area. There is evidence that the Skopska Crna Gora road was used by the "terrorist" groups to transport weapons, drugs and people. The casualties as a result of armed clashes and violent incidents throughout the months of January and February resulted in the deaths of at least four police officers.

213. The month of March saw an increase of armed clashes between the FYROM forces, both army and police, and the NLA consisting of sporadic shooting, the use by the NLA of landmines, small scale fire fights, the bombarding by Macedonian forces of NLA positions, attacks with automatic weapons and the NLA firing upon police convoys. * * * The President issued a number of decisions on the use of the security forces of FYROM, which ordered the Macedonian army to respond to the "armed attacks" of "diversion-terrorist groups"; mobilized the 1st and 4th Guardist Battalion; engaged the Artillery Battalion of the 1st Infantry Brigade; put all the units of the army in full combat readiness; specifically ordered an operation to "destroy the terrorists" in the area of Tetovo in order to regain control over the territory; and [launched] another specific operation to "destroy the terrorists" in the area of Kumanovo. Army reserves as well as police reserves were mobilized. Operation Ramno was set up in early March in order to coordinate and direct activities in reaction to the crisis. The UN Security Council on 12 March issued a Presidential Statement condemning the violence by "ethnic Albanian armed extremists" and expressing concern about the threat this caused to the stability and security of FYROM and the wider region. * * *

217. On 22 May, the "Prizren Agreement" was signed by Ali Ahmeti as "political representative" of the NLA, Arben Xaferi, President of the Democratic Party of Albanians (DPA) and Imer Imeri, President of the Party for Democratic Prosperity (PDP), both ethnic Albanian political parties in FYROM, setting out agreed common action with regard to resolving the concerns of the ethnic Albanian population in FYROM. * * * There is evidence that around this time, Macedonian authorities arrested 66 people, 32 of whom were charged with terrorist offences, 28 with illegal possession of weapons, one with organising an armed rebellion and one with attack on the constitutional order. The offensives and armed clashes throughout the month of May resulted in the deaths of a number of NLA and members of FYROM forces, as well as civilians. On 29 May, the Minister of the Interior, the Accused, Ljube Boškoski, established a working group to gather evidence on war crimes committed in the territory of FYROM.

218. * * * The month of June marked a continuation and increase in the frequency of offensive attacks both by the Macedonian forces and the NLA and an expansion in the geographic scope of areas of fighting beyond Tetovo and Kumanovo into Araščinovo, and the surrounding area. As a result of a surge of attacks in the beginning of June, Prime Minister Georgievski threatened on 6 June, again, to seek a parliamentary decision declaring a state of war. * * * KFOR forces [NATO-led international forces in Kosovo] were reported to have detained 19 suspected NLA members and seized 27 anti-personnel mines, 40 machine-guns, six rocket-propelled grenades, 13 mortars, eight pistols and ammunition, uniforms, cash, food and water, and medical supplies. . * * *

233. On 13 August, the Ohrid Framework Agreement was signed by the main ethnic Macedonian and ethnic Albanian parliamentary parties, as well as the U.S. and the European Union as guarantors. The NLA was not a party to the Agreement. This Agreement established a "general, unconditional and open-ended cease fire" based on the principle of finding "peaceful political solutions." It also laid down the obligations on parties to facilitate refugee return, rehabilitation and reconstruction and provided fundamental changes in the constitution of Macedonia, including its preamble as well as a number of important provisions related to the use of the Albanian language, educational rights in the native language, proportional representation in the bodies of power, as well as the rearrangement of certain functions and administrative powers at the municipal level. * * *

234. On 14 August, the NLA issued a communiqué that it had signed an agreement with NATO to disarm and disband, in accordance with the Ohrid Agreement. Fourteen persons detained in relation to the Ljuboten operation were taken before the Lower Court Skopje II and charged with the criminal offence of "terrorism" and decisions were issued to extend custody over the detainees for another 30 days. On or

around 26 September, these terrorism charges were changed to "service in an Enemy Army," a charge that only applies "during war or during an armed conflict" on the basis that the accused persons had allegedly "participated in armed conflict as combatants against the Republic of Macedonia" during which they had been involved in "intensive military actions using infantry and weapons and ammunition." * * *

238. On 8 October 2001, the President declared that the government would grant an amnesty to all persons who had committed or who were accused of having committed criminal acts related to the conflict in the year 2001 up to 26 September, with the exception of those acts falling within the jurisdiction of the ICTY. On 26 October, President Boris Trajkovski wrote to the Prosecutor of the ICTY seeking an investigation into serious violations of international humanitarian law committed "in parts of the territory of the Republic of Macedonia, not under the control of the Macedonian security forces." * * * In December, the President issued a number of decisions pardoning members of the NLA who were deprived of liberty, including all those involved in the Ljuboten events. An amnesty law to this effect was issued on 8 March 2002, which was passed for the "promotion of peace and overcoming the crisis." The decree gave a full amnesty to all those "persons that have participated in the conflict," with the exemption of those persons who have committed crimes falling within the jurisdiction of the ICTY.

239. The Chamber received differing evidence as to the total numbers of casualties as a result of the events of 2001. Varying sources indicate that 15 to 24 police officers and 35 to 43 to 60 members of the army were killed. Gzim Ostreni [reportedly the NLA's Chief of Staff] testified that around 68 members of the NLA had been killed. The "White Book" documents 10 civilians killed, while the "Report on the activities of the Ministry of Interior for 2001" states that 16 civilians were killed. Some 150 to 174 police officers and 119 to 211 to 270 army members were injured, while 61 to 75 to 100 civilians were injured, and 20 to 36 civilians reportedly went missing. Although none of these figures are absolutely reliable, the Chamber takes note of them as a broad indication of the numbers of casualties produced by the events of 2001, the majority of which appeared to occur in June and August.

240. In terms of the numbers of persons displaced by the conflict, by the end of August, the United Nations Refugee Agency estimated that there were around 64,000 Macedonian refugees in Kosovo or southern Serbia, and around 70,000 internally displaced persons in Macedonia, 15,000 of whom were "micro-displaced" very short distances from original residence or sleeping in a location different from day time residence. Evidence suggests that most of the displacement occurred in late March, around 8 June, and in late July and early to mid-August. FYROM sources put the number of Macedonian refugees at 80,000 and the number of internally displaced persons at over 86,000. * * *

242. The Chamber received varying analyses of whether the NLA exercised control over territory during 2001. This was complicated by the fact that different definitions of "control" were used by various sources.[1076] The "Report on the activities of the Ministry of the Interior of Macedonia" dated April 2002 indicates that the NLA were thought by the Ministry of the Interior ["MoI"] to have "temporarily occupied" up to 20 per cent of the north-west part of Macedonia. While the NLA did not control any of the large towns or cities, the Chamber heard evidence that much of the mountainous areas with predominantly ethnic-Albanian villages were under the "control" of the NLA. The OSCE estimated that 135 to 140 villages were under NLA control, meaning that the police were unable to perform their jobs there. The degree of control did not reach the level of the exercise of governmental control, but the Macedonian forces were unable to enter these villages for prolonged periods of time. * * *

243. While NLA armed actions had occurred at times during the first months of 2001, particularly in the more mountainous areas in the north west bordering Albania and the Kosovo region, the evidence described above attests to a significant escalation in the intensity of the events in Macedonia from May to mid-August 2001, when the Ohrid Framework Agreement was signed, although it does not always follow from the evidence that the "terrorist groups" involved in all the events were, in fact, the NLA. There was an increase in armed clashes to the point of almost daily incidents of violence, shooting and provocations by the NLA and the standard military response to these by the army or police or both. There was also a geographical expansion of areas of fighting from Tetovo, to Kumanovo-Lipkovo, around Skopje, and in Gostivar. Other relevant factors were the distribution and use of heavy weaponry by the Macedonian forces including combat helicopters and tanks; the growing variety of weapons used by the NLA; the mobilization of the army and units of the police to combat readiness; the calling up of reserve forces; the number of orders for military offensives to "destroy terrorists"; the besieging of towns; the use of cease fires; the appeals to and intervention of international actors to help resolve the crisis by both sides; the institution of a peace agreement to end active hostilities; and the large number of displaced persons and refugees caused by the conflict. Some other indicative factors of armed conflict were also present: these included the attention of the UN Security Council which adopted a resolution in March condemning the "terrorist activities" and a further resolution in September welcoming the signing of the Ohrid Agreement; facilitation by the ICRC for the release of detainees on both sides and to pass messages to families of detainees; the prosecution by FYROM authorities of persons for service in the aid of an enemy army and other offences only applicable during armed conflict; and the granting of a

[1076] It is recalled that there is no specific definition of "control" of territory under the international humanitarian law instruments. The ICTR Trial Chamber in *Akayesu* found that territory in an armed group's control is usually that which has eluded the control of the government forces. *Akayesu* Trial Judgement, para. 626.

broad amnesty to all those who participated in the conflict, with the explicit exception of those accused of war crimes who would come within the jurisdiction of the ICTY.

244. The Chamber takes into account that despite this clear escalation there remained relatively few casualties on both sides and to civilians (the highest estimates put the total number of those killed during 2001 as a result of the armed clashes at 168), and material damage to property and housing was of a relatively small scale. These low figures may indicate that, despite the use of heavy weaponry by the FYROM forces, there was generally restraint in the way in which it was used, which could suggest that the operations of the police and army were more directed to law enforcement. However, another factor relevant to the low casualties is that the armed clashes that occurred usually involved small numbers of forces and tended to be localised. While, as indicated earlier, the evidence does not always fully establish whether incidents or clashes were attributable to the "NLA" or to some independently acting groups of individuals, it is noted that in general the tactics favoured by the NLA were of a guerrilla nature in that often they involved a quick strike by a small force making full use of the terrain. Against such tactics there was limited scope for a massive military offensive which would normally produce greater casualties.

245. The evidence received reveals an inconsistency in the legal framework applied to the FYROM security forces in 2001. This may have been a reflection of a certain degree of confusion and even disagreement among different branches of government in regard to how best to deal with the situation. The Chamber takes into account the Order of the President to the army in early August—the period of the highest intensity during 2001—to use force only in response to an attack by the "self-styled NLA" or in self defence, which might indicate that a law enforcement framework was being applied. However, in many regards, the legal and administrative framework that the Government of FYROM applied to its actions in 2001 reflected that which would be applicable during an armed conflict. Every order of the President in this year was issued pursuant to Article 79(2) of the Constitution, meaning that the President was acting in his capacity of Commander in Chief of the armed forces. The orders repeatedly called for the mobilization of police units, including reservists, which, according to the Official Book of Rules on the way of summoning and engaging members of the reserve ranks of the MoI, may be engaged "in military or emergency state" to protect the security of FYROM or to maintain public peace and order when "it has been disturbed to a greater extent." The Law on Internal Affairs proscribes similar conditions under which the MoI may establish special units of the police, which were established on several occasions in 2001.

* * *

247. A degree of ambiguity in the applicable legal framework may also be found in the way that captured NLA members were treated by

the FYROM authorities. Although one order of the Ministry of Defence was issued to treat "military captured persons" in accordance with "the Geneva Convention," the Chamber received no evidence that this was applied or whether it was supposed to apply to members of the NLA. The Chamber takes into account the fact that large numbers of male ethnic Albanians suspected of terrorism, including those from Ljuboten, were arrested and charged with criminal offences rather than merely detained without charge for the duration of the conflict as is the more usual practice in armed conflict. However, these persons were often charged with offences that would normally only apply during an armed conflict. Moreover, the Amnesty Law that was passed on 8 March 2002 that absolved from prosecution all those persons who had "participated in the conflict," with the exception of those who were accused of crimes within the jurisdiction of the ICTY, is an indication that the situation was one of armed conflict.

248. A significant consideration in support of a conclusion that the situation in FYROM had reached the level of an armed conflict is the extent of the civil disruption being experienced as evidenced by the extensive displacement of persons from their homes and villages, at least 64,000 of whom became refugees and 70,000 of whom were internally displaced.

249. The Chamber is satisfied that at the times material to the Indictment, the conflict in FYROM had reached the required level of intensity.

(b) Organisation of the Armed Group * * *

252. The Prosecution has submitted that the evidence shows that the NLA was an organised and hierarchically structured armed group, with a functioning chain of command and logistics, able to engage in an internal armed conflict. Both Defences have disputed this claim. The Boškoski Defence has argued that the evidence does not establish that the NLA had the necessary organisational, fighting and logistical abilities to be regarded as a party to an armed conflict, in particular, because, it is argued, the NLA did not have the ability of an organised group to plan and carry out sustained and concerted military operations and to guarantee the implementation of humanitarian standards. The Tarčulovski Defence has argued that there is no credible documentary evidence to support the contention that the NLA was an organised armed group, and that the evidence of events on the ground does not indicate the actions of an organised military force. * * *

266. With these considerations in mind the Chamber has reviewed the evidence and has been able to reach the following conclusions. In June 2001 the NLA had approximately 2,000 to 2,500 fighters with some non-military support (food, lodging, transport, etc.) being provided by another 1,000. By August 2001 the NLA had four functioning, though not fully manned, Brigades—the 112th, 113th, 114th, and 115th—and two (the 111th and 116th Brigades) still in the process of becoming

operational. The 112th Brigade operated in the area of Tetovo, the 113th in the Kumanovo area, the 114th in the Skopje area, and the 115th in the Raduša area.

268. Ali Ahmeti was the leader of the NLA. Although the manner in which he assumed this position was not fully verified in evidence, members of the NLA regarded him as the leader, as did members of the international community, as indicated by the fact that communications to the NLA were directed to him and that negotiations for cease fires, the withdrawal of troops, and disarmament were carried out with Mr. Ahmeti. Gzim Ostreni was NLA's Chief of Staff; he was regarded as the deputy leader of the organisation and the military director.

269. The NLA issued a number of communiqués during the course of 2001, most of them signed by Ali Ahmeti. These communiqués were the NLA's primary vehicle of communication to the public. A communiqué of 9 March set out the goals of the group. One dated 9 May informed about the NLA's structure and hierarchy. The weaponry and manpower of the NLA was communicated in a communiqué of 10 May signed by Ostreni. A communiqué was issued proclaiming the appointment of Mevlud Aliu as NLA political representative in Turkey and the Middle East. There is no further evidence as to the existence of this political representative or any activities undertaken in Turkey or the Middle East, although Gzim Ostreni testified that almost all the countries of Europe as well as the United States had had political representatives appointed to them. * * *

271. Nazim Bushi and Gzim Ostreni testified that under the Brigades, there existed battalions, companies, platoons and squads, and that there was a functioning chain of command from Ali Ahmeti and Gzim Ostreni down to the individual member of the organisation in the field. NLA regulations prepared by Gzim Ostreni refer to a complex hierarchical structure, including units from the level of detachment to squad. While the Chamber cannot accept the entirety of this evidence, the existence of a hierarchical command structure is supported by Exhibit P493, a NATO document containing extracts from the "NLA Handbook," which details the structures of Brigades, the NLA political leadership, the NLA military command (general headquarters), and the NLA command and control. NLA regulations prepared by Gzim Ostreni refer to functions of legal advisors, media and information officers. * * *

272. To establish a functioning organisational system the Prosecution seeks to rely on a number of the rules and regulations which are said to have been applicable to the NLA in 2001. These informal regulations and rules, *inter alia*, purport to establish a chain of command defining the duties of each level; oblige unit commanders to ensure implementation of the regulations; lay down provisions on disciplinary measures such as detention or arrest; inform the Brigade commanders of their duty to respect civilians and civilian property as well as the obligation to observe the laws of war and international conventions

during any military engagements; and recognise the jurisdiction of the ICTY over any crimes committed by NLA members. Gzim Ostreni, who says he created the documents in March, April and May 2001, testified that he did indeed use KLA, Kosovo Protection Force ("KPC"), Albanian and the former Yugoslavia regulations as sources. * * *

274. What remains pertinent to the Chamber is whether or to what extent these rules and regulations had actually been applied in practice by the NLA Brigades. In this regard, Nazim Bushi, the commander of the 114th Brigade, testified that he was familiar with the regulations and Gzim Ostreni testified that the Brigades followed the instructions by the General Staff and the NLA regulations. Although, apart from this, there is no direct evidence that these rules and regulations were distributed and implemented throughout the NLA units and structures, the NLA has been described in a NATO document prepared in 2001 and accepted as reliable as "a well-armed, well-disciplined and a highly motivated organisation" with "a highly developed basic level of organisation and discipline" which allows the group to function effectively at the tactical level. This suggests that while the full content of the purported "Rules" and "Regulations" of the NLA does not credibly reflect the degree of organisation of the NLA, there was nonetheless a basic system of discipline within the NLA that allowed it to function with some effectiveness. * * *

277. Indicative of the level of organisation of an armed group is its ability to carry out military operations, including troop movements and logistics. As discussed earlier, the Chamber is satisfied that there was a marked increase in hostilities from May 2001, for the most part concentrated in the north-western part of the country. Most of these hostile incidents consisted of small-scale attacks on police patrols or police stations. Like other ethnic Albanian armed groups in the formative stages of an insurgency such as the KLA in Kosovo in 1998, the tactics of the NLA consisted in large part of hit and run maneuvers as demonstrated in the number of ambushes carried out in 2001. More serious or prolonged incidents also occurred, such as the 10 day NLA "occupation" of Araščinovo in June, and heavy clashes in Tetovo and Radušsa in August. * * *

280. There are also some examples when at least some NLA troops on the ground appeared to fail to act in accordance with the position expressed by the NLA General Staff. On at least three occasions in June 2001 the NLA announced unilaterally, or agreed to, a cease fire; despite this fighting continued. * * * According to the Crisis Management Centre, a body set up by the FYROM government, a total of 788 cease fire violations by the NLA were observed between 6 and 24 July. * * * The general effect of this evidence may be seen to be that the NLA had developed some capacity to implement a cease fire, although its results were far from uniform or always successful. The lack of respect for cease fires could also be indicative of the fact that incidents and clashes at

times did not involve NLA but instead other groups or individuals who for various reasons wanted to resort to violence and cause disruption. It is to be observed that there were also significant cease fire violations by Macedonian forces in the same period or other prohibited behaviour, even though these were conventionally organised and disciplined army and police forces.

281. Gzim Ostreni testified that the NLA was able to supply its units with weaponry and equipment, even though this was only achieved with difficulty. A number of sources pointed to the NLA having financial support from the ethnic Albanian diaspora, which funded the weaponry for most of the Brigades. Over the course of 2001, KFOR routinely intercepted large amounts of weaponry and other supplies being smuggled over the border into FYROM from Kosovo, as well as hundreds of suspected NLA members. According to Ostreni, the NLA had a variety of weapons, including "Strela-2M" AA portable missiles (used against aircraft), 60 millimetre, 82 millimetre and 120 millimetre mortars, 12.7 millimetre AA machine guns, sniper rifles, anti-tank rocket launchers, rocket propelled grenades and 120 millimetre howitzers. * * * In Operation Essential Harvest, NATO received 3,875 weapons from NLA members, but this is likely to be significantly less than the actual numbers possessed by the NLA at the height of the conflict. An email of the OSCE spill-over mission indicated that the NLA routinely used anti-tank mines and maybe anti-personnel mines.

282. The NLA lacked large scale transportation means, and largely relied on tractors or transported weapons and supplies by foot or with the use of donkeys and mules over the mountainous terrain.

283. Evidence suggests that new recruits were to have an inauguration ceremony and be given a military identification card. * * * An order was issued in August by the Chief of General Staff according to which proof of membership in the NLA was to be established via a central commission. There is no evidence suggesting that this was carried out before the NLA was disbanded.

284. NLA recruits underwent short military training. There is evidence that there were a higher number of training centres in FYROM, which is confirmed by a report of the MoI Department of Analytics, Investigation and Information Sector, and also a training centre abroad which is not independently confirmed.

285. Further, there is some evidence that NLA members were required to wear uniforms during operations, although not all NLA members had a uniform. Some wore black clothing or other civilian clothes. There is also evidence that some NLA members would wear as a minimum the NLA Brigade insignia, but this could be impractical especially if civilian clothes were worn.

286. Notwithstanding particular deficiencies in some evidence which have been discussed, there remains a body of evidence, the general

effect of which is to demonstrate that while initially, in January and February 2001, the NLA mainly composed individually formed and organised smaller local groups, struggling to secure appropriate weapons and armament and operating substantially on local initiative, there was progressively a development and maturing of the NLA. It grew significantly in membership, both by local recruitment and as volunteers came from abroad. The supply and distribution of weapons and armament became progressively more planned and coordinated and the quantity and variety of weaponry more extensive. Gradually and progressively, uniforms and other equipment were becoming available. A limited system of basic training was implemented.

287. The evidence suggests that other local "terrorist"-type groups existed and functioned, probably independently of the NLA. Indeed the NLA appears to have drawn heavily on these as it formed and developed. It is clear that after the Ohrid agreement a splinter formation continued with armed aggression. The growing strength and organisation of the NLA had the effect, however, of limiting the number and effectiveness of sub-groups, especially by mid-2001. In the Chamber's finding the NLA was making significant progress toward the full and effective establishment and implementation of a command structure and the organisation of its localised volunteer groups into Brigades and other more subordinate units. This substantial undertaking had not, however, been fully achieved by August 2001. * * *

289. It is not the case that the NLA at any time was a modern, well-organised and supplied, trained and disciplined, efficient fighting force. What is established by an extensive body of evidence from FYROM governmental, army and police sources was that the NLA managed to compel the government to commit the full weight of its substantial army including reserves, and the large police force including reserves, to the fight against the NLA. The NLA was seen by the Macedonian government as presenting a most grave threat to the very survival of the country. As contemporary assessments indicate, the country was on the verge of a civil war. The government sought the assistance of international agencies including NATO and diplomatic activity became intense, diplomatic activity which reached out to and involved the leadership of the NLA in negotiating a peaceful political resolution to the crisis. The NLA was sufficiently organised to enter into cease fire agreements using international bodies as intermediaries, to negotiate and sign a political agreement setting out its common goals with ethnic Albanian political groups in FYROM, and to enter into and abide by an agreement with NATO to gradually disarm and disband.

290. The Chamber is persuaded that the effect produced by the NLA by August 2001, and the level of military success it had achieved against the much larger and better equipped Macedonian army and police force, together with its ability to speak with one voice, and to recruit and arm its members, are sufficient in the particular circumstances being

considered, to demonstrate that the NLA had developed a level of organisation and coordination quite markedly different and more purposed from that which existed in the early months of 2001. This had enabled it to conduct military activities and to achieve a measure of military success over more than three months at a level which could not have been expected at the beginning of 2001. It is also of some relevance that it had come to be recognised and applied by the legal system of FYROM that a state of armed conflict existed at the times relevant to this Indictment. In respect of those times, and earlier, there were judicial investigations, charges, and convictions in respect of offences that depended on the existence of an armed conflict.

291. In the Chamber's finding therefore the evidence demonstrates that the NLA possessed by August 2001 sufficient of the characteristics of an organised armed group or force to satisfy the requirements in this respect of the jurisprudence of the Tribunal set out earlier in this Judgement.

292. Having regard to the law applicable and the analysis of the evidence made above, the Chamber is persuaded that in August 2001, at the times material to the Indictment, there was a state of internal armed conflict in FYROM involving FYROM security forces, both army and police, and the NLA.

NOTES & QUESTIONS

1. Case History and Outcome

In the pre-trial period, the defendants made a number of unsuccessful challenges to the jurisdiction of the Tribunal. In addition to the argument that they could not be charged with war crimes, they also argued that the temporal jurisdiction of the Tribunal ceased in 1999 as a result of the promulgation of the peace agreements ending the war in Bosnia-Herzegovina and that the Tribunal could not exercise jurisdiction over events in the FYROM since that political entity did not exist at the time the Security Council created the ICTY. *See Prosecutor v. Boškoski*, Case No. IT–04–82–PT, Decision on Johan Tarčulovski's Motions Challenging Jurisdiction (June 1, 2005). The Trial Chamber acquitted Boškoski—who had been charged with superior responsibility for the alleged violations—on the ground that he took adequate means within his material ability to ensure that criminal conduct was investigated, but was in essence a political figurehead with no real power. Tarčulovski, on the other hand, was convicted of the war crimes of murder, wanton destruction, and cruel treatment and was sentenced to twelve years' imprisonment.

The conviction and sentence survived the defendant's appeal. The ICTY originally exercised primacy over five cases concerning crimes committed in the FYROM by requesting that they be sent to the ICTY; however, only this indictment issued, and the other three cases returned to domestic courts. Why would the Prosecutor not indict the defendants' NLA counterparts?

Why would the Prosecutor charge only war crimes and not crimes against humanity under the circumstances?

2. Tadić and the Definition of Armed Conflict

In *Tadić*, the Trial Chamber determined that an armed conflict exists:

> whenever there is a resort to armed force between States or protracted armed violence between governmental authorities and organized armed groups or between such groups within a State. International humanitarian law applies from the initiation of such armed conflicts and extends beyond the cessation of hostilities until a general conclusion of peace is reached; or, in the case of internal conflicts, a peaceful settlement is achieved. Until that moment, international humanitarian law continues to apply in the whole territory of the warring States or, in the case of internal conflicts, the whole territory under the control of a party, whether or not actual combat takes place there.

Prosecutor v. Tadić, Case No. IT–94–1–A, Decision on the Defence Motion for Interlocutory Appeal on Jurisdiction, para. 70 (October 2, 1995). Note that the *Tadić* Trial Chamber defines "armed conflict" and not "war." This is in keeping with the lexicon of the International Committee of the Red Cross as well. Why might this be so? Is the definition of armed conflict formulated by the *Tadić* Appeals Chamber a useful one? What violent situations might it exclude?

What is the test employed by the Trial Chamber in determining the existence of an armed conflict in the FYROM? Do you agree with the Trial Chamber that an armed conflict existed in the territory of the FYROM? What evidence was most dispositive in your eyes? Was there a particular moment in the timeline presented by the Trial Chamber when you became convinced that an armed conflict was underway and IHL applied?

3. Declarations of War

Today, wars are rarely declared. The power of the United States to declare war rests with Congress, under Article I, Section 8 of the U.S. Constitution. Despite the fact that the United States has been involved in scores of armed conflicts throughout its history, it has only declared war eleven times (against the United Kingdom, Mexico, Spain, Germany (twice), Austria-Hungary, Japan, Italy, Bulgaria, Hungary, and Romania), and in the context of five conflicts (the War of 1812, the Mexican-American War, the Spanish-American War, World War I, and World War II). Today, the law of armed conflict applies regardless of whether there has been a formal declaration of war. Historically, this was not always the case. The Hague Convention III of 1907 (Opening of Hostilities) required that war be declared before a state could commence hostilities. This requirement arose out of the doctrine of *de jure* war, which linked the existence of a legal state of war to the intention of at least one of the parties to be at war. Such a subjective test was rightly criticized. For example, Ian Brownlie called the doctrine "absurd," as it made a state of war dependent on the whim of a party that may or may not admit that a state of war exists for reasons having nothing to do with the magnitude of hostilities. *See* I. Brownlie, INTERNATIONAL LAW

AND THE USE OF FORCE BY STATES 26 (1963). This subjective test weakened during the twentieth century with efforts to outlaw—and then when such efforts failed, to regulate—war.

4. IHL in Domestic Courts

Domestic courts are becoming increasingly adept at adjudicating international humanitarian and criminal law. Indeed, the conflict in Syria has in many respects revitalized the principle of universal jurisdiction in Europe, with cases proceeding in a number of European states. Such cases are also facilitated by the establishment of specialized war crimes units and increasingly seamless processes for mutual legal assistance. Domestic prosecutors are also pursuing a number of historical justice cases when perpetrators are found within reach.

A Swiss court, for example, recently had to determine whether the situation in Algeria in 1992–94 constituted an armed conflict for the purpose of applying that country's international crimes statute. The defendant, former Algerian Minister of Defence Khaled Nezzar, was charged with war crimes and crimes against humanity. The Office of the Attorney General had closed its investigation, reasoning that armed conflicts involve heavy weaponry, but such weapons were not in use in Algeria. On appeal, the Federal Criminal Court (FCC) reversed and concluded that the confrontations between the regime and Islamist militants were sufficiently intense, and the opposition was sufficiently organized, to constitute an armed conflict. *A. v. Public Ministry of the Confederation*, BB.2017.9-11 (May 30, 2018). The Swiss court cited jurisprudence from the ICTY, and specifically the above-excerpted case, extensively.

In the course of this case, the FCC also ruled that Nezzar was not entitled to immunity from prosecution because (a) any immunity *rationae personae* (personal immunity) he might have enjoyed while in office lapsed when he stepped down in 2003 and (b) he was not entitled to immunity *rationae materiae* (functional immunity) as a former minister of defense for the commission of international crimes, which cannot constitute an "official" act. The court also determined that the *ex post facto* prohibition did not bar the prosecution because the relevant articles expanding jurisdiction over international crimes were procedural in nature. *See A. v. Public Ministry of the Confederation*, BB.2011.140 (July 25, 2012) (Switz.). The relevant provisions of the *Code Pénal Suisse du 21 Décembre 1937* are: Article 7 (allowing extraterritorial jurisdiction if the offender has committed a felony prescribed by the international community), Article 101 (providing no statute of limitations for international crimes), and Articles 264 et seq. (defining international crimes). The case was initiated by a Swiss NGO, TRIAL (Track Impunity Always) International.

5. Conflict Classification

Before proceeding to the next section on conflict classification, compare how the four Geneva Conventions and their Protocols define their respective material fields of application:

- 1949 Geneva Conventions, Common Article 2: "In addition to the provisions which shall be implemented in peacetime, the present Convention shall apply to all cases of declared war or of any other armed conflict which may arise between two or more of the High Contracting Parties, even if the state of war is not recognized by one of them. The Convention shall also apply to all cases of partial or total occupation of the territory of a High Contracting Party, even if the said occupation meets with no armed resistance."

- 1949 Geneva Conventions, Common Article 3: "In the case of armed conflict not of an international character occurring in the territory of one of the High Contracting Parties, each Party to the conflict shall be bound to apply, as a minimum, the following provisions. . ."

- 1977 Protocol I, Article 1:

  3. This Protocol, which supplements the Geneva Conventions of 12 August 1949 for the protection of war victims, shall apply in the situations referred to in Article 2 common to those Conventions.

  4. The situations referred to in the preceding paragraph include armed conflicts which peoples are fighting against colonial domination and alien occupation and against racist regimes in the exercise of their right of self-determination, as enshrined in the Charter of the United Nations and the Declaration on Principles of International Law concerning Friendly Relations and Co-operation among States in accordance with the Charter of the United Nations.

- 1977 Protocol II, Article 1:

  1. This Protocol, which develops and supplements Article 3 common to the Geneva Conventions of 12 August 1949 without modifying its existing conditions or application, shall apply to all armed conflicts which are not covered by Article 1 of the Protocol Additional to the Geneva Conventions of 12 August 1949, and relating to the Protection of Victims of International Armed Conflicts (Protocol I) and which take place in the territory of a High Contracting Party between its armed forces and dissident armed forces or other organized armed groups which, under responsible command, exercise such control over a part of its territory as to enable them to carry out sustained and concerted military operations and to implement this Protocol.

  2. This Protocol shall not apply to situations of internal disturbances and tensions, such as riots, isolated and sporadic acts of violence and other acts of a similar nature, as not being armed conflicts.

From these provisions, can you construct a conflict classification typology? How many different types of conflict are contemplated? What contribution do the Protocols (drafted in the 1970s) make to the definition of an international armed conflict? Revisit this typology at the end of the next Section.

B. INTERNATIONAL & NON-INTERNATIONAL CONFLICTS

If a situation meets the definition of an armed conflict, thus triggering the application of international humanitarian law, the next question is whether the armed conflict is an "international" or "non-international" one. The law of armed conflict has historically made a distinction between international (IACs) and non-international armed conflicts (NIACs), with the former having a more rigorous prescriptive and enforcement regime than the latter. For example, the four Geneva Conventions of 1949, supplemented by two Protocols in 1977,* primarily apply to IACs, defined at Article 2—common to all four Conventions—as "all cases of declared war or of any other armed conflict which may arise between two or more of the High Contracting Parties." The treaties provide specific protections to four classes of "protected persons": the wounded and the sick in the field (Geneva Convention I); the wounded and sick at sea (Geneva Convention II); prisoners of war (Geneva Convention III); and civilians (Geneva Convention IV). Certain forms of injurious conduct committed against these protected persons (such as acts of murder, torture, inhuman treatment, causing great suffering, destruction of property, unlawful confinement, denials of due process, and hostage-taking) constitute so-called "grave breaches" of the treaties and are punishable as war crimes.

During the negotiations around the four Geneva Conventions, the ICRC and a handful of state delegates sought to include rules governing internal armed conflicts within the four Geneva Conventions. In the face of stiff resistance from other participants, these advocates were only able to obtain a cryptic reference to armed conflicts "not of an international character" in Article 3, which is also common to the four Geneva Conventions. "Common Article 3" is a convention-in-miniature, setting forth a minimum set of rules governing NIACs. Note that commentators often speak of "international" or "internal" armed conflicts. The drafters of the Geneva Conventions, however, deliberately chose the formulation "non-international armed conflict." As you review the materials that follow, consider whether this distinction is significant and why drafters adopted a negative definition for armed conflicts that do not qualify as international conflicts.

In 1977, the international community adopted two Protocols to the Geneva Conventions in response to the changing nature of armed conflict. Protocol I provides a detailed set of rules concerning the obligation to discriminate between military and civilian targets; defines *international* conflicts as including, "armed conflicts in which people are fighting against colonial domination and alien occupation and against

---

* A third Protocol, adopted in 2005, added a new and entirely secular distinctive emblem (a red diamond) to mark protected objects.

racist regimes in the exercise of their right of self-determination"; expands the category of lawful combatants to include some members of guerrilla movements; and further defines and clarifies rules governing mercenaries. Protocol II elaborates on the minimum rules in Common Article 3 governing non-international armed conflicts and reflects a growing trend toward minimizing the differences between the rules that govern international and non-international armed conflicts.

Neither Common Article 3 nor Protocol II by their own terms contains a penal regime on the theory that crimes committed by individual combatants within non-international armed conflicts would be prosecutable under domestic law. Nonetheless, when the U.N. Security Council created the Statutes governing the first two *ad hoc* international tribunals for Yugoslavia and Rwanda, it contemplated that war crimes could be charged under international law in non-international armed conflicts. Article 2 of the Statute of the International Criminal Tribunal for the Former Yugoslavia (ICTY) contained a composite of the grave breaches regime of the Geneva Conventions. Article 3 of the ICTY Statute extended the jurisdiction of the Tribunal to other "violations of the laws and customs of war" including a non-exhaustive list of violations of the Fourth Hague Convention. The Tribunal interpreted this latter provision expansively to penalize violations of common Article 3 as well as other prohibitions within the Geneva Conventions and their Protocols, finding authority for this assertion in customary international law rather than treaty law. Because the conflict in the former Yugoslavia had both international and internal aspects, Article 3 of the ICTY Statute became increasingly important as the work of the tribunal progressed.

By contrast, the armed conflict in Rwanda was primarily internal. Accordingly, the Statute of the International Criminal Tribunal for Rwanda (ICTR) expressly granted that Tribunal jurisdiction over serious violations of common Article 3 and of Protocol II, including violence to life, torture, collective punishments, hostage-taking, terrorism, rape, pillage, and "the passing of sentences and the carrying out of executions without previous judgement pronounced by a regularly constituted court, affording all the judicial guarantees which are recognised as indispensable by civilised peoples." By conceptualizing violations of Common Article 3 and Protocol II as war crimes in the ICTR Statute, the Security Council furthered the trend toward applying the same rules to both classes of conflict.

Resistance to this conflation of the rules that apply to international and non-international conflicts re-emerged in the context of the "war on terror," which challenged the traditional conflict classification system and other penal aspects of international humanitarian law. Aspects of this debate will be discussed in greater length later in the next chapter and in Chapter 12 on Terrorism. Despite the modern trend toward a convergence in IHL rules, the question of whether conduct constitutes a war crime is still determined by whether IHL is even applicable, whether the conflict is considered to be international or non-international, whether the victim is granted protection under IHL, and whether the acts in question have a sufficient nexus to an armed conflict.

These issues are exemplified in the opinion below, which involves the situation in the Ituri region of the Democratic Republic of the Congo (DRC), one of the first situations to come before the then-fledgling International Criminal Court by way of a 2004 self-referral. As was the case in Rwanda, ethnic tensions in the DRC region span decades but were exacerbated by colonial rule and the Belgian practice of favoring one group over others. The immediate trigger for hostilities, however, concerned land disputes.

The events discussed below are part of the "Second Congo War," a complicated series of conflicts-within-conflicts. The map of the DRC in the Map Appendix is useful to consult to get a sense of the geographic scope of the conflict. The armed actors include an array of armed groups claiming to be fighting on behalf of the Hema or the Lendu ethnic groups that rapidly formed factions and switched alliances as political interests shift. Although some militia groups at times had only a couple of hundred active members, they were able to inflict enormous harm upon the civilian population by exploiting the area's vast natural resources, obtaining various forms of support from neighboring states engaged in proxy wars, and taking advantage of the proliferation of small arms in the country. The war in Ituri was devastating. It resulted in the deaths of over 60,000 people and the displacement of many thousands more. The conflict officially ended in 2003 when a new transitional government took power in Kinshasa, the DRC capital, although hostilities continued.

Thomas Lubanga Dyilo was the founder and leader of the *Union des Patriotes Congolais* (UPC) and the *Forces Patriotiques pour la Libération du Congo* (FPLC). He was arrested by Congolese authorities in 2005 and became the first suspect to be transferred to the ICC. He had originally been charged under Article 8(2)(e)(vii) of the ICC Statute with the war crimes of conscripting and enlisting children under the age of fifteen years into "armed forces or groups" and using them to participate actively in hostilities. In so charging, the Prosecutor implicitly characterized the relevant conflict as a NIAC. (Virtually the same crime involving recruitment into "the national armed forces" could be charged in connection with an international armed conflict pursuant to Article 8(2)(b)(xxvi)). As you will see, the Pre-Trial Chamber disagreed with this assessment of the conflict and confirmed charges under both provisions, finding that there was both an IAC and a NIAC. In the judgment below, however, the Trial Chamber reversed the Pre-Trial Chamber's conflict classification analysis. As you read the excerpt, consider how you would classify this conflict given the treaty standards set forth above and the facts described below.

Prosecutor v. Thomas Lubanga Dyilo, Case No. ICC–01/04–01/06, Judgment Pursuant to Article 74 of the Statute (March 14, 2012)

In Trial Chamber I

The Armed Conflict And Its Nature

503. It is necessary to determine whether there was a relevant armed conflict, and if so, whether it was international or non-international in character.

504. The existence of an armed conflict, be it international or non-international, is a fundamental requirement of the charges under Articles 8(2)(b)(xxvi) and 8(2)(e)(vii) of the Statute, which provide, *inter alia*:

> 2. For the purpose of this Statute, "war crimes" means: [. . .]
>
> b) Other serious violations of the laws and customs applicable in international armed conflict, within the established framework of international law [. . .]
>
> e) Other serious violations of the laws and customs applicable in armed conflicts not of an international character, within the established framework of international law [. . .]

It follows that if the prosecution has failed to prove the existence of a relevant armed conflict in Ituri from early September 2002 until 13 August 2003, it will have failed to prove the charges against the accused.

1. Prosecution Submissions

505. The prosecution submits it is undisputed that a significant and protracted armed conflict occurred in Ituri during the relevant period.

506. Relying on jurisprudence from the Pre-Trial Chambers and the International Criminal Tribunal for the former Yugoslavia ("ICTY"), the prosecution suggests an international armed conflict exists "whenever there is resort to armed force between States." It is argued a non-international armed conflict is established when States have not resorted to armed force and i) the violence is sustained and has reached a certain degree of intensity, and ii) armed groups with some degree of organisation, including the capability of imposing discipline and the ability to plan and carry out sustained military operations, are involved. Additionally, Article 8(2)(f) of the Statute stipulates that the conflict must be "protracted" for these purposes.

507. It is argued non-international conflicts only cease with a "peaceful settlement" and that a mere reduction in the extent of the hostilities is insufficient. The prosecution submits the evidence demonstrates that a settlement of this kind did not exist prior to 13 August 2003 because many organised armed groups continued to operate in Ituri during this period, including the *Le Front des Nationalistes et*

Intégrationnistes (FNI), which allegedly perpetrated massacres in June and July 2003; *Le Parti pour l'Unité et la Sauvegarde de l'Intégrité du Congo* (PUSIC), in its opposition to Lubanga's Union of Congolese Patriots and the Patriotic Forces for the Liberation of Congo (UPC/FPLC) in Tchomia in November 2003; and the *Forces Armées du Peuple Congolais* (FAPC), as regards its fight with the FNI and *Forces Populaires pour la Démocratie au Congo* (FPDC) in order to take control of Mahagi in June 2003. It is the prosecution's contention that members of the UPC/FPLC attacked MONUC several times.*

508. The prosecution alleges the UPC/FPLC fought the Rally for Congolese Democracy Liberation Movement (RCD-ML), the FNI and its ally the Patriotic Front for Resistance in Ituri (FRPI), and that each of these groups was armed and had a sufficient degree of organisation (demonstrated by their leadership structure and participation in the political process). Furthermore, it is suggested these armed groups had the ability to undertake sustained operations, as revealed by their ability to train troops and participate in numerous battles.

509. The prosecution submits the conflict was non-international in character, notwithstanding the conclusion of the Pre-Trial Chamber that it was international until Uganda withdrew from Ituri on 2 June 2003.

510. It is the prosecution submission that there can be simultaneous conflicts within a particular territory that involve different forces, and that Uganda's involvement (even if it is found to have constituted occupation), would not automatically mean the armed conflict relevant to the charges was international in character. The prosecution submits the key issue is the nature of the conflict to which the particular army or militia is a party (*viz.* the conflict "to which Lubanga's militia was a party during the relevant times").

511. The prosecution suggests that even if Uganda can be said to have been occupying certain areas of Ituri, such as Bunia airport, there is insufficient evidence that it occupied Bunia as a whole during the relevant timeframe. In addition, the prosecution submits that although there is some evidence of assistance provided by Rwanda and Uganda, applying the overall control test, as adopted by the ICC and ICTY (see below), it falls short of the threshold for indirect intervention. Equally, it is submitted that neither the presence of multi-national forces nor the direct intervention by Ugandan military forces were sufficient to constitute an international conflict, as the part played by these forces did not result in two states opposing each other. Finally, the prosecution

* Eds.: MONUC (the United Nations Organization Mission in the Democratic Republic of the Congo) was the original name of the U.N. peacekeeping force in the DRC created by the Security Council with Resolution 1279 following the signing of the Lusaka Ceasefire Agreement in July 1999 by the DRC and five regional states. MONUC was renamed the United Nations Organization Stabilization Mission in the Democratic Republic of the Congo (MONUSCO) by Resolution 1925 in May 2010. In 2005, nine Bangladeshi MONUC peacekeepers were killed by the FNI and the UCP—then the highest U.N. casualties among peacekeepers other than during the Rwandan genocide.

argues that even if Ugandan involvement did create an international armed conflict, the UPC/FPLC was involved in a distinct, simultaneous non-international armed conflict.

2. Defence Submissions

512. The defence, as part of its analysis of armed conflicts that are non-international in character, relies on the approach adopted by Pre-Trial Chamber I. Referring to the provisions of Article 8(2)(f) of the Statute, it submits the violence must reach a particular level of intensity. Armed conflicts not of an international character are conflicts that take place in the territory of a State when there is a protracted conflict between the government and organised armed groups, or between armed groups.

513. It is suggested by the defence that Additional Protocol II to the Geneva Conventions of 8 June 1977 operates to restrict this definition by stipulating that armed conflicts in this category

> take place in the territory of a High Contracting Party between its armed forces and dissident armed forces or other organized armed groups which, under responsible command, exercise such control over a part of its territory as to enable them to carry out sustained and concerted military operations and to implement this Protocol.

514. The defence argues the prosecution has failed to demonstrate that the FNI, the FRPI, PUSIC, and the FAPC were "organized armed groups" under international humanitarian law. It is submitted it has not been proven that these organisations were under responsible command or exercised sufficient control over a part of the relevant territory, thereby enabling them to carry out sustained and concerted military operations and to implement the provisions of international humanitarian law.

515. The approach of the Pre-Trial Chamber is referred to by the defence in this regard:

> Thus, in addition to the requirement that the violence must be sustained and have reached a certain degree of intensity, Article 1(1) of Additional Protocol II provides that armed groups must: i) be under responsible command implying some degree of organisation of the armed groups, capable of planning and carrying out sustained and concerted military operations and imposing discipline in the name of a de facto authority, including the implementation of the Protocol; and ii) exercise such control over territory as to enable them to carry out sustained and concerted military operations.

516. The defence supports the conclusion of the Pre-Trial Chamber that the conflict in Ituri in the period between September 2002 and June 2003 was an armed conflict of an international character (it is suggested that the conflict only extended until late May 2003). The defence argues

that whilst sporadic acts of violence occurred in Ituri after May 2003, these did not involve organised armed groups exercising territorial control and they should be treated as instances of internal disturbance and tension. It is suggested there was no conflict of any kind in Ituri between the end of May 2003 and August 2003.

517. The defence emphasises the evidence of P-0041, who testified as to arms being provided to the FPLC by Rwanda and the decision of the United Nations to maintain Ugandan troops in the DRC. The defence also highlights the testimony of a number of other witnesses: P-0017, concerning alleged training given by Rwanda to the FPLC and his reference to the Ugandan army as an occupying force; P-0055, as to the presence of the Ugandan army as an occupying force in Bunia and the provision of weapons and uniforms by Rwanda; P-0012, relating to Ugandan arms deliveries to PUSIC; and the expert Gérard Prunier (P-0360), on Uganda's role as an occupying force in Ituri, the involvement of the Kinshasa government in the conflict either directly or through the RCD-ML, and what he described as a "war by proxy between the states of the DRC, Uganda, and Rwanda." However, the defence observes that Mr. Prunier stressed that the available information on the events in Ituri in 2002–2003 is not particularly reliable. In addition, the defence submits that some of the views expressed in this witness's report are partial, although it accepts he is reliable on certain identified subjects.

3. Victims Submissions

518. The V01 group of legal representatives of victims contends it is undisputed that one or more armed conflicts occurred in Ituri between 1 September 2002 and 13 August 2003. The V01 group submits that the conflict cannot properly be considered as a situation of internal disturbance or tension, given the duration and intensity of the hostilities, the number of victims and the manner in which the forces were organised and armed.

519. The V01 team argues that during the period between September 2002 and June 2003, an international armed conflict and a non-international armed conflict existed simultaneously in the territory of Ituri.

520. * * * It advances by way of further evidence in this regard the Security Council's Resolution 1493 (pursuant to Chapter VII of the United Nations Charter), and the latter's decision to remain actively seized of the Ituri situation throughout the period of the charges. * * *

521. The V02 team maintains that the armed conflict can be classified as international due to its intensity, duration and character. It is suggested the UPC/FPLC was an organised armed group within the meaning of Article 8(2)(f) of the Statute, as it was capable of carrying out large-scale military operations for a protracted period of time. It also relies on the testimony of several witnesses as to the highly structured nature of the UPC and its chain of command.

522. The Office of Public Counsel for Victims (OPCV) has not advanced submissions as to whether there was an armed conflict, arguing that the prosecution is better placed to address this issue. Similarly, it has not presented arguments as to the appropriate characterisation of the conflict. Instead, the OPCV stresses that Articles 8(2)(b)(xxvi) and 8(2)(e)(vii) of the Statute criminalise the same conduct regardless of the characterisation of the armed conflict. The V02 team advanced a similar submission.

The Chamber's Conclusions

1. The Law

Characterisation of the Armed Conflict (International Armed Conflict vs. Non-International Armed Conflict)

523. In the Decision on the confirmation of charges, the Pre-Trial Chamber, having considered the evidence as to Rwanda's involvement in the armed conflict, concluded there was insufficient evidence to establish substantial grounds to believe that Rwanda played a role that could be described as direct or indirect intervention in the armed conflict in Ituri.

524. In its final analysis, the Pre-Trial Chamber held:

> On the evidence admitted for the purpose of the confirmation hearing, the Chamber considers that there is sufficient evidence to establish substantial grounds to believe that, as a result of the presence of the Republic of Uganda as an occupying Power, the armed conflict which occurred in Ituri can be characterised as an armed conflict of an international character from July 2002 to 2 June 2003, the date of the effective withdrawal of the Ugandan army. [. . .] There are substantial grounds to believe that between 2 June and late December 2003, the armed conflict in Ituri involved, inter alia, the UPC/FPLC, PUSIC and the FNI; that the UPC and FNI fought over control of the gold-mining town of Mongbwalu; that various attacks were carried out by the FNI in Ituri during this period. * * *

525. In determining that the relevant conflict was international between September 2002 and 2 June 2003 and non-international between 2 June 2003 and 13 August 2003, the Pre-Trial Chamber confirmed the charges against the accused on the basis of Articles 8(2)(b)(xxvi) and 8(2)(e)(vii) of the Statute, although the prosecution had only charged the accused with the conscription and enlistment of children under the age of fifteen years, and their use to participate actively in hostilities, within the context of a non-international armed conflict under Article 8(2)(e)(vii) of the Statute.

526. The prosecution and the defence applications for leave to appeal were refused by the Pre-Trial Chamber, which observed:

> [P]ursuant to Regulation 55 of the Regulations of the Court, the Trial Chamber may "change the legal characterisation of facts

> to accord with the crimes under articles 6, 7 or 8, or to accord with the form of participation of the accused." Indeed, there is nothing to prevent the Prosecution or the Defence from requesting that the Trial Chamber reconsider the legal characterisation of the facts described in the charges against Thomas Lubanga Dyilo and as confirmed by the Chamber.

527. Following submissions from the parties after the transfer of the case to the Trial Chamber, the latter gave notice, in accordance with Regulation 55 of the Regulations of the Court, that the legal characterisation of the facts may be subject to change. The Chamber instructed the parties and participants to:

> [. . .] prepare their cases on the basis that the Bench may decide that the first group of three charges encompass both international and internal armed conflicts.[1624]

528. Accordingly, the prosecution submitted as follows:

> Consistent with the Trial Chamber's decision of 13 December 2007 and the amended document containing the charges, the Prosecution will present the totality of its evidence relating to both international and non-international aspects of the conflict. The evidence will enable the Chamber to determine whether the Ugandan occupation of Ituri between the 1st of September 2002 and early June 2003 transformed the character of the conflict into an international armed conflict. * * *

530. The parties and the participants have not challenged the procedure followed by the Chamber as regards a possible legal recharacterisation of the facts under Regulation 55 of the Regulations of the Court, although they addressed in their submissions whether it would be appropriate for any modification to occur.

Definition of Armed Conflict

531. The relevant Elements of Crimes require that the alleged criminal conduct "took place in the context of and was associated with an [. . .] armed conflict." There is no definition of armed conflict in the Statute or in the Elements of Crimes. The introduction to the Elements of Crimes sets out that:

> The elements for war crimes under article 8, paragraph 2, of the Statute shall be interpreted within the established framework of the international law of armed conflict [. . .]

532. As with the Rome Statute, neither the Geneva Conventions nor their Additional Protocols explicitly define "armed conflict."

[1624] Decision on the Statute before the Trial Chamber of the Evidence Heard by the Pre-Trial Chamber and the Decisions of the Pre-Trial Chamber in Trial Proceedings, and the Manner in which Evidence shall be Submitted, ICC–01/04–01/06–1084 (Dec. 13, 2007), para. 49.

533. The definition of this concept has been considered by other international tribunals and the Chamber has derived assistance from the jurisprudence of the ICTY:

> 70. [. . .] an armed conflict exists whenever there is a resort to armed force between States or protracted violence between governmental authorities and organized armed groups or between such groups within a State. International humanitarian law applies from the initiation of such armed conflicts and extends beyond the cessation of hostilities until a general conclusion of peace is reached; or, in the case of internal conflicts, a peaceful settlement is achieved. Until that moment, international humanitarian law continues to apply in the whole territory of the warring States or, in the case of internal conflicts, the whole territory under the control of a party, whether or not actual combat takes place there.[1629]

Armed Conflict Not of an International Character

534. As to the definition of an armed conflict not of an international character, Article 8(2)(f) of the Statute provides:

> Paragraph 2(e) applies to armed conflicts not of an international character and thus does not apply to situations of internal disturbances and tensions, such as riots, isolated and sporadic acts of violence or other acts of a similar nature. It applies to armed conflicts that take place in the territory of a State when there is protracted armed conflict between governmental authorities and organized armed groups or between such groups.[1630]

535. Relying on Additional Protocol II to the Geneva Conventions and the ICTY *Tadić* Interlocutory Appeal Decision cited above, Pre-Trial Chamber I determined that "the involvement of armed groups with some

---

[1629] ICTY, *Prosecutor v. Tadić*, Case No. IT–94–1–AR72, Appeals Chamber, Decision on the Defence Motion for Interlocutory Appeal on Jurisdiction, 2 October 1995 ("*Tadić* Interlocutory Appeal Decision").

[1630] Common Article 3 to the Geneva Conventions of 12 August 1949 provides: "In the case of an armed conflict not of an international character occurring in the territory of one of the High Contracting parties, [. . .]"; Article 1(1) of Additional Protocol II reads:

> This Protocol, which develops and supplements Article 3 common to the Geneva Conventions of 12 August 1949 without modifying its existing conditions of application, shall apply to all armed conflicts which are not covered by Article 1 of the Protocol Additional to the Geneva Conventions of 12 August 1949, and relating to the Protection of Victims of International Armed Conflicts (Protocol I) and which take place in the territory of a High Contracting Party between its armed forces and dissident armed forces or other organized armed groups which, under responsible command, exercise such control over a part of its territory as to enable them to carry out sustained and concerted military operations and to implement this Protocol."

Article 1(2) of Additional Protocol II provides as follows: "This Protocol shall not apply to situations of internal disturbances and tensions, such as riots, isolated and sporadic acts of violence and other acts of a similar nature, as not being armed conflicts." Whereas Common Article 2 is limited to international armed conflicts between signatories, Common Article 3 affords minimal protection to organised armed groups involved in any conflict not of an international character.

degree of organisation and the ability to plan and carry out sustained military operations would allow for the conflict to be characterised as an armed conflict not of an international character."[1631]

536. The Trial Chamber agrees with this approach, and notes that Article 8(2)(f) of the Statute only requires the existence of a "protracted" conflict between "organised armed groups." It does not include the requirement in Additional Protocol II that the armed groups need to "exercise such control over a part of [the] territory as to enable them to carry out sustained and concerted military operations." It is therefore unnecessary for the prosecution to establish that the relevant armed groups exercised control over part of the territory of the State. Furthermore, Article 8(2)(f) does not incorporate the requirement that the organised armed groups were "under responsible command," as set out in Article 1(1) of Additional Protocol II. Instead, the "organized armed groups" must have a sufficient degree of organisation, in order to enable them to carry out protracted armed violence.[1635]

537. When deciding if a body was an organised armed group (for the purpose of determining whether an armed conflict was not of an international character), the following non-exhaustive list of factors is potentially relevant: the force or group's internal hierarchy; the command structure and rules; the extent to which military equipment, including firearms, are available; the force or group's ability to plan military operations and put them into effect; and the extent, seriousness, and intensity of any military involvement. None of these factors is individually determinative. The test, along with these criteria, should be applied flexibly when the Chamber is deciding whether a body was an organised armed group, given the limited requirement in Article 8(2)(f) of the Statute that the armed group was "organized."

538. The intensity of the conflict is relevant for the purpose of determining whether an armed conflict that is not of an international character existed,[1637] because under Article 8(2)(f) the violence must be more than sporadic or isolated. The ICTY has held that the intensity of the conflict should be "used solely as a way to distinguish an armed conflict from banditry, unorganized and short-lived insurrections, or terrorist activities, which are not subject to international humanitarian law." In order to assess the intensity of a potential conflict, the ICTY has indicated a Chamber should take into account, *inter alia*,

> the seriousness of attacks and potential increase in armed clashes, their spread over territory and over a period of time, the

---

[1631] *Prosecutor v. Thomas Lubanga Dyilo*, Case No. ICC–01/04–01/06, Decision on the Confirmation of Charges (Public Redacted Version), para. 233 (Jan. 29, 2007).

[1635] The inclusion of the additional requirements set out in Additional Protocol II that the armed groups are under responsible command and exercise control over a part of the territory appears to have been deliberately rejected by the drafters of the Rome Statute.

[1637] The requirement set out in Article 8(2)(f) is also a jurisdictional requirement because if the necessary level of intensity is not reached, the alleged crimes do not fall within the jurisdiction of the Court.

> increase in the number of government forces, the mobilisation and the distribution of weapons among both parties to the conflict, as well as whether the conflict has attracted the attention of the United Nations Security Council, and, if so, whether any resolutions on the matter have been passed.

The Chamber is of the view that this is an appropriate approach.

The Distinction Between International and Non-International Armed Conflicts

539. It is to be observed at the outset that some academics, practitioners, and a line of jurisprudence from the *ad hoc* tribunals have questioned the usefulness of the distinction between international and non-international armed conflicts, particularly in light of their changing nature. In the view of the Chamber, for the purposes of the present trial the international/non-international distinction is not only an established part of the international law of armed conflict, but more importantly it is enshrined in the relevant statutory provisions of the Rome Statute framework, which under Article 21 must be applied. The Chamber does not have the power to reformulate the Court's statutory framework.

540. The Appeals Chamber of the ICTY has recognised that, depending on the particular actors involved, conflicts taking place on a single territory at the same time may be of a different nature. The Chamber endorses this view and accepts that international and non-international conflicts may coexist.

International Armed Conflict

541. The Rome Statute framework does not define an "international armed conflict." Relying on Common Article 2 of the Geneva Conventions, the International Committee of the Red Cross ("ICRC") Commentary thereto, and the ICTY *Tadić* Appeals Judgment, Pre-Trial Chamber I determined that an armed conflict is international:

> if it takes place between two or more States; this extends to the partial or total occupation of the territory of another State, whether or not the said occupation meets with armed resistance. In addition an internal armed conflict that breaks out on the territory of a State may become international—or depending upon the circumstances, be international in character alongside an internal armed conflict—if (i) another State intervenes in that conflict through its troops (direct intervention), or if (ii) some of the participants in the internal armed conflict act on behalf of that other State (indirect intervention).

It is widely accepted that when a State enters into conflict with a non-governmental armed group located in the territory of a neighbouring State and the armed group is acting under the control of its own State, "the fighting falls within the definition of an international armed conflict between the two States." However, if the armed group is not acting on behalf of a government, in the absence of two States opposing each other, there is no international armed conflict. Pre-Trial Chamber II, when considering this issue, concluded that "an international armed conflict exists in case of armed hostilities between States through their respective armed forces or other actors acting on behalf of the State." As regards the necessary degree of control of another State over an armed group acting on its behalf, the Trial Chamber has concluded that the "overall control" test is the correct approach. This will determine whether an armed conflict not of an international character may have become internationalised due to the involvement of armed forces acting on behalf of another State. A State may exercise the required degree of control when it "has a role in organising, coordinating or planning the military actions of the military group, in addition to financing, training and equipping or providing operational support to that group."[1649] Pre-Trial Chamber I adopted this approach.

542. Moreover, footnote 34 of the Elements of Crimes stipulates that the term "international armed conflict" includes a "military occupation," for all of the crimes coming within Article 8(2)(a) of the Statute. Pre-Trial Chamber I held that a "territory is considered to be occupied when it is actually placed under the authority of the hostile army, and the occupation extends only to the territory where such authority has been established and can be exercised."[1651] The Chamber agrees with this definition. The Chamber notes the reference in Article 8(2)(b) to "the established framework of international law," which applies equally to the crimes set out in Article 8(2)(b). The crime of "conscripting or enlisting children under the age of fifteen years into the national armed forces or using them to participate actively in hostilities" as set out in Article 8(2)(b)(xxvi) of the Statute falls within "the established framework of international law" as one of the "other serious violations of the laws and customs applicable in international armed conflict." The prohibition is based on Article 77(2) of Additional Protocol I to the Geneva Conventions of 12 August 1949. This Protocol applies to armed conflicts between States, as indicated by Common Article 2 of the Geneva Conventions.[1653] It follows that for the purposes of Article 8(2)(b)(xxvi) of the Statute, "international armed conflict" includes a military occupation.

[1649] *Tadić* Appeal Judgement, para. 137 (emphasis in the original); see also: "[C]ontrol by a State over subordinate armed forces or militias or paramilitary units may be of an overall character (and must comprise more than the mere provision of financial assistance or military equipment or training)." Ibid., para. 137.

[1651] Articles 42 and 43, Regulations Concerning the Laws and Customs of War on Land, annexed to Convention (IV) respecting the Laws and Customs of War on land, 18 October 1907. Article 42 reads: "Territory is considered occupied when it is actually placed under the authority of the hostile army. The occupation extends only to the territory where such authority has been established and can be exercised." Article 43 reads: "The authority of the legitimate power having in fact passed into the hands of the occupant, the latter shall take all the measures in his power to restore, and ensure, as far as possible, public order and safety, while respecting, unless absolutely prevented, the laws in force in the country."

[1653] Article 1(3) of Additional Protocol I reads: "This Protocol, which supplements the Geneva Conventions of 12 August 1949 for the protection of war victims, shall apply in the situations referred to in Article 2 common to those Conventions."

2. The Facts

543. The evidence in the case demonstrates beyond reasonable doubt that during the entirety of the period covered by the charges there were a number of simultaneous armed conflicts in Ituri and in surrounding areas within the DRC, involving various different groups. Some of these armed conflicts, which included the UPC, involved protracted violence. The military wing of the UPC, known as the FPLC, was established by September 2002. * * * [F]rom the beginning of September 2002 at the latest, the UPC/FPLC as a political and military organisation was in control of Bunia. The takeover of Bunia [the regional capital] by the UPC/FPLC marked the turning point in the Ituri conflict. From then onwards, the "rapidity of the alliance switches," the "multi-directionality" of the fighting and the nature of the violence against the civilian population reached unprecedented extremes. The UPC/FPLC was organised with a leadership structure that was capable of training troops as well as imposing discipline, and it carried out sustained military operations in Ituri during the relevant timeframe.

544. In addition to the FPLC, there were a number of significant political and military groups in operation in Ituri in 2002. The RCD-ML, whose army was the APC, was defeated in August 2002 in Bunia and thereafter it supported the Lendu militias and engaged in fighting against the UPC/FPLC. As set out above, the Lendu formed a group called the FNI and the Ngiti created the FRPI. Other significant militias at the time included, *inter alia*, PUSIC, headed by Chief Kahwa Panga Mandro after his departure from the UPC/FPLC near the end of 2002, and Jérôme Kakwavu's FAPC.

545. On the basis of the evidence presented in this case, it has been established that the APC, the armed wing of the RCD-ML, was an organised armed group capable of carrying out prolonged hostilities within the period of the charges. During this time, the RCD-ML/APC also supported various Lendu armed militias, including the FRPI, in combat against the UPC/FPLC.

546. From March 2003, at the latest, the FRPI was an organised armed group as it had a sufficient leadership and command structure, participated in the Ituri Pacification Commission, carried out basic training of soldiers and engaged in prolonged hostilities, including the battles in Bogoro and Bunia (between March and May 2003).

547. Extensive evidence has been given during the trial concerning the UPC/FPLC's involvement in the fighting involving rebel militias (namely the RCD-ML and Lendu militias, including the FRPI) that took place in Ituri between September 2002 and August 2003. The Chamber heard evidence that the UPC/FPLC, assisted by the Ugandan Peoples Defense Force (UPDF), fought the RCD-ML in Bunia in August 2002. In November 2002, the UPC/FPLC fought Lendu combatants and the APC in Mongbwalu. The UPC/FPLC fought the APC and Lendu militias in Bogoro (March 2003), and it was in conflict with Lendu militias in Lipri,

Bambu and Kobu (in February and March 2003), Mandro (March 2003), and Mahagi, among other areas. In early March 2003, fighting between the UPC/FPLC and the UPDF and several Lendu militias, including the FRPI, ended in the withdrawal of the UPC/FPLC from Bunia. However, in May 2003 the UPC/FPLC army returned to Bunia where it clashed with Lendu militias, again including the FRPI, resulting in a number of casualties.

548. Although Ugandan forces withdrew from Bunia in May 2003, the evidence indicates that there was no "peaceful settlement" prior to 13 August 2003. Documentary evidence establishes that in June 2003, the Hema village of Katoto was attacked twice by Lendu militia members, resulting in many casualties. In addition, Lendu militia and APC soldiers attacked Tchomia in July 2003, killing up to eleven civilians. Scores more civilians were killed in July 2003, when Lendu combatants carried out attacks on Fataki. During the summer of 2003, the U.N. Security Council authorised the deployment to Ituri of a European Union-led Interim Emergency Multinational Force (Operation Artemis) in order to restore security in the area, and on 28 July 2003 MONUC was given a Chapter VII mandate authorising it to take the necessary measures to protect civilians. Despite these and other efforts, the evidence clearly indicates that during the period between the end of May 2003 and 13 August 2003, a peaceful settlement had not been reached in Ituri. * * *

550. The Chamber finds that the evidence on this issue leaves no reasonable doubt that the UPC/FPLC, as an armed force or group, participated in protracted hostilities and was associated with an armed conflict throughout the relevant timeframe of the charges.

551. In situations where conflicts of a different nature take place on a single territory, it is necessary to consider whether the criminal acts under consideration were committed as part of an international or a non-international conflict. In these circumstances, the question arises as to whether the military involvement by one or more of the DRC's neighbours on its territory internationalised the relevant conflict or conflicts.

552. In accordance with the test set out above, to determine whether the UPC/FPLC was a party to an international armed conflict in Ituri, the relevant inquiry is whether between September 2002 and 13 August 2003, the UPC/FPLC, the APC and the FRPI were used as agents or "proxies" for fighting between two or more states (namely Uganda, Rwanda, or the DRC).

553. As to the role of the DRC, there is some evidence that authorities in Kinshasa [the capital of the DRC] sent trainers and weapons to the APC. The U.N. Special Report on the events in Ituri contains allegations that in the last three months of 2002, "some military supplies may have also been sent directly to the Lendu militia" in Rethy, within the Djugu territory. However, the limited support provided by the Congolese government to the RCD-ML and potentially to Lendu militias

during this time is insufficient to establish the DRC government's overall control over these armed groups. Critically, there is no sustainable suggestion that the DRC had a role in organising, coordinating or planning the military actions of the UPC/FPLC during the period relevant to the charges.

554. Regarding the role of Rwanda, there is ample evidence it provided support to the UPC/FPLC. There is evidence that Rwanda supplied uniforms and weapons to the UPC/FPLC, including dropping weapons by air to Mandro, and it provided training to UPC/FPLC soldiers, in the DRC and in Rwanda. P-0017, a former UPC/FPLC member, testified that he went to Rwanda with a group of soldiers to receive heavy-weapons training in late 2002. Around January 2003, the UPC/FPLC reportedly signed an agreement with the RCD-G, which was supported by Kigali. Documentary evidence establishes that after the UPDF expelled the UPC/FPLC from Bunia in March 2003, Thomas Lubanga and others were evacuated to Rwanda.

555. P-0055 testified that he had been told, with regard to the UPC/FPLC's objective of taking military control of the town of Mongbwalu, "they had received orders from Rwanda" and Rwanda had indicated "if they took the town of Mongbwalu it would be a good thing and they were going to receive everything they needed. And so the objective of taking Mongbwalu was to obey an order issued by Rwanda, and in order to receive assistance from Rwanda as a result." There is no corroboration of this statement.

556. Furthermore, there is no evidence that Rwanda supported either the APC or the FRPI. Therefore, it is unnecessary for the Chamber to consider this issue further.

557. There is considerable material regarding the presence of Ugandan troops in Ituri between September 2002 and 13 August 2003, although the overall number involved was decreasing during the period covered by the charges. For instance, Gérard Prunier indicated that although the UPDF once deployed 13,000 troops in the DRC, at the time the all-inclusive peace agreement was signed on 17 December 2002, 10,000 had been withdrawn. Similarly, reports from the U.N. set out that between 10 September 2002 and 18 October 2002, 2,287 UPDF troops withdrew from Ituri, leaving a reinforced battalion in Bunia and troops patrolling the Ruwenzori Mountains. Notwithstanding that reduction, there was, on occasion, substantial activity on the part of Ugandan forces: for instance, the UPDF was in occupation of areas in Bunia, such as the airport, for considerable periods of time (in the latter case, from 1 September 2002 until 6 May 2003).

558. Additionally, there is evidence of Ugandan support for UPC/FPLC troops in the form of training and providing weapons.

559. Documentary evidence demonstrates the FRPI was supported by individual UPDF commanders, and the FRPI (and other militias) assisted in removing the UPC/FPLC from Bunia in March 2003.

560. Gérard Prunier testified that the DRC, Uganda, and Rwanda fought through "proxies," and at one point in his evidence, he asserted that a proxy war between Kinshasa and Uganda continued until the final departure of Ugandan troops (which he suggested was in 2004). However, as discussed above, the evidence in this case concerning the DRC's role in the relevant conflict has essentially been limited to the way it provided support to the APC. As to Uganda's involvement, according to Gérard Prunier, the UPDF initially had supported "the Hemas against the Lendu" before switching sides and lending assistance to the Lendu. As to Uganda's control over the FRPI and other militias, Mr. Prunier testified that the Ugandans were "unable to control their agents on the ground." In his report to the Chamber, Mr. Prunier asserted "[a]fter August 2002 the UPDF obviously lost control of its proxies." He also suggested that at some point Kampala may not even have had control of its own forces in the DRC. * * *

563. Similarly, although there is evidence of direct intervention on the part of Uganda, this intervention would only have internationalized the conflict between the two states concerned (viz. the DRC and Uganda). Since the conflict to which the UPC/FPLC was a party was not "a difference arising between two states" but rather protracted violence carried out by multiple non-state armed groups, it remained a non-international conflict notwithstanding any concurrent international armed conflict between Uganda and the DRC.

564. As discussed above, there is evidence that during the relevant timeframe the UPDF occupied certain areas of Bunia, such as the airport. However, it is unnecessary to analyse whether territory came under the authority of the Ugandan forces, thereby amounting to a military occupation, because the relevant conflict or conflicts concern the UPC and other armed groups.

565. Focusing solely on the parties and the conflict relevant to the charges in this case, the Ugandan military occupation of Bunia airport does not change the legal nature of the conflict between the UPC/FPLC, RCD-ML/APC and FRPI rebel groups since this conflict, as analysed above, did not result in two states opposing each other, whether directly or indirectly, during the time period relevant to the charges. In any event, the existence of a possible conflict that was "international in character" between the DRC and Uganda does not affect the legal characterisation of the UPC/FPLC's concurrent non-international armed conflict with the APC and FRPI militias, which formed part of the internal armed conflict between the rebel groups.

566. For these reasons and applying Regulation 55 of the Regulations of the Court, the Chamber changes the legal

characterisation of the facts to the extent that the armed conflict relevant to the charges was non-international in character.

567. The Trial Chamber therefore finds that the armed conflict between the UPC/FPLC and other armed groups between September 2002 and 13 August 2003 was non-international in nature.

NOTES & QUESTIONS

1. Conflict Classification

As discussed, the applicability of the IHL treaties and the sub-parts of Article 8 of the ICC depends on the characterization of a conflict as international or non-international. Have modern geopolitical realities and the conflicts to which they give rise, especially during and since the Cold War, challenged this distinction between the two types of conflict? Did the conflict in central Africa fit cleanly in this binary distinction? When does a conflict that began as an internal armed conflict become an international one and vice versa? In the *Lubanga* decision above, what were the facts and types of evidence relied upon by the tribunal to determine that the conflict in the region in question was not an international one as the Pre-Trial Chamber had found? On what authority did the Trial Chamber rely in formulating the test it employed? Is the occupation by Uganda of parts of Ituri relevant to the classification of the conflict? What about the presence of peacekeepers serving as part of MONUC (later denominated MONUSCO) or Operation Artemis? The latter was authorized by Security Council Resolution 1484 and involved the temporary deployment of a French-led Interim Multilateral Emergency Force to secure Bunia, the regional capital, while MONUC was being reinforced. It marked the first EU military mission outside of Europe.

2. Effective v. Overall Control

In *Military and Paramilitary Activities in and against Nicaragua (Nicaragua v. United States)*, the International Court of Justice (ICJ) was faced with the question of whether the violations of international humanitarian law committed by the Nicaraguan *Contras* were attributable to the United States which was, at the time, "training, arming, equipping, financing and supplying the *contra* forces or otherwise encouraging, supporting and aiding military and paramilitary activities in and against Nicaragua." If such actions were attributed to the United States, it could be held responsible for any acts of the *Contras*—a non-state actor—that violated international law. The Court concluded that for the United States to be legally responsible for the alleged violations, it would have to be proved that it had "effective control" of the operations in the course of which the alleged violations were committed. The Court found that, notwithstanding the high degree of support provided to the *Contras* by the United States, this test of "effective control" was not met. Thus, Nicaragua could not hold the United States accountable for the actions of the *Contras*. How does the test applied in *Lubanga* compare to that employed in the *Nicaragua* case? How do you explain the differences? What is the difference between a standard of effective control versus overall control? Does it make sense to have both tests?

3. Armed Activities on the Territory of the Congo

Elsewhere in the opinion, the ICC cites another ICJ case—the 2005 *Case Concerning Armed Activities on the Territory of the Congo (DRC v. Uganda)*. Upon assuming power over the DRC (formerly Zaire) in May 1997, President Laurent-Désiré Kabila allowed Ugandan troops into the eastern regions of the country to help maintain security. A year later, however, when Kabila called for the withdrawal of these troops, Uganda refused and in fact began providing support to various Congolese militias opposed to the regime in Kinshasa. Uganda claimed it was exercising its right of self-defense against cross-border attacks emanating from anti-Ugandan insurgent, Congolese, and Sudanese forces.

The ICJ determined that Ugandan troops acted unlawfully by remaining on DRC territory and substituting their own authority in Ituri for that of the Congolese government. How is this case relevant to the *Lubanga* case? Does the question of whether Uganda's presence in the DRC was lawful have a bearing on the qualification of the acts committed as war crimes? Should it? What standard of proof is applied by the ICJ in determining state responsibility? This ruling laid the foundation for further findings that the government of Uganda was responsible for violations of human rights and international humanitarian law, not only by its own troops but also by various other non-state actors present in the occupied territory. What level of involvement by a foreign state is enough to internationalize what would otherwise be a NIAC? Should the level of involvement necessary to internationalize a NIAC be the same as the level of involvement necessary to ascribe state responsibility?

4. Occupation

The law governing belligerent occupation dates back as least as far as the 1899 and 1907 Hague Regulations Respecting the Laws and Customs of War on Land. These rules apply from the time a state establishes what amounts to effective control over another sovereign's territory until it relinquishes control to the indigenous authorities. Thus, the mere presence of foreign troops on the territory of another state does not *ipso facto* constitute an occupation. Whether a situation of occupation exists is not dependent upon any declaratory act or subjective intent; rather, it is the objective facts on the ground that govern. An over-arching obligation of the occupying power is to restore and maintain public order on the occupied territory while respecting the laws in force. To this end, Article 43 of the 1907 Hague Regulations states:

> The authority of the legitimate power having in fact passed into the hands of the occupant, the latter shall take all measures in his power to restore, and ensure, as far as possible, public order and safety, while respecting, unless absolutely prevented, the laws in force in the country.

World War II—and the mistreatment of the civilian population it occasioned—made it clear that the Hague Convention's provisions did not provide adequate protection to civilians in situations of occupation. Accordingly, the Fourth Geneva Convention imposes more detailed—and rigorous—obligations on the occupying power (*see, e.g.*, Part III of the treaty). Persons who find themselves in the territory that is under the control of an occupying power are considered protected persons within the meaning of the Fourth Geneva Convention. Article 4 of this treaty defines its "protected persons" as:

> those who, at a given moment and in any manner whatsoever, find themselves, in case of a conflict or occupation, in the hands of a Party to the conflict or Occupying Power of which they are not nationals.

For a discussion, *see Prosecutor v. Naletilić & Martinović*, Case No IT–88–34–T, Judgement (March 31, 2003). Consider the way in which a situation of occupation might impact international criminal law and its enforcement. For example, would a situation of occupation bear on who might be charged and for what crimes? The law of belligerent occupation does not apply to non-international armed conflicts. Why not?

5. Regulation 55

When drafting the Regulations of the ICC in 2004, the judges included Regulation 55, which states:

> 1. In its decision under article 74 [relating to the final judgment of the Trial Chamber], the [Trial] Chamber may change the legal characterisation of facts to accord with the crimes under articles 6, 7 or 8, or to accord with the form of participation of the accused under articles 25 and 28, without exceeding the facts and circumstances described in the charges and any amendments to the charges.
>
> 2. If, at any time during the trial, it appears to the Chamber that the legal characterisation of facts may be subject to change, the Chamber shall give notice to the participants of such a possibility and having heard the evidence, shall, at an appropriate stage of the proceedings, give the participants the opportunity to make oral or written submissions. The Chamber may suspend the hearing to ensure that the participants have adequate time and facilities for effective preparation or, if necessary, it may order a hearing to consider all matters relevant to the proposed change. * * *

The Regulation thus allows the Trial Chamber to convict an accused of a crime or on the basis of a theory of liability that is other than that with which he was originally charged so long as the recharacterization does not exceed the facts or circumstances described in the charges as confirmed by the Pre-Trial Chamber.

The judges have invoked Regulation 55 to alter the substantive charges, as was done in *Lubanga*, and also the forms of responsibility. In *Katanga*, Pre-Trial Chamber I confirmed charges against the accused on a joint co-perpetration theory. The Trial Chamber subsequently indicated (over Judge Christine Van den Wyngaert's strong dissent) that his responsibility should also be considered under a common purpose theory. *Prosecutor v. Katanga and Chui*, Case No. ICC–01/04–01/07, Decision on the implementation of regulation 55 of the Regulations of the Court and Severing the Charges against the Accused Persons, para. 45 (ICC Trial Chamber II, Nov. 21, 2012). A group of victims unsuccessfully invoked Regulation 55 in the *Lubanga* case in an effort to add charges of sexual violence. *See Prosecutor v. Lubanga*, Case No. ICC–01/04/04–01/06, Decision on the Legal Representatives' Joint Submissions Concerning the Appeals Chamber's Decision on 8 December 2009 on Regulation 55 of the Regulations of the Court (Jan. 8, 2010).

Regulation 55 has been controversial, in part because there are questions about whether the judges were empowered to adopt it in the first place given that the treaty contains a set of procedures for advancing and confirming charges that does not envision any sort of judicial recharacterization. The Regulation also raises acute concerns about the rights of the defense (e.g., to be informed of the charges, to have adequate time to prepare, to enjoy a speedy trial etc.). For a strong critique of Regulation 55, *see* Dov Jacobs, *A Shifting Scale of Power: Who is in Charge of the Charges at the International Criminal Court and the Uses of Regulation 55, in* THE ASHGATE RESEARCH COMPANION TO INTERNATIONAL CRIMINAL LAW 205 (W. Schabas, et al. eds., 2013). *See also* American University War Crimes Research Office, *Regulation 55 and the Rights of the Accused at the International Criminal Court* (October 2013). Regulation 55 is discussed in greater detail in Chapter 13 on charging.

6. Children Associated with Armed Groups or Forces (So-Called "Child-Soldiers")

Many conflicts, notably but not exclusively in Africa, involve the recruitment, enlistment, and deployment of child soldiers. Rebel groups, civil defense groups, and government forces have forcibly abducted children for use in their respective militaries. Some children have joined such forces voluntarily for ideological, political, or economic reasons or to seek retaliation for harms committed against their communities. Many child soldiers are used in combat; others play support roles as porters, spotters, couriers, spies, looters, and cooks. Girls are particularly, but not exclusively, vulnerable to many forms of sexual and gender-based violence (SGBV).

In 2000, the U.N. General Assembly adopted an Optional Protocol to the Convention on the Rights of the Child on the Involvement of Children in Armed Conflict. *See* G.A. Res. A/RES/54/263 (May 25, 2000). The Protocol, which entered into force in 2002 and governs only national armed forces, sets eighteen as the minimum age for recruitment and direct participation in hostilities, although youth may enlist at age sixteen or above so long as certain safeguards (such as parental and informed consent) are in place. In this regard, the Protocol seeks to raise the age of recruitment and participation; Additional Protocols I and II to the Geneva Conventions and the Convention on the Rights of the Child all set fifteen as the minimum age, although states are to give priority to older youth. Similarly, the ICC Statute only criminalizes the recruitment and use of children under fifteen. The Child Soldiers Protocol also obliges States Parties to approach child soldiers with an ethos of rehabilitation rather than retribution. In particular, pursuant to Article 6(3), States Parties agree to take all feasible measures to ensure that persons within their jurisdiction who are recruited or used in hostilities contrary to the present Protocol are demobilized or otherwise released from service. States Parties shall, when necessary, accord to such persons all appropriate assistance for their physical and psychological recovery and their social reintegration.

The Special Court for Sierra Leone (SCSL) was the first tribunal to litigate the crime of recruiting and using child soldiers. In its decision in the case against Sam Hinga Norman, the Court concluded for the first time that the crime entailed individual criminal responsibility under customary international law and indicted Norman for recruiting children under 15. *Prosecutor v. Sam Hinga Norman*, Case No. SCSL–2003–14–AR72(E), Decision on Preliminary Motion Based on Lack of Jurisdiction (May 31, 2004). (For more on the *Norman* case see Chapter 17.) The Court subsequently prosecuted several individuals for the same crime, including, most recently, Charles Taylor, Liberia's former president. See *Prosecutor v. Charles Ghankay Taylor*, Case No. SCSL–03–01–T, Judgement (May 18, 2012).

For a nuanced discussion of the phenomenon of child soldiers, and the way in which they tend to be characterized as either hapless victims or violent sociopaths, *see* Mark Drumbl, REIMAGINING CHILD SOLDIERS IN INTERNATIONAL LAW AND POLICY (2012). The CRC and its Child Soldiers Protocol are directed at states; what rules govern, or should govern, the participation of young people in non-state armed groups? The non-governmental organization Geneva Call regularly enters into deeds of commitment with non-state armed actors in which they pledge not to recruit children in their ranks.

7. Peacekeeping and International Justice

All but one of the International Criminal Court's DRC indictees is in custody, in trial, or pursuing an appeal. The lone DRC fugitive is Sylvestre Mudacumura, a commander in the FDLR. He is reportedly hiding somewhere in eastern DRC. The Hutu-dominated FDLR is composed of ex-*génocidaires* who fled Rwanda when the Rwandan Patriotic Front (RPF) assumed control of the country following the 1994 genocide. For many years the FDLR has controlled territory and preyed on the civilian population in the DRC, particularly those of Tutsi ancestry. A rival armed group, the M23 Movement—led by ICC defendant Bosco Ntaganda—was allegedly supported by the current Rwandan Government in part as a proxy force against the FDLR. M23 is also alleged to be responsible for abuses against the civilian population in DRC. The M23 was defeated by the *Forces Armées de la République Démocratique du Congo* (FARDC), with the crucial assistance of the UN Stabilization Mission in the DRC (MONUSCO). It is now expected that the FARDC and MONUSCO will turn their attention toward the FDLR. Additionally, there are reports that Mudacumura may be injured or ill. (Indeed, a bit of a scandal ensued when rumors emerged in 2009 that MONUC had offered medical and transportation assistance to Mudacumura). Whatever his circumstances, it cannot be gainsaid that his presence in the region is a source of continued regional instability. The Security Council has called expressly for his arrest; such arrest would demonstrate that the DRC and MONUSCO are as committed to curtailing Rwanda's enemies as they are its allies, the M23.

The situation in the DRC benefits from a Security Council peacekeeping mandate that is the most robust yet when it comes to capturing fugitives. When the Security Council renewed the mandate of MONUSCO in 2013, it created an Intervention Brigade (IB) to address the continued instability and threat posed by numerous armed groups (including the FDLR, M23, LRA, and various local and loosely connected Mai Mai groups) in the region. Resolution 2098 of 2013 included language to the effect that MONUSCO may "take all necessary measures" to protect civilians, neutralize armed groups through the IB, and

> support and work with the Government of the DRC to arrest and bring to justice those responsible for war crimes and crimes against humanity in the country, including through cooperation with States of the region and the ICC.

It also requests the Government of the DRC to arrest and hold accountable those responsible for international crimes, including Mudacumura, in cooperation with the ICC. Should peacekeeping mandates be written so as to support international justice efforts? What might counsel against having peacekeepers engage in the arrest of suspects?

PROBLEM

As you consider the facts set forth below, how would you classify the various stages of the armed conflict in Afghanistan along the conflict spectrum? (See the Appendix for a map of Afghanistan.) What are the implications of the conflict being an international or non-international conflict? Which IHL treaties applied to the conflicts at the various times?

Afghanistan has been a nation in conflict for centuries. A landlocked rural country with numerous rival tribes and ethnicities, it stands in Asia at the crossroads between East and West. Though ruled as a monarchy since 1747, King Mohammed Zahir Shah in 1964 instituted a new constitution affording limited democratic representation. He hoped to bring socio-economic modernization to vast swaths of rural territory, and to stall political rivals within the royal family. Unfortunately, corruption plagued the new government, which did not adequately address national economic needs or respond to growing resentment over the nobility's privileges—particularly access to education. In particular, university students began to organize anti-government groups with Communist or militant Muslim ideologies. By 1972 (and before the Arab oil boom), severe drought and job shortages brought tensions to crisis levels.

In 1973, while the King sought medical treatment in Italy, his cousin Mohammad Daoud Khan seized power. Daoud, a former Prime Minister and senior Army officer, had allied with Marxist student groups to affect the near-bloodless coup, but slowly began purging them from government and military ranks. He jailed dissident Muslim activists, rejected calls for political reform, and failed to deliver prosperity. By 1977, Daoud had promulgated a new constitution which concentrated most state power in a single party he controlled, and openly cultivated ties with Western-leaning states such as Iran, Pakistan, and Egypt. (In 1978, Shah Pahlavi still ruled

Iran, India's communist leanings caused the U.S. to court Pakistan, and a Sadat-led Egypt had reconciled with Israel). The Soviet Union feared its neighbor was tilting toward the West.

In 1978, Marxist organizers brought down Daoud's government. A decapitation strike by Afghan air assault and artillery units loyal to the Communists gunned down the President and most of his family, and swiftly moved to seize power in Kabul. The new leaders immediately opened a dialogue with the Soviet Union and signed a treaty of friendship, including military and economic aid. Communist officials at all levels also swiftly moved to liquidate the nobility, political enemies, and educated elites, destabilizing Afghan society. Infighting and murders between Marxist factions caused power to shift hands over 18 months, with mixed results. Finally, after months of internal wrangling, the Soviet Union fatefully chose to intervene, using as a pretext enforcement of the friendship treaty to counter U.S. infiltration and propaganda. (Ironically, the Afghan government had increasingly requested Soviet military support to fight Muslim radicals). In late December 1979, the Soviets invaded Afghanistan and installed a new government.

The Soviet occupation inflamed nationalist and Islamic sentiments, but popular uprisings were met by brutal repression. Loosely-aligned Afghan opposition groups, known as the *Mujahedeen* ("those who struggle"), battled Soviet troops in a war that drew Muslims from all over the world, including Saudi-born Osama bin Laden. An estimated one million Afghans died during this time, and one third of the population became refugees in Pakistan and elsewhere. Against all odds, and with covert support from multiple nations, including U.S. aid funneled through the U.S. Central Intelligence Agency (CIA) and Pakistan's Inter-Service Intelligence Agency (ISI), the *Mujahedeen*'s attrition strategy eventually caused the Soviets to withdraw troops when Mikhail Gorbachev convinced the Politburo that the enormous cost in blood and treasure was no longer politically justifiable in an era of *glasnost*. To end the war, Afghanistan and Pakistan signed the Geneva Accords in 1988, which promised mutual non-interference and non-intervention (with the U.S.A. and U.S.S.R. as guarantors). The agreement also provided a timetable for Soviet troop withdrawal from Afghanistan, which was completed in 1989.

Following the Soviet withdrawal, the United States and its allies abandoned efforts to establish a peace process between Afghanistan's still-surviving Communist government and the *Mujahedeen*. The latter were not party to the Geneva Accords and rejected the agreement. A long, internal struggle ensued until—as everyone expected—elements of the *Mujahedeen* finally took control of the capital, Kabul, in 1992 and ousted the Communist-backed regime. Old tribal and ethnic rivalries, however, divided the new government led by Burhanuddin Rabbani, and generated internal fighting and dysfunction. In 1994, a village *mullah* (a religiously educated man), Mohammed Omar, began organizing a new armed movement in the south that eventually earned Pakistan's backing. The movement became known as the Taliban, meaning "Students of Islam."

Over time, the Taliban expanded their reach throughout the country. Pakistan allowed hundreds of armed Taliban supporters from Afghan refugee camps in Pakistan to re-cross the border and join in attacks on the weak central government and any opposing tribes. They also received financial and other assistance from Osama bin Laden, one of the founders of al Qaeda, and welcomed him back to Afghanistan after his expulsion from Sudan.

In 1996, the Taliban took Kabul, the nation's capital and most developed city. By the late 1990s, they controlled over ninety percent of Afghanistan and became the *de facto* government. The Taliban imposed a harsh version of *shar'ia* law within the country, resulting in human rights violations among the populace. These policies especially targeted the country's women, who previously enjoyed a fair amount of autonomy under communist rule. The same year, Afghanistan welcomed Osama bin Laden, who had been expelled from the Sudan.

With the aim of toppling the Taliban government, Afghan warlords and their militias banded together in 1996–1997 to form a multi-ethnic anti-Taliban force. This coalition became known as the Northern Alliance, because it retained control of the northernmost parts of the country. Although the Taliban controlled the capital and most of the country, only Pakistan, Saudi Arabia, and the United Arab Emirates recognized the Taliban as the official government of Afghanistan. The rest of the international community treated President Rabbani and the Northern Alliance as the legitimate government of Afghanistan.

The situation in Afghanistan took center stage following the attacks of September 11, 2001. The next day, the Security Council, acting under Chapter VII, passed Resolution 1368, condemning the attacks and recognizing the inherent right of individual or collective self-defense in accordance with Article 51 of the U.N. Charter. In a joint session of the U.S. Congress on September 20, 2001, President Bush issued a non-negotiable demand to the Taliban to turn over bin Laden and the leaders of al Qaeda in Afghanistan, close the terrorist training camps, and give the United States full access to the country. The Taliban rejected these demands.

On October 7, 2001, the U.S. launched Operation Enduring Freedom (OEF), which originally focused on destroying terrorist training camps and capturing suspected terrorists. Soon after, the United States and its allies aligned with the Northern Alliance. By mid-October, the U.S. escalated its operations and introduced CIA and military Special Forces. With air support and allied partners, the Northern Alliance retook Kabul on November 13, 2001. The Bonn Agreement, signed on December 5, created the Afghan Interim Authority (AIA) until a *loya jirga* (grand council) could formally establish a new government. The Taliban formally surrendered Kandahar, their seat of power and last stronghold, on December 7–9. U.N. Security Council Resolution 1386 created the International Security Assistance Force (ISAF) to aid the new government, as contemplated by the Bonn Agreement. On December 22, 2001, the AIA took power, with Hamid Karzai as chairman. A *loya jirga* elected Karzai as interim head of state on June 13, 2002.

In 2003, NATO troops assumed continuous command of the ISAF. NATO troops remained in Afghanistan with U.N. authorization and at the Afghan government's invitation, to aid in attacks against the resurgent Taliban, who controlled parts of the country and staged regular attacks against coalition and government forces. The Taliban also crossed into Pakistan and controlled parts of that country, having displaced Pakistani authorities in certain tribal areas. The United States separately commanded an OEF mission in Afghanistan targeting the Taliban and al Qaeda remnants, citing the right of national self-defense recognized by the U.N. Charter. Between ISAF and OEF, the United States maintained a large ground presence in Afghanistan, with varying levels of local support. In more recent years, the United States stepped up ground attacks against Taliban strongholds and increased unmanned drone attacks against suspected Taliban and al Qaeda militants. While ISAF ceased combat activities in Afghanistan at the end of 2014, hostilities continue on both sides of the Afghan/Pakistani border.

The Taliban continued to launch attacks on major cities and elsewhere throughout the country. It has remained relatively cohesive as an insurgency, although breakaway groups formed after the death of its leader Mullah Mohammad Omar in 2013. Some, such as the Hezb-e-Islami group, have since signed peace deals with the Afghan government and ceased combat operations. The Islamic State also gained a toehold starting in 2015 (calling itself the "Islamic State in Khorasan Province"), at first under the leadership of Rauf Khadem, who was released from Guantánamo in 2007 but killed in a drone strike in 2015. It has engaged Taliban forces for control of parts of the country. By September 2018, about a dozen districts remained under the Taliban's control (comprising 4% of the country); the group is active in an additional 200-plus districts. Hostilities continue to the present day on both sides of the Afghan/Pakistani border. A faltering peace process is underway, including controversial efforts to conclude an agreement between the United States and the Taliban.

How would you classify the various stages of the armed conflict in Afghanistan and Pakistan? Afghanistan is a party to the Geneva Conventions, Protocol II thereto, and—since 2003—the Rome Statute establishing the International Criminal Court.

C. NEXUS TO ARMED CONFLICT

When does a violent or unlawful act—such as an act of murder or the theft of property—constitute a war crime as opposed to a simple domestic crime? This conundrum is addressed in the Judgment below, which was rendered by Trial Chamber II of the ICTR. The Tribunal was established by U.N. Security Council Resolution 955 of November 8, 1994, in which the Security Council found that widespread violations of international law committed in Rwanda constituted a threat to international peace and security within the meaning of Chapter VII of the U.N. Charter. (See the Appendix for a map of Rwanda.)

The history and sociology of ethnicity in Rwanda is a complex one that will be considered in further detail below in Chapter 9 on Genocide. To summarize briefly, however, since the colonial era in Rwanda, tensions and power struggles between individuals designated as Tutsi and Hutu have waxed and waned in part as a result of manipulation of these ethnic identities by the colonial and post-colonial powers. A large Tutsi diaspora swelled in neighboring countries as Tutsi individuals were driven or forced to flee from the country in the face of repression and violence. Many were subsequently denied re-entry. Eventually, Tutsi expatriots formed the Rwandan Patriotic Front (RPF), which served as a focal point for organized Tutsi resistance to Hutu domination and repression. The RPF began launching attacks from neighboring countries against government targets and forces. Various attempted ceasefires culminated in the Arusha Accords, signed on August 4, 1993, which were aimed at settling the political and military crisis facing the country.

Meanwhile, Hutu political groups, such as the Mouvement Républicain National Pour La Démocratie et le Développement (the National Revolutionary Movement for Democracy and Development or MRND) and the Coalition pour la Défense de la République (the Coalition for the Defense of the Republic or CDR), had begun to form and train paramilitary units, such as the *interahamwe* ("those who stand together") and *impuzamugambi* ("those who share a single goal"). Between 1992 and 1994, these groups stepped up their anti-Tutsi rhetoric and violence, effectively flouting the Arusha Accords. As Rwandan President Juvénal Habyarimana was returning on April 6, 1994, from a meeting in Tanzania on the implementation of the Arusha Accords, his plane was shot down over Kigali airport by a pair of surface-to-air missiles (SAMs). The identity and the precise motive of the assassins remain unknown notwithstanding the work of several investigative commissions.* Radios immediately announced the end of the ceasefire, and massacres of Tutsi and moderate Hutu individuals began. Militia groups went house-to-house to round up and eliminate individuals identified as Tutsi or sympathetic to Tutsis.

In Kibuyu prefecture, one of eleven political subdivisions located in the west of the country, Tutsi civilians congregated in several churches when the violence erupted. When the churches overflowed, the displaced moved into the local stadium. These traditional safe havens soon proved lethal when militia, members of the *Gendarmerie Nationale* (the national police), commune (local) police, and armed civilians began massacring trapped individuals. In the case whose opinion is excerpted below,

---

* The report commissioned by Rwanda, the Mutsinzi Report, suggests that the Hutu Power movement, which wanted to derail the peace process, was behind the assassination. By contrast, a French anti-terrorism judge sought to indict close associates of Rwandan President Paul Kagame affiliated with the RPF, prompting Rwanda to break diplomatic relations with France. The case fell apart and the diplomatic rift was repaired. France has been long accused of supporting the genocidal regime.

pathologists testified that the majority of the victims died from force trauma by machetes or other agricultural tools.

The ICTR indicted Clément Kayishema, the prefect of Kibuye, for genocide, crimes against humanity, and war crimes in connection with massacres at four main sites. His co-defendant, Obed Ruzindana, was a commercial trader in the capital city of Kigali who was indicted for his role in one of the four massacres. The charges against Kayishema were brought under Article 6(1) of the ICTR Statute for direct responsibility and Article 6(3) for superior responsibility on the theory that he had command and control over the *Gendarmerie Nationale*, the *interahamwe*, and the communal police. At the time he was indicted, Kayishema had fled to then-Zaire; he was later arrested in Zambia and transferred to the Tribunal. At his trial, Kayishema offered the defense of alibi, although he had not provided adequate notice to the Prosecution of his intent to do so prior to the commencement of trial as required by Rule 67 of the Rules of Procedure and Evidence. Nonetheless, witnesses at trial placed him at the massacres commanding militia, directing events with a megaphone, and even participating in abuses. He also argued that the acts for which he was charged did not constitute war crimes because they were unconnected with the war between the RPF and the Hutu-led government. The Trial Chamber's discussion on this last point follows.

Prosecutor v. Clément Kayishema & Obed Ruzindana, Case No. ICTR–95–1–T, Judgement (21 May 1999)

In the Trial Chamber

Link Between the Accused and the Armed Forces * * *

174. Violations of Common Article 3 and Protocol II could be committed during, or as a result of, military operations. This means that the Parties to an armed conflict should be responsible for such breaches. In the instant case, this would constitute the [Rwandan Armed Forces (FAR)] and the RPF. The ability of the RPF as a dissident armed force to implement legally binding international instruments is considered in Protocol II as a fundamental criteria in order to recognise the non-international character of the armed conflict. The ability of the governmental armed forces to comply with the provisions of such instruments is axiomatic. In the instant case, the two armies were well organised and participated in the military operations under responsible military command. Therefore, based on Article 6(1) of the ICTR Statute, it could be concluded that the appropriate members of the FAR and RPF shall be responsible individually for violations of Common Article 3 and Protocol II, if factually proven.

175. Thus, individuals of all ranks belonging to the armed forces under the military command of either of the belligerent Parties fall

within the class of perpetrators. If individuals do not belong to the armed forces, they could bear criminal responsibility only when there is a link between them and the armed forces. It cannot be disregarded that the governmental armed forces are under the permanent supervision of public officials representing the government who had to support the war efforts and fulfill a certain mandate. On this issue, in the *Akayesu* Judgement, Trial Chamber I was correct to include in the class of perpetrators, "individuals who were legitimately mandated and expected as public officials or agents or persons otherwise holding public authority or *de facto* representing the Government to support or fulfill the war efforts."

176. Thus, the Trial Chamber is of the opinion that the laws of war apply not only to the members of the armed forces but, in certain cases, to civilians as well, if so established factually. In this case, the accused persons could fall within the class of individuals who may be held responsible for serious violations of Common Article 3 and Protocol II. Violations of these international instruments could be committed outside the theatre of combat. For example, the captured members of the RPF may be brought to any location within the territory of Rwanda and could be under the control or in the hands of persons who are not members of the armed forces. Therefore, every crime should be considered on a case-by-case basis taking into account the material evidence presented by the Prosecution. In other words, the evidence needs to show, beyond a reasonable doubt, that there was a link between the accused and the armed forces. * * *

Nexus Requirement Between the Armed Conflict and the Crime

185. It is important to establish whether all the crimes committed during the non-international armed conflict should be considered as crimes connected with serious violations of Common Article 3 and Protocol II. The Chamber is of the opinion that only offences which have a nexus with the armed conflict fall within this category. If there is not a direct link between the offences and the armed conflict there is no ground for the conclusion that Common Article 3 and Protocol II are violated.

186. The jurisprudence in this area of the law requires such a link between the armed conflict and the offence. The ICTY Trial Chamber in the Judgement of *Prosecutor v. Zejnil Delalić, Zdravko Mucić, Hazim Delić and Esad Landžo* (*Čelebici* Judgement) stated that "there must be an obvious link between the criminal act and the armed conflict." The same point of view is reflected in the *Tadić* Judgement. In *Tadić*, the Trial Chamber remarked that "the only question to be determined in the circumstances of each individual case was whether the offences were closely related to the armed conflict as a whole."[106] In the *Akayesu* Judgement, the Trial Chamber found that ". . . it has not been proved

---

[106] *Prosecutor v. Tadić*, Case No. IT–94–1–T, Opinion & Judgement, para. 573 (July 15, 1999).

beyond reasonable doubt that the acts perpetrated by Akayesu . . . were committed in conjunction with the armed conflict." Such a conclusion means that, in the opinion of that Chamber, such a connection is necessary. * * *

188. Thus the term "nexus" should not be understood as something vague and indefinite. A direct connection between the alleged crimes, referred to in the Indictment, and the armed conflict should be established *factually*. No test, therefore, can be defined *in abstracto*. It is for the Trial Chamber, on a case-by-case basis, to adjudge on the facts submitted as to whether a nexus existed. It is incumbent upon the Prosecution to present those facts and to prove, beyond a reasonable doubt, that such a nexus exists.

189. The nexus requirement between the offence and the armed conflict is of crucial significance, taking into account that Common Article 3 and Protocol II are designed to protect the victims of the armed conflict. War crimes are inevitably connected with violations of Common Article 3 and Protocol II. Whether there is a nexus between the alleged crimes and the armed conflict in the instant case is an issue of legal findings which will be addressed [later in] the Judgement. At this stage it should be highlighted that the consideration of the applicability of the provisions of Common Article 3 and Protocol II would be proper if such a nexus is established. * * *

Common Article 3 and Additional Protocol II

590. Counts 5, 11 and 17 of the Indictment charge Kayishema with violations of Common Article 3 and Counts 6, 12 and 18 charge Kayishema with violations of Protocol II. * * *

592. During the trial, evidence was produced that between about 10 April and 30 June 1994 thousands of men, women and children were killed and numerous persons injured as a result of massacres at the Catholic Church and Home St. Jean Complex, at the Stadium in Kibuye Town, at the Church in Mubuga and in the area of Bisesero in the *Prefecture* of Kibuye, Republic of Rwanda.

593. These men, women and children were unarmed and were predominantly Tutsis seeking protection from attacks that had occurred throughout various regions in Rwanda and Kibuye *Prefecture*. The Prosecution considers the massacred people as victims of the armed conflict and charges Kayishema and Ruzindana with serious violations of Common Article 3 and Protocol II. * * *

598. Therefore, the question which should be addressed is * * * whether these instruments were applicable to the alleged crimes at the four sites referred to in the Indictment. It is incumbent on the Prosecutor to prove the applicability of these international instruments to the above-mentioned crimes.

599. However, the Prosecution limited itself to state, "in order to hold Clement Kayishema and Obed Ruzindana criminally responsible for

the above-mentioned counts, the Prosecutor must prove that the alleged crimes must have been committed *in the context* of a non-international armed conflict."

600. The Prosecutor did not specify the meaning of the words "in the context." If she meant "during" an internal armed conflict, there is nothing to prove as it was recognised, and this matter was not in dispute, that in this period of time Rwanda was in a state of armed conflict not of [an] international character. Therefore, in this case the words "in the context" are too general in character and do not clarify the situation in a proper way. When the country is in a state of armed conflict, crimes committed in this period of time could be considered as having been committed in the context of this conflict. However, it does not mean that all such crimes have a direct link with the armed conflict and all the victims of these crimes are victims of the armed conflict.

601. There is recognition, nevertheless, in the Prosecutor's Closing Brief that "the Prosecutor must also establish a nexus between the armed conflict and the alleged offence." The following paragraph of this document was intended to prove such a nexus,

> In the present case, the Prosecutor submits that the evidence shows, beyond a reasonable doubt, that for each of the alleged violations there was a nexus between the crimes and the armed conflict that was underway in Rwanda. The Tutsis who were massacred in Kibuye went to the four sites seeking refuge from attacks that were occurring on the Tutsis throughout Kibuye and Rwanda. These attacks were occurring because hostilities had broken out between the RPF and the FAR and the Tutsis were being sought out on the pretext that they were accomplices of the RPF, were "the enemy" and/or were responsible for the death of the President.

602. It is true that "the Tutsis went to the four sites seeking refuge from attacks that were occurring on the Tutsis throughout Kibuye and Rwanda." However, the Tutsi were attacked by neither the RPF nor the FAR in the places where they sought refuge in Kibuye. It was proved through witness testimony that these attacks were undertaken by the civilian authorities as a result of a campaign to exterminate the Tutsi population in the country. Therefore, there is no ground to assert that there was a nexus between the committed crimes and the armed conflict, because "the Tutsis went to the four sites seeking refuge from attacks. . . ." The Prosecutor's next allegation is that "these attacks were occurring because hostilities had broken out between the RPF and the FAR and the Tutsis were being sought out on the pretext that they were accomplices of the RPF, were 'the enemy' and/or were responsible for the death of the President."

603. It is true that "hostilities had broken out between the RPF and the FAR" in this period of time. However, evidence was not produced that the military operations occurred in Kibuye *Prefecture* when the alleged

crimes were committed. Furthermore, it was not shown that there was a direct link between crimes committed against these victims and the hostilities mentioned by the Prosecutor. It was also not proved that the victims were accomplices of the RPF and/or were responsible for the death of the President. The Prosecutor herself recognised that the Tutsis were being sought out *on the pretext* that they were accomplices etc. These allegations show only that the armed conflict had been used as pretext to unleash an official policy of genocide. Therefore, such allegations cannot be considered as evidence of a direct link between the alleged crimes and the armed conflict. * * *

608. Article 13 of Protocol II is more pertinent to the case before the Trial Chamber, since it is devoted to the protection of the civilian population during armed conflicts. This Article, entitled "Protection of the Civilian Population" stipulates,

> 1. The civilian population and individual civilians shall enjoy general protection against the dangers arising from military operations. To give effect to this protection, the following rules shall be observed in all circumstances.
>
> 2. The civilian population as such, as well as individual civilians, shall not be the object of attack. Acts or threats of violence the primary purpose of which is to spread terror among the civilian population are prohibited.

609. From these two paragraphs of Article 13 it could be understood that military operations in all circumstances should be conducted in such a way not to create dangers for the civilian population, as well as individual civilians, and in any case this category of persons shall not be the object of attacks during military operations.

610. The Prosecutor emphasised that the attacks against the Tutsis at the four sites, referred to in the Indictment, "were occurring because hostilities had broken out between the RPF and the FAR." It is true that such hostilities had broken out in different parts of the country. In accordance with Article 13, as well as Articles 14 to 18 of Protocol II, each Party in the conflict was obliged to conduct the hostilities without affecting the civilian population and individual civilians or creating dangers for them. The Prosecutor claimed, and the witnesses confirmed, that there were no military operations in Kibuye Town nor in the area of Bisesero in this period of time. There is also no evidence that the civilian population, at the four sites in question, was affected by military operations which were under way in other regions of Rwanda.

611. On the basis of the foregoing, it could not be asserted *pleno jure* ["on full authority"] that Articles 5, 7, 9 or 13 to 18 of Protocol II were violated in the case of the alleged crimes. * * *

615. Since the Prosecutor did not produce evidence of a nexus between the alleged crimes and the armed conflict, the Trial Chamber is of the opinion that there is no ground to consider the applicability to the

instant case of Article 4(a) of the Statute which covers Common Article 3 and Article 4(2)(a) of Protocol II.

616. It has already been illustrated that the FAR and the RPF were Parties in the internal armed conflict in Rwanda during the period of time in question. Pursuant to the [stated] requirement of the Prosecution, Kayishema and Ruzindana must be connected to one of these Parties and bound by the respective regime. In other words, to hold both accused criminally responsible for serious violations of Common Articles 3 and Protocol II it should be proved that there was some sort of a link between the armed forces and the accused.

617. It was shown that both accused were not members of the armed forces. However, it was recognised earlier in this Judgement that civilians could be connected with the armed forces if they are directly engaged in the conduct of hostilities or the alleged civilians were legitimately mandated and expected, as persons holding public authority or *de facto* representing the Government, to support or fulfill the war effort.

618. However, the Prosecution did not produce any evidence to show how and in what capacity Kayishema and in particular Ruzindana, who was not a public official, were supporting the Government efforts against the RPF.

619. Presenting her case, the Prosecutor pointed out that Kayishema and Ruzindana carried rifles and participated in the massacres alleged in the Indictment. However, the Prosecutor herself recognised that the FAR or the RPF were not involved in these massacres, which were organised and directed by the civilian authorities of the country. She further recognised that the overwhelming majority of the attackers were civilians, armed with traditional weapons. This was proved through witness testimony, and also recognised by the Prosecutor in her Closing Brief, when she stated "the Hutu civilian population was mobilised to attack and kill the Tutsi population under the guise of the Civilian Defence Program." Therefore, these men, women and children were killed not as a result of the military operations between the FAR and the RPF but because of the policy of extermination of the Tutsi, pursued by the official authorities of Rwanda. Therefore, it does not follow from the participation of the accused in these massacres that they were connected with the armed forces of the FAR or the RPF.

620. The struggle for power between the FAR and the RPF, which was underway in 1994, meant that each Party in this armed conflict, in all circumstances, had to treat humanely all persons belonging to the adverse Party. In this period of time, Rwanda had been invaded by the armed forces of the RPF and, in accordance with international law, the Government of this country was undoubtedly entitled to take all necessary measures to resist these attacks. * * *

621. However, the crimes committed at the four sites, referred to in the Indictment, were not crimes against the RPF and its members. They were committed by the civilian authorities of this country against their own civilian population of a certain ethnicity and this fact was proven beyond a reasonable doubt during the trial. It is true that these atrocities were committed during the armed conflict. However, they were committed as part of a distinct policy of genocide; they were committed parallel to, and not as a result of, the armed conflict. Such crimes are undoubtedly the most serious of crimes which could be committed during or in the absence of an armed conflict. In any event, however, these crimes are beyond the scope of Common Article 3 and Protocol II which aim to protect victims of armed conflict.

622. In this respect, it is important to recall a recent statement of the ICRC that, "It should be stressed that in war time international humanitarian law coexists with human rights law, certain provisions of which cannot be derogated from. Protecting the individual *vis-à-vis* the enemy (as opposed to protecting the individual *vis-à-vis* his own authorities) is one of the characteristics of the law of armed conflicts. A state at war cannot use the conflict as a pretext for ignoring the provisions of that law . . ." This is just what happened in Rwanda with only one clarification. The armed conflict there was used not only as a pretext for ignoring the provisions of human rights laws but, moreover, as a pretext for committing extremely serious crimes.

623. Considering the above, and based on all the evidence presented in this case, the Trial Chamber finds that it has not been proved, beyond a reasonable doubt, that the crimes alleged in the Indictment were committed in direct conjunction with the armed conflict. The Trial Chamber further finds that the actions of Kayishema and Ruzindana, in the alleged period of time, had no direct connection with the military operations or with the victims of the armed conflict. It has not been shown that there was a direct link between the accused and the armed forces. Moreover, it cannot be concluded *pleno jure*, that the material provisions of Common Article 3 and Protocol II have been violated in this particular case. Thus both accused persons, *ipso facto et ipso jure* ["by that very fact and by right itself"], cannot be individually responsible for violations of these international instruments.

624. The Trial Chamber finds, therefore, that Kayishema did not incur individual criminal responsibility for breaches of Article 4 of the Statute and neither Kayishema nor Ruzindana incurred liability under counts 23 and 24.

NOTES & QUESTIONS

1. Case Outcome

The Trial Chamber convicted Kayishema of genocide, but exonerated him on the other counts. The Chamber sentenced him to life imprisonment, a sentence which was upheld on appeal. In 2001, he was transferred to Mali to serve his sentence. The Tribunal convicted Ruzindana of genocide and sentenced him to twenty-five years' imprisonment. The Trial Chamber acquitted the defendants of crimes against humanity, reasoning that these charges overlapped with the genocide charges. (The issue of cumulation of charges is addressed in Chapter 13 on Charging International Crimes). The Prosecutor's appeal was considered time-barred. The defendants appealed and the judgment was affirmed. *Prosecutor v. Kayishema & Ruzindana*, Case No. ICTR–95–1–A, Judgement (Reasons) (June 1, 2001).

2. Prosecutorial Burden

What was the Prosecutor's burden in determining a nexus to the armed conflict as set forth by the Trial Chamber in *Kayishema*? Why did the Prosecution fail to meet this burden? What evidence would the Prosecution have needed to present in order to satisfy the Trial Chamber's formulation of the nexus requirement? In a subsequent case, the ICTR Trial Chamber cited to the *Kayishema* opinion to emphasize the burden placed on the Prosecution:

> 104. In addition to the offence being committed in the context of an armed conflict not of an international character satisfying the material requirements of Common Article 3 and Additional Protocol II, there must be a nexus between the offence and the armed conflict for Article 4 of the Statute to apply. By this it should be understood that the offence must be closely related to the hostilities or committed in conjunction with the armed conflict.

The Prosecutor v. Rutaganda, Case No. ICTR–96–3, Trial Chamber Judgement and Sentence (Dec. 6, 1999).

3. Nexus and Causation

Should it be necessary to show a causal relationship between an armed conflict and an alleged war crime? In a decision involving the prosecution of three Serbian military officials for war crimes in the Foča area of the former Yugoslavia, the Appeals Chamber noted that such a causal relationship was not necessary:

> 58. What ultimately distinguishes a war crime from a purely domestic offence is that a war crime is shaped by or dependent upon the environment—the armed conflict—in which it is committed. It need not have been planned or supported by some form of policy. The armed conflict need not have been causal to the commission of the crime, but the existence of an armed conflict must, at a minimum, have played a substantial part in the perpetrator's ability to commit it, his decision to commit it, the manner in which it was committed or the purpose for which it was committed. Hence, if it can be established, as in the present case, that the perpetrator acted in furtherance of or under the guise of the armed conflict, it would be sufficient to conclude that his acts were closely related to the armed conflict. * * *
>
> 59. In determining whether or not the act in question is sufficiently related to the armed conflict, the Trial Chamber may

> take into account, *inter alia*, the following factors: the fact that the perpetrator is a combatant; the fact that the victim is a non-combatant; the fact that the victim is a member of the opposing party; the fact that the act may be said to serve the ultimate goal of a military campaign; and the fact that the crime is committed as part of or in the context of the perpetrator's official duties.
>
> 60. The Appellants' proposition that the laws of war only prohibit those acts which are specific to an actual wartime situation is not right. The laws of war may frequently encompass acts which, though they are not committed in the theatre of conflict, are substantially related to it. The laws of war can apply to both types of acts. The Appeals Chamber understands the Appellants' argument to be that if an act can be prosecuted in peacetime, it cannot be prosecuted in wartime. This betrays a misconception about the relationship between the laws of war and the laws regulating a peacetime situation. The laws of war do not necessarily displace the laws regulating a peacetime situation; the former may add elements requisite to the protection which needs to be afforded to victims in a wartime situation.

Prosecutor v. Kunarac, Case No. IT–96–23 & IT–96–23/1–A, Judgement (June 12, 2002).

4. Alternative Formulations of Required Nexus

The Trial Chamber in *Semanza* stated that the issue is whether the act was either "closely related to the hostilities" *or* "committed in conjunction with them." *Prosecutor v. Semanza*, Case No. ICTR 97–20–T, Trial Chamber Decision, para. 14 (May 15, 2003). In the *Akayesu* case, the Trial Chamber stated that only acts "committed in conjunction with the armed conflict" will qualify as war crimes. *Prosecutor v. Akayesu*, Case No. ICTR–96–4–T, Judgement, para. 643 (Sept. 2, 1998). Further elaborating upon the test articulated in *Kunarac*, the Appeals Chamber in *Rutaganda* stated:

> It is only necessary to explain two matters. First, the expression "under the guise of the armed conflict" does not mean simply "at the same time as an armed conflict" and/or "in any circumstances created in part by the armed conflict." For example, if a non-combatant takes advantage of the lessened effectiveness of the police in conditions of disorder created by an armed conflict to murder a neighbor he has hated for years, that would not, without more, constitute a war crime under Article 4 of the Statute. By contrast, the accused in *Kunarac*, for example, were combatants who took advantage of their positions of military authority to rape individuals whose displacement was an express goal of the military campaign in which they took a part. Second, as paragraph 59 of the *Kunarac* Appeal Judgement indicates, the determination of a close relationship between particular offences and an armed conflict will usually require consideration of several factors, not just one. Particular care is needed when the accused is a non-combatant.

Prosecutor v. Rutaganda, Case No. ICTR–96–3–A, Judgement, para. 570 (May 26, 2003). Are these statements different ways of articulating the same test, or do they establish different tests? If so, which is the best test? Would these Trial Chambers have convicted defendant Kayishema of war crimes on the facts set forth above? Article 8 of the ICC Statute addressing War Crimes contains no mention of any war nexus. The ICC's Elements of Crimes—drafted to "assist the Court in the interpretation and application" of the crimes within the Court's jurisdiction—list as an element of each enumerated war crime that "the conduct took place in the context of and was associated with" an armed conflict. In addition, the U.S. Manual for Military Commissions (MMC) requires, as an individual element of every substantive offense (not including conspiracy), that "[t]he conduct [take] place in the context of and [be] associated with armed conflict." *See* MMC, Part IV, Crimes and Elements (1)–(27). How do these formulations compare to the formulations utilized by the ICTR and ICTY? Would *Kayishima & Ruzindana* come out the same way?

5. Relationship Between Genocide and Armed Conflict

Why would the Prosecution pursue both war crimes and genocide counts against the defendant with respect to the same conduct? The Trial Chamber assumes that the genocide and the armed conflict in Rwanda are parallel phenomena, unrelated to each other. Alternatively, the Trial Chamber suggests that the armed conflict was used as a pretext to unleash the genocide (para. 603). What was the relationship between the genocide against the Tutsi population and the elimination of their "sympathizers," on the one hand, and the armed conflict between the government forces (the RAF) and the Tutsi rebel forces (the RPF), on the other? What is the *legal significance* of that relationship? Did the Trial Chamber get it right? How is the relationship between the Holocaust and the aggressive armed conflict waged by Germany generally characterized? Are war and internal oppression inevitably linked within state policy or might they proceed independently of, or even at odds with, each other? How might the pursuit of a genocidal policy actually undermine a war effort, as has been argued occurred in Nazi Germany?

6. "Chapeau" Elements of War Crimes

The existence of an armed conflict, the classification of that armed conflict, and the nexus between the impugned conduct and the underlying armed conflict are foundational elements of any war crimes charge. In addition, and as will be considered in greater depth in the next chapter, the victim must be a so-called "protected person." These *chapeau* elements must be adequately proven before a tribunal will consider whether the defendant committed any enumerated war crime (which will be subject to its own set of elements). Accordingly, the ICC's Elements of Crimes for Article 8 state that the Prosecutor must prove that the conduct took place in the context of and was associated with an international or non-international armed conflict and that the perpetrator was aware of the factual circumstances that established the existence of an armed conflict. In addition:

- There is no requirement for a legal evaluation by the perpetrator as to the existence of an armed conflict or its character as international or non-international;
- In that context there is no requirement for awareness by the perpetrator of the facts that established the character of the conflict as international or non-international;
- There is only a requirement for the awareness of the factual circumstances that established the existence of an armed conflict that is implicit in the terms "took place in the context of and was associated with."

International Criminal Court, *Elements of Crimes*, ISBN No. 92-9227-232-2 (2011). What is the impact of these provisions on the Prosecutor's burden of proof in a war crimes prosecution?

PROBLEM

A non-international armed conflict existed in a particular state for years, flaring up and cooling down depending on the status of political negotiations between the government and insurgents and the harsh winter weather, which often made fighting impossible. Many insurgents adhered to the classic model of farming by day and fighting by night. One particular battalion of rebels became known for engaging in assault-and-withdraw attacks against government targets. The government, in an effort to halt the attacks, pulled troops from elsewhere in the country and launched a major assault against a region known to be a rebel stronghold. Government troops went door-to-door searching homes for weapons and other evidence of rebel activity.

In this process, they knocked on the door of a young couple. The wife answered and denied that her husband was at home. The soldiers insisted on searching the house. The wife became obviously nervous when the soldiers entered the couple's bedroom. Pressed up against a dresser, she insisted repeatedly that her husband was not at home and that the soldiers should leave them alone. The soldiers, increasingly suspicious, searched the room thoroughly and eventually found covered by the bureau a loose panel behind which the husband was hiding. As the husband was being arrested, he shouted angrily at his wife for giving away his location.

The husband was detained, interrogated, and harshly treated for several months before he was released. One leg was permanently disabled as a result of the treatment he received while in custody. When he returned home, he beat his wife severely, blaming her for his having been discovered. Because he had provided government officials with some information about the rebels during his interrogation, he was shunned by his former rebel comrades. His injuries prevented him from practicing his profession as a farmer. He never forgave his wife for his capture, and eventually the wife fled the marriage and his brutality.

Years later, the war finally came to a close and the state authorities established special chambers within the domestic court system to bring war crimes charges arising out of the war. Prior to the war, the legislature had adopted a war crimes statute that penalizes grave breaches of the Geneva Conventions as well as the provisions of Common Article 3. There is no statute of limitations associated with these offenses, although the analogous domestic crimes (assault, battery) have become time barred. The wife has come to you, a local lawyer, because she wants to press war crimes charges against her husband. Can she proceed? If charges are brought, what arguments would you make to get the charges dismissed if you represented the husband?

CHAPTER 7

WAR CRIMES

I. INTRODUCTION

Historically, the law of armed conflict (i.e., international humanitarian law (IHL)) evolved along parallel tracks. One set of treaties emerging from international conferences in The Hague and elsewhere concerned the means and methods of warfare. These treaties sought to limit the tactics of war and prohibit the use of certain weapons that cause excessive suffering ("Hague Law"). The most important of the Hague treaties is the Fourth Convention Respecting the Laws and Customs of War on Land (1907) and its annexed regulations, which take as a basic premise that the means and methods of warfare are not without limits. Subsequent treaties in this tradition regulate or prohibit particular weapons systems, such as the 1925 Protocol for the Prohibition of the Use in War of Asphyxiating, Poisonous or Other Gases, and of Bacteriological Methods of Warfare; the 1993 Chemical Weapons Convention; and the 1997 Convention on the Prohibition of the Use, Stockpiling, Production and Transfer of Anti-Personnel Mines and on Their Destruction.

A second set of treaties sponsored by the International Committee of the Red Cross in Geneva ("Geneva Law") established protections for individuals uniquely impacted by war (so-called "protected persons"), especially those who do not—or who no longer—participate directly in hostilities, such as the shipwrecked, prisoners of war (POWs), and civilians. In addition, while the law of war originally and almost exclusively addressed international armed conflicts, with notable exceptions such as the Lieber Code governing the Union Forces during the U.S. Civil War, it increasingly applies to a wide variety of non-international armed conflicts as well. Over time, these various strands of IHL have converged to create a more complete corpus of law. Article 8 of the Statute of the ICC reflects this gradual merging of the penal aspects of Hague and Geneva Law and of the law applicable in international and non-international armed conflicts. This chapter considers the penal aspects of these two bodies of law.

II. "HAGUE LAW": THE MEANS & METHODS OF WARFARE

International humanitarian law places limits on the use of force in pursuit of military objectives. The Hague treaties and their progeny regulate the use of force within an armed conflict with reference to the principles of humanity, necessity, distinction, and proportionality. While these four principles obviously overlap, they each provide distinct guidance to the regulation of armed conflict. The principle of humanity requires that those means and methods of warfare that produce the least unnecessary suffering be employed. The principle of necessity requires that armed attacks be designed and intended to defeat the opponent militarily. Thus, Article 52(2) of Protocol I states:

> Attacks shall be limited strictly to military objectives. In so far as objects are concerned, military objectives are limited to those objects which by their nature, location, purpose or use make an effective contribution to military action and whose total or partial destruction, capture or neutralization, in the circumstances ruling at the time, offers a definite military advantage.

The definition of military objects has two elements: (a) they must make an effective contribution to military action, and (b) their destruction must offer a definite military advantage in the circumstances at the time. Civilian objects lose their protected status if they are used to make an effective contribution to military action.

The principle of distinction requires that parties to an armed conflict distinguish between legitimate military targets and illegitimate targets, such as civilians. It has also been interpreted to prohibit certain types of weapons that, by their very nature, do not discriminate among lawful and unlawful targets. Indiscriminate attacks are thus prohibited under international law. Article 48 of Protocol I provides that "Parties to the conflict shall at all times distinguish between the civilian population and combatants." Article 51 of Protocol I defines indiscriminate attacks to include attacks that

> employ a method or means of combat the effects of which cannot be limited as required by this Protocol; and consequently, in each such case, are of a nature to strike military objectives and civilians or civilian objects without distinction; [and]
>
> may be expected to cause incidental loss of civilian life, injury to civilians, damage to civilian objects, or a combination thereof, which would be excessive in relation to the concrete and direct military advantage anticipated.

Article 57 requires that those who plan or decide upon an attack must "do everything feasible to verify that the objectives to be attacked are neither civilians nor civilian objects."

The principle of proportionality states that when military force is used against a proper military objective, parties may employ only that level of force that is proportional to the military objective to be gained. If a choice of weaponry, tactics, or force levels is available, the commander or combatant must choose those that will cause the least incidental harm. Civilian casualties—euphemistically referred to as "collateral damage"—in and of themselves are thus not necessarily unlawful. Rather, IHL only prohibits deliberate attacks and attacks that cause damage to civilian objects that is excessive in relation to the anticipated military advantage. This is a sliding scale to a certain degree; the greater the degree of military advantage anticipated, the more likely "collateral damage" will be permitted.

These principles from Hague Law find expression as war crimes in Article 3 of the ICTY Statute concerning "Violations of the Laws or Customs of War," which include, but are not limited to:

(a) employment of poisonous weapons or other weapons calculated to cause unnecessary suffering;

(b) wanton destruction of cities, towns or villages, or devastation not justified by military necessity;

(c) attack, or bombardment, by whatever means, of undefended towns, villages, dwellings, or buildings;

(d) seizure of, destruction or wilful damage done to institutions dedicated to religion, charity and education, the arts and sciences, historic monuments and works of art and science;

(e) plunder of public or private property.

Consider the application of these principles and Article 3 of the ICTY Statute in the following case. Milan Martić was the president of the self-proclaimed Serb Republic of Krajina (RSK), in Croatia near the border with Bosnia-Herzegovina. (See the Appendix for a map of Yugoslavia.) When Croatia commenced secession from the former Yugoslavia in 1991, Serb militants within Krajina announced their secession from Croatia. The original indictment against Martić contained four counts charging him with violations of the laws and customs of war under Article 3 of the ICTY Statute for having knowingly and willfully ordered an unlawful attack against the civilian population and individual civilians of Zagreb (the capital of Croatia) causing at least five deaths and numerous injuries to the civilian population and individual civilians of Zagreb on two occasions in May 1995, allegedly in retaliation to Operation Flash, a Croatian military offensive in RSK launched in May 1995. *Prosecutor v. Martić*, Case No. IT–96–11, Indictment (July 25, 1995) (charging Martić with unlawful attacks against the civilian population).

In May 2002, Martić surrendered to the ICTY and the indictment was amended to allege that Martić was a co-perpetrator in a joint criminal enterprise (JCE), the purpose of which was to forcibly remove a majority of the Croat, Muslim, and other non-Serb population from approximately a third of the territory of Croatia and large parts of the territory of the Republic of Bosnia and Herzegovina to create a new Serb-dominated republic. *See Prosecutor v. Martić,* Case No. IT–95–11–PT, Amended Indictment (Dec. 9, 2005) (charging various crimes against humanity and war crimes as part of a joint criminal enterprise and pursuant to the doctrine of superior responsibility). The Trial Chamber convicted Martić on 16 counts of the indictment including persecutions, murder, torture, deportation, attacks on civilians, wanton destruction of civilian areas and other crimes against humanity and violations of laws and customs of war. He was acquitted of one count concerning extermination, and was sentenced to 35 years' imprisonment. With respect to the Zagreb attack, the Trial Chamber found that the use of twelve M-87 Orkan rockets constituted a widespread attack against the civilian population. The Trial Chamber concluded that given the indiscriminate character of the weapon employed in the attack on Zagreb, especially at the range at which it was fired, its use in a densely populated area constituted a *per se* indiscriminate attack, notwithstanding the presence of any lawful military targets. *Id.* at para. 461. Both Martić and the Prosecution appealed.

Prosecutor v. Milan Martić, Case No. IT–95–11–A, Decision (October 8, 2008)

In the Appeals Chamber

Alleged Errors regarding the Shelling of Zagreb (Milan Martić's Eighth Ground of Appeal)

Discussion

246. From Martić's * * * submissions, the Appeals Chamber can discern the following challenges: the Trial Chamber allegedly erred (i) when it considered the M-87 Orkan rocket to be an indiscriminate weapon incapable of hitting specific targets; (ii) when it found that the shelling of Zagreb was a widespread attack directed against the civilian population of which Martić had knowledge; (iii) when it found that the civilian population was wilfully made the object of attack by Martić; (iv) when it rejected the argument that the shelling was a lawful reprisal or justified by self-defence; and (v) when it did not consider the obligations allegedly incumbent on Croatia in protecting her civilians.

The M-87 Orkan Rocket as an Indiscriminate Weapon Incapable of Hitting Specific Targets

247. The Trial Chamber concluded that the M-87 Orkan was used as an indiscriminate weapon. It found that the distance from which the rockets were fired was close to the maximum range (50 km) of the M-87 Orkan, at which the dispersion error is about 1,000m in every direction, with the area of the dispersion of the bomblets on the ground being about 2 hectares. The Trial Chamber reasoned that the M-87 Orkan, "by virtue of its characteristics and the firing range in the specific instance" was "incapable of hitting specific targets." Using the M-87 Orkan from such a range in a densely populated urban area like Zagreb "will result in the infliction of severe casualties." The Trial Chamber elaborated that considering the indiscriminate character of the M-87 Orkan, the presence of military targets in Zagreb was irrelevant. * * *

250. Martić further argues that the Trial Chamber erred when it "failed to note that, due to its technical characteristics, Orkan is precise

even fired from a maximum range." In support of this argument, he refers generally to Exhibit 776, which contains the firing tables for the M-87 Orkan, but without pointing to any particular piece of information in this exhibit. The Appeals Chamber notes that the Trial Chamber admitted into evidence not the whole of Exhibit 776, but only the firing tables contained in it and that expert Witness Jožef Poje prepared his report on the basis of those tables. During his testimony, the Witness described in detail how he came to the conclusion that when fired from a range of 49 km, the dispersion error of the M-87 Orkan is about 1000m in each direction. The Trial Chamber relied on this evidence. As a challenge to the Trial Chamber's findings, Martić merely refers to the Expert Report of Theunens (Exhibits 6) and a memorandum from the United Nations Military Observers ("UNMO") headquarters dated 6 May 1995 (Exhibit 94), which state that in relation to the M-87 Orkan "[a] typical dispersion error for a warhead at payload release height would be an ellipse of 180m x 165m." However, the Appeals Chamber notes that these numbers are devoid of any detail as to how they were calculated. This is especially important since the dispersion pattern depends on a number of factors, including the firing range. Moreover, even if accepting Martić's figures, a dispersion pattern of such proportion would hardly make the finding of the Trial Chamber that the M-87 Orkan was incapable of hitting specific targets unreasonable. In this context, Martić's reliance on the purported fact that the M-87 Orkan "was the most sophisticated rocket launcher produced by Yugoslavia" is beside the point.

251. The Appeals Chamber considers that Martić's reference to expert Witness Jožef Poje's statement that certain governmental and military buildings and facilities in Zagreb were "possible targets which you could target with the Orkan system" is misguided. The Witness was explicit in stating that "the Orkan is not principally suitable for use in populated areas" and because of its characteristics "is not intended for deployment in populated areas." He also testified that "because of the high dispersion that kind of targeting [hitting a military target] was not suited. . . ." The Trial Chamber took this evidence into account. Consequently, the Appeals Chamber is satisfied that the Trial Chamber, given its findings on the nature of the M-87 Orkan, could disregard the presence of military targets in Zagreb. The Appeals Chamber finally rejects Martić's argument that "many armies had and used in the recent past similar weapons" as irrelevant.

252. For the foregoing reasons, Martić has not demonstrated that the Trial Chamber erred when it found that the M-87 Orkan was an indiscriminate weapon, incapable of hitting specific targets in the circumstances of the case as presented before the Trial Chamber. This sub-ground of appeal is accordingly dismissed.

The Shelling of Zagreb as a Widespread Attack Directed Against the Civilian Population of Which Martić Had Knowledge

253. The Trial Chamber held that the shelling of Zagreb was a widespread attack against the civilian population. It reached this conclusion on the basis of the large-scale nature of the attack and the indiscriminate nature of the M-87 Orkan. It considered that it was proven beyond reasonable doubt that Martić was aware of this attack.

254. The Appeals Chamber notes that Martić seems to confuse the notion of a widespread attack on the civilian population (as a threshold requirement [to charge crimes against humanity] under Article 5 of the Statute) with the [war] crime of attacks on civilians (pursuant to Article 3 of the Statute). The Appeals Chamber will nevertheless address Martić's arguments in relation to both issues. In this Section, it will deal with the question of whether the Trial Chamber erred when it found that the shelling of Zagreb was part of a widespread attack against the civilian population, in the sense of Article 5 of the Statute, of which Martić had knowledge. After this, the Appeals Chamber will deal with alleged errors committed by the Trial Chamber when assessing Martić's responsibility for the crime of attack against civilians under Article 3 of the Statute.

255. The Appeals Chamber recalls that the Trial Chamber reasonably found that Martić had ordered the shelling of Zagreb. The Trial Chamber, when setting out the applicable law, correctly stated that in order for criminal responsibility to arise under Article 5 of the Statute, "the acts of the accused must have formed part of a widespread or systematic attack directed against any civilian population." Martić has not challenged the high number of civilian casualties caused by the shelling of Zagreb with the M-87 Orkan. Likewise, he does not object to the Trial Chamber's finding that of the purported military targets, only one was hit. The Appeals Chamber has already found that the Trial Chamber did not err when it found that the M-87 Orkan was an indiscriminate weapon, incapable of hitting specific targets. Thus, Martić has failed to show that the Trial Chamber erred when it found that "due to the characteristics of the M-87 Orkan and due to the large-scale nature of the attack" the shelling of Zagreb was a widespread attack directed against the civilian population of Zagreb.

256. The heart of Martić's arguments in relation to his *mens rea* is that he did not have the appropriate military knowledge of the effects of the M-87 Orkan. To support his claim, Martić refers to the testimony of expert Witness Jožef Poje that "not everyone is familiar with the consequences of the use of the Orkan." The Appeals Chamber notes that the Trial Chamber made reference to this statement in the Trial Judgement. The Appeals Chamber further notes the Trial Chamber's finding that "the effects of firing the M-87 Orkan on Zagreb were known to those involved." The Trial Chamber *inter alia* referred to a letter from Martić to Slobodan Milošević of 9 June 1993 in which he informed the latter that the P-65 Luna rocket system had been moved "to prevent

aggression or to carry out possible attacks on Zagreb." The Trial Chamber also quoted Witness Peter Galbraith who testified that Martić on 24 October 1993 had "in effect [said] that attacking civilian targets in Zagreb, attacking the city itself was an option. . ." It further mentioned the cable by a United Nations envoy, who reported that Martić "spoke of massive rocket attacks on Zagreb which would leave 100,000 people dead." Martić also argues that he relied on his advisors and articles published in Serbian newspapers. However, given the evidence before the Trial Chamber which pointed to Martić's involvement in matters concerning the weaponry in the possession of the RSK, his statements in relation to the shelling itself and his position as President of the RSK and leader of the Serbian Army of Krajina (*Srpska Vojska Krajine*, SVK), the Appeals Chamber is satisfied that a reasonable Trial Chamber could have come to the conclusion beyond reasonable doubt that Martić knew about the effects of the M-87 Orkan when he ordered the shelling of Zagreb.

257. Moreover, the Appeals Chamber finds that the Trial Chamber reasonably concluded that because of the extensive media coverage of the shelling of 2 May 1995, the impact of the M-87 Orkan was known before the second round of shelling on 3 May 1995. Martić's argument that little "structural damage" was caused by the first shelling, and that he had the right to assume that even if the M-87 Orkan had missed the military targets once again, the Croatian authorities would take the measures necessary for the protection of the civilian population fails to address this finding by the Trial Chamber.

258. Consequently, this sub-ground of appeal is dismissed.

The Civilian Population Was Wilfully Made the Object of Attack by Martić

259. Based on its finding that the M-87 Orkan was an indiscriminate weapon and that Martić knew of its effects, the Trial Chamber found that Martić wilfully made the civilian population of Zagreb the object of the attack under Article 3 of the Statute.

260. In relation to this crime, the Appeals Chamber considers that the Trial Chamber correctly stated the applicable law when it held that "a direct attack against civilians can be inferred from the indiscriminate weapon used." The Trial Chamber also stated the requirement that "the attacks resulted in death or serious bodily injury within the civilian population at the time of such attacks." Contrary to Martić's submissions, the Trial Chamber was not required to establish that the attack on Zagreb was one with "the primary purpose [. . .] to spread terror among the civilian population." The Appeals Chamber notes that such a requirement only applies to the distinct crime of acts or threats of violence the primary purpose of which is to spread terror among the civilian population.

261. As stated above, the Trial Chamber correctly found that Martić had ordered the shelling of Zagreb, which resulted in the death and serious injury of numerous civilians. Considering that the Trial Chamber did not err when it found that the M-87 Orkan was an indiscriminate weapon, Martić's arguments as to the purported targeting of military objects in Zagreb fail. In relation to Martić's *mens rea*, the Appeals Chamber recalls that the Trial Chamber reasonably found that he knew about the effects of the M-87 Orkan, yet ordered the shelling nevertheless.

262. Consequently, this sub-ground of appeal is dismissed. * * *

Precautions Pursuant to Article 58 Additional Protocol I

270. The Trial Chamber did not address the question of whether or not Croatia had obligations to take precautions against the effects of attacks according to Article 58 of Additional Protocol I. Martić argues that the Trial Chamber was required to find a violation of Article 58 of Additional Protocol I by Croatia because "if preventive measures were taken, there would have been no civilian casualties." The Appeals Chamber squarely rejects this argument. It is one of the pillars of international humanitarian law that its provisions have to be applied in all circumstances. One side in a conflict cannot claim that its obligations are diminished or non-existent just because the other side does not respect all of its obligations. Consequently, Martić's arguments as to alleged violations of Article 58 of Additional Protocol I by Croatia are irrelevant when assessing his individual criminal responsibility for violating international humanitarian law, in this case the prohibition to make the civilian population the object of attack. This sub-ground of appeal is thus dismissed.

271. For the foregoing reasons, the Appeals Chamber dismisses Martić's eighth ground of appeal.

NOTES & QUESTIONS

1. Case Update

The Appeals Chamber affirmed Martić's 35-year sentence, and on June 26, 2009, Martić was transferred to Estonia to serve out his sentence. The Appeals Chamber largely affirmed the Trial Chamber's findings, determining that Martić knew about the effects of the M-87 Orkan when he ordered the shelling of Zagreb. It also confirmed that the attack could not be characterized as a lawful reprisal or an exercise of self-defense. *Id.* at paras. 249–261.

2. Cluster Bombs

The Orkan rockets in question in *Martić* were Yugoslav-manufactured, non-guided, high-dispersion missiles containing cluster bomb warheads—so-called cluster bombs. Yugoslavia jointly developed the M-87 Orkan rocket with Iraq. The treaty prohibiting the use of cluster bombs was not in existence at the time this opinion was rendered; nonetheless, the Trial

Chamber found the bombs' use in a densely populated area of Zagreb to be presumptively unlawful under general IHL principles. Cluster bombs are weapons that, when dropped from the air or launched from land-based artillery, eject a payload of sub-munitions (bomblets or other fragmentation weapons) from a dispenser upon contact or just prior to contact. The Trial Chamber found that the cluster bombs fired on Zagreb each contained 288 bomblets. At a height of 800–1,000m above the targeted area, the rocket ejected the bomblets, which exploded upon impact, releasing the pellets. The maximum firing range of the M-87 Orkan is 50 kilometers, and the dispersion error (i.e., the distance from the point of impact to the mean point of impact) increases with the firing range. Expert testimony adduced by the Prosecution indicated that when fired from a range of 50 km, the dispersion error of the Orkan is about 1000m in each direction.

Cluster munitions can be used against "soft" targets, such as enemy personnel or civilians, or can be designed to destroy runways, scatter landmines, penetrate armor, start fires (so-called "firebombs"), and deliver chemical weapons. Although the United States and others have developed guided cluster munitions (such as the CBU-97 ("Cluster Bomb Unit 97") that automatically fires at the first heat source it finds using infrared technology), cluster bombs generally distribute their sub-munitions randomly over a "footprint" of up to one square kilometer.

Besides their indiscriminate nature, a major critique of cluster bomb use concerns the fact that up to 40% of the payload may remain unexploded (so-called unexploded ordnance (UXO)), causing harm many years after the initial use. Cluster bombs were used by both Israel and Hezbollah during the 2006 armed conflict in Lebanon. The United Nations estimates that Israel fired cluster bombs containing over 4 million sub-munitions into Lebanon, close to 90% of them during the last 72 hours of the conflict. The U.N. also estimates that over 100,000 of these sub-munitions did not explode, posing an enormous threat to the local civilian population. Human Rights Watch confirmed that Hezbollah also used Chinese-made cluster bombs to attack Israel during the Lebanese conflict. Over seventy countries in the world stockpile cluster munitions; thirty-four countries produce 210 types of cluster bombs; and at least twelve countries, including the United States, sell or transfer cluster munitions to other countries.

In 2007, Norway launched an initiative to negotiate and adopt an international treaty prohibiting cluster munitions. The 2008 Convention on Cluster Munitions bans the use, production, stockpiling, and transfer of cluster munitions. The treaty entered into force on August 1, 2010, and as of July 2019, has 106 state parties and fourteen signatories.

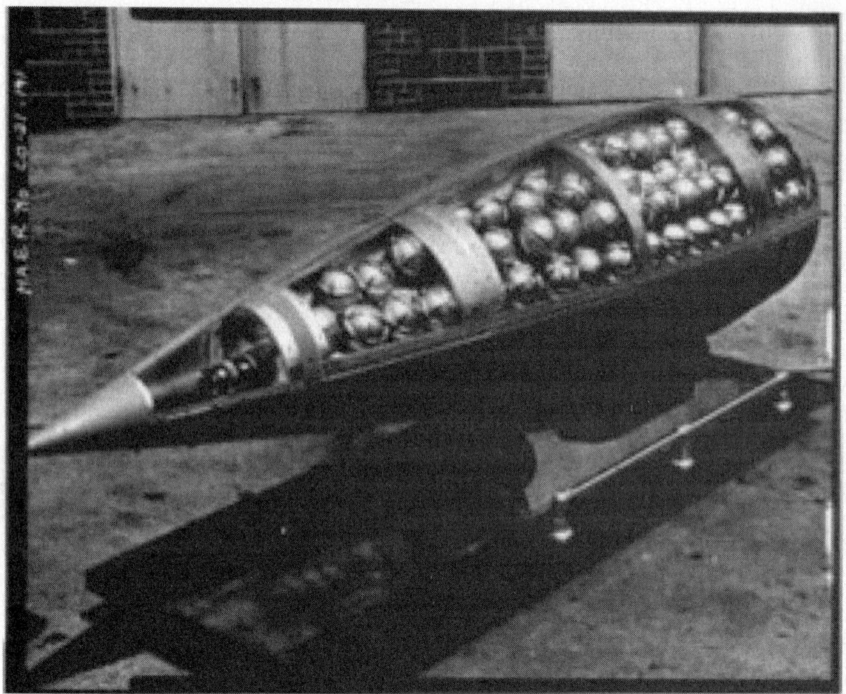

3. Landmines

Other weapons with indiscriminate effects are the subject of specific treaties prohibiting or restricting their use. These weapon-specific treaties complement and reinforce the general rules of international humanitarian law applicable in armed conflict. For example, there is now a treaty dedicated to regulating the use of landmines. *See* Convention on the Prohibition of the Use, Stockpiling, Production and Transfer of Anti-Personnel Mines and on their Destruction ("Ottawa Treaty"). As of this writing, 164 states are parties to the 1997 Ottawa Treaty, and most of the non-parties do not use or produce antipersonnel mines. Three of the five permanent members of the Security Council—China, Russia, and the United States—are neither parties nor signatories to the treaty. These states have refused to sign the treaty on the theory that landmines, particularly more modern high-tech ones, can be used without endangering civilians. The United States in particular has indicated that maintaining the demilitarized zone (DMZ) between North and South Korea depends on the use of landmines. In September 2014, the United States indicated that it would henceforth abide by the Ottawa Treaty except on the Korean Peninsula. Given the high degree of support for the Ottawa Treaty, can it be said that any use of landmines is now contrary to international law? In answering this question, consider that Israel and Syria continue to lay landmines, and that Egypt, and North and South Korea have continued to oppose any effort to ban landmines. Would the contemporary use of landmines give rise to individual criminal responsibility? Should it? How could such conduct be charged under the ICC Statute?

4. Other Prohibited Weapons

Other weapons have been declared to be inherently illegal. For example, early treaties codified the prohibition against the use of "dum-dum" (expanding) bullets and poisonous gas. (Dum dum bullets take their name from the Indian arsenal that first produced the munition for the British Indian Army). On the prohibition of expanding bullets, *see* the 1899 Hague Declaration Concerning Expanding Bullets, and the 1998 ICC Statute Article 8(2)(b)(xix). On prohibition of poisoned weapons, *see* 1899 Hague Convention, Article 23(a); 1907 Hague Convention, Article 23(a); the 1925 Geneva Gas Protocol; and the 1998 ICC Statute, Article 8(2)(b)(xvii). More recent treaties prohibit the use of biological and chemical weapons and blinding laser weapons. *See* the 1972 Biological Weapons Convention; 1993 Convention on the Prohibition of the Development, Production, Stockpiling and Use of Chemical Weapons and on Their Destruction; and Protocol IV to the 1980 Convention on Prohibitions or Restrictions on the Use of Certain Conventional Weapons which may be deemed to be Excessively Injurious or to have Indiscriminate Effects (prohibiting certain uses of laser weapons).

The Rome Statute criminalized some of these prohibitions in Article 8, but only in the context of international armed conflicts. States from the developing world wanted a provision criminalizing resort to nuclear weapons; states from the developed world wanted a similar provision on chemical and biological weapons. This gulf between the poor man's and the rich man's weapons of mass destruction has long bedeviled disarmament efforts. The stalemate was resolved by excluding explicit reference to both categories of weapons and adding a placeholder that might one day allow for their piecemeal inclusion. The ICC Statute at Article 8(2)(b)(xx) governing international conflicts thus would allow for the prosecution of individuals shown to have employed "weapons, projectiles and material and methods of warfare which are of a nature to cause superfluous injury or unnecessary suffering or which are inherently indiscriminate in violation of the international law of armed conflict." However, this provision will not be activated until "such weapons, projectiles and material and methods of warfare are the subject of a comprehensive prohibition and are included in an annex to this Statute, by an amendment in accordance with the relevant provisions set forth in articles 121 and 123." This Annex has never been created.

During the Kampala Review Conference in 2010, states adopted a Belgian proposal to amend the ICC Statute to penalize the use of poison weapons, asphyxiating gases, and expanding bullets in non-international armed conflicts, further harmonizing the law governing the two classes of conflict. Other proposals to specifically penalize the use of chemical weapons, biological weapons, anti-personnel landmines, blinding laser weapons, cluster munitions, and nuclear weapons again failed. In 2017 the Assembly of State Parties passed a resolution adding prohibitions on microbial and biological weapons; weapons that injure by fragments and escape x-ray detection; and laser weapons to be used against the naked eye. The amendments were made pursuant to Art. 121(5), so these new prohibitions only apply to those state parties that expressly agree to them. *See* Assembly of State Parties, *Resolution on Amendments to Article 8 of the Rome Statute of the International Criminal Court*, ICC-ASP/16/Res.4 (Dec. 14, 2017).

5. Chemical Weapons Use in Syria

Given Syria's extensive pre-war stockpiles, the threat of chemical weapons use was ever-present as the conflict unfolded. It appears that chemical weapons were first used in December 2012 in Homs and then in March 2013 in the form of a sarin gas attack that killed twenty-six people in Khan al-Assal. As these threats began to materialize, with rumors circulating that there was activity at chemical weapons storage sites or even that the regime had begun mixing the precursors required to make sarin nerve gas, U.S. President Barack Obama, in impromptu remarks, announced that the use of chemical weapons would cross a "red line" and change his calculus towards the conflict. Specifically, he stated: "We have been very clear to the Assad regime—but also to other players on the ground—that a red line for us is we start seeing a whole bunch of chemical weapons moving around or being utilized. That would change my calculus; that would change my equation." In August 2013, in Ghouta, a rebel-held suburb of Damascus, hundreds suffocated in another presumed attack, also involving sarin gas. Following the emergence of graphic images of victims convulsing and foaming at the mouth, Obama began the process of seeking Congressional approval to respond militarily. When it became clear from Congressional debates that this authority would not be forthcoming, Obama—not without controversy—withdrew this threat and backed a deal brokered by Russia. Obama's decision to turn the decision over to Congress was criticized once it became clear that his red line remark had been interpreted as a green light by the Assad regime. Others have argued that Obama's threat of force spurred a massive multilateral mobilization that ultimately led to the elimination of much of Assad's chemical weapon stockpiles and was an example of the effective use of coercive diplomacy. *See* Derek Chollet, *Obama's Red Line, Revisited*, POLITICO (July 19, 2016).

As part of the Russia-brokered Framework Agreement for the Elimination of Syrian Chemical Weapons, Assad agreed to turn over the country's chemical weapons stockpiles for destruction and ratify the Convention on the Prohibition of the Development, Production, Stockpiling and Use of Chemical Weapons and on their Destruction (CWC). Months later, the Organization for the Prohibition of Chemical Weapons (OPCW) certified that 1,300 metric tons of chemical weapons and their precursors were destroyed, and the facilities for their replacement rendered inoperative. Nonetheless, the accuracy of Assad's declaration of existing stocks, the thoroughness of this removal process, and the genuineness of Assad's commitment to renounce these weapons have been repeatedly called into question as chemical weapons attacks continued. Indeed, in August 2015 and several times thereafter, Assad reportedly attacked civilians with chlorine gas, an agent that was not part of the OPCW's weapons elimination program though its use in combat is prohibited by the CWC. The Islamic State in the Levant (ISIL) also appeared to have acquired either mustard gas stockpiles that escaped elimination under the OPCW process or developed the capacity to weaponize these chemicals, given their confirmed use in 2015 near Aleppo (and also in Iraq in the vicinity of U.S. and Kurdish forces). Investigations under the purview of the United Nations, the Commission of Inquiry, and the OPCW have confirmed attacks and allocated responsibility.

An airborne nerve gas attack in Khan Sheikhoun in April 2017 appeared to implicate Syria or Russia as they were the only states with planes in the air at the time. Newly-elected President Donald Trump responded soon after with air strikes on the Al Shayrat airbase where the attack was presumed to have originated. Renewed US strikes on what were identified as fundamental elements of Syria's chemical weapon infrastructure followed an apparent chemical weapon attack in the suburb of Douma in April 2018. At first, the Trump Administration did not provide an international law justification other than to indicate the intent to "prevent and deter the spread and use of deadly chemical weapons." *Statement by President Trump on Syria*, THE WHITE HOUSE (Apr. 6, 2017). The administration later asserted inherent domestic legal authority for such strikes under Article II of the U.S. Constitution to advance important national interests in "averting a worsening catastrophe in Syria, and specifically deterring the use and proliferation of chemical weapons." Department of Defense, *Statement by Secretary James N. Mattis on Syria* (Apr. 13, 2018). The Department of Justice's Office of Legal Counsel finally issued an official opinion on the legality of the airstrikes in May 2018, citing the convergence of domestic and international legal justifications for the use of force, including humanitarian concerns and the need to deter the proliferation of chemical weapons. Office of Legal Counsel, *Memorandum Opinion for the Counsel to the President, April 2018 Airstrikes Against Syrian Chemical-Weapons Facilities* (May 31, 2018). The United Kingdom invoked the ancient doctrine of humanitarian intervention as its legal basis for also acting in response to Syrian chemical weapons attacks. Prime Minister's Office, *Syria-Action—UK Government Legal Position* (Apr. 14, 2018).

The international community's response to these developments has been largely (but not exclusively) positive, suggesting an increased acceptance of the use of force for humanitarian reasons, at least in response to serious breaches of international law. Some of the states on record indicated that the strikes were legal; a broader geographic set of states expressed their general approval (indicating that the operations were justified, necessary, appropriate, and/or legitimate) without addressing the question of legality, *per se*. Others, expressed vague concerns without fully condemning the United States' actions. Only a handful of states expressed outright disapproval, with Russia calling the strikes an act of aggression. Russia was not, however, able to garner any support for a Security Council resolution that would have condemned the attacks. Notwithstanding this effort at enforcement and deterrence through targeted air strikes, the use of chemical weapons in Syria has continued.

Imagine that the situation in Syria were finally referred to the ICC by the Security Council. Could chemical weapon use be prosecuted under Article 8 of the Rome Statute? Should the judges consider the treaty's legislative history or only look to the plain text of Article 8? Does the genus crime of employing asphyxiating and poisonous weapons encompass the use of chemical weapons? Could an *ad hoc* tribunal devoted to Syria prosecute chemical weapons use more easily?

6. Nuclear Weapons

Do nuclear weapons inherently or necessarily violate the principles of proportionality and distinction? Some commentators argue that because nuclear weapons and other weapons of mass destruction cannot distinguish between civilians and combatants, they should be considered inherently illegal. *See, e.g.*, INGRID DETTER, THE LAW OF WAR 146 (2nd ed. 2000). At the request of the U.N. General Assembly, the International Court of Justice issued an advisory opinion on the legality of nuclear weapons. By a tie vote broken by the President of the Court, the Court held that the threat or use of nuclear weapons "would generally be contrary to the rules of international law applicable in armed conflict," but that in view of the current state of international law, and of the facts at its disposal, the Court could not conclude definitively whether the threat or use of force of nuclear weapons would be lawful or unlawful in an extreme circumstance of self-defense, in which the very survival of a State would be at stake. *Legality of the Threat or Use of Nuclear Weapons*, 1996 I.C.J. Reports 226, at para. 105 (2)(E) (July 8). In that opinion, the ICJ stated that in ascertaining whether a particular military action is proportional, states must consider impact to the environment. *Id.* at 30. Judges Koroma (Sierra Leone) and Weeramantry (Sri Lanka) argued in their dissenting opinions that the use of nuclear weapons would be illegal in all circumstances. *Id.* at 429, 556.

On July 7, 2017, the UN General Assembly adopted the Treaty on the Prohibition on Nuclear Weapons. The rounds of negotiations that led to the adoption were boycotted by all nuclear weapons possessing states, most NATO countries, and many military allies of nuclear weapons states. As of this writing, twenty-five states have ratified the treaty and seventy have signed it. Significant ratifying states include South Africa, New Zealand, Mexico, and Austria. For an overview of the treaty and the events leading up to it, *see* Daniel Rietiker, *Wind of Change in Nuclear Disarmament: The Treaty on the Prohibition of Nuclear Weapons as a New Example of Humanitarian, Victim-Centered Arms Control*, 51 SUFFOLK U. L. REV. ONLINE 1 (2018).

7. Robotics and Warfare

Advanced armed forces are increasingly developing and employing unmanned and remotely-operated vehicles and other robotic equipment for warfare. Indeed, in Operation Enduring Freedom (Afghanistan) and Operation Iraqi Freedom, the U.S. military and Central Intelligence Agency have employed unmanned aerial vehicles (UAVs), including remote-operated drones, and other more sophisticated robotic equipment. The utility of robots for surveillance, intelligence gathering, explosive ordnance disposal, and the neutralization of improvised explosive devices (IEDs) is obvious and relatively uncontroversial. More troubling, weaponized robots can be employed for destroying enemy air defenses, for engaging in targeted killings, or on attack missions in high-risk scenarios. Already, drones and other UAVs mounted with Hellfire missiles, laser-guided bombs, and G.P.S.-

enhanced Joint Direct Attack Munitions (JDAMs) have been used to kill high-value terrorist targets in Afghanistan, Yemen, Pakistan and elsewhere, at times causing civilian casualties, although the exact number remains contested.

Although most modern robotic equipment still requires a human operator (albeit one who may be thousands of miles from the theatre of war), technology that is capable of greater decisional autonomy is on the horizon, including—perhaps—even machines with the ability to make independent targeting decisions and proportionality calculi. Is the increased use of robotics in warfare likely to impact when (per the *jus ad bellum*) and how (per the *jus in bello*) states and non-state actors wage war? Might such equipment permanently alter the fundamentals of war? Is it likely to impact the ability of a fighting force to discriminate and utilize proportionate force? Can the existing IHL rules regulate the use of such equipment or do we need new rules? For an argument that the Martens Clause applies to the use of fully autonomous weapons, *see* Russell Christian, *Heed the Call: A Moral and Legal Imperative to Ban Killer Robots* (Human Rights Watch, 2018). For more information, *see, e.g.*, Vik Kanwar, Book Review, *Post-Human Humanitarian Law: The Law of War in the Age of Robotic Weapons*, 2 HARV. NAT'L SEC. J. 616 (2011); Michael N. Schmitt & Jeffrey Thurner, *'Out of the Loop': Autonomous Weapon Systems and the Law of Armed Conflict*, 4 HARV. NAT'L SEC. J. 231 (2013); Mary Ellen O'Connell, *Banning Autonomous Killing: The Legal & Ethical Requirement that Humans Make Near-Time Legal Decisions*, *in* THE AMERICAN WAY OF BOMBING: CHANGING ETHICAL & LEGAL NORMS, FROM FLYING FORTRESSES TO DRONES (Matthew Evangelista & Henry Shue eds., 2014).

8. Martić's Article 58 Argument

As part of his appeal, Martić argued that Croatian officials failed to take the necessary precautions to protect the civilian population from the attack as required by Article 58 of Additional Protocol I. *Id.* at paras. 240, 244. That Article provides that

> The Parties to the conflict shall, to the maximum extent feasible:
>
> (a) Without prejudice to Article 49 of the Fourth Convention [concerning forcible transfers and deportations of civilians], endeavour to remove the civilian population, individual civilians and civilian objects under their control from the vicinity of military objectives;
>
> (b) Avoid locating military objectives within or near densely populated areas;
>
> (c) Take the other necessary precautions to protect the civilian population, individual civilians and civilian objects under their control against the dangers resulting from military operations.

The Trial and Appeals Chamber summarily dismissed this argument. Do you agree that Martić's argument concerning Croatia's potential breach of Article 58 is irrelevant to his responsibility? Or should this be a fact in mitigation? Suppose government officials established civilian shields around a target or subtly encouraged civilians to congregate in an area known to be subject to an impending attack. Would that make a difference? Suppose civilians were transported to be near a military target in the hope that their presence would deter an attack? Do city planners take into account the possibility of future warfare in locating military and civilian installations? Should an enemy be held responsible where military objects are placed in close proximity to civilian objects long before war was contemplated?

9. Implementing the Principle of Distinction

Article 57 of Protocol I requires that commanders "do everything feasible to verify that the objectives to be attacked are neither civilians nor civilian objects." This provision requires a military commander to set up an effective intelligence-gathering system to collect and evaluate information concerning potential targets and to direct forces to use available technical means to properly identify targets. How much discretion should commanders and troops engaged in military operations have to determine which available resources to use in any particular military engagement? Should an evaluation of the efforts made to distinguish between military objectives and civilians or civilian objects focus on specific incidents? Or, rather, should the fact that precautionary measures worked in a high or a low percentage of cases be taken into account in determining their adequacy? Consider this opinion:

> [R]egard might be had to considerations such as the cumulative effect of attacks on military objectives causing incidental damage to civilians. In other words, it may happen that single attacks on military objectives causing incidental damage to civilians, although they may raise doubts as to their lawfulness, nevertheless do not appear on their face to fall foul *per se* of the loose prescriptions of Articles 57 and 58 (or of the corresponding customary rules). However, in case of repeated attacks, all or most of them falling within the grey area between indisputable legality and unlawfulness, it might be warranted to conclude that the cumulative effect of such acts entails that they may not be in keeping with international law. Indeed, this pattern of military conduct may turn out to jeopardise excessively the lives and assets of civilians, contrary to the demands of humanity.

Prosecutor v. Kupreškić, Case No. IT–95–16–T, Judgement, para. 526 (Jan. 14, 2000). Where individual (and legitimate) attacks on military objectives are concerned, may the accumulation of such instances, all of which are deemed to have been individually lawful, amount to a crime?

10. Military Objectives

Protocol I defines "military objective" as:

> In so far as objects are concerned, military objectives are limited to those objects which by their nature, location, purpose or use make an effective contribution to military action and whose total or partial destruction, capture or neutralization, in the circumstances ruling at the time, offers a definite military advantage.

This definition is simple to apply with respect to obvious military assets, such as a munitions factory or barracks. It becomes more difficult to apply with respect to dual-use objects, such as communications systems, transportation systems, energy sources, and manufacturing plants. In 1956, the International Committee of the Red Cross (ICRC) drew up the following proposed list of categories of legitimate military targets:

> (1) Armed forces, including auxiliary or complementary organisations, and persons who, though not belonging to the above-mentioned formations, nevertheless take part in the fighting.
>
> (2) Positions, installations or constructions occupied by the forces indicated in sub-paragraph 1 above, as well as combat objectives (that is to say, those objectives which are directly contested in battle between land or sea forces including airborne forces).
>
> (3) Installations, constructions and other works of a military nature, such as barracks, fortifications, War Ministries (e.g. Ministries of Army, Navy, Air Force, National Defence, Supply) and other organs for the direction and administration of military operations.
>
> (4) Stores of army or military supplies, such as munition dumps, stores of equipment or fuel, vehicle parks.
>
> (5) Airfields, rocket launching ramps and naval base installations.
>
> (6) Those of the lines and means of communications (railway lines, roads, bridges, tunnels and canals) which are of fundamental military importance.
>
> (7) The installations of broadcasting and television stations; telephone and telegraph exchanges of fundamental military importance.
>
> (8) Industries of fundamental importance for the conduct of the war:
>
> > (a) industries for the manufacture of armaments such as weapons, munitions, rockets, armoured vehicles, military aircraft, fighting ships, including the manufacture of accessories and all other war material;
> >
> > (b) industries for the manufacture of supplies and material of a military character, such as transport and communications material, equipment of the armed forces;
> >
> > (c) factories or plants constituting other production and manufacturing centres of fundamental importance for the conduct of war, such as the metallurgical, engineering and chemical industries, whose nature or purpose is essentially military;
> >
> > (d) storage and transport installations whose basic function it is to serve the industries referred to in (a)–(c);

(e) installations providing energy mainly for national defence, e.g. coal, other fuels, or atomic energy, and plants producing gas or electricity mainly for military consumption.

(9) Installations constituting experimental, research centres for experiments on and the development of weapons and war material.

ICRC, *Draft Rules for the Limitation of the Dangers incurred by the Civilian Population in Time of War*, Annex (1956).

Should determinations of the lawfulness of a target consider its war-sustaining capability? For a detailed and critical discussion of the definition of "military object," *see* W. Hays Parks, *Air War and the Law of War*, 32 AIR FORCE L. REV. 1, 135–45 (1990). Might attacks on even legitimate military objects be unlawful where they cause excessive long-term damage to an enemy's economic infrastructure? *See* Judith G. Gardam, *Proportionality and Force in International Law*, 87 AM. J. INT'L L. 391, 404–10 (1993).

11. The Martens Clause

Many of the early IHL treaties contain the so-called Martens Clause, named after the Russian delegate to the first Hague Conferences. The Clause appears in the preamble of the Hague Conventions of 1899 and 1907, in a modified form in the 1949 Geneva Conventions, and in the main text of Protocol I of 1977 of the Geneva Conventions. The clause provides that:

> Until a more complete code of the laws of war is issued, * * * populations and belligerents remain under the protection and empire of the principles of international law, as they result from the usages established between civilized nations, from the laws of humanity and the requirements of the public conscience.

Martens introduced the declaration after delegates at the Peace Conference failed to agree on the status of civilians who took up arms against an occupying force. Large military powers argued that such individuals should be treated as *francs-tireurs*—a term used to describe irregular military formations who had taken up arms during the Franco-Prussian War (1870–1871) and from then on used to refer more generally to guerrilla fighters. Conversely, smaller states contended that these irregular fighters should be treated as lawful combatants. Although the clause was originally formulated to resolve this particular dispute, it has subsequently reappeared with some modifications in later treaties regulating armed conflicts.

The clause highlights the legal and moral bases of humanitarian obligations by making reference not only to law, but also to "pre-juridical principles [and] to the sentiments of humanity." As such, the Martens Clause also provides a principle of interpretation. If "faced with two interpretations—one in keeping with the principles of humanity and moral standards, and one which is against these principles—then we should of course give priority to the former interpretation." Antonio Cassese, *The Attitude of States toward the Development of Humanitarian Law*, *in* THE NEW HUMANITARIAN LAW OF ARMED CONFLICT: PROCEEDINGS OF THE 1976 AND 1977 CONFERENCES 221, 257 (Antonio Cassese ed., 1980). One of the military commissions in the post-WWII period noted that the Clause

> is much more than a pious declaration. It is a general clause, making the usages established among civilized nations, the laws of humanity, and the dictates of public conscience into the legal yardstick to be applied if and when the specific provisions of the [Hague] Convention and the Regulations annexed to it do not cover specific cases occurring in warfare, or concomitant to warfare.

U.S. v. Krupp, 9 TRIALS OF WAR CRIMINALS BEFORE THE NUREMBURG MILITARY TRIBUNALS UNDER CONTROL COUNCIL NO. 10, at 1327, 1341 (1950). The ICJ invoked the Martens Clause somewhat cryptically in its Nuclear Weapons Opinion, stating that "it has proved to be an effective means of addressing the rapid evolution of military technology." *Legality of the Threat or Use of Nuclear Weapons*, 1996 I.C.J. Reports 226 at para. 78 (July 8). Given the substantial codification of international humanitarian law, is the Martens Clause now obsolete? If it still has some force, what is its relevance, if any, to international criminal law? Is it sufficient to impose individual criminal responsibility?

12. Implementing the Principle of Proportionality

The principle of proportionality requires the weighing of military advantage gained against potential or actual civilian harm caused. As a practical matter, how are combatants to assign relevant values to the military advantage gained or to the injury to non-combatants or to civilian objects? How are judges to do so when they rule on war crimes charges? The judges who convicted Martić at the trial level were Bakone Justice Moloto of South Africa, a former Judge of the Land Claims Court and the High Court; Janet Nosworthy of Jamaica, a former Prosecutor and Defense Counsel in Jamaica; and Frank Höpful of Austria, a former law professor who also practiced criminal law in Austria and appeared before the European Court of Human Rights. None of these judges had any apparent military experience (nor do the judges who heard the appeal).

Might such judges assign different values to these factors than a combatant in the field, a commander at headquarters, or a country's Minister of Defense? Can such civilian judges accurately evaluate what measures were "feasible" in a conflict situation? Are judges from varied legal and cultural backgrounds likely to have different intuitions about how to balance the strategic value of a target and the moral cost of harm to civilians? Will they necessarily undertake the same assessment *ex post* that the defendant undertook *ex ante*? Should international criminal tribunals adopt the notion of the "reasonable military commander?" How might expert testimony be of use in this context? To what extent is a military commander obligated to expose his own forces to danger in order to limit civilian casualties or damage to civilian objects?

13. Implementing the Principle of Distinction

In the case that follows involving Ante Gotovina, Ivan Čermak, and Mladen Markač, the ICTY used expert testimony to establish a bright line test to determine whether specific artillery attacks satisfied the principle of distinction. Gotovina was the Commander of the Split Military District of the Croatian Army (HV) from October 9, 1992, to March 1996. Čermak was the

Assistant Minister of Defense in the Croatian Government from 1991–1993, and from August 5, 1995 he was the Commander of the Knin Garrison at the rank of Colonel General. Markač was Commander of the Special Police of the Ministry of the Interior of the Republic of Croatia from February 18, 1994. All three were indicted in connection with Operation Storm, a military offensive undertaken by Croatia to retake the Krajina region of the country from the self-proclaimed Serb Republic of Krajina. (The events leading up to the establishment of the Serb Republic of Krajina was the subject of the Martić case excerpted above.) All three were indicted as participants in a joint criminal enterprise (JCE) to permanently remove the Serb population from the Krajina region. Specifically, the indictment alleged violations of the laws and customs of war, and crimes against humanity, including persecution, deportations, forcible transfers, murder, inhuman acts, and cruel treatment aimed at the Serb population in the region.

The Trial Chamber acquitted Čermak of all charges, and convicted both Gotovina and Markač as members of a JCE for persecution, deportation, murder and inhuman acts as a crime against humanity; and plunder of private and public property, wanton destruction, murder, and cruel treatment in violation of the laws and customs of war. Gotovina was sentenced to twenty-four years' and Markač to eighteen years' imprisonment. Both Gotovina and Markač appealed their convictions. Much of the discussion in the Appeals judgment concerned artillery attacks against Knin, Benkovac, Obrovac, and Gračac (the "Four Towns"), and whether the attack was aimed at a military objective and thus consistent with the principles of distinction and proportionality.

Prosecutor v. Ante Gotovina & Ivan Markač, Case No. IT–06–90–A, Decision (November 16, 2012)

In the Appeals Chamber

28. Gotovina submits, *inter alia*, that the Trial Chamber erred in finding that unlawful artillery attacks took place, and that, "without a finding of unlawful attacks resulting in mass-deportation," the Trial Chamber's finding that a JCE existed should be reversed. Markač joins Gotovina in these contentions.

29. More specifically, Gotovina submits, *inter alia*, that the Trial Chamber erred in convicting him because the indiscriminate nature of the artillery attacks was not pled in the Indictment. He asserts that he lacked notice of three material elements underlying the Trial Chamber's conclusions, namely: i) the presumption of unlawfulness with respect to shells falling more than 200 meters from a lawful target; ii) the projectile-by-projectile assessment of the artillery attacks rather than an assessment of the attacks as a whole; and iii) the conclusion that the HV was unable to fire at targets of opportunity. Gotovina maintains that the Trial Chamber erred by not putting "its case" to the various expert witnesses appearing at trial and, accordingly, submits that he was

deprived of the opportunity to challenge and fully litigate relevant issues related to the theory underpinning his convictions. * * *

33. Gotovina submits that, absent this erroneous analysis, the Trial Chamber could not have concluded that the impact sites demonstrated that unlawful artillery attacks took place. More specifically, he suggests that absent the assumptions implicit in the 200 Metre Standard, there is no relevant evidence on the record regarding attacks on the Four Towns, as the Prosecution failed to introduce evidence of civilian casualties or damage to civilian infrastructure in the Four Towns. Gotovina further maintains that estimates of artillery ranges of error greater than 200 metres would result in many fewer areas being classified as "civilian" and suggests that this illustrates the problematic nature of the Trial Chamber's reliance on an arbitrary rule like the 200 Metre Standard. He also asserts that using a 400 metre range of error, as suggested by Prosecution Witness Andrew Leslie, would result in only 13 of the identified impacts falling outside the permissible zone. * * *

39. The Prosecution maintains, *inter alia*, that the Trial Chamber correctly concluded that Gotovina ordered artillery attacks on the Four Towns, which involved indiscriminate shelling. The Prosecution submits that Gotovina overstates the significance of the 200 Metre Standard, and contends that, in any event, it was a reasonable finding based on the evidence before the Trial Chamber. It maintains that the Trial Chamber noted evidence it received concerning margins of error for artillery weapons when it derived the 200 Metre Standard, including evidence from Witness Rajčić that the range of error for 130-millimetre guns was 70–75 metres and evidence from Prosecution Witness Harry Konings [a lieutenant-colonel in the Dutch Royal Army and expert witness] that artillery weapons similar to those used by the HV had margins of error between 18 and 60 metres. The Prosecution further maintains that the Trial Chamber reasonably rejected Witness Leslie's testimony that HV projectiles would have a 400 metre range of error. In this context, the Prosecution suggests that the Trial Chamber reasonably considered additional factors which could reduce accuracy, and on that basis created the 200 Metre Standard, a measure that functioned as "a presumption applied against the Prosecution that was generous and favourable to Gotovina." * * *

The 200 Metre Standard

The Trial Chamber's Findings

52. The Trial Chamber observed that, in shelling Knin, the HV deployed 130-millimetre guns at distances of 25 to 27 kilometres from the town and 122-millimetre BM-21 Multi Barrel Rocket Launchers ("BM-21") at distances of 18 to 20 kilometres from the town. The Trial Chamber explicitly considered the testimony of three witnesses concerning the accuracy of this weaponry. Witness Konings testified in his capacity as a Lieutenant Colonel in the Royal Netherlands Army and as an expert in the use of artillery in military operations. Witness Rajčić testified in his

capacity as the chief of artillery of the Split MD from April 1993 to June 1996. As part of his responsibilities in this role, he was involved in implementing the 2 August Order.* Witness Leslie testified in his capacity as Chief of Staff of UNCRO Sector South in Knin from 1 March 1995 to 7 August 1995 and as a military officer with extensive experience in artillery.**

53. More specifically, the Trial Chamber considered Witness Konings's evidence that, with respect to an unguided 155-millimetre shell fired from a distance of 14.5 kilometres, variations caused by internal factors can affect "locations of impacts of up to 55 metres in range and five metres in deflection; while a number of external factors (such as muzzle velocity, wind speed, air temperature and density) can lead to variations in the locations of impacts of between 18 and 60 metres per factor." Witness Konings explained that guns firing 155-millimetre shells are comparable to those firing 130-millimetre shells. The Trial Chamber noted Witness Konings's view that BM-21 launchers cover a broader area than 130-millimetre guns. The Trial Chamber also noted Witness Konings's view that "probable errors increase the further the target is from the fire unit."

54. The Trial Chamber summarised Witness Rajčić's relevant testimony as stating that a 130-millimetre gun at a distance of 26 kilometres "has an error range of about 15 metres along the axis, and about 70 to 75 metres in distance, with the normal scattering dispersion of a 130-millimetre shell being an area with a diameter of 35 metres." The Trial Chamber further understood Witness Rajčić to have testified that BM-21 launchers cover a broader area than 130-millimetre guns. Additionally, the Trial Chamber noted Witness Leslie's view that "landing within a 400-metre radius of the target with the first shot" would be acceptable with respect to, *inter alia*, 130-millimetre guns and BM-21s.

55. The Trial Chamber observed that it understood "primarily from [Witness] Konings's evidence that the variation in the locations of impacts of the artillery weaponry employed by the HV is difficult to delimit precisely, as it depends on a number of factors on which the Trial Chamber has not received detailed evidence." The Trial Chamber further observed that Witness Leslie "was not called as an artillery expert" and that it was "not clear which of the factors described by [Witness] Konings [Witness] Leslie took into account." The Trial Chamber concluded that a reasonable interpretation of this evidence was that "those artillery projectiles which impacted within a distance of 200 metres of an identified artillery target were deliberately fired at that artillery target."
* * *

---

* Eds.: The Trial Chamber found that on August 2, Gotovina and Rajčić ordered the formation of artillery units to support Operation Storm.

** Eds.: UNCRO was the United Nations Confidence Restoration Operation deployed to Croatia to help implement a 1994 ceasefire and replace UNPROFOR, the U.N. Protection Force.

57. The Trial Chamber's Impact Analysis never deviated from the 200 Metre Standard. With respect to all Four Towns, it found that all impact sites within 200 metres of a target it deemed legitimate could have been justified as part of an attack offering military advantage to HV forces. By contrast, the Trial Chamber found that all impact sites more than 200 metres from a target it deemed legitimate served as indicators of an indiscriminate artillery attack.

Analysis

58. The Appeals Chamber observes that the Trial Chamber did not explain the specific basis on which it arrived at a 200 metre margin of error as a reasonable interpretation of evidence on the record. The Trial Judgement contains no indication that any evidence considered by the Trial Chamber suggested a 200 metre margin of error. The Trial Chamber appears to have accepted Witness Konings's testimony that the range of error for artillery weapons depends on a number of factors, such as wind speed and air temperature, but concluded that it did not receive detailed evidence on these factors. However, the Trial Chamber made no attempt to justify the 200 Metre Standard with respect to the factors Witness Konings identified, despite rejecting Witness Leslie's proposed 400 metre range of error partly because it did not explicitly account for these factors. * * *

61. The Trial Chamber's failure to make crucial findings and calculations may be partially explained by its observation that it did not receive detailed evidence on the factors identified by Witness Konings as affecting artillery shells' range of error. However, the Prosecution's failure to proffer relevant evidence did not justify the Trial Chamber's insufficient analysis in this regard. The Appeals Chamber finds that there was a need for an evidentiary basis for the Trial Chamber's conclusions, particularly because these conclusions relate to a highly technical subject: the margin of error of artillery weapons in particular conditions. However, the Trial Chamber adopted a margin of error that was not linked to any evidence it received; this constituted an error on the part of the Trial Chamber. The Trial Chamber also provided no explanation as to the basis for the margin of error it adopted; this amounted to a failure to provide a reasoned opinion, another error. * * *

83. In these circumstances, the Appeals Chamber, Judge Agius and Judge Pocar dissenting, finds that the reversal of the Impact Analysis undermines the Trial Chamber's conclusion that artillery attacks on the Four Towns were unlawful. The Trial Chamber's reliance on the Impact Analysis was so significant that even considered in its totality, the remaining evidence does not definitively demonstrate that artillery attacks against the Four Towns were unlawful. In view of the foregoing, the Appeals Chamber, Judge Agius and Judge Pocar dissenting, considers that no reasonable trier of fact could conclude beyond reasonable doubt that the Four Towns were subject to unlawful artillery attacks. The Appeals Chamber thus need not consider the Appellants'

remaining arguments challenging the Trial Chamber's findings on the unlawful nature of artillery attacks against the Four Towns. * * *

Dissenting Opinion of Judge Fausto Pocar

2. Given the sheer volume of errors and misconstructions in the Majority's reasoning and the fact that the Appeal Judgement misrepresents the Trial Chamber's analysis, I will not discuss everything in detail. Instead, I will limit my dissenting opinion to discussing the reasons of my disagreement with the three most fatal errors in the Majority's approach and conclusions with respect to: (i) the error relating to the 200 Metre Standard; (ii) the other evidence on the unlawfulness of the artillery attacks on the towns of Knin, Benkovac, Obrovac, and Gračac ("Four Towns"); and (iii) the JCE. * * *

200 Metre Standard

5. In my view, the Majority's approach is wholly erroneous and in violation of our standard of review on appeal for various reasons.

6. In its analysis, the Majority seems to identify two distinct errors. One of them is the adoption of a margin of error of artillery weapons, which according to the Majority is "not linked to any evidence". However, the Majority falls short of identifying what type of error it is. The second error identified by the Majority is the failure to provide a reasoned opinion as to the basis for the margin of error of artillery weapons, which it correctly characterizes as an error of law. Having found that the Trial Chamber committed an error of law by failing to provide a reasoned opinion as to the basis for the margin of error of artillery weapons and that the Trial Chamber's findings do not support the Trial Chamber's conclusion to adopt the 200 Metre Standard, the Majority states that, "[i]n view of this legal error, [it] will consider *de novo* the remaining evidence on the record to determine whether the conclusions of the Impact Analysis are still valid." However, the Majority's subsequent analysis is erroneous, fails to do what it enounces, and is in violation of our standard of review on appeal.

7. The Majority states that, "[a]bsent an established range of error", it cannot exclude the possibility that:

> all of the impact sites considered in the Trial Judgement were the results of shelling aimed at targets that the Trial Chamber considered to be legitimate. The fact that a relatively large number of shells fell more than 200 metres from fixed artillery targets could be consistent with a much broader range of error. The spread of shelling across Knin is also plausibly explained by the scattered locations of fixed artillery targets, along with the possibility of a higher margin of error.

The Majority continues further and states:

> Although evidence on the record suggests that individual units of the HV aimed artillery in the general direction of the Four

> Towns rather than at specific targets, the Trial Chamber found that this evidence was not wholly conclusive when considered alone and was indicative of an unlawful attack only in the context of the Trial Chamber's application of the 200 Metre Standard. The Appeals Chamber [. . .] considers that absent the 200 Metre Standard, this latter evidence is inconclusive.

Finally, in the second paragraph of its analysis, the Majority states:

> The Trial Judgement suggests that in Knin, a few impacts occurred particularly far from identified legitimate artillery targets, and could not be justified by any plausible range of error. In view of its finding that the Trial Chamber erred in deriving the 200 Metre Standard, however, the Appeals Chamber [. . .] does not consider that this conclusion is adequately supported. In any event, the Appeals Chamber [. . .] has found that in Knin, the Trial Chamber erred in excluding the possibility of mobile targets of opportunity such as military trucks and tanks. The possibility of shelling such mobile targets, combined with the lack of any dependable range of error estimation, raises reasonable doubt about whether even artillery impact sites particularly distant from fixed artillery targets considered legitimate by the Trial Chamber demonstrate that unlawful shelling took place.

Based on this cursory analysis of only two paragraphs, the Majority concludes that "after reviewing the relevant evidence, the Trial Chamber's errors with respect to the 200 Metre Standard and targets of opportunity are sufficiently serious that the conclusions of the Impact Analysis cannot be sustained."

8. I find the Majority's reasoning flawed as it is in violation of our standard of review on appeal, but also because it fails to conduct the review of the evidence it enounced it would do.

9. First, the Majority's reasoning fails to apply the standard that it previously and correctly enounced in the section of the Appeal Judgement setting the standard of review. According to our appellate standard of review, where the Appeals Chamber finds an error of law in the trial judgement arising from the application of an incorrect legal standard, the Appeals Chamber will articulate the correct legal standard and review the relevant factual findings of the trial chamber accordingly. In so doing, the Appeals Chamber not only corrects the legal error, but, when necessary, also applies the correct legal standard to the evidence contained in the trial record and determines whether it is itself convinced beyond reasonable doubt as to the factual finding challenged by the appellant before that finding may be confirmed on appeal.

10. Although the 200 Metre Standard was, according to the Majority, "not linked to any evidence", it is not a simple error of fact. The Trial Chamber used the 200 Metre Standard in its consideration of the

explanation given by the chief of artillery of the Split Military District during Operation Storm and subordinate of Gotovina, Marko Rajčić, that Gotovina's and his subordinates' orders to the HV artillery to put the towns under artillery fire should not be interpreted as treating the Four Towns as targets when firing projectiles during Operation Storm but that these orders meant that previously selected targets with specific coordinates in those towns should be put under constant disruptive artillery fire. The Trial Chamber, having evaluated all of the evidence, considered "that those artillery projectiles which impacted within a distance of 200 metres of an identified artillery target [offering a definite military advantage] were deliberately fired at that artillery target." Thus, in its assessment of the evidence, the Trial Chamber used the 200 Metre Standard as a presumption of legality—which was generous and to the benefit of Gotovina—to analyse in part the evidence of the shelling attacks and the artillery impacts. In my view, there is therefore no doubt that, while the error was allegedly founded on a factual basis, the establishment of the 200 Metre Standard and its use ultimately constitutes an error of law. The 200 Metre Standard was, as its name indicates, a *standard* or a legal tool that the Trial Chamber used in order to determine that Rajčić was not credible when he claimed that Gotovina's attack order was understood as directing his subordinates only to target designated military objectives.

11. Having found that the 200 Metre Standard was erroneous and that the Trial Chamber committed an error of law in deriving and applying an incorrect legal standard, the Appeals Chamber had, in accordance with the standard of appellate review, two obligations. First, to identify and articulate the correct legal standard and, second, to apply this standard to the evidence contained in the trial record or, in the alternative, to remand the case back to the Trial Chamber to apply the correct legal standard to the evidence. However, in contravention of our well-established appellate standard of review, the Majority followed neither of these requirements. As reflected by the wording used at the beginning of the Majority's two-paragraph analysis—"[a]bsent an established range of error"—the Majority pretends to review the evidence in the trial record without having first determined the correct legal standard. It therefore starts on a wrong premise.

12. Second, although the Majority enounces that, "[i]n view of this legal error, [it] will consider *de novo* the remaining *evidence* on the record", it does not consider the *evidence in the trial record* to determine whether the conclusion of the Trial Chamber is still valid, but limits its assessment to the *Trial Chamber's analysis and findings*. The correct approach for the Majority in accordance with the appellate standard of review would have been to consider the evidence in the trial record in light of the legal standard it should have announced. Unfortunately, the Majority fails to do so.

13. By not articulating the correct legal standard, the Majority falls short of correcting any legal errors in the Trial Judgement and clarifying the law the Trial Chamber should have applied when assessing the legality of an attack directed on civilians and civilian objects. It also fails to consider whether the artillery attacks on the Four Towns were lawful or not when the evidence is assessed in light of the principles of international humanitarian law ("IHL"). First, the Majority fails to give any indication as to what the correct legal standard was. Does the Majority consider that the correct legal standard was a 400-metre standard? A 100-metre standard? A 0-metre standard? The Appeal Judgement provides no answer to this question. Second, the Majority also fails to clarify on which basis the correct legal standard should have been established. Does the Majority consider that a legal standard can be established on a margin of error of artillery weapons? Does the Majority consider that a trial chamber is entitled in law to establish a presumption of legality to assess the evidence of the shelling attacks and the artillery impacts in order to establish the lawfulness of the attack? Is a trial chamber not limited in its analysis to the strict application of IHL principles? Here again, the Appeal Judgement is mute on these issues. Third, if the Majority considers that applying a presumption of legality to analyse the evidence of the shelling attacks and the artillery impacts in order to establish its lawfulness is incorrect, it further fails to articulate which legal principles the Trial Chamber should have applied. Does the Majority consider that the Trial Chamber should have applied the principles of customary IHL in its analysis? If so, which exact IHL principles should the Trial Chamber have applied in assessing whether the artillery attack was lawful? Does the Majority consider that the minimum applicable legal standard was to analyse whether the shelling was aimed at targeting military objectives offering a definite military advantage, whether it was done in respect of the principle of proportionality and after all precautionary measures had been taken? Silence.

14. Unfortunately, the paucity of the legal analysis in the Majority's reasoning opens more questions than it provides legal answers. The Appeals Chamber fails in its mission to clarify the correct legal standard, finding errors without providing the necessary guidance to other trial chambers. By failing to articulate a legal standard, the Majority further omits to assess whether the shelling of the Four Towns was done in respect of IHL principles and, therefore, whether the attack on the Four Towns was lawful or not. In that sense, the Majority's approach does not leave a good legacy in terms of respecting IHL principles when assessing the legality of an attack on towns where civilians and civilian objects are present. The Majority imputes to the Trial Chamber the failure to provide a reasoned opinion regarding the standard adopted and reverses its conclusions while simultaneously failing to articulate the standard that should have been applied. Finally, I do not believe that justice is done when findings of guilt not lightly entered by the Trial Chamber in

more than 1300 pages of analysis are sweepingly reversed in just a few paragraphs, without careful consideration of the trial record and a proper explanation. In light of the above, I fundamentally dissent.

Other Evidence on the Unlawfulness of the Artillery Attacks on the Four Towns

15. Contrary to the Majority's mischaracterization of the Trial Chamber's analysis, the Trial Chamber did not base its conclusion on the unlawfulness of the artillery attacks on the Four Towns only on the 200 Metre Standard nor was this standard "the cornerstone and the organising principle" of the Trial Chamber's analysis of the evidence of unlawful attacks on civilians and civilian objects as the Majority claims.

16. In its assessment of the various underlying acts of persecutions as a crime against humanity, the Trial Chamber entered its finding on the unlawfulness of the attacks on the Four Towns after considering the following mutually reinforcing evidence: (i) the Brioni Meeting held on 31 July 1995 and the Brioni Transcript of this meeting, where Croatian political and military leaders—including Gotovina and Markač—agreed on a common plan to remove Serb civilians from the Krajina region through force or threat of force; (ii) the attack orders given by Gotovina and his subordinates—including Rajčić—to the HV artillery to put the Four Towns under artillery fire as well as the testimonies of expert witnesses who interpreted these attack orders; (iii) the HV artillery reports relating to the HV units' implementation of orders; (iv) the evidence of the shelling attacks as well as the location of artillery impacts, including from international and military eyewitnesses; and (vi) the disproportionate attacks on Milan Martić.

17. If the Majority wishes to reverse Gotovina's and Markač's convictions for one of the underlying acts of persecutions as a crime against humanity, namely unlawful attacks on civilians and civilian objects, it needs to demonstrate that *all* the other remaining findings of the Trial Chamber establishing the unlawfulness of the attacks *cannot stand* in the face of the quashing of the Trial Chamber's application of the 200 Metre standard.

18. Unfortunately, here again the Majority's reasoning is far from being convincing. The Majority uses the error of the 200 Metre Standard to quash—in simply seven paragraphs—all the other remaining findings of the Trial Chamber establishing the unlawfulness of the attacks. The Majority concludes that, "[i]n these circumstances, [. . .] the reversal of the Impact Analysis [due to the error of the 200 Metre Standard] undermines the Trial Chamber's conclusion that artillery attacks on the Four Towns were unlawful." Similar to its analysis on the evidence following the error of the 200 Metre Standard, the Majority again fails to articulate the correct legal standard and to apply it to the evidence contained in the trial record. Moreover, the Majority fails to explain how the Trial Chamber's findings based on evidence not at all linked to the

200 Metre Standard—such as the Brioni Meeting or the disproportionate attacks on Martić—do not stand. Thus, I must dissent.

NOTES & QUESTIONS

1. Case Update

The Appeals Chamber thus reversed the convictions of both Gotovina and Markač. The Appeals Chamber went on to hold that the Trial Chamber's JCE conviction was premised on the assumption that the artillery attacks were unlawful. In finding that the Trial Chamber failed to establish that the attacks were unlawful, the Appeals Chamber reversed all of the other convictions as they were based on the existence of a JCE of forcible deportation of a civilian population, which was in turn premised upon unlawful artillery attacks (para. 91). In addition to the dissenting opinion excerpted above, Judge Carmel Agius (Malta) also issued a dissent, and Judges Patrick Robinson (Jamaica) and Theodore Meron (USA) issued concurring opinions. The decision was greeted with anger and disbelief in Serbia, and fueled the argument among some Serbs that the ICTY was biased against the Serbian people and was a form of victor's justice because many Western governments had supported Croatia during the war, and indeed had played a role in training the individuals involved in Operation Storm. Gotovina was cheered upon his return home to Croatia as a national hero and patriot. The Trial Chamber judgment exceeded 1,300 pages, while the Appeals Chamber's majority decision was slightly under sixty pages, leading the dissenters to criticize, among other things, what they perceived as the failure of the majority to engage with the rich record produced at trial. One commentator has called the Appeals Chamber opinion "the most radical reversal in the ICTY's history." Henri Decoeur, *The ICTY Appeals Judgment in* Prosecutor v. Gotovina and Markač: *Scratching Below the Surface*, CAMBRIDGE J. INT'L & COMP. L. (Nov. 19, 2012). Do you agree that the reversal was "radical?" Should the judges have taken into account the Serb perception of bias in crafting their judgment? Do you think they did?

In a bizarre twist to the *Gotovina* case, an ICTY judge not involved in the proceedings, Frederik Harhoff (Denmark), circulated an email to fifty-six of his "closest friends" (which was quickly leaked to the press) claiming that Judge Meron was "corrupted" by the U.S. Government to pressure his fellow judges to acquit, among others, the defendants in this case. Judge Harhoff cited no evidence supporting this claim, and no such evidence has since emerged. Nevertheless the email, once it was leaked, caused a firestorm of protest and discussion in the blogosphere. In the letter, Judge Harhoff notes that the Court has begun to depart from its "set practice" of convicting military commanders. The defendant in another case being heard by Judge Harhoff, Vojislav Šešelj, successfully argued that Judge Harhoff should be disqualified from his case as he had demonstrated a bias in favor of conviction. *Prosecutor v. Vojislav Šešelj*, Case No. IT–03–67–T, Decision on Defense Motion for Disqualification of Judge Frederik Harhoff and Report to the Vice President (Aug. 28, 2013). This controversy emerged again in connection with the *Perišić* case, discussed in Chapter 15 on Direct and Indirect Responsibility.

2. Error of Law or Fact?

Judge Pocar (Italy) (along with Judge Agius in his separate dissent) criticized the majority for not clearly stating whether the Trial Chamber's error with respect to the 200 meter standard is an error of law or fact. Which one is it? The Majority concludes that the 200-meter standard is not the correct legal standard—why does it not provide the correct standard? What do you think should be the correct standard? Consider the following from Professor Ohlin:

> This might have been a situation where the Trial Chamber said too much, making themselves subject to reversal because they articulated a legal standard (if it even was a legal standard) that was not defensible. But what if they had articulated no legal standard at all? What then?
>
> How is this possible, you ask? It is very possible. The Trial Chamber could have examined the entire spectrum of facts, including the known location of military targets, the known location of civilian deaths, the number of civilian deaths, and then stated that these facts amounted to a legal conclusion of an indiscriminate attack against civilians or even a disproportionate attack against civilians. Period. Had the Trial Chamber done this, their decision would have been subject to less scrutiny, and might even have withstood the appeal.
>
> There's an irony here, of course, and one that I often point out to my students in other contexts. When a court applies the law to the facts, they are obligated to state reasons for their decisions (although juries do not). In announcing that decision, they justifiably feel compelled to articulate standards that explain the basis for that decision. But when they do so, they often get reversed if the standard or legal theory is ill advised.
>
> This creates a law of perverse incentives. Trial Chambers (and courts generally) should be as terse as possible with their explanations if they want to be successful. Although this renders their decision-making process comparatively opaque, it might immunize them from eventual reversal on appeal. But that's not the type of judicial decision-making we want to encourage.

Jens David Ohlin, *Why the* Gotovina *Judgement Matters*, EJIL: TALK! (Dec. 21, 2012).

3. Competing Narratives

With respect to the two-day Operation Storm, two narratives emerged from the evidence presented at trial. It is clear that the lightning-fast operation coincided with a massive exodus of the Serbian population from the area four years after many of its Croatian inhabitants had themselves been pushed from the area by Serbian forces. Was this a case of retaliatory ethnic cleansing and persecution, as alleged in the indictment and believed by some observers, or a natural response to armed conflict conditions and an evacuation order by the Serb leadership, as others have argued? The

Operation also occasioned looting and plunder. But by whom: soldiers under Gotovina's command and control; civilians; or retreating Serbian forces?

In its Judgment, the Trial Chamber squarely adopted the ethnic-cleansing narrative. In so doing, it relied heavily on Gotovina's operations order, which directed his forces to "place [Knin] under attack," and the fact that approximately 5% of the projectiles employed struck farther than 200 meters from any identifiable military objective. The entire opinion is ultimately premised on the view that Gotovina ordered a direct attack on civilians in the Krajina. The rest of the Judgment largely balances on this finding like an inverted pyramid. This finding thus served as the basis for the wanton-destruction war crimes charge. The crimes against humanity convictions relied on the indiscriminate attack as the predicate widespread/systematic attack against a civilian population. The attack also served as a key *actus reus* for the persecution count and the other inhumane acts count. The attack was conceived of as one of the means by which the Croatian forces effectuated the deportation of the Serbian population (the other being the subsequent acts of plunder). Finally, the attack served as one of two "substantial contributions" made by the defendant to the apparent joint criminal enterprise. (The other was an omission; that is, the failure to take the necessary and reasonable measures to prevent and punish foreseeable crimes committed in connection with effectuating the joint criminal enterprise). When the direct attack finding was reversed on appeal, the whole conviction pyramid came tumbling down.

4. Targeting Martić

In his dissent, Judge Pocar refers to the targeting of Milan Martić by the Croatian military. With respect to this incident, the Trial Chamber observed,

> As commander in chief and President of the RSK, Martić was a lawful military objective, and although the probability of killing or disabling Martić by artillery attack was limited, if Gotovina believed Martić to be an important component in SVK decision-making, the potential operational advantage in disrupting the SVK command and control structure would be substantial.

Trial Chamber, Judgement, para. 1175. The Trial Chamber nevertheless found that some of the attacks aimed at killing Martić were disproportionate, given the risk of civilian casualties:

> The Trial Chamber considers that Martić's apartment was located in an otherwise civilian apartment building and that both the apartment and the area marked R on P2337 [a map] were in otherwise predominantly civilian residential areas. The Trial Chamber has considered this use of artillery in light of the evidence on the accuracy of artillery weapons reviewed above and the testimony of expert Konings on the blast and fragmentation effects of artillery shells. At the times of firing, namely between 7:30 and 8 a.m. and in the evening on 4 August 1995, civilians could have reasonably been expected to be present on the streets of Knin near Martić's apartment and in the area marked R on P2337. Firing

> twelve shells of 130 millimetres at Martić's apartment and an unknown number of shells of the same calibre at the area marked R on P2337, from a distance of approximately 25 kilometres, created a significant risk of a high number of civilian casualties and injuries, as well as of damage to civilian objects. The Trial Chamber considers that this risk was excessive in relation to the anticipated military advantage of firing at the two locations where the HV believed Martić to have been present. This disproportionate attack shows that the HV paid little or no regard to the risk of civilian casualties and injuries and damage to civilian objects when firing artillery at a military target on at least three occasions on 4 August 1995.

Id. at para. 1910.

Do you think it was lawful for the Croatian forces to target Milan Martić, the "president" of the self-proclaimed Republic of Serbian Krajina (RSK)? If so, was he a legitimate target while asleep in his residence in a civilian neighborhood? Did Martić himself violate IHL by embedding himself within a civilian neighborhood (see the discussion above about Article 58 of Protocol I)?

5. Assassination v. Targeted Killing

In the wake of revealed assassination plots against foreign leaders, U.S. Presidents Gerald Ford, Jimmy Carter, and Ronald Reagan issued executive orders (E.O. 11905 (1976), E.O. 12036 (1978), and E.O. 12333 (1981), respectively) banning assassination. E.O. 12333, for example, provides: "No person employed by or acting on behalf of the United States Government shall engage in, or conspire to engage in, assassination." These orders have been interpreted to recognize exceptions in conventional military, counterinsurgency, and counter-terrorism operations. *See* Col. W. Hays Parks, *Memorandum on Executive Order 12233 and Assassination* (Nov. 2, 1989). Parks, former Special Assistant to the Judge Advocate General of the Army and Senior Associate Deputy General Counsel for International Affairs at the U.S. Department of Defense, concludes:

> clandestine, low visibility or overt use of military force against legitimate targets in time of war, or against similar targets in time of peace where such individuals or groups pose an immediate threat to United States citizens or the national security of the United States, as determined by competent authority, does not constitute assassination or conspiracy to engage in assassination, and would not be prohibited by the proscription in EO 12333 or by international law.

In Operation Enduring Freedom (Afghanistan), the United States engaged in targeted killing of high-value al Qaeda and Taliban operatives, at times using remotely-piloted Predator and Reaper drone aircraft. Do such killings run afoul of these executive orders, which have never been publicly repealed or repudiated? Would it be preferable if wars were waged as a series of assassinations rather than through large-scale loss of combatant life on more traditional battlefields or through military strikes? Are such assassinations lawful under IHL and international human rights law, or may they constitute willful or treacherous killings of a protected person, the denial of quarter, or a summary execution? Is there a duty to capture such individuals where possible rather than kill them? *See* Elizabeth B. Bazan, *Assassination Ban and E.O. 12333: A Brief Summary,* Congressional Research Service RS21037 (Jan. 2002). Some literature suggests that removing leaders is an effective counter-insurgency tool. *See* Patrick B. Johnson, *The Effectiveness of Leadership Decapitation in Combating Insurgencies*, INT'L SEC. (June 2012).

6. Proportionality

The principle of proportionality requires those who plan and implement attacks to balance the anticipated military advantage with the anticipated harm to civilians and to civilian objects. How would you formulate the proportionality calculus likely employed by Gotovina, particularly as it relates to the attack on President Martić's residence? How does your application of proportionality change given the testimony that Gotovina knew he was unlikely to actually kill Martić? Does the objective of disorienting Martić, and potentially severing or at least impeding his command over the RSK forces, offer a weighty enough military advantage to the Croatian forces to justify the potential harm to civilians by firing into a civilian area?

The record was unclear as to how many civilians were in fact present in Knin at the time of the attack; how was Gotovina to do a proper proportionality analysis under the circumstance without this knowledge? Who bears the burden of proving the number of civilians in the area at the time of the attack? Is the failure to obtain definitive information a war crime? Gotovina's chief of artillery testified that the Croatian troops were highly trained and skilled at engaging in precision targeting; should they be subjected to a more rigorous proportionality calculus as a result? As it turns out, there were no civilian casualties in Knin. What, then, is the crime for which the Trial Chamber convicted Gotovina?

7. Direct Participation in Hostilities

Civilians are entitled to immunity "unless and for such time as they take a direct part in hostilities." *See* Article 51(3), Additional Protocol I (applicable in international armed conflicts); Article 13(3), Protocol II (applicable in non-international armed conflicts). Thus, someone charged with willfully killing a civilian in the context of an armed conflict can, as a defense, put on proof that the victim was directly participating in hostilities. *See Prosecutor v. Strugar*, Case No. IT–01–42–A, Judgement, paras. 164–186 (July 17, 2008). How is a tribunal to determine when a civilian is directly participating in hostilities (DPH)?

The International Committee of the Red Cross undertook a consultative process to develop interpretive guidance concerning when individuals lose their civilian protection for the purposes of targeting. *See* International Committee of the Red Cross, *Interpretive Guidance on the Notion of Direct Participation in Hostilities Under International Humanitarian Law*, 90 INT'L REV. OF THE RED CROSS 991 (2008). According to this guidance, individuals who are members of organized armed groups and who undertake a continuous combat function are targetable at any time. In addition, individuals may lose protection while committing acts that are "likely to adversely affect the military operations or military capacity of a party to an armed conflict or, alternatively, to inflict death, injury, or destruction" on protected persons or objects when there is a direct causal link between the act and the harm likely to result. *Id.* at 995–6.

8. NATO Intervention in Kosovo

Kosovo was a province in southern Serbia with a majority ethnic Albanian population that declared its independence in February 2008. (See the map of Yugoslavia in the Appendix.) The province of Kosovo enjoyed a high degree of autonomy within the former Yugoslavia until 1989. In that year, Serbian leader Slobodan Milošević eliminated Kosovo's formal autonomy and brought it under the direct control of Belgrade, the Yugoslav capital. In 1998, an armed conflict erupted in Kosovo province between the Kosovo Liberation Army (KLA) and the Yugoslav military and police forces resulting in the deaths of over 1,500 Kosovar Albanians and the displacement of 400,000 people. The United Nations Security Council and the Organization for Security and Cooperation in Europe (OSCE) sponsored diplomatic efforts to diffuse tensions and bring about a political solution to the conflict. Nonetheless, at the beginning of 1999, the situation in Kosovo flared up again following a number of acts of provocation on both sides and the use of excessive force by the Serbian military. President Milošević rejected a proposed peace agreement signed by the KLA.

In March 1999, the North Atlantic Treaty Organization (NATO)—a military alliance of European and North American states—launched an air campaign against Yugoslavia in an effort to halt that country's attack on its minority Albanian population. It did so without Security Council approval. The goals were, *inter alia*, to force the Yugoslav military, police, and paramilitary forces to withdraw from Kosovo; station in Kosovo an international military presence; ensure the unconditional and safe return of all refugees and displaced persons and unhindered access to them by humanitarian aid organizations; and establish a political framework agreement for Kosovo. In the campaign, NATO aircraft from thirteen countries flew 38,400 sorties, including 10,484 strike sorties in which 26,614 air munitions were released. In its first days, the campaign struck military targets including Yugoslav defense installations, such as military airports and landing strips. This succeeded in grounding the Yugoslav air force, but did not neutralize its air defense capability. NATO planes were then placed under orders to fly above 15,000 feet to avoid this continuing threat. NATO planes attempted to target Yugoslavia's air defense system from this altitude, but a number of decoys limited the NATO pilots' abilities to make positive visual identification before an attack. In addition, Yugoslav forces apparently located air defense systems and decoys near schools and hospitals.

After four weeks of bombing, the Yugoslav leadership continued to reject negotiation proposals. At a NATO summit in April 1999, NATO leaders decided to intensify the air campaign by expanding the target set to include elements of the military-industrial infrastructure. As a result of this effort, most of the main telecommunications transmitters, fifty-nine bridges, nine major highways, two-thirds of the main industrial plants, 70% of the electricity production capacity, and 80% of the oil refinery capacity were destroyed or severely compromised. The United States employed the Cluster Bomb Unit 97 (CBU-97) alongside new anti-electrical cluster weapons—the CBU-94/B and CBU-102/B (so-called "blackout bombs"). The dispensers of these munitions contain reels of fine conductive fiber that disrupt and damage electrical power transition systems by producing short circuits. Reports indicate that it took 500 people fifteen hours to get a transformer back on line after being disabled by one of these bombs. NATO's campaign lasted from March 24, 1999, to June 9, 1999. In total, between 488 and 527 Yugoslav non-combatants were killed by these air strikes because they were located in or near targets. NATO never introduced ground troops and suffered no casualties, with the exception of two non-combat deaths from the crash of an Apache AH-84 on a training mission.

The ICTY Prosecutor received numerous requests to investigate allegations that senior political and military figures from NATO countries committed serious violations of international humanitarian law during the air campaign. If the Prosecutor's investigation found evidence of serious violations, she had the power to indict pursuant to the ICTY Statute. Criticism of the NATO bombing campaign included allegations that: a) as the resort to force was illegal, all NATO actions were illegal, b) the NATO forces deliberately attacked civilian infrastructure targets (and that such attacks were unlawful), and c) NATO recklessly attacked the civilian population and caused excessive civilian casualties in disregard of the rule of proportionality by trying to fight a "zero casualty" war for their own side. Allegations concerning the "zero casualty" war involved suggestions that, for example, NATO aircraft operated at heights that enabled them to avoid attack by Yugoslav defenses and, consequently, made it impossible for them to properly distinguish between military or civilian objects on the ground.

On May 14, 1999, the Prosecutor established a committee to assess the allegations and material accompanying them, and to advise the Prosecutor and Deputy Prosecutor whether there was a sufficient basis to proceed with an investigation into some or all the allegations related to the NATO bombing. The Committee Established to Review the NATO Bombing Campaign against the Federal Republic of Yugoslavia (Committee) made certain factual findings below with respect to particular incidents it investigated:

Final Report to the Prosecutor by the Committee Established to Review the NATO Bombing Campaign Against the Federal Republic of Yugoslavia

The Attack on a Civilian Passenger Train at the Grdelica Gorge on 12/4/99

58. On 12 April 1999, a NATO aircraft launched two laser guided bombs at the Leskovac railway bridge over the Grdelica gorge and Juzna Morava River, in eastern Serbia. A 5-carriage passenger train, traveling from Belgrade to Ristovac on the Macedonian border, was crossing the bridge at the time, and was struck by both missiles. The various reports made of this incident concur that the incident occurred at about 11:40 a.m. At least ten people were killed in this incident and at least 15 individuals were injured. The designated target was the railway bridge, which was claimed to be part of a re-supply route being used for Serb forces in Kosovo. After launching the first bomb, the person controlling the weapon, at the last instant before impact, sighted movement on the bridge. The controller was unable to dump the bomb at that stage and it hit the train, the impact of the bomb cutting the second of the passenger coaches in half. Realising the bridge was still intact, the controller picked a second aim point on the bridge at the opposite end from where the train had come and launched the second bomb. In the meantime the train had slid forward as a result of the original impact and parts of the train were also hit by the second bomb.

59. * * * U.S. Deputy Defense Secretary John Hamre stated that "one of our electro-optically guided bombs homed in on a railroad bridge just when a passenger train raced to the aim point. We never wanted to destroy that train or kill its occupants. We did want to destroy the bridge and we regret this accident." The substantive part of the explanation, both for the failure to detect the approach of the passenger train and for firing a second missile once it had been hit by the first, was given by General Wesley Clark, NATO's Supreme Allied Commander for Europe and is here reprinted [in part].

> [T]his was a case where a pilot was assigned to strike a railroad bridge that is part of the integrated communications supply network in Serbia. He launched his missile from his aircraft that was many miles away, he was not able to put his eyes on the bridge, it was a remotely directed attack. And as he stared intently at the desired target point on the bridge, and I talked to the team at Aviano who was directly engaged in this operation, as the pilot stared intently at the desired aim point on the bridge and worked it, and worked it and worked it, and all of a sudden at the very last instant with less than a second to go he caught a flash of movement that came into the screen and it was the train coming in. * * * He realised when it had

happened that he had not hit the bridge, but what he had hit was the train. He had another aim point on the bridge, it was a relatively long bridge and he believed he still had to accomplish his mission, the pilot circled back around. He put his aim point on the other end of the bridge from where the train had come, by the time the bomb got close to the bridge it was covered with smoke and clouds and at the last minute again in an uncanny accident, the train had slid forward from the original impact and parts of the train had moved across the bridge, and so that by striking the other end of the bridge he actually caused additional damage to the train.

General Clark showed the cockpit video of the plane which fired on the bridge:

> The pilot in the aircraft is looking at about a 5-inch screen, he is seeing about this much and in here you can see this is the railroad bridge which is a much better view than he actually had, you can see the tracks running this way. Look very intently at the aim point, concentrate right there and you can see how, if you were focused right on your job as a pilot, suddenly that train appeared. It was really unfortunate.
>
> Here, he came back around to try to strike a different point on the bridge because he was trying to do a job to take the bridge down. Look at this aim point—you can see smoke and other obscuration there—he couldn't tell what this was exactly.
>
> Focus intently right at the centre of the cross. He is bringing these two crosses together and suddenly he recognises at the very last instant that the train that was struck here has moved on across the bridge and so the engine apparently was struck by the second bomb. (Press Conference, NATO HQ, Brussels, 13 April).

60. Some doubt has since been cast on this version of events by a comprehensive technical report submitted by a German national, Mr. Ekkehard Wenz, which queries the actual speed at which the events took place in relation to that suggested by the video footage of the incident released by NATO. The effect of this report is to suggest that the reaction time available to the person controlling the bombs was in fact considerably greater than that alleged by NATO. Mr. Wenz also suggests the aircraft involved was an F15E Strike Eagle with a crew of two and with the weapons being controlled by a Weapons Systems Officer (WSO) not the pilot. * * *

The Bombing of the RTS (Serbian TV and Radio Station) in Belgrade on 23/4/99

71. On 23 April 1999, at 0220, NATO intentionally bombed the central studio of the RTS (state-owned) broadcasting corporation at 1 Aberdareva Street in the centre of Belgrade. The missiles hit the

entrance area, which caved in at the place where the Aberdareva Street building was connected to the Takovska Street building. While there is some doubt over exact casualty figures, between 10 and 17 people are estimated to have been killed.

72. The bombing of the TV studio was part of a planned attack aimed at disrupting and degrading the C3 (Command, Control and Communications) network. In coordinated attacks, on the same night, radio relay buildings and towers were hit along with electrical power transformer stations. At a press conference on 27 April 1999, NATO officials justified this attack in terms of the dual military and civilian use to which the FRY communication system was routinely put, describing this as a

> very hardened and redundant command and control communications system [which . . .] uses commercial telephone, [. . .] military cable, [. . .] fibre optic cable, [. . .] high frequency radio communication, [. . .] microwave communication and everything can be interconnected. There are literally dozens, more than 100 radio relay sites around the country, and [. . .] everything is wired in through dual use. Most of the commercial system serves the military and the military system can be put to use for the commercial system [. . .].

Accordingly, NATO stressed the dual-use to which such communications systems were put, describing civilian television as "heavily dependent on the military command and control system and military traffic is also routed through the civilian system."

73. At an earlier press conference on 23 April 1999, NATO officials reported that the TV building also housed a large multi-purpose communications satellite antenna dish, and that "radio relay control buildings and towers were targeted in the ongoing campaign to degrade the FRY's command, control and communications network." In a communication of 17 April 1999 to Amnesty International, NATO claimed that the RTS facilities were being used "as radio relay stations and transmitters to support the activities of the FRY military and special police forces, and therefore they represent legitimate military targets" (Amnesty International Report, *NATO/Federal Republic of Yugoslavia: Violations of the Laws of War by NATO during Operation Allied Force,* June 2000, p. 42).

74. Of the electrical power transformer stations targeted, one transformer station supplied power to the air defence co-ordination network while the other supplied power to the northern-sector operations centre. Both these facilities were key control elements in the FRY integrated air-defence system. In this regard, NATO indicated that

> we are not targeting the Serb people as we repeatedly have stated nor do we target President Milošević personally, we are

> attacking the control system that is used to manipulate the military and security forces.

More controversially, however, the bombing was also justified on the basis of the propaganda purpose to which it was employed:

> [We need to] directly strike at the very central nerve system of Milošević's regime. These of course are those assets which are used to plan and direct and to create the political environment of tolerance in Yugoslavia in which these brutalities can not only be accepted but even condoned. [. . .] Strikes against TV transmitters and broadcast facilities are part of our campaign to dismantle the FRY propaganda machinery which is a vital part of President Milošević's control mechanism.

In a similar statement, British Prime Minister Tony Blair was reported as saying in *The Times* that the media is the apparatus that keeps [Milošević] in power and we are entirely justified as NATO allies in damaging and taking on those targets (24 April, 1999). In a statement of 8 April 1999, NATO also indicated that the TV studios would be targeted unless they broadcast 6 hours per day of Western media reports: "If President Milošević would provide equal time for Western news broadcasts in its programmes without censorship 3 hours a day between noon and 1800 and 3 hours a day between 1800 and midnight, then his TV could be an acceptable instrument of public information." * * *

77. * * * Although NATO alleged that it made every possible effort to avoid civilian casualties and collateral damage, some doubts have been expressed as to the specificity of the warning given to civilians by NATO of its intended strike, and whether the notice would have constituted "effective warning * * * of attacks which may affect the civilian population, unless circumstances do not permit" as required by Article 57(2) of Additional Protocol I. Evidence on this point is somewhat contradictory. On the one hand, NATO officials in Brussels are alleged to have told Amnesty International that they did not give a specific warning as it would have endangered the pilots (Amnesty International Report, *ibid,* June 2000, at p. 47 * * *). On this view, it is possible that casualties among civilians working at the RTS may have been heightened because of NATO's apparent failure to provide clear advance warning of the attack, as required by Article 57(2). On the other hand, foreign media representatives were apparently forewarned of the attack. As Western journalists were reportedly warned by their employers to stay away from the television station before the attack, it would also appear that some Yugoslav officials may have expected that the building was about to be struck. Consequently, UK Prime Minister Tony Blair blamed Yugoslav officials for not evacuating the building, claiming that "[t]hey could have moved those people out of the building. They knew it was a target and they didn't. . . . [I]t was probably for . . . very clear propaganda reasons." Although knowledge on the part of Yugoslav officials of the impending attack would not divest NATO of its obligation to forewarn civilians

under Article 57(2), it may nevertheless imply that the Yugoslav authorities may be partially responsible for the civilian casualties resulting from the attack and may suggest that the advance notice given by NATO may have in fact been sufficient under the circumstances.

78. Assuming the RTS building to be a legitimate military target, it appeared that NATO realised that attacking the RTS building would only interrupt broadcasting for a brief period. Indeed, broadcasting allegedly recommenced within hours of the strike. * * * The FRY command and control network was alleged by NATO to comprise a complex web and that could thus not be disabled in one strike. As noted by General Wesley Clark, NATO "knew when we struck that there would be alternate means of getting the Serb Television. There's no single switch to turn off everything but we thought it was a good move to strike it and the political leadership agreed with us." At a press conference on 27 April 1999, another NATO spokesperson similarly described the dual-use Yugoslav command and control network as "incapable of being dealt with in 'a single knock-out blow.' " * * *

The Attack on the Chinese Embassy on 7/5/99

80. On 7/5/99, at 2350, NATO aircraft fired several missiles which hit the Chinese Embassy in Belgrade, killing 3 Chinese citizens, injuring an estimated 15 others, and causing extensive damage to the embassy building and other buildings in the immediate surrounds. At the moment of the attack, fifty people were reported to have been in the embassy buildings. By the admission of U.S. Government sources, the Chinese Embassy compound was mistakenly hit. The bombing occurred because at no stage in the process was it realised that the bombs were aimed at the Chinese Embassy. The Embassy had been wrongly identified as the Yugoslav Federal Directorate for Supply and Procurement (Yugoimport FDSP) at 2 Umetnosti Boulevard in New Belgrade. The FDSP was deemed by the CIA to be a legitimate target due to its role in military procurement: it was selected for its role in support of the Yugoslav military effort.

81. Under Secretary of State Thomas Pickering offered the following explanation for what occurred:

> The bombing resulted from three basic failures. First, the technique used to locate the intended target—the headquarters of the Yugoslav Federal Directorate for Supply and Procurement (FDSP)—was severely flawed. Second, none of the military or intelligence databases used to verify target information contained the correct location of the Chinese Embassy. Third, nowhere in the target review process was either of the first two mistakes detected. No one who might have known that the targeted building was not the FDSP headquarters—but was in fact the Chinese Embassy—was ever consulted.

According to U.S. Government sources, the street address of the intended target, the FDSP headquarters, was known as Bulevar Umetnosti 2 in New Belgrade. During a mid-April "work-up" of the target to prepare a mission folder for the B-2 bomber crew, three maps were used in an attempt to physically locate this address within the neighborhood: two local commercial maps from 1989 and 1996, and one U.S. government (National Imagery and Mapping Agency or NIMA) map produced in 1997. None of these maps had any reference to the FDSP building and none accurately identified the current location of the Chinese Embassy. * * *

83. Finally, reviewing elements in, *inter alia,* the Joint Staff did not uncover either the inaccurate location of the FDSP headquarters or the correct location of the Chinese Embassy. The data base reviews were limited to validating the target data sheet geographic coordinates and the information put into the data base by the NIMA analyst. Such a circular process did not serve to uncover the original error and highlighted the system's susceptibility to a single point of data base failure. The critical linchpin for both the error in identification of the building and the failure of the review mechanisms was thus the inadequacy of the supporting data bases and the mistaken assumption the information they contained would necessarily be accurate.

84. The building hit was clearly a civilian object and not a legitimate military objective. NATO, and subsequently various organs of the U.S. Government, including the CIA, issued a formal apology, accepted full responsibility for the incident and asserted that the intended target, the Federal Directorate for Supply and Procurement, would have been a legitimate military objective. The USA has formally apologized to the Chinese Government and agreed to pay $28 million in compensation to the Chinese Government and $4.5 million to the families of those killed or injured. The CIA has also dismissed one intelligence officer and reprimanded six senior managers. The U.S. Government also claims to have taken corrective actions in order to assign individual responsibility and to prevent mistakes such as this from occurring in the future. * * *

NOTES & QUESTIONS

1. Investigation Outcome

In the course of its review, the Prosecutor's Committee applied two criteria to determine whether to open an investigation:

a. Are the alleged prohibitions sufficiently well-established as violations of international humanitarian law to form the basis of a prosecution? Does the application of the law to the particular facts reasonably suggest that a violation of these prohibitions may have occurred?

b. Upon the reasoned evaluation of the information by the Committee, is the information credible and does it tend to show that crimes within the jurisdiction of the Tribunal may have been committed by individuals during the NATO bombing campaign?

The Committee also noted that as a practical matter the Prosecutor, before deciding to open an investigation in any case, also takes into account other factors concerning the prospects for obtaining evidence sufficient to prove that the crime has been committed by an individual who merits prosecution in an international forum. The Committee ultimately determined that none of the incidents, in its opinion, merited further investigation by the Office of the Prosecution. In this regard, it concluded:

> On the basis of the information reviewed, the Committee is of the opinion that neither an in-depth investigation related to the bombing campaign as a whole nor investigations related to specific incidents are justified. In all cases, either the law is not sufficiently clear or investigations are unlikely to result in the acquisition of sufficient evidence to substantiate charges against high level accused or against lower accused for particularly heinous offences.

Are these appropriate grounds to decline an investigation? Do you agree with the final recommendation of the Committee?

2. Particular Incidents

Consider the following questions with respect to the particular incidents discussed.

a. With respect to the attack on the Grdelica Gorge Bridge, is it relevant whether the person controlling the bomb was a pilot or the Weapons Systems Officer (WSO)? Accepting Mr. Wenz's estimate of the operative reaction time, the person controlling the bombs still had a very short period of time, less than seven or eight seconds, to react. Was their response adequate? Was the bridge a legitimate military objective? Does your assessment of this incident vary with respect to the first and second bomb dropped? Was either the pilot or WSO reckless? GlobalSecurity.org and YouTube have short video images (of 4 and 6 seconds) of the two bridge strikes, although the U.S. Department of Defense later admitted that the short videos were condensed and accelerated from an original real-time 15-second video.

b. Was the radio/television station (Radio-Television Serbia, "RTS") a legitimate military objective? Were the civilian casualties disproportionate to any military advantage gained in the attack? Was the attack legitimate if the aim was to disrupt the ability of the regime to incite the population to violence or dismantle the Yugoslav propaganda machine? Does an attack on a civilian facility on such grounds alone meet the "effective contribution to military action" and "definite military advantage" criteria required by the Additional Protocol? Does your perspective change if the attack on the RTS building formed part of an integrated attack against numerous C3 targets, including electricity grids and transformer stations, command posts, transmission towers, and control buildings of the Yugoslav radio relay network that enabled Milošević to direct and control his army and special police forces in Kosovo and activate the Yugoslav air-defense network? What about the fact that the station resumed broadcasting in a matter of hours? Did NATO properly warn civilians that the station would be an object of attack? Does the international human right to freedom of speech impact IHL with respect to targeting media outlets?

c. The attack on the Chinese Embassy seems to be the result of "garbage in/garbage out" intelligence gathering. Should such errors give rise to criminal responsibility? Who should be held responsible? The person who designed the database or maps used? The aircrew who dropped the bomb? The superior in charge of target selection? Article 57 of Protocol I sets forth an affirmative duty on commanders to verify that targets are proper military objectives. Did NATO adequately conform to this duty in this incident?

If you were a member of the Committee, would you recommend further investigation or prosecution of any of the incidents described above? In considering the various incidents separately or collectively, which facts or factors do you find most compelling? In deciding whether to recommend an additional investigation, would you take into account any extra-legal factors, such as the fact that the ICTY was established by the Security Council, three members of which are also members of NATO; that NATO was engaged in an ostensible humanitarian intervention; or that the Tribunal's judicial resources are limited? If the Prosecutor did decide to undertake her own investigation, what obstacles might she have encountered? How readily could she obtain the documents and witness testimony she would need to do her work? Is the Committee's report likely to increase or decrease the perceived legitimacy of the Tribunal in the eyes of people in the former Yugoslavia? Would a formal investigation or indictment have eased complaints about "victor's justice" or asymmetrical prosecutions?

3. Jurisdiction

As a threshold question, why would the ICTY have jurisdiction over crimes committed by NATO forces in the former Yugoslavia at all? Which IHL treaties apply to the NATO intervention in Kosovo? Is NATO, an international organization, obligated to observe the Geneva Conventions even though those treaties have only states as parties? Does the NATO action in Kosovo qualify as an international conflict? Apply the test set forth above.

4. Crime of Aggression

In the course of its work, the Committee did not address the issue of the legality of the use of force by NATO members against the former Yugoslavia on the grounds that the ICTY has no jurisdiction over the crime of aggression. The legitimacy of the recourse to force by NATO was, however, before the International Court of Justice (ICJ) in a series of cases brought by the State Union of Serbia and Montenegro (the name for the former Yugoslavia from 2002–6) against various NATO countries. The basis for the Union's claim of illegality was that NATO had intervened without the blessing of the Security Council after Russia exercised its veto in the face of a proposal for military action to force the withdrawal of Yugoslav troops.

All of the cases were dismissed for lack of jurisdiction after the Court concluded that, at the time of the filing of the complaint, the Union of Serbia and Montenegro was not a member of the United Nations, and thus was not a party to the Statute of the ICJ. *See Legality of Use of Force (Serbia and Montenegro v. Belgium)* (Judgment of December 15, 2004). The Court based its ruling on the fact that the Union of Serbia and Montenegro was not treated as the successor state of the former Yugoslavia and so had to re-apply for U.N. membership in 2000. Montenegro later declared its independence following a referendum in 2006; Serbia thus became the legal successor of the prior Union. The crime of Aggression and the Kosovo intervention in particular will be considered in the next chapter.

5. Weapons Use: Depleted Uranium and Cluster Bombs

Other incidents investigated by the ICTY include NATO's use of depleted uranium (DU) projectiles during the bombing campaign. DU is a highly dense and pyrophoric material (meaning it can ignite spontaneously) that can be used both defensively and offensively (e.g., to pierce armor or demobilize tanks). The US allegedly used DU weapons in both Iraq and Syria in 2015. *See* Samuel Oakford, *The United States Used Depleted Uranium in Syria*, FOREIGN POLICY (Feb. 14, 2017). Although there is no specific treaty ban on the use of DU projectiles, and the substance is only weakly radioactive, there are concerns about long-term health effects following exposure. The Committee concluded:

> There is a developing scientific debate and concern expressed regarding the impact of the use of such projectiles and it is possible that, in future, there will be a consensus view in international legal circles that use of such projectiles violate general principles of the law applicable to use of weapons in armed conflict. No such consensus exists at present

With respect to NATO's use of cluster bombs in Kosovo, the ICTY OTP Committee concluded as follows:

> There is no specific treaty provision which prohibits or restricts the use of cluster bombs although, of course, cluster bombs must be used in compliance with the general principles applicable to the use of all weapons. Human Rights Watch has condemned the use of cluster bombs alleging that the high "dud" or failure rate of the sub-munitions (bomblets) contained inside cluster bombs converts these sub-munitions into antipersonnel landmines which, it asserts, are now prohibited under customary international law. Whether antipersonnel landmines are prohibited under current customary law is debatable, although there is a strong trend in that direction. There is, however, no general legal consensus that cluster bombs are, in legal terms, equivalent to antipersonnel landmines.
>
> It should be noted that the use of cluster bombs was an issue of sorts in *Martić*. In that decision, the Chamber stated there was no formal provision forbidding the use of cluster bombs as such but it regarded the use of the Orkan rocket with a cluster bomb warhead in that particular case as evidence of the intent of the

> accused to deliberately attack the civilian population because the rocket was inaccurate, it landed in an area with no military objectives nearby, it was used as an antipersonnel weapon launched against the city of Zagreb, and the accused indicated he intended to attack the city as such. The Chamber concluded that "the use of the Orkan rocket in this case was not designed to hit military targets but to terrorise the civilians of Zagreb." There is no indication cluster bombs were used in such a fashion by NATO. It is the opinion of the Committee, based on information presently available, that the OTP should not commence an investigation into use of cluster bombs as such by NATO.

Why did the Kosovo Committee reach a different conclusion about the use of cluster bombs in the Kosovo intervention than the ICTY did in the *Martić* opinion set forth above? Is the new breed of cluster bombs employed by the United States in Kosovo sufficiently advanced to avoid the concerns raised in *Martić*? Is Human Rights Watch correct in arguing that cluster bombs are the equivalent to landmines? If the Committee were considering this attack today, would its conclusions differ given the enactment of the 2008 Convention on Cluster Munitions?

6. Banković v. Belgium

Citizens of the former Yugoslavia whose loved ones were killed in the attack on the RTS attempted to bring suit before the European Court of Human Rights against NATO member states that are also parties to the European Convention on Human Rights (ECHR). The applicants alleged violations of the right to life set forth in Article 2 of the ECHR on the grounds that the attack on RTS was not for a proper purpose, such as the defence of any person from unlawful violence, and was not proportionate. The European Court ruled that the application was inadmissible because it dealt with extra-territorial actions by the respondent states that were not governed by the ECHR. *See Banković v. Belgium*, App. No. 52207/99, Eur. Ct. H.R., Judgment (2001), reprinted in 123 I.L.R. 94 (2001). For a strongly critical discussion of the decision, *see* Erik Roxstrom et al., *The NATO Bombing Case* (Banković et al. v. Belgium et al.) *and the Limits of Western Human Rights Protection*, 23 BOSTON U. INT'L L. J. 55 (2005) (declaring the decision "the most egregious decision in the history of the European Court of Human Rights").

In subsequent opinions, the European Court has all but limited this ruling to its facts. *Issa v. Turkey*, for example, involved the abduction and extrajudicial killing of Iraqi shepherds, allegedly by Turkish forces operating in northern Iraq—another state outside the *espace juridique* of the European Convention. The Court confirmed that:

> According to the relevant principles of international law, a State's responsibility may be engaged where, as a consequence of military action—whether lawful or unlawful—that State in practice exercises effective control of an area situated outside its national territory.

Issa and Others v. Turkey, App. No. 31821/96, Eur. Ct. H.R., Judgment, para. 69 (30 Mar. 2005). Even more on point is *Pad & Others v. Turkey*, brought on behalf of families of Iranian individuals killed by fire from a Turkish helicopter patrolling the border. It was unclear whether the events in question occurred on Turkish or Iranian soil; in either case, the Court found Turkey responsible since the deaths were caused by Turkish personnel. *Pad & Others v. Turkey*, App. No. 60167/00, Eur. Ct. H.R. (2007).

7. The Relativity of IHL

Do the duties of states and other warring parties under IHL vary according to the fighting forces' level of technological development? Does (or should) advanced technological capability raise the bar for belligerents? Does the use of terms such as "all feasible measures" suggest a margin of appreciation for less developed states or heightened duties for developed states? Should NATO members—possessing or having access to the most advanced technology available—be held to a higher standard than more technologically-deficient states? Does the principle of distinction favor more organized and resourced military organizations over insurgencies or vice versa? Should a revolutionary force engaged in a just struggle (such as the wars waged against colonialism and the struggle against apartheid in South Africa) against a technologically-advanced national military be held to the same standard as its opponent with respect to the core IHL principles? Is it fair to hold formal armed forces to higher standards, or is this the equivalent of forcing once side to fight with one hand tied behind its back?

8. Negligence v. Recklessness

Did NATO's conduct rise to the level of negligence or recklessness in whole or in part with respect to the incidents discussed above? What *mens rea* would be required to show culpability in these instances? What significance should be given to the fact that after the bombing of a convoy of civilians, NATO issued new guidelines about target selection? Should international tribunals adopt a rule similar to U.S. Federal Rule of Evidence 407 that excludes evidence of subsequent remedial measures as proof of an admission of fault? The rationale for the rule in the tort context is two-fold: (1) subsequent remedial measures are not an admission, since such conduct is equally consistent with injury by mere accident, and (2) a social policy desire to encourage, rather than discourage, actors to take steps to increase safety. Do such rationales apply in ICL?

9. Humanitarian Intervention

The NATO bombing campaign has been hailed as an example of humanitarian intervention—the intervention into the territorial state by another state or a collective of states, with or without authorization from the United Nations Security Council, for the promotion or protection of basic human rights when the territorial state is perpetuating abuses or is unable or unwilling to provide the necessary protection to its inhabitants. Should humanitarian missions be entitled to greater leeway in terms of breaches of IHL? Should we be more willing to trust the intentions of parties engaged in a humanitarian intervention? Should humanitarian interventions trigger a Good Samaritan doctrine as in tort law, which applies when individuals voluntarily provide assistance, for which they are not legally obligated to provide, in an emergency situation? According to this doctrine, where individuals intervene in good faith, they are immune from liability unless they cause intentional harm or unless their actions constitute gross negligence. Should individuals involved in operations like the NATO operation be liable only for acts of intentional harm or reckless actions? Was NATO, in effect, given such a presumption in this situation? Alternatively, should such operations be held to a higher standard because they are pursuing a humanitarian purpose to safeguard civilians, rather than attempting to achieve military victory? The concept of humanitarian intervention will be discussed again in Chapter 8 on Aggression.

10. Kosovar War Crimes

At the time of the intervention, the focus was on Serbian war crimes rather than on crimes committed by Kosovar Albanians. In 2011, the European Union Rule of Law Mission in Kosovo (EULEX) appointed Clint Williamson—former U.S. Ambassador-at-Large for War Crimes Issues—to lead a Special Investigative Task Force (SITF) into alleged crimes committed by Albanian rebels, including potential organ trafficking. The European Union next established a hybrid judicial mechanism to focus on such crimes during the 1998–99 conflict with Serbia. The model arrived upon, as set forth in agreement between Kosovo and the EU, and Kosovo and the Netherlands, involves "Specialist Chambers" located in the Netherlands but headquartered in Kosovo and operating under Kosovar jurisdiction as an extension of EULEX. The Hague was chosen because of concerns about witness intimidation, which hampered cases involving Kosovo Liberation Army defendants before the ICTY. The Lockerbie Court—which was a Scottish court established on a former American military base in the Netherlands governed by Scots law—is being cited as a model.

PROBLEM

The situation in Israel and Palestine has come before the Court in several incarnations. (See the Appendix for a map of Israel.) Consider the following: The Palestinian National Authority (PNA) governs the Gaza Strip and the West Bank pursuant to the 1993 Declaration of Principles on Interim Self-Government Arrangements (Oslo Accord I) between the Palestine Liberation Organization (PLO) and Israel. The Accord indicates that disputes arising out of the interpretation of the agreement are to be resolved by negotiations or conciliation. The 1995 Interim Agreement on the West Bank and the Gaza Strip (Oslo II) contains provisions allocating, to a certain degree, penal jurisdiction to Israel over certain territory and Israeli citizens. Following elections in 2006, Gaza has been controlled by Hamas, a Palestinian Islamic socio-political party and paramilitary force that is considered by some to be a terrorist organization. Following this election, Israel and Egypt established a blockade around Gaza. Peace, formal ceasefires, and informal "lulls" in fighting between Hamas and Israel were shattered over the next two years by the launch of mortars and rockets from Gaza into Israel by Hamas and other Palestinian factions.

In response to escalating rocket fire from Gaza, suggestions that a tunnel into Israel was under construction, and evidence of weapons smuggling into Gaza, Israel launched Operation Cast Lead in December 2008 with air strikes in the Gaza Strip. On January 3, 2009, the Israeli Defense Forces (IDF) began the second stage of Operation Cast Lead with a ground offensive; Israel also imposed a naval blockade. The third stage of Operation Cast Lead commenced on January 11, 2009, when IDF ground forces entered Gaza City. After another week of combat, the IDF declared a unilateral ceasefire on January 17 and withdrew its forces. The Palestinian Ministry of Health, a Gaza governmental office, puts the death toll of Operation Cast Lead at over 1300 Palestinian individuals, although other estimates are lower. There were 13 confirmed Israeli deaths (four from friendly fire). The reported use by Israel of air-burst white phosphorus, an incendiary agent used to create smokescreens, over populated areas has drawn particular criticism.

On January 22, 2009, the PNA lodged an Article 12(3) Declaration with the Registrar of the ICC stating that it recognizes:

> The jurisdiction of the Court for the purpose of identifying, prosecuting and judging the authors and accomplices of acts committed on the territory of Palestine since 1 July 2002.

Such a declaration is not the equivalent of a referral of a situation to a Court, but rather satisfies the preconditions for jurisdiction contained in Article 12 absent full ratification. Over the years, the OTP has reportedly received over 400 communications concerning crimes allegedly committed in the Palestinian territories. As is customary, the OTP opened a preliminary examination into the situation to consider whether there was a reasonable basis to proceed with a full investigation.

On April 3, 2009, the U.N. Human Rights Council established the United Nations Fact-Finding Mission on the Gaza Conflict to examine alleged violations of international human rights and international humanitarian law committed in Gaza during the conflict with Israel from December 27, 2008, to January 18, 2009. In that three-week period, approximately 1,400 people were killed when Israel launched Operation Cast Lead. The Commission was headed by the South African jurist and former Chief Prosecutor of the *ad hoc* international criminal tribunals, Richard Goldstone. Israel refused to cooperate with the Mission. The Mission found violations of international humanitarian law and international criminal law (war crimes and potentially crimes against humanity) were committed by both Israel and the Palestinians. *See Report of the United Nations Fact-Finding Mission on the Gaza Conflict*, U.N. Doc. A/HRC/12/48 (Sept. 25, 2009).

With respect to Israel, the Mission found numerous violations including, *inter alia*, 1) a military plan directed "at least in part" at the people of Gaza as a whole; 2) a failure to take reasonable precautions to avoid or minimize incidental loss of civilian life, injury to civilians, and damage to civilian objects; 3) the targeting of civilian infrastructure, including food supply installations, water sanitation systems, concrete factories, and residential houses; 4) the use of civilians as human shields; 5) the detention and ill treatment, including beatings and confinement in inhuman conditions, of numerous persons not justified under international law; and 6) the following grave breaches of the Geneva Conventions: willful killings, torture or inhuman treatment, willfully causing great suffering or serious injury to body or health, and extensive destruction of property not justified by military necessity and carried out unlawfully and wantonly.

With respect to Palestinian armed groups, the Mission also found numerous violations including, *inter alia*, 1) intentional failure to distinguish between civilian and military targets; 2) the failure to take precautions to protect the civilian population and the deliberate use of civilian objects to launch attacks; and 3) extrajudicial executions, arbitrary arrest, detention and ill treatment of people, in particular political opponents, by the Gaza authorities. It recommended that the Security Council refer the situation to the ICC if the domestic authorities do not undertake credible investigations of the crimes committed. See also the reports by Richard Falk, the Special Rapporteur on the situation of human rights in the Palestinian territories occupied since 1967, which discuss potential crimes against the peace as well as war crimes. Human Rights Situation in Palestine and Other Occupied Arab Territories, U.N. Doc. No. A/HRC/10/20 (Feb. 11, 2009).

In May 2010, activists and NGOs launched a "Freedom Flotilla" to challenge the naval blockade and deliver humanitarian aid to the Gaza Strip. The ships of the flotilla included the MV *Mavi Marmara*, which was registered in the Union of Comoros. Along with Jordan, Tunisia, and Djibouti, the Comoros is one of the few League of Arab States members that has ratified the ICC Statute. Other ships involved in the flotilla were registered in ICC member states—Greece and Cambodia—and in non-member states Turkey and the United States.

Although the precise facts remain in dispute, when ships of the flotilla refused to reroute to the Port of Ashdod for inspection, they were boarded on May 31, 2010, in international waters by Israeli naval forces. On the *Mavi Marmara*, Israeli forces faced resistance from a group of activists. Nine activists (all Turkish nationals, including one dual Turkish-U.S. national) were killed, and ten Israeli forces were wounded. These events formed the subject of several commissions of inquiry by, *inter alia*: the UN Secretary-General (the Palmer Report), Israel (the Turkel Report and Lindenstrauss Report), Turkey, and the U.N. Human Rights Council. The reports reach differing conclusions as to when lethal weaponry was employed and by whom.

In April 2011, Justice Goldstone penned an op-ed in which he withdrew some of his conclusions as to whether Israel targeted civilians as a matter of policy on the ground that he had learned more about what happened in Gaza, including the degree to which Israel had investigated its own potential "operational misconduct" during Operation Cast Lead. *See* Richard Goldstone, *Reconsidering the Goldstone Report on Israel and War Crimes*, WASH. POST (April 1, 2011). The op-ed followed upon indications that Justice Goldstone had come under tremendous pressure (which reportedly included efforts to prevent him from attending his grandson's *bar mitzvah*) following the release of the Report.

In the meantime, the Palestinians gradually assumed additional indicia of statehood. On October 31, 2011, the PNA was admitted to the United Nations Educational, Scientific, and Cultural Organization (UNESCO), a U.N. specialized agency that allows any state to become a member upon a two-thirds majority vote of all members. Over 100 members of the organization supported the bid for Palestinian membership, including China, France, and Russia—all permanent members of the Security Council (the United Kingdom abstained, and the United States voted no). On March 22, 2012, the Human Rights Council dispatched another fact-finding mission devoted to the region, this time focused on the impact of Israeli settlements in the Occupied Territories. The United States cast the sole "no" vote on the resolution, arguing that the effort was "politicized" and "one-sided" and would not advance the peace process. The mission's report, issued in January 2013, concluded that the settlements are in breach of Israel's international humanitarian law obligations. Back at the Court, in April 2012, the then-Chief Prosecutor, Luis Moreno Ocampo, in one of his final acts in office, finally issued his decision declining to move forward with an investigation into events on the Palestinian Territories in connection with Operation Cast Lead on the grounds that he was not empowered to determine whether Palestine is a "state" within the meaning of Article 12(3). He explained that

> it is for the relevant bodies at the United Nations or the Assembly of States Parties to make the legal determination whether Palestine qualifies as a State for the purpose of acceding to the Rome Statute and thereby enabling the exercise of jurisdiction by the Court under article 12(1).

On November 29, 2012, the U.N. General Assembly by way of Resolution 67/19 accorded Palestine Non-Member Observer State status in the United Nations (an upgrade from participation as a mere "observer"). Some European states reportedly traded a "yes" vote for assurances that Palestine would not rush to join the ICC. Palestine is unlikely to be accorded full U.N.-membership, however, since that would require a decision of the General Assembly upon the recommendation of the Security Council (Article 4 of the U.N. Charter). That said, over 130 states had by this point established bilateral relations with Palestinian officials. Weeks prior, the Israeli Air Force conducted a targeted air strike against Ahmed al-Jabari, a commander of the military wing of Hamas prior to and during Operation Cast Lead. The Air Force operation was part of Operation Pillar of Defense, an eight-day offensive that Israel commenced in response to the launch of over 100 rockets and other attacks originating from the Gaza Strip. Following an April 2013 speech in Paris, Chief Prosecutor Fatou Bensouda was asked about the potential membership of Palestine in the ICC. She indicated that now that the General Assembly has weighed in on Palestinian statehood, it is for the Palestinians to return to the ICC if they are interested in the Court moving forward. In her estimation, any acceptance of jurisdiction would extend back only to November 2012 and not earlier.

In May 2013, the Union of the Comoros submitted a referral of the flotilla incident on its flagship, as well as similar incidents on a Greek and Cambodian flagship, to the Court. The Prosecutor opened a preliminary examination. Later that year, the Prosecutor released her decision not to proceed with an investigation on grounds of insufficient gravity. The Comoros appealed and Pre-Trial Chamber I asked the Prosecutor to reconsider her decision. The Appeals Chamber dismissed the Prosecutor's appeal of this decision. In November 2017, the Prosecutor reiterated her decision not to proceed. The PTC granted the Comoros's further application for judicial review and again ordered reconsideration. The Prosecutor again appealed. The Appeals Chamber is slated to rule in the fall 2019. Meanwhile, in April 2014, as Israel moved to expand settlements in contested areas and peace talks again collapsed, Palestinian President Mahmoud Abbas indicated an intention to join a range of multilateral treaties. The United Nations Secretary General accepted the Palestinians' instruments of accession to fourteen multilateral treaties for which he serves as depository, including the Convention on the Rights of the Child, the International Covenant on Civil and Political Rights, the Convention Against Torture, and the Genocide Convention. All states parties to the respective treaties have been notified and may raise issues of concern, including declaring that they do not recognize the Palestinian accession and thus no legal obligations are created between the opposing state and Palestine. The PNA also indicated an intention to join the Geneva Conventions of 1949, for which the Swiss Government serves as depository, and the 1907 Hague Convention (IV) Respecting the Laws and Customs of War on Land and its Annex, for which the government of the Netherlands is depository. These treaties indicate that they are open to "all states." Back in 1989, the PLO attempted to join the Geneva Conventions and their Protocols; at that time, the Swiss Federal Department of Foreign Affairs rejected the effort due to the uncertainty within the international community as to the existence or non-existence of the State of Palestine. This time around, the Swiss accepted the instruments of accession and indicated that the treaties have taken immediate effect per their terms (the Netherlands followed suit). In response, Samantha Power, U.S. Ambassador to the United Nations, announced that the United States opposes unilateral actions with respect to the Palestinian territories because they undermine the possibility of achieving a negotiated settlement. Palestine ratified the Rome Statute in April 2015 and submitted another Article 12(3) declaration, accepting jurisdiction over alleged crimes on Palestinian territories since June 13, 2014. In May 2018, Palestine referred itself to the ICC with a focus on settlements. *See* The State of Palestine, *Referral by the State of Palestine Pursuant to Articles 13(a) and 14 of the Rome Statute* (May 15, 2018).

If you were Chief Prosecutor of the ICC, how would you handle the referral and Article 12(3) declaration filed by the Palestinian authorities? How would you handle the Comoros referral? Neither Cambodia nor Greece referred the incidents on their flagships to the Court. How would you argue that the Court nevertheless has jurisdiction over incidents on the Greek and Cambodian flagships? What is the legal basis for the PTC to order the OTP to reconsider its decision not to proceed with a full investigation? What impact would a new preliminary examination have on events on the ground, including the faltering peace process? Would the impact on the peace process affect your decision on whether to proceed or not with an investigation? If so, what legal authority, if any, could the Prosecutor cite to support such a decision?

III. "GENEVA LAW": PROTECTED PERSONS AND THINGS

One of the primary goals of international humanitarian law (IHL) is to protect particularly vulnerable types of property and classes of people whose destruction or injury serves no legitimate military purpose. In this regard, the Fourth Geneva Convention is devoted to protecting civilians and civilian property during armed conflicts and in situations of occupation. By contrast, the Third Geneva Convention creates a regime to protect prisoners of war (POWs). By implication, it also sets forth the requirements for an individual to be considered a privileged combatant, i.e., someone authorized to use lethal force in the context of an armed conflict. Absent such authorization, an individual using lethal force may run afoul of domestic criminal law, such as the prohibitions against treason, murder, mayhem, or assault (although they do not violate IHL *per se*). In addition, the 1954 Convention for the Protection of Cultural Property in the Event of Armed Conflict and its Protocols specifically protect cultural property in times of war, a set of rules implicated by recent events in Mali and the referral of that situation to the ICC.

A. CIVILIANS AS PROTECTED PERSONS

Throughout history, wars have resulted in huge numbers of civilian casualties and terrible devastation to civilian infrastructure. Commentators do not agree on the actual numbers of civilians killed during each war, but there is broad acceptance that the risk to civilians from armed conflict has increased dramatically. For example, the percentage of civilians to military personnel killed from World War I to World War II increased from thirteen to seventy percent according to one commentator. The total number of British civilians killed during World War II is estimated to be 51,509 from bombing by aircraft; 6,184 from flying bombs, 2,754 from rockets, and forty-eight from cross-channel guns. The bombing of Germany by the United States and Britain during World War II destroyed 485,000 residential buildings and seriously damaged another 415,000, the total of which constituted 20% of all of the residential buildings in Germany. The Allied firebombing of Dresden is estimated to have killed 25,000 civilians, and of Tokyo, 85,000. The atomic bombings of Hiroshima and Nagasaki are estimated to have killed 105,000 to 125,000 civilians immediately, not to mention the thousands who died later from radiation poisoning and other collateral effects. The Soviet Union is estimated to have lost over ten million civilians because of the war. Some estimates place the total number of civilians killed by aerial bombardment alone during World War II at twelve million. For these and other statistics, see Thomas Michael McDonnell, *Cluster Bombs Over Kosovo: A Violation of International Law?*, 44 ARIZONA L. REV. 31, 62–3 (2002). *See also* W. Hays Parks, *Air War and the Law of War*, 32 AIR FORCE L. REV. 1, n.1 (1990).

The protection of civilians from the effects of armed conflict is a central goal of IHL. Thus, the principle of proportionality requires that military commanders choose a course of conduct that results in the least number of civilian casualties or harm to civilian objects. *See* Article 52 of Additional Protocol I. Likewise, the principle of distinction requires that militaries distinguish between military objectives and civilian objects and target only the former. Per Article 4 of the Third Geneva Convention, combatants must wear a "fixed distinctive sign recognizable at a distance" in order to better distinguish themselves from civilians for targeting purposes. Belligerents are prohibited from targeting civilians in conflict by, *inter alia*, Article 51(2) of Protocol I. Civilians can lose this protection, however, if they directly participate in hostilities (DPH). *See* Article 51(3), Additional Protocol I ("Civilians shall enjoy the protection afforded by this Section, unless and for such time as they take a direct part in hostilities"); Article 13(3), Protocol II (same with respect to non-international armed conflicts).

The Fourth Geneva Convention is devoted to the protection of civilian populations. These protections are supplemented and expanded within Protocols I and II. None of these instruments, however, contains a precise definition of the term "civilian." Rather, Protocol I defines civilians in the negative as individuals who are not members of an armed force or an organized military group. Article 50 thus provides that "a civilian is any person who does not belong to one of the categories of persons referred to in Article 4(A)(1), (2), (3) and (6) of the Third Geneva Convention and in Article 43 of Protocol I." The Fourth Geneva Convention also identifies a discrete subset of civilians as "protected persons," whose protection is specifically guaranteed by the treaty. The vague definition of the population protected by the Fourth Geneva Convention is found in Article 4:

> Persons protected by the Convention are those who, at a given moment and in any manner whatsoever, find themselves, in case of a conflict or occupation, in the hands of a Party to the conflict or Occupying Power of which they are not nationals. Nationals of a State which is not bound by the Convention are not protected by it. Nationals of a neutral State who find themselves in the territory of a belligerent State, and nationals of a co-belligerent State, shall not be regarded as protected persons while the State of which they are nationals has normal diplomatic representation in the State in whose hands they are.

That Article also notes that the Fourth Convention does not apply if the individual is protected by one of the other three Geneva Conventions (addressed to the wounded and sick on land (Geneva I), the shipwrecked

(Geneva II), or POWs (Geneva III)) or if the nationality requirements are not met.

Although the protected population is ambiguously defined, the consequences triggered by violating the rules protecting civilians are clear. The Fourth Geneva Convention at Articles 146–147 identifies certain "grave breaches" of the treaty that are subject to universal jurisdiction when they are committed against persons protected by the treaty. Article 147 lists the following crimes that contracting states are obliged to prosecute:

> Grave breaches * * * shall be those involving any of the following acts, if committed against persons or property protected by the present Convention: wilful killing, torture or inhuman treatment, including biological experiments, wilfully causing great suffering or serious injury to body or health, unlawful deportation or transfer or unlawful confinement of a protected person, compelling a protected person to serve in the forces of a hostile Power, or wilfully depriving a protected person of the rights of fair and regular trial prescribed in the present Convention, taking of hostages and extensive destruction and appropriation of property, not justified by military necessity and carried out unlawfully and wantonly.

This list of crimes has been incorporated into the Statutes of the ICTY (Article 2), the Extraordinary Chambers in the Courts of Cambodia (ECCC) (Article 6), and the ICC (Article 8(2)(a)). The ICC's Elements of Crimes indicate that the Prosecutor must show that the victim in question was protected under one or more of the Geneva Conventions of 1949—i.e., that the victim belonged to or was a national of an adverse party; was a POW, a civilian or a medical or religious personnel taking no active part in hostilities; was in the power of an adverse party; or was *hors de combat*—and that the perpetrator was aware of the factual circumstances that established the victim's status.

Given the formulation of the Fourth Geneva Convention's grave breaches regime, are all civilians affected by armed conflicts equally protected? Because the drafters of the Geneva Conventions primarily envisioned that the treaties would govern classical conflicts between two distinct nation-states, it is not clear how, or if at all, their protective provisions would apply to conflicts that are not so neatly defined, such as occurred within the former Yugoslavia. This conundrum is demonstrated by the following case from the ICTY, the so-called Čelebići case. The case was the first collective trial and the first case concerning the detention, torture, and killing of predominantly Bosnian Serbs by forces controlled by Bosnian Muslims and Croats.

Prosecutor v. Delalić et al., Case No. IT–96–21–A, Judgement (Feb. 20, 2001)

In the Appeals Chamber

1. The Indictment against Zejnil Delalić, Zdravko Mucić, Hazim Delić and Esad Landžo, confirmed on 21 March 1996, alleged serious violations of humanitarian law that occurred in 1992 when Bosnian Muslim and Bosnian Croat forces took control of villages within the Konjic municipality in central Bosnia and Herzegovina. The present appeal concerns events within the Konjic municipality, where persons were detained in a former Yugoslav People's Army (JNA) facility: the Čelebići camp. The Trial Chamber found that detainees were killed, tortured, sexually assaulted, beaten and otherwise subjected to cruel and inhumane treatment by Mucić, Delić and Landžo. Mucić was found to have been the commander of the Čelebići camp, Delić the deputy commander and Landžo a prison guard. * * *

Whether the Bosnian Serbs Detained in the Čelebići Camp Were Protected Persons Under Geneva Convention IV

52. Delalić, Mucić, Delić and Landžo[70] submit that the Trial Chamber erred in law in finding that the Bosnian Serb detainees at the Čelebići camp could be considered not to be nationals of Bosnia and Herzegovina for the purposes of the category of persons protected under Geneva Convention IV. They contend that the Trial Chamber's conclusions are inconsistent with international law and Bosnian law. The appellants request that the Appeals Chamber enter judgements of acquittal on all counts based on Article 2 of the Statute.

53. The Prosecution submits that the appellants' grounds of appeal have no merit and that the Appeals Chamber should follow its previous jurisprudence on the issue, as set out in the *Tadić* Appeal Judgement, and confirmed by the *Aleksovski* Appeal Judgement. It submits that it is now settled in that jurisprudence that in an international conflict victims may be considered as not being nationals of the party in whose hands they find themselves, even if, as a matter of national law, they were nationals of the same State as the persons by whom they are detained. Further, the Prosecution submits that the test applied by the Trial Chamber is consistent with the *Tadić* Appeal Judgement. * * *

---

[70] Delalić's Ground of Contention 3, as set out in the Delalić Brief, reads: "The Trial Chamber committed errors of both law and fact in its determination that the Čelebići detainees were persons protected by the Geneva Conventions of 1949." Mucić's Ground 4 reads: "Whether the Trial Chamber erred at [*sic*] holding that Bosnian citizens of Serbian ethnicity should be treated as non-nationals of the Republic of Bosnia and Herzegovina and were therefore protected persons as defined in Article 4 of the Geneva Convention IV." Delić's Ground 4 reads: "Whether the Trial Chamber erred in holding that Bosnian citizens of Serbian ethnicity should be treated as non-nationals of the Republic of Bosnia and Herzegovina and were therefore protected persons as defined in Article 4 of the Geneva Convention Relative to the Protection of Civilian Persons in Time of War." Landžo's Ground 6 reads: "The Trial Chamber erred in law by finding that the victims of the alleged crimes were protected persons for the purpose of the Geneva Conventions."

What Is the Applicable Law?

56. Article 2 of the Statute of the Tribunal provides that it has the power to prosecute persons who committed grave breaches of the Geneva Conventions "against persons or property protected under the provisions of the relevant Geneva Conventions." The applicable provision to ascertain whether Bosnian Serbs detained in the Čelebići camp can be regarded as victims of grave breaches is Article 4(1) of Geneva Convention IV on the protection of civilians, which defines protected persons as those in the hands of a Party to the conflict or Occupying Power of which they are not nationals. The Appeals Chamber in *Tadić* found that:

> [. . .] the Convention intends to protect civilians (in enemy territory, occupied territory or the combat zone) who do not have the nationality of the belligerent in whose hands they find themselves, or who are stateless persons. In addition, as is apparent from the preparatory work, the Convention also intends to protect those civilians in occupied territory who, while having the nationality of the Party to the conflict in whose hands they find themselves, are refugees and thus no longer owe allegiance to this Party and no longer enjoy its diplomatic protection. . . .

57. The Appeals Chamber held that "already in 1949 *the legal bond of nationality was not regarded as crucial* and allowance was made for special cases."[73] Further, relying on a teleological approach, it continued:

> [. . .] Article 4 of Geneva Convention IV, if interpreted in the light of its object and purpose, is directed to the protection of civilians to the maximum extent possible. It therefore does not make its applicability dependent on formal bonds and purely legal relations. [. . .] In granting its protection, Article 4 intends to look to the substance of relations, not to their legal characterisation as such.

58. The Appeals Chamber in *Aleksovski* endorsed the *Tadić* reasoning holding that Article 4 may be given a wider construction so that a person may be accorded protected status, notwithstanding the fact that he is of the same nationality as his captors.

59. The appellants submit that the Appeals Chamber decisions in *Tadić* and *Aleksovski* wrongly interpreted Article 4 of Geneva Convention IV, and that the *Tadić* and *Aleksovski* Trial Chamber Judgements are correct. It is essentially submitted that in order for victims to gain "protected persons" status, Geneva Convention IV requires that the person in question be of a different nationality than the perpetrators of the alleged offence, based on the national law on citizenship of Bosnia and Herzegovina. This interpretation is based on a "strict" interpretation

---

73 * * * In this context, the Appeals Chamber referred to the situation of refugees and nationals of neutral States who do not enjoy diplomatic protection.

of the Convention which is, in the appellants' view, mandated by the "traditional rules of treaty interpretation."

60. The Prosecution contends that the Appeals Chamber in *Aleksovski* already adopted the approach used in the *Tadić* Appeal Judgement, and that the appellants in this case have not demonstrated any cogent reasons in the interests of justice that could justify a departure by the Appeals Chamber from its previous decisions on the issue. * * *

65. The appellants submit that "the traditional rules of treaty interpretation" should be applied to interpret strictly the nationality requirement set out in Article 4 of Geneva Convention IV. The word "national" should therefore be interpreted according to its natural and ordinary meaning. The appellants submit in addition that if the Geneva Conventions are now obsolete and need to be updated to take into consideration a "new reality," a diplomatic conference should be convened to revise them.

66. The Prosecution on the other hand contends that the Vienna Convention on the Law of Treaties of 1969 provides that the ordinary meaning is the meaning to be given to the terms of the treaty in their context and in the light of their object and purpose. It is submitted that the Appeals Chamber in *Tadić* found that the legal bond of nationality was not regarded as crucial in 1949, *i.e.,* that there was no intention at the time to determine that nationality was the sole criteria. In addition, adopting the appellants' position would result in the removal of protections from the Geneva Conventions contrary to their very object and purpose.

67. The argument of the appellants relates to the interpretative approach to be applied to the concept of nationality in Geneva Convention IV. The appellants and the Prosecution both rely on the Vienna Convention in support of their contentions. The Appeals Chamber agrees with the parties that it is appropriate to refer to the Vienna Convention as the applicable rules of interpretation, and to Article 31 in particular, which sets forth the general rule for the interpretation of treaties. The Appeals Chamber notes that it is generally accepted that these provisions reflect customary rules. The relevant part of Article 31 reads as follows:

> A treaty shall be interpreted in good faith in accordance with the ordinary meaning to be given to the terms of the treaty in their context and in the light of its object and purpose.

68. The Vienna Convention in effect adopted a textual, contextual *and* a teleological approach of interpretation, allowing for an interpretation of the natural and ordinary meaning of the terms of a treaty in their context, while having regard to the object and purpose of the treaty.

69. In addition, Article 32 of the Vienna Convention, entitled "Supplementary means of interpretation," provides that:

> Recourse may be had to supplementary means of interpretation, including the preparatory work of the treaty and the circumstances of its conclusion, in order to confirm the meaning resulting from the application of article 31, or to determine the meaning when the interpretation according to article 31:
>
> (a) leaves the meaning ambiguous and obscure; or
>
> (b) leads to a result which is manifestly absurd or unreasonable.

70. Where the interpretative rule set out in Article 31 does not provide a satisfactory conclusion recourse may be had to the *travaux préparatoires* [drafting history] as a subsidiary means of interpretation.

71. In finding that ethnicity may be taken into consideration when determining the nationality of the victims for the purposes of the application of Geneva Convention IV, the Appeals Chamber in *Tadić* concluded:

> Under these conditions, the requirement of nationality is even less adequate to define protected persons. In such conflicts, *not only the text and the drafting history of the Convention but also, and more importantly, the Convention's object and purpose* suggest that allegiance to a Party to the conflict and, correspondingly, control by this Party over persons in a given territory, may be regarded as the crucial test.

72. This reasoning was endorsed by the Appeals Chamber in *Aleksovski*:

> The Appeals Chamber considers that this extended application of Article 4 *meets the object and purpose of Geneva Convention IV*, and is particularly apposite in the context of present-day inter-ethnic conflicts.

73. The Appeals Chamber finds that this interpretative approach is consistent with the rules of treaty interpretation set out in the Vienna Convention. Further, the Appeals Chamber in *Tadić* only relied on the *travaux préparatoires* to reinforce its conclusion reached upon an examination of the overall context of the Geneva Conventions. The Appeals Chamber is thus unconvinced by the appellants' argument and finds that the interpretation of the nationality requirement of Article 4 in the *Tadić* Appeals Judgement does not constitute a rewriting of Geneva Convention IV or a re-creation of the law. The nationality requirement in Article 4 of Geneva Convention IV should therefore be ascertained within the context of the object and purpose of humanitarian law, which "is directed to the protection of civilians to the maximum extent possible." This in turn must be done within the context of the changing nature of the armed conflicts since 1945, and in particular of the development of conflicts based on ethnic or religious grounds. * * *

78. Relying on the ICRC Commentary to Article 4 of Geneva Convention IV, the appellants further argue that international law cannot interfere in a State's relations with its own nationals, except in cases of genocide and crimes against humanity. In the appellants' view, in the situation of an internationalised armed conflict where the victims and the perpetrators are of the same nationality, the victims are only protected by their national laws.

79. The purpose of Geneva Convention IV in providing for universal jurisdiction only in relation to the grave breaches provisions was to avoid interference by domestic courts of other States in situations which concern only the relationship between a State and its own nationals. The ICRC Commentary (GC IV), referred to by the appellants, thus stated that Geneva Convention IV is "faithful to a recognised principle of international law: it does not interfere in a State's relations with its own nationals." The Commentary did not envisage the situation of an internationalised conflict where a foreign State supports one of the parties to the conflict, and where the victims are detained because of their ethnicity, and because they are regarded by their captors as operating on behalf of the enemy. In these circumstances, the formal national link with Bosnia and Herzegovina cannot be raised before an international tribunal to deny the victims the protection of humanitarian law. It may be added that the government of Bosnia and Herzegovina itself did not oppose the prosecution of Bosnian nationals for acts of violence against other Bosnians based upon the grave breaches regime.

80. It is noteworthy that, although the appellants emphasised that the "nationality" referred to in Geneva Convention IV is to be understood as referring to the legal citizenship under domestic law, they accepted at the hearing that in the former Yugoslavia "nationality," in everyday conversation, refers to ethnicity.

81. The Appeals Chamber agrees with the Prosecution that depriving victims, who arguably are of the same nationality under domestic law as their captors, of the protection of the Geneva Conventions solely based on that national law would not be consistent with the object and purpose of the Conventions. Their very object could indeed be defeated if undue emphasis were placed on formal legal bonds, which could also be altered by governments to shield their nationals from prosecution based on the grave breaches provisions of the Geneva Conventions. A more purposive and realistic approach is particularly apposite in circumstances of the dissolution of Yugoslavia, and in the emerging State of Bosnia and Herzegovina where various parties were engaged in fighting, and the government was opposed to a partition based on ethnicity, which would have resulted in movements of population, and where, ultimately, the issue at stake was the final shape of the State and of the new emerging entities.

82. In *Tadić*, the Appeals Chamber, relying on a teleological approach, concluded that formal nationality may not be regarded as

determinative in this context, whereas ethnicity may reflect more appropriately the reality of the bonds:

> This legal approach, hinging on substantial relations more than on formal bonds, becomes all the more important in present-day international armed conflicts. While previously wars were primarily between well-established States, in modern inter-ethnic armed conflicts such as that in the former Yugoslavia, new States are often created during the conflict and ethnicity rather than nationality may become the grounds for allegiance. Or, put another way, ethnicity may become determinative of national allegiance.

83. As found in previous Appeals Chamber jurisprudence, Article 4 of Geneva Convention IV is to be interpreted as intending to protect civilians who find themselves in the midst of an international, or internationalised, conflict to the maximum extent possible. The nationality requirement of Article 4 should therefore be ascertained upon a review of "the substance of relations" and not based on the legal characterisation under domestic legislation. In today's ethnic conflicts, the victims may be "assimilated" to the external State involved in the conflict, even if they formally have the same nationality as their captors, for the purposes of the application of humanitarian law, and of Article 4 of Geneva Convention IV specifically. The Appeals Chamber thus agrees with the *Tadić* Appeal Judgement that even if in the circumstances of the case the perpetrators and the victims were to be regarded as possessing the same nationality, Article 4 would still be applicable. * * *

NOTES & QUESTIONS

1. Case Outcome

The Trial Chamber judgment from which the above appeal was taken acquitted Delalić of violations of the laws of armed conflict, holding that he did not have sufficient command and control over the Čelebići camp and its guards to justify imposing command responsibility. Mucić was found guilty of various violations of the laws of war, including murder, torture, inhuman treatment and unlawful detention, both as a superior and for his direct participation in some of these acts. Mucić was sentenced to seven years' imprisonment, which was increased on appeal to nine years. Delić and Landžo were found guilty of violations of the laws of war for their direct participation in murder, torture, and inhuman treatment. Delić was sentenced to eighteen years, and Landžo to fifteen years. Both Delić and Landžo were transferred to a detention facility in Finland to serve their sentences. Mucić, who had been in custody since March 18, 1996, was granted early release effective July 18, 2003. In 2006, the ICTY ultimately commuted Landžo's sentence on the ground that he was entitled to early release under Finnish Law because he had shown remorse and positive signs of rehabilitation. Delić was granted early release on June 24, 2008 based on credit given for time he had served in detention since May 2, 1996. The superior responsibility aspects of the case are discussed *infra* in Chapter 14.

2. Nationality Test

The International Court of Justice in the *Nottebohm Case (Liech. v. Guat.)* 1955 I.C.J. Reports 4 (April 6), established a case-by-case test for determining the nationality of an individual. In that case, Liechtenstein brought a claim against Guatemala for restitution and compensation for Guatemala's seizure of Nottebohm's property. Guatemala challenged whether Nottebohm was in fact a national of Liechtenstein, and thus whether Liechtenstein had standing to espouse his claim. (Guatemala argued that Nottebohm was either a national of Germany or Guatemala.) The appellants in the *Čelebići* case urged the Appeals Chamber to adopt the test developed in *Nottebohm* for determining nationality. That test requires that the court look to the following factors on a case-by-case basis to determine nationality: place of birth, education, marriage, habitual residence, and where the individual votes. The Appeals Chamber rejected this argument as follows:

> The *Nottebohm* case was concerned with ascertaining the effects of the national link for the purposes of the exercise of diplomatic protection, whereas in the instant case, the Appeals Chamber is faced with the task of determining whether the victims could be considered as having the nationality of a foreign State involved in the conflict, for the purposes of their protection under humanitarian law. It is thus irrelevant to demonstrate, as argued by the appellants, that the victims and their families had their habitual residence in Bosnia and Herzegovina, or that they exercised their activities there. Rather, the issue at hand, in a situation of internationalized armed conflict, is whether the victims can be regarded as not sharing the same nationality as their captors, for the purposes of the Geneva Conventions, even if arguably they were of the same nationality from a domestic legal point of view.

Prosecutor v. Delalić, Case No. IT–96–21–A, Judgement, para. 101 (Feb. 20, 2001). Was the Appeals Chamber correct in rejecting the *Nottebohm* test for nationality in the context of the case? Should international criminal law employ a standard for nationality that is different from that in force in public international law?

3. *Stare Decisis*

There is no strong tradition of stare decisis in international law. The International Court of Justice, for example, specifically disclaims any precedential value of its prior decisions. ICJ Statute, Article 59. Nonetheless, the international criminal tribunals have acknowledged the importance of stability and predictability in the law. Before the ICTY, the Appeals Chamber has indicated that it can depart from a prior decision for only "cogent reasons." *Prosecutor v. Aleksovski*, Case No. IT–95–14/1–A, Judgement, paras. 107, 110, 111, 125 (March 24, 2000). In the instant case, defendants tried to avoid prior rulings in Tadić and Aleksovski on the question of whether a defendant could be guilty of grave breaches of the Geneva Conventions when he shares the victim's nationality (although are of different ethnicities). Should the Appeals Chamber have entertained the appeal and ruled on its merits as it did, or should it have simply affirmed the ruling below based upon stare decisis? .

4. Civilians as Perpetrators

While civilians are provided special protections under international humanitarian law, they may also be held liable for violations of the laws of war. Thus, civilians who commit law-of-war violations themselves, or assist others in committing violations, may be criminally liable under international humanitarian law. *See Prosecutor v. Musema*, Case No. ICTR–96–13–T, Judgement, paras. 264–75 (January 27, 2000) (confirming that civilians may be liable as perpetrators of IHL, although acquitting the defendant).

B. COMBATANTS AS PROTECTED PERSONS

In addition to protecting civilians, international humanitarian law regulates, and provides protections to, those who employ lethal force. An individual is authorized to use lethal force within an armed conflict if (1) the target and means of the attack are lawful (see above); and (2) if the individual employing such force has the privilege of combatant status. Non-combatants or unprivileged combatants who use force within an armed conflict may be prosecuted for their conduct under domestic laws prohibiting the use of violence or, potentially, under the laws of war if war crimes are committed. Such acts do not, in and of themselves and in the absence of a violation of the principles of distinction or proportionality, constitute war crimes under IHL.

Early treaties concluded at The Hague provide a set of criteria for determining who is entitled to combatant status within armed conflicts. Thus the 1899 and 1907 Hague Conventions appear to define those entitled to combatant or belligerent status as members of armies, militias, and volunteer corps who fulfill the following requirements:

> To be commanded by a person responsible for his subordinates;
>
> To have a fixed distinctive emblem recognizable at a distance;
>
> To carry arms openly; and
>
> To conduct their operations in accordance with the laws and customs of war.

Article 1, Convention With Respect to the Laws and Customs of War on Land, Annex I, 36 Stat. 2277, 2295–96.

The Geneva Conventions of 1949 do not specifically define who constitutes a privileged combatant, although the practice has been to consider combatants to be those individuals who are entitled to prisoner-of-war status under the Third Geneva Convention. Article 4 of the Third Geneva Convention defines the categories of individuals entitled to prisoner-of-war status as follows:

1. Members of the armed forces of a Party to the conflict as well as members of militias or volunteer corps forming part of such armed forces.

2. Members of other militias and members of other volunteer corps, including those of organized resistance movements, belonging to a Party to the conflict and operating in or outside their own territory, even if this territory is occupied, provided that such militias or volunteer corps, including such organized resistance movements, fulfill the following conditions:

(a) That of being commanded by a person responsible for his subordinates;

(b) That of having a fixed distinctive sign recognizable at a distance;

(c) That of carrying arms openly;

(d) That of conducting their operations in accordance with the laws and customs of war.

3. Members of regular armed forces who profess allegiance to a government or an authority not recognized by the Detaining Power.

4. Persons who accompany the armed forces without actually being members thereof, such as civilian members of military aircraft crews, war correspondents, supply contractors, members of labour units or of services responsible for the welfare of the armed forces, provided that they have received authorization from the armed forces which they accompany, who shall provide them for that purpose with an identity card similar to the annexed model. * * *

6. Inhabitants of a non-occupied territory, who on the approach of the enemy spontaneously take up arms to resist the invading forces, without having had time to form themselves into regular armed units, provided they carry arms openly and respect the laws and customs of war [the so-called "*levée en masse*"].

Prisoners of war are thus combatants who have lawfully engaged in hostilities and have fallen into the hands of an enemy power. So long as they have complied with the law of armed conflict, prisoners of war are not considered criminals and are entitled to certain rights and protections. Their detention during the duration of the hostilities is expressly preventative rather than punitive, and they are entitled to combat immunity for lawful acts of war and to be released at the close of hostilities. (Chapter 17 contains a fuller discussion of the defense of combat immunity). If prisoners of war have committed war crimes, domestic crimes, or other infractions, however, they may be prosecuted for such conduct. Among the rights and protections afforded to prisoners of war is the right set forth in Article 102 to be tried in the same courts and by the same procedures as members of the armed forces of the Detaining Power.

The Third Geneva Convention also protects POWs from war crimes. Article 130 thus obliges signatories to prosecute the following grave breaches when committed against someone who falls within the protections of the treaty:

> Grave breaches to which the preceding Article relates shall be those involving any of the following acts, if committed against persons or property protected by the Convention: wilful killing, torture or inhuman treatment, including biological experiments, wilfully causing great suffering or serious injury to body or health, compelling a prisoner of war to serve in the forces of the hostile Power, or wilfully depriving a prisoner of war of the rights of fair and regular trial prescribed in this Convention.

As you read the next excerpt, consider whether the victims discussed constitute "protected persons" within the meaning of the Third Geneva Convention. The judgment that follows concerns Bosco Ntaganda ("Ntaganda"). In 1997, Laurent-Désiré Kabila overthrew Mobutu Sese Seko in the country then known as Zaire. Kabila renamed the country the Democratic Republic of Congo and ruled for only four years until he was assassinated by one of his bodyguards. He was succeeded by his son, Joseph Kabila, who inherited a country beset by multiple armed conflicts being waged by nine national armies and nineteen irregular armed forces. Six of the conflicts were in Orientale Province, which includes the Ituri district, an area rich in natural resources that borders Uganda (see the map of the DRC in the Appendix). The war in Ituri (1999–2003) pitted rebel groups from the Hema and Lendu ethnic groups against each other. According to a report from the U.N. peacekeeping mission, then called MONUC (the United Nations Organization Mission in the Congo):

> The competition for the control of natural resources by combatant forces, exacerbated by an almost constant political vacuum in the region, [was] a major factor in prolonging the crisis in Ituri.

Special Report on the Events in Ituri, Jan 2002–Dec 2003, U.N. Doc. S/2004/573, para. 7 (July 16, 2004). The same report suggested that the local ethnic problems "would not have turned into massive slaughter without the involvement of national and foreign players" including the Ugandan and Rwandan armies. *Id.* at para. 18.

Ntaganda, who is of Tutsi ethnicity, was born in Rwanda but raised in North Kivu in the DRC. Ntaganda became a high-level official of the *Union des Patriots Congolais* (UPC) (later renamed *Union des Patriotes Congolais/Réconcilation et Paix*—Union of Congolese Patriots/ Reconciliation and Peace (UPC/RP)) and its armed military wing, the

Forces Patriotiques pour la Libération du Congo (FPLC). The Trial Chamber in the decision excerpted below found that Ntaganda held the position of Deputy Chief of Staff in charge of Operations and Organization of the UPC/FPLC from early September 2002 to December 8, 2003, by virtue of which he was in charge of the troops' deployment and operations, and that he "was personally involved in the organization's recruitment activities." The Trial Chamber further found that Ntaganda established the Mandro training center, which was the first training center created by the UPC/FPLC; that he was responsible for the training of recruits; and that he regularly paid visits to the training camps, including Mandro, to inspect the training process and to participate in the teaching of recruits.

Ntaganda was charged with the direct perpetration of numerous counts of war crimes and crimes against humanity, including the murder of Priest Boniface Bwanalonga (Ntaganda is alleged to have shot him several times in the head); the war crime of intentionally directing attacks against civilians; the crime of humanity of persecution; the war crime of pillaging; the war crime of enlistment and use of child soldiers; and the war crime of intentionally attacking protected objects (a hospital and a church). He was also charged as an indirect perpetrator as part of a common plan with members of the UPC/FPLC to assume military and political control over Ituri by, *inter alia*, forcibly expelling the non-Hema civilian population, particularly those who identify as Lendu, from Ituri. Please be advised that the facts are quite disturbing.

Prosecutor v. Ntaganda, Case No. ICC–01/04–02/06, Judgment (July 8, 2019)

787. In June 2002, during a meeting held in Kampala where they discussed how they would take control of Ituri, Thomas Lubanga and other political leaders of the emerging UPC/FPLC decided that each person present at the meeting should mobilise the children in their community in order to join the UPC. * * *[L]arge-scale recruitment efforts followed.

788. The Chamber also recalls that some political and military leaders of the UPC/FPLC, including Mr. Ntaganda, had children under the age of 15 in their immediate vicinity, most notably, as part of their personal escorts. These individuals accompanied them everywhere, including to the front, as part of military operations. The demobilisation efforts, notably made by Mr. Ntaganda and the other leaders of the UPC/FPLC, were isolated initiatives throughout the period of the charges, while the recruitment and reliance on individuals under the age of 15 continued.

789. In order to grow in strength as an army, and to be able to chase away the RCD/ML from Ituri, and to fight its well-armed and organised military wing, the UPC/FPLC had a strict and violent disciplinary

system within its ranks. Recruits were told that they would be killed in case of desertion. Those who tried to escape were brought back to face other recruits before being seriously beaten up. More generally, the Chamber considers that members of the organisation knew that they would be punished if they did not obey orders.

790. The military leaders of the organisation employed various methods to ensure that their commands would be obeyed. With regard to the recruits, the Chamber observes that the commanders subjected them to violent treatment and instilled fear in them. It was found that Mr. Ntaganda, notably, inspired fear amongst the troops. Life in the UPC/FPLC for recruits, including for the youngest ones, meant harsh living conditions, threats, including to their life, monitoring of their movements, and severe punishments, including beatings and executions. While ensuring that the recruits obeyed their orders, the actual orders given to them, including to the youngest ones, directed them to be engaged in violent acts, such as killing the enemy, namely the Lendu, regardless of their sex, age and whether they were soldiers or civilians. * * *

792. In addition to these conditions, its young female recruits and soldiers were additionally subjected to a continuous exposure to the risk of sexual abuses, including rape, accompanied by severe physical violence. The Chamber found that female members of the UPC/FPLC, including those under 15 years of age, were regularly raped or subjected to sexual violence by male members of the UPC/FPLC. These crimes were left largely unpunished and the Chamber considers that no effective measures were taken by Mr. Ntaganda or Floribert Kisembo [Chief of staff of the FPLC] to restrain or prevent this practice within their respective groups of escorts. Moreover, some of the UPC/FPLC commanders themselves subjected some members of the UPC/FPLC to sexual violence. The Chamber finds that this practice could occur due to the circumstances in which these vulnerable young girls were kept, notably not being able to leave. In this regard, the Chamber emphasises the fact that the military leaders did not create the necessary conditions to ensure a safe environment for the female members of the UPC/FPLC, in which they would not be sexually abused by other members of the group. * * *

[The Chamber then sets out evidence of the plan to cleanse the region of members of the Lendu community, and recounts some of the specific actions taken to implement this plan.]

810. In the view of the Chamber, the co-perpetrators, by virtue of this agreement to drive out all the Lendu from the localities that they attacked, meant beyond reasonable doubt: (i) for civilians to be attacked and killed (Counts 1, 2 and 3); (ii) for their property to be appropriated and destroyed (Counts 11 and 18); (iii) for civilians to be raped and subjected to sexual slavery (Counts 4, 5, 7 and 8); (iv) for civilians to be forcibly displaced (Counts 12 and 13); and (v) for protected objects to be

attacked (Count17). Moreover, the Chamber finds beyond reasonable doubt that the co-perpetrators meant for the abovementioned conduct to be targeted towards the Lendu civilian population as such (Count 10).

811. The Chamber also concludes that, as of at least the beginning of August 2002, the co-perpetrators were virtually certain that the implementation of their plan to drive out all the Lendu from the localities targeted during the course of their military campaign against the RCD-K/ML would lead to: (i) the recruitment and active use in hostilities of children under the age of 15 within the UPC/FPLC (Counts 14, 15 and 16); and (ii) the rape and sexual slavery of these children (Counts 6 and 9). Indeed, the Chamber finds that, in the circumstances prevailing in Ituri at the time, the occurrence of these crimes was not simply a risk that they accepted, but crimes they foresaw with virtual certainty. * * *

Findings of the Chamber on the Crimes Charged * * *

Rape as a Crime against Humanity and as a War Crime (Counts 4 and 5) (1)

930. The crime against humanity of rape is laid down in Article 7(1)(g) of the Statute. The war crime of rape is laid down in Article 8(2)(e)(vi) of the Statute.

931. The legal elements of the crime against humanity of rape are:

> 1. The perpetrator invaded the body of a person by conduct resulting in penetration, however slight, of any part of the body of the victim or of the perpetrator with a sexual organ, or of the anal or genital opening of the victim with any object or any other part of the body.
>
> 2. The invasion was committed by force, or by threat of force or coercion, such as that caused by fear of violence, duress, detention, psychological oppression or abuse of power, against such person or another person, or by taking advantage of a coercive environment, or the invasion was committed against a person incapable of giving genuine consent.
>
> 3. The conduct was committed as part of a widespread or systematic attack directed against a civilian population.
>
> 4. The perpetrator knew that the conduct was part of or intended the conduct to be part of a widespread or systematic attack directed against a civilian population.
>
> 5. The perpetrator's conduct was deliberate and the perpetrator: (i) meant to cause the consequence; or (ii) was aware that it would occur in the ordinary course of events.

932. The legal elements of the war crime of rape are:

> 1. The perpetrator invaded the body of a person by conduct resulting in penetration, however slight, of any

> part of the body of the victim or of the perpetrator with a sexual organ, or of the anal or genital opening of the victim with any object or any other part of the body.
>
> 2. The invasion was committed by force, or by threat of force or coercion, such as that caused by fear of violence, duress, detention, psychological oppression or abuse of power, against such person or another person, or by taking advantage of a coercive environment, or the invasion was committed against a person incapable of giving genuine consent.
>
> 3. The conduct took place in the context of and was associated with an armed conflict not of an international character.
>
> 4. The perpetrator was aware of factual circumstances that established the existence of an armed conflict.
>
> 5. The perpetrator's conduct was deliberate and the perpetrator: (i) meant to cause the consequence; or (ii) was aware that it would occur in the ordinary course of events.

933. The concept of 'invasion' is intended to be broad enough to be gender neutral. Accordingly, 'invasion', in the Court's legal framework, includes same-sex penetration, and encompasses both male and/or female perpetrators and victims.

934. Save for the very specific situation of a person whose 'incapacity' was 'tak[en] advantage of', the Elements of Crimes do not refer to the victim's lack of consent, and therefore this need not be proven. The Elements of Crimes clearly seek to punish any act of penetration where committed under threat of force or coercion, such as that caused by the threat of violence, duress, detention, psychological pressure or abuse of power or, more generally, any act of penetration taking advantage of a coercive environment. The establishment of at least one of the coercive circumstances or conditions set out in the second element is therefore sufficient alone for penetration to amount to rape within the meaning of Articles 7(1)(g) and 8(2)(e)(vi) of the Statute.

935. Coercive circumstances need not be evidenced by a show of physical force. Threats, intimidation, extortion, and other forms of duress which prey on fear or desperation may constitute coercion, and coercion may be inherent in certain circumstances, such as armed conflict or the military presence of hostile forces amongst the civilian population. Several factors may contribute to creating a coercive environment, such as, for instance, the number of people involved in the commission of the crime, or whether the rape is committed during or immediately following a combat situation, or is committed together with other crimes. In addition, in relation to the requirement of the existence of a 'coercive environment,' it must be proven that the perpetrator's conduct involved 'taking advantage' of such a coercive environment. * * *

940. As established above, the Chamber found that:

- during and in the immediate aftermath of the UPC/FPLC assault on Mongbwalu, PC/FPLC soldiers forced women and girls to have sexual intercourse with them, including at the Appartements camp;
- in Kilo, some UPC/FPLC soldiers used their influence on girls in Kilo to have sexual intercourse with them, and in one instance, forced a detainee to insert his hand into P-0022's vagina;
- in Kobu, UPC/FPLC soldiers raped detained women and girls; and also anally penetrated men with their penises or by using 'bits of wood';
- in Sangi, UPC/FPLC soldiers raped women, and
- in Buli a UPC/FPLC soldier raped P-0113.

Penetration

941. The Chamber found that all incidents described above resulted in an invasion of the victim's body through an act of penetration, as required by the Elements of Crimes. It is therefore satisfied that the first material elements of the crime against humanity of rape and of the war crime of rape are met. * * *

Use of force, threat of force or coercion, or taking advantage of a coercive environment

943. Turning to the second legal element of rape, the Chamber notes that, in many instances, the perpetrators used force against the victims or other individuals present, both before and during the invasion of their body. Notably, one girl was violently undressed and, because she was screaming, the UPC/FPLC soldier who was on top of her and penetrating her put a cloth over her mouth and continued to penetrate her. She suffered serious injuries as a result of the conduct of the two UPC/FPLC soldiers who successively raped her, and required subsequent medical intervention. P-0022 was hit and thrown in an underground makeshift prison before she was raped. Other victims were also captured, physically restrained, and hurt by their perpetrators. The Chamber also notes that some victims were crying or screaming for help before, during, or immediately after the invasion of their body.

944. In addition, the Chamber finds that UPC/FPLC soldiers used implicit threats of force when carrying their arms in front of their victims, thereby intimidating these persons, or, in some instances, took out their weapons to show them to the victims, apparently to scare them. Other UPC/FPLC soldiers also plainly told their victims that they would be killed if they cried out or refused to cooperate. After the 'pacification meeting', when the soldiers were taking women to the bush to rape them, they carried out their threats and killed at least two individuals in front

of some of the victims, notably killing one woman who had tried to defend herself.

945. Finally, the Chamber notes that the UPC/FPLC soldiers engaged in the conduct described above in the immediate aftermath of the group's takeover of, respectively, Mongbwalu and Kilo, or in the context of its military assaults on villages in the Walendu-Djatsi collectivité. In these circumstances, the perpetrators' status as UPC/FPLC soldiers placed them in a position of authority vis-à-vis the local population, particularly considering the young age of many of the victims, as well as the fact that the rapes coincided with the commission of other crimes by UPC/FPLC soldiers against the inhabitants of these villages. For this reason, even for the incidents where the use of violence or threats was not established, notably when soldiers were calling girls from the road in front of their camp in Kilo, the Chamber considers that the UPC/FPLC soldiers abused their power and took advantage of a coercive environment to have sexual intercourse with girls or women.

946. Accordingly, the Chamber concludes that at least one, often more, of the coercive circumstances or conditions set out in the second legal element of the crime against humanity and of the war crime of rape is proven for all incidents listed at paragraph 940 above. * * *

Sexual slavery as a crime against humanity and as a war crime (Counts 7 and 8)

949. The crime against humanity of sexual slavery is laid down in Article 7(1)(g) of the Statute. The war crime of sexual slavery is laid down in Article 8(2)(e)(vi) of the Statute.

950. The legal elements of the crime against humanity of sexual slavery are:

> 1. The perpetrator exercised any or all of the powers attaching to the right of ownership over one or more persons, such as by purchasing, selling, lending or bartering such a person or persons, or by imposing on them a similar deprivation of liberty.
>
> 2. The perpetrator caused such person or persons to engage in one or more acts of a sexual nature.
>
> 3. The conduct was committed as part of a widespread or systematic attack directed against a civilian population.
>
> 4. The perpetrator knew that the conduct was part of or intended the conduct to be part of a widespread or systematic attack directed against a civilian population.
>
> 5. The perpetrator's conduct was deliberate and the perpetrator: (i) meant to cause the consequence; or (ii) was aware that it would occur in the ordinary course of events.

951. The legal elements of the war crime of sexual slavery are:

1. The perpetrator exercised any or all of the powers attaching to the right of ownership over one or more persons, such as by purchasing, selling, lending or bartering such a person or persons, or by imposing on them a similar deprivation of liberty.

2. The perpetrator caused such person or persons to engage in one or more acts of a sexual nature.

3. The conduct took place in the context of and was associated with an armed conflict not of an international character.

4. The perpetrator was aware of factual circumstances that established the existence of an armed conflict.

5. The perpetrator's conduct was deliberate and the perpetrator: (i) meant to cause the consequence; or (ii) was aware that it would occur in the ordinary course of events.

952. There is no exhaustive list of situations or circumstances which reflect the exercise of a power of ownership. In determining whether the perpetrator exercised such a power, the Chamber must take into account various factors, such as control of the victim's movement, the nature of the physical environment, psychological control, measures taken to prevent or deter escape, use of force or threats of use of force or other forms of physical or mental coercion, duration, assertion of exclusivity, subjection to cruel treatment and abuse, control of sexuality, forced labour, and the victim's vulnerability. The exercise of the right of ownership over someone need not entail a commercial transaction. Imposition of 'similar deprivation of liberty' may take various forms; it may cover situations in which the victims may not have been physically confined, but were otherwise unable to leave as they would have nowhere else to go and fear for their lives. * * *

Findings of the Chamber

954. As established above, the Chamber found that during the course of the Second Operation, in Kobu, Sangi, Buli, and Jitchu, UPC/FPLC soldiers detained P-0018, P-0019, P-0113, and an 11-year-old girl, for certain periods, in some instances for several days, during which they raped them on one or more occasions, and forced them to carry items and/or prepare food.

955. On the basis of its finding that the victims referred to above were raped on one or more occasions, the Chamber is satisfied that the second material element of the crime of sexual slavery, i.e. that the perpetrator cause the person to engage in one or more acts of a sexual nature, is met.

956. The Chamber notes that the alleged victims, including P-0018, P-0019, P-0113, and an 11-year-old girl, were captured by UPC/FPLC soldiers and subsequently taken to other locations.

957. P-0018 was captured in Jitchu and made to carry items to Buli. The next morning, she was raped, together with other women, and UPC/FPLC soldiers shot her. While she was captured against her will and forced to carry items the day before she was raped, the Chamber has not received any evidence to indicate that any or all of the powers attaching to the right of ownership were exercised by the soldiers who raped her the next day, or anyone involved in allowing the rape to occur, nor has it received evidence to assess whether a similar deprivation of liberty was imposed on her. The Chamber therefore cannot conclude that the first element of sexual slavery is fulfilled. The Chamber has already made a positive findings above on the crimes of rape and attempted murder having been committed against P-0018, but its findings on what happened to P-0018 during the day prior does not allow the sexual violence suffered by P-0018 to be qualified as another charged crime than rape. Although her capture and having been made to carry items were not lawful, this conduct is not separately charged. * * *

959. P-0113 was captured by the UPC/FPLC in the bush surrounding Buli. After being taken to Buli, she was forced together with three other women to cook for the UPC/FPLC soldiers and told to fetch water. From there, she was made to carry a mattress to Kobu. When she was made to fetch water and on the way to Kobu, she was raped by UPC/FPLC soldiers. In Kobu, she was brought to the place where a named UPC/FPLC commander was staying. During the night, a soldier woke her up, telling her that the commander was calling for her. The commander told her that she would be spending the night with him and raped her. The commander later told P-0113 to come with him to Bunia to live in his house. Although she did not want to, she felt that she to obey him and go to Bunia in order not to be killed by the UPC/FPLC soldiers in Kobu. The commander made her to carry a mattress to Bunia, where she stayed one night in his house, before being sent away by the commander's wife.

960. The Chamber considers that the aforementioned circumstances show that the deprivation of liberty of P-0113 was such that the some of the powers of the right of ownership were exercised over her by members of the UPC/FPLC, including after she was brought to the location where he was staying in Kobu, by the named UPC/FPLC commander. During this period she was raped various times, only to afterwards be made to carry on with what she was forced to do by the UPC/FPLC, such as cooking or carrying goods. The Chamber therefore considers that the first element of the crime of sexual slavery is established with regard to P-0113. Although the Chamber also made a finding above on the crime of rape having been committed against P-0113, it considers that the circumstances of P-0113's prolonged deprivation of liberty are such that

the period during which she was deprived of her liberty is in addition appropriately qualified as the crime of sexual slavery. * * *

965. The Chamber further recalls * * * that, provided there is a nexus to the armed conflict, rape and sexual slavery against any person is prohibited, and that therefore members of the same armed force are not per se excluded as potential victims of the war crimes of rape and sexual slavery under Article 8(2)(e)(vi), which was upheld by the Appeals Chamber. The Chamber further recalls its indication, and the Appeals Chamber's finding in this regard, that for a proper delineation between war crimes and ordinary crimes, the nexus between the conduct in question and the armed conflict must be satisfied. * * *

984. The Chamber notes the Defence's submissions that 'sexual abuse [is] widespread in armed forces around the world', but emphasises that it is not generally pronouncing on whether such sexual abuse, while criminal, constitutes a war crime. Sexual abuse within armed forces may or may not take place at a time that the relevant armed force is a party to an armed conflict, and may or may not take place in the context of or be associated with such an armed conflict. The facts before the Chamber concern the two victims referred to above. The rapes and sexual slavery of these girls took place during training at one of the UPC/FPLC camps and during the assignment as an escort to a UPC/FPLC commander, respectively, during a period in which the UPC/FPLC was actively engaged in military operations and fought opposing armed actors. The UPC/FPLC's recruitment campaign at the relevant time was aimed at building up its military strength—which was required to achieve the desired control over Ituri.

985. The Chamber further recalls the link between the recruitment campaign of soldiers and the related recruitment of individuals under the age of 15, as a result of the absence of measures to exclude such persons and the UPC/FPLC's acceptance that individuals under the age of 15 would therefore become part of the UPC/FPLC, and the UPC/FPLC's engagement in the non-international armed conflict in Ituri.

986. The Chamber is therefore satisfied that the conduct discussed above, and amounting to the rape and/or sexual slavery of individuals under the age of 15, was associated with a non-international armed conflict and therefore fulfils the requisite nexus requirement. * * *

Cumulative Convictions

1202. The Chamber agrees with trial chambers at this Court that cumulative convictions are permissible under the Court's framework. The Chamber can enter multiple convictions under different provisions of the Statute for the same conduct only if each statutory provision at stake has a 'materially distinct' element not contained in the other, i.e. an element which requires proof of a fact not required by the other. It is the legal elements of each statutory provision and not the acts and/or omissions of the accused that must be considered when applying the aforementioned test. Further, for the purpose of this determination, all elements, including the contextual elements, should be taken into account. Where the offences are not materially distinct, only a conviction under the more specific provision should be entered as the more specific offence subsumes the less specific one. Such a test ensures that an accused is convicted only for distinct offences and, at the same time, that the convictions entered fully reflect his or her criminality. However, where the same conduct underlies multiple convictions, this ought to be taken into account at the sentencing stage. * * *

1204. The Chamber further recalls that its findings on sexual slavery are, in part, based on the same underlying conduct as its findings of rape. In this respect, the Chamber notes that rape requires the invasion of the body of a person by conduct resulting in penetration, however slight, committed under certain specific circumstances, while the act(s) of a sexual nature required for the crimes of sexual slavery do not require penetration. Moreover, the crimes of sexual slavery require that the perpetrator exercised any or all of the powers attaching to the right of ownership over the victim; an element not required for the crime of rape to have been committed. Convicting for rape as a war crime and as a crime against humanity and for sexual slavery as a war crime and as a crime against humanity, when based on the same underlying conduct, is therefore legally permissible.

1205. However, the Chamber is mindful of the Appeals Chamber's consideration that a bar to multiple convictions could also arise in situations where the same conduct fulfils the elements of two offences, even if these offences have different legal elements, such as where one offence is fully consumed by the other offence or is viewed as subsidiary to it. In this regard, the Chamber recalls that its findings on the second legal element of sexual slavery, both as a crime against humanity and as a war crime, are based on its findings that the victims concerned had been subjected to rape by members of the UPC/FPLC. For the purpose of sentencing, the Chamber will thus take into account that some of the conduct underlying the convictions for rape and sexual slavery is the same.

NOTES & QUESTIONS

1. Case Update

Ntaganda was convicted of a total of 18 counts of war crimes and crimes against humanity, the highest number of counts by which any individual has been convicted before the ICC. Ntaganda was the first person to be convicted of sexual slavery before the ICC, and the first to be convicted of multiple crimes of sexual violence. Ntaganda has filed a notice of appeal, and a single judge has been designated to oversee the reparations proceedings arising from his conviction.

2. Sexual Violence Before the ICC

At the urging of Fatou Bensouda (initially as Deputy Prosecutor and then as Prosecutor of the ICC), the Office of the Prosecutor issued a Policy Paper on Sexual and Gender-Based Crimes, the first such document produced by an international court or tribunal. The need for such a policy was underscored by Professor Valerie Oosterveld: "Between 2002–2014, the Office of the Prosecutor brought fifty-seven charges for sexual and gender-based violence in twenty cases. * * * Thirty-five of these charges proceeded to the preliminary Confirmation of Charges stage, but only twenty of those charges were actually confirmed. At the judgment stage, the Prosecutor failed to secure a single conviction on these charges." This failure was attributed in part, according to Professor Oosterveld, to "narrow and inadequate conceptions of gender amongst staff, inadequate investigations and evidence-gathering processes, weak case strategies, and weak evidence." *See* Valerie Oosterveld, *The ICC Policy Paper on Sexual and Gender-Based Crimes: A Crucial Step for International Criminal Law*, 24 WM. & MARY J. WOMEN & L. 443 (2018).

The *Lubanga* case is illustrative. In March 2012, the Congolese militia leader Thomas Lubanga became the first person to be tried and convicted by the ICC. (For more on the *Lubanga* case, see Chapter 18 for discussion of sentence and reparations, Chapter 15 for the child soldiers aspect of the case, and Chapter 6 for the classification of the conflict.) He was convicted of the crime of enlisting, conscripting and using child soldiers, and sentenced to fourteen years' imprisonment. While testimony of sexual- and gender-based violence against girl soldiers was presented at trial, Lubanga was not charged with, nor convicted of, sexual- or gender-based violence. While the Trial Chamber tried to remedy this at the reparations phase, the Appeals Chamber held in March 2015 that although reparations would be available to former child soldiers, there would be no specific reparations for sexual- and gender-based crimes.

The case against the Congolese militia leader Germain Katanga was the first case in which sexual violence was part of the indictment. While the court found evidence of rape and sexual slavery in the aftermath of attacks led by Katanga, insufficient evidence was submitted to connect him to these crimes. Thus while he was convicted of murder and other acts which constituted a crime against humanity, he was acquitted of rape and sexual slavery. (For more on the *Katanga* case see Chapter 13.)

Finally, Jean-Pierre Bemba Gombo was convicted in March 2016 of rape as a war crime and as a crime against humanity in his role as a militia leader in the conflict in the Central African Republic, resulting in a sentence of imprisonment of eighteen years. On June 8, 2018, the Appeals Chamber reversed Bemba's convictions, acquitting him of all charges. (For more on the *Bemba* case see Chapters 13 and 14.)

3. Inter-Unit Rape and the War Crimes Nexus Requirement

In its closing brief, Mr. Ntaganda's defense argued that rape of child soldiers and women within Mr. Ntanganda's own unit did not satisfy the war crimes nexus requirement: "The alleged rapes were also not sufficiently related to the armed conflict to constitute a war crime. . . [One victim] was not a non-combatant; not a member of the opposing party; and not raped in circumstances that served any goal of the military campaign. The rapes occurred in camp, and not during operations. The circumstances are typical of the type of sexual abuse widespread in armed forces around the world, but that is not properly a matter of international war crimes jurisdiction as currently defined." *Prosecutor v. Ntaganda,* Case No. ICC–01/04–02/06, Public Redacted Version, Annex 1 to filing ICC–01/04–02/06–2298, para. 1546–1547 (Nov. 8, 2018). How does the ICC distinguish the rapes in Ntaganda's unit as meeting the war crimes nexus requirement? By charging rapes against people within the perpetrators' own units as war crimes, do you think the ICC unduly expanded the nexus requirement? The defense pointed out that sexual abuse in armed forces around the world is "widespread." In the United States, for instance, the U.S. Department of Defense reported that approximately 20,500 armed forces service members experienced some kind of sexual assault in 2018. Department of Defense Annual Report on Sexual Assault in the Military, Fiscal Year 2018. Under what conditions should rapes within armed forces units constitute war crimes?

4. Cumulative Charging and Sexual Violence

The sexual violence against soldiers and civilians perpetrated by those under Mr. Ntaganda's command underlie the war crime of rape, crime against humanity of rape, war crime of sexual slavery, and crime against humanity of sexual slavery charges. Do you think it is fair for the Court to charge Mr. Ntaganda for multiple crimes for the same conduct? In the *Bemba* case, the ICC judges declined to convict the defendant for sexual slavery and rape arising from the same set of facts. Here, the Court acknowledged that several charges relied in part on some of the same incidents, but allowed their separate prosecution anyway, saying they would take the overlapping factual predicates into consideration in sentencing. What standard did the Court set for determining the permissibility of multiple criminal charges for the same underlying conduct? (For more on cumulative charging, see Chapter 13.)

5. War Crimes Prosecutions Involving Syria and Iraq

As the war wages on in Syria, domestic courts—particularly in Europe—have emerged as fertile grounds for justice given the failure of the ICC referral effort, the lack of multilateral support for a hybrid or *ad hoc* tribunal devoted to Syria, and the perceived legal impediments to building international justice institutions outside the Security Council. The Syrian Commission of Inquiry has expressly called upon states to utilize universal jurisdiction to "investigate and prosecute persons and groups implicated in egregious violations." Report of the Independent International Commission of Inquiry on the Syrian Arab Republic, U.N. Doc. A/HRC/28/69, ¶ 145(a) (Feb. 5, 2015). Individual states have begun to oblige, leading to the revival of the concept of universal jurisdiction after a period of retrenchment and the activation of diverse principles of jurisdiction. Indeed, TRIAL International estimates that universal jurisdiction cases worldwide are up 18% since 2018.

See Trial International, EVIDENTIARY CHALLENGES IN UNIVERSAL JURISDICTION CASES, UNIVERSAL JURISDICTION ANNUAL REVIEW 2019, at 11.

As a result, a number of domestic trials involving events and actors in Syria are underway featuring a range of criminal charges and fact patterns. These cases fall into two general buckets. One set of cases involves foreign fighters who have returned home to face charges under anti-terrorism legislation or laws criminalizing their participation in foreign wars. States are highly motivated to prosecute such cases because they perceive these defendants as posing an acute national security threat, both from the perspective of bringing the violence home but also as potential recruiters and radicalizers. In addition, by virtue of Security Council Resolution 2178, states are under U.N. Charter-based duties to comprehensively address the phenomenon of foreign terrorist fighters. S.C. Res. 2178, U.N. Doc. S/RES/2178 (Sept. 24, 2014). The Council has defined this concept as: "individuals who travel to a State other than their States of residence or nationality for the purpose of the perpetration, planning, or preparation of, or participation in, terrorist acts or the providing or receiving of terrorist training, including in connection with armed conflict." *Id.* at para. 5. Many states have accordingly enacted legislation enhancing their ability to prosecute terrorism, raising concerns among rights groups and advocates about the misuse of such laws.

A second subset of cases involves individuals who stand accused of committing international crimes *stricto sensu*. These latter prosecutions are enabled by the incorporation of international criminal law into domestic penal codes, a global legislative trend occasioned in part by the ratification of the Rome Treaty (even though that treaty technically does not require domestic incorporation of ICC crimes). Although most domestic cases involving Syria feature some combination of these two sets of criminal charges, sometimes states are only able to resort to immigration remedies for lack of evidence or other legal impediments—a last-ditch option for accountability. (Recall the discussion of immigration remedies in Note 13 after the discussion of the Spanish universal jurisdiction case in Chapter 3.) Facilitating these cases is the proliferation of special prosecutorial units dedicated to investigating international crimes; global mutual legal assistance arrangements (such as INTERPOL); the formation of multinational "joint investigative teams" focused on the prosecution of transnational crimes; training programs dedicated to investigating international crimes by such groups as the Institute for International Criminal Investigations (IICI); and Europe-wide institutions such as EUROPOL, the European Arrest Warrant (EAW), and the Eurojust Genocide Network. *See* Human Rights Watch, THE LONG ARM OF JUSTICE: LESSONS FROM SPECIALIZED WAR CRIMES UNITS IN FRANCE, GERMANY, AND THE NETHERLANDS (2014). In addition, domestic prosecutors have benefited from institutional learning and assistance from non-governmental investigative efforts that jumpstart domestic processes and render these cases less daunting.

6. War Crimes Against Combatants

Although there is political will to bring these cases, they are difficult to prove. In particular, absent an eye witness, evidence of battlefield conduct is hard to come by. That said, prosecutors are moving forward with what charges they can, which are often undergird by the defendant's own social media profile. For example, Aria Ladjedvardi, a German national, became radicalized and subsequently travelled to Syria to fight against the Assad regime. Upon his return, Ladjedvardi was convicted of the war crime of subjecting a protected person to humiliating and degrading treatment by posing with the heads of executed members of President Bashar al-Assad's forces. *See Prosecutor v. Aria Ladjedvardi*, OLG Frankfurt Am Main, Az.: 5-3 StE 2/16-4-1/16 (July 12, 2016). He was identified from trophy photographs found on Facebook. The court held that it is a war crime to mistreat enemy fighters who are *hors de combat*—including prisoners of war in an international armed conflict and captured fighters of the opposing party in non-international armed conflicts—even when such individuals were already deceased. *Id.* at III, §§ 1–2. The court cited ICTY and ICTR jurisprudence (*The Prosecutor v. Brđanin*, Case No. T–99–36–T, Judgement (Sept. 1, 2004) and *The Prosecutor v. Bagasora et al.*, Case No. ICTR–98–41–T, Judgement (May 8, 2012)) for this proposition. Ladjedvardi was sentenced to two years' imprisonment, which included mitigation for his youth, the fact that someone else uploaded the photographs (although he approved of them), and his confession. The defendant appealed the conviction, but the appeal was denied by the Federal High Court of Justice.

7. A Uniform Standard

Professor Derek Jinks has argued that international humanitarian law should provide a uniform standard of treatment to all combatants, whether they are categorized as privileged or not. Rather than use status categories to determine protection—that is, to provide different protections for civilians, combatants, and others—Professor Jinks argues for a legal regime that focuses on individual action, rather than collective identity, and thus punishes individuals for their bad acts, such as war crimes, rather than their failure to meet the requirements of a particular status category. How would this impact individuals detained by the United States in connection with the "war on terror"? *See* Derek Jinks, *Symposium: The Changing Laws of War: Do We Need a New Legal Regime after September 11?: Protective Parity and the Laws of War*, 79 NOTRE DAME L. REV. 1493 (2004).

PROBLEMS

1. War Crimes Act of 1996 and Its Amendments

Review the two versions of the U.S. War Crimes Act set forth below with reference to the penal enforcement provisions of the 1949 Geneva Conventions (see Part IV on Execution of the Conventions) and the war crimes provisions in the ICC Statute (Art. 8). Congress passed the first draft of the Act in 1996 with amendments in 1997. The second major iteration contains amendments made pursuant to the Military Commission Act of 2006. As you review these materials, consider the following questions: Was the 1996/7 version consistent with the United States' obligations to implement the 1949 Geneva Conventions? Is the 2006 version? What are the effects of the amendments adopted in 2006? Was the United States obligated to continue to make criminal any violation of Common Article 3 or was it free to, in effect, decriminalize parts of that Article? Do the Common Article 3 crimes defined in the Act match the customary and judicial definitions of them? In some ways, has the United States gone further than required by the Conventions in these pieces of legislation? Why would Congress make the amendments it did in 2006?

U.S. War Crimes Act of 1996, 18 U.S.C. § 2441

(a) Offense. Whoever, whether inside or outside the United States, commits a war crime, in any of the circumstances described in subsection (b), shall be fined under this title or imprisoned for life or any term of years, or both, and if death results to the victim, shall also be subject to the penalty of death.

(b) Circumstances. The circumstances referred to in subsection (a) are that the person committing such war crime or the victim of such war crime is a member of the Armed Forces of the United States or a national of the United States (as defined in section 101 of the Immigration and Nationality Act).

(c) Definition. As used in this section the term "war crime" means any conduct—

(1) defined as a grave breach in any of the international conventions signed at Geneva 12 August 1949, or any protocol to such convention to which the United States is a party;

(2) prohibited by Article 23, 25, 27, or 28 of the Annex to the Hague Convention IV, Respecting the Laws and Customs of War on Land, signed 18 October 1907;

(3) which constitutes a violation of Common Article 3 of the international conventions signed at Geneva, 12 August 1949, or any protocol to such convention to which the United States is a party and which deals with non-international armed conflict; or

(4) of a person who, in relation to an armed conflict and contrary to the provisions of the Protocol on Prohibitions or Restrictions on the Use of Mines, Booby-Traps and Other Devices as amended at Geneva on 3 May 1996 (Protocol II as amended on 3 May 1996), when the United States is a party to such Protocol, willfully kills or causes serious injury to civilians.

18 U.S.C. § 2441, as Amended by the Military Commission Act of 2006

(a) Offense. Whoever, whether inside or outside the United States, commits a war crime, in any of the circumstances described in subsection (b), shall be fined under this title or imprisoned for life or any term of years, or both, and if death results to the victim, shall also be subject to the penalty of death.

(b) Circumstances. The circumstances referred to in subsection (a) are that the person committing such war crime or the victim of such war crime is a member of the Armed Forces of the United States or a national of the United

States (as defined in section 101 of the Immigration and Nationality Act [8 USCS § 1101]).

(c) Definition. As used in this section the term "war crime" means any conduct—

(1) defined as a grave breach in any of the international conventions signed at Geneva 12 August 1949, or any protocol to such convention to which the United States is a party;

(2) prohibited by Article 23, 25, 27, or 28 of the Annex to the Hague Convention IV, Respecting the Laws and Customs of War on Land, signed 18 October 1907;

(3) which constitutes a grave breach of Common Article 3 (as defined in subsection (d)) when committed in the context of and in association with an armed conflict not of an international character; or

(4) of a person who, in relation to an armed conflict and contrary to the provisions of the Protocol on Prohibitions or Restrictions on the Use of Mines, Booby-Traps and Other Devices as amended at Geneva on 3 May 1996 (Protocol II as amended on 3 May 1996), when the United States is a party to such Protocol, willfully kills or causes serious injury to civilians.

(d) Common Article 3 violations.

(1) Prohibited conduct. In subsection (c)(3), the term "grave breach of common Article 3" means any conduct (such conduct constituting a grave breach of common Article 3 of the international conventions done at Geneva August 12, 1949), as follows:

(A) Torture. The act of a person who commits, or conspires or attempts to commit, an act specifically intended to inflict severe physical or mental pain or suffering (other than pain or suffering incidental to lawful sanctions) upon another person within his custody or physical control for the purpose of obtaining information or a confession, punishment, intimidation, coercion, or any reason based on discrimination of any kind.

(B) Cruel or inhuman treatment. The act of a person who commits, or conspires or attempts to commit, an act intended to inflict severe or serious physical or mental pain or suffering (other than pain or suffering incidental to lawful sanctions), including serious physical abuse, upon another within his custody or control. * * *

(D) Murder. The act of a person who intentionally kills, or conspires or attempts to kill, or kills whether intentionally or unintentionally in the course of committing any other offense under this subsection, one or more persons taking no active part in the hostilities, including those placed out of combat by sickness, wounds, detention, or any other cause.

(E) Mutilation or maiming. The act of a person who intentionally injures, or conspires or attempts to injure, or injures whether intentionally or unintentionally in the course of committing any other offense under this subsection, one or more persons taking no active part in the hostilities, including those placed out of combat by sickness, wounds, detention, or any other cause, by disfiguring the person or persons by any mutilation thereof or by permanently disabling any member, limb, or organ of his body, without any legitimate medical or dental purpose.

(F) Intentionally causing serious bodily injury. The act of a person who intentionally causes, or conspires or attempts to cause, serious bodily injury to one or more persons, including lawful combatants, in violation of the law of war.

(G) Rape. The act of a person who forcibly or with coercion or threat of force wrongfully invades, or conspires or attempts to invade, the body of a person by penetrating, however slightly, the anal or genital opening of the victim with any part of the body of the accused, or with any foreign object.

(H) Sexual assault or abuse. The act of a person who forcibly or with coercion or threat of force engages, or conspires or attempts to engage, in sexual contact with one or more persons, or causes, or conspires or attempts to cause, one or more persons to engage in sexual contact.

(I) Taking hostages. The act of a person who, having knowingly seized or detained one or more persons, threatens to kill, injure, or continue to detain such person or persons with the intent of compelling any nation, person other than the hostage, or group of persons to act or refrain from acting as an explicit or implicit condition for the safety or release of such person or persons.

(2) Definitions. In the case of an offense under subsection (a) by reason of subsection (c)(3)—

(A) the term "severe mental pain or suffering" shall be applied for purposes of paragraphs (1)(A) and (1)(B) in accordance with the meaning given that term in section 2340(2) of this title [18 USCS § 2340(2)];

(B) the term "serious bodily injury" shall be applied for purposes of paragraph (1)(F) in accordance with the meaning given that term in section 113(b)(2) of this title [18 USCS § 113(b)(2)];

(C) the term "sexual contact" shall be applied for purposes of paragraph (1)(G) in accordance with the meaning given that term in section 2246(3) of this title [18 USCS § 2246(3)];

(D) the term "serious physical pain or suffering" shall be applied for purposes of paragraph (1)(B) as meaning bodily injury that involves—

(i) a substantial risk of death;

(ii) extreme physical pain;

(iii) a burn or physical disfigurement of a serious nature (other than cuts, abrasions, or bruises); or

(iv) significant loss or impairment of the function of a bodily member, organ, or mental faculty; and

(E) the term "serious mental pain or suffering" shall be applied for purposes of paragraph (1)(B) in accordance with the meaning given the term "severe mental pain or suffering" (as defined in section 2340(2) of this title [18 USCS § 2340(2)]), except that—

(i) the term "serious" shall replace the term "severe" where it appears; and

(ii) as to conduct occurring after the date of the enactment of the Military Commissions Act of 2006 [enacted Oct. 17, 2006], the term "serious and non-transitory mental harm (which need not be prolonged)" shall replace the term "prolonged mental harm" where it appears.

(3) Inapplicability of certain provisions with respect to collateral damage or incident of lawful attack. The intent specified for the conduct stated in subparagraphs (D), (E), and (F) or paragraph (1) precludes the applicability of those subparagraphs to an offense under subsection (a) by reasons of subsection (c)(3) with respect to—

(A) collateral damage; or

(B) death, damage, or injury incident to a lawful attack.

(4) Inapplicability of taking hostages to prisoner exchange. Paragraph (1)(I) does not apply to an offense under subsection (a) by reason of subsection (c)(3) in the case of a prisoner exchange during wartime.

(5) Definition of grave breaches. The definitions in this subsection are intended only to define the grave breaches of common Article 3 and not the full scope of United States obligations under that Article.

2. War Crimes Under the Military Commission Act of 2006

Review the war crimes that are prosecutable under the Military Commission Act of 2006 (and as amended in 2009) as set forth below. Which of these war crimes finds expression in the Geneva Conventions, in the U.S. War Crimes Act (in either the 1996/7 or 2006 version), or in Article 8 of the ICC Statute? Are there enumerated war crimes that are *sui generis*? What are the implications of the United States prosecuting individuals before military commissions for crimes that were not historically or are not currently considered to be war crimes under international humanitarian law? What is the impact of §§ 948b and 950p(c) and (d), below? Can the perpetrators of the attacks of September 11th be lawfully tried under the MCA? What about the perpetrators of the 1998 embassy bombings in Kenya or the 2000 U.S.S. Cole attack in Yemen?

Military Commissions Act of 2006, Public Law 109–366, Pub. L. 109–366 (Oct. 17, 2006), as amended by the National Defense Authorization Act for Fiscal Year 2010, Public Law 111–84

§ 948b. Military commissions generally

(a) Purpose. This chapter establishes procedures governing the use of military commissions to try alien unprivileged enemy belligerents* engaged in hostilities against the United States for violations of the law of war and other offenses triable by military commission. * * *

(f) Geneva Conventions Not Establishing Private Right of Action—No alien unprivileged enemy belligerent subject to trial by military commission under this chapter may invoke the Geneva Conventions as a basis for a private right of action.**

§ 950p. Definitions; construction of certain offenses; common circumstances

(a) Definitions—In this subchapter:

(1) The term 'military objective' means combatants and those objects during an armed conflict which, by their nature, location, purpose, or use, effectively contribute to the war-fighting or war-sustaining capability of an opposing force and whose total or partial destruction, capture, or neutralization would constitute a definite military advantage to the attacker under the circumstances at the time of an attack.

(2) The term 'protected person' means any person entitled to protection under one or more of the Geneva Conventions, including civilians not taking an active part in hostilities, military personnel placed out of combat by sickness, wounds, or detention, and military medical or religious personnel.

(3) The term 'protected property' means any property specifically protected by the law of war, including buildings dedicated to religion, education, art, science, or charitable purposes, historic monuments, hospitals, and places where the sick and wounded are collected, but only if and to the extent such property is not being used for military purposes or is not otherwise a military objective. The term includes objects properly identified by one of the distinctive emblems of the Geneva Conventions, but does not include civilian property that is a military objective.

(b) Construction of Certain Offenses—The intent required for offenses under paragraphs (1), (2), (3), (4), and (12) of section 950t of this title precludes their applicability with regard to collateral damage or to death, damage, or injury incident to a lawful attack.

---

* Eds.: The 2009 amendments changed this terminology from "alien unlawful enemy combatants."

** Eds.: The 2006 version of this provision stated: "No alien unlawful enemy combatant subject to trial by military commission under this chapter may invoke the Geneva Conventions as a source of rights."

(c) Common Circumstances—An offense specified in this subchapter is triable by military commission under this chapter only if the offense is committed in the context of and associated with armed conflict.*

(d) Effect—The provisions of this subchapter codify offenses that have traditionally been triable by military commission. This chapter does not establish new crimes that did not exist before the date of the enactment of this subchapter, as amended by the National Defense Authorization Act for Fiscal Year 2010, but rather codifies those crimes for trial by military commission. Because the provisions of this subchapter codify offenses that have traditionally been triable under the law of war or otherwise triable by military commission, this subchapter does not preclude trial for offenses that occurred before the date of the enactment of this subchapter, as so amended. * * *

§ 950t. Crimes triable by military commission

The following offenses shall be triable by military commission under this chapter at any time without limitation:

(1) MURDER OF PROTECTED PERSONS—Any person subject to this chapter who intentionally kills one or more protected persons shall be punished by death or such other punishment as a military commission under this chapter may direct.

(2) ATTACKING CIVILIANS—Any person subject to this chapter who intentionally engages in an attack upon a civilian population as such, or individual civilians not taking active part in hostilities, shall be punished, if death results to one or more of the victims, by death or such other punishment as a military commission under this chapter may direct, and, if death does not result to any of the victims, by such punishment, other than death, as a military commission under this chapter may direct.

(3) ATTACKING CIVILIAN OBJECTS—Any person subject to this chapter who intentionally engages in an attack upon a civilian object that is not a military objective shall be punished as a military commission under this chapter may direct. * * *

(5) PILLAGING—Any person subject to this chapter who intentionally and in the absence of military necessity appropriates or seizes property for private or personal use, without the consent of a person with authority to permit such appropriation or seizure, shall be punished as a military commission under this chapter may direct. * * *

(8) EMPLOYING POISON OR SIMILAR WEAPONS—Any person subject to this chapter who intentionally, as a method of warfare, employs a substance or weapon that releases a substance that causes death or serious and lasting damage to health in the ordinary course of events, through its asphyxiating, bacteriological, or toxic properties, shall be punished, if death results to one or more of the victims, by death or such other punishment as a military commission under this chapter may direct, and, if death does not result to any of the victims, by such

* Eds.: This article was added to the 2009 legislation.

punishment, other than death, as a military commission under this chapter may direct. * * *

(11) TORTURE—

(A) OFFENSE—Any person subject to this chapter who commits an act specifically intended to inflict severe physical or mental pain or suffering (other than pain or suffering incidental to lawful sanctions) upon another person within his custody or physical control for the purpose of obtaining information or a confession, punishment, intimidation, coercion, or any reason based on discrimination of any kind, shall be punished, if death results to one or more of the victims, by death or such other punishment as a military commission under this chapter may direct, and, if death does not result to any of the victims, by such punishment, other than death, as a military commission under this chapter may direct.

(B) SEVERE MENTAL PAIN OR SUFFERING DEFINED—In this section, the term 'severe mental pain or suffering' has the meaning given that term in section 2340(2) of title 18 [the torture statute].

(12) CRUEL OR INHUMAN TREATMENT—

(A) OFFENSE—Any person subject to this chapter who commits an act intended to inflict severe or serious physical or mental pain or suffering (other than pain or suffering incidental to lawful sanctions), including serious physical abuse, upon another within his custody or control shall be punished, if death results to the victim, by death or such other punishment as a military commission under this chapter may direct, and, if death does not result to the victim, by such punishment, other than death, as a military commission under this chapter may direct.

(B) DEFINITIONS—In this paragraph:

(i) The term 'serious physical pain or suffering' means bodily injury that involves—

(I) a substantial risk of death;

(II) extreme physical pain;

(III) a burn or physical disfigurement of a serious nature (other than cuts, abrasions, or bruises); or

(IV) significant loss or impairment of the function of a bodily member, organ, or mental faculty. * * *

(13) INTENTIONALLY CAUSING SERIOUS BODILY INJURY—

(A) OFFENSE—Any person subject to this chapter who intentionally causes serious bodily injury to one or more persons, including privileged belligerents, in violation of the law of war shall be punished, if death results to one or more of the victims, by death or such other punishment as a military commission under this chapter may direct, and, if death does not result to any of the victims, by such punishment, other than death, as a military commission under this chapter may direct.

(B) SERIOUS BODILY INJURY DEFINED—In this paragraph, the term 'serious bodily injury' means bodily injury which involves—

(i) a substantial risk of death;

(ii) extreme physical pain;

(iii) protracted and obvious disfigurement; or

(iv) protracted loss or impairment of the function of a bodily member, organ, or mental faculty. * * *

(15) MURDER IN VIOLATION OF THE LAW OF WAR—Any person subject to this chapter who intentionally kills one or more persons, including privileged belligerents, in violation of the law of war shall be punished by death or such other punishment as a military commission under this chapter may direct. * * *

(17) USING TREACHERY OR PERFIDY—Any person subject to this chapter who, after inviting the confidence or belief of one or more persons that they were entitled to, or obliged to accord, protection under the law of war, intentionally makes use of that confidence or belief in killing, injuring, or capturing such person or persons shall be punished, if death results to one or more of the victims, by death or such other punishment as a military commission under this chapter may direct, and, if death does not result to any of the victims, by such punishment, other than death, as a military commission under this chapter may direct. * * *

(21) RAPE—Any person subject to this chapter who forcibly or with coercion or threat of force wrongfully invades the body of a person by penetrating, however slightly, the anal or genital opening of the victim with any part of the body of the accused, or with any foreign object, shall be punished as a military commission under this chapter may direct.

(22) SEXUAL ASSAULT OR ABUSE—Any person subject to this chapter who forcibly or with coercion or threat of force engages in sexual contact with one or more persons, or causes one or more persons to engage in sexual contact, shall be punished as a military commission under this chapter may direct.

(23) HIJACKING OR HAZARDING A VESSEL OR AIRCRAFT—Any person subject to this chapter who intentionally seizes, exercises unauthorized control over, or endangers the safe navigation of a vessel or aircraft that is not a legitimate military objective shall be punished, if death results to one or more of the victims, by death or such other punishment as a military commission under this chapter may direct, and, if death does not result to any of the victims, by such punishment, other than death, as a military commission under this chapter may direct.

(24) TERRORISM—Any person subject to this chapter who intentionally kills or inflicts great bodily harm on one or more protected

persons, or intentionally engages in an act that evinces a wanton disregard for human life, in a manner calculated to influence or affect the conduct of government or civilian population by intimidation or coercion, or to retaliate against government conduct, shall be punished, if death results to one or more of the victims, by death or such other punishment as a military commission under this chapter may direct, and, if death does not result to any of the victims, by such punishment, other than death, as a military commission under this chapter may direct.

(25) PROVIDING MATERIAL SUPPORT FOR TERRORISM—

(A) OFFENSE—Any person subject to this chapter who provides material support or resources, knowing or intending that they are to be used in preparation for, or in carrying out, an act of terrorism (as set forth in paragraph (24)), or who intentionally provides material support or resources to an international terrorist organization engaged in hostilities against the United States, knowing that such organization has engaged or engages in terrorism (as so set forth), shall be punished as a military commission under this chapter may direct.

(B) MATERIAL SUPPORT OR RESOURCES DEFINED—In this paragraph, the term 'material support or resources' has the meaning given that term in section 2339A(b) of title 18.

(26) WRONGFULLY AIDING THE ENEMY—Any person subject to this chapter who, in breach of an allegiance or duty to the United States, knowingly and intentionally aids an enemy of the United States, or one of the co-belligerents of the enemy, shall be punished as a military commission under this chapter may direct.

(27) SPYING—Any person subject to this chapter who, in violation of the law of war and with intent or reason to believe that it is to be used to the injury of the United States or to the advantage of a foreign power, collects or attempts to collect information by clandestine means or while acting under false pretenses, for the purpose of conveying such information to an enemy of the United States, or one of the co-belligerents of the enemy, shall be punished by death or such other punishment as a military commission under this chapter may direct. * * *

(29) CONSPIRACY—Any person subject to this chapter who conspires to commit one or more substantive offenses triable by military commission under this subchapter, and who knowingly does any overt act to effect the object of the conspiracy, shall be punished, if death results to one or more of the victims, by death or such other punishment as a military commission under this chapter may direct, and, if death does not result to any of the victims, by such punishment, other than death, as a military commission under this chapter may direct. * * *

3. Charging War Crimes

Imagine an armed conflict in a nation that involves a foreign power aligned with the host government against an insurgent force. The insurgents seek to unseat the government and replace it with a fundamentalist theocracy. They exercise control over parts of the country beyond the capital city and engage in frequent guerilla attacks within urban areas where the foreign troops are congregated. The defendant in question traveled to the war zone from his native country in order to take a job clearing mines. He was captured fleeing the scene of a grenade attack that seriously injured two foreign soldiers and their interpreter. He was taken into custody by the foreign government and accused of tossing one of the grenades into the window of a jeep carrying the three victims. The defendant apparently confessed to the crime, but later recanted, arguing that his confession was the result of torture. The foreign government has agreed not to utilize the confession in any subsequent prosecution. Consider how you would charge this defendant under the law of war as it is contained within the Geneva Conventions, under the 2009 Military Commission Act, under domestic U.S. law (Title 18), and before the ICC. Assuming the facts presented above are true and that the evidence shows the defendant did in fact participate in the grenade attack, what war crime(s), if any, did he commit?

CHAPTER 8

AGGRESSION

> The charges in the Indictment that the defendants planned and waged aggressive wars are charges of the utmost gravity. * * * To initiate a war of aggression, therefore, is not only an international crime; it is the supreme international crime differing only from other war crimes in that it contains within itself the accumulated evil of the whole.
>
> —Nuremberg Judgment

I. INTRODUCTION

We take up in this chapter the crime of aggression, an area of law that implicates the *jus ad bellum* (the law or justice *of* war). The *jus ad bellum* encompasses the set of rules regulating the decision to use force. These rules are distinct from the *jus in bello* (the law or justice *in* war), covered more fully in Chapters 6 and 7, which discuss the legal regulation of armed conflict, including the legality of the means and methods employed once the decision to go to war has been made. The idea of distinguishing between the legality, or justice, of resorting to armed force and the legality, or justice, of what is done in an armed conflict is not a new one. This chapter concerns itself with the former question.

Historically, and in many human societies, a distinction was made between just and unjust wars. In ancient India, a ruler was entitled to go to war only after due deliberation and only for a serious issue, which did not include territorial acquisition. Similar distinctions were made in ancient China, Babylon, Greece, and are found within the Islamic tradition. The Roman Empire formally adopted the idea of a just war, though there were perennial debates over its content. St. Augustine (CE 354–430), and later St. Thomas Aquinas (CE 1225–74), developed the idea of a just war within Christian theology at a time when the power and legitimacy of the State was linked to the power and legitimacy of the Church. St. Augustine observed that "unjust war is no more than robbery on a majestic scale." *De Civitate Dei*, Book 4, Ch. 1. St. Thomas Aquinas built upon Augustine's work to develop further the theory of just war. In his *Summa Theologicae,* Aquinas set forth the following requirements for a war to be considered just: 1) it must be authorized by a legitimate sovereign; 2) it must be necessary for the achievement of a just cause; and 3) it must be for a "right intention," that is the restoration of a good and just order and not in furtherance of injustice. Self-defense against an unjust act of aggression, punishment of an unjust act of aggression, or recovery of something wrongly taken all qualified as just causes for Aquinas.

Under early just-war theory, what could be done in the pursuit of war depended on the reason for resorting to war, and whether the war was considered just. This meant that the body of rules that today we would call *jus in bello* varied among belligerents, depending on the apparent legitimacy of their decision to resort to force. Under this theory, if a war was just, then everything done in its name was itself just: the ends justified the means. The reverse was also true: if a war was deemed unjust, then every act of violence was itself unlawful. As we saw in the previous chapter, the contemporary law of armed conflict rejects this view and instead asserts that a specific act of warfare is to be judged independently of whether it is in furtherance of a just cause.

An important step in this process of untangling the *jus ad bellum* and the *jus in bello* was the abandonment of the notion that a set of factors could distinguish a just from an unjust war; this concept was replaced by a more blanket norm against aggressive war containing some discrete exceptions. War remained "lawful" if it was undertaken in self-defense or in response to a breach of international law. In 1899 and 1907, two international peace conferences were convened in The Hague. The goal was to "seek the most effective means of guaranteeing the peoples a secure peace." By the close of each Conference, however, more attention had been paid to drafting rules governing the means and methods of war (the *jus in bello*) than to rules governing the use of force. It was not until the post-World War I and II periods that the international community gave renewed attention to developing rules governing the use of force in the first place. The following excerpt presents a short history of how the just-war theory gave rise to the crime of aggression (then called "crimes against the peace") following these two world wars.

Jonathan A. Bush, "The Supreme . . . Crime" and Its Origins: The Lost Legislative History of the Crime of Aggressive War, 102 COLUM. L. REV. 2324, 2324–2369 (2002)

To the Allied lawyers and planners around 1940 who began to contemplate war crimes trials, there was little precedent for the notion that aggressive war itself might be a crime. The historical examples on which international law always relied offered no support. The nineteenth century had witnessed the birth of the modern law of war in so many areas—the first general treaties governing war at sea, guaranteeing humanitarian access to the Red Cross, and prohibiting specific weapons all date from the middle decades of that century, as does the "Lieber Code," the first modern code of land warfare—but no nation or jurist even proposed that war was wrong, much less presumptively unjust or a crime. On the contrary, the great eighteenth-century international lawyer Vattel had expressed the prevailing view: "The first rule . . . is that regular war, as to its effects, is to be accounted just on both sides . . ." A century later, little had changed; the Lieber Code (1863) explained that the law of war sought to ameliorate the excesses of battle, but that war itself was legally neutral. War could be a test of national glory, and for good causes or bad. As Secretary of State and War Henry Stimson later put it—intending no compliment—international law "attempt[ed] to moderate the excesses of war without controlling war itself."

In academic circles a few lawyers and theologians still wrote about the medieval tradition of the so-called Just War, but that tradition had exhausted its political appeal and intellectual power. What began in Augustine's writings as a narrow canonical doctrine allowing Christian princes to defend their lands and the faithful, and sometimes to use force to extend the faith, had grown to justify centuries of Crusades against Muslims and Baltic pagans, internal and domestic Crusades against dissidents like the Albigensians, wars of reconquest against breakaway Protestant kingdoms, systematic atrocities against Jews, and wars of expansion against indigenous peoples in the New World, Africa, and Asia. In short, in the secular, protestant, optimistic world of the nineteenth-century West, Just War theory was discredited by its loopholes and the self-serving uses to which it had been put for the better part of a millennium, and also, it must be said, by its historical links with Catholic political theology. The prevailing attitude to the legal status of war was best illustrated by the organization of the grand peace conferences that met in 1899 and 1907 in The Hague: The Armament and Arbitration Commissions attempted to make war less likely and the Laws of War Commissions for land and sea warfare sought to make it less destructive, but there was no serious thought to making war a criminal act or its authors international felons.

The terrible war that began in August 1914 seemed to make a mockery of these legal rules from the previous half century, but it also fueled a demand on the Allied side for war crimes trials for culpable Germans. Most of the attention centered on specific, widely publicized atrocities such as the rape of Belgian women, the machine gunning by U-boat crews of lifeboat victims, the burning of the Louvain library and the destruction of the Soissons and Senlis cathedrals, the executions of British Captain Fryatt and Nurse Edith Cavell, the mistreatment of Allied POWs, and, for American audiences, the sinking of the Lusitania. But a few commentators included the demand that Kaiser Wilhelm II and his senior ministers be punished for planning and initiating a war of aggression and, regardless of whether the war was aggressive, for the clear violation of the neutrality of Belgium and Luxembourg. Predictably, the press and public appeared to have been less interested in liability for aggressive war than in the atrocities. If so, it was but the first example of a consistent pattern found also in World War II and the Vietnam and Bosnia wars, wherein the public's interest in war crimes focused on graphic atrocities rather than abstruse points of international law and treaty interpretation and the seeming "he said, she said" of which side started the fight. Nevertheless, soon after the Armistice, at a preliminary session at Versailles, a Commission on the Responsibility of the Authors of the War and on Enforcement of Penalties was established, and that Commission in turn created subcommittees with overlapping jurisdiction to consider the causes of the war and the potential legal liability of its authors.

A few weeks later, Sub-Commission I on criminal acts reported that Germany and its allies had used the pretext of the assassination in Sarajevo [of Archduke Ferdinand of Austria] to launch a long-planned war, involving the intentional violation of treaties of neutrality. The conclusion was hardly a surprise, since the overwhelming sentiment of the conferees at Versailles was to punish Germany and its allies for the war. Even so, this Sub-Commission did a hurried job, examining no official records but nonetheless concluding: "The responsibility for [the war and violations of neutrality] lies wholly upon the Powers which declared war in pursuance of a policy of aggression, the concealment of which gives to the origin of this war the character of a dark conspiracy against the peace of Europe." Remarkably, though, Sub-Commission II, charged with assessing whether charges should be levied for the initiation of war, reported unanimously that "[w]e . . . do not advise that the acts which provoked the war should be charged against their authors and made the subject of proceedings before a tribunal." Unlike the favorable recommendation for punishment of combat atrocities, which came with American and Japanese dissents, the recommendation not to proceed with trials of the war's political authors was formally unanimous. Sir Ernest Pollock, the British Solicitor-General and member of the Sub-Commission, preserved that unanimity by siding with the Americans against liability, and all the public saw was a report concluding that

> by reason of the purely optional character of the institutions at The Hague for the maintenance of peace . . . a war of aggression may not be considered as an act directly contrary to positive law, or one which can be successfully brought before a tribunal such as the Commission is authorized to consider . . . [and therefore] no criminal charge can be made against the responsible . . . individuals (and notably the ex-Kaiser).

The final text of the Versailles Treaty [ending World War I between Germany and the Allied Powers] equivocated on this positivistic conclusion, for Article 227 "publicly arraign[ed] William II . . . for a supreme offence against international morality and the sanctity of treaties"—language that might have allowed charges for planning or initiating war. But the loose language was never put to the test, for the Kaiser had fled to the Netherlands, which refused to extradite him for what it deemed political charges. Neither the Kaiser nor royal princes nor senior generals and ministers, all of whom the French and Belgians continued to request at least in part for planning and initiating war, were ever tried.

Immediately, ferocious public anger was directed against the Germans for successfully sabotaging the dozen trials that were conducted by the German Supreme Court under Allied auspices at Leipzig of their lower-level officers for ordinary battlefield atrocities. But there is no record of anger at, or even public memory of, the forgotten notion of charging the Kaiser for starting the war. Within a few years, opinion in Britain and the United States came to feel that Versailles had been too harsh, that the demand for trials had obviously been a political mistake, and that the far more important issue of "war guilt" and reparations had also been mishandled, with Allied demands that were politically unrealistic, fiscally excessive, or both. By the time of the Locarno treaty (1925) [which normalized relations with Germany and established its boundaries], even the French seemed to agree. Given that prevailing mood, the idea of imposing new criminal liability on aggressors was forgotten by all but a tiny fringe.

But if trials were seen as a false path, diplomats and lawyers replied to the demonstrated failure of legal mechanisms before and during World War I with a variety of new regulatory treaties and frameworks. In response to the new weapons systems deployed during the war, agreements were proposed regulating the use of airplanes (1923) and submarines (1922, 1936), and prohibiting altogether the use of gas (1925). A successful naval disarmament conference was held and concluded in Washington, D.C. (1922). The Permanent Court of International Justice was established (1920), with the hope that among its cases would be those especially contentious issues that, in the past, had led to war. Various combinations of the great powers of the day were brought or enticed into collective and regional security pacts—even those nations such as the United States, the Soviet Union, and Germany that otherwise had opted or were kept out of the international League of Nations system.

At least theoretically, the high-water mark of this regulatory drive was the Pact of Paris, or Kellogg-Briand Pact (1928), by which signatories sought to foreswear or even outlaw war altogether. To its framers, Kellogg-Briand stood atop other legal efforts in the same direction. Among other instruments, the Preamble to the League of Nations 1924 Protocol for the Pacific Settlement of International Disputes (the Geneva Protocol) had stated that "a war of aggression constitutes a violation of this [international] solidarity and is an international crime." On September 24, 1927, the Assembly of the League of Nations had declared that "all wars of aggression are, and shall always be prohibited." A few months later, in February 1928, delegates at the Sixth Pan-American Conference at Havana went further by resolving that "war of aggression" was "an international crime against the human species" and was both "illicit" and "prohibited." But the Geneva Protocol failed to win ratification, and its preamble would have been weak law anyway; League resolutions were viewed, like U.N. General Assembly resolutions today, as "soft law;" and the Havana language was contained also in a preamble, and was at best merely hemispheric in scope. Kellogg-Briand, by contrast, was seen as hard treaty law, explicitly ratified and made binding. The Pact had originated as a bilateral agreement between the United States and France and might well have merely led to another familiar treaty of friendship and commerce between old allies. But a number of American academics and peace activists began to say that the French overture could be an opportunity to do more than cement the prickly Franco-American relationship. In time, both nations' foreign ministers agreed to make the treaty a general instrument open to all. After American Secretary of State Frank Kellogg gave a series of explicit reassurances that the treaty allowed unilateral determinations of self-defense (and therefore posed no threat to national interests or sovereignty), it soon attracted the ratification or adherence of almost all nations of the day. The operative language of the treaty provided that the parties

> condemn recourse to war for the solution of international controversies, and renounce it as an instrument of national policy in their relations with one another . . . [and] agree that the settlement or solution of all disputes or conflicts of whatever nature or of whatever origin they may be, which may arise among them, shall never be sought except by pacific means.

In total, over sixty nations, including Germany and all other major combatants in World War II, ratified or adhered to the treaty. And after Kellogg-Briand, throughout the last decade of peace, there grew a dense web of bilateral and regional treaties of friendship, security, peaceful settlement, and neutrality.

A generation later, in the summer of 1945—in London, where the framework of the Nuremberg trials was negotiated, and then at Nuremberg itself—the argument was raised that the charges relating to aggressive war were violations of one or another version of the "legality principle" or the rule against retroactivity in criminal law—*nullum crimen sine lege*, *nulla poena sine lege*, as the civil law put it. In response, lawyers relied heavily on the Kellogg-Briand Pact, the more explicit regional affirmations of the Pact, and the treaties of neutrality, friendship, arbitration, and collective security to demonstrate that Crimes against Peace was already clear law by the 1930s, and not new to Nuremberg. If it was implicit in Kellogg-Briand, little significance was attached to that fact when the treaty was first opened for ratification in 1928. On the contrary, in response to realists and critics concerned about sovereignty, it was said that the treaty was only hortatory, or expressive of national goals and aspirations, or political rather than legal in character. The treaty was praised for the possibility it held out of helping mold a political and moral consensus against war, and attacked for being unrealistic and holding international law in ridicule. Neither friend nor foe mentioned the possibility of criminal trials for individual aggressors. * * *

Within a few years of its ratification, the entire question of the treaty was moot, or so it seemed until the sudden postwar revival of interest, for by the late 1930s Kellogg-Briand was no longer an achievement of pride. Historian and isolationist writer Charles A. Beard termed it a "gibbering ghost," but across the political spectrum, few Americans would have disagreed. By the time of the Spanish Civil War, the issue for many was no longer how to lock pacifist or even-handed neutrality into foreign policy, but how to find a neutrality that could permissibly tip toward the victims of Axis aggression. Now the treaty was an embarrassment, proof of how naïve the West had been in believing that German and Italian (and soon, Soviet) signatures were worth anything at all. * * * If placing the blame on Germany by requiring war crimes trials and reparations payments had backfired by leading the humiliated Germans to look to demagogues as leaders, it seemed that treating the Germans as equals with whom one could reach an agreement for peace also led nowhere.

So it was that in the two and a half years between *Anschluss* [the 1938 annexation of Austria] and Munich (1938) [when Britain and Germany signed a non-aggression pact] and the [London] Blitz (1940), as world war threatened and then came, there was almost no public discussion of the legal issues of war crimes. The summary acquittals at Leipzig, the disengagement of the United States from Versailles and the League of Nations, the complete breakdown of the regulatory regimes for submarines and aerial bombing, and the mockery of Kellogg-Briand, all suggested that the so-called law of war was bad policy, law, and politics. The mood was summarized by another émigré international lawyer, Wolfgang Friedmann * * *. Addressing a roomful of international lawyers who must have been desperate to hear a learned speaker tell them their field still had relevance, Friedmann began: "[A] large body of what we know as positive international law no longer exists, because its basis has been shattered. . . . In particular . . . the bulk of the rules of warfare have ceased to have any validity. . . ." After a dark speech surveying the terrain and noting small exceptions, Friedmann concluded:

> [M]ost of the laws of warfare are to all intents and purposes eliminated from the sphere of international law although they survive on paper. The essential notions and conditions which underlie the rules of warfare have lost meaning and certainty. There is always room for humanitarian feelings, even in the present war. But it is far better to leave it in the sphere of ethics. * * *

For most other observers, if the law of war had any relevance whatsoever, it could only be after victory over the Axis. * * *

Not surprisingly, it was common in both popular and scholarly literature to denounce the Nazi leaders for starting the war, as well as for their brutal means of waging it, and occasionally to speak of the need for Nazis to face a reckoning for starting the war. Typically aggression, war-making, expansionism, militarism, or the like was used as a description and a political charge, to which responses—political or military, but possibly legal—would be required. Sometimes these authors employed terms with legal overtones like "crime" and "aggression," and some writers resurrected the Kellogg-Briand Pact and related instruments to argue that Germany had criminally initiated the war. * * * But very few of the wartime authors, even the lawyers, took that next step of calling for trials for an identifiable legal crime of planning, initiating, or waging aggressive war. There are obvious reasons why they did not. For one thing, aggressive war as a triable crime was essentially as lacking in precedent in 1943 as it had been in 1919, when it was rejected as being without precedent, unless one thought that the discredited Kellogg-Briand Pact had sufficiently changed the law. And because there was no explicit precedent criminalizing aggression, most authors concluded in a formulaic manner that after victory there should be judicial punishment for those who had committed atrocities, and a harsh but not necessarily legal response to aggression, based on joint Allied decision. Those who only a few years before had hoped for more, putting their faith in a strong prohibition of aggression under Versailles and Kellogg-Briand, saw that those texts, and their vision, had manifestly failed, and presumably they were loathe to propose again the same failed solutions. In fact, some commentators now looked back ruefully and said they should have endorsed not peace or neutrality but aggressive intervention against Germany as early as 1934. In a telling sign of the mood, they did not call it humanitarian intervention, but aggression—aggression as virtue. * * *

The few experts who thought that aggression was internationally prohibited generally concluded that inclusion of aggression for planned trials against the Axis leaders was premature in the absence of a clear sign of Allied political will or new legal institutions. In addition to general caution, there were also subtler pressures at work. Trials for aggression might have been politically imprudent—risking the dilution of public attention, permitting Nazi defendants to bring up the ambiguities of diplomatic relations, or leaving atrocities unavenged. * * * There was, finally, the failure of imagination. Even those who thought aggression was a crime, the utility of which was unfairly maligned, must have despaired in 1943 that criminal courts, even international courts, were the answer to Nazi war-making; surely that smacked of the failed legalisms of the League of Nations and the collective security pacts of the 1930s. Only someone seasoned in criminal law and courtroom practice could possibly imagine that the entirety of Nazi evil could best be encompassed in the notion of a crime of planning aggression and world domination. * * *

Until around [Autumn 1944], whatever American government planning there was for war crimes trials seems to have occurred in the

Army Judge Advocate General's office (JAG). The JAG favored trying culpable Germans in military tribunals conducted by JAG prosecutors under the traditional "laws and customs of war," which meant that most cases would probably involve mistreatment of American or Allied POWs. But now, with victory on the horizon and keen public and congressional interest developing in issues relating to war crimes, it was increasingly difficult to limit planning to the prosecution of murderous POW camp guards. So beginning in the autumn of 1944, State, Justice, Navy, and, less obviously, Treasury, joined the War Department as the great departments of state in which planning staffs were at work on postwar occupation issues, including possible war crimes trials. * * * Some of the senior staff * * * worried that the traditional laws and customs of war would allow the trial of few of the most horrific Nazi perpetrators.

Once criminal aggression was made part of the American agenda, the path of its development and inclusion in international agreement and Nuremberg indictment can be traced with clarity. * * * President Truman accepted the need for a full-time American viceroy for war crimes policy to unify American policy and to negotiate with the Allies. * * * In late April, he selected Supreme Court Associate Justice Robert H. Jackson, who turned out to be extremely enthusiastic about the theory of criminal aggression. * * * Within days of his appointment, Jackson revealed and began to act on his enthusiasm for the inclusion of criminal aggression in trial planning. He read the January 22 memorandum and various American drafts that included jurisdiction over the crime of aggression, and was briefed by the drafters. * * * Throughout May [1945], Jackson made sure that aggression, in one form or another, stayed in the American draft proposals for the international tribunal. And, not least, he advised President Truman—over the initial reservations of staff newcomer Telford Taylor—that aggressive war-making should be the central element of the American trial plan. * * *

The negotiations that were held in London from late June to early August 1945 were famously contentious, and one of the most difficult areas was the definition of criminal aggression. But the difficulties centered on whether the substantive definition of aggression would specify Nazi or Axis aggression (the Soviet position), or would define the crime in a clean, universal way that might, in another era, even include American acts (the Jackson position). After early French and Russian skepticism was dispelled, there was no serious prospect that aggression or Crimes against Peace, as it was now called, would not be included in the jurisdiction of the new court. That was the measure of Jackson's determination, and his success. In the end, the Charter for the new tribunal embodied Jackson's view, and defined individual responsibility for: "Crimes Against Peace: namely, planning, preparation, initiation or waging of a war of aggression, or a war in violation of international treaties, agreements or assurances, or participation in a common plan or conspiracy for the accomplishment of any of the foregoing."

II. PROSECUTING AGGRESSION: NUREMBERG AND TOKYO

The Charters of the Nuremberg and Tokyo Tribunals thus defined the crime of aggression. The Nuremberg and Tokyo Tribunals were the first, and to date only, international tribunals to find individuals guilty of the crime of aggression. The excerpt below sets forth the Nuremberg Tribunal's judgment on Count Two of the Indictment: Crimes Against the Peace. Count One alleged a common plan or conspiracy among the defendants; Count Three concerned war crimes, and Count Four concerned crimes against humanity.

The United States of America, et al. v. Hermann Wilhelm Goering, et al. Opinion and Judgment (October 1, 1946), *reprinted in* 41 AM. J. INT'L L. 172, 186

On 8 August 1945, the Government of the United Kingdom of Great Britain and Northern Ireland, the Government of the United States of America, the Provisional Government of the French Republic, and the Government of the Union of Soviet Socialist Republics entered into an Agreement establishing this Tribunal for the Trial of War Criminals whose offenses have no particular geographical location. In accordance with Article 5, the following Governments of the United Nations have expressed their adherence to the Agreement:

> Greece, Denmark, Yugoslavia, the Netherlands, Czechoslovakia, Poland, Belgium, Ethiopia, Australia, Honduras, Norway, Panama, Luxembourg, Haiti, New Zealand, India, Venezuela, Uruguay, and Paraguay.

By the Charter annexed to the Agreement, the constitution, jurisdiction, and functions of the Tribunal were defined. The Tribunal was invested with power to try and punish persons who had committed Crimes against Peace, War Crimes, and Crimes against Humanity as defined in the Charter. The Charter also provided that at the Trial of any individual member of any group or organization the Tribunal may declare (in connection with any act of which the individual may be convicted) that the group or organization of which the individual was a member was a criminal organization.

In Berlin, on 18 October 1945, in accordance with Article 14 of the Charter, an Indictment was lodged against the defendants named in the caption above, who had been designated by the Committee of the Chief Prosecutors of the signatory Powers as major war criminals. A copy of the Indictment in the German language was served upon each defendant in custody, at least 30 days before the Trial opened. This Indictment charges the defendants with Crimes against Peace by the planning, preparation, initiation, and waging of wars of aggression, which were also wars in violation of international treaties, agreements, and assurances; with War Crimes; and with Crimes against Humanity. The defendants are also charged with participating in the formulation or execution of a common plan or conspiracy to commit all these crimes. The Tribunal was further asked by the Prosecution to declare all the named groups or organizations to be criminal within the meaning of the Charter. * * *

The Tribunal now turns to the consideration of the crimes against peace charged in the Indictment. * * * The first acts of aggression referred to in the Indictment are the seizure of Austria and Czechoslovakia and the first war of aggression charged in the Indictment is the war against Poland begun on the 1st September, 1939. * * *

[T]he aggressive designs of the Nazi Government were not accidents arising out of the immediate political situation in Europe and the world; they were a deliberate and essential part of Nazi foreign policy. From the beginning, the National Socialist movement claimed that its object was to unite the German people in the consciousness of their mission and destiny, based on inherent qualities of race, and under the guidance of the Fuehrer. For its achievement, two things were deemed to be essential: the disruption of the European order as it had existed since the Treaty of Versailles, and the creation of a Greater Germany beyond the frontiers of 1914. This necessarily involved the seizure of foreign territories. War was seen to be inevitable, or at the very least, highly probable, if these purposes were to be accomplished. The German people, therefore, with all their resources were to be organized as a great political-military army, schooled to obey without question any policy decreed by the State. * * *

The Charter defines as a crime the planning or waging of war that is a war of aggression or a war in violation of international treaties. The Tribunal has decided that certain of the defendants planned and waged aggressive wars against twelve nations, and were therefore guilty of this series of crimes. This makes it unnecessary to discuss the subject in further detail, or even to consider at any length the extent to which these aggressive wars were also wars in violation of international treaties, agreements or assurances. * * * Those [treaties] of principal importance are the following.

Hague Conventions

In the 1899 Convention the signatory powers agreed: "before an appeal to arms . . . to have recourse, as far as circumstances allow, to the good offices or mediation of one or more friendly powers." A similar clause was inserted in the Convention for Pacific Settlement of International Disputes of 1907. In the accompanying Convention Relative to Opening of Hostilities Article I contains this far more specific language:

> "The Contracting Powers recognize that hostilities between them must not commence without a previous and explicit

> warning, in the form of either a declaration of war, giving reasons, or an ultimatum with a conditional declaration of war."

Germany was a party to these conventions.

Versailles Treaty * * *

Breaches of certain provisions of the Versailles Treaty are also relied on by the Prosecution—not to fortify the left bank of the Rhine (Art. 42–44); to "respect strictly the independence of Austria" (Art. 80), renunciation of any rights in Memel (Art. 99), and the Free City of Danzig (Art. 100), the recognition of the independence of the Czecho-Slovak State; and the Military, Naval and Air Clauses against German rearmament found in Part V. There is no doubt that action was taken by the German Government contrary to all these provisions. * * *

Treaties of Mutual Guarantee, Arbitration and Non-Aggression

It is unnecessary to discuss in any detail the various treaties entered into by Germany with other powers. Treaties of Mutual Guarantee were signed by Germany at Locarno in 1925, with Belgium, France, Great Britain and Italy, assuring the maintenance of the territorial status quo. Arbitration treaties were also executed by Germany at Locarno with Czechoslovakia, Belgium and Poland.

Article I of the latter treaty is typical, providing:

> All disputes of every kind between Germany and Poland . . . which it may not be possible to settle amicably by the normal methods of diplomacy, shall be submitted for decision either to an arbitral tribunal or to the Permanent Court of International Justice. . . .

Conventions of Arbitration and Conciliation were entered into between Germany, the Netherlands and Denmark in 1926; and between Germany and Luxemburg in 1929. Non-aggression treaties were executed by Germany with Denmark and Russia in 1939.

Kellogg-Briand Pact

The Pact of Paris was signed on the August 27, 1928, by Germany, the United States, Belgium, France, Great Britain, Italy, Japan, Poland and other countries; and subsequently by other powers. The Tribunal has made full reference to the nature of this Pact and its legal effect in another part of this judgment. It is therefore not necessary to discuss the matter further here, save to state that in the opinion of the Tribunal this Pact was violated by Germany in all the cases of aggressive war charged in the Indictment. It is to be noted that on January 26, 1930, Germany signed a Declaration for the Maintenance of Permanent Peace with Poland, which was explicitly based on the Pact of Paris, and in which the use of force was outlawed for a period of ten years. * * *

The Law of the Charter * * *

The Charter makes the planning or waging of a war of aggression or a war in violation of international treaties a crime, and it is therefore not strictly necessary to consider whether and to what extent aggressive war was a crime before the execution of the London Agreement. But in view of the great importance of the questions of law involved, the Tribunal has heard full argument from the Prosecution and the Defense, and will express its view on the matter.

It was urged on behalf of the defendants that a fundamental principle of all law—international and domestic—is that there can be no punishment of crime without a pre-existing law. "*Nullum crimen sine lege. Nulla poena sine lege.*" It was submitted that *ex post facto* punishment is abhorrent to the law of all civilized nations, that no sovereign power had made aggressive war a crime at the time the alleged criminal acts were committed, that no statute had defined aggressive war, that no penalty had been fixed for its commission, and no court had been created to try and punish offenders.

In the first place, it is to be observed that the maxim *nullum crimen sine lege* is not a limitation of sovereignty, but is in general a principle of justice. To assert that it is unjust to punish those who in defiance of treaties and assurances have attacked neighboring states without warning is obviously untrue, for in such circumstances the attacker must know that he is doing wrong, and so far from it being unjust to punish him, it would be unjust if his wrong were allowed to go unpunished. Occupying the positions they did in the government of Germany, the defendants, or at least some of them must have known of the treaties signed by Germany, outlawing recourse to war for the settlement of international disputes; they must have known that they were acting in defiance of all international law when in complete deliberation they carried out the designs of invasion and aggression. On this view of the case alone, it would appear that the maxim has no application to the present facts.

This view is strongly reinforced by a consideration of the state of international law in 1939, so far as aggressive war is concerned. The General Treaty for the Renunciation of War of 27th August, 1928, more generally known as the Pact of Paris or the Kellogg-Briand Pact, was binding on sixty-three nations, including Germany, Italy and Japan at the outbreak of war in 1939. * * *

The question is, what was the legal effect of this Pact? The nations who signed the Pact or adhered to it unconditionally condemned recourse to war for the future as an instrument of policy, and expressly renounced it. After the signing of the Pact, any nation resorting to war as an instrument of national policy breaks the Pact. In the opinion of the Tribunal, the solemn renunciation of war as an instrument of national policy necessarily involves the proposition that such a war is illegal in international law; and that those who plan and wage such a war, with its inevitable and terrible consequences, are committing a crime in so doing. War for the solution of international controversies undertaken as an instrument of national policy certainly includes a war of aggression, and such a war is therefore outlawed by the Pact. * * *

But it is argued that the Pact does not expressly enact that such wars are crimes, or set up courts to try those who make such wars. To that extent the same is true with regard to the laws of war contained in the Hague Convention. The Hague Convention of 1907 prohibited resort to certain methods of waging war. These included the inhumane treatment of prisoners, the employment of poisoned weapons, the improper use of flags of truce, and similar matters. Many of these prohibitions had been enforced long before the date of the Convention; but since 1907 they have certainly been crimes, punishable as offences against the laws of war; yet the Hague Convention nowhere designates such practices as criminal, nor is any sentence prescribed, nor any mention made of a court to try and punish offenders. For many years past, however, military tribunals have tried and punished individuals guilty of violating the rules of land warfare laid down by this Convention. In the opinion of the Tribunal, those who wage aggressive war are doing that which is equally illegal, and of much greater moment than a breach of one of the rules of the Hague Convention. In interpreting the words of the Pact, it must be remembered that international law is not the product of an international legislature, and that such international agreements as the Pact have to deal with general principles of law, and not with administrative matters of procedure. The law of war is to be found not only in treaties, but in the customs and practices of states which gradually obtained universal recognition, and from the general principles of justice applied by jurists and practiced by military courts. This law is not static, but by continual adaptation follows the needs of a changing world. Indeed, in many cases treaties do no more than express and define for more accurate reference the principles of law already existing.

The view which the Tribunal takes of the true interpretation of the Pact is supported by the international history which preceded it. In the year 1923, the draft of a Treaty of Mutual Assistance was sponsored by the League of Nations. In Article I, the Treaty declared "that aggressive war is an international crime," and that the parties would "undertake that no one of them will be guilty of its commission." The draft treaty was submitted to twenty-nine States, about half of whom were in favor of accepting the text. The principal objection appeared to be in the difficulty of defining the acts which would constitute "aggression," rather than any doubt as to the criminality of aggressive war. The preamble to the League of Nations 1924 Protocol for the Pacific Settlement of International Disputes ("Geneva Protocol"), after "recognizing the solidarity of the members of the international community," declared that "a war of aggression constitutes a violation of this solidarity and is an international crime." It went on to declare that the contracting parties were "desirous of facilitating the complete application of the system provided in the Covenant of the League of Nations for the pacific settlement of disputes between the states and of ensuring the repression of international crimes." The Protocol was recommended to the members of the League of Nations by a unanimous resolution in the Assembly of the forty-eight members of the League. These members included Italy and Japan, but Germany was not then a member of the League. Although the Protocol was never ratified, it was signed by the leading statesmen of the world, representing the vast majority of the civilized states and peoples, and may be regarded as strong evidence of the intention to brand aggressive war as an international crime. * * *

All these expressions of opinion, and others that could be cited, so solemnly made, reinforce the construction which the Tribunal placed upon the Pact of Paris, that resort to a war of aggression is not merely illegal, but is criminal. The prohibition of aggressive war demanded by the conscience of the world, finds its expression in the series of pacts and treaties to which the Tribunal has just referred. * * *

It was submitted that international law is concerned with the action of sovereign States, and provides no punishment for individuals; and further, that where the act in question is an act of state, those who carry it out are not personally responsible, but are protected by the doctrine of the sovereignty of the State. In the opinion of the Tribunal, both these submissions must be rejected. That international law imposes duties and liabilities upon individuals as well as upon States has long been recognized. * * * Many other authorities could be quoted, but enough has been said to show that individuals can be punished for violations of international law. Crimes against international law are committed by men, not by abstract entities, and only by punishing individuals who commit such crimes can the provisions of international law be enforced. * * *

Goering

Goering is indicted on all four counts. The evidence shows that after Hitler he was the most prominent man in the Nazi Regime. He was Commander-in-Chief of the Luftwaffe [the air force], Plenipotentiary for the Four Year Plan, and had tremendous influence with Hitler, at least until 1943 when their relationship deteriorated, ending in his arrest in 1945. He testified that Hitler kept him informed of all important military and political problems.

From the moment he joined the Party in 1922 and took command of the street-fighting organization, the SA [*Sturm Abteilung*, meaning "Storm Section" or "Stormtroopers"], Goering was the adviser, the active agent of Hitler and one of the prime leaders of the Nazi movement. As Hitler's political deputy, he was largely instrumental in bringing the National Socialists to power in 1933, and was charged with consolidating this power and expanding German armed might. He developed the Gestapo, and created the first concentration camps, relinquishing them to Himmler in 1934. * * * Shortly after the Pact of Munich, he announced that he would embark on a five-fold expansion of the Luftwaffe and speed rearmament with emphasis on offensive weapons.

Goering was one of the five important leaders present at the Hoszbach Conference of November 5, 1937, and he attended the other important conferences already discussed in this Judgment. In the Austrian *Anschluss*, he was indeed the central figure, the ringleader. He said in Court: "I must take 100 percent responsibility.... I even overruled objections by the Fuehrer and brought everything to its final development." In the seizure of the Sudetenland, he played his role as Luftwaffe chief, by planning an air offensive which proved unnecessary, and his role as a politician, by lulling the Czechs with false promises of friendship. The night before the invasion of Czechoslovakia and the absorption of Bohemia and Moravia, at a conference with Hitler and President Hacha he threatened to bomb Prague if Hacha did not submit. This threat he admitted in his testimony.

Even if he opposed Hitler's plans against Norway and the Soviet Union, as he alleged, it is clear that he did so only for strategic reasons; once Hitler had decided the issue, he followed him without hesitation. He made it clear in his testimony that these differences were never ideological or legal. He was "in a rage" about the invasion of Norway, but only because he had not received sufficient warning to prepare the Luftwaffe offensive. He admitted he approved of the attack: "My attitude was perfectly positive." He was active in preparing and executing the Yugoslavian and Greek campaigns, and testified that "Plan Marita," the attack on Greece, had been prepared long beforehand. The Soviet Union he regarded as the "most threatening menace to Germany," but said there was no immediate military necessity for the attack. Indeed, his only objection to the war of aggression against the U.S.S.R. was its timing; he wished for strategic reasons to delay until Britain was conquered. He testified: "My point of view was decided by political and military reasons only."

After his own admissions to this Tribunal, from the positions which he held, the conferences he attended, and the public words he uttered, there can remain no doubt that Goering was the moving force for aggressive war second only to Hitler. He was the planner and prime mover in the military and diplomatic preparation for war which Germany pursued. * * * The Tribunal finds the defendant Goering guilty on all four counts of the Indictment.

Schacht

Schacht is indicted under Counts One and Two of the Indictment. Schacht served as Commissioner of Currency land President of the Reichsbank from 1923 to 1930; was reappointed President of the bank on 17th March, 1933; Minister of Economics in August, 1934; and Plenipotentiary General for War Economy in May, 1935. * * * Schacht was an active supporter of the Nazi Party before its accession to power on January 30, 1933, and supported the appointment of Hitler to the post of Chancellor. After that date he played an important role in the vigorous rearmament program which was adopted, using the facilities of the Reichsbank to the fullest extent in the German rearmament effort. The Reichsbank, in its traditional capacity as financial agent for the German Government, floated long-term Government loans, the proceeds of which were fused for rearmament. He devised a system under which five-year notes, known as M.E.F.O. bills, guaranteed by the Reichsbank and backed, in effect, by nothing more than its position as a bank of issue, were used to obtain large sums for rearmament from the short-term money market. As Minister of Economics and as Plenipotentiary General for War Economy he was active in organizing the German economy for war. He made detailed plans for industrial mobilization and the coordination of the Army with industry in the event of war. He was particularly concerned with shortages of raw materials and started a scheme of stock-piling and a system of exchange control designed to prevent Germany's weak foreign exchange position from hindering the acquisition abroad of raw materials needed for rearmament. On May 3, 1935, he sent a memorandum to Hitler stating that "the accomplishment of the armament program with speed and in quantity is the problem of German politics, that everything else therefore should be subordinated to this purpose." * * *

It is clear that Schacht was a central figure in Germany's rearmament program, and the steps which he took, particularly in the early days of the Nazi regime, were responsible for Nazi Germany's rapid rise as a military power, but rearmament of itself is not criminal under the Charter. To be a crime against peace under Article 6 of the Charter it must be shown that Schacht carried out this rearmament as part of the Nazi plans to wage aggressive wars.

Schacht has contended that he participated in the rearmament program only because he wanted to build up a strong and independent Germany which would carry out a foreign policy which would command respect on an equal basis with other European countries; that when he discovered that the Nazis were rearming for aggressive purposes he attempted to slow down the speed of rearmament, and that after the dismissal of von Fritsch and von Blomberg he participated in plans to get rid of Hitler, first by deposing him and later by assassination

Schacht, as early as 1936, began to advocate a limitation of the rearmament program for financial reasons. Had the policies advocated by him been put into effect, Germany would not have been prepared for a general European war. Insistence on his policies led to his eventual dismissal from all positions of economic significance in Germany. On the other hand, Schacht, with his intimate knowledge of German finance, was in a peculiarly good position to understand the true significance of Hitler's frantic rearmament, and to realize that the economic policy adopted was consistent only with war as its object. * * *

Schacht was not involved in the planning of any of the specific wars of aggression charged in Count Two. His participation in the occupation of Austria and the Sudetenland (neither of which are charged as aggressive wars) was on such a limited basis that it does not amount to participation in the common plan charged in Count One. He was clearly not one of the inner circle around Hitler which was most closely involved with this common plan. He was regarded by this group with undisguised hostility. The testimony of Speer shows that Schacht's arrest on 23rd July, 1944, was based as much on Hitler's enmity towards Schacht growing out of his attitude before the war as it was on suspicion of his complicity in the bomb plot. The case against Schacht therefore depends on the inference that Schacht did in fact know of the Nazi aggressive plans.

On this all important question evidence has been given for the prosecution, and a considerable volume of evidence for the defense. The Tribunal has considered the whole of this evidence with great care, and comes to the conclusion that this necessary inference has not been established beyond a reasonable doubt. The Tribunal finds that Schacht is not guilty on this Indictment, and directs that he shall be discharged by the Marshal, when the Tribunal presently adjourns. * * *

Doenitz

Doenitz is indicted on Counts One, Two and Three. In 1935 he took command of the first U-boat flotilla commissioned since 1918, became in 1936 commander of the submarine arm, was made Vice-Admiral in 1940, Admiral in 1942, and on 30th January, 1943, Commander-in-Chief of the German Navy. On 1st May, 1945, he became the Head of State, succeeding Hitler [after Hitler committed suicide]. * * *

Although Doenitz built and trained the German U-boat arm, the evidence does not show he was privy to the conspiracy to wage aggressive wars or that he prepared and initiated such wars. He was a line officer performing strictly tactical duties. He was not present at the important conferences when plans for aggressive wars were announced, and there is no evidence he was informed about the decisions reached there. Doenitz did, however, wage aggressive war within the meaning of that word as used by the Charter. Submarine warfare which began immediately upon the outbreak of war, was fully coordinated with the other branches of the Wehrmacht. It is clear that his U-boats, few in number at the time, were fully prepared to wage war.

It is true that until his appointment in January, 1943, as Commander-in-Chief he was not an "Oberbefehlshaber". But this statement underestimates the importance of Doenitz' position. He was no mere Army or division commander. The U-boat arm was the principal part of the German fleet and Doenitz was its leader. The High Seas fleet made a few minor, if spectacular, raids during the early years of the war but the real damage to the enemy was done almost exclusively by his submarines as the millions of tons of allied and neutral shipping sunk will testify. Doenitz was solely in charge of this warfare. The Naval War Command reserved for itself only the decision as to the number of submarines in each area. In the invasion of Norway, for example, Doenitz made recommendations in October, 1939, as to submarine bases, which he claims were no more than a staff study, and in March, 1940, he made out the operational orders for the supporting U-boats, as discussed elsewhere in this Judgment.

That his importance to the German war effort was so regarded is eloquently proved by Raeder's recommendation of Doenitz as his successor and his appointment by Hitler on 30th January, 1943, as Commander-in-Chief of the Navy. Hitler too knew that submarine warfare was the essential part of Germany's naval warfare.

From January, 1943, Doenitz was consulted almost continuously by Hitler. The evidence was that they conferred on naval problems about 120 times during the course of the war.

As late as April, 1945, when he admits he knew the struggle was hopeless, Doenitz as its Commander-in-Chief urged the Navy to continue its fight. On 1st May, 1945, he became the Head of State and as such ordered the Wehrmacht to continue its war in the East, until capitulation on 9th May, 1945. Doenitz explained that his reason for these orders was to insure that the German civilian population might be evacuated and the Army might make an orderly retreat from the East.

In the view of the Tribunal, the evidence shows that Doenitz was active in waging aggressive war [and guilty on Count Two].

NOTES & QUESTIONS

1. The Elements of Crimes Against the Peace

Can you glean the elements of crimes against the peace from the Nuremberg Charter and the Judgment? How would you define the *mens rea* and *actus reus* of that crime? Does the Schacht case suggest a specific intent requirement? What attendant circumstances or jurisdictional elements, if any, does the Tribunal identify?

2. Outcome

Twelve of nineteen defendants indicted for crimes against the peace (Count 2) were convicted of that crime. Although the Prosecution indicted all twenty-four original defendants for engaging in a common plan or conspiracy to commit crimes against peace (Count 1), the Tribunal only convicted eight defendants for this crime. Of these, four were military men (Göring, Keitel, Raeder, and Jodl), two were Foreign Ministers (von Neurath and Ribbentrop), and two were high in Nazi circles (Hess and Rosenberg). Many of the defendants argued that they lacked knowledge that acts of aggression were under contemplation and thought Germany was engaging in rearmament for security and defensive purposes. Could Schacht, who financed the rearmament, not know he was helping Germany down the road to war? Was the Tribunal right to acquit him? What explanation would you give for his acquittal?

3. Dönitz and Heads of State in the Dock

At the time of his suicide, Hitler had become estranged from both Goering (also spelled Göring) and SS chief Heinrich Himmler, and so tapped Admiral Karl Dönitz (also spelled Doenitz), head of the German Navy, as his successor. It was thus left to Dönitz to negotiate Germany's surrender. Dönitz was only charged with aggression and the commission of war crimes, stemming mainly from the use of unrestricted submarine warfare with the famous U-boats—i.e., targeting Allied merchant ships without warning rather than making attacks pursuant to the law of prize. Dönitz's defense counsel, *Flottenrichter* ["Navy Judge"] Otto Kranzbuhler, submitted deposition testimony from U.S. Admiral Chester Nimitz to the Nuremberg Tribunal that admitted that Nimitz had utilized the same tactics during the war against Japan. The potency of Dönitz's *tu quoque* ("you also") defense may explain his comparatively low sentence (10 years).

Although many Nuremberg observers believe he should have been exonerated, Dönitz was convicted. Some speculate that this was because of the widespread belief that the last German head of state should not walk free. Dönitz continued to claim he was Germany's head of state into the 1950s, even while imprisoned. He thus technically qualifies as the first head of state to stand trial before an international criminal tribunal. He was followed by Jean Kambanda (the former Prime Minister of Rwanda who pled guilty to genocide and conspiracy to commit genocide in 1998), Slobodan Milošević of Yugoslavia (who died while on trial before the ICTY), Charles Taylor of Liberia, and Hissène Habré of Chad. Taylor was convicted by the Special Court for Sierra Leone, sitting in The Hague for security reasons. He was sentenced to fifty years' imprisonment for aiding rebels who committed atrocities in neighboring Sierra Leone. Habré was convicted by a hybrid international tribunal established in Senegal with African Union backing. President Omar Al-Bashir of the Sudan is the subject of two ICC arrest warrants, but remains in custody in the Sudan. The President and Deputy President of Kenya were also indicted by the ICC (though their indictments were issued before they were elected to those positions), but those cases have been suspended amidst widespread allegations of witness tampering and intimidation. Former heads of state Saddam Hussein of Iraq, José Efraín Ríos Montt of Guatemala, and Alberto Fujimori of Peru were all prosecuted for human rights abuses by their home courts. The issue of head of state immunity has emerged as a source of international controversy as discussed in Chapter 17 on Defenses.

4. Crimes Against the Peace at Tokyo

The Charter for the Tokyo Tribunal differed from the Nuremberg Charter in that it required that all defendants be charged with crimes against the peace. The indictment thus centered on crimes against the peace and various interlocking conspiracies to commit aggressive war; the war crimes and crimes against humanity charges appear as afterthoughts. The Tokyo Tribunal convicted 26 out of 28 defendants for waging aggressive war.

Justice Röling, who was one of the dissenters in the Tokyo judgment, disagreed with the conviction of some of the Japanese officials. According to Röling, Foreign Minister Tōgō, for example, assumed his position before hostilities had begun with the intention of preventing war, and Shigemitsu became Foreign Minister after the start of the war but with the intention of ending hostilities. He wrote:

> The rules as applied by the Tokyo Tribunal condemn acceptance of a responsible post, even if this is done with the design to acquit an advantageous position to promote peace.

See Bert V.A. Röling, *Crimes Against Peace in* THE CURRENT LEGAL REGULATION OF THE USE OF FORCE (Antonio Cassese, ed., 1986). Should the Tribunal have considered Tōgō's or Shigemitsu's motives for assuming their positions as relevant to the *mens rea* element of the charge? As mitigation in sentencing?

5. Crimes Against the Peace in Subsequent Proceedings

Control Council Law No. 10, which governed prosecutions before U.S. military tribunals of lesser war criminals in Germany, also provided for jurisdiction over crimes against the peace. Only a handful of defendants were convicted of aggression, however. *See* "The Ministries Case," *United States v. von Weizsaecker*, 12 TRIALS OF WAR CRIMINALS BEFORE THE NUERNBERG MILITARY TRIBUNALS UNDER CONTROL COUNCIL LAW NO. 10 (1949) (convicting three defendants of crimes against the peace). The tribunals in other cases acquitted the defendants, either because the evidence against them was lacking (i.e., the defendants were deemed to have aided the war effort but not to have planned or led it) or because it was determined that the defendants did not operate on a policy-making level. Even the defendants in the so-called High Command Case were acquitted on this latter basis, although they were convicted of war crimes and crimes against humanity. *See* "The High Command Trial," *United States v. von Leeb*, 11 TRIALS OF WAR CRIMINALS BEFORE THE NUERNBERG MILITARY TRIBUNALS UNDER CONTROL COUNCIL LAW NO. 10 (1949). There, the military tribunal ruled that

> Somewhere between the Dictator and Supreme Commander of the Military Forces of the nation and the common soldier is the boundary between the criminal and the excusable participation in the waging of an aggressive war by an individual engaged in it.

Id. at 67. Further, the tribunal required a showing that the defendant had knowledge that aggressive war was intended and was "in a position to shape or influence the policy that brings about its initiation or its continuance after initiation." *Id.* at 68. For a discussion of these historical cases and others, *see* Secretariat for the Preparatory Commission for the International Criminal Court, Working Group on the Crime of Aggression, *Historical Review of Developments Relating to Aggression*, U.N. Doc. PCNICC/2002/WGCA/L.1 (Jan. 24, 2002). Recall these cases when you review the leadership clause in the contemporary definition of the crime of aggression.

6. *Nullum Crimen Sine Lege*

How convincing is the Tribunal's response to the argument that the crimes against the peace provisions in the Charter constituted *ex post facto* law? The Right Honorable Lord Justice Lawrence, one of the Justices presiding over the Nuremberg Trial, in 1946 defended the inclusion of, and convictions for, the crime of aggression. He argued first, that the crime of aggression had already been established under international law at the time the Germans initiated their wars of aggression. And second, he argued that "the maxim *nullum crimen* is not a limitation of sovereignty but merely a general rule of justice to which there may be exceptions of which the present in any event was one. . . ." The Right Honorable Lord Justice Lawrence (The Lord Oaksey), *The Nuremberg Trial*, 23 INT'L AFF. 151, 155 (1947). Is the principle of *nullum crimen sine lege* one that should yield to the interests of justice? Would it have been preferable to simply execute the defendants—as was first advocated by the British and the Soviets—rather than subject them to what many view was a juridically imperfect process? If so, who should have been executed, who should have decided, and by what process?

7. Victor's Justice

One of the frequent criticisms of the Nuremberg and Tokyo Tribunals is that they meted out victor's justice. Justice Jackson, in his famous opening statement at the Nuremberg Tribunal, observed

> Unfortunately the nature of these crimes is such that both prosecution and judgment must be by victor nations over vanquished foes. The worldwide scope of the aggressions carried out by these men has left but few real neutrals. Either the victors must judge the vanquished or we must leave the defeated to judge themselves.

Second Day, Wednesday, 11/21/1945, Part 04, in 2 TRIAL OF THE MAJOR WAR CRIMINALS BEFORE THE INTERNATIONAL MILITARY TRIBUNAL, NUREMBERG, 14 NOVEMBER 1945–1 OCTOBER 1946, at 101. Now that the ICC can exercise jurisdiction over the crime of aggression, will the prosecution of the crime inevitably constitute a form of victor's justice? For general criticism of the Nuremberg and Tokyo trials as victor's justice, *see* Reinhold Niebuhr, *Victor's Justice: The War Crimes Trial*, 15 COMMON SENSE 6 (1946); Richard H. Minear, VICTOR'S JUSTICE: THE TOKYO WAR CRIMES TRIAL (1971).

8. The Separation of the *Jus in Bello* and the *Jus ad Bellum*

Why would contemporary law separate these two bodies of law? Should the protections of the *jus in bello* be linked to the legality of the underlying conflict? Are civilians offered greater protections if the two systems are linked or uncoupled? What protections do combatants have under the *jus in bello*? Would international law offer combatants greater protections if it developed a more robust system for the prohibition of aggressive war? For a discussion, *see* Gabriella Blum, *The Dispensable Lives of Soldiers*, 2(1) J. LEG. ANALYSIS 115 (2010).

III. THE UNITED NATIONS AND THE PROHIBITION ON THE USE OF FORCE

The offense of crimes against the peace was the centerpiece of the Nuremberg Trial, which was to be the "trial to end all wars." Indeed, the

Nuremberg Tribunal reasoned that aggressive war was the proximate cause of the other crimes within the court's jurisdiction—war crimes and crimes against humanity. Notwithstanding its prominence in the postwar period, the crime of aggression all but disappeared in the pantheon of international criminal law after World War II. Instead, the postwar architects of the United Nations enshrined a prohibition on the use of force directed at states in the U.N. Charter. Article 2(4) of the Charter reads:

> All Members shall refrain in their international relations from the threat or use of force against the territorial integrity or political independence of any state, or in any other manner inconsistent with the Purposes of the United Nations.

Although the U.N. Charter contains some key human rights provisions—most notably Articles 55 and 56 in which states pledge to take joint and several action to promote universal respect for human rights—the Charter is principally a document concerned with the maintenance of international peace and security. The U.N. Security Council bears primary responsibility for maintaining international peace, through identifying threats to the peace and acts of aggression (Article 39) and deciding on measures, including the use of armed force, on how to respond to them (Articles 41 and 42). Significantly, the Council is the only U.N. body with the express power to pass resolutions that are legally binding on all states. As briefly outlined below, however, all U.N. bodies may play a role in this regard.

The terms "crimes against the peace" and "just war" have, in modern parlance, given way to the concept of the lawful use of force and debates about when the use of force is legal or, as some have argued, an obligation in humanitarian crises. In addition to express U.N. Security Council approval, self-defense and humanitarian intervention are the two most common justifications for the use of force internationally. The former enjoys explicit mention in the U.N. Charter; the latter does not, although scholars have argued that a right to engage in humanitarian intervention survived the promulgation of the Charter and finds new life in the Responsibility to Protect ("R2P") doctrine. States have also justified the use of force to protect their own nationals outside of their territory and to support claims of self-determination. There is a large body of literature concerning each of these justifications of which we provide only a sample.

Nico Schrijver, The Use of Force Under the U.N. Charter: Restrictions and Loopholes (2003)

One of the most significant developments of the 20th century was the outlawing of the use of force as a legitimate instrument of national policy. For centuries, the right to resort to war, the *jus ad bellum*, had been considered the sovereign right of each State. But warfare deteriorated frequently into cruelties, as the Great War, which we now call the First World War, showed us: too cruel and too bloody for soldiers, too total and too dramatic for civilians. * * *

After the Great War, the League of Nations was established, the very first intergovernmental political organization in world history. This was one of the arrangements in the series of peace treaties concluded at Versailles and elsewhere during 1919–1920. One of the primary goals of the League was the maintenance of the *status quo* as it existed at the time, but based on a collective system that guaranteed peace and security. * * * Article 11 stated:

> any war, or threat of war, whether immediately affecting any of the Members of the League or not, is hereby declared a matter of concern to the whole League, and the League shall take any action that may be deemed wise and effectual to safeguard the peace of nations.

A cornerstone of this collective system was what at first glance appeared to be a unique ban on war: the High Contracting Parties wanted to achieve international peace and security "by the acceptance of obligations not to resort to war" (preamble, see also Art. 10). * * * However, this ban on the use of war had been formulated in the League's Covenant rather loosely and certainly not in an absolute way. In essence, it amounted to a cooling-off period, a moratorium, of three months and an attempt to resolve disputes by peaceful methods, such as arbitration, a judicial process or through the League's Council. But if parties did not cool off, or chose to put aside arbitral or judicial decisions, then they still had the right "to take such action as they shall consider necessary for the maintenance of right and justice" (Art. 15.7). * * *

During the time of the League of Nations various attempts were made to close the loopholes in the new law. The most impressive attempt was the Kellogg-Briand Pact of August 1928, a joint initiative of the American Secretary of State and his French colleague. In their view, the time was ripe for a "frank renunciation of war as an instrument of national policy". * * * While this Pact was not watertight, it excluded at least the so-called aggressive war. As such it gave expression to the increasing aversion to war. As early as July 25th 1929, this Pact entered into force and, quite interestingly, is still in effect today. During the post-1945 international criminal war tribunals, this Pact was invoked when accusing and convicting German and Japanese politicians of waging an aggressive war. Earlier Japan had called its invasion of Manchuria not a war but "an incident" and Italy had called its annexation of Abyssinia/ Ethiopia an "expedition." Obviously, opinions differed considerably as to what constituted war and aggression under Article 1 of the Pact.

Taking a Close Look at Article 2(4) of the U.N. Charter

Obviously, for these reasons the "founding fathers" of the United Nations opted in 1945 for the word "force" as a more encompassing term [than "war"]. After first having stipulated that all members of the new

United Nations shall settle their international disputes peacefully, Article 2, paragraph 4 of the U.N. Charter unequivocally stipulates:

> All Members shall refrain in their international relations from the threat or use of force against the territorial integrity or political independence of any state, or in any other manner inconsistent with the Purposes of the United Nations.

Hence, in principle every use of force became prohibited but solely in the relations among States. International law vests in principle each state with the monopoly of force over its own territory. From this provision in the U.N. Charter, it follows that the parties to the U.N. Charter, like the parties to the League of Nations Covenant, aimed at the maintenance of the *status quo*. The prohibition to use force was imposed to protect the territorial integrity and political independence of sovereign States. Existing boundaries would be inviolable. In rather broadly sketched terms, Article 2(4) adds that no force may be used against the purposes of the United Nations. Similarly, it ensures that "armed force will not be used, save in the common interest." Nevertheless, there can be no misunderstanding that, as the records of the San Francisco conference also show, the aim in 1945 was "to state in the broadest terms an all-inclusive prohibition without loopholes." In contrast to the Kellogg-Briand Pact, the use of force had now been embedded, at least in principle, in the Charter's collective security system that provided for the possibility of collective sanctions against an aggressor state. It may be noted that the composition and the right of veto in the Security Council make it unlikely that measures will ever be taken which are against the interests of the Permanent Five. Nonetheless, the principle of decision-making by a qualified majority, and in a Council with a limited number of members, contrasts sharply with the League of Nations where voting by unanimity was the rule and hence every member state had a veto right.

Article 2(4) can be said to be the pivot of the U.N. Charter and serves as the backbone of the envisaged system of collective security and peaceful relations among states. It has been most notably confirmed and elaborated in the 1970 U.N. General Assembly Declaration on Principles of International Law Concerning Friendly Relations and the 1974 Definition of Aggression. Article 2(4) has also been the subject of many extensive and learned analyses as well as judicial scrutiny, including at the ICJ in the *Nicaragua* case (1986); the *Advisory Opinion on Legality of Nuclear Weapons* rendered upon request of U.N. General Assembly (1996); *Yugoslavia v. NATO* (1999), and *Congo v. Uganda* (2000). Notwithstanding all of this, its interpretation is still not devoid of ambiguities. While there can be little doubt that the term "force" is meant to refer to "armed force," the scope of the prohibition of "the threat of force" is not entirely clear and perhaps also not easy to capture in precise legal rules. For example, to what extent is an ultimatum announcing recourse to military measures if certain demands are not accepted or adhered to, lawful or unlawful under Article 2(4)? Moreover, who can provide us with the ultimate interpretation of what exactly is meant by its phrase "*or* in any other manner inconsistent with the Purposes of the United Nations"?

Furthermore, in this multi-actor world one should note that the prohibition of Article 2(4) is incumbent on states only and merely applicable in '*international* relations'. Would there be a reason to seek its extension as well as that of international humanitarian law to other subjects of international law, most notably international organizations such as NATO, internationally-recognized representatives of peoples with some *de facto* control in an area or even to multinational corporations? In my view, in all cases the answer should be affirmative.

Exceptions in the Charter

The Charter itself provides for a few exceptions to the prohibition to use force. The most important one is the right to self-defense. This is called an "inherent right," in the French text "*droit naturel*," thus reflecting that it emanates from customary international law. However, the Charter qualifies the right to self-defense in a considerable way. First, it only applies "upon an armed attack." Secondly, States are under a duty to report to the Security Council when exercising their right to self-defense, a requirement that always has been taken rather lightly by both the States concerned and the Council itself. Thirdly, the right to self-defense will be suspended as soon as the Security Council has taken measures "as it deems necessary in order to maintain or restore international peace and security." This has to do with the second main exception, an order or—as is more common in the practice of the U.N.—an authorization to use force under Article 42, following a determination under Article 39 that a threat to peace, breach of peace or act of aggression has occurred. Following the end of the Cold War, the Security Council made use of this competence on a number of occasions, mainly through authorization resolutions. These cases include Somalia, East Timor and Afghanistan.

Extra-Charter Exceptions as Difficult Issues: New Directions or Deviations?

As stated earlier, the intention in 1945 was to formulate the prohibition to use force in as absolute terms as possible. Yet, in life we are not always entirely sound in the faith. A number of what we could perhaps call Charter-related and a number of extra-Charter exceptions arose.

As to the first category of Charter-related exceptions, I will discuss two. First, a central issue has been whether, next to the Charter, some customary international law could be said to survive. Does Article 51 incorporate the full law of self-defense? Yes, in case of contradictions Charter law takes priority (see Art. 103 U.N. Charter), but does not Article 51 itself refer to "*Nothing* in the Charter shall impair the *inherent* right. . ."? This issue is still important, for example with respect to the concept of pre-emption. In my view a right of anticipatory self-defense can still be said to exist as long as it meets the Webster criteria formulated on the occasion of *The Caroline* incident in 1838, that is "a necessity of self-defense, instant, overwhelming, leaving no choice of means, and no moment for deliberation." Israel called on this during the Six-Day War in 1967. This aspect of the law of self-defense may also still have relevance in a contemporary context when we are faced with serious and imminent threats of international terrorism or weapons of mass destruction. Of course, this right can easily be subject to abuse, and a mere presumption that an attack might take place is insufficient. However, it is better to recognize and if possible qualify the operation of a right to anticipatory self-defense rather than simply deny its existence, as some prefer to do.

Furthermore, in the practice of the United Nations—I am not quite sure whether I can say in the law of the United Nations—two further exceptions emerged. First, the Uniting for Peace Resolution, enabling the General Assembly in case of a breach of peace or act of aggression to recommend even military action should the Security Council be paralyzed due to a lack of agreement. There has been a full-fledged and interesting doctrinarian battle on the issue of whether or not Uniting for Peace can be viewed as to be in accordance with the Charter. Is it "Disuniting for War" rather than "Uniting for Peace," as the Soviet Union claimed it to be? It is notable that the Uniting for Peace-procedure has not often been invoked in the practice of the United Nations, despite frequent speculations. * * *

A second claimed exception, equally controversial, is the right of National Liberation Movements to use force in their legitimate struggle against colonialism, racist regimes or foreign occupation. Such a right, advocated especially during the 1970s at the level of the General Assembly, was always controversial. With the disappearance, fortunately, of the last remnants of colonialism and the apartheid regime, and with the gradual but steady recognition of the right of the Palestinian people, this claimed exception might no longer be relevant.

More relevant are two extra-Charter exceptions. Thus, it has convincingly been argued that the right of a State to rescue its nationals, if necessary by military coercion, is unaffected by the U.N. Charter. Well-known examples include the Entebbe Operation in Uganda in 1976, the failed U.S. attempt to liberate the American hostages in Tehran in 1980 and a British military action to rescue peacekeepers in Sierra Leone in 2002. Such actions raised little protest. Practice and an absence of protest, together with a widely-held conviction that a State has a right, if not a duty to protect the life of its nationals, may be another exception to Article 2(4) which cannot comfortably be placed under the scope of self-defense.

The doctrine of "humanitarian intervention" is also quoted as an extra-Charter exception. At stake here is not the protection of a State's own nationals but rather the nationals of third States. This doctrine seeks to legitimize the use of force in case of flagrant violations of human rights, without the consent of the Government of the state in which the intervention takes place and in some cases without prior authorization of the U.N. Security Council. A rather genuine and successful example is *Operation Provide Comfort* relating to the Kurdish people and Shi'ites in Northern Iraq in April 1991. A more complicated example is the NATO action in Kosovo in Spring 1999, in response to the suppression of the Albanian minority in Kosovo by the Serbs in power. My personal opinion is that there was a necessity to act militarily, but I am not quite sure whether the NATO bombing campaign can stand the test of proportionality, observance of international humanitarian law and effectiveness. Obviously, the issue of humanitarian intervention touches the very core of contemporary international law. There is a tension, if not a clash among the key principles.

On the one hand, there is the classical international law of State sovereignty, non-intervention and the cardinal principle of the prohibition to use force. On the other hand, there is the modern international law of respect for universally accepted human rights and the organization of the world as an international community, meaning more than just a "world of States." We can note that the Security Council has identified increasingly serious violations of human rights, humanitarian disasters and breaches of international humanitarian law as threats to peace. Yet, often the Security Council is divided. Does this mean that one can then conclude that States should take matters into their own hands? Preferably not, but in genuine humanitarian emergencies one cannot and should not exclude it, as a lack of protest, or acquiescence, shows in e.g. Operation Comfort, and as also recent normative developments reflect, such as the new African Union Treaty.
* * *

The challenge now is how to adapt and strengthen this system to the new reality of life after the terrorist attacks of September 11th instead of weakening it. This demands foremost a thorough appreciation of non-military means to achieve internationally agreed goals, such as more effective ("smart") sanctions, early deployment of U.N. troops with a robust mandate, weapon inspections, demobilization and disarmament. In the last few years, encouraging progress has been made on all these points, despite occasional setbacks.

The use of force can never be excluded as a final resort. This has been proven by the Security Council's decisions in the cases of Somalia, Haiti, East Timor and Afghanistan. In these cases, the "old" international law of sovereignty and non-intervention had to give way to the "new" international law aimed at preventing genocide, crimes against humanity, international terrorism, and the use of weapons of mass destruction.

Final Observations: Article 2(4) U.N. Charter, Still a Straitjacket or Are the Fences Coming Down? * * *

There are repeatedly signs that States consider the prohibition to use force under Article 2(4) to be a straitjacket. Hence all of the attempts to unravel the strings. These attempts have taken various forms and range from stretched interpretations of the Charter concepts of "armed attack" and "self-defense," through claims of emerging new U.N. law under the Uniting for Peace-procedure and claims with respect to the legitimacy of the struggle of national liberation movements, through a revival of old doctrines such as "humanitarian intervention" and "pre-emptive strikes" for whatever noble motives. These motives include promoting respect for human rights, regime change, democracy, anti-terrorism and disarmament of weapons of mass destruction. * * *

Should we in international law cross out Article 2(4) from the list of principles with the status of *jus cogens*, i.e. peremptory norm of general international law accepted and recognized by the international community of States as a whole from which no derogation is permitted and which can be modified only by a subsequent norm of general international law having the same character (Art. 53 Vienna Convention on the Law of Treaties)? These views are too harsh and too premature. While I do not subscribe to the opposite view that the use of force ought to become completely obsolete in international relations, I do believe that the current reappraisal of the use of force is a dangerous one. It can easily lead to replacing the law of the Charter by the right of the mighty, however kind-hearted the gunmen may be. But it can never be the case that new rules are made by a few militarily powerful states and their allies and then forced down the throats of other nations. Acceptance demands negotiations and final decision-making in the political nerve centre of the U.N., imperfect as that may be. *International law should not be through the barrel of a gun.* If we are not careful, we may face a dangerous appreciation of the unilateral use of force in a world that already is suffering from great discrepancies between rich and poor countries, civilizations and religions.

In sum, we should not overestimate the role of the use of force in international relations and underestimate what can be achieved by non-forcible measures. We should not neglect, let alone belittle, the notable progress in the latter field, through strengthened human rights monitoring, smart sanctions regimes, international inspection, weapon destruction, conflict prevention and pro-democratic action. Development assistance and human rights policy can play an important role in the maintenance or restoration of peace and security, either preventive or after a conflict.

NOTES & QUESTIONS

1. The U.N. Charter and Aggression

Review the provisions of the U.N. Charter concerning the use of force, especially Articles 2(4), 11, 12, 51, and Chapter VII. What, if any, guidance does the U.N. Charter provide in defining unlawful uses of force or acts of aggression? Are all unlawful acts of force as envisioned by the Charter scheme equivalent to the crime of aggression as understood at Nuremberg and Tokyo? During the debates around the ICC aggression amendments, some argued that the Security Council has the *exclusive* power to determine what constitutes aggression. *See* W. Michael Reisman, *The Definition of Aggression and the ICC*, 96 AM. SOC'Y INT'L L. PROC. 181 (2002). That same volume includes other views on the issue that differ from those expressed by Professor Reisman.

The Security Council has rarely provided any concrete standards for what constitutes an unlawful use of force under international law. Indeed, the Council's practice of declaring that a particular use of force constitutes "aggression" is somewhat checkered. On the one hand, the Council has classified conduct as "aggression" on multiple occasions over the years (most notably in connection with events in Southern Africa). These aggression determinations, however, at times employed somewhat ambiguous or inconclusive rhetoric. Sometimes members of the P-5 (the five permanent members of the Security Council) have abstained in these determinations, for example when Israel was the target of condemnation; on other occasions, the target state was an easily denounced pariah. Even the invasion of Kuwait by Iraq was only deemed "a breach of international peace and security" rather than an act of aggression. *See* U.N. Doc. S/RES/660 (Aug. 2, 1990). Nor did the Council denounce Turkey's action in Cyprus as aggression *per se*. *See* U.N. Doc. S/RES/353 (July 20, 1974) (demanding an end to foreign intervention in Cyprus and the withdrawal of foreign troops).

This haphazard practice was cited during the Review Conference of the Assembly of State Parties of the ICC in Kampala (the main agenda of which was to draft a definition of the crime of aggression) as evidence that the Council could not be trusted to make unbiased, principled, or even consistent aggression determinations. It was also argued that in cases in which potential acts of aggression were under debate, the Council would be paralyzed by political dissension, which would, in turn, immobilize the Court. Would it have been preferable to provide that the ICC could only prosecute the crime of aggression if there had been a prior Council determination that a state had committed an act of aggression?

2. The General Assembly and Aggression

While the Security Council clearly has the power to order or authorize the use of force against, among other things, an act of aggression, there is also support for the argument that the General Assembly may have similar powers. While the United States opposes this position today, it was in fact the United States that pushed for such General Assembly authority during the Korean War in 1950. After North Korea invaded South Korea, the U.S. was unable to get a resolution from the Security Council authorizing the use of force to assist South Korea because of a threatened veto by the Soviet Union. Faced with deadlock at the Security Council, the U.S. sponsored a resolution before the General Assembly giving that body power to decide issues otherwise reserved for the Security Council if the latter is unable to act. As mentioned in the excerpt above, the so-called "Uniting for Peace Resolution" provided that

> if the Security Council because of lack of unanimity of the permanent members, fails to exercise its primary responsibility for the maintenance of international peace and security in any case where there appears to be a threat to the peace, breach of the peace, or act of aggression, the General Assembly shall consider the matter immediately with a view to making appropriate recommendations to Members for collective measures, including in the case of a breach of the peace or act of aggression, the use of armed force when necessary, to maintain or restore international peace and security. If not in session at the time, the General Assembly may meet in emergency special session within twenty-four hours of the request therefor. Such emergency special session shall be called if requested by the Security Council on the vote of any seven members, or by a majority of the Members of the United Nations.

G.A. Res. 377(V) (Nov. 3, 1950). Is this Resolution consistent with the separation of powers delineated in the U.N. Charter? John Foster Dulles, who at the time was a member of the U.S. delegation to the United Nations and who eventually served as Secretary of State under President Dwight D. Eisenhower, defended the resolution as follows:

> Although the Charter gave the [Security Council (SC)] the "primary responsibility" to maintain peace and the power of the "veto," the Charter gave the Assembly the power to make recommendations, even where the SC has used the "veto" power. Article 10 gave the Assembly the power to make recommendations to Members on any matter within the scope of the Charter, excluding matters which the SC was dealing with at that time. In fact, the "veto" was approved on the condition that the Assembly would be able to make recommendations in the event that the SC was unable to discharge its primary responsibility. In addition, a recommendation does not have the full effect of a decision from the SC, but sometimes a recommendation is more effective than an "order."

Uniting for Peace: How the General Assembly Arrived at its Momentous Resolution, with the Text of the Resolution, Excerpts from the Debate, and the Conclusions of the Collective Measures Committee (U.N. Department of Public Information, 1952).

So far, the General Assembly has invoked the Uniting for Peace resolution to, *inter alia*, impose voluntary sanctions on South Africa and to provide assistance to freedom fighters (1981), to establish a commission of inquiry to consider Cold War foreign intervention in Hungary (1956), to ask the International Court of Justice to determine the legality of Israel's border wall (2003), and to establish and sustain peacekeeping forces (1956, 1960). There was talk that the Assembly could invoke this mechanism to respond to political paralysis in the Security Council over the war in Syria, but this has yet come to pass.

3. The General Assembly's Definition of Aggression

In 1974, ostensibly in order to guide the work of the Security Council, the U.N. General Assembly passed by consensus a resolution in 1974 defining aggression as follows:

United Nations General Assembly Resolution 3314 (XXIX): Definition of Aggression

> Article 1. Aggression is the use of armed force by a State against the sovereignty, territorial integrity or political independence of another State, or in any other manner inconsistent with the Charter of the United Nations, as set out in this Definition. * * *
>
> Article 2. The First use of armed force by a State in contravention of the Charter shall constitute *prima facie* evidence of an act of aggression although the Security Council may, in conformity with the Charter, conclude that a determination that an act of aggression has been committed would not be justified in the light of other relevant circumstances, including the fact that the acts concerned or their consequences are not of sufficient gravity.
>
> Article 3. Any of the following acts, regardless of a declaration of war, shall, subject to and in accordance with the provisions of article 2, qualify as an act of aggression:
>
> (a) The invasion or attack by the armed forces of a State of the territory of another State, or any military occupation, however temporary, resulting from such invasion or attack, or any annexation by the use of force of the territory of another State or part thereof;
>
> (b) Bombardment by the armed forces of a State against the territory of another State or the use of any weapons by a State against the territory of another State;
>
> (c) The blockade of the ports or coasts of a State by the armed forces of another State;
>
> (d) An attack by the armed forces of a State on the land, sea or air forces, or marine and air fleets of another State;
>
> (e) The use of armed forces of one State which are within the territory of another State with the agreement of the receiving State, in contravention of the conditions provided for in the agreement or any extension of their presence in such territory beyond the termination of the agreement;
>
> (f) The action of a State in allowing its territory, which it has placed at the disposal of another State, to be used by that other State for perpetrating an act of aggression against a third State;

(g) The sending by or on behalf of a State of armed bands, groups, irregulars or mercenaries, which carry out acts of armed force against another State of such gravity as to amount to the acts listed above, or its substantial involvement therein.

Article 4. The acts enumerated above are not exhaustive and the Security Council may determine that other acts constitute aggression under the provisions of the Charter.

Article 5.

1. No consideration of whatever nature, whether political, economic, military or otherwise, may serve as a justification for aggression.

2. A war of aggression is a crime against international peace. Aggression gives rise to international responsibility.

3. No territorial acquisition or special advantage resulting from aggression is or shall be recognized as lawful.

Article 6. Nothing in this Definition shall be construed as in any way enlarging or diminishing the scope of the Charter, including its provisions concerning cases in which the use of force is lawful.

Article 7. Nothing in this Definition, and in particular article 3, could in any way prejudice the right to self-determination, freedom and independence, as derived from the Charter, of peoples forcibly deprived of that right and referred to in the Declaration on Principles of International Law concerning Friendly Relations and Cooperation among States in accordance with the Charter of the United Nations, particularly peoples under colonial and racist regimes or other forms of alien domination: nor the right of these peoples to struggle to that end and to seek and receive support, in accordance with the principles of the Charter and in conformity with the above-mentioned Declaration.

Definition of Aggression, G.A. Res. 3314 (XXIX), U.N. GAOR, 6th Comm., 29th Sess., 2319th plen. mtg. (Dec. 14, 1974). The definition never really served its intended purpose, however, and it has made little appreciable impact on Security Council deliberations. It is, however, generally accepted as an accurate interpretation of the Charter. For example, the International Court of Justice in the *Nicaragua* decision stated that the definition in Article 3 reflected customary international law. *Case Concerning Military and Paramilitary Activities in and against Nicaragua (Nicar. v. U.S.),* Merits, 1986 I.C.J. Reports 14, 103. Can the elements of a penal offense be discerned from the definition of aggression set forth in Resolution 3314? Does the definition cover all situations that in your view qualify as aggression? What acts, if any, would you add? Does the definition leave any room for a doctrine of humanitarian intervention? Recall this Resolution when you review modern attempts to define the crime of aggression in the next part of this chapter.

4. The ICJ and the Prohibition Against Aggression

The excerpt above notes that the International Court of Justice (ICJ), among other bodies, has repeatedly stated that the prohibition against unlawful uses of force and acts of aggression is an obligation *erga omnes*—an obligation in which all states have an interest. The ICJ has considered alleged violations of these rules a number of times since its establishment. The first involved a case brought by Nicaragua against the United States, in which the Court found that the financing and arming of paramilitary forces active against Nicaragua (the *Contras*) constituted a violation of the prohibition against the use of force under international law. *Military and Paramilitary Activities in and Against Nicaragua* 1986 I.C.J. Reports 14 (Merits judgment of June 27, 1986). More recently, the Democratic Republic of the Congo (DRC) brought claims against Rwanda, Uganda, and Burundi alleging unlawful uses of force. (See the Appendix for a map of the DRC situating it in the region.) The case against Burundi was withdrawn by the DRC, *Armed Activities on the Territory of the Congo (Democratic Republic of the Congo v. Burundi)*, 2001 I.C.J. Reports 3 (Order of January 30, 2001); the case against Rwanda was dismissed for lack of jurisdiction, *Armed Activities on the Territory of the Congo (Democratic Republic of the Congo v. Rwanda)*, 2006 I.C.J. Reports 6 (Judgment of February 3, 2006); the case against Uganda resulted in a finding that Uganda had violated the prohibition against the use of force, although its conduct did not rise to the level of aggression, *Armed Activities on the Territory of the Congo (Democratic Republic of the Congo v. Uganda)*, 2005 I.C.J. Reports 168 (Judgment of December 19, 2005).

Serbia and Montenegro brought claims of aggression against ten NATO states for their military intervention in Kosovo in 1999. (See the Appendix for a map of Yugoslavia showing Serbia, Montenegro, and Kosovo.) The cases were dismissed for lack of jurisdiction. *See Legality of Use of Force (Serbia and Montenegro v. Belgium at al.)* (Judgment of December 15, 2004). Iran brought a claim against the United States for military attacks against certain oil platforms, alleging a violation of international law generally as well as of a Treaty of Amity, Economic Relations, and Consular Relations between the two countries. *Oil Platforms (Islamic Republic of Iran v. United States of America)* (Judgment of November 6, 2003). While the Court concluded there was no violation of the treaty, it also found that the U.S. attack against the oil platforms was not a legitimate act of self-defense. To what extent might this jurisprudence guide the ICC in adjudicating cases involving allegations of the crime of aggression?

5. Self-Defense

Most of the debate concerning self-defense centers on the application and interpretation of Article 51 of the U.N. Charter. Article 51 codifies the long-held position that a state may use force either individually or collectively in self-defense against an "armed attack"—a term that does not seem to encompass all threats and uses of force prohibited by Article 2(4). The drafters of Article 51 of the U.N. Charter deliberately chose the phrase "armed attack" instead of "aggression" to describe the precondition for acting in legitimate self-defense. Why do you think this choice was made? If a state is invaded by another state, there is no question that the invaded state and its allies may use force to repel the invading army. The invasion of Kuwait by Iraq in 1990 is a classic example of an act of aggression that triggered a collective response in self-defense. When self-defense may be utilized against activities that fall short of a full-scale invasion remains a point of contention. Although there is a growing consensus that states may utilize self-defense against non-state actors situated outside of a state's territory, this position is not yet uniformly espoused.

Furthermore, a state is not required to wait until it is actually invaded before using force in self-defense. A state may use force in anticipation of an invasion if the threat to which it is responding is instant, overwhelming, and leaves no choice of means and no time for deliberation. This formulation of *anticipatory self-defense* is derived from the case of *The Caroline*, which involved an attack in 1837 against The Caroline, a U.S. flag ship, near the Canadian border by British forces claiming to be acting preemptively in self-defense. The legal formulation of anticipatory self-defense that derives from this incident is found in a 1842 letter from the U.S. Secretary of State, Daniel Webster, to the British Foreign Ministry.

In 2002, the Administration of President George W. Bush articulated a new doctrine of *preventative self-defense* in the face of more remote threats based upon a lesser showing of imminence. Under this doctrine, the U.S. asserted the right to attack preemptively a state or other entity that posed a threat to the United States. Does Article 51 allow for anticipatory self-defense or preventative war? How should the ICC treat claims of preemptive or preventative self-defense? Will the ICC have the institutional capacity to consider such claims?

6. Libya

As the Arab Spring unfolded around the region, demonstrations in Libya quickly devolved into a full-scale civil war. After Muammar Gaddafi threatened to slaughter his opponents in Benghazi—the epicenter of the rebellion—the Security Council, acting under Chapter VII, issued Resolution 1970 on February 26, 2011, which referred the situation in Libya since February 13, 2011, to the International Criminal Court. The resolution purported to limit the ICC's personal jurisdiction as follows:

> [N]ationals, current or former officials or personnel from a State outside the Libyan Arab Jamahiriya which is not a party to the Rome Statute of the International Criminal Court shall be subject to the exclusive jurisdiction of that State for all alleged acts or omissions arising out of or related to operations in the Libyan Arab Jamahiriya established or authorized by the Council, unless such exclusive jurisdiction has been expressly waived by the State.

Less than a month later, the Council passed Resolution 1973, noting that while Libya bore the primary responsibility for protecting its populace, widespread and systematic attacks continued to be committed against the civilian population and may amount to crimes against humanity. In addition, it demanded an immediate ceasefire and no-fly zone and authorized member states,

> acting nationally or through regional organizations or arrangements . . . to take all necessary measures . . . to protect civilians and civilian populated areas under threat of attack . . . while excluding a foreign occupation force of any form on any part of Libyan territory.

Russia and China, among other Council members, abstained during the vote.

"All necessary measures" is a standard formulation indicating an authorization to use military force. Accordingly, on March 19, 2011, members of NATO and other coalition members launched attacks against Libyan air defense systems and other military targets to enforce the no-fly zone and disrupt ongoing attacks against civilians. Gaddafi's announcement of a ceasefire was greeted with profound skepticism. Attacks on Libyan forces as well as Gaddafi's compound gave rise to criticism among some states that the coalition had "taken sides" and, in so doing, gone beyond the Security Council mandate to protect civilians in favor of regime change. After being charged by the ICC, Gaddafi was executed by rebels after being captured while hiding in a storm drain.

If the ICC had been able to assert jurisdiction over the crime of aggression at the time of the Libya operation, under what circumstances (if ever) would aggression charges be appropriate against coalition members? The Russian Foreign Minister stated that the ICC should look into cases of NATO airstrikes that resulted in civilian deaths. Would Resolution 1970 preclude such an investigation into NATO actions?

IV. CONTEMPORARY DEFINITION OF THE CRIME OF AGGRESSION

As discussed above, aggression was one of the first crimes prosecuted at the international level under the definition set forth in the Nuremberg and Tokyo Charters. None of the modern *ad hoc* international criminal tribunals asserted jurisdiction over the crime of aggression, however, even though the crime was arguably relevant to the Yugoslavian, Sierra Leonean, and East Timorese contexts. There is one exception: the Iraqi Special Tribunal, which had jurisdiction over designated Iraqi laws, could assert jurisdiction over "the abuse of position and the pursuit of policies that may lead to the threat of war or the use of the armed forces of Iraq against an Arab country" (Article 14(c)). President Saddam Hussein was executed for crimes against humanity committed in the village of Dujail before he could be prosecuted under this provision for launching the First Gulf War.

The crime of aggression has been central to the efforts since World War II to establish a permanent international criminal court. In the immediate postwar period, the General Assembly charged the International Law Commission (ILC) with promulgating a Draft Code of Offenses Against the Peace and Security of Mankind. It was contemplated that this Code could be applied by national courts pending the establishment of an international court. The ILC's project stalled in

1954, however, when the General Assembly postponed further work until a new special committee on aggression finalized its work.* The U.N. General Assembly ultimately convened several such committees, which eventually generated the consensus definition contained in General Assembly Resolution 3314 (1974) that was meant to guide the Security Council in implementing its peace and security mandate. After a period of Cold War quiescence, the General Assembly invited the ILC to resume work on the Draft Code in the 1980s. This, coupled with the establishment of the first *ad hoc* criminal tribunals in the 1990s, helped revive the idea of a permanent international criminal court (ICC).

During the negotiations that ensued surrounding the establishment of the ICC, the crime of aggression again emerged as a sticking point. The definition of aggression in Resolution 3314 was influential, but many delegates took the view that it did not easily lend itself to a penal context. As a result, other options were explored.** Delegates attending six sessions of Preparatory Committees in 1996–1998 and the 1998 Rome Conference—where the ICC Statute was finally opened for signature—were again unable to agree on the definition of aggression or on a jurisdictional regime to govern the crime's prosecution. And so, at the last minute, delegates agreed to punt, listing the crime of aggression in the Court's jurisdiction but delaying consideration of the details to a mandatory Review Conference to be convened in seven years' time per Article 123 of the Statute. The only guidance the negotiators in Rome offered their successors was the cryptic declaration in Article 5(2) that any pre-conditions for the exercise of jurisdiction over the crime of aggression should be "consistent with the relevant provisions of the Charter of the United Nations." A series of Preparatory Committees (1999–2002), Special Working Groups (2003–2009), and informal gatherings held at Princeton University (2004–2007) then took up the task in the period leading up to the 2010 Review Conference of the Assembly of State Parties in Kampala, Uganda.

During this time, delegates came back full circle. By 2008, they had agreed upon a definition of the crime of aggression based largely on Resolution 3314 and the U.N. Charter:

Article 8*bis*: Crime of Aggression

1. For the purpose of this Statute, "crime of aggression" means the planning, preparation, initiation or execution, by a person in a position effectively to exercise control over or to direct the political or military action of a State, of an act of

---

* Draft Code of Offences Against the Peace and Security of Mankind, G.A. Res. 897 (IX), U.N. Doc. A/RES/897(IX) (Dec. 4, 1954) (postponing work on the Draft Code in light of the convening of a Special Committee of representatives from nineteen member states to consider the crime of aggression).

** *See, e.g.*, Int'l Criminal Court, Assembly of States Parties, Special Working Grp. on the Crime of Aggression, 5th Sess., Nov. 23–Dec. 1, 2006, *Informal Inter-Sessional Meeting of the Special Working Group on the Crime of Aggression*, U.N. Doc. ICC-ASP/5/SWGCA/INF.1 (Sept. 5, 2006).

> aggression which, by its character, gravity and scale, constitutes a manifest violation of the Charter of the United Nations.
>
> 2. For the purpose of paragraph 1, "act of aggression" means the use of armed force by a State against the sovereignty, territorial integrity or political independence of another State, or in any other manner inconsistent with the Charter of the United Nations. Any of the following acts, regardless of a declaration of war, shall, in accordance with United Nations General Assembly resolution 3314 (XXIX) of 14 December 1974, qualify as an act of aggression . . . .

The text goes on to list all the acts enumerated in Resolution 3314 as acts of aggression:

> (a) The invasion or attack by the armed forces of a State of the territory of another State, or any military occupation, however temporary, resulting from such invasion or attack, or any annexation by the use of force of the territory of another State or part thereof;
>
> (b) Bombardment by the armed forces of a State against the territory of another State or the use of any weapons by a State against the territory of another State;
>
> (c) The blockade of the ports or coasts of a State by the armed forces of another State;
>
> (d) An attack by the armed forces of a State on the land, sea or air forces, or marine and air fleets of another State;
>
> (e) The use of armed forces of one State which are within the territory of another State with the agreement of the receiving State, in contravention of the conditions provided for in the agreement or any extension of their presence in such territory beyond the termination of the agreement;
>
> (f) The action of a State in allowing its territory, which it has placed at the disposal of another State, to be used by that other State for perpetrating an act of aggression against a third State;
>
> (g) The sending by or on behalf of a State of armed bands, groups, irregulars or mercenaries, which carry out acts of armed force against another State of such gravity as to amount to the acts listed above, or its substantial involvement therein.

Although this definition enjoyed a shaky consensus going into Kampala, several states remained ill at ease. Most vocal was the United States once it began participating in the aggression negotiations as an observer in November 2009.* Although the definition of the crime resisted amendment from this point forward, the United States did manage to massage the definition in Kampala with several interpretive Understandings that are contained in the final Resolution adopting the amendments. These read:

6. It is understood that aggression is the most serious and dangerous form of the illegal use of force; and that a determination whether an act of aggression has been committed requires consideration of all the circumstances of each particular case, including the gravity of the acts concerned and their consequences, in accordance with the Charter of the United Nations.
7. It is understood that in establishing whether an act of aggression constitutes a manifest violation of the Charter of the United Nations, the three components of character, gravity and scale must be sufficient to justify a "manifest" determination. No one component can be significant enough to satisfy the manifest standard by itself.

In Kampala, the State Parties also adopted elements of the crime of aggression:

1. The perpetrator planned, prepared, initiated or executed an act of aggression.
2. The perpetrator was a person in a position effectively to exercise control over or to direct the political or military action of the State which committed the act of aggression.
3. The act of aggression—the use of armed force by a State against the sovereignty, territorial integrity or political independence of another State, or in any other manner inconsistent with the Charter of the United Nations—was committed.
4. The perpetrator was aware of the factual circumstances that established that such a use of armed force was inconsistent with the Charter of the United Nations.
5. The act of aggression, by its character, gravity and scale, constituted a manifest violation of the Charter of the United Nations.
6. The perpetrator was aware of the factual circumstances that established such a manifest violation of the Charter of the United Nations.

The majority of the negotiations during the Review Conference focused almost exclusively on the jurisdictional regime to govern the crime. This regime is different depending on the trigger mechanism by

* By way of disclosure, one author of this casebook (Prof. Van Schaack) was the Academic Adviser to the U.S. interagency delegation involved in these negotiations.

which the situation is brought before the Court. For situations subject to a state referral or *proprio motu* investigation, the following provisions apply:

Article 15*bis*: Exercise of Jurisdiction over the Crime of Aggression

4. The Court may, in accordance with article 12, exercise jurisdiction over a crime of aggression, arising from an act of aggression committed by a State Party, unless that State Party has previously declared that it does not accept such jurisdiction by lodging a declaration with the Registrar. The withdrawal of such a declaration may be effected at any time and shall be considered by the State Party within three years.
5. In respect of a State that is not a party to this Statute, the Court shall not exercise its jurisdiction over the crime of aggression when committed by that State's nationals or on its territory.
6. Where the Prosecutor concludes that there is a reasonable basis to proceed with an investigation in respect of a crime of aggression, he or she shall first ascertain whether the Security Council has made a determination of an act of aggression committed by the State concerned. The Prosecutor shall notify the Secretary-General of the United Nations of the situation before the Court, including any relevant information and documents.
7. Where the Security Council has made such a determination, the Prosecutor may proceed with the investigation in respect of a crime of aggression.
8. Where no such determination is made within six months after the date of notification, the Prosecutor may proceed with the investigation in respect of a crime of aggression, provided that the Pre-Trial Division has authorized the commencement of the investigation in respect of a crime of aggression in accordance with the procedure contained in article 15, and the Security Council has not decided otherwise in accordance with article 16.
9. A determination of an act of aggression by an organ outside the Court shall be without prejudice to the Court's own findings under this Statute.

By contrast, per Article 15ter, a Security Council referral does not require any prior determination that a state committed an act of aggression by either the Council or the Pre-Trial Division. Nor is any opt-out available.

Although the Assembly of State Parties in Kampala agreed to amendments to the Rome Statute defining the crime of aggression, two conditions were required for them to come into effect. First, the crime of aggression could not be prosecuted until one year after the amendments were ratified or accepted by thirty States Parties. On June 26, 2016, the State of Palestine became the thirtieth state to ratify the amendments on the crime of aggression. As of July 1, 2019, thirty-eight states had ratified the Kampala amendments. Second, the Assembly of States Parties (ASP) had to decide to activate them no sooner than January 1, 2017. On December 14, 2017, the Assembly of State Parties adopted by consensus a resolution activating jurisdiction over the crime of aggression as of July 17, 2018 (twenty years to the day of the adoption of the ICC Statute in Rome in 1998).

NOTES & QUESTIONS

1. Definition

Are there interpretive concerns raised by the definition of the crime of aggression as adopted in Kampala? What does "manifest" modify? What does the term signify in this context? One group of delegates wanted no such threshold at all on the theory that every act of aggression should be subject to prosecution. A second group of delegates wanted a higher threshold, one that would limit prosecutions to "flagrant" breaches of the Charter, wars of aggression, "unlawful" uses of force, or acts of aggression aimed at the occupation or annexation of territory. What is the relationship between an "act of aggression" and the "crime of aggression" in Article 8*bis*, the Elements, and the Understandings? Would attempts to commit aggression be prosecutable?

2. Leadership Clause

As a result of the aggression amendments, Article 25(3) of the Statute has been amended to read:

> 3*bis*. In respect of the crime of aggression, the provisions of this article shall apply only to persons in a position effectively to exercise control over or to direct the political or military action of a State.

What caliber of defendant will this limitation leave subject to prosecution? How does this provision compare with the approach adopted at Nuremberg and Tokyo? Is this language consistent with the Nuremberg precedent as you understand it?

3. Jurisdictional Filters

What role does the Security Council play in prosecutions for the crime of aggression? What about the Pre-Trial Division (composed of the Pre-Trial judges sitting *en banc*)? The question of whether prosecutions for the crime of aggression should be subject to a jurisdictional filter remained contentious throughout the aggression negotiations. The P-5 and several other states favored designating the Security Council as an exclusive and determinative filter. Under this system, in the absence of a prior Security Council determination that the state in question had committed an act of aggression, prosecution for the crime would be barred. This approach would have required the Council not only to muster the necessary majority but also to gain the affirmative vote or abstention of the P-5 per U.N. Charter, Art. 27(3):

> Decisions of the Security Council on all other matters shall be made by an affirmative vote of nine members including the concurring votes of the permanent members. . . .

If the Security Council did not make the necessary determination, no aggression charges could be brought, although the Prosecution could investigate other ICC crimes committed within the same situation. This approach was premised on the argument that the Council enjoys the primary, if not exclusive, role of addressing threats to and breaches of the peace in the U.N. Charter system.

Opponents of an exclusive role for the Security Council proposed alternative or back-up filter mechanisms in the event that the Council failed, or was unable, to make the necessary aggression determination. These alternative filters were designed to ensure that Security Council inaction would not be fatal to an investigation into potential crimes of aggression. Candidates for this back-up filter included the General Assembly, the International Court of Justice (ICJ), and the Court itself. Beyond these alternative filters, several delegations advanced two more permissive options: first, no filter whatsoever; and second, no back-up filter in the event of Security Council inaction.

Which position would you have favored and why? What logistical problems can you foresee had delegates chosen to empower the General Assembly or ICJ with a filter role? How exactly will the tandem filters work in practice? Why is there no filter for Security Council referrals per Article 15*ter*?

4. The Jurisdictional Regime

What is the impact of Article 15*bis*(4)? Article 15*bis*(5)? Why would the ASP members agree to such gaps in the jurisdictional regime? How will the opt-out work in practice? The text states that the opt-out must be lodged "previously", but previously to what? Must states opt-out prior to or at the time of ratification, or can they opt-out later? Must they opt-out prior to the commission of the putative act of aggression or only prior to the exercise of jurisdiction by the Court? The main drafter of the provision, Stefan Barriga, has stated that "previously" means prior to an act of aggression. Stefan Barriga, *Exercise of Jurisdiction and Entry into Force of the Amendments on the Crime of Aggression*, *in* FROM ROME TO KAMPALA: THE FIRST 2 AMENDMENTS TO THE ROME STATUTE 31 (Gérad Dive, Benjamin Goes & Damien Vandermeersch eds., 2012). In addition, can a state file a "partial opt-out" with respect to a single situation (such as when they are participating in a peacekeeping operation, intervening on humanitarian grounds, or engaged in hot pursuit)? Or, could a state opt-out of any exercise of jurisdiction arising out of a situation triggered by the Security Council, or by the *proprio motu* powers of the Prosecutor?

As of July 1, 2019, only two states have lodged a declaration under Article 15*bis*(4) opting out of the ICC's jurisdiction over crimes of aggression: Kenya and Guatemala. In its resolution, Kenya raised concerns about paragraph 2(f) of Article 8*bis* (reproduced above), claiming that this paragraph will "constrain states' right to request [the] intervention of neighboring states in order to restore peace and security within its territory." The Guatemalan declaration stated that Guatemala would not accept the jurisdiction over the crime of aggression until it had completed its own internal process of ratification of the amendments.

5. Negotiating Dynamics

The negotiating dynamics in Kampala were considerably more complex than they had been at the initial Rome Conference. In Rome, the so-called "Like-Minded States," overwhelmingly supported by the non-governmental organization (NGO) community, were able to garner a large and disparate alliance in favor of a strong and largely independent Court. In Kampala, by contrast, the negotiations over the crime of aggression splintered along more diverse fault lines. Prominent in one camp were the P-5, along with a few key allies, who sought to limit the prosecution of the crime of aggression. In addition, this camp insisted that the U.N. Charter and policy considerations required that the Security Council have the exclusive power to control prosecutions for the crime of aggression.

A second camp—featuring many members of the group of Latin American and Caribbean Countries (GRULAC), the so-called "African Group" of States Parties, a handful of European states and other smaller States Parties—defended the expansive definition of the crime. They also pushed for a jurisdictional regime that would apply without requiring state consent and would be unfettered by the Security Council (or at least no more fettered than it was vis-à-vis the original core crimes of genocide, crimes against humanity, and war crimes). A third group of diverse States Parties were wary of according the Security Council hegemony over the question of aggression but did not share the larger coalition's preference for an expansive aggression regime. They sought alternative ways to cabin the Court's jurisdiction over the crime that would not alienate the Council's permanent members.

NGOs were also split. Some remained agnostic toward the crime on the ground that evaluating the use of force ostensibly fell outside their mandate; others opposed the inclusion of the crime in the ICC Statute out of fear that it would distract the Court from the atrocity crimes; and still others supported including the crime as a way to prevent the commission of other crimes within the Court's jurisdiction and bring about a more peaceful world. Which group would you say prevailed in Kampala? Are there obvious compromises in the provisions adopted? For a discussion of the negotiation dynamics, *see* Beth Van Schaack, *Negotiating at the Interface of Power & Law: The Crime of Aggression*, 49 COLUM. J. TRANSNAT'L L. 505 (2011); Jennifer Trahan, *The Rome Statute's Amendment on the Crime of Aggression: Negotiations at the Kampala Review Conference*, 11 INT'L CRIM. L. REV. 49 (2011); THE CRIME OF AGGRESSION—A COMMENTARY (Claus Kreß & Stefan Barriga eds., 2016). The P-5 had difficulty asserting their full influence in Kampala. With China, Russia, and the United States all serving as observers during the negotiations, and the United States a latecomer at that, it was left to France and the United Kingdom (the P-2) to formally defend Security Council privileges.

What are the most compelling legal arguments in favor of Security Council exclusivity in the aggression realm? Are there policy arguments in favor of granting the Security Council a central role in any aggression prosecution? What are the countervailing arguments? How might the Security Council's past practice have limited its permanent members' ability to assert their interests in Kampala? Review the Understandings above that were pushed by the United States. Why do you think the United States advocated this language? For a detailed discussion of the U.S. position at Kampala, *see* Harold Hongju Koh & Todd F. Buchwald, *The Crime of Aggression: The United States Perspective*, 109 AM. J. INT'L L. 257 (2015). Professor Koh was the co-head, and Mr. Buchwald was the co-deputy head, of the U.S. delegation to the Kampala Conference.

6. Complementarity and the Crime of Aggression

How will the principle of complementarity apply in the aggression context? Most domestic penal codes do not include a crime of aggression. *See* Astrid Reisinger Coracini, *Evaluating Domestic Legislation on the Customary Crime of Aggression Under the Rome Statute's Complementarity Regime*, *in* THE EMERGING PRACTICE OF THE INTERNATIONAL CRIMINAL COURT 735 (Carsten Stahn & Göran Sluiter eds., 2009) (cataloging approximately two dozen national codes containing a version of the crime of aggression). Most definitions that do exist date from the immediate post-World War II period, and it appears that none has been invoked in an actual prosecution. Similarly, most domestic crimes would not cover the same conduct at issue in an aggression charge, viz. "the planning, preparation, initiation or execution . . . of an act of aggression." If a domestic system is unable to prosecute an individual suspect for the crime of aggression, but can assert jurisdiction over other atrocity crimes, would a case involving an act of aggression be admissible under Article 17 of the ICC Statute? Should the ICC assert jurisdiction under these circumstances?

7. Domesticating the Crime of Aggression

In addition to the Understandings set forth above concerning the definition of the crime, the ASP also adopted two Understandings on the exercise of domestic jurisdiction over the crime.

> 4. It is understood that the amendments that address the definition of the act of aggression and the crime of aggression do so for the purpose of this Statute only. The amendments shall, in accordance with article 10 of the Rome Statute, not be interpreted as limiting or prejudicing in any way existing or developing rules of international law for purposes other than this Statute.
>
> 5. It is understood that the amendments shall not be interpreted as creating the right or obligation to exercise domestic jurisdiction with respect to an act of aggression committed by another State.

What is the intent of these Understandings? Are States Parties obliged to harmonize their penal codes with the substantive law of the ICC Statute? Consider the language of the ICC Statute's Preamble in this regard. Should

States Parties include the crime of aggression, as defined by Article 8*bis*, in their domestic law? Should the ASP encourage States Parties to prosecute the crime of aggression domestically? Under what circumstances? Does universal jurisdiction apply to the crime of aggression?

8. The Understandings

What legal authority should the Court accord the Understandings? Are they binding on States Parties? Article 21, which lists applicable sources of law, says nothing about such provisions. Article 21 reads:

> The Court shall apply:
>
> (a) In the first place, this Statute, Elements of Crimes and its Rules of Procedure and Evidence;
>
> (b) In the second place, where appropriate, applicable treaties and the principles and rules of international law, including the established principles of the international law of armed conflict;
>
> (c) Failing that, general principles of law derived by the Court from national laws of legal systems of the world including, as appropriate, the national laws of States that would normally exercise jurisdiction over the crime, provided that those principles are not inconsistent with this Statute and with international law and internationally recognized norms and standards.

The Vienna Convention on the Law of Treaties—a treaty on treaties—contains the following rules on treaty interpretation:

> Article 31: General rule of interpretation
>
> 1. A treaty shall be interpreted in good faith in accordance with the ordinary meaning to be given to the terms of the treaty in their context and in the light of its object and purpose.
>
> 2. The context for the purpose of the interpretation of a treaty shall comprise, in addition to the text, including its preamble and annexes:
>
>   (a) any agreement relating to the treaty which was made between all the parties in connection with the conclusion of the treaty;
>
>   (b) any instrument which was made by one or more parties in connection with the conclusion of the treaty and accepted by the other parties as an instrument related to the treaty.
>
> 3. There shall be taken into account, together with the context:
>
>   (a) any subsequent agreement between the parties regarding the interpretation of the treaty or the application of its provisions;

(b) any subsequent practice in the application of the treaty which establishes the agreement of the parties regarding its interpretation;

(c) any relevant rules of international law applicable in the relations between the parties.

Article 32: Supplementary means of interpretation

Recourse may be had to supplementary means of interpretation, including the preparatory work of the treaty and the circumstances of its conclusion, in order to confirm the meaning resulting from the application of article 31, or to determine the meaning when the interpretation according to article 31:

(a) leaves the meaning ambiguous or obscure; or

(b) leads to a result which is manifestly absurd or unreasonable.

Where do the Understandings fit within this interpretive scheme? If the ASP wanted to guarantee the binding nature of the Understanding, what should it do? For a discussion, *see* Kevin Jon Heller, *The Uncertain Legal Status of the Aggression Understandings*, 10 J. INT'L CRIM. JUSTICE 229 (2012).

9. Humanitarian Intervention

Humanitarian intervention involves the involvement of a state or a collective of states, with or without authorization from the U.N. Security Council, in the territory of another state for the promotion or protection of basic human rights in situations in which the territorial state is perpetuating abuses or is unable or unwilling to provide the necessary protection to vulnerable individuals. Humanitarian intervention boasts a long pedigree—Grotius argued in 1625 that " 'war for the subjects of another [is] just, for the purpose of defending them from injuries inflicted by their ruler' [if the] 'tyrant . . . practices atrocities toward his subjects which no just man can approve.' " Malvina Halberstam, *The Legality of Humanitarian Intervention*, 3 CARDOZO J. INT'L & COMP. L. 1, 2–3 (1995) (quoting Grotius, VINDICAE CONTRA TYNRANNOS (1625)).

The legality, morality, and wisdom of humanitarian intervention in modern times remains contested. Whereas the concept of self-defense is well established under international law, the right to use force in defense of others is less so. Advocates of an emerging norm in favor of humanitarian intervention raise a host of arguments, including textual ones that attempt to carve out an exception for humanitarian intervention from the language of Article 2(4) of the Charter; moral claims drawing on natural law theory; and customary international law-based theories looking to state practice. The Genocide Convention provides some positive law in support of humanitarian intervention, as it speaks of an obligation to "prevent" acts of genocide, which some scholars and activists point to as providing a legal justification for the use of military force in the face of genocide. The failure of the world's strongest military powers to intervene in, *inter alia*, (1) Cambodia, to stop the crimes against humanity committed by the Khmer Rouge regime from 1975–1979; (2) Bosnia and Herzegovina, to stop the ethnic cleansing and other crimes against humanity that commenced there in 1991; and (3) Rwanda, to stop the genocide of 1994, led to increasing calls for a recognition of the right, and for some an obligation, to intervene to stop the worst international crimes.

In part due to these past failures, NATO forces attacked the Federal Republic of Yugoslavia in 1998 in response to alleged atrocities committed by that government's military forces in the province of Kosovo. The intervention occurred without express Security Council authorization. An independent commission of experts brought together by the Swedish Prime Minister, Goran Persson, concluded that there was not yet a basis under international law for humanitarian intervention. Independent International Commission on Kosovo, THE KOSOVO REPORT: CONFLICT, INTERNATIONAL RESPONSE, LESSONS LEARNED (Oxford University Press, 2000). The Commission controversially concluded that while the intervention was illegal (as it did not enjoy Security Council approval), it was nonetheless legitimate. Allegations of violations of *jus in bello* committed by NATO troops in Kosovo were discussed in Chapter 7 on War Crimes. The Kosovo precedent was not uniformly praised, however. The Group of 77 issued a statement in April 2000, stressing

> The need to maintain a clear distinction between humanitarian assistance and other activities of the United Nations. We reject the so-called "right" of humanitarian intervention, which has no legal basis in the United Nations Charter or in the general principles of international law.

Responding to a plea from then Secretary-General Kofi Annan to explore the "responsibility to protect" as a basis for collective action in the face of atrocities, Canada convened an International Commission on Intervention and State Sovereignty (ICISS). The Commission's 2001 report concluded that a responsibility to protect (R2P) existed under international law. The report noted the need to strike a balance between, on the one hand, not undermining the U.N. system and international order by sanctioning unilateral interventions and, on the other hand, not allowing atrocities to continue when the Security Council fails to act. *See* International Commission on Intervention and State Sovereignty, THE RESPONSIBILITY TO PROTECT (2001). In the meantime, the African Union's Constitutive Act (2000) preserved the "right of the Union to intervene in a Member State pursuant to a decision of the Assembly in respect of grave circumstances, namely war crimes, genocide and crimes against humanity."

In a major initiative, the U.N. subsequently recognized:

> The emerging norm that there is a collective international responsibility to protect, exercisable by the Security Council authorizing military intervention as a last resort, in the event of genocide and other large-scale killing, ethnic cleansing or serious violations of international humanitarian law which sovereign Governments have proved themselves powerless or unwilling to prevent.

The U.N. Secretary-General's High-Level Panel on Threats, Challenges and Change, *A More Secure World: Our Shared Knowledge*, ¶ 202, U.N. Doc. A/59/565 (Dec. 2, 2004). The High-Level Panel focused on five criteria for legitimacy: the seriousness of the threat, the right purpose of the interveners, the exhaustion of other options (diplomacy or sanctions), the proportionality of the response, and the balance of the consequences. *Id.* at 207. In the 2005 World Summit Outcome document, states pledged their support to the R2P concept:

> 138. Each individual State has the responsibility to protect its populations from genocide, war crimes, ethnic cleansing and crimes against humanity. This responsibility entails the prevention of such crimes, including their incitement, through appropriate and necessary means. We accept that responsibility and will act in accordance with it. The international community should, as appropriate, encourage and help States to exercise this responsibility and support the United Nations in establishing an early warning capability.
>
> 139. The international community, through the United Nations, also has the responsibility to use appropriate diplomatic, humanitarian and other peaceful means, in accordance with Chapters VI and VIII of the Charter, to help protect populations from genocide, war crimes, ethnic cleansing and crimes against humanity. In this context, we are prepared to take collective action, in a timely and decisive manner, through the Security Council, in accordance with the Charter, including Chapter VII, on a case-by-case basis and in cooperation with relevant regional organizations as appropriate, should peaceful means be inadequate and national authorities manifestly fail to protect their populations from genocide, war crimes, ethnic cleansing and crimes against humanity. * * * We also intend to commit ourselves, as necessary and appropriate, to helping States build capacity to protect their populations from genocide, war crimes, ethnic cleansing and crimes against humanity and to assisting those which are under stress before crises and conflicts break out.

This formulation contains three pillars: (1) states bear the primary responsibility to protect their populations from international crimes, (2) the wider international community should assist states in meeting this obligation, but (3) stand ready to "take collective action, in a timely and decisive manner, through the Security Council" in the event that the state has "manifestly fail[ed]" in this regard.

Interested parties continue to grapple with the specifics of identifying substantive criteria to evaluate interventions, mechanisms for doing so within and without the U.N. institutional framework, operational considerations, and means to protect against abuses of the doctrine. Do the proposed amendments on the crime of aggression and the contemporaneous Understandings exclude military actions under R2P from the ambit of the crime of aggression? To what extent should the drafters of the aggression amendments have carved out an explicit exception to the definition of aggression for military actions taken to protect individuals from the commission of other Rome Statute crimes: genocide, crimes against humanity, or war crimes? The potential criminality of humanitarian actions involving military force under the new amendments is posed by the Kosovo and Syria Problems below.

PROBLEMS

1. Kosovo

Revisit the facts of NATO's 1999 intervention in Kosovo presented in the Problem in the prior chapter on War Crimes. Consider also the following. The Security Council condemned the situation in Kosovo as a threat to international peace and security in a number of resolutions. *See, e.g.*, S.C. Res. 1160, S/RES/1160 (Mar. 31, 1998); S.C. Res. 1199, S/RES/1199 (Sept. 23, 1998); S.C. Res. 1239, S/RES/1239 (May 14, 1999); S.C. Res. 1244, S/RES/1244 (June 10, 1999). In these Resolutions, the Council acknowledged Kosovo as a humanitarian tragedy; demanded a cessation of violence on all sides and a political solution to the conflict; reaffirmed the territorial integrity of the former Yugoslavia, and called for an international civil and security presence in Kosovo. It did not, however, use the word "aggression" or authorize states to deploy "all necessary means" in response. Yugoslavia did not comply with these resolutions.

Many members of the Security Council apparently favored a more robust intervention, but Russia—which had ethnic and other affiliations with the Yugoslav leadership—and China would not support a resolution to this effect. NATO thus undertook the intervention without express Security Council approval. The intervention was met with general acquiescence or even support by most, but by no means all, members of the international community. A resolution before the Security Council to condemn the action was defeated, and the Council subsequently engaged in conflict management and other activities following the intervention. It has been argued that the Council subsequently ratified NATO's intervention in Kosovo in Resolution 1244 (1999) when it approved the Kosovo settlement and international security intervention (but without mention of NATO's intervention). Neither the U.N. General Assembly nor the U.N. Commission on Human Rights (now the Human Rights Council) censured NATO members for intervening.

Would the Kosovo intervention constitute the crime of aggression under the aggression amendments? Assume the ICC Statute was in force at the time, and you were the Chief Prosecutor, would you initiate an investigation? If so, what sort of evidence would you seek to amass in order to satisfy each element of the crime? Given the proposed leadership clause, whom might you seek to prosecute for the crime? How might such a case come to the Court? If Yugoslavia or some other state made a referral of the situation to the Court for investigation and prosecution, would you be compelled to go forward or could you exercise prosecutorial discretion and decline to prosecute? (See Article 53 of the ICC Statute). Might proceedings before the ICC contribute to the crystallization of a norm in favor or opposed to humanitarian interventions? How?

2. North Korea

After a long occupation dating from the first Sino-Japanese War (1894–96), Japan ruled the Korean peninsula as a quasi-colony from 1910 until the conclusion of World War II. (See the Appendix for a map of Korea.) At that time, the victorious Allies divided the peninsula along the 38th parallel. United States troops occupied the south, which established a government under the leadership of Syngman Rhee in 1948. In the meantime, Soviet troops occupied the north, which eventually established a communist government under Kim Il-Sung. Reunification negotiations failed, and tensions along the border between the two halves of the peninsula intensified as the two sides launched raids and skirmishes.

On June 25, 1950, North Korean forces invaded South Korea across the 38th parallel. The U.N. Security Council condemned the invasion in Resolution 82 as a breach of international peace and recommended that member states provide military assistance in Resolution 83. The Soviet Union did not participate in the proceedings, as it was boycotting the Council in protest of the fact that the Republic of China (Taiwan) and not the People's Republic of China held the permanent seat in the Council. The United States—with U.N. backing—launched a counter-offensive, which the United States described as a "police action." Mirroring Cold War alliances, China entered the war on the side of North Korea and the Soviet Union. After a series of defeats, U.S. forces held the advancing North Koreans at the southern port city of Pusan. The armies remained in a standoff until U.S. forces landed behind North Korean lines at Inchon taking North Korean forces by surprise. The U.S. forces pursued the retreating North Koreans across the 38th parallel up to the Yalu River. Once at the Yalu, the Chinese army intervened, engaging U.S. forces and driving them back across the 38th parallel. U.S. forces launched a counter-offensive, slowly pushing the North Korean and Chinese forces back across the 38th parallel, where the two armies remained in a stalemate for two years.

An armistice signed on July 27, 1953, ended the active conflict although a full peace agreement has never been reached. The two countries remain separated by a two-mile-wide Demilitarized Zone (DMZ). Tensions on the Peninsula have waxed and waned over the years. In particular, several disputes have erupted over the location of the maritime border between North and South Korea, known as the Northern Limit Line. The North has refused to accept the location of the border, drawn unilaterally by U.S.-led forces at the end of the Korean War. In June of 1999, after a naval standoff in which North Korean ships repeatedly crossed the Northern Limit Line, South Korea sank a North Korean torpedo boat and damaged several others, killing 30 North Koreans. The two navies again traded gunfire in June of 2002 resulting in six South Korean and thirteen North Korean deaths. Another exchange of fire between North and South Korean ships in November 2009 reportedly left a North Korean patrol boat retreating in flames.

On March 26, 2010 the Cheonan Warship, a 1,200-tonne gunboat flying a South Korean flag, split in two and sank after an explosion close to the Northern Limit Line. Forty-six crew members were killed. No civilians were injured. Drawing on eye witness accounts, an examination of the damage to the vessel, an analysis of seabed evidence, and the recovered torpedo, a joint military/civilian multinational team concluded that the ship was sunk by a North Korean torpedo. There was "no other plausible explanation." North Korea denied responsibility and argued that the evidence against it was fabricated and that the sinking was faked by Seoul. China did not accept the investigative results and blocked the U.N. Security Council resolution condemning the North Korea for the attack.

In March 2013 the Human Rights Council established a commission of inquiry (COI) with Resolution 22/13 for the purpose of "investigating the systematic, widespread and grave violations of human rights" in the state of North Korea "with a view to ensuring full accountability, in particular, for violations that may amount to crimes against humanity." The COI cataloged a whole range of human rights violations attributed to the state and its instrumentalities, including arbitrary arrest and detention, torture and inhuman treatment, enforced disappearances, and murder. It concluded that North Korea had committed crimes against humanity pursuant to policies established at the highest level of the state. The report does not address the sinking of the Cheonan to any extent.

South Korea deposited its instrument of ratification of the Rome Statute in 2002; North Korea is not a party to the treaty. The Office of the Prosecutor of the International Criminal Court conducted a preliminary examination into the situation on the territory of South Korea. Would you consider the attack on the Cheonan to constitute the crime of aggression within the ICC definition? If the aggression amendments had been in place, how might this incident come before the Court? Assuming the Court's jurisdiction had been properly triggered, should the Prosecutor move forward? Are there countervailing considerations? What other charges might be brought? In June 2014, the Prosecutor closed her preliminary examination into these matters. Can you envisage why?

3. Stuxnet

The Islamic Republic of Iran began its first nuclear program in the 1960s under the last Shah, Mohammad Reza Pahlavi, but abandoned it after the 1979 revolution. In the mid-1990s, Iran resurrected its program and began building nuclear reactors to enrich uranium for medical reactors and nuclear power. It justified its nuclear program on the ground that it preferred to sell its oil on the more lucrative world market than to use it domestically. Under the Nuclear Non-Proliferation Treaty, to which Iran is a party, Iran has the right to enrich uranium for peaceful purposes. Western nations and Israel believe, however, that Iran is processing uranium to develop a nuclear weapon.

In 2002, an Iranian exile group obtained documents showing that Iran had in fact been running a clandestine nuclear program. The international community responded by threatening to impose sanctions on Iran. To prevent sanctions, the government of Mohammed Khatami suspended uranium enrichment in 2003 and allowed inspections by the International Atomic Energy Agency (IAEA). In elections held in January 2005, Mr.

Khatami was replaced as President of Iran by Mr. Mahmoud Ahmadinejad, who ordered the resumption of the enrichment work. The IAEA called for a halt to the program until questions regarding the alleged clandestine program were answered. Iran defied the IAEA, prompting the Security Council to impose sanctions on the country.

In 2007, the United States estimated that Iran would likely be able to produce a nuclear weapon between 2010 and 2015. In 2008, Israel secretly requested specialized bunker-busting bombs from the United States, presumably for an attack on Iran's main nuclear complex at Natanz, which is eight kilometers underground. President Bush denied the request as well as Israel's request to fly over Iraq to reach Natanz, stating that he had authorized new covert action intended to sabotage Iran's nuclear program. In September 2009, the United States, France and the United Kingdom revealed the existence of a secret Iranian underground plant. An article by Dan Williams of Reuters, published in July of that year, stated that Israel was looking into non-military options, such as cyber-warfare, to prevent a nuclear Iran.

In February of 2010, the IAEA stated that they had extensive evidence of "past or current undisclosed activities" by Iran's military to develop a nuclear warhead. *See* IAWA, Implementation of the NPT Safeguards Agreement and Relevant Provision of Security Council Resolutions 1737 (2006), 1747 (2007), 1803 (2008) and 1835 (2008) in the Islamic Republic of Iran, GOV/2010/10 (Feb. 18, 2010). In April, the United States estimated that Iran could produce enough weapons-grade material for a nuclear bomb within a year, but would need two to five years to manufacture a workable nuclear weapon. In June, the Security Council voted to impose a fourth round of sanctions on Iran after international inspectors detailed how they had been denied access to facilities in Iran.

In July 2010, Iran discovered a computer worm in the computers of its nuclear plant in Natanz. The Stuxnet worm had reportedly been in place undetected since January, most likely delivered to the plant by an infected USB drive. The particular worm is the first of its kind: a highly complex program that infects only industrial systems created by a single company, Siemens of Germany. While the worm has been found in industrial systems in other countries, over 60% of the computers affected are in Iran. The worm reprograms centrifuges, causing them to change speeds rapidly. Such precipitous fluctuations, experts say, can cause the centrifuges to blow apart. Iran stated that only a limited number of centrifuges were affected, but inspectors reveal that since 2009, hundreds of centrifuges were removed from Iran's main nuclear plant. Cyber-security experts state that the worm's complexity means that it would have taken six to ten highly skilled programmers a period of six months to create it, suggesting some form of government sponsorship. The United States denies any involvement. Experts speculate that Israel's equivalent of the U.S. National Security Agency, Unit 8200, would have the capability and motivation to create and deliver the worm.

Assuming a state sponsored the Stuxnet attack, are the elements of the crime of aggression satisfied on the above facts? How would this case come before the International Criminal Court? Should the Prosecutor and Court pursue this case? If this attack had taken place within the context of an armed conflict, how would it be evaluated under international humanitarian law in terms of the principles of distinction, proportionality, and humanity?

4. Syria

The civil war in Syria began in April 2011 when the Syrian Government deployed its army to quell popular demonstrations demanding the resignation of Syrian President Bashar al-Assad, whose family has ruled the country since 1971. An armed opposition coalesced and clashes intensified. The International Committee of the Red Cross declared the existence of a full-scale civil war in July 2012, triggering the application of international humanitarian law across Syria. A year later, the death toll had surpassed 100,000.

On August 20, 2012, in remarks to the White House press corps, President Obama warned the Syrian government not to use chemical weapons. He stated:

> We cannot have a situation where chemical or biological weapons are falling into the hands of the wrong people. . . . We have been very clear to the Assad regime—but also to other players on the ground—that a red line for us is we start seeing a whole bunch of chemical weapons moving around or being utilized. That would change my calculus; that would change my equation.

In May 2013, the General Assembly invoked the Responsibility to Protect with respect to Syria in Resolution 67/262 in which it condemned "the failure of the Government of the Syrian Arab Republic to protect its population" and demanded that the authorities "meet their responsibility to protect the population." Action in the Security Council, however, was blocked due to Russia's exercise of its veto. In response to a draft resolution (S/2011/612) condemning the violence in Syria and threatening more coercive measures, Russia at one point invoked Libya:

> The situation in Syria cannot be considered in the Council separately from the Libyan experience. The international community is alarmed by statements that compliance with Security Council resolutions on Libya in the NATO interpretation is a model for the future actions of NATO in interpreting the responsibility to protect. . . . [I]t is very important to know how the resolution was implemented and how a Security Council resolution turned into its opposite. . . . The . . . no-fly zone has morphed into the bombing of oil refineries, television stations and other civilian sites.

A year after President Obama issued his "red line," and as later confirmed by a United Nations inspection team, the government of Syria launched surface-to-surface rockets containing sarin gas into opposition-controlled areas around the city of Ghouta—the deadliest chemical weapon attack since the Iran-Iraq war (1980–88). Sarin is a highly volatile nerve agent that causes a whole range of physiological reactions upon exposure, including blurred vision, nausea, respiratory problems and asphyxiation, confusion and neurological damage, paralysis, headaches, and metabolic changes. Hundreds of individuals were killed, and thousands more were exposed to the toxin during the attack. The attack was widely condemned. The U.N. Advisers on the Responsibility to Protect and the Prevention of Genocide issued a joint statement on August 22, 2013, stating that "there was never any military justification for the use of chemical weapons . . . given their horrific and indiscriminate impact" and calling for accountability for those responsible. NATO condemned the attack and indicated that the use of chemical weapons is a threat to international peace and security.

On August 29, 2013, the United Kingdom issued a Legal Memorandum on its position regarding the legality of military action in Syria:

> If action in the Security Council is blocked, the UK would still be permitted under international law to take exceptional measures in order to alleviate the scale of the overwhelming humanitarian catastrophe in Syria by deterring and disrupting the further use of chemical weapons by the Syrian regime. Such a legal basis is available under the doctrine of humanitarian intervention. . .

Days later, President Obama indicated that he would seek authorization from Congress to strike Syria, although he made clear that he believed he had constitutional authority to act without Congressional approval. On September 4, 2013, the U.S. Senate Foreign Relations Committee approved a joint resolution authorizing a limited use of force against military objectives within Syria to respond to its apparent use of chemical weapons in Ghouta. The resolution set forth four objectives: (1) to respond to the use of weapons of mass destruction; (2) to deter future uses of such weapons; (3) to degrade Syria's capacity to use such weapons; and (4) to prevent their transfer to terrorist groups. Similar language is contained in a Joint Statement on Syria issued at the G20 Summit on September 6, 2013. In public remarks, the U.S. Permanent Representative to the United Nation, Samantha Power, argued that

> the international system that was founded in 1945 . . . has not lived up to its promise or its responsibilities in the case of Syria. . . . Syria is one of those occasions—like Kosovo—when the Council is so paralyzed that countries have to act outside it if they are to prevent the flouting of international laws and norms.

Despite this high-level support for the use of military force, various Congressional whip counts suggested that the full Congress would not pass the resolution.

At this point, President Vladimir Putin of Russia suggested a diplomatic solution: Syria would put its chemical arsenals under international control and consent to their destruction. A Syrian spokesperson welcomed the Russian proposal as a means to "avert American aggression" against the Syrian people. On September 14, 2013, and as part of the Russian-brokered deal, Syria joined 190 other state parties in acceding to the Convention on the Prohibition of the Development, Production, Stockpiling and Use of Chemical Weapons and on their Destruction, an arms control treaty that outlaws the production, stockpiling, or use of chemical weapons and their precursors. The Russian-United States Framework for Elimination of Syrian Chemical Weapons was blessed in Security Council Resolution 2118. In it, the Council decided to impose measures under Chapter VII in the event of non-compliance, although was silent on what measures were contemplated.

Beyond an ambiguous counter-terrorism resolution involving the Islamic State, the Security Council has never authorized the use of force in Syria, leaving states to find their own legal justifications for their kinetic involvement in the conflict. On April 4, 2017, the town of Khan Sheikhoun in Idlib province experienced a devastating chemical attack—the deadliest since Ghouta—with a sarin-like substance. Days later, the U.S. Administration of Donald Trump unilaterally launched cruise missiles against Syria's Sahyrat air base from which the attack was thought to have been unleashed. The Council called an emergency meeting at which time Russia exercised its veto (for the eighth time since the war began) in response to a draft resolution initiated by the United States that would have condemned the chemical weapons attack and called for full and free inspections. In its justifying its veto, Russia insisted that voting for the resolution would have legitimized the illegal U.S. air strikes. France expressed support for the United States' operation as a "legitimate response to a mass crime that could not go unpunished."

A 2019 chemical weapon attack in the Damascene suburb of Douma provoked a second major round of air strikes involving the United States, France, and the United Kingdom. Russia immediately called for an emergency session of the Council. U.N. Secretary-General António Guterres opened the session with an admonition that any use of chemical weapons is "abhorrent," but in the same breath reminded all member states of their Charter obligations. The Russian Permanent Representative introduced a draft resolution that would have condemned the coalition operation as an act of aggression and read a statement from President Putin to this effect. The United States rejected this conclusion and explained that it had acted "to deter the future use of chemical weapons by holding the Syrian regime responsible for its crimes against humanity" in a way that was "justified, legitimate and proportionate." U.N. Ambassador Nikki Haley blamed Russia for defending Assad's use of "barbaric weapons." She also warned that the United States stood ready to act again if necessary: "When our President draws a red line, our President enforces the red line."

In addition to a deterrence rationale, the United Kingdom invoked the doctrine of humanitarian intervention. It reasoned: "Any State is permitted under international law, on an exceptional basis, to take measures in order to alleviate overwhelming humanitarian suffering" so long as there is convincing evidence of extreme humanitarian distress, there is no practicable alternative, and the use of force is necessary and proportionate to the underlying humanitarian aid. France noted that the use of chemical weapons constitutes a war crime within the Rome Statute and, in an explanation sounding of reprisals, justified its participation as necessary to address the Syrian regime's repeated violations of international law. Poland overtly supported the action, whereas the Netherlands described the response as "understandable" and "measured." A number of states reiterated calls for the perpetrators of the chemical attacks to be held accountable, including via action outside the Security Council. Other members did not express their views on the strikes other than to counsel restraint, express their condemnation of the use of chemical weapons, and urge a political resolution to the conflict. Russia's proposed draft resolution gained the support of only three states: Bolivia, China, and Russia.

At the time of publication, the situation in Syria is not before the ICC. Although a number of states, non-governmental organizations, and U.N. officials have urged the Security Council to refer the situation to the Court, Russia and China vetoed a draft referral resolution in 2014. Would the U.S.-led airstrikes constitute the crime of aggression as formulated within the ICC Statute? If the referral resolution had passed, might these strikes have opened up U.S. personnel to prosecution for the crime of aggression in the event that the ICC would have jurisdiction over the situation in Syria? Would the aggression amendments have deterred the Trump Administration? Are the articulated justifications for the use of force in Syria consistent with the R2P doctrine? Are the aggression amendments likely to deter, or over-deter, military solutions to situations such as Syria?

CHAPTER 9

GENOCIDE

I. INTRODUCTION

It has been said that "genocide is a modern word for an old crime." When the Allies liberated the Nazi concentration camps, revealing the horrific scope of the Nazi "Final Solution," the world community was faced with the challenge of how to understand the enormity of the Holocaust. As an initial response, and in reply to Winston Churchill's portrayal of the Nazi extermination program as a "crime without a name," the Polish scholar and jurist Raphaël Lemkin coined the term "genocide" from the Greek word *genos* (race, tribe) and the Latin word *caedere* (to kill). For Lemkin, who had fled Poland upon the German invasion, the critical elements of genocide were not the individual acts, though they may be crimes in themselves, but the broader aim to destroy entire human collectivities. *See* Raphaël Lemkin, AXIS RULE IN OCCUPIED EUROPE 79 (1944).

The Nuremberg Charter did not include the crime of genocide as a prosecutable crime. Nonetheless, the indictment of October 8, 1945, against the major Nazi war criminals was the first international document to employ this neologism, albeit only in passing and not as a charged offense. The indictment accused the defendants of conducting

> deliberate and systemic genocide, *viz.*, the extermination of racial and national groups, against the civilian populations of certain occupied territories in order to destroy particular races and classes of people and national, racial or religious groups. . . .

Indictment of Herman Göring et al., 1 TRIAL OF THE MAJOR WAR CRIMINALS BEFORE THE INTERNATIONAL MILITARY TRIBUNAL 43–44 (1947). In their closing arguments, Nuremberg prosecutors argued that the defendants had engaged in

> the scientific and systematic extermination of millions of human beings and more especially of certain national or religious groups whose existence hampered the hegemony of the German race. This is a crime so monstrous, so undreamt of in history . . . that the term "genocide" has had to be coined to define it.

19 TRIAL OF THE MAJOR WAR CRIMINALS BEFORE THE INTERNATIONAL MILITARY TRIBUNAL 531 (1948) (final statement of Chief Prosecutor for the French Republic M. Auguste Champetier De Ribes).

Lemkin was the first to advocate the promulgation of a comprehensive convention condemning genocide. On November 9, 1946, in its first session, the U.N. General Assembly referred a draft resolution condemning the crime of genocide to the Sixth (Legal) Committee of the

General Assembly. The Committee returned the following resolution, which the General Assembly unanimously adopted:

> Genocide is a denial of the right of existence of entire human groups, as homicide is the denial of the right to live of individual human beings; such denial of the right of existence shocks the consciences of mankind, results in great losses to humanity in the form of cultural and other contributions represented by these human groups, and is contrary to moral law and the spirit and aims of the United Nations.
>
> Many instances of such crimes of genocide have occurred when racial, religious, political and other groups have been destroyed, entirely or in part.
>
> The punishment of the crime of genocide is a matter of international concern.
>
> The General Assembly, therefore,
>
> Affirms that genocide is a crime under international law which the civilized world condemns . . . whether the crime is committed on religious, racial, political or any other grounds.

G.A. Res. 96 (IX), at 188–89, U.N. Doc. A/64/Add. 1 (Dec. 11, 1946).

From this start, an *ad hoc* Committee of the Economic and Social Council drafted a Convention on Genocide that was forwarded to the Sixth Committee. The draft Convention announced that its express purpose was "to prevent [the] destruction of racial, national, linguistic, religious, or political groups of human beings," because genocide "inflicts irreparable loss on humanity by depriving it of the cultural and other contributions of the group so destroyed." Convention on the Prevention and Punishment of the Crime of Genocide, Secretariat Draft, U.N. Doc. E/447 (May 1947). The Sixth Committee formulated the final treaty text, which defines the crime of genocide in Article II of the Genocide Convention as:

> In the present Convention, genocide means any of the following acts committed with intent to destroy, in whole or in part, a national, ethnical, racial or religious group, as such:
>
> (a) Killing members of the group;
>
> (b) Causing serious bodily or mental harm to members of the group;
>
> (c) Deliberately inflicting on the group conditions of life calculated to bring about its physical destruction in whole or in part;
>
> (d) Imposing measures intended to prevent births within the group;

(e) Forcibly transferring children of the group to another group.

This definition has been incorporated verbatim into the statutes of the *ad hoc* criminal tribunals and the International Criminal Court (ICC). While there have been some prosecutions for genocide before the International Criminal Tribunal for the Former Yugoslavia (ICTY), all the defendants before the International Criminal Tribunal for Rwanda (ICTR) have been charged with participation of one sort or another in this "crime of crimes."

II. PROTECTED GROUPS

The Genocide Convention protects four delineated groups: national, ethnic, racial, and religious groups. This limitation was contentious at the time of the drafting of the Convention and remains a major source of criticism of the Convention today. The implication of a closed list of protected persons arose in the first international genocide prosecution and judgment since the promulgation of the Convention. Jean-Paul Akayesu was the *bourgmestre* (principal magistrate) of Taba commune during the Rwandan genocide. As *bourgmestre*, Akayesu was responsible for

> the performance of executive functions and the maintenance of public order within his commune, subject to the authority of the prefect. He had exclusive control over the communal police, as well as any *gendarmes* [police officers] put at the disposition of the commune. He was responsible for the execution of laws and regulations and the administration of justice, also subject only to the prefect's authority.

Prosecutor v. Akayesu, Case No. ICTR–96–4–T, Indictment, para. 4 (Sept. 2, 1998). Akayesu was charged with individual criminal responsibility and superior responsibility for genocide against Tutsi individuals within his commune. The judgment against him follows. (For a brief history of the Rwandan genocide, see Chapter 6 on the Legal Regulation of Armed Conflict. See the Appendix for a map of Rwanda.)

The Prosecutor v. Akayesu, Case No. ICTR–96–4–T, Judgement (Sept. 2, 1998)

In the Trial Chamber

Historical Context of the Events in Rwanda in 1994

78. It is the opinion of the Chamber that, in order to understand the events alleged in the Indictment, it is necessary to say, however briefly, something about the history of Rwanda, beginning from the pre-colonial period up to 1994.

79. Rwanda is a small, very hilly country in the Great Lakes region of Central Africa. Before the events of 1994, it was the most densely populated country of the African continent (7.1 million inhabitants for 26,338 square kilometres). Ninety per cent of the population lives on agriculture. Its per capita income is among the lowest in the world, mainly because of a very high population pressure on land. * * *

81. Rwanda [during colonial rule] had some eighteen clans defined primarily along lines of kinship. The terms Hutu and Tutsi were already in use but referred to individuals rather than to groups. In those days, the distinction between the Hutu and Tutsi was based on lineage rather than ethnicity. Indeed, the demarcation line was blurred: one could move from one status to another, as one became rich or poor, or even through marriage.

82. Both German and Belgian colonial authorities, if only at the outset as far as the latter are concerned, relied on an elite essentially composed of people who referred to themselves as Tutsi, a choice which, according to Dr. Alison Desforges [an expert witness from Human Rights Watch], was born of racial or even racist considerations. In the minds of the colonizers, the Tutsi looked more like them, because of their height and colour, and were, therefore, more intelligent and better equipped to govern.

83. In the early 1930s, Belgian authorities introduced a permanent distinction by dividing the population into three groups which they called ethnic groups, with the Hutu representing about 84% of the population, while the Tutsi (about 15%) and Twa (about 1%) accounted for the rest. In line with this division, it became mandatory for every Rwandan to carry an identity card mentioning his or her ethnicity. The Chamber notes that the reference to ethnic background on identity cards was maintained, even after Rwanda's independence and was, at last, abolished only after the tragic events the country experienced in 1994. * * *

85. From the late 1940s, at the dawn of the decolonization process, the Tutsi became aware of the benefits they could derive from the privileged status conferred on them by the Belgian colonizers and the Catholic church. They then attempted to free themselves somehow from Belgian political stewardship and to emancipate the Rwandan society from the grip of the Catholic church. The desire for independence shown by the Tutsi elite certainly caused both the Belgians and the church to shift their alliances from the Tutsi to the Hutu, a shift rendered more radical by the change in the church's philosophy after the second world war, with the arrival of young priests from a more democratic and egalitarian trend of Christianity, who sought to develop political awareness among the Tutsi-dominated Hutu majority.

86. Under pressure from the United Nations Trusteeship Council and following the shift in alliances just mentioned, Belgium changed its policy by granting more opportunities to the Hutu to acquire education

and to hold senior positions in government services. This turn-about particularly angered the Tutsi, especially because, on the renewal of its mandate over Rwanda by the United Nations, Belgium was requested to establish representative organs in the Trust territory, so as to groom the natives for administration and, ultimately, grant independence to the country. The Tutsi therefore began the move to end Belgian domination, while the Hutu elite, for tactical reasons, favoured the continuation of the domination, hoping to make the Hutu masses aware of their political weight in Rwanda, in a bid to arrive at independence, which was unavoidable, at least on the basis of equality with the Tutsi. Belgium particularly appreciated this attitude as it gave it reason to believe that with the Hutu, independence would not spell a severance of ties.

87. In 1956, in accordance with the directives of the United Nations Trusteeship Council, Belgium organized elections on the basis of universal suffrage in order to choose new members of local organs, such as the grassroots representative Councils. With the electorate voting on strictly ethnic lines, the Hutu of course obtained an overwhelming majority and thereby became aware of their political strength. The Tutsi, who were hoping to achieve independence while still holding the reins of power, came to the realization that universal suffrage meant the end of their supremacy; hence, confrontation with the Hutu became inevitable.
* * *

89. The dreaded political unrest broke out in November 1959, with increased bloody incidents, the first victims of which were the Hutu. In reprisal, the Hutu burnt down and looted Tutsi houses. Thus became embedded a cycle of violence which ended with the establishment on 18 October 1960, by the Belgian authorities, of an autonomous provisional Government headed by Grégoire Kayibanda, President of MDR Parmehutu [a Hutu political party], following the June 1960 communal elections that gave an overwhelming majority to Hutu parties. After the Tutsi monarch fled abroad, the Hutu opposition declared the Republic of Gitarama, on 28 January 1961, and set up a legislative assembly. On 6 February 1961, Belgium granted self-government to Rwanda. Independence was declared on 1 July 1962, with Grégoire Kayibanda at the helm of the new State, and, thus, President of the First Republic.

90. The victory of Hutu parties increased the departure of Tutsi to neighbouring countries from where Tutsi exiles made incursions into Rwanda. The word *Inyenzi,* meaning cockroach, came to be used to refer to these assailants. Each attack was followed by reprisals against the Tutsi within the country and in 1963, such attacks caused the death of at least ten thousand of them, further increasing the number of those who went into exile. Concurrently, at the domestic level, the Hutu regime seized this opportunity to allocate to the Hutu the lands abandoned by Tutsi in exile and to redistribute posts within the Government and the civil service, in favour of the Hutu, on the basis of a quota system linked to the proportion of each ethnic group in the population.

91. The dissensions that soon surfaced among the ruling Hutu led the regime to strengthen the primacy of the MDR Parmehutu party over all sectors of public life and institutions, thereby making it the *de facto* sole party. * * * From then onwards, a rift took root within the Hutu political Establishment, between its key figures from the Centre and those from the North and South who showed great frustration. Increasingly isolated, President Kayibanda could not control the ethnic and regional dissensions. The disagreements within the regime resulted into anarchy, which enabled General Juvénal Habyarimana, Army Chief of Staff, to seize power through a coup on 5 July 1973. General Habyarimana dissolved the First Republic and established the Second Republic. Scores of political leaders were imprisoned and, later, executed or starved to death, as was the case with the former President, Grégoire Kayibanda.

92. Following a trend then common in Africa, President Habyarimana, in 1975, instituted the one-party system with the creation of the Mouvement révolutionnaire national pour le développement (MRND), of which every Rwandan was a member *ipso facto*, including the newborn. Since the party encompassed everyone, there was no room for political pluralism. A law passed in 1978 made Rwanda officially a one-party State with the consequence that the MRND became a "State-party," as it formed one and the same entity with the Government. * * *

93. Like his predecessor, Grégoire Kayibanda, Habyarimana strengthened the policy of discrimination against the Tutsi by applying the same quota system in universities and government services. * * * On 1 October [1991], an attack was launched from Uganda by the Rwandan Patriotic Front (RPF) whose forebear, the Alliance rwandaise pour l'unité nationale ("ARUN"), was formed in 1979 by Tutsi exiles based in Uganda. The attack provided a pretext for the arrest of thousands of opposition members in Rwanda considered as supporters of the RPF.

94. Faced with the worsening internal situation that attracted a growing number of Rwandans to the multi-party system, and pressured by foreign donors demanding not only economic but also political reforms in the form of much greater participation of the people in the country's management, President Habyarimana was compelled to accept the multi-party system in principle. * * *

95. At the same time, Tutsi exiles, particularly those in Uganda organized themselves not only to launch incursions into Rwandan territory but also to form a political organization, the Rwandese Patriotic Front (RPF), with a military wing called the Rwandan Patriotic Army (RPA). The first objective of the exiles was to return to Rwanda. But they met with objection from the Rwandan authorities and President Habyarimana, who is alleged to have said that land in Rwanda would not be enough to feed all those who wanted to return. On these grounds, the exiles broadened their objectives to include the overthrow of Habyarimana.

96. The above-mentioned RPF attack on 1 October 1991 sent shock waves throughout Rwanda. Members of the opposition parties formed in 1991 saw this as an opportunity to have an informal alliance with the RPF so as to further destabilize an already weakened regime. The regime finally accepted to share power between the MRND and the other political parties and, around March 1992, the Government and the opposition signed an agreement to set up a transitional coalition government headed by a Prime Minister from the MDR [Parmehutu]. Out of the nineteen ministries, the MRND obtained only nine. Pressured by the opposition, the MRND accepted that negotiations with the RPF be started. The negotiations led to the first cease-fire in July 1992 and the first part of the Arusha Accords. The July 1992 cease-fire tacitly recognized RPF control over a portion of Rwandan territory in the north-east. The protocols signed following these accords included the October 1992 protocol establishing a transitional government and a transitional assembly and the participation of the RPF in both institutions. The political scene was now widened to comprise three blocs: the Habyarimana bloc, the internal opposition and the RPF. Experience showed that President Habyarimana accepted these accords only because he was compelled to do so, but had no intention of complying with what he himself referred to as "un chiffon de papier," meaning a scrap of paper.

97. Yet, the RPF did not drop its objective of seizing power. It therefore increased its military attacks. The massive attack of 8 February 1993 seriously undermined the relations between the RPF and the Hutu opposition parties, making it easy for Habyarimana supporters to convene an assembly of all Hutu. Thus, the bond built on Hutu kinship once again began to prevail over political differences. The three blocs mentioned earlier gave way to two ethnic-based opposing camps: on the one hand, the RPF, the supposed canopy of all Tutsi and, on the other hand, the other parties said to be composed essentially of the Hutu. * * *

102. On 4 August 1993, the Government of Rwanda and the RPF signed the final Arusha Accords and ended the war which started on 1 October [1991]. The Accords provided, *inter alia*, for the establishment of a transitional government to include the RPF, the partial demobilization and integration of the two opposing armies (13,000 RPF and 35,000 FAR troops), the creation of a demilitarized zone between the RPF-controlled area in the north and the rest of the country, the stationing of an RPF battalion in the city of Kigali, and the deployment, in four phases, of a UN peace-keeping force, the United Nations Assistance Mission for Rwanda (UNAMIR), with a two-year mandate. * * *

106. At the end of March 1994, the transitional government was still not set up and Rwanda was on the brink of bankruptcy. International donors and neighbouring countries put pressure on the Habyarimana government to implement the Arusha Accords. On 6 April 1994, President Habyarimana and other heads of State of the region met in Dar-es-Salaam (Tanzania) to discuss the implementation of the peace

accords. The aircraft carrying President Habyarimana and the Burundian President, Ntaryamirai, who were returning from the meeting, crashed around 8:30 pm near Kigali airport. All aboard were killed.

107. The Rwandan army and the militia immediately erected roadblocks around the city of Kigali. Before dawn on April 7, 1994, in various parts of the country, the Presidential Guard and the militia started killing the Tutsi as well as Hutu known to be in favour of the Arusha Accords and power-sharing between the Tutsi and the Hutu. Among the first victims, were a number of ministers of the coalition government* * *. The constitutional vacuum thus created cleared the way for the establishment of the self-proclaimed Hutu-power interim government, mainly under the aegis of retired Colonel Théoneste Bagosora.

108. Soldiers of the Rwandan Armed Forces (FAR) executed ten Belgian blue helmets, thereby provoking the withdrawal of the Belgian contingent which formed the core of UNAMIR. On April 21, 1994, the UN Security Council decided to reduce the peace-keeping force to 450 troops.

109. In the afternoon of 7 April 1994, RPF troops left their quarters in Kigali and their zone in the north, to resume open war against the Rwandan Armed Forces. Its troops from the north moved south, crossing the demilitarized zone, and entered the city of Kigali on April 12, 1994, thus forcing the interim government to flee to Gitarama.

110. On April 12, 1994, after public authorities announced over Radio Rwanda that "we need to unite against the enemy, the only enemy and this is the enemy that we have always known . . . it's the enemy who wants to reinstate the former feudal monarchy," it became clear that the Tutsi were the primary targets. During the week of 14 to 21 April 1994, the killing campaign reached its peak. The President of the interim government, the Prime Minister and some key ministers traveled to Butare and Gikongoro, and that marked the beginning of killings in these regions which had hitherto been peaceful. Thousands of people, sometimes encouraged or directed by local administrative officials, on the promise of safety, gathered unsuspectingly in churches, schools, hospitals and local government buildings. In reality, this was a trap intended to lead to the rapid extermination of a large number of people.

111. The killing of Tutsi which henceforth spared neither women nor children, continued up to 18 July 1994, when the RPF triumphantly entered Kigali. The estimated total number of victims in the conflict varies from 500,000 to 1,000,000 or more.

112. As regards the massacres which took place in Rwanda between April and July 1994, * * * the question before this Chamber is whether they constitute genocide. [The Tribunal concludes that genocide writ large occurred in Rwanda in 1994.] * * *

127. [I]n response to the question * * * as to whether the tragic events that took place in Rwanda in 1994 occurred solely within the context of the conflict between the RAF and the RPF, the Chamber replies in the negative, since it holds that the genocide did indeed take place against the Tutsi group, alongside the conflict. The execution of this genocide was probably facilitated by the conflict, in the sense that the fighting against the RPF forces was used as a pretext for the propaganda inciting genocide against the Tutsi, by branding RPF fighters and Tutsi civilians together, through dissemination via the media of the idea that every Tutsi was allegedly an accomplice of the *Inkotanyi* [a term connoting 19th century Tutsi feudal militia and used to describe the RPF]. Very clearly, once the genocide got under way, the crime became one of the stakes in the conflict between the RPF and the RAF. In 1994, General Kagame, speaking on behalf of the RPF, declared that a cease fire could possibly not be implemented until the massacre of civilians by the government forces had stopped.

128. In conclusion, it should be stressed that although the genocide against the Tutsi occurred concomitantly with the above-mentioned conflict, it was, evidently, fundamentally different from the conflict. The accused himself stated during his initial appearance before the Chamber, when recounting a conversation he had with one RAF officer and Silas Kubwimana, a leader of the *Interahamwe* [a Hutu militia], that the acts perpetrated by the *Interahamwe* against Tutsi civilians were not considered by the RAF officer to be of a nature to help the government armed forces in the conflict with the RPF. Note is also taken of the testimony of witness KK which is in the same vein. This witness told the Chamber that while she and the children were taken away, an RAF soldier allegedly told persons who were persecuting her that "instead of going to confront the *Inkotanyi* at the war front, you are killing children, although children know nothing; they have never done politics." The Chamber's opinion is that the genocide was organized and planned not only by members of the RAF, but also by the political forces who were behind the "Hutu-power," that it was executed essentially by civilians including the armed militia and even ordinary citizens, and above all, that the majority of the Tutsi victims were non-combatants, including thousands of women and children, even foetuses. The fact that the genocide took place while the RAF was in conflict with the RPF, can in no way be considered as an extenuating circumstance for it.

129. This being the case, the Chamber holds that the fact that genocide was indeed committed in Rwanda in 1994 and more particularly in Taba, cannot influence it in its decisions in the present case. Its sole task is to assess the individual criminal responsibility of the accused for the crimes with which he is charged, the burden of proof being on the Prosecutor.[61] In spite of the irrefutable atrocities committed in Rwanda,

[61] In the opinion of the Chamber, it is not only obvious that an accused person could be declared innocent of the crime of genocide even when it is established that genocide had indeed

the judges must examine the facts adduced in a most dispassionate manner, bearing in mind that the accused is presumed innocent. Moreover, the seriousness of the charges brought against the accused makes it all the more necessary to examine scrupulously and meticulously all the inculpatory and exonerating evidence, in the context of a fair trial and in full respect of all the rights of the Accused. * * *

170. Paragraph 7 of the indictment alleges that the victims in each paragraph charging genocide were members of a national, ethnic, racial or religious group. The Chamber notes that the Tutsi population does not have its own language or a distinct culture from the rest of the Rwandan population. However, the Chamber finds that there are a number of objective indicators of the group as a group with a distinct identity. Every Rwandan citizen was required before 1994 to carry an identity card which included an entry for ethnic group (*ubwoko* in Kinyarwanda and *ethnie* in French), the ethnic group being Hutu, Tutsi or Twa. The Rwandan Constitution and laws in force in 1994 also identified Rwandans by reference to their ethnic group. Article 16 of the Constitution of the Rwandan Republic, of 10 June 1991, reads, "All citizens are equal before the law, without any discrimination, notably, on grounds of race, colour, origin, ethnicity, clan, sex, opinion, religion or social position." Article 57 of the Civil Code of 1988 provided that a person would be identified by "sex, ethnic group, name, residence and domicile." Article 118 of the Civil Code provided that birth certificates would include "the year, month, date and place of birth, the sex, the ethnic group, the first and last name of the infant." The Arusha Accords of 4 August 1993 in fact provided for the suppression of the mention of ethnicity on official documents (see Article 16 of the Protocol on diverse questions and final dispositions).

171. Moreover, customary rules existed in Rwanda governing the determination of ethnic group, which followed patrilineal lines of heredity. The identification of persons as belonging to the group of Hutu or Tutsi (or Twa) had thus become embedded in Rwandan culture. The Rwandan witnesses who testified before the Chamber identified themselves by ethnic group, and generally knew the ethnic group to which their friends and neighbours belonged. Moreover, the Tutsi were conceived of as an ethnic group by those who targeted them for killing.

172. As the expert witness, Alison Desforges, summarised:

> The primary criterion for [defining] an ethnic group is the sense of belonging to that ethnic group. It is a sense which can shift over time. In other words, the group, the definition of the group to which one feels allied may change over time. But, if you fix any given moment in time, and you say, how does this population divide itself, then you will see which ethnic groups

---

taken place, but also, in a case other than that of Rwanda, a person could be found guilty of genocide without necessarily having to establish that genocide had taken place throughout the country concerned.

are in existence in the minds of the participants at that time. The Rwandans currently, and for the last generation at least, have defined themselves in terms of these three ethnic groups. In addition reality is an interplay between the actual conditions and peoples' subjective perception of those conditions. In Rwanda, the reality was shaped by the colonial experience which imposed a categorisation which was probably more fixed, and not completely appropriate to the scene. But, the Belgians did impose this classification in the early 1930's when they required the population to be registered according to ethnic group. The categorisation imposed at that time is what people of the current generation have grown up with. They have always thought in terms of these categories, even if they did not, in their daily lives have to take cognizance of that. This practice was continued after independence by the First Republic and the Second Republic in Rwanda to such an extent that this division into three ethnic groups became an absolute reality. * * *

510. Since the special intent to commit genocide lies in the intent to "destroy, in whole or in part, a national, ethnical, racial or religious group, as such," it is necessary to consider a definition of the group as such. Article 2 of the Statute, just like the Genocide Convention, stipulates four types of victim groups, namely national, ethnical, racial or religious groups.

511. On reading through the *travaux préparatoires* of the Genocide Convention, it appears that the crime of genocide was allegedly perceived as targeting only "stable" groups, constituted in a permanent fashion and membership of which is determined by birth, with the exclusion of the more "mobile" groups which one joins through individual voluntary commitment, such as political and economic groups. Therefore, a common criterion in the four types of groups protected by the Genocide Convention is that membership in such groups would seem to be normally not challengeable by its members, who belong to it automatically, by birth, in a continuous and often irremediable manner.

512. Based on the *Nottebohm* decision[97] rendered by the International Court of Justice, the Chamber holds that a national group is defined as a collection of people who are perceived to share a legal bond based on common citizenship, coupled with reciprocity of rights and duties.

513. An ethnic group is generally defined as a group whose members share a common language or culture.

514. The conventional definition of racial group is based on the hereditary physical traits often identified with a geographical region, irrespective of linguistic, cultural, national or religious factors.

---

[97] [*Liechtenstein v. Guatemala*, 1955 I.C.J. Reports 4 (April 6, 1955).]

515. The religious group is one whose members share the same religion, denomination or mode of worship.

516. Moreover, the Chamber considered whether the groups protected by the Genocide Convention, echoed in Article 2 of the Statute, should be limited to only the four groups expressly mentioned and whether they should not also include any group which is stable and permanent like the said four groups. In other words, the question that arises is whether it would be impossible to punish the physical destruction of a group as such under the Genocide Convention, if the said group, although stable and membership is by birth, does not meet the definition of any one of the four groups expressly protected by the Genocide Convention. In the opinion of the Chamber, it is particularly important to respect the intention of the drafters of the Genocide Convention, which according to the *travaux préparatoires*, was patently to ensure the protection of any stable and permanent group. * * *

702. In the light of the facts brought to its attention during the trial, the Chamber is of the opinion that, in Rwanda in 1994, the Tutsi constituted a group referred to as "ethnic" in official classifications. Thus, the identity cards at the time included a reference to *"ubwoko"* in Kinyarwanda or *"ethnie"* (ethnic group) in French which, depending on the case, referred to the designation Hutu or Tutsi, for example. The Chamber further noted that all the Rwandan witnesses who appeared before it invariably answered spontaneously and without hesitation the questions of the Prosecutor regarding their ethnic identity. Accordingly, the Chamber finds that, in any case, at the time of the alleged events, the Tutsi did indeed constitute a stable and permanent group and were identified as such by all.

NOTES & QUESTIONS

1. Genocide in Rwanda

On what basis did the Trial Chamber find that genocide was committed in Rwanda given the fact that the Hutu and Tutsi people of Rwanda share the same language, culture, and religion? Does the Tribunal reach a definitive decision on whether the Hutu and Tutsi people are separate ethnic groups or is its genocide finding based on the recognition that the Hutu and Tutsi identities were "stable and permanent" within Rwandan society in 1994? Is ethnicity in Rwanda (or anywhere else) a stable phenomenon? Should social constructs and institutions, such as the Rwandan identity card, be sufficient to establish the existence of a protected group? Was the killing of moderate Hutus, seeking to protect the Tutsi population, genocide? Does the fact that moderate Hutus were killed alongside Tutsis detract from a finding of genocidal intent on the part of perpetrators? For a brief discussion of the question of ethnicity under the Genocide Convention and an argument that the *Akayesu* Chamber sidestepped the issue of ethnic identity, *see* Harvard Law Review, *Developments in the Law: IV. Defining Protected Groups under the Genocide Convention*, 114 HARV. L. REV. 2007 (2001).

In the *Kayishema* case, the ICTR more clearly concluded that the Tutsi were a distinct ethnic group. *Prosecutor v. Kayishema*, Case No. ICTR–95–1–T, Judgement, para. 291 (May 21, 1999). Paul Magnarella argues that the *Akayesu* Chamber "significantly expanded the kinds of populations that will be protected by [the Genocide] Convention." Paul Magnarella, *Some Milestones and Achievements at the International Criminal Tribunal for Rwanda: The 1998 Kambanda and Akayesu Cases*, 11 FLA. J. INT'L L. 517 (1997). Do you agree? Should the kinds of populations protected by the Genocide Convention be expanded?

2. Protected Groups

Why would the drafters of the Genocide Convention provide protection for national, ethnic, racial, and religious groups and not other groups that had been identified by the earlier General Assembly resolution or draft versions of the treaty (such as political, economic, or social groups)? Is there a principled reason to exclude these groups? What is the common principle that links the four protected groups and not others? Immutability? The *Akayesu* Chamber identifies the common themes as stability and permanence. Does that adequately identify a common characteristic of the four enumerated groups? What about groups defined by age, gender, or sexual orientation? If membership in other groups is considered "immutable" by a perpetrator, should their destruction be deemed a genocide? In some contexts, once an individual becomes affiliated with a political group or ideology, that designation may be considered an indelible stain. If political affiliation is considered permanent and stable by a perpetrator, why shouldn't an attempt to destroy that group be considered genocide? Are religious groups different from political, or other excluded groups, in terms of their immutability? Should people have to give up or suppress fundamental rights—like the right to a political opinion or to assembly—to avoid destruction? How might the drafting of the Convention been influenced by the commencement of the Cold War? Could a campaign to eliminate al Qaeda constitute genocide? For a discussion of the elimination of political groups from the Convention, *see* Beth Van Schaack, *The Crime of Political Genocide: Repairing the Genocide Convention's Blind Spot*, 106 YALE L. J. 2259 (1997).

3. Objective v. Subjective Considerations

How should the enumerated groups be conceptualized in contemporary genocide prosecutions—with reference to historical definitions, scientific "reality," contemporary understandings, or the perpetrator's beliefs and assumptions? For example, race remains a powerful and meaningful social construct. Should courts insist upon the existence of an "objective" racial or ethnic group to find genocide, or are "subjective" perceptions of difference along these dimensions sufficient? Is it genocide where the perpetrator denies the existence of the victim group? Consider the approach of the Trial Chamber to this issue in the *Jelisić* case in the passage below (this opinion is excerpted more fully in the next sub-section):

> 66. It is in fact the *mens rea* which gives genocide its speciality and distinguishes it from an ordinary crime and other

crimes against international humanitarian law. The underlying crime or crimes must be characterised as genocide when committed with the intent to destroy, in whole or in part, a national, ethnical, racial or religious group as such. Stated otherwise, "[t]he prohibited act must be committed against an individual because of his membership in a particular group and as an incremental step in the overall objective of destroying the group." Two elements which may therefore be drawn from the special intent are:

— that the victims belonged to an identified group;

— that the alleged perpetrator must have committed his crimes as part of a wider plan to destroy the group as such. * * *

70. Although the objective determination of a religious group still remains possible, to attempt to define a national, ethnical or racial group today using objective and scientifically irreproachable criteria would be a perilous exercise whose result would not necessarily correspond to the perception of the persons concerned by such categorisation. Therefore, it is more appropriate to evaluate the status of a national, ethnical or racial group from the point of view of those persons who wish to single that group out from the rest of the community. The Trial Chamber consequently elects to evaluate membership in a national, ethnical or racial group using a subjective criterion. It is the stigmatisation of a group as a distinct national, ethnical or racial unit by the community which allows it to be determined whether a targeted population constitutes a national, ethnical or racial group in the eyes of the alleged perpetrators. * * *

71. A group may be stigmatised in this manner by way of positive or negative criteria. A "positive approach" would consist of the perpetrators of the crime distinguishing a group by the characteristics which they deem to be particular to a national, ethnical, racial or religious group. A "negative approach" would consist of identifying individuals as not being part of the group to which the perpetrators of the crime consider that they themselves belong and which to them displays specific national, ethnical, racial or religious characteristics. Thereby, all individuals thus rejected would, by exclusion, make up a distinct group. The Trial Chamber concurs here with the opinion already expressed by the Commission of Experts[97] and deems that it is consonant with the object and the purpose of the Convention to consider that its

---

[97] *Report of the Commission of Experts*, UN Doc. S/1994/674, para. 96, p. 25: "If there are several or more than one victim groups, and each group as such is protected, it may be within the spirit and purpose of the Convention to consider all the victim groups as a larger entity. The case being, for example, that there is evidence that group A wants to destroy in whole or in part groups B, C and D, or rather everyone who does not belong to the national, ethnic, racial or religious group A. In a sense, group A has defined a pluralistic non-A group using national, ethnic, racial and religious criteria for the definition. It seems relevant to analyse the fate of the non-A group along similar lines as if the non-A group had been homogenous."

> provisions also protect groups defined by exclusion where they have been stigmatised by the perpetrators of the act in this way.

Prosecutor v. Jelisić, Case No. IT–95–10–T, Judgement (Dec. 14, 1999). Does this approach, in effect, reify or ratify what may be erroneous, irrational, obsolete, or even offensive assumptions about a group? Should international criminal law permit prosecution for genocide against a group that has no objective existence, so-called "imagined communities"? Should it be enough to define a group in the negative as not part of the perpetrator group? Reconsider this point when you read the ICC's *Al Bashir* opinion below.

4. Original Intent of the Drafters

The *travaux préparatoires* (the documents making up the drafting history) of the Genocide Convention make it clear that the intent of the drafters was to exclude efforts to eliminate political, social, and economic groups from the definition of genocide. During the treaty's drafting, many states raised substantive arguments in favor of the exclusion of these groups based on debatable assumptions that an individual's membership in these groups is neither immutable nor ascribed. Other states, in contrast, seemed more concerned with avoiding international scrutiny of their own responses to internal dissension. For example, the Soviet Union, which under Joseph Stalin had engaged in wide-ranging political purges, was a vocal critic of the inclusion of political groups. Does the incorporation of such overt political concerns by states decrease the legitimacy of the restrictive definition of protected group? Is the *Akayesu* Tribunal faithful to the original intent of the drafters of the Genocide Convention in its determination that efforts to destroy the Tutsi group constituted genocide? Should it be?

Consider Article 32 of the 1969 Vienna Convention on the Law of Treaties May 23, 1969, 1155 U.N.T.S. 331, which provides that

> Recourse may be had to supplementary means of interpretation, including the preparatory work of the treaty and the circumstances of its conclusion, in order to confirm the meaning resulting from the application of article 31 [requiring courts to look to the text and to subsequent practice for interpretive assistance], or to determine the meaning when the interpretation according to article 31:
>
> a. leaves the meaning ambiguous or obscure; or
>
> b. leads to a result which is manifestly absurd or unreasonable.

According to the Vienna Convention—which sets forth rules on drafting, interpreting, enforcing, and exiting treaties—should tribunals consult the drafting history of the Genocide Convention when determining whether a particular group qualifies as a protected group? The source of law for the ICTR is its Statute, which in turn adopts the same definition of genocide found in the Genocide Convention. What authority, if any, does the drafting history of the Genocide Convention have before the ICTR? By adopting the Convention's definition of genocide, does the Statute necessarily import all of the Convention's drafting history? Should international criminal tribunals reify the original intent of drafters of such iconic treaties, or should the drafters of tribunal statutes be allowed to incorporate their own preferences with respect to, for example, the definition of protected groups under the Genocide Convention?

5. National Definitions of Genocide

While most states have simply copied the Genocide Convention's definition of genocide into their criminal codes after ratification, some have made more substantive changes to this definition. For example, Bangladesh, Costa Rica, Ethiopia, and Panama at one point extended coverage to political groups. Other states, such as France, Canada, and Finland, make the list of groups more open-ended. For national legislation on genocide, *see* John Quigley, THE GENOCIDE CONVENTION: AN INTERNATIONAL LAW ANALYSIS 15–20 (2006) (compiling statutes); William A. Schabas, GENOCIDE IN INTERNATIONAL LAW 350–353 (2003) (same). How do, or should, these variations affect the development of international criminal law? The 1973 Penal Code of Spain defined genocide as follows at Article 137 *bis*:

> Those who, with the intent to destroy in whole or in part, a national ethnic [sic], social, or religious group, perpetrate any of the following acts, will be punished:
>
> 1. With life imprisonment, if they cause the death of any members of the group.
> 2. With lengthy imprisonment, if they cause castration, sterilization, mutilation or any other grave harm.
> 3. With the lesser imprisonment, if they submit the group or any of its members to conditions of existence that place their life in danger or gravely harm their health.
>
> The same punishment will be given to those who forcibly displace the group or its members, adopt any method that would tend to impede their way of life or reproduction, or transfer members of a group to another group by force.

This definition was in place during the "dirty wars" in Latin America in the 1970s and 1980s. The Spanish *Audencia Nacionale*, the court that asserted extraterritorial jurisdiction over Chilean General Augusto Pinochet, considered whether the persecution of other Chileans by members of Pinochet's regime constituted genocide:

> Referring to Chile's conduct alleged in the criminal investigation that has resulted in this appeal, the Office of the Public Prosecutor argues that such conduct cannot constitute genocide, for the repression in Chile during the military regime, as of 11 September 1973 [the day of Pinochet's coup], was not directed at any national, ethnic, racial, or religious group. The plural and pluripersonal acts alleged, in the terms in which they appear in the criminal investigation, were acts against a group of Chileans or residents of Chile that could be differentiated, and which no doubt [were] differentiated by those who organized the persecution and harassment. * * * The idea is clearly present in the facts alleged in the criminal investigation of the extermination of a group which, while highly heterogeneous, is differentiated. The persecuted and

harassed group was composed of those citizens who did not fit the type pre-established by the promoters of the repression as necessary for the new order to be installed in the country. The group was made up of citizens opposed to the military regime of 11 September, contrary to the understanding of national identity, of the national value, embraced by the new rulers, but also those citizens who were indifferent to the regime and to their understanding of the nation. The repression was not aimed at changing the group's attitude, but at destroying the group by means of detention, torture, disappearance, death, and instilling fear in the members of the group, which was clearly defined—identifiable—by the repressors. It was not a random, indiscriminate action. * * *

The acts alleged herein constitute the crime of genocide. We know why the 1948 Convention does not include the term "political" or the words "or others" when it lists, at Article 2, the characteristics of the groups targeted for genocidal destruction. Yet silence is not perforce equivalent to exclusion. Whatever intent the drafters of the text may have had, the Convention takes on life by virtue of the successive signatures and accessions to the treaty by members of the United Nations who share the idea that genocide was an odious scourge that they should commit to preventing and punishing. Article 137 *bis* of the Spanish Criminal Code, now derogated, and Article 607 of the current Criminal Code, [were] inspired by the worldwide concern that was the basis for acts such as those alleged in this case. The extent of the need felt by the countries that are parties to the 1948 Convention to criminalize genocide, by preventing impunity and considering it a horrendous crime of international law, requires that the term "national group" not mean "group made up of persons who belong to the same nation," but simply, a national human group, a differentiated human group, characterized by some trait, and integrated into a larger collectivity. The restrictive understanding of the criminal definition of genocide that the appellants (in this motion, a single appellant) defend would make it difficult to characterize as genocide actions as odious as systematic elimination, by the authorities or by a band, of AIDS patients, as a differentiated group, or the elderly, also as a differentiated group, or of all foreigners who live in a country, who, despite being of different nationalities, can be understood as a national group in relation to the country in which they live, differentiated precisely by the fact of not being nationals of that State. This social conception of genocide—felt, understood by the collectivity, and the basis of society's rejection of and horror at the crime—would not allow for exclusions such as those indicated. The prevention and punishment of genocide in these terms, i.e. as an international crime, as an evil that affects the international community directly, based on the intent of the 1948 Convention readily inferable from the text, cannot exclude certain differentiated national groups, discriminating against them in respect of others, which would be unreasonable in the logic of the system. Neither the 1948 Convention nor our Criminal Code, nor the previous Criminal Code, expressly excludes this necessary integration.

In these terms, the acts alleged in the criminal investigation constitute genocide, and consequently Article 23(4) of the Organic Law on the Judicial Branch [allowing for universal jurisdiction] applies to the case. At the time of the acts and in the country where they took place an effort was made to destroy a differentiated national group, those who did not fit in the project of national reorganization, or those who the persons who carried out the persecution considered did not fit. The victims included foreigners, among them Spaniards. All the victims, real or potential Chileans or foreigners, made up a differentiated group, in the nation, that was targeted for extermination.

Audencia Nacionale—Criminal Chamber En Banc Appeal 173/98 (November 5, 1998), *reprinted in* THE PINOCHET PAPERS: THE CASE OF AUGUSTO PINOCHET IN SPAIN AND BRITAIN 95 (Reed Brody & Michael Ratner eds., 2000).

On the basis of this ruling, Spain issued an indictment against General Pinochet and sought his extradition from the United Kingdom. The genocide charge was not among those allowed in the extradition proceedings by application of the double criminality rule, because genocide was not part of British law. Is the *Audencia Nacionale*'s reasoning on the genocide characterization convincing or defensible? If you were representing General Pinochet in this case, what arguments would you raise to challenge the court's reasoning? In 1983, Spain amended Article 137 *bis* to conform to the definition of genocide in the Genocide Convention by replacing "social" with "racial." The genocide prohibition is now codified at Article 607. *See* 2007 Código Penal (Sp.).

6. Codification

The codification of customary international law into treaties and other international instruments ensures uniformity and certainty with respect to the principles of international law. Yet codification may also have the effect of "freezing" international norms and potentially hindering the progressive development of international law. The ICC Statute addresses this tendency directly at Article 10: "Nothing in this Part [on jurisdiction, admissibility, and applicable law] shall be interpreted as limiting or prejudicing in any way existing or developing rules of international law for purposes other than this Statute." Does the codification of norms within binding treaties provide the best means of ensuring rigorous and enforceable international rules? Or does codification open the way for political compromises that might weaken or retard norms? Are there issues specific to international criminal law that affect your view of the utility of codification? Would contemporary efforts to prosecute mass violence be more effective under the definition contained in the General Assembly Resolution on genocide as compared with the definition eventually adopted within the binding Genocide Convention?

The definition of genocide under international law has remained constant since its inception. This is despite calls and opportunities to amend the definition or recognize a more expansive crime that would reach violence against political or other groups or relax the intent requirement to cover acts undertaken with knowledge that the destruction of the group would result. The high threshold of specificity has been maintained to recognize a conceptual distinction between acts taken to destroy a particular type of human group and other acts of violence that may not be directed at the total destruction of a group. It also avoids a collapse of the concept of genocide into crimes against humanity. Given that the prohibition against genocide excludes many instances of mass violence (contrary to popular understanding), should the international community revisit the definition of genocide? If so, should states seek to amend the treaty itself or to draft a separate protocol?

7. A "One-Man Genocide Mission"

The *Akayesu* Tribunal opines at footnote 61 that an individual could be convicted of genocide even if genocide "writ large" had not occurred in the region in which he acted. In other words, the Tribunal assumed that a conviction is theoretically possible where a single perpetrator killed a single individual with genocidal intent. (One should query whether one victim alone is enough—the Genocide Convention employs "members" in the plural, whereas the ICC Elements of Crimes mentions "one or more persons.") Under this theory, a genocide conviction would be possible if the perpetrator would not have had the capacity to achieve even the partial destruction of a protected group so long as he intended to do so. Is this appropriate? Consider this scenario in the context of the *Jelisić* case below.

III. THE SPECIFIC INTENT TO COMMIT GENOCIDE

The specific intent of the crime of genocide—the intent to destroy a protected group in whole or in part—sets genocide apart from other international crimes. The concept of specific intent acts as a mental element that is required above and beyond the mental state required as to the *actus reus* of the crime. The case that follows explores the way in which a prosecutor can prove that a defendant was acting with the specific intent to destroy a protected group.

Goran Jelisić was indicted by the ICTY for the murder, torture and inhuman treatment of Muslim detainees in Luka camp in the town of Brčko on the border of Bosnia-Herzegovina and Croatia. (See the Appendix for a map of Yugoslavia.) He had adopted the sobriquet "the Serb Adolf," and the testimony at trial revealed that on numerous occasions he had publicly articulated his desire to eliminate the Muslim population (so-called "Bosniaks"). He pled guilty to 31 counts alleging violations of the laws or customs of war and crimes against humanity, but pled not guilty to a genocide count. The trial thus proceeded on the genocide count alone. Once the Prosecution rested, however, the Trial Chamber—after deliberations—announced the acquittal of the defendant on this count pursuant to Rule 98 *bis*, which obliges the Trial

Chamber to pronounce the acquittal of the accused when the evidence presented by the Prosecution was insufficient to sustain a conviction. The Trial Chamber imposed a 40-year sentence for the crimes to which Jelisić had already pled guilty. The Trial Chamber's opinion on the genocide acquittal appears below followed by an explanation of the Appeals Chamber's partial reversal—the result of an appeal filed by the Prosecution on the genocide acquittal.

Prosecutor v. Jelisić, Case No. IT–95–10–T, Judgement (Dec. 14, 1999)

In the Trial Chamber

61. In accordance with the principle *nullum crimen sine lege*, the Trial Chamber means to examine the legal ingredients of the crime of genocide taking into account only those which beyond all doubt form part of customary international law. Several sources have been considered in this respect. First, the Trial Chamber takes note of the Convention on whose incontestable customary value it has already remarked. It interprets the Convention's terms in accordance with the general rules of interpretation of treaties set out in Articles 31 and 32 of the Vienna Convention on the Law of Treaties. In addition to the normal meaning of its provisions, the Trial Chamber also considered the object and purpose of the Convention and could also refer to the preparatory work and circumstances associated with the Convention's coming into being. The Trial Chamber also took account of subsequent practice grounded upon the Convention. Special significance was attached to the Judgements rendered by the Tribunal for Rwanda, in particular to the *Akayesu* and *Kayishema* cases which constitute to date the only existing international case-law on the issue. The practice of States, notably through their national courts, and the work of international authorities in this field have also been taken into account. The ILC report commenting upon the "Articles of the Draft Code of Crimes Against the Peace and Security of Mankind"* which sets out to transcribe the customary law on the issue appeared especially useful.

62. Genocide is characterised by two legal ingredients according to the terms of Article 4 of the Statute:

— the material element of the offence, constituted by one or several acts enumerated in paragraph 2 of Article 4;

— the *mens rea* of the offence, consisting of the special intent to destroy, in whole or in part, a national, ethnical, racial or religious group, as such. * * *

* Eds.: The ILC is the International Law Commission. The General Assembly charged it with drafting a Draft Code of Crimes, which was a precursor to the ICC Statute.

The Intent to Destroy, in Whole or in Part, the Group as Such

78. In examining the intentionality of an attack against a group, the Trial Chamber will first consider the different concepts of the notion of destruction of a group as such before then reviewing the degree of intent required for a crime to be constituted. In other words, the Trial Chamber will have to verify that there was both an intentional attack against a group and an intention upon the part of the accused to participate in or carry out this attack. Indeed, the intention necessary for the commission of a crime of genocide may not be presumed even in the case where the existence of a group is at least in part threatened. The Trial Chamber must verify whether the accused had the "special" intention which, beyond the discrimination of the crimes he commits, characterises his intent to destroy the discriminated group as such, at least in part.

79. Apart from its discriminatory character, the underlying crime is also characterised by the fact that it is part of a wider plan to *destroy*, in whole or in part, the group *as such*. As indicated by the ILC, "the intention must be to destroy the group 'as such,' meaning as a separate and distinct entity, and not merely some individuals because of their membership in a particular group." By killing an individual member of the targeted group, the perpetrator does not thereby only manifest his hatred of the group to which his victim belongs but also knowingly commits this act as part of a wider-ranging intention to destroy the national, ethnical, racial or religious group of which the victim is a member. The Tribunal for Rwanda notes that "[t]he perpetration of the act charged therefore extends beyond its actual commission, for example, the murder of a particular individual, for the realisation of an ulterior motive, which is to destroy, in whole or in part, the group of which the individual is just one element." Genocide therefore differs from the crime of persecution in which the perpetrator chooses his victims because they belong to a specific community but does not necessarily seek to destroy the community as such.

80. Notwithstanding this, it is recognised that the destruction sought need not be directed at the whole group which, moreover, is clear from the letter of Article 4 of the Statute. The ILC also states that "[i]t is not necessary to intend to achieve the complete annihilation of a group from every corner of the globe." The question which then arises is what proportion of the group is marked for destruction and beyond what threshold could the crime be qualified as genocide? In particular, the Trial Chamber will have to verify whether genocide may be committed within a restricted geographical zone.

81. The Prosecution accepts that the phrase "in whole or in part" must be understood to mean the destruction of a significant portion of the group from either a quantitative or qualitative standpoint. The intention demonstrated by the accused to destroy a part of the group would therefore have to affect either a major part of the group or a representative fraction thereof, such as its leaders.

82. Given the goal of the Convention to deal with mass crimes, it is widely acknowledged that the intention to destroy must target at least a *substantial* part of the group.[110] The Tribunal for Rwanda appears to go even further by demanding that the accused have the intention of destroying a "considerable" number of individual members of a group.[111] In a letter addressed to the United States Senate during the debate on Article II of the Convention on genocide, Raphaël Lemkin explained in the same way that the intent to destroy "in part" must be interpreted as a desire for destruction which "must be of a substantial nature [. . .] so as to affect the entirety."[112] A targeted part of a group would be classed as substantial either because the intent sought to harm a large majority of the group in question or the most representative members of the targeted community. The Commission of Experts specified that "[i]f essentially the total leadership of a group is targeted, it could also amount to genocide. Such leadership includes political and administrative leaders, religious leaders, academics and intellectuals, business leaders and others—the totality per se may be a strong indication of genocide regardless of the actual numbers killed. A corroborating argument will be the fate of the rest of the group. The character of the attack on the leadership must be *viewed in the context of the fate or what happened to the rest of the group*. If a group has its leadership exterminated, and at the same time or in the wake of that, has a relatively large number of the members of the group killed or subjected to other heinous acts, for example deported on a large scale or forced to flee, the cluster of violations ought to be considered in its entirety in order to interpret the provisions of the Convention in a spirit consistent with its purpose."[113] Genocidal intent may therefore be manifest in two forms. It may consist of desiring the extermination of a very large number of the members of the group, in which case it would constitute an intention to destroy a group en masse. However, it may also consist of the desired destruction of a more limited number of persons selected for the impact that their disappearance would have upon the survival of the group as such. This would then constitute an intention to destroy the group "selectively." The Prosecutor did not actually choose between these two options.

---

[110] The ILC Draft Articles [and] Nehemia Robinson's commentary indicate that the perpetrators of genocide must be seeking to destroy a "substantial part" of the group (ILC Draft Articles, p. 89; Nehemia Robinson, THE GENOCIDE CONVENTION, New York, 1949 (1st edition), 1960, p. 63); the U.S. Senate's "understanding" of Article II of the Convention also states that the U.S. interprets "partial destruction" as the destruction of a "*substantial* part" of the group (*Genocide Convention, Report of the Committee on Foreign Relations*, U.S. Senate, 18 July 1981, p. 22).

[111] *Kayishema* Judgement, para. 97.

[112] Raphaël Lemkin in *Executive Session of the Senate Foreign Relations Committee, Historical Series*, 1976, p. 370. In the same vein, the implementing legislation proposed by the Nixon and Carter administrations stated that " 'substantial part' means a part of a group of such numerical significance that the destruction or loss of that part would cause the destruction of the group as a viable entity," S Exec. Rep. No. 23, 94th Cong., 2nd Sess. (1976), pp. 34–35.

[113] *Report of the Commission of Experts*, UN Doc. S/1994/674, para. 94 (emphasis added).

83. The Prosecution contends, however, that the geographical zone in which an attempt to eliminate the group is made may be limited to the size of a region or even a municipality. The Trial Chamber notes that it is accepted that genocide may be perpetrated in a limited geographic zone. Furthermore, the United Nations General Assembly did not hesitate in characterising the massacres at Sabra and Shatila[117] as genocide, even if it is appropriate to look upon this evaluation with caution due to its undoubtedly being more of a political assessment than a legal one. Moreover, the Trial Chamber adopted a similar position in its Review of the Indictment Pursuant to [Rule] 61 filed in the *Nikolić* case. In this case, the Trial Chamber deemed that it was possible to base the charge of genocide on events which occurred only in the region of Vlasenica. In view of the object and goal of the Convention and the subsequent interpretation thereof, the Trial Chamber thus finds that international custom admits the characterisation of genocide even when the exterminatory intent only extends to a limited geographic zone.

The Degree of Intention Required

84. The accused is charged with committing genocide or aiding and abetting therein. These charges are grounded on Article 7(1) of the Statute according to which any person who has either committed a crime or instigated, ordered or otherwise aided and abetted in the commission of the crime without having himself directly committed it must be held responsible for the crime.

85. The Prosecutor proposes a broad understanding of the intention required under Article 7(1) of the Statute and submits that an accused need not *seek* the destruction in whole or in part of a group. Instead, she claims that it suffices that he *knows* that his acts will inevitably, or even only probably, result in the destruction of the group in question. Furthermore, she states that premeditation is not required.

86. The Trial Chamber notes that, contrary to the Prosecutor's contention, the Tribunal for Rwanda in the *Akayesu* case considered that any person accused of genocide for having committed, executed or even only aided and abetted must have had "the specific intent to commit genocide," defined as "the intent to destroy, in whole or in part, a national, ethnical, racial or religious group as such." The *Akayesu* Trial Chamber found that an accused could not be found guilty of genocide if he himself did not share the goal of destroying in part or in whole a group even if he knew that he was contributing to or through his acts might be contributing to the partial or total destruction of a group. It declared that such an individual must be convicted of complicity in genocide.

87. Before even ruling on the level of intention required, the Trial Chamber must first verify whether an act of genocide has been committed as the accused cannot be found guilty of having aided and

---

[117] U.N. Off. Doc. AG/Res. 37/123 D (16 December 1982), para. 2.

abetted in a crime of genocide unless that crime has been established. * * *

The Intention to Commit "All-Inclusive" Genocide

88. As has already been seen, the collection of the population in centres located at different points around the town, their subsequent transfer to detention camps and the interrogations always conducted in an identical manner over a short period of time demonstrate that the operation launched by the Serbian forces against the Muslim population of Brčko was organised. Consequently, whether this organisation meant to destroy in whole or in part the Muslim group must be established. * * *

91. The Prosecutor tendered lists of names of persons who were reputedly killed at the time of the acts ascribed to the accused. In particular, the Prosecutor submitted a list of thirty-nine persons who for the most part were either members of the local administrative or political authorities, well-known figures in town, members of the Muslim Youth Association, members of the SDA [Party for Democratic Action, the primarily Bosniak party] or simply SDA sympathisers.

92. One witness described how the police detectives who interrogated the detainees at Luka camp appeared to decide which detainees were to be executed upon the basis of a document. Another detainee claimed at the hearing to have seen a list of numbered names headed "people to execute" in one of the administrative building offices in Luka camp. According to this witness, about fifty names appeared on the list and they were mostly Muslim.

93. However, the reason for being on these lists and how they were compiled is not clear. Nor has it been established that the accused relied on such a list in carrying out the executions. One witness stated *inter alia* that Goran Jelisić seemed to select the names of persons at random from a list. Other witnesses suggested that the accused himself picked out his victims from those in the hangar. In no manner has it been established that the lists seen by Witness K or by Witness R at Luka camp correspond to that submitted by the Prosecutor. It is not therefore possible to conclude beyond all reasonable doubt that the choice of victims arose from a precise logic to destroy the most representative figures of the Muslim community in Brčko to the point of threatening the survival of that community. * * *

95. It has also not been established beyond all reasonable doubt whether the accused killed at Luka camp [pursuant to higher] orders. Goran Jelisić allegedly presented himself to the detainees as the Luka camp commander. The detainees believed that he was the chief or at least a person in authority because he gave orders to the soldiers at the camp who appeared to be afraid of him. The Trial Chamber does not doubt that the accused exercised a *de facto* authority over the staff and detainees at the camp. * * *

97. The Trial Chamber thus considers it possible that Goran Jelisić acted beyond the scope of the powers entrusted to him. Some of the testimony heard would appear to confirm this conclusion since it describes the accused as a man acting as he pleased and as he saw fit. One witness even recounted that Goran Jelisić had an altercation with a guard and told him that he should not subject the detainees to such treatment.

98. In consequence, the Trial Chamber considers that, in this case, the Prosecutor has not provided sufficient evidence allowing it to be established beyond all reasonable doubt that there existed a plan to destroy the Muslim group in Brčko or elsewhere within which the murders committed by the accused would allegedly fit.

Jelisić's Intention to Commit Genocide

99. It is therefore only as a perpetrator that Goran Jelisić could be declared guilty of genocide.

100. Such a case is theoretically possible. The murders committed by the accused are sufficient to establish the material element of the crime of genocide and it is *a priori* possible to conceive that the accused harboured the plan to exterminate an entire group without this intent having been supported by any organisation in which other individuals participated.[147] In this respect, the preparatory work of the Convention of 1948 brings out that premeditation was not selected as a legal ingredient of the crime of genocide, after having been mentioned by the *ad hoc* committee at the draft stage, on the grounds that it seemed superfluous given the special intention already required by the text and that such precision would only make the burden of proof even greater. It ensues from this omission that the drafters of the Convention did not deem the existence of an organisation or a system serving a genocidal objective as a legal ingredient of the crime. In so doing, they did not discount the possibility of a lone individual seeking to destroy a group as such.

101. The Trial Chamber observes, however, that it will be very difficult in practice to provide proof of the genocidal intent of an individual if the crimes committed are not widespread and if the crime charged is not backed by an organisation or a system.[150]

102. Admittedly, the testimony makes it seem that during this period Goran Jelisić presented himself as the "Serbian Adolf" and

---

[147] Pieter N. Drost, THE CRIME OF STATE, GENOCIDE, A.W. Sythoff, Leyden, 1959, p. 85: "both as a question of theory and as a matter of principle nothing in the present Convention prohibits its provisions to be interpreted and applied to individual cases of murder by reason of the national, racial, ethnical or religious qualities of the single victim if the murderous attack was done with the intent to commit similar acts in the future and in connection with the first crime."

[150] The International Criminal Tribunal for Rwanda noted similarly in the *Kayishema* case that "although a specific plan to destroy does not constitute an element of genocide, it would appear that it is not easy to carry out a genocide without such a plan, or organisation" (para. 94).

claimed to have gone to Brčko to kill Muslims. He also presented himself as "Adolf" at his initial hearing before the Trial Chamber on 26 January 1998. He allegedly said to the detainees at Luka camp that he held their lives in his hands and that only between 5 to 10% of them would leave there. According to another witness, Goran Jelisić told the Muslim detainees in Luka camp that 70% of them were to be killed, 30% beaten and that barely 4% of the 30% might not be badly beaten. Goran Jelisić remarked to one witness that he hated the Muslims and wanted to kill them all, whilst the surviving Muslims could be slaves for cleaning the toilets but never have a professional job. He reportedly added that he wanted "to cleanse" the Muslims and would enjoy doing so, that the "*balijas*"* had proliferated too much and that he had to rid the world of them. Goran Jelisić also purportedly said that he hated Muslim women, that he found them highly dirty and that he wanted to sterilise them all in order to prevent an increase in the number of Muslims but that before exterminating them he would begin with the men in order prevent any proliferation.

103. The statements of the witnesses bring to light the fact that, during the initial part of May, Goran Jelisić regularly executed detainees at Luka camp. According to one witness, Goran Jelisić declared that he had to execute twenty to thirty persons before being able to drink his coffee each morning. The testimony heard by the Trial Chamber revealed that Goran Jelisić frequently informed the detainees of the number of Muslims that he had killed. Thus, on 8 May 1992 he reputedly said to one witness that it was his sixty-eighth victim, on 11 May that he had killed one hundred and fifty persons and finally on 15 May to another witness following an execution that it was his "eighty-third case."

104. Some witnesses pointed out that Goran Jelisić seemed to take pleasure from his position, one which gave him a feeling of power, of holding the power of life or death over the detainees and that he took a certain pride in the number of victims that he had allegedly executed. According to another testimony, Goran Jelisić spoke in a bloodthirsty manner, he treated them like animals or beasts and spittle formed on his lips because of his shouts and the hatred he was expressing. He wanted to terrorise them.

105. The words and attitude of Goran Jelisić as related by the witnesses essentially reveal a disturbed personality. Goran Jelisić led an ordinary life before the conflict. This personality, which presents borderline, anti-social and narcissistic characteristics and which is marked simultaneously by immaturity, a hunger to fill a "void" and a concern to please superiors, contributed to his finally committing crimes.[163] Goran Jelisić suddenly found himself in an apparent position of authority for which nothing had prepared him. It matters little

* Eds.: A derogatory term for Bosnian Muslims and ethnic Bosnians.

[163] The Trial Chamber notes that the presence of a woman at Goran Jelisić's side also seems to have encouraged him to commit certain murders in order to impress the young woman.

whether this authority was real. What does matter is that this authority made it even easier for an opportunistic and inconsistent behaviour to express itself.

106. Goran Jelisić performed the executions randomly. In addition, Witness R, an eminent and well-known figure in the Muslim community was allegedly forced to play Russian roulette with Goran Jelisić before receiving a *laissez-passer* [a pass] directly from him. Moreover, on his own initiative and against all logic, Goran Jelisić issued *laissez-passer* to several detainees at the camp, as shown *inter alia* by the case of Witness E whom Goran Jelisić released after having beaten.

107. In conclusion, the acts of Goran Jelisić are not the physical expression of an affirmed resolve to destroy in whole or in part a group as such.

108. All things considered, the Prosecutor has not established beyond all reasonable doubt that genocide was committed in Brčko during the period covered by the indictment. Furthermore, the behaviour of the accused appears to indicate that, although he obviously singled out Muslims, he killed arbitrarily rather than with the clear intention to destroy a group. The Trial Chamber therefore concludes that it has not been proved beyond all reasonable doubt that the accused was motivated by the *dolus specialis* [specific intent] of the crime of genocide. The benefit of the doubt must always go to the accused and, consequently, Goran Jelisić must be found not guilty on this count.

Prosecutor v. Jelisić, Case No. IT–95–10–A, Judgement (July 5, 2001)

In the Appeals Chamber

Prosecution's Third Ground of Appeal: Intent to Commit Genocide

53. It now remains to consider the second part of the prosecution's third ground of appeal. Assuming the meaning of intent set out above [that the defendant specifically intended to destroy the Muslim group], the prosecution contended that the Trial Chamber was in error in holding that its evidence was insufficient to sustain a conviction for genocide. In particular, it pointed to several items of evidence to which the Trial Chamber had not referred. * * *

57. Having reviewed the evidence in the appeal record, the Appeals Chamber cannot validate the Trial Chamber's conclusion that it was not sufficient to sustain a conviction. It is not necessary in explaining reasons for this conclusion that the Appeals Chamber evaluates every item of evidence in the record. Rather, the Appeals Chamber can first assess the Trial Chamber's own reasons for its conclusion that acquittal was required in light of the evidence on record which was relevant to those reasons and, secondly, the Appeals Chamber can assess other evidence

on the record which was not specifically referred to by the Trial Chamber but to which it has been directed in the course of the appeal. * * *

66. The Appeals Chamber turns first to evidence on the record that was presented by the prosecution during the appeal to demonstrate both that the respondent believed himself to be following a plan sent down by superiors to eradicate the Muslims in Brčko and that, regardless of any such plan, he was himself a one-man genocide mission, intent upon personally wiping out the protected group in whole or part. Some of this evidence was specifically cited by the Trial Chamber itself and summarised in its Judgement: threats by the respondent to kill 70%, to beat 30%, and spare only 5–10% of the Muslim detainees, statements by the respondent that he wanted to rid the world of the Muslims, announcements of his quota of daily killings, and his desire to sterilise Muslims in order to prevent proliferation of the group.

67. However, during the appeal the prosecution has also pointed to other material on the record which in its view supplements this evidence considerably, including extended interviews with the respondent himself which, though often contradictory, contained critical evidence as to his state of mind in committing the murders. A lengthy Annex A compiled by the prosecution contains citations from the evidence that the respondent operated from lists designating prominent Muslims to be killed; he referred to a "plan" for eradicating them; he wanted to "cleanse [. . .] the extremist Muslims and *balijas* like one cleans the head of lice." Witness I said of him: "[h]e carried out orders but he also selected his victims through his own free will" and that "[h]e could have not shot dead someone even if he were told to do so, but he did quite a few things on his own." There is additional evidence of the regular visits of a Bimeks refrigerated truck to the camp to pick up 10–20 dead bodies a day; nightly killings in which the respondent commented after each one "[a]nother *balija* less"; his repeated references to himself as the "Adolf the second" and comments like "I've killed 80 Muslims so far, and I'll finish all of you too" and "as many Muslims as possible had to be killed and that Brčko should become a Serbian town."

68. The Appeals Chamber considers that this evidence and much more of a similar genre in the record could have provided the basis for a reasonable Chamber to find beyond a reasonable doubt that the respondent had the intent to destroy the Muslim group in Brčko. To reiterate, the proper lens through which the Appeals Chamber must view such evidence is not whether it is convinced that the respondent was guilty of genocide beyond reasonable doubt but whether, giving credence to such evidence, no reasonable Trial Chamber could have found that he had such an intent. The Appeals Chamber is not able to conclude that that was the case.

69. The Appeals Chamber also considers whether the Trial Chamber reasonably concluded that, even on the basis of the evidence it

cited and discussed, the respondent should be acquitted for lack of the requisite intent by any reasonable trier of fact.

70. The Trial Chamber essentially relied on the following evidence for its reasonable doubt conclusion: that the respondent had a disturbed personality; that he was immature, narcissistic, desirous of pleasing superiors and that, when placed in a position of authority, those traits manifested themselves in an obsession with power over the lives of those he commanded. This, the Trial Chamber said, was not the same as "an affirmed resolve" to destroy a protected group, in this case the Brčko Muslims. It bears noting that the psychiatric underpinnings of this conclusion come from expert reports prepared for the purpose of deciding whether the respondent was competent to stand trial (he was found to be) and in particular not for evaluating his mental capacity to commit the crimes with which he was charged. He did not plead a defence of insanity and indeed the Trial Chamber itself found him capable of a discriminatory intent in a separate finding. It is sufficient for our purposes here to point out that there is no *per se* inconsistency between a diagnosis of the kind of immature, narcissistic, disturbed personality on which the Trial Chamber relied and the ability to form an intent to destroy a particular protected group. Indeed, as the prosecution points out, it is the borderline unbalanced personality who is more likely to be drawn to extreme racial and ethnical hatred than the more balanced modulated individual without personality defects. The Rules visualise, as a defence, a certain degree of mental incapacity and in any event, no such imbalance was found in this case.

71. The Trial Chamber also placed heavy reliance on the randomness of the respondent's killings. It cited examples of where he let some prisoners go, played Russian roulette for the life of another, and picked his victims not just off lists allegedly given to him by others, but according to his own whim. Entitled though it may have been to consider such evidence, the Trial Chamber, in the view of the Appeals Chamber, was not entitled to conclude that these displays of "randomness" negated the plethora of other evidence recounted above as to the respondent's announced intent to kill the majority of Muslims in Brčko and his quotas and arrangements for so doing. A reasonable trier of fact could have discounted the few incidents where he showed mercy as aberrations in an otherwise relentless campaign against the protected group. Similarly, the fact that he took "pleasure" from the killings does not detract in any way from his intent to perform such killings; as has been mentioned above, the Tribunal has declared in the *Tadić* appeal judgement the irrelevance and "inscrutability of motives in criminal law" insofar as liability is concerned, where an intent—including a specific intent—is clear.

72. Thus, even if the Trial Chamber's conclusion that there was insufficient evidence to show an intent to destroy the group on the respondent's part is examined on the basis of the evidence specifically

referred to by the Trial Chamber itself, it does not pass the approved standard for acquittal under Rule 98*bis*(B) and, consequently, this part of the prosecution's third ground of appeal is sustained.

73. With regard to remedy, counsel for the respondent argues that the Appeals Chamber has discretion, and that, in all the circumstances of this case, there should be no retrial. The Appeals Chamber agrees that the choice of remedy lies within its discretion. Article 25 of the Statute (relating to appellate proceedings) is wide enough to confer such a faculty; this discretion is recognised as well in the wording of Rule 117(C) of the Rules which provides that in "appropriate circumstances the Appeals Chamber may order that the accused be retried according to law." Similarly, national case law gives discretion to a court to rule that there should be no retrial. The discretion must of course be exercised on proper judicial grounds, balancing factors such as fairness to the accused, the interests of justice, the nature of the offences, the circumstances of the case in hand and considerations of public interest. These factors (and others) would be determined on a case by case basis. The question arises as to how the Appeals Chamber should exercise its discretion in this case.

74. For the purpose of determining that question, the Appeals Chamber considers the following factors to be of relevance. The respondent pleaded guilty to certain criminal conduct that was set out in the agreed factual basis. On the basis of that criminal conduct he was found guilty of 31 counts of violations of the laws or customs of war and crimes against humanity. The Trial Chamber imposed a sentence of 40 years' imprisonment. A potential retrial would deal with a count of genocide, charging the respondent with genocide by killing. In respect of this count, the prosecution has brought no further charges of killing. The genocide count is therefore based on the killings to which he has already pleaded guilty. Accordingly, a retrial would be limited to the question of whether he possessed the special intent to destroy in whole or in part, a national, ethnical, racial or religious group, as such. The definition of specific intent has been clarified in the context of the prosecution appeal above.

75. Also, it was through no fault of the accused that the Trial Chamber erred in law—it was not the case that arguments advanced by the defence led to the Trial Chamber's decision to enter a judgement of acquittal. Considerable time will have elapsed between the date that the offences were committed in May 1992 and the date of any potential retrial. The *ad hoc* nature of the International Tribunal which, unlike a national legal system, means resources are limited in terms of manpower and the uncertain longevity of the Tribunal.

76. Furthermore, the respondent has been in the detention of the Tribunal since 22 January 1998. The Trial Chamber recommended that the respondent receive "psychological and psychiatric follow-up treatment." Such treatment is currently provided by the United Nations

Detention Unit. However, a prison would generally be in a better position to provide long-term consistent treatment.

77. Rule 117(C) of the Rules provides that in "appropriate circumstances the Appeals Chamber may order that the accused be retried according to law." The Appeals Chamber recognizes the prosecution's right to request a retrial as a remedy on appeal. However, as has been stated above, whether or not such a request is granted lies within the discretion of the Appeals Chamber based on the facts of the case before it. It is not obliged, having identified an error, to remit for retrial. Considering the exceptional circumstances of the present case, the Appeal Chamber considers that it is not in the interests of justice to grant the prosecution's request and accordingly declines to reverse the acquittal entered by the Trial Chamber and remit the case for further proceedings. In this regard, the Appeals Chamber does not consider that the facts of this case constitute appropriate circumstances, as referred to in Rule 117(C) of the Rules.

NOTES & QUESTIONS

1. Case Outcome

Although the Appeals Chamber reversed the Trial Chamber's Rule 98 ruling, it nonetheless declined to reverse the acquittal. *Prosecutor v. Jelisić*, Case No. IT–95–10–A, Judgement, para. 4 (July 5, 2001). In 2002, Jelisić's counsel lodged a confidential request for a revision of his client's forty-year sentence, one of the stiffest imposed at the time. The request was denied, and Jelisić was transferred to Italy to serve out the remainder of his sentence. In 2002, the Italian Supreme Court issued a decision reducing Jelisić sentence to thirty years. Based on this reduction in his sentence, Jelisić in 2016 formally requested early release from the Mechanism for International Criminal Tribunals (MICT), as the ICTY's residual mechanism was then known. Under the MICT's statute, an individual is eligible for early release if they have served two-thirds of their sentence, which would be the case for Jelisić if the sentence reduction ordered by the Italian Court were recognized by the MICT. President Theodor Meron of the MICT refused to grant early release, citing a number of factors and noting that it was in the discretion of the MICT to recognize the sentence reduction ordered by the Italian court. *Prosecutor v. Jelisić*, Case No. MICT-14-63-ES, Decision of the President on Recognition of Commutation of Sentence, Remission of Sentence, and Early Release of Goran Jelisić (Public Redacted Version) (Aug. 11, 2017).

2. The Genocide Count

As a matter of prosecutorial strategy, why would the Prosecution proceed with the genocide count after Jelisić pled guilty to war crimes and crimes against humanity? Conversely, why would Jelisić plead guilty *only* to those crimes and still seek to defend against the genocide count? Should the Prosecution have dropped the genocide count and accepted the forty-year sentence, which amounts to a life sentence for a man of Jelisić's age? Consider this view:

> The ICTY's role is to contribute to peace, accountability, and ultimately reconciliation within a context of collective atrocity. Directing its fire at what are really no more than isolated social deviants can only distort the historical record in an unnecessarily provocative fashion. If Serb militias did not, in a collective sense, commit genocide during the Bosnian war, such genocide convictions may not assist the Tribunal in its restorative function and may ultimately prove to be counterproductive. * * * [A] responsible international prosecutor, conscious of the need to focus precious resources on genuinely significant cases, ought to discourage prosecution of individual maniacs who seem to possess preposterous and unrealistic genocidal plans that are not shared by others.

William A. Schabas, *Was Genocide Committed in Bosnia and Herzegovina? First Judgments of the International Criminal Tribunal for the Former Yugoslavia (ICTY)*, 25 FORDHAM INT'L L. J. 23, 35–6 (2001). Do you agree with Professor Schabas that if Jelisić's special intent was an anomaly, scarce international prosecutorial resources should not have been expended on him? Should lower-level defendants ever be charged with genocide? Or, should that highly stigmatizing charge be reserved for those superiors who design a campaign of persecution? What prosecutorial strategy might be furthered by charging individuals with genocide at all levels of a chain of command? Does such a strategy contribute to creating a more complete story about how violence was employed within a particular region? Is the creation of such a historical narrative of events a proper goal of international prosecutions?

3. Prosecutorial Discretion

The Prosecution's decision to go forward with the genocide count may reflect the influence of the civil law notion of "compulsory prosecution." Consider the excerpt below, which uses Germany as an example to discuss the way in which prosecutorial discretion in civil law countries is more constrained when it comes to declining to prosecute, reducing charges, or engaging in plea bargaining.

> The practice of [civil law] prosecutors today is an outgrowth of the civil law tradition of "compulsory prosecution," which demands that a prosecutor file criminal charges whenever the evidence is strong enough to support such charges. While the doctrine of compulsory prosecution has softened with the passage of time and the realities of modern caseloads, it still remains fair to say that a prosecutor's charging discretion in non-minor criminal cases remains limited. In the first place, the tradition of compulsory prosecution encourages prosecutors to "play it safe" in close cases and file criminal charges. Secondly, a decision not to prosecute someone with a crime will have to face review by prosecutorial superiors who tend to be conservative in matters of discretion not to prosecute.

> And, finally, if a prosecutor decides not to file criminal charges because the prosecutor believes that the evidence in the case is insufficient to support the filing of criminal charges, civil law systems usually afford victims the right to challenge such decisions unless the crime involved is rather minor. Sometimes this challenge is administrative in the form of a complaint about the prosecutor's actions, but sometimes the victim's challenge can be brought directly in court seeking reversal of the decision not to prosecute or even through a form of private prosecution. If review of the prosecutor's decision reveals a violation of the duty of compulsory prosecution, this would be entered in the prosecutor's file and could have a negative impact on the speed with which the prosecutor advances up the hierarchical career path typical of civil law systems. * * * If an American prosecutor decides not to file a criminal charge, there usually is no mechanism that would permit judicial review of that decision and, even when there is a statute permitting review, judicial approval is given perfunctorily. Thus [American] prosecutors have tremendous discretion in deciding whether to charge someone with a crime, even when the evidence is strong.

William T. Pizzi, *Understanding Prosecutorial Discretion in the United States: The Limits of Comparative Criminal Procedure as an Instrument of Reform*, 54 OHIO ST. L.J. 1325, 1332, 1337 (1993).

4. Jelisić on a "One-Man Genocide Mission"

The ICTY seems to accept that an individual could be convicted of genocide on the basis of acts perpetrated only by that one individual against a single member of a protected group if the requisite intent is present. Absent weapons of mass destruction, a low-level individual such as Jelisić would rarely be capable of destroying an entire group, or even a significant part of a group. Should such an individual still be found guilty of genocide where his intended outcome was impossible to achieve? How would a prosecutor prove the intent to destroy the entire group where the defendant killed only a single individual and had little possibility of killing more? Is attempted genocide a more appropriate charge in these circumstances?

5. Inferring Intent

Absent a confession of intent or a written genocidal policy, the intent to destroy a group must usually be inferred. How is a tribunal to do this? What evidence is appropriate to use to infer that a defendant was acting with genocidal intent? On which factors did the ICTY rely in the *Jelisić* case? The *Akayesu* Trial Chamber has observed that "it is possible to deduce the genocidal intent inherent in a particular act charged from the general context of the perpetration of other culpable acts systematically directed against that same group, whether these acts were committed by the same offender or by others." *Prosecutor v. Akayesu*, Judgement, Case No. ICTR–96–4–T, para. 523 (Sept. 2, 1998).

How would the actions of other individuals not before the court bear on the determination of a particular defendant's own *mens rea*? How might evidence of genocidal intent be obscured where alternative motives, intents, or purposes can be identified, hypothesized, or claimed? For example, where violence is occurring within the context of a civil war or a counter-insurgency movement with ethnic dimensions, attacks on a particular group, or sub-set of a group, can be framed as part of an armed conflict reflecting political or other discord in an effort to deflect attention from a genocidal policy. How would defense counsel make such arguments on behalf of a client charged with genocide? Keep these questions in mind when you read the excerpt from the *Al Bashir* case below. For a criticism of the tendency to use the existence of a nationwide campaign of genocide to infer genocidal intent, *see* Kevin Jon Heller, *International Decision: Prosecutor v. Karemera, Ngirumpatse, & Nzirorera*, 101 AM. J. INT'L L. 157, 161 (2007).

6. Premeditation

Is premeditation an element of genocide? Can genocidal intent form spontaneously or must it be the result of prior contemplation and planning? If not an element of the offense, should proof of premeditation be an aggravating factor at sentencing? Should international criminal law recognize a notion of "escalation" to genocide, where the specific intent for genocide is formed at a stage later than the onslaught of an initial operation not amounting to genocide?

7. Knowledge of the Inevitability of Destruction

In this case as in others (e.g., the *Prosecutor v. Sikirica*, excerpted *infra*), the Prosecutor argued in pre-trial proceedings that genocide could be found where the accused knew that his acts would "inevitably, or even only probably" lead to the partial destruction of the group. *Prosecutor v. Jelisić*, Case No. IT–95–10–A, Judgement, para. 85 (Dec. 14, 1999). In support of this more relaxed *mens rea* standard, the Prosecution maintained that proof of any of the following three alternative forms of intent would satisfy the *mens rea* requirement of Article 4 of the ICTY Statute:

> (a) the accused consciously desired the acts to result in the destruction, in whole or in part, of the group, as such; or
>
> (b) the accused knew his acts were destroying, in whole or in part, the group, as such; or
>
> (c) the accused knew that the likely consequence of his acts would be to destroy, in whole or in part, the group, as such.

Prosecutor v. Sikirica, Case No. IT–95–8–T, Judgement on Defense Motions to Acquit, para. 27 (Sept. 3, 2001). In *Sikirica*, the Prosecution argued that requiring proof of option (a) alone "reduces the scope of application of the genocide prohibition in a way that undermines the object and purpose of the [ICTY] Statute." *Id.* at para. 27. The Prosecutor also invoked Article 30 of the ICC Statute, which contains a definition of intent that is satisfied with a showing of knowledge:

> 1. Unless otherwise provided, a person shall be criminally responsible and liable for punishment for a crime within the jurisdiction of the Court only if the material elements are committed with intent and knowledge.

2. For the purposes of this article, a person has intent where: (a) In relation to conduct, that person means to engage in the conduct; (b) In relation to a consequence, that person means to cause that consequence or is aware that it will occur in the ordinary course of events.

3. For the purposes of this article, "knowledge" means awareness that a circumstance exists or a consequence will occur in the ordinary course of events. "Know" and "knowingly" shall be construed accordingly.

In *Sikirica*, the Tribunal refused the Prosecution's invitation to amend the *mens rea* requirement of genocide with the following reasoning:

58. In the Trial Chamber's opinion, the submissions by the Prosecution on this question have for the most part complicated what is a relatively simple issue of interpretation of the *chapeau* of Article 4(2). In contradistinction to the manner in which many crimes are elaborated in treaties and, indeed, in the domestic law of many States, Article 4 expressly identifies and explains the intent that is needed to establish the crime of genocide. This approach follows the 1948 Genocide Convention and is also consistent with [Article 6 of] the ICC Statute. It is an approach that is necessary if genocide is to be distinguished from other species of the *genus* to which it belongs. Genocide is a crime against humanity, and it is easy to confuse it with other crimes against humanity, notably, persecution. Both genocide and persecution have discriminatory elements, some of which are common to both crimes. Thus, Article 5(h) of the Statute proscribes "persecutions on political, racial and religious grounds," while, in respect of genocide, what is required is an "intent to destroy, in whole or in part, a national, ethnical, racial or religious group, as such."

60. The first rule of interpretation [set out in Article 31 of the Vienna Convention] is to give words their ordinary meaning where the text is clear. Here, the meaning of intent is made plain in the *chapeau* to Article 4(2). Beyond saying that the very specific intent required must be established, particularly in the light of the potential for confusion between genocide and persecution, the Chamber does not consider it necessary to indulge in the exercise of choosing one of the three standards identified by the Prosecution. In the light, therefore, of the explanation that the provision itself gives as to the specific meaning of intent, it is unnecessary to have recourse to theories of intent. It is, however, important to understand the part of the *chapeau* that elaborates on and explains the required intent, that is "intent to destroy, in whole or in part, a national, ethnical, racial or religious group, as such."

For an argument in favor of the Prosecution's approach, *see* Alexander K.A. Greenawalt, *Rethinking Genocidal Intent: The Case for a Knowledge-Based Interpretation*, 99 COLUM. L. REV. 2259 (1999). Greenawalt argues:

> [I]n cases where a perpetrator is otherwise liable for a genocidal act, the requirement of genocidal intent should be satisfied if the perpetrator acted in furtherance of a campaign targeting members of a protected group and knew that the goal or manifest effect of the campaign was the destruction of the group in whole or in part. Drawing upon the Genocide Convention's core concern for the permanent losses to humanity that result from the annihilation of enumerated groups, this approach emphasizes the destructive result of genocidal acts instead of the specific reasons that move particular individuals to perform such acts. . . . [I]t seeks to assert a more objective and principled standard of liability than that offered by the specific intent interpretation.

Id. at 2288.

The Prosecutor's argument was not a specious one. In many criminal justice systems, a trier of fact can find that a person intentionally caused the social harm of an offense if (1) it was within the defendant's desire to cause the social harm or (2) the defendant acted with knowledge that the social harm was virtually certain to occur as a result of the conduct. Note, however, that in the United States, the Model Penal Code—which rejects entirely the concept of specific intent—makes a cleaner distinction between intentional conduct and conduct undertaken knowingly:

> § 2.02. General Requirements of Culpability
>
> (a) *Purposely*. A person acts purposely with respect to a material element of an offense when:
>
> (i) if the element involves the nature of his conduct or a result thereof, it is his conscious object to engage in conduct of that nature or to cause such a result; and
>
> (ii) if the element involves the attendant circumstances, he is aware of the existence of such circumstances or he believes or hopes that they exist.
>
> (b) *Knowingly*. A person acts knowingly with respect to a material element of an offense when:
>
> (i) if the element involves the nature of his conduct or the attendant circumstances, he is aware that his conduct is of that nature or that such circumstances exist; and
>
> (ii) if the element involves a result of his conduct, he is aware that it is practically certain that his conduct will cause such a result.

If you could redraft the *mens rea* of genocide, which approach would you adopt?

8. Proof of Genocide

In ruling on the criminal liability of particular individuals indicted for genocide, the *ad hoc* tribunals have generally proceeded in two steps. First, they have undertaken a threshold inquiry of whether genocide occurred in the region in which the individual was operating. Then, the tribunals consider whether the particular defendant possessed genocidal intent. Is a defendant prejudiced by this two-step methodology, especially if the court concludes that genocide writ large was in fact occurring in the area in which the defendant operated? Inversely, does this approach unnecessarily prolong the proceedings or increase the prosecution's burden of proof by requiring the prosecution to prove the existence of genocide before proving the defendant's role therein? If a defendant is found to have acted with genocidal intent, the defendant may be convicted as a perpetrator. Compare *Prosecutor v. Akayesu*, Case No. ICTR–96–4–T, Judgement, paras. 112–129 and 726–734 (Sept. 2, 1998) (concluding that genocide occurred in Rwanda and determining that the accused acted with genocidal intent) with *Prosecutor v. Jelisić*, Case No. IT–95–10–A, Judgement (July 5, 2001) (determining that genocide did not occur in Brčko, but finding defendant may have committed genocide nonetheless because he possessed genocidal intent). If the Tribunal concludes that the defendant is not acting with genocidal intent, the defendant may still be convicted as an accomplice to genocide, so long as he knew that the primary perpetrator possessed genocidal intent and knew that his own actions would assist the commission of genocide. *See Prosecutor v. Krstić*, Case No. IT–98–33–A, Judgement, para. 142 (Apr. 19, 2004). Is it appropriate to hold someone guilty of genocide if they do not possess genocidal intent? Complicity liability is the subject of Chapter 15.

9. Ethnic Cleansing and Genocide in Yugoslavia

Does ethnic cleansing always amount to genocide? The term "genocide" was not universally applied with respect to the internecine war in the former Yugoslavia, notwithstanding that the conflict was characterized by massive rights violations against Bosnian Muslims, and to a lesser extent other ethnic groups, clearly singled out on the basis of their ethnic and religious identity. Instead, the term "ethnic cleansing" was coined to describe acts of violence incidental to efforts to obtain territory from one ethnic group by another ethnic group. The theory was that the perpetrators did not intend to destroy the victim group, in whole or in part, they simply wanted to obtain the victim group's territory and thus used persecutory violence to effectuate this outcome. In this way, ethnic cleansing has become a defense to genocide. Helsinki Watch was the first organization to officially equate the concepts of ethnic cleansing and genocide in the context of the former Yugoslavia. *See* Helsinki Watch, WAR CRIMES IN BOSNIA AND HERZEGOVINA, at 1 (1992) ("The findings in this report . . . provide at the very least *prima facie* evidence that genocide is taking place"). Likewise, the U.N. General Assembly suggested that "the abhorrent policy of 'ethnic cleansing' . . . is a form of genocide." The Situation in Bosnia and Herzegovina, G.A. Res. 47/121, at 44, U.N. GAOR, 47th. Sess., Supp. No. 49, U.N. Doc. A/Res/47/121 (Apr. 7, 1993).

Nonetheless, the ICTY has determined that genocide, as a matter of state policy, did not occur universally throughout the various republics of the former Yugoslavia as seen in the principal case above. At the same time, the ICTY has convicted particular individuals of genocide based on findings that the defendants acted with genocidal intent, and determined that certain massacres, notably at Srebrenica, constituted acts of genocide. This latter ruling is reproduced in the next Section. *See Prosecutor v. Krstić*, Case No.

IT–98–33–T, Judgement, para. 643 (Aug. 2, 2001). Over time, Carla Del Ponte (Switzerland), when she was Chief Prosecutor, dropped several genocide charges against defendants from the former Yugoslavia. Why might she have done this? What weight should international or domestic criminal tribunals give pronouncements of non-governmental organizations, such as Helsinki Watch, in determining whether or not genocide had occurred in a particular region? Should a similar statement by the General Assembly be given greater weight?

10. Genocidal Intent in Darfur

Sudan has been plagued by conflict for the majority of its fifty-year existence. (See the Appendix for a map of Sudan.) The primary civil war has been one between the Northern government and rebels in the South. Just as peace negotiations were proceeding between the North and South in 2002, a new conflict flared up in the Western region of Darfur. In February 2003, loosely federated rebel groups, calling themselves the Sudan Liberation Movement/Army (SLM/A) and the Justice and Equality Movement (JEM), declared open rebellion against the government because they were excluded from the power- and wealth-sharing agreements emerging from the North-South negotiations. The government responded with a counterinsurgency campaign directed primarily at civilian targets. This coincided with the emergence in the international lexicon of the *janjaweed*—roving militia on camel- and horseback with deniable ties to the central authorities.

In response to the high levels of violence, the Security Council by Resolution 1564 in 2004 directed the U.N. Secretary-General to form a Commission of Inquiry to investigate reports of violations of international criminal law by all parties to the conflict. *See* Report of the Commission of Inquiry on Darfur to the Secretary-General Pursuant to Security Council Resolution 1564 of 18 September 2004, UN Doc. S/2005/60 (February 1, 2005). The Commission of Inquiry concluded that even though some Sudanese officials may have acted with genocidal intent, there was insufficient evidence to prove a Sudanese government policy of committing genocide. Shortly thereafter on March 31, 2005, the Security Council adopted Resolution 1593 under its Chapter VII powers and referred, pursuant to Article 13(b) of the Rome Statute, the situation in Darfur to the Prosecutor of the ICC to investigate crimes committed since July 1, 2002. This was the first referral by the Security Council to the Court. The Prosecutor subsequently sought to indict President Al Bashir.

Prosecutor v. Omar Hassan Ahmad Al Bashir, Case No. ICC–02/05–01/09, Decision on the Prosecution's Application for a Warrant of Arrest Against Omar Hassan Ahmad Al Bashir (March 4, 2009)

Pre-Trial Chamber I

1. On 31 March 2005, the United Nations Security Council, acting under Chapter VII of the Charter of the United Nations, adopted Resolution 1593 referring the situation in Darfur, Sudan since 1 July

2002 ("the Darfur situation") to the Prosecutor of the International Criminal Court, in accordance with article 13(b) of the Statute. * * *

4. On 14 July 2008, the Prosecution filed an application under article 58 ("the Prosecution Application") requesting the issuance of a warrant of arrest against Omar Hassan Ahmad Al Bashir (hereinafter referred to as "Omar Al Bashir") for his alleged criminal responsibility in the commission of genocide, crimes against humanity and war crimes against members of the Fur, Masalit and Zaghawa groups in Darfur from 2003 to 14 July 2008. * * *

8. On 11 January 2009, the Sudan Workers Trade Unions Federation and the Sudan International Defence Group filed the "Application on behalf of Citizens' Organisations of The Sudan in relation to the Prosecutor's Applications for Arrest Warrants of 14 July 2008 and 20 November 2008" whereby they requested, pursuant to rule 103 of the Rules, the leave of the Chamber to make written and oral submissions on the following matters:

> The Applicants request that no arrest warrants be issued by the Pre-Trial Chamber at this time on grounds that (1) issuing such warrants would have grave implications for the peace building process in Sudan and that deference must be given to considerations of national interest and security; (2) that the interests of justice will not be served particularly in light of the Prosecutor's conduct in bringing these applications; (3) that such warrants could entrench the negative perceptions of the ICC and thus contribute to a deterioration of the situation in Sudan; and, (4) that alternative means of transitional justice and resolution are being and will [be] pursued without the need for any consideration of involvement of the ICC at this stage. * * *

15. On 5 February 2009, the Chamber issued the "Decision on Application under Rule 103," in which the Chamber rejected the request made by the Sudan Workers Trade Unions Federation and the Sudan International Defence Group pursuant to rule 103 of the Rules as, according to the Statute and the Rules, "the Chamber neither has the power to review, nor is it responsible for, the Prosecution's assessment that, under the current circumstances in Sudan, the initiation of a case against Omar Al Bashir and three alleged commanders of organised armed groups would not be detrimental to the interests of justice." * * *

Whether the Common Requirements Under Article 58(1) of the Statute for the Issuance of a Warrant of Arrest Have Been Met

52. As the Chamber has already held: according to the Statute and the Elements of Crimes, the definition of every crime within the jurisdiction of the Court includes both contextual and specific elements.

53. Hence, the Chamber will first analyse whether there are reasonable grounds to believe that the contextual elements of the crimes

alleged by the Prosecution in the Prosecution Application are present, and only if the answer is in the affirmative, will the Chamber turn its attention to the question as to whether there are reasonable grounds to believe that the specific elements of any such crime have been met.

54. Moreover, although the Prosecution Application focuses, for the most part, on the three counts of genocide, the Chamber observes that, according to the Prosecution, the alleged crimes were committed as part of a counter-insurgency campaign launched in March 2003 by the Government of Sudan ("the GoS"). Hence, the Chamber will first analyse the Prosecution's allegations concerning war crimes and crimes against humanity, and only then will the Chamber turn its attention to the Prosecution's allegations relating to the crime of genocide. * * *

[The Chamber goes on to conclude that there are reasonable grounds for believing that there is an armed conflict not of an international character in the Sudan; that there are reasonable grounds to believe that the specific elements of at least one war crime are present; that there are reasonable grounds to believe that crimes against humanity have been committed; and that there are reasonable grounds to believe that the specific elements of at least one crime against humanity are present, including extermination.]

Genocide

110. The Prosecution submits that there are reasonable grounds to believe that Omar Al Bashir bears criminal responsibility under article 25(3)(a) of the Statute for the crime of genocide as a result of:

i. the killing of members of the Fur, Masalit and Zaghawa ethnic groups (article 6(a)—Count 1);

ii. causing serious bodily or mental harm to members of the Fur, Masalit and Zaghawa ethnic groups (article 6(b)—Count 2); and

iii. deliberately inflicting on the Fur, Masalit and Zaghawa ethnic groups conditions of life calculated to bring about the groups physical destruction (article 6(c)—Count 3).

111. Nevertheless, the Prosecution acknowledges that (i) it does not have any direct evidence in relation to Omar Al Bashir's alleged responsibility for the crime of genocide; and that therefore (ii) its allegations concerning genocide are solely based on certain inferences that, according to the Prosecution, can be drawn from the facts of the case. * * *

113. The Majority notes that the Elements of Crimes elaborate on the definition of genocide provided for in article 6 of the Statute, establishing that the three following elements must always be fulfilled for the existence of the crime of genocide under the Statute:

i. the victims must belong to the targeted group;

ii. the killings, the serious bodily harm, the serious mental harm, the conditions of life, the measures to prevent births or the forcible transfer of children must take place "in the context of a manifest pattern of similar conduct directed against that group or was conduct that could itself effect such destruction"; and

iii. the perpetrator must act with the intent to destroy in whole or in part the targeted group. * * *

123. The Majority * * * observes that * * * the conduct for which the suspect is allegedly responsible must have taken place in the context of a manifest pattern of similar conduct directed against the targeted group or must have had such a nature so as to itself effect the total or partial destruction of the targeted group.

124. In the view of the Majority, according to this contextual element, the crime of genocide is only completed when the relevant conduct presents a concrete threat to the existence of the targeted group, or a part thereof. In other words, the protection offered by the penal norm defining the crime of genocide—as an *ultima ratio* ["last resort"] mechanism to preserve the highest values of the international community—is only triggered when the threat against the existence of the targeted group, or part thereof, becomes concrete and real, as opposed to just being latent or hypothetical.

125. The Majority is aware that there is certain controversy as to whether this contextual element should be recognised. * * *

126. In this regard, the Majority recalls that, according to article 21(1)(a) of the Statute, the Court must apply "in the first place" the Statute, the Elements of Crimes and the Rules. Moreover, as already held in the previous section on jurisdiction, those other sources of law provided for in paragraphs (1)(b) and (1)(c) of article 21 of the Statute [treaties, other international principles, and general principles of law derived from national law], can only be applied when the following two conditions are met: (i) there is a lacuna in the written law contained in the Statute, the Elements of Crimes and the Rules; and (ii) such lacuna cannot be filled by the application of the criteria provided for in articles 31 and 32 of the Vienna Convention on the Law of the Treaties and article 21(3) of the Statute. * * *

131. The Majority considers that this interpretation is also supported by the object and purpose of article 9(1) of the Statute, which consists of furthering the *nullum crimen sine lege* principle embraced in article 22 of the Statute, by providing *a priori* legal certainty on the content of the definition of the crimes provided for in the Statute. In the Majority's view, had the application of the Elements of Crimes been fully discretionary for the competent Chamber, the safeguards provided for by the article 22 *nullum crimen sine lege* principle would be significantly eroded.

132. In the case at hand, the Majority does not observe any irreconcilable contradiction between the definition of the crime of genocide provided for in article 6 of the Statute and the contextual element provided for in the Elements of Crimes with regard to the crime of genocide.

133. Quite the contrary, the Majority considers that the definition of the crime of genocide, so as to require for its completion an actual threat to the targeted group, or a part thereof, is (i) not per se contrary to article 6 of the Statute; (ii) fully respects the requirements of article 22(2) of the Statute that the definition of the crimes "shall be strictly construed and shall not be extended by analogy" and "[i]n case of ambiguity, the definition shall be interpreted in favour of the person being investigated, prosecuted or convicted"; and (iii) is fully consistent with the traditional consideration of the crime of genocide as the "crime of the crimes."

134. The Majority observes that, in addition to the above-mentioned contextual element, the Elements of Crimes provide for the following two elements, which are common to the above-mentioned five categories of genocidal acts provided for in article 6 of the Statute: (i) the victims must belong to a particular national, ethnic, racial or religious group; and (ii) the perpetrator must act with the intent to destroy in whole or in part that particular group.

135. In relation to the first element, the Majority is of the view that the targeted group must have particular positive characteristics (national, ethnic, racial or religious), and not a lack thereof. In this regard, it is important to highlight that the drafters of the 1948 Genocide Convention gave "close attention to the positive identification of groups with specific distinguishing well-established, some said immutable, characteristics." It is, therefore, a matter of who the targeted people are, not who they are not. As a result, the Majority considers that negative definitions of the targeted group do not suffice for the purpose of article 6 of the Statute.

136. The Majority considers that there are no reasonable grounds to believe that nationality, race and/or religion are a distinctive feature of any of the three different groups—the Fur, the Masalit and the Zaghawa—that, according to the Prosecution, have been targeted. In this regard, the Majority highlights that the members of these three groups, as well as others in the region, appear to have Sudanese nationality, similar racial features, and a shared Muslim religion.

137. As a result, the question arises as to whether any of the three said groups is a distinct ethnic group. In this regard, the Majority finds that there are reasonable grounds to believe that this question must be answered in the affirmative as there are reasonable grounds to believe that each of the groups (the Fur, the Masalit and the Zaghawa) has its own language, its own tribal customs and its own traditional links to its lands.

138. In relation to the second element, the crime of genocide is characterised by the fact that any of the five categories of genocidal acts provided for in article 6 of the Statute must be carried out with the "intent to destroy, in whole or in part, a national, ethnic, racial or religious group." In the view of the Majority, this introduces a subjective element that is additional to the general intent and knowledge requirement provided for in article 30 of the Statute.

139. As a result, the Majority considers that the crime of genocide is comprised of two subjective elements:

i. a general subjective element that must cover any genocidal act provided for in article 6(a) to (e) of the Statute, and which consists of article 30 intent and knowledge requirement; and

ii. an additional subjective element, normally referred to as "*dolus specialis*" or specific intent, according to which any genocidal acts must be carried out with the "intent to destroy in whole or in part" the targeted group. * * *

147. The Prosecution highlights that it relies exclusively on proof by inference to substantiate its allegations concerning Omar Al Bashir's alleged responsibility for genocide. In particular, the Prosecution relies on inferences to prove the existence of Omar Al Bashir's *dolus specialis*/specific intent to destroy in whole or in part the Fur, Masalit and Zaghawa groups.

148. In this regard, the Majority observes that, according to the Prosecution, Omar Al Bashir was in full control of the "apparatus" of the State of Sudan, including the Sudanese Armed Forces and their allied Janjaweed Militia, the Sudanese Police Forces, the National Intelligence and Security Services (NISS) and the Humanitarian Aid Commission (HAC), and used such State apparatus to carry out a genocidal campaign against the Fur, Masalit and Zaghawa groups.

149. As a result, the Majority considers that if the materials provided by the Prosecution support the Prosecution's allegations in this regard, the existence of reasonable grounds to believe that Omar Al Bashir had a genocidal intent would automatically lead to the conclusion that there are also reasonable grounds to believe that a genocidal campaign against the Fur, Masalit and Zaghawa groups was a core component of the GoS counter-insurgency campaign.

150. However, the situation would be different if the materials provided by the Prosecution show reasonable grounds to believe that Omar Al Bashir shared the control over the "apparatus" of the State of Sudan with other high-ranking Sudanese political and military leaders. In this situation, the Majority is of the view that the existence of reasonable grounds to believe that one of the core components of the GoS counter-insurgency campaign was a genocidal campaign against the Fur, Masalit and Zaghawa groups would be dependent upon the showing of

reasonable grounds to believe that those who shared the control of the "apparatus" of the State of Sudan with Omar Al Bashir agreed that the GoS counter-insurgency campaign would, *inter alia*, aim at the destruction, in whole or in part, of the Fur, Masalit and Zaghawa groups.

151. It is for this reason that the Majority refers throughout the rest of the present decision to "the GoS's genocidal intent" as opposed to "Omar Al Bashir's genocidal intent."

152. Moreover, regardless of whether Omar Al Bashir had full control, or shared control with other high-ranking Sudanese political and military leaders, over the apparatus of the State of Sudan, the mental state of mid-level superiors and low-level physical perpetrators is irrelevant for the purpose of determining whether the materials provided by the Prosecution show reasonable grounds to believe that the crime of genocide against the Fur, Masalit and Zaghawa groups was part of the GoS counter-insurgency campaign. * * *

153. The Majority observes that, according to the Prosecution, an inference of the GoS's genocidal intent "may properly be drawn from all evidence taken together, even where each factor on its own may not warrant such an inference."

154. Furthermore, the Prosecution submits that, in order for such an inference to be drawn, the existence of the GoS's genocidal intent "must be the only reasonable inference available on the evidence."

155. The Majority also notes that the Prosecution, in support of its submissions on the applicable law concerning the proof by inference, places particular reliance on the case law of the Appeals Chamber of the ICTY. In this regard, the Prosecution emphasises that, in applying the law on the proof by inference at the current stage of the proceedings, the Chamber must take into consideration that (i) the ICTY's case law refers to a "beyond reasonable doubt" standard; and that (ii) "for the purpose of an Art. 58 application the lower standard of reasonable grounds will instead be applicable."

156. The Majority finds the Prosecution's submissions to be a correct statement of the law on the proof by inference applicable before this Court. * * *

157. In this regard, the Majority recalls that, according to the consistent interpretation of article 58 of the Statute by this Chamber, a warrant of arrest or a summons to appear shall only be issued in relation to a specific crime if the competent Chamber is satisfied that there are reasonable grounds to believe that the relevant crime has been committed and the suspect is criminally liable for it under the Statute.

158. In applying the law on the proof by inference to the article 58 evidentiary standard in relation to the existence of a GoS's genocidal intent, the Majority agrees with the Prosecution in that such a standard would be met only if the materials provided by the Prosecution in support of the Prosecution Application show that the only reasonable conclusion

to be drawn therefrom is the existence of reasonable grounds to believe in the existence of a GoS's *dolus specialis*/specific intent to destroy in whole or in part the Fur, Masalit and Zaghawa groups.

159. As a result, the Majority considers that, if the existence of a GoS's genocidal intent is only one of several reasonable conclusions available on the materials provided by the Prosecution, the Prosecution Application in relation to genocide must be rejected as the evidentiary standard provided for in article 58 of the Statute would not have been met. * * *

162. In the absence of direct evidence, the Prosecution submits that:

> In the instant case, the Prosecution respectfully submits that Al Bashir's intent to destroy the target groups as such in substantial part is the only available inference from a comprehensive consideration of [a number of] factors.

163. The Majority observes that the Prosecution, at paragraphs 366 et seq. of the Prosecution Application, provides for nine different factors from which to infer the existence of a GoS's genocidal intent.

164. In the Majority's view, they can be classified into the following categories:

i. the alleged existence of a GoS strategy to deny and conceal the crimes allegedly committed in the Darfur region against the members of the Fur, Masalit and Zaghawa groups;

ii. some official statements and public documents, which, according to the Prosecution, provide reasonable grounds to believe in the (pre) existence of a GoS genocidal policy;

iii. the nature and extent of the acts of violence committed by GoS forces against the Fur, Masalit, and Zaghawa civilian population.

165. In relation to the alleged existence of a GoS strategy to deny and conceal the alleged commission of crimes in Darfur, the Majority considers that, even if the existence of such strategy was to be proven, there can be a variety of other plausible reasons for its adoption, such as the intention to conceal the commission of war crimes and crimes against humanity. * * *

167. [With regard to documents submitted by the Prosecution, i]n the Majority's view, the first documents * * * do not provide, by themselves, any indicia of a GoS's genocidal intent. In this regard, the Majority considers that they provide, at best, indicia of the GoS's intent to discriminate against the members of the Fur, Masalit and Zaghawa groups by excluding them from federal government and implementing political arrangements aimed at limiting their power in their homeland (Darfur). * * *

169. In the Majority's view, evidence [in other documents] of close coordination provides indicia of the existence of a well organised

governmental structure through which decisions taken in the upper levels of the GoS can be effectively implemented. Nevertheless, considering the ongoing armed conflict between the SLM/A, the JEM and other armed groups (which appear to have broad social support in Darfur) and the GoS, the Majority sees no indicia of unlawfulness in securing a close coordination among the military, the police, the intelligence services and the civil administration, as well as among the federal, the state and the local levels of government.

170. The Prosecution places particular reliance on two statements allegedly made by Omar Al Bashir in March/April 2003, at a time in which peace talks with the SLM/A and the JEM broke off, and the GoS preparations for its counter-insurgency campaign were starting:

i. In March 2003, Omar Al Bashir is said to have declared in front of a number of members of the Sudanese Armed Forces in El Facher that the rebellion is to be quelled in two weeks and that no prisoners or wounded are to be brought back;

ii. In April 2003, Omar Al Bashir, again in El Facher, is said to have stated in front of Northern Darfur State officials and members of the Sudanese Armed Forces officials that he "did not want any villages or prisoners, only scorched earth."

171. The Prosecution also relies on a statement allegedly given on national television by Omar Al Bashir in January 2004. According to the Prosecution, Omar Al Bashir is said to have confirmed the concept of the operation in Darfur and is said to have told the Sudanese public that he had given the Sudanese Armed Forces *carte blanche* in Darfur not to take prisoners or inflict injuries.

172. The Majority is of the view that the above-mentioned statements allegedly made by Omar Al Bashir do not provide, by themselves, any indicia of a GoS's genocidal intent. In this regard, the Majority considers that they provide, at best, indicia of Omar Al Bashir's alleged individual criminal responsibility, pursuant to article 25(3)(a) of the Statute, for those war crimes and crimes against humanity that were allegedly a core component of the GoS counter-insurgency campaign. Whether a different conclusion is merited when assessed in light of the rest of the materials provided by the Prosecution in support of the Prosecution Application is a question that shall be analysed below by the Majority. * * *

177. As a result of previous findings, and as the Prosecution itself acknowledges, the Prosecution's allegations concerning the existence of reasonable grounds to believe in a GoS's genocidal intent are essentially based on the inference that can be drawn from the alleged clear pattern of mass-atrocities committed by GoS forces between 2003 and 2008

against the Fur, Masalit and Zaghawa civilian population throughout Darfur region.

178. In particular, the Majority observes that, in order to show the existence of a GoS's genocidal intent, the Prosecution relies heavily on what the Prosecution considers to be a key component of an alleged GoS genocidal campaign: the subjection of a substantial part of the Fur, Masalit and Zaghawa civilian population of Darfur (up to 2,700,000 individuals) to unbearable conditions of life within IDP [Internally Displaced Person] camps due to the: (i) insufficient allocation of resources by the GoS for IDPs within Sudan; (ii) acts of violence (including murder, rape and mistreatment) committed by GoS forces within the IDP Camps; (iii) unlawful arrest of community leaders and subsequent mistreatment/torture in the facilities of HAC (which was allegedly comprised of former members of the NISS); and (iv) the GoS hindrance of access to international aid.

179. In relation to the alleged insufficient resources allocated by the GoS to ensure adequate conditions of life in IDP camps in Darfur, the Majority considers that the Prosecution's allegation is vague in light of the fact that, in addition to the Prosecution's failure to provide any specific information as to what possible additional resources could have been provided by the GoS, there existed an ongoing armed conflict at the relevant time and the number of IDPs, according to the United Nations, was as high as two million by mid-2004, and as high as 2.7 million today.

180. In relation to conditions inside the IDP camps, the Majority finds that the materials provided by the Prosecution in support of the Prosecution Application reflect a situation within the IDP camps which significantly differs from the situation described by the Prosecution in the Prosecution Application. The Majority reaches this conclusion as a result of an overall assessment of the materials provided by the Prosecution—including [an] * * * account of the conditions since February 2004 in one of the largest IDP camps in Darfur ("the Kalma Camp") given in the latest report issued on 23 January 2009 by the United Nations High Commissioner for Human Rights on the situation in Sudan, which indicates, *inter alia*, that during the relevant period in the Kalma Camp: (i) several violent exchanges between armed elements within the Camp and GoS forces took place; (ii) several sources referred to by the United Nations African Union Mission in Darfur (UNAMID) as "credible, independent sources," reported on the presence in the Camp of "light and heavy arms"; (iii) the conflict between the GoS forces and the armed elements within the Camp was a very important factor in exacerbating the tension between the IDP community and the GoS; and (iv) poor living conditions in the Camps were not systematically, but only "at times," exacerbated by measures introduced by the GoS on security grounds, and, in some circumstances, such measures were lifted at the intervention of UNAMID. * * *

181. In relation to the Prosecution's allegations concerning the alleged GoS hindrance of medical and other humanitarian assistance in the IDP Camps in Darfur, the Majority considers that hindrance of humanitarian assistance, as well as cutting off supplies of food and other essential goods, can be carried out for a variety of reasons other than intending to destroy in whole or in part the targeted group. As a result, the Prosecution's claim must be assessed in light of the extent and systematicity, duration and consequences of the alleged GoS obstruction.

* * *

184. In relation to the extent, systematicity, duration and consequences of the alleged GoS hindrance of medical and other humanitarian assistance needed to sustain life in the IDP Camps in Darfur, the Majority observes that in the additional materials provided by the Prosecution, at the request of the Chamber on 18 November 2008, the Prosecution included a chronology on the evolution of this alleged GoS practice from 2003 to the end of 2007.

185. According to the reports included in this chronology, the higher level of obstruction to humanitarian aid took place during the first year of the conflict until June 2004, at a time in which GoS forces appear to have launched their two main offensives (summer 2003 and January 2004). The lack of humanitarian assistance is explained in some reports by the GoS's attempt to hide the magnitude of the crisis. Yet, in one of the reports, the United Nations Office for Humanitarian Affairs emphasised the late reaction and lack of coordination of the international community.

186. The reports provided by the Prosecution also underline that, after the conclusion of the Moratorium on Restrictions (July 2004), access to the IDP Camps improved substantially and permitted Darfur to eventually become the site of "the largest world humanitarian effort."

187. Finally, the said reports also highlight that bureaucratic barriers and difficulties in accessing a number of areas increased again in 2006. Nevertheless, despite increasing difficulties it appears that aid programmes continued to operate.

188. This, in the Majority's view, is consistent with the account given by the latest report of the United Nations High Commissioner for Human Rights in relation to the Kalma Camp, where it is stressed that the poor living conditions existing in the Kalma Camp since its establishment in February 2004 "at times have been exacerbated by measures introduced by government on security grounds."

189. As a result, the Majority considers that the materials submitted by the Prosecution in support of the Prosecution Application provide reasonable grounds to believe that the extent, systematicity and consequences of the GoS hindrance of medical and humanitarian assistance in IDP Camps in Darfur varied greatly over time. Consequently, the Majority finds that such materials reflect a level of

GoS hindrance of medical and humanitarian assistance in IDP Camps in Darfur which significantly differs from that described by the Prosecution in the Prosecution Application.

190. The Majority observes that the second component of the Prosecution's submissions in relation to the inference of the existence of a GoS's genocidal intent from the clear pattern of mass-atrocities allegedly committed by GoS forces between 2003 and 2008 against the Fur, Masalit and Zaghawa civilian population, is based on the underlying facts of the Prosecution's allegations for war crimes and crimes against humanity that have been discussed in previous sections.

191. In this regard, the Majority notes that the Chamber has already found that there are reasonable grounds to believe that a core component of the GoS counterinsurgency campaign, which started soon after the April 2003 attack on the El Fasher airport and lasted for well over five years, was the unlawful attack on that part of the civilian population of Darfur—belonging largely to the Fur, Masalit and Zaghawa groups—perceived by the GoS as being close to the SLM/A, the JEM and other armed groups opposing the GoS in the ongoing conflict in Darfur.

192. In particular, the majority observes that there are reasonable grounds to believe that as part of the GoS counter-insurgency campaign, GoS forces:

i. carried out numerous unlawful attacks, followed by systematic acts of pillage, on towns and villages, mainly inhabited by civilians belonging to the Fur, Masalit and Zaghawa groups;

ii. subjected thousands of civilians belonging primarily to the Fur, Masalit and Zaghawa groups to acts of murder, as well as to acts of extermination;

iii. subjected thousands of civilian women, belonging primarily to the said groups, to acts of rape;

iv. subjected hundreds of thousands of civilians belonging primarily to the said groups to acts of forcible transfer; and

v. subjected civilians belonging primarily to the said groups to acts of torture.

193. Nevertheless, the Majority considers that the existence of reasonable grounds to believe that GoS forces carried out such serious war crimes and crimes against humanity in a widespread and systematic manner does not automatically lead to the conclusion that there exist reasonable grounds to believe that the GoS intended to destroy, in whole or in part, the Fur, Masalit and Zaghawa groups.

194. In this regard, the Majority observes that a similar approach has recently been taken by the ICJ in its Judgment on Genocide, in which, leaving aside the specific events following the fall of Srebrenica, the ICJ declined to infer that the Bosnian Serb leadership acted with a

genocidal intent from the existence of a clear pattern of mass atrocities affecting hundreds of thousands of Bosnian Muslims for a period of five years. * * *

195. Moreover, the Majority finds that there are a number of additional factors, resulting from the materials provided by the Prosecution, that must be taken into consideration in determining whether the existence of reasonable grounds to believe that the GoS acted with genocidal intent is the only reasonable conclusion from the commission by GoS forces, in a widespread and systematic manner, of the abovementioned war crimes and crimes against humanity.

196. First, in relation to the attacks conducted by the GoS forces on towns and villages primarily inhabited by members of the Fur, Masalit and Zaghawa groups, the Majority finds that there are reasonable grounds to believe that in most of such attacks, the large majority of their inhabitants were neither killed nor injured despite the fact that the attackers, in addition to often counting on aerial support, either had previously encircled the targeted village or came to such village with tens or hundreds of vehicles and camels forming a wide line.

197. Second, the Majority observes that the Prosecution does not claim that GoS forces established in Darfur long-lasting detention camps where inmates were systematically mistreated, tortured and executed.

198. Third, in relation to forcible displacement resulting from the attacks, the Majority is of the view that there are reasonable grounds to believe that GoS forces did not attempt to prevent civilians belonging to the Fur, Masalit and Zaghawa groups from crossing the border to go to refugee camps in Chad, and that the great majority of those who left their villages after the attacks by GoS forces reached IDP Camps in Darfur or refugee camps in Chad.

199. Fourth, in the view of the Majority, the Prosecution has failed to substantiate its claim that the materials that it submitted provide reasonable grounds to believe that Janjaweed militiamen were stationed around IDP Camps for the purpose of raping those women and killing those men who ventured outside the camps. * * *

201. As a result, the Majority considers that the existence of reasonable grounds to believe that the GoS acted with genocidal intent is not the only reasonable conclusion of the alleged commission by GoS forces, in a widespread and systematic manner, of the particularly serious war crimes and crimes against humanity mentioned above. * * *

204. In this regard, the Majority recalls that the above-mentioned analysis of the Prosecution's allegations concerning the GoS's genocidal intent and its supporting materials has led the Majority to make the following findings:

i. even if the existence of an alleged GoS strategy to deny and conceal the crimes committed in Darfur was to be proven, there can be a variety of plausible reasons for its adoption, including the intention to conceal the commission of war crimes and crimes against humanity;

ii. the Prosecution's allegations concerning the alleged insufficient resources allocated by the GoS to ensure adequate conditions of life in IDP Camps in Darfur are vague in light of the fact that, in addition to the Prosecution's failure to provide any specific information as to what possible additional resources could have been provided by the GoS, there existed an ongoing armed conflict at the relevant time and the number of IDPS, according to the United Nations, was as high as two million by mid-2004, and as high as 2.7 million today;

iii. the materials submitted by the Prosecution in support of the Prosecution Application reflect a situation within the IDP Camps which significantly differs from the situation described by the Prosecution in the Prosecution Application itself;

iv. the materials submitted by the Prosecution in support of the Prosecution Application reflect a level of GoS hindrance of medical and humanitarian assistance in IDP Camps in Darfur which significantly differs from that described by the Prosecution in the Prosecution Application;

v. despite the particular seriousness of those war crimes and crimes against humanity that appeared to have been committed by GoS forces in Darfur between 2003 and 2008, a number of materials provided by the Prosecution point to the existence of several factors indicating that the commission of such crimes can reasonably be explained by reasons other than the existence of a GoS's genocidal intent to destroy in whole or in part the Fur, Masalit and Zaghawa groups;

vi. the handful of GoS official statements (including three allegedly made by Omar Al Bashir himself) and public documents relied upon by the Prosecution provide only indicia of a GoS's persecutory intent (as opposed to a genocidal intent) against the members of the Fur, Masalit and Zaghawa groups; and

vii. as shown by the Prosecution's allegations in the case of *The Prosecutor v. Ahmad Harun and Ali Kushayb,* the Prosecution has not found any indicia of genocidal intent on the part of Ahmad Harun, in spite of the fact that the harsher language contained in the above-mentioned GoS official statements and documents comes allegedly from him.

205. In the view of the Majority, when all materials provided by the Prosecution in support of the Prosecution Application are analysed together, and consequently, the above-mentioned findings are jointly assessed, the Majority cannot but conclude that the existence of reasonable grounds to believe that the GoS acted with a *dolus specialis*/specific intent to destroy in whole or in part the Fur, Masalit and Zaghawa groups is not the only reasonable conclusion that can be drawn therefrom. * * *

207. Nevertheless, the Majority considers that, if, as a result of the ongoing Prosecution's investigation into the crimes allegedly committed by Omar Al Bashir, additional evidence on the existence of a GoS's genocidal intent is gathered, the Majority's conclusion in the present decision would not prevent the Prosecution from requesting, pursuant to article 58(6) of the Statute, an amendment to the arrest warrant for Omar Al Bashir so as to include the crime of genocide.

208. In addition, the Prosecution may always request, pursuant to article 58(6) of the Statute, an amendment to the arrest warrant for Omar Al Bashir to include crimes against humanity and war crimes which are not part of the Prosecution Application, and for which the Prosecution considers that there are reasonable grounds to believe that Omar Al Bashir is criminally liable under the Statute.

NOTES & QUESTIONS

1. Case Update

The Appeals Chamber reversed and remanded, reasoning that the PTC had applied the wrong standard of proof:

> 30. In the view of the Appeals Chamber, the evidentiary threshold of "reasonable grounds to believe" for the issuance of a warrant of arrest must be distinguished from the threshold required for the confirmation of charges ("substantial grounds to believe", article 61(7) of the Statute) and the threshold for a conviction ("beyond reasonable doubt", article 66(3) of the Statute). It is evident from the wording of the provisions that the standards of "substantial grounds to believe" and "beyond reasonable doubt" are higher standards of proof than "reasonable grounds to believe". Accordingly, when disposing of an application for a warrant of arrest under article 58(1) of the Statute, a Pre-Trial Chamber should not require a level of proof that would be required for the confirmation of charges or for conviction.
>
> 33. In the view of the Appeals Chamber, requiring that the existence of genocidal intent must be the *only* reasonable conclusion amounts to requiring the Prosecutor to disprove any other reasonable conclusions and to eliminate any reasonable doubt. If the only reasonable conclusion based on the evidence is the existence of genocidal intent, then it cannot be said that such a

finding establishes merely "reasonable grounds to believe". Rather, it establishes genocidal intent "beyond reasonable doubt". * * *

39. * * * The Appeals Chamber finds that, although the Pre-Trial Chamber appreciated the appropriate standard to be "reasonable grounds to believe", it applied this standard erroneously. The standard it developed and applied in relation to 'proof by inference' was higher and more demanding than what is required under article 58(1)(a) of the Statute. This amounted to an error of law. * * *

42. The Appeals Chamber notes that the Prosecutor has requested the Appeals Chamber to "apply the correct standard to the facts found by the Pre-Trial Chamber, entering a finding that there are reasonable grounds to believe that President Omar Al Bashir is criminally responsible for genocide". He also requests the Appeals Chamber to "direct the Pre-Trial Chamber to issue a warrant of arrest on those counts". The Appeals Chamber is of the view that the substance of the matter should be considered by the Pre-Trial Chamber, and not by the Appeals Chamber. Therefore, the matter is remanded to the Pre-Trial Chamber for a new decision, using the correct standard of proof.

Prosecutor v. Omar Hassan Ahmad Al Bashir, Case No. ICC–02/05–01/09–OA, Judgment on the Appeal of the Prosecutor Against the "Decision on the Prosecution's Application for a Warrant of Arrest Against Omar Hassan Ahmad Al Bashir" (Feb. 3, 2010).

Following the Appeals Chamber remand, the Pre-Trial Chamber determined that there were reasonable grounds to believe that Al Bashir was criminally responsible under Article 23(3)(a) as an indirect perpetrator, or as an indirect co-perpetrator, for genocide committed by governmental forces as part of a counter-insurgency campaign. *See Prosecutor v. Al Bashir,* Case No. ICC–02/05–01/09, Second Warrant of Arrest for Omar Hassan Ahmad Al Bashir (July 12, 2010). (For more on the al Bashir case, see Note 4 in Chapter 1 after the excerpt from Miriam J. Aukerman, and Chapter 17 on Defenses.)

2. Security Council Referral

Sudan is not a party to the Rome Statute. The Sudan situation is the first example of the Security Council triggering jurisdiction before the ICC. Up until this point, all of the situations before the Court came with the consent of the States on whose territory the alleged crimes had occurred. The Council's actions have been controversial in some quarters, particularly given its lack of follow up. In addition three of the five permanent members of the Security Council (China, Russia, and the United States) are not parties. Does the lack of consent by the Sudan (and the involvement of non-State parties in imposing jurisdiction on the Sudan), lessen the legitimacy of the ICC's Darfur proceedings? Should the Prosecutor and Court approach matters brought to it through the Security Council differently than those based upon state consent?

3. Al Bashir on the Road

Notwithstanding the warrants against him, Al Bashir visited a whole range of countries (including Chad, China, Djibouti, Egypt, Eritrea, Ethiopia, Iran, Iraq, Kenya, Libya (pre- and post-Qaddafi), Jordan, Qatar, Russia, and South Sudan), where he often enjoyed a dignitary's welcome. Many of these destinations are ICC member states; Russia is a member of the P-5. Al Bashir's radius diminished considerably in recent years, however. In 2013, for example, he fled an African Union Special Summit on HIV/AIDS, Tuberculosis, and Malaria in Nigeria after being in the country less than twenty-four hours and following an effort by members of the local NGO community to serve a summons on him. This happened amidst expressions of concern about the visit from influential states and rumors that foreign powers might actually arrest him. It also followed upon the issuance of a request to Nigeria by ICC Pre-Trial Chamber II to immediately take him into custody and indications that Nigeria was "considering the necessary steps to be taken in respect of his visit in line with [its] international obligations."

Prior to that, and following a visit to Kenya, a Kenyan NGO went to court and secured a ruling indicating that Kenya was under an obligation to arrest Al Bashir if he returned to the country. Al Bashir subsequently did not attend the inauguration of the newly elected Kenyan President, Uhuru Kenyatta in 2013. Chad postponed its 2013 Greenbelt Conference of the Community of Sahel-Saharan States upon learning Al Bashir would attend on Sudan's behalf. Even in advance of his 2011 trip to China—a non-party state that is ambivalent, at best, towards international justice efforts—Al Bashir reportedly felt the need to confirm that he would not be arrested if he stepped off a plane. He has not attended the annual meeting of the U.N. General Assembly in New York City, notwithstanding that he has an argument that he enjoys immunity under the U.N. Headquarters Agreement.

Other states that once allowed him to visit have since withdrawn their welcome, including Malawi, which hosted Al Bashir in October 2011 for a summit of the Common Market for Eastern and Southern Africa (COMESA). When confronted with a finding of non-cooperation by the Court, Malawi replied that it had accorded him all the immunities and privileges guaranteed to every visiting Head of State and Government; these privileges and immunities include freedom from arrest and prosecution within the territories of Malawi. Following his visit, Malawi's \$350M compact with the Millennium Challenge Corporation (MCC), a foreign aid agency dedicated to alleviating global poverty, was suspended by the United States at the urging of former Representative Frank Wolf (R-VA), a long-time critic of the Sudanese government. Malawi's approach changed dramatically under the newly-installed administration of Joyce Banda, who relinquished the opportunity to host an African Union Summit in June 2012 when Al Bashir indicated his intention to represent Sudan at the Summit—losing tens of thousands of dollars in income for its hotels and other benefits in the process. The MCC compact was re-instated following President Banda's decision. Malawi subsequently received a number of favorable loans from the International Monetary Fund and the World Bank as well as a visit from

Hillary Rodham Clinton and later her husband and daughter. Even Saudi Arabia, Tajikistan and Turkmenistan, ICC non-parties, refused permission for Al Bashir's plane to cross into their air space when Al Bashir sought to attend the Iranian inauguration and meetings with China, respectively. Al Bashir feared flying over Afghanistan because of the NATO presence there.

What obligations of cooperation do States Parties owe the Court (see Part 9 of the Statute)? What remedies exist in the event that States Parties fail to execute ICC arrest warrants? What role should the Security Council play in the Darfur context given that it referred the situation to the Court in the first place? On several occasions, the Court notified the Security Council of the failure of States Parties to arrest Al Bashir while he was in country. So far, the Council has yet to respond to these notifications. The Prosecutor, in her reports to the Council on the two referred situations, regularly asks for greater assistance from the Council in effectuating the Court's mandate.

For more on the efforts by the ICC to pressure member states to honor their commitment to cooperating with the Court by handing over fugitives like Al Bashir, *see* Chapter 17 on Defenses the discussion of the ICC Appeals Chamber decision concerning Jordan's failure to arrest Al Bashir when he visited that country.

4. Contextual Elements

The Majority read into the definition of genocide several contextual elements, including requiring proof of a manifest pattern of similar conduct and an actual threat of destruction against a protected group. The Majority drew these contextual elements from the Elements of Crimes of the ICC, and not from the definition of genocide in the Statute itself (which as noted is the same as the definition contained in the Genocide Convention and in the Statutes of the two *ad hoc* tribunals). The Majority reasoned that the Elements of Crimes must be applied unless there is "an irreconcilable contradiction between those documents on the one hand and the Statute on the other hand" (para. 128). Review Articles 9 and 21 of the ICC Statute. What is the proper relationship between the Statute and the Elements of Crimes? Does the introduction of these contextual elements change the definition of genocide? For discussion of the opinion, including the controversy surrounding the contextual elements, *see* Robert Cryer, *The Definitions of International Crimes in the Al Bashir Arrest Warrant Decision*, 7 J. INT'L CRIM. JUST. 283 (2009). For an argument in support of the contextual elements, though somewhat critical of its application by the Pre-Trial Chamber, *see* Claus Kreß, *The Crime of Genocide and Contextual Elements: A Comment on the ICC Pre-Trial Chamber's Decision in the Al Bashir Case*, 7 J. INT'L CRIM. JUST. 297 (2009). *See also* Jennifer Trahan, *Why the Killing in Darfur is Genocide*, 31 FORDHAM INT'L L.J. 990 (2008); Andrew T. Cayley, *The Prosecutor's Strategy in Seeking the Arrest of Sudanese President Al Bashir on Charges of Genocide*, 6 J. INT'L CRIM. JUST. 829 (2008) (Cayley was the former Co-Prosecutor before the ECCC).

5. Policy or Plan?

Does the Pre-Trial Chamber require a genocidal policy or plan? In other words, does the opinion foreclose a genocide indictment against a single individual or an individual who had no recourse to the apparatus of a state? Professor Cryer, *supra*, criticizes the majority on this point, noting that the requirement of a "manifest pattern of similar conduct" found in the Elements is not the same as a plan or policy. Kress, *supra*, argues that a lone *génocidaires* could still be found liable, but only if, pursuant to the Elements, he had the ability to effect the destruction of the targeted group, either in whole or in part. Does this effectively foreclose prosecutions against individuals like Jelisić? Does the Pre-Trial Chamber render genocide a result crime rather than a crime of intent? The ICTY Appeals Chamber admonished its Trial Chamber for adopting the "manifest pattern of similar conduct" as a contextual element of genocide, concluding that the elaboration in the ICC's Element of Crimes did not reflect customary international law at the time of the atrocities in the former Yugoslavia. *Prosecutor v. Krstić*, Case No. IT–98–33–A, Judgement, para. 223 *et seq.* (April 19, 2004).

6. Intent

Determining whether individuals are acting with genocidal intent—the intent to destroy a protected group in whole or in part—does not lend itself to easy determination. Criminal intent is an inherently individualistic inquiry, so determining governmental responsibility for genocide raises particular questions about whose intent matters: The intent of members of the central authorities who may be designing a genocidal policy, or that of the "foot soldiers" responsible for implementing it? Absent a confession of intent or a revealed genocidal policy, the intent to destroy a group—either as a matter of individual *mens rea* or a governmental plan—must usually be inferred. The international criminal tribunals for the former Yugoslavia and Rwanda have developed a set of criteria for this purpose, but the result of particular inquiries always turn on their own facts. For example, the tribunals have looked to statements or propaganda condemning the group, acts of violence against cultural symbols associated with the group, other policies of discrimination against members of the group, racial or other epithets used in connection with violence, the sheer number of victims, whether children are included within the victims, patterns and systematicity of violence, the brutality or gratuity of the violence employed, etc. How did the ICC conceptualize the relationship between individual intent and governmental policy? If one government official has genocidal intent but others who control the government with him do not, is a genocide conviction possible under the ICC's approach? Can two accomplices responsible for the same act be subject to different charges because only one has specific intent (with one responsible for genocide and the other for crimes against humanity)? We will discuss the unique issues of genocidal *mens rea* and complicity in Chapter 15.

7. Protected Groups

The Pre-Trial Chamber opinion included a dissent by Judge Anita Ušacka (Latvia). In her dissent, Judge Ušacka identified the relevant group as "African tribes" basing this conclusion in part on statements by Government officials using this language to describe the groups. The majority identified three protected groups: the Fur, Masalit, and Zaghawa. Does the majority adopt a subjective or objective test? The majority also seems to reject the "negative" approach to group membership discussed above. Are tribal groups, which are defined primarily through lineage and territoriality, protected groups under the Genocide Convention?

8. *Actus Reus*

Does the Majority place too much stock in the need to show physical violence against the victim group? The Genocide Convention purposefully reaches acts that fall short of murder but that will lead to the destruction of a group, reflecting the concentration camp "death through work" phenomenon of World War II. The international tribunals have recognized the concept of genocide by "slow death," where certain conditions of life are inflicted upon a protected group that may not lead to the immediate death of members of the group, but will eventually lead to that result if implemented over a long period of time. Accordingly, the tribunals have emphasized the importance of examining the cluster of abuses suffered by members of the group and the collective impact of those actions on the survival of the group. This broader conception of genocide reflects the fact that eliminating the members of an entire race or religion, or a substantial part thereof, through outright extermination is difficult work. If that is the goal, it may be much easier to deprive people of their livelihoods, homes, medical care, humanitarian assistance, etc. Implementing such a policy in Sudan would enable the government to blame any subsequent deaths on the harsh Sudanese conditions or external factors such as famine and deflect attention away from a program of extermination.

9. Genocide in Darfur?

The U.N. Security Council established the International Commission of Inquiry on Darfur (COI) under Chapter VII with Resolution 1564 (2004) in order to: investigate reports of violations of international humanitarian and human rights law, determine whether acts of genocide had occurred, and identify perpetrators "with a view to ensuring that those responsible are held accountable." The COI determined that the victim tribes constituted protected groups under the Genocide Convention; however, the Commission was not able to definitively identify a governmental policy aimed at destroying these protected groups in whole or in part. The COI noted that not all individuals in attacked regions were killed (although most were abused) and that it was primarily young men who were executed. It also noted that sometimes when people surrendered their property, they were spared. Why might the COI have reached a different conclusion than the ICC? Are the COI's methodology and conclusions consistent with the genocide jurisprudence? For a discussion, *see* Beth Van Schaack, *Darfur and the Rhetoric of Genocide*, 26 WHITTIER L. REV. 1101 (2004).

Mahmood Mamdani has been quite critical of the characterization of the events in Darfur as genocide, arguing that most analysts do not understand Sudanese history, culture, and politics, and impose on the Sudan their own notions of race and ethnicity. He finds the use of the term genocide to be not only wrong, but counter-productive:

> Calling the violence in Darfur genocide has had three consequences. First, it has postponed any discussion of context

> while imposing the view of one party in the 1987–89 civil war in the name of stopping the "genocide." Second, it has conferred impunity on those same partisans by casting them as resisters to genocide. Finally, the description of the violence as genocide—racial killing—has served to further racialize the conflict and give legitimacy to those who seek to punish rather than to reconcile.

Mahmood Mamdani, SAVIORS AND SURVIVORS: DARFUR, POLITICS, AND THE WAR ON TERROR 7 (2009). Might the concept of genocide racialize political or economic conflicts?

10. ICC Article 16, Peace and Justice

A group of Sudanese petitioned the Court not to indict President Al Bashir, arguing that it would endanger peace efforts. Upon his indictment, President Al Bashir immediately expelled most of the major international aid organizations that had been operating in the country providing much-needed food, health care, and other assistance to the Sudanese.

Although African states were instrumental in the formation of the ICC Statute and its entry into force, the indictment of Al Bashir, as a sitting head of state, caused a *volte face*, at least among some African Union members. Some elements within the A.U. also rallied around President Kenyatta when he was subject to a summons to appear. On their behalf, the A.U. has several times attempted to prompt the Security Council to invoke Article 16 of the ICC Statute, which allows the Council to defer ICC proceedings for a year in the exercise of its Chapter VII powers. Although Article 16 language has been floated in the Council for both the Sudan and Kenya cases, it has been continually blocked by the United Kingdom, France, the United States, and other Council members. When the Council did not act upon one such request other than to take note of it in Resolution 1828 and pledge to consider matters further, the A.U. adopted a decision in 2009 calling on its members to withhold cooperation with the Court pursuant to Article 98 of the Rome Statute with respect to the arrest or surrender of Al Bashir.

Elements within the A.U. have tried to foment a broader anti-ICC campaign, as reflected in an Extraordinary Summit devoted to the ICC hosted in Addis Ababa in 2013; however, A.U. members that remain supportive of the Court have managed to temper these impulses. Although the Extraordinary Summit was poorly attended, the A.U. did decide to seek the postponement of the Kenya and Sudan cases until the two heads of state were no longer in office, although this decision was mooted with respect to the Kenya cases. Although it was doubtful that the Council would defer the Sudan cases in light of Sudan's recalcitrance vis-à-vis the Court and the international community, the Kenya cases may have presented a different set of considerations. Given this larger political context, do you think it was wise for the Prosecutor to seek an indictment against President Al Bashir?

IV. IN WHOLE OR IN PART

As defined by the Genocide Convention and elsewhere, the crime of genocide is committed with the intent to destroy a protected group "in whole or in part." The meaning of this latter phrase is somewhat difficult to ascertain in practice. It seems clear that it modifies the defendant's intent, such that conviction is appropriate where the defendant intended to destroy only a "part" of the group. At the same time, the phrase "in whole or in part" may also be applied to the outcome or result of the defendant's actions, such that some threshold number of victims must be targeted before genocide is found. This element—or sub-element—became an issue in the case that follows, in which an ICTY Trial Chamber was confronted with the question of whether the massacres at Srebrenica, in which upwards of 8,000 Bosniak men and boys were killed, constituted an act of genocide. (See the Appendix for a map of Yugoslavia showing the location of Srebrenica.)

The Trial Chamber made the following factual findings in the principal case (see paras. 1–70): The city of Srebrenica sits in eastern Bosnia, a mere 15 kilometers from the border with Serbia. During the war, the city occupied part of an island between two Bosnian Serbian regions, so its capture was vital to the Bosnian Serb forces (VRS) engaged in ethnic gerrymandering to create the envisioned Greater Serbia ("Republika Srpska"). As a military expert for the defense stated during the trial, "Without [Srebrenica], there would be no Republic Srpska, there would be no territorial integrity of Serb ethnic territories; instead the Serb population would be forced to accept the so-called enclave status of their ethnic territories." *Prosecutor v. Krstić*, Case No. IT–98–33–T, Judgement, para. 12 (Aug. 2, 2001). During the fighting within the surrounding region, rural Muslims sought shelter in the city, doubling its population.

The Security Council, acting under Chapter VII, issued a resolution demanding "that all parties and others concerned treat Srebrenica and its surroundings as a safe area which should be free from any armed attack or any other hostile act" and the "immediate cessation of armed attacks by Bosnian Serb paramilitary units against Srebrenica and their immediate withdrawal from the areas surrounding Srebrenica." S.C. Res. 819, para. 1–2, U.N. Doc. S/RES/819 (Apr. 16, 1993). Thus, Srebrenica became one of five cities designated as "U.N. safe havens." Bosnian Serb Commander-in-Chief Radko Mladić and Bosnian Muslim General Emar Halilović signed a truce calling for the enclave to be disarmed. The city was placed under the protection of a rotating UNPROFOR ("United Nations Protection Force") command that was authorized to use force in self-defence against attacks against these areas, and to coordinate with the North Atlantic Treaty Organization (NATO) to use air power in support of its activities. In a 1993 visit to the enclave, the Commander of UNPROFOR at the time, General Philippe Morillon of France, told residents that the town was under the protection of the United Nations and would not be abandoned. Evacuations of Bosnian Muslims from the city under the auspices of the U.N. High Commissioner for Refugees were criticized by the Muslim government as contributing to the ethnic cleansing of the region. Both sides—the VRS and the Bosnian Army

(ABiH)—were found to have violated the safe haven status of the city, although the city did remain relatively stable for two years.

In 1995, the 600 or so UNPROFOR troops guarding Srebrenica and stationed at the central U.N. base at Potočari, a city suburb, were from the Netherlands and were known as Dutchbat. (UNPROFOR named deploying battalions after their country of origin.) In March 1995, Radovan Karadžić, the self-proclaimed President of Republika Srpska, ordered the city to be cut off from humanitarian assistance. In early July, Bosnian Serb forces began to advance on the city, taking several UNPROFOR observation posts. Dutchbat soldiers either surrendered to the advancing forces or retreated into the enclave. On July 9, 1995, President Karadžić issued a new order authorizing the Drina Corps, a formation of the Bosnian Serb Army, to capture the town of Srebrenica. On July 11, 1995, Bosnian Serb forces ransacked and took the city. Thousands of residents sought refuge in the U.N.'s compound at Potočari. The Dutch commanding officer, Colonel Thomas Karremans, apparently requested NATO air support, but the response to the request was delayed for reasons that remain unclear. After limited air strikes, NATO retreated in the face of threats by the Bosnian Serbs to kill Dutch troops held hostage or shell the U.N. compound. The ABiH response was limited as well, and rumors of a "deal" struck between the Muslim government and the Serbian forces to trade Srebrenica for parts of Sarajevo later swirled at trial.

On July 12 and 13, the Bosnian Serb forces began separating the men and boys from the women and children. Approximately 25,000 women and children were bused out of the city to internally displaced person (IDP) camps or to Muslim-held territory. Ten to fifteen thousand men, including ABiH soldiers, decided to leave the enclave rather than risk capture. Their column was attacked and dispersed by Serb forces. The men who remained behind were transferred between detention centers where they were joined by men captured from among the escapees. It has been estimated that 7,000–8,000 captives were then executed by firing squads and buried in mass graves with earth-moving equipment. A few men miraculously survived and later testified at trial. Many of the bodies were moved to different mass graves as peace negotiations at Dayton began in 1995, which complicated official exhumations and the identification of the bodies.

General Krstić was commander of the Drina Corps, the VRS forces involved in the attack on Srebrenica. In 1998, NATO-led Stabilization Force troops (SFOR) ambushed and forcibly arrested Krstić, who had been the subject of a sealed indictment. When his trial began, he was the highest-ranking military officer to stand trial at the ICTY. The occurrence of the massacres was not in dispute at trial. Krstić's main defense was that he did not actually become commander of the Drina Corps until after the massacre, and at the time he was directing a military campaign around Žepa, another U.N. safe haven. He also argued that General Mladić had set up an alternative chain of command for the executions that did not involve the Drina Corps. Krstić claimed to have only heard of the massacre weeks later. However, footage and witness testimony placed him nearer to the events in question as did intercepted telephone conversations in which he coordinated the arrival of buses to remove the women and children and received information of the capture of Muslim men.

In the course of its investigations, the ICTY conducted a number of exhumations. These confirmed that most of the men had been blindfolded and shot in the head with their hands tied behind their backs, negating revisionist accounts that they had been combat victims. For an account of the fall of Srebrenica and its aftermath, *see* Elizabeth Neuffer, A KEY TO MY NEIGHBOR'S HOUSE (2001). For a first-hand account of the trial by the United States judge on the panel, *see* Patricia M. Wald, *General Radislav Krstić: A War Crimes Case Study*, 16 GEO. J. LEGAL ETHICS 445 (2003).

Prosecutor v. Krstić, Case No. IT–98–33–T, Judgement (Aug. 2, 2001)

In the Trial Chamber

541. The Trial Chamber must interpret Article 4 of the Statute taking into account the state of customary international law at the time the events in Srebrenica took place. Several sources have been considered in this respect. The Trial Chamber first referred to the codification work undertaken by international bodies. The Convention on the Prevention and Punishment of the Crime of Genocide (hereinafter "the Convention"), adopted on 9 December 1948, whose provisions Article 4 adopts *verbatim*, constitutes the main reference source in this respect. Although the Convention was adopted during the same period that the term "genocide" itself was coined, the Convention has been viewed as codifying a norm of international law long recognised and which case-law would soon elevate to the level of a peremptory norm of general international law (*jus cogens*). The Trial Chamber has interpreted the Convention pursuant to the general rules of interpretation of treaties laid down in Articles 31 and 32 of the Vienna Convention on the Law of Treaties. As a result, the Chamber took into account the object and purpose of the Convention in addition to the ordinary meaning of the terms in its provisions. As a supplementary means of interpretation, the Trial Chamber also consulted the preparatory work and the circumstances which gave rise to the Convention. Furthermore, the Trial Chamber considered the international case-law on the crime of genocide, in particular, that developed by the ICTR. The Report of the International Law Commission (ILC) on the Draft Code of Crimes against Peace and Security of Mankind received particular attention. Although the report was completed in 1996, it is the product of several years of reflection by the Commission

whose purpose was to codify international law, notably on genocide: it therefore constitutes a particularly relevant source for interpretation of Article 4. The work of other international committees, especially the reports of the Sub-Commission on Prevention of Discrimination and Protection of Minorities of the UN Commission on Human Rights, was also reviewed. Furthermore, the Chamber gave consideration to the work done in producing the Rome Statute on the establishment of an international criminal court, specifically, the finalised draft text of the elements of crimes completed by the Preparatory Commission for the International Criminal Court in July 2000. Although that document post-dates the acts involved here, it has proved helpful in assessing the state of customary international law which the Chamber itself derived from other sources. In this regard, it should be noted that all the States attending the conference, whether signatories of the Rome Statute or not, were eligible to be represented on the Preparatory Commission. From this perspective, the document is a useful key to the *opinio juris* of the States. Finally, the Trial Chamber also looked for guidance in the legislation and practice of States, especially their judicial interpretations and decisions. * * *

558. Whereas the indictment in this case defined the targeted group as the Bosnian Muslims, the Prosecution appeared to use an alternative definition in its pre-trial brief by pleading the intention to eliminate the "Bosnian Muslim population of Srebrenica" through mass killing and deportation. In its final trial brief, the Prosecution chose to define the group as the Bosnian Muslims of Srebrenica, while it referred to the Bosnian Muslims of Eastern Bosnia in its final arguments. The Defence argued in its final brief that the Bosnian Muslims of Srebrenica did not form a specific national, ethnical, racial or religious group. In particular, it contended that "one cannot create an artificial 'group' by limiting its scope to a geographical area." According to the Defence, the Bosnian Muslims constitute the only group that fits the definition of a group protected by the Convention.

559. Originally viewed as a religious group, the Bosnian Muslims were recognised as a "nation" by the Yugoslav Constitution of 1963. The evidence tendered at trial also shows very clearly that the highest Bosnian Serb political authorities and the Bosnian Serb forces operating in Srebrenica in July 1995 viewed the Bosnian Muslims as a specific national group. Conversely, no national, ethnical, racial or religious characteristic makes it possible to differentiate the Bosnian Muslims residing in Srebrenica, at the time of the 1995 offensive, from the other Bosnian Muslims. The only distinctive criterion would be their geographical location, not a criterion contemplated by the Convention. In addition, it is doubtful that the Bosnian Muslims residing in the enclave at the time of the offensive considered themselves a distinct national, ethnical, racial or religious group among the Bosnian Muslims. Indeed, most of the Bosnian Muslims residing in Srebrenica at the time of the

attack were not originally from Srebrenica but from all around the central Podrinje region. Evidence shows that they rather viewed themselves as members of the Bosnian Muslim group.

560. The Chamber concludes that the protected group, within the meaning of Article 4 of the Statute, must be defined, in the present case, as the Bosnian Muslims. The Bosnian Muslims of Srebrenica or the Bosnian Muslims of Eastern Bosnia constitute a part of the protected group under Article 4. The question of whether an intent to destroy a part of the protected group falls under the definition of genocide is a separate issue that will be discussed below. * * *

581. Since in this case primarily the Bosnian Muslim men of military age were killed, a second issue is whether this group of victims represented a sufficient part of the Bosnian Muslim group so that the intent to destroy them qualifies as an "intent to destroy the group in whole or in part" under Article 4 of the Statute.

582. Invoking the work of the ILC and the *Jelisić* Judgement [relevant parts of which are excerpted above], the Prosecution interprets the expression "in whole or in part" to mean a "substantial" part in quantitative or qualitative terms. However, the Prosecution states that "it is not necessary to consider the global population of the group. The intent to destroy a multitude of persons because of their membership in a particular group constitutes genocide even if these persons constitute only part of a group either within a country or within a region or within a single community." The Prosecution relies on, *inter alia*, the *Akayesu* Judgement which found the accused guilty of genocide for acts he committed within a single commune and the *Nikolić* Decision taken pursuant to Rule 61, which upheld the characterisation of genocide for acts committed within a single region of Bosnia-Herzegovina, in that case, the region of Vlasenica. The Prosecution further cites the *Jelisić* Judgement which declared that "international custom admit[ted] the characterization of genocide even when the exterminatory intent only extend[ed] to a limited geographic zone."

583. The Defence contends that the term "in part" refers to the scale of the crimes actually committed, as opposed to the intent, which would have to extend to destroying the group as such, *i.e.* in its entirety. The Defence relies for this interpretation on the intention of the drafters of the Convention, which it contends was confirmed by the subsequent commentary of Raphaël Lemkin in 1950 before the American Congress during the debates on the Convention's ratification and by the implementing legislation proposed by the United States during the Nixon and Carter administrations. That is, any destruction, even if only partial, must have been carried out with the intent to destroy the entire group, as such.

584. The Trial Chamber does not agree. Admittedly, by adding the term "in part," some of the Convention's drafters may have intended that actual destruction of a mere part of a human group could be characterised

as genocide, only as long as it was carried out with the intent to destroy the group as such. The debates on this point during the preparatory work are unclear, however, and a plain reading of the Convention contradicts this interpretation. Under the Convention, the term "in whole or in part" refers to the intent, as opposed to the actual destruction, and it would run contrary to the rules of interpretation to alter the ordinary meaning of the terms used in the Convention by recourse to the preparatory work which lacks clarity on the issue. The Trial Chamber concludes that any act committed with the intent to destroy a part of a group, as such, constitutes an act of genocide within the meaning of the Convention.

585. The Genocide Convention itself provides no indication of what constitutes intent to destroy "in part." The preparatory work offers few indications either. The draft Convention submitted by the Secretary-General observes that "the systematic destruction even of a fraction of a group of human beings constitutes an exceptionally heinous crime." Early commentaries on the Genocide Convention opined that the matter of what was substantial fell within the ambit of the Judges' discretionary evaluation. Nehemia Robinson was of the view that the intent to destroy could pertain to only a region or even a local community if the number of persons targeted was substantial.[1297] Pieter Drost remarked that any systematic destruction of a fraction of a protected group constituted genocide.[1298]

586. A somewhat stricter interpretation has prevailed in more recent times. According to the ILC, the perpetrators of the crime must seek to destroy a quantitatively substantial part of the protected group:

> It is not necessary to intend to achieve the complete annihilation of a group from every corner of the globe. None the less the crime of genocide by its very nature requires the intention to destroy at least a substantial part of a particular group.

The *Kayishema and Ruzindana* Judgement stated that the intent to destroy a part of a group must affect a "considerable" number of individuals. The Judgement handed down on Ignace Bagilishema, on 7

[1297] Nehemia Robinson, THE GENOCIDE CONVENTION, p. 63: "the intent to destroy a multitude of persons of the same group must be classified as genocide even if these persons constitute only part of a group either within a country or within a region *or within a single community*, provided the number is substantial." The writer also noted before the Foreign Relations Commission of the American Senate: "the intent to destroy a multitude of persons of the same group must be classified as genocide even if these persons constitute only part of a group either within a country or within a single community, provided the number is substantial because the aim of the convention is to deal with action against large numbers, not individual events if they happen to possess the same characteristics. It will be up to the court to decide in every case whether such intent existed." (The Genocide Convention—Its Origins and Interpretation, *reprinted in* Hearings on the Genocide Convention Before a Subcomm. of the Senate Comm. on Foreign Relations, 81st Cong., 2nd Sess., 487, 498 (1950)).

[1298] Pieter Drost, THE CRIME OF STATE, BOOK II, GENOCIDE, Sythoff, Leyden, p. 85: "Acts perpetrated with the intended purpose to destroy various people as members of the same group are to be classified as genocidal crimes although the victims amount to only a small part of the entire group present within the national, regional or local community."

June 2001, also recognised that the destruction sought must target at least a substantial part of the group.

587. Benjamin Whitaker's 1985 study on the prevention and punishment of the crime of genocide holds that the partial destruction of a group merits the characterisation of genocide when it concerns a large portion of the entire group or a significant section of that group.

> "In part" would seem to imply a reasonably significant number, relative to the total of the group as a whole, or else a significant section of a group, such as its leadership.

The "Final Report of the Commission of Experts established pursuant to Security Council resolution 780 (1992)" (hereinafter "Report of the Commission of Experts") confirmed this interpretation, and considered that an intent to destroy a specific part of a group, such as its political, administrative, intellectual or business leaders, "may be a strong indication of genocide regardless of the actual numbers killed." The report states that extermination specifically directed against law enforcement and military personnel may affect "a significant section of a group in that it renders the group at large defenceless against other abuses of a similar or other nature." However, the Report goes on to say that "the attack on the leadership must be viewed *in the context of the fate of what happened to the rest of the group*. If a group suffers extermination of its leadership and in the wake of that loss, a large number of its members are killed or subjected to other heinous acts, for example deportation, the cluster of violations ought to be considered in its entirety in order to interpret the provisions of the Convention in a spirit consistent with its purpose." * * *

589. Several other sources confirm that the intent to eradicate a group within a limited geographical area such as the region of a country or even a municipality may be characterised as genocide. The United Nations General Assembly characterised as an act of genocide the murder of approximately 800 Palestinians detained at Sabra and Shatila, most of whom were women, children and elderly.[1307] The *Jelisić* Judgement held that genocide could target a limited geographic zone. Two Judgements recently rendered by German courts took the view that genocide could be perpetrated within a limited geographical area. The Federal Constitutional Court of Germany, in the *Nikola Jorgić* case, upheld the Judgement of the Düsseldorf Supreme Court, interpreting the intent to destroy the group "in part" as including the intention to destroy a group within a limited geographical area.[1310] In a Judgement against

---

[1307] UN Doc. AG/Res.37/123D (16 December 1982), para. 2. It should however be noted that the resolution was not adopted unanimously, notably, the paragraph characterising the massacre as an act of genocide was approved by 98 votes to 19, with 23 abstentions. *See* UN Doc. A/37/PV.108, para. 151.

[1310] Federal Constitutional Court, 2BvR 1290/99, 12 December 2000, par. 23: "The courts also do not go beyond the possible meaning of the text by accepting that the intent to destroy may relate to a geographically limited part of the group. There is support for that interpretation

Novislav Djajic on 23 May 1997, the Bavarian Appeals Chamber similarly found that acts of genocide were committed in June 1992 though confined within the administrative district of Foča.

590. The Trial Chamber is thus left with a margin of discretion in assessing what is destruction "in part" of the group. But it must exercise its discretionary power in a spirit consonant with the object and purpose of the Convention which is to criminalise specified conduct directed against the existence of protected *groups*, as such. The Trial Chamber is therefore of the opinion that the intent to destroy a group, even if only in part, means seeking to destroy a distinct part of the group as opposed to an accumulation of isolated individuals within it. Although the perpetrators of genocide need not seek to destroy the entire group protected by the Convention, they must view the part of the group they wish to destroy as a distinct entity which must be eliminated as such. A campaign resulting in the killings, in different places spread over a broad geographical area, of a finite number of members of a protected group might not thus qualify as genocide, despite the high total number of casualties, because it would not show an intent by the perpetrators to target the very existence of the group as such. Conversely, the killing of all members of the part of a group located within a small geographical area, although resulting in a lesser number of victims, would qualify as genocide if carried out with the intent to destroy the part of the group as such located in this small geographical area. Indeed, the physical destruction may target only a part of the geographically limited part of the larger group because the perpetrators of the genocide regard the intended destruction as sufficient to annihilate the group as a distinct entity in the geographic area at issue. In this regard, it is important to bear in mind the total context in which the physical destruction is carried out.

591. The parties have presented opposing views as to whether the killings of Bosnian Muslim men in Srebrenica were carried out with intent to destroy a substantial part of the Bosnian Muslim group. It should be recalled that the Prosecution at different times has proposed different definitions of the group in the context of the charge of genocide. In the Indictment, as in the submission of the Defence, the Prosecution referred to the group of the Bosnian Muslims, while in the final brief and arguments it defined the group as the Bosnian Muslims of Srebrenica or the Bosnian Muslims of Eastern Bosnia. The Trial Chamber has previously indicated that the protected group, under Article 4 of the Statute, should be defined as the Bosnian Muslims.

592. The Prosecution first argues that "causing at least 7,475 deaths of mainly Bosnian Muslim men in Srebrenica, the destruction of this part of the group, which numbered in total approximately 38,000 to 42,000 prior to the fall," constitutes a substantial part of the group not only

---

in the fact that STGB para. 220a [the national law integrating the Convention] penalises the intent to destroy partially as well as entirely."

because it targeted a numerically high number of victims, but also because the victims represented a significant part of the group. It was common knowledge that the Bosnian Muslims of Eastern Bosnia constituted a patriarchal society in which men had more education, training and provided material support to their family. The Prosecution claims that the VRS [Bosnian Serb] troops were fully cognisant that by killing all the military aged men, they would profoundly disrupt the bedrock social and cultural foundations of the group. The Prosecution adds that the mass executions of the military aged men must be viewed in the context of what occurred to the remainder of the Srebrenica group. The offensive against the safe area aimed to ethnically cleanse the Bosnian Muslims and progressively culminated in the murder of the Bosnian Muslim men as well as the evacuation of the women, children and elderly. In the Prosecution's view, the end result was purposeful, as shown by the longstanding plan of Republika Srpska to eliminate the Bosnian Muslims from the area. Specifically, Radovan Karadžić, in Directive 7 of 7 March 1995, ordered the Drina Corps to "create an unbearable situation of total insecurity with no hope of further survival or life for the inhabitants of Srebrenica and Žepa." General Krstić and his superiors also manifested genocidal intent by using inflammatory rhetoric and racist statements that presented the VRS as defending the Serbian people from a threat of genocide posed by "Ustasha-Muslim hordes." According to the Prosecution, "by killing the leaders and defenders of the group and deporting the remainder of it, the VRS and General Krstić had assured that the Bosnian Muslim community of Srebrenica and its surrounds would not return to Srebrenica nor would it reconstitute itself in that region or indeed, anywhere else." The Prosecution points us to the terrible impact the events of 11–16 July had upon the Bosnian Muslim community of Srebrenica: "what remains of the Srebrenica community survives in many cases only in the biological sense, nothing more. It's a community in despair; it's a community clinging to memories; it's a community that is lacking leadership; it's a community that's a shadow of what it once was." The Prosecution concludes that "the defendant's crimes have not only resulted in the death of thousands [of] men and boys, but have destroyed the Srebrenica Muslim community."

593. The Defence argues in rejoinder that, "although the desire to condemn the acts of the Bosnian Serb Army at Srebrenica in the most pejorative terms is understandably strong," these acts do not fall under the legal definition of genocide because it was not proven that they were committed with the intent to destroy the group as an entity. First, the killing of up to 7,500 members of a group, the Bosnian Muslims, that numbers about 1.4 million people, does not evidence an intent to destroy a "substantial" part of the group. To the Defence, the 7,500 dead are not even substantial when compared to the 40,000 Bosnian Muslims of Srebrenica. The Defence also points to the fact that the VRS forces did not kill the women, children and elderly gathered at Potočari but

transported them safely to Kladanj, as opposed to all other genocides in modern history, which have indiscriminately targeted men, women and children. The Defence counters the Prosecution's submission that the murder of all the military aged men would constitute a selective genocide, as the VRS knew that their death would inevitably result in the destruction of the Muslim community of Srebrenica as such. According to the Defence, had the VRS actually intended to destroy the Bosnian Muslim community of Srebrenica, it would have killed all the women and children, who were powerless and already under its control, rather than undertaking the time and manpower consuming task of searching out and eliminating the men of the column. The Defence rejects the notion that the transfer of the women, children and elderly can be viewed cynically as a public relations cover-up for the planned execution of the men. First, it says the decision to transfer the women, children and elderly was taken on 11 July, *i.e.* before the VRS decided to kill all the military aged men. Further, the Defence points out, by the time the evacuation started, the world community was already aware of, and outraged by, the humanitarian crisis caused by the VRS in Srebrenica, and the VRS was not concerned with covering up its true intentions. The Defence also argues that the VRS would have killed the Bosnian Muslims in Žepa, a neighbouring enclave, as well, if its intent was to kill the Bosnian Muslims as a group. Furthermore, the Defence claims that none of the military expert witnesses "could attribute the killings to any overall plan to destroy the Bosnian Muslims as a group." To the Defence, a true genocide is almost invariably preceded by propaganda that calls for killings of the targeted group and nothing similar occurred in the present case. Inflammatory public statements made by one group against another—short of calling for killings—are common practice in any war and cannot be taken as evidence of genocidal intent. The Defence argues that, despite the unprecedented access to confidential material obtained by the Prosecution, none of the documents submitted, not even the intercepted conversations of VRS Army officers involved in the Srebrenica campaign, show an intent to destroy the Bosnian Muslims as a group. The Defence contends that the facts instead prove that the VRS forces intended to kill solely all potential fighters in order to eliminate any future military threat. The wounded men were spared. More significantly, 3,000 members of the column were let through after a general truce was concluded between the warring parties. The Defence concludes that the killings were committed by a small group of individuals within a short period of time as a retaliation for failure to meet General Mladić's demand of surrender to the VRS of the BiH Army units in the Srebrenica area. The Defence recognises that "the consequences of the killings of 7,500 people on those who survived are undoubtedly terrible." However, it argues that these consequences would remain the same, regardless of the intent underlying the killings and thus "do not contribute to deciding and determining what the true intent of the killing was." The Defence concludes that "there is no proof and evidence upon which this Trial Chamber could conclude beyond all reasonable doubt that the killings were carried out with the intent to destroy, in whole or in part, the Bosnian Muslims as an ethnic group."

594. The Trial Chamber concludes from the evidence that the VRS forces sought to eliminate all of the Bosnian Muslims in Srebrenica as a community. Within a period of no more than seven days, as many as 7,000–8,000 men of military age were systematically massacred while the remainder of the Bosnian Muslim population present at Srebrenica, some 25,000 people, were forcibly transferred to Kladanj. The Trial Chamber previously described how the VRS attempted to kill all the Bosnian Muslim men of military age, regardless of their civilian or military status; wounded men were spared only because of the presence of UNPROFOR and the portion of the column that managed to get through to government-held territory owed its survival to the fact that the VRS lacked the military resources to capture them.

595. Granted, only the men of military age were systematically massacred, but it is significant that these massacres occurred at a time when the forcible transfer of the rest of the Bosnian Muslim population was well under way. The Bosnian Serb forces could not have failed to know, by the time they decided to kill all the men, that this selective destruction of the group would have a lasting impact upon the entire group. Their death precluded any effective attempt by the Bosnian Muslims to recapture the territory. Furthermore, the Bosnian Serb forces had to be aware of the catastrophic impact that the disappearance of two or three generations of men would have on the survival of a traditionally patriarchal society, an impact the Chamber has previously described in detail. The Bosnian Serb forces knew, by the time they decided to kill all of the military aged men, that the combination of those killings with the forcible transfer of the women, children and elderly would inevitably result in the physical disappearance of the Bosnian Muslim population at Srebrenica. Intent by the Bosnian Serb forces to target the Bosnian Muslims of Srebrenica as a group is further evidenced by their destroying homes of Bosnian Muslims in Srebrenica and Potočari and the principal mosque in Srebrenica soon after the attack.

596. Finally, there is a strong indication of the intent to destroy the group as such in the concealment of the bodies in mass graves, which were later dug up, the bodies mutilated and reburied in other mass graves located in even more remote areas, thereby preventing any decent burial in accord with religious and ethnic customs and causing terrible distress to the mourning survivors, many of whom have been unable to come to a closure until the death of their men is finally verified.

597. The strategic location of the enclave, situated between two Serb territories, may explain why the Bosnian Serb forces did not limit themselves to expelling the Bosnian Muslim population. By killing all the military aged men, the Bosnian Serb forces effectively destroyed the

community of the Bosnian Muslims in Srebrenica as such and eliminated all likelihood that it could ever re-establish itself on that territory.

598. The Chamber concludes that the intent to kill all the Bosnian Muslim men of military age in Srebrenica constitutes an intent to destroy in part the Bosnian Muslim group within the meaning of Article 4 and therefore must be qualified as a genocide.

NOTES & QUESTIONS

1. Case Outcome

The *Krstić* case marks the ICTY's first formal genocide conviction. For his involvement in the massacre at Srebrenica, Krstić was convicted of genocide; persecution through acts of murder, cruel and inhumane treatment, terrorizing the civilian population, and forcible transfer and destruction of personal property; and murder as a violation of the laws or customs of war. The Prosecution argued for life imprisonment, on the ground that the most serious penalty was deserved for a finding of genocide. The Trial Chamber ultimately sentenced Krstić to 46 years, relying in part on the sentencing practice of the former Yugoslavia. Krstić appealed his conviction. The Appeals Chamber did not reverse any of the factual or legal findings concerning the commission of genocide at Srebrenica. *Prosecutor v. Krstić*, Case No. IT–98–33–A, Judgement, paras. 6–38 (Apr. 19, 2004). However, it did conclude that General Krstić himself did not possess genocidal intent and, as such, could not be convicted of committing genocide:

> As has been demonstrated, all that the evidence can establish is that Krstić was aware of the intent to commit genocide on the part of some members of the VRS Main Staff, and with that knowledge, he did nothing to prevent the use of Drina Corps personnel and resources to facilitate those killings. This knowledge on his part alone cannot support an inference of genocidal intent. Genocide is one of the worst crimes known to humankind, and its gravity is reflected in the stringent requirement of specific intent. Convictions for genocide can be entered only where that intent has been unequivocally established. There was a demonstrable failure by the Trial Chamber to supply adequate proof that Radislav Krstić possessed the genocidal intent. Krstić, therefore, is not guilty of genocide as a principal perpetrator.

Prosecutor v. Krstić, *supra*, at para. 134. The Appeals Chamber accordingly substituted a conviction for aiding and abetting genocide on the ground that Krstić acted with knowledge that others involved in the fall of Srebrenica possessed genocidal intent and reduced his sentence to thirty-five years. *Id.* at paras. 135–143.

The distinction between committing genocide and complicity in genocide as it relates to the *mens rea* element will be discussed in greater detail in Chapter 15. For now, consider whether an individual should be convicted of aiding and abetting genocide notwithstanding the fact that a court found that the individual did not possess the intent to commit genocide. General Krstić is serving his sentence in Great Britain. Prior to the fall of Srebrenica, the city's population had been mostly Muslim. Despite the international condemnation of the siege and the massacres, the Dayton Peace Accord that ended the war granted Srebrenica to Republika Srpska. Its residents are now mostly of Serbian descent. Under strong pressure from the international community, the Republika Srpska government established a Commission, including Bosnian Muslim representatives, to inquire into the events that occurred in July 1995 around Srebrenica. That Commission issued a report which for the first time officially acknowledged government responsibility for the killing of close to 8,000 Bosnian Muslims.

2. Krstić in Prison

In 2004 Krstić was transferred to the United Kingdom to serve his sentence. On May 7, 2010, three Muslim inmates attacked and seriously wounded Krstić. The three inmates were convicted of "wounding with intent to commit grievous bodily harm" but acquitted of attempted murder. They were given sentences of six to twelve years. Shortly thereafter Krstić was transferred back to the Netherlands, and then in 2014 to a prison in Poland where he is currently serving his sentence.

3. The Responsibility of Dutchbat

In 2002, in a belated act of penance, the Dutch government (headed by Prime Minister Wim Kok) resigned after an internal investigation into their responsibility for the massacres at Srebrenica. The report, completed by the Netherlands Institute of War Documentation (NIOD), accused political leaders of carrying out an "ill-conceived plan" to boost Dutch international prestige by participating in the mission and sending unprepared troops on a "mission impossible" to defend 30,000 refugees. It also indicated that vital information about the massacre was withheld from the government by the army. It charged: "[the] Army had different priorities and not much political sensitivity, with the result that the Minister was generally not informed in time and/or properly of matters which the Army were well aware of; in some cases, indeed, he was not informed at all." (Part IV, Chap. 7, Sec. 13, *see also* Management Report Part IV, Chap. 7, Sec. 5). The report also noted that the Dutch government and military had refrained from using the term "genocide" until the Dutch soldiers were out of Bosnia and criticized a Dutch politician that had gone to Bosnia and described the situation as genocide. (Part IV, Chap. 5, Sec. 19). The report states that there is no evidence that Milošević, or his government in Belgrade, was involved in the massacre and that most of the men killed in Srebrenica were members of the ABiH. Colonel Thom Karremans, the former commander of Dutchbat, later testified as a defence witness in the case of Vidoje Blagojević, the former head of a Bosnian Serb army brigade. Defence counsel tried to elicit testimony that the situation in Srebrenica was "complex" and not a one-sided massacre.

Do the members of Dutchbat or the United Nations bear any legal or moral responsibility for the Srebrenica massacres? Victims' families filed civil suits against both the United Nations and the Dutch Government in The Hague District Court seeking compensation for failing in their duty to protect. Almost twenty years after the massacre, the District Court found the Dutch government liable for the loss suffered by relatives of the over 300 men who were deported from the Dutchbat compound in Potočari on the afternoon of July 13, 1995, the majority of whom were then killed. The Court ruled that the peacekeepers should have known that the men deported from the Dutch compound would be killed or mistreated. The Court declined to find the Dutch government liable for acts prior to the fall of Srebrenica, including the failure to provide air support. While the Court also found that Dutchbat failed to report to the United Nations war crimes it observed, it also concluded that even if such crimes had been reported it would not have led to direct military intervention by the United Nations, and thus the Dutch government is not liable to the families for this failure. The case against the U.N. was dismissed on immunity grounds. *Mothers of Srebrenica v. The State of the Netherlands and the United Nations,* Case No. C/09/295247, The Hague District Court, Judgment (July 16, 2014) (ECLI:NL:RBDHA:2014: 8562). Under what circumstances could peacekeepers be responsible for abuses committed by warring sides? Does the "good Samaritan" doctrine apply to such situations? Consider these questions further when you review the materials in Chapter 15 on complicity liability.

4. "In Part"

How should the term "in part" be interpreted? Note the difficulty the Prosecution had in defining the "part" of the Bosnian Muslim population that Krstić allegedly intended to destroy. The Prosecution had alternatively argued that the targeted group was the Bosnian Muslim population of Srebrenica or of Eastern Bosnia. *Krstić* Trial Judgement, *supra*, at para. 558. The Tribunal sided with the defense in finding that the relevant group was in fact all 1.5 million Bosnian Muslims, rather than the 37,000 or so in Srebrenica. Does the intent to kill 7–8,000 members of a 1.5 million member group manifest an intent to eliminate "a part" of a protected group? Is it appropriate to call both the massacre at Srebrenica and the Rwandan violence, which resulted in the deaths of at least 800,000 persons, by the same term? Krstić's defense counsel argued that "while in no way justifying the events at Srebrenica, it cannot be ignored that its scale pales in comparison with the three *bona fide* genocides recognized in modern history: the Armenia [sic] genocide, the Holocaust, and the Rwandan genocide." *Prosecutor v. Krstić*, Case No. IT–98–33–A, Defence Response to Prosecution Appeal Brief, para. 58 (Dec. 21, 2001).

Should the term "genocide" be "saved" for massacres on the order of the Holocaust, which resulted in the death of over 6 million people? By that measure, should Rwanda even qualify? Or, should we look to proportional numbers rather than to absolute numbers? In Rwanda, 75% of the Tutsi population were killed. *See* Philip Verwimp, *Death and Survival during the 1994 Genocide in Rwanda,* 58 POPULATION STUD. 233 (2004). According to Philip Gourevitch, "[t]he dead of Rwanda accumulated at nearly three times the rate of Jewish dead during the Holocaust." Philip Gourevitch, WE WISH TO INFORM YOU THAT TOMORROW WE WILL BE KILLED WITH OUR FAMILIES 4 (1997). The ICTY also characterized the Srebrenica massacre as an act of extermination (*Krstić* Trial Judgement, *supra*, at para. 505) and persecution (*id.* at para. 538); should it have stopped there?

The *Krstić* opinion hinges, in part, on the recognition that the Muslim population of Eastern Bosnia was a "patriarchal" society in which men and boys provided "the bedrock social and cultural foundations of the group." *Krstić* Trial Judgement, *supra*, at para. 595. Does this mean that if only women had been killed at Srebrenica, no genocide would have occurred? What if only the elderly had been eliminated? Should a finding of genocide depend on whether a protected group is "traditionally patriarchal"? *Id.* at para. 595. Is the Defense's notion (substantially accepted by the Trial Chamber) of "selective genocide" (*id.* at para. 593) tenable within the terms or the object and purpose of the Convention? Is it appropriate for a criminal tribunal to make such judgments about the relative importance of different strata within a society to the group?

5. Attempted Genocide

Article III(d) of the Genocide Convention makes the "attempt to commit genocide" a punishable act. While the inclusion of attempt as a punishable offense was unanimously adopted by the drafting committee, a proposed provision prohibiting "preparatory acts" was voted down. These preparatory acts were originally defined as

(a) studies and research for the purpose of developing the technique of genocide;

(b) setting up installations, manufacturing, obtaining, possessing or supplying of articles or substances with the knowledge that they are intended for genocide;

(c) issuing instructions or orders, and distributing tasks with a view to committing genocide.

UN Doc. E/447, Art. II.I.2 (1947). Why would the committee reject the notion of preparatory acts as punishable offenses? The Rome Statute of the ICC also assigns individual criminal responsibility for "attempts to commit such a crime by taking action that commences its execution by means of a substantial step, but the crime does not occur because of circumstances independent of the person's intentions." Art. 25(3)(f). The Rome Statute, however, offers no useful guidance on what constitutes a "substantial step." When should preparatory acts be considered criminal? How should the ICC determine when acts constitute a "substantial step" towards the execution of a crime? The Statutes of the ICTY and ICTR include other forms of participation in genocide, but exclude the notion of attempt for all crimes. Professor Schabas opines that there was "hardly a need" to include attempt as a crime in the *ad hoc* tribunals, since they were created *ex post facto* to the offenses in question. William A. Schabas, GENOCIDE IN INTERNATIONAL LAW 281 (2003). Do you agree? Should defendants such as Jelisić and Krstić be convicted of attempt to commit genocide instead of the commission of genocide? What type of conduct would constitute attempted genocide?

PROBLEM

The Yanomami

The Yanomami are an indigenous group residing in the Amazon rainforest in parts of Brazil and Venezuela. They subsist by hunting, fishing, gathering, and tending gardens. In the 1980s, gold was discovered in the territories in which they reside. This brought an influx of mining interests—legal and illegal. The Yanomami suffered through the introduction of foreign diseases, alcohol, prostitution, and the destruction of the local environment through surface mining practices and mercury pollution (mercury is used to separate gold from soil and rock). Between 1987 and 1990, loss of territory, epidemiological shock, ecological damage, and physical violence resulted in the death of approximately 13% of the Yanomami people. The Brazilian and Venezuelan governments have since protected parts of the Yanomami land in national parks, although the Yanomami hold no formal title to the land. Nonetheless, gold prospectors continue to enter the area illegally. The Yanomami often fight back, attacking miners and stealing their equipment.

In one instance in 1993, after an attack on a Yanomami community in which four men were killed, a group of Yanomami people sought revenge, killing two miners. Sometime later, other miners from the same expedition attacked and massacred residents of the Yanomami village of Haximú. They killed men, women, and children.

The Brazilian authorities brought genocide charges against the miners under a Brazilian law that tracks the Genocide Convention's definition. The court convicted the defendants of genocide and sentenced them to 19–20 years' imprisonment. *See* Recurso Especial No. 222,653 (Roraima) (1999/0061733–9), Superior Tribunal of Justice (May 22, 2001) (Braz.). Several years later, however, an appeals court overturned the verdicts on the grounds that murder charges must be tried before a jury. The Public Prosecutor appealed. In 2006, the Supreme Court upheld the sentences against some of the miners for the Haximú massacre.

On what grounds might the prosecution have argued that the defendants committed genocide? How might the accused have defended themselves against the genocide charge?

V. THE CONSTITUTIVE ACTS OF GENOCIDE

The *actus reus* of genocide includes more than the killing of members of the group. Indeed, Article II of the Genocide Convention lists several general categories of acts that may also lead to a finding of genocide: causing serious bodily or mental harm to members of the group, subjecting members of the group to adverse conditions of life, impairing the reproductive capacities of members of the group, and transferring children from the group. Another excerpt from the *Akayesu* case appears below. In it, the Trial Chamber discusses the question of whether rape constitutes an *actus reus* of genocide, even though rape is not mentioned in the definition of the crime. Specifically, the Indictment against Akayesu alleged:

12A. Between April 7 and the end of June 1994, hundreds of civilians (hereinafter "displaced civilians") sought refuge at the bureau communal. The majority of these displaced civilians were Tutsi. While seeking refuge at the bureau communal, female displaced civilians were regularly taken by armed local militia and/or communal police and subjected to sexual violence, and/or beaten on or near the bureau communal premises. Displaced civilians were also murdered frequently on or near the bureau communal premises. Many women were forced to endure multiple acts of sexual violence which were at times committed by more than one assailant. These acts of sexual violence were generally accompanied by explicit threats of death or bodily harm. The female displaced civilians lived in constant fear and their physical and psychological health deteriorated as a result of the sexual violence and beatings and killings.

12B. Jean Paul Akayesu knew that the acts of sexual violence, beatings and murders were being committed and was at times present during their commission. Jean Paul Akayesu facilitated the commission of the sexual violence, beatings and murders by allowing the sexual violence and beatings and murders to occur on or near the bureau communal premises. By virtue of his presence during the commission of the sexual violence, beatings and murders and by failing to prevent the sexual violence, beatings and murders, Jean Paul Akayesu encouraged these activities.

Prosecutor v. Akayesu, Case No. ICTR–96–4–T, Judgement (Sept. 2, 1998)

In the Trial Chamber

416. Allegations of sexual violence first came to the attention of the Chamber through the testimony of Witness J [during trial], a Tutsi woman, who stated that her six-year-old daughter had been raped by three *Interahamwe* when they came to kill her father. On examination by the Chamber, Witness J also testified that she had heard that young girls were raped at the bureau communal. Subsequently, Witness H, a Tutsi woman, testified that she herself was raped in a sorghum field and that, just outside the compound of the bureau communal, she personally saw other Tutsi women being raped and knew of at least three such cases of rape by *Interahamwe*. Witness H testified initially that the Accused, as well as commune police officers, were present while this was happening and did nothing to prevent the rapes. However, on examination by the Chamber as to whether Akayesu was aware that the rapes were going on, she responded that she didn't know, but that it happened at the bureau communal and he knew that the women were there. Witness H stated that some of the rapes occurred in the bush area

nearby but that some of them occurred "on site." On examination by the Chamber, she said that the Accused was present during one of the rapes, but she could not confirm that he saw what was happening. While Witness H expressed the view that the *Interahamwe* acted with impunity and should have been prevented by the commune police and the Accused from committing abuses, she testified that no orders were given to the *Interahamwe* to rape. She also testified that she herself was beaten but not raped at the bureau communal.

417. On 17 June 1997, the Indictment was amended to include allegations of sexual violence and additional charges against the Accused under Article 3(g), Article 3(i) and Article 4(2)(e) of the ICTR Statute. In introducing this amendment, the Prosecution stated that the testimony of Witness H motivated them to renew their investigation of sexual violence in connection with events which took place in Taba at the bureau communal. The Prosecution stated that evidence previously available was not sufficient to link the Accused to acts of sexual violence and acknowledged that factors to explain this lack of evidence might include the shame that accompanies acts of sexual violence as well as insensitivity in the investigation of sexual violence. The Chamber notes that the Defence in its closing statement questioned whether the Indictment was amended in response to public pressure concerning the prosecution of sexual violence. The Chamber understands that the amendment of the Indictment resulted from the spontaneous testimony of sexual violence by Witness J and Witness H during the course of this trial and the subsequent investigation of the Prosecution, rather than from public pressure. Nevertheless, the Chamber takes note of the interest shown in this issue by non-governmental organizations, which it considers as indicative of public concern over the historical exclusion of rape and other forms of sexual violence from the investigation and prosecution of war crimes. The investigation and presentation of evidence relating to sexual violence is in the interest of justice.

418. Following the amendment of the Indictment, Witness JJ, a Tutsi woman, testified about the events which took place in Taba after the plane crash. She [testified] that she was driven away from her home, which was destroyed by her Hutu neighbours who attacked her and her family after a man came to the hill near where she lived and said that the bourgmestre had sent him so that no Tutsi would remain on the hill that night. Witness JJ saw her Tutsi neighbours killed and she fled, seeking refuge in a nearby forest with her baby on her back and her younger sister, who had been wounded in the attack by a blow with an axe and two machete cuts. As she was being chased everywhere she went, Witness JJ said she went to the bureau communal. There she found more than sixty refugees down the road and on the field nearby. She testified that most of the refugees were women and children. * * *

420. Witness JJ testified that she spent the night in the rain in a field. The next day she said she returned to the bureau communal and

went to the Accused, in a group of ten people representing the refugees, who asked that they be killed as the others had been because they were so tired of it all. She said the Accused told them that there were no more bullets and that he had gone to look for more in Gitarama but they had not yet been made available. He asked his police officers to chase them away and said that even if there were bullets they would not waste them on the refugees. As the refugees saw that death would be waiting for them anywhere else, Witness JJ testified they stayed at the bureau communal.

421. Witness JJ testified that often the *Interahamwe* came to beat the refugees during the day, and that the policemen came to beat them at night. She also testified that the *Interahamwe* took young girls and women from their site of refuge near the bureau communal into a forest in the area and raped them. Witness JJ testified that this happened to her—that she was stripped of her clothing and raped in front of other people. At the request of the Prosecutor and with great embarrassment, she explicitly specified that the rapist, a young man armed with an axe and a long knife, penetrated her vagina with his penis. She stated that on this occasion she was raped twice. Subsequently, she told the Chamber, on a day when it was raining, she was taken by force from near the bureau communal into the cultural center within the compound of the bureau communal, in a group of approximately fifteen girls and women. In the cultural center, according to Witness JJ, they were raped. She was raped twice by one man. Then another man came to where she was lying and he also raped her. A third man then raped her, she said, at which point she described herself as feeling near dead. Witness JJ testified that she was at a later time dragged back to the cultural center in a group of approximately ten girls and women and they were raped. She was raped again, two times. Witness JJ testified that she could not count the total number of times she was raped. She said, "each time you encountered attackers they would rape you,"—in the forest, in the sorghum fields. Witness JJ related to the Chamber the experience of finding her sister before she died, having been raped and cut with a machete.

422. Witness JJ testified that when they arrived at the bureau communal the women were hoping the authorities would defend them but she was surprised to the contrary. In her testimony she recalled lying in the cultural center, having been raped repeatedly by *Interahamwe*, and hearing the cries of young girls around her, girls as young as twelve or thirteen years old. On the way to the cultural center the first time she was raped there, Witness JJ said that she and the others were taken past the Accused and that he was looking at them. The second time she was taken to the cultural center to be raped, Witness JJ recalled seeing the Accused standing at the entrance of the cultural center and hearing him say loudly to the *Interahamwe*, "Never ask me again what a Tutsi woman tastes like," and "Tomorrow they will be killed." * * * According to

Witness JJ, most of the girls and women were subsequently killed, either brought to the river and killed there, after having returned to their houses, or killed at the bureau communal. Witness JJ testified that she never saw the Accused rape anyone, but she, like Witness H, believed that he had the means to prevent the rapes from taking place and never even tried to do so. In describing the Accused and the statement he made regarding the taste of Tutsi women, she said he was "talking as if someone were encouraging a player" and suggested that he was the one "supervising" the acts of rape. Witness JJ said she did not witness any killings at the bureau communal, although she saw dead bodies there.

423. When Witness JJ fled from the bureau communal, she left her one-year-old child with a Hutu man and woman, who said they had milk for the child and subsequently killed him. Witness JJ spoke of the heavy sorrow the war had caused her. She testified to the humiliation she felt as a mother, by the public nudity and being raped in the presence of children by young men. She said that just thinking about it made the war come alive inside of her. Witness JJ told the Chamber that she had remarried but that her life had never been the same because of the beatings and rapes she suffered. She said the pain in her ribs prevents her from farming because she can no longer use a hoe, and she used to live on the food that she could grow. * * *

442. Defence Witness Matata, called as an expert witness, noted only one case he had heard of in Taba, an attempted rape of two girls aged fourteen and fifteen. He expressed his opinion that the bourgmestre would not have been aware of this case as it was in a region, Buguri sector, which the bourgmestre had never gone to. Witness Matata noted that there is a cultural factor which prevented people from talking about rape, but also suggested that the phenomenon of rape was introduced afterwards for purposes of blackmail. He said he had come across incidents of rape in other parts of the country but suggested that cases of rape were not frequent and not related to an ethnic group. Witness Matata expressed the opinion that rapists were more interested in satisfying their physical needs, that there were spontaneous acts of desire even in the context of killing. He noted that Tutsi women, in general, are quite beautiful and that raping them is not necessarily intended to destroy an ethnic group, but rather to have a beautiful woman. * * *

446. The Accused himself testified that he was completely surprised by the allegations of rape in Taba during the events which took place. He asserted that anyone saying that even a single woman was raped at the bureau communal was lying. While he acknowledged that some witnesses had testified that they were raped at the bureau communal, he swore, in the name of God, that the charge was made up. He said he never saw, and never heard from his policemen, that any woman was raped at the bureau communal. He said that he heard about rape accusations over Radio Rwanda and that women's associations had organized

demonstrations and a march from Kigali to Taba. He suggested that perhaps this was intended to make the Chamber understand that in Taba women were raped at the bureau communal, but he insisted that women were never raped within the premises of the bureau communal or on land belonging to the bureau communal or the commune.

448. On examination by the Chamber, the Accused stated that he did hear about rapes in Kigali but only after he was out of the country. When asked by the Chamber for a reaction to the testimony of sexual violence, the Accused noted that rape was not mentioned in the pre-trial statements of Witness J and Witness H, although Witness H said on examination by the Chamber that she had mentioned her rape to investigators. The Accused suggested that his Indictment was amended because of pressure from the women's movement and women in Rwanda, whom he described as "worked up to agree that they have been raped." On examination by the Chamber, the Accused acknowledged that it was possible that rape might have taken place in the commune of Taba, but he insisted that no rape took place at the bureau communal. He said he first learned of the rape allegations in Taba at the Chamber and maintained that the charges were an "invented accusation."

Factual Findings

449. Having carefully reviewed the testimony of the Prosecution witnesses regarding sexual violence, the Chamber finds that there is sufficient credible evidence to establish beyond a reasonable doubt that during the events of 1994, Tutsi girls and women were subjected to sexual violence, beaten and killed on or near the bureau communal premises, as well as elsewhere in the commune of Taba. Witness H, Witness JJ, Witness OO, and Witness NN all testified that they themselves were raped, and all, with the exception of Witness OO, testified that they witnessed other girls and women being raped. Witness J, Witness KK and Witness PP also testified that they witnessed other girls and women being raped in the commune of Taba. Hundreds of Tutsi, mostly women and children, sought refuge at the bureau communal during this period and many rapes took place on or near the premises of the bureau communal* * *. Many other instances of rape in Taba outside the bureau communal—in fields, on the road, and in or just outside houses—were described by Witness J, Witness H, Witness OO, Witness KK, Witness NN and Witness PP. Witness KK and Witness PP also described other acts of sexual violence which took place on or near the premises of the bureau communal—the forced undressing and public humiliation of girls and women. The Chamber notes that much of the sexual violence took place in front of large numbers of people, and that all of it was directed against Tutsi women. * * *

452. On the basis of the evidence set forth herein, the Chamber finds beyond a reasonable doubt that the Accused had reason to know and in fact knew that sexual violence was taking place on or near the premises of the bureau communal, and that women were being taken away from

the bureau communal and sexually violated. There is no evidence that the Accused took any measures to prevent acts of sexual violence or to punish the perpetrators of sexual violence. In fact there is evidence that the Accused ordered, instigated and otherwise aided and abetted sexual violence. * * *

Genocide (Article 2 of the Statute)

494. The definition of genocide, as given in Article 2 of the Tribunal's Statute, is taken verbatim from Articles 2 and 3 of the Convention on the Prevention and Punishment of the Crime of Genocide. * * *

496. The Chamber notes that Rwanda acceded, by legislative decree, to the Convention on Genocide on 12 February 1975. Thus, punishment of the crime of genocide did exist in Rwanda in 1994, at the time of the acts alleged in the Indictment, and the perpetrator was liable to be brought before the competent courts of Rwanda to answer for this crime.

497. Contrary to popular belief, the crime of genocide does not imply the actual extermination of [a] group in its entirety, but is understood as such once any one of the acts mentioned in Article 2(2)(a) through 2(2)(e) is committed with the specific intent to destroy "in whole or in part" a national, ethnical, racial or religious group. * * *

499. Thus, for a crime of genocide to have been committed, it is necessary that one of the acts listed under Article 2(2) of the Statute be committed, that the particular act be committed against a specifically targeted group, it being a national, ethnical, racial or religious group. Consequently, in order to clarify the constitutive elements of the crime of genocide, the Chamber will first state its findings on the acts provided for under Article 2(2)(a) through Article 2(2)(e) of the Statute, the groups protected by the Genocide Convention, and the special intent or *dolus specialis* necessary for genocide to take place.

Causing Serious Bodily or Mental Harm to Members of the Group

502. Causing serious bodily or mental harm to members of the group does not necessarily mean that the harm is permanent and irremediable.

503. In the Adolf Eichmann case, who was convicted of crimes against the Jewish people, genocide under another legal definition, the District Court of Jerusalem stated in its judgement of 12 December 1961, that serious bodily or mental harm of members of the group can be caused

> by the enslavement, starvation, deportation and persecution [. . .] and by their detention in ghettos, transit camps and concentration camps in conditions which were designed to cause their degradation, deprivation of their rights as human beings, and to suppress them and cause them inhumane suffering and torture.[95]

[95] *Attorney General of the Government of Israel v. Adolph Eichmann*, District Court of Jerusalem, 12 December 1961, quoted in 36 I.L.R. 340 (1968).

504. For purposes of interpreting Article 2(2)(b) of the Statute, the Chamber takes serious bodily or mental harm, without limiting itself thereto, to mean acts of torture, be they bodily or mental, inhumane or degrading treatment, persecution. * * *

Imposing Measures Intended to Prevent Births Within the Group

507. For purposes of interpreting Article 2(2)(d) of the Statute, the Chamber holds that the measures intended to prevent births within the group, should be construed as sexual mutilation, the practice of sterilization, forced birth control, separation of the sexes and prohibition of marriages. In patriarchal societies,* where membership of a group is determined by the identity of the father, an example of a measure intended to prevent births within a group is the case where, during rape, a woman of the said group is deliberately impregnated by a man of another group, with the intent to have her give birth to a child who will consequently not belong to its mother's group.

508. Furthermore, the Chamber notes that measures intended to prevent births within the group may be physical, but can also be mental. For instance, rape can be a measure intended to prevent births when the person raped refuses subsequently to procreate, in the same way that members of a group can be led, through threats or trauma, not to procreate.

Forcibly Transferring Children of the Group to Another Group

509. With respect to forcibly transferring children of the group to another group, the Chamber is of the opinion that, as in the case of measures intended to prevent births, the objective is not only to sanction a direct act of forcible physical transfer, but also to sanction acts of threats or trauma which would lead to the forcible transfer of children from one group to another. * * *

731. With regard, particularly, to the acts described in paragraphs 12(A) and 12(B) of the Indictment, that is, rape and sexual violence, the Chamber wishes to underscore the fact that in its opinion, they constitute genocide in the same way as any other act as long as they were committed with the specific intent to destroy, in whole or in part, a particular group, targeted as such. Indeed, rape and sexual violence certainly constitute infliction of serious bodily and mental harm on the victims and are even, according to the Chamber, one of the worst ways [to] inflict harm on the victim as he or she suffers both bodily and mental harm. In light of all the evidence before it, the Chamber is satisfied that the acts of rape and sexual violence described above, were committed solely against Tutsi women, many of whom were subjected to the worst public humiliation, mutilated, and raped several times, often in public, in the Bureau Communal premises or in other public places, and often by more than one assailant. These rapes resulted in physical and psychological

* Eds.: Here, the tribunal probably means "patrilineal," which denotes a system in which descent is traced through the paternal line.

destruction of Tutsi women, their families and their communities. Sexual violence was an integral part of the process of destruction, specifically targeting Tutsi women and specifically contributing to their destruction and to the destruction of the Tutsi group as a whole.

732. The rape of Tutsi women was systematic and was perpetrated against all Tutsi women and solely against them. A Tutsi woman, married to a Hutu, testified before the Chamber that she was not raped because her ethnic background was unknown. As part of the propaganda campaign geared to mobilizing the Hutu against the Tutsi, the Tutsi women were presented as sexual objects. Indeed, the Chamber was told, for an example, that before being raped and killed, Alexia, who was the wife of the Professor, Ntereye, and her two nieces, were forced by the *Interahamwe* to undress and ordered to run and do exercises "in order to display the thighs of Tutsi women." The *Interahamwe* who raped Alexia said, as he threw her on the ground and got on top of her, "let us now see what the vagina of a Tutsi woman takes like." As stated above, Akayesu himself, speaking to the *Interahamwe* who were committing the rapes, said to them: "don't ever ask again what a Tutsi woman tastes like." This sexualized representation of ethnic identity graphically illustrates that Tutsi women were subjected to sexual violence because they were Tutsi. Sexual violence was a step in the process of destruction of the Tutsi group—destruction of the spirit, of the will to live, and of life itself. * * *

733. On the basis of the substantial testimonies brought before it, the Chamber finds that in most cases, the rapes of Tutsi women in Taba, were accompanied with the intent to kill those women. Many rapes were perpetrated near mass graves where the women were taken to be killed. A victim testified that Tutsi women caught could be taken away by peasants and men with the promise that they would be collected later to be executed. Following an act of gang rape, a witness heard Akayesu say "tomorrow they will be killed" and they were actually killed. In this respect, it appears clearly to the Chamber that the acts of rape and sexual violence, as other acts of serious bodily and mental harm committed against the Tutsi, reflected the determination to make Tutsi women suffer and to mutilate them even before killing them, the intent being to destroy the Tutsi group while inflicting acute suffering on its members in the process.

734. In light of the foregoing, the Chamber finds firstly that the acts described *supra* are indeed acts as enumerated in Article 2(2) of the Statute, which constitute the factual elements of the crime of genocide, namely the killings of Tutsi or the serious bodily and mental harm inflicted on the Tutsi. The Chamber is further satisfied beyond reasonable doubt that these various acts were committed by Akayesu with the specific intent to destroy the Tutsi group, as such. * * * [H]ence, the Chamber finds Akayesu individually criminally responsible for genocide.

NOTES & QUESTIONS

1. Rape as Genocide

Are you convinced that rape without killing satisfies the *actus reus* of genocide? How does the rape of a woman from a protected group contribute to the destruction of the group in whole or in part? Does this depend on the stigmatization associated with rape in a particular society and the concomitant long-term psychic harm experienced by those who are raped? Does it depend on whether the intent is to impregnate the victim? Would the rape of a man also constitute genocide? Does focusing on rape as a form of genocide obscure the gendered nature of the crime? Consider this perspective:

> The elision of genocide and rape in the focus on "genocidal rape" as a means of emphasizing the heinousness of [rape] is dangerous. Rape and genocide are each atrocities. Genocide is an effort to debilitate or destroy a people based on its identity as a people, while rape seeks to degrade and destroy a woman based on her identity as a woman. Both are grounded in total contempt for and dehumanization of the victim. And both give rise to unspeakable brutalities. * * * But to emphasize as unparalleled the horror of genocidal rape is factually dubious and risks rendering rape invisible once again. When the ethnic war ceases or is forced back into the bottle, will the crimes against women matter? * * * Or will condemnation be limited to this seemingly exceptional case? * * * [W]e must surface gender in the midst of genocide at the same time that we avoid dualistic thinking. We must examine critically the claim that rape as a tool of "ethnic cleansing" is unique, worse than, or incomparable to other forms of rape in war or in peace—even while we recognize that rape coupled with genocide inflicts multiple, intersectional harms. * * * To exaggerate the distinctiveness of genocidal rape obviates the atrocity of common rape.

Rhonda Copelon, *Gendered War Crimes: Reconceptualizing Rape in a Time of War*, *in* WOMEN'S RIGHTS HUMAN RIGHTS 199, 204 (Julie Peters & Andrea Wolper eds., 1995).

The ICTR subsequently indicted Pauline Nyiramasuhuko, the former Rwandan Minister of Family and Women's Development, for genocide and rape as a crime against humanity. Nyiramasuhuko reportedly supervised attacks against Tutsi individuals and ordered that Tutsi women be raped before they were killed. Nyiramasuhuko is the first woman to be indicted by the ICTR and the first women in the history of international criminal law to be indicted for rape. Her trial, as part of the so-called "Butare 6," was completed on April 30, 2009—one of the longest in the history of the ICTR. She was found guilty of, *inter alia*, genocide, and extermination and rape as a crime against humanity. *Prosecutor v. Nyiramasuhuko et al.*, Case No. ICTR–98–42–T, Judgement (June 24, 2011). For further reading, *see* Catharine MacKinnon, *Defining Rape Internationally: A Comment on* Akayesu, 44 COLUM. J. TRANSNAT'L L. 940 (2006); Sherrie L. Russell-Brown,

Rape as an Act of Genocide, 21 BERKELEY J. INT'L L. 350 (2003); Mark Drumbl, *"She Makes Me Ashamed to be a Woman": The Genocide Conviction of Pauline Nyiramasuhuko*, 34 MICH. J. INT'L L. 559 (2013).

2. Rape Under International Law

The *Akayesu* case for the first time defined rape under international law. Note that rape is not a free-standing crime under the statutes of the international criminal tribunals; rather, it must be charged as a war crime, a crime against humanity, or an act of genocide. The rape counts were not included in the first Indictment against Akayesu. It was only when trial witnesses began testifying to having been raped that the Prosecution moved to amend the Indictment. This amendment is largely credited to Judge Navanethem Pillay (a judge from South Africa, a long-time women's rights activist, and the United Nations High Commissioner for Human Rights from September 1, 2008 to August 31, 2014), and to an *amicus* brief filed mid-trial by a consortium of women's rights organizations urging the Trial Chamber to call upon the Prosecution to amend the indictment. *See* Brief for the Coalition of Women's Human Rights in Conflict Situations in Support of Amending Indictment as *Amicus Curiae*, *Prosecutor v. Akayesu*, Case No. ICTR–96–4–T, Judgement (Sept. 2, 1998). For a discussion of this behind-the-scenes story, *see* Beth Van Schaack, *Engendering Genocide:* Akayesu *and the Affirmation of Genocidal Rape*, *in* HUMAN RIGHTS ADVOCACY STORIES 193 (D. Hurwitz ed., 2008).

3. Slow Death

As discussed above, the international tribunals have recognized the concept of genocide by "slow death," where conditions of life are inflicted upon a protected group that may not lead to the immediate death of members of the group, but will eventually lead to that result if implemented over a long period of time. Consider the following passage, which defines "slow death" as:

> methods of destruction by which the perpetrator does not necessarily intend to immediately kill the members of the group, but which are, ultimately, aimed at their physical destruction. The Chamber holds that the means of deliberately inflicting on the group conditions of life calculated to bring about its physical destruction, in whole or in part, include subjecting a group of people to a subsistence diet, systematic expulsion from their homes and deprivation of essential medical supplies below a minimum vital standard.

Prosecutor v. Rutaganda, Case No. ICTR–96–3–T, Judgement, para. 52 (Dec. 6, 1999). The Tribunals have emphasized the importance of examining the cluster of abuses suffered by members of the group and the collective impact of those actions on the survival of the group. Would it be easier to eliminate a group through starvation, deportation, and neglect than through outright murder? Would such a policy enable a plausible deniability on the part of perpetrators who might blame any subsequent deaths on the harsh conditions or external factors such as famine? Is there any limiting principle to this idea of genocide by slow death? For example, a large percentage of the deaths that occurred during the Khmer Rouge era in Cambodia were due to starvation and disease caused by the Khmer Rouge's implementation of a radical—and ultimately disastrous—agrarian policy. How is a criminal tribunal to distinguish between misguided economic policies, negligence, indifference, and genocide?

4. Mental Harm

Compare the ICTR's conception of the applicability of mental harm in paras. 502 and 508 with the Proxmire Act, implementing the Genocide Convention into United States law. Genocide Convention Implementation Act, 18 U.S.C. § 1091 (2005). That Act requires proof of the "permanent impairment of the mental faculties" arising out of physical intrusion of the body (such as through the injection of drugs, acts of torture, electric shock, etc.). Which is the better approach? In many respects, mental harm was included within the Genocide Convention at the insistence of the Chinese delegation to the drafting proceedings who invoked the Japanese use of narcotics to pacify the Chinese populace during the Japanese occupation of China in World War II.

5. Preventative Action

The full title of the Genocide Convention is: "The Convention on the Prevention and Punishment of the Crime of Genocide." Article I of the Convention announces that "[t]he Contracting Parties confirm that genocide, whether committed in time of peace or in time of war, is a crime under international law which they undertake to prevent and to punish." In addition to defining the crime of genocide, the Convention contains a series of articles setting forth mechanisms to channel inter-governmental responses to genocide. For example, Article VIII empowers contracting parties to

> call upon the competent organs of the United Nations to take such action under the Charter of the United Nations as they consider appropriate for the prevention and suppression of acts of genocide or any of the other acts enumerated in article III.

The United States Congress invoked this provision when it called upon the U.N. "to assert leadership by calling the atrocities being committed in Darfur by their rightful name: genocide." H.R. Con. Res. 467, 108th Cong. (2004). Is the definition of genocide determinate enough to enable these preventative mechanisms to work? What action would be appropriate for the prevention or suppression of genocide? Does the Genocide Convention provide a sufficient justification for acts of humanitarian intervention? On the legality of military intervention for humanitarian purposes, *see* Chapter 8 on Aggression.

6. Judicial Notice

Which aspects or elements, if any, of the crime of genocide are susceptible to judicial notice? Recall the practice of the *ad hoc* tribunals is to determine the existence of genocide first and then adjudicate the defendant's role therein. Should one Trial Chamber be able to take judicial notice of the perpetration of genocide in a country or region when another court has already adjudicated this question or where such facts are "common knowledge"? Or, must the prosecution prove the commission of genocide over and over again with respect to each defendant? Is taking judicial notice of the perpetration of genocide prejudicial to a defendant? Consider the relevant provision from the ICTR's Rules of Procedure and Evidence:

Rule 94: Judicial Notice

(A) A Trial Chamber shall not require proof of facts of common knowledge but shall take judicial notice thereof.

(B) At the request of a party or *proprio motu* [on its own motion] a Trial Chamber, after hearing the parties, may decide to take judicial notice of adjudicated facts or documentary evidence from other proceedings of the Tribunal relating to the matter at issue in the current proceedings.

To what use might this provision be put in a genocide prosecution before the ICTR? In *Prosecutor v. Karemera,* the Appeals Chamber of the ICTR ruled that the Trial Chamber did not err in taking judicial notice of the fact that the Tutsi and Hutu people constitute protected groups within the meaning of the genocide prohibition. It also ruled that the Trial Chamber had erred in not taking judicial notice of the existence of widespread or systematic attacks against a civilian population based on their Tutsi ethnic identification, the existence of a non-international armed conflict, and the existence of genocide in Rwanda in the relevant period. *Prosecutor v. Karemera,* Case No. ICTR–98–44–AR73(C), Decision on Prosecutor's Interlocutory Appeal of Decision on Judicial Notice (June 16, 2006). Has this ruling relieved the prosecution of its burden of proof or prejudiced defendants?

7. State Responsibility for Genocide

Although genocide is a crime, the Genocide Convention also envisions state (civil) responsibility for acts of genocide. Article IX of the Genocide Convention provides that disputes "between the Contracting Parties relating to the interpretation, application or fulfillment of the present Convention, including those relating to the responsibility of a State for genocide or any of the other acts enumerated in article III [conspiracy, incitement, attempt, complicity], shall be submitted to the International Court of Justice." Pursuant to Article IX, Bosnia-Herzegovina sued the Federal Republic of Yugoslavia (Serbia and Montenegro) for committing genocide. Bosnia-Herzegovina obtained injunctive relief pursuant to Article 41 of the ICJ Statute, which empowers the Court to issue provisional measures. *Application of the Convention on the Prevention and Punishment of the Crime of Genocide* (*Bosn. & Herz. v. Yugo.*), 1993 I.C.J. Reports 3 (Order of the Court Indicating Provisional Measures of April 16).

In 2007, the Court largely exonerated Serbia and Montenegro. The Court did not find that the applicant had established "the existence of [genocidal] intent on the part of the Respondent, either on the basis of a concerted plan, or * * * a consistent pattern of conduct which could only point to the existence of such intent." *Application of the Convention on the*

Prevention and Punishment of the Crime of Genocide (Bosn. & Herz. v. Serbia & Montenegro), 2007 I.C.J. Reports 1, para. 376 (Feb. 26, 2007). Largely tracking the ICTY's jurisprudence, the Court declined to find acts of genocide beyond Srebrenica. Thus, the respondent State was found liable only for its conventional obligations to "prevent" genocide, and no reparations were awarded. It was later revealed that many documents that might have further implicated Serbia had been kept from the ICTY's public records on grounds of "national security" and thus were not before the ICJ. Should the ICJ have ordered the production of the documents, which it knew existed?

Professor Ruth Wedgwood opined that the case posthumously exonerated Slobodan Milošević. Ruth Wedgwood, Op-Ed., *Slobodan Milošević's Last Waltz*, N.Y. TIMES, March 12, 2007. Yugoslavia, in turn, had earlier sued NATO countries under the same provision arguing that NATO committed genocide against a protected national group. *Legality of the Use of Force (Yugo. v. Belg. et al.)*, 1999 I.C.J. Reports 124 (Request for the Indication of Provisional Measures of June 2). The Respondents similarly argued that they lacked genocidal intent. The Court dismissed the cases because Serbia-Montenegro was not a party to the Court's Statute at the time the case was filed. *Legality of Use of Force (Serb. & Mont. v. Belg. et al.)*, Preliminary Objections, Judgment, 2004 I.C.J. Reports 279 (Dec. 15).

Prior to this conflict, Article IX was invoked for the first time by Pakistan against India in 1973 concerning the threatened prosecution of Pakistani POWs for genocide following the War of Liberation in East Pakistan (now Bangladesh), but that claim was withdrawn. Trial of Pakistani Prisoners of War (*Pak. v. India*), 1973 I.C.J 347 (Order of Dec. 15). What relevance should such proceedings before the International Court of Justice have before the international criminal tribunals and *vice versa*? What might be the impact of contradictory rulings on whether or not genocide occurred in the former Yugoslavia emerging from the ICJ and ICTY?

8. Burden of Proof?

In ruling on the applicable burden of proof in the case against Serbia-Montenegro, the ICJ noted:

> 209. The Court has long recognized that claims against a State involving charges of exceptional gravity must be proved by evidence that is fully conclusive. The Court requires that it be fully convinced that allegations made in the proceedings, that the crime of genocide or the other acts enumerated in Article III have been committed, have been clearly established. The same standard applies to the proof of attribution for such acts.

Is this the equivalent of a criminal law standard? Prof. Wedgwood further opined that the ICJ opinion limited the charges that could be brought against the Bosnian Serb leaders Radovan Karadžić and Ratko Mladić. Do you agree? May only victim states initiate suit before the ICJ or could any state party to the Genocide Convention bring suit against another party? For a discussion of the Yugoslav genocide cases and the problem of Serbia and Montenegro's membership in the Court, *see* Maria Chiara Vitucci, *Has Pandora's Box Been Closed? The Decisions on the Legality of Use of Force*

Cases in Relation to the Status of the Federal Republic of Yugoslavia (Serbia and Montenegro) Within the United Nations, 19 LEIDEN J. INT'L L. 105 (2006).

9. Genocide and Crimes Against Humanity

Compare the ICC's Elements of Crimes for genocide and crimes against humanity. Undertaking an elemental analysis, is genocide an aggravated crime against humanity as is often stated?

10. For Further Reading

The best compendiums on genocide are John Quigley, THE GENOCIDE CONVENTION: AN INTERNATIONAL LAW ANALYSIS (2006) and William A. Schabas, GENOCIDE IN INTERNATIONAL LAW (2000). *See also* Diane Marie Amann, *Group Mentality, Expressivism, and Genocide*, 2 INT'L CRIM. L. REV. 93 (2002); Nina H.B. Jörgensen, *The Definition of Genocide: Joining the Dots in Light of Recent Practice*, 1 INT'L CRIM. L. REV. 285 (2001); Johan D. van der Vyver, *Prosecution and Punishment of the Crime of Genocide,* 23 FORDHAM INT'L L. J. 286 (1999–2000). On the protected groups, *see Developments in the Law—International Criminal Law: IV Defining Protected Groups Under the Genocide Convention*, 114 HARV. L. REV. 2007 (2001). On genocidal intent, *see* David L. Nersessian, *The Contours of Genocidal Intent: Troubling Jurisprudence from the International Criminal Tribunals*, 37 TEX. INT'L L. J. 231 (2002). For a discussion of the ICTY's jurisprudence from two insiders, *see* Michelle Jarvis & Alan Tieger, *Applying the Genocide Convention at the ICTY*, 14 J. INT'L CRIM. JUST. 857 (2016).

PROBLEMS

1. Cambodia

Can an individual be prosecuted for intending to destroy a group of which he is part? Consider this brief account of the Khmer Rouge era in Cambodia. (See the Appendix for a map of Cambodia.) The Khmer Rouge, otherwise known as the Party of Democratic Kampuchea, seized power in Cambodia from the American-backed Lon Nol government on April 17, 1975. The Khmer Rouge encountered a nation destabilized by a still fresh civil war, frequent invasions by neighbors, periodic *coups d'état*, and a full-scale American incursion that had dropped over 250,000 tons of bombs in an effort to disrupt the Ho Chi Minh trail during the Vietnam War. Under the leadership of Pol Pot, the Khmer Rouge immediately dismantled Cambodian society and installed a brutally repressive state. This marked "year zero" in what turned out to be a four-year campaign to create a "New Cambodia"—a radical project of social reorganization drawing upon communist and Maoist thought to construct an idealized vision of a rural proletariat.

The draconian measures instituted by the Khmer Rouge regime in the quest to remake Cambodian society included the liquidation of the Lon Nol army and members of the former regime; the extermination of the elite and educated; a complete evacuation of the urban centers; the incineration of books, libraries, banks, places of worship, and university facilities; the criminalization of the usage of foreign languages; the abolition of money, private property, markets, and salaries; the dissolution of families and the separation of children from their parents; the execution of ethnic minorities;

conviction? In 2009, the Co-Investigating Judges of the ECCC announced charges of genocide in Case 002/02 involving the surviving Khmer Rouge leaders. The charges related to the regime's violence toward the Cham Muslims and ethnic Vietnamese minorities but not toward the Buddhist majority. For a discussion, *see* Ryan Park, *Proving Genocidal Intent: International Precedent and ECCC Case 002*, 63 RUTGERS L. REV. 129 (2010). The defendants were convicted.

2. Genocide Elsewhere

Consider the following historical scenarios and come up with a position of whether these events constitute genocide. If they do not, how would they be characterized under existing international criminal law or the international law in place at the time of the events in question?

- The treatment of Native Americans by European settlers to the United States.
- African slavery as practiced in antebellum United States.
- Stalin's starvation of up to seven million Ukrainians during the imposition of a command economy in the Soviet Union in the 1930s.
- The creation of a "Lost Generation" of aboriginal children in Australia starting in the late nineteenth century by removing them from their homes and placing them in orphanages or with white families.
- The internment of Japanese Americans during World War II.
- The bombing of Nagasaki and Hiroshima to end World War II.
- China's one-child policy.
- Saddam Hussein's gassing of Kurdish regions in 1988 during the Iran-Iraq War.
- The first or second Intifadas launched by Palestinians against Israeli occupation.
- The attacks of September 11th.
- The "targeted killing" of al Qaeda leaders and operatives.
- The use by a state of nuclear weapons against another state.
- Ethnic cleansing by the Islamic State of Iraq and the Levant (ISIL) in Iraq, particularly given that ISIL has offered captured victims the option of conversion to Islam over death.
- The treatment of the Rohingya Muslims in Myanmar/Burma (recall the facts in Chapter 5 on the ICC).

CHAPTER 10

CRIMES AGAINST HUMANITY

I. HISTORY OF THE OFFENSE OF CRIMES AGAINST HUMANITY

Although crimes against humanity are as old as humanity, the concept of a cognizable offense first surfaced during the World War I period. The offense traces its roots to the so-called Martens Clause, which appears in the preamble to the 1907 Hague Convention (IV) Respecting the Laws and Customs of War on Land and in subsequent humanitarian law conventions. As discussed in Chapter 7 on War Crimes, the Martens Clause first articulated the notion that international law encompasses transcendental humanitarian principles that exist beyond conventional (treaty) law. This clause provides that:

> Until a more complete code of the laws of war has been issued, the High Contracting Parties deem it expedient to declare that, in cases not included in the Regulations adopted by them, the inhabitants and the belligerents remain under the protection and the rule of the principles of the laws of nations, as they result from the usages established among civilized peoples, from the laws of humanity, and the dictates of the public conscience.

Convention Respecting the Laws and Customs of War on Land, preamble. Oct. 18, 1907, 36 Stat. 2277, 1 Bevans 631. Some of the Allies invoked these "laws of humanity" after World War I in connection with the proposed trials of war criminals from Germany and its allies. In particular, the deportation and massacre of the Armenian population of the Ottoman Empire prompted the Allied governments of France, Great Britain, and Russia to issue in 1915 a joint Declaration to the Ottoman Empire denouncing these acts as "crimes against humanity and civilization for which all the members of the Turkish Government will be held responsible together with its agents implicated in the massacres."

The Allied governments attending the Preliminary Peace Conference of Paris in January 1919 formed a Commission on the Responsibilities of the Authors of War and on Enforcement of Penalties for Violations of the Law and Customs of War with representatives from the "Great Powers"—the United States, the United Kingdom, France, Italy, and Japan—and the "Lesser Powers"—Belgium, Greece, Poland, Romania, and Serbia—to report on violations of international law committed in World War I and a procedure for trying such offenses. The majority of the Commission called for the establishment of a Tribunal that would try "[a]ll persons belonging to enemy countries, however high their position may have been, without distinction of rank, including Chiefs of States, who have been guilty of offences against the laws and customs of war or the laws of humanity." Commission on the Responsibility of the Authors of the War and on Enforcement of Penalties, *Report Presented to the Preliminary Peace Conference (Mar. 29, 1919), reprinted in* 14 AM. J. INT'L L. 95, 177 (1920).

The U.S. delegation dissented from this recommendation, however, insofar as such a tribunal would exercise jurisdiction over violations of the "laws of humanity." The delegation noted that the duty of the Commission would be to investigate violations or breaches of the laws and customs of war, not violations of the laws or principles of humanity. In its interventions, the U.S. delegation distinguished between moral and legal responsibilities and argued that the former were not justiciable by an international tribunal regardless of how iniquitous the challenged acts were. The U.S. delegate further explained that:

> The laws and customs of war are a standard certain, to be found in books of authority and in the practice of nations. The laws and principles of humanity vary with the individual, which, if for no other reason, should exclude them from consideration in a court of justice, especially one charged with the administration of criminal law.

Id. at 134. The U.S. position ultimately prevailed, and the 1919 Treaty of Versailles excluded reference to "crimes against humanity" in the relevant provisions (Articles 228–29). *See* 1919 Versailles Treaty of Peace Between the Allied and Associated Powers and Germany, June 28, 1919, 225 Consol. T.S. 188.

After this brief but abortive appearance, the juridical history of this offense really begins at Nuremberg. The term "crimes against humanity" first entered positive international law in Article 6(c) of the Nuremberg Charter, which defined crimes against humanity as a constellation of prohibited acts:

> [M]urder, extermination, enslavement, deportation, and other inhumane acts committed against any civilian population, before or during the war, or persecutions on political, racial, or religious grounds in execution of or in connection with any crime within the jurisdiction of the Tribunal, whether or not in violation of the domestic law of the country where perpetrated.

A similar provision appeared in the Tokyo Charter, although crimes against humanity were less central to those proceedings. The category of crimes against humanity was added to the Nuremberg Charter because it was feared that under the traditional formulation of war crimes many of the defining acts of the Nazis would go unpunished. In particular, the crimes against humanity count in the Nuremberg Indictment encompassed acts committed by Nazi perpetrators against German victims, who were thus of the same nationality as their oppressors, or against citizens of a state allied with Germany. At the time the Nuremberg Tribunal was viewed as "the Trial to End All Wars," and, thus, the crime of aggression—deemed "the greatest menace of our times"—was the centerpiece of the Charter and the trial. The notion of crimes against humanity, however, has so far proven to be the real substantive law legacy of Nuremberg, albeit with chronic definitional confusion.

Consider the excerpt from the Nuremberg Judgment below in connection with the more modern jurisprudence that follows. Count 1 of the Nuremberg Indictment covered the common plan or conspiracy allegations, and Count 2 addressed alleged crimes against the peace. The war crimes allegations appeared in Count 3, and the crimes against humanity allegations appeared in Count 4.

International Military Tribunal (Nuremberg), Judgment and Sentences, October 1, 1946, Reprinted in 41 AM. J. INT'L L. 172 (Jan. 1947)

The individual defendants are indicted under Article 6 of the Charter. * * * These provisions are binding upon the Tribunal as the law to be applied to the case. * * *

The Law Relating to War Crimes and Crimes Against Humanity
* * *

The Tribunal is of course bound by the Charter, in the definition which it gives both of War Crimes and Crimes against Humanity. * * * With regard to Crimes against Humanity there is no doubt whatever that political opponents were murdered in Germany before the war, and that many of them were kept in concentration camps in circumstances of great horror and cruelty. The policy of terror was certainly carried out on a vast scale, and in many cases was organized and systematic. The policy of persecution, repression, and murder of civilians in Germany before the war of 1939, who were likely to be hostile to the Government, was most ruthlessly carried out. The persecution of Jews during the same period is established beyond all doubt. To constitute Crimes against Humanity, the acts relied on before the outbreak of war must have been in execution of, or in connection with, any crime within the jurisdiction of the Tribunal. The Tribunal is of the opinion that revolting and horrible as many of these crimes were, it has not been satisfactorily proved that they were done in execution of, or in connection with, any such crime. The Tribunal therefore cannot make a general declaration that the acts before 1939 were Crimes against Humanity within the meaning of the Charter, but from the beginning of the war in 1939 War Crimes were committed on a vast scale, which were also Crimes against Humanity; and insofar as the inhumane acts charged in the Indictment, and committed after the beginning of the war, did not constitute War Crimes, they were all committed in execution of, or in connection with, the aggressive war, and therefore constituted Crimes against Humanity. * * * [Later in the judgment, the tribunal considered the guilt of particular defendants for crimes against humanity.]

Wilhelm Keitel

Keitel is indicted on all four Counts. He was Chief of Staff to the then Minister of War Von Bomberg from 1935 to 4 February 1938; on that day Hitler took command of the Armed Forces, making Keitel Chief of the High Command of the Armed Forces [*Oberkommando der Wehrmacht* or OKW]. * * * OKW was in effect Hitler's military staff. * * *

On 4 August 1942 Keitel issued a directive that paratroopers were to be turned over to the SD [*Sicherheitsdienst*, the intelligence service]. On 18 October Hitler issued the Commando Order [an order stating that all commandos captured in Europe and Africa should be executed, even if they attempted to surrender] which was carried out in several instances. After the landing in Normandy, Keitel reaffirmed the order, and later extended it to Allied missions fighting with partisans. He admits he did not believe the order was legal but claims he could not stop Hitler from decreeing it. * * *

Lahousen testified that Keitel told him on 12 September 1939, while aboard Hitler's headquarters train, that the Polish intelligentsia, nobility, and Jews were to be liquidated. On 20 October, Hitler told Keitel the Intelligentsia would be prevented from forming a ruling class, the standard of living would remain low, and Poland would be used only for labor forces. Keitel does not remember the Lahousen conversation, but admits there was such a policy and that he had protested without effect to Hitler about it.

On 16 September 1941 Keitel ordered that attacks on soldiers in the East should be met by putting to death 50 to 100 Communists for one German soldier, with the comment that human life was less than nothing in the East. On 1 October he ordered military commanders always to have hostages to execute when soldiers were attacked. When Terboven, the Reich Commissioner in Norway, wrote Hitler that Keitel's suggestion that workmen's relatives be held responsible for sabotage, could work only if firing squads were authorized, Keitel wrote on this memorandum "Yes, that is the best."

On 12 May 1941, five weeks before the invasion of the Soviet Union, OKW urged upon Hitler a directive of OKH [Army High Command] that political commissars [i.e., captured political officers appointed by the Communist Party] be liquidated by the Army, Keitel admitted the directive was passed on to field commanders. And on 13 May Keitel signed an order that civilians suspected of offenses against troops should be shot without trial, and that prosecution of German officers for offenses against civilians was unnecessary. On 27 July all copies of this directive were ordered destroyed without affecting its validity. Four days previously he had signed another order that legal punishment was inadequate and troops should use terrorism.

On 7 December 1941, the so-called "Nacht und Nebel" ["night and fog"] Decree, over Keitel's signature, provided that in occupied territories civilians who had been accused of crimes of resistance against the army of occupation would be tried only if a death sentence was likely; otherwise they would be handed to the Gestapo for transportation to Germany. Keitel directed that Russian POW's be used in German war industry. On 8 September 1942 he ordered French, Dutch, and Belgian citizens to work on the construction of the Atlantic Wall. He was present on 4 January 1944 when Hitler directed Sauckel to obtain 4 million new workers from occupied territories.

In the face of these documents Keitel does not deny his connection with these acts. Rather, his defense relies on the fact that he is a soldier, and on the doctrine of "superior orders," prohibited by Article 8 of the Charter as a defense. There is nothing in mitigation. Superior orders, even to a soldier, cannot be considered in mitigation where crimes as shocking and extensive have been committed consciously, ruthlessly, and without military excuse or justification. The Tribunal finds Keitel guilty on all four Counts. * * *

Hans Frank

Frank is indicted under Counts One, Three, and Four. Frank joined the Nazi Party in 1927. * * * Frank was appointed Chief Civil Administration Officer for occupied Polish territory and, on 12 October 1939, was made Governor General of the occupied Polish territory. On 3 October 1939 he described the policy which he intended to put into effect by stating: "Poland shall be treated like a colony; the Poles will become the slaves of the Greater German World Empire." The evidence establishes that this occupation policy was based on the complete destruction of Poland as a national entity, and a ruthless exploitation of its human and economic resources for the German war effort. All opposition was crushed with the utmost harshness. A reign of terror was instituted, backed by summary police courts which ordered such actions as the public shootings of groups of 20 to 200 Poles, and the widespread shootings of hostages. The concentration camp system was introduced in the General Government by the establishment of the notorious Treblinka and Maidaneck camps. As early as 6 February 1940, Frank gave an indication of the extent of this reign of terror by his cynical comment to a newspaper reporter on Von Neurath's poster announcing the execution of the Czech students: "If I wished to order that one should hang up posters about every seven Poles shot, there would not be enough forests in Poland with which to make the paper for these posters." On 30 May 1940 Frank told a police conference that he was taking advantage of the offensive in the West which diverted the attention of the world from Poland to liquidate thousands of Poles who would be likely to resist German domination of Poland, including "the leading representatives of the Polish intelligentsia." Pursuant to these instructions the brutal A.B. action [a German acronym for "Extraordinary Peace-Bringing Action"] was begun under which the Security Police and SD carried out these exterminations which were only partially subjected to the restraints of legal procedure. On 2 October 1943 Frank issued a decree under which any non-German hindering German construction in the General Government were to be tried by summary courts of the Security Police and SD and sentenced to death.

The economic demands made on the General Government were far in excess of the needs of the army of occupation, and were out of all proportion to the resources of the country. The food raised in Poland was shipped to Germany on such a wide scale that the rations of the population of the occupied territories were reduced to the starvation level, and epidemics were widespread. Some steps were taken to provide for the feeding of the agricultural workers who were used to raise the crops, but the requirements of the rest of the population were disregarded. It is undoubtedly true, as argued by counsel for the Defense, that some suffering in the General Government was inevitable as a result of the ravages of war and the economic confusion resulting therefrom. But the suffering was increased by a planned policy of economic exploitation.

Frank introduced the deportation of slave laborers to Germany in the very early stages of his administration. On 25 January 1940 he indicated his intention of deporting 1 million laborers to Germany, suggesting on 10 May 1940 the use of police raids to meet this quota. On 18 August 1942 Frank reported that he had already supplied 800,000 workers for the Reich, and expected to be able to supply 140,000 more before the end of the year.

The persecution of the Jews was immediately begun in the General Government. The area originally contained from 2 1/2 million to 3 1/2 million Jews. They were forced into ghettos, subjected to discriminatory laws, deprived of the food necessary to avoid starvation, and finally systematically and brutally exterminated. On 16 December 1941 Frank told the Cabinet of the Governor General: "We must annihilate the Jews, wherever we find them and wherever it is possible, in order to maintain there the structure of the Reich as a whole." By 25 January 1944, Frank estimated that there were only 100,000 Jews left.

At the beginning of his testimony, Frank stated that he had a feeling of "terrible guilt" for the atrocities committed in the occupied territories. But his defense was largely devoted to an attempt to prove that he was not in fact responsible; that he ordered only the necessary pacification measures; that the excesses were due to the activities of the police which were not under his control; and that he never even knew of the activities of the concentration camps. It had also been argued that the starvation was due to the aftermath of the war and policies carried out under the Four Year Plan; that the forced labor program was under the direction of Sauckel; and that the extermination of the Jews was by the police and

SS [the Nazi *Schutzstaffel*, an elite paramilitary organization within the Nazi party] under direct orders from Himmler.

It is undoubtedly true that most of the criminal program charged against Frank was put into effect through the police, that Frank had jurisdictional difficulties with Himmler over the control of the police, and that Hitler resolved many of these disputes in favor of Himmler. It therefore may well be true that some of the crimes committed in the General Government were committed without the knowledge of Frank, and even occasionally despite his opposition. It may also be true that some of the criminal policies put into effect in the General Government did not originate with Frank but were carried out pursuant to orders from Germany. But it is also true that Frank was a willing and knowing participant in the use of terrorism in Poland; in the economic exploitation of Poland in a way which led to the death by starvation of a large number of people; in the deportation to Germany as slave laborers of over a million Poles; and in a program involving the murder of at least 3 million Jews. The Tribunal finds that Frank is not guilty on Count One but guilty under Counts Three and Four. * * *

Baldur von Schirach

Von Schirach is indicted under Counts One and Four. He joined the Nazi Party and the SA in 1925. In 1929 he became the leader of the National Socialist Students Union. In 1931 he was made Reichs Youth Leader of the Nazi Party with control over all Nazi youth organization including the Hitler Jugend. In 1933, after the Nazis had obtained control of the Government, Von Schirach resigned as head of the Hitler Jugend and Leader of Youth in the German Reich, but retained his position as *Reichsleiter* with control over the Youth education. * * *

In July 1940 Von Schirach was appointed Gauleiter of Vienna. At the same time he was appointed Reichs Governor for Vienna and Reichs Defense Commissioner. * * * As Reichs Defense Commissioner, he had control of the civilian war economy. As Reichs Governor he was head of the municipal administration of the City of Vienna, and under the supervision of the Minister of the Interior, in charge of the governmental administration of the Reich in Vienna.

Von Schirach is not charged with the commission of War Crimes in Vienna, only with the commission of Crimes against Humanity. As has already been seen, Austria was occupied pursuant to a common plan of aggression. Its occupation is, therefore, a "crime within the jurisdiction of the Tribunal," as that term is used in Article 6(c) of the Charter. As a result, "murder, extermination, enslavement, deportation, and other inhumane acts" and "persecutions on political, racial, or religious grounds" in connection with this occupation constitute a Crime against Humanity under that Article. * * *

When Von Schirach became Gauleiter of Vienna the deportation of the Jews had already been begun, and only 60,000 out of Vienna's original 190,000 Jews remained. On 2 October 1940 he attended a conference at Hitler's office and told Frank that he had 50,000 Jews in Vienna which the General Government would have to take over from him. On 3 December 1940 Von Schirach received a letter from Lammers stating that after the receipt of the reports made by Von Schirach, Hitler had decided to deport the 60,000 Jews still remaining in Vienna to the General Government because of the housing shortage in Vienna. The deportation of the Jews from Vienna was then begun and continued until the early fall of 1942. On 15 September 1942 Von Schirach made a speech in which he defended his action in having driven "tens of thousands upon tens of thousands of Jews into the ghetto of the East" as "contributing to European culture."

While the Jews were being deported from Vienna, reports, addressed to him in his official capacity, were received in Von Schirach's office from the office of the Chief of the Security Police and SD which contained description of the activities of *Einsatzgruppen* [death squads] in exterminating Jews. Many of these reports were initialed by one of Von Schirach's principal deputies. On 30 June 1944 Von Schirach's office also received a letter from Kaltenbrunner informing him that a shipment of 12,000 Jews was on its way to Vienna for essential war work and that all those who were incapable of work would have to be kept in readiness for "special action."

The Tribunal finds that Von Schirach, while he did not originate the policy of deporting Jews from Vienna, participated in this deportation after he had become Gauleiter of Vienna. He knew that the best the Jews could hope for was a miserable existence in the ghettos of the East. Bulletins describing the Jewish extermination were in his office. * * * The Tribunal finds that Von Schirach is not guilty on Count One. He is guilty under Count Four.

NOTES & QUESTIONS

1. IMT Outcome

Of the twenty-two indicted Nazi leaders, nineteen were convicted, sixteen of crimes against humanity under Count 4 of the indictment. The Tribunal convicted two defendants of a single count of crimes against humanity (Julius Streicher and Baldur von Schirach). Neither had been charged with war crimes under Count 3. Although the Nuremberg judges may have limited and even downplayed the crimes against humanity charge, all those sentenced to hang were found guilty of crimes against humanity. In contrast, the defendants found guilty of waging aggressive war were accorded life sentences even though the Tribunal had indicated that "to initiate a war of aggression is the supreme international crime, differing only from other war crimes in that it contains within itself the accumulated evil of the whole." Thus, the judges "revealed their true sentiment by meting out their most severe punishment, the death penalty, only to those who had been found guilty of those quite uncommon atrocities that actually constituted a 'crime against humanity.' " Hannah Arendt, EICHMANN IN JERUSALEM 257 (1963).

2. The Role of the Crimes Against Humanity Count at Nuremburg

Why did the architects of the Nuremberg Charter need the crimes against humanity charge? Why not rely on the well-established prohibition against war crimes to address the atrocities committed by Nazi Germany? Consider the cases of defendants Keitel and Frank—what did the crimes against humanity charge add to the judgments against them? Which of the crimes proven by the prosecution constituted crimes against humanity versus war crimes? Why was defendant Von Schirach not charged with war crimes?

3. A New Crime

Why would the drafters of the Charter limit the prosecution of crimes against humanity to such acts committed "in execution of or in connection with any crime within the jurisdiction of the Tribunal"? What effect was given to the phrase "before or during the war" in the Charter's definition? It is generally understood that this so-called "war nexus" was added to counter the claim that the Allies were legislating retroactively. How would you argue that the addition of such language addressed that concern? Does the enormity of the crimes of the Nazis justify overlooking such legal technicalities in keeping with the maxim *in delictis atrocissimus jura transgredi liceat* ("with atrocious crimes, legal rules can be relaxed")? How did the crimes against humanity committed by German officials relate to Germany's plans to commit aggressive war in Europe? Did the acts that constituted the Holocaust advance the Nazi war effort or might they have distracted the Nazis from the war? Consider the judgment against Von Schirach—how was the war nexus satisfied in his case? With the war nexus as an element of the offense, how could Von Schirach be guilty under Count 4 but acquitted under Count 1?

4. Crimes Against Humanity at Tokyo

The Charter of the Tokyo Tribunal was nearly identical to that of the Nuremberg Tribunal. Article 5(c) of the Tokyo Charter defined crimes against humanity as:

> [M]urder, extermination, enslavement, deportation, and other inhumane acts committed against any civilian population, before or during the war, or persecutions on political or racial grounds in execution of or in connection with any crime within the jurisdiction of the Tribunal, whether or not in violation of the domestic law of the country where perpetrated.

Charter of the International Military Tribunal for the Far East art. 5(c), Jan. 19, 1946. T.I.A.S. No. 1589.

While the wording of the article is substantially similar to that of the Nuremberg Tribunal, the Prosecution pursued the crimes against humanity charges less vigorously in Tokyo. In this respect, Professor Paik Choong-Hyun has commented, "while the Nuremberg trial placed great emphasis on crimes against humanity, the Tokyo trial apparently failed to recognize the importance of these crimes." THE TOKYO WAR CRIMES TRIAL 53 (C. Hosoya et al. eds., 1986). Professor Paik identifies a number of untried crimes committed by or with the acquiescence of the Japanese government against minority populations in Japan, Korea, Manchuria, China, the Philippines, and other Asian regions. His view is echoed in the same volume by other Asian scholars. Professor Onuma Yasuaki explains this difference as one of relativity. He argues that the Nazis' slaughter of Jews was more appalling than any atrocities committed by the Japanese:

> [T]he scale and degree of these acts were a little different from the crimes against humanity committed by the Nazis. To lump the Japanese war crimes together with Nazi war crimes would be ludicrous.

Id. at 187. Do you agree? What about the literal and figurative "Rape of Nanking," which witnessed the murder of over 300,000 Chinese citizens and the rape of thousands more in several weeks? What other crimes committed in the Pacific theater deserved to be prosecuted internationally as crimes against humanity? What about the use of opium addiction during the Japanese occupation? The activities of the covert biological and chemical unit of the Japanese military, Unit 731?

II. THE CONTEMPORARY DEFINITION OF CRIMES AGAINST HUMANITY

After its debut in the Nuremberg and Tokyo Charters, the offense of crimes against humanity did not become the subject of a comprehensive treaty, although the International Law Commission included crimes against humanity in their Draft Code of Offenses Against the Peace and Security of Mankind (which served as a precursor to the ICC Statute). This is notwithstanding that the international community drafted various multilateral conventions in the post-war period criminalizing other international crimes such as genocide, torture, apartheid, and various forms of terrorism. In addition, the International Committee of the Red Cross sponsored the drafting and ratification of the four Geneva Conventions of 1949 and two Optional Protocols in 1977 elaborating on the prohibition against war crimes in international humanitarian law. Why would the international community not be more motivated to codify and universalize the prohibition against crimes against humanity? (As noted below, a number of international lawyers and scholars have recently initiated a campaign to draft a treaty dedicated to crimes against humanity.) Finally, in the mid-1990s, the Security Council included crimes against humanity within the subject matter jurisdiction of the two *ad hoc* criminal tribunals, although it defined the crime slightly differently in each:

ICTY, Article 5

> The International Tribunal shall have the power to prosecute persons responsible for the following crimes when committed in

armed conflict, whether international or internal in character, and directed against any civilian population:

(a) Murder;

(b) Extermination;

(c) Enslavement;

(d) Deportation;

(e) Imprisonment;

(f) Torture;

(g) Rape;

(h) Persecutions on political, racial and religious grounds;

(i) Other inhumane acts.

ICTR, Article 3

The International Tribunal for Rwanda shall have the power to prosecute persons responsible for the following crimes when committed as part of a widespread or systematic attack against any civilian population on national, political, ethnic, racial or religious grounds: [virtually same list of enumerated crimes as the ICTY].

It was not until the promulgation of the ICC statute that a consensus negotiated definition of the offense emerged:

ICC, Article 7

1. For the purpose of this Statute, "crimes against humanity" means any of the following acts when committed as part of a widespread or systematic attack directed against any civilian population, with knowledge of the attack:

(a) Murder;

(b) Extermination;

(c) Enslavement;

(d) Deportation or forcible transfer of population;

(e) Imprisonment or other severe deprivation of physical liberty in violation of fundamental rules of international law;

(f) Torture;

(g) Rape, sexual slavery, enforced prostitution, forced pregnancy, enforced sterilization, or any other form of sexual violence of comparable gravity;

(h) Persecution against any identifiable group or collectivity on political, racial, national, ethnic, cultural, religious, gender . . . , or other grounds that are universally recognised as impermissible under international law, in connection with any act referred to in this paragraph or any crime within the jurisdiction of the Court;

(i) Enforced disappearance of persons;

(j) The crime of apartheid;

(k) Other inhumane acts of a similar character intentionally causing great suffering, or serious injury to body or to mental or physical health.

2. For the purpose of paragraph 1:

(a) "Attack against any civilian population" means a course of conduct involving the multiple commission of acts referred to in paragraph 1 against any civilian population, pursuant to or in furtherance of a state or organizational policy to commit such attack;

(b) "Extermination" includes the intentional infliction of conditions of life, *inter alia* the deprivation of access to food and medicine, calculated to bring about the destruction of part of a population; * * *

(g) "Persecution" means the intentional and severe deprivation of fundamental rights contrary to international law by reason of the identity of the group or collectivity * * *

Academics, former United Nations officials, and international lawyers are in the process of drafting a convention dedicated to the prohibition of crimes against humanity. The current draft incorporates the ICC definition of the crime, provides for state responsibility and universal jurisdiction, allows for the prosecution of incitement to commit crimes against humanity, and establishes a treaty monitoring mechanism. The U.N. International Law Commission—dedicated to the codification and progressive development of international law—added the treaty project to its active agenda and appointed Sean Murphy (United States) as Special Rapporteur. As you complete this chapter, consider whether the ICC definition reflects customary international law and whether a comprehensive treaty devoted to crimes against humanity is warranted.

NOTES & QUESTIONS

1. The Elements of Crimes Against Humanity

In reviewing the definitions above, consider the following questions: What are the elements of crimes against humanity in each of these definitions? How does the burden on the prosecutor change under each definition? Why would the Security Council define the crimes differently in the ICTY and ICTR Statutes, which were drafted so close in time to each other? Why would the drafters of the ICC Statute make the amendments they did? How has the formulation of *actus reus*, *mens rea* and circumstantial elements been defined and clarified in the ICC Statute? What remains of the war nexus in the three definitions? If a jury were adjudicating a crimes against humanity case, how would you draft jury instructions for the offense? For more on the drafting history of the crimes against humanity provision in the ICC Statute, *see* Darryl Robinson, *Defining "Crimes Against Humanity" at the Rome Conference*, 93 AM. J. INT'L L. 43 (1999). American courts have looked to Article 7 of the ICC Statute for the definition of crimes against humanity. *See Doe v. Qi*, 349 F. Supp. 2d 1258, 1308 (N.D.Cal. 2004).

2. Crimes Against Humanity Within the ICTY

Many of the defendants before the ICTY were charged with crimes against humanity in connection with efforts of the warring parties to ethnically cleanse particular regions. The events that are the subject of the judgment below concern the Muslim-Croat conflict of 1992–1993 that took place in central Bosnia during the war triggered by the dissolution of the former Yugoslavia. Croat and Muslim citizens ("Bosniacs") of Bosnia-Herzegovina initially fought side-by-side in 1992 to resist Serb and Yugoslav attacks in eastern and western Bosnia-Herzegovina.

> As the conflict with the Serbs wore on, however, 'ethnic cleansing' by Serb forces in Bosnia and Herzegovina drove Croat and Bosniac refugees into the interior of Bosnia, creating overcrowding and tension between the two nationalities and leading to a conflict between these former allies. The Muslim-Croat conflict ended only with the signing of the Washington Agreement on 2 March 1994, which created the Muslim-Croat Federation, an entity which exists to this day in the form of the Federation of Bosnia and Herzegovina, one of the two entities of Bosnia and Herzegovina under the Dayton Peace Agreement.

Prosecutor v. Kupreškić, et al., Case No. IT–95–16–T, Judgement, para. 38 (Jan. 14, 2000). During this conflict, the village of Ahmići-Šantići was attacked on April 16, 1993, as part of a campaign of "ethnic cleansing" undertaken by Croat forces to create an ethnically homogenous canton in central Bosnia that could be annexed to Croatia. (See the Appendix for a map of Yugoslavia.) The village was destroyed and over 100 Muslim individuals were killed; others were wounded and displaced. The attack apparently started with bombardment from a distance; soldiers then went house to house purging inhabitants and seizing their belongings. The defendants adjudged below were six members of the Croatian military (the HVO) who were allegedly affiliated with the "Jokers," a "special ops" paramilitary unit of the Croatian Military Police. The Prosecution alleged that the accused, including Vladimir Santić who commanded the First Company of the 4th Battalion of the military police, helped prepare, organize, and implement the attack on Ahmići. Defendants were charged with crimes against humanity (murder, persecution, and other inhumane acts) and war crimes (murder and cruel treatment). Several of the defendants gave themselves up voluntarily on October 6, 1997, and were transferred to the ICTY on the same day. Defendant Vlatko Kupreškić was supposed to surrender as well, but apparently changed his mind at the last minute. SFOR—the NATO-led

Stabilization Force in Bosnia—eventually arrested him on December 18, 1997. Kupreškić was wounded resisting arrest.

Prosecutor v. Zoran Kupreškić et al., Case No. IT–95–16–T, Judgement (Jan. 14, 2000)

In the Trial Chamber

Objective and Subjective Elements of the Crimes Under Article 5

543. Article 5 of the Statute of the International Tribunal deals with crimes against humanity. The essence of these crimes is a systematic policy of a certain scale and gravity directed against a civilian population. In the *Nikolić* Rule 61 decision, the Trial Chamber set forth in broad terms three distinct components of crimes against humanity under the ICTY Statute:[798]

> First, the crimes must be directed at a civilian population, specifically identified as a group by the perpetrators of those acts. Secondly, the crimes must, to a certain extent, be organised and systematic. Although they need not be related to a policy established at State level, in the conventional sense of the term, they cannot be the work of isolated individuals alone. Lastly, the crimes, considered as a whole, must be of a certain scale and gravity.

544. The following elements can be identified as comprising the core elements of crimes against humanity: first, the existence of an armed conflict; second, that the acts were part of a widespread or systematic occurrence of crimes directed against a civilian population (the requirement that the occurrence of crimes be widespread or systematic being a disjunctive one) and finally, that the perpetrator had knowledge of the wider context in which his act occurs.

The Requirement of an Armed Conflict

545. By requiring that crimes against humanity be committed in either internal or international armed conflict, the Security Council, in establishing the International Tribunal, may have defined the crime in Article 5 more narrowly than is necessary under customary international law.[801] It is nevertheless sufficient for the purposes of Article 5 that the act occurred in the course or duration of any armed conflict. The type and nature of such conflict—whether international or internal—is therefore immaterial. An armed conflict can be said to exist whenever there is a resort to armed force between States or protracted armed violence

---

798 *Prosecutor v. Nikolić*, Rule 61 Decision, Trial Chamber, 20 Oct. 1995, at para. 26.

801 See *Prosecutor v. Tadić*, (IT–94–1–AR72), Decision on Defence Motion for Interlocutory Appeal on Jurisdiction, Appeals Chamber, 2 Oct. 1995 at para. 141: "It is by now a settled rule of customary international law that crimes against humanity do not require a connection to international armed conflict. Indeed . . . customary international law may not require a connection between crimes against humanity and any conflict at all."

between governmental authorities and organized armed groups or between such groups within a State.

546. The nature of the nexus required under Article 5 of the Statute is merely that the act be linked geographically as well as temporally with the armed conflict.

Directed Against a Civilian Population

547. It would seem that a wide definition of "civilian" and "population" is intended. This is warranted first of all by the object and purpose of the general principles and rules of humanitarian law, in particular by the rules prohibiting crimes against humanity. The latter are intended to safeguard basic human values by banning atrocities directed against human dignity. One fails to see why only civilians and not also combatants should be protected by these rules (in particular by the rule prohibiting persecution), given that these rules may be held to possess a broader humanitarian scope and purpose than those prohibiting war crimes. However, faced with the explicit limitation laid down in Article 5, the Trial Chamber holds that a broad interpretation should nevertheless be placed on the word "civilians," the more so because the limitation in Article 5 constitutes a departure from customary international law.

548. The above proposition is borne out by the case law. Of particular relevance to the present case is the finding in *Barbie* (admittedly based on general international law) that "inhumane acts and persecution committed in a systematic manner," in the name of a State practising a policy of ideological supremacy, not only against persons by reason of their membership of a racial or religious community but also against the opponents of that policy, whatever the form of their opposition, could be considered a crime against humanity.[806] In the *Vukovar* Rule 61 Decision of 3 April 1996, a Trial Chamber held that crimes against humanity may be committed even where the victims at one time bore arms.[807] * * *

The Policy Element

551. With regard to the "form of governmental, organisational or group policy" which is to direct the acts in question, the Trial Chamber has noted that although the concept of crimes against humanity

---

[806] The *Barbie* case, French *Court of Cassation* (Criminal Chamber), 20 Dec. 1985, 78 ILR 125, 137.

[807] On this point, the Trial Chamber held that "[a]lthough according to the terms of Article 5 of the Statute of this Tribunal [. . .] combatants in the traditional sense of the term cannot be victims of a crime against humanity, this does not apply to individuals who, at one particular point in time, carried out acts of resistance." As the Commission of Experts, established pursuant to Security Council Resolution 780 noted, "it seems obvious that Article 5 applies first and foremost to civilians, meaning people who are not combatants. This, however, should not lead to any quick conclusions concerning people who at one particular point in time did bear arms.... Information of the overall circumstances is relevant for the interpretation of the provision in a spirit consistent with its purpose." *Report of the Commission of Experts established pursuant to Security Council Resolution 780*, Doc. S/1994/674, para. 78.

necessarily implies a policy element, there is some doubt as to whether it is strictly a *requirement,* as such, for crimes against humanity. In any case, it appears that such a policy need not be explicitly formulated, nor need it be the policy of a State.[811]

552. The need for crimes against humanity to have been at least tolerated by a State, Government or entity is also stressed in national and international case-law. The crimes at issue may also be State-sponsored or at any rate may be part of a governmental policy or of an entity holding *de facto* authority over a territory.

553. National case-law tends, in particular, to emphasise that crimes against humanity are usually the manifestation of a criminal governmental policy. As observed by the Canadian Supreme Court in the case of *Finta:*[813]

> The central concern in the case of crimes against humanity is with such things as state-sponsored or sanctioned persecution, not the private individual who has a particular hatred against a particular group or the public generally.

554. The aforementioned judgements and others on the same matter implicitly illustrate the nature and implications of the link between an offence and a large-scale or systematic practice of abuses necessary in order for the offence to be characterised as a crime against humanity. In particular, they enable us to answer the question of whether the offence must be perpetrated by organs or agents of a State or a governmental authority or on behalf of such bodies, or whether it may be committed by individuals not acting in an official capacity, and in the latter case, whether the offence must be approved of or at least condoned or countenanced by a governmental body for it to amount to a crime against humanity.

555. While crimes against humanity are normally perpetrated by State organs, i.e. individuals acting in an official capacity such as military commanders, servicemen, etc., there may be cases where the authors of such crimes are individuals having neither official status nor acting on behalf of a governmental authority. The available case-law seems to indicate that in these cases some sort of explicit or implicit approval or endorsement by State or governmental authorities is required, or else that it is necessary for the offence to be clearly

---

[811] *Prosecutor v. Tadić*, Trial Chamber Judgement, 7 May 1997, at para. 653, where the Trial Chamber noted that "[t]he reason that crimes against humanity so shock the conscience of mankind and warrant intervention by the international community is because they are not isolated, random acts of individuals but rather result from a deliberate attempt to target a civilian population." It went on to explain that although traditionally this requirement was understood to mean that there must be some form of State policy to commit these acts occurred during this period, this was no longer the case (*ibid.*, at para. 654). *See also Prosecutor v. Nikolić*, Rule 61 decision, at para. 26: "Although [the crimes in question] need not be related to a policy established at State level, in the conventional sense of the term, they cannot be the work of isolated individuals alone."

[813] *R v. Finta* [1994] 1 S.C.R. 701 at 733.

encouraged by a general governmental policy or to clearly fit within such a policy. In addition to many decisions concerning crimes against humanity perpetrated by individuals acting in a private capacity, the *Weller* case may prove to be of some relevance to this issue. This case gave rise to six different judgements by German courts after World War II and involved the ill-treatment of Jewish civilians by two persons under the command of Weller, a member of the SS, who was at the time not in uniform and was acting on his own initiative. After the injured parties reported to the Jewish community, which in turn complained to the local Gestapo [the German Secret Police], the head of the Gestapo informed the wronged Jews that Weller's actions were an isolated event which would in no way be approved. Thereafter Weller was summoned by the Gestapo and strongly taken to task by the district leader of the Nazi party. On appeal to the Supreme Court for the British zone, it was held that the offence did indeed constitute a crime against humanity, on the grounds that it was sufficient for the attack on human dignity to be connected to the national-socialist system of power and hegemony.[816]

Knowledge of the Context Within Which the Perpetrator's Actions Are Taken: the *Mens Rea* Requirement

556. The determination of the elements comprising the *mens rea* of crimes against humanity has proved particularly difficult and controversial. Nevertheless, the requisite *mens rea* for crimes against humanity appears to be comprised by (1) the *intent* to commit the underlying offence, combined with (2) *knowledge* of the broader context in which that offence occurs.

557. With regard to the latter requirement (knowledge), the ICTR in *Prosecutor v. Kayishema* noted as follows:[818]

> [t]he perpetrator must knowingly commit crimes against humanity in the sense that he must understand the overall context of his act. Part of what transforms an individual's act(s) into a crime against humanity is the inclusion of the act within a greater dimension of criminal conduct; therefore an accused

---

[816] In this regard the Supreme Court noted that "[a]ctions which seemingly or actually originated from quite personal decisions were also often and readily put by the national-socialist leadership at the service of its criminal goals and plans. This held true even for actions which outwardly were even disapproved of. [. . .] The link, in this sense, with the national-socialist system of power and tyranny does in the case at issue manifestly exist [as] the actions of the accused fitted into the numerous persecutory measures which were then imposed against the Jews in Germany or could at any time be imposed against them. [. . .] [Th]e link with the national-socialist system of power and tyranny does not exist only in the case of those actions which are ordered and approved by the holders of hegemony; that link exists also when those actions can only be explained by the atmosphere and conditions created by the authorities in power. The trial court was [thus] wrong when it attached decisive value to the fact that the accused after his action was "rebuked" and that even the Gestapo disapproved of the excess as an isolated infringement. That this action nevertheless fitted into the persecution of Jews effected by the State and the party, is shown by the fact that the accused . . . was not held criminally responsible . . . in proportion to the gravity of his guilt. . . ." (See *Entscheidungen* des Obersten Gerichtshofes für die Britische Zone in Strafsachen, Vol. I, pp. pp. 206–207). * * *

[818] *Prosecutor v. Kayishema and Ruzindana*, Case No. ICTR–95–1–T, Judgement, paras. 133–4 (21 May 1999).

should be aware of this greater dimension in order to be culpable thereof. Accordingly, actual or constructive knowledge of the broader context of the attack, meaning that the accused must know that his act(s) is part of a widespread or systematic attack on a civilian population and pursuant to some sort of policy or plan, is necessary to satisfy the requisite *mens rea* element of the accused. * * *

The Constituent Offences

559. The instant case involves counts of murder under Article 5(a) (counts 2, 4, 6, 8, 12 and 16), persecutions under Article 5(h) (count 1) and inhumane acts under Article 5(i) (counts 10, 14 and 18). * * *

Article 5(i): Other Inhumane Acts

562. The expression "other inhumane acts" was drawn from Article 6(c) of the London Agreement [establishing the Nuremburg Tribunal] and Article II(1)(c) of Control Council Law No. 10.

563. There is a concern that this category lacks precision and is too general to provide a safe yardstick for the work of the Tribunal and hence, that it is contrary to the principle of the "specificity" of criminal law. It is thus imperative to establish what is included within this category. The phrase "other inhumane acts" was deliberately designed as a residual category, as it was felt to be undesirable for this category to be exhaustively enumerated. An exhaustive categorization would merely create opportunities for evasion of the letter of the prohibition. The importance of maintaining such a category was elucidated by the International Committee of the Red Cross (ICRC) when commenting on what would constitute a violation of the obligation to provide "humane treatment" contained in common Article 3 of the Geneva Conventions:[825]

> [I]t is always dangerous to try to go into too much detail—especially in this domain. However great the care taken in drawing up a list of all the various forms of infliction, it would never be possible to catch up with the imagination of future torturers who wished to satisfy their bestial instincts; and the more specific and complete a list tries to be, the more restrictive it becomes. The form of wording adopted is flexible and, at the same time, precise.

564. In interpreting the expression at issue, resort to the *ejusdem generis* [of the same kind or class] rule of interpretation does not prove to be of great assistance. Under this rule, that expression would cover *actions similar* to those specifically provided for. Admittedly such a rule of interpretation has been relied upon by various courts with regard to Article 6(c) of the London Agreement [defining crimes against humanity]. Thus, for instance, in the *Tarnek* case, the District Court of Tel-Aviv held in a decision of 14 December 1951 that the definition of "other inhumane

---

[825] *ICRC Commentary on the IVth Geneva Convention Relative to the Protection of Civilian Persons in Time of War* (1958, repr. 1994), p. 39.

acts" laid down in the Israeli Law on Nazi and Nazi Collaborators (Punishment) of 1950, which reproduced the definition of Article 6(c), was to apply only to such other inhumane acts as resembled in their nature and their gravity those specified in the definition.[826] This interpretative rule lacks precision, and is too general to provide a safe yardstick for the work of the Tribunal.

565. The Statute of the International Criminal Court (ICC) (Article 7(k)) provides greater detail than the ICTY Statute as to the meaning of other inhumane acts: "other inhumane acts of a similar character intentionally causing great suffering, or serious injury to the body or to mental or physical health."[827] However, this provision also fails to provide an indication, even indirectly, of the legal standards which would allow us to identify the prohibited inhumane acts.

566. Less broad parameters for the interpretation of "other inhumane acts" can instead be identified in international standards on human rights such as those laid down in the Universal Declaration on Human Rights of 1948 and the two United Nations Covenants on Human Rights of 1966. Drawing upon the various provisions of these texts, it is possible to identify a set of basic rights appertaining to human beings, the infringement of which may amount, depending on the accompanying circumstances, to a crime against humanity. Thus, for example, serious forms of cruel or degrading treatment of persons belonging to a particular ethnic, religious, political or racial group, or serious widespread or systematic manifestations of cruel or humiliating or degrading treatment with a discriminatory or persecutory intent no doubt amount to crimes against humanity: inhuman or degrading treatment is prohibited by the United Nations Covenant on Civil and Political Rights (Article 7), the European Convention on Human Rights of 1950 (Article 3), the Inter-American Convention on Human Rights of [of 1969] (Article 5) and the 1984 Convention against Torture (Article 1).[829] Similarly, the expression

---

[826] *See* 18 ILR, 1951, p. 540. * * *

[827] With regard to a similar concept, that of "inhuman treatment" under Art. 2(b) (grave breaches), the ICTY Trial Chamber in *Delalić et al.* noted that "inhuman treatment" was constituted by "an intentional act or omission [. . .] which causes serious mental or physical suffering or injury or constitutes a serious attack on human dignity" (*Prosecutor v. Delalić et al.*, (IT–96–21–T), Judgement, Trial Chamber, 16 Nov. 1998 at para. 543). The Trial Chamber also suggested a negative definition, namely that inhuman treatment is treatment which causes severe mental or physical suffering but which falls short of torture, or lacks one of the elements of torture (e.g. a prohibited purpose or official sanction). (*Ibid.* at para. 542). Whether a given conduct constitutes inhuman treatment will be determined on a case-by-case basis and appears ultimately to be a question of fact (*ibid.*, at para. 544). * * *

[829] As for the specification of what constitutes cruel, debasing, humiliating or degrading treatment, resort can of course be had to the important case-law of the relevant international bodies, chiefly to the United Nations Torture Committee and the European Commission and Court of Human Rights. It is worth adding that resort to the standards laid down in the Universal Declaration of Human Rights has already been made in 1950 by a Belgian court. The *Conseil de Guerre* of Brussels, in a judgment of 8 Feb. 1950, held that Art. 5 of the Universal Declaration, prohibiting torture and inhuman treatment can be utilised for the application of the so-called Martens clause in the IVth Hague Convention of 1899. It noted that "in searching for the principles of the law of nations as they result from the usages established among civilized peoples, from the laws of humanity and the dictates of public conscience, the Court-Martial is

at issue undoubtedly embraces the forcible transfer of groups of civilians (which is to some extent covered by Article 49 of the 4th [Geneva] Convention of 1949 and Article 17(1) of the Additional Protocol II of 1977), enforced prostitution (indisputably a serious attack on human dignity pursuant to most international instruments on human rights), as well as the enforced disappearance of persons (prohibited by General Assembly Resolution 47/133 of 18 December 1992 and the Inter-American Convention of 9 June 1994). Plainly, all these, and other similar acts, must be carried out in a systematic manner and on a large scale. In other words, they must be as serious as the other classes of crimes provided for in the other provisions of Article 5. Once the legal parameters for determining the content of the category of "inhumane acts" are identified, resort to the *ejusdem generis* rule for the purpose of comparing and assessing the gravity of the prohibited act may be warranted.

Persecution as a Crime Against Humanity

567. Persecution under Article 5(h) [of the ICTY Statute] has never been comprehensively defined in international treaties. Furthermore, neither national nor international case law provides an authoritative single definition of what constitutes "persecution." Accordingly, considerable emphasis will be given in this judgement to elucidating this important category of offences.

568. It is clear that persecution may take diverse forms, and does not necessarily require a physical element. * * * Under Article 5 of the Statute, a key constituent of persecution appears to be the carrying out of any prohibited conduct, directed against a civilian population, and motivated by a discriminatory *animus* ["attitude" or "intention"] (political, racial or religious grounds). Beyond these brief observations, however, much uncertainty exists. * * *

572. From the submissions of the parties, it appears that there is agreement between the parties that (a) persecution consists of the occurrence of a persecutory act or omission, and (b) a discriminatory basis is required for that act or omission on one of the listed grounds. Two questions remain in dispute: (a) must the crime of persecution be linked to another crime in the Statute, or can it stand alone? (b) what is the *actus reus* of persecution and how can it be defined? Each of these issues will be addressed in turn. [With respect to the first question, the Chamber concluded that there was no textual support in the ICTY statute that required acts of persecution to be linked to other crimes in the Statute. The Chamber concluded that although the World War II tribunals required such a link, and the fact that the ICC statute also has a similar requirement, such a requirement has not risen to the level of customary international law and thus cannot trump the plain language

presently guided by the Universal Declaration of Human Rights . . . " * * * (30 *Revue de droit pénal et de criminologie*, 1949–50, p. 566).

of the ICTY statute. The Chamber's discussion of the second issue follows.]

The *Actus Reus* of Persecution * * *

591. [I]n resolving matters in dispute on the scope of persecution, the Trial Chamber must of necessity turn to customary international law. Indeed, any time the Statute does not regulate a specific matter, and the Report of the Secretary-General does not prove to be of any assistance in the interpretation of the Statute, it falls to the International Tribunal to draw upon (i) rules of customary international law or (ii) general principles of international criminal law; or, lacking such principles, (iii) general principles of criminal law common to the major legal systems of the world; or, lacking such principles, (iv) general principles of law consonant with the basic requirements of international justice. It must be assumed that the draftspersons intended the Statute to be based on international law, with the consequence that any possible *lacunae* ["gaps"] must be filled by having recourse to that body of law.

592. In its discussion, the Trial Chamber will focus upon two distinct issues: (a) can the acts covered by the other subheadings of Article 5 fall within the notion of persecution? And (b) can persecution cover acts not envisaged in one of the other subheadings of Article 5?

Can the Acts Covered by the Other Subheadings of Article 5 Fall Within the Notion of Persecution? * * *

594. With regard to the question of whether persecution can include acts laid out in the other subheadings of Article 5, and particularly the crimes of murder and deportation, the Trial Chamber notes that there are numerous examples of convictions for the crime of persecution arising from the Second World War. The IMT in its findings on persecution included several of the crimes that now would fall under other subheadings of Article 5. These acts included mass murder of the Jews by the *Einsatzgruppen* [death squads] and the SD [*Sicherheitsdienst*, the Nazi intelligence service], and the extermination, beatings, torture and killings which were widespread in the concentration camps. Similarly, the judgements delivered pursuant to Control Council Law No. 10 included crimes such as murder, extermination, enslavement, deportation, imprisonment and torture in their findings on the persecution of Jews and other groups during the Nazi era. Thus the Military Tribunal sitting at Nuremberg found that persecution could include those crimes that now would be covered by the other subheadings of Article 5 of the Statute. * * *

596. At Nuremberg, organisations as well as individual defendants were convicted of persecution for acts such as deportation, slave labour, and extermination of the Jewish people pursuant to the "Final Solution." Moreover, several individual defendants were convicted of persecution in the form of discriminatory economic acts. An example is the defendant Frick who had "drafted, signed, and administered many laws designed to

eliminate Jews from German life and [the] economy," and thus "paved the way for the Final Solution [. . .]." * * *

604. These findings emphasise the conclusion of international tribunals and national courts that the crime of persecution both during and since the Second World War did not consist only of those acts not covered by the other types of crimes against humanity. On the contrary, these Tribunals and courts specifically included crimes such as murder, extermination and deportation in their findings on persecution.

605. The Trial Chamber finds that the case-law referred to above reflects, and is indicative of, the notion of persecution as laid down in customary international criminal law. The Trial Chamber therefore concludes that acts enumerated in other sub-clauses of Article 5 can thus constitute persecution. Persecution has been used to describe some of the most serious crimes perpetrated during Nazi rule. A narrow interpretation of persecution, excluding other sub-headings of Article 5, is therefore not an accurate reflection of the notion of persecution which has emerged from customary international law.

606. It should be added that if persecution was given a narrow interpretation, so as not to include the crimes found in the remaining sub-headings of Article 5, a *lacuna* would exist in the Statute of the Tribunal. There would be no means of conceptualising those crimes against humanity which are committed on discriminatory grounds, but which, for example, fall short of genocide, which requires a specific intent "to destroy, in whole or in part, a national, ethnical, racial, or religious group." An example of such a crime against humanity would be the so-called "ethnic cleansing," a notion which, although it is not a term of art, is particularly germane to the work of this Tribunal.

607. Although the *actus reus* of persecution may be identical to other crimes against humanity, what distinguishes the crime of persecution is that it is committed on discriminatory grounds. The Trial Chamber therefore accepts the submission of the Prosecution that "[p]ersecution, which can be used to charge the conduct of ethnic cleansing on discriminatory grounds is a serious crime in and of itself and describes conduct worthy of censure above and apart from non-discriminatory killings envisioned by Article 5."

Can Persecution Cover Acts Not Envisaged in One of the Other Subheadings of Article 5?

608. The Prosecution argues that persecution can also involve acts other than those listed under Article 5. * * * By contrast, the Defence submits that the two basic elements of persecution are (a) the occurrence of a persecutory act or omission, and (b) a discriminatory basis for that act or omission on one of the listed grounds. As mentioned above, the Defence argues that persecution should be narrowly construed.

609. The Trial Chamber is thus called upon to examine what acts not covered by Article 5 of the Statute of the International Tribunal may

be included in the notion of persecution. Plainly, the Trial Chamber must set out a clear-cut notion of persecution, in order to decide whether the crimes charged in this case fall within its ambit. In addition, this notion must be consistent with general principles of criminal law such as the principles of legality and specificity. First, the Trial Chamber will examine what types of acts, aside from the other categories of crimes against humanity have been deemed to constitute persecution. Secondly, it will examine whether there are elements underlying these acts which assist in defining persecution.

610. The Judgement of the IMT included in the notion of persecution a variety of acts which, at present, may not fall under the Statute of the International Tribunal, such as the passing of discriminatory laws, the exclusion of members of an ethnic or religious group from aspects of social, political, and economic life, the imposition of a collective fine on them, the restriction of their movement and their seclusion in ghettos, and the requirement that they mark themselves out by wearing a yellow star. Moreover, and as mentioned above, several individual defendants were convicted of persecution in the form of discriminatory economic acts.

611. It is also clear that other courts have used the term persecution to describe acts other than those enumerated in Article 5. A prominent example is the trial of *Josef Altstötter et al.* (the *Justice* trial). Altstötter and the other accused were former German Judges, Prosecutors or officials of the Reich Ministry of Justice. They were charged with a common design, conspiracy, plan and enterprise which "embraced the use of the judicial process as a powerful weapon for the persecution and extermination of all opponents of the Nazi regime regardless of nationality and for the persecution and extermination of races."

612. The U.S. Military Tribunal in the *Justice* case held that the national pattern or plan for racial persecution was one of actual extermination of Jewish and Polish people, but that "lesser forms of racial persecution were universally practiced by governmental authority and constituted an integral part in the general policy of the Reich." These lesser forms of persecution included the passing of a decree by which Jews were excluded from the legal profession; the prohibition of intermarriage between Jews and persons of German blood and the severe punishment of sexual intercourse between these groups; and decrees expelling Jews from public services, educational institutions, and from many business enterprises. Furthermore, upon the death of a Jew his property was confiscated, and under an amendment to the German Citizenship Law, the Security Police and the SD could also confiscate property of Jews who were alive. Jews were subject to more severe punishments than Germans; the rights of defendants in court were severely circumscribed; courts were empowered to impose death sentences on Poles and Jews even if not prescribed by law; and the police were given *carte blanche* in the punishment of Jews without resort to the judicial process. In summary, what was considered to be persecution in

the *Justice* case was the use of a legal system to implement a discriminatory policy. * * *

614. The Trial Chamber is thus bolstered in its conclusion that persecution can consist of the deprivation of a wide variety of rights. A persecutory act need not be prohibited explicitly either in Article 5 or elsewhere in the Statute. Similarly, whether or not such acts are legal under national laws is irrelevant. It is well-known that the Nazis passed many discriminatory laws through the available constitutional and legislative channels which were subsequently enforced by their judiciary. This does not detract from the fact that these laws were contrary to international legal standards. The Trial Chamber therefore rejects the Defence submission that persecution should not include acts which are legal under national laws. * * *

The Definition of Persecution

616. In the Judgement of *Prosecutor v. Tadić,* Trial Chamber II held that persecution is a form of discrimination on grounds of race, religion or political opinion that is intended to be, and results in, an infringement of an individual's fundamental rights. It is not necessary to have a separate act of an inhumane nature to constitute persecution, but rather, the discrimination itself makes the act inhumane. The Trial Chamber held that the crime of persecution encompasses a wide variety of acts, including, *inter alia,* those of a physical, economic, or judicial nature that violate an individual's basic or fundamental rights. The discrimination must be on one of the listed grounds to constitute persecution. * * *

618. However, this Trial Chamber holds the view that in order for persecution to amount to a crime against humanity it is not enough to define a core assortment of acts and to leave peripheral acts in a state of uncertainty. There must be clearly defined limits on the types of acts which qualify as persecution. Although the realm of human rights is dynamic and expansive, not every denial of a human right may constitute a crime against humanity.

619. Accordingly, it can be said that at a minimum, acts of persecution must be of an equal gravity or severity to the other acts enumerated under Article 5. This legal criterion has already been resorted to, for instance, in the *Flick* case.[897]

---

[897] In this case, the U.S. Military Tribunal sitting at Nuremberg held that "[n]ot even under a proper construction of the section of Control Council Law No. 10 relating to crimes against humanity, do the facts [compulsory taking of Jewish industrial property] warrant conviction. The 'atrocities and offences' listed therein, 'murder, extermination,' etc., are all offences against the person. Property is not mentioned. Under the doctrine of *ejusdem generis* the catch-all words 'other persecutions' must be deemed to include only such as affect the life and liberty of the oppressed peoples. Compulsory taking of industrial property, however reprehensible, is not in that category." (*United States v. Flick et al.*, VI TRIALS OF WAR CRIMINALS BEFORE THE NUREMBERG MILITARY TRIBUNALS UNDER CONTROL COUNCIL LAW NO. 10 1212, 1215). This statement was taken up and used by the U.S. Military Tribunal in *U.S. v. Krauch et al.*, (*Farben* case) (TRIALS OF WAR CRIMINALS BEFORE THE NUREMBERG MILITARY TRIBUNALS UNDER CONTROL COUNCIL LAW NO. 10, 1129–1130). *See also* Notes on the Case, U.N. War Crimes Commission, Vol. IX, which states at p. 50, that the judgement in the *Flick* case

620. It ought to be emphasised, however, that if the analysis based on this criterion relates only to the level of seriousness of the act, it does not provide guidance on what types of acts can constitute persecution. The *ejusdem generis* criterion can be used as a supplementary tool, to establish whether certain acts which generally speaking fall under the proscriptions of Article 5(h), reach the level of gravity required by this provision. The only conclusion to be drawn from its application is that only gross or blatant denials of fundamental human rights can constitute crimes against humanity.

621. The Trial Chamber, drawing upon its earlier discussion of "other inhumane acts," holds that in order to identify those rights whose infringement may constitute persecution, more defined parameters for the definition of human dignity can be found in international standards on human rights such as those laid down in the Universal Declaration on Human Rights of 1948, the two United Nations Covenants on Human Rights of 1966 and other international instruments on human rights or on humanitarian law. Drawing upon the various provisions of these texts it proves possible to identify a set of fundamental rights appertaining to any human being, the gross infringement of which may amount, depending on the surrounding circumstances, to a crime against humanity. Persecution consists of a severe attack on those rights, and aims to exclude a person from society on discriminatory grounds. The Trial Chamber therefore defines persecution as the gross or blatant denial, on discriminatory grounds, of a fundamental right, laid down in international customary or treaty law, reaching the same level of gravity as the other acts prohibited in Article 5.

622. In determining whether particular acts constitute persecution, the Trial Chamber wishes to reiterate that acts of persecution must be evaluated not in isolation but in context, by looking at their cumulative effect. Although individual acts may not be inhumane, their overall consequences must offend humanity in such a way that they may be termed "inhumane." This delimitation also suffices to satisfy the principle of legality, as inhumane acts are clearly proscribed by the Statute.

623. The Trial Chamber does not see fit to identify which rights constitute fundamental rights for the purposes of persecution. The interests of justice would not be served by so doing, as the explicit inclusion of particular fundamental rights could be interpreted as the implicit exclusion of other rights (*expressio unius est exclusio alterius*). This is not the approach taken to crimes against humanity in customary international law, where the category of "other inhumane acts" also allows courts flexibility to determine the cases before them, depending

declared that "A distinction could be made between industrial property and the dwellings, household furnishings and food supplies of a persecuted people" and thus left open the question whether such offences against personal property as would amount to an assault upon the health and life of a human being (such as the burning of his house or depriving him of his food supply or his paid employment) would not constitute a crime against humanity.

on the forms which attacks on humanity may take, forms which are ever-changing and carried out with particular ingenuity. Each case must therefore be examined on its merits. * * *

626. The Trial Chamber observes that in the light of its broad definition of persecution, the Prosecution cannot merely rely on a general charge of "persecution" in bringing its case. This would be inconsistent with the concept of legality. To observe the principle of legality, the Prosecution must charge particular acts (and this seems to have been done in this case). These acts should be charged in sufficient detail for the accused to be able to fully prepare their defence. * * *

The Application of the Definition Set Out Above to the Instant Case

628. The Trial Chamber will now examine the specific allegations in this case, which are the "deliberate and systematic killing of Bosnian Muslim civilians," the "organised detention and expulsion of the Bosnian Muslims from Ahmići-Šantići and its environs," and the "comprehensive destruction of Bosnian homes and property." Can these acts constitute persecution?

629. In light of the conclusions above, the Trial Chamber finds that the "deliberate and systematic killing of Bosnian Muslim civilians" as well as their "organised detention and expulsion from Ahmići" can constitute persecution. This is because these acts qualify as murder, imprisonment, and deportation, which are explicitly mentioned in the Statute under Article 5.

630. The Trial Chamber next turns its attention to the alleged comprehensive destruction of Bosnian Muslim homes and property. The question here is whether certain property or economic rights can be considered so fundamental that their denial is capable of constituting persecution. The Trial Chamber notes that in the Judgement of the IMT, several defendants were convicted of economic discrimination. For example, Göring "persecuted the Jews . . . and not only in Germany where he raised the billion mark fine . . . this interest was primarily economic—how to get their property and how to force them out of economic life in Europe." Defendants Funk and Seyss-Inquart were also charged with acts of economic discrimination.

631. The Trial Chamber finds that attacks on property can constitute persecution. To some extent this may depend on the type of property involved: in the passage from *Flick* cited above the Tribunal held that the compulsory taking of industrial property could not be said to affect the life and liberty of oppressed peoples and therefore did not constitute persecution. There may be certain types of property whose destruction may not have a severe enough impact on the victim as to constitute a crime against humanity, even if such a destruction is perpetrated on discriminatory grounds: an example is the burning of someone's car (unless the car constitutes an indispensable and vital asset

to the owner). However, the case at hand concerns the comprehensive destruction of homes and property. Such an attack on property in fact constitutes a destruction of the livelihood of a certain population. This may have the same inhumane consequences as a forced transfer or deportation. Moreover, the burning of a residential property may often be committed with a recklessness towards the lives of its inhabitants. The Trial Chamber therefore concludes that this act may constitute a gross or blatant denial of fundamental human rights, and, if committed on discriminatory grounds, it may constitute persecution.

The *Mens Rea* of Persecution * * *

636. As set forth above, the *mens rea* requirement for persecution is higher than for ordinary crimes against humanity, although lower than for genocide. In this context the Trial Chamber wishes to stress that persecution as a crime against humanity is an offence belonging to the same *genus* as genocide. Both persecution and genocide are crimes perpetrated against persons that belong to a particular group and who are targeted because of such belonging. In both categories what matters is the intent to discriminate: to attack persons on account of their ethnic, racial, or religious characteristics (as well as, in the case of persecution, on account of their political affiliation). While in the case of persecution the discriminatory intent can take multifarious inhumane forms and manifest itself in a plurality of actions including murder, in the case of genocide that intent must be accompanied by the intention to destroy, in whole or in part, the group to which the victims of the genocide belong. Thus, it can be said that, from the viewpoint of *mens rea,* genocide is an extreme and most inhuman form of persecution. To put it differently, when persecution escalates to the extreme form of wilful and deliberate acts designed to destroy a group or part of a group, it can be held that such persecution amounts to genocide.

NOTES & QUESTIONS

1. Case Outcome

On January 14, 2000, the Trial Chamber pronounced Zoran Kupreškić guilty of one count of crimes against humanity (persecutions on political, racial or religious grounds) and sentenced him to 10 years in prison. The Appeals Chamber revoked this sentence and ordered the defendant's immediate release on the grounds that the evidence did not support the conviction and the principal witness lacked credibility. A number of witnesses who assisted in the investigation ultimately did not testify at trial. This was the first time that the Appeals Chamber had overturned a verdict.

Zoran's brothers—Vlatko and Drago Kupreškić—were also convicted on one persecution count; on appeal, the former was acquitted as a result of the introduction of new evidence and the latter's sentence was reduced from 15 to 12 years. Defendant Santić's sentence was also reduced on appeal from 25 to 18 years on the ground that the evidence did not prove that he played a strategic role in the attack on Ahmići, although the Appeals Chamber upheld his conviction for three counts of crimes against humanity: murder, persecution, and other inhumane acts. Defendant Papić was declared not guilty by the Trial Chamber and released. The convicted defendants served their sentences in Villahierro prison in Spain; they were granted early release in 2006 and 2009.

2. Crimes Against Humanity v. Domestic Crimes

How does the Trial Chamber formulate the elements of crimes against humanity? Which elements serve to distinguish the various crimes against humanity—murder, torture, cruel treatment—from domestic crimes of the same nature? The definition of crimes against humanity in the two *ad hoc* tribunals requires a showing that the acts occurred within the context of a widespread *or* systematic attack against a civilian population. How should these terms be interpreted? This disjunctive formulation was a matter of great debate during the drafting of the ICC Statute. Many delegates preferred a conjunctive formulation ("widespread *and* systematic"). How would this have changed the definition of the crimes? Proponents of the disjunctive formulation prevailed—or did they? Review the full ICC definition again closely with this question in mind. How should the ICC definition be interpreted in light of this contested "legislative" history?

3. The Definition of Persecution

Does the construction of the ICTY Statute support the interpretation of persecution advocated by the Prosecution and adopted by the Trial Chamber? Or is the Defense's proposed construction more logical? If persecution constitutes acts not enumerated in Article 5, what purpose is served by the designation "other inhumane acts," which the Chamber earlier in the opinion (para. 563) identified as a residual clause? If the crime of persecution includes acts already enumerated elsewhere as crimes against humanity, why include a separate designation of persecution? What is the *lacuna* in the statute the Trial Chamber is trying to avoid (para. 606) in its construction of the persecution provision? How should the Prosecution charge individuals accused of committing multiple acts under Article 5? How else could an international criminal tribunal address this apparent *lacuna*? Is there any remedy were the Security Council to disagree with the Trial Chamber's expansive construction of the Statute?

The definition of persecution in the ICTY Statute contains a shorter list of prohibited discriminatory grounds ("political, racial and religious") than that found in the ICC Statute ("any identifiable group or collectivity on political, racial, national, ethnic, cultural, religious, gender . . . , or other grounds that are universally recognised as impermissible under international law"). Why would the Security Council not list gender as a discriminatory ground in the statute of the *ad hoc* tribunals given the prevalence of rape and other sexual violence in the conflicts in both the former Yugoslavia and Rwanda? The ICC Statute at Article 7(3) defines "gender" as "the two sexes, male and female, within the context of society. The term 'gender' does not indicate any meaning different from the above." This language was included at the insistence of certain states (mainly Middle Eastern states) and the Holy See. Why might they advocate for this awkward phraseology? What notions of gender does this definition encompass and exclude? Could discrimination based upon sexual orientation rise to the level of criminal persecution under any of these formulations? The ILC in their crimes against humanity treaty project have generally followed the ICC Statute's formulation of the offense, but have dropped this definition at the urging of civil society organizations. *See* Human Rights & Gender Justice Clinic, CUNY School of Law, *Letter to Secretary-General António Guterres re: The Definition of Gender in the Draft Crimes Against Humanity Convention* (Dec. 1, 2018).

The ICC Statute contains language akin to the war nexus when it provides that persecution may be charged "in connection with any act referred to in this paragraph or any crime within the jurisdiction of the Court." Why would the drafters of the ICC Statute adopt this formula? Was Kupreškić entitled to this formulation of the offense, as argued by the Defense, since it represents the most recent articulation of persecution by the international community and a consensus definition? Would this definition have exonerated the defendants in this case?

4. Persecution in Refugee Law

The concept of persecution is central to refugee law. Article 1A(2) of the Convention Relating to the Status of Refugees of 1951, as supplemented by the 1967 Protocol, defines a refugee as someone who:

> owing to a well-founded fear of being persecuted for reasons of race, religion, nationality, membership of a particular social group or political opinion is outside the country of his nationality and is unable or, owing to such fear, is unwilling to avail himself of the protection of that country; or who * * * is unwilling to return to it.

Art. 33 of the same Convention states:

> No Contracting State shall expel or return ('*refouler*') a refugee in any manner whatsoever to the frontiers of territories where his life or freedom would be threatened on account of his race, religion, nationality, membership of a particular social group or political opinion.

Should the concept of persecution from refugee law, or asylum jurisprudence, inform international criminal law? In the opinion excerpted above, the ICTY largely rejected this approach:

> 587. It has been argued that further elaboration of what is meant by the notion of persecution is provided by international refugee law. In its comments on the Draft Code presented in 1991, the government of the Netherlands stated: "It would be desirable to interpret the term 'persecution' in the same way as the term embodied in the Convention on refugees is interpreted." The concept of persecution is central to the determination of who may claim refugee status under the.
>
> 588. However, the corpus of refugee law does not, as such, offer a definition of persecution. Nor does human rights law provide such a definition. The European Commission and the Court have

> on several occasions held that exposing a person to a risk of persecution in his or her country of origin may constitute a violation of Article 3 of the European Convention on Human Rights [which provides that "[n]o one shall be subjected to torture or to inhuman or degrading treatment or punishment."]. * * *
>
> 589. The Trial Chamber finds, however, that these cases cannot provide a basis for individual criminal responsibility. It would be contrary to the principle of legality to convict someone of persecution based on a definition found in international refugee law or human rights law. In these bodies of law the central determination to be made is whether the person claiming refugee status or likely to be expelled or deported has a "well-founded fear of being persecuted for reasons of race, religion, nationality, membership of a particular social group or political opinion." The emphasis is more on the state of mind of the person claiming to have been persecuted (or to be vulnerable to persecution) than on the factual finding of whether persecution has occurred or may occur. In addition, the intent of the persecutor is not relevant. The result is that the net of "persecution" is cast much wider than is legally justified for the purposes of imposing individual criminal responsibility. The definition stemming from international refugee law or human rights law cannot therefore be followed here.

Do you agree or should we strive for congruence between these bodies of law as originally argued by the delegate from the Netherlands?

5. Klaus Barbie

The Trial Chamber cites the *Barbie* case for the proposition that crimes against humanity can be committed against combatants (para. 548). Klaus Barbie was the head of the Gestapo in Lyon, France, from November 1942 to August 1944. Shortly after the war, the Tribunal Permanent des Forces Armées de Lyon—one of eight tribunals created throughout France for the purpose of prosecuting international law violations committed by the military—twice sentenced him to death *in absentia*. Years later, Barbie was discovered living in Bolivia. In 1983, the Bolivian government expelled him for obtaining citizenship through the use of a false identity. Barbie was immediately thereafter arrested in French Guyana and sent to France to stand trial for alleged crimes against humanity. The charge included allegations of murder, torture and arbitrary arrests, detentions, and imprisonments. Barbie applied for release, claiming that his transfer from Bolivia was illegal and the forthcoming trial invalid. He further argued the statute of limitations of the domestic French crime of crimes against humanity had lapsed. All these applications were rejected.

On appeal, the Court of Cassation in 1984 disallowed his statute of limitations appeal on the grounds that the European Convention on Human Rights and the International Covenant on Civil and Political Rights did not allow "any derogation from the rule that the prosecution of crimes against humanity was not subject to statutory limitation." Finally, and most relevant to the *Kupreškić* excerpt, Barbie's original indictment included allegations of crimes committed against both members of the Jewish community and the French Resistance. The Examining Magistrate of Lyons determined that a charge of crimes against humanity could only include alleged crimes against Jewish persons on racial or religious grounds, on the reasoning that the persecution of a hostile enemy combatant is not a crime against humanity, which has no statute of limitations, but a war crime, which was barred by the statute of limitations. To this end, the *Chambre d'accusation* (the court of first instance) stated the following:

> Only the persecution of persons who are non-combatants, committed in furtherance of a deliberate State policy and for racial, religious, or political motives, is of such a nature as to constitute a crime against humanity [. . .]. On the other hand a war crime, even if it may be committed by the same means, is characterized, in contrast to a crime against humanity, by the fact that it appears to assist the conduct of war.

Fédération Nationale des Déportés et Internés Résistants et Patriotes and Others v. Barbie, Cass. Crim., 78 ILR 124, 137 (Dec. 20, 1985) (Fr.). Furthermore, the examining magistrate noted:

> The combatants in the Resistance were motivated firstly by the desire to chase out the invader of their country and give freedom to their children. Their political ideology, by comparison with their patriotism, was merely a secondary impetus for their action, inseparable from their patriotism. On the other hand, when the Nazis took into account the political philosophies of their adversaries, they classified them without distinction as "Judéo-Bolsheviks and Communists" in order to render their fight against these "combatants of darkness" more effective.

Id. at 139.

Several individuals and organizations representing members of the French Resistance appealed this decision. In 1986, the Court of Cassation critically examined the lower court's judgment. The Court reasoned that the lower court had given improper weight to the intent of the victims participating in the Resistance. In addition to the passage cited in *Kupreškić*, the French decision states: "[n]either the driving force which motivated the victims, nor their possible membership in the Resistance, excludes the possibility that the accused acted with the element of intent necessary for the commission of crimes against humanity." *Id.* Accordingly, the Court of Cassation quashed the lower court's decision to exclude those crimes allegedly committed against members of the Resistance and remanded the case for reconsideration of which charges to add to the indictment. Mr. Barbie's trial concluded on July 4, 1987. He was found guilty on all 340 counts of the seventeen crimes against humanity with which he was charged and sentenced to life imprisonment. He died in 1991.

6. War Crimes v. Crimes Against Humanity

Did the *Barbie* Court of Cassation, in effect, collapse the distinction between war crimes and crimes against humanity? Does the *Barbie* opinion leave any room for a charge of war crimes in conflicts arising from racial or religious conflict or will all such charges inevitably be brought as crimes against humanity? Does war, by definition, involve persecution of an enemy? Consider the following analogy, argued by Advocate General Dontenwille during the *Barbie* proceedings, "[c]rimes against humanity are to war crimes what assassination is to murder. The premeditation involved is simply of another order. On one side stands not simply an individual but a state with all its resources. On the other side is not merely a single victim but humanity." *Id.* at 146. Why would crimes against humanity, but not war crimes, have no statute of limitation, per the French Court of Cassation?

7. Combatant Victims of Crimes Against Humanity

How are tribunals to determine which combatants may be the victims of crimes against humanity and which may be the victims of war crimes only? The *Tadić* case considered the issue of combatant victims of crimes against humanity in greater depth:

> 638. [I]t is clear that the targeted population must be of a predominantly civilian nature. The presence of certain non-civilians in their midst does not change the character of the population.
>
> 639. [D]etermining which individual[s] of the targeted population qualify as civilians for purposes of crimes against humanity, is not, however, quite as clear. Common Article 3, the language of which reflects "elementary considerations of humanity" which are "applicable under customary international law to any armed conflict," provides that in an armed conflict "not of an international character," Contracting States are obliged "as a minimum" to comply with the following: "Persons taking no active part in the hostilities, including members of armed forces who have laid down their arms and those placed *hors de combat* [outside of combat] by sickness, wounds, detention, or any other cause, shall in all circumstances be treated humanely. . . ." Protocol Additional to the Geneva Conventions of 12 August 1949, and Relating to the Protection of Victims in International Armed Conflicts (Protocol I) defines civilians by the exclusion of prisoners of war and armed forces, considering a person a civilian in case of doubt. However, this definition of civilians contained in Common Article 3 is not immediately applicable to crimes against humanity because it is a part of the laws or customs of war and can only be applied by analogy. The same applies to the definition contained in Protocol I and the Commentary, Geneva Convention IV, on the treatment of civilians, both of which advocate a broad interpretation of the term "civilian." They, and particularly Common Article 3, do, however, provide guidance in answering the most difficult question: specifically, whether acts taken against an individual who cannot be considered a traditional "non-combatant" because he is actively involved in the conduct of hostilities by membership in some form of resistance group can nevertheless constitute crimes against humanity if they are committed in furtherance or as part of an attack directed against a civilian population.

640. In this regard the United Nations War Crimes Commission stated in reference to Article 6(c) of the Nürnberg Charter that "[t]he words '*civilian* population' appear to indicate that 'crimes against humanity' are restricted to inhumane acts committed against civilians as opposed to members of the armed forces. . . ." In contrast, the Supreme Court of the British zone determined that crimes against humanity were applicable in all cases where the perpetrator and the victim were of the same nationality, regardless of whether the victim was civilian or military. * * * The Commission of Experts Established Pursuant to Security Council Resolution 780 [to consider international law violations in the former Yugoslavia] observed: "It seems obvious that article 5 applies first and foremost to civilians, meaning people who are not combatants. This, however, should not lead to any quick conclusions concerning people who at one particular point in time did bear arms." The Commission of Experts then provided an example based on the situation in the former Yugoslavia and concluded: "A Head of a family who under such circumstances tries to protect his family gun-in-hand does not thereby lose his status as a civilian. Maybe the same is the case for the sole policeman or local defence guard doing the same, even if they joined hands to try to prevent the cataclysm." * * *

643. Despite the limitations inherent in the use of these various sources, from Common Article 3 to the *Barbie* case, a wide definition of civilian population, as supported by these sources, is justified. Thus the presence of those actively involved in the conflict should not prevent the characterization of a population as civilian and those actively involved in a resistance movement can qualify as victims of crimes against humanity. As noted by Trial Chamber I of the International Tribunal in its Review of the Indictment Pursuant to Rule 61 of the Rules of Procedure and Evidence in *Prosecutor v. Msksić* ("*Vukovar Hospital Decision*"), although crimes against humanity must target a civilian population, individuals who at one time performed acts of resistance may in certain circumstances be victims of crimes against humanity. In the context of that case, patients in a hospital, either civilians or resistance fighters who had laid down their arms, were considered victims of crimes against humanity.

Prosecutor v. Tadić, Case No. IT–94–1–T, Opinion and Judgement (May. 7, 1997). Consider the situation of the so-called *levée en masse* ["mass uprising"], whereby citizens spontaneously rise up against invading or occupying foreign troops. Could such individuals be the victims of crimes against humanity? Recall from the chapter on War Crimes that designating an individual as a combatant or a civilian has implications for whether the individual is entitled to combat immunity for participating in lawful acts of war or can be subject to either status-based preventative detention (as a POW) or security detention.

8. *Mens Rea*

What is the *mens rea* of crimes against humanity? Note that in many international crimes, there will be two required mental states. The first relates to the particular constitutive offense. For example, the *mens rea* of murder is intent to kill. The second relates to the so-called *chapeau* ("hat") elements that apply to all constitutive offenses (e.g., knowledge of the existence of a widespread or systematic attack). Review the formulation of crimes against humanity in the ICC Statute and glean what exactly the prosecutor's burden of proof is with respect to *mens rea*—must the defendant know the attack is widespread or systematic? Pursuant to a policy? Pursuant to a policy of a particular state or organization? Likewise, is the defendant's motive an element of crimes against humanity? Should it be?

9. The Longevity of the War Nexus

The ICTY Appeals Chamber ruled in an early opinion that the definition of crimes against humanity under customary international law no longer required a link to war as an element. Specifically, the Appeals Chamber opined:

> 140. [T]he nexus between crimes against humanity and either crimes against peace or war crimes, required by the Nuremberg Charter, was peculiar to the jurisdiction of the Nuremberg Tribunal. Although the nexus requirement in the Nuremberg Charter was carried over to the 1948 General Assembly resolution affirming the Nuremberg principles, there is no logical or legal basis for this requirement and it has been abandoned in subsequent State practice with respect to crimes against humanity. Most notably, the nexus requirement was eliminated from the definition of crimes against humanity contained in Article II(1)(c) of Control Council Law No. 10 of 20 December 1945. The obsolescence of the nexus requirement is evidenced by international conventions regarding genocide and apartheid, both of which prohibit particular types of crimes against humanity regardless of any connection to armed conflict. (Convention on the Prevention and Punishment of the Crime of Genocide, 9 December 1948, art. 1, 78 U.N.T.S. 277, Article 1 (providing that genocide, "whether committed in time of peace or in time of war, is a crime under international law"); International Convention on the Suppression and Punishment of the Crime of Apartheid, 30 November 1973, 1015 U.N.T.S. 243, arts. 1–2.).

Prosecutor v. Tadić, Case No. IT–94–1–I, Decision on the Defence Motion for Interlocutory Appeal on Jurisdiction (Oct. 2, 1995). If the ICTY is right that customary international law no longer considers a nexus to an armed conflict to be an element of crimes against humanity, why would the Security Council nonetheless reproduce the war nexus in the ICTY Statute (but not the ICTR Statute)?

When did the evolution of the definition of crimes against humanity with respect to the war nexus occur? How would a prosecutor or defense counsel argue this point? The preceding set of questions is not purely academic. The Statute of the Extraordinary Chambers in the Courts of Cambodia for the Prosecution of Crimes Committed during the Period of Democratic Kampuchea (ECCC) includes subject matter jurisdiction over genocide and crimes against humanity, among other crimes. Article 5 of the Statute of the Extraordinary Chambers provides that crimes against humanity, which have no statute of limitations, are any listed acts committed as part of a widespread or systematic attack directed against any civilian population, on national, political, ethnical, racial or religious grounds. As discussed in the last chapter, many of the defining acts of the Khmer Rouge do not constitute genocide under the prevailing conventional definition despite common assumptions to the contrary. May those same acts be charged as crimes against humanity? This may turn on whether the war nexus was in place in 1975–79 when the Khmer Rouge were in power.

For the most part, the violence in Cambodia during this period was not linked to an armed conflict; rather, this violence consisted of internal repression against civilians and Khmer Rouge cadre. There was, however, a low-intensity border war between Cambodia and Vietnam in 1975–77, which escalated in 1977. Vietnam eventually occupied parts of the Eastern Zone of Cambodia. The Khmer Rouge regime was finally halted when Vietnam undertook a full-scale invasion of Cambodia that reached Phnom Penh in early January 1979 and installed the People's Republic of Kampuchea. How would the Nuremberg Tribunal have interpreted these facts under the framework it employed in adjudicating the crimes against humanity count in the Nuremberg Indictment? How would the ICTY?

10. The Policy Element

Is the fact that the constitutive acts were undertaken pursuant to a policy an element of crimes against humanity within the ICTY jurisprudence? Is this a true element or simply a factor of evidentiary significance? Likewise, is state action an element of crimes against humanity within the ICTY jurisprudence? In other words, must the policy be that of a state or state-like organization, or would the policy of a non-state actor qualify? Compare the ICTY's treatment of this issue with the definition of the offense in the ICC Statute. Several defendants in U.S. Alien Tort Statute litigation have argued that the plaintiffs pleading crimes against humanity should have to demonstrate the existence of a policy. They cite in support the French legislation on crimes against humanity, which governed the domestic cases discussed in the previous Notes. That legislation required a showing that the acts were performed "in the name of a State practicing by such means a policy of Ideological Supremacy." Professor Leila Sadat has convincingly argued that this element was inserted to absolve members of the Vichy collaborationist government as well as French colonial officials in Algeria from liability. Leila Sadat Wexler, *Interpretation of the Nuremberg Principles by the French Court of Cassation: From* Touvier *to* Barbie *and Back Again*, 32 COLUM. J. TRANSNAT'L L. 289 (1994).

Review the language in Article 7 of the ICC Statute concerning crimes against humanity. Does it require an organizational policy? If so, what form of organization is required? The next case addresses these and other questions arising out of the ICC definition of crimes against humanity.

11. The *Chapeau* Elements of Crimes Against Humanity Within the ICC

The decision below from an ICC Pre-Trial Chamber (PTC) arises out of the situation in Kenya. On March 31, 2010, a PTC granted the request of the Prosecutor to open an investigation into violations of international criminal law committed in connection with the Kenyan election in December 2007. Following that contested election, over 1,100 people were killed in a spate of violence that spread throughout six of the eight provinces. In March 2011, the Court issued summonses to appear (as opposed to arrest warrants) against six prominent Kenyans for alleged involvement in planning or implementing the post-election violence. Each of the six was charged with committing acts that constituted crimes against humanity under Article 7 of the Rome Statute. (See the Appendix for a map of Kenya.)

The six suspects were divided into two groups of three based upon their political affiliation during the post-election violence. Case One involved those individuals associated with the then-incumbent Party of National Unity (PNU); Case Two involved those individuals associated with the Orange Democratic Movement (ODM). While such generalizations are always imprecise and politically fraught, most members of the Kikuyu ethnic group supported the PNU and most members of the Kalenjin and Luo group supported the ODM. Included within the so-called Ocampo Six were two men later elected President and Deputy President of Kenya: Uhuru Kenyatta and William Ruto. (While President Kenyatta and Deputy President Ruto ran for office on a common ticket in 2013, they were political opponents during the 2007 election and thus were the subject of separate cases before the ICC). One other suspect, Joshua arap Sang, was the head of operations of a radio station in Kenya, and stood accused of using the media to encourage listeners to engage in acts of violence against political and ethnic opponents by, among other things, broadcasting hate messages to fan the violence, disseminating false news to inflame the atmosphere surrounding the violence, and providing information to perpetrators directing them to attack designated targets.

The Prosecutor alleged that the PNU defendants worked closely with a shadowy group known as the *Mungiki* to organize and perpetrate violence against their political opponents, particularly those associated with the ODM. The *Mungiki* were formed by Kikuyu victims of ethnic political clashes, particularly in the early 1990s in the Rift Valley, drawing their inspiration in part from the anti-colonial Mau movement, and evolved into a closely-knit organization that many allege terrorized individuals from other ethnic groups. The excerpt below is from the decision concerning the Confirmation of Charges in the case against President Kenyatta; a similar opinion was issued in the case involving Deputy President Ruto and Joshua arap Sang. Judge Kaul issued a dissent in both cases.

Situation in the Republic of Kenya in the Case of the Prosecutor v. Francis Kirimi Muthaura, Uhuru Muigai Kenyatta and Mohammed Hussein Ali, Case No. ICC–01/09–02/11, Decision on the Confirmation of Charges Pursuant to Article 61(7)(a) and (b) of the Rome Statute (January 23, 2012) (Public Redacted Version)

Pre-Trial Chamber II

109. The Chamber will not engage in an in-depth discussion of the interpretation of contextual elements of crimes against humanity, as it considers that they are well settled in the jurisprudence of the Court. The Chamber will address only those aspects of the interpretation that are subject to dispute between the parties or are otherwise significant for the present decision.

110. First, the Chamber notes that the qualifier "any civilian population" has been previously interpreted to mean "groups distinguishable by nationality, ethnicity or other distinguishing features". In the view of the Chamber, the civilian population targeted can include a group defined by its (perceived) political affiliation.

111. With respect to the requirement that the attack take place pursuant to a "policy", the Chamber recalls that it has been held previously that "an attack which is planned, directed or organized—as opposed to spontaneous or isolated acts of violence—will satisfy this criterion."

112. Further, as concerns the proper interpretation of the term "organization", this Chamber has held previously that "the formal nature of a group and the level of its organization should not be the defining criterion. Instead, [. . .] a distinction should be drawn on whether a group has the capability to perform acts which infringe on basic human values." In addition, the Chamber recalls its previous finding that "had the drafters intended to exclude non-State actors from the term 'organization', they would not have included this term in article 7(2)(a) of the Statute."

113. The Defence of Mr. Kenyatta asserts that this interpretation "is incorrect and does not reflect the intention of the drafters of the Statute." In particular, the Defence argues that under the principle of *nullum crimen sine lege* enshrined in article 22 of the Statute, the term "organizational policy" must be strictly construed. It submits that the drafters of the Statute "intended to create a clear boundary between crimes against humanity and national crimes, and for this boundary to be dependent not on the abhorrent nature of the crimes but on the entity and policy behind them." Further, the Defence avers that because the Statute refers to an 'organization' and not to " 'groups', 'bodies' or other less clearly defined entities," the drafters of the Statute "clearly intended

the formal nature of the group and the level of its organization to be a defining criterion." The Defence of Mr. Kenyatta, thus, requests the Chamber to adopt a narrower interpretation of the term "organization" and to determine, upon examination of the evidence presented against such narrow definition, that the statutory requirement at issue is not met in the present case. * * *

The Targeted Population

142. Upon review of the evidence, the Chamber considers that the Prosecutor's description of the targeted civilian population as "perceived ODM supporters" appropriately captures the nature of the Mungiki attack in Nakuru and Naivasha.

143. First, there is evidence to support the conclusion that the attack in Nakuru and Naivasha was politically motivated and directed against the opponents of the PNU Coalition. Witness OTP-2 avers that the violence in Naivasha was politically motivated. Witness OTP-11 similarly states that "what [was] being planned [were] retaliatory attacks [. . .] to fight any other person who [was] not supporting Kikuyus." Furthermore, Witness OTP-12 explains:

> [The attack occurred] because the members of the Kikuyu wanted to retain the seat, the presidential seat. [. . .] [B]ecause it was announced that Kibaki had won the elections. Now, the people who were against the Kikuyus winning started complaining that it was not fair, and these people were the Kalenjins and the Luos. Now, the Kikuyus now had to retaliate and they were prepared to fight back because they also claimed that they had won the elections, so it was as a result of the outcome of the presidential announcement, of the results.

144. Second, in the view of the Chamber the evidence equally indicates that the attackers chose their individual targets based upon the assumed political allegiance of particular ethnic groups. As laid out in the preceding section, the evidence establishes that the perceived ODM supporters consisted predominantly of Luo, Luhya and Kalenjin residents of Nakuru and Naivasha. However, the Chamber considers that this does not diminish the fact that the identification of the targeted population was essentially on political grounds.

145. Finally, the Chamber finds substantial grounds to believe that the attack in or around Nakuru and Naivasha resulted in a large number of killings, displacement of thousands of people, rape, severe physical injuries, mental suffering and destruction of property. The Chamber refers to its analysis of the evidence and its findings below in sections relating to the individual crimes charged. * * *

The Mungiki Organization

186. The Chamber shall analyze in this section the evidence with respect to a series of facts that support its conclusion that the Mungiki qualified as an organization within the meaning of article 7(2)(a) of the

Statute at the time of the events under consideration. In particular, the Chamber finds that the following facts are of relevance to its conclusion: (i) the Mungiki was a hierarchically structured organization under the control of Maina Njenga; (ii) there existed an effective system of ensuring compliance by the members with the rules and orders imposed by higher levels of command; (iii) the Mungiki was a large organization and included a trained quasi-military wing; and (iv) it controlled and provided, in certain parts of Kenya, essential social services, including security. * * *

189. * * * [T]he Chamber now turns to the analysis of the evidence relevant to demonstrating that at the relevant time the Mungiki qualified as an organization within the meaning of article 7(2)(a) of the Statute.

190. First, the Chamber notes that several independent sources in the evidence before it show that the Mungiki operated at the relevant time as a hierarchical organization with defined roles for members at different levels. The evidence also indicates that Maina Njenga possessed exclusive control over the Mungiki organization.

191. Witness OTP-4 explains that "[t]he Mungiki hierarchy works around one main centre of power—Maina Njenga." The same witness clarifies that although "Ndungu" was the Chairman of the organization, he was under Maina Njenga and could not take important decisions on his own. In his second statement to the Prosecutor, Witness OTP-4 confirms that "[i]t is Maina Njenga who has all the real power. The other leaders can have different titles, but all the decisions and powers come from Maina Njenga."

192. Witness OTP-9 provides a corroborating account of the structure of the Mungiki, referring to Maina Njenga as on "the top" and a hierarchical command structure below him. He confirms that during the post-election violence, although he was in prison, Maina Njenga was still making decisions on behalf of the Mungiki. * * *

194. Witness OTP-12 refers to Maina Njenga as "the most powerful man in the movement". According to the witness, when Maina Njenga was in prison, Charles Ndungu Wagacha was representing him, receiving his orders by going to prison to visit Maina Njenga or through the telephone. Witness OTP-12 continues:

> Only Maina can issue orders. The big orders, like those pertaining to national issues are given by Maina. No one else can do that. Small things can be done at the local level, but not the things that pertain to national issues. These are only for one man. If you are outside the movement and there is something that you want the Mungiki to do, you first approach the local Mungiki leaders. If the local leaders agree, they will take you to the next level. Eventually you can reach Maina Njenga. * * *

196. Turning more specifically to individual Mungiki leaders that, as clarified below, are alleged to have played key roles in the commission of the crimes with which the Suspects are charged in the present case, the Chamber first notes that according to Witness OTP-4, Maina Diambo, [redacted] and [redacted] were members of the "Higher Office"—the highest group in the Mungiki ranking after Maina Njenga and Charles Ndungu Wagacha—and, as such, were "very close to Maina Njenga," and "in charge of sending information from Maina Njenga to the local branches of the Mungiki." * * *

198. Witness OTP-12 explains that [redacted] commonly known as [redacted] was the Nairobi coordinator of the Mungiki. Witness OTP-11 similarly states that [redacted] was one of the top leaders of the Mungiki. In addition, the NSIS Situation Report for 21 January 2008 refers to him as "Acting National Coordinator" in the context of information on the planning of retaliatory attacks by the Mungiki. Importantly, the Chamber notes that the individual himself, interviewed by the Defence of Mr. Muthaura, confirms his identity as the "Mungiki Coordinator for Nairobi."

199. Moreover, according to Witness OTP-11, [redacted] was the treasurer of the organization and a confidant of Maina Njenga. Witness OTP-12 refers to [redacted] as the "Executive Officer" and the link to the lawyer representing the interests of the Mungiki. This individual, who states his name as [redacted] is also Witness D12-37. He states that he was a Mungiki member between 1999 and 2006, but denies involvement in the planning of violence in Naivasha and Nakuru. The Chamber, however, reiterates that, due to the level of involvement of this individual as shown by the evidence, it does not find the denial of [redacted] about any association with the Mungiki at the time of the alleged crimes decisive for the findings of the Chamber on the point at issue. * * *

201. Furthermore, the evidence indicates that the Mungiki is territorially organized. Witness OTP-4 states:

> The Mungiki is organized into local and regional branches. In every local area, there is a local Chairman who has his own office and his own people. There is a Chairman for every region. The Chairmen of the different regions are equals in the hierarchy. They are the next level after the Higher Office. The Chairmen would get orders from the Higher Office which got its orders from Maina Njenga. The Chairmen could independently take some decisions at the local level as they were seen as the "eyes" of Maina Njenga on the ground at that level. However, the Chairmen were bound by general or common rules for the organization which I do not think are written. Nevertheless, the Chairmen must follow instructions given by [Maina Njenga].

202. Witness OTP-4 also states that "[i]nformation flowed well in the organization [. . .]; [t]he communication and orders were given through mobile phones". Witness OTP-11 confirms this particular point,

stating that "[i]t is through phones and the message can reach in the grass roots within a period of 15 minutes."

203. Witness OTP-11 also confirms that the Mungiki were, at the relevant time, territorially organized in regions with their own coordinators. Witness OTP-12 provides a similar account, explaining that the Mungiki were organized in territorially defined units, at village, location and division level.

204. The Chamber considers that although the witnesses give diverging estimates of the size of the Mungiki membership, the evidence in total nevertheless supports the conclusion that the Mungiki was at the time of events under consideration a large organization, capable of carrying out complex operations without depending on the will of the individual members.

205. The Chamber notes the argument of the Defence of Mr. Kenyatta that the Mungiki is "far from being under responsible command with an established hierarchy," because it is "no more than an amorphous group with disparate aims, shifting politically, as its changing aspirations dictate." In its final written observations, the Defence of Mr. Kenyatta reiterates its argument that the Mungiki lack a coherent ideology, as evidenced by the transient support for different religious movements of members of the Mungiki. The Defence highlights that the political alliances of Mungiki members have changed over time, which shows their lack of ability to act in a uniform manner with a coherent purpose, subject to an established hierarchy.

206. Upon examination of the Defence argument, the Chamber does not consider that the evidence of the changing political alliances of the Mungiki—a fact on which the Prosecutor appears to agree—stands in contradiction with its nature as a hierarchical organization and the fact that it was, at the relevant time, under the control of a single leader, Maina Njenga. For this reason, the Chamber does not find the Defence challenge conclusive.

207. In the view of the Chamber, the evidence further demonstrates the existence, at the relevant time, of an effective system of ensuring compliance by the members of the Mungiki with the rules of the organization.

208. One such mechanism was the Mungiki oath, which is described in detail by those witnesses who are (former) Mungiki members. In this respect, Witness OTP-4 states, referring to his own experience of being forcefully recruited into the Mungiki, that the content of the oath was to "abide by the rules of the Kikuyu organization," and never to "betray the Kikuyu community." The witness states that he was told that he would be killed if he did not respect the oath.

209. Witness OTP-9, who voluntarily took the Mungiki oath, refers to it as a promise of secrecy. Witness OTP-10 also confirms having taken the Mungiki oath. Witness OTP-11 describes the Mungiki oath as

"degrading" and its purpose as being to "instill fear" in the new members, further confirming that a pledge of secrecy forms part of this oath. Witness OTP-12 also confirms that oathing rituals were used by the Mungiki. Further corroboration is provided by Mungiki members interviewed by the Defence teams. (D12-37) states that he underwent a "cleansing process" in order to become a member of the Mungiki. (D12-48) in turn refers to being "baptized" to join the Mungiki.

210. More generally on the matter of discipline within the Mungiki, Witness OTP-4 states:

> The Mungiki do not tolerate dissidence. People who disobeyed the Mungiki and the Chairman would disappear. [. . .] It is even worse for members. If a member disobeys, they would cut that member's head off and put the head in public view at the place where they had a problem with that member.

211. Similarly, Witness OTP-12 states that not to follow orders was "a crime in the movement."

212. The Chamber is also informed by the evidence of Witnesses OTP-9 and OTP-10, who provide independent testimony about their own hesitation to leave the Mungiki, for fear of punishment by death. Witnesses OTP-11 and OTP-12 confirm that in the Mungiki defectors were killed.

213. In addition, the witnesses relied upon by the Prosecutor provide extensive evidence describing a quasi-judicial system of enforcement of Mungiki rules. Witness OTP-4 explains that "before a person is killed, he is taken before the Mungiki judicial system, where the Chairman is the judge." Witness OTP-11 provides similar testimony in relation to Mungiki courts, stating that the judges in these courts (also referred to as *mzebu/wazebu*) had their "own policemen who can come and arrest you" and even "their own cells where you will be put." Finally, Witness OTP-12 also refers to what he calls "kangaroo courts" operated by the Mungiki, while also describing the sanctions applied, including the death penalty.

214. Furthermore, the Chamber finds relevant the evidence which establishes that the Mungiki organization possessed, at the relevant time, quasi-military capabilities.

215. Witness OTP-4 refers to the existence of "radical members," or "militants," who were "the ones that kill" and "the ones who control people in the slums." They were at the centre of Mungiki operations and carried out the violence and killings. According to the witness, Maina Diambo had control over the militants. Witness OTP-9 corroborates the existence of a special class of Mungiki members, who were used for killings and received training in martial arts, self-defence and shooting. Witness OTP-11 explains that within the Mungiki, there was a "military group." Furthermore, the witness states that there was a weapons management system and certain members were given training in the use

of these weapons. Additionally, Witness OTP-12 refers to the existence of a military wing within the Mungiki. According to the witness, its members received special training in military skills, marching, martial arts and the handling of guns.

216. Moreover, the Chamber is cognizant of the evidence of Mungiki activities as approximating those of a public authority in certain slums in Nairobi as well as in Central Province.

217. In this respect, the Chamber refers first to the above discussion of the evidence in relation to a system of courts operated by the Mungiki and notes that the evidence establishes that this system was applied not only to members of the organization but to the general population of slum areas where the Mungiki was present.

218. Furthermore, Witness OTP-4 explains that the Mungiki provided basic services in the slums, such as security, electricity, water and public toilets. Witness OTP-11 independently provides identical information to the effect that the Mungiki provided security, water and electricity in certain slum areas. Witness OTP-12 similarly states that in the slums, the Mungiki kept security in exchange for small payments, agreed with or imposed on the local population.

219. The evidence also shows that the Mungiki granted protection from competing cartels to *matatu* (minibus) drivers, and imposed fees in exchange. * * * Witness OTP-10 stated more generally that in Nairobi, the Mungiki generated income from taxation of local businesses.

220. The Defence of Mr. Kenyatta maintains that the Mungiki have sought to alleviate crime in Nairobi slums and invested in social programmes and campaigned against "drunkenness, rent hikes, drug use, prostitution." On this basis, the Defence argues that the Mungiki do not have criminal activities against the civilian population as a primary purpose, and that, therefore, they do not qualify as an organization under article 7(2)(a) of the Statute. The Chamber does not accept this argument. First, it is predicated on an improper interpretation of the Chamber's previous articulation of the considerations which may guide the determination of whether a given organization meets the requirements of article 7(2)(a) of the Statute. The Chamber has emphasized that "while these considerations may assist the Chamber in its determination, they do not constitute a rigid legal definition, and do not need to be exhaustively fulfilled." Second, the evidence indicates clearly that Mungiki activities must generally be seen as criminal, because they involve acts of violence and extortion of the population in areas of Mungiki activity. In fact, such is also the submission of the Defence of Mr. Kenyatta.

221. A similar conclusion must be reached with respect to the Defence argument that the Mungiki does not exercise control over part of the territory of a State. The Defence of Mr. Kenyatta argues that Mungiki activities "remain limited in nature and are territorially

restricted, in particular to the slums of Nairobi." More specifically, the Defence of Mr. Kenyatta asserts that such activities are to be qualified as "criminal extortion and cannot be considered evidence of the entity having *de facto* control over the territory so as to be endowed with a capability to provide an organizational policy." The Chamber observes that it is nowhere alleged by the Prosecutor that the Mungiki exercise control over part of the Kenyan territory. Indeed, in the 31 March 2010 Decision, the Chamber clarified that, whilst territorial control is among the various factors that may guide its determination as to the existence of "organization," it is not a rigid legal criterion. For this reason, the Chamber is not persuaded by the argument of the Defence teams of Mr. Kenyatta and Mr. Ali.

222. Further, the Chamber notes the Defence of Mr. Kenyatta's assertion that "the Mungiki did not have the means at its disposal to commit a large-scale attack directed against the civilian population" as demonstrated by the Prosecutor's allegation that the group relied on external funds and logistics. In this respect, the Defence of Mr. Kenyatta, in its final written observations, refers to the live testimony of Lewis Nguyai (D13-26), who stated that he had been regularly asked for small amounts of money by two Mungiki members. However, in view of the above analysis of the evidence and the determination that the Mungiki is a large, hierarchically structured organization with a trained military wing, and with access to regular income, the Chamber does not consider the issues of whether the Mungiki relied on external funding in the commission of the particular crimes alleged in this case, or whether two members of the Mungiki individually requested financial assistance of Lewis Nguyai, to be relevant to the determination of whether the Mungiki qualifies as an organization under article 7(2)(a) of the Statute.

223. Finally, the Chamber recalls that the Defence of Mr. Kenyatta seeks to challenge the qualification of the Mungiki as an organization under article 7(2)(a) of the Statute by asserting that no link exists between Mr. Kenyatta and the Mungiki. The Chamber however recalls that, for the purposes of the determination of contextual elements of crimes against humanity, the attack within the meaning of article 7(2)(a) of the Statute need not, as a matter of law, be attributed to the person charged, neither does the person charged need to be the leader, or even a member, of the organization within the meaning of the same provision. This follows from the language of article 7(1) of the Statute, which refers to "knowledge of the attack" as a legal requirement of crimes against humanity, thereby making clear that examination of any tighter link between the person charged and the organization bearing the policy to commit a widespread or systematic attack is unnecessary. Therefore, the Chamber shall not further address this particular aspect of the Defence objections to the charges. * * *

227. The above analysis of the evidence provides substantial grounds to believe that the Mungiki carried out a planned and

coordinated attack against perceived ODM supporters in or around Nakuru and Naivasha between 24 and 28 January 2008, which involved the commission of a number of crimes perpetrated on a large scale.

228. The Chamber further finds that there are substantial grounds to believe that the Mungiki qualified at the relevant time as an "organization" within the meaning of article 7(2)(a) of the Statute. This is established by sufficient evidence supporting that: (i) the Mungiki was a hierarchically structured organization; (ii) there existed an effective system of ensuring compliance by the members with the rules and orders imposed by higher levels of command; (iii) the Mungiki was a large organization and included a trained quasi-military wing; and (iv) it controlled and provided, in certain parts of Kenya, essential social services, including security.

229. In light of the above the Chamber is therefore satisfied that there are substantial grounds to believe that the events in or around Nakuru and Naivasha between 24 and 28 January 2008 constitute an attack within the meaning of article 7(2)(a) of the Statute, since they qualify as a course of conduct involving the multiple commission of acts referred to in article 7(1) of the Statute against a civilian population, pursuant to an organizational policy to commit such attack. Furthermore, the Chamber finds that there are substantial grounds to believe that this attack was widespread and systematic.

Dissenting Opinion by Judge Hans-Peter Kaul

2. I am unable to accept this decision of the Majority and the analysis that underpins it. I continue to believe—and after having heard the arguments of all parties and participants at the hearing I am even more firmly convinced—that the International Criminal Court lacks jurisdiction *ratione materiae* in the situation in the Republic of Kenya, including in the present case. Contrary to the Majority's findings, I am not satisfied that the crimes allegedly committed by Mr. Muthaura and Mr. Kenyatta occurred pursuant to or in furtherance of a policy of an *organization* within the meaning of article 7(2)(a) of the Rome Statute. Thus, I am not satisfied that the crimes charged constitute crimes against humanity as set out in article 7 of the Statute. * * *

7. My fundamental disagreement with the Majority stems from the differing interpretation of the notion of 'organization' within the meaning of article 7(2)(a) of the Statute. It is worth recalling that under the Statute crimes alleged to be part of an attack against any civilian population must be committed pursuant to the policy of a State or 'organization." In my 31 March 2010 dissenting opinion on the Majority's "Decision Pursuant to Article 15 of the Rome Statute on the Authorization of an Investigation into the Situation in the Republic of Kenya," I set out in appropriate detail my understanding of the applicable law governing this constitutive contextual requirement. Lacking any definition in the Statute, I was duty-bound to give meaning and clarity to the indeterminate legal term "organizational policy"

through *lege artis* ["the law of the art"] interpretation in conformity with article 31 of the Vienna Convention on the Law of Treaties. The relevant parts of my interpretation of this specific statutory legal requirement are briefly rehearsed below:

> 51. I read the provision such that the juxtaposition of the notions 'State' and 'organization' in article 7(2)(a) of the Statute are an indication that even though the constitutive elements of statehood need not be established those 'organizations' should partake of some characteristics of a State. Those characteristics eventually turn the private 'organization' into an entity which may act like a State or has quasi-State abilities. These characteristics could involve the following: (a) a collectivity of persons; (b) which was established and acts for a common purpose; (c) over a prolonged period of time; (d) which is under responsible command or adopted a certain degree of hierarchical structure, including, as a minimum, some kind of policy level; (e) with the capacity to impose the policy on its members and to sanction them; and (f) which has the capacity and means available to attack any civilian population on a large scale.
>
> 52. In contrast, I believe that non-state actors which do not reach the level described above are not able to carry out a policy of this nature, such as groups of organized crime, a mob, groups of (armed) civilians or criminal gangs. They would generally fall outside the scope of article 7(2)(a) of the Statute. To give a concrete example, violence-prone groups of persons formed on an *ad hoc* basis, randomly, spontaneously, for a passing occasion, with fluctuating membership and without a structure and level to set up a policy are not within the ambit of the Statute, even if they engage in numerous serious and organized crimes. Further elements are needed for a private entity to reach the level of an 'organization' within the meaning of article 7 of the Statute. For it is not the cruelty or mass victimization that turns a crime into a *delictum iuris gentium* but the constitutive contextual elements in which the act is embedded.
>
> 53. In this respect, the general argument that any kind of non-state actors may be qualified as an 'organization' within the meaning of article 7(2)(a) of the Statute on the grounds that it "has the capability to perform acts which infringe on basic human values" without any further specification seems unconvincing to me. In fact, this approach may expand the concept of crimes against humanity to any infringement of human rights. I am convinced that a distinction must be upheld between human rights violations on the one side and international crimes on the other side, the latter forming the nucleus of the most heinous violations of human rights

representing the most serious crimes of concern to the international community as a whole.

14. The Majority argues that the Mungiki fulfill all the requirements of an 'organization' on the grounds that (1) they are a hierarchically structured organisation under the exclusive control of Maina Njenga with defined roles for members at different levels; (2) there exists an effective system of ensuring compliance by the members of the Mungiki with the rules of the organisation, such as taking an oath and sanctions; (3) the organisation has "quasi-military capabilities"; and (4) "Mungiki activities [approximate] those of a public authority in certain slums of Nairobi as well as in Central Province."

15. I must differ. I am still unable to see, how the Mungiki can qualify overall as an 'organization' within the meaning of article 7(2)(a) of the Statute. As I previously held in my 15 March 2011 Dissenting Opinion:

> 32. Even if, for the sake of argument, and taking into consideration the Majority's finding to that effect, the Mungiki gang alone were to be considered as the entity which had established a policy of attacking the civilian population, I hold that the Mungiki gang *as such* does not qualify as an 'organisation' within the meaning of article 7(2)(a) of the Statute. Admittedly, the Mungiki gang appears to control core community activities and to provide services, such as electricity, water and sanitation, and transport. However, the activities of the Mungiki gang remain limited in nature and are territorially restricted, in particular, to the slums of Nairobi. Moreover, as noted above, the evidence reveals that a series of police operations were directed against the Mungiki gang before and after the 2007/2008 violence and that it could only have committed the crimes alleged with the support of certain individuals within the Kenyan political elite and the police apparatus. That said, I doubt whether the Mungiki gang had the capacity and the means at its disposal to attack any civilian population on a large scale. In light of the foregoing, I therefore do not find that the Mungiki gang, a criminal organisation, could have qualified as a 'organisation' within the meaning of article 7(2)(a) of the Statute.

16. At the hearing, no sufficiently compelling new argument, fact or piece of evidence was presented for me to reconsider my previous assessment of the facts in this case. Even had I followed the Majority's factual findings on the Mungiki, I simply cannot conclude that the Mungiki reach the level of a State-like 'organization' within the meaning of article 7(2)(a) of the Statute. I remain convinced that the Mungiki, a violent and organised criminal gang operating mainly in the slums of Nairobi, primarily engage in illegal economic activities and organised crime just like any other well-known criminal organisation in other

countries. The provision of illegal electricity connections, sanitation and protection in certain slums, however, does not place them on a par with a State which provides a broad range of services to its population. Furthermore, so-called "Mungiki courts" cannot be equated in any way with a State's judicial apparatus, which covers all aspects of litigation for the entire population. Moreover, the Mungiki are normally subjected to severe crackdowns by the Kenyan Police. Regardless of questions as to their legality, these are police operations as conducted against any criminal gang. In this context, the Mungiki arguably required the extra-judicial killings and arrests to cease in order to be able to operate outside their very limited sphere of influence (mainly the slums of Nairobi). This is a further clear indication that their capacity to act is far more limited than that of a State. Consequently, all of the above considerations militate against the assumption that the Mungiki are a State-like 'organization.'

17. During the Hearing, I noted another aspect of the Prosecutor's presentation of the facts. According to the Prosecutor, the Mungiki apparently required substantial assistance from others in order to commit the crimes in Naivasha and Nakuru town: they purportedly received funding, uniforms and weapons, and had to be transported to different parts of the country. According to the Prosecutor, the Mungiki benefited from a "free zone," allegedly facilitated by the Kenyan Police, for the purposes of the attack, which was vital—almost a *conditio sine qua non*—for the success of their operations. In this connection, it is noteworthy that the Mungiki apparently successfully negotiated a temporary end to extra-judicial killings of Mungiki members by Government forces in order to perform their activities unhindered.

18. The foregoing leads me to conclude that had the Kenyan Police allegedly not abstained, had the Mungiki not received money, uniforms and weapons, and had they not been transported to different parts of the country, they would not have been able to launch the alleged large-scale attack against Kenyan civilians over a large geographical area. Even if, *arguendo,* the Mungiki "relied on external funding in the commission of particular crimes," their need for financial support, regardless of its extent, shows that they do not have sufficient means to commit crimes on a large scale. Therefore, I am at pains to understand how this 'organization', heavily dependent on outside logistical support, could satisfy the criteria I set out in my 31 March 2010 Dissenting Opinion to the extent of qualifying as a State-like 'organization' or any other 'organization' *with the capability, including the means*, to target the civilian population on a large scale. More importantly, in light of the Majority's finding excluding the Kenyan Police from the 'organization,' I have serious doubts whether, having been deprived of the second pillar in the 'organization' structure, the Mungiki could have launched on their own a widespread or systematic attack against civilians, as the Prosecutor maintains. If this indispensable and quintessential element

of the 'organization' structure is excluded, I remain doubtful whether this case, thus amputated, can be argued and sustained at all.

19. I therefore reaffirm my previous finding that the Mungiki, like many other criminal gangs in Kenya or elsewhere, remain a somewhat structured, outlawed, violent criminal gang engaged in organised crime and deriving revenues from the illegal provision of certain community services to the local population, mainly in the slums of Nairobi. In light of the foregoing, I take the view that the Mungiki cannot qualify as an 'organization' within the meaning of article 7(2)(a) of the Statute. Accordingly, they fall outside the scope of the Statute.

20. In conclusion, I am not satisfied to the 'degree of certainty' that the crimes were committed pursuant to the policy of a State-like 'organisation,' which is an indispensable constitutive contextual element and inherent characteristic of crimes against humanity under article 7 of the Statute. Without the crimes alleged having been embedded in an "organizational policy", I maintain that the Court has no jurisdiction *ratione materiae* over the situation in the Republic of Kenya, including in the present case.

21. Finally, apart from my disagreement on fundamental issues of law, I wish to add some more thoughts to the Majority's finding in relation to the Mungiki gang. I underline my deep concern with regard to the fact that the Majority has set an unfortunate precedent in accepting, with far-reaching consequences, the activities of a mafia-like criminal gang to fall under the ambit of article 7(2)(a) of the Statute. Since criminal gangs, with the capability to perform acts which infringe on basic human values, operate not only in the Republic of Kenya but in most parts of the world, all their activities would, according to the Majority, fall under the Court's jurisdiction *ratione materiae.* Is this what the drafters of the Rome Statute intended? And what may be the consequences of this unfortunate precedent, if maintained, for the future work of the International Criminal Court? As I have explained my carefully considered approach as far back as on 31 March 2010:

> (. . .) It is neither appropriate nor possible to examine and explain in this opinion all the potential negative implications and risks of a gradual downscaling of crimes against humanity towards serious ordinary crimes. As a Judge of the ICC, I feel, however, duty-bound to point at least to the following: such an approach might infringe on State sovereignty and the action of national courts for crimes which should not be within the ambit of the Statute. It would broaden the scope of possible ICC intervention almost indefinitely. This might turn the ICC, which is fully dependent on State cooperation, in a hopelessly overstretched, inefficient international court, with related risks for its standing and credibility. Taken into consideration the limited financial and material means of the institution, it might be unable to tackle all the situations which could fall under its

jurisdiction with the consequence that the selection of the situations under actual investigation might be quite arbitrary to the dismay of the numerous victims in the situations disregarded by the Court who would be deprived of any access to justice without any convincing justification.

NOTES & QUESTIONS

1. Case Outcome and Update

The Chamber confirmed a number of crimes against humanity charges against the accused (murder, deportation or forcible transfer of population, rape, other inhumane acts, and persecution). The Defense in both cases appealed the decision confirming the charges, relying heavily on the arguments in Judge Kaul's dissent concerning the organization requirement. The Appeals Chamber affirmed the confirmation of charges in both cases for all four suspects. *See Prosecutor v. Francis Kirimi Muthaura and Uhuru Muigai Kenyatta*, Case No. ICC–01/09–02/11 OA 4, Decision on the Appeal of Mr. Francis Kirimi Muthaura and Mr. Uhuru Muigai Kenyatta against the Decision of Pre-Trial Chamber II of 23 January 2012 entitled 'Decision on the Confirmation of Charges Pursuant to Article 61(7)(a) and (b) of the Rome Statute' (May 24, 2012). Eventually, the Kenya cases all collapsed. But before that happened, they produced a record number of filings and decisions. This was not only because the suspects vigorously defended themselves before the Court, but also because other interested parties—including victims, Kenyan and international civil society groups, and the Government of Kenya—filed multiple motions before the Court. The Government of Kenya, for example, submitted numerous filings, many of which (including twenty-two annexes of over 900 pages) challenged the admissibility of the cases, unsuccessfully as it turned out.

The Prosecutor withdrew a number of the charges voluntarily, arguing that the evidence available did not provide a reasonable prospect of securing proof of his guilty beyond a reasonable doubt. *See* Statement of the Prosecutor of the International Criminal Court, Fatou Bensouda, on the Notice to withdraw charges against Mr. Muthaura (Mar. 11, 2013). In her statement, the Prosecutor complained that the Kenyan government had not lived up to its public pledges to cooperate with the Court in the investigation and described the scale of witness intimidation as "unprecedented." She also noted that important witnesses in the case had been killed, had died, or had refused to speak with the Prosecution. Another key witness (so-called Witness 4) had recanted part of his incriminating evidence and admitted to accepting money to withdraw his testimony. Witness 4 had produced an affidavit in connection with an asylum application that suggested he had not actually attended a key meeting at which Prosecutors allege that violence was being organized; this affidavit was not provided to the Defense.

The Defense took the opportunity to criticize the prosecution for withholding exculpatory evidence and proceeding on weak inculpatory evidence:

> This development this morning is presented to you in a way of responsible prosecution. It is anything but responsible prosecution that has gone on in this case. Let's face the fact, this Confirmation of Charges hearing was determined upon false evidence, evidence that was concealed from the Defence, and the facts underlying the charges have been put utterly and fully in doubt. Let us consider the matter now. The Kenyatta case has been put into this Court on a series of allegations and charges that at the time we said were fundamentally flawed. We were in this courtroom for three weeks telling the Pre-Trial Chamber about that matter. We were ignored. We were overridden. The Prosecution have now conceded, in relation to one accused, the withdrawal of charges. * * * [T]he practices that have gone on in relation to the Confirmation of Charges hearing have been utterly shameful and the conduct thereafter. * * * [T]he Prosecution know exactly the fate of their case. It's attempted to be dressed up in front of you in relation to other issues, but they are a mere smokescreen.

This marked the first, though not the last, time that the Prosecution withdrew charges against a suspect. The Prosecution subsequently withdrew the charges against Kenyatta, also for lack of sufficient evidence. The cases against the other remaining Kenyan suspects, Deputy President William Ruto and the radio announcer Joshua arap Sang, were vacated by a two-to-one vote of the Trial Chamber without prejudice with respect to possible future proceedings. While the Prosecutor could reopen each of these three cases—against Uhuru Kenyatta, William Ruto, and Joshua arap Sang—if sufficient evidence were discovered to support the indictments, there is no indication that the Prosecution will be requesting to open these cases in the near future.

2. Interpretation of the Organizational Policy Requirement

Judge Kaul, who passed away in 2014, sets out in his dissent his definition of "organization" for the purposes of satisfying the requirement of an "organizational policy" in Article 7(2)(a). How would you distinguish between the majority's approach and that of Judge Kaul? Given Judge Kaul's interpretation of "organizational policy," what elements are missing in the case of the Mungiki? How does the approach of the ICC compare with that of the ICTY as set out above in the *Kupreškić* case? For a thoughtful critique of the dissent's approach to the organizational policy requirement, *see* Leila Nadya Sadat, *Crimes Against Humanity in the Modern Age*, 107 AM. J. INT'L L. 334 (2013).

The more recent articulation of the organization and policy requirements under Article 7 is provided by Pre-Trial Chamber I in confirming charges of crimes against humanity against the former President of Côte d'Ivoire, Laurent Gbagbo (who was ultimately acquitted at trial). In that decision the Chamber opined as follows:

> 214. As clarified by the Elements of Crimes, the "policy", for the purposes of the Statute, must be understood as the active promotion or encouragement of an attack against a civilian

population by a State or organisation. The Chamber observes that neither the Statute nor the Elements of Crimes include a certain rationale or motivations of the policy as a requirement of the definition. Establishing the underlying motive may, however, be useful for the detection of common features and links between acts. Furthermore, in accordance with the Statute and the Elements of Crimes, it is only necessary to establish that the person had knowledge of the attack in general terms. Indeed, the Elements of Crimes clarify that the requirement of knowledge "should not be interpreted as requiring proof that the perpetrator had knowledge of all characteristics of the attack or the precise details of the plan or policy of the State or organization."

215. The Chamber also observes that in accordance with the established jurisprudence of the Court, an attack which is planned, directed or organized—as opposed to spontaneous or isolated acts of violence—will satisfy the policy criterion, and that there is no requirement that the policy be formally adopted.

216. Furthermore, the Chamber is of the view, consistent with the jurisprudence of the Court, that the concept of "policy" and that of the "systematic" nature of the attack under article 7(1) of the Statute both refer to a certain level of planning of the attack. In this sense, evidence of planning, organisation or direction by a State or organisation may be relevant to prove both the policy and the systematic nature of the attack, although the two concepts should not be conflated as they serve different purposes and imply different thresholds under article 7(1) and (2)(a) of the Statute.

217. Finally, in accordance with article 7(2)(a) of the Statute, the policy to carry out the attack against the civilian population must be attributed to a State or an organisation. With respect to the latter, Chambers of the Court have consistently held that the policy may be linked to groups that govern a specific territory or to an organisation that has the capability to commit a widespread or systematic attack against the civilian population. A view has also been expressed that the organisation within the meaning of article 7(2)(a) of the Statute must partake of some characteristics of a State, which "eventually turn the private 'organization' into an entity which may act like a State or has quasi-State abilities." In the present case, the Chamber is of the view that the organisation alleged by the Prosecutor and satisfactorily established by the available evidence would meet the threshold under either interpretation and that, accordingly, it is unnecessary for the Chamber to dwell any further on this point. In any case, the Chamber considers that, regardless of the interpretation of the notion of organisation, it is important that, as part of the analysis of the facts before it, the Chamber is able to understand how the organisation operates (for instance in terms of whether a chain of command or certain internal reporting lines exist) in order to

determine whether the policy to carry out the attack is attributable to the organisation.

Prosecutor v. Laurent Gbagbo, Case No. ICC–02/11–01/11, Decision on the Confirmation of Charges against Laurent Gbagbo (Public Redacted) (June 12, 2014). Judge Christine Van den Wyngaert issued a dissent, arguing that the evidence was insufficient to show Laurent Gbagbo's individual criminal responsibility for the crimes alleged. Her dissent did not take issue with the approach of the majority concerning the interpretation of organization and policy under Article 7.

In his dissent, Judge Kaul also warned of the far-reaching negative implications of the Majority's finding that acts committed by organizations like the Mungiki may fall within the jurisdiction of the Court. Do you think Judge Kaul's concerns are well-founded? The Kenyan post-election violence that is the subject of the ICC cases left over 1,100 dead; tens of thousands were assaulted and raped, and it is estimated that over 300,000 individuals were displaced. As of this writing, some of the displaced are still living in make-shift camps, including some as refugees in Uganda. Despite the Kenyan government's promise to investigate and prosecute vigorously those responsible for the violence, there has been no significant prosecutions, much less convictions, related to the post-election violence.

Since the confirmation of charges in the Kenya cases, the Court has taken up a number of additional situations, including Côte d'Ivoire (*proprio motu*); Libya (Security Council referral); and Mali and Central African Republic II (self-referrals). Do these situations support Judge Kaul's concern of an overly expansive interpretation of the Court's jurisdiction?

3. Targeted Population

The Chamber identifies the targeted population as "perceived ODM supporters" (para. 142) and that "the identification of the targeted population was essentially on political grounds." (para. 144) Why does it matter that the population was targeted on political grounds? Does this suggest that a discriminatory purpose or intent is required for crimes against humanity? Recall that the drafters of the ICTR Statute expressly included such a requirement in the applicable definition of crimes against humanity, a formulation that was not followed in drafting the definition found in the ICC Statute. Why then does the Chamber require that those targeted be perceived as sharing a common political identity? The ICC affirmed this approach by identifying "perceived Ouattara supporters" as the population targeted by crimes against humanity committed in Côte d'Ivoire. *Prosecutor v. Laurent Gbagbo*, Case No. ICC–02/11–01/11, Decision on the Confirmation of Charges against Laurent Gbagbo (Public Redacted), para. 211 (June 12, 2014).

III. CONSTITUTIVE ACTS

A. SEXUAL VIOLENCE

Control Council Law No. 10 (governing post-Nuremberg prosecutions), the statutes of all the *ad hoc* tribunals, and the ICC

Statute designate rape as a crime against humanity. Article 12 of the Law of the Iraqi Higher Criminal Court and Article 2 of the Statute for the Special Court for Sierra Leone also allow "sexual slavery, enforced prostitution, forced pregnancy and any other form of sexual violence as crimes against humanity" to be charged. To this list, Section 5 of the regulation that governed prosecutions before the East Timor Special Panels added enforced sterilization. *See* U.N. Transitional Administration in East Timor, Regulation No. 2000/15 on the Establishment of Panels with Exclusive Jurisdiction Over Serious Criminal Offences, U.N. Doc. No. UNTAET/REG/2000/15 (June 6, 2000). Under the authority of these provisions, the international tribunals have issued a number of important rulings recognizing the existence of multiple crimes of gender violence.*

Below is an excerpt from one such opinion emanating from the Appeals Chamber of the Special Court for Sierra Leone (SCSL). The case involved senior members of the Armed Forces Revolutionary Council (AFRC), a military *junta* aligned with the Revolutionary United Front (RUF) rebels that briefly controlled the country after the Sierra Leonean Army (SLA) overthrew the government of President Ahmad Tejan Kabbah in 1997. (A military intervention by the Economic Community of West African States (ECOWAS) led to President Kabbah's reinstatement as President, a position he held until 2007. See the Appendix for a map of Sierra Leone.)

The original Indictment alleged various crimes against humanity and war crimes, including rape, sexual slavery, enslavement, outrages upon personal dignity, and other forms of sexual violence. In 2004, the Prosecution added Count 8 to the Indictment, alleging the commission of the crime against humanity of "forced marriage" pursuant to Article 2(i), the residual clause prohibiting "other inhumane acts." *See Prosecutor v. Brima et al.*, Case No. SCSL–2004–16–PT, Decision on Prosecution Request for Leave to Amend the Indictment (May 6, 2004); *Prosecutor v. Brima et al.* Case No. SCSL–16–PT, Amended Consolidated Indictment (May 13, 2004). The Prosecutor defined "forced marriage" as consisting of

> words or other conduct intended to confer a status of marriage by force or threat of force or coercion, such as that caused by fear of violence, duress, detention, psychological oppression or abuse of power against the victim, or by taking advantage of a coercive environment, with the intention of conferring the status of marriage.

In its judgment, the Trial Chamber struck the count concerning sexual slavery on technical grounds (the count alleged two separate

* This text will generally employ the term "gender violence" to refer to violence committed on the basis of a person's sex or gender. Although much gender violence is sexual violence, the latter term excludes acts of persecution that are not sexual in nature but that are still based upon sex or gender discrimination.

crimes at once, violating the one count/one crime pleading rule) and struck the count concerning forced marriage as duplicative of other counts in the indictment. *See Prosecutor v. Brima et al.*, Case No. SCSL–04–16–T, Judgement (June 20, 1997) ("*Brima* Trial Judgement"). The Trial Chamber ruled that as a matter of statutory construction, the residual clause "other inhumane acts" must be interpreted "as applying only to acts of a non-sexual nature amounting to an affront to human dignity." *Id.* at para. 697. Taking the evidence as a whole, the Trial Chamber ruled that the evidence adduced by the Prosecution did not establish the elements of a non-sexual crime of forced marriage independent of the crime of sexual slavery. *Id.* at paras. 704–714. The Prosecutor appealed these rulings. The Seventh Ground of the Prosecution's Appeal challenged the Trial Chamber's dismissal of Count 8 concerning forced marriage as an "other inhumane act." The decision of the Appeals Chamber follows.

Prosecutor v. Brima, Kamara & Kanu, Case No. SCSL–2004–16–A, Judgement (Feb. 22, 2008)

In the Appeals Chamber

182. The first issue for the Appeals Chamber's determination relates to the scope of "Other Inhumane Acts" under Article 2.i of the Statute. The Trial Chamber concluded that in light of the exhaustive categorisation of sexual crimes under Article 2.g, the offence of "Other Inhumane Acts" must be restrictively interpreted so as to exclude offences of a sexual nature. The Appeals Chamber considers that it is implicit in the Trial Chamber's finding that it considered forced marriage as a sexual crime.

183. In order to assess the correctness of the Trial Chamber's finding, regard must be given to the objective of the prohibition of "Other Inhumane Acts" in international criminal law. First introduced under Article 6.c of the Nuremberg Charter, the crime of "Other Inhumane Acts" is intended to be a residual provision so as to punish criminal acts not specifically recognised as crimes against humanity, but which, in context, are of a comparable gravity to the listed crimes against humanity. It is therefore inclusive in nature, intended to avoid unduly restricting the Statute's application to crimes against humanity. The prohibition against "Other Inhumane Acts" is now included in a large number of international legal instruments and forms part of customary international law.

184. The jurisprudence of the international tribunals shows that a wide range of criminal acts, including sexual crimes, have been recognised as "Other Inhumane Acts." These include forcible transfer, sexual and physical violence perpetrated upon dead human bodies, other serious physical and mental injury, forced undressing of women and marching them in public, forcing women to perform exercises naked, and

forced disappearance, beatings, torture, sexual violence, humiliation, harassment, psychological abuse, and confinement in inhumane conditions. Case law at these tribunals further demonstrates that this category has been used to punish a series of violent acts that may vary depending upon the context. In effect, the determination of whether an alleged act qualifies as an "Other Inhumane Act" must be made on a case-by-case basis taking into account the nature of the alleged act or omission, the context in which it took place, the personal circumstances of the victims including age, sex, health, and the physical, mental and moral effects of the perpetrator's conduct upon the victims.

185. The Trial Chamber therefore erred in law by finding that "Other Inhumane Acts" under Article 2.i must be restrictively interpreted. A tribunal must take care not to adopt too restrictive an interpretation of the prohibition against "Other Inhumane Acts" which, as stated above, was intended to be a residual provision. At the same time, care must be taken not to make it too embracing as to make a surplusage of what has been expressly provided for, or to render the crime nebulous and incapable of concrete ascertainment. An over-broad interpretation will certainly infringe the rule requiring specificity of criminal prohibitions.

186. Furthermore, the Appeals Chamber sees no reason why the so-called "exhaustive" listing of sexual crimes under Article 2.g of the Statute should foreclose the possibility of charging as "Other Inhumane Acts" crimes which may among others have a sexual or gender component. As an ICTY Trial Chamber has recognised, "[h]owever much care [was] taken in establishing a list of all the various forms of infliction, one would never be able to catch up with the imagination of future torturers who wish to satisfy their bestial instincts; and the more specific and complete a list tries to be, the more restrictive it becomes."[285] The Trial Chamber therefore erred in finding that Article 2.i of the Statute excludes sexual crimes.

The Nature of "Forced Marriage" in the Sierra Leone Conflict and Its Distinction from Sexual Slavery

187. The Appeals Chamber recalls the Trial Chamber's findings that the evidence adduced by the Prosecution did not establish the elements of a non-sexual offence of forced marriage independent of the crime of sexual slavery under Article 2.g of the Statute; and that the evidence is completely of the crime of sexual slavery, leaving no lacuna in the law that would necessitate a separate crime of forced marriage as an "Other Inhumane Act."[287]

---

[285] [*Prosecutor v. Blaškić*, Case No. IT–95–14–T, Judgement, para. 237 (Mar. 3, 2000), citing with approval J. Pictet, COMMENTARY ON THE 1ST GENEVA CONVENTION OF 12 AUGUST 1949 54 (1952).]

[287] The Trial Chamber held that sexual slavery had the following elements: (i) The perpetrator exercised any or all of the powers attaching to the right of ownership over one or more persons, . . . or by imposing on them a similar deprivation of liberty; (ii) the perpetrator caused such person or persons to engage in one or more acts of a sexual nature; (iii) the

188. The Trial Chamber defined sexual slavery as the perpetrator's exercising any or all of the powers attaching to the right of ownership over one or more persons by imposing on them a deprivation of liberty, and causing them to engage in one or more acts of a sexual nature. In finding that the evidence of forced marriage was completely of the crime of sexual slavery, the Trial Chamber found that the relationship of the perpetrators to their "wives" was one of ownership, and that the use of the term "wife" was indicative of the perpetrator's intent to exercise ownership rights over the victim. Implicitly, the Trial Chamber found that evidence of forced marriage was predominantly sexual in nature.

189. According to the Prosecution, the element that distinguishes forced marriage from other forms of sexual crimes is a "forced conjugal association by the perpetrator over the victim. It represents forcing a person into the appearance, the veneer of a conduct (i.e. marriage), by threat, physical assault or other coercion." The Prosecution adds that while acts of forced marriage may in certain circumstances amount to sexual slavery, in practice they do not always involve the victim being subjected to non-consensual sex or even forced domestic labour. Therefore, the Prosecution contends that forced marriage is not a sexual crime.

190. The trial record contains ample evidence that the perpetrators of forced marriage intended to impose a forced conjugal association upon the victims rather than exercise an ownership interest and that forced marriage is not predominantly a sexual crime. There is substantial evidence in the Trial Judgement to establish that throughout the conflict in Sierra Leone, women and girls were systematically abducted from their homes and communities by troops belonging to the AFRC and compelled to serve as conjugal partners to AFRC soldiers. They were often abducted in circumstances of extreme violence, compelled to move along with the fighting forces from place to place, and coerced to perform a variety of conjugal duties including regular sexual intercourse, forced domestic labour such as cleaning and cooking for the "husband," endure forced pregnancy, and to care for and bring up children of the "marriage." In return, the rebel "husband" was expected to provide food, clothing and protection to his "wife," including protection from rape by other men, acts he did not perform when he used a female for sexual purposes only. As the Trial Chamber found, the relative benefits that victims of forced marriage received from the perpetrators neither signifies consent to the forced conjugal association, nor does it vitiate the criminal nature of the perpetrator's conduct given the environment of violence and coercion in which these events took place.

perpetrator committed such conduct intending to engage in the act of sexual slavery or in the reasonable knowledge that it was likely to occur. *Prosecutor v. Brima*, Case No. SCSL–2004–16–T, Judgement, para. 708 (June 20, 2007). *See also* Rome Statute, Elements of Crimes, Article 7(1)(k).

191. The Trial Chamber findings also demonstrate that these forced conjugal associations were often organised and supervised by members of the AFRC or civilians assigned by them to such tasks. A "wife" was exclusive to a rebel "husband," and any transgression of this exclusivity such as unfaithfulness, was severely punished. A "wife" who did not perform the conjugal duties demanded of her was deemed disloyal and could face serious punishment under the AFRC disciplinary system, including beating and possibly death.

192. In addition to the Trial Chamber's findings, other evidence in the trial record shows that the perpetrators intended to impose a forced conjugal association rather than exercise mere ownership over civilian women and girls. In particular, the Appeals Chamber notes the evidence and report of the Prosecution expert Ms. Zainab Bangura which demonstrates the physical and psychological suffering to which the victims of forced marriage were subjected during the civil war in Sierra Leone. According to the Prosecution expert:

> the most devastating effect on women of the war was the phenomenon called "bush wife", rebel wife or jungle wife. This was a phenomenon adopted by rebels whereby young girls or women were captured or abducted and forcibly taken as wives. . . . The use of the term "wife" by the perpetrator was deliberate and strategic. The word "wife" demonstrated a rebel's control over a woman. His psychological manipulations of her feelings rendered her unable to deny him his wishes. . . . By calling a woman "wife", the man or "husband" openly staked his claim and she was not allowed to have sex with any other person. If she did, she would be deemed unfaithful and the penalty was severe beating or death. "Bush wives" were expected to carry out all the functions of a wife and more. . . . [S]he was expected to show undying loyalty to her husband for his protection and reward him with "love and affection.". . . "Bush wives" were constantly sexually abused, physically battered during and after pregnancies, and psychologically terrorised by their husbands, who thereby demonstrated their control over their wives. Physically, most of these girls experienced miscarriages, and received no medical attention at the time. . . . Some now experience diverse medical problems such as severe stomach pains. . . some have had their uterus removed; menstrual cycles are irregular; some were infected with sexually transmitted diseases and others tested HIV positive.

193. In light of all the evidence at trial, Judge Doherty, in her Partly Dissenting Opinion, expressed the view that forced marriage involves "the imposition, by threat or physical force arising from the perpetrator's words or other conduct, of a forced conjugal association by the perpetrator

over the victim."[302] She further considered that this crime satisfied the elements of "Other Inhumane Act" because victims were subjected to mental trauma by being labeled as rebel "wives"; further they were stigmatised and found it difficult to reintegrate into their communities. According to Judge Doherty, forced marriage qualifies as an "Other Inhumane Acts" causing mental and moral suffering, which in the context of the Sierra Leone conflict, is of a comparable seriousness to the other crimes against humanity listed in the Statute.

194. Furthermore, the Appeals Chamber also notes that in their respective Concurring and Partly Dissenting Opinions, both Justice Sebutinde and Justice Doherty make a clear and convincing distinction between forced marriages in a war context and the peacetime practice of "arranged marriages" among certain traditional communities, noting that arranged marriages are not to be equated to or confused with forced marriage during armed conflict. Justice Sebutinde goes further to add, correctly in our view, that while traditionally arranged marriages involving minors violate certain international human rights norms such as the Convention on the Elimination of all Forms of Discrimination against Women (CEDAW), forced marriages which involve the abduction and detention of women and girls and their use for sexual and other purposes is clearly criminal in nature.

195. Based on the evidence on record, the Appeals Chamber finds that no tribunal could reasonably have found that forced marriage was subsumed in the crime against humanity of sexual slavery. While forced marriage shares certain elements with sexual slavery such as non-consensual sex and deprivation of liberty, there are also distinguishing factors. First, forced marriage involves a perpetrator compelling a person by force or threat of force, through the words or conduct of the perpetrator or those associated with him, into a forced conjugal association with another person resulting in great suffering, or serious physical or mental injury on the part of the victim. Second, unlike sexual slavery, forced marriage implies a relationship of exclusivity between the "husband" and "wife," which could lead to disciplinary consequences for breach of this exclusive arrangement. These distinctions imply that forced marriage is not predominantly a sexual crime. The Trial Chamber, therefore, erred in holding that the evidence of forced marriage is subsumed in the elements of sexual slavery.

196. In light of the distinctions between forced marriage and sexual slavery, the Appeals Chamber finds that in the context of the Sierra Leone conflict, forced marriage describes a situation in which the perpetrator through his words or conduct, or those of someone for whose actions he is responsible, compels a person by force, threat of force, or

---

[302] *Prosecutor v. Brima*, Case No. SCSL–2004–16–T, Partly Dissenting Opinion of Justice Doherty on Count 7 (Sexual Slavery) and Count 8 ("Forced Marriages"), para. 53 (June 20, 2007).

coercion to serve as a conjugal partner resulting in severe suffering, or physical, mental or psychological injury to the victim.

Does Forced Marriage Satisfy the Elements of "Other Inhumane Acts"?

197. The Prosecution submits that the crime charged under Count 8 is "Other Inhumane Acts," which forms part of customary international law, and therefore, does not violate the principle of *nullum crimen sine lege*. Therefore, the Prosecution submits that the only question on appeal is whether forced marriage satisfies the elements of "Other Inhumane Acts." The Prosecution argues that forced marriage amounts to an "Other Inhumane Act" and that the imposition of a forced conjugal association is as grave as the other crimes against humanity such as imprisonment, causing great suffering to its victims. In particular, the Prosecution argues that the mere fact of forcibly requiring a member of the civilian population to remain in a conjugal association with one of the participants of a widespread or systematic attack directed against the civilian population is at least of sufficient gravity to make this conduct an "Other Inhumane Act."

198. The Appeals Chamber agrees with the Prosecution that the notion of "Other Inhumane Acts" contained in Article 2.i of the Statute forms part of customary international law. As noted above, it serves as a residual category designed to punish acts or omissions not specifically listed as crimes against humanity provided these acts or omissions meet the following requirements:

(i) inflict great suffering, or serious injury to body or to mental or physical health;

(ii) are sufficiently similar in gravity to the acts referred to in Article 2.a to Article 2.h of the Statute; and

(iii) the perpetrator was aware of the factual circumstances that established the character of the gravity of the act.

The acts must also satisfy the general *chapeau* requirements of crimes against humanity.

199. The Appeals Chamber finds that the evidence before the Trial Chamber established that victims of forced marriage endured physical injury being subjected to repeated acts of rape and sexual violence, forced labour, corporal punishment, and deprivation of liberty. Many were psychologically traumatized by being forced to watch the killing or mutilation of close family members, before becoming "wives" to those who committed these atrocities and from being labeled rebel "wives" which resulted in them being ostracised from their communities. In cases where they became pregnant from the forced marriage, both they and their children suffered long-term social stigmatisation.

200. In assessing the gravity of forced marriage in the Sierra Leone conflict, the Appeals Chamber has taken into account the nature of the

perpetrators' conduct especially the atmosphere of violence in which victims were abducted and the vulnerability of the women and girls especially those of a very young age. Many of the victims of forced marriage were children themselves. Similarly, the Appeals Chamber has considered the effects of the perpetrators' conduct on the physical, moral, and psychological health of the victims. The Appeals Chamber is firmly of the view that acts of forced marriage were of similar gravity to several enumerated crimes against humanity including enslavement, imprisonment, torture, rape, sexual slavery and sexual violence.

201. The Appeals Chamber is also satisfied that in each case, the perpetrators intended to force a conjugal partnership upon the victims, and were aware that their conduct would cause serious suffering or physical, mental or psychological injury to the victims. Considering the systematic and forcible abduction of the victims of forced marriage, and the prevailing environment of coercion and intimidation, the Appeals Chamber finds that the perpetrators of these acts could not have been under any illusion that their conduct was not criminal. This conclusion is fortified by the fact that the acts described as forced marriage may have involved the commission of one or more international crimes such as enslavement, imprisonment, rape, sexual slavery, abduction among others.

202. The Appeals Chamber has carefully given consideration to whether or not it would enter fresh convictions for "Other Inhumane Acts" (forced marriage). The Appeals Chamber is fully aware of the Prosecution's submission that entering such convictions would reflect the full culpability of the Appellant. The Appeals Chamber is also aware that the Trial Chamber relied upon the evidence led in support of sexual slavery and forced marriage to enter convictions against the Appellants for "Outrages upon Personal Dignity" under Count 9 of the Indictment. Since "Outrages upon Personal Dignity" and "Other Inhumane Acts" have materially distinct elements (in the least, the former is a war crime, and the latter a crime against humanity) there is no bar to entering cumulative convictions for both offences on the basis of the same facts. However, in this case the Appeals Chamber is inclined against such cumulative convictions. The Appeals Chamber is convinced that society's disapproval of the forceful abduction and use of women and girls as forced conjugal partners as part of widespread or systematic attack against the civilian population, is adequately reflected by recognising that such conduct is criminal and that it constitutes an "Other Inhumane Act" capable of incurring individual criminal responsibility in international law.

203. The Appeals Chamber therefore grants Ground Seven of the Prosecution's Appeal.

NOTES & QUESTIONS

1. Case Outcome and Subsequent Cases

After considering a number of mitigating and aggravating factors, the Trial Chamber convicted the defendants on eleven counts and sentenced them to forty-five and fifty years' imprisonment. *Prosecutor v. Brima et al.*, Case No. SCSL–04–16–T, Sentencing Judgement (July 19, 2007). Although the Appeals Chamber overturned the Trial Chamber's rulings on forced marriage in the opinion reproduced above, it declined to enter new convictions and upheld the original sentences. Why would the Appeals Chamber overturn the Trial Chamber but not alter the convictions? Bear in mind that entering convictions on appeal has been a controversial practice before the *ad hoc* tribunals. In a subsequent case concerning Civilian Defense Force (CDF) defendants, the SCSL determined that allegations of forced marriage were not supported by the charges set forth in the indictment and, as such, evidence of sexual violence would be excluded to avoid prejudice to the accused. *Prosecutor v. Moinina and Kondewa*, Case No. SCSL–04–14–A, Judgement, paras. 430–434 (May 28, 2008). Given the *ad hoc* nature of the SCSL, and the existence of a domestic amnesty, the responsibility of CDF members for forced marriage may never be adjudicated. The SCSL finally entered convictions for forced marriage in a subsequent case involving RUF defendants. *Prosecutor v. Sesay et al.*, Case No. SCSL–04–15–T, Judgement (Mar. 2, 2009). The Trial Chamber determined that the RUF's invocation of the concept of marriage and the term "wife" was deliberately and strategically undertaken "with the aim of enslaving and psychologically manipulating the women and with the purpose of treating them like possessions." *Id.* at para. 1466.

2. The Origins of the Charge

The concept of forced marriage was not a theory originally conceived of by feminist academics or advocates; rather, it came from victims themselves. As the story goes, prosecutors interviewing victims of the brutal civil war in Sierra Leone heard innumerable stories of gang-rape and other forms of sexual violence by all sides of the country's complex conflict. Other women, however, described their experience using the vocabulary of marriage.

The trial testimony of witness TF1–094 is indicative. TF1–094 was about 12 when her village was raided by rebels. Her parents were killed. She survived because one Andrew intervened to "save her." Saving her meant first raping her and then taking her along with him to act as his "wife" (also known by the term "bush wife")—doing laundry, carrying his things, performing other chores, and traveling with his unit as the theatre of war shifted. On cross-examination, she admitted that Andrew generally "care[d] for her." Andrew was ultimately killed in combat. Other women stayed with their "husbands" post-conflict, often because they had borne children, knew no other life, and had no other life to return to.

Forced marriages are not unique to Sierra Leone. *See* Monikia Satya Kalra, *Forced Marriage: Rwanda's Secret Revealed*, 7 U.C. DAVIS J. INT'L L. & POL'Y 197 (2001). The representatives of civil parties appearing in the trials before the Extraordinary Chambers in the Courts of Cambodia

("ECCC") have successfully pushed prosecutors to add charges of forced marriage against Khmer Rouge defendants based on allegations that the Khmer Rouge hosted hundreds of group marriages as part of their effort to entirely remake Cambodian society by destroying prior allegiances (including familial). *See* Neha Jain, *Forced Marriage as a Crime Against Humanity*, 6 J. INT'L CRIM. JUST. 1013 (2008) (comparing forced marriage in Sierra Leone and in Cambodia under the Khmer Rouge).

In September 2011 the Trial Chamber of the ECCC severed Case 002 (the prosecution of the former head of state Khieu Samphan and former Prime Minister—also known as "Brother Number Two"—Nuon Chea) to better manage the large number of allegations. The first half of the severed case, Case 002/01, focused on alleged crimes against humanity arising from forced movement of populations and the alleged execution of Khmer Republic soldiers immediately after the Khmer Rouge takeover in 1975. Case 002/02 included allegations of forced marriages. The defendants were convicted and sentenced them to life imprisonment in both cases. Nuon Chea died in August 2019; although he admitted to "mistakes," he never accepted responsibility for the deaths during the Khmer Rouge era.

3. Forced Marriage v. Arranged Marriage

In his defense, one of the defendants (Santigie Borbor Kanu) argued that the "bush wife" phenomenon was simply a war-time adaptation of customary arranged marriages practices. Can a distinction be made between the crime against humanity of forced marriage discussed in *Brima* and non-consensual forms of arranged marriage endemic to many cultures whereby parents coordinate the marriage of their children, often while their children are minors or without their children's express consent? Both the Prosecution and the Defense tendered expert testimony about the phenomenon of forced marriage in the Sierra Leonean context. The Prosecution's witness—Zainab Bangura, a social activist and politician who became Sierra Leone's Foreign Minister in 2007 and the second United Nations Secretary General's Special Representative on Sexual Violence in Conflict—argued for a distinction in her expert's report:

> The fundamental difference between an early or arranged marriage in times of peace and a forced "marriage" during the war is that family members were not involved in the arrangement of the latter so-called "marriage," no official ceremony of any form took place and nor was the consent of the parents sought. * * * Because it was a marriage without consent and no intermediaries were present, the "wives" had no protection or family support they could count on. * * * Forced marriage during the conflict had no security. The "husband" could abandon his "wife" whenever he wanted to and get a new one whenever he felt like it. The "wives" were led to believe that their "husbands" had the right to kill them, without fear of any repercussions. There were no formal or informal institutions available to address the brutality of the "husbands." * * * The use of the term "wife" by the perpetrator was deliberate and strategic. The word "wife" demonstrated a rebel's control over a woman.

Does the involvement of fiduciaries or the execution of formalities or marriage rituals mitigate the non-consensual nature of the practice? In a separate opinion, Judge Sebutinde (Uganda) agreed, reasoning that

> a clear distinction should be drawn between traditional or religious marital unions involving minors (early or arranged marriages), during times of peace; and the forceful abduction and holding in captivity of women and girls ("bush wives") against their will, for purposes of sexual gratification of their "bush husbands" and for gender-specific forms of labour including cooking, cleaning, washing clothes (conjugal duties). In my view, while the former is proscribed as a violation of human rights under international human rights instruments or treaties like CEDAW, it is not recognized as a crime in international humanitarian law. The latter conduct on the other hand, is clearly criminal in nature and is liable to attract prosecution.

Prosecutor v. Brima et al., Case No. SCSL–2004–16–T, Separate Concurring Opinion of the Hon. Justice Julia Sebutinde Appended to Judgement Pursuant to Rule 88(C), para. 12 (June 20, 2007). (Judge Sebutinde joined the majority opinion in arguing that forced marriage was subsumed in charges of sexual slavery. *Id.* at paras. 15–18.) Are these distinctions convincing? Even if it is assumed that customary marriage in Sierra Leone often amounted to forced marriage, is that fact relevant to the prosecution of the accused for acts committed in the context of an armed conflict?

4. Sexual Violence

Do you agree with the Appeals Chamber's reasoning that forced marriage is not predominantly a sexual crime and that it is fully distinct from sexual slavery? Judge Sebutinde in her separate opinion to the trial judgment argued that "the sexual element inherent in these acts tends to dominate the other elements therein such as forced labour and other forced conjugal duties" such that forced marriage bears all the hallmarks of sexual slavery. *See Prosecutor v. Brima et al.*, Case No. SCSL–04–16–T, Separate Concurring Opinion of the Hon. Justice Julia Sebutinde Appended to Judgement Pursuant to rule 88(C), para. 6 (June 20, 2007). The then-Special Rapporteur on Contemporary Forms of Slavery, Gay J. McDougall, reported that sexual slavery "also encompasses situations where women and girls are forced into 'marriage', domestic servitude or other forms of labor that ultimately involves forced sexual activity, including rape by their captors." *See* Contemporary Forms of Slavery, Systematic Rape, Sexual Slavery and Slavery-Like Practices During Armed Conflict, U.N. Doc. No. E/CN.4/Sub.2/1998/13, para 30 (June 22, 1998). By contrast, Judge Teresa Doherty (Northern Ireland) considered the crime primarily one of mental and moral suffering. *See Prosecutor v. Brima, et al.*, Case No. SCSL–2004–16–T, Partly Dissenting Opinion of Justice Doherty on Count 7 (Sexual Slavery) and Count 8 ("Forced Marriages"), paras. 53, 70 (June 20, 2007). In his pleadings, the Prosecutor originally characterized the crime of forced marriage as a sexual crime; he later argued that it should be considered a non-sexual offense. *See* RUF Judgement, *supra*, paras. 466–467.

5. Sierra Leonean Law

In 2007–9, Sierra Leone passed three laws, known as the Gender Bills, which included the Domestic Violence Act, the Registration of Customary Marriages and Divorce Act, and the Devolution of Estates Act. *See* Sierra Leone Court Monitoring Programme, *Sierra Leone Parliament Passes the Gender Bills into Law* (June 15, 2007). In addition, the Child Rights Act set the minimum age of marriage at eighteen and prohibited forced marriage and dowry transactions. Can this legislation be considered part of the legacy of the Special Court for Sierra Leone?

6. Forced Marriage as Slavery

Is the recognition of a crime of "forced marriage" ultimately beneficial to women? Does calling this conduct "marriage" ratify the perpetrators' characterization of the relationship and understate the slavery element of the practice? Might it raise the bar for challenging other forms of non-consensual marriage under international human rights law, such as the Convention on the Elimination of Discrimination Against Women (Article 16 of which guarantees men and women the same rights to enter into marriage with their free and full consent)? *See also* Convention on Consent to Marriage, Minimum Age for Marriage and Registration of Marriages, G.A. Res. 1763 A (XVII) (Nov. 7, 1962). This treaty provides at Article 1.1:

> No marriage shall be legally entered into without the full and free consent of both parties, such consent to be expressed by them in person after due publicity and in the presence of the authority competent to solemnize the marriage and of witnesses, as prescribed by law.

For a declaration condemning early and forced marriages, *see* the Ouagadougou Declaration on Early and Forced Marriage. Certain forms of non-consensual marriage are treated as analogous to slavery in Article 1 of the Supplementary Convention on the Abolition of Slavery, the Slave Trade, and Institutions and Practices Similar to Slavery, 226 U.N.T.S. 3 (1957), which has about 100 parties and obliges State Parties to "take all practicable and necessary legislative . . . measures to bring about progressively and as soon as possible the complete abolition or abandonment of the following institutions and practices." The treaty prohibits:

> (c) Any institution or practice whereby:
>
> (i) A woman, without the right to refuse, is promised or given in marriage on payment of a consideration in money or in kind to her parents, guardian, family or any other person or group; or
>
> (ii) The husband of a woman, his family, or his clan, has the right to transfer her to another person for value received or otherwise; or
>
> (iii) A woman on the death of her husband is liable to be inherited by another person.

7. Gravity

The Defense argued that forced marriage, even if cognizable as an offense separate and apart from the enumerated crime of sexual slavery, was not of a similar gravity to other acts referred to in Articles 2(a) to (h) of the Statute. As a result, the Defense reasoned, acts of forced marriage could not be charged as "Other Inhumane Acts," which require proof that the act in question is of similar gravity to other enumerated crimes against humanity. The Appeals Chamber rejected this argument, reasoning that the phenomenon of forced marriage in the Sierra Leone conflict was "of similar gravity to several enumerated crimes against humanity including enslavement, imprisonment, torture, sexual slavery and sexual violence." *Brima* Appeals Judgment, *supra*, at para. 200. Do you agree? Where should the law draw the line between forced marriages that violate international human rights law and forced marriages that constitute prosecutable crimes? Or, should there be such a distinction?

8. Forced Marriage Before the ICC

Gender-based violence features prominently in all of the situations under consideration by the International Criminal Court. The ICC Statute does not enumerate forced marriage as a crime against humanity; rather, the crimes against humanity provision allows for the prosecution of the crimes of "rape, sexual slavery, enforced prostitution, forced pregnancy, enforced sterilization, or any other form of sexual violence of comparable gravity" (Article 7(g)) as well as "other inhumane acts of a similar character intentionally causing great suffering, or serious injury to body or to mental or physical health" (Article 7(k)). Based on the SCSL's reasoning, could the ICC Prosecutor charge forced marriage as a crime against humanity? The Prosecution has charged Dominic Ongwen with forced marriage in connection with the Uganda situation. *See The Prosecutor v. Dominic Ongwen*, Decision on the Confirmation of Charges against Dominic Ongwen, Case No. ICC–02/04–01/15–422-Red (Mar. 23, 2016). For a discussion of the way in which the Lord's Resistance Army methodically organized and regulated forced marriage in the Ugandan context, *see* Khristopher Carlson & Dyan Mazurnana, FORCED MARRIAGE WITHIN THE LORD'S RESISTANCE ARMY (May 2008).

9. Sexual Violence in International Criminal Law

For most of human history, the rape and sexual abuse of women associated with the enemy was an expected spoil, inevitable by-product, or legitimate tactic of war. In response, one of the first efforts to codify the law of war—the Lieber Code, which was drafted to govern the Union forces during the Civil War—specifically designated rape as a war crime, providing that:

> [c]rimes punishable by all penal codes, such as arson, murder, maiming, assaults, highway robbery, theft, burglary, fraud, forgery, and rape, if committed by an American soldier in a hostile country against its inhabitants, are not only punishable as at home, but in all cases in which death is not inflicted, the severer punishment shall be preferred.

See INSTRUCTIONS FOR THE GOVERNMENT OF ARMIES OF THE UNITED STATES IN THE FIELD 17, 18 (Francis Lieber ed., Washington, Government Printing Office 1898) (1863).

Subsequent humanitarian law treaties did not follow suit. More contemporary international humanitarian law—which in many respects reflects the male experience with armed conflict—conceptualized sexual violence as an offense against a woman's dignity or a family's honor. For example, the regulations annexed to the 1907 Hague Convention on Land Warfare (IV) euphemistically indicated that "family honour and rights . . . must be respected." *See* Article 46, Hague Convention Respecting the Laws and Customs of War on Land, Oct. 18, 1907, 36 Stat. 2277, 1 Bevans 631. Even though sexual violence was rampant during World War II, the 1949 Geneva Conventions do not expressly categorize rape and other acts of sexual violence as "grave breaches" of the treaties giving rise to a duty of state parties to prosecute such crimes pursuant to principles of universal jurisdiction. *See id.* Articles 146–47. Rather, such acts are specifically prohibited elsewhere in the treaties in provisions that give rise to state responsibility only. For example, Article 27 of the Fourth Geneva Convention states that women shall be protected against "any attack on their honor, in particular rape, enforced prostitution, or any form of sexual assault." *Id.* The grave breaches regime does penalize a number of violent acts—including torture, inhuman treatment, and willfully causing great suffering or serious injury to body or health—that easily could be (and have been) interpreted to encompass acts of rape and other forms of sexual violence. *See id.* Article 147. The 1977 Protocols to the four Geneva Conventions prohibit various forms of sexual assault, but do not mandate penal consequences for such breaches.

The Statute of the Yugoslavia Tribunal, which reproduced the grave breaches regime at Article 2, thus did not enumerate acts of sexual violence as war crimes. By contrast, the Rwanda Tribunal's Statute did designate rape, enforced prostitution, and other forms of indecent assault as war crimes with reference to Protocol II governing non-international armed conflicts. International criminal law now treats gender violence as a prosecutable crime against the physical and mental integrity of the victim. Indeed, with the promulgation of the Statute of the ICC and the jurisprudence of the *ad hoc* criminal tribunals, there is now strong law on the books enabling gender crimes to be prosecuted as war crimes, crimes against humanity, and the predicate acts of genocide. (The cognizability of genocidal rape is discussed in Chapter 9 on Genocide). *See generally* PROSECUTING CONFLICT-RELATED SEXUAL VIOLENCE AT THE ICTY (Serge Brammertz & Michelle Jarvis eds., 2016).

10. Prosecutorial Policy

Although the substantive law concerned with gender violence is now well established, significant obstacles remain to ensuring a robust system of gender justice in international criminal law. These obstacles are less visible than defects in positive law because they emerge in the practice of international criminal law at crucial yet shrouded stages of the penal process: investigation, charging, pre-trial plea negotiations, trial preparation, the provision of protective measures, and appeals. Most importantly, strong positive law is irrelevant where a commitment to gender justice does not infuse all stages of the development and implementation of a prosecutorial strategy. For example, the Office of the Prosecutor of the Rwanda Tribunal, especially under the leadership of Swiss jurist Carla del Ponte, was criticized for neglecting gender crimes.

Can you identify any special challenges presented by prosecuting superiors for acts of sexual violence committed by their subordinates? For a discussion of gender-based violence in ICL and prosecutorial policy, *see* Kelly D. Askin, *Prosecuting Wartime Rape and Other Gender-Related Crimes Under International Law: Extraordinary Advances, Enduring Obstacles*, 21 BERKELEY J. INT'L L. 288, 317 (2003) (noting that investigation, indictment, and prosecution for gender crimes in the Rwanda and Yugoslav Tribunals occurred only after widespread lobbying by women's rights organizations and feminist scholars); Beth Van Schaack, *Obstacles On The Road To Gender Justice: The International Criminal Tribunal for Rwanda As Object Lesson*, 17 AM. UNIV. J. GENDER, SOCIAL POL. & L. 355 (2009) (critiquing prosecutorial policy before the ICTR).

B. EXTERMINATION

Extermination is another crime frequently included within the list of crimes against humanity. As you review the case below, consider how extermination differs from other crimes against humanity (e.g., of murder) or genocide.

Prosecutor v. Krstić, Case No. IT–98–33–T, Judgement (April 19, 2004)

In the Trial Chamber

490. The indictment charges extermination under Article 5(b) based on [the massacre at Srebrenica]. The Trial Chamber will first set out a legal definition of extermination, before moving to consider whether the elements required to establish the crime of extermination are met in this case.

491. Article 5 of the Statute which covers crimes against humanity states:

> [t]he International Tribunal shall have the power to prosecute persons responsible for the following crimes when committed in an armed conflict, whether international or national in character, and directed against any civilian population: [. . .] (b) extermination.

492. Extermination is also widely recognised as a crime against humanity in many international and national instruments. Nevertheless, it has rarely been invoked by national courts and it has not yet been defined by this Tribunal. The term "extermination" appeared in a number of post-war decisions by the Nuremberg Military Tribunal and

the Supreme National Tribunal of Poland. However, although the crime of extermination was alleged, the judgements generally relied on the broader notion of crimes against humanity and did not provide any specific definition of the term "extermination."[1132] Only the ICTR has defined, on several occasions, the requisite elements of the offence:[1133]

1. the accused or his subordinate participated in the killing of certain named or described persons;
2. the act or omission was unlawful and intentional.
3. the unlawful act or omission must be part of a widespread or systematic attack;
4. the attack must be against the civilian population[.]

493. The Prosecutor submits that the crime of extermination must, by its very nature, be directed against a group of individuals, that it requires an element of mass destruction and that it embraces situations where a large number of people who do not share any common characteristic are killed. No discriminatory element is required.

494. The pre-trial Brief of the Defence argues that the act of extermination is distinguishable from genocide by the fact that it is not committed on account of a person's national, ethnical, racial or religious affiliation and that, moreover, the commission of the act does not require any special intention, that is, the intent to destroy the group in whole or in part.

495. The offences of murder and extermination have a similar element in that they both intend the death of the victims. They have the same *mens rea*, which consists of the intention to kill or the intention to cause serious bodily injury to the victim which the perpetrator must have reasonably foreseen was likely to result in death. The Trial Chamber will now identify what extermination further involves and whether the requirements of that crime are met in this case. * * *

497. [T]he International Law Commission insists on the element of mass destruction in defining extermination:

[1132] *See* the following judgements. *Josef Altstötter and others*, U.S. Military Tribunal, Nuremberg (1947), LAW REPORTS OF TRIALS OF WAR CRIMINALS BY THE U.N. WAR CRIMES COMMISSION, VOL. VI. The accused were found guilty of crimes against humanity. The expression "racial extermination of the Poles" is used in the judgement to define the programme implemented nation-wide, p. 75; *Amon Leopold Goeth (Hauptsturmführer)*, Supreme National Tribunal of Poland (1946), LAW REPORTS OF TRIALS OF WAR CRIMINALS, VOL. VII. The judgement uses the term "extermination" broadly to justify genocide. The Tribunal notes that a policy of extermination was applied in order to destroy the Jewish and Polish nations (unofficial translation), p. 9. * * *

[1133] Judgement, *The Prosecutor v. Jean-Paul Akayesu*, Case No. ICTR–96–4–T, 2 September 1998, paras. 591–592; Judgement, *The Prosecutor v. Kambanda*, Case No. ICTR–97–23, 4 September 1998; Judgement, *The Prosecutor v. Kayishema/Ruzindana*, Case No. ICTR–95–1–T, 21 May 1999, paras. 141–147; Judgement, *The Prosecutor v. Rutaganda*, Case No. ICTR–96–3–T, 6 December 1999, paras. 82–84; Judgement, *The Prosecutor v. Musema*, Case No. ICTR–96–13–T, 27 January 2000.

> [Extermination is a] crime which by its very nature is directed against a group of individuals. In addition, the act used to carry out the offence of extermination involves an element of mass destruction which is not required for murder. In this regard, extermination is closely related to the crime of genocide [. . .][1143]

498. Given the limited precedents in the matter, it is useful to refer further to Article 7(2)(b) of the Statute of the International Criminal Court, which goes into more detail on the definition of the term "extermination" and specifies that:

> Extermination includes the intentional infliction of conditions of life, *inter alia* the deprivation of access to food and medicine, calculated to bring about the destruction of part of the population.

From the insertion of this provision, we surmise that the crime of extermination may be applied to acts committed with the intention of bringing about the death of a large number of victims either directly, such as by killing the victim with a firearm, or less directly, by creating conditions provoking the victim's death. The Report of the ICC Preparatory Commission on the elements of the crimes provides further guidance. It indicates that "the perpetrator [should have] killed one or more persons" and that the conduct should have taken place "as part of a mass killing of members of a civilian population."[1145] * * *

500. According to the commentary on the ILC Draft Code, extermination distinguishes itself from the crime of genocide by the fact that the targeted population does not necessarily have any common national, ethnical, racial or religious characteristic, and that it also covers situations where "some members of a group are killed while others are spared." For this reason, extermination may be retained when the crime is directed against an entire group of individuals even though no discriminatory intent nor intention to destroy the group as such on national, ethnical, racial or religious grounds has been demonstrated; or where the targeted population does not share any common national, ethnical, racial or religious characteristics.

501. The very term "extermination" strongly suggests the commission of a massive crime, which in turn assumes a substantial degree of preparation and organisation. It should be noted, though, that "extermination" could also, theoretically, be applied to the commission of a crime which is not "widespread" but nonetheless consists in eradicating an entire population, distinguishable by some characteristic(s) not

---

[1143] *See* in particular the commentary on the ILC Draft Code of Crimes against the Peace and Security of Mankind (hereinafter, "ILC Draft Code"), *Report of the International Law Commission on the work of its 48th session, 6 May–26 July 1996*, Official Documents of the United Nations General Assembly's 51st session, Supplement no. 10 (A/51/10), Article 18, p. 118.

[1145] Report of the Preparatory Commission for the International Criminal Court, Finalized draft text of the Elements of Crimes, PCNICC/2000/1/Add.2, 2 November 2000 (footnotes omitted).

covered by the Genocide Convention, but made up of only a relatively small number of people. In other words, while extermination generally involves a large number of victims, it may be constituted even where the number of victims is limited.

502. In this respect, the ICC definition of extermination indicates that it would be sufficient that the criminal acts be "calculated to bring about the destruction of *part* of the population." The Trial Chamber notes that this definition was adopted after the time the offences in this case were committed. In accordance with the principle that where there is a plausible difference of interpretation or application, the position which most favours the accused should be adopted, the Chamber determines that, for the purpose of this case, the definition should be read as meaning the destruction of a numerically significant part of the population concerned.

503. In sum, the Trial Chamber finds that for the crime of extermination to be established, in addition to the general requirements for a crime against humanity, there must be evidence that a particular population was targeted and that its members were killed or otherwise subjected to conditions of life calculated to bring about the destruction of a numerically significant part of the population.

504. Although there is evidence that a small number of killings in Potočari [a suburb of Srebrenica] and afterwards involved women, children and elderly,[1149] virtually all of the persons killed in the aftermath of the fall of Srebrenica were Bosnian Muslim males of military age. The screening process at Potočari, the gathering of those men at detention sites, their transportation to execution sites, the opportunistic killings of members of the column along the Bratunac-Milici road as they were apprehended, demonstrate beyond any doubt that all of the military aged Bosnian Muslim males that were captured or fell otherwise in the hands of the Serb forces were systematically executed. The result was that the majority of the military aged Bosnian Muslim males who fled Srebrenica in July 1995 were killed.

505. A crime of extermination was committed at Srebrenica. * * *

Criminal Responsibility of General Krstić * * *

600. The Trial Chamber will now turn to the criminal responsibility of General Krstić for the crimes proved at trial. * * *

619. The Trial Chamber has made findings that, as of 13 July, the plan to ethnically cleanse the area of Srebrenica escalated to a far more insidious level that included killing all of the military-aged Bosnian Muslim men of Srebrenica. A transfer of the men after screening for war criminals—the purported reason for their separation from the women,

---

[1149] One witness testified about the slaughtering of a baby. Expert reports on the exhumations show that a small number of the victims were under the age of fifteen [or] over sixty-five year old. Although those victims may not legally qualify as "military aged men," the[y] were obviously treated by the Bosnian Serb forces as if of military age.

children and elderly—to Bosnian Muslim held territory or to prisons to await a prisoner exchange was at some point considered an inadequate mode for assuring the ethnic cleansing of Srebrenica. Killing the men, in addition to forcibly transferring the women, children and elderly, became the object of the newly elevated joint criminal enterprise of General Mladić and VRS [Bosnian Serb] Main Staff personnel. The Trial Chamber concluded that this campaign to kill all the military aged men was conducted to guarantee that the Bosnian Muslim population would be permanently eradicated from Srebrenica and therefore constituted genocide. * * *

685. Extermination requires an intentional killing of one or more persons as part of the mass killing of a civilian population. Genocide, though it might also be committed by a single or a few murders, needs proof that the perpetrator intended to destroy a national, ethnical, racial or religious group, or part of the group, as such. Thus, while neither crime has a substantiality threshold as such in term of the actual killings perpetrated, both require that the killings be part of an extensive plan to kill a substantial part of a civilian population. But genocide has a distinct additional requirement, in terms of the nature of the group targeted. In extermination, the killings may be indiscriminate. Thus, in this case, at least, where genocide is committed by killings, it cannot be supplemented by extermination for the same underlying acts. [Thus,] it is impermissible to convict the accused of the two offences of extermination and genocide based on the same conduct. * * * Genocide requires a highly specialised intent in the destruction of a characterised group or part of a group, extermination does not. Genocide, the most specific crime, is to be retained.

NOTES & QUESTIONS

1. Genocide and Crimes Against Humanity

In the excerpt above, the count in the Indictment alleging the crime against humanity of extermination is dismissed on the ground that the attack in question is better characterized as genocide. When do acts of persecution and extermination become genocide? If international criminal law recognizes the crime of extermination (and persecution for that matter), why do we need the crime of genocide? Does genocide capture a special type of criminal conduct that is qualitatively different from the crimes against humanity of either persecution or extermination?

The crime of extermination seems to presuppose mass killings. How many killings are required to reach the necessary threshold to transform mere murder into extermination? Here, the massacre of 7–8,000 Muslim men was deemed sufficient. Would 700–800 men be enough? 70–80? 7–8? How should international criminal tribunals approach such questions? Is this inquiry inherently a relative one, dependent upon the size of the targeted population?

2. Crimes Against Humanity and United States Law

There is no crimes against humanity statute in the federal penal code, although it does designate torture, war crimes, genocide, terrorism, trafficking, slavery, and the use of child soldiers as prosecutable international crimes subject to expansive forms of jurisdiction, including universal jurisdiction. Why would the U.S. Congress not include crimes against humanity in this list? Are there any consequences for its absence? According to the Department of Homeland Security, over 1000 potential perpetrators have been found in the United States.

While there is no federal law covering crimes against humanity directly, both California (CA CIV PRO § 354.8) and Puerto Rico (33 L.P.R.A. § 4934) do have such statutes. Why would California and Puerto Rico enact such a statute? Do they raise preemption issues?

In 2009, Senator Dick Durban (D-Ill.)—the author of statutes addressed to genocide, the use of child soldiers, and trafficking—introduced legislation that would make it a violation of U.S. law to commit a crime against humanity. The draft legislation provided:

§ 519. Crimes against humanity

(a) OFFENSE.—It shall be unlawful for any person to commit or engage in, as part of a widespread and systematic attack directed against any civilian population, and with knowledge of the attack—

(1) conduct that, if it occurred in the United States, would violate—

(A) section 1111 of this title (relating to murder);

(B) section 1581(a) of this title (relating to peonage);

(C) the first undesignated paragraph of section 1583 of this title (relating to kidnapping or carrying away individuals for involuntarily servitude or slavery);

(D) section 1584 of this title (relating to sale into involuntary servitude);

(E) section 1589 of this title (relating to forced labor); or

(F) section 1590 of this title (relating to trafficking with respect to peonage, slavery, involuntary servitude, or forced labor);

(2) conduct that, if it occurred in the special maritime and territorial jurisdiction of the United States, would violate—

(A) section 1591(a) of this title (relating to sex trafficking of children or by force, fraud, or coercion);

(B) section 2241(a) of this title (relating to aggravated sexual abuse by force or threat); or

(C) section 2242 of this title (relating to sexual abuse);

(3) conduct that, if it occurred in the special maritime and territorial jurisdiction of the United States, and without regard to

whether the offender is the parent of the victim, would violate section 1201(a) of this title (relating to kidnapping);

(4) conduct that, if it occurred in the United States, would violate section 1203(a) of this title (relating to hostage taking), notwithstanding any exception under subsection (b) of section 1203;

(5) conduct that, if the alleged offender were a national of the United States, would violate section 2340A of this title (relating to torture);

(6) extermination;

(7) national, ethnic, racial, or religious cleansing;

(8) arbitrary detention; or

(9) imposed measures intended to prevent births.

(b) PENALTY.—Any person who violates subsection (a), or attempts or conspires to violate subsection (a)—

(1) shall be fined under this title, imprisoned not more than 20 years, or both; and

(2) if the death of any person results from the violation of subsection (a), shall be fined under this title and imprisoned for any term of years or for life.

(c) JURISDICTION.—There is jurisdiction over a violation of subsection (a), and any attempt or conspiracy to commit a violation of subsection (a), if—

(1) the alleged offender is a national of the United States or an alien lawfully admitted for permanent residence;

(2) the alleged offender is a stateless person whose habitual residence is in the United States;

(3) the alleged offender is present in the United States, regardless of the nationality of the alleged offender; or

(4) the offense is committed in whole or in part within the United States.

(d) NONAPPLICABILITY OF CERTAIN LIMITATIONS.—Notwithstanding section 3282 of this title [establishing a five year statute of limitations for non-capital offenses], in the case of an offense under this section, an indictment may be found, or information instituted, at any time without limitation.

How does this definition compare to the international criminal law definition? Why would Senator Durbin have defined the crime as such? For a discussion of the need, *vel non*, for such a statute, *see* Brian W. Walsh & Steven Groves, *The Crimes Against Humanity Act: Another Step Toward "Universal Jurisdiction*, The Heritage Foundation (April 21, 2010); Beth Van Schaack, *Crimes Against Humanity: Repairing Title 18's Blind Spots*, *in* ARCS OF GLOBAL JUSTICE: ESSAYS IN HONOUR OF WILLIAM A. SCHABAS, 341

(Margaret M. deGuzman & Diane Marie Amann eds., 2018). The proposed bill did not move forward.

PROBLEMS

1. Female Genital Cutting

According to UNICEF, more than 130 million women and girls have been subjected to female genital cutting (FGC), while every year millions of additional girls are at risk of some form of the practice. Almost half of the countries in Africa practice FGC in one form or another. In Kenya, for example, approximately 27% of females have been cut, although the practice is more prevalent within certain groups, such as the Maasai. The practice is not criminalized in Kenya, but the Children's Code does prohibit it. In Egypt and Somalia, among other places, over 90% of women have been subjected to some form of FGC.

FGC is unlawful in some countries of the world where it has traditionally been practiced, and in some of these countries the practice carries criminal penalties. However, enforcement of these laws remains lax where governments have little interest in antagonizing the community elders who are guardians of the tradition or families intent on continuing a custom they consider important. As a result of migration, women who have been cut exist in every country of the world, and the practice is found in global diaspora communities. UNICEF compiles detailed data about the prevalence of, and changing attitudes toward, the practice around the world.

Section 116 of Title 18 makes it a criminal offense to "knowingly circumcise[ ], excise[ ], or infibulate[ ] the whole or any part of the labia majora or labia minora or clitoris of another person who has not attained the age of 18 years. . . . [No] account shall be taken of the effect on the person on whom the operation is to be performed of any belief on the part of that person, or any other person, that the operation is required as a matter of custom or ritual." 18 U.S.C. § 116. In addition, the Transport for Female Genital Mutilation Act, P.L. 112-239 (Jan. 2, 2013), makes it a crime to knowingly transport a girl outside of the United States for the purpose of committing FGM. *See* 18 U.S.C. § 116(d). Review these statutes and consider the fact patterns below.

- Rachel Taher, a member of the Dawoodi Bohra community (a Shia subsect), was 7 when she went on vacation with her parents from Michigan to Mumbai, India. During the journey, she was told she was going on a "girls' trip" with her aunties. Together, she and her aunts visited an apartment where she was eventually placed on the floor and a woman removed part of her clitoris with a knife that had been heated on a gas stove. After the procedure, she was bandaged and given cake and gifts. When she returned to the United States, she was told not to tell anyone about her special day. There is no specific legislation in India banning the practice, but the Indian Supreme Court has taken up the question of its legality under the Indian Constitution and child abuse statutes.

- Fatna Musa, whose family came to the United States from Eritrea during the Ethiopia-Eritrean War, was 7 when her mother took her from her hometown in Connecticut to a clinic in New York City. She was given anesthesia and then her external genitalia were removed with a scalpel by a woman in surgical clothing. She was given a painkiller and antibiotics upon her release. In 2007, Eritrea passed Proclamation 158/2007 outlawing the practice in all its forms.
- The practice has been illegal in Egypt since 2008, but it continues nonetheless. Indeed, UNICEF estimates that over 90% of married women in Egypt have been cut, 70% of them by licensed doctors who see the practice as a source of income. The Minister of Health and Population has pledged to eliminate the practice by 2030, in part by educating doctors.

Who could be prosecuted in the United States under § 116 on these facts? Are there potential constitutional infirmities you can identify? Could the crime be prosecuted under the ICC Statute? How would you frame an indictment of any responsible individuals before the Court? Given the prevalence of the practice, and the dearth of criminal laws in practicing states, should foreign states prosecute individual perpetrators if they are found in their midst? Is the criminalization of such practices on either the domestic or international level an appropriate or effective response? Is it likely to embolden or impede activists working to eradicate the practice from the grassroots? Will the criminalization of the practice contribute to norm shifts within communities that practice FGC or will it entrench the practice?

2. Lebanon

As part of the process of establishing the Special Tribunal for Lebanon (see Chapter 12 on Terrorism), the Secretary General of the United Nations, then Kofi Annan of Ghana, was asked to report to the Security Council on the nature and scope of international assistance needed to prosecute individuals charged with the February 14, 2005, terrorist attack that killed former Lebanese Prime Minister Rafik Hariri and other such attacks committed between October 1, 2004, and December 21, 2005, that were connected to the Hariri assassination. In his second such report, the Secretary General appended a draft statute for the proposed mixed (hybrid) tribunal. Although he noted in his report that only terrorism and related common crimes under the Lebanese Criminal Code were contemplated for the subject matter jurisdiction of the tribunal, he indicated that he had considered including crimes against humanity as well. In the report, Annan explained his theory of the applicability of the prohibition against crimes against humanity as follows:

> Mindful of the differences in scope and number of victims between the series of terrorist attacks committed in Lebanon and the killings and executions perpetrated on a large and massive scale in other parts of the world subject to the jurisdiction of any of the existing international criminal jurisdictions, it was nevertheless considered that the 14 attacks committed in Lebanon could meet

> the *prima facie* definition of [crimes against humanity], as developed in the jurisprudence of international criminal tribunals. The attacks that occurred in Lebanon since 1 October 2004 could reveal a "pattern" or "methodical plan" of attacks against a civilian population, albeit not in its entirety. They could be "collective" in nature, or "a multiple commission of acts" and, as such, exclude a single, isolated or random conduct of an individual acting alone. For the crime of murder, as part of a systematic attack against a civilian population, to qualify as a "crime against humanity", its massive scale is not an indispensable element.

See Report of the Secretary-General on the Establishment of a Special Tribunal for Lebanon, U.N. Doc. No. S/2006/893 (Nov. 15, 2006). There was not, however, sufficient support within the Security Council for the inclusion of crimes against humanity within the Statute ultimately enacted. As a result, the Tribunal now has jurisdiction over the following domestic crimes: acts of terrorism (arts. 314–316), crimes and offences against life and personal integrity (arts. 547–568); illicit associations (arts. 335–339); and failure to report crimes and offences (arts. 398–400).

Imagine that you were a representative of a state with a seat on the Security Council while these debates were transpiring. What legal, policy, and political arguments would have been made for or against the inclusion of crimes against humanity in the Special Tribunal's statute? Do you agree with the decision to restrict the prosecutable crimes to terrorism-related offenses?

CHAPTER 11

TORTURE

I. INTRODUCTION

The prohibition against torture is one of the most widely codified proscriptions under international law. Torture is the subject of its own multilateral treaty—the Convention Against Torture and Other Cruel, Inhuman or Degrading Treatment or Punishment ("Torture Convention"). Prohibitions against torture can be found in every omnibus international human rights and humanitarian law treaty, as well as in each of the three regional human rights conventions, and is an enumerated war crime and crime against humanity. The prohibition against torture is now accepted as a *jus cogens* norm of international human rights law. It has been so recognized by both international criminal tribunals for Rwanda and the former Yugoslavia; by all three regional human rights regimes; by the Committee Against Torture (established to monitor compliance with the Torture Convention); by judges in numerous domestic jurisdictions; by authoritative statements of international law, including the Restatement (Fourth) of Foreign Relations Law of the United States; and by the Universal Islamic Declaration of Human Rights. The prohibition against torture is an absolute one; torture is prohibited in all circumstances, even in cases of war or national emergency. Not only are states prohibited from committing torture, they are also forbidden to extradite or otherwise send an individual to a place where there are substantial grounds for believing that the person will be tortured (the principle of *non-refoulement*). Almost every codified prohibition of torture is accompanied by a bar on other forms of cruel, inhuman or degrading treatment or punishment (CIDT), although such acts are not criminalized as extensively as torture.

Most states criminalize and can prosecute acts of torture under their domestic laws, making torture probably the most prosecuted international crime under domestic law. Indeed, the Convention Against Torture expects states to exercise expansive forms of jurisdiction over the crime. While torture is not a separate stand-alone offense within any of the international criminal tribunals, the act of torture is prosecutable as a war crime, when committed in the context of an armed conflict, and as a crime against humanity, when committed in the context of a widespread or systematic attack against a civilian population. It can also serve as the basis for a genocide charge.

As this chapter discusses, torture has a long and complex history, having evolved from being the cornerstone of proof for some criminal legal systems to a significant focus of the international human rights movement and modern international criminal law. Indeed, no government today officially or publicly condones the use of torture. And yet, acts that violate the Torture Convention and related prohibitions have been recorded in almost all states of the world. Notwithstanding the near universal acceptance of the definition of torture under international law and of its prohibition, strong disagreements persist with respect to whether certain specific practices meet the definition, enabling states to claim that their police, detention practices, interrogation techniques, or systems of punishment do not run afoul of these prohibitions.

The potential for equivocation around the scope of the prohibition against torture is exemplified by the revelations that the U.S. government during the presidency of George W. Bush sanctioned the development and use of so called "enhanced interrogation techniques" in the "war on terror" that many observers consider to be torture and/or CIDT. Critics contend that the United States justified the use of coercive techniques by exploiting the apparent "gap" between torture and CIDT in international law. Critics also charge that the United States' use of these techniques has undermined the torture prohibition and given "cover" for other states to adopt similar techniques against their own war-time detainees, criminal suspects, prisoners, and others who find themselves in the custody of state agents. The events of September 11, 2001—and the subsequent detention of suspected terrorists in Guantánamo, Abu Ghraib, and elsewhere—prompted a public debate in the United States concerning the morality, legality, and utility of torture. This chapter engages these issues with reference to caselaw emerging from the international criminal tribunals and domestic courts as well as memoranda generated by departments of the U.S. government and international reactions thereto.

Before introducing the current debates on torture, we start with some historical context. The universal condemnation of torture is a relatively modern development. Indeed, at certain points in history, not only was torture not prohibited, it was viewed as a crucial element of a justice system.

John Langbein, The Legal History of Torture, in TORTURE: A COLLECTION, at 93 (Sanford Levinson ed., 2004)

European law of proof emerged in the city-states of northern Italy in the thirteenth century. It spread across the Continent together with the rest of Roman-canon criminal and civil procedure as part of the broader movement known as the reception of Roman law. Investigation under torture was reserved for cases of serious crime, for which the sanction was death or maiming. * * *

The largest chapter of the European law of torture concerned the prerequisites for examination under torture. European jurists devised what modern American lawyers would call a standard of probable cause, designed to ensure that only persons highly likely to be guilty would be examined under torture. Torture was permitted only when a so-called half proof had been established against the suspects. That meant either one eyewitness, or circumstantial evidence that satisfied elaborate requirements of gravity. In the example in which a suspect was caught with the dagger and the loot, each of those indicia would have been reckoned as a quarter proof, which, cumulated to a half proof, would have been sufficient to permit the authorities to examine the suspect under torture. * * *

Alas, because torture tests endurance rather than veracity, innocent persons might (as one sixteenth-century handbook on criminal procedure warned) yield to "the pain and torment and confess things that they never did." For a variety of reasons, the safeguards never proved adequate. If the examining magistrate engaged in suggestive questioning, even accidentally, his lapse could not always be detected or prevented. If the accused knew something about the crime but was still innocent, what he did know might be enough to give his confession verisimilitude. In some jurisdictions the requirement of verification was not enforced or was enforced indifferently.

In order to achieve a verbal or technical reconciliation with the requirement of the formal law of proof that the confession be voluntary, the law treated a confession extracted under torture as involuntary, hence ineffective, unless the accused repeated it free from torture at a hearing held a day or so later. Sometimes the accused who had confessed under torture did recant when asked to confirm his confession. But seldom to avail: The examination under torture could thereupon be repeated. When an accused confessed under torture, recanted, and was then tortured anew, he learned quickly enough that only a "voluntary" confession at the ratification hearing would save him from further agony in the torture chamber. Thus, Johannes Julius, the seventeenth-century burgomaster of Bamburg, Germany, writing from his dungeon cell where he was awaiting execution, told his daughter why he had confessed to witchcraft "for which I must die. It is all falsehood and invention, so help me God. . . . They never cease to torture until one says something." Against the coercive force of the engines of torture, no safeguards were ever found that could protect the innocent and guarantee the truth. The agony of torture created an incentive to speak, but not necessarily to speak the truth.

These shortcomings in the law of torture were identified even in the Middle Ages and were the subject of emphatic complaint in Renaissance and early modern times. Cases arose recurrently in which the real culprit was detected after an innocent accused had confessed under torture and been convicted and executed. In the eighteenth century, as the law of torture was finally about to be abolished, along with the system of proof that had required it, Beccaria [an Italian philosopher and the author of *On Crimes and Punishments* (1764)] and Voltaire [a French enlightenment thinker] became famous as critics of judicial torture by pointing to such cases, but they were latecomers to a critical legal literature nearly as old as the law of torture itself. Judicial torture survived the centuries not because its defects had been concealed but in spite of their having been long revealed. * * *

The European states abolished the system of judicial torture within about two generations. Frederick the Great all but abolished torture within a month of his accession to the Prussian throne in 1740; torture was used for the last time in Prussia in 1752 and was definitely abolished in 1754. In 1770, Saxony and Denmark abolished torture; in 1776, Poland and Austria-Bohemia; in 1780, France; in 1786, Tuscany; in 1787, the Austrian Netherlands (Belgium); and in 1789, Sicily. Early in the nineteenth century, abolition reached the last corners of the Continent.

II. DEFINING TORTURE IN INTERNATIONAL CRIMINAL LAW

In developing jurisprudence related to torture, the international criminal tribunals have drawn upon international human rights treaties and the work of human rights bodies defining and interpreting the prohibition against torture at the international and regional levels. The most cited and replicated treaty definition of torture is that found in the 1984 Convention Against Torture and Other Cruel, Inhuman, or Degrading Treatment or Punishment. Article 1(1) of that treaty provides:

> For the purposes of this Convention, the term "torture" means any act by which severe pain or suffering, whether physical or mental, is intentionally inflicted on a person for such purposes as obtaining from him or a third person information or a confession, punishing him for an act he or a third person has committed or is suspected of having committed, or intimidating or coercing him or a third person, or for any reason based on discrimination of any kind, when such pain or suffering is inflicted by or at the instigation of or with the consent or acquiescence of a public official or other person acting in an official capacity. It does not include pain or suffering arising only from, inherent in or incidental to lawful sanctions.

The Convention further provides that

> Each State Party shall undertake to prevent in any territory under its jurisdiction other acts of cruel, inhuman or degrading treatment or punishment which do not amount to torture as defined in article 1, when such acts are committed by or at the instigation of or with the consent or acquiescence of a public official or other person acting in an official capacity. In particular, the obligations contained in articles 10 [duty to train law enforcement, military, etc. personnel], 11 [duty to review interrogation practices], 12 [duty to ensure prompt and impartial investigation] and 13 [right to complain] shall apply

> with the substitution for references to torture or references to other forms of cruel, inhuman or degrading treatment or punishment.

Article 1 is qualified by the statement that it is "without prejudice to any international instrument or national legislation which does or may contain provisions of wider application."

There are four elements to proving the crime of torture under the Convention definition: (1) severe pain or suffering (2) intentionally inflicted (3) for one of the enumerated purposes (4) by someone acting on behalf of a state. CIDT is not separately defined. Article 16 of the Torture Convention, simply states:

> Each State Party shall undertake to prevent in any territory under its jurisdiction other acts of cruel, inhuman or degrading treatment or punishment which do not amount to torture as defined in article 1, when such acts are committed by or at the instigation of or with the consent or acquiescence of a public official or other person acting in an official capacity.

The Torture Convention definition may be contrasted with that of the 1987 Inter-American Convention to Prevent and Punish Torture, which defines torture at Article 2 as:

> For the purposes of this Convention, torture shall be understood to be any act intentionally performed whereby physical or mental pain or suffering is inflicted on a person for purposes of criminal investigation, as a means of intimidation, as personal punishment, as a preventive measure, as a penalty, or for any other purpose. Torture shall also be understood to be the use of methods upon a person intended to obliterate the personality of the victim or to diminish his physical or mental capacities, even if they do not cause physical pain or mental anguish.

Article 3 indicates that the treaty applies to public servants or employees as well as those who act at the instigation of a public servant or employee. About half of the eligible states are members of this regional treaty; the United States is not a party.

As you review the materials in this chapter, consider the way in which these definitions of torture, which have their origins in human rights treaties, have been adapted and applied in international criminal law. Pay particular attention to which elements of the above definitions have been retained and which have been abandoned and why. In addition, endeavor to formulate a definition of CIDT and consider when such conduct should give rise to criminal penalties under international or domestic law.

The International Criminal Tribunal for the Former Yugoslavia (ICTY) compared the elements of the crime of torture in human rights law and international criminal law in a case involving the 1992 take-over by the Bosnian Serb Army and paramilitaries of the municipality of Foča.

This case generated the first indictment exclusively addressing sexual violence (torture, rape, outrages upon dignity, and enslavement charged as war crimes and crimes against humanity). The charges stemmed from abuses committed in various improvised detention centers (some in hotels and private homes) where Muslim girls and women were repeatedly raped by occupation forces. Kunarac, the commander of a special reconnaissance unit of the Bosnian Serb Army, voluntarily surrendered to the ICTY in 1998; the multinational Stabilization Force in Bosnia (SFOR) arrested his co-defendants—Zoran Vuković and Radomir Kovač—in 1999. In the opinion below, the Trial Chamber sets forth the elements of torture under the ICTY Statute. The Appeals Chamber's opinion on rape as torture follows.

Prosecutor v. Kunarac, et al., Case No. IT–96–23 & 23–1, Judgement (Feb. 22, 2001)

In the Trial Chamber

465. Torture has been charged against the three accused as a violation of the laws or customs of war under Article 3 of the Statute and as a crime against humanity under Article 5 of the Statute. * * *

466. Torture is prohibited under both conventional and customary international law and it is prohibited both in times of peace and during an armed conflict. The prohibition can be said to constitute a norm of *jus cogens*. However, relatively few attempts have been made at defining the offence of torture outside of human rights instruments. * * *

467. Because of the paucity of precedent in the field of international humanitarian law, the Tribunal has, on many occasions, had recourse to instruments and practices developed in the field of human rights law. Because of their resemblance, in terms of goals, values and terminology, such recourse is generally a welcome and needed assistance to determine the content of customary international law in the field of humanitarian law. With regard to certain of its aspects, international humanitarian law can be said to have fused with human rights law.

468. The Trial Chamber in *Furundžija* held that "[i]nternational law, while outlawing torture in armed conflict, does not provide a definition of the prohibition." That Trial Chamber consequently turned to human rights law to determine the definition of torture under customary international law. The Trial Chamber, however, pointed out that it should "identify or spell out some specific elements that pertain to torture as considered from the specific viewpoint of international criminal law relating to armed conflicts."

469. The Trial Chamber agrees with this approach. The absence of an express definition of torture under international humanitarian law does not mean that this body of law should be ignored altogether. The definition of an offence is largely a function of the environment in which

it develops. Although it may not provide its own explicit definition of torture, international humanitarian law does provide some important definitional aspects of this offence.

470. In attempting to define an offence under international humanitarian law, the Trial Chamber must be mindful of the specificity of this body of law. In particular, when referring to definitions which have been given in the context of human rights law, the Trial Chamber will have to consider two crucial structural differences between these two bodies of law:

(i) Firstly, the role and position of the state as an actor is completely different in both regimes. Human rights law is essentially born out of the abuses of the state over its citizens and out of the need to protect the latter from state-organized or state-sponsored violence. Humanitarian law aims at placing restraints on the conduct of warfare so as to diminish its effects on the victims of the hostilities. In the human rights context, the state is the ultimate guarantor of the rights protected and has both duties and a responsibility for the observance of those rights. In the event that the state violates those rights or fails in its responsibility to protect the rights, it can be called to account and asked to take appropriate measures to put an end to the infringements.

In the field of international humanitarian law, and in particular in the context of international prosecutions, the role of the state is, when it comes to accountability, peripheral. Individual criminal responsibility for violation of international humanitarian law does not depend on the participation of the state and, conversely, its participation in the commission of the offence is no defense to the perpetrator.[1175] Moreover, international humanitarian law purports to apply equally to and expressly bind all parties to the armed conflict whereas, in contrast, human rights law generally applies to only one party, namely the state involved, and its agents. * * *

(ii) Secondly, that part of international criminal law applied by the Tribunal is a penal law regime. It sets one party, the prosecutor, against another, the defendant. In the field of international human rights, the respondent is the state. Structurally, this has been expressed by the fact that human rights law establishes lists of protected rights whereas international criminal law establishes lists of offences.

471. The Trial Chamber is therefore wary not to embrace too quickly and too easily concepts and notions developed in a different legal context. The Trial Chamber is of the view that notions developed in the field of human rights can be transposed in international humanitarian law only if they take into consideration the specificities of the latter body of law.

[1175] Art. 7(2) of the [ICTY] Statute states that: "The official position of any accused person, whether as Head of State or Government or as a responsible Government official, shall not relieve such person of criminal responsibility nor mitigate punishment."

The Trial Chamber now turns more specifically to the definition of the crime of torture.

472. The Trial Chamber in the *Delalić* case considered that the definition contained in the Torture Convention reflects a consensus which the Trial Chamber considers to be representative of customary international law. The Trial Chamber in the *Furundžija* case shared that view and held that there was general acceptance of the main elements contained in the definition set out in Article 1 of the Torture Convention.

473. This Trial Chamber notes, however, that Article 1 of the Torture Convention makes it abundantly clear that its definition of torture is limited in scope and was meant to apply only "for the purposes of this Convention." In addition, paragraph 2 of Article 1 of the Torture Convention states that this Article is "without prejudice to any international instrument or national legislation which does or may contain provisions of wider application." Therefore, insofar as other international instruments or national laws give the individual broader protection, he or she shall be entitled to benefit from it. This, and the fact that the definition was meant to apply only in the context of the Convention, are elements which should be kept in mind when considering the possibility that the definition of the Torture Convention produced an extra-conventional effect. * * *

478. Article 3 of the 1950 European Convention for the Protection of Human Rights and Fundamental Freedoms ("European Convention" or "Convention") provides that no one shall be subjected to torture or to inhuman or degrading treatment or punishment. The European Court of Human Rights ("ECHR") held that the concept of torture attaches a special stigma to deliberate inhuman treatment causing very serious and cruel suffering. The European Commission of Human Rights held that torture constitutes an aggravated and deliberate form of inhuman treatment which is directed at obtaining information or confessions, or at inflicting a punishment. The three main elements of the definition of torture under the European Convention are thus the level of severity of the ill-treatment, the deliberate nature of the act, and the specific purpose behind the act. The requirement that the state or one of its officials take part in the act is a general requirement of the Convention—not a definitional element of the act of torture—which applies to each and every prohibition contained in the Convention. Article 1 of the Convention, which provides that the High Contracting Parties shall secure to everyone within their jurisdiction the rights and freedoms defined in Section I of the Convention, is clearly addressed to member states, not to individuals. The ECHR is not a criminal court, which determines individual criminal responsibility, but an organ whose mandate is to determine state compliance with its obligations under the Convention.

479. The Trial Chamber notes, however, the ECHR's jurisprudence which has held that Article 3 of the Convention may also apply in

situations where organs or agents of the state are *not* involved in the violation of the rights protected under Article 3. For example, in *HLR v. France*, the Court held that

> Owing to the absolute character of the right guaranteed, the Court does not rule out the possibility that Article 3 of the Convention may also apply where the danger emanates from persons or groups of persons who are not public officials.[1191]

480. Article 7 of the 1966 International Covenant on Civil and Political Rights ("ICCPR") provides that no one shall be subject to torture or to cruel, inhuman or degrading treatment or punishment. The Human Rights Committee held that the protection offered by Article 7 of the ICCPR was not limited to acts committed by or at the instigation of public officials but that it also possessed horizontal effects, and that states should therefore protect individuals from interference by private parties. The Committee stated the following: "It is also the duty of public authorities to ensure protection by law against such treatment even when committed by persons acting outside or without any official authority." * * *

482. The Trial Chamber in *Furundžija* held that a conventional provision could have an extra-conventional effect to the extent that it codifies or contributes to developing or crystallizing customary international law. In view of the international instruments and jurisprudence reviewed above, the Trial Chamber is of the view that the definition of torture contained in the Torture Convention cannot be regarded as the definition of torture under customary international law which is binding regardless of the context in which it is applied. The definition of the Torture Convention was meant to apply at an inter-state level and was, for that reason, directed at the states' obligations. The definition was also meant to apply only in the context of that Convention, and only to the extent that other international instruments or national laws did not give the individual a broader or better protection. The Trial Chamber, therefore, holds that the definition of torture contained in Article 1 of the Torture Convention can only serve, for present purposes, as an interpretational aid.

483. Three elements of the definition of torture contained in the Torture Convention are, however, uncontentious and are accepted as representing the status of customary international law on the subject:

(i) Torture consists of the infliction, by act or omission, of severe pain or suffering, whether physical or mental.

(ii) This act or omission must be intentional.

(iii) The act must be instrumental to another purpose, in the sense that the infliction of pain must be aimed at reaching a certain goal.

[1191] *HLR v. France*, 29 Apr. 1997, Reports 1997–III, p. 758, para. 40.

484. On the other hand, three elements remain contentious:

(i) The list of purposes the pursuit of which could be regarded as illegitimate and coming within the realm of the definition of torture.

(ii) The necessity, if any, for the act to be committed in connection with an armed conflict.

(iii) The requirement, if any, that the act be inflicted by or at the instigation of or with the consent or acquiescence of a public official or other person acting in an official capacity.

485. The Trial Chamber is satisfied that the following purposes have become part of customary international law: (a) obtaining information or a confession, (b) punishing, intimidating or coercing the victim or a third person, (c) discriminating, on any ground, against the victim or a third person. There are some doubts as to whether other purposes have come to be recognised under customary international law. The issue does not need to be resolved here, because the conduct of the accused is appropriately subsumable under the above-mentioned purposes.

486. There is no requirement under customary international law that the conduct must be solely perpetrated for one of the prohibited purposes. As was stated by the Trial Chamber in the *Delalić* case, the prohibited purpose must simply be part of the motivation behind the conduct and need not be the predominant or sole purpose.

487. Secondly, the nature of the relationship between the underlying offence—torture—and the armed conflict depends, under the Tribunal's Statute, on the qualification of the offence, as a grave breach, a war crime or a crime against humanity. If, for example, torture is charged as a violation of the laws or customs of war under Article 3 of the Statute, the Trial Chamber will have to be satisfied that the act was closely related to the hostilities. If, on the other hand, torture is charged as a crime against humanity under Article 5 of the Statute, the Trial Chamber will have to be convinced beyond reasonable doubt that there existed an armed conflict at the relevant time and place.

488. Thirdly, the Torture Convention requires that the pain or suffering be inflicted by or at the instigation of or with the consent or acquiescence of a public official or other person acting in an official capacity. As was already mentioned, the Trial Chamber must consider each element of the definition "from the specific viewpoint of international criminal law relating to armed conflicts." In practice, this means that the Trial Chamber must identify those elements of the definition of torture under human rights law which are extraneous to international criminal law as well as those which are present in the latter body of law but possibly absent from the human rights regime.

489. The Trial Chamber draws a clear distinction between those provisions which are addressed to states and their agents and those

provisions which are addressed to individuals. Violations of the former provisions result exclusively in the responsibility of the state to take the necessary steps to redress or make reparation for the negative consequences of the criminal actions of its agents. On the other hand, violations of the second set of provisions may provide for individual criminal responsibility, regardless of an individual's official status. While human rights norms are almost exclusively of the first sort, humanitarian provisions can be of both or sometimes of mixed nature. This has been pointed out by the Trial Chamber in the *Furundžija* case:

> Under current international humanitarian law, in addition to individual criminal liability, State responsibility may ensue as a result of State officials engaging in torture or failing to prevent torture or to prevent torturers. If carried out as an extensive practice of State officials, torture amounts to a serious breach on a widespread scale of an international obligation of essential importance for safeguarding the human being, thus constituting a particularly wrongful act generating State responsibility.[1202]

490. Several humanitarian law provisions fall within the first category of legal norms, expressly providing for the possibility of state responsibility for the acts of its agents: thus, Article 75 ("Fundamental Guarantees") of Additional Protocol I provides that acts of violence to the life, health, or physical or mental well-being of persons such as murder, torture, corporal punishment and mutilation, outrages upon personal dignity, the taking of hostages, collective punishments and threats to commit any of those acts when committed by civilian or by military agents of the state could engage the state's responsibility. The requirement that the acts be committed by an agent of the state applies equally to any of the offences provided under paragraph 2 of Article 75 and in particular, but no differently, to the crime of torture.

491. This provision should be contrasted with Article 4 ("Fundamental Guarantees") of Additional Protocol II. The latter provision provides for a list of offences broadly similar to that contained in Article 75 of Additional Protocol I but does not contain any reference to agents of the state. The offences provided for in this Article can, therefore, be committed by any individual, regardless of his official status, although, if the perpetrator is an agent of the state he could additionally engage the responsibility of the state. The Commentary to Additional Protocol II dealing specifically with the offences mentioned in Article 4(2)(a) namely, violence to the life, health, or physical or mental wellbeing of persons in particular murder and cruel treatment such as torture, states:

> The most widespread form of torture is practiced by public officials for the purpose of obtaining confessions, but torture is not only condemned as a judicial institution; *the act of torture is*

[1202] *Prosecutor v. Furundžija*, Case IT–95–17/1–T, Judgement, para. 142 (Dec. 10, 1998).

> *reprehensible in itself, regardless of its perpetrator*, and cannot be justified in any circumstances.[1204]

492. The Trial Chamber also notes Article 12 ("Protection and Care") of 1949 Geneva Convention I for the Amelioration of the Condition of the Wounded and Sick in Armed Forces in the Field, which provides that members of the armed forces and other defined persons who are wounded or sick shall be respected and protected in all circumstances. In particular, paragraph 2 of this Article provides that the wounded or sick shall not be tortured. The Commentary to this paragraph adds the following:

> The obligation [of respect and protection mentioned in paragraph 1] applies to all combatants in an army, whoever they may be, and also to non-combatants. *It applies also to civilians*, in regard to whom Article 18 specifically states: "The civilian population shall respect these wounded and sick, and in particular abstain from offering them violence." A clear statement to that effect was essential in view of the special character which modern warfare is liable to assume (dispersion of combatants, isolation of units, mobility of fronts, etc.) and which may lead to closer and more frequent contacts between military and civilians. It was necessary, therefore, and more necessary today than in the past, that the principle of the inviolability of wounded combatants should be brought home, *not only to the fighting forces, but also to the general public*. That principle is one of the fine flowers of civilization, and should be implanted firmly in public morals and in the public conscience.[1207]

493. A violation of one of the relevant articles of the Statute will engage the perpetrator's individual criminal responsibility. In this context, the participation of the state becomes secondary and, generally, peripheral. With or without the involvement of the state, the crime committed remains of the same nature and bears the same consequences. The involvement of the state in a criminal enterprise generally results in the availability of extensive resources to carry out the criminal activities in question and therefore greater risk for the potential victims. It may also trigger the application of a different set of rules, in the event that its involvement renders the armed conflict international. However, the involvement of the state does not modify or limit the guilt or responsibility of the individual who carried out the crimes in question.

[1204] Sandoz, Swinarski and Zimmermann (eds.), COMMENTARY ON THE ADDITIONAL PROTOCOLS OF 8 JUNE 1977 TO THE GENEVA CONVENTIONS OF 12 AUGUST 1949, 1373–1374 (1987).

[1207] Pictet, COMMENTARY TO 1949 GENEVA CONVENTION I FOR THE AMELIORATION OF THE CONDITION OF THE WOUNDED AND THE SICK IN ARMED FORCES IN THE FIELD 135 (1952) (emphasis added).

This principle was clearly stated in the *Flick* judgment [against German industrialists]:

> But the International Military Tribunal [at Nuremburg] was dealing with officials and agencies of the State, and it is argued that individuals holding no public offices and not representing the State, do not, and should not, come within the class of persons criminally responsible for a breach of international law. It is asserted that international law is a matter wholly outside the work, interest and knowledge of private individuals. The distinction is unsound. International law, as such, binds every citizen just as does ordinary municipal law. Acts adjudged criminal when done by an officer of the Government are criminal also when done by a private individual. The guilt differs only in magnitude, not in quality. The offender in either case is charged with personal wrong and punishment falls on the offender in *propria persona* ["in his own person"]. The application of international law to individuals is no novelty. [. . .] There is no justification for a limitation of responsibility to public officials.[1208] * * *

495. The Trial Chamber also points out that those conventions, in particular the human rights conventions, consider torture *per se* while the Tribunal's Statute criminalizes it as a form of war crime, crime against humanity or grave breach. The characteristic trait of the offence in this context is to be found in the nature of the act committed rather than in the status of the person who committed it.[1210]

496. The Trial Chamber concludes that the definition of torture under international humanitarian law does not comprise the same elements as the definition of torture generally applied under human rights law. In particular, the Trial Chamber is of the view that the presence of a state official or of any other authority-wielding person in

---

[1208] *Trial of Friedrich Flick and Five Others* ("Flick Trial"), U.S. Military Tribunal, 20 Apr.–22 Dec. 1947, IX LAW REPORTS OF THE TRIALS OF WAR CRIMINALS, 1, 18 (1948).

[1210] The Trial Chamber also notes the definition of torture contained in Art. 7(e) of the International Criminal Court Statute, Rome Statute of the International Criminal Tribunal, 17 July 1998, PCNICC/1999/INF/3, ("ICC Statute"), which provides: "'Torture' means the intentional infliction of severe pain or suffering, whether physical or mental, upon a person in the custody or under the control of the accused; except that torture shall not include pain or suffering arising only from, inherent in or incidental to, lawful sanctions." See also Arts. 7(1)(f) (crimes against humanity) and 8(2)(a)(ii)–1 (war crimes), of the Finalized Draft Text of the Elements of the Crimes for the International Criminal Court, Report of the Preparatory Commission for the International Criminal Court, 6 July 2000, PCNICC/2000/INF/3/Add.2. Article 27(1) ("Irrelevance of the official capacity") of the ICC Statute further states that the Statute shall apply "equally to all persons without any distinction based on official capacity." Although the ICC Statute does not necessarily represent the present status of international customary law, it is a useful instrument in confirming the content of customary international law. These provisions obviously do not necessarily indicate what the state of the relevant law was at the time relevant to this case. However, they do provide some evidence of state *opinio juris* as to the relevant customary international law at the time at which the recommendations were adopted. See, e.g., *Prosecutor v. Furundžija*, Case No. IT–95–17/1–T, Judgement, para. 227 (Dec. 10, 1998); *Prosecutor v. Tadić*, Case No. IT–94–A, Judgement, para. 223 (July 15, 1999).

the torture process is not necessary for the offence to be regarded as torture under international humanitarian law.

497. On the basis of what has been said, the Trial Chamber holds that, in the field of international humanitarian law, the elements of the offence of torture, under customary international law are as follows:

(i) The infliction, by act or omission, of severe pain or suffering, whether physical or mental.

(ii) The act or omission must be intentional.

(iii) The act or omission must aim at obtaining information or a confession, or at punishing, intimidating or coercing the victim or a third person, or at discriminating, on any ground, against the victim or a third person.

Prosecutor v. Kunarac, et al., Case No. IT–96–23 & 23–1A, Judgement (June 12, 2002)

In the Appeals Chamber

134. Neither Appellant challenges the Trial Chamber's definition of torture. Indeed, the Appellants seem to accept the conclusions of the Trial Chamber identifying the crime of torture on the basis of three elements, these being respectively an intentional act, inflicting suffering, and the existence of a prohibited purpose. Nonetheless, they assert that these three constitutive elements of the crime of torture have not been proven beyond reasonable doubt in relation to either Kunarac or Vuković and that their convictions were thus ill-founded.

135. With regard to the first element of the crime of torture, the Appellant Kunarac contends that he committed no act which could inflict severe physical or mental pain or suffering and that the arguments raised by the Prosecutor, as well as the case-law to which she refers, are not sufficient to justify the findings of the Trial Chamber that some of Kunarac's victims experienced such mental pain or suffering. Kunarac states that he never asserted that rape victims, in general, could not suffer, but rather that, in the instant case, no witness showed the effects of physical or mental pain or suffering. In Kunarac's view, therefore, the first element of the crime of torture—the infliction of severe pain or suffering—is not met in his case.

136. * * * Appellant Vuković further challenges his conviction for torture through rape in the form of vaginal penetration on the basis that [victim] FWS-50, who was allegedly raped by Vuković, did not mention the use of force or threats. The Appellant appears to conclude from the absence of evidence of the use of physical force that the alleged rape of FWS-50 could not have resulted in severe *physical* pain or suffering on the part of FWS-50. The Appellant thus asserts that the first element of the crime of torture will only be satisfied if there is evidence that the alleged rape resulted in severe *mental* pain or suffering on the part of

FWS-50. In this regard, the Appellant first contends that FWS-50 did not claim to have been inflicted with severe mental pain or suffering. Secondly, the Appellant seems to argue that, objectively, FWS-50 would not have experienced severe mental pain or suffering as a result of the alleged rape, as she had been raped on previous occasions by other perpetrators. Thirdly, the Appellant notes that two Defence expert witnesses testified that they did not find that the victims of the alleged rapes had suffered severe consequences. Finally, the Appellant states that the Prosecutor failed to prove beyond reasonable doubt that FWS-50 was inflicted with severe physical or mental pain or suffering. For these reasons, the Appellant Vuković contends that the first element of the crime of torture—the infliction of severe pain or suffering—is not met in his case and that the Trial Chamber erred in its application of the law and in finding him guilty of the crime of torture.

137. The Appellants also submit that they did not intend to inflict pain or suffering, rather that their aims were purely sexual in nature. The Appellants, therefore, argue that the second element of the crime of torture—the deliberate nature of the act or omission—has not been proven in either of their cases.

138. Both Appellants deny having pursued any of the prohibited purposes listed in the definition of the crime of torture, in particular, the discriminatory purpose. Kunarac further states that he did not have sexual relations with any of the victims in order to obtain information or a confession or to punish, intimidate or coerce the victim or a third person, or to discriminate on any ground whatsoever. Vuković seeks to demonstrate that the Trial Chamber erred when it established that his acts were committed for a discriminatory purpose because the victim was Muslim. Both Appellants thus conclude that the third constitutive element of the crime of torture—the pursuance of a prohibited purpose—was not established in their cases and that the Trial Chamber erroneously applied the law and committed an error in finding each guilty of the crime of torture.

139. The [Prosecutor] Respondent claims that the pain and suffering inflicted on FWS-50 through the Appellant Vuković's sexual acts was established. She asserts that, after leaving Foča, FWS-50 went to a physician who noted physiological and psychological symptoms resulting from rape, that she felt the need to go to a psychiatrist, and that she testified to having experienced suffering and pain when orally raped by Vuković.

140. The Respondent asserts that the crime of torture, as defined by customary international law, does not require that the perpetrator committed the act in question with the intent to inflict severe physical or mental suffering, but rather that the perpetrator committed an intentional act for the purpose of obtaining information or a confession, or to punish, intimidate or coerce the victim or a third person, or to discriminate on any ground whatsoever, and that, as a consequence, the

victim suffered. There is thus no need to establish that the Appellants committed such acts with the knowledge or intention that those acts would cause severe pain or suffering.

141. According to the Respondent and as noted by the Trial Chamber, there is no requirement under customary international law for the act of the perpetrator to be committed *solely* for one of the prohibited purposes listed in the definition of torture. The Respondent also claims that the Trial Chamber reasonably concluded that the Appellant Vuković intended to discriminate against his victim because she was Muslim. She further submits that, in this case, all the acts of torture could be considered to be discriminatory, based on religion, ethnicity or sex. Moreover, all the acts of sexual torture perpetrated on the victims resulted in their intimidation or humiliation.

142. With reference to the Torture Convention and the case-law of the Tribunal and the International Criminal Court for Rwanda (ICTR), the Trial Chamber adopted a definition based on the following constitutive elements:

(i) The infliction, by act or omission, of severe pain or suffering, whether physical or mental.

(ii) The act or omission must be intentional.

(iii) The act or omission must aim at obtaining information or a confession, or at punishing, intimidating or coercing the victim or a third person, or at discriminating, on any ground, against the victim or a third person. * * *

149. Torture is constituted by an act or an omission giving rise to "severe pain or suffering, whether physical or mental," but there are no more specific requirements which allow an exhaustive classification and enumeration of acts which may constitute torture. Existing case-law has not determined the absolute degree of pain required for an act to amount to torture.

150. The Appeals Chamber holds that the assumption of the Appellants that suffering must be visible, even long after the commission of the crimes in question, is erroneous. Generally speaking, some acts establish *per se* the suffering of those upon whom they were inflicted. Rape is obviously such an act. The Trial Chamber could only conclude that such suffering occurred even without a medical certificate. Sexual violence necessarily gives rise to severe pain or suffering, whether physical or mental, and in this way justifies its characterisation as an act of torture.

151. Severe pain or suffering, as required by the definition of the crime of torture, can thus be said to be established once rape has been proved, since the act of rape necessarily implies such pain or suffering. The Appeals Chamber thus holds that the severe pain or suffering, whether physical or mental, of the victims cannot be challenged and that the Trial Chamber reasonably concluded that that pain or suffering was

sufficient to characterise the acts of the Appellants as acts of torture. The Appellants' grounds of appeal in this respect are unfounded and, therefore, rejected.

152. The argument that the Appellant Vuković has not been charged with any act inflicting severe pain or suffering, whether physical or mental, is erroneous since he is charged with the crime of torture arising from rape. Moreover, the fact alleged in the Appeal Brief, that [the] Indictment does not refer to the use of physical force, does not mean that there was none.

153. The Appellants argue that the intention of the perpetrator was of a sexual nature, which, in their view, is inconsistent with an intent to commit the crime of torture. In this respect, the Appeals Chamber wishes to assert the important distinction between "intent" and "motivation." The Appeals Chamber holds that, even if the perpetrator's motivation is entirely sexual, it does not follow that the perpetrator does not have the intent to commit an act of torture or that his conduct does not cause severe pain or suffering, whether physical or mental, since such pain or suffering is a likely and logical consequence of his conduct. In view of the definition, it is important to establish whether a perpetrator intended to act in a way which, in the normal course of events, would cause severe pain or suffering, whether physical or mental, to his victims. The Appeals Chamber concurs with the findings of the Trial Chamber that the Appellants did intend to act in such a way as to cause severe pain or suffering, whether physical or mental, to their victims, in pursuance of one of the purposes prohibited by the definition of the crime of torture, in particular the purpose of discrimination.

154. The Appellant Kunarac claims that the requisite intent for torture, alleged by the Prosecutor, has not been proven. Vuković also challenges the discriminatory purpose ascribed to his acts. The Appeals Chamber finds that the Appellants have not demonstrated why the conclusions of the Trial Chamber on this point are unreasonable or erroneous. The Appeals Chamber considers that the Trial Chamber rightly concluded that the Appellants deliberately committed the acts of which they were accused and did so with the intent of discriminating against their victims because they were Muslim. Moreover, the Appeals Chamber notes that in addition to a discriminatory purpose, the acts were committed against one of the victims with the purpose of obtaining information. The Appeals Chamber further finds that, in any case, all acts were committed for the purpose of intimidating or coercing the victims.

155. Furthermore, in response to the argument that the Appellant's avowed purpose of sexual gratification is not listed in the definition of torture, the Appeals Chamber restates the conclusions of the Trial Chamber that acts need not have been perpetrated solely for one of the purposes prohibited by international law. If one prohibited purpose is

fulfilled by the conduct, the fact that such conduct was also intended to achieve a non-listed purpose (even one of a sexual nature) is immaterial.

156. The Appeals Chamber thus finds that the legal conclusions and findings of the Trial Chamber are well-founded and rejects all grounds of appeal relating to the crime of torture.

NOTES & QUESTIONS

1. Case Outcome

The three co-accused were convicted of many of the crimes charged, including cumulative crimes against humanity convictions for rape, enslavement, and torture with respect to two defendants. The enslavement charge relates to evidence that Kovač detained and then "sold" his victims to other soldiers. In regard to the cumulative convictions, the Tribunal reasoned:

> Applying the approach adopted by the Appeals Chamber in the *Delalić* case, convictions for rape and torture under either Article 3 [the laws and customs of war] or Article 5 [crimes against humanity] based on the same conduct would be permissible. Comparing the elements of rape and torture under either Article 3 or Article 5, a materially distinct element of rape *vis-à-vis* torture is the sexual penetration element. A materially distinct element of torture *vis-à-vis* rape is the severe infliction of pain or suffering aimed at obtaining information or a confession, punishing, intimidating, coercing or discriminating against the victim or a third person.

Kunarac Trial Chamber Judgement, *supra*, at para. 557. The theory behind cumulative convictions will be taken up in Chapter 13. The *Kunarac* case is also notable as the first decision by the ICTY convicting a defendant for rape and enslavement as a crime against humanity. Indeed, the Tribunal concluded that the systemic rape of women from another ethnic group was used as a "weapon of war" and an "instrument of terror." The defendants' convictions and sentences were affirmed on appeal in the second opinion excerpted above. The defendants are serving the remainder of their sentences (ranging from 10–28 years) in Norway and Germany. Vuković was granted early release in March 2008 and Kovač in June 2013. Why would the Office of the Prosecutor not charge genocide under these facts, especially given the *Akayesu* precedent?

2. State and Non-State Actors

The defendants were part of the Bosnian Serb Army, an ethnically-based militia fighting on behalf of the self-proclaimed Republika Srpska against the Bosnian Army and seeking the accession of parts of the newly independent Bosnia-Herzegovina with the rump Yugoslavia. The Serb enclave in Bosnia (the Republika Srpska) exhibited many features of a state, including a legislative body, an elected head of state (Radovan Karadžić), control of territory, an army, and a constitution. Article 1 of the 1933 Montevideo Convention on the Rights and Duties of States offers one articulation of the elements of statehood: a permanent population, a defined territory, a government, and the capacity to enter into relations with other states. The Convention does not include international recognition as required for a finding of statehood. Given their affiliation with Republika Srpska, should the Trial Chamber's opinion concerning non-state actors be considered *dicta*? Was Republika Srpska a state even though it was not formally recognized as such by any other state?

Following the Dayton Peace Accords, Republika Srpska became a political-territorial division within Bosnia-Herzegovina. In a civil suit in the Second Circuit under the Alien Tort Statute (ATS), Karadžić argued that the court had no jurisdiction over him for claims of war crimes and genocide because international law norms bind only states and persons acting under color of state law, not private actors. At the same time, Karadžić asserted that he was the president of the self-proclaimed Republika Srpska and thus was entitled to head-of-state immunity. The Second Circuit ruled that some international law rules are actionable against both state and non-state actors, including the prohibitions against war crimes and genocide. At the same time, the court held that the plaintiffs were entitled to prove that Karadžić's regime satisfied the criteria for a state, or that he and his subordinates were acting in concert with the state of Yugoslavia, in order to prevail on those international law violations that do require state action. His head-of-state immunity claim was denied. *See Kadić v. Karadžić*, 70 F.3d 232 (2d Cir. 1995). The *Kadić* case in many respects opened the door for suits under the ATS against corporations. Can you see why?

3. State Action

The ICTY has not been consistent in its rulings on the state action requirement for torture charges. Both the Trial Chamber in *Prosecutor v. Delalić*, Case No. IT–96–21–T, Judgement, para. 494 (Nov. 16, 1998), and the Appeals Chamber in *Prosecutor v. Furundžija*, Case No. IT–95–17/1, Judgement, para. 111 (Dec. 10, 1998), required a showing of the involvement of a public official or, in the words of the Appeals Chamber in *Furundžija*, someone acting in a non-private capacity. While the definition of torture adopted by the *Kunarac* Trial Chamber was not contested on appeal, the Appeals Chamber did agree (in a paragraph we did not excerpt above) that "the public official requirement is not a requirement under customary international law in relation to the criminal responsibility of an individual for torture outside of the framework of the Torture Convention." *Prosecutor v. Kunarac*, Case No. IT–96–23 and IT–96–23/1–A, Judgement, para. 148 (Feb. 22, 2002). *See also Prosecutor v. Kvočka*, Case No. IT–98–30/1–T, para. 139 (Nov. 2, 2001). Does the *Kunarac* decision mean that any non-state actor who intentionally inflicts severe pain or suffering on an individual in furtherance of one of the prohibited purposes is liable for torture under international criminal law? Given that the Torture Convention defines torture in terms of state action, does this opinion violate the principle of legality and the prohibition against *ex post facto* law?

4. The Committee Against Torture and State Action

The Committee Against Torture is the body created to monitor compliance with the Convention Against Torture. State parties are required to submit periodic reports to the Committee, and individuals may bring petitions under the Convention against states that have agreed to be the subject of such claims. The Committee Against Torture has relaxed the state action requirement of the definition of torture in cases involving countries without an effective government. Thus, in the context of a claim brought by a Somali citizen challenging an Australian decision to return him to Somalia, the Committee found that a fear of severe ill treatment at the hands of groups that have set up "quasi-governmental institutions" that "*de facto* . . . exercise certain prerogatives that are comparable to those normally exercised by legitimate governments" triggered Australia's *non-refoulement* obligations. *Elmi v. Australia*, CAT/C/22/D/120/1998 (1999), para. 6.5. A few years later, the Committee found that the recent creation of a Transitional National Government in Somalia precluded a finding that acts committed by non-state actors like those at issue in *Elmi* could qualify as torture under the Convention definition. *H.M.H.I. v. Australia*, CAT/C/28/D/177/2001 (2002), para. 6.4.

In addition, states may bear responsibility for acts of torture committed by private actors when public authorities fail to "exercise due diligence to prevent, investigate, prosecute and punish" such non-state actors. Committee Against Torture, General Comment 2, Implementation of Article 2 by State Parties, U.N. Doc. CAT/C/GC/2/CRP.1/rev. 4 (2007). (In human rights law, General Comments are authoritative interpretations of a treaty by the expert bodies charged with overseeing its implementation). Similarly, the European Court of Human Rights has held that the prohibition against *refoulement* still applies even if the risk of mistreatment emanates from private groups or individuals. *HLR v. France,* III Eur. Ct HR 745; 26 EHRR 29 (1997).

5. A Feminist Critique

Should the law on torture distinguish between "private" and "public" acts or motivations? Feminist scholars have long argued that the distinction between the public and private spheres privileges men and discriminates against women. This discrimination is reflected in the different treatment of assaults against individuals within private homes (which are predominantly directed against women and children), and assaults against individuals within state custody (which affect women and men, but is the primary place where men are the objects of such violence). For a discussion of the discriminatory impact of this distinction under international human rights law in the context of torture and its purpose requirement, *see* Rhonda Copelon, *Recognizing the Egregious in the Everyday: Domestic Violence as Torture*, 25 COLUM. HUM. RTS. L. REV. 291 (1994). Ela Grdinić argues that domestic violence qualifies as torture under the jurisprudence of the European Court of Human Rights and the now-defunct European Commission of Human Rights. Ela Grdinić, *Application of the Elements of Torture and Other Forms of Ill-Treatment, as Defined by the European Court and Commission of Human Rights, to the Incidents of Domestic Violence*, 23

HASTINGS INT'L & COMP. L. REV. 217 (2000). If the distinction between acts of torture by state actors and acts of torture by private actors were eliminated, would every act of domestic torture implicate international criminal law? For a more general treatment of the feminist critique of the public/private distinction and international human rights law, *see* Celina Romany, *Women as Aliens: A Feminist Critique of the Public/Private Distinction in International Human Rights Law*, 6 HARV. HUM. RTS. J. 87 (1993).

6. Prohibited Acts

Why does the Torture Convention include a general definition without a list (exemplary or closed) of acts deemed torture *per se*? As you review the materials in this chapter consider what acts you would include on such a list. In 1985, the United Nations established a Special Rapporteur on Torture with a mandate to examine allegations of torture in any state in the world. In a 1986 report, the Special Rapporteur identified the following acts as constituting torture: beatings; extraction of nails, teeth, etc.; burns; electric shocks; suspension; suffocation; exposure to excessive light or noise; sexual aggression; administration of drugs in detention or psychiatric institutions; prolonged denial of rest or sleep; prolonged denial of food; prolonged denial of sufficient hygiene; prolonged denial of medical assistance; total isolation and sensory deprivation; being kept in constant uncertainty in terms of space and time; threats to torture or kill relatives; total abandonment; and simulated executions. Report of the Special Rapporteur on Torture, U.N. Doc. No. E/CN.4 /1986/15, para. 119 (1986).

7. Purpose

What justification is there for including a purpose element in the definition of torture? Should this element be removed? Restricted? Expanded? The language of the requirement, "for such purposes as," raises the question of whether the listed purposes are exhaustive. If the list is read exclusively, what types of torture are excluded from the Convention's definition? The ICTY has held that the Torture Convention's list of purposes is not exhaustive:

> 470. The use of the words "for such purposes" in the customary definition of torture, indicate that the various listed purposes do not constitute an exhaustive list, and should be regarded as merely representative. Further, there is no requirement that the conduct must be solely perpetrated for a prohibited purpose. Thus, in order for this requirement to be met, the prohibited purpose must simply be part of the motivation behind the conduct and need not be the predominating or sole purpose.
>
> 471. A fundamental distinction regarding the purpose for which torture is inflicted is that between a "prohibited purpose" and one which is purely private. The rationale behind this distinction is that the prohibition on torture is not concerned with private conduct, which is ordinarily sanctioned under national law. In particular, rape and other sexual assaults have often been labeled as "private," thus precluding them from being punished

under national or international law. However, such conduct could meet the purposive requirements of torture as, during armed conflicts, the purposive elements of intimidation, coercion, punishment or discrimination can often be integral components of behavior, thus bringing the relevant conduct within the definition. Accordingly,

> [o]nly in exceptional cases should it therefore be possible to conclude that the infliction of severe pain or suffering by a public official would not constitute torture . . . on the ground that he acted for purely private reasons.

Prosecutor v. Delalić, Case No. IT–96–21–T, Judgement (Nov. 16, 1998) (citing J. Herman Burgess & Hans Danelius, A HANDBOOK ON THE CONVENTION AGAINST TORTURE AND OTHER CRUEL, INHUMAN OR DEGRADING TREATMENT OR PUNISHMENT 119 (1988)).

8. Specific Intent, General Intent and Motive

Recall that the concept of specific intent encompasses the intent to produce a particular consequence or harm as a result of the crime. For example, the domestic crime of larceny/theft involves the taking of personal property with the intent to permanently deprive its rightful owner of it. In order to convict a person of larceny, the prosecutor must prove that the defendant intended to keep the property permanently, not just that the defendant took the property. In international criminal law, genocide is the classic specific intent crime—it requires the specific intent to destroy in whole or in part a protected group. By contrast, a general intent crime only requires a showing that the defendant intended to commit the act that is prohibited by the law. Both forms of intent are thus distinct from an individual's motive, which is the reason that a person acts (or fails to act). Domestic systems that recognize the concept of specific intent allow the trier of fact to infer the intent from the facts in the case. In particular, the doctrine of presumed intent holds that individuals are presumed to intend the natural and probable consequences of their acts. Does the Torture Convention define torture in terms of specific intent, general intent, motive or some combination of the three? How is this question answered by the *Kunarac* case? Is the Appeals Chamber clear on the distinction between intent and motive? Does the Trial Chamber significantly alter the Torture Convention's definition of torture with its analysis?

9. Torture Before the ICC

The prohibition against torture appears in the ICC Statute as a crime against humanity (Article 7(1)(f)) and a war crime that may be committed within an international (Article 8(2)(a)(ii)) or non-international (Article (2)(c)(i)) armed conflict. The Elements of Crimes also make clear that torture can constitute "serious bodily harm" for the purpose of genocide (Article 6(b)). The Elements of Crimes list the following elements for proving torture as a crime against humanity:

1) The perpetrator inflicted severe physical or mental pain or suffering upon one or more persons.

2) Such person or persons were in the custody or under the control of the perpetrator.

3) Such pain or suffering did not arise only from, and was not inherent in or incidental to, lawful sanctions.

4) The conduct was committed as part of a widespread or systematic attack directed against a civilian population.

5) The perpetrator knew that the conduct was part of or intended the conduct to be part of a widespread or systematic attack directed against a civilian population.

The notes indicate that "[i]t is understood that no specific purpose need be proved for this crime." When torture is charged as a grave breach under the Geneva Conventions pursuant to Article 8(2)(a)(ii), the following elements are applicable per the ICC Elements of Crimes:

1) The perpetrator inflicted severe physical or mental pain or suffering upon one or more persons.

2) The perpetrator inflicted the pain or suffering for such purposes as: obtaining information or a confession, punishment, intimidation or coercion or for any reason based on discrimination of any kind.

3) Such person or persons were protected under one or more of the Geneva Conventions of 1949.

4) The perpetrator was aware of the factual circumstances that established that protected status.

5) The conduct took place in the context of and was associated with an international armed conflict.

6) The perpetrator was aware of factual circumstances that established the existence of an armed conflict.

When torture is charged in connection with a non-international armed conflict governed by common Article 3, the victim must be *hors de combat*, a civilian, or a member of the medical or religious personnel taking no active part in the hostilities. The other elements are comparable to those governing torture as a grave breach. What do the Elements of Crimes say about some of the outstanding issues concerning the definition of torture, such as whether it is a specific intent crime? Would any of the cases above come out differently if they had been prosecuted before the ICC?

10. Severity: Torture v. Cruel, Inhuman or Degrading Treatment

The Convention Against Torture prohibits both torture and "other cruel, inhuman, or degrading treatment" (CIDT), but only requires that states criminalize torture (Articles 4 and 5). International humanitarian law also contains prohibitions of torture and other forms of cruel treatment, and these acts also constitute enumerated crimes against humanity. The Rwanda Tribunal Statute thus criminalizes "cruel treatment," "outrages upon personal dignity, in particular humiliating and degrading treatment," and "other inhumane acts." *See* ICTR Statute, Articles 3(i) ("other inhumane acts" constituting crimes against humanity), 4(a) (cruel treatment as a violation of common Article 3 of the Geneva Conventions and Protocol II), and 4(e) (outrages upon personal dignity as a violation of common Article 3 of the Geneva Conventions and Protocol II). *See also* ICTY Statute, Articles 2(b) (torture and inhuman treatment as grave breaches of the Geneva Conventions) and 5 (torture and "other inhumane acts" as constituting crimes against humanity). How should international criminal law distinguish between acts of torture, other acts of cruel treatment that fall short of torture, and other harmful conduct that does not rise to the level of an international crime? Where along this continuum of mistreatment should the line be drawn between human rights violation and international crime?

Consider the following excerpt. Radomir Kovač was convicted by the ICTY of crimes against humanity as part of the *Kunarac* case excerpted above. Kovač, a member of a militia known as the "Dragan Nikolić unit," was charged with acts of rape, enslavement, and outrages upon personal dignity committed against a number of young women whom he kept in an apartment. The Trial Chamber found that the young women, who ranged in age from 15 to 25, "were frequently sexually assaulted and that they were beaten, threatened, psychologically oppressed and kept in constant fear," were required to "take care of the household chores, the cooking and the cleaning," were forced to dance naked, and their diet and hygiene were "completely neglected." *Prosecutor v. Kunarac, et al.*, Case No. IT–96–23 & 23–1, Judgement, paras. 746–782 (Feb. 22, 2001). On appeal, Kovač challenged, among other things, his conviction for outrages upon personal dignity, arguing that the Trial Chamber did not adequately define the acts that would qualify as the crime in question and that the Prosecution had neglected to establish his specific intent to humiliate or degrade the victims. The Appeals Chamber upheld Kovač's conviction and commented on the crime of outrages upon personal dignity as set forth below.

Prosecutor v. Kunarac, et al., Case No. IT–96–23 & 23–1A, Judgement (June 12, 2002)

In the Appeals Chamber

157. The Appellant Kovač submits that, since every humiliating or degrading act is not necessarily an outrage upon personal dignity, the acts likely to be outrages upon personal dignity must be defined, and he further argues that the Trial Chamber did not do so.

158. Moreover, the Appellant asserts that to find a person guilty of outrages upon personal dignity, a specific intent to humiliate or degrade the victim must be established. In his opinion, the Trial Chamber did not prove beyond any reasonable doubt that he acted with the intention to humiliate his victims, as his objective was of an exclusively sexual nature.

159. In response to the Appellant's claim that the Trial Chamber did not state which acts constituted outrages upon personal dignity, the Respondent recalls that the Trial Chamber considered that it had been proved beyond any reasonable doubt that, during their detention in

Kovač's apartment, the victims were repeatedly raped, humiliated and degraded. That the victims were made to dance naked on a table, that they were "lent" and sold to other men and that [witnesses] FWS-75 and FWS-87 were raped by Kovač while he was playing "Swan Lake" were all correctly characterised by the Trial Chamber as outrages upon personal dignity. * * *

161. The Trial Chamber ruled that the crime of outrages upon personal dignity requires:

> (i) that the accused intentionally committed or participated in an act or an omission which would be generally considered to cause serious humiliation, degradation or otherwise be a serious attack on human dignity, and (ii) that he knew that the act or omission could have that effect.

162. Contrary to the claims of the Appellant, the Appeals Chamber considers that the Trial Chamber was not obliged to define the specific acts which may constitute outrages upon personal dignity. Instead, it properly presented the criteria which it used as a basis for measuring the humiliating or degrading character of an act or omission. The Trial Chamber, referring to the *Aleksovski* case, stated that the humiliation of the victim must be so intense that any reasonable person would be outraged. In coming to its conclusion, the Trial Chamber did not rely only on the victim's purely subjective evaluation of the act to establish whether there had been an outrage upon personal dignity, but used objective criteria to determine when an act constitutes a crime of outrages upon personal dignity.

163. In explaining that outrages upon personal dignity are constituted by "any act or omission which would be *generally* considered to cause serious humiliation, degradation or otherwise be a serious attack on human dignity," the Trial Chamber correctly defined the objective threshold for an act to constitute an outrage upon personal dignity. It was not obliged to list the acts which constitute outrages upon personal dignity. For this reason, this ground of appeal is dismissed.

164. According to the Trial Chamber, the crime of outrages upon personal dignity requires that the accused knew that his act or omission *could* cause serious humiliation, degradation or otherwise be a serious attack on human dignity. The Appellant, however, asserts that this crime requires that the accused knew that his act or omission *would have* such an effect.

165. The Trial Chamber carried out a detailed review of the case-law relating to the *mens rea* of the crime of outrages upon personal dignity. The Trial Chamber was never directly confronted with the specific question of whether the crime of outrages upon personal dignity requires a specific intent to humiliate or degrade or otherwise seriously attack human dignity. However, after reviewing the case-law, the Trial Chamber properly demonstrated that the crime of outrages upon

personal dignity requires only knowledge of the "possible" consequences of the charged act or omission. The relevant paragraph of the Trial Judgement reads as follows:

> As the relevant act or omission for an outrage upon personal dignity is an act or omission which would be generally considered to cause serious humiliation, degradation or otherwise be a serious attack on human dignity, an accused must know that his act or omission is of that character—i.e., that it could cause serious humiliation, degradation or affront to human dignity. This is not the same as requiring that the accused knew of the *actual* consequences of the act.

166. Since the nature of the acts committed by the Appellant * * * undeniably reaches the objective threshold for the crime of outrages upon personal dignity set out in the Trial Judgement, the Trial Chamber correctly concluded that any reasonable person would have perceived his acts "to cause serious humiliation, degradation or otherwise be a serious attack on human dignity." Therefore, it appears highly improbable that the Appellant was not, at the very least, aware that his acts could have such an effect. Consequently this ground of appeal is rejected.

NOTES & QUESTIONS

1. Other Outrages upon Personal Dignity

In other cases, the ICTY found the following to also constitute outrages upon personal dignity: (1) subjecting individuals to inappropriate conditions of confinement, forcing individuals to engage in subservient acts or to relieve bodily functions in their clothing; and placing someone in fear of being subjected to physical, mental, or sexual violence (*Prosecutor v. Miroslav Kvočka et al.*, Case No. IT–98–30/1T, Judgement, para. 173 (Nov. 2, 2001)); and (2) using detainees as human shields or trench diggers (*Prosecutor v. Aleksovski*, Case No. IT–95–14/1T, Judgement, para. 229 (June 25, 1999); *Prosecutor v. Blaškić,* Case No. IT–95–14–A, Judgement, paras. 653, 669 (July 29, 2004)). Would such acts constitute torture or CIDT under the Torture Convention or the Inter-American Convention on Torture? The International Criminal Court's Elements of Crimes provides further guidance on the definition of outrages upon personal dignity:

- The perpetrator humiliated, degraded or otherwise violated the dignity of one or more persons.
- The severity of the humiliation, degradation and other violation was of such a degree as to be generally recognized as an outrage upon personal dignity.

Does this formulation give sufficient notice to potential defendants of the prohibited conduct?

2. Lasting Impact of Harm

Should it matter whether the effect of the harm inflicted is long-lasting, or is a temporary impact sufficient? Consider the following ruling of the Trial

Chamber in *Prosecutor v. Aleksovski*, Case No. 95–14/1T, Judgement, para. 56 (June 25, 1999):

> An outrage against personal dignity is an act which is animated by contempt for the human dignity of another person. The corollary is that the act must cause serious humiliation or degradation to the victim. It is not necessary for the act to directly harm the physical or mental well-being of the victim. It is enough that the act causes real and lasting suffering to the individual arising from the humiliation or ridicule.

The Trial Chamber in *Prosecutor v. Kunarac et al.*, Case No. 96–23 & 23/1–T, Judgement, para. 501 (Feb. 22, 2001), disagreed with the *Aleksovski* decision on this point:

> Insofar as [*Aleksovski*] provides that an outrage upon personal dignity is an act which "cause[s] serious humiliation or degradation to the victim," the Trial Chamber agrees with it. However, the Trial Chamber would not agree with any indication from the passage above that this humiliation or degradation must cause "lasting suffering" to the victim. So long as the humiliation or degradation is real and serious, the Trial Chamber can see no reason why it would also have to be "lasting." In the view of the Trial Chamber, it is not open to regard the fact that a victim has recovered or is overcoming the effects of such an offence as indicating of itself that the relevant acts did not constitute an outrage upon personal dignity. Obviously, if the humiliation and suffering caused is only fleeting in nature, it may be difficult to accept that it is real and serious. However this does not suggest that any sort of minimum temporal requirement of the effects of an outrage upon personal dignity is an element of the offence.

How do you think the disagreement between the two Trial Chambers should be resolved? Should the requirement of lasting impact be the same as for torture, or should "outrages upon personal dignity" be treated differently? Why?

3. Torture v. CIDT

The Committee Against Torture, which monitors compliance with the Torture Convention, has affirmed the obligations to prevent torture and CIDT are "interdependent, indivisible and interrelated." Committee Against Torture, General Comment 2, Implementation of Article 2 by State Parties, U.N. Doc. CAT/C/GC/2/CRP.1/rev. 4 (2007). Nigel Rodley, a former U.N. Special Rapporteur on Torture, identified three elements distinguishing torture from CIDT: (1) the relative intensity of the pain or suffering inflicted; (2) the purpose for inflicting the pain or suffering; and (3) the status of the perpetrator as a state or private actor. Sir Nigel Rodley, *The Definition(s) of Torture in International Law*, *in* CURRENT LEGAL PROBLEMS 467 (Michael Freedman ed., 2002).

How should an adjudicative body measure severity? Should there be an objective test or a subjective test (along the lines of the famous "eggshell skull" rules from torts) given that the long-term effects of such conduct can vary from person-to-person, depending upon the individual's personal circumstances, age and general state of physical and mental health, support network, length of detention, etc.? Rodley has argued that it is "virtually impossible" to ascertain the level of severity required for an act to qualify as torture. Nigel Rodley, THE TREATMENT OF PRISONERS UNDER INTERNATIONAL LAW 98 (2d ed. 1999). The ICTY has created a case-by-case test that combines objective and subjective elements, further complicating the issue:

> In assessing the seriousness of any mistreatment, the objective severity of the harm inflicted must be considered, including the nature, purpose and consistency of the acts committed. Subjective criteria, such as the physical or mental condition of the victim, the effect of the treatment and, in some cases, factors such as the victim's age, sex, state of health and position of inferiority will also be relevant in assessing the gravity of the harm. Permanent injury is not a requirement for torture; evidence of the suffering need not even be visible after the commission of the crime.

Prosecutor v. Brđanin, Case No. IT–99–36–T, Judgement, para. 484 (Sept. 1, 2004). Compare the test articulated by the Trial Chamber in *Brđanin* with that of a different Trial Chamber:

> With respect to the assessment of the seriousness of the acts charged as torture, previous jurisprudence of the Tribunal has held that this should take into account all circumstances of the case and in particular the nature and context of the infliction of pain, the premeditation and institutionalization of the ill-treatment, the physical condition of the victim, the manner and the method used and the position of inferiority of the victim. Also relevant to the Chamber's assessment is the physical or mental effect of the treatment on the victim, the victim's age, sex, or state of health. Further, if the mistreatment has occurred over a prolonged period of time, the Chamber would assess the severity of the treatment as a whole. Finally, this Chamber concurs with the finding of the *Čelebići* Trial Chamber, made specifically in the context of rape, that in certain circumstances the suffering can be exacerbated by social and cultural conditions and it should take into account the specific social, cultural and religious background of the victims when assessing the severity of the alleged conduct.

Prosecutor v. Limaj, Case No. IT–03–66–T, Judgement, para. 237 (Nov. 30, 2005). Likewise, consider this approach, which reasoned that the subjective element of an outrage

> must be tempered by objective factors; otherwise, unfairness to the accused would result because his/her culpability would depend not on the gravity of the act but wholly on the sensitivity of the victim. Consequently, an objective component to the *actus reus* is apposite: the humiliation to the victim must be so intense that the reasonable person would be outraged.

Prosecutor v. Aleksovski, Case No. IT–95–14/1, Judgement, para. 56 (June 25, 1999).

4. Torture's Effects

There is a sophisticated body of medical literature on the short- and long-term effects of torture and other forms of ill-treatment, both physical and psychological on victims. One study found that torture survivors experienced various forms of trauma, including a state of psychosis, with long-lasting aftereffects. John Conroy, UNSPEAKABLE ACTS, ORDINARY PEOPLE: THE DYNAMICS OF TORTURE (2000); Stefan Priebe & Michael Bauer, *Inclusion of Psychological Torture in PTSD [Post Traumatic Stress Disorder] Criterion A*, 152 AM. J. PSYCHIATRY 1691–2 (1995). A report produced by 75 experts organized by the Human Rights Foundation of Turkey and Physicians for Human Rights listed the following physical and psychological effects of torture:

> Common somatic complaints include headache, back pain, gastrointestinal symptoms, sexual dysfunction, and muscle pain. Common psychological symptoms include depressive affect, anxiety, insomnia, nightmares, flashbacks, and memory difficulties.

Istanbul Protocol, para. 170, U.N. Doc. HR/P/PT/8 (1999). In a study of the effect of psychological torture by U.S. forces against detainees, Physicians for Human Rights listed the following possible impacts of psychological torture:

> memory impairment, reduced capacity to concentrate, somatic complaints such as headache and back pain, hyperarousal, avoidance, and irritability. Additionally, victims often experience severe depression with vegetative symptoms, nightmares, and 'feelings of shame and humiliation' associated with sexual violations, among others.

Physicians for Human Rights, *Break Them Down: Systematic Use of Psychological Torture by U.S. Forces* (2005). For an extensive discussion of the medical effects of torture, *see* the three-part series by Ole V. Rasmussen et al., *Medical, Physical Examination in Connection with Torture*, in 14 TORTURE J. 46 (2004) (Section 1); 15 TORTURE J. 37 (2005) (Section 2); and 16 Torture Journal 48 (2006) (Section 3). For a profound philosophical and cultural treatment of torture and pain that draws upon literature, art, documentation of torture from Amnesty International, and the writings of Clausewitz, Churchill, and Kissinger, *see* Elaine Scarry, THE BODY IN PAIN: THE MAKING AND UNMAKING OF THE WORLD (1985). For a longitudinal study of individuals who had been detained on Guantánamo, *see* Laurel E. Fletcher & Eric Stover, THE GUANTÁNAMO EFFECT (2009).

Little research exists on the impact of torture on torturers. Why might this be so? The limited research available suggests that participating in human rights abuses can exert a negative psychological impact on perpetrators. The concept of "moral injury" describes the adverse impact on soldiers and others of being personally involved in an experience that violates core values and principles. *See* WAR AND MORAL INJURY: A READER (Robert Emmet Meagher & Douglas A. Pryer eds., 2018). Moral injury involves a cluster of symptoms that are similar to PTSD but also has a spiritual component linked to the sanctity of life. Michael D. Matthews, *Moral Injury: Toxic Leadership, Maleficent Organizations, and Psychological Distress*, PSYCHOL. TODAY (Mar. 10, 2018). Some transitional justice programs have endeavored to address this moral injury by providing opportunities for perpetrators to "pay their dues" in order to be re-absorbed into society. In Timor-Leste, for example, perpetrators of less serious crimes were able to enter into agreements (which were filed in court) to undertake community service as part of community reconciliation procedures. Geoffrey Gunn & Reyko Huang, *Reconciliation as State-building in East Timor*, 11 LUSOTOPIE 19, 32 (2004).

5. "Torture Lite"

Interrogation techniques such as sleep deprivation, stress positions (so-called "self-inflicted pain"), isolation and sensory deprivation, temperature and dietary manipulation, noise bombardment, psychological humiliations (forced nudity, prevention of personal hygiene, forced grooming, denial of privacy, and infested surroundings), threats against self or family, attacks on cultural values or religious beliefs, and mock execution, have been described as "torture lite," because they do not at first consideration bear the hallmarks of brutality associated with ancient forms of torture—such as those described by Professor Langbein—or of today's notorious authoritarian regimes. These forms of abuse—which are often called "clean" or "stealth" torture—do not physically mutilate or maim the victim's body, leave permanent physical traces, require direct contact between the victim and the individual utilizing the particular technique, or cause pain immediately.

And yet, are such techniques truly less severe than the rack and screw of yesteryear? Detainees in U.S. custody have died as a result of these techniques: for example, one individual reportedly froze to death in a CIA "black site" prison in Afghanistan, and another died after being beaten and then placed in a stress position in Abu Ghraib. How would the special characteristics of "torture lite" alter the way in which victims, perpetrators, policymakers, or the general public might interpret the legality, efficacy, and morality of these techniques? Might the combined effects of such techniques be more disruptive and damaging than a short but brutal beating? A 2007 study of victims of torture compared the long-term psychological effects of "torture lite" techniques and more physically violent torture. The authors conclude:

> Ill treatment during captivity, such as psychological manipulations, humiliating treatment, and forced stress positions, does not seem to be substantially different from physical torture in terms of the severity of mental suffering they cause, the underlying mechanism of traumatic stress, and their long-term psychological outcome. * * * These findings suggest that physical pain *per se* is not the most important determinant of traumatic stress in survivors of torture. * * * These findings [also] imply that various psychological manipulations, ill treatment, and torture during interrogation share the same psychological mechanism in exerting their traumatic impact. All three types of acts are geared toward creating anxiety or fear in the detainee while at the same time

> removing any form of control from the person to create a state of total helplessness.

See Metin Başoğlu, Maria Livanou, & Cvetana Crnobarić, *Torture vs. Other Cruel, Inhuman, and Degrading Treatment: Is the Distinction Real or Apparent?*, 64(3) ARCHIVES GEN. PSYCHIATRY 277, 284 (2007). According to these researchers, what mattered most in terms of long-term effects were subjective factors, such as the victim's level of distress, feelings of helplessness, stressor interactions, and the perceived degree of uncontrollability of the situation. Indeed, declassified CIA-funded research from the 1950s and 1960s found that such techniques could be very effective at breaking prisoners. *See* KUBARK COUNTERINTELLIGENCE INTERROGATION (1963) (available at https://nsarchive2.gwu.edu/NSAEBB/NSAEBB27/docs/doc01.pdf).

On the basis of self-reporting by detainees in the former Yugoslavia and Turkey, Başoğlu concludes that acts of CIDT are ranked as more severe than acts of physical torture and are more often associated with Post-Traumatic Stress Disorder (PTSD). Should the assessment of whether conduct constitutes torture or CIDT turn on whether the conduct causes long-term physical or psychological effects or is the degree of immediate suffering by a victim more relevant? On "torture lite," consider this perspective:

> [T]he use of terms like "torture lite" and the nature of such techniques encourage a moral psychology in which the violence and cruelty of torture is denied, the victim's suffering is hidden, minimized and doubted, and the torturer's responsibility is diminished. As such, the use of torture lite techniques is likely to encourage the normalization of torture. * * * The distinction between the methods referred to as torture lite and so-called real torture serves a further aim: it is sometimes used to distinguish not only between types of torture methods but also between the *moral character* of torturers and their *motivations*. According to this view, torturers who use such methods as beatings and mutilations are clearly brutal and sadistic, whereas those who use torture lite techniques can be portrayed as professionals motivated by the need to gain intelligence essential for saving lives. * * * By creating a false distinction between *torture* (understood as violent, brutal, and physically mutilating) and torture *lite* (with its connotations of minimal harm, minimal force, and minimal violence), those who authorize the use of torture and those who carry it out are able to portray their actions (to themselves and to observers) as something other than *real* torture, with all the negative connotations of that word. * * * Terms such as "torture lite" and "enhanced interrogation" neutralize the violence of these techniques and downplay the suffering they cause. Such euphemisms can also have a strong impact on how those using these terms (interrogators, public officials, and the general public) perceive the morality of the techniques thus described.

Jessica Wolfendale, *The Myth of "Torture Lite,"* 23 ETHICS & INT'L AFFAIRS 47 (2009).

6. *Incommunicado* Detention

Might *incommunicado* detention, even in luxurious conditions, constitute torture, CIDT, or some other international crime? How would you make such an argument within the framework of the Torture Convention or the ICC Statute?

PROBLEMS

1. Criminal Abortion

Prior to 2008, Nicaraguan law permitted "therapeutic abortions" only for those women and girls whose life or health was threatened by the continuation of their pregnancy and, in some cases, for victims of rape. The revised penal code (which came into force in 2008), repealed this provision. *See* Law No. 164, Penal Code of the Republic of Nicaragua. Nicaraguan law now completely prohibits abortion, regardless of the circumstances and even if the woman has been raped, is the victim of incest, or is at physical risk from the continuation of the pregnancy. Abortion is also prohibited if the baby is unviable as in cases of anencephaly—a neural tube defect in which the fetus fails to develop a brain or skull vault and is born with dramatic physical defects. The condition is uniformly fatal; the baby is literally born dying and usually survives only a few days.

A violation of this law can result in prison terms for both doctors and women or girls who carry out, or seek, an abortion (Article 143) and for doctors who cause unintentional harm to a fetus while administering medically-necessary treatment to a pregnant women or girl (Articles 145, 148, and 149). Even women who miscarry may be investigated. Article 143 provides:

> Whosoever causes an abortion with the consent of the woman shall be sanctioned with a penalty of one to three years in prison. If the person is a medical professional or health worker, the penalty will simultaneously include being prohibited from working in medicine or as a health worker for two to five years. The woman who intentionally causes her own abortion or agrees with someone else to provide an abortion will face a penalty of one to two years in prison.

In a submission to the Committee Against Torture—the body charged with ensuring state compliance with the Convention Against Torture—Amnesty International argued that the penal legislation violated Nicaragua's obligations under the treaty. *See* Amnesty International, *Nicaragua: The Impact of the Complete Ban of Abortion in Nicaragua: Briefing to the United Nations Committee Against Torture*, Index No. AMR 43/005/2009 (April 29, 2009). How would you make such an argument? If you were a lawyer within the Foreign Ministry of Nicaragua, how would you defend against such charges? Do such laws rise to the level of crimes against humanity?

2. Child Separation Policy

In March 2017, John Kelly, then Secretary of the Department of Homeland Security, indicated in a media interview that the Trump administration was considering taking children from their parents at the border "to deter more movement along this terribly dangerous network." In April, then-Attorney General Jeff Sessions issued a memorandum to all U.S. Attorneys' offices announcing a nationwide policy to prosecute all adults who crossed the border "illegally." The misdemeanor in question, codified at 8 U.S.C. § 1325(a), makes it a crime to "improper[ly]" enter, or attempt to enter, the United States without appearing before an immigration officer or through the making of willfully false or misleading representations. The Trump administration claimed that the new "zero tolerance" policy was necessary to respond to a "crisis" on the border and the "flood" of migrants, drugs, gang members, and other contraband coming into this country. And yet, the policy applied to anyone improperly entering the country—even those requesting political asylum who have a legal right to press their claim for refuge. Government documents as well as statements from multiple U.S. officials reveal that the core purpose of the separation policy was actually to punish individuals who crossed the border improperly and to deter others from following suit.

Under the administration's policy, it was envisioned that when a parent and child arrived at the border or a port of entry, the parent would be criminally prosecuted for his or her unlawful border crossing and placed in a detention center while awaiting a hearing. Because children cannot be incarcerated with their parents for more than 20 days, they were rendered—in essence—unaccompanied under U.S. law. The now "unaccompanied minor" would fall within the jurisdiction of Department of Health and Human Services (HHS)' Office of Refugee Resettlement (ORR) pursuant to the Homeland Security Act of 2002. HHS/ORR would then be responsible for the child's shelter and care until he or she could be placed with another caregiver or sponsor.

ORR ended up housing children in shelters all over the country, sometimes thousands of miles away from where their parents were being detained. Many children were placed in makeshift centers, such as retrofitted big box stores, warehouses, and tent cities managed by private contractors. Adults, by contrast, were held in criminal detention by Immigration and Customs Enforcement (ICE). As a result of the policy, over 2,300 children were separated from their parents between the beginning of the policy and June 20, 2019, when President Donald Trump ordered a halt to it. This included infants, toddlers, disabled children, and at least one child with Down's Syndrome. Very few of these children were able to adequately advocate for themselves or even tell U.S. authorities the full names of their parents. Journalists have reported heart-breaking stories of children being separated for so long that they did not immediately recognize their parents when they were finally reunited. Advocates have also indicated that many parents thought that they would be separated from their children for a matter of hours, not months or even indefinitely. Parents were also pressured to sign voluntary departure forms out of desperation to be reunited with their children. This generally results in a waiver of any asylum claims.

In response to the sharp and unrelenting domestic and international outcry over the policy of family separation, Trump hastily issued an executive order (E.O. 13841) on June 20, 2019, announcing the ostensible end of the family separation policy (belying his earlier protestations that congressional action was necessary for it to end) and directing DHS to detain family units together. Even as court-ordered reunifications began, the Trump administration could not indicate how many children were still separated from their parents. Reunions were hampered by the fact that some parents had been released from custody into the United States, were already deported, were already serving criminal sentences, or had been accused of serious criminal violations. DNA tests were also deemed necessary to ensure accurate reunions.

Allegations have emerged of children having been abused in these detention facilities, including claims that children were sexually assaulted by facility employees. Lawyers representing children held in some Customs & Border Protection (CBP) centers have compiled copious evidence revealing that their clients have been subjected to unsanitary and inhumane conditions of detention. This includes receiving inadequate food, experiencing enforced dehydration and sleep deprivation, being denied privacy in overcrowded facilities, and being kept in artificially cold temperatures. Media have reported that children were kept in cages. In addition, there appear to be little to no educational services to speak of. Several children have died after receiving inadequate medical care. A court also found that children in detention were being over-medicated and administered psychotropic drugs without parental consent or judicial authorization through a court order. These medications, which react with the central nervous system, can have long-term side effects (hallucinations, self-harm, suicidal ideation, etc.) when administered to adolescents or children. Many of these drugs are not approved for use on children by the Food & Drug Administration. Lawyers have alleged that detention facility personnel administered these medications solely to control the behavior and "pacify" the children and not because the children had a psychiatric disorder in need of treatment.

Child advocates are concerned about the long-term harm of this policy on the children and parents involved. As a general matter, experiencing any form of traumatic event during childhood can have lasting effects on children's psychological health and neurological functioning. C. Heim & C.B. Nemeroff, *The Role of Childhood Trauma in the Neurobiology of Mood and Anxiety Disorders: Preclinical and Clinical Studies*, 49(12) BIOL. PSYCHOLOGY 1023 (2001). Children who have experienced trauma are at a significantly elevated risk of developing enduring mental health problems, including emotional and behavioral problems as well as posttraumatic stress disorder (PTSD), mood disorders, anxiety disorders, learning disorders, and personality disorders. R. Lubit, et al., *Impact of Trauma on Children,* 9(2) J. PSYCHIATR. PRACT. 128 (Mar. 2003). Emotional and behavioral problems seen in survivors of early childhood trauma include fearfulness, nervousness, restlessness, impulsivity and disobedience. Children also manifest other symptoms of trauma-related disorders including depressed mood, anhedonia or an inability to feel happiness or pleasure, changes in appetite/weight, panic symptoms, excessive worry, difficulty concentrating, insomnia, fatigue, emotional numbing, negative changes in cognitions, intrusive thoughts, nightmares, muscle tension, feelings of guilt or worthlessness, psychomotor agitation or retardation, experiential avoidance, and suicidal thoughts.

Exposure to childhood trauma may also contribute to the development of personality disorders that disrupt the child's development of his or her sense of self, as well as their ability to regulate emotions and form positive interpersonal relationships. In addition to these psychological forms of harm, trauma experienced during childhood is also related to deleterious psychosocial outcomes, such as increased risk of self-harm, substance use, domestic violence, and suicide. Bessel A. van der Kolk, *Developmental Trauma Disorder: Towards a Rational Diagnosis for Children with Complex Trauma Histories*, 35(5) PSYCHIATRIC ANNALS 401 (April 2005). Childhood exposure to abuse has been linked to disrupted attachments, poor social skills, difficulties with trust and security in relationships, and poor interpersonal effectiveness. As a result, trauma exposure in childhood is commonly associated with functional impairment including social isolation, impaired security and stability in relationships, and risk for further trauma or victimization. Wendy D'Andrea et al., *Understanding Interpersonal Trauma in Children: Why We Need a Developmentally Appropriate Trauma Diagnosis*, 82 AM. J. ORTHOPSYCHIATRY 187 (2012).

An experience of trauma alters the child's development by prioritizing tasks of survival. This, in turn, interferes with other developmental tasks by diverting cognitive and other resources away from learning and growth. A child exposed to abuse, violence, and threats will utilize his or her survival skills (i.e., fight/flight) more than his or her executive control and emotional regulation skills. A child living in chronic fight/flight mode will continue to allocate their resources to survival, rather than to developing other cognitive or executive functioning skill. At the same time, the child may receive input that efforts to make the world a safer place have failed. As a result, the child can develop dissociative responses as the best means of self-preservation. In addition, children often assume that they are responsible for the traumas they experience, leading to lasting feelings of guilt, self-blame, shame, and worthlessness.

There is a special trauma associated with childhood separation from parents, especially in a child's early years. Early separation from parents is associated with a range of psychiatric symptoms that can persist even into adulthood. This is confirmed by a longitudinal study of Finnish children separated from their parents during World War II. This research shows that the loss of a parent, and especially one who is of the same sex as the child, during early childhood can impact the severity and course of depressive symptoms and personality disorders throughout the child's lifespan. This holds true even for temporary separations from parents in childhood. Temporary separations are also associated with increased rates of substance abuse. Hiroshi Takeuchi et al., *Childhood Parental Separation Experiences and Depressive Symptomatology in Acute Major Depression*, 57(2) PSYCHIATRY & CLINICAL NEUROSCIENCES 215 (April 2003).

The long-term impact of early childhood separation is attributable to physiological changes that occur in children. Such separations often lead to a significant impairment in the ability of the child's central nervous system to respond to and recover from stress. The psychiatric and neurological effects of being separated from their parents appear to be the most pronounced in children who are separated after infancy and before the age of five. In other words, children's brains are physically changed in connection with these sorts of trauma, and thus this harm is not easily remedied. Indeed, increases in depressive symptoms related to childhood parental separation have been demonstrated nearly sixty years post-separation. Heidemarie K. Laurent, *Child Anxiety Symptoms Related to Longitudinal Cortisol Trajectories and Acute Stress Responses: Evidence of Developmental Stress Sensitization*, 124(1) J. ABNORM. PSYCHOL. 68 (2015). In essence, parents serve as a buffer for children from the adverse effects of a toxic stressor—a traumatic experience that engages the prolonged activation of the body's stress management system.

These negative outcomes are compounded in situations in which children experience repeated, or prolonged, traumas, including immigration detention and family separation. Research has found that the duration of detention is positively correlated with deterioration of mental health and overall functioning. Further, the separation from family enhances the uncertainty and distress, leading to further psychological harm. Prompt access to appropriate physical and psychological health services is critical to mitigating the harmful effects of immigration detention. Damion Grasso, *Cumulative Trauma in Childhood*, *in* TREATING COMPLEX TRAUMATIC STRESS DISORDERS IN CHILDREN AND ADOLESCENTS: SCIENTIFIC FOUNDATIONS AND THERAPEUTIC MODELS (C. Greene et al. eds., 2013). All told, the medical research is unequivocal that immigration detention puts children—even when they are accompanied by their parents—at significant risk for negative mental health outcomes and overall poorer socioemotional functioning. These impacts become more acute when accompanied by indefinite family separation.

Does the family separation policy constitute a form of state-sanctioned torture of children and their parents? Are each of the elements of the definition of torture under international law satisfied? What about the idiosyncratic definition of torture in U.S. law (see more on this below)? Would this policy implicate the definition of crimes against humanity under international law? Or the definition of cruel, inhuman, or degrading treatment or punishment?

III. UNITED STATES' DEFINITIONS OF TORTURE

The United States came under increasing scrutiny for certain interrogation practices undertaken at the U.S. military base in Guantánamo Bay, Cuba, and other U.S. military detention centers throughout the world. While U.S. officials continually proclaimed that the United States neither practices nor condones torture, evidence of the severe mistreatment of detainees emerged. In addition, legal memoranda prepared by government lawyers have been made public that discuss when and how detainees may be interrogated using so-called "enhanced interrogation techniques" ("EITs"). In these memoranda, government lawyers offered a number of controversial interpretations of what constitutes torture under the international definition of the offense as well as the prohibition in U.S. law (18 U.S.C. § 2340). These memoranda have been posted on the website of the ACLU, which obtained them through the use of litigation, the Freedom of Information Act (FOIA), and other advocacy. Government officials initially claimed that these memoranda were drafted in advance of the use of EITs; careful chronological research has revealed that some of these legal opinions were actually issued after particular techniques had already been employed.

The memoranda take as their starting point the RUDS—reservations, understandings, and declarations—issued by the United States when it ratified the Convention Against Torture in 1994 and the criminal prohibition against torture codified at 18 U.S.C. § 2340. *See* U.S. Reservations, Declarations, and Understandings, Convention Against Torture and Other Cruel, Inhuman or Degrading Treatment of Punishment, Cong. Rec. S17486–01 (daily ed., Oct. 27, 1990). One reservation states that

> the United States considers itself bound by the obligation under Article 16 to prevent 'cruel, inhuman or degrading treatment or punishment,' only insofar as the term 'cruel, inhuman or degrading treatment or punishment' means the cruel, unusual and inhumane treatment or punishment prohibited by the Fifth, Eighth, and/or Fourteenth Amendments to the Constitution of the United States.

An "understanding" states that a form of specific intent is required for an act to constitute torture and sets forth a closed list of forms of punishable mental torture:

> [W]ith reference to Article 1 [defining torture], the United States understands that, in order to constitute torture, an act must be specifically intended to inflict severe physical or mental pain or suffering and that mental pain or suffering refers to prolonged mental harm caused by or resulting from (1) the intentional infliction or threatened infliction of severe physical pain or suffering; (2) the administration or application, or threatened administration or application, of mind altering substances or other procedures calculated to disrupt profoundly the senses or the personality; (3) the threat of imminent death; or (4) the threat that another person will imminently be subjected to death, severe physical pain or suffering, or the administration or application of mind altering substances or

> other procedures calculated to disrupt profoundly the senses or personality.

Upon ratification, the United States defined torture in its penal code as follows:

> an act committed by a person acting under the color of law specifically intended to inflict severe physical or mental pain or suffering (other than pain or suffering incidental to lawful sanctions) upon another person within his custody or physical control.

18 U.S.C. § 2340(1). Severe mental pain or suffering is defined as:

> the prolonged mental harm caused by or resulting from
>
> (A) the intentional infliction or threatened infliction of severe physical pain or suffering;
>
> (B) the administration or application, or threatened administration or application, of mind-altering substances or other procedures calculated to disrupt profoundly the senses of the personality;
>
> (C) the threat of imminent death; or
>
> (D) the threat that another person will imminently be subjected to death, severe physical pain or suffering, or the administration or application of a mind-altering substance or other procedures calculated to disrupt profoundly the senses or personality.

18 U.S.C. § 2340(2).

An August 1, 2002, memorandum drafted by then-Assistant Attorney General Jay S. Bybee (a former professor of law and now a judge on the Ninth Circuit Court of Appeals) to the then Counsel to the President, Alberto Gonzalez, interpreted the definition of torture under § 2340 as follows:

> *Specific Intent*: "To violate Section 2340A, the statute requires that severe pain and suffering must be inflicted with specific intent. In order for a defendant to have acted with specific intent, he must expressly intend to achieve the forbidden act. * * * As a result, the defendant had to act with the express 'purpose to disobey the law' in order for the *mens rea* element to be satisfied. * * * [A] defendant [must] act with the specific intent to inflict severe pain, [and] the infliction of such pain must be the defendant's precise objective. * * * If the defendant acted knowing that severe pain or suffering was reasonably likely to result from his actions, but no more, he would have acted only with general intent. * * * As a theoretical matter, therefore, knowledge alone that a particular result is certain to occur does not constitute specific intent. * * * While as a theoretical matter such knowledge does not constitute

specific intent, juries are permitted to infer from the factual circumstances that such intent is present. * * * [A] showing that an individual acted with a good faith belief that his conduct would not produce the result that the law prohibits negates specific intent. * * * Where a defendant acts in good faith, he acts with an honest belief that he has not engaged in the proscribed conduct. * * * A good faith belief need not be a reasonable one. * * * Where a defendant holds an unreasonable belief, he will confront the problem of proving to the jury that he actually held that belief."

Severe Pain or Suffering: "[To qualify as severe pain, an act must cause damage that rises to] the level that would ordinarily be associated with a sufficiently serious physical condition or injury such as death, organ failure, or serious impairment of body functions."

Severe Mental Pain or Suffering: "In order to prove 'severe mental pain or suffering,' the statute requires proof of 'prolonged mental harm.' * * * [T]he acts giving rise to the harm must cause some lasting, though not necessarily permanent, damage. For example, the mental strain experienced by an individual during a lengthy and intense interrogation—such as the one that state or local police might conduct upon a criminal suspect—would not meet this requirement. On the other hand, the development of a mental disorder such as post-traumatic stress disorder, which can last months or even years, or even chronic depression, which also can last for a considerable period of time if untreated, might satisfy the prolonged harm requirement." * * *

"A defendant must specifically intend to cause prolonged mental harm for the defendant to have committed torture. It could be argued that a defendant needs to have specific intent only to commit the predicate acts that give rise to prolonged mental harm. Under that view, so long as the defendant specifically intended to, for example, threaten a victim with imminent death, he would have had sufficient *mens rea* for a conviction. According to this view, it would be further necessary for a conviction to show only that the victim factually suffered prolonged mental harm, rather than that the defendant intended to cause it. We believe that this approach is contrary to the text of the statute. The statute requires that the defendant specifically intend to inflict severe mental pain or suffering. Because the statute requires this mental state with respect to the infliction of severe mental pain, and because it expressly defines severe mental pain in terms of prolonged mental harm, that mental state must be present with respect to prolonged mental harm. * * * A defendant could negate a

> showing of specific intent to cause severe mental pain or suffering by showing that he had acted in good faith that his conduct would not amount to the acts prohibited by the statute. Thus if a defendant has a good faith belief that his actions will not result in prolonged mental harm, he lacks the mental state necessary for his action to constitute torture. Because the presence of good faith would negate the specific intent element of torture, it is a complete defense to such a charge."

Dept. of Justice, Memorandum for Alberto R. Gonzales, Counsel to the President, *Standards of Conduct for Interrogation under 18 U.S.C. §§ 2340–2340A* (Aug. 1, 2002) (citations removed).

The August 2002 memo reflected the official U.S. policy on the definition of torture under U.S. law until it was leaked in the summer of 2004, the same summer during which reports, including photographs, of torture and other abuses by U.S. military personnel at the Abu Ghraib prison in Iraq were made public. The Bybee memo was "withdrawn" on June 22, 2004, and replaced in December 2004 by a Memorandum written by Acting Assistant Attorney General Daniel Levin to the then Deputy Attorney General James B. Comey. That memo re-interpreted the definition of torture in 18 U.S.C. § 2340 as follows:

> *Severe*: "Although Congress defined 'torture' * * * to require conduct specifically intended to cause 'severe' pain or suffering, we do not believe Congress intended to reach only conduct involving 'excruciating and agonizing' pain or suffering. * * * Drawing distinctions among gradations of pain (for example, severe, mild, moderate, substantial, extreme, intense, excruciating, or agonizing) is obviously not an easy task, especially given the lack of any precise, objective scientific criteria for measuring pain. * * * We conclude that under some circumstances 'severe physical suffering' may constitute torture even if it does not involve 'severe physical pain.' * * * To constitute '*severe* physical suffering' [as distinct from pain] would have to be a condition of some extended duration or persistence as well as intensity."
>
> *Severe Mental Pain or Suffering*: "[W]e do not believe that Congress intended the definition [of the crime] to create a presumption that any time one of the predicate acts occurs, prolonged mental harm is deemed to result. Turning to the question of what constitutes 'prolonged mental harm caused by or resulting from' a predicate act, we believe that Congress intended this phrase to require mental 'harm' that is caused by or that results from a predicate act, and that has some lasting duration. * * * This damage need not be permanent, but it must continue for a 'prolonged' period of time."
>
> *Special Intent*: "[T]he [specific intent] cases are inconsistent. Some suggest that only a conscious desire to

> produce the proscribed result constitutes specific intent; others suggest that even reasonable foreseeability suffices. * * * In light of the President's directive that the United States not engage in torture, it would not be appropriate to rely on parsing the specific intent element of the statute to approve as lawful conduct that might otherwise amount to torture. Some observations, however, are appropriate. It is clear that the specific intent element would be met if a defendant performed an act and 'consciously desired' that act to inflict severe physical or mental pain or suffering. Conversely, if an individual acted in good faith, and only after reasonable investigation establishing that his conduct would not inflict severe physical or mental pain or suffering, it appears unlikely that he would have the specific intent necessary to violate section 2340. Such an individual could be said neither consciously to desire the proscribed result, nor to have 'knowledge or notice' that his act 'would likely have resulted in' the proscribed outcome.
>
> Two final points on the issue of specific intent. First, specific intent must be distinguished from motive. There is no exception under the statute permitting torture to be used for a 'good reason.' Thus a defendant's motive (to protect national security, for example) is not relevant to the question whether he has acted with the requisite specific intent under the statute. Second, specific intent to take a given action can be found even if the defendant will take the action only conditionally. Thus, for example, the fact that a victim might have avoided being tortured by cooperating with the perpetrator would not make permissible actions otherwise constituting torture under the statute. Presumably that has frequently been the case with torture, but that fact does not make the practice of torture any less abhorrent or unlawful."

Dept. Of Justice, Memorandum for James B. Comey, Deputy Attorney General, *Legal Standards Applicable Under 18 U.S.C. §§ 2340–2340A* (Dec. 30, 2004) (citations removed).

NOTES & QUESTIONS

1. Comparing the Memos

Do you agree with either interpretation of § 2340? In what ways did the Levin memo alter the views contained within the Bybee memo? In what ways is it consistent with those views? In a footnote, Levin concludes that he has "reviewed this Office's prior opinions addressing issues involving treatment of detainees and [does] not believe that any of their conclusions would be different under the standards set forth in this memorandum." *Id.* at 2, n.8. Do you agree?

2. The United States' Understanding

Is the United States' "understanding" of specific intent in the statute consistent with your understanding of the concept as it applies to ordinary domestic law, the crime of torture under the Torture Convention, or the jurisprudence of the ICTY in *Kunarac*? Several states formally objected to the United States' "understanding" of the definition of torture. The Netherlands and Sweden, for example, declared that such an understanding should not affect the obligations of the United States under the treaty. The Netherlands stated the following:

> The Government of the Kingdom of the Netherlands considers the [above-quoted] understanding to have no impact on the obligations of the United States of America under the Convention [as it] . . . appears to restrict the scope of the definition of torture under Article 1 of the Convention.

Do you agree with this assertion that the U.S.'s "understanding" improperly narrows the definition of torture? How?

3. Specific Intent

In the Torture Convention, which element of the definition is modified by the terms "intentionally inflicted"? What arguments might a defendant make to avoid a finding of specific intent under the various formulations? What is the effect of the Bybee and Levin formulations of specific intent? Would it constitute an act of torture if an individual did not intend to inflict severe pain or suffering but did in fact do so? What if the perpetrator knew there was a high likelihood that severe pain or suffering would result from her actions? Can a finding of specific intent be based on willful indifference, which exists where an actor is subjectively aware of the high probability of the fact in question? How might one prove this subjective state of mind? Would the fact that an individual thought in good faith that his or her actions would not cause severe pain or suffering exonerate him if his actions in fact caused serious suffering? How would an individual demonstrate that they were acting "in good faith?" Could an interrogator consult a lawyer for a legal opinion on whether a particular act would cause severe pain or suffering, whether physical or mental?

4. Additional Memoranda

Upon taking office in 2009, President Barack Obama declassified additional "torture memos" (containing varying degrees of redaction). Further memos were released as a result of litigation. Consider the following excerpt from a May 10, 2005, memorandum written by Stephen G. Bradbury, then a Deputy Assistant Attorney General for the Office of Legal Council (OLC) of the Department of Justice. (As of this writing Bradbury is General Counsel of the U.S. Department of Transportation in the Trump Administration). The OLC provides legal advice to the Executive Branch under the leadership of an Assistant Attorney General.

Stephen Bradbury, U.S. Department of Justice Office of Legal Counsel

MEMORANDUM FOR JOHN A. RIZZO SENIOR DEPUTY GENERAL COUNSEL, CENTRAL INTELLIGENCE AGENCY

Re: Application of 18 U.S.C. §§ 2340–2340A to Certain Techniques That May Be Used in the Interrogation of a High Value al Qaeda Detainee

You have asked us to address whether certain specified interrogation techniques designed to be used on a high value al Qaeda detainee in the War on Terror comply with the federal prohibition on torture, codified at 18 U.S.C. §§ 2340–2340A. * * * Because you have asked us to address the application of sections 2340–2340A to specific interrogation techniques, the present memorandum necessarily includes discussion of the applicable legal standards and their application to particular facts. * * *

Torture is abhorrent both to American law and values and to international norms. The universal repudiation of torture is reflected not only in our criminal law, *see e.g.* 18 U.S.C. §§ 2340–2340A, but also in international agreements, in centuries of Anglo-American law, and in the longstanding policy of the United States, repeatedly and recently reaffirmed by the President. Consistent with these norms, the President has directed unequivocally that the United States is not to engage in torture.

The task of interpreting and applying sections 2340–2340A is complicated by the lack of precision in the statutory terms and the lack of relevant case law. In defining the federal crime of torture, Congress required that the defendant "*specifically intend*" to inflict "*severe* physical or mental pain or suffering," and Congress narrowly defined "severe mental pain or suffering" to mean "the *prolonged* mental harm caused by" enumerated predicate acts, including "the threat of *imminent* death" and "procedures *calculated* to disrupt *profoundly* the senses or personality." 18 U.S.C. § 2340 (emphases added). These statutory requirements are consistent with U.S. obligations under the United Nations Convention Against Torture ["CAT"], the treaty that obligates the United States to ensure that torture is a crime under U.S. law and that is implemented by sections 2340–2340A. The requirements in sections 2340–2340A closely track the understandings and reservations required by the Senate when it gave its advice and consent to ratification of the Convention Against Torture. They reflect a clear intent by Congress to limit the scope of the prohibition on torture under U.S. law. However, many of the key terms used in the statute (for example, "severe," "prolonged," "suffering") are imprecise and necessarily bring a degree of uncertainty to addressing the reach of sections 2340–2340A. Moreover, relevant judicial guidance, coupled with the President's clear directive that the United States does not condone or engage in torture, counsel great care in applying the statute to specific conduct. We have attempted to exercise such care throughout this memorandum.

With these considerations in mind, we turn to the particular question before us: whether certain specified interrogation techniques may be used by the Central Intelligence Agency ("CIA") on a high value al Qaeda detainee consistent with the federal statutory prohibition on torture, 18 U.S.C. §§ 2340–2340A.[5] For the reasons discussed below, and based on the representations we have received from you (or officials of your Agency) about the particular techniques in question, the circumstances in which they are authorized for use, and the physical and psychological assessments made of the detainee to be interrogated, we conclude that the separate authorized use of each of the specific techniques at issue, subject to the limitations and safeguards described herein, would not violate sections 2340–2340A. Our conclusion is straightforward with respect to all but two of the techniques discussed herein. As discussed below, use of sleep deprivation as an enhanced technique and use of the waterboard involve more substantial questions, with the waterboard presenting the most substantial question. * * *

I.

In asking us to consider certain specific techniques to be used in the interrogation of a particular al Qaeda operative, you have provided background information common to the use of all of the techniques. You have advised that these techniques would be used only on an individual who is determined to be a "High Value Detainee," defined as:

> a detainee who, until time of capture, we have reason to believe: (1) is a senior member of al-Qai'da or an al-Qai'da associated terrorist group (Jemaah Islamiyyah, Egyptian Islamic Jihad, al-Zarqawi Group, etc.); (2) has knowledge of imminent terrorist threats against the USA, its military forces, its citizens and organizations, or its allies; or that has/had direct involvement in planning and preparing terrorist actions against the USA or its allies, or assisting the al-Qai'da leadership in planning and preparing such terrorist actions; and (3) if released, constitutes a clear and continuing threat to the USA or its allies.

Fax for Daniel Levin, Acting Assistant General, Office of Legal Counsel, from [REDACTED] Assistant General Counsel, CIA, at 3 (Jan. 4, 2005) (*"January 4 [REDACTED] Fax"*). * * *

---

[5] We have previously advised you that the use by the CIA of the techniques of interrogation discussed herein is consistent with the Constitution and applicable statutes and treaties. In the present memorandum, you have asked us to address only the requirements of 18 U.S.C §§ 2340–2340A. Nothing in this memorandum or in our prior advice to the CIA should be read to suggest that the use of these techniques would conform to the requirements of the Uniform Code of Military Justice that governs members of the Armed Forces or to United States obligations under the Geneva Conventions in circumstances in which those Conventions would apply. We do not address the possible application of article 16 of the CAT [prohibiting cruel, inhuman, or degrading treatment or punishment], nor do we address any question relating to conditions of confinement or detention, as distinct from the interrogation of detainees. * * *

You have also explained that, prior to interrogations, each detainee is evaluated by medical and psychological professionals from the CIA's Office of Medical Services ("OMS") to ensure that he is not likely to suffer any severe physical or mental pain or suffering as a result of interrogation.

> [T]echnique-specific advanced approval is required for all "enhanced" measures and is conditional on on-site medical and psychological personnel confirming from direct detainee examination that the enhanced technique(s) is not expected to produce "severe physical or mental pain or suffering." As a practical matter, the detainee's physical condition must be such that these interventions will not have lasting effect, and his psychological state strong enough that no severe psychological harm will result.

OMS Guidelines on Medical and Psychological Support to Detainee Rendition, Interrogation and Detention at 9 (Dec. 2004) (*"OMS Guidelines"*). * * * In addition, "subsequent medical rechecks during the interrogation period should be performed on a regular basis." *Id.* As an additional precaution, and to ensure the objectivity of their medical and psychological assessments, OMS personnel do not participate in administering interrogation techniques; their function is to monitor interrogations and the health of the detainee. * * *

We understand that, when approved, interrogation techniques are generally used in an escalating fashion, with milder techniques used first. Use of the techniques is not continuous. Rather, one or more techniques may be applied—during or between interrogation sessions—based on the judgment of the interrogators and other team members and subject always to the monitoring of the on-scene medical and psychological personnel. Use of the techniques may be continued if the detainee is still believed to have and to be withholding actionable intelligence. The use of these techniques may not be continued for more than 30 days without additional approval from CIA Headquarters. *See generally* George J. Tenet, Director of Central Intelligence, *Guidelines on Interrogations Conducted Pursuant to the* [REDACTED] at 1–2 (Jan 28, 2003) (describing approval procedures required for use of enhanced interrogation techniques). Moreover, even within that 30-day period, any further use of these interrogation techniques is discontinued if the detainee is judged to be consistently providing accurate intelligence or if he is no longer believed to have actionable intelligence. This memorandum addresses the use of these techniques during no more than one 30-day period. We do not address whether the use of these techniques beyond the initial 30-day period would violate the statute.

Medical and psychological personnel are on-scene throughout (and, as detailed below, physically present or otherwise observing during the application of many techniques, including all techniques involving physical contact with detainees), and "[d]aily physical and psychological evaluations are continued throughout the period of [enhanced interrogation technique] use." CIA Inspector General, *Counterterrorism Detention and Interrogation Activities* (September 2001–October 2003), No. 2003–7123–IG (May 7, 2004) 30 n. 35 ("IG Report"). * * * In addition, "[i]n each interrogation session in which an Enhanced Technique is employed, a contemporaneous record shall be created setting forth the nature and duration of each such technique employed." *Interrogation Guidelines* at 3. At any time, any on-scene personnel (including the medical or psychological personnel, the chief of base, substantive experts, security officers, and other interrogators) can intervene to stop the use of any technique if it appears that the technique is being used improperly, and on-scene medical personnel can intervene if the detainee has developed a condition making the use of the technique unsafe. More generally, medical personnel watch for signs of physical distress or mental harm so significant as possibly to amount to the "severe physical or mental pain or suffering" that is prohibited by sections 2340–2340A. * * *

These techniques have all been imported from military Survival, Evasion, Resistance, Escape ("SERE") training, where they have been used for years on U.S. military personnel, although with some significant differences described below. *See IG Report* at 13–14. Although we refer to the SERE experience below, we note at the outset an important limitation on reliance on that experience. Individuals undergoing SERE training are obviously in a very different situation from detainees undergoing interrogation; SERE trainees know it is part of a training program, not a real-life interrogation regime, they presumably know it will last only a short time, and they presumably have assurance that they will not be significantly harmed by the training.

You have described the specific techniques at issue as follows:

1. Dietary manipulation. This technique involved the substitution of commercial liquid meal replacements for normal food, presenting detainees with a bland, unappetizing, but nutritionally complete diet. You have informed us that the CIA believes dietary manipulation makes other techniques, such as sleep deprivation, more effective. * * * Calories are provided using commercial liquid diets (such as Ensure Plus), which also supply other essential nutrients and make for nutritionally complete meals.[11] * * *

2. *Nudity.* This technique is used to cause psychological discomfort, particularly if a detainee, for cultural or other reasons, is especially modest. When the technique is employed, clothing can be

---

[11] While detainees subject to dietary manipulation are obviously situated differently from individuals who voluntarily engage in commercial weight-loss programs, we note that widely available commercial weight-loss programs in the United States employ diets of 1000 kcal/day for sustained periods of weeks or longer without requiring medical supervision. While we do not equate commercial weight loss programs and this interrogation technique, the fact that these calorie levels are used in the weight-loss programs, in our view, is instructive in evaluating the medical safety of the interrogation technique.

provided as an instant reward for cooperation. During and between interrogation sessions, a detainee may be kept nude, provided that ambient temperatures and the health of the detainee permit. For this technique to be employed, ambient temperature must be at least 68°F. No sexual abuse or threats of sexual abuse are permitted. Although each detention cell has full-time closed circuit video monitoring, the detainee is not intentionally exposed to other detainees or unduly exposed to the detention facility staff. We understand that interrogators "are trained to avoid sexual innuendo or any acts of implicit or explicit sexual degradation." Letter from [REDACTED] Associate General Counsel, CIA, to Dan Levin, Acting Assistant Attorney General, OLC (October 12, 2004) at 2 (*"October 12 [REDACTED] Letter"*). Nevertheless, interrogators can exploit the detainee's fear of being seen naked. In addition, female officers involved in the interrogation may see the detainees naked; and for purposes of our analysis, we will assume that detainees subjected to nudity as an interrogation technique are aware that they may be seen naked by females. * * *

4. *Walling*. This technique involves the use of a flexible, false wall. The individual is placed with his heels touching the flexible wall. The interrogator pulls the individual forward and then quickly and firmly pushes the individual into the wall. It is the individual's shoulder blades that hit the wall. During this motion, the head and neck are supported with a rolled hood or towel that provides a C-collar effect to help prevent whiplash. To reduce further the risk of injury, the individual is allowed to rebound from the flexible wall. You have informed us that the false wall is also constructed to create a loud noise when the individual hits it in order to increase the shock or surprise of the technique. We understand that walling may be used when the detainee is uncooperative or unresponsive to questions from interrogators. Depending on the extent of the detainee's lack of cooperation, he may be walled one time during an interrogation session (one impact with the wall) or many times (perhaps 20 or 30 times) consecutively. We understand that this technique is not designed to, and does not, cause severe pain, even when used repeatedly as you have described. Rather, it is designed to wear down the detainee and to shock or surprise the detainee and alter his expectations about the treatment he believes he will receive. In particular, we specifically understand that the repetitive use of the walling technique is intended to contribute to the shock and drama of the experience, to dispel a detainee's expectations that interrogators will not use increasing levels of force, and to wear down his resistance. It is not intended to—and based on experience you have informed us that it does not—inflict any injury or cause severe pain. Medical and psychological personnel are physically present or otherwise observing whenever this technique is applied (as they are with any interrogation technique involving physical contact with the detainee). * * *

6. *Facial slap or insult slap.* With this technique, the interrogator slaps the individual's face with fingers slightly spread. The hand makes contact with the area directly between the tip of the individual's chin and the bottom of the corresponding earlobe. The interrogator thus "invades" the individual's "personal space." We understand that the goal of the facial slap is not to inflict physical pain that is severe or lasting. Instead, the purpose of the facial slap is to induce shock, surprise, or humiliation. Medical and psychological personnel are physically present or otherwise observing whenever this technique is applied. * * *

8. *Cramped confinement.* This technique involves placing the individual in a confined space, the dimensions of which restrict the individual's movement. The confined space is usually dark. The duration of confinement varies based upon the size of the container. For the larger confined space, the individual can stand up or sit down; the smaller space is large enough for the subject to sit down. Confinement in the larger space may last no more than 8 hours at a time for no more than 18 hours a day; for the smaller space, confinement may last no more than two hours.[13] * * *

10. *Stress positions.* There are three stress positions that may be used. You have informed us that these positions are not designed to produce the pain associated with contortions or twisting of the body. Rather, like wall standing, they are designed to produce the physical discomfort associated with temporary muscle fatigue. The three stress positions are (1) sitting on the floor with legs extended straight out in front and arms raised above the head, (2) kneeling on the floor while leaning back at a 45 degree angle, and (3) leaning against a wall generally about three feet away from the detainee's feet, with only the detainee's head touching the wall, while his wrists are handcuffed in front of him or behind his back, and while an interrogator stands next to him to prevent injury if he loses his balance. As with wall standing, we understand that these positions are used only to induce temporary muscle fatigue.

11. *Water dousing.* Cold water is poured on the detainee either from a container or from a hose without a nozzle. This technique is intended to weaken the detainee's resistance and persuade him to cooperate with interrogators. The water poured on his head must be potable, and the interrogators must ensure that water does not enter the detainee's nose, mouth, or eyes. A medical officer must observe and monitor the detainee throughout application of this technique, including for signs of hypothermia. Ambient temperatures must remain about 64°F. If the detainee is lying on the floor, his head is to remain vertical, and a poncho, mat, or other material must be placed between him and the floor to

[13] In *Interrogation Memorandum*, we also addressed the use of harmless insects placed in a confinement box and concluded that it did not violate the statute. We understand that—for reasons unrelated to any concern that it might violate the statute—the CIA never used that technique and has removed it from the list of authorized interrogation techniques; accordingly, we do not address it again here.

minimize the loss of body heat. At the conclusion of the water dousing session, the detainee must be moved to a heated room if necessary to permit his body temperature to return to normal in a safe manner. To ensure an adequate margin of safety, the maximum period of time that a detainee may be permitted to remain wet has been set at two-thirds the time at which, based on extensive medical literature and experience, hypothermia could be expected to develop in healthy individuals who are submerged in water of the same temperature. * * *

The minimum permissible temperature of the water used in water dousing is 41°F, though you have informed us that in practice the water temperature is generally not below 50°F, since tap water rather than refrigerated water is generally used. We understand that a version of water dousing routinely used in SERE training is much more extreme in that it involved complete immersion of the individual in cold water (where water temperatures may be below 40°F) and is usually performed outdoors where ambient air temperatures may be as low as 10°F. Thus, the SERE training version involves a far greater impact on body temperature; SERE training also involves a situation where the water may enter the trainee's nose and mouth. * * *

12. *Sleep deprivation (more than 48 hours).* This technique subjects a detainee to an extended period without sleep. You have informed us that the primary purpose of this technique is to weaken the subject and wear down his resistance.

The primary method of sleep deprivation involves the use of shackling to keep the detainee awake. In this method, the detainee is standing and is handcuffed, and the handcuffs are attached by a length of chain to the ceiling. The detainee's hands are shackled in front of his body, so that the detainee has approximately a two to three-foot diameter of movement. The detainee's feet are shackled to a bolt in the floor. Due care is taken to ensure that the shackles are neither too loose nor too tight for physical safety. We understand from discussions with OMS that the shackling does not result in any significant physical pain for the subject. The detainee's hands are generally between the level of his heart and his chin. In some cases, the detainee's hands may be raised above the level of his head, but only for a period of up to two hours. All of the detainee's weight is borne by his legs and feet during standing sleep deprivation. You have informed us that the detainee is not allowed to hang from or support his body weight with the shackles. Rather, we understand that the shackles are only used as a passive means to keep the detainee standing and thus to prevent him from falling asleep; should the detainee begin to fall asleep, he will lose his balance and awaken, either because of the sensation of losing his balance or because of the restraining tension of the shackles. The use of this passive means for keeping the detainee awake avoids the need for using means that would require interaction with the detainee and might pose a danger of physical harm.

We understand from you that no detainee subjected to this technique by the CIA has suffered any harm or injury, either by falling down and forcing the handcuffs to bear his weight or in any other way. You have assured us that detainees are continuously monitored by closed-circuit television, so that if a detainee were unable to stand, he would immediately be removed from the standing position and would not be permitted to dangle by his wrists. We understand that standing sleep deprivation may cause edema, or swelling, in the lower extremities because it forces detainees to stand for an extended period of time. OMS has advised us that this condition is not painful, and that the condition disappears quickly once the detainee is permitted to lie down. * * *

We understand that a detainee undergoing sleep deprivation is generally fed by hand by CIA personnel so that he need not be unshackled; however, "if progress is made during interrogation, the interrogators may unshackle the detainee and let him feed himself as a positive incentive." *October 12 [REDACTED] Letter* at 4. If the detainee is clothed, he wears an adult diaper under his pants. Detainees subject to sleep deprivation who are also subject to nudity as a separate interrogation technique will at times be nude and wearing a diaper. If the detainee is wearing a diaper, it is checked regularly and changed as necessary. The use of the diaper is for sanitary and health purposes of the detainee; it is not used for the purpose of humiliating the detainee, and it is not considered to be an interrogation technique. The detainee's skin condition is monitored, and diapers are changed as needed so that the detainee does not remain in a soiled diaper. You have informed us that to date no detainee has experienced any skin problems resulting from use of diapers.

The maximum allowable duration for sleep deprivation authorized by the CIA is 180 hours, after which the detainee must be permitted to sleep without interruption for at least eight hours. You have informed us that to date, more than a dozen detainees have been subjected to sleep deprivation of more than 48 hours, and three detainees have been subjected to sleep deprivation of more than 96 hours; the longest period of time for which any detainee has been deprived of sleep by the CIA is 180 hours. * * *

13. *The "waterboard."* In this technique, the detainee is lying on a gurney that is inclined at an angle of 10 to 15 degrees to the horizontal, with the detainee on his back and his head toward the lower end of the gurney. A cloth is placed over the detainee's face, and cold water is poured on the cloth from a height of approximately 6 to 18 inches. The wet cloth creates a barrier through which it is difficult—or in some cases not possible—to breathe. A single "application" of water may not last for more than 40 seconds, with the duration of an "application" measured from the moment when water—of whatever quantity—is first poured on to the cloth until the moment the cloth is removed from the subject's face. *See* Letter from [REDACTED] Associate General Counsel, CIA, to Dan

Levin, Acting Assistant Attorney General, OLC (August 19, 2004) at 1 (*"August 19 [REDACTED] Letter"*). When the time limit is reached, the pouring of water is immediately discontinued and the cloth is removed. We understand that if the detainee makes an effort to defeat the technique (e.g., by twisting his head to the side and breathing out of the corner of his mouth), the interrogator may cup his hands around the detainee's nose and mouth to dam the runoff, in which case it would not be possible for the detainee to breathe during the application of the water. In addition, you have informed us that the technique may be applied in a manner to defeat efforts by the detainee to hold his breath by, for example, beginning an application of water as the detainee is exhaling. Either in the normal application, or where countermeasures are used, we understand that water may enter and may accumulate in the detainee's mouth and nasal cavity, preventing him from breathing. * * *

We understand that the effect of the waterboard is to induce a sensation of drowning. This sensation is based on a deeply rooted physiological response. Thus, the detainee experiences this sensation even if he is aware that he is not actually drowning. We are informed that based on extensive experience the process is not physically painful but that it usually does cause fear and panic. The waterboard has been used many thousands of times in SERE training provided to American military personnel, though in that context it is usually limited to one or two applications of no more than 40 seconds each.

You have explained that the waterboard technique is used only if: (1) the CIA has credible intelligence that a terrorist attack is imminent; (2) there are "substantial and credible indicators the subject has actionable intelligence that can prevent, disrupt or delay this attack"; and (3) other interrogation methods have failed or are unlikely to yield actionable intelligence in time to prevent the attack. You have also informed us that the waterboard may be approved for use with a given detainee only during, at most, one single 30-day period, and that during that period, the waterboard technique may be used on no more than five days. We further understand that in any 24-hour period, interrogators may use no more than two "sessions" of the waterboard on a subject—with a "session" defined to mean the time that the detainee is strapped to the waterboard—and that no session may last more than two hours. Moreover, during any session, the number of individual applications of water lasting 10 seconds or longer may not exceed six. As noted above, the maximum length of any application of water is 40 seconds (you have informed us that this maximum has rarely been reached). Finally, the total cumulative time of all applications of whatever length in a 24-hour period may not exceed 12 minutes. * * *

Your medical personnel have explained that the use of the waterboard does pose a small risk of certain potentially significant medical problems and that certain measures are taken to avoid or address such problems. First, a detainee might vomit and then aspirate the emesis [vomit]. To reduce this risk, any detainee on whom this technique will be used is first placed on a liquid diet. Second, the detainee might aspirate some of the water, and the resulting water in the lungs might lead to pneumonia. To mitigate this risk, a potable saline solution is used in the procedure. Third, it is conceivable (though, we understand from OMS, highly unlikely) that a detainee could suffer spasms of the larynx that would prevent him from breathing even when the application of water is stopped and the detainee is returned to an upright position. In the event of such spasms, a qualified physician would immediately intervene to address the problem, and, if necessary, the intervening physician would perform a tracheotomy. * * *

As noted, all of the interrogation techniques described above are subject to numerous restrictions, many based on input from OMS. Our advice in this memorandum is based on our understanding that there will be careful adherence to all of these guidelines, restrictions, and safeguards, and that there will be ongoing monitoring and reporting by the team, including OMS medical and psychological personnel, as well as prompt intervention by a team member, as necessary, to prevent physical distress or mental harm so significant as possibly to amount to the "severe physical or mental pain or suffering" that is prohibited by sections 2340–2340A. Our advice is also based on our understanding that interrogators who will use these techniques are adequately trained to understand that the authorized use of the techniques is not designed or intended to cause severe physical or mental pain or suffering, and also to understand and respect the medical judgment of OMS and the important role that OMS personnel play in the program. * * *

III.

In the discussion that follows, we will address each of the specific interrogation techniques you have described. Subject to the understandings, limitations, and safeguards discussed herein, including ongoing medical and psychological monitoring and team intervention as necessary, we conclude that the authorized use of each of these techniques, considered individually, would not violate the prohibition that Congress has adopted in sections 2340–2340A. This conclusion is straightforward with respect to all but two of the techniques. Use of sleep deprivation as an enhanced technique and use of the waterboard, however, involve more substantial questions, with the waterboard presenting the most substantial question. Although we conclude that the use of these techniques—as we understand them and subject to the limitations you have described—would not violate the statute, the issues raised by these two techniques counsel great caution in their use, including both careful adherence to the limitations and restrictions you have described and also close and continuing medical and psychological monitoring. * * *

1. *Dietary manipulation.* Based on experience, it is evident that this technique is not expected to cause any physical pain, let alone pain that is extreme in intensity. * * * Nor could this technique reasonably be thought to induce "severe physical suffering." Although dietary manipulation may cause some degree of hunger, such an experience is far from extreme hunger (let alone starvation) and cannot be expected to amount to "severe physical suffering" under the statute. * * * This technique presents no issue of "severe mental pain or suffering" within the meaning of sections 2340–2340A, because the use of this technique would involve no qualifying predicate act. * * *

2. *Nudity.* * * * Even if this technique involves some physical discomfort, it cannot be said to cause "suffering," let alone "severe physical pain or suffering," and we therefore conclude that its authorized use by an adequately trained interrogator could not reasonably be considered specifically intended to do so. Although some detainees might be humiliated by this technique, especially given possible cultural sensitivities and the possibility of being seen by female officers, it cannot constitute "severe mental pain or suffering" under the statute because it does not involve any of the predicate acts specified by Congress. * * *

4. *Walling.* Although the walling technique involves the use of considerable force to push the detainee against the wall and may involve a large number of repetitions in certain cases, we understand that the false wall that is used is flexible and that this technique is not designed to, and does not, cause severe physical pain to the detainee. We understand that there may be some pain or irritation associated with the collar, which is used to help avoid injury such as whiplash to the detainee, but that any physical pain associated with the use of the collar would not approach the level of intensity needed to constitute severe physical pain. * * * We also do not believe that the use of this technique would involve a threat of infliction of severe physical pain or suffering or other predicate act for purposes of severe mental pain or suffering under the statute. Rather, this technique is designed to shock the detainee and disrupt his expectations that he will not be treated forcefully and to wear down his resistance to interrogation. Based on these understandings, we conclude that the authorized use of this technique by adequately trained interrogators could not reasonably be considered specifically intended to cause severe physical or mental pain or suffering in violation of sections 2340–2340A.[38] * * *

[38] In *Interrogation Memorandum,* we did not describe the walling technique as involving the number of repetitions that we understand may be applied. Our advice with respect to walling in the present memorandum is specifically based on the understanding that the repetitive use of walling is intended only to increase the drama and shock of the technique, to wear down the detainee's resistance, and to disrupt expectations that he will not be treated with force, and that such use is not intended to, and does not in fact, cause severe physical pain to the detainee. Moreover, our advice specifically assumes that the use of walling will be stopped if there is any indication that the use of the technique is or may be causing severe physical pain to a detainee.

6. *Facial slap or insult slap.* Although this technique involves a degree of physical pain, the pain associated with a slap to the face, as you have described it to us, could not be expected to constitute severe physical pain. We understand that the purpose of this technique is to cause shock, surprise, or humiliation not to inflict physical pain that is severe or lasting; we assume it will be used accordingly. * * * Therefore, the authorized use of this technique by adequately trained interrogators could not reasonably be considered specifically intended to cause severe physical or mental pain or suffering in violation of sections 2340–2340A.[39] * * *

8. *Cramped confinement.* This technique does not involve any significant physical pain or suffering. It also does not involve a predicate act for purposes of severe mental pain or suffering. Specifically, we do not believe that placing a detainee in a dark, cramped space for the limited period of time involved here could reasonably be considered a procedure calculated to disrupt profoundly the senses so as to cause prolonged mental harm. Accordingly, we conclude that its authorized use by adequately trained interrogators could not reasonably be considered specifically intended to cause severe physical or mental pain or suffering in violation of sections 2340–2340A. * * *[40] * * *

11. *Water dousing.* OMS has advised that, based on the extensive experience in SERE training, the medical literature, and the experience with detainees to date, water dousing as authorized is not designed or expected to cause significant physical pain, and certainly not severe physical pain. Although we understand that prolonged *immersion* in very cold water may be physically painful, as noted above, this interrogation technique does not involve immersion and a substantial margin of safety is built into the time limitation on the use of the CIA's water dousing technique—use of the technique with water of a given temperature must be limited to no more than two-thirds of the time in which hypothermia could be expected to occur from *total immersion* in water of the same temperature. * * *

12. *Sleep deprivation.* We understand from OMS, and from our review of the literature on the physiology of sleep, that even very extended sleep deprivation does not cause physical pain, let alone severe

---

[39] Our advice about both the facial slap and the abdominal slap assumes that the interrogators will apply those techniques as designed and will not strike the detainee with excessive force or repetition in a manner that might result in severe physical pain.

[40] A stress position that involves such contortion or twisting, as well as one held for so long that it could not be aimed only at producing temporary muscle fatigue, might raise more substantial questions under the statute. *Cf. Army Field Manual 34–52: Intelligence Interrogation* at 1–8 (1992) (indicating that "[f]orcing an individual to stand, sit, or kneel in abnormal positions for prolonged periods of time" may constitute "torture" within the meaning of the Third Geneva Convention's requirement that "[n]o physical or mental torture, nor any other form of coercion, may be inflicted on prisoners of war," but not addressing 18 U.S.C. §§ 2340–2340A); United Nations General Assembly, *Report of the Special Rapporteur on Torture and Other Cruel, Inhumane or Degrading Treatment or Punishment*, U.N. Doc. A/59/150 at 6 (Sept. 1, 2004) (suggesting that "holding detainees in painful and/or stressful positions" might in certain circumstances be characterized as torture).

physical pain.[44] * * * Although it is a more substantial question, particularly given the imprecision in the statutory standard and the lack of guidance from the courts, we also conclude that extended sleep deprivation, subject to the limitations and conditions described herein, would not be expected to cause "severe physical suffering." * * * Nevertheless, because extended sleep deprivation could in some cases result in substantial physical distress, the safeguards adopted by the CIA, including ongoing medical monitoring and intervention by the team if needed, are important to ensure that the CIA's use of extended sleep deprivation will not run afoul of the statute. * * * Moreover, we emphasize our understanding that OMS will intervene to alter or stop the course of sleep deprivation for a detainee if OMS concludes in its medical judgment that the detainee is or may be experiencing extreme physical distress. The team, we understand, will intervene not only if the sleep deprivation itself may be having such effects, but also if the shackling or other conditions attendant to the technique appear to be causing severe physical suffering. * * *

Finally, we also conclude that extended sleep deprivation cannot be expected to cause "severe mental pain or suffering" as defined in sections 2340–2340A, and that its authorized use by adequately trained interrogators could not reasonably be considered specifically intended to do so. First, we do not believe that use of the sleep deprivation technique, subject to the conditions in place, would involve one of the predicate acts necessary for "severe mental pain or suffering" under the statute. * * * It may be questioned whether sleep deprivation could be characterized as a "procedure calculated to disrupt profoundly the senses or personality" within the meaning of sections 2340(2)(B), since we understand from OMS and from the scientific literature that extended sleep deprivation might induce hallucinations in some cases. * * * Even assuming, however, that the extended use of sleep deprivation may result in hallucinations that could fairly be characterized as a "profound" disruption of the senses, we do not believe it tenable to conclude that in such circumstances the use of sleep deprivation could be said to be "calculated" to cause such profound disruption to the senses, as required by the statute. The term "calculated" denotes something that is planned or thought out beforehand. * * * Here, it is evident that the potential for any hallucinations on the part of a detainee undergoing sleep deprivation is not something that would be a "calculated" result of the use of this technique, particularly given that the team would intervene immediately to stop the technique if there were signs the subject was experiencing hallucinations.

Second, even if we were to assume, out of an abundance of caution, that extended sleep deprivation could be said to be a "procedure

[44] Although sleep deprivation is not itself physically painful, we understand that some studies have noted that extended total sleep deprivation may have the effect of reducing tolerance to some forms of pain in some subjects. * * *

calculated to disrupt profoundly the senses or personality" of the subject within the meaning of sections 2340(2)(B), we do not believe that this technique would be expected to—or that its authorized use by adequately trained interrogators could reasonably be considered specifically intended to—cause "*prolonged* mental harm" as required by the statute, because, as we understand it, any hallucinatory effects of sleep deprivation would dissipate rapidly. * * *

13. *Waterboard.* We previously concluded that the use of the waterboard did not constitute torture under sections 2340–2340A. We must reexamine the issue, however, because the technique, as it would be used, could involve more applications in longer sessions (and possibly using different methods) than we earlier considered.[51] * * *

However frightening the experience may be, OMS personnel have informed us that the waterboard technique is not physically painful. * * * As you have informed us, the CIA has previously used the waterboard repeatedly on two detainees, and, as far as can be determined, these detainees did not experience physical pain or, in the professional judgment of doctors, is there any medical reason to believe they would have done so. * * * We also conclude that the use of the waterboard, under the strict limits and conditions imposed, would not be expected to cause "severe physical suffering" under the statute. * * * To the extent that in some applications the use of the waterboard could cause choking or similar physical—as opposed to mental—sensations, those physical sensations might well have an intensity approaching the degree contemplated by the statute. However, we understand that any such physical—as opposed to mental—sensations caused by the use of the waterboard end when the application ends. Given the limits imposed, and the fact that any physical distress (as opposed to possible mental suffering, which is discussed below) would occur only during the actual application of water, the physical distress caused by the waterboard would not be expected to have the duration required to amount to severe physical suffering. * * *

The most substantial question raised by the waterboard relates to the statutory definition of "severe mental pain or suffering." The sensation of drowning that we understand accompanies the use of the waterboard arguably could qualify as a "threat of imminent death" within the meaning of section 2340(2)(C) and thus might constitute a

---

[51] The *IG report* noted that in some cases the waterboard was used with far greater frequency than initially indicated, *see IG Report* at 5, 44, 46, 103–04, and also that it was used in a different manner. *See id.* at 37 ("[T]he waterboard technique . . . was different from the technique described in the DoJ opinion and used in the SERE training. The difference was in the manner in which the detainee's breathing was obstructed. At the SERE school and in the DoJ opinion, the subject's airflow is disrupted by the firm application of a damp cloth over the air passages; the interrogator applies a small amount of water to the cloth in a controlled manner. By contrast, the Agency interrogator . . . applied large volumes of water to a cloth that covered the detainee's mouth and nose. One of the psychologists/interrogators acknowledged that the Agency's use of the technique is different from that used in SERE training because it is 'for real' and is more poignant and convincing.") * * *

predicate act for "severe mental pain or suffering" under the statute.[56] * * *

Nevertheless, the statutory definition of "severe mental pain or suffering" also requires that the predicate act produce "prolonged mental harm." As we understand from OMS personnel familiar with the history of the waterboard technique, as used both in SERE training (though in a substantially different manner) and in the previous CIA interrogations, there is no medical basis to believe that the technique would produce any mental effect beyond the distress that directly accompanies its use and the prospect that it will be used again. * * * But the physicians and psychologists at the CIA familiar with the facts have informed us that in the case of the two detainees who have been subjected to more extensive use of the waterboard technique, no evidence of prolonged mental harm has appeared in the period since the use of the waterboard on those detainees, a period which now spans at least 25 months for each of these detainees. * * * The technique may be designed to create fear at the time it is used on the detainee, so that the detainee will cooperate to avoid future sessions. Furthermore, we acknowledge that the term "prolonged" is imprecise. Nonetheless, without in any way minimizing the distress caused by this technique, we believe that the panic brought on by the waterboard during the very limited time it is actually administered, combined with any residual fear that may be experienced over a somewhat longer period, could not be said to amount to the "prolonged mental harm" that the statute covers. * * *

Assuming adherence to the strict limitations discussed herein, including the careful medical monitoring and available intervention by the team as necessary, we conclude that although the question is substantial and difficult, the authorized use of the waterboard by adequately trained interrogators and other team members could not reasonably be considered specifically intended to cause severe physical or mental pain or suffering and thus would not violate sections 2340–2340A.

In sum, based on the information you have provided and the limitations, procedures, and safeguards that would be in place, we conclude that—although extended sleep deprivation and use of the waterboard present more substantial questions in certain respects under the statute and the use of the waterboard raises the most substantial issue—none of these specified techniques, considered individually, would violate the prohibition in sections 2340–2340A. The universal rejection of torture and the President's unequivocal directive that the United States not engage in torture warrant great care in analyzing whether particular interrogation techniques are consistent with the requirements

[56] It is unclear whether a detainee being subjected to the waterboard in fact experiences it as a "threat of imminent death." We understand that the CIA may inform a detainee on whom this technique is used that he would not be allowed to drown. Moreover, after multiple applications of the waterboard, it may become apparent to the detainee that, however frightening the experience may be, it will not result in death.

of sections 2340–2340A, and we have attempted to employ such care throughout our analysis. * * * As is apparent, our conclusion is based on the assumption that close observation, including medical and psychological monitoring of the detainees, will continue during the period when these techniques are used; that the personnel present are authorized to, and will, stop the use of a technique at any time if they believe it is being used improperly or threatens a detainee's safety or that a detainee may be at risk of suffering severe physical or mental pain or suffering; that the medical and psychological personnel are continually assessing the available literature and ongoing experience with detainees, and that, as they have done to date, they will make adjustments to techniques to ensure that they do not cause severe physical or mental pain or suffering to the detainees; and that all interrogators and other team members understand the proper use of the techniques, that the techniques are not designed or intended to cause severe physical or mental pain or suffering, and that they must cooperate with OMS personnel in the exercise of their important duties.

Please let us know if we may be of further assistance.

NOTES & QUESTIONS

1. Obama Administration Response

As one of his first acts upon taking office in January 2009, President Obama issued Executive Order (EO) 13491 ("Ensuring Lawful Interrogations"), which revoked an earlier EO issued by President Bush (EO 13440) that had asserted that members of al Qaeda, the Taliban, and associated forces were not entitled to the protections provided under the Third Geneva Convention (concerning prisoners of war) and that the CIA Detention and Interrogation Program would satisfy Common Article 3 of the Geneva Conventions so long as the program complied with the US definition of torture as provided under U.S. law and thus as such laws were interpreted by the OLC and Department of Defense. EO 13491 mandated that all detention centers ensure that individuals subject to U.S. custody enjoy the protections of Common Article 3, at a minimum, and refrain from any interrogation technique not authorized by the applicable Army Field Manual (FM 2–22.3, Human Intelligence Collector Operations). The order also directed the CIA to close all detention facilities. The EO also made clear that any government employee or agent of the U.S. government could not rely upon any interpretation of the law governing interrogation issued by the Department of Justice between September 11, 2001, and January 20, 2009. One area of lingering controversy concerns Appendix M of F.M. 2–22.3, which allows isolation, sleep deprivation, and sensory deprivation. *See* Amnesty International, *The Army Field Manual: Sanctioning Cruelty* (Mar. 19, 2009).

2. Implementing the Memos

These memoranda provide highly detailed, almost choreographed, instructions on how to utilize particular techniques without running afoul of prohibition against torture. How, as a practical matter, might such limitations have been arrived at? Are the opinions within the memoranda about whether particular techniques constitute torture within the competency of the lawyers providing the legal analysis? How are such instructions likely to be implemented in the context of a real-life interrogation? What would happen, for example, if a detainee refused to stand up to be hung by his hands or wrists? What if a detainee continued to resist questioning after 180 hours of sleep deprivation?

3. Combined Techniques

The excerpted memo considers each technique in turn and explicitly does not consider their concurrent or consecutive use. In 2005, Bradbury authored another memorandum ("the Combined Use Memo") to Rizzo on the application of § 2340 to the "Combined Use of Certain Techniques in the Interrogation of High Value al Qaeda Detainees." Bradbury cautioned that "[t]he issue of the combined effects of interrogation techniques raises complex and difficult questions and comes to us in a less precisely defined form than the questions treated in our earlier opinions about individual techniques." Bradbury also noted that

> it is possible that the application of certain techniques might render the detainee unusually susceptible to physical or mental pain or suffering," such that careful monitoring is necessary to prevent the infliction of "severe physical or mental pain or suffering.

Nonetheless, he concluded that "the use of the techniques in combination as . . . described . . . would" not "be expected to inflict 'severe physical or mental pain or suffering' within the meaning of the statute," although he cautioned that extended sleep deprivation and the waterboard may present "more substantial risk of physical distress." Under Bradbury's reasoning, so long as the interrogator did not specifically intend to cause severe pain or suffering, would it constitute torture if he or she did in fact do so with a combined set of techniques? Research has demonstrated that

> The cumulative impact of torture stressors is also determined by the interactions among them. The distressing or helplessness-inducing effect of a particular stressor might be compounded when combined with another stressor. * * * Thus, the relative impact of each stressor needs to be considered in the context of its interactions with other concurrent stressors. A measure of mere exposure to torture stressors fails to capture such important information.

Metin Başoğlu, Maria Livanou, & Cvetana Crnobarić, *Torture vs. Other Cruel, Inhuman, and Degrading Treatment: Is the Distinction Real or Apparent?*, 64(3) ARCHIVES GEN. PSYCHIATRY 277, 283 (2007).

4. Interrogation Theory

Also in 2005, Bradbury prepared a memo addressing the question of whether the particular techniques under review violated Article 16 of the Torture Convention concerning cruel, inhuman, or degrading treatment or punishment (CIDT) . In addition to setting forth arguments as to why the prohibition against CIDT did not apply to law-of-war interrogations abroad or to conduct that does not "shock the conscience" in a constitutional sense (*Rochin v. California*, 342 U.S. 165, 172 (1952)), the memo, explicated a taxonomy of the various techniques. First, there are "conditioning techniques" (nudity, dietary manipulation, and sleep deprivation), which are used to "demonstrate to the [detainee] that he has no control over basic human needs" so that he will "value his personal welfare, comfort, and immediate needs more than the information he is protecting." Second, there are "corrective techniques" (the insult slap, abdominal slap, facial hold, and attention grasp) that "condition a detainee to pay attention to the interrogator's questions and dislodge expectations that the detainee will not be touched." Finally, there are "coercive techniques" (walling, water dousing, stress positions, wall standing, cramped confinement, and the waterboard) that "place the detainee in more physical and psychological stress." In the Combined Use Memo, Bradbury described the prototypical phases of an interrogation:

- "Initial Conditions": this involves a medical examination, sensory deprivation, transportation to the interrogation site, and being shaved and photographed, which confronts the detainee with a sudden change of environment to create uncertainty and dread as to what will happen next.
- "Transition to Interrogation": this involves an initial interview in a relatively benign environment to ascertain the detainee's willingness to cooperate. This phase continues so long as the detainee is providing information on "actionable threats" and the location of "High-Value Targets." If the detainee is not cooperative, then interrogators draft a detailed interrogation plan to the CIA for approval.
- "Interrogation": at this point, the enhanced techniques are employed interchangeably, in succession, and simultaneously over a number of sessions for up to thirty days to frighten, wear down, and ultimately gain compliance from the detainee. As the detainee begins to cooperate, the interrogation techniques are decreased.

5. "The Waterboard"

As acknowledged by the memo excerpted above, one of the more controversial interrogation techniques used by the United States against suspected terrorists and other detainees is waterboarding. "Waterboarding" consists of using water to suffocate an individual, either by placing a wet towel, or pouring water, over a person's face to create the feeling of drowning. The declassified U.S. memoranda admitted that at least three individuals have been waterboarded by U.S. agents: Abu Zubaydah (a "senior lieutenant" in al Qaeda captured in March 2002 who apparently wrote al Qaeda's manuals on resistance techniques and ran training camps) and Khalid Sheikh Mohammed (considered a primary architect of the 9/11 attacks) were waterboarded 83 and 183 times, respectively, in some instances before the practice was officially sanctioned. The third is Abd al-Rahim al-Nashiri, alleged to be the mastermind of the bombing of the U.S.S. Cole in the Yemeni port of Aden in 2000 in which seventeen sailors were killed and thirty-nine others were injured.

A footnote in the CIDT Memo indicates that the use of waterboarding may have been "unnecessary" on Zubaydah as the on-scene interrogation team judged him to be compliant, but "elements within CIA Headquarters still believed he was withholding information." CIDT Memo, *supra*, at 31 n.28. Reports are inconclusive as to whether actionable intelligence was revealed as a result of these techniques; some reports suggest that Zubaydah had revealed useful information prior to the harsh methods being used. Do you agree with the conclusion of the legal memoranda discussed above that waterboarding does not constitute torture or CIDT under the Torture Convention or U.S. law? If you think it does constitute torture, is it physical or mental torture? How would you characterize it under the Torture Convention and 18 U.S.C. § 2340?

6. Waterboarding Through the Ages

According to Professor Alfred McCoy, the first reference to waterboarding appears in a 1541 French judicial handbook called TORTURAE GALLICAE ORDINARIAE. Alfred McCoy, *The U.S. has a History of Using Torture*, HISTORY NEWS NETWORK (Dec. 4, 2006).

Fig. 341.—The Water Torture.—Fac-simile of a Woodcut in J. Damhoudère's "Praxis Rerum Criminalium:" in 4to, Antwerp, 1556.

As the woodcut above indicates, waterboarding was a practice used in Europe at least as early as the 16th century. Japan used waterboarding and other similar techniques against U.S. soldiers during World War II. At both the Tokyo war crimes trials as well as in subsequent war crimes trials conducted by the United States, Japanese citizens were prosecuted and convicted of torture for such actions committed against U.S. and other Allied personnel. For example, Yukio Asano was sentenced by a U.S. court to fifteen years hard labor for the war crime of subjecting a U.S. citizen to a form of waterboarding. *United States of America v. Hideji Nakamura, Yukio Asano, Seitara Hata, and Takeo Kita,* U.S. Military Commission, Yokohama, May 1–28, 1947, NARA Records, NND 735027 RG 153, Entry 143 Box 1025. Waterboarding was also practiced by the United States in Vietnam, as illustrated by the below photograph from 1968 that was originally published in *The Washington Post.* Within one month of the appearance of the photograph, court martial proceedings were initiated against one of the soldiers. For more on this case and the history of the prosecution of waterboarding by U.S. courts, *see* Evan Wallach, *Drop by Drop: Forgetting the History of Water Torture in U.S. Courts*, 45 COLUM. J. TRANS'L L. 468 (2007).

7. Conditions of Confinement

Bradbury also wrote an August 31, 2006, letter to Rizzo evaluating conditions of confinement (specifically: the practice of blocking detainees' vision during transport around the facility, the use of *incommunicado* and solitary confinement, the playing of white noise in walkways to prevent communication, the constant illumination in cells, the use of shackling, and the policy of forcibly shaving detainees upon arrival) in CIA detention centers against the proscriptions in common Article 3. With respect to the prohibition against "outrages upon personal dignity," he opined as follows:

> [S]ubparagraph (c)'s use of the phrase "outrages upon personal dignity" should be understood to mean a relatively significant form of ill-treatment. In this context, "outrage" appears to carry the

> meaning of "an act or condition that violated accepted standards." * * * [A]n act must violate some relatively clear and objective standard of behavior or acceptable treatment; it must be something that does not merely insult the dignity of the victim, but does so in an obvious or particularly significant manner. * * * Importantly, the text is clear that humiliating and degrading treatment is merely a subset of "outrages upon personal dignity." This text stands in contrast to provisions in other treaties, such as Article 16 of the Convention Against Torture, in which prohibitions on "degrading" treatment stand alone. * * * The prohibition does not reach trivial slights or insults, but instead reaches only those that represent a more fundamental assault on the dignity of the victim. * * * Certain activities may well be intended solely to humiliate and to degrade in certain settings, but may be undertaken for a legitimate purpose in others. For example, a systematic practice of marching detainees blindfolded in public with the intent to humiliate may so evince a "hostility to human dignity" as to run afoul of common Article 3. In contrast, obstructing the vision of the detainee during transport, with no needless exposure to the public, for the purpose [of] maintaining the security of the facility would not trigger the same concerns.

Letter from Bradbury to Rizzo (Aug. 31, 2006). The same conditions were evaluated under the Detainee Treatment Act in a subsequent memorandum. *See* Dept. of Justice, Memorandum for John H. Rizzo, Acting General Counsel, Central Intelligence Agency, *Application of the Detainee Treatment Act to Conditions of Confinement at Central Intelligence Agency Detention Facilities* (Aug. 31, 2006). Compare this interpretation of what constitutes outrages upon personal dignity with the ICYT's interpretation of the crime in *Kunarac*.

8. The Committee Against Torture and the United States

Parties to the Torture Convention must periodically submit reports to the Committee Against Torture, a body of experts charged with enforcing the treaty. The Committee considered the United States' second periodic report in 2006. Acknowledging the allegations of torture against detainees, the United States' report emphasized that the Bush Administration prohibits torture and prosecutes substantiated allegations. The report included an Annex of relevant proceedings. In response, the Committee in its Concluding Observations welcomed the United States' comprehensive submission, but raised the following concerns and recommendations, among others:

- The U.S. should enact a domestic torture statute rather than rely on ordinary crimes of murder and assault to prosecute domestic torture. (18 U.S.C. § 2340 only applies to acts committed outside the United States.)
- U.S. law should reflect the fact that acts of psychological manipulation need not cause "prolonged mental harm" to constitute torture.

- The U.S. should ensure that the Convention applies at all times, even in armed conflict, in any area under the party's jurisdiction, defined as areas under the state's *de facto* effective control.
- The U.S. should register all persons it detains anywhere in the world as a safeguard against acts of torture and ensure that no one is detained in any secret detention facility. No secret detention facilities should be utilized.
- The U.S. should apply the *non-refoulement* guarantee to all detainees in its custody, even those detained outside U.S. territory, and refrain from relying on "diplomatic assurances" when it sends detainees to states that systematically violate the Convention.
- The U.S. should close the Guantánamo detention facility and charge or return individuals to a place where they do not face a risk of torture.
- Interrogation techniques such as water-boarding or the use of dogs should be ceased.
- Victims of torture should have the opportunity to obtain redress.
- All allegations of torture or CIDT should be investigated.

U.N. Committee Against Torture, Consideration of Reports Submitted by States Parties under Article 19 of the Convention: Conclusions and Recommendations of the Committee Against Torture, U.N. Doc. CAT/C/USA/CO/2 (July 25, 2006).

9. Extraterritorial Application

A recurring issue in human rights law concerns the question of the degree to which treaty obligations of states apply in extraterritorial contexts. The Committee Against Torture in a General Comment on the Torture Convention emphasized that the Convention applies to "any territory under [a state's] jurisdiction," which protects any person "subject to the *de jure* or *de facto* control of a State party," including when persons are in the hands of individuals acting at the behest of a State party. *See* Committee Against Torture, General Comment No. 2: Implementation of article 2 by States parties, U.N. Doc., No. CAT/C/GC/2, para. 7 (Jan. 24, 2008). The last few U.S. administrations have resisted the extraterritorial application of U.S. human rights treaty obligations, although it was clear that this was an issue of intense debate during the Obama Administration. Several memoranda were leaked setting forth the position of Harold Hongju Koh, then Legal Adviser to the U.S. State Department, arguing that some human rights treaties that the US has ratified do apply extraterritorially in some circumstances. *See* Harold Hongju Koh, *Memorandum Opinion on the Geographic Scope of the Convention Against Torture and Its Application in Situations of Armed Conflict* (Jan. 21, 2013).

10. SERE Training

Under the Survival, Evasion, Resistance, Escape (SERE) program, U.S. military personnel have voluntarily participated in survival training that includes tactics to resist physical and psychological interrogations if captured. The goal of the program is to prepare soldiers for the types of abuse they might suffer if captured by hostile forces. The U.S. Air Force established the program at the end of the Korean War based upon the experiences of U.S. and allied prisoners of war. It was expanded after the Vietnam War to cover other branches of the military.

In an article on the program, THE NEW YORKER magazine reported that psychologists who helped develop and implement the SERE program had been advising detention and interrogation personnel at Guantánamo Bay and elsewhere on how the results of SERE might be "re-engineered" for the purpose of developing effective interrogation and counter-resistance programs, especially against individuals who may have received resistance training themselves. In addition, Behavioral Science Consultation Teams ("biscuits" in military jargon) from the military intelligence units were apparently also employed to develop interrogation strategies, some individually tailored to particular detainees. *See* Jane Mayer, *The Experiment*, THE NEW YORKER (July 11, 2005). For what purpose is the SERE program invoked in the excerpted memorandum? How relevant to the question of the legality of the techniques discussed is the fact that members of the U.S. armed forces were subjected to waterboarding and other authorized interrogation techniques in connection with the SERE program?

11. Doctors and Psychologists

The memo above references the CIA's Office of Medical Services (OMS), a division of the Agency tasked in part to ensure the physical and mental wellbeing of CIA employees and their families as well as to produce psychiatric and medical intelligence. Other memoranda, a report from the International Committee of the Red Cross (ICRC), and the testimony of detainees reveals that medical personnel, particularly psychologists, were aware of, designed, supervised, and were in some cases involved in, the abuse of detainees. In some cases, it appears medical personnel collected aggregate data on detainees' reactions to particular techniques, suggesting some level of medical experimentation.

The World Medical Association, a membership organization representing physicians around the world including those in the United States, issued in 1975 the Declaration of Tokyo, Guidelines for Physicians Concerning Torture and other Cruel, Inhuman or Degrading Treatment or Punishment in Relation to Detention and Imprisonment. The Declaration prohibits medical personnel from participating in any way in torture or other forms of abuse, even as monitors. In particular, the Declaration states that a physician "shall not use nor allow to be used, as far as he or she can, medical knowledge or skills, or health information specific to individuals, to facilitate or otherwise aid any interrogation, legal or illegal, of those individuals." Both the American Medical Association and the American Psychiatric Association had ethics statements prohibiting healthcare personnel from participating in the interrogation or torture of others. The American Psychological Association did not, although it has since adopted one in response to criticism. *See* APA, ETHICS CODE STANDARD 3.04.

In 2006, the Pentagon released new guidelines ("Medical Program Support for Detainee Operations," Instruction No. 2310.08E) prohibiting doctors charged with the medical care of detainees from participating in interrogations, but allowing the participation of non-treating health care personnel (i.e., individuals not involved in giving care) such as behavioral science consultants. Such a policy is acceptable to the American Psychological Association, many of whose members view psychology as not only a mental health profession, but also a science of human behavior. For more on evolving policies around the use of psychologists in detention and interrogation, *see* Carroll H. Greene III & L. Morgan Banks, *Ethical Guideline Evolution In Psychological Support To Interrogation Operations*, 61 CONSULTING PSYCHOLOGY J.: PRAC. & RES. 25–32 (2009). For a discussion of doctors and torture, *see* Elena Nightingale, THE BREAKING OF BODIES AND MINDS (1985); Steven Miles, OATH BETRAYED: TORTURE, MEDICAL COMPLICITY, AND THE WAR ON TERROR (2006). In addition to potential violations of ethical guidelines, may criminal sanctions attach where doctors or others from the healing professions participate in abusive interrogations? *See Reisner v. Leso*, No. 115400/2010 (Aug. 11, 2011) (professional complaint against psychologist involved in torture at Guantánamo).

12. Advice-of-Counsel and Reliance Defenses

Given the existence of the "Torture Memos," might a CIA agent subject to prosecution raise either the defense of advice of counsel or reasonable reliance on official interpretation? The advice-of-counsel doctrine works to establish a defendant's good faith and can negate the *scienter* requirement of a particular crime or cause of action (i.e., the intent to engage in, or the knowledge of, wrongdoing). The advice-of-counsel doctrine is generally employed with respect to offenses defined by an intent to defraud, willfulness, or bad faith. The defendant who relies upon the advice of counsel may thus be able to prove that he had a good faith belief that his actions were legal prior to when he acted.

Because the doctrine does not require that the defendant admit any aspect of the accuser's case, advice-of-counsel is not technically an affirmative defense that results in exoneration notwithstanding that all elements of the claim or crime have been established. Likewise, the reliance defense applies more often in situations involving regulatory crimes rather than intrinsically wrong (*malum in se*) acts. The U.S. Model Penal Code at § 2.04 treats these defenses under the heading "Ignorance or Mistake:"

> (1) Ignorance or mistake as to a matter of fact or law is a defense if:
>
> > (a) the ignorance or mistake negatives the purpose, knowledge, belief, recklessness or negligence required to establish a material element of the offense * * *

(3) A belief that conduct does not legally constitute an offense is a defense to a prosecution for that offense based upon such conduct when: . . .

(b) [the defendant] acts in reasonable reliance upon an official statement of the law, afterward determined to be invalid or erroneous, contained in

(i) a statute or other enactment;

(ii) a judicial decision, opinion or judgment;

(iii) an administrative order or grant of permission; or

(iv) an official interpretation of the public officer or body charged by law with responsibility for the interpretation, administration or enforcement of the law defining the offense.

Both defenses rely on basic moral principles of, and utilitarian rationales for, criminal responsibility and punishment that consider it odious or useless to punish someone who manifested a clear intent not to break the law formed in reliance on legal or official advice. If you represented a hypothetical CIA interrogator who employed enhanced interrogation techniques, how would you argue that these defenses were applicable to your client? Are either *scienter* or willfulness elements of torture as it is defined in the Torture Convention or the Torture Memos? Is the degree of pain caused by a particular technique something on which a lawyer can provide an expert opinion? Would it be reasonable to rely upon one of the torture memos in determining whether particular interrogation techniques were lawful?

Professor David Luban testified to Congress that the Torture Memos had been drafted to "reverse engineer" a defense for illegal actions already committed. *See* Testimony of David Luban, Senate Judiciary Committee, "What Went Wrong: Torture and the Office of Legal Counsel in the Bush Administration" (May 13, 2009). Do you agree? For a discussion of the reliance on counsel defense, *see* Mark W.S. Hobel, Note, *"So Vast an Area of Legal Responsibility"? The Superior Orders Defense and Good Faith Reliance on Advice of Counsel*, 111 COLUM. L. REV. 574 (2011).

13. Extraordinary Rendition

The United States and other states engaged in a secret program known as "extraordinary rendition," whereby an individual suspected of terrorism is transferred from one state to another for purposes of interrogation, detention, and possible prosecution. Critics of the program contend that its purpose is to transfer suspects to places where torture is regularly practiced, and thus is—in effect—a program for "outsourcing torture." For one of the early stories revealing the U.S. extraordinary rendition program, *see* Jane Mayer, *Annals of Justice: Outsourcing Torture*, THE NEW YORKER (Feb. 14, 2005); *see also* Meg Satterthwaite, *Rendered Meaningless: Extraordinary Rendition and the Rule of Law*, 75 GEO. WASH. L. REV. 1333 (2007).

One of the stories highlighted in the Mayer article is that of Maher Arar, a Canadian citizen who was born in Syria, but moved to Canada with his family when he was 17. While traveling through the United States on his way home to Canada, Arar was detained by U.S. immigration officials for thirteen days and questioned about possible links to terrorism. After his interrogation, he was flown by plain-clothed officials via Jordan to Syria, where he was beaten and tortured for one year. A year later, the Syrian government released him, claiming they were unable to find any connection of Arar to terrorism. The Canadian government established a Commission of Inquiry into its own complicity in Arar's detention and rendition to Syria. The commission concluded that there was no credible evidence linking Arar to any form of terrorism. Although Canadian officials did provide false information to the United States government concerning Arar, the Commission was unable to conclude that the Canadian government participated in or supported Arar's detention and subsequent rendition to Syria by U.S. officials. Canada paid upwards of $10 million to Arar by way of reparation.

Arar sued the U.S. Government alleging he had been wrongfully detained and should be compensated, but the U.S. courts refused to hear the case, reasoning that the claim was based upon state secrets that, if revealed, would threaten U.S. foreign relations and national security. *Arar v. Ashcroft*, 585 F.3d 559 (2nd. Cir. 2009) (*en banc*), *cert. den.* 560 U.S. 978 (2010).

14. Extraordinary Rendition and the European Justice System

While the cases concerning extraordinary rendition filed in U.S. courts have been unsuccessful, individuals claiming to have been wrongly subjected to the practice have received more success in Europe. The case of Khaled El-Masri was the first such case to come before the European Court of Human Rights (ECHR). El-Masri, a German national, was detained by Macedonian border security officials on December 31, 2003. He was handed over to the CIA and transferred to an infamous secret prison in Kabul, Afghanistan known as the "Salt Pit," where he was detained for five months and subjected to regular interrogations, physical abuse, and humiliation. In April 2004, the then-CIA Director George Tenet learned that El-Masri was being held wrongfully. In early May, then-National Security Adviser Condoleezza Rice ordered his release. El-Masri was finally released on May 28, 2004. Rather than being returned to his home country of Germany, however, El-Masri was released at night on a desolate road in Albania with no funds to return home. Albanian border guards detained him, believing him to be a terrorist given his unkempt appearance. He was eventually released and returned home to Germany on May 29, 2004.

Like Arar, El-Masri brought a case against the U.S. Government in the U.S. court system, and as with the case of Arar, the suit was dismissed based on the state secrets doctrine. Indeed, the court noted that the very subject of the litigation was a state secret. A similar case brought in the German judicial system requesting the extradition of U.S. officials was also dismissed, though arrest warrants for the CIA employees involved in the rendition were issued by the Munich District Court on January 31, 2007.

El-Masri brought a claim against the Macedonian Government before the ECHR. In December 2012, the ECHR unanimously held that Macedonia had violated multiple rights enshrined in the European Convention on

Human Rights including Article 3, which prohibits torture and CIDT. The European Court also held, given information available to the Macedonian government at the time concerning the U.S. detention and interrogation program, that by transferring El-Masri into U.S. custody, "the Macedonian authorities knowingly exposed him to a real risk of ill-treatment and to conditions of detention contrary to Article 3 of the [European] Convention." *Case of El-Masri v. The Former Yugoslav Republic of Macedonia,* E. Ct. H.R. Application No. 39630/09, Judgment (December 13, 2012), para. 220. Macedonia was ordered to pay El-Masri €60,000.

Poland was the subject of a similar suit brought by Abd al-Rahim al-Nashiri, mentioned above in connection with waterboarding, who was detained in a CIA "black site" in Poland. The ECHR ruled that Poland had violated, *inter alia,* Articles 3 and 5 (arbitrary detention) of the European Convention and ordered it to pay €100,000. *Al Nashiri v. Poland,* E. Ct. H. R., Application No. 28761/11, Judgment (July 24, 2014). Will such judgments dissuade European states from participating in renditions in the future?

15. Does Torture "Work"

Many consequentialist arguments about torture (which are premised on the belief that torture is justified in extreme situations in order to save the lives of others) hinge on the assumption that torture "works" to force subjects to divulge true and actionable information. In one of his first major interviews as President, Trump announced that he would return to the practices of the Bush Administration because torture works. According to the "one percent doctrine," attributed to former Vice President Dick Cheney, so long as there is a one percent chance that torture will produce useful intelligence, torture should be employed. "Proof" of torture's effectiveness, however, is often lacking or deemed to be a state secret, unable to be divulged. On the other hand, anti-torture absolutists insist—with equally little empirical data for support—that torture does not work and is counter-productive. Given the absolute prohibition against torture under international law, is any debate about its efficacy valid? How would a judge determine the veracity of statements made by subjects under torture? Even if some useful information was revealed, how would one judge determine whether the use of torture was "worth" the costs associated with such a practice? For a discussion that torture has not worked in any historical context in which it has been systematically employed, *see* Lisa Hajjar, *Does Torture Work? A Sociological Assessment of the Practice in Historical and Global Perspective*, 5 ANN. REV. L. SOC. SCIENCE 11.1 (2009).

PROBLEMS

1. Force-Feeding

Starting in 2002, detainees on Guantánamo began staging non-violent hunger strikes to protest their detention and conditions of confinement. The strikes (or "non-religious fasts" in the Guantánamo lexicon) have occurred, off and on, since then, occasionally involving up to 200 men participating in shifts. At least 30 men detained on Guantánamo have been force-fed in response to these hunger-strikes. Force-feeding involves strapping the detainee in a six-point restraint chair (marketed by the vender as "a padded cell on wheels") or on a bed with Velcro straps (at times after a forcible extraction from their cells). A tube, alleged to be as thick as a finger, is inserted into the nostril of the detainee, and upwards of 1.5 liters of liquid food, such as Ensure Plus, is administered by either medics or, it is alleged, untrained guards or riot squad personnel. The individuals remain strapped down for up to an hour after the feeding in order to prevent them from regurgitating the foodstuff. Reports from Guantánamo indicated that guards would at times leave the feeding tube in place between feedings in order to avoid having to re-insert them each time. It has also been alleged that the tubes are not sterilized between detainees and that the liquid food was laced with laxatives.

Force-feeding can cause complications such as infections, dizziness, "dumping syndrome" (an expulsion reaction caused by over-feeding), inflammation, internal bleeding, infected or occluded nostrils, bloating, vomiting blood, and gastrointestinal disorders (such as nausea and diarrhea). Muhammad Ahmad Abdallah Salih (a.k.a. Al-Hanashi) allegedly committed suicide during a hunger strike when he was being enterally fed (through a feeding tube), although how he accomplished this has not been revealed and others have opined that he was killed. Another detainee, Farhan Abdul Latif, attempted to cover himself with his own excrement in order to avoid being force fed, but the tube was allegedly inserted through the excrement covering his nostrils. Latif—a Yemeni who had been cleared for release and suffered from mental illness—later died in 2012 for reasons that have not been revealed. One detainee explained his resort to a hunger strike as follows:

> This hunger strike is the only way I have to speak out. I do not strike because I enjoy hunger, thirst, fever, fatigue, pain, lightheadedness, or my body consuming itself. I do it to protest the injustice all the prisoners endure—the attacks on my religion, the disrespect shown to the Qur'an, the denial of medical treatment, the torture, and the cruelty of the interrogators. My strike is a form of peaceful protest against this injustice.

This quote and the above accounts are drawn from a formal communication filed by several human rights groups against U.S. Army General Bantz John Craddock, then U.S. Southern Command Commander in charge of Guantánamo and former NATO Supreme Allied Commander Europe (SACEUR). The communication was filed with the United Nations Special Rapporteurs on Torture, Health, and the Promotion of Human Rights while Countering Terrorism. *See* Center for Constitutional Rights et al., *Formal Communication for Consideration and Action* (April 2, 2009).

Does the practice of force-feeding hunger strikers constitute torture or cruel, inhuman or degrading treatment under U.S. or international law? Is it a violation of common Article 3, which requires detaining authorities to treat prisoners humanely and to refrain from acts of cruel treatment and from degrading or humiliating treatment? Are there parallels between force-feeding and the dietary manipulation authorized by the excerpted memorandum? Is it relevant that standing guidelines used by the U.S.

Bureau of Prisons and the Immigration and Customs Enforcement's Office of Detention and Removal allow prison/ICE officials to force prisoners to eat when the individual's life or health is at risk? *See, e.g.*, 28 C.F.R. § 549.65 (Refusal to Accept Treatment). By way of comparison, the World Medical Association's Guidelines for Physicians Concerning Torture and other Cruel, Inhuman or Degrading Treatment or Punishment in Relation to Detention and Imprisonment ("Declaration of Tokyo") states:

> Where a prisoner refuses nourishment and is considered by the physician as capable of forming an unimpaired and rational judgment concerning the consequences of such a voluntary refusal of nourishment, he or she shall not be fed artificially. The decision as to the capacity of the prisoner to form such a judgment should be confirmed by at least one other independent physician. The consequences of the refusal of nourishment shall be explained by the physician to the prisoner.

Should U.S. detention officers allow hunger strikers to die as the British did with Irish Republican Army captives in the 1980s?

In May 2014, District Court Judge Gladys Kessler, issued a temporary restraining order (TRO) to halt the force-feeding of Abu Wa'el Dhiab (of Syria) through the use of a restraint chair. She also ordered the government to produce videos depicting the petitioner's forcible cell extractions and subsequent force-feedings. *Abu Wa'el (Jihad) Dhiab v. Obama et al.*, Civil Action No. 05–1457 (GK), Order (May 16, 2014). The Department of Defense refused to allow Dhiab to be fed in the Guantánamo Bay hospital without a restraint chair. At a subsequent hearing, and facing what she described as "an anguishing Hobson's choice," Judge Kessler ruled that the U.S. military could continue to force-feed Dhiab to prevent him from dying despite credible allegations that the force-feeding practices cause him acute suffering. *Abu Wa'el (Jihad) Dhiab v. Obama et al.*, Civil Action No. 05–1457 (GK), Order (May 22, 2014). Dhiab, who has been cleared for release since 2009, is not opposed to voluntary enteral feeding.

2. Prosecute or Praise

Imagine a multi-ethnic country in Southeast Asia where a separatist movement in the north of the country, predominantly populated by an ethnic minority, is increasingly shattering the sense of peace and security. Historically, members of the movement employed the political process, a savvy media campaign, and non-violent direct-action tactics to achieve change. In recent years, however, a wing of the movement has grown increasingly frustrated with the slow pace of change and has begun resorting to terrorist methods to bring attention to its cause. These methods have primarily involved delivering, on a weekly basis, incendiary devices disguised as harmless letters and packages to prominent members of the ethnic majority group. At the beginning of each week, the entire country is on edge awaiting the next attack.

Following up on a tip, the country's criminal investigative agency apprehended an individual (Operative X) who turned out to be a relatively senior operative of the movement. In her possession was a laptop with a number of coded files that seemed to detail past and potentially future attacks. After thoroughly searching the remote safe house where Operative X and a confederate (Operative Y) were captured, the investigative agents staged a firefight that destroyed the building. The central government then announced that Operative X had been killed in the firefight and that no important leads had been discovered.

Meanwhile, Operative X's captors began secretly interrogating her in an effort to fully break the code and identify the victims and modalities of future attacks. After she refused to cooperate, the agents escalated the harshness of tactics used on her. In addition to being kept for long periods of time in various stress positions, Operative X was deprived of sleep, kept in an excessively cold and then hot cell, interrogated and photographed naked by male interrogators, and denied immediate medical attention for wounds received upon capture (although she was eventually treated). She was repeatedly subjected to strip and bodily cavity searches, ostensibly because she might have come into possession of prohibited items. Operative Y, captured with her, was subjected to similar conduct. Individuals in lab coats observed these sessions, occasionally recording the captives' vital signs.

After the rebels staged an attack on the country's Constitutional Court, the Prime Minister convened a secret meeting of senior national security, intelligence, and foreign ministry cabinet members and a few key deputies to address the growing terrorism threat in the country. In an effort to more effectively halt and prevent the attacks, the Prime Minister asked the team to design a program to capture and interrogate members of the separatist group who were prone to violence. He insisted that the program be consistent with the country's international law obligations and domestic law, which includes a statute penalizing torture and cruel, inhuman and degrading treatment that copies verbatim the formulation of those offenses contained within the Torture Convention. The group—dubbed the Senior National Security Advisors (SNSA)—eventually approved a classified interrogation program for captured terrorists that authorized the techniques already used on the senior operative and her confederate in addition to other enhanced tactics, such as prolonged solitary confinement, the manipulation of ethnic loyalties or cultural beliefs, the exploitation of phobias, and mock executions. In support of the program, several law professors who had short term appointments with the Ministry of Justice presented research on the legality of the proposed tactics. In addition, several physicians and psychologists were contracted from the private sector to provide advice on the design and implementation of the program. Members of the Ministry of Defense reportedly raised strong objections to some of the more harsh tactics, but the SNSA ultimately unanimously signed off on the program. The Prime Minister did not attend the meetings, but he was briefed on their contours and results in a series of classified memoranda. Senior interrogators were instructed on elements of the program in confidential training sessions.

After an extensive interrogation by intelligence officials that followed 180 hours of sleep deprivation, Operative Y eventually revealed the key to break the code on the seized laptop. Two subsequent attacks were successfully thwarted, and additional members of the separatist movement were captured and detained. They too were interrogated by intelligence agents in accordance with the program devised by the SNSA. In most cases, interrogators followed the instructions they had received in their training. On several occasions, however, when it was suspected that a subject was not being cooperative, interrogators exceeded the limits imposed on them by the program with respect to certain tactics.

The next national election resulted in the ouster of several members of parliament, including the Prime Minister. The reconfigured parliament passed new legislation that amended the torture/CIDT statute to prohibit a number of enumerated interrogation tactics, including sleep deprivation for more than 48 hours, mock executions, and the use of any nudity, dogs, or prolonged stress positions (exceeding 5 hours) in interrogations. Nothing in the legislative record reveals whether the legislation is to be applied retroactively.

You are a recently appointed senior official in the Ministry of Justice tasked with determining whether to bring charges against anyone involved in the design and implementation of the SNSA interrogation policy. How would you approach your mandate? Who—if anyone—would you target for investigation and possible prosecution? Would you prosecute individuals who stayed within the "four corners" of the original program or only those who exceeded the limits placed on them in training? Assuming you decide to go forward with prosecutions, what theories of liability would you employ to charge the different participants in the program? Besides criminal charges, are there other potential responses to the program?

CHAPTER 12

TERRORISM

I. INTRODUCTION

Terrorism has not historically been clearly defined as a crime under international law. Nor is it among the international crimes over which the International Criminal Court (ICC) has jurisdiction. Yet, the list of acts of terrorism committed during the last century is a long one, and one can find references to what we would today call terrorism throughout human history. Moreover, acts of terrorism—and their severity—have increased in recent years. Besides the catastrophic attacks of September 11, 2001, particularly visible acts of terrorism have occurred in the Madrid commuter train system on March 11, 2004 (killing 191 and wounding upwards of 2,000), in central London on July 7, 2005 (killing over 50 people and wounding over 700), in the Mumbai (Bombay) train system on July 11, 2006 (killing 209 and injuring more than 700), and in a mall in Nairobi on September 21, 2013 (killing over 60 and wounding 175). Civilians and combatants are regularly the victims of improvised explosive device (IED) and suicide bomber attacks in the two active war zones of Iraq and Afghanistan. All these attacks—terrible in their impact—share one characteristic: they were launched by organizations with the intent of terrorizing a people, often with little concern as to the identities of the victims. While we may think we know terrorism when we see it, the label remains contentious. Which events should be labeled as terrorism, as opposed to some other term (such as an act of war or justified violence as part of a liberation struggle), is at the heart of the debate over the evolving international definition of terrorism.

As you become familiar with the definitional challenges inherent to the concept of terrorism, consider the following events:

- A car bomb detonated in a market in downtown Baghdad, killing 48 civilians in 2002. The same act occurred in 2004 after the U.S. invasion of Iraq (2003).
- A car bomb detonated next to a U.S. Army Humvee in downtown Baghdad, killing three U.S. soldiers, in 2004 while U.S. troops occupied Iraq.
- Snipers surrounding Sarajevo killed residents of that city during the civil war in Bosnia-Herzegovina.
- The atomic bombings of Hiroshima and Nagasaki, which led to the immediate deaths of over 100,000 people, and innumerable injuries and subsequent fatalities.

- The World War II fire-bombings of Dresden and Tokyo, which resulted in estimated deaths of 25,000 and 85,000, respectively.
- The 1995 bombing of a federal building in Oklahoma City that killed 168 people, including a number of children.
- The destruction of a village by government forces in Darfur in 2008.
- The 1996 detonation of a truck bomb in front of a military barracks in Saudi Arabia housing foreign troops involved in a peacetime deployment.
- The same truck bomb is detonated in front of a military barracks housing members of the Royal Saudi Land Force, the Saudi army.
- The attack on a tavern frequented by off-duty military personnel in South Africa during the apartheid era, in which a number of civilians were injured and killed.
- The 2002 bombing of a night club in Bali in a tourist district.

As you read through the following materials, ask yourself which of these acts qualify, or should qualify, as "terrorism" under international law. How else might international criminal law characterize these acts? Are any of these acts essentially unregulated by *international* law? Should such acts more properly be addressed under domestic law? Which standard domestic crimes might be implicated by these events? Which state(s) could prosecute such acts?

As these introductory materials reveal, one of the biggest challenges facing any attempt to craft a legal response to terrorism has been that of definition. Is terrorism defined by its target? For example, as any act of violence aimed at a civilian population. Or is it defined by its purpose? For example, as any act intended to provoke fear and terror or to influence a government. Can states commit acts of terrorism, or is terrorism something that by definition is only committed by non-state entities? How does one distinguish between acts of terrorism and legitimate efforts to further self-determination in the face of a racist regime, a colonial power, or a hostile occupying force in a situation of asymmetrical warfare? How does one distinguish between acts of terrorism and legitimate acts of war? Can privileged combatants fall victim to terrorism, or may only civilians be the victims of terrorism?

The effort to draft an omnibus definition of terrorism has been a long one. The League of Nations in 1937 adopted a definition of terrorism—the first major attempt in the modern era to codify the crime of terrorism under international law. The treaty—the Convention for the Prevention and Punishment of Terrorism—was motivated by the 1934 assassination of King Alexander of Yugoslavia, the French foreign minister Louis

Barthou, and two bystanders, in France, by a Bulgarian nationalist working in coordination with Croatian separatists. This treaty required states to criminalize acts of terrorism under their own laws. The treaty attracted twenty-four state signatories. Only one of the signatories, India, ultimately ratified the Convention, and it thus never came into effect. The treaty defined terrorism as follows:

> All criminal acts directed against a State and intended or calculated to create a state of terror in the minds of particular persons or a group of persons or the general public.

For more on the circumstances surrounding the 1937 Convention on Terrorism and other subsequent efforts, *see* Thomas M. Franck & Bert B. Lockwood, Jr., *Preliminary Thoughts Towards an International Convention on Terrorism*, 68 AM. J. INT'L L. 69 (1974); and Ben Saul, *The Legal Response of the League of Nations to Terrorism*, 4 J. INT'L CRIM. JUST. 78 (2006).

The onset of World War II scuttled any further efforts to bring the treaty into effect, and with the dissolution of the League of Nations, the treaty was never revived. Efforts to codify and define terrorism have, however, persisted. In the 1960s and 1970s, a series of high-profile airplane hijackings led to specific treaties aimed at this form of terrorism:

- Convention on Offences and Certain Other Acts Committed on Board Aircraft, Sept. 14, 1963, 3 U.S.T. 2941 (the Tokyo Convention of 1963);
- Convention for the Suppression of Unlawful Seizure of Aircraft, Dec. 16, 1970, 22 U.S.T. 1641 (the Hague Convention of 1970); and
- Convention for the Suppression of Unlawful Acts against the Safety of Civil Aviation, Sept. 23, 1971 (the Montreal Convention of 1971).

Additional treaties prohibit other particular manifestations of terrorism, such as

- Attacks on internationally protected persons: Convention on the Prevention and Punishment of Crimes Against Internationally Protected Persons, Including Diplomatic Agents, G.A. Res. 3166, U.N. GAOR 6th Comm., 27th Sess., 2202nd plen. mtg., Supp. No. 30, U.N. Doc A/9407 (1973);
- The theft of nuclear materials: Convention on the Physical Protection of Nuclear Material, T.I.A.S. 11080 (Feb. 8, 1997);
- The taking of hostages: International Convention Against the Taking of Hostages, G.A. Res. 34/146, U.N. GAOR 6th Comm., 34th Sess., 105th mtg., Supp. No. 46, U.N. Doc. A/34/819 (1979);

- Acts that interfere with maritime navigation, including attacks on ships and attacks that damage maritime navigation facilities: Convention for the Suppression of Unlawful Acts Against the Safety of Maritime Navigation, 27 I.L.M. 668 (1988);
- Terrorist bombings: International Convention for the Suppression of Terrorist Bombings, 37 I.L.M. 249 (1998);
- The financing of terrorism: International Convention for the Suppression of the Financing of Terrorism, G.A. Res. 109, U.N. GAOR 6th Comm., 54 Sess., 76th mtg., Agenda Item 160, U.N. Doc. A/54/109 (1999); and
- Nuclear terrorism: International Convention for the Suppression of Acts of Nuclear Terrorism (2005).

In addition, a number of General Assembly resolutions and other international pronouncements have condemned various acts of terrorism. So far, however, efforts to draft a Comprehensive Convention on International Terrorism have deadlocked over definitional issues.

Consider the following definitions of terrorism or terrorist acts. Are they overly broad such that they cover acts that you think should not qualify as international terrorism? Or are they too narrow such that they fail to capture acts that should clearly generate international opprobrium and prosecution? How do you explain the differences in these definitions? How are they influenced by the history, politics, and culture of the institutions that formulated them? How would these definitions be employed in a criminal proceeding? Can you discern elements of crimes from these definitions?

U.N. General Assembly Resolution 51/210 (1999) ("Measures to Eliminate International Terrorism"):

> Criminal acts intended or calculated to provoke a state of terror in the general public, a group of persons or particular persons for political purposes are in any circumstance unjustifiable, whatever the considerations of a political, philosophical, ideological, racial, ethnic, religious or other nature that may be invoked to justify them.

International Convention for the Suppression of Terrorist Bombings, Art. 2, 37 I.L.M. 249, 253 (1998):

> Any person commits an offence within the meaning of this Convention if that person unlawfully and intentionally delivers, places, discharges or detonates an explosive or other lethal device in, into or against a place of public use, a State or government facility, a public transportation system or an infrastructure facility:
>
> a. With the intent to cause death or serious bodily injury; or

b. With the intent to cause extensive destruction of such a place, facility or system, where such destruction results in or is likely to result in major economic loss.

International Convention for the Suppression of the Financing of Terrorism, G.A. Res. 109, U.N. GAOR 6th Comm., 54 Sess., 76th mtg., Agenda Item 160, U.N. Doc. A/54/109 (1999), Art. 2(1)(b):

> Any . . . act intended to cause death or serious bodily injury to a civilian, or to any other person not taking an active part in the hostilities in a situation of armed conflict, when the purpose of such act, by its nature or context, is to intimidate a population, or to compel a Government or an international organization to do or to abstain from doing any act.

Council of Europe, Parliamentary Assembly Recommendation 1426 (1999):

> Any offence committed by individuals or groups resorting to violence or threatening to use violence against a country, its institutions, its population in general or specific individuals which, being motivated by separatist aspirations, extremist ideological conceptions, fanaticism or irrational and subjective factors, is intended to create a climate of terror among official authorities, certain individuals or groups in society, or the general public.

Convention of the Organization of the Islamic Conference on Combating International Terrorism (1999):

> "Terrorism" means any act of violence or threat thereof notwithstanding its motives or intentions perpetrated to carry out an individual or collective criminal plan with the aim of terrorizing people or threatening to harm them or imperiling their lives, honor, freedoms, security or rights or exposing the environment or any facility or public or private property to hazards or occupying or seizing them, or endangering a national resource, or international facilities, or threatening the stability, territorial integrity, political unity or sovereignty of independent States. * * * Peoples struggle including armed struggle against foreign occupation, aggression, colonialism, and hegemony, aimed at liberation and self-determination in accordance with the principles of international law shall not be considered a terrorist crime.

Organization of African Unity Convention on the Prevention and Combating of Terrorism (1999):

> Any act which is a violation of the criminal laws of a State Party and which may endanger the life, physical integrity or freedom of, or cause serious injury or death to, any person, any number or group of persons or causes or may cause damage to public or

private property, natural resources, environmental or cultural heritage and is calculated or intended to:

(i) intimidate, put in fear, force, coerce or induce any government, body, institution, the general public or any segment thereof, to do or abstain from doing any act, or to adopt or abandon a particular standpoint, or to act according to certain principles; or

(ii) disrupt any public service, the delivery of any essential service to the public or to create a public emergency; or

(iii) create general insurrection in a State.

United States Annual Country Reports on Terrorism, 22 U.S.C.A. § 2656f(d)(2):

[Terrorism for the purpose of this report is defined as] premeditated, politically motivated violence perpetrated against noncombatant targets by sub-national groups or clandestine agents.

Pakistan Anti-Terrorism (Amendment) Ordinance (1999):

A person is said to commit a terrorist act if he,

(a) in order to, or if the effect of his actions will be to, strike terror or create a sense of fear and insecurity in the people, or any section of the people, does any act or thing by using bombs, dynamite or other explosive or inflammable substances, or such fire-arms or other lethal weapons as may be notified, or poisons or noxious gases or chemicals, in such a manner as to cause, or be likely to cause, the death of, or injury to, any person or persons, or damage to, or destruction of, property on a large scale, or a widespread disruption of supplies of services essential to the life of the community, or threatens with the use of force public servants in order to prevent them from discharging their lawful duties; or

(b) commits a scheduled offence, the effect of which will be, or be likely to be, to strike terror, or create a sense of fear and insecurity in the people, or any section of the people, or to adversely affect harmony among different sections of the people; or

(c) commits an act of gang rape, child molestation, or robbery coupled with rape as specified in the Schedule to this Act; or

(d) commits an act of civil commotion.

Alex P. Schmid, *The Response Problem as a Definition Problem*, *in* WESTERN RESPONSES TO TERRORISM 8 (Alex P. Schmid & Ronald D. Crelinsten eds., 1993):

> Terrorism is an anxiety-inspiring method of repeated violent action, employed by (semi-) clandestine individual, group or state actors, for idiosyncratic, criminal or political reasons, whereby—in contrast to assassination—the direct targets of violence are not the main targets. The immediate human victims of violence are generally chosen randomly (targets of opportunity) or selectively (representative or symbolic targets) from a target population, and serve as message generators. Threat-and violence-based communication processes between terrorist (organization), (imperiled) victims, and main targets are used to manipulate the main target (audience(s)), turning it into a target of terror, a target of demands, or a target of attention, depending on whether intimidation, coercion, or propaganda is primarily sought.

Draft Comprehensive Convention Against International Terrorism (Article 2):

> Any person commits an offence within the meaning of the present Convention if that person, by any means, unlawfully and intentionally, causes:
>
> (a) Death or serious bodily injury; or
>
> (b) Serious damage to public or private property, including a place of public use, a State or government facility, a public transportation system, an infrastructure facility or to the environment; or
>
> (c) Damage to [such] property, places, facilities or systems . . . resulting in or likely to result in major economic loss,
>
> when the purpose of the conduct, by its nature or context, is to intimidate a population, or to compel a Government or an international organization to do or to abstain from doing any act.

NOTES & QUESTIONS

1. A Separate Crime

Should terrorism be treated as a separate international crime, or is it better dealt with as a subset of war crimes or crimes against humanity? What is the difference between a war crime and an act of terrorism? Between a crime against humanity and an act of terrorism? Ordinary acts of murder and an act of terrorism? Many of the treaties mentioned above focus on a specific terrorist tactic, such as hijackings or hostage-taking. This approach has been criticized as a piecemeal and incomplete solution to a more comprehensive problem. Do you agree with this criticism? A draft Comprehensive Convention Against International Terrorism (quoted above) has been in the works since the 1970s. *See* Mahmoud Hmoud, *Negotiating the Draft Comprehensive Convention on International Terrorism: Major Bones of Contention*, 4 J. INT'L CRIM. JUST. 1031 (2006). Which of the existing terrorism treaties would apply to the events of September 11th? What are the advantages and disadvantages of adopting either a piecemeal approach or a comprehensive approach? Why might the international community not yet have adopted an omnibus definition of the crime of terrorism? Is the draft Convention's definition sufficient?

2. Asymmetrical Warfare

Is terrorism inevitable in situations of asymmetrical warfare where one party (usually a state actor) possesses military capabilities that vastly exceed those of the other party (usually a non-state actor)? Likewise, is it inevitable that once one party begins utilizing terrorism as a tactic of war or otherwise, the other party will follow suit?

3. Terrorism and Acts of War

Several of the terrorism treaties do not seem to apply to the actions of military forces. For example, the Terrorist Bombing Convention states as follows:

> [T]he activities of military forces of States are governed by rules of international law outside the framework of this Convention and * * * the exclusion of certain actions from the coverage of this Convention does not condone or make lawful otherwise unlawful acts, or preclude prosecution under other laws. (Preamble). * * *
>
> "Military forces of a State" means the armed forces of a State which are organized, trained and equipped under its internal law for the primary purpose of national defence or security and persons acting in support of those armed forces who are under their formal command, control and responsibility. (Article 1(4)). * * *
>
> The activities of armed forces during an armed conflict, as those terms are understood under international humanitarian law, which are governed by that law, are not governed by this Convention, and the activities undertaken by military forces of a State in the exercise of their official duties, inasmuch as they are governed by other rules of international law, are not governed by this Convention. (Article 19(2)).

What is the impact of these provisions? Why might treaty drafters have included such language? How would such provisions apply in an international versus a non-international armed conflict? Several states (such as Pakistan, Egypt, Jordan, and the Syrian Arab Republic) have entered controversial reservations to certain terrorism treaties to the effect that

> nothing in this Convention shall be applicable to struggles, including armed struggles, for the realization of [the] right of self-determination launched against any alien or foreign occupation or domination, in accordance with the rules of international law.

Should struggles of self-determination be exempt from the prohibition against terrorism? Should the law of terrorism, unlike the laws of armed conflict, take account of the justness of the cause pursued?

4. Law Enforcement, Trials, Efficiency and Efficacy

Since the invasion of Afghanistan in 2001, the United States has adopted two approaches toward individuals who are accused of participating in acts of terrorism in armed conflicts in Afghanistan, Iraq, and elsewhere: a law-of-war approach (targeting individuals with lethal force or preventatively detaining them) and a law enforcement approach (prosecuting them as criminals). These competing approaches played out in 2004 in the pages of FOREIGN POLICY magazine in a debate between Kenneth Roth, the Executive Director of Human Rights Watch, and Ruth Wedgwood, a law professor and adviser to President George W. Bush. Roth in his submission argued that

> [U]sing war rules when law-enforcement rules could reasonably be followed is dangerous. . . . If law-enforcement rules are used, a mistaken arrest can be rectified at trial. But if war rules apply, the government is never obliged to prove a suspect's guilt. Instead, a supposed terrorist can be held for however long it takes to win the "war" against terrorism. And the consequences of error are even graver if the supposed combatant is killed. . .

Prof. Wedgwood countered that terrorism trials are ineffective and inefficient:

> [A] war is in fact raging, and criminal law is too weak a weapon. . . . The law of armed conflict . . . allows measures, such as the preventive internment of enemy combatants during the conflict, that do not require the full-dress procedure of criminal trials.

Which side has the stronger argument? Is efficiency the primary value by which we should judge whether to adopt an armed conflict or law enforcement approach to terrorism? What about justice? Due process? Even if one is concerned about justice and due process, is there a point at which adherence to such values endangers the very existence of society? President Lincoln famously stated that those who asserted that the Constitution did not allow him to suspend the writ of *habeas corpus* would allow "all the laws, but one, to go unexecuted, and the government itself go to pieces, lest that one be violated." *See* William H. Rehnquist, ALL THE LAWS BUT ONE: CIVIL LIBERTIES IN WARTIME 38 (1998).

Human Rights First, a non-profit human rights organization, has published a report demonstrating that prosecutions for terrorism in federal courts have been successful, garnering a conviction rate of over 90%. *See* Richard B. Zabel & James J. Benjamin, Jr., IN PURSUIT OF JUSTICE: PROSECUTING TERRORISM CASES IN THE FEDERAL COURTS (2009). The report examined over 100 international terrorism cases (involving almost 300 defendants) that have been prosecuted in U.S. federal courts. The report reaches four broad conclusions:

1) The criminal justice system is not sufficient to address international terrorism alone. The Government must adopt a

multi-faceted approach in combating terrorism, drawing upon military, intelligence, diplomatic, economic, and law enforcement resources.

2) Major terrorism cases produce strains and burdens on the criminal justice system. Terrorism cases are extremely complex, and present thorny legal issues and challenging practical problems.

3) The criminal justice system is not perfect. It is prone to errors of all kinds, and can be too slow, too fast, too harsh, too lenient, too subtle, too blunt, too opaque and too transparent.

4) Despite these shortcomings, the criminal justice system has adapted to such challenges and remained workable and credible.

5. International v. Domestic Terrorism

Several of the treaties also include language requiring a transnational element in order to have the act fall within the terms of the treaty. For example, the Terrorist Bombing Convention provides at Article 3:

> This Convention shall not apply where the offence is committed within a single State, the alleged offender and the victims are nationals of that State, the alleged offender is found in the territory of that State and no other State has a basis under [territorial or active/passive nationality jurisdiction] to exercise jurisdiction [and the offense was not committed to compel another state to act].

What is the impact of this language? Why might drafters have included it in the treaty?

6. *Mens Rea*

Is terrorism a crime, like genocide, that is defined by its mental state? Like many international crimes, formulations of terrorism envision multiple mental states as defining elements. The primary *mens rea* is that associated with the underlying *actus reus* element and usually involves intentional conduct. The Bombing Convention, for example, identifies the relevant *mens rea* as intentionality when it prohibits enumerated acts undertaken with

> the intent to cause death or serious bodily injury; or . . . the intent to cause extensive destruction of [a] place [of public use], facility or system, where such destruction results in or is likely to result in major economic loss.

By contrast, the Financing Convention also prohibits knowingly providing or collecting funds to be used to carry out acts of terrorism. In addition, many definitions of terrorism, especially in domestic law or the regional instruments, require proof of the existence of some secondary mental state over and above the general intent to commit prohibited acts of violence. In some cases, this mental element is aimed at the civilian population (the intent to cause terror) or a government (the intent to influence a government). For example, U.S. law defines "international terrorism" as acts that

> appear to be intended (i) to intimidate or coerce a civilian population; (ii) to influence the policy of a government by intimidation or coercion; or (iii) to affect the conduct of a government by mass destruction, assassination, or kidnapping.

18 U.S.C. § 2331(1)(B). Is this supplemental mental state best conceived of as a form of specific intent or motive? What purpose do these provisions serve?

7. Bases of Jurisdiction over Terrorism

Does international law allow for the exercise of universal jurisdiction over acts of terrorism? Most of the terrorism treaties provide for expansive forms of extraterritorial jurisdiction. For example, the draft Comprehensive Convention states that:

> 1. Each State Party shall take such measures as may be necessary to establish its jurisdiction over the offences set forth in article 2 of the present Convention when:
>
>   (a) The offence is committed in the territory of that State; or
>
>   (b) The offence is committed on board a vessel flying the flag of that State or an aircraft which is registered under the laws of that State at the time the offence is committed; or
>
>   (c) The offence is committed by a national of that State.
>
> 2. A State Party may also establish its jurisdiction over any such offence when:
>
>   (a) The offence is committed by a stateless person who has his or her habitual residence in the territory of that State; or
>
>   (b) The offence is committed wholly or partially outside its territory, if the effects of the conduct or its intended effects constitute or result in, within its territory, the commission of an offence set forth in article 2; or
>
>   (c) The offence is committed against a national of that State; or
>
>   (d) The offence is committed against a State or government facility of that State abroad, including an embassy or other diplomatic or consular premises of that State; or
>
>   (e) The offence is committed in an attempt to compel that State to do or to abstain from doing any act; or
>
>   (f) The offence is committed on board an aircraft which is operated by the Government of that State. * * *
>
> 4. Each State Party shall likewise take such measures as may be necessary to establish its jurisdiction over the offences referred to in article 2 in cases where the alleged offender is present in its territory and it does not extradite that person to any of the States Parties that have established their

jurisdiction in accordance with paragraph 1 or 2 of the present article.

5. When more than one State Party claims jurisdiction over the offences set forth in article 2, the relevant States Parties shall strive to coordinate their actions appropriately, in particular concerning the conditions for prosecution and the modalities for mutual legal assistance.

Given that a number of terrorism treaties contain similar formulas, can it be said that acts of terrorism are subject to universal jurisdiction as a matter of customary international law?

In a case involving a conspiracy to bomb commercial airlines and the February 1993 bombing of the World Trade Center in New York City, a U.S. court found otherwise. *United States v. Yousef*, 327 F.3d 56, 96 (D.C. Cir. 2003). In particular, the court ruled that the jurisdictional rule contained in the Montreal Convention for the Suppression of Unlawful Acts Against the Safety of Civil Aviation

> creates a basis for the assertion of jurisdiction that is moored in a process of formal lawmaking and that is binding only on the States that accede to it. The jurisdiction thus created is not a species of universal jurisdiction, but a jurisdictional agreement among contracting States to extradite or prosecute offenders who commit the acts proscribed by the treaty—that is, the agreements between contracting States create *aut dedere aut punire* ("extradite or prosecute") jurisdiction.

Do you agree? Could you argue more broadly for a customary-law right to assert universal jurisdiction over acts of terrorism?

II. PROSECUTING TERRORISM AT THE INTERNATIONAL LEVEL

Acts of terrorism have most often been prosecuted at the national level using domestic anti-terrorism legislation. An exceptional prosecution took place in the Netherlands at a decommissioned U.S. military base using Scottish law. The prosecution involved two Libyan defendants accused of contributing to the bombing of a civilian airliner (Pan Am flight 103) that was downed over the Scottish town of Lockerbie, killing all 259 passengers and crew. After extensive negotiations, and the imposition by the United Nations Security Council of economic sanctions against Libya, the two officials were delivered to the Netherlands for trial. One of the defendants, Al Amin Khalifa Fhimah, was acquitted, and returned to Libya; the other, Abdel Basset Ali al-Megrahi, was convicted and sentenced to life imprisonment with a minimum sentence of twenty-seven years before parole. He was granted compassionate release in 2009, having served ten of his mandatory twenty-seven year sentence, on the ground that he was dying of cancer (he died in 2012).

We focus briefly here on the prosecution of terrorism at the *international* level under international law. Few of the international criminal tribunals created to date specifically include jurisdiction over the crime of terrorism. As discussed in more detail below, the Special Tribunal for Lebanon (STL) asserts jurisdiction over domestic terrorism crimes. The Statutes of the International Criminal Tribunal for Rwanda (Article 4(d)) and the Special Court for Sierra Leone (Article 3(d)) are unique in listing "acts of terrorism" as war crimes. These provisions are drawn from Protocol II, which along with Protocol I prohibits inflicting terror on a civilian population (Art. 51(2), Protocol I and Article 13(2), Protocol II). The Fourth Geneva Convention on civilians also contains the following prohibition with respect to civilians and other protected persons: "Collective penalties and likewise all measures of intimidation or of terrorism are prohibited." (Art. 33). These acts, however, are not designated as grave breaches of that treaty. These references to terror and terrorism opened the door for the prosecution as war crimes of some acts that would qualify as terrorism under many of the definitions listed above. Consider the following case prosecuted before the International Criminal Tribunal for the former Yugoslavia (ICTY). Compare the formulation of the crime by the ICTY in the opinion below to the opinion by the STL that follows it.

Prosecutor v. Galić, Case No. IT–98–29–T, Judgement (Dec. 5, 2003)

In the Trial Chamber

Terror Against the Civilian Population as a Violation of the Laws or Customs of War * * *

64. The first count of the Indictment reads:

> Count 1: Violations of the Laws or Customs of War (unlawfully inflicting terror upon civilians as set forth in Article 51 of Additional Protocol I and Article 13 of Additional Protocol II to the Geneva Conventions of 1949) punishable under Article 3 of the Statute of the Tribunal.

65. The paragraph introducing Count 1 alleges that the Accused, General Galić, as commander of the SRK [a branch of the Bosnian Serb military forces], "conducted a protracted campaign of shelling and sniping upon civilian areas of Sarajevo and upon the civilian population thereby inflicting terror and mental suffering upon its civilian population." * * * [I]t will transpire in the course of the Majority's discussion that "Infliction of terror" is not an appropriate designation of the offence considered here because actual infliction of terror is not a required element of the offence. The Majority will henceforth refer to the offence charged in Count 1 as "the crime of terror against the civilian population," or simply "the crime of terror," a purported violation of the laws or customs of war.

66. The charge, as such, of terror against the civilian population is one that until now has not been considered in a Tribunal judgement, although evidence of terrorization of civilians has been factored into convictions on other charges.[114] This is also the first time an international tribunal has pronounced on the matter.[115] After considering the arguments of the Parties, the Majority will examine in detail the legal foundations and other essential characteristics of the charge.

Prosecution * * *

70. The Prosecution submitted that the following elements constitute the crime of terror:

1. Unlawful acts or threats of violence.
2. Which caused terror to spread among the civilian population.
3. The acts or threats of violence were carried out with the primary purpose of spreading terror among the civilian population.

In addition, according to the Prosecution's proposal, there must be a nexus between the acts or threats of violence and the armed conflict, and the Accused must bear responsibility for the acts or threats under Article 7 of the Statute.

71. The Prosecution submitted that the first element in the list above, which is part of the *actus reus* of the offence, is "broad," because it encompasses both acts and threats of violence. The Prosecution sees the acts of violence in the present case as consisting of systematic shelling and sniping of civilians. The Prosecution's case is thus limited to these acts. As for "threats," the alleged shelling and sniping of civilians created, according to the Prosecution, a constant threat that more such acts would be perpetrated at any moment. The "threats" in the present case are said

---

[114] In the *Čelebići* case, acts of intimidation creating an "atmosphere of terror" in prison camps were punished as grave breaches of the Geneva Conventions (torture or inhuman treatment) and as violations of Article 3 common to the Geneva Conventions (torture or cruel treatment). In the *Blaškić* case "the atmosphere of terror reigning in the detention facilities" was part of the factual basis leading to the Accused in that case being convicted for the crimes of inhuman treatment (a grave breach) and cruel treatment (a violation of the laws or customs of law). Blaškić's additional conviction for "unlawful attack" on civilians was based in part upon the finding that his soldiers "terrorised the civilians by intensive shelling, murders and sheer violence." And in the *Krstić* case, General Krstić was accused of persecutions, a crime against humanity, on the basis of his alleged participation in "the terrorising of Bosnian Muslim civilians". The Trial Chamber found that a "terror campaign" was in existence: "Numerous witnesses gave evidence that, during Operation Krivaja 95, the VRS [Bosnian Serbs] shelled the Srebrenica enclave intensively with the apparent intent to terrify the populace." Moreover: "On 12 and 13 July 1995, upon the arrival of Serb forces in Potocari, the Bosnian Muslim refugees taking shelter in and around the compound were subjected to a terror campaign comprised of threats, insults, looting and burning of nearby houses, beatings, rapes, and murders." The Trial Chamber in *Krstić* characterized "the crimes of terror", and the forcible transfer of the women, children, and elderly at Potočari as constituting persecution and inhumane acts. * * *

[115] The Special Court for Sierra Leone has issued several indictments containing counts of "acts of terrorism" ("terrorizing the civilian population") brought pursuant to Article 3 common to the Geneva Conventions and to Additional Protocol II.

to be of a kind implicit in the acts of violence. The Trial Chamber is thus not called upon to determine liability for threats that are not implicit, in the Prosecution's sense.

72. The "special intent requirement" (element 3) is, according to the Prosecution, the distinguishing feature of the crime of terror. The Prosecution has interpreted "primary purpose" as requiring that "the infliction of terror upon the civilian population was the predominant purpose served by the acts or threats of violence. It need not be established that the broader campaign in the Sarajevo theatre had this as its sole or only objective." Where the special intent, or *mens rea*, cannot be proven directly, it may be "inferred from the nature, manner, timing, frequency and duration of the shelling and sniping of civilians."

73. "As an element of the offence of terror [. . . i]t must [. . .] be established that terror *was in fact caused*." In addition to proof of actual infliction of terror, the Prosecution requires a causal connection between the first and second elements ("2. Which caused . . ."). That is, there must have been not only unlawful acts and actual terror experienced by the population, but also a causal link between the acts and the terror. "[T]he offence of unlawfully inflicting terror [. . .] is distinguished also by its *effect*, which in the present case was the profound psychological impact on the population." The Prosecution does not cite any authority for these submissions.

74. "Population," according to the Prosecution, does not just mean any number of Sarajevo civilians: "the unlawful shelling and sniping campaigns [had] the result that *much of the civilian population* lived in a state of terror." The implication that "population" is to be understood to mean the *majority* of the population, or at least a large segment of it, is found also in the following: "The requirement that terror be spread among the civilian population is satisfied even if certain civilians, or sectors of the population, were not so affected."

75. In its preliminary submissions the Prosecution did not provide a legal definition of "terror" (i.e. of the emotional effect which figures in the purported second element of the offence), except to refer in a footnote to a dictionary definition of the word as "extreme fear." In the course of trial, when the Prosecution's expert on terror (a psychologist) was heard, terror was again rendered as extreme fear. The Prosecution later explicitly adopted its expert's definition. * * *

Defence

77. The Defence in its preliminary submissions termed the Prosecution's stand on the applicable law "unacceptable," but did not dismiss outright the availability of the charge. It acknowledged that Article 51 of Additional Protocol I, which prohibits (in the Defence's words) "illegal terror inflicted on civilians," was binding upon the parties to the conflict.

78. The Defence stated that the intent to inflict terror must be demonstrable: "If the Prosecution is charging General Galić with having conducted a long-lasting shelling and sniping campaign designed to terrorize [the] civilian population [. . .] it must be established that there existed the intent to inflict terror on [the] civilian population by shelling and sniping." Lastly, the Defence did not take issue with the *actus reus* element "of the criminal act of inflicting terror, as the Prosecution has qualified it," namely acts of violence causing civilian casualties.

79. Thus, from the beginning of the case, the Defence joined the Prosecution in understanding that the scope of the *actus reus* of terror would be limited to the acts underlying Counts 4 and 7 of the Indictment (killing or severe injury of civilians through unlawful attacks), and that "threats" would not be a significant factor. The Defence's only comment on threats was on a theoretical plane, when it stated that for threats of violence to come within the offence of terror they had to be specifically directed against the civilian population. "[The threat] must be serious. It must be real. And it must be capable to cause terror or spread terror among [the] civilian population." * * *

81. [T]he Defence notes the Prosecution's position that "the civilian population was the subject of illegal attacks and terror [etc.]," and then states:

> In order to accept the above mentioned, unfounded Prosecution's conclusions, the Defence's viewpoint is that the Prosecution must prove the following:
>
> a) The exact military actions that were conducted against the illegal targets and by which means (i.e. shelling or sniping), including the exact time and place,
>
> b) That, as part of these illegal actions, there was intention of targeting the civilians with the aim to terrorize,
>
> c) That the intention to kill the civilians existed,
>
> d) That the intention to inflict injuries, other than killings existed.

The difference between this list (which may or may not have been intended by the Defence as an alternative definition of the offence) and the Prosecution's definition of the elements of the crime of terror is that the Defence does not seem to require proof that the civilian population did, in fact, experience terror (the second element in the Prosecution's list), but does require proof of the perpetrator's intent to kill or injure civilians.

82. In yet another part of [its brief], however, the Defence does demand proof of actual infliction of terror, as well as a causal link between actual terror and unlawful violent acts:

> The prosecutor should have proven several things:
>
> 1. that there was terror

2. that this terror was not simply the result of war in an urban theatre, led in a legitimate way

3. that this terror was the result of illegitimate acts

4. performed by troops commanded by the Accused

5. following his orders

6. (alternatively) that the Accused was aware of the facts and (if he had not given the orders himself) that he had not punished them

7. finally that the result was hoped for as such within the scope of a global plan.

If this was meant as a definition of the crime of terror, the Defence did not cite any authority for it.

83. On the experiential aspect of terror, the Defence said: "It is underestimating the meaning of 'terror' to say that if an individual (or individuals) feels 'extreme fear' he feels terror." Later, in its oral submissions at the trial's end, the Defence asserted: "Inflicting of terror as an element of a criminal offence [. . .] cannot be causing of any kind of terror or causing terror of any intensity. [. . .] It has to be of the highest intensity. It has to be long term. It has to be direct. And it has to be capable of causing long-term consequences." * * *

Discussion

86. While the Parties have not raised the question of jurisdiction *ratione materiae* [subject matter jurisdiction], the Majority will consider it *ex officio*, for it is fundamental to the exercise of competence.

87. The Majority must decide whether the Tribunal has jurisdiction over the crime of terror against the civilian population, but only to the extent relevant to the charge in this case. That is to say, the Majority is not required to decide whether an offence of terror in a *general* sense falls within the jurisdiction of the Tribunal, but only whether a *specific* offence of killing and wounding civilians in time of armed conflict with the intention to inflict terror on the civilian population, as alleged in the Indictment, is an offence over which it has jurisdiction.[150] * * *

---

[150] The Majority is aware that several international instruments exist outlawing "terrorism" in various forms. The Majority necessarily limits itself to the legal regime that has been developed with reference to conventional armed conflict between States, or between governmental authorities and organized armed groups, or between such groups within a State. In other words, the Majority proceeds on the understanding that the present case will have a basis, if at all, in the legal regime of the Geneva Conventions and the Additional Protocols and not in international efforts directed against "political" varieties of terrorism. The Majority would also note that "terrorism" has never been singly defined under international law. * * * [T]he international community has followed a thematic approach to the characterization of international terrorism. * * * The prohibition of terror against the civilian population in times of war, which (as discussed below) is given expression in Geneva Convention IV and the Additional Protocols, is another example of the thematic, subject-specific, approach to "terrorism."

89. As noted in the preceding section, in the *Tadić* decision on jurisdiction the Appeals Chamber said that four conditions (the *Tadić* conditions) must be met for an offence to be subject to prosecution under Article 3 of the Statute (violations of the laws or customs of law): (i) the violation must constitute an infringement of a rule of international humanitarian law; (ii) the rule must be customary in nature or, if it belongs to treaty law, the required conditions must be met; (iii) the violation must be serious, that is to say, it must constitute a breach of a rule protecting important values and the breach must involve grave consequences for the victim; and (iv) the violation must entail, under customary or conventional law, the individual criminal responsibility of the person breaching the rule.

90. The discussion below begins with preliminary remarks on the Majority's approach to treaty interpretation and the paramount importance of the *nullum crimen sine lege* principle. The Majority will then consider each of the *Tadić* conditions. The elements of the crime of terror are developed as part of the discussion of the fourth *Tadić* condition. * * *

93. The principle known as *nullum crimen sine lege* is meant to prevent the prosecution and punishment of a person for acts which were reasonably, and with knowledge of the laws in force, believed by that person not to be criminal at the time of their commission. In practice this means "that penal statutes must be strictly construed" and that the "paramount duty of the judicial interpreter [is] to read into the language of the legislature, honestly and faithfully, its plain and rational meaning and to promote its object." Moreover, the effect of strict construction of the provisions of a criminal statute is that where an equivocal word or ambiguous sentence leaves a reasonable doubt of its meaning which the canons of construction fail to solve, the benefit of the doubt should be given to the subject and against the legislature which has failed to explain itself.[156]

First and Second *Tadić* Conditions

94. The Indictment is not explicit as to which part of Article 51 of Additional Protocol I, or which part of Article 13 of Additional Protocol II, Count 1 is referenced to. Article 51 is an extensive provision in Part IV of the Protocol concerned with the protection of the civilian population. Yet it is clear from the submissions in this case that the intended reference of Count 1 is to sub-paragraph 2 of Article 51, which states:

> The civilian population as such, as well as individual civilians, shall not be the object of attack. Acts or threats of violence the primary purpose of which is to spread terror among the civilian population are prohibited.

---

[156] *Čelebići* Trial Judgement, para. 413.

The second sentence of this excerpt will henceforth be referred to as the "second part" of the second paragraph of Article 51, or simply as the "second part of 51(2)."

95. The quoted passage is identical to sub-paragraph 2 of Article 13 of Additional Protocol II. Since the Trial Chamber has found that certain parts of Additional Protocol I, including Article 51 thereof, applied to the armed conflict in Sarajevo during the relevant time, the Majority takes Additional Protocol I to be the basis of Count 1. It is not necessary to decide whether Additional Protocol II was also applicable to the conflict. Moreover, the Majority is not called upon to decide whether Additional Protocol I came at any time into effect in the State of Bosnia-Herzegovina through fulfilment of the Protocol's inherent conditions of application (Article 1 of the Protocol). The implementing instrument, on the evidence in this case, was the 22 May Agreement.*

96. Thus the first two *Tadić* conditions are met: Count 1 bases itself on an actual rule of international humanitarian law, namely the rule represented by the second part of the second paragraph of Article 51 of Additional Protocol I. * * *

97. The Majority emphasizes that it is not required to pronounce on whether the rule in question is also customary in nature. As stated above, it belongs to "treaty law." This is enough to fulfil the second *Tadić* condition as articulated by the Appeals Chamber. Nevertheless, the Majority will proceed with additional caution here to avoid any possible misunderstanding of its position on this important question.

98. [In the *Tadić* jurisdictional appeal, t]he Appeals Chamber has said "that the International Tribunal is authorised to apply, in addition to customary international law, any treaty which: (i) was unquestionably binding on the parties at the time of the alleged offence; and (ii) was not in conflict with or derogating from peremptory norms of international law, as are most customary rules of international humanitarian law." In relation to the first point, the Majority understands that it stems from the unqualified imperative of respect for the *nullum crimen sine lege* principle. The fact that the 22 May Agreement was binding on the parties to the conflict, and that certain provisions of Additional Protocol I had thereby undoubtedly been brought into effect, means that in this general sense there is no affront to the principle of *nullum crimen sine lege* by the Majority's determination. In relation to the Appeals Chamber's second point, this raises the question of whether the second part of 51(2) in any way conflicts with, or derogates from, peremptory norms of international law. In the Majority's view, it does not. What the second paragraph of Article 51, read as a whole, intends to say is that the prohibition against terror is a specific prohibition within the general prohibition of attack on

* Eds.: An agreement was entered into by the parties to the conflict under the auspices of the International Committee of the Red Cross concerning adherence to international humanitarian law, including a pledge to punish all of those found to violate such law. The parties agreed to bring Articles 35–42 and 48–58 of Protocol I into force between them.

civilians.[160] The general prohibition is a peremptory norm of customary international law.[161] It could be said that the specific prohibition also shares this peremptory character, for it protects the same value. However, to reiterate, the Majority is not required to decide this question. What is clear is that, by exemplifying and therefore according with the general norm, the rule against terror neither conflicts with nor derogates from peremptory norms of international law.

99. The following considerations are also relevant. The Additional Protocols were debated and finalized at the 1974–1977 Diplomatic Conference under the auspices of the ICRC. A summary record of the proceedings has been preserved. The ICRC's delegate to the committee to which Article 51(2) of Additional Protocol I was assigned in draft form said that the rule "merely reaffirmed existing international law," without making a distinction between the provision's first and second parts. This was the consistent attitude at the Conference. States' concerns were for the most part limited to whether the object of the prohibition against terror should be the actor's intent or the capacity of the methods employed to spread violence. Several States simply put on record their approval of the draft provision without proposing changes. * * *

103. Explicit reference to the terror clause is found twice in the States' explanations of their votes on Article 51. In both cases the endorsement of the prohibition is strong and unqualified. The Byelorussian Soviet Socialist Republic noted the "criminal" character of conduct which the prohibition aimed to counteract:

> Also very important from the standpoint of increasing the protection afforded to the civilian population is the provision in Article [51] concerning the prohibition of the use of force or threat of the use of force for the purpose of intimidating the civilian population. Intimidating peaceful citizens and spreading terror among the civilian population is well known to be one of the infamous methods widely resorted to by aggressors seeking to attain their criminal ends at whatever price.

104. The plenary adopted Additional Protocol I in whole by consensus on 8 June 1977. Following this, many States provided further explanations of their positions, but there was no further reference to the terror clause of Article 51(2). There were no treaty reservations of any relevance to this provision. A perusal of the *travaux préparatoires* of the

---

[160] *See* ICRC Commentary, para. 4785: "Attacks aimed at terrorizing *are just one type of attack*, but they are particularly reprehensible. Attempts have been made for a long time to prohibit such attacks, for they are frequent and inflict particularly cruel suffering upon the civilian population." (Emphasis added.) While the second part of 51(2) uses the expression "acts or threats of violence," and not "attacks," the concept of "attack" is defined in Article 49 of Additional Protocol I as "acts of violence."

[161] The Trial Chamber also notes that in a 1995 decision on the applicability of Additional Protocol II to the conflict in Colombia, the Constitutional Court of Colombia accepted the customary-law status of Article 13 of the Protocol, including the prohibition against terror: Ruling No. C-225/95, excerpted in translation in M. Sassòli and A. A. Bouvier (eds.), HOW DOES LAW PROTECT IN WAR? 1366 (1999).

Diplomatic Conference thus satisfies the Majority that all participating States condemned the strategy of terrorizing civilians as, in Byelorussia's words, an "infamous method" of warfare.[176]

105. These observations further support the view that the second part of 51(2) neither conflicts with nor derogates from peremptory norms of international law. It was meant, on the contrary, to be an exemplification of the general principle.

Third *Tadić* Condition

106. The Majority now considers the third *Tadić* condition, namely that the violation must be serious—that is to say, that it must constitute a breach of a rule protecting important values and the breach must involve grave consequences for the victim.

107. In the Majority's opinion, this third condition, correctly interpreted, is not that the *rule* must be inherently "serious," which would mean that every violation of it would also be serious, but that the alleged *violation* of the rule—that is, of a recognized humanitarian rule—must be serious for the violation to come within the jurisdiction of the Tribunal.

108. In the present case, acts of violence of a very serious nature are alleged in the Indictment. In particular, Count 1 alleges a protracted campaign of shelling and sniping of civilians. A campaign of this nature cannot but cause death and injury to civilians over time, and allegedly this was the result of the Accused's actions in this case. There is no doubt that making the civilian population or individual civilians the object of attack, with resulting death and injury to civilians, is a very serious violation of a basic rule of international humanitarian law. It would even qualify as a grave breach of Additional Protocol I.

109. Since doing that much is a serious violation, doing the same with the primary purpose of spreading terror among the civilian population can be no less serious, nor can it make the consequences for the victims any less grave. It is clear moreover from the *travaux préparatoires* of the Diplomatic Conference that the participating States without exception regarded the deliberate taking of measures to terrorize the civilian population as reprehensible as any attack upon the civilian population. Therefore the alleged violation is serious and the third condition is met.

110. The Majority has not neglected the question of whether threats of violence, as opposed to acts of violence, could also involve grave consequences for the victim. However, because the question is not at issue in this case, the Majority is not required to address it.[179]

---

[176] By 1992, when there were around 191 countries in the world, 118 States had ratified Additional Protocol I and five had signed the treaty without ratifying it. The State of Bosnia-Herzegovina succeeded to the Protocol on 31 December 1992.

[179] Certain threats of violence would undoubtedly involve grave consequences. For example, a credible and well-publicized threat to bombard a civilian settlement

111. It is perhaps worth reiterating Article 1 of the Tribunal's Statute ("Competence of the International Tribunal"), that "The International Tribunal shall have the power to prosecute persons responsible for serious violations of international humanitarian law committed in the territory of the former Yugoslavia since 1991 [. . .]"—the key notion for the purposes of this discussion is the seriousness of an offence.

112. The Majority has demonstrated the seriousness of the violations alleged in this case.

Fourth *Tadić* Condition

113. The Majority now comes to examine the fourth *Tadić* condition, namely whether a serious violation of the prohibition against terrorizing the civilian population entails, under customary or conventional law, the individual criminal responsibility of the person breaching the rule. The issue here, in particular, is whether the intent to spread terror had already been criminalized by 1992. The Majority reiterates that it takes no position on whether a customary basis exists for a crime of terror as a violation of the laws or customs of war. Its discussion below amounts to a survey of statutory and conventional law relevant to the fulfilment of the fourth *Tadić* condition.

114. To the Majority's knowledge, the first conviction for terror against a civilian population was delivered in July 1947 by a court-martial sitting in Makassar in the Netherlands East-Indies (N.E.I.). The offences alleged in *Motomura et al.* were charged in the indictment as "systematic terrorism against persons suspected by the Japanese of punishable acts [. . .] this systematic terrorism taking the form of repeated, regular and lengthy torture and/or ill-treatment, the seizing of men and women on the grounds of wild rumours, repeatedly striking them [. . .] the aforesaid acts having led or at least contributed to the death, severe physical and mental suffering of many." The court-martial's jurisdiction was conferred by statute, Article 1 of which read, in relevant part:

> Under war crimes are understood acts which constitute a violation of the laws and usages of war committed in time of war by subjects of an enemy power or by foreigners in the service of the enemy, such as: [. . .]
>
> 2. Systematic terror. [. . .]
>
> 4. Torture of civilians. [. . .]
>
> 34. Indiscriminate mass arrests.
>
> 35. Ill-treatment of interned civilians or prisoners. [. . .]

---

indiscriminately, or to attack with massively destructive weapons, will most probably spread extreme fear among civilians and result in other serious consequences, such as displacement of sections of the civilian population.

115. The *Motomura* court-martial convicted 13 of the 15 accused of "systematic terrorism practiced against civilians" for acts including unlawful mass arrests. The court found that those arrests had the effect of terrorizing the population, "for nobody, even the most innocent, was any longer certain of his liberty, and a person once arrested, even if absolutely innocent, could no longer be sure of health and life." The associated torture and ill-treatment of interned civilians was also found to be a form of systematic terror. Seven of those convicted were sentenced to death and the rest to prison sentences ranging from 1 to 20 years.

116. The list of war crimes in the aforementioned N.E.I. statute reproduced with minor changes a list of war crimes proposed in March 1919 by the so-called Commission on Responsibilities, a body created by the Preliminary Peace Conference of Paris to inquire into breaches of the laws and customs of war committed by Germany and its allies during the 1914–1918 war. The Commission reported that it had found evidence of multiple violations of the rights of civilians and combatants, as well as a carefully planned and executed "system of terrorism." It claimed that: "Not even prisoners, or wounded, or women, or children have been respected by belligerents who deliberately sought to strike terror into every heart for the purpose of repressing all resistance." The Commission's list of war crimes had "Murders and massacres; systematic terrorism" of civilians as one item (the first in the list). The few trials held in 1921–1922 in Leipzig pursuant to the Treaty of Versailles are generally considered to have been a failure. In any event, they did not advance the concept of systematic terrorism created by the Commission.
* * *

119. The next relevant appearance of a prohibition against terror was in Article 33 of the 1949 Geneva Convention IV, which article states in part: "No protected person may be punished for an offence he or she has not personally committed. Collective penalties and likewise all measures of intimidation or of terrorism are prohibited." This protection extends only to persons "in the hands of a Party to the conflict" (Article 4 of the Convention). Thus, purely by operation of Article 33, civilians in territory not occupied by the adversary are not protected against "measures of intimidation or of terrorism" which the adversary might decide to direct against them.

120. The most important subsequent development on the international stage was the unopposed emergence of Article 51(2) of Additional Protocol I (and of the identical provision in the second Protocol) in the Diplomatic Conference of 1974–1977, as described above. Additional Protocol I elaborated and extended the protections of the Geneva Conventions, including those of the fourth Convention on the protection of civilians in times of war. The Majority recalls that the scope of application of Additional Protocol I is given in its first Article, which states that the Protocol "shall apply in the situations referred to in Article 2 common to [the Geneva] Conventions." Article 2 of the Conventions

states, *inter alia*, that the Convention "shall also apply to all cases of partial or total occupation of the territory of a High Contracting Party, even if the said occupation meets with no armed resistance." Consequently Additional Protocol I applies to the aforementioned situations to the extent feasible, as well as to situations such as that which the present Indictment is concerned with, in which civilians not in the hands of an attacking force allegedly become victims of attacks by that force. In other words, whereas the cited part of Article 33 of Geneva Convention IV brought protection from intimidation or terrorism to only a subset of civilians in the context of armed conflict (those in the hands of a Party to the conflict), Article 51(2) of the Protocol elaborated and extended the protection from terror to civilians whether or not in the hands of the Party to the conflict conducting the attack, to the extent consistent with a purposeful and logical interpretation of Additional Protocol I. * * *

124. The 22 May 1992 Agreement states in its section on "Implementation" that each party "undertakes, when it is informed, in particular by the ICRC, of any allegation of violations of international humanitarian law, to open an enquiry promptly and pursue it conscientiously, and to take the necessary steps to put an end to the alleged violations or prevent their recurrence *and to punish those responsible* in accordance with the law in force." Clearly the parties intended that serious violations of international humanitarian law would be prosecuted as criminal offences committed by individuals.

125. The developments reviewed so far demonstrate that, by the time the second part of 51(2) was added verbatim to the 22 May Agreement it already had a significant history of usage by direct or indirect reference in the region of the former Yugoslavia. * * *

127. Finally, the fact that there existed, by 1992, individual criminal responsibility for serious violations of the rule against terror under at least conventional law, is evident from the content and context of Additional Protocol I. If a violation charged against the Accused in the present case is of the same nature as that which States at the Diplomatic Conference collectively considered a grave breach, individual criminal responsibility for the charge would thereby have been established. Terror in the present Indictment is not charged as a grave breach of Additional Protocol I. But with regard to whether there was, in 1992, individual criminal responsibility for a person committing a serious violation of the rule prohibiting terror, this can be answered in the affirmative where the serious violation took the form of serious injury or death caused to civilians. In such cases the acts of violence qualified, in themselves, as grave breaches of Additional Protocol I. Therefore the violation seen in all its elements (attack plus intent to terrorize) could not have been qualified as less criminal than a grave breach.

128. The same conclusion is reached by another line of reasoning. Article 85 of Additional Protocol I is addressed to States, yet it delineates

crimes, and legal elements of crimes, for which there is individual criminal responsibility. The Majority finds in Article 85's universal acceptance in the Diplomatic Conference clear proof that certain violations of Article 51(2) of Additional Protocol I had been criminalized. In particular, as already explained in the preceding section, there was individual criminal responsibility for "making the civilian population or individual civilians the object of attack," "when committed wilfully, in violation of the relevant provisions of this Protocol, and causing death or serious injury to body or health." Alongside this component should be considered the unanimous and unqualified condemnation by the Diplomatic Conference of attacks against civilians intended to spread terror. That is, this specific intentional state—having the intent to spread terror—was also condemned. The serious violations alleged in the present case include both of the above components (wilfully attacking civilians resulting in death or serious injury plus the intent to terrorize them).

129. Because the alleged violations would have been subject to penal sanction in 1992, both internationally and in the region of the former Yugoslavia including Bosnia-Herzegovina, the fourth *Tadić* condition is satisfied.

130. Since all four conditions have now been satisfied, the Majority finds that serious violations of the second part of Article 51(2), and specifically the violations alleged in this case causing death or injury, entailed individual criminal responsibility in 1992. The Majority expresses no view as to whether the Tribunal also has jurisdiction over other forms of violation of the rule, such as the form consisting only of threats of violence, or the form comprising acts of violence not causing death or injury. This is not a question it has been called upon to decide.
* * *

133. In conclusion, the crime of terror against the civilian population in the form charged in the Indictment is constituted of the elements common to offences falling under Article 3 of the Statute, as well as of the following specific elements:

1. Acts of violence directed against the civilian population or individual civilians not taking direct part in hostilities causing death or serious injury to body or health within the civilian population.

2. The offender wilfully made the civilian population or individual civilians not taking direct part in hostilities the object of those acts of violence.

3. The above offence was committed with the primary purpose of spreading terror among the civilian population.[222]

[222] As stated * * * earlier, the Majority has not considered it necessary to enter into [a] discussion of "political" terrorist violence and of attempts to regulate it through international conventions. Nevertheless, for comparative purposes, it may be of interest that the 1999

134. The Majority rejects the Parties' submissions that actual infliction of terror is an element of the crime of terror. The plain wording of Article 51(2), as well as the *travaux préparatoires* of the Diplomatic Conference exclude this from the definition of the offence. Since actual infliction of terror is not a constitutive legal element of the crime of terror, there is also no requirement to prove a causal connection between the unlawful acts of violence and the production of terror, as suggested by the Parties.

135. With respect to the "acts of violence," these do not include legitimate attacks against combatants but only unlawful attacks against civilians.

136. "Primary purpose" signifies the *mens rea* of the crime of terror. It is to be understood as excluding *dolus eventualis* or recklessness from the intentional state specific to terror. Thus the Prosecution is required to prove not only that the Accused accepted the likelihood that terror would result from the illegal acts—or, in other words, that he was aware of the possibility that terror would result—but that that was the result which he specifically intended. The crime of terror is a specific-intent crime.

137. The meaning of "civilian population" was given in the section discussing the crime of attack on civilians. The Majority accepts the Prosecution's rendering of "terror" as "extreme fear." The *travaux préparatoires* of the Diplomatic Conference do not suggest a different meaning.

138. The Majority is of the view that an offence constituted of acts of violence wilfully directed against the civilian population or individual civilians causing death or serious injury to body or health within the civilian population with the primary purpose of spreading terror among the civilian population—namely the crime of terror as a violation of the laws or customs of war—formed part of the law to which the Accused and his subordinates were subject to during the Indictment period. The Accused knew or should have known that this was so. Terror as a crime within international humanitarian law was made effective in this case by treaty law. The Tribunal has jurisdiction *ratione materiae* by way of Article 3 of the Statute. Whether the crime of terror also has a foundation in customary law is not a question which the Majority is required to answer.

International Convention for the Suppression of the Financing of Terrorism, 39 I.L.M. 270 (2000), defines terrorism as including: "Art. 2(b) Any other act intended to cause death or serious bodily injury to a civilian, or to any other person not taking an active part in the hostilities in a situation of armed conflict, when the purpose of such act, by its nature or context, is to intimidate a population, or to compel a government or an international organization to do or to abstain from doing any act."

Dissent of Judge Nieto-Navia * * *

Terror Against the Civilian Population as a Violation of the Laws or Customs of War

108. The Majority finds that the Trial Chamber has jurisdiction by way of Article 3 of the Statute to consider the offence constituted of "acts of violence wilfully directed at a civilian population or against individual civilians causing death or serious injury to body or health of individual civilians[,] with the primary purpose of spreading terror among the civilian population." I respectfully dissent from this conclusion because I do not believe that such an offence falls within the jurisdiction of the Tribunal.

109. In his Report to the Security Council regarding the establishment of the Tribunal, the Secretary-General explained that "the application of the [criminal law] principle of *nullum crimen sine lege* requires that the international tribunal should apply rules which are beyond any doubt part of customary law." The Secretary-General's Report therefore lays out the principle that the Tribunal cannot create new criminal offences, but may only consider crimes already well-established in international humanitarian law. Such a conclusion accords with the imperative that "under no circumstances may a court create new criminal offences after the act charged against an accused either by giving a definition to a crime which had none so far, thereby rendering it prosecutable or punishable, or by criminalizing an act which had not until the present time been regarded as criminal."

110. In [the *Ojdanić* Interlocutory Appeal] decision, the Appeals Chamber considered this principle to determine the circumstances under which an offence will fall within the jurisdiction of the Tribunal. It concluded that "the scope of the Tribunal's jurisdiction *ratione materiae* may . . . be said to be determined both by the Statute, insofar as it sets out the jurisdictional framework of the International Tribunal, and by customary international law, insofar as the Tribunal's power to convict an accused of any crime listed in the Statute depends on its existence *qua* custom at the time this crime was allegedly committed." With respect to *ratione personae* or personal jurisdiction, the Appeals Chamber found that the Secretary-General's Report did not contain any express limitation concerning the nature of the law which the Tribunal may apply, but concluded "that the principle of legality demands that the Tribunal shall apply the law which was binding upon individuals at the time of the acts charged. And, just as is the case in respect of the Tribunal's jurisdiction *ratione materiae*, that body of law must be reflected in customary international law."

111. Thus, an offence will fall within the jurisdiction of the Tribunal only if it existed as a form of liability under international customary law. When considering an offence, a Trial Chamber must verify that the provisions upon which a charge is based reflect customary law. Furthermore, it must establish that individual criminal liability attaches

to a breach of such provisions under international customary law at the time relevant to an indictment in order to satisfy the *ratione personae* requirement. Once it is satisfied that a certain act or set of acts is indeed criminal under customary international law, a Trial Chamber must finally confirm that this offence was defined with sufficient clarity under international customary law for its general nature, its criminal character and its approximate gravity to have been sufficiently foreseeable and accessible.

112. The Accused is charged pursuant to Article 3 of the Statute with "unlawfully inflicting terror upon civilians as set forth in Article 51 of Additional Protocol I and Article 13 of Additional Protocol II to the Geneva Conventions of 1949." Since such an offence has never been considered before by this Tribunal, it would seem important to determine whether this offence existed as a form of liability under international customary law in order to confirm that it properly falls within the jurisdiction of this Trial Chamber. The Majority repeatedly retreats from pronouncing itself though on the customary nature of this offence and, in particular, does not reach any stated conclusion on whether such an offence would attract individual criminal responsibility for acts committed during the Indictment Period under international customary law. Instead, it argues that such individual criminal responsibility attaches by operation of conventional law. In support of this conclusion, it observes that the parties to the conflict had entered into an agreement dated 22 May 1992 in which they had committed to abide by Article 51 of the Additional Protocol I, particularly with respect to the second part of the second paragraph of that article which prohibits "acts or threats of violence the primary purpose of which is to spread terror among the civilian population."

113. The signing of the 22 May Agreement does not suffice though to satisfy the jurisdictional requirement that the Trial Chamber may only consider offences which are reflected in international customary law. Even if I accepted—*quod non* [but it is not]—that the Trial Chamber has the necessary *ratione materiae* to consider the offence of inflicting terror on a civilian population by virtue of the signing of the 22 May Agreement, the *ratione personae* requirement would still have to be satisfied, meaning that this offence must have attracted individual criminal responsibility under international customary law for acts committed at the time of the Indictment period. The Prosecution and the Majority cited few examples indicating that the criminalization of such an offence was an admitted state practice at such a time. In my view, these limited references do not suffice to establish that this offence existed as a form of liability under international customary law and attracted individual criminal responsibility under that body of law. I therefore conclude that the offence of inflicting terror on a civilian population does not fall within the jurisdiction of this Trial Chamber. By concluding otherwise without establishing that the offence of inflicting

terror on a civilian population attracted individual criminal responsibility under international customary law, the Majority is furthering a conception of international humanitarian law which I do not support.

NOTES & QUESTIONS

1. Case Outcome

The Trial Chamber found Galić guilty on one war crimes count (terror) and four crimes against humanity counts (murder and inhumane acts) for his role in the 1992–1994 sniping and shelling campaign in Sarajevo. It sentenced the defendant to twenty years' imprisonment. The Appeals Chamber upheld the convictions in the face of objections from the defendant that (1) the Trial Chamber had effectively convicted him of an offense for which he was not charged, (2) the terrorization of the civilian population is inherent to urban warfare, and (3) the charge violated the principle of legality (see Note 2 below). *Prosecutor v. Galić*, Case No. IT–98–29–A, Judgement, paras. 70–75, 79 (Nov. 30, 2006). The Appeals Chamber also narrowly granted the Prosecution's appeal of the sentence on the ground that "the sentence of only 20 years was so unreasonable and plainly unjust, in that it underestimated the gravity of Galić's criminal conduct." The Appeals Chamber substituted a life sentence. In January 2009, the Tribunal transferred Galić to Germany to serve his sentence.

2. *Nullum Crimen Sine Lege* and Terrorism

The majority relies upon treaty law to establish the crime of terrorizing a civilian population, and does not address whether such a crime exists as a matter of customary international law. Why does the Tribunal examine the *travaux préparatoires* of the Additional Protocol I to establish the position of states on the crime? Do the *travaux préparatoires* adequately support the majority's position? Why does the dissent (a Colombian professor and judge on the Inter-American Court of Human Rights who was later considered for a seat on the International Court of Justice) argue that it is necessary to establish the offense as a matter of customary international law and not just treaty law? The Appeals Chamber in considering defendant's appeal on this point ruled that a treaty-based provision is sufficient to satisfy the requirements of *nullum crimen sine lege*. *Id.* at para. 82. At the same time, it concluded by majority that the crime found expression in customary international law as well. *Id.* at paras. 87–98.

Judge Schomburg (Germany) dissented on this point, arguing that while the conduct was prohibited under international law, it was not penalized. *Prosecutor v. Galić*, Case No. IT–98–29–A, Separate and Partially Dissenting Opinion of Judge Wolfgang Schomburg (Nov. 30, 2006). He concluded that a trend in domestic law toward prohibiting and criminalizing such action was insufficient to establish its customary basis at the time the defendant acted, especially in light of the crime's absence in the ICC Statute. *Id.* at paras. 12 and 20–21. Judge Schomburg noted:

> It would be detrimental not only to the Tribunal but also to the future development of international criminal law and international

> criminal jurisdiction if our jurisprudence gave the appearance of inventing crimes—thus highly politicizing its function—where the conduct in question was not without any doubt penalized at the time when it took place.

Id. at para. 21. Did the ICTY effectively "make law" in convicting the defendant of the crime of committing acts and threats of violence the primary purpose of which is to spread terror among the civilian population?

3. Terrorism Defined

Is the crime discussed by the Tribunal in *Galić* the same as the crime of terrorism discussed in the scenarios presented at the start of this chapter or the treaties excerpted above? The majority in *Galić* expressly does not address the question of whether threats to terrorize a civilian population would constitute a crime under the ICTY Statute. Based upon the above decision, could you argue that such a crime should be recognized by the Tribunal? Would such a crime be sufficiently grave to satisfy the third *Tadić* condition as discussed above? What about acts of terror committed against combatants? Is it, or should it be, a crime to terrorize combatants?

4. The *Actus Reus* of the Crime

Does prosecution of this crime require proof that the defendant participated in an attack resulting in death or serious injury to civilians? In a subsequent case, a Trial Chamber ruled that it did. *See Prosecutor v. Dragomir Milošević*, Case No. IT–98–29/1–T, Judgement, para. 875 (Dec. 12, 2007). The Appeals Chamber considered this an error of law, reasoning that "[c]ausing death or serious injury to body or health represented only one of the possible modes of commission of the crime of terror, and thus is not an element of the offense *per se*." *Prosecutor v. Dragomir Milošević*, Case No. IT–98–29/1–A, Judgement, para. 33 (Nov. 12, 2009). In other words, the physical element of the crime is satisfied by acts or threats of violence, irrespective of whether these acts or threats ultimately cause death or serious injury. Does this mean that terrorism is an inchoate crime?

5. Prosecuting Terrorism Within U.S. Military Commissions

The U.S. Military Commission Act of 2006 (MCA), which governs the establishment and operation of military commissions to prosecute "unlawful enemy combatants," lists the crime of terrorism as a punishable offense. Terrorism is defined as:

> [I]ntentionally kill[ing] or inflict[ing] great bodily harm on one or more protected persons, or intentionally engag[ing] in an act that evinces a wanton disregard for human life, in a manner calculated to influence or affect the conduct of government or civilian population by intimidation or coercion, or to retaliate against government conduct.

Military Commissions Act, Pub. L. No. 109–366, 120 Stat. 2600 (Oct. 17, 2006). The Act also criminalizes providing material support for terrorism with reference to 18 U.S.C. § 2339A. In *Hamdan v. Rumsfeld*, a plurality of the Supreme Court (Justices Stevens, Souter, Ginsburg, and Breyer) ruled that military commissions have jurisdiction over offenses against the law of war. *Hamdan v. Rumsfeld*, 548 U.S. 557, 598 (2006). In arguing that the standalone crime of conspiracy was not triable before a military commission, the plurality reasoned that the crime of conspiracy was rarely, if ever, tried before a military commission and does not appear in any of the major treaties on the law of war. Does terrorism qualify as an offense triable by a military commission under this framework? How might the *Galić* opinion reproduced above impact this determination? Can the crime be committed against U.S. combatants in Afghanistan or Iraq as conceptualized by the ICTY?

6. Terrorism and the ICC

Although early drafts contemplated the inclusion of the crime of terrorism, the ICC Statute (finalized in 1998) does not list terrorism as a separate crime over which it has subject matter jurisdiction. Nor is the crime of inflicting terror on the civilian population listed as a war crime in Article 8. Nonetheless, delegates who supported the inclusion of terrorism managed to pass Resolution E, which recommended that the Review Conference (ultimately convened in 2010) consider the inclusion of the crime of terrorism. The Netherlands submitted a formal proposal to this effect, but it was not considered at the 2010 Review Conference. Why do you think terrorism was excluded from the ICC Statute? What arguments do you imagine delegates might raise in support of or in opposition to the inclusion of terrorism as a core crime? Would delegates have reached a different decision if the treaty had been finalized after the attacks of 9/11? Do you think acts of terrorism can still be prosecuted before the ICC? For an argument that they can, *see* Lucy Martinez, *Prosecuting Terrorists at the International Criminal Court: Possibilities and Problems*, 34 RUTGERS L.J. 1 (2002) (arguing that some acts of terrorism would qualify as war crimes or crimes against humanity, provided that the other elements of those crimes are satisfied); Vincent-Joël Proulx, *Rethinking the Jurisdiction of the International Criminal Court in the Post-September 11th Era: Should Acts of Terrorism Qualify as Crimes Against Humanity?*, 19 AM. U. INT'L L. REV. 1009 (2004) (arguing that attacks on September 11, 2001 qualify as a crime against humanity).

7. The Special Tribunal for Lebanon

The United Nations and Lebanon created a hybrid tribunal—the Special Tribunal for Lebanon (STL)—in The Hague to address political violence in Lebanon. (See the Appendix for a map of Lebanon.) The precipitating event was the car-bomb assassination on February 14, 2005, of former Lebanese Prime Minister Rafiq Hariri and twenty-two others. An investigation initiated shortly thereafter implicated Hezbollah, a Shi'a political party and group with ties to the Syrian government and designated as "terrorist" by many states. Subsequently, the U.N. Security Council sent a fact-finding mission to Lebanon to observe the Lebanese investigation. That mission reported that the investigatory "process suffers from serious flaws and has neither the capacity nor the commitment to reach a satisfactory and credible conclusion." Security Council Resolution 1595, S/Res/1595 (Apr. 7, 2005). The U.N. subsequently initiated its own investigation, under the auspices of an International Independent Investigation Commission (IIIC), for the purposes of assisting the Lebanese authorities in identifying the perpetrators. The IIIC's initial report concluded that

> given the infiltration of Lebanese institutions and society by the Syrian and Lebanese intelligence services working in tandem, it would be difficult to envisage a scenario whereby such a complex assassination plot could have been carried out without their knowledge.

Detlev Mehlis, *Report of the International Independent Investigation Commission Established Pursuant to Security Council Resolution 1595*, para. 5, U.N. Doc. S/2005/662 (Oct. 20, 2005).

Following the investigation into the Hariri assassination, Lebanese Prime Minister Fouad Siniora requested an extension of the IIIC's mandate. Specifically, Siniora requested that the IIIC investigate *all* terrorist attacks having taken place in Lebanon since October 1, 2004. Furthermore, he requested the establishment of a "tribunal of an international character" to try all those whom the IIIC found responsible. The Security Council obliged on all accounts, requesting that the Secretary General help the Lebanese government identify the nature and scope of the international assistance needed. In 2012, the mandate for the STL was extended another three years.

During this time, an agreement was reached between the Lebanese government and the United Nations as memorialized in a 2006 report of the Secretary-General and a Security Council resolution, which activated the new Tribunal. *See Report of the Secretary-General on the Establishment of a Special Tribunal for Lebanon*, U.N. Doc. S/2006/893 (Nov. 15, 2006); S.C. Res. 1757 (2007). For all practical purposes, the IIIC was transformed into the Office of the Prosecutor of the new Tribunal. The Tribunal is adjudicating the terrorist bombing that killed Mr. Hariri and other related attacks that occurred between October 1, 2004, and December 12, 2005, of similar gravity. In terms of subject matter jurisdiction, the Lebanese government demanded that the applicable law be largely based on Lebanese domestic law. As such, according to Article 2 of its statute, the Tribunal can assert jurisdiction over

> (a) The provisions of the Lebanese Criminal Code relating to the prosecution and punishment of acts of terrorism, crimes and offences against life and personal integrity, illicit associations and failure to report crimes and offences, including the rules regarding the material elements of a crime, criminal participation and conspiracy; and
>
> (b) Articles 6 and 7 of the Lebanese law of 11 January 1958 on "Increasing the penalties for sedition, civil war and interfaith struggle."

The Tribunal's personal jurisdiction is broad, including all those responsible for perpetrating, organizing, and sponsoring the alleged crimes. This could, and likely will, include members of the Syrian intelligence services. As for the location of the Tribunal, the Secretary General said security concerns required it to be established outside Lebanon and so it sits in a suburb of The Hague. With regard to personnel, the tribunal is composed of both Lebanese and international judges and an international prosecutor (Canadian Norman

Farrell) assisted by a Lebanese Deputy Prosecutor (Joyce F. Tabet). The international prosecutor and judges are appointed by the Secretary-General from among those recommended by the Lebanese government and member states. Fifty-one percent of the costs of the Special Tribunal are borne by voluntary contributions from states; the Lebanese Government finances the rest.

In August 2011, Pre-Trial Judge Daniel Fransen of Belgium made public an amended indictment that had issued on June 10, 2011, and confirmed on June 28, 2011, against four Lebanese co-accused associated with Hezbollah: Salim Jamil Ayyash, Mustafa Amine Badreddine, Hussein Hassan Oneissi, and Assad Hassan Sabra. Prior to that point, the indictment had, at the request of the Prosecutor, been kept under seal in order to "ensure the integrity of the judicial procedure" and enable the search for and apprehension of the accused. The nine-count indictment—which concerns the assassination of Hariri, the death of twenty-one others, and the injury of 231 others—charges:

- Conspiracy aimed at committing a terrorist act;
- Committing a terrorist act by means of an explosive device;
- Intentional homicide with premeditation using explosive materials;
- Attempted intentional homicide with premeditation by using explosive materials; and
- Being an accomplice to the above.

Much of the evidence against the accused is circumstantial and involves call data records from a number of networked mobile phones that show surveillance on Hariri in advance of his death as well as coordination leading up to the assassination and the purchase of the Mitsubishi van that carried the explosives.

When the Prosecutor submitted the first indictment for confirmation, the Pre-Trial Judge certified several preliminary questions relating to the charged offenses and modes of responsibility to the Appeals Chamber. By way of an interlocutory decision, the Appeals Chamber—headed by the late Italian jurist Antonio Cassese—replied to these questions in February 2011. The panel's unanimous decision is excerpted below.

Interlocutory Decision on the Applicable Law: Terrorism, Conspiracy, Homicide, Perpetration, Cumulative Charging, Case No. STL–11–01/I/AC/R176*bis* (Feb. 16, 2011)

In the Appeals Chamber

1. The Pre-Trial Judge of the Special Tribunal for Lebanon ("Tribunal") is currently seized with an indictment filed by the Tribunal's Prosecutor on 17 January 2011. On 21 January 2011, the Pre-Trial Judge submitted to the Appeals Chamber 15 questions of law raised by this

indictment, pursuant to Article 68(G) of the Tribunal's Rules of Procedure and Evidence ("Rules").[2] The Pre-Trial Judge has asked the Appeals Chamber to resolve these questions *ab initio* (from the outset) to ensure that this and any future indictments are confirmed—if they are confirmed—on sound and well-founded grounds. On the basis of the President's Scheduling Order of the same day, the Office of the Prosecutor ("Prosecution") and the Head of the Defence Office ("Defence Office") filed written submissions on these questions and presented oral arguments at a public hearing on 7 February 2011. * * *

42. We turn first to this Tribunal's principal *raison d'être:* the crime of terrorism. The Pre-Trial Judge has asked:

> (i) Taking into account the fact that Article 2 of the Statute refers exclusively to the relevant provisions of the Lebanese Criminal Code in order to define the notion of terrorist acts, should the Tribunal also take into account the relevant applicable international law?
>
> (ii) Should the question raised in paragraph (i) receive a positive response, how, and according to which principles, may the definition of the notion of terrorist acts set out in Article 2 of the Statute be reconciled with international law? In this case, what are the constituent elements, intentional and material, of this offence?
>
> (iii) Should the question raised in paragraph (i) receive a negative response, what are the constituent elements, material and intentional, of the terrorist acts that must be taken into consideration by the Tribunal, in the light of Lebanese law and case law pertaining thereto?
>
> (iv) If the perpetrator of terrorist acts aimed at creating a state of terror by the use of explosives intended to commit those acts to kill a particular person, how is his criminal responsibility to be defined in the event of death of or injury caused to persons who may be considered not to have been personally or directly targeted by such acts? * * *

44. The clear language of Article 2, which is unaffected by other contextual factors, therefore leads us to conclude that the Tribunal must apply the provisions of the Lebanese Criminal Code, and not those of international treaties ratified by Lebanon or customary international law to define the crime of terrorism.

45. We note, however, that international conventional and customary law can provide guidance to the Tribunal's interpretation of the Lebanese Criminal Code. It is not a question of untethering the Tribunal's law from the Lebanese provisions referred to in Article 2. It is

---

[2] Rule 68(G) provides: "The Pre-Trial Judge may submit to the Appeals Chamber any preliminary question, on the interpretation of the Agreement, Statute and Rules regarding the applicable law that he deems necessary in order to examine and rule on the indictment."

rather that as domestic law those Lebanese provisions may be *construed* in the light and on the basis of the relevant international rules. Thus when applying the law of terrorism, the Tribunal may "take into account the relevant applicable international law," but only as an aid to interpreting the relevant provisions of the Lebanese Criminal Code. * * *

The Notion of Terrorism Under the Lebanese Criminal Code

47. Article 314 of the Lebanese Criminal Code states:

> Terrorist acts are all acts intended to cause a state of terror and committed by means liable to create a public danger such as explosive devices, inflammable materials, toxic or corrosive products and infectious or microbial agents. * * *

49. It is clear from these provisions, as all parties agree, that the elements of terrorism under Lebanese law are as follows: (i) an *act*, whether constituting an offence under other provisions of the Criminal Code or not, which is (ii) intended "to cause a state of terror"; and (iii) the use of a means "liable to create a public danger (*un danger commun*)".

50. These relevant means are indicated in an illustrative enumeration preceded by the expression "such as" (in French: *tels que):* explosive devices, inflammable materials, poisonous or incendiary products, or infectious or microbial agents. * * *

51. Some Lebanese courts have propounded a strict interpretation of Article 314. According to the Lebanese Military Court of Cassation in Case no. 125/1964, decision of 17 September 1964, it is not the conduct, but the *means or instrument or device used* that must be such as to create a public danger. If the means used is apt to create a public danger, then the act can be defined as terrorism. Thus, for instance, in the *Karami* case, the Court of Justice held that the use of explosive devices in a flying helicopter created a public danger and was therefore to be considered as a terrorist act.

52. Lebanese courts appear to have further concluded that the definition of (terrorist) "means" is limited to those means which *as such* are likely to create a public danger, namely a danger to the general population. It would follow that the definition does not embrace any non-enumerated means referred to in Article 314 ("means such as . . .") unless these means are similar to those enumerated in their effect of creating a public danger *per se*. The means or implements which under this approach are not envisaged in Article 314 include a gun, a semi-automatic or automatic machine gun, a revolver, or a knife and perhaps even a letter-bomb. This construction was applied by the Court of Justice in the *Assassination of Sheikh Nizar Al-Halabi* case, in which an act that would be considered terrorism under most national legislation and international treaties was instead categorized as simple murder. In this case, Sheikh Nizar al-Halabi was killed (on 31 August 1995) by means of Kalashnikov assault rifles by masked men in broad daylight and in a crowded street, as he was leaving his home to go to his offices in Beirut.

The Sheikh was murdered because he was the leader of the Al-Ahbash movement, regarded by the killers, who belonged to another Islamic movement (Wahhabi), as deviating from the precepts of Islam and perverting the verse of the Quran. Nevertheless, according to the Court the murder in question did *not* amount to a terrorist act because the materials or devices used were not those required by Article 314.

53. In the *Homicide of Engineer Dany Chamoun and others* case, the same Court also held that the murder of Mr. Chamoun, his wife and his two sons was not a terrorist act, but "simply" murder, because of the means used:

> While it may be true that the crime that is being prosecuted was intended and succeeded in creating panic, *it was not perpetrated by any of the means referred to* in the Article [314 of the Criminal Code], *and the means used* (handguns and submachine guns), the place in which they were used, a private and closed apartment, and the persons targeted *were not designed to bring about a public emergency.*

Thus, according to Lebanese courts the means that may cause a "public danger" include only those means which may harm innocent victims who are not specifically targeted but are injured by mere chance, for they happen to be on the place where the terrorist means is used.

54. From these interpretations of Article 314, it would follow among other things that—under Lebanese legislation as applied by Lebanese courts—attacks on a Head of State or Prime Ministers, or on persons enjoying diplomatic immunity, including ambassadors and diplomats serving in or accredited to the State, as well as on their spouses and families, would not be considered "terrorist acts" if such attacks were carried out by means (for instance, rifles or handguns) which are not likely *per se* to cause a danger to the general population or, more precisely, to third parties falling victim to the terrorist act without being intended in any way to be involved in the actions leading to it (such as passers-by, onlookers, and so on). * * *

56. Likewise, as Lebanese courts have applied Article 314, a terrorist act is punishable even if it does not achieve its intended physical goal (for instance, a person plants a bomb under the car of a political leader but the bomb explodes prematurely, before any person gets into or even approaches the car). Lebanese legislation is grounded in the notion that terrorist conduct is so reprehensible that it must be punished regardless of whether or not the intended consequences of the criminal conduct actually materialize—it is in other terms a *crime of danger* (as opposed to a "crime of harm"). The act in question is punishable not because and insofar as it creates actual damage, but because it puts in jeopardy the protected value. Terrorist acts are thus punished by Lebanese law on account of their social relevance, even when they exhibit the features and the nature of an *inchoate* crime.

57. As for the *subjective elements* of the crime or *mens rea*, the Prosecution and the Defence Office are likewise in agreement, as are we, that, since the Lebanese Criminal Code (unlike other national legislation or international treaties) does not require the act in question to amount to an offence punished by other statutory provisions, the *mens rea* of the underlying offence is not a requisite element of the crime of terrorism. What is required is a deliberate act (throwing a bomb, spreading toxic substances, and so on) intended to cause a state of terror. Thus, if the terrorist act consists of killing one or more persons, Lebanese law does not require the *mens rea* of murder for the act to amount to terrorism, as long as the act which resulted in death was intentional. However, the perpetrator may be responsible both for terrorism and murder—two distinct crimes—if it is proved that he had the intent both to cause terror and to bring about the death of the victim. The essential subjective element required under Article 314 for the crime of terrorism is the special intent *(dolus specialis)* of spreading terror or panic among the population. * * *

60. As to how the requisite special intent to spread terror may be proved, the Court of Justice held in *Attempted Assassination of Minister Michel Murr* in 1997 that the existence of the special intent could be inferred because the murder attempt had been conducted by means of explosive devices causing a public danger. On the other hand, the special intent to spread terror will not suffice, by itself, to make an offence terrorist in nature, if the means used are not those required by Article 314. * * * As the Prosecution has summarized, Lebanese courts have considered the following factors as relevant to establishing this special intent to spread terror: "the social or religious status of the principal target; the commission of the attack in daylight in a street full of people; the collateral killing of bystanders; the use of explosives; and the destruction of residential and commercial buildings." In general, this determination will have to be made on a case-by-case basis.

The Notion of Terrorism in International Rules Binding upon Lebanon

61. The Appeals Chamber will now consider the definition of terrorism under treaties and customary international law binding on Lebanon. We have noted that both the Prosecutor and the Defence Office hold the view that international law, either conventional in nature or (assuming it exists, which both deny) customary, is not material to the interpretation or application of the Lebanese law on terrorism. According to the Prosecutor, in principle reliance on international law may be had when national legislation contains gaps; however, in the case at issue no such gaps exist. The Defence Office takes a more radical view. In its opinion international law must not be taken into account, for Lebanese law is sufficiently clear and would better guarantee the rights of potential defendants. Nevertheless, the Defence Office argues, international rules

could exceptionally be taken into consideration to the extent, and to such extent only, that they grant or ensure broader rights to the defendants.

62. We conclude instead that although the Tribunal may not apply those international sources of law directly because of the clear instructions of Article 2 of the Tribunal's Statute, it may refer to them to assist in *interpreting* and *applying* Lebanese law.

63. The only international treaty *ratified by Lebanon* that provides a general definition of terrorism is the Arab Convention for the Suppression of Terrorism of 22 April 1998 ("Arab Convention).[90] * * *

64. The Arab Convention is different from other conventions on judicial cooperation such as the 1948 Convention on Genocide or the 1984 Convention against Torture, which impose on the Contracting Parties an obligation to adopt in their domestic legal systems the definition of the crime laid down in the Convention. In contrast, the Arab Convention defines terrorism for the purposes of judicial cooperation, while carefully stressing that it does not intend to replace the contracting parties' national laws of terrorism.

65. In Article 1(2) the Arab Convention defines terrorist acts as follows:

> Any act or threat of violence, whatever its motives or purposes, that occurs in the advancement of an individual or collective criminal agenda and seeking to sow panic among people, causing fear by harming them, or placing their lives, liberty or security in danger, or seeking to cause damage to the environment or to public or private installations or property or to occupying or seizing them, or seeking to jeopardise a national resource.

66. Article 1(3) adds that States parties shall also consider as terrorism any act provided for in a host of listed international conventions, to the extent that the States in question have ratified such conventions. Furthermore, Article 2(a) excludes from the category of terrorist acts some acts performed in the course of conflicts for national liberation, unless the armed conflict is designed to jeopardise the territorial integrity of an Arab country. It provides that:

> [a]ll cases of struggle by whatever means, including armed struggle, against foreign occupation and aggression for liberation and self-determination, in accordance with the principles of international law, shall not be regarded as an offence. This provision shall not apply to any act prejudicing the territorial integrity of any Arab State.

67. In addition, Article 2(b) provides that some offences shall be considered as terrorist acts and not as political acts (clearly, with a view

[90] League of Arab States, Arab Convention for the Suppression of Terrorism ("Arab Convention"), 22 April 1998 (entered into force on 7 May 1999).

to allowing the extradition of alleged terrorists, given that normally treaties on judicial cooperation ban the extradition of persons accused of political offences):

> 1. Attacks on the kings, Heads of State or rulers of the contracting States or on their spouses and families;
>
> 2. Attacks on crown princes, vice-presidents, prime ministers or ministers in any of the Contracting States;
>
> 3. Attacks on persons enjoying diplomatic immunity, including ambassadors and diplomats serving in or accredited to the Contracting States;
>
> 4. Premeditated murder or theft accompanied by the use of force directed against individuals, the authorities or means of transport and communications;
>
> 5. Acts of sabotage and destruction of public property and property assigned to a public service, even if owned by another Contracting State;
>
> 6. The manufacture, illicit trade in or possession of weapons, munitions or explosives, or other items that may be used to commit terrorist offences.

68. It is clear from these provisions that the two notions of terrorism, one contained in the Lebanese Criminal Code, the other enshrined in the Arab Convention, have in common some elements, in particular that they both require a special intent which may be to spread terror or fear (although the Convention also envisages other possible purposes, namely "seeking to cause damage to the environment or to public or private installations or property or to occupying or seizing them, or seeking to jeopardise a national resources").

69. In some respects, the Convention's definition is broader than that of Lebanese law. The Arab Convention requires that the act be intended to sow panic and fear (or to damage the environment, or property or natural resources), without mention of particular means as Article 314 does. It follows that, *inter alia,* under the Arab Convention, any attack on a Head of State, Prime Minister, or persons enjoying diplomatic immunity (including ambassadors and diplomats serving in or accredited to the State, as well as on their spouses and families), can be defined as "terrorism" whatever the means by which the attack is carried out, provided that the intent be that required by the Convention.

70. In other respects the Arab Convention's notion of terrorism is narrower: it requires the terrorist act to be actually (rather than only potentially) violent in nature. Further it excludes acts performed in the course of a *war of national liberation* (as long as such war is not conducted against an Arab country). The provisions of Article 314 of the Lebanese Criminal Code do not distinguish between times of peace and *times of war or armed conflict.* On the face of these articles, anybody

engaging in acts of terrorism, as defined by Article 314, may be found guilty and punished, whatever his status (civilian or military), and regardless of whether, in the event of an armed conflict, he is engaged in a war of national liberation or in any other armed conflict involving so-called "freedom fighters."

Implementation of Treaties Under Lebanese Law

71. States are duty bound by international law to adopt the necessary implementing legislation once they become parties to international treaties (that is, when such legislation is needed to give effect to international rules at the domestic level). * * * In certain States, including Lebanon, the mere publication of the treaty in the *Official Gazette* renders the treaty provisions applicable within the Lebanese legal system. While other Arab countries lay down this principle in their constitutions, in Lebanon the principle, although not explicit, has been recognized by the Lebanese Governmental authorities in their initial report to the UN Human Rights Committee:

> All treaties duly ratified by Lebanon acquire mandatory force of law within the country simply [. . .] upon the deposit of the instruments of ratification or accession [. . .] *No further procedure is required for their incorporation into internal legislation. The provisions of those treaties which are sufficiently specific and concrete will therefore be immediately applied.* * * *

72. Lebanese case law corroborates this view of the law. Thus, for instance, the Single Judge of Beirut, Civil Section, in the decision no. 818 of 2 June 1950 stated that:

> [T]he purpose of the publication of a law is to disseminate it and to make the public aware of it. This purpose has been achieved through the publication of the law on ratification of the Convention. * * * [A]fter publication, its provisions prevail over those of the domestic law which may be inconsistent with them, on the strength of the principle: the external law trumps the domestic law. * * *

78. The Arab Convention includes a clear definition intended to complement Lebanon's national legislation and to take precedence in instances of judicial cooperation with other Arab States that have ratified the Convention. It does not create a new crime in Lebanon but expands in some foreseeable ways the definition of an existing crime, although solely with regard to and in the area of judicial cooperation with other Arab countries. * * *

83. The Defence Office and the Prosecutor both forcefully assert that there is currently no settled definition of terrorism under customary international law. However, although it is held by many scholars and other legal experts that no widely accepted definition of terrorism has evolved in the world society because of the marked difference of views on

some issues, closer scrutiny demonstrates that in fact such a definition has gradually emerged. * * *

85. As we shall see, a number of treaties, UN resolutions, and the legislative and judicial practice of States evince the formation of a general *opinio juris* in the international community, accompanied by a practice consistent with such *opinio,* to the effect that a customary rule of international law regarding the international crime of terrorism, at least *in time of peace,* has indeed emerged. This customary rule requires the following three key elements: (i) the perpetration of a criminal act (such as murder, kidnapping, hostage-taking, arson, and so on), or threatening such an act; (ii) the intent to spread fear among the population (which would generally entail the creation of public danger) or directly or indirectly coerce a national or international authority to take some action, or to refrain from taking it; (iii) when the act involves a transnational element. * * *

88. Let us first consider international and multilateral instruments that include a definition of the crime of international terrorism. Numerous regional treaties have defined terrorism as *criminal* acts intended to *terrorize populations* or *coerce an authority.* By the same token, UN General Assembly resolutions have, since 1994, insisted that "*criminal* acts intended or calculated to *provoke a state of terror* in the general public, a group of persons or particular persons for political purposes are *in any circumstance* unjustifiable." Likewise, in 2004 the Security Council, by a *unanimous* decision taken under Chapter VII of the UN Charter, "recall[ed]" in Resolution 1566 that: *criminal acts,* including against civilians, committed with the intent to cause death or serious bodily injury, or taking of hostages, with the *purpose to provoke a* state *of terror in the general public* or in a group of persons or particular person, intimidate a population *or compel a government or an international organization to do or to abstain from doing any act,* which constitute offences within the scope of and as defined in the international conventions and protocols relating to terrorism, are *under no circumstances* justifiable. A similar definition has found a large measure of approval in the *Ad Hoc* Committee tasked to draft a Comprehensive Convention on Terrorism. For now, the 1999 International Convention for the Suppression of the Financing of Terrorism ("Financing Convention") provides the UN's clearest definition of terrorism, which includes the elements of (i) a criminal act (ii) intended to intimidate a population or compel an authority, and is limited to those crimes containing (iii) a transnational aspect. * * *

89. The Financing Convention and most of the regional and multilateral conventions regarding terrorism incorporate into their definition of terrorism the specific offences criminalized in a long line of terrorism-related conventions. Among the terrorist offences so criminalized are the taking of hostages, the hijacking of planes, and the harming of diplomatic representatives. For political expediency at the

time of their drafting, the earliest of these conventions focus solely on particular conduct that is universally condemned and do not require a particular intent (*e.g.,* to terrorize or to coerce). Such an intent element, however, has been specified in the most recent conventions. Further, all of these conventions also require—through the definition of the *actus reus* (the material element of a crime) or by additional provision—a transnational element to the crime. Indeed, the three most recent universal conventions share a nearly identical Article 3, which states:

> This Convention shall not apply where the offence is committed within a single State, the alleged offender and the victims are nationals of that State, the alleged offender is found in the territory of that State and no other State has a basis [under subsequent articles of the Convention] to exercise jurisdiction. . . .

It is to be emphasized that the requirement of a cross-border element goes not to the definition of terrorism but to its character as *international* rather than *domestic.* The two elements of (i) criminal act and (ii) intention to intimidate a population or compel an authority are common to both domestic and international terrorism.

90. Regarding this transnational element, it will typically be a connection of perpetrators, victims, or means used across two or more countries, but it may also be a significant impact that a terrorist act in one country has on another—in other words, when it is foreseeable that a terrorist attack that is planned and executed in one country will threaten international peace and security, at least for neighboring countries. The requirement of a transnational element serves to exclude from the definition of *international* terrorism those crimes that are purely domestic, in planning, execution, and direct impact. However, such purely domestic crimes may be equally serious in terms of human loss and social destruction. The exclusion of the transnational element from the *domestic* crime of terrorism, as defined by most countries' criminal codes, does not detract from the essential communality of the concept of terrorism in international and domestic criminal law. The exclusion allows those countries to apply the heightened investigative powers, deterrence mechanisms, punishment, and public condemnation that attach with the label "terrorism" to serious crimes that may not have international connections or a direct "spill over" effect in other countries.

91. Other than the exclusion of this transnational element, however, the national legislation of countries around the world consistently defines terrorism in similar if not identical terms to those used in the international instruments just surveyed. Consistent national legislation can be another important source of law indicative of the emergence of a customary rule. * * * Reference must not be made to one national legal system only—for example, either common law or civil law to the exclusion of the other—although the distillation of a shared norm does not require a comprehensive survey of all legal systems of the world.

* * * However, the mere existence of concordant laws does not prove the existence of a customary rule, "for it may simply result from an identical view that States freely take and can change at any moment." Thus, for instance, the fact that all States of the world punish murder through their legislation does not entail that murder has become an international crime. To turn into an international crime, a domestic offence needs to be regarded by the world community as an attack on universal values (such as peace or human rights) or on values held to be of paramount importance in that community; in addition, it is necessary that States and intergovernmental organizations, through their acts and pronouncements, sanction this attitude by clearly expressing the view that the world community considers the offence at issue as amounting to an international crime.

92. In this instance, there is more than a mere concordance of laws. The Security Council, acting under Chapter VII of the UN Charter, has instructed member States to adopt laws outlawing terrorism and related crimes (such as the financing or incitement of terrorism), to ratify the recent anti-terrorism conventions, and to report periodically to the Council's Counter-Terrorism Committee on steps taken to bring national law into conformity with international standards in this field. In the last ten years, many States have reported back to the Counter-Terrorism Committee not only their success in doing so, but also their understanding that terrorism is an international crime and/or that their laws increasingly align with a global standard. That the attitude taken in these laws is concordant and not subject to transient national interests evinces a widespread stand on and a shared view of terrorism. * * *

97. It is indeed not startling that these laws, despite peripheral variations normally motivated by national exigencies, share a core concept: terrorism is a criminal action that aims at spreading terror or coercing governmental authorities and is a threat to the stability of society or the State. This notion is so deeply embedded in the legislation of so many diverse countries, that one is warranted to conclude that those countries share the same basic view of terrorism and are not in the least likely to depart from it.

98. We have mentioned the requirement, in the legislation of a number of common law states and civil law states, as well as in some of the UN Terrorism Conventions and the draft Comprehensive Convention, for a political, religious, racial or ideological purpose. However, the overwhelming weight of state opinion, reinforced by the international and multilateral instruments, to which these states are party, does not yet contain that element. * * *

100. In recent years courts have reached concordant conclusions about the elements of an international crime of terrorism. They have either explicitly referred to a customary international rule on the matter, as noted above, or have advanced or upheld a general definition of terrorism that is broadly accepted. Judicial decisions stating instead that

no generally accepted definition of terrorism exists are far and few between, and their number diminishes each year. Furthermore, those courts that have upheld a shared definition of terrorism have done so with consistency. They have therefore met and exceeded the test propounded by the International Court of Justice, in the *Nicaragua* case, where the Court did not consider discrepancies to be fatal to the formation of a rule of customary law,[195] but that practice instead "should, in general, be consistent with such rules". We are satisfied that the additional requirement of political, religious, racial or ideological purpose found in legislation of some states and UN instruments is a discrepancy covered by the *Nicaragua* principle. Indeed, those national courts dealing with terrorism have shown more than a mere consistent tendency to take the same view of terrorism. * * * In sum, those judgments, viewed in combination with national legislation and the international attitude of States as taken in international fora, evince that the courts thereby intend to apply at the domestic level a notion that is commonly accepted at the international level. In other words, those decisions reflect a legal opinion *(opinio juris)* as to the fundamental elements of the crime of terrorism. * * *

103. The Appeals Chamber acknowledges that the existence of a customary rule outlawing terrorism does not automatically mean that terrorism is a criminal offence under international law. According to the legal parameters suggested by the ICTY Appeals Chamber in the *Tadić* Interlocutory Decision with regard to war crimes, to give rise to individual criminal liability at the international level it is necessary for a violation of the international rule to entail the individual criminal responsibility of the person breaching the rule.[202] The criteria for determining this issue were again suggested by the ICTY in that seminal decision: the intention to criminalize the prohibition must be evidenced by statements of government officials and international organizations, as well as by punishment for such violations by national courts. Perusal of these elements of practice will establish whether States intend to criminalize breaches of the international rule.

104. In the case of terrorism, demonstrating the requisite practice and *opinio juris sive necessitatis,* namely the legal view that it is necessary and indeed obligatory to bring to trial and punish the perpetrators of terrorist acts, is relatively easy. * * * [C]riminalization of terrorism has begun at the domestic level, with many countries of the world legislating against terrorist acts and bringing to court those allegedly responsible for such acts. This trend was internationally strengthened by the passing of robust resolutions by the UN General

---

[195] *Military and Paramilitary Activities in and against Nicaragua (Nicaragua v United States),* Judgment, I.C.J. Reports (1986) 14, at 98, para. 186: "The Court does not consider that, for a rule to be established as customary, the corresponding practice must be in absolutely rigorous conformity with the rule."

[202] *Prosecutor v. Tadić,* Decision on the Defence Motion for Interlocutory Appeal on Jurisdiction, 2 October 1995, para 94.

Assembly and Security Council condemning terrorism, and the conclusion of a host of international treaties banning various manifestations of terrorism and enjoining the contracting parties to cooperate for the repression of those manifestations. As a result, those States which had not already criminalized terrorism at the domestic level have increasingly incorporated the emerging criminal norm into domestic penal legislation and case-law, often acting out of a sense of international obligation. * * *

107. [T]he Appeals Chamber takes the view that, while the customary rule of an international crime of terrorism that has evolved so far only extends to terrorist acts *in times of peace,* a broader norm that would outlaw terrorist acts *during times of armed conflict* may also be emerging. As the ICTY and the SCSL have found, acts of terrorism can constitute war crimes,[208] but States have disagreed over whether a distinct crime of terrorism should apply during armed conflict. Indeed, both within the drafting committee of the Comprehensive Convention on Terrorism and in reservations to the UN Convention for the Suppression of the Financing of Terrorism, some members of the Islamic Conference have expressed strong disagreement with the notion of considering as terrorist those acts of "freedom fighters" in time of armed conflict (including belligerent occupation and internal armed conflict) which are directed against innocent civilians. They have insisted both on the need to safeguard the right of peoples to self-determination and on the necessity to also punish "State terrorism."

108. Nevertheless, it is necessary to emphasize three circumstances. First, the very high number of States that have not only ratified the Convention for the Suppression of the Financing of Terrorism (currently numbering 173), but also refrained from making any reservation with regard to its definition of terrorism, a definition that refers to armed conflicts without any reference to a "freedom fighters" exception (these States currently number 170).[211] Second, the unique content of this Convention, namely the fact that unlike other Conventions on terrorism it deals with conduct that is not criminal *per se,* and in addition is conduct preliminary or prodromic to violent terrorist acts; it follows that criminalizing such conduct as terrorism is crucial in time of armed conflict, because the financing of attacks on civilians not taking an active part in hostilities is not per se forbidden under the laws of war. In other

---

[208] The crime of "acts or threats of violence the primary purpose of which is to spread terror," see for instance *Prosecutor v. Galić,* Trial Judgment, December 2003, paras. 91–138; *Prosecutor v. Galić,* Appeals Judgment, 30 November 2006, paras. 81–104. * * *

[211] Article 2 of the Convention provides that "1. Any person commits an offence within the meaning of this Convention if that person by any means, directly or indirectly, unlawfully and wilfully, provides or collects funds with the intention that they should be used or in the knowledge that they are to be used, in full or in part, in order to carry out:[. . .] (b) Any [. . .] act intended to cause death or serious bodily injury to a Civilian, *or to any other person not taking an active part in the hostilities in a situation of armed conflict,* when the purpose of such act, by its nature or context, is to intimidate a population, or to compel a government or an international organization to do or to abstain from doing any act" (emphasis added).

words, the Convention, more than any other treaty on the matter, is a turning point in the fight against terrorism, for it reaches out to activities that otherwise would go unpunished (either by criminal law or by international humanitarian law). Since it covers such a wide range of activities, the Convention is a veritable litmus test for the attitude of States towards criminalizing terrorism. Third, the 170 States that have undertaken by ratification or accession to comply with the Convention and have not made any reservation to the provision on armed conflict are widely representative of the world community: they include not only the five permanent members of the Security Council but also such major countries as Brazil, India, Pakistan, Indonesia, Saudi Arabia, Turkey and Nigeria. Furthermore, and strikingly, eleven Arab countries that are parties to the Arab Convention on Terrorism (a Convention that, as noted above, excepts from the category of terrorists the class of "freedom fighters") have ratified the Convention for the Suppression of the Financing of Terrorism without making any reservation, thereby accepting the notion that the financing of persons or groups attacking innocent civilians in time of armed conflict, as well as, in consequence, the perpetration of such attacks, may be categorized as "terrorism." These three circumstances warrant the proposition that an overwhelming majority of States currently takes the view that acts of terrorism may be repressed even in time of armed conflicts to the extent that such acts target civilians who do not take an active part in armed hostilities; these acts, in addition, could also be classified as war crimes (whereas the same acts, if they are directed against combatants or civilians participating in hostilities, may *not* be defined as either terrorist acts or war crimes, unless the requisite conditions for war crimes were met). * * *

109. Thus, the conclusion is warranted that a customary rule is incipient *(in statu nascendi)* which also covers terrorism in time of armed conflict (or rather, the contention can be made that the current customary rule on terrorism is being gradually amended). * * *

111. In sum, the subjective element of the crime under discussion is twofold, (i) the intent or *dolus* of the underlying crime and (ii) the special intent (*dolus specialis*) to spread fear or coerce an authority. The objective element is the commission of an act that is criminalized by other norms (murder, causing grievous bodily harm, hostage taking, etc.). The crime of terrorism at international law of course requires as well that the terrorist act be transnational. * * *

113. A comparison between the crime of terrorism as defined under the Lebanese Criminal Code and that envisaged in customary international law shows that the latter notion is much *broader* with regard to the means of carrying out the terrorist act, which are not limited under customary international law, whereas it is *narrower* in that (i) it only deals with terrorist acts in time of peace, (ii) it requires

both an underlying criminal act and an intent to commit that act,[223] and (iii) it involves a transnational element. * * *

123. However, despite the existence of a customary international law definition of the crime of terrorism in time of peace, and its binding force on Lebanon, it cannot be *directly* applied by this Tribunal to the crimes of terrorism perpetrated in Lebanon and falling under our jurisdiction. As we have previously noted, the text of Article 2 of the Tribunal's Statute makes clear that codified Lebanese law, not customary international law, should be applied to the substantive crimes that will be prosecuted by the Tribunal.

124. The above conclusion does not, however, mean that the Tribunal will completely disregard international law when construing the relevant provisions of Lebanese law mentioned in the Statute. That domestic legislation deals with terrorist acts occurring in Lebanon regardless of whether or not they have a transnational dimension—that is, whether or not they are acts of national or international terrorism. But the allegations falling under the jurisdiction of the Tribunal have been uniquely regarded by the UN Security Council as a "threat to international peace and security" and have also justified the establishment of an international Tribunal entrusted with the task of prosecuting and trying the alleged authors of those facts. This patently proves that those terrorist attacks were considered by the Security Council as particularly grave acts of terrorism with international implications. Thus, faced with this criminal conduct and the Security Council's response to it, the Tribunal, while fully respecting Lebanese jurisprudence relating to cases of terrorism brought before Lebanese courts, cannot but take into account the unique gravity and transnational dimension of the facts at issue, which by no coincidence have been brought before an international court. The Tribunal therefore holds that it is justified in interpreting and applying Lebanese law on terrorism in light of international legal standards on terrorism, given that these standards specifically address transnational terrorism and are also binding on Lebanon. The issue under this score that the Appeals Chamber will address in particular is that of the instrumentalities used to carry out a terrorist act.

The Question of the Means or Instrumentalities Used for Carrying out a Terrorist Act * * *

126. What Article 314 requires is that the means used to carry out a terrorist act be capable of causing a "public danger," namely that the means, in addition to injuring the physical target of the act, be such as to expose other persons to adverse consequences. This may occur even when

[223] Further, under the customary definition of terrorism, the requisite special intent may be to coerce an authority instead of to terrorize a population (as required by Lebanese law), but since a terrorist generally coerces *by spreading fear,* these two articulations of the special intent required for the crime of terrorism, in practical terms, largely overlap with each other. The additional basis for finding special intent under international law (*e.g.* the intent to coerce an authority) is thus not a critical distinction.

a terrorist shoots at a person in a public road, thereby imperiling a large number of other persons simply because they are present at the same location.

127. Moreover, a "public danger" may also occur when a prominent political or military leader is killed or wounded, even if this occurs in a house or in any other closed place with no other persons present. In such cases, the danger may consist in other leaders belonging to that same faction or group being assassinated or in causing a violent reaction by other factions. These consequences are undoubtedly capable of causing a common or "public danger," as required by Article 314 of the Lebanese Criminal Code, regardless of the weapon used.

128. Furthermore, it is difficult not to see the close link between the aim of the crime (to "cause a state of terror") and the result of the terrorist act (to create a "public danger"). Clearly, the two concepts are closely intertwined: often a terrorist can be said to aim at causing panic and terror *because* he uses means that endanger the broader population; or, a terrorist act may create a public danger by spreading terror, for instance by killing a political leader and thereby alarming a portion of the population that will foreseeably respond with violent protests, riots, or retaliations against opposing factions—all of which, especially in the context of political instability, may create a public danger. In particular, in contemporary societies—where media are swift to bring attention to the smallest act of violence against political targets around the globe, thus arousing passions and tensions—the expression "liable to create a public danger" has to be interpreted differently than in the 1940s.

129. This interpretation of the "means" element, in addition to appearing better suited to address contemporary forms of terrorism than the more restrictive approach employed by some Lebanese courts, is also warranted by the need to interpret national legislation as much as possible in such a manner as to bring it into line with binding relevant international law. We have seen above that both the Arab Convention and the customary international rule on terrorism do not envisage any restriction based on the kind of weapons or means used to carry out a terrorist attack. To construe Article 314 in this way would render this provision more consonant with the international rules just mentioned, rules that are binding on Lebanon at the international level even if not yet explicitly implemented through domestic legislation.

130. However, this interpretation may *broaden* one of the objective elements of the crime as it has been applied in prior Lebanese cases. We must therefore consider whether this is permissible under the principle of legality (*nullum crimen sine lege*). * * *

132. According to the principle of legality, everybody must know in advance whether specific conduct is consonant with, or a violation of, penal law. In addition to Article 8 of the Lebanese Constitution, the preamble of the Constitution incorporates the principle of legality as set out in the ICCPR, according to Article 15 of which no breach of the

nullum crimen principle exists when the act was criminal "under national or *international* law, at the time when it was committed."*

133. This provision does not necessarily entail, however, that the authorities of a State party to the ICCPR may try and convict a person for a crime that is provided for in international law but not yet codified in the domestic legal order: in criminal matters, international law cannot substitute itself for national legislation; in other words, international criminalization alone is not sufficient for domestic legal orders to punish that conduct. Nevertheless, Article 15 of the ICCPR allows at the very least that fresh national legislation (or, where admissible, a binding case) defining a crime that was already contemplated in international law may be applied to offences committed *before* its enactment without breaching the *nullum crimen* principle. This implies that individuals are *expected and required to know* that a certain conduct is criminalized in international law: at least from the time that the same conduct is criminalized also in a national legal order, a person may thus be punished by domestic courts even for conduct predating the adoption of national legislation.

134. * * * [I]n the *Ojdanić* case, when determining the question of "foreseeability" of a criminal offence, the ICTY Appeals Chamber held that non-codified international customary law could give an individual "reasonable notice" of conduct that could entail criminal liability.[241] This facet of the *nullum crimen* principle should not be surprising: international crimes are those offences that are considered so heinous and contrary to universal values that the whole community condemns them through customary rules. Individuals are therefore required and expected to know that, as soon as national authorities take all the necessary legislative (or judicial) measures necessary to punish those crimes at the national level, they may be brought to trial even if their breach is prior to national legislation (or judicial pronouncements). The same applies to crimes punished at the international level by way of bilateral or multilateral treaties.

135. Furthermore, the principle of legality does not preclude the progressive development of the law by the court. * * * Thus the ICTY Appeals Chamber has held that the principle of legality does not prevent a court from interpreting and clarifying the elements of a particular crime. Further, the application of these elements to new circumstances may in some instances better align domestic practice with a nation's international obligations. At times, domestic and international courts have even come to the conclusion that conduct previously considered legal can be construed as embraced within an existing offence, for

---

* Eds.: This article reads in full: "Nothing in this article shall prejudice the trial and punishment of any person for any act or omission which, at the time when it was committed, was criminal according to the general principles of law recognized by the community of nations."

[241] *Prosecutor v. Milutinovic et al.,* Decision on Dragoljub Ojdanic's Motion Challenging Jurisdiction—Joint Criminal Enterprise, at para. 41 (21 May 2003).

instance if it relates to "an area where the law has been subject to progressive development and there are strong indications that still wider interpretation by the courts of the inroads on the immunity was probable"—that is, as long as the circumstances made this criminalization foreseeable. This principle would be better expressed by saying that the *application* of the law may be subject to development as social conditions change, as long as this application was foreseeable.

136. What matters is that an accused must, at the time he committed the act, have been able to understand that what he did was criminal, even if "without reference to any specific provision." Similarly, "[a]lthough the immorality or appalling character of an act is *not* a sufficient factor to warrant its criminalization under customary international law," it may nevertheless be used to "refute any claim by the Defence that it did not know of the criminal nature of the acts." * * *

138. With these principles in mind, we conclude that it was foreseeable for a Lebanese national or for anybody living in Lebanon that any act designed to spread terror would be punishable, regardless of the kind of instrumentalities used as long as such instrumentalities were likely to cause a public danger.

139. This proposition is borne out by the fact that neither the Arab Convention nor customary international law, both applicable within the Lebanese legal order, restrict the means used to perpetrate terrorism, and both of these sources of law are binding on Lebanon. Furthermore, Lebanon's legislature has gradually authorized or approved ratification of or accession to a number of international treaties against terrorist action, which likewise do *not* contain any such limitation as to the means to be used for a terrorist act. * * *

142. Finally, Lebanon is not a country where a formal doctrine of binding precedent (*stare decisis*) is adopted. Thus, there is no general expectation that individuals will rely definitively on the prior interpretations of Article 314 by Lebanese courts. Different circumstances could lead Lebanese courts in the future to different conclusions regarding the scope of Article 314. This is something to be taken into account by the Tribunal when interpreting the Lebanese Criminal Code.

143. On the basis of the considerations above, the Appeals Chamber concludes that the aforementioned interpretation of Article 314 by the Tribunal is permissible because it meets the requisite conditions: (i) it is consistent with the offence as explicitly defined under Lebanese law; (ii) it was accessible to the accused, especially given the publication of the Arab Convention and other international treaties ratified by Lebanon in the *Official Gazette;* (iii) hence, it was reasonably foreseeable by the accused.

144. Thus, the approach taken here—to provide a modern interpretation to the "means" element—does not amount to adding a new

crime to the Lebanese Criminal Code or a new element to an existing crime. The Appeals Chamber simply allows a reasonable interpretation of the existing crime that takes into account significant legal developments within the international community (as well as in Lebanon). This interpretation is not binding *per se* on courts other than the Special Tribunal for Lebanon, although it may of course be used as an interpretation of the applicable legal provisions in other cases where terrorism is charged.

NOTES & QUESTIONS

1. Advisory Opinion?

The opinion above was not issued in the context of adversarial proceedings, but rather in response to a request from a lower court. Is this an advisory opinion, controlling precedent, or something in between? What would the Prosecutor and Defense argue in this regard? Indeed, the Appeals Chamber notes at para. 7 that "neither the Appeals Chamber nor the Defence Office has seen the indictment (which is currently under seal), much less the evidence submitted by the Prosecutor to the Pre-Trial Judge to support the indictment's confirmation." This form of appellate intervention is the result of new rules introduced by the judges in November 2010. In particular, the interlocutory opinion was issued pursuant to Rule 68G, which provides:

> The Pre-Trial Judge may submit to the Appeals Chamber any preliminary question, on the interpretation of the Agreement, Statute and Rules regarding the applicable law, that he deems necessary in order to examine and rule on the indictment.

Article 26 of the Tribunal's Statute, by contrast, limits the Appeals Chamber to hearing appeals from the parties on questions of law or fact. Does this render the Rule *ultra vires*? Should judges be empowered to draft their own rules and assume new powers? Does this rule disempower the Trial Chamber, which was not given the chance to consider these questions in the context of an actual trial? Can the Defence Office—an independent organ mandated to manage and provide assistance to defense counsel—adequately represent the rights of the accused, who played no role in the litigation? The other international tribunals have rejected such an advisory function. Judge Sidwa (Pakistan) of the ICTY wrote:

> The courts have no inherent powers to create appellate provisions or acquire jurisdiction where none is granted. . . . A tribunal having international criminal jurisdiction should be careful not to convert itself into a free or general advisory body. Its enunciation of the law must be on a case by case basis and limited to the *lis* [suit] before it. A matter which should normally be decided on the basis of law and evidence should not be foreclosed by an enunciation of law by a superior tribunal which may have the effect of pre-empting the rights of the parties to have the matter properly appraised by the lower chamber.

Prosecutor v. Tadić, Separate Opinion of Judge Sidwa on the Defence Motion for Interlocutory Appeal on Jurisdiction, Case No. IT–94–1–AR72, 6, 109

(Oct. 2, 1995). Which is the better approach? For a discussion, *see* Matthew Gillett & Matthias Schuster, *Fast-Track Justice: The Special Tribunal for Lebanon Defines Terrorism*, 9 J. INT'L CRIM. JUST. 989 (2011).

2. Methodology

How would you evaluate the Tribunal's methodology in addressing the questions presented to it? Is its reasoning persuasive? At one point, the STL notes that all adjudication is interpretation—do you agree? Was it correct for the Appeals Chamber to rely on international law to interpret Lebanese law, even in the absence of any gaps or inconsistencies in domestic law and contrary to the views of the parties, who largely agreed on how the law should be interpreted? Has the STL adopted the equivalent of the *Charming Betsy* principle from U.S. law, whereby the U.S. Supreme Court ruled that "an act of Congress ought never to be construed to violate the law of nations if any other possible construction remains." *Murray v. The Charming Betsy*, 6 U.S. (2 Cranch) 64 (1804). Does the fact that the STL is a hybrid tribunal, which includes national court judges, alter the validity of its approach? Incidentally, Judge and Vice President of the Tribunal Ralph Riachi (Lebanon) joined the above opinion and yet sat on the bench in the domestic case involving the assassination of Sheikh Nizar Al-Halabi, which resulted in the narrow interpretation of Article 314 that had been rejected by the STL.

3. *Nullum Crimen Sine Lege*

Do you agree that anyone living in Lebanon could have reasonably foreseen that acts designated to spread terror could be punishable, regardless of the instrumentality employed? Interlocutory Decision, at para. 138. In other words, is this decision fair to the accused who, per the *nullum crimen sine lege* maxim, are entitled to be prosecuted under the law that existed at the time they acted? Does the fact that Lebanon, like many civil law jurisdictions, does not adhere to a strict doctrine of *stare decisis* affect your evaluation of the opinion? This decision foreshadows one of the cases that may come before the Tribunal: Pierre Gemayel, the Lebanese Minister of Industry and an opponent of Syria, was killed by gunfire as the STL Statute was being finalized in 2006. Would this act fall within the STL's jurisdiction?

4. Terrorism Under Customary International Law

How did the tribunal identify the elements of the offense of terrorism under customary international law? Do you find its approach convincing? Could a state prosecute someone for the offense identified by the STL in the absence of domestic legislation? Was this ruling necessary to resolve the questions presented? As indicated earlier in this chapter, the international community has struggled for years to devise an omnibus definition of terrorism. How influential is this opinion likely to be in that effort? For a discussion of the controversy surrounding this opinion, *see* Ben Saul, *Legislating from a Radical Hague: The United Nations Special Tribunal for Lebanon Invents an International Crime of Transnational Terrorism*, 24 LEIDEN J. INT'L L. 667 (2011); Stefan Kirsch & Anna Oehmichen, *Judges Gone Astray—The Fabrication of Terrorism as an International Crime by the Special Tribunal for Lebanon*, 1 DURHAM L. REV. 1 (2011). Note that Judge

Cassese prior to the establishment of the STL had written an influential law review article arguing that a prohibition against terrorism could be identified in customary international law. Antonio Cassese, *The Multifaceted Criminal Notion of Terrorism in International Law*, 4 J. INT'L CRIM. JUST. 933 (2006).

5. Terrorism and Armed Conflict

Do you agree with the Tribunal's exclusion of a prohibition of terrorism in armed conflict? Is the lingering unwillingness to apply the prohibition against terrorism to acts of freedom fighters enough to support the Tribunal's reasoning? Should attacks by unprivileged combatants against a state's armed forces be considered crimes of terrorism?

6. *In Absentia* Proceedings

Many of the procedural features of the STL are drawn from civil law traditions, including the expectation of more proactive judges, the admissibility of written evidence, and an allowance for *in absentia* proceedings. After Lebanese authorities failed to locate and apprehend the accused (following the surveillance of last known addresses, service on neighborhood leaders (*mukhtars*), the issuance of advertisements and public service announcements, the release of an Interpol red notice, and the establishment of a hotline), the Tribunal ruled that it would proceed *in absentia*. Unlike the Statutes of the other international tribunals, Article 22 of the Tribunal's Statute (along with Rule 106) allows such proceedings if the accused has absconded and "all reasonable steps have been taken to secure his or her appearance before the Tribunal and to inform him or her of the charges. . ." Closing arguments in the STL case concluded in September 2018. As of this writing no decision has been issued.

The trial proceeded *in absentia*, marking the first such trial before an international tribunal since the Nuremberg Tribunal sentenced Martin Bormann, Hitler's Chief of Staff, to death. At first, it was believed that Bormann had gone into exile in South America at the close of World War II (and it was rumored that he underwent plastic surgery in order to conceal his identity). Others believe that he died in Germany in the waning days of the Nazi regime, an end seemingly confirmed by genetic testing on a set of remains found in 1972. In any case, Bormann was declared dead by a German court in 1973.

Although barred in the United States unless the defendant absconds after trial has commenced (Fed. R. Crim. Proc. 43), many civil law jurisdictions allow for *in absentia* proceedings, a practice that largely has the blessing of human rights institutions so long as the defendant has the right to a retrial. *See* U.N. Human Rights Comm., General Comment No. 32, 90th Sess., U.N. Doc. CCPR/C/GC/32, para. 36 (Aug. 23, 2007); *Sejdovic v. Italy*, App. No. 56581/00, Eur. Ct. Hum. Rts. (Nov. 10, 2004). How would the retrial right be guaranteed if the STL winds down before the *in absentia* defendants are apprehended?

For more on *in absentia* proceedings, *see* Maggie Gardner, *Reconsidering Trials* in Absentia *at the Special Tribunal for Lebanon: An Application of the Tribunal's Early Jurisprudence*, 43 GEO. WASH. INT'L L. REV. 91 (2011);

Ralph Riachi, *Trials* in Absentia *in the Lebanese Judicial System and at the Special Tribunal for Lebanon: Challenge or Evolution?*, 8 J. INT'L CRIM. JUST. 1295 (2010); Chris Jenks, *Notice Otherwise Given: Will* in Absentia *Trials at the Special Tribunal for Lebanon Violate Human Rights?*, 33 FORDHAM INT'L L. J. 57 (2009).

7. Forms of Responsibility

In another part of this opinion, the Appeals Chamber indicated that the STL is empowered to apply all customary international law modes of responsibility, including joint criminal enterprise (JCE), to the crimes within its jurisdiction (for more on JCE liability, see Chapter 15). Departing from the precedent of the other *ad hoc* tribunals—which have convicted individuals for being part of a JCE that resulted in the commission of genocide—the Tribunal rejected the applicability of the third form of joint criminal enterprise to the crime of terrorism. It reasoned that terrorism is a specific intent crime, and that JCE III allows liability to attach where the defendant exhibited mere recklessness. The Appeals Chamber noted that it would treat secondary offenders as aiders and abettors rather than as principals. Interlocutory Decision, at para. 249. The Tribunal also noted that the co-perpetration doctrine, which is so prevalent in the charging instruments before the International Criminal Court, "is not recognized in customary international law." Interlocutory Decision, at para. 255–56.

8. El Sayed

The first individual in the custody of the STL was Jamil El Sayed, who was arrested in 2005, apparently upon the recommendation of the then IIIC Commissioner, Detlev Mehlis. Soon after the files were transferred to the STL in early 2009, the Prosecutor indicated that he had in his possession insufficient evidence to justify the continued detention of El Sayed and three other individuals and requested their release. In so doing, he admitted that there were inconsistencies in witness testimony and that several witnesses had retracted their prior testimony. *See In the Matter of El Sayed*, Case No. CH/PRES/2010/01, Order Assigning Matter to Pre-Trial Judge (Apr. 4, 2010).

Since then, El Sayed has endeavored to get the underlying evidentiary material released so that he may commence a suit for libel and arbitrary detention. Although the Prosecutor argued that the STL was without jurisdiction over the application, the Tribunal relied upon its "inherent" powers to allow the application since it is "closely linked" to the Tribunal's mandate and "must be settled in the interests of fairness of the proceedings and good administration of justice." *In the Matter of El Sayed*, Case No. CH/AC/2010/02, Decision on Appeal of Pre-Trial Judge's Order Regarding Jurisdiction and Standing (Nov. 10, 2010). A Pre-Trial Judge ordered more than 270 documents (mostly witness statements submitted to the IIIC) to be released to El Sayed. On the Prosecutor's appeal, the Appeals Chamber ordered certain documents to be released, subject to redaction, and ordered that the Victim & Witnesses Unit be consulted on other documents and potential redactions. *See In the Matter of El Sayed*, Case No. CH/AC/2011/02, Order Allowing in Part and Dismissing in Part the Appeal by the Prosecutor

Against the Pre-Trial Judge's Decision of 2 September 2011 and Ordering the Disclosure of Documents (Oct. 7, 2011).

9. Security Concerns

The STL is operating in an extremely insecure and tumultuous political environment. At first, the judges were not publicly named; investigators have been harassed; and individuals who gave testimony to the IIIC were later killed. The IIIC was plagued by allegations that witnesses gave false testimony, and there have been successive leaks of confidential documents. The new ruling majority in Lebanon has declared its hostility toward the Tribunal. Indeed, in 2011, a prior national unity government led by Hariri's son, Saad Hariri, collapsed in part due to its support for the Tribunal. The conflict in Syria has only exacerbated the situation. These problems have done little to instill confidence in the process. For more, *see* Nidal Nabil Jurdi, *Falling Between the Cracks: The Special Tribunal for Lebanon's Jurisdictional Gaps as Obstacles to Achieving Justice & Public Legitimacy*, 17 U.C. DAVIS J. INT'L L. & POL'Y 253 (2011).

10. For Further Reading

THE SPECIAL TRIBUNAL FOR LEBANON: LAW & PRACTICE (Amal Alamuddin et al. eds., 2014); Nidal Nabil Jurdi, *The Subject-Matter Jurisdiction of the Special Tribunal for Lebanon*, 5 J. INT'L CRIM. JUST. 1125 (2007); Cecile Aptel, *Some Innovation in the Statute of the Special Tribunal for Lebanon*, 5 J. INT'L CRIM. JUST. 1107 (2007); Sandra Hodgkinson, *Are Ad Hoc Tribunals an Effective Tool for Prosecuting International Terrorism Cases?*, 24 EMORY INT'L L. REV. 515 (2010).

PROBLEM

Consider the following scenarios and determine whether the violent acts in question would constitute a punishable act of terrorism under the Terrorist Bombing Convention, whose text you can find online. If these acts do not constitute an act of terrorism pursuant to that treaty, would they implicate other international criminal prohibitions? Would they qualify as an act of terrorism under the definition found in the STL Statute as interpreted in the Interlocutory Decision above? If the acts do not violate international law, would they likely violate the domestic law of either one of the referenced states? Assume both states are parties to the Terrorist Bombing Convention, the Geneva Conventions, and the Additional Protocols and that the national legislatures have incorporated the penal provisions of these treaties into their domestic law.

1) In an international armed conflict involving states Alpha and Beta, Alpha's troops attack Beta's military barracks using grenade launchers, leading to the death of dozens of Betan troops.

2) In an international armed conflict involving states Alpha and Beta, Alpha's troops attack a civilian hamlet with no military presence using grenade launchers. Dozens of Betan citizens are killed.

3) Alpha and Beta are at peace. A radical group based in Alpha whose members share the ethnicity of an oppressed minority group in Beta launch four cluster bombs into a civilian neighborhood in Beta populated by the Beta majority ethnic group. Homes and a bridge are destroyed, and dozens of Betan citizens are killed or injured.

4) Alpha and Beta are at peace. A radical group based in Beta who seeks the overthrow of the Betan government launches a cluster bomb attack in a civilian neighborhood in Beta. Homes and a bridge are destroyed, and dozens of Betan citizens are killed or injured.

5) Beta is engaged in a civil war with a separatist group seeking independence. Members of the rebel group attack a civilian hamlet with no military presence and a military barracks where Betan troops are billeted. They employ tactical ballistic missiles that they obtained on the international weapons black market. The attack destroys the targets and kills or wounds their occupants.

6) Beta is engaged in a civil war with a separatist group seeking independence. Betan troops attack a civilian hamlet in rebel territory and a rebel camp using tactical ballistic missiles. The attack destroys the targets and kills or wounds their occupants.

CHAPTER 13

CHARGING INTERNATIONAL CRIMES

As the preceding chapters indicate, the elements of international law offenses overlap considerably. For one, a single act may implicate multiple international crimes (so-called "inter-article offenses"). For example, an act of murder can constitute a war crime (when a protected person is intentionally killed within the context of an armed conflict), a crime against humanity (when a person is intentionally killed within the context of a widespread or systematic attack against a civilian population), or an act of genocide (when a member of a protected group is killed with the specific intent to destroy the person's group, in whole or in part). Likewise, the same act or course of conduct can implicate multiple constitutive crimes (so-called "intra-article offenses"), such as the crimes against humanity of imprisonment, enslavement, disappearances, and persecution. In addition, an individual may be indicted under several theories of liability: for committing, ordering, inciting, instigating and being complicit in a crime. Consider, for example, the multiple counts the following event could generate: a protected person from a minority ethnic group is intentionally killed using a prohibited weapon in the context of the bombardment of an undefended town involving excessive force in relation to any military advantage that was ordered by a regional military commander.

The overlap of international crimes (*concursus delictorum*) raises multiple questions about the administration of justice. These include questions about how a prosecutor should charge defendants whose conduct implicates multiple prohibitions, how a tribunal should construct its verdict in light of multiple and overlapping counts in an indictment, and how a defendant should be sentenced where multiple crimes are proven. This chapter considers the first two phenomena. Sentencing shall be considered independently in Chapter 18. To start, consider the two opinions below from the ICTY (the Trial Chamber and Appeals Chamber decisions in *Kunarac*, excerpts of which were presented in the chapter on Torture). Kunarac and his co-defendants were charged with a combination of crimes, including torture and rape, as crimes against humanity and war crimes, and enslavement as a crime against humanity. Thus, the decisions address both inter- and intra-article charging and convictions.

Prosecutor v. Kunarac, Case No. IT–96–23–T & IT–96–23/1–T, Judgement (Feb 22, 2001)

In the Trial Chamber

Cumulative Convictions

544. The issue of cumulative convictions centers on the question whether an accused may be convicted of more than one offence for the same conduct.

545. With respect to the present case, in several instances the accused are charged with more than one offence under a single Article, like torture and rape under Article 5 of the Statute, based on the same conduct. The accused are also charged with offences under two Articles, like torture under Article 5 and torture and/or rape under Article 3 of the Statute, again based on the same conduct.

546. The Prosecutor submits that an accused may be indicted, convicted and sentenced on cumulative charges emanating from the same conduct under the following circumstances: where the offences have different elements; where the provisions creating the offences protect different interests; or where it is necessary to record a conviction for both offences in order to fully describe what the accused did. The Defence submits that an accused cannot be indicted and convicted for more than one offence for the same act.

547. Although the Appeals Chamber in the *Delalić* case rendered its judgement only very recently,[1347] this Trial Chamber applies the approach of the majority in that judgement to the issue of cumulative convictions, without the assistance of the parties, in the present case.

548. The Appeals Chamber in the *Delalić* case held that cumulative charging is to be allowed. The primary reason is that it is impossible for the Prosecutor to determine with certainty, prior to the presentation of all the evidence, which of the charges brought against an accused will be proved. A Trial Chamber is in a better position, after the parties' presentation of the evidence, to evaluate which charges should be retained.

549. The Appeals Chamber in the *Delalić* case held that cumulative convictions are permissible only in certain circumstances. It is worth quoting the relevant section of that judgement in full:

> 412. [. . .] [t]his Appeals Chamber holds that reasons of fairness to the accused and the consideration that only distinct crimes may justify multiple convictions, lead to the conclusion that multiple criminal convictions entered under different statutory provisions but based on the same conduct are permissible only if each statutory provision involved has a

---

[1347] *Prosecutor v. Delalić*, Case No. IT–96–21–A, Judgement (Feb 20, 2001) [a.k.a. "*Čelebići*"].

materially distinct element not contained in the other. An element is materially distinct from another if it requires proof of a fact not required by the other.

413. Where this test is not met, the Chamber must decide in relation to which offence it will enter a conviction. This should be done on the basis of the principle that the conviction under the more specific provision should be upheld. Thus, if a set of facts is regulated by two provisions, one of which contains an additional materially distinct element, then a conviction should be entered only under that provision.

550. Accordingly, once all the evidence has been assessed, before deciding which convictions, if any, to enter against an accused, a Trial Chamber first has to determine whether an accused is charged with more than one statutory offence based upon the same conduct. Secondly, if there is evidence to establish both offences, but the underlying conduct is the same, the Trial Chamber has to determine whether each relevant statutory provision has a materially distinct element not contained in the other. This involves a comparison of the elements of the relevant statutory provisions—the facts of a specific case play no role in this determination. Thirdly, if the relevant provisions do not each have a materially distinct element, the Trial Chamber should select the more specific provision.

551. As to the impact that cumulative convictions based on the same conduct will have on sentencing, the Appeals Chamber in the *Delalić* case held that it must be ensured that the final or aggregate sentence reflects the totality of the criminal conduct and overall culpability of the offender. The prejudice that an offender will or may suffer because of cumulative convictions based on the same conduct has to be taken into account when imposing the sentence.

552. The Appeals Chamber in the *Delalić* case dealt with the matter of cumulative convictions in the context of Articles 2 [grave breaches of the Geneva Conventions] and 3 [other violations of the laws and customs of war] of the Statute. This Trial Chamber considers the approach identified in that judgement must also be applied in the present case, which relates to Articles 3 and 5 [crimes against humanity] of the Statute. It would be inappropriate to apply different approaches to different cumulations of charges.

553. The Prosecutor charges Dragoljub Kunarac for torture under Articles 5 and 3 and for rape under Articles 5 and 3, based upon the same criminal conduct. She also charges Dragoljub Kunarac and Radomir Kovać with enslavement under Article 5 and outrages upon personal dignity under Article 3 based upon the same conduct. Based upon the same criminal conduct, Zoran Vuković has been indicted under Articles 5 and 3 on counts of torture and counts of rape.

554. The Prosecutor does not submit that convictions for rape and enslavement under Article 5 based on the same conduct should be entered against the accused. The alleged repeated violations of the sexual integrity of the victims, by various means, is one of the main factors to be considered when determining whether enslavement was committed. She states that

> The main characteristic of the enslavement exercised by the accused Kunarac and Kovać was the sexual exploitation of the girls and women. All the controls exerted served that purpose. Repeated violations of the victim's sexual integrity, through rape and other sexual violence, were some of the most obvious exercises of the powers of ownership by the accused.

Furthermore, with regards to rape and outrages upon personal dignity, the Prosecutor charges rape and outrages upon personal dignity separately in this case, although, in her view, rape clearly could have and has been classified as an outrage upon personal dignity. In view of these submissions, the cumulative convictions problem in relation to rape and enslavement and rape and outrages upon personal dignity does not arise, because these charges are not based on the same conduct.

555. Having regard to the Indictments and the Prosecutor's submissions, what is to be determined here, therefore, are the following questions. First, would convictions for an Article 3 offence and an Article 5 offence, based on the same conduct, be permissible? Secondly, would convictions for rape and torture under one Article based on the same conduct be permissible?

Convictions Under Articles 3 and 5 of the Statute

556. Applying the approach adopted by the Appeals Chamber in the *Delalić* case, convictions for both an Article 3 offence and an Article 5 offence based on the same conduct would be permissible. That is so because each Article has at least one materially distinct element that does not appear in the other. A materially distinct element in Article 3 *vis-à-vis* Article 5 is the nexus requirement, which holds that there must be a close link between the acts of an accused and the armed conflict. A materially distinct element in Article 5 *vis-à-vis* Article 3 is the requirement of a widespread or systematic attack directed against a civilian population. In other words, regardless of the enumerated or specific offences charged under Articles 3 and 5, convictions under both Articles based on the same conduct will be permissible. With reference to the present case, convictions based on the same conduct would be permissible: convictions for rape under both Articles; convictions for torture under both Articles; convictions for enslavement under Article 5 and outrages upon personal dignity under Article 3; convictions for rape under Article 5 and torture under Article 3; convictions for rape under Article 3 and torture under Article 5; and convictions for enslavement under Article 5 and rape under Article 3.

Torture and Rape Under Articles 3 or 5 of the Statute

557. Applying the approach adopted by the Appeals Chamber in the *Delalić* case, convictions for rape and torture under either Article 3 or Article 5 based on the same conduct would be permissible. Comparing the elements of rape and torture under either Article 3 or Article 5, a materially distinct element of rape *vis-à-vis* torture is the sexual penetration element. A materially distinct element of torture *vis-à-vis* rape is the severe infliction of pain or suffering aimed at obtaining information or a confession, punishing, intimidating, coercing or discriminating against the victim or a third person.

Prosecutor v. Kunarac, Case No. IT–96–23–A & IT–96–23/1–A, Judgement (June 12, 2002)

In the Appeals Chamber

Cumulative Charging

167. The Appellants argue that they were inappropriately cumulatively charged. The Appeals Chamber has consistently rejected this argument and it is not necessary to rehearse this settled jurisprudence here. These grounds of appeal are, hereby, rejected.

Cumulative Convictions

168. The Appeals Chamber accepts the approach articulated in the *Čelebići* Appeal Judgement [a.k.a. *Delalić*],* an approach heavily indebted to the *Blockburger* decision of the Supreme Court of the United States.[226] * * *

169. Care, however, is needed in applying the *Čelebići* test for, as Judges Hunt and Bennouna observed in their separate and dissenting opinion in the same case, cumulative convictions create "a very real risk of . . . prejudice" to the accused.[228] At the very least, such persons suffer the stigma inherent in being convicted of an additional crime for the same conduct. In a more tangible sense, there may be such consequences as losing eligibility for early release under the law of the state enforcing the sentence. Nor is such prejudice cured, as the U.S. Supreme Court warned in *Rutledge v. U.S.*,[230] by the fact that the second conviction's concomitant sentence is served concurrently. On the other hand, multiple convictions

---

* Eds.: *Prosecutor v. Delalić*, Case No. IT–96–21–A, Judgement, paras. 412–13 (Feb. 20, 2001).

226 *Blockburger v. United States*, 284 U.S. 299, 304 (1932) ("The applicable rule is that, where the same act or transaction constitutes a violation of two distinct statutory provisions, the test to be applied to determine whether there are two offenses or only one is whether each provision requires proof of an additional fact which the other does not.").

228 *Prosecutor v. Delalić*, Case No. IT–96–21–A, Separate and Dissenting Opinion of Judge David Hunt and Judge Mohamed Bennouna, para. 23 (Feb. 20, 2001).

230 *Rutledge v. United States*, 517 U.S. 292 (1996).

serve to describe the full culpability of a particular accused or provide a complete picture of his criminal conduct.[232]

170. Typically, the issue of multiple convictions or cumulative convictions arises in legal systems with a hierarchy of offences in which the more serious offences within a category require proof of an additional element or even require a specific *mens rea*. It is, however, an established principle of both the civil and common law that punishment should not be imposed for both a greater offence and a lesser included offence. Instead, the more serious crime subsumes the less serious (*lex consumens derogat legi consumptae*). The rationale here, of course, is that the greater and the lesser included offence constitute the same core offence, without sufficient distinction between them, even when the same act or transaction violates two distinct statutory provisions. Indeed, it is not possible to commit the more serious offence without also committing the lesser included offence.

171. In national laws, this principle is easier to apply because the relative gravity of a crime can normally be ascertained by the penalty imposed by the law. The Statute, however, does not provide a scale of penalties for the various crimes it proscribes. Nor does the Statute give other indications as to the relative gravity of the crimes. Indeed, the Tribunal has explicitly rejected a hierarchy of crimes, concluding instead that crimes against humanity are not inherently graver than war crimes.[235]

172. The *Čelebići/Blockburger* test serves to identify distinct offences within this constellation of statutory provisions. While subscribing to this test, the Appeals Chamber is aware that it is deceptively simple. In practice, it is difficult to apply in a way that is conceptually coherent and promotes the interests of justice.

173. For this reason, the Appeals Chamber will scrutinise with the greatest caution multiple or cumulative convictions. In so doing, it will be guided by the considerations of justice for the accused: the Appeals Chamber will permit multiple convictions only in cases where the same act or transaction clearly violates two distinct provisions of the Statute and where each statutory provision requires proof of an additional fact which the other does not. * * *

---

[232] *Prosecutor v. Jelisić*, Case No. IT–95–10–A, Partial Dissenting Opinion of Judge Shahabuddeen, *Jelisić* Appeal Judgement, para. 34 (July 5, 2001) ("To record the full criminality of his conduct, it may be necessary to convict of all the crimes, overlapping in convictions being adjusted through penalty.").

[235] *Prosecutor v. Tadić*, Case No. IT–94–1–A and IT–94–1–A*bis*, Judgement in Sentencing Appeals, para. 69 (Jan. 26, 2000) ("After full consideration, the Appeals Chamber takes the view that there is in law no distinction between the seriousness of a crime against humanity and that of a war crime. The Appeals Chamber finds no basis for such a distinction in the Statute or the Rules of the International Tribunal construed in accordance with customary international law; the authorized penalties are also the same, the level in any particular case being fixed by reference to the circumstances of the case.").

The Instant Convictions

1. Inter-Article Convictions Under Articles 3 and 5 of the Statute

175. The Appeals Chamber will now consider the argument of the Appellants that the Trial Chamber erred in convicting them for the same conduct under Articles 3 and 5 of the Statute.

176. The Appeals Chamber agrees with the Trial Chamber that convictions for the same conduct under Article 3 of the Statute (violations of the laws or customs of war) and Article 5 of the Statute (crimes against humanity) are permissible and dismisses the appeals on this point. Applying the *Čelebići* test, subsequent judgements of the Appeals Chamber have consistently held that crimes against humanity constitute crimes distinct from crimes against the laws or customs of war in that each contains an element that does not appear in the other. The Appeals Chamber sees no reason to depart from this settled jurisprudence.

177. As a part of this analysis, the Appeals Chamber reaffirms that the legal prerequisites describing the circumstances of the relevant offences as stated in the *chapeaux* of the relevant Articles of the Statute constitute elements which enter the calculus of permissibility of cumulative convictions. The contrary view would permit anomalous results not intended by the Statute.

178. The Appeals Chamber notes that the permissibility of multiple convictions ultimately turns on the intentions of the lawmakers. The Appeals Chamber believes that the Security Council intended that convictions for the same conduct constituting distinct offences under several of the Articles of the Statute be entered. Surely the Security Council, in promulgating the Statute and listing in it the principal offences against International Humanitarian Law, did not intend these offences to be mutually exclusive. Rather, the *chapeaux* elements disclose the animating desire that all species of such crimes be adequately described and punished.

2. Intra-Article Convictions Under Article 5 of the Statute

(a) Rape and Torture

179. The Appeals Chamber will now consider the Appellants' arguments regarding intra-Article convictions. The Appellants contend that the Trial Chamber erred by entering convictions for both torture under Article 5(f) and rape under Article 5(g) of the Statute on the theory that neither the law nor the facts can reasonably be interpreted to establish distinct crimes. The Trial Chamber found that the crimes of rape and torture each contain one materially distinct element not contained in the other, making convictions under both crimes permissible. As its earlier discussion of the offences of rape and torture make clear, the Appeals Chamber agrees. The issue of cumulative convictions hinges on the definitions of distinct offences under the Statute which are amplified in the jurisprudence of the Tribunal. That

torture and rape each contain a materially distinct element not contained by the other disposes of this ground of appeal. That is, that an element of the crime of rape is penetration, whereas an element for the crime of torture is a prohibited purpose, neither element being found in the other crime. * * *

181. In the *Čelebići* Trial Judgement, the Trial Chamber considered the issue of torture through rape. The Appeals Chamber overturned the Appellant's convictions under Article 3 of the Statute as improperly cumulative in relation to Article 2 of the Statute, but the Trial Chamber's extensive analysis of torture and rape remains persuasive. Grounding its analysis in a thorough survey of the jurisprudence of international bodies, the Trial Chamber concluded that rape may constitute torture. Both the Inter-American Commission on Human Rights and the European Court of Human Rights have found that torture may be committed through rape. And the United Nations Special Rapporteur on Torture listed forms of sexual assault as methods of torture.[246]

182. For rape to be categorised as torture, both the elements of rape and the elements of torture must be present. Summarising the international case-law, the Trial Chamber in the *Čelebići* case concluded that "rape involves the infliction of suffering at a requisite level of severity to place it in the category of torture." By way of illustration, the Trial Chamber discussed the facts of two central cases, *Fernando and Raquel Mejía v. Peru* from the Inter-American Commission and *Aydin v. Turkey* from the European Commission for Human Rights.[248] * * *

(b) Rape and Enslavement

186. Equally meritless is the Appellants' contention that Kunarac's and Kovać's convictions for enslavement under Article 5(c) and rape under Article 5(g) of the Statute are impermissibly cumulative. That the Appellants also forced their captives to endure rape as an especially odious form of their domestic servitude does not merge the two convictions. As the Appeals Chamber has previously explained in its discussion of enslavement, it finds that enslavement, even if based on sexual exploitation, is a distinct offence from that of rape. The Appeals Chamber, therefore, rejects this ground of appeal.

---

246 * * * The United Nations Special Rapporteur on Torture introduced his 1992 Report to the Commission on Human Rights by stating: "Since it was clear that rape or other forms of sexual assault against women held in detention were a particularly ignominious violation of the inherent dignity and right to physical integrity of the human being, they accordingly constituted an act of torture" (para. 35).

248 *Fernando and Raquel Mejía v. Peru*, Case No. 10,970, Judgment of 1 March 1996, Report No. 5/96, INTER-AMERICAN YEARBOOK ON HUMAN RIGHTS, 1996, p. 1120, and *Aydin v. Turkey*, Opinion of the European Commission of Human Rights, 7 March 1996, *reprinted in* EUROPEAN COURT OF HUMAN RIGHTS, ECHR 1997–VI, p. 1937, paras. 186 and 189.

Article 3 of the Statute * * *

1. Intra-Article Convictions Under Article 3 of the Statute

188. The Appellants' argument against convictions for rape and torture are made also with regard to intra-Article convictions under Article 3 of the Statute. As with intra-Article convictions for rape and torture under Article 5 of the Statute, the Appellants argue that in the "absence of described distinct infliction of physical or mental pain . . . the infliction of physical or mental pain is brought down only to the very act of sexual intercourse, without the consent of the victim" and that the convicted person's conduct "cannot be deemed to be both the case of a criminal offence of rape and the criminal offence of torture, because one act excludes the other."

189. * * * [I]n the context of cumulative convictions under Article 3 of the Statute, which imports Common article 3 of the Geneva Conventions, the Appeals Chamber acknowledges a specific problem, namely that Common article 3 refers to "cruel treatment and torture" (3(1)(a)), and "outrages upon personal dignity, in particular humiliating and degrading treatment" (3(1)(c)), but does not refer to rape.

190. The Appeals Chamber finds the invocation and the application of Common article 3, by way of a *renvoi* ["sending back," a doctrine of conflicts of law involving reference to another source of law] through Article 3 of the Statute, entirely appropriate. The Trial Chamber attempted to ground the rape charges in Common article 3 by reference to outrages upon personal dignity. Although the Appeals Chamber agrees that rape may be charged in this manner, it notes that grounding the charge in Common article 3 imposes certain limitations with respect to cumulative convictions. This is because, where it is attempted to charge rape as an outrage upon personal dignity, the rape is only evidence of the outrage; the substantial crime is not rape but the outrage occasioned by the rape. This leaves open the argument that an outrage upon personal dignity is substantially included in torture, with the consequence that convictions for both may not be possible. However, as will be shown below, rape was not in fact charged as an outrage upon personal dignity in this case.

191. Where the Trial Chamber (or indeed the Prosecutor) chooses to invoke Common article 3, it is bound by the text. In other words, each offence must be hanged, as it were, on its own statutory hook. In the present case, a statutory hook for rape is absent in Common article 3. The Indictments acknowledge the absence of an express statutory provision. The Prosecutor charged Kunarac, for instance, with both torture and rape under Article 3 of the Statute but the language of the counts diverges:

> Count 3: Torture, a VIOLATION OF THE LAWS OR CUSTOMS OF WAR, punishable under Article 3 of the Statute of the

> Tribunal and recognised by Common Article 3(1)(a)(torture) of the Geneva Conventions.
>
> Count 4: Rape, a VIOLATION OF THE LAWS OR CUSTOMS OF WAR, punishable under Article 3 of the Statute of the Tribunal.

In the case of torture, there is an express statutory provision, while in the case of rape, there is not.

192. Whether rape is considered to constitute torture under Common article 3(1)(a) or an outrage upon personal dignity under Common article 3(1)(c) depends on the egregiousness of the conduct. The Appeals Chamber notes that in the *Furundžija* Trial Judgement, the Trial Chamber found sexual abuse to constitute an outrage upon personal dignity under Article 3 of the Statute (incorporating Common article 3). The Trial Chamber pronounced the accused guilty of one criminal offence, outrages upon personal dignity, including rape. However, whether one regards rape as an instrument through which torture is committed (Common article 3(1)(a)) or one through which outrages upon personal dignity are committed (Common article 3(1)(c)), in either case, a separate conviction for rape is not permitted under Common article 3, given the absence of a distinct statutory hook for rape.

193. This statutory limitation does not, however, dispose of the matter. As the Appeals Chamber has noted, the Indictments charged Kunarac and Vuković with rape under Article 3 of the Statute without reference to Common article 3. In its discussion of the charges under Article 3 of the Statute, the Trial Chamber noted that the Prosecutor "submitted that the basis for the rape charges under Article 3 lies in both treaty and customary international law, including common Article 3." Notwithstanding its exhaustive analysis of Common article 3 in connection to the charged offences under Article 3 of the Statute, the Trial Chamber's disposition makes no mention of Common article 3.

194. Article 3 of the Statute, as the Appeals Chamber has previously observed, also prohibits other serious violations of customary international law. The Appeals Chamber in the *Tadić* Jurisdiction Decision outlined four requirements to trigger Article 3 of the Statute: (i) the violation must constitute an infringement of a rule of international humanitarian law; (ii) the rule must be customary in nature . . . ; (iii) the violation must be "serious," that is to say, it must constitute a breach of a rule protecting important values . . . ; (iv) the violation of the rule must entail, under customary or conventional law, the individual criminal responsibility of the person breaching the rule. Therefore, so long as rape is a "serious" war crime under customary international law entailing "individual criminal responsibility," separate convictions for rape under Article 3 of the Statute and torture under that Article, by reference to Common article 3(1)(a), are not impermissibly cumulative.

195. In keeping with the jurisprudence of the Tribunal, the Appeals Chamber concludes that rape meets these requirements and, therefore, constitutes a recognised war crime under customary international law, which is punishable under Article 3 of the Statute. The universal criminalisation of rape in domestic jurisdictions, the explicit prohibitions contained in the fourth Geneva Convention and in the Additional Protocols I and II, and the recognition of the seriousness of the offence in the jurisprudence of international bodies, including the European Commission on Human Rights and the Inter-American Commission on Human Rights, all lead inexorably to this conclusion.

196. In summary, under Article 3 of the Statute, a conviction for rape can be cumulated with a conviction for torture for the same conduct. A question of cumulativeness assumes the validity of each conviction standing independently; it asks only whether both convictions may be made where they relate to the same conduct. The answer to that question will depend on whether each of the two crimes has a materially distinct element not contained in the other. An element is materially distinct from another if it requires proof of a fact not required by the other. Without being exhaustive and as already noted, an element of the crime of rape is penetration, whereas an element for the crime of torture is a prohibited purpose, neither element being found in the other crime. From this, it follows that cumulative convictions for rape and torture under Article 3 of the Statute are permissible though based on the same conduct. Furthermore, * * * relating to the question of cumulation in respect of intra-Article 5 crimes, the rapes and sexual abuses amount to torture in the circumstances of this case. The Appeals Chamber, therefore, dismisses the Appellants' grounds of appeal relating to cumulative convictions with regard to the intra-Article 3 convictions.

NOTES & QUESTIONS

1. Cumulative Charging

In *Delalić*, the ICTY Appeals Chamber ruled that cumulative charging is permissible where "prior to the presentation of all the evidence, it is not possible to determine to a certainty which of the charges brought against an accused will be proved. The Trial Chamber is better poised, after the parties' presentation of the evidence, to evaluate which of the charges may be retained, based upon the sufficiency of the evidence." *Prosecutor v. Delalić*, Case No. IT–96–21–A, Judgement, para. 400 (Feb. 20, 2001). The two dissenters (Judges David Hunt from Australia and Mohamed Bennouna from Morocco) generally agreed with this approach:

> It is not possible to know with precision, prior to that time, which offenses among those charged the evidence will prove, particularly in relation to the proof of differing jurisdictional pre-requisites—such as, for example, the requirement that an international armed conflict be proved for Article 2 offences but not for those falling under Article 3. Further, * * * the offenses in the Statute do not

> refer to specific categories of well-defined acts, but to broad groups of offences, the elements of which are not always clearly defined and which may remain to be clarified in the Tribunal's jurisprudence.

Prosecutor v. Delalić, Case No. IT–96–21–A, Separate And Dissenting Opinion Of Judge David Hunt And Judge Mohamed Bennouna, para. 12 (Feb. 20, 2001). Are defendants prejudiced by a system that allows the prosecutor to cumulatively charge and then take a "wait and see" attitude toward what the evidence will adduce as practiced by the ICTY? Is it true, as argued by Judges Hunt and Bennouna in their Separate and Dissenting Opinion in the *Delalić* case, that "there is no prejudice to an accused in permitting cumulative charging and in determining the issues arising from accumulation of offenses after all of the evidence has been presented?" *Id.* For a discussion of cumulative charging in the *ad hoc* tribunals, *see* Attila Bogdan, *Cumulative Charges, Convictions and Sentencing at the* Ad Hoc *International Tribunals for the Former Yugoslavia and Rwanda*, 3 MELB. J. INT'L L. 1 (2002).

2. Cumulative Charging at the ICC

Jean-Pierre Bemba Gombo is a citizen of the Democratic Republic of Congo (DRC), once a member of its Senate, who was implicated in crimes committed within the Central African Republic (CAR) in 2002–3. (See the Appendix for a map of the Central African Republic.) Bemba—one of the richest men in the DRC—led the Movement for the Liberation of Congo (MLC or *Mouvement de Libération du Congo*) in the DRC, a rebel group turned opposition political party. In 2002, the former President of the CAR, Ange-Félix Patassé, invited the MLC to CAR to help him resist a coup attempt. MLC troops under Bemba's command allegedly went on a rampage in which mass sexual violence featured more prominently than mass murder. The President was subsequently ousted by General François Bozizé. In December 2004, the new CAR government referred the situation in that country to the ICC.

In 2006, the Cour de Cassation of CAR ruled that the country was unable to investigate or prosecute the alleged crimes, in part because it could not gain custody of the accused. In 2007, Bemba traveled to Europe, ostensibly for medical treatment, but most likely to avoid prosecution in the DRC for treason. He was arrested in Belgium in 2008 and transferred to The Hague. The opinion below addresses questions of cumulative charging by the prosecution and/or cumulative convictions by the court. Bemba's arrest warrant indicated that (1) there were reasonable grounds to believe that troops under Bemba's command and acting with a common purpose committed rape, torture, outrages upon human dignity and pillage, and (2) Bemba knew that the implementation of the common plan with Patassé would, in the normal course of events, lead to the commission of crimes and that he accepted this risk through his decision to send MLC combatants to the Central African Republic. *Prosecutor v. Jean-Pierre Bemba Gombo*, Case No. ICC–01/05–01/08, Warrant of Arrest for Jean-Pierre Bemba Gombo (May 23, 2008). So far, Bemba has not been indicted for crimes committed in his own country. The ICC Appeals Chamber acquitted Bemba in an opinion discussed in Chapter 14.

Prosecutor v. Jean-Pierre Bemba Gombo, Case No. ICC–01/05–01/08, Decision Pursuant to Article 61(7)(a) and (b) of the Rome Statute on the Charges of the Prosecutor Against Jean-Pierre Bemba Gombo (June 15, 2009)

Pre-Trial Chamber II

Crimes Against Humanity

71. In the Amended Document Containing the Charges ("DCC")* the Prosecutor charges Mr. Jean-Pierre Bemba with murder (article 7(1)(a) of the Statute), rape (article 7(1)(g) of the Statute) and torture (article 7(1)(f) of the Statute) as crimes against humanity falling within the jurisdiction of the Court.

72. Having reviewed the Disclosed Evidence as a whole, the Chamber finds that there is sufficient evidence to establish substantial grounds to believe that acts of murder and rape constituting crimes against humanity within the meaning of articles 7(1)(a) and 7(1)(g) of the Statute were committed as part of a widespread attack directed against the civilian population carried out in the Central African Republic (CAR) from on or about 26 October 2002 to 15 March 2003. However, the Chamber rejects the cumulative charging approach of the Prosecutor and declines to confirm count 3 of torture as a crime against humanity within the meaning of article 7(1)(f) of the Statute. The Chamber bases this finding on the following considerations. * * *

Specific Elements of the Act of Rape as a Crime Against Humanity (Count I)

159. In the Amended DCC, the Prosecutor alleges that:

> [f]rom on or about 26 October 2002 to 15 March 2003, Jean-Pierre Bemba committed, jointly with another, Ange-Félix Patassé, crimes against humanity through acts of rape upon civilian men, women and children in the Central African Republic, in violation of [article] 7(1)(g) (. . .) of the Rome Statute.

160. The Chamber finds that there is sufficient evidence to establish substantial grounds to believe that acts of rape constituting crimes against humanity directed against CAR civilians were committed by Movement for the Liberation of Congo (MLC) soldiers [Bemba's forces] as part of the widespread attack against the CAR civilian population from

* Eds.: In the ICC, the DCC is the equivalent of an indictment.

on or about 26 October 2002 to 15 March 2003, with the knowledge of the attack by MLC soldiers. * * *

161. The Elements of Crimes with regard to article 7(1)(g) of the Statute require that:

(1) The perpetrator invaded the body of a person by conduct resulting in penetration, however slight, of any part of the body of the victim or of the perpetrator with a sexual organ, or of the anal or genital opening of the victim with any object or any other part of the body;

(2) The invasion was committed by force, or by threat of force or coercion, such as that caused by fear of violence, duress, detention, psychological oppression or abuse of power, against such person or another person, or by taking advantage of a coercive environment, or the invasion was committed against a person incapable of giving genuine consent.

162. With regard to the term "coercion," the Chamber notes that it does not require physical force. Rather, "threats, intimidation, extortion and other forms of duress which prey on fear or desperation may constitute coercion, and coercion may be inherent in certain circumstances, such as armed conflict or military presence."

163. With regard to the mental element, the perpetrator must have committed the act of rape with intent and knowledge within the meaning of article 30 of the Statute. * * *

165. Having reviewed the Disclosed Evidence, and in particular, the statements of direct witnesses, the Chamber finds that they consistently describe the multiple acts of rape they directly suffered from and detail the invasion of their body by the sexual organ of MLC soldiers, resulting in vaginal or anal penetration. The evidence shows that direct witnesses were raped by several MLC perpetrators in turn, that their clothes were ripped off by force, that they were pushed to the ground, immobilised by MLC soldiers standing on or holding them, raped at gunpoint, in public or in front of or near their family members. The element of force, threat of force or coercion was thus a prevailing factor.

166. The evidence also shows that the perpetrators of the said acts of rape were identified as MLC soldiers. All witnesses who were either victims of rape or witnessed the rape of others, indicate distinguishing features of MLC perpetrators, such as the language spoken by the MLC soldiers, Lingala [primarily a Congolese language], often mixed with a "little bit of French," their inability to communicate properly with the witnesses and/or their families in Sango [the local CAR language], and their military clothing, which allows the Chamber to conclude that the perpetrators were MLC soldiers. * * *

188. Finally, as to the nexus requirement, the Chamber finds that the acts of rape were committed as part of the widespread attack directed against the CAR population from on or about 26 October 2002 to 15

March 2003. Rapes occurred when civilians resisted the looting of their goods by MLC soldiers. Repeated acts of rape were used as a method to terrorise the population. The evidence shows that rapes occurred as MLC troops advanced into CAR territory or withdrew from the CAR. In addition, the Disclosed Evidence shows that rapes occurred in localities, such as PK 12, Fouh, Boy-Rabe and Mongoumba, which were localities under attack by MLC soldiers at the said period.

Specific Elements of the Act of Torture as a Crime Against Humanity (Count 3)

189. In the Amended DCC, the Prosecutor alleges that:

> From on or about 26 October 2002 to 15 March 2003, Jean-Pierre BEMBA committed, jointly with another, Ange-Félix Patassé, crimes against humanity by inflicting severe physical or mental pain or suffering through acts of rape or other forms of sexual violence, upon civilian men, women and children in the Central African Republic, in violation of Articles 7(1)(f) (. . .) of the Rome Statute. * * *

191. Article 7(2)(e) of the Statute defines torture as:

> the intentional infliction of severe pain or suffering, whether physical or mental, upon a person in the custody or under the control of the accused; except that torture shall not include pain or suffering arising only from, inherent in or incidental to, lawful sanctions.

192. The Elements of Crimes add with regard to article 7(1)(f) of the Statute that:

(1) [t]he perpetrator inflicted severe physical or mental pain or suffering upon one or more persons;

(2) [s]uch person or persons were in the custody or under control of the perpetrator;

(3) [s]uch pain or suffering did not arise only from, and was not inherent in or incidental to, lawful sanctions.

193. As to the objective element, the *actus reus*, the Chamber is of the view that, although there is no definition of the severity threshold as a legal requirement of the crime of torture, it is constantly accepted in applicable treaties and jurisprudence that an important degree of pain and suffering has to be reached in order for a criminal act to amount to an act of torture.

194. The subjective element, the *mens rea*, is the intent as expressly mentioned in article (2)(e) of the Statute. Bearing in mind that article 30(1) of the Statute is applicable "unless otherwise provided," and taking into account that the infliction of pain or suffering must be "intentional," the Chamber finds that this excludes the separate requirement of knowledge as set out in article 30(3) of the Statute. In this respect, the Chamber believes that it is not necessary to demonstrate that the

perpetrator knew that the harm inflicted was severe. This interpretation is consistent with paragraph 4 of the General Introduction to the Elements of Crimes. To prove the mental element of torture, it is therefore sufficient that the perpetrator intended the conduct and that the victim endured severe pain or suffering.

195. The Chamber notes that under the Statute, the definition of torture as a crime against humanity, unlike the definition of torture as a war crime, does not require the additional element of a specific purpose. This is also clarified in the Elements of Crimes. * * *

197. The Chamber recalls that the Prosecutor framed count 3 of the Amended DCC as torture "through acts of rape or other forms of sexual violence." At the Hearing, the Prosecutor presented evidence showing not only (a) acts of rape that would allegedly amount to torture, but also (b) material facts other than acts of rape which he legally characterised as acts of torture. In his closing statement, the Prosecutor highlighted that "[t]he main physical acts underpinning the charges of rape, torture and outrages upon personal dignity is rape in this case."

199. The Prosecutor used a cumulative charging approach by characterising count 3 of the Amended DCC as "[torture] through acts of rape or other forms of sexual violence." He avers that the same criminal conduct can be prosecuted under two different counts, namely the count of torture as well as the count of rape, the acts of rape being the instrument of torture.

200. The Chamber acknowledges that the cumulative charging approach is followed by national courts,[275] and international tribunals under certain conditions.[276]

201. The Chamber deems it necessary to recall paragraph 25 of the Decision of 10 June 2008 [concerning the issuance of the arrest warrant] in which the following was clearly stated:

> the Prosecutor appears on occasion to have presented the same facts under different legal characterizations. [The Chamber] wishes to make it clear that the Prosecutor should choose the most appropriate characterization. The Chamber considers that the Prosecutor is risking subjecting the Defence to the burden of responding to multiple charges for the same facts and at the same time delaying the proceedings. It is for the Chamber to characterize the facts put forward by the Prosecutor. The Chamber will revisit this issue in light of the evidence submitted to it by the Prosecutor during the period prior to the confirmation of charges, having regard to the rights of the

---

[275] * * * *Blockburger v. United States*, 284 U.S. 299, 304 (1932).

[276] For example, *Prosecutor v. Delalić et al.*, Case No. IT–96–21–A, Judgement (20 February 2001). * * *

Defence and to the need to ensure the fair and expeditious conduct of the proceedings.*

202. By its decision, the Chamber intended to make it clear that the prosecutorial practice of cumulative charging is detrimental to the rights of the Defence since it places an undue burden on the Defence. The Chamber considers that, as a matter of fairness and expeditiousness of the proceedings, only distinct crimes may justify a cumulative charging approach and, ultimately, be confirmed as charges. This is only possible if each statutory provision allegedly breached in relation to one and the same conduct requires at least one additional material element not contained in the other.

203. In addition, the Chamber further recalls that the ICC legal framework differs from that of the *ad hoc* tribunals, since under regulation 55 of the Regulations, the Trial Chamber may re-characterise a crime to give it the most appropriate legal characterisation. Therefore, before the ICC, there is no need for the Prosecutor to adopt a cumulative charging approach and present all possible characterisations in order to ensure that at least one will be retained by the Chamber.

204. The Chamber considers that in this particular case, the specific material elements of the act of torture, namely severe pain and suffering and control by the perpetrator over the person, are also the inherent specific material elements of the act of rape. However, the act of rape requires the additional specific material element of penetration, which makes it the most appropriate legal characterisation in this particular case.

205. The Chamber, after having carefully reviewed the factual circumstances submitted by the Prosecutor, concludes that the evidence he presented reflects the same conduct which underlies the count of rape, as identified in the statements of witnesses 22, 23, 29, 68, 80, 81, 87 and Unidentified Victims 1 to 35. The Chamber therefore considers that the act of torture is fully subsumed by the count of rape. * * *

208. The Chamber notes article 61(3) of the Statute [concerning charging] and regulation 52(b) of the Regulations and highlight the basic principles on framing a document containing the charges. These principles establish, *inter alia*, that a DCC must state the material facts underpinning the charges and that the material facts underpinning the charges shall be specific enough to clearly inform the suspect of the charges against him or her, so that he or she is in a position to prepare properly his or her defence. The Chamber believes that it is the duty of the Prosecutor to furnish all facts underpinning the charges. Any deficiencies cannot be compensated by the Chamber. In addition, the Chamber considers that, where the Prosecutor is able to do so, he should

---

* Eds.: *Prosecutor v. Jean-Pierre Bemba Gombo*, Case No. ICC–01/05–01/08, Decision on the Prosecutor's Application for a Warrant of Arrest against Jean-Pierre Bemba Gombo, para. 25 (June 10, 2008).

identify the method of commission of the crime or the manner in which it was committed.

209. Applying these principles, the Chamber is of the view that in the Amended DCC, the Prosecutor neither detailed the material facts of torture other than acts of rape nor the method of commission of the alleged acts of torture. As a consequence, Mr. Jean-Pierre Bemba was not in a position to properly identify the facts underpinning the act of torture and adequately prepare his defence. Therefore, the Chamber declines to confirm count 3 of torture as a crime against humanity through other acts of torture, other than acts of rape.

NOTES & QUESTIONS

1. Case Updates

In November 2013, and just days after the defense finished presenting its case, the authorities of the Netherlands, the DRC, Belgium, and France staged a coordinated arrest operation against Bemba's lead defense counsel, his case manager, a defense witness, and a member of the DRC parliament in connection with charges of witness intimidation and forging evidence under Article 70 of the ICC Statute. Bemba himself was also charged with offenses against the administration of justice. Although Bemba himself was acquitted in the main case, all the defendants were convicted in the Article 70 case. Even if defendants are accused of multiple Article 70 offenses, the Trial Chamber determined that the maximum sentence is 5 years (for the Article 5 crimes, the maximum punishment is 30 years at the ICC).

CAR has been beset by renewed violence since December 2012 when a group of rebels calling themselves *Séléka* ("Alliance") launched a coup. The predominantly Muslim *Séléka* ultimately ousted President Francois Bozizé in March 2013. Since then, there have been waves of sectarian violence between loosely-affiliated Muslim forces and predominantly Christian *anti-balaka* ("anti-machete") civil defense forces that have taken on genocidal undertones. The Security Council by way of Resolution 2127 authorized French and African Union troops to use force as necessary to protect civilians throughout the country. The ICC Prosecutor, Fatou Bensouda, opened a new investigation (CAR II) with respect to these events. For a discussion of the ICC's decision in *Bemba* above, *see* American University, War Crimes Research Office, THE PRACTICE OF CUMULATIVE CHARGING AT THE INTERNATIONAL CRIMINAL COURT (May 2010).

2. Prosecutorial v. Judicial Discretion in Charging

These two sets of decisions from the ICTY and the ICC reveal disparate approaches to the allocation of roles between the prosecutor and the bench in the criminal process. In most legal systems of the common law tradition, the court is bound by the prosecutor's legal characterization of the charges. As such, and pursuant to the *ne ultra petita* principle ("not more than asked"), the court can only convict the defendant of a charged crime. That said, some systems do allow for conviction to be entered for a wholly-subsumed lesser included offense without amendment to the indictment. *See, e.g.*, the Criminal Procedure Code of the Republic of Zambia (1996), Art. 181. By contrast, civil law systems are more inclined toward the *iura novit curia* principle—"the judge knows the law." Accordingly, the judge is bound by the prosecutor's selection of cases and conduct, but is free to conduct her own legal evaluation of those facts and to amend the charges as she deems appropriate. The charges in the charging document are thus little more than recommendations by the prosecutor. As a prosecutor, which system would you prefer? As a defense counsel? The International Court of Justice in the *Fisheries (Jurisdiction) Case* ruled that international organs are free to consider the applicable legal rules, independent of the arguments of the parties:

> The Court [. . .], as an international judicial organ, is deemed to take judicial notice of international law and is therefore required [. . .] to consider on its own initiative all rules of international law which may be relevant to the settlement of the dispute. It being the duty of the Court itself to ascertain and apply the relevant law in the given circumstances of the case, the burden of establishing or proving rules of international law cannot be imposed upon any of the parties, for the law lies within the judicial knowledge of the Court.

Fisheries Jurisdiction Case (Fed. Rep. of Germany v. Iceland), Merits, Judgment 1974 I.C.J. Reports 175, 181, para. 18 (July 25, 1974). Do the policies underlying and justifying this approach also apply in the case of international criminal law? The ICTY has ruled that this general approach of international tribunals was not appropriate for the ICTY given that the law was underdeveloped and in flux at the time of the creation of the Tribunal. In light of the strain it would put on defendants, the ICTY did not allow for the reclassification of offenses other than with respect to lesser included offenses. *See Prosecutor v. Kupreškić*, Case No. IT–95–16–T, Judgement, para. 740 (Jan. 14, 2000). Which is the better approach from the perspective of the victims, the defense, the prosecution, and the international justice system?

3. Fairness to the Accused?

Are defendants more prejudiced by a system that allows the court itself to alter the charges, as was done in the ICC? Does the ICC system, in which cumulative charging by the prosecutor appears to be limited, adequately address the concerns of the defense under the ICTY regime of more liberal cumulative charging? Consider this view:

> The [ICC's] restrictive approach to cumulative charging is to be welcomed. This practice, which is one of the common-law legacies of the *ad hoc* tribunals, blows up the prosecution case unnecessarily and creates a difficult situation for the defense. In fact, this practice is incompatible with the information and delimitation functions of charging rules, since it entails an imprecise "overcharging" which makes it difficult, if not impossible, for the defense to prepare adequately a defense case. While cumulative charging may be considered indispensable from a prosecution perspective if it runs

> the risk of "losing" offenses it has not (properly) charged in the first place, such a risk does not exist if the judge has the ultimate word on the "correct" legal classification anyway—that is, in a system governed by the *iura novit curia* principle.

Kai Ambos, *Critical Issues in the* Bemba *Confirmation Decision*, 22 LEIDEN J. INT'L L. 715, 724 (2009). Do you agree?

4. Cumulative Convictions

Although they were with the majority on cumulative charging, the dissenters in *Delalić* objected to the entering of cumulative convictions for the same conduct under Articles 2 (penalizing grave breaches of the Geneva Conventions) and 3 (penalizing violations of the laws and customs of war) of the ICTY Statute (inter-article convictions), which both address war crimes. (They also noted that their analysis would prohibit cumulative convictions for war crimes and crimes against humanity for the same conduct, even where the elements of each crime are distinct). They reasoned:

> As to the "test" to be applied in order to avoid cumulative convictions, we agree with the majority that an accused may only be convicted of more than one offence in respect of the same conduct where each offence has a unique element that the other offence or offences do not. * * * The majority has elected to include in that consideration the legal prerequisites relating to the circumstances of the relevant offences, or the *chapeaux* to the Articles, as well as the elements of the crimes which go to the *actus reus* and *mens rea* of the offences. * * *
>
> [T]he fundamental consideration arising from charges relating to the same conduct is that an accused should not be penalised more than once for the same conduct. The purpose of applying this test is therefore to determine whether the conduct of the accused genuinely encompasses more than one crime. For that reason, we believe that it is not meaningful to consider for this purpose legal prerequisites or contextual elements which do not have a bearing on the accused's conduct, and that the focus of the test should therefore be on the substantive elements which relate to an accused's conduct, including his mental state. * * * Although matters such as protected person status or the internationality of the armed conflict provide the context in which the offence takes place, it is, we believe, artificial to suggest that the precise nature of the conflict or the technical status of the victim (i.e. classification as a protected person as opposed to a person taking no active part in hostilities) has any bearing on the accused's conduct. * * *
>
> We believe that taking into account such abstract elements creates the danger that the accused will also be convicted—with, as discussed, the penalty inherent in that conviction alone—in respect of additional crimes which have a distinct existence only as a purely legal and abstract matter, effectively through the historical accidents of the way in which international humanitarian law has developed in streams having distinct contextual requirements. * * *

> Under the "different elements" test as we believe it should be applied, only those elements relating to the conduct and mental state of the accused would be taken into account.

Id. at paras. 24–27, 33. They further reasoned that when there are multiple potential convictions to be entered, the tribunal should choose

> the crime which more specifically describes what the accused actually did in the circumstances of the particular case [given] the totality of the circumstances of the particular case and of the evidence given in relation to the crimes charged, in order to * * * arrive at the closest fit between the conduct and the provision violated. This would involve a consideration of all of the elements of the offences.

Id. at para. 37. Do you agree that this approach is preferable to the approach adopted by the ICTY, whereby all the elements of the charged offenses are considered when entering cumulative convictions? Do cumulative convictions better reflect the reality of the atrocities committed, or do they instead confuse the historical record? Does it matter?

5. Convicting Uncharged Crimes

When the evidence at trial reveals that additional crimes or more serious crimes may have been committed, should a defendant be convicted of an offense for which she or he was not charged? If so, is the defendant entitled to an amended indictment or a continuance to prepare a more specific defense? Some national courts are so empowered so long as the facts charged remain the same. For a discussion of several such national codes of criminal procedure, *see* Carsten Stahn, *Modification of the Legal Characterization of Facts in the ICC System: A Portrayal of Regulation 55*, 16 CRIM. L. FOR. 1 (2005). The European Court of Human Rights has upheld this practice in principle notwithstanding the right of criminal defendants to be informed of the charges against them. *See Case of Abramyan v. Russia*, Application No 10709/02, Eur. Ct. H.R., Judgment (Jan. 9, 2009) (finding a violation of petitioner's human rights where he was not fully informed of the nature of the charges against him or allowed adequate time to prepare his defense).

6. Regulation 55

The *Bemba* decision refers to the power of the ICC Chamber under Regulation 55 to change the legal characterization of the facts pursuant to the Court's regulations. Regulation 55 provides:

> Authority of the Chamber to modify the legal characterisation of facts
>
> 1. In its decision under article 74, the Chamber may change the legal characterisation of facts to accord with the crimes under articles 6, 7 or 8, or to accord with the form of participation of the accused under articles 25 and 28, without exceeding the facts and circumstances described in the charges and any amendments to the charges.

2. If, at any time during the trial, it appears to the Chamber that the legal characterisation of facts may be subject to change, the Chamber shall give notice to the participants of such a possibility and having heard the evidence, shall, at an appropriate stage of the proceedings, give the participants the opportunity to make oral or written submissions. The Chamber may suspend the hearing to ensure that the participants have adequate time and facilities for effective preparation or, if necessary, it may order a hearing to consider all matters relevant to the proposed change.

3. For the purposes of sub-regulation 2, the Chamber shall, in particular, ensure that the accused shall:

   (a) Have adequate time and facilities for the effective preparation of his or her defence in accordance with article 67, paragraph 1 (b); and

   (b) If necessary, be given the opportunity to examine again, or have examined again, a previous witness, to call a new witness or to present other evidence admissible under the Statute in accordance with article 67, paragraph 1 (e).

See Regulations of the Court, ICC–BD/01–02–07.

This has proven to be a controversial practice, as illustrated by the next case, which involves changing the mode of liability of an accused at a late stage in the proceedings. Germain Katanga surrendered to the Court in October 2007. His trial lasted almost three years (from November 2009 to May 2012). Upon the conclusion of the trial testimony and the submission of written arguments by the parties, the Trial Chamber informed the parties that, after examining the evidence, it was providing notice of a change in the legal characterization of facts related to Katanga's mode of participation to include complicity in the commission of a crime by a group of persons acting with a common purpose under Article 25(3)(d), in addition to indirect co-perpetration under Article 25(3)(a) as set out earlier in the confirmed charges. *Prosecutor v. Katanga and Chui*, Case No. ICC–01/04–01/07, Decision on the Implementation of Regulation 55 of the Regulations of the Court and Severing the Charges against the Accused Persons, para. 7 (Nov. 21, 2012). (Judge Christine van den Wyngaert (Belgium) dissented, arguing that such a change was not consistent with Regulation 55, and that it could not be implemented in a way that would not violate Katanga's right to a fair trial.)

This change in the legal characterization of the mode of liability did not apply to Katanga's co-accused, Mathieu Ngudjolo Chui, who in fact was acquitted of all charges and released from custody a month later. For a summary of the background facts of the cases, see Chapter 5 on the ICC. In the decision excerpted below, the Appeals Chamber held that changes in the legal characterization of the facts under Regulation 55 could occur as late as the deliberations stage of the proceedings so long as the trial remained fair.

Prosecutor v. Germain Katanga, Case No. ICC–01/04–01/07 OA 13, Judgment on the Appeal of Mr. Germain Katanga Against the Decision of Trial Chamber II of 21 November 2012 Entitled "Decision on the Implementation of Regulation 55 of the Regulations of the Court and Severing the Charges Against the Accused Persons" (March 27, 2013)

In the Appeals Chamber

10. * * * [T]he Appeals Chamber, in determining whether the Impugned Decision is materially affected by an error, will address the following essential questions that arise out of the arguments raised on appeal by Mr. Katanga, namely: whether the timing of the Impugned Decision (see below, section A) and the scope of the change in the legal characterisation of the facts that is envisaged (see below, section B) are in conformity with regulation 55 of the Regulations of the Court; and whether the Impugned Decision violates the rights of Mr. Katanga to a fair trial (see below, section C).

A. Timing of the Impugned Decision * * *

14. The Impugned Decision was rendered on 21 November 2012, after the Trial Chamber had begun its deliberations on Mr. Katanga's guilt or innocence. This was more than one year after the last evidence was presented (11 November 2011), and several months after the formal close of the evidence (7 February 2012) and the hearing of closing statements (15 to 23 May 2012). * * *

17. Pursuant to regulation 55(2) of the Regulations of the Court, notice of a possible re-characterisation may be given "at any time during the trial." The Appeals Chamber observes that, at the time the Impugned Decision was rendered, the trial was at the deliberations stage and that no decision under article 74 of the Statute had yet been rendered. Furthermore, nothing in the Statute, the Rules of Procedure and Evidence, or the Regulations of the Court prevents the Trial Chamber from re-opening the hearing of evidence at the deliberations stage of the proceedings. The Appeals Chamber therefore concludes that, for the purposes of regulation 55 of the Regulations of the Court, the trial is ongoing at the present time. The timing of the Impugned Decision was therefore not incompatible with regulation 55 of the Regulations of the Court.

18. The Appeals Chamber is not persuaded by Mr. Katanga's argument that there is an unspecified temporal limit as to when notice of a possible re-characterisation can be given by the Trial Chamber under regulation 55(2) of the Regulations of the Court, by reason of that provision's reference to the "appropriate stage of the proceedings." The Appeals Chamber considers, as was pointed out by the Prosecutor, that the reference to the "appropriate stage of the proceedings" relates to the

opportunity to be given to the participants to make oral or written submissions. In other words, the participants must be given an opportunity to make submissions at an appropriate stage of the proceedings, following notice of a possible re-characterisation, but this does not limit the Trial Chamber's power to give such notice "at any time during the trial."

19. As to Mr. Katanga's argument that the phrase "and having heard the evidence" within the first sentence of regulation 55(2) of the Regulations of the Court suggests that notice must be given before the conclusion of the evidence, the Appeals Chamber accepts that this is a possible reading of that sentence. However, for the reasons set out below, and having regard to the regulation as a whole, the Appeals Chamber is not persuaded by this argument.

20. First, as pointed out above, it is clear from the opening words of regulation 55(2) of the Regulations of the Court that the Trial Chamber can give notice "at any time during the trial."

21. Second, the interpretation put forward by Mr. Katanga is inconsistent with the purpose of the provision. The Appeals Chamber observes that changing the legal characterisation of the facts may become necessary not only in the course of the hearing of evidence as, for example, an immediate reaction thereto, but also thereafter. At that latter stage, the Trial Chamber may realise, upon carefully analysing the material and evidence that was presented in its totality, that the legal characterisation on the basis of which the charges were confirmed may be subject to change. That this may be necessary at the deliberations stage is particularly the case in light of the length, complexity and evidentially voluminous nature of the proceedings that come before this Court. As the Prosecutor correctly points out, if regulation 55 of the Regulations of the Court were inapplicable at the deliberations stage of the proceedings, the Trial Chamber would have to acquit the accused in such a situation, even if the evidence presented clearly established his or her guilt based upon the appropriate legal characterisation of the facts.

22. In this context, the Appeals Chamber recalls that it has previously held that "a principal purpose of Regulation 55 is to close accountability gaps, a purpose that is fully consistent with the Statute." The Appeals Chamber found that failing to permit a Trial Chamber to re-visit the legal characterisation that was confirmed by the Pre-Trial Chamber at the end of the confirmation procedure:

> bears the risk of acquittals that are merely the result of legal qualifications confirmed in the pre-trial phase that turn out to be incorrect, in particular based on the evidence presented at trial. This would be contrary to the aim of the Statute to "put an end to impunity" (fifth paragraph of the Preamble)

23. Third, the last sentence of regulation 55(2) of the Regulations of the Court provides that the Trial Chamber may, when considering a

possible change in the legal characterisation of facts and having given notice, either suspend the hearing or, "if necessary," "order a hearing to consider all matters relevant to the proposed change." The Appeals Chamber interprets this to mean that the hearing may be suspended to enable effective preparation if notice is given during a hearing; but that there is also provision for a hearing to be ordered "if necessary," which implies that notice can be given, *inter alia,* after the hearing of evidence has been concluded, such as at the deliberations stage.

24. The Appeals Chamber therefore concludes that, while it is preferable that notice under regulation 55(2) of the Regulations of the Court should always be given as early as possible, Mr. Katanga's argument that the timing of the Impugned Decision is incompatible with the terms of regulation 55(2) of the Regulations of the Court is not persuasive.

B. Scope of the Envisaged Change in the Legal Characterization of Facts * * *

26. In the Amended Document Containing the Charges, the Prosecutor alleged that Mr. Katanga and Mr. Ngudjolo, together with other Front for Patriotic Resistance in Ituri (FRPI, the group to which Mr. Katanga was alleged to belong) and Nationalist and Integrationist Front (FNI, the group to which Mr. Ngudjolo was alleged to belong) commanders, agreed on a common plan to carry out a joint attack to "wipe out" Bogoro. Mr. Katanga was alleged, in his capacity as military chief of the FRPI, to have made "an essential contribution to the common plan and the crimes it furthered," including by providing weapons to commanders of the FRPI and the FNI, overseeing and ensuring that the attack on Bogoro was executed by the FNI and FRPI forces in a coordinated and joint manner, communicating the details of the common plan to all FRPI and FNI commanders, and ordering subordinates to carry out the plan. It was alleged that Mr. Katanga and Mr. Ngudjolo, in contributing to the common plan, were aware of their essential roles, which gave them joint control over the implementation of the common plan and that they, "as well as the other co- perpetrators," were all mutually aware that implementing the common plan may result in the commission of the various crimes charged.

27. In the Decision on the Confirmation of Charges, it is mentioned that, even if the attack on Bogoro was intended to "target a military objective," it was also intended to be directed against the Hema civilian population. The section on the criminal responsibility of the suspects commenced with a detailed exposition of the Pre-Trial Chamber's interpretation of the notion of joint responsibility as a principal perpetrator under article 25(3)(a) of the Statute. The Pre-Trial Chamber then assessed whether there was sufficient evidence to establish substantial grounds to believe that Mr. Katanga and Mr. Ngudjolo were responsible for the crimes with which they were charged, by reference to each of the legal elements it had defined. The Pre-Trial Chamber found

that, at all material times, Mr. Katanga was the supreme commander of the FRPI and had *de facto* ultimate control over its commanders, that the FRPI was a hierarchically organised group, with FRPI commanders having the ability to communicate with each other, and that compliance with Mr. Katanga's orders was ensured. The Pre-Trial Chamber further considered that Mr. Katanga and Mr. Ngudjolo agreed upon a common plan to attack Bogoro and that Mr. Katanga made an essential contribution to the plan. More specifically, the Pre-Trial Chamber found, *inter alia,* that Mr. Katanga had responsibility for implementing the plan, including by ordering militias to "wipe out" Bogoro, distributing the plan of attack to commanders and distributing weapons and ammunition; and that Mr. Katanga had a coordinating role in implementing the common plan, including by having contacts with other participants in implementing the plan, and obtaining and distributing weapons and ammunition. The Decision on the Confirmation of Charges mentioned that other FRPI and FNI commanders were also involved in the planning and/or execution of the attack. The Pre-Trial Chamber, however, found that, without the agreement of Mr. Katanga and Mr. Ngudjolo on, and their participation in the implementation of, the common plan, the crimes would not have been committed as planned and concluded that Mr. Katanga and Mr. Ngudjolo implemented the plan in a coordinated manner and had "joint control over the implementation of the plan, insofar as their essential overall coordinating roles gave to them, and only to them, the power to frustrate the implementation of the plan." It was further alleged that Mr. Katanga and Mr. Ngudjolo "were aware of the factual circumstances enabling them to exercise joint control over the crimes" and that crimes would be committed in the implementation of the common plans. * * *

29. In the Impugned Decision, the Trial Chamber stated that, further to its receipt of "the written and oral summaries of the parties and participants," it noted that, "both during his testimony and his defence, Germain Katanga emphasised his contribution as coordinator of preparations for the attack on Bogoro while maintaining that its aim was to dislodge the Union of Congolese Patriots (UPC) and asserting that it had been carried out by a group of local combatants linked to the [Army of the Congolese People (APC)]." The Trial Chamber further noted that a number of witnesses called by both parties had also highlighted Mr. Katanga's "contribution to the attack, albeit in different terms." * * *

35. In respect of the subjective elements of liability under the proposed re-characterisation, the Trial Chamber recalled that Mr. Katanga had defended himself at the trial in relation to crimes committed in the attack on Bogoro by a group comprising commanders and combatants of the Walendu-Bindi *collectivité,* whose criminal intent had been assessed in the Decision on the Confirmation of Charges. The Trial Chamber was of the view that:

> The facts underlying Germain Katanga's knowledge of the alleged criminal intent of the group pursuant to article (25(3)(d)(ii)) are, in the Majority's view, necessarily included in the Pre-Trial Chamber's description, of the Accused's intent and the knowledge of the fact that the realisation of the crimes "would result in the implementation of the common plans" (25(3)(a)).

36. The Trial Chamber accepted that it was arguable that it was suggesting an amended narrative of the charges, by proposing to focus on certain facts to the exclusion of others, yet emphasised that it was "confining itself to proposing a different assessment of the facts" without amending the statement of facts set out in the Decision on the Confirmation of Charges. The Trial Chamber further stated that Mr. Katanga was able fully to express himself during the trial in relation to the facts that would form the basis for the re-characterisation and that he had already, during the course of his defence, addressed the majority of the factual and legal issues that arose under article 25(3)(d) of the Statute. * * *

39. Mr. Katanga * * * argues that his alleged role as a coordinator and his contribution to the plan to attack Bogoro by permitting the town of Aveba to be used for the transmission of weapons and troops "are clearly secondary to his alleged joint planning with Ngudjolo of this attack and his direct responsibility for its implementation." He argues that these are significantly different roles, with "the latter being the material role for the purposes of the existing charges." Mr. Katanga further argues that those who executed the crimes are now to be viewed as individuals who harboured a common plan to wipe out Bogoro, to which he contributed by facilitating preparations for the attack, as opposed to individuals who automatically complied with his orders and through whom he acted, also directly quoting a passage from the Dissenting Opinion in this respect. By reference to his role and that of the perpetrators of the crimes, Mr. Katanga argues that the proposed re-characterisation would "alter, in a fundamental way, the fabric of the story," thereby exceeding the facts and circumstances contained in the charges. He points out that this was also the view expressed in the Dissenting Opinion. Given the role attributed to him in the Decision Confirming the Charges, Mr. Katanga avers that changing his role "from that of an essential contribution to that of a significant but not necessarily essential contribution" alters the circumstances described in the charges.

40. Mr. Katanga submits that crucial facts are clearly missing from the charges in respect of article 25(3)(d) of the Statute as neither the group, nor its common purpose, were previously identified. Mr. Katanga argues that what the Trial Chamber proposes "is a categorical change" and that he would now have to move his attention from his alleged actions undertaken jointly with Mr. Ngudjolo to whether there were

"meetings between other groups in other places, who were there and what was discussed etc." He submits that there "is a risk of having to restart the whole trial process." * * *

46. [A]t this stage of the proceedings, the Appeals Chamber is not called upon to determine whether the legal characterisation of the facts actually can be changed from article 25(3)(a) of the Statute to article 25(3)(d) of the Statute without exceeding the facts and circumstances described in the charges. By issuing the Impugned Decision, the Trial Chamber has merely given notice pursuant to regulation 55(2) of the Regulations of the Court. The Appeals Chamber therefore has to review whether the Trial Chamber erred in relation to whether "it appears [. . .] that the legal characterisation of facts may be subject to change," pursuant to regulation 55(2) of the Regulations of the Court. Hence, the review that the Appeals Chamber can undertake at this stage of the proceedings is a limited one, in that the Impugned Decision would be erroneous only if it were immediately apparent to the Appeals Chamber, at this stage, that the change in the legal characterisation contemplated by the Trial Chamber would exceed the facts and circumstances described in the charges. * * *

50. The Appeals Chamber is not persuaded by Mr. Katanga's argument that, necessarily, only "material facts," but not "subsidiary or collateral facts" may be the subject of a change in the legal characterisation. There is no indication of any such limitation in the text of article 74(2) of the Statute or regulation 55(1) of the Regulations of the Court. Rather, those provisions stipulate that any change cannot exceed the "facts and circumstances." To the extent that Mr. Katanga relies on the *Lubanga* Judgment, where the Appeals Chamber indicated at footnote 163 that "facts" must be distinguished from the evidence put forward by the Prosecutor, as well as from background or other information contained in the document containing the charges or the decision confirming the charges, the Appeals Chamber notes that it did not determine in that judgment how narrowly or how broadly the term "facts and circumstances described in the charges" as a whole should be understood. The Appeals Chamber will not, in the abstract, address this matter any further.

51. The Appeals Chamber recalls that the contemplated change in the characterisation is from the form of participation charged (co-perpetration under article 25(3)(a) of the Statute) to contribution to the commission of a crime by a group acting with a common purpose under article 25(3)(d) of the Statute.

52. Article 25(3) of the Statute provides, in relevant part, as follows:

> In accordance with this Statute, a person shall be criminally responsible and liable for punishment for a crime within the jurisdiction of the Court if that person:

(a) Commits such a crime, whether as an individual, jointly with another or through another person, regardless of whether that other person is criminally responsible; [. . .]

(d) In any other way contributes to the commission or attempted commission of such a crime by a group of persons acting with a common purpose. Such contribution shall be intentional and shall either:

(i) Be made with the aim of furthering the criminal activity or criminal purpose of the group, where such activity or purpose involves the commission of a crime within the jurisdiction of the Court; or

(ii) Be made in the knowledge of the intention of the group to commit the crime;

53. Article 25(3)(d)(ii) of the Statute requires, on its face, that one or more crimes are committed by a group of persons, that this group acts with a common purpose, and that the accused intentionally contributes to the commission of the crime in the knowledge of the group's intention to commit the crime. * * *

56. Having reviewed the Impugned Decision in light of the documents describing the charges, the Appeals Chamber concludes that, at the present stage of the proceedings, it is not immediately apparent that the contemplated change in the legal characterisation of the facts would exceed the facts and circumstances described in the charges. The Appeals Chamber emphasises that, in reaching that conclusion, it is not expressing any view about the correct legal interpretation of article 25(3)(d) of the Statute. To do so would be premature at this stage of the proceedings. In this regard, the Appeals Chamber observes that the Trial Chamber expressly stated that it remained to be considered whether a common plan was required for the purposes of article 25(3)(d) of the Statute, and that it has requested submissions, *inter alia,* on the interpretation of article 25(3)(d) of the Statute.

57. The Appeals Chamber does, however, make the following further observations in relation to the arguments that Mr. Katanga has raised. The Appeals Chamber does not accept that it is obviously impermissible to re-characterise the facts so that the role of Mr. Katanga changes from, in his words, "that of an essential contribution to that of a significant but not necessarily essential contribution." Any change from, for example, being alleged to be a principal to being alleged to have in fact been an accessory will always necessarily involve a change in the characterisation of the role. Were such a change not to be permissible, it would defeat the purpose of regulation 55 of the Regulations of the Court. The Trial Chamber would be constrained exclusively to using the precise characterisations established by the Pre-Trial Chamber at a much earlier

stage of the proceedings and with a necessarily more restricted view of the case as a whole.

58. The Appeals Chamber also does not accept that a change in the narrative exceeds *per se* the facts and circumstances described in the charges. As pointed out by the Trial Chamber, focusing on certain facts to the exclusion of others will necessarily alter the narrative: indeed, it would appear inevitable that a change in characterisation would result in a change of narrative to a certain extent. Whether the change of narrative is of such an extent or nature that it does, in fact, exceed the facts or circumstances is something on which the Appeals Chamber will only be able to rule if and when the Trial Chamber has changed the legal characterisation in its decision under article 74 of the Statute.

Alleged Violations of Mr. Katanga's Fair Trial Rights * * *

67. Mr. Katanga submits that his right to be informed promptly of the charges and to have adequate time and facilities to prepare his defence is compromised because he a) should have been informed prior to the defence case, or in any event in a much more timely fashion, that there may be a change in the legal characterisation, b) his defence strategy, including his decision to testify, may have been different, had he known that the alleged form of participation may change, thereby infringing his right not to be compelled to testify.

68. In elaborating upon these arguments, Mr. Katanga avers that early notice of the charges determines the defence strategy in an adversarial trial: "what evidence to challenge, whether to call any evidence and, in particular, whether to testify." He argues, including by reference to views expressed in the Dissenting Opinion, that he did not anticipate that the charges "would be changed in this manner," and that he would have conducted his case significantly differently had he had early notice of the re-characterisation. He states that he would have "been contesting a different case"; that he may not have put forward a positive defence case and that it is unlikely that he would have given evidence. He further submits that the focus of the defence case could have been different. He avers that article 25(3)(d) of the Statute is not "a lesser included mode of liability" of article 25(3)(a) of the Statute as "[p]roof of an essential contribution to a common plan does not necessarily mean proof of a non-essential contribution to a crime" (footnote omitted). Mr. Katanga argues in addition that, at this late stage of the proceedings, he is "left in doubt as to the nature and extent of the charge it is proposed he faces": specifically, no Trial Chamber has yet defined the "unclear" form of participation provided for in article 25(3)(d) of the Statute—and that he will not now have the benefit of having its scope "raised, discussed and if necessary, reviewed in the Confirmation process." * * *

71. The Prosecutor generally argues that:

> Whether in fact prejudice will result cannot be determined at this stage. Rather, due to the limited scope of the Decision, these

arguments are premature. They are made in the abstract and are speculative as they overlook the range of measures that are available to the Chamber to ensure the fairness of the proceedings as well as other factors that are relevant for the assessment of any claim of unfairness.

72. The Prosecutor further submits that it was reasonably foreseeable to Mr. Katanga that notice to re-characterise the facts might be given. She submits that, in devising its strategy, the defence must bear the existence of regulation 55 of the Regulations of the Court in mind. She further submits that the re-characterisation now proposed would be, as said by the Trial Chamber, a "relatively limited step." * * *

Determination by the Appeals Chambers

86. The Appeals Chamber has had specific regard to, and emphasises the importance of, the rights of the accused to a fair trial, as detailed in article 67 of the Statute. The Appeals Chamber further underlines that, pursuant to article 21(3) of the Statute, the application and interpretation of the law of the Court "must be consistent with internationally recognized human rights."

87. The Appeals Chamber underscores that regulation 55(2) and (3) of the Regulations of the Court make specific provision, *inter alia,* for notice of a possible re-characterisation to be given to the parties and for the receipt of their submissions thereon, in particular ensuring that the accused has adequate time and facilities to prepare the defence in accordance with article 67(1)(b) of the Statute and has the opportunity to examine witnesses or to present other evidence in accordance with article 67(1)(e) of the Statute.

88. The Appeals Chamber further recalls that, in the *Lubanga* Judgment, it held that:

> [. . .] human rights law demands that the modification of the legal characterisation of facts in the course of the trial must not render that trial unfair. The Appeals Chamber notes in this context that article 67(1)(b) of the Statute provides for the right of the accused person to "have adequate time and facilities for the preparation of the defence." It is to avoid violations of this right that Regulation 55(2) and (3) set out several stringent safeguards for the protection of the rights of the accused. How these safeguards will have to be applied to protect the rights of the accused fully and whether additional safeguards must be implemented has not been fully considered in the context of the present appeal and will depend on the circumstances of the case. [Footnote omitted.]

89. The Appeals Chamber notes that, in the Impugned Decision, the Trial Chamber specifically considered the relevant rights of Mr. Katanga under article 67(1) of the Statute * * *, thereby making it clear that it was aware of the various rights that could potentially be violated in the

course of making a re-characterisation pursuant to regulation 55 of the Regulations of the Court. Furthermore, the Trial Chamber expressly took into account the protections guaranteed by regulation 55(2) and (3) of the Regulations of the Court by making specific provision for submissions to be made, including by Mr. Katanga in relation to those matters set out in regulation 55(3) of the Regulations of the Court.

90. The Appeals Chamber further emphasises that, when leave to appeal the Impugned Decision was granted, those submissions had not yet been received (and, considering that the proceedings have been in suspension thereafter, have still not been received). At the present stage of the proceedings, the Appeals Chamber is not called upon to, and cannot, rule on the measures that the Trial Chamber may take in the future to ensure the continued fairness of the proceedings, should the re-characterisation proceed.

91. In these circumstances, the Appeals Chamber cannot determine conclusively now whether the trial as a whole will remain fair if the re-characterisation proceeds. Whether it will depends to a large extent upon how the Trial Chamber conducts the further proceedings and, in particular, on the measures it will take to protect Mr. Katanga's rights. Nevertheless, the Appeals Chamber will briefly address the arguments of Mr. Katanga that the Impugned Decision has rendered the trial unfair. Any such assessment is without prejudice to any ruling that it may be called upon to make in the future as to whether the trial in fact remained fair, should the Trial Chamber proceed to re-characterise the facts in this case in its decision under article 74 of the Statute.

[The Appeals Chamber concludes this discussion by finding that, at this stage, the re-characterization of the facts does not violate Katanga's right to an effective defense, the right to be tried without undue delay, the right to be informed of the charges in detail, or the right to an impartial trial.]

NOTES & QUESTIONS

1. Case Outcome

Katanga was the first ICC accused to take the stand in his own defense. Katanga tried to argue that the attack on Bogoro was the responsibility of regional parties (Uganda and Rwanda) or other local militias, such as the Union of Congolese Patriots (UPC), led by ICC defendant Thomas Lubanga-Dyilo. Nonetheless, the Trial Chamber issued its judgment on March 7, 2014, finding Katanga guilty under Article 25(3)(d) of crimes against humanity (murder) and war crimes (murder, attacking a civilian population, destruction of property, and pillaging). On May 23, 2014, Katanga was sentenced to twelve years in prison, from which time was deducted for his period in detention from September 18, 2007, to May 23, 2014. While both the Prosecutor and the Defence initially appealed the judgment, both appeals were discontinued on June 25, 2014. The judgment is now final.

2. Dissent

Judge Cuno Tarfusser (Italy) dissented from the above decision, arguing that Regulation 55 did not apply to changes of the kind contemplated here (from indirect co-perpetration under Article 25(3)(a) to contribution to a crime committed by a group acting with a common purpose under Article 25(3)(d)). He also concluded that the re-characterization at this late stage violated Katanga's right to be informed in detail of the nature, cause and content of the charges as set out in Article 67(1). The recharacterization of the facts generated a good deal of criticism and academic debate. For a thoughtful discussion of the issues raised by Regulation 55 in the *Katanga* case among others, *see* the following web post: Jennifer Easterday, *A Closer Look at Regulation 55 at the ICC*, INT'L JUST. MONITOR (May 28, 2013).

3. Sources of Authority Before the ICC

Part of the controversy around Regulation 55 concerns the fact that it is a regulation rather than a statutory provision. Article 52 of the ICC Statute empowers the judges to adopt regulations for the "routine functioning" of the Court. As in any administrative law system, regulations cannot be inconsistent with the statutory scheme under which they are promulgated.

The Appeals Chamber addresses the compatibility of Regulation 55 with the fair trial rights found in Article 67(1) of the Rome Statute. Consider also Article 61(9), which provides:

> After the charges are confirmed and before the trial has begun, the Prosecutor may, with the permission of the Pre-Trial Chamber and after notice to the accused, amend the charges. If the Prosecutor seeks to add additional charges or to substitute more serious charges, a hearing under this article to confirm those charges must be held. After commencement of the trial, the Prosecutor may, with the permission of the Trial Chamber, withdraw the charges.

Does this provision suggest that any changes to the charges must come from the Prosecutor, and then be subject to review by the appropriate Pre-Trial or Trial Chamber, rather than initiated by the Chamber itself? What other provisions of the Rome Statute are in tension with Regulation 55? For a discussion of the origins and function of Regulation 55, *see* Carsten Stahn, *Modification of the Legal Characterization of Facts in the ICC System: A Portrayal of Regulation 55*, 16 CRIM. L. FOR. 1 (2005).

4. Defense Strategy and Right to a Fair Trial

How does the possibility of the recharacterization of the facts at such a late stage of the proceedings affect defense strategy? The Trial Chamber decided to change the legal characterization of the facts after, and in part based upon, testimony given by the defendant himself. Does this use of the defendant's testimony concerning a mode of liability for which he was not originally charged violate his right against self-incrimination (Article 67(1)(g) of the Rome Statute)? The Trial Chamber in fact addressed this concern, arguing that Katanga freely chose to testify and there were no suggestions that he had been subjected to any pressure or duress to do so. It reasoned:

> 52. Arguably, the Accused might have expressed himself differently had he known beforehand that his statements would be used under article 25(3)(d). However, it should be recalled once again that Germain Katanga elected of his own free will to testify, that he expressed himself freely and that he answered the questions put to him equally freely, with his counsel ever at his side. It should also be recalled that the parties to the case at bar were fully aware of the existence of regulation 55 insofar as, firstly, it was mentioned in the aforementioned 21 October 2009 Decision on the Filing of a Summary of the Charges by the Prosecutor and, secondly, it was the subject of filings made in anticipation, among other things, of a possible application on the nature of the armed conflict. Finally, the Appeals Chamber stipulated the conditions of its application in its public judgment of 8 December 2009 in Lubanga. Moreover, as has been amply demonstrated above, it is worth recalling that the application of regulation 8(2) and 8(3) affords Germain Katanga the opportunity to make any submissions he considers necessary on the proposed recharacterisation and on points of law and fact as well as, among other things, to provide any clarifications he wishes regarding statements he has made.

Do you find the Trial Chamber's reasoning compelling? For a discussion, *see* Margaux Dastugue, Note, *The Faults in "Fair" Trials: An Evaluation of Regulation 55 at the International Criminal Court*, 48 VAND. J. TRANSNAT'L L. 273 (2015).

5. Regulation 55 and Victims

In July 2009, and pursuant to a mid-trial request from the legal representatives of the victims, an ICC Trial Chamber gave notice to the parties and participants that the legal characterization of the facts may be subject to change in the *Lubanga* case. *Prosecutor v. Lubanga*, Decision Giving Notice To The Parties And Participants That The Legal Characterisation Of The Facts May Be Subject To Change In Accordance With Regulation 55(2) of the Regulations of the Court, Case No. ICC–01/04–01/06–2049 (July 14, 2009). (See Chapters 6, 15, and 18 for more on the *Lubanga* case.) In particular, the victims wanted the Chamber to re-characterize the facts described in the charges and the evidence adduced at trial as "sexual slavery" as a crime against humanity and a war crime and as the war crimes of inhuman (8(2)(a)(ii)) and cruel treatment (8(2)(c)(i)).

Not surprisingly, the Defence opposed the request, arguing that the facts relied upon by the victims exceeded the framework of facts described in the charges, which did not allege the existence of a widespread or systematic attack against a civilian population, the commission of sexual violence, or the imposition of pain or suffering other than a reference to the strict discipline accorded to child soldiers. The Defence further argued that the war crimes charges concerning the enlistment of child soldiers do not implicitly include sexual violence charges. The Defence warned that allowing the proposed re-characterization would prejudice the Article 61 rights of the accused to be informed of the charges against them, to have adequate time to prepare their defense, and to be tried without undue delay. Judge Adrian

Fulford (United Kingdom) dissented, arguing that absent a withdrawal of charges by the Prosecution, only the Pre-Trial Chamber can affect any changes to the charges pursuant to Article 61(9). *Prosecutor v. Lubanga*, Case No. ICC–01/04–01/06–2054, Minority Opinion On The 'Decision Giving Notice To The Parties And Participants That The Legal Characterisation of Facts May Be Subject To Change In Accordance With Regulation 55(2) of The Regulations of The Court' (July 17, 2009).

The Appeals Chamber reversed the Trial Chamber's attempt to change the legal characterization of the facts to incorporate the crime of sexual slavery and other uncharged crimes. In particular, the Appeals Chamber disagreed with the Trial Chamber's assertion that it could consider additional facts introduced into trial through a change of their legal characterization under Regulation 55, as this would be in conflict with Article 74(2) of the Statute, which provides that "The decision [of the Trial Chamber at the end of the trial] shall not exceed the facts and circumstances described in the charges and any amendments to the charges." *Prosecutor v. Lubanga*, Case No. ICC–01/04–01/06 OA 15 OA 16, Judgment on the appeals of Mr. Lubanga Dyilo and the Prosecutor against the Decision of Trial Chamber I of 14 July 2009 entitled "Decision giving notice to the parties and participants that the legal characterisation of the facts may be subject to change in accordance with Regulation 55(2) of the Regulations of the Court" (Dec. 8, 2009). Does this development affect your view of which approach to cumulative charging is better, that of the ICC or the ICTY?

6. Changes to Modes of Responsibility at the ICTY

The issue of changing modes of responsibility of an accused is not unique to the ICC. While the ICTY rejected the ability to reclassify the substantive offense, it ruled that it could reclassify the form of responsibility (e.g., the entering of a conviction for complicity rather than direct commission). Consider this holding:

> Since the Prosecution has not charged any specific head of criminal responsibility under Article 7(1) of the Statute, it is within the discretion of the Trial Chamber to convict the Accused under the appropriate head within the limits of the Indictment and fair notice of the charges and insofar as the evidence permits. * * * The Prosecution "also, or alternatively" alleges that General Krstić incurs "command responsibility" for the crimes charged in the Indictment pursuant to Article 7(3) of the Statute. * * * The facts pertaining to the commission of a crime may establish that the requirements for criminal responsibility under both Article 7(1) and Article 7(3) are met. However, the Trial Chamber adheres to the belief that where a commander participates in the commission of a crime *through his subordinates*, by "planning," "instigating" or "ordering" the commission of the crime, any responsibility under Article 7(3) is subsumed under Article 7(1). The same applies to the commander who incurs criminal responsibility under the joint criminal enterprise doctrine through the physical acts of his subordinates.

Prosecutor v. Krstić, Case No. IT–98–33–T, Judgement, paras. 602–5 (Aug. 2, 2001). Is there a domestic equivalent to this practice?

7. Charging v. Sentencing

Does any of this matter, so long as the sentence is adjusted to assure that the accused is not being penalized more than once in relation to the underlying conduct? That said, how should the various forms of cumulative charging impact sentencing? Should a defendant be sentenced on the basis of the underlying conduct or the ultimate legal characterization? When should an individual's sentence run consecutively versus concurrently?

8. *Concursus Delictorum* in International Criminal Law

Criminal law doctrine recognizes two forms of concurrence. The first is real or true concurrence (*concours idéal*), which occurs when the same conduct by the accused fulfils multiple distinct offenses. The second is apparent or false concurrence (*concours apparent*), which occurs when one offense is completely subsumed within another. Why has international criminal law developed with such a high degree of overlap of offenses? How does this compare with the domestic criminal law system? Does the *Blockburger* test translate well into international criminal law? In international criminal law, the offenses are often distinguished by their *chapeau* elements rather than by the core elements of the crimes. The underlying predicate offenses (e.g., murder, torture, unlawful detention) are often the same or similar.

PROBLEMS

1. Charging War Crimes and Crimes Against Humanity

A civil war has broken out in a country pitting the government against two loosely affiliated rebel groups vying for the support of the civilian population. The belligerents are roughly associated with different ethnic groups, although the conflict is more political than ethnic in nature. Once the conflict erupted, the national military enlisted local civilian defense forces to operate as vigilantes of sorts alongside the regular police forces to help protect communities against attacks by the rebels and to collect intelligence about where the rebels had obtained traction within the country. These defense forces were encouraged to increase their numbers through recruitment and initiation drives and to participate in government-organized military training, which included training in the law of war. The government distributed some arms to the defense forces and passed a law allowing them to carry and use weapons in defense. In particular operations, the military often engaged the rebels side-by-side with the defense forces. After each deployment, the defense forces would return to their respective communities.

In the beginning of the civil war, the rebels were largely billeted far from the capital city. They occasionally made incursions closer to the capital to attack and pillage areas considered to be loyal to the government. In these raids, the rebels stole weapons and food and generally destroyed the civilian infrastructure. Civilians who did not remain under cover were often killed or wounded in these attacks. At a certain point, the conflict escalated. The rebels began pushing closer and closer toward the capital before retreating. Finally, defense forces in the field reported to the central government that rebels had occupied a medium-sized town in a region bordering the capital city. In so doing, the rebels killed a number of police officers considered loyal to the local government. The central government immediately dispatched an army battalion to a nearby town as a base of operations.

On August 14, 2010, the government and defense forces launched a joint attack on the town occupied by the rebels in an attempt to re-take it and re-assert governmental control. A battle ensued over several days, pitting rebels against the joint government forces. Dozens of civilians fleeing the battle or taking cover were killed or injured in the crossfire. The government eventually pushed the rebel forces out of the town and destroyed a rebel encampment on the outskirts of the town. The rebels disbursed into the surrounding forest. The joint government forces then occupied the town and sent bands of soldiers and defense forces around town to root out any remaining rebels. In their house-to-house raids, these forces discovered a number of individuals whom they suspected of collaboration with the rebels by virtue of their possession of weapons, military boots, rebel ideological tracts or paraphernalia, or of their proximity to the rebel encampment. These presumed collaborators were tortured for information about the rebels and then executed. Their homes were looted and then destroyed. A number of civilians attempting to flee the town to the south were stopped by government forces. The soldiers told the captured civilians to identify any rebels amongst them. The individuals so identified were shot. Individuals who admitted to, or who were identified as, having engaged in commerce or otherwise aided the rebels were also killed.

The rebels eventually regrouped outside of the town. They managed to capture a unit of government troops and defense forces who had been patrolling the outskirts of the town. The rebels took the detainees to a makeshift rebel camp, where the captives were tortured for information about the strength and location of government forces in the region and the identities of members of the defense forces in nearby towns. The soldiers were then killed and their heads were placed on stakes outside the town.

In the crime base described above, which acts of violence could be charged as crimes against humanity? If such acts do not constitute crimes against humanity, are there other charges available under international criminal law? If you were representing the prosecution or defense in a subsequent prosecution of government forces, defense forces, or rebels, how would you argue the applicability of the prohibition against crimes against humanity to these facts? Are there circumstances in which proving crimes against humanity will be easier against state actors as opposed to non-state actors?

2. Extermination and Genocide

Review the Darfur problem in Chapter 9 on Genocide. Imagine that the ICC has charged a high-level defendant from the Government of Sudan in connection with international crimes committed in Darfur. The defendant was a Major General in the Sudanese Army in charge of the western region.

He was accused of orchestrating air and ground attacks against the civilian population in Darfur. The Indictment charged the defendant with Genocide, Crimes Against Humanity (extermination), and Crimes Against Humanity (murder) in connection with these allegations, and the Trial Chamber entered a conviction on all three counts with a concurrent sentence of thirty years total. The Prosecution led the same evidence to prove each of these offenses. You are defense counsel. Construct an argument for the Appeals Chamber as to why cumulative charging and conviction should not have been allowed in this case.

PART IV

INDIVIDUAL CRIMINAL RESPONSIBILITY FOR INTERNATIONAL CRIMES

> "Crimes against international law are committed by men, not by abstract entities, and only by punishing individuals who commit such crimes can the provisions of international law be enforced."

So wrote the Nuremberg Tribunal in its historic judgment. Modern international criminal law is premised on individual—as opposed to state or collective—responsibility. This focus was not inevitable. Most early manifestations of what we now consider international criminal law involved state (civil) responsibility. In addition, and as will be discussed more fully in Chapter 15, *infra*, the drafters of the Nuremberg Charter designed a regime of collective responsibility in an effort to respond to the massive and systematic nature of the Nazi crimes and account for the involvement of thousands of rank-and-file party members. This experiment in collective justice proved to be short-lived, and modern international criminal law efforts have by and large mirrored the domestic criminal law model of ascribing individual criminal responsibility.

In this part, we discuss various ways in which an individual can be held responsible for the commission of international crimes. Some forms and theories of responsibility employed in international criminal law—like complicity and incitement—trace their origins to familiar domestic law principles. Other forms of responsibility—like superior responsibility—developed within military law or international criminal law. Accessorial and other forms of liability that ascribe responsibility based upon the defendant's relationship or association with others have become increasingly important in international criminal law, because the crimes in question often involve the participation of multiple individuals over vast distances of time and space. As one commentator has noted:

> Recourse to generous—and at times somewhat vicarious—liability theories becomes eminently understandable insofar as these theories permit the tribunals to ascribe individual guilt in cases where violence has several, and often murky, organic sources.

Mark A. Drumbl, *Pluralizing International Criminal Justice*, 99 MICH. L. REV. 1295, 1309 (2005). In addition, where a state or organization is involved at various stages of the crime, there may be some individuals designing and orchestrating an international crime and others actually carrying it out.

As you know from your courses in criminal law, there are multiple ways in which individuals can be held individually, jointly, and vicariously liable for the commission of crimes. These liability theories may be principal or accessorial. Thus, a defendant can be found directly liable if she committed, planned, co-perpetrated, or ordered a crime. Likewise, she may be culpable if she instigated, incited, aided and abetted, or was otherwise complicit in a crime. It is well established that domestic criminal law recognizes various forms of complicity liability during the life of a crime, including the concepts of accessory before- and after-the-fact. Conspiracy doctrines are less common. Under expansive forms of conspiracy liability found in the United States and elsewhere, a person may be found liable not only for the commission of crimes that were the object of the conspiracy, but also for the commission of unintended crimes executed by co-conspirators, so long as those crimes were reasonably foreseeable in the execution of the conspiracy. Many of these forms of liability inevitably involve two or more perpetrators: the direct perpetrators (who personally commit the crime and are directly liable) and the accessories (who are responsible for making substantial contributions to the commission of the crime). This designation may or may not be relevant for sentencing purposes. United States law, for example, contains an expansive definition of principal: 18 U.S.C. § 2 considers individuals who participate in the commission of a crime via various forms of complicity to be a principal to the offense. To a certain extent, all these forms of liability exist in international criminal law as well.

An important form of responsibility in international criminal law is superior (or command) responsibility. This doctrine originated in international humanitarian law, although it is often invoked in domestic military justice proceedings and has domestic analogs in doctrines of *respondeat superior*. With the movement around the codification of international crimes occasioned by the ICC ratification process, many domestic systems now allow prosecutors to charge this form of liability in civilian courts. Generally—but not exclusively—considered a form of accessorial liability, the doctrine of superior responsibility provides that a superior may be liable for the criminal acts of a subordinate if the superior knew (or should have known) of those acts and failed to fulfill a duty to prevent or punish them.

In addition to these forms of liability that assume the commission of a crime, many domestic criminal law systems also recognize forms of inchoate liability (conspiracy, solicitation, and attempt) whereby an individual may be criminally liable for acts that precede the commission of an object crime. Facilitation doctrines, which ascribe liability where an individual knowingly provides general assistance to groups or individuals who intend to commit some future crime, reach even farther. The line between these various forms of participation and theories of responsibility is not always a sharp one. The Rome Statute also contains forms of responsibility that may be less familiar to a common law lawyer, such as the many permutations of co-perpetration.

A number of these doctrines find expression in multilateral treaties. For example, the Genocide Convention at Article III states that individuals shall be punished for conspiracy to commit genocide, direct and public incitement to commit genocide, and attempt to commit genocide (whether or not genocide is actually committed), in addition to the direct commission of genocide and acts of complicity therein. Likewise, the Torture Convention at Article 4(1) obliges states to punish attempts to commit torture and complicity (or "participation") in torture. Superior responsibility first found treaty expression in Protocol I to the Geneva Conventions at Article 86(2), which states:

> The fact that a breach of the Conventions or of this Protocol was committed by a subordinate does not absolve his superiors from penal or disciplinary responsibility, as the case may be if they knew, or had information which would have enabled them to conclude in the circumstances at the time, that he was committing or was going to commit such a breach and if they did not take all feasible measures within their power to prevent or repress the breach.

Protocol Additional to the Geneva Conventions of 12 August 1949 and Relating to the Protection of Victims of International Armed Conflicts, Dec. 12, 1977, 1125 U.N.T.S. 3 (Protocol I). The U.N. Security Council later codified the doctrine of superior responsibility in the statutes of the *ad hoc* war crimes tribunals; it also finds expression in the ICC Statute. *See, e.g.*, Article 7(3) of the ICTY Statute, Article 6(3) of the ICTR Statute, and Article 28 of the ICC Statute. Some of the terrorism treaties allow for the prosecution of individuals who contribute to the commission of terrorist offenses by a group of persons acting with a common purpose. *See, e.g.,* Article 2 of the International Convention for the Suppression of Terrorist Bombing, G.A. Res. 164, U.N. GAOR, 52nd Sess., Supp. No. 49, at 389, U.N. Doc. A/52/49 (1998).

Although these treaties identify applicable forms and theories of responsibility, they provide little in the way of concrete standards for determining when the participation of an individual in the principal crime rises to the level of complicity, conspiracy, co-perpetration, or attempt. For this, the modern international criminal tribunals have had to rely upon national law traditions and World War II precedents to identify more precise standards of liability. The result is a veritable international common law of individual criminal responsibility. As you read the materials that follow, consider whether the standards of liability being developed in international criminal law are consistent with domestic criminal law. Where international criminal law departs from domestic law, ask yourself whether this distinction is attributable to something special about international criminal law and whether judges are adequately explaining the divergence. In particular, pay special attention to whether international criminal law judges are departing too far from the principle of individual criminal responsibility, a fundamental precept of the penal law, as they develop doctrines of criminal responsibility. You might also consider whether the focus of international criminal law on individual actions and motivations is overly reductionist and has hindered the development of viable theories of collective responsibility (including concepts of state or corporate responsibility) in the face of collective violence.

CHAPTER 14

THE RESPONSIBILITY OF SUPERIORS

I. INTRODUCTION

Military or civilian superiors are rarely on the battlefield or in detention centers committing international crimes. Yet, many argue that international criminal tribunals should focus on the leaders and architects of international crimes. While the statutes of the *ad hoc* tribunals did not initially specify whether the focus should be on superiors or subordinates, the tribunals' Security Council-mandated Completion Strategies required them to concentrate their prosecutorial efforts on the senior leaders who were deemed "most responsible" for the crimes within their jurisdiction. As we noted in Chapter 2, this focus is expressly mandated in the statutes of other tribunals; the Cambodian tribunal, for example, is directed to prosecute "senior leaders" and "those most responsible" for the crimes within its jurisdiction. The ICC Statute, by contrast, does not take this approach, but instead speaks of "the most serious crimes," rather than those individuals who are most responsible. Nevertheless, there is a general acceptance that international tribunals should focus on leaders rather than subordinates. Do you agree that preference should always be given to prosecuting superiors over those subordinates who, in many cases, "pulled the trigger?"

Superiors can be held liable for the criminal acts of their subordinates through several distinct modes of liability. Two will be considered here: the ordering of subordinates to commit offenses and the failure to prevent abuses or to punish subordinates who have committed abuses. Other applicable forms of liability derived from doctrines of co-perpetration, complicity, and conspiracy that may reach leaders will be addressed in the next chapters.

Individuals who order a crime to be committed are individually culpable if the order achieves its purpose. Ordering the commission of a crime is thus a form of direct, rather than vicarious, liability. Superior responsibility attaches if the defendant had actual or constructive knowledge that his subordinates were committing abuses and he did not take necessary and reasonable measures to prevent these abuses or to punish the perpetrators. The theory of liability is thus premised on the commander's failure to exercise powers of command and control over subordinates in the face of a duty to act. Although originally developed in the military context, the doctrine of superior responsibility applies to both military and civilian superiors. These two doctrines are considered in greater detail below.

II. ORDERING OFFENSES

In order to understand the distinction between ordering offenses and being liable for offenses pursuant to the doctrine of command responsibility, consider the case against General Tihomir Blaškić. With respect to coordinated attacks on the villages of Ahmići, Šantići, Pirići, and Nadioci by Bosnian Croat forces, the Prosecution indicted General Blaškić on two theories of liability: the theory of superior responsibility and for ordering the underlying crimes. By way of background, the Croatian Community of Herzeg-Bosna ("HZHB") proclaimed its existence on November 18, 1991 as a separate or distinct "political, cultural, economic and territorial whole" within the borders of Bosnia-Herzegovina. It aimed to establish closer ties and eventually accession with Croatia, as evidenced by the use by many in HZHB of Croatian currency and the Croatian dialect. These aspirations were supported by Croatia, which granted automatic Croatian citizenship to Bosnian Croats. The Constitutional Court of Bosnia-Herzegovina declared the HZHB illegal on September 14, 1992, and HZHB was never internationally recognized. And yet, HZHB purported to imbue all executive, administrative, and defensive authority within the Croatian Defense Council ("HVO"). The events giving rise to the case concern the conflict between HVO forces and the official Bosnian Army ("ABiH") in the Lašva Valley of Central Bosnia.

General Blaškić was appointed commander of the HVO armed forces headquarters in central Bosnia on June 27, 1992. The Prosecution indicted General Blaškić on twenty counts, including grave breaches of the Geneva Conventions, violations of the laws and customs of war, and crimes against humanity. *Prosecutor v. Blaškić*, Case No. IT–95–14, Second Amended Indictment (April 25, 1997). The crimes alleged in the Indictment were purportedly committed in the context of "serious violations of international humanitarian law against Bosnian Muslims" by members of the armed forces of the Croatian Defence Council between May 1992 and January 1994 in various municipalities in Bosnia-Herzegovina, including the villages of Ahmići, Šantići, Pirići, and Nadioci. According to the last official census taken in 1991, the municipality had 27,859 inhabitants, made up of 45.5% Croats, 5.4% Serbs, 41.3% Muslims and 2.8% other nationalities. These attacks were purportedly part of an effort to create a Greater Croatia involving areas within Bosnia-Herzegovina with Croatian majorities.

Pursuant to Article 7(1) of the Statute, General Blaškić was accused of having, in concert with members of the HVO, planned, instigated, ordered, or otherwise aided and abetted in the planning, preparation, or execution of each of the crimes alleged. The Trial Chamber agreed with the Prosecution's theory that defendant ordered the crimes charged. At issue in particular was an order submitted into evidence by the defense (designated D269), which was described as follows:

> 435. A third order [D269], which again referred to "planned terrorist activities" on the part of the enemy and to the risk of its engaging in an open offensive designed to destroy everything Croatian, was given on 16 April at 01:30 hours and addressed to the Viteška brigade and to the Tvrtko independent units. That "combat command order to prevent attack activity by the enemy" ordered Commander Čerkez and the Tvrtko independent units "to occupy the defence region, blockade villages and prevent all entrances to and exits from the villages." The order stated that "in the event of open attack activity by the Muslims," those units should "neutralize them and prevent their movement with precise fire" in counterattack. That order indicated that the forces of the Military Police Fourth Battalion, the N.Š. Zrinski unit and the civilian police would also take part in the combat. The order required the forces to be ready to open fire at 05:30 hours and, by way of combat formation, provided for blockade (observation and ambush), search and attack forces. General Blaškić stated in that order that "the commander of the Vitez HVO brigade, Mario Čerkez, is personally responsible to me for the performance of this mission." The order closed by saying that the "instruction given previously [should be] complied with," although the Trial Chamber was not able to establish what that instruction was.

The Trial Chamber interpreted this order as an order to attack the villages:

> 437. The Trial Chamber finds that the third order [D269], dated 16 April at 01:30 hours is very clearly an order to attack. That order, which was addressed in particular to the Viteška brigade, also expressly mentions other units, such as the Military Police Fourth Battalion, the forces of the N.Š. Zrinski unit and the forces of the civilian police which were recognised on the ground as being those which had carried out the attack. The time to commence hostilities which is set out in that order corresponds very precisely to the start of fighting on the ground. Admittedly, the order is presented as "a combat command order to prevent attack activity by the enemy." Accordingly, the attack purportedly formed part of a defensive rather than offensive strategy. However the Trial Chamber has already concluded that no military objective justified that attack. It is therefore unnecessary here to go back over the reasons given for the issue of that order, which, in any event, remains an order to attack. The Trial Chamber considers that that evidence sufficed to show that all those troops, acting in concert, attacked on the accused's order. * * *

> 470. The Trial Chamber further notes that those orders recommend the modes of combat that were actually used on the ground on 16 April. In this way, order D268 stresses co-ordination among the different units. It also asks the forces to take care to ensure that they have total control over fuel consumption, which was one of the main weapons used by the Croatian forces during the attack on 16 April. It is hard to image how the systematic use of petrol as a combat weapon could have been possible in that period of fuel shortage without the approval of the military and/or civilian authorities. Order D269 refers to blocking (observation and ambush), search and offensive forces. The main (mountain and valley) roads between Vitez and Zenica were in fact blocked by HVO blocking forces on the morning of 16 April, in particular by the Viteška brigade. According to witness Landry, the area was subjected to a so-called "cleansing" operation, which was carried out by establishing a cordon outside the village by means of check points on the roads leading to the villages, whilst lighter, more mobile troops, notably search troops, carried out the "cleansing" of the village. * * *
>
> 472. The testimony of the victims of the massacres tended to show that the civilians were killed in response to orders. Accordingly, witness Fatima Ahmic testified that she heard an HVO soldier in a van say by walkie-talkie: "Yes, the operation was successful, they are lying in front of houses like pigs." When she asked them why they had killed her son, the soldiers said that "it was the *force majeure* who ordered it . . . the orders came from above." Witness Abdullah Ahmic testified that he saw a soldier say to another soldier who refused to kill a man: "do as you are ordered." Witness Cazim Ahmic testified to what an officer, Ibrica Kupreškić, said to him: "go and run for your life. No Muslim may stay here. If they learn that I let you go, I will be executed." According to witness F, the Dzokeri and the Vitezovi said that they had been given orders to kill all the Muslims so that Muslims would never ever live there again. Witness A said that he heard a person named Cicko speak in these terms with regard to the events of 16 April: "everyone is washing their hands now as regards Ahmići, but we all know that Blaškić has ordered that no prisoners of war were of interest to him, only dead bodies."

The Trial Chamber also determined that even if the order could not be interpreted as an attack order, the defendant was nonetheless reckless in issuing the order he did:

> 474. Even if doubt were still cast in spite of everything on whether the accused ordered the attack with the clear intention that the massacre would be committed, he would still be liable

> under Article 7(1) of the Statute for ordering the crimes. [A]ny person who, in ordering an act, knows that there is a risk of crimes being committed and accepts that risk, shows the degree of intention necessary (recklessness) so as to incur responsibility for having ordered, planned or incited the commitment of the crimes. In this case, the accused knew that the troops which he had used to carry out the order of attack of 16 April had previously been guilty of many crimes against the Muslim population of Bosnia. The order given by the accused on 4 November 1992 expressly prohibiting the troops from burning the houses proves this. Moreover, the accused admitted before the Trial Chamber that he had been informed about the crimes committed by troops acting in the area for which he was responsible. In particular, the disciplinary reports were forwarded to him. Likewise, the accused stated that he asked the Commander of the main general staff and the head of the Defence Department in January 1993 that the independent units be withdrawn from the Central Bosnia Operative Zone on account of the troubles they were causing. Furthermore, the accused was aware that there were criminals acting in the ranks of the Military Police. Witness Marin, who was a subordinate of the accused at the time, himself acknowledged that there were criminals in the ranks of the Military Police. Admittedly, the accused did give an order on 18 January 1993 for the attention of the regular units of the HVO, the independent units and the Military Police Fourth Battalion instructing them to make sure that all soldiers prone to criminal conduct were not in a position to do any harm. However, that order remained without effect, even though the accused issued a reminder on 6 February 1993. On the contrary, according to the witness Marin the situation deteriorated thereafter. The Defence also presented an order issued by the accused on 17 March 1993 requiring the commanders of all HVO brigades to identify their members who were prone to criminal conduct. Nevertheless, the Trial Chamber finds that the accused did not ensure himself, before calling on their services on 16 April, that measures had indeed been taken so as to be sure that those criminal elements were not in a position to do any harm. On the contrary, according to the accused it was not until he received the letter from Colonel Stewart [commander of the British battalion of the U.N. forces] on 22 April 1993 that he realised that he could not rely on the reports sent to him by the Military Police commander Ljubišcić. It was not until 30 April that the accused asked the commander of the main staff to replace Paško Ljubišcić and to change the structure of that unit. * * *

The Trial Chamber thus concluded that "[i]n the final analysis, the Trial Chamber is convinced that General Blaškić ordered the attacks that gave rise to these crimes. In any event, it is clear that he never took any reasonable measure to prevent the crimes being committed or to punish those responsible for them." *Prosecutor v. Blaškić*, Case No. IT–95–14–T, Judgement, para. 495 (March 3, 2000).

The Appeals Chamber opinion follows:

Prosecutor v. Blaškić, Case No. IT–95–14–A, Judgement (July 29, 2004)

In the Appeals Chamber

Whether there was Circumstantial Evidence that the Appellant Ordered the Commission of the Crimes

309. The Appellant submits that the Trial Chamber committed four errors in convicting him in the absence of direct evidence concerning the crimes in Ahmići. First, the Trial Chamber erroneously concluded that D269 was an order directing attacks against Muslim civilians in Ahmići. Second, the finding of the Trial Chamber, not disputed by the Appellant, that the attack on Ahmići was planned and organised, does not mean that it was planned or organised by him, as found by the Trial Chamber. Further, the Trial Chamber relied on the testimony of one witness without supporting evidence to find that the Appellant ordered the crimes in question on the basis of the "scale and uniformity" of the attack and the crimes. Third, the Trial Chamber erroneously found the Appellant responsible for the crimes in question by presuming that the orders in the period from 1 May 1992 to 31 January 1994, which were not presented to the Trial Chamber, must have directed the crimes. Fourth, he claims that the Trial Chamber erred in finding that the Viteška Brigade participated in the crimes in question and that the Military Police was under the effective control of the Appellant.

310. The Prosecution submits that: (i) the finding that D269 was not a defensive order was reasonable, as the trial evidence showed that there was no significant ABiH presence in the area proximate to Ahmići and there was no justification for the extent of the attack; and (ii) the Appellant issued D269 whose timing corresponded to the commencement of the attacks, and it was thus open to the Trial Chamber to conclude that he ordered the attacks. The Prosecution notes that the Appellant does not challenge the finding that the attacks were planned, that Bosnian Croat civilians were forewarned, that the attacks were on a large scale, and that the Appellant had control over the artillery that was used on Ahmići. In response to the Appellant's argument that the Trial Chamber erred in convicting him in the absence of evidence, the Prosecution asserts that the argument lacks merit, as the Trial Chamber heard evidence of a practice of issuing oral orders.

311. In reply, the Appellant argues that the pertinent issue is not *whether* the crimes in question were planned and ordered, but rather *who*

planned and ordered them, and that no evidence at trial allowed the Trial Chamber to conclude beyond reasonable doubt that he planned and ordered the crimes. He challenges the Prosecution's emphasis on the use of artillery by stating that there was no evidence that the NORA howitzer, which was under his *de jure* control, was used in Ahmići, and that it is unreasonable to premise his guilt on the use of unspecified artillery in the village. He also disputes the Prosecution's reliance upon the testimony of Witness A * * *, because, he says, Witness A's testimony was a multiple hearsay statement with the ultimate source-declarant unidentified * * *.

The Appeals Chamber's Findings * * *

332. The Appeals Chamber considers that the Trial Chamber's assessment of D269, as reflected in the Trial Judgement, diverges significantly from that of the Appeals Chamber following its review. The Appeals Chamber considers that the Trial Chamber's assessment was "wholly erroneous."

333. The Appeals Chamber considers that the trial evidence does not support the Trial Chamber's conclusion that the ABiH forces were not preparing for combat in the Ahmići area. In addition, the Appeals Chamber notes that additional evidence admitted on appeal shows that there was a Muslim military presence in Ahmići and the neighbouring villages, and that the Appellant had reason to believe that the ABiH intended to launch an attack along the Ahmići-Šantići-Dubravica axis. Consequently, the Appeals Chamber considers that there was a military justification for the Appellant to issue D269.

334. The Appeals Chamber further notes that in light of the planned nature, scale, and manner in which crimes were committed in the Vitez municipality on 16 April 1993, the Trial Chamber concluded that D269 corresponded to the start of fighting in the Ahmići area, and that it instructed all the troops mentioned therein to coordinate an offensive attack and commit the crimes in question. The Appeals Chamber has failed to find evidence in the record which shows that the Appellant issued D269 with the "clear intention that the massacre would be committed" during its implementation, or evidence that the crimes against the Muslim civilian population in the Ahmići area were committed in response to D269. * * *

Whether the Appellant was Aware of the Substantial Likelihood that Civilians Would be Harmed

344. The Trial Chamber concluded that since the Appellant knew that some of the troops engaged in the attack on Ahmići and the neighbouring villages had previously participated in criminal acts against the Muslim population of Bosnia or had criminals within their ranks, when ordering those troops to launch an attack on 16 April 1993 pursuant to D269, the Appellant deliberately took the risk that crimes

would be committed against the Muslim civilian population in the Ahmići area and their property. * * *

345. The Appeals Chamber has articulated the *mens rea* applicable to ordering a crime under Article 7(1) of the Statute, in the absence of direct intent. It has stated that a person who orders an act or omission with the awareness of the substantial likelihood that a crime will be committed in the execution of that order, has the requisite *mens rea* for establishing responsibility under Article 7(1) pursuant to ordering. Ordering with such awareness has to be regarded as accepting that crime. The Trial Chamber did not apply this standard in relation to the finding outlined above. Therefore, the Appeals Chamber will apply the correct legal standard to determine whether the Appellant is responsible under Article 7(1) of the Statute for ordering the crimes which occurred in the Ahmići area on 16 April 1993. * * *

347. The Appeals Chamber considers that the orders and reports outlined above, may be regarded at most, as sufficient to demonstrate the Appellant's knowledge of the mere possibility that crimes could be committed by some elements. However, they do not constitute sufficient evidence to prove, under the legal standard articulated by the Appeals Chamber, awareness on the part of the Appellant of a substantial likelihood that crimes would be committed in the execution of D269.

348. Therefore, the Appeals Chamber is not satisfied that the relevant trial evidence and the additional evidence admitted on appeal prove beyond reasonable doubt that the Appellant is responsible under Article 7(1) of the Statute for ordering the crimes committed in the Ahmići area on 16 April 1993.

NOTES & QUESTIONS

1. Ordering Crimes

Liability for ordering the commission of a crime seems to presume that the defendant is the superior of the individual who actually commits the crime. Indeed, the Trial Chamber in the *Akayesu* case so presumed when it held: "Ordering implies a superior-subordinate relationship between the person giving the order and the one executing it. In other words, the person in a position of authority uses it to convince another to commit an offense." *Prosecutor v. Akayesu*, Case No. ICTR–96–4–T, Judgement, para. 483 (Sept. 2, 1998). In *Prosecutor v. Kordić & Čerkez*, however, a Trial Chamber ruled that "no formal superior-subordinate relationship is required for a finding of 'ordering' so long as it is demonstrated that the accused possessed the authority to order." *Prosecutor v. Kordić & Čerkez*, Case No. IT–95–14/2, Judgement, para. 388 (Feb. 26, 2001). Which is the better approach? May a superior be found liable for issuing an order that is not executed? Under what circumstances? Is it unlawful to convey patently illegal orders down a chain of command? What about orders that are not patently illegal, but that the middleman knows to be illegal? As to criminal responsibility of commanders for passing on criminal orders, the military commission in the *High*

Command case held: "to find a field commander criminally responsible for the transmittal of such an [illegal] order, he must have passed the order to the chain of command and the order must be one that is criminal upon its face, or one which he is shown to have known was criminal." *U.S.A. v. Wilhelm von Leeb et al.*, in VII TRIALS OF WAR CRIMINALS BEFORE THE NUREMBERG MILITARY TRIBUNALS UNDER CONTROL COUNCIL LAW NO. 10, 74 (1947–8).

2. *Mens Rea*

What is the *mens rea* for ordering the commission of a crime according to the *Blaškić* case? The Trial Chamber and Appeals Chamber articulate a slightly different *mens rea* standard—which is the better approach? Is it necessary to demonstrate that the accused intended for the crime ordered to be committed, or is it enough that the accused was reckless—or even negligent—as to whether the order would lead to the commission of crimes? It seems clear a defendant should be liable for issuing an order he knows to be unlawful. What about an order that a superior should know is unlawful? Under what circumstances would such a lesser *mens rea* suffice?

3. Joinder and Severance

The original Indictment against General Blaškić joined Dario Kordić and four other Bosnian Croats in connection with crimes committed in the Lašva Valley. The indictment against two defendants was withdrawn. Croatian cooperation in securing the presence of the remainder of the accused was inconsistent. Accordingly, the defendants arrived in The Hague at different times, necessitating separate trials. The case against defendant Kupreškić and others (excerpted elsewhere in this text) concerns the same attack on Ahmići. Witnesses in the *Blaškić* case revealed Kupreškić's role in the killing of civilians there. Judge Almiro Rodrigues (Portugal) has estimated that each hour of a trial before the Tribunal costs $30,000. Requiring separate trials for individuals indicted for the same events is thus an expensive proposition.

At the same time, should individuals within the same chain of command, albeit at different levels, be prosecuted together? Superiors and subordinates were charged and prosecuted in the same proceedings in the *Čelebići* case (excerpted below). Are such joint trials likely to complicate defense strategy or even lead to prejudicial conflicts of interest? In a multi-tiered hierarchy, may multiple defendants be held liable for the same acts of a subordinate? How should responsibility be allocated between individuals with immediate command authority and individuals more distant from the battlefield?

4. Obeying Orders

It is essential that soldiers follow orders to ensure the effective functioning of a military force. Where an order is illegal, however, soldiers are required to repudiate the order. Is it clear that D269 is an illegal order? On its face? Given the context? Is there a reasonable interpretation of the order that makes it legal, and thus reasonable both to issue and to follow? The circumstances in which following superior orders operates as a defense will be taken up in Chapter 17.

III. THE DOCTRINE OF SUPERIOR RESPONSIBILITY

A. HISTORY

The doctrine of superior responsibility has as its backbone the duty of responsible command. This duty is set forth in Article 1 of the Regulations annexed to the two Hague Conventions on the Laws and Customs of War on Land:

> The laws, rights, and duties of war apply not only to armies, but also to militia and volunteer corps fulfilling the following conditions:
>
> 1. To be commanded by a person responsible for his subordinates;
> 2. To have a fixed distinctive emblem recognizable at a distance;
> 3. To carry arms openly; and
> 4. To conduct their operations in accordance with the laws and customs of war.

Annex to the Convention Respecting the Laws and Customs of War on Land, Oct. 18, 1907, 36 Stat. 2277, 2295. Hague Convention IV also imposes an obligation on commanders to issue instructions concerning the law of land warfare and makes belligerent states responsible for the acts committed by their armed forces.

These early humanitarian law treaties did not contain penal provisions. Instead, it was envisioned that compliance would be primarily enforced through state responsibility or states' military justice systems. It was only later that the doctrine of superior responsibility emerged as a parallel mechanism for enforcing the duties of responsible command and, derivatively, international humanitarian law. This evolution happened primarily through judicial proceedings; codification in international treaties came later.

The doctrine of superior responsibility was contemplated in the post-WWI period. For example, the Commission on the Responsibility of the Authors of the War and on Enforcement of Penalties recommended that the German ex-Kaiser be tried for war crimes because he and others

> were cognizant of and could at least have mitigated the barbarities committed during the course of the war. A word from them would have brought about a different method in the action of their subordinates on land, at sea and in the air.

See Report Presented to the Preliminary Peace Conference, in 1 THE LAW OF WAR: A DOCUMENTARY HISTORY 842, 853–54 (Leon Friedman ed., 1972); Christopher N. Crowe, *Command Responsibility in the Former Yugoslavia: The Chances for Successful Prosecution*, 29 U. RICH. L. REV. 191, 193 (1994).

These trials of responsible WWI leaders, however, never came to fruition. So, it was not until the post-WWII period that international and quasi-international courts first adjudicated the doctrine of superior responsibility, although neither the Nuremberg nor the Tokyo Charter set forth the elements of the doctrine. With respect to the International Military Tribunal at Nuremberg ("IMT"), a United States proposal to refer to the responsibility for the "omission of a superior officer to prevent war crimes when he knows of, or is on notice as to, their commission or contemplated commission and is in a position to prevent them" was not included in the IMT Charter. Nonetheless, the Nuremberg Tribunal invoked superior responsibility without enunciating the precise elements of the doctrine—no doubt because the direct responsibility of the accused for designing and implementing the atrocities that were the subject of the Indictment was so manifest. In contrast, the International Military Tribunal for the Far East ("the Tokyo Tribunal") was much more diligent in applying the theory of liability to each defendant pursuant to Count 55 of the Indictment:

> The Defendants Dohihara, Hata, Hoshino, Itagaki, Kaya, Kido, Kimura, Koiso, Muto, Nagano, Oka, Oshima, Sato, Shigemitsu, Shimada, Suzuki, Togo, Tojo and Umezu, between the 7th December, 1941 and the 2nd September, 1945, being by virtue of their respective offices responsible for securing the observance of the said Conventions and assurances and the Laws and Customs of War in respect of the armed forces in the countries hereinafter named and in respect of many thousands of prisoners of war and civilians then in the power of Japan belonging to the United States of America, the British Commonwealth of Nations, the Republic of France, the Kingdom of the Netherlands, the Commonwealth of the Philippines, the Republic of China, the Republic of Portugal and the Union of Soviet Socialist Republics, deliberately and recklessly disregarded their legal duty to take adequate steps to secure the observance and prevent breaches thereof, and thereby violated the laws of war.

Both military and civilian superiors, including high-level members of the Japanese Cabinet, were convicted by the Tokyo Tribunal solely on the basis of the activities of their subordinates.

The case that follows, brought against Japanese General Tomoyuki Yamashita before a United States Military Commission, is the most important superior responsibility case of this era. As two commentators have noted, "in many ways, the evolution of command responsibility doctrine has consisted of reactions and counter-reactions to *Yamashita*." Allison Marston Danner & Jenny S. Martinez, *Guilty Associations: Joint Criminal Enterprise, Command Responsibility, and the Development of International Criminal Law*, 93 CALIF. L. REV. 75, 124 (2005). Consider this observation as you proceed through this chapter.

Tomoyuki Yamashita was commanding general of the Fourteenth Army Group of the Japanese Army in the Philippines Islands. He surrendered to the United States on September 3, 1945, and was held for a time as a prisoner of war. Although plans had been laid for the Tokyo Tribunal to begin operations in May 1946, General Douglas MacArthur moved forward with plans for a United States Military Commission to try General Yamashita. The Commission leveled the following charge against General Yamashita on September 25, 1945:

> Tomoyuki Yamashita, General Imperial Japanese Army, between 9 October 1944 and 2 September 1945, at Manila and other places in the Philippine Islands, while commander of armed forces of Japan at war with the United States of America and its allies, unlawfully disregarded and failed to discharge his duty as commander to control the operations of the members of his command, permitting them to commit brutal atrocities and other high crimes against people of the United States and of its allies and dependencies, particularly in the Philippines; and he, General Tomoyuki Yamashita, thereby violated the laws of war.

The Prosecution filed a bill of particulars containing sixty-four specifications and, on the first day of trial, a supplemental bill of particulars of fifty-nine additional specifications. The excerpt below is a summary of the military commission proceedings against General Yamashita prepared by the United Nations War Crimes Commission, which was charged with recording the trials of "minor war criminals" (those not indicted by the international tribunals at Nuremberg or Tokyo) before United States military commissions and British military courts. In many of these cases, the commissions in question did not issue a reasoned judgment, so the rapporteur has had to summarize the parties' positions and evidence in order to glean the foundation for the final verdict.

Trial of General Tomoyuki Yamashita, United States Military Commission, Manila, 8th October–7th December, 1945 IV LAW REPORTS OF TRIALS OF WAR CRIMINALS 1 (1948)

The Court which tried Yamashita was a United States Military Commission established under, and subject to, the provisions of the Pacific Regulations of 24th September, 1945, Governing the Trial of War Criminals. Acting under authority from General MacArthur, Commander-in-Chief, United States Army Forces, Pacific Theatre, General Styer, Commanding General, United States Army Forces, Western Pacific, appointed the Commission, and instructed it to meet in the City of Manila, Philippine Islands, "at the call of the President thereof." The Commission was convened on 8th October, 1945, at the High Commissioner's Residence in Manila. * * *

The classification of alleged offences made by the President of the Commission in delivering judgment may be reproduced at this point. He pointed out that:

> The crimes alleged to have been permitted by the accused in violation of the laws of war may be grouped into three categories:
>
> (1) Starvation, execution or massacre without trial and maladministration generally of civilian internees and prisoners of war;
>
> (2) Torture, rape, murder and mass execution of very large numbers of residents of the Philippines, including women and children and members of religious orders, by starvation, beheading, bayoneting, clubbing, hanging, burning alive, and destruction by explosives;
>
> (3) Burning and demolition without adequate military necessity of large numbers of homes, places of business, places of religious worship, hospitals, public buildings, and educational institutions. In point of time, the offences extended throughout the period the accused was in command of Japanese troops in the Philippines. In point of area, the crimes extended throughout the Philippine Archipelago, although by far the most of the incredible acts occurred on Luzon. * * *

Those stated to have been the victims of these atrocities were unarmed non-combatant civilians, civilian internees and prisoners of war, and unspecified hospital patients. The civilians included Austrian, French, Russian, Chinese and German nationals as well as United States citizens. * * *

The Second Motion to Dismiss the Case * * *

The present motion was addressed to the Charge as supplemented by the original Bill of Particulars and by the Supplemental Bill of Particulars, and the claim was again made that it failed to set forth a violation of the Laws of War by the accused and that the Commission did not have jurisdiction to try the cause. It was the contention of Defence that the Bill of Particulars did not cure the defects of the Charge. On the contrary, it provided further reasons for allowing the motion.

The Bill of Particulars detailed sixty-four instances in which members of the accused's command were alleged to have committed war crimes. In no instance was it alleged that the accused committed or aided in the commission of a crime or crimes. In no instance was it alleged that the accused issued an order, expressly or impliedly, for the perpetration of the crime or crimes charged. Nor was it alleged that the accused authorised the crimes prior to their commission or condoned them thereafter.

The Charge alleged that the accused failed in his duty to control his troops, permitting them to commit certain alleged crimes. The Bill of Particulars, however, set forth no instance of neglect of duty by the accused. Nor did it set forth any acts of commission or omission by the accused as amounting to a "permitting" of the crimes in question. What then was the substance of the Charge against the accused? It was submitted by the Defence that, on the three documents now before the Commission, the Charge and the two Bills of Particulars, the accused was not accused of having done something or having failed to do something, but solely of having been something, namely commander of the Japanese forces. It was being claimed that, by virtue of that fact alone, he was guilty of every crime committed by every soldier assigned to his command.

American jurisprudence recognised no such principle so far as its own military personnel were concerned. The Articles of War denounced and punished improper conduct by military personnel, but they did not hold a commanding officer responsible for the crimes committed by his subordinates. No one would even suggest that the Commanding General of an American occupation force became a criminal every time an American soldier violated the law. It was submitted that neither the Laws of War nor the conscience of the world upon which they were founded would countenance any such charge. It was the basic premise of all civilised criminal justice that it punished not according to status but according to fault, and that one man was not held to answer for the crime of another. * * *

Before introducing evidence, the Defence made a short opening statement summarising the facts which they hoped to prove, and making the following claims in particular:

> Defence will show that the accused never ordered the commission of any crime or atrocity; that the accused never gave permission to anyone to commit any crimes or atrocities; that the accused had no knowledge of the commission of the alleged crimes or atrocities; that the accused had no actual control of the perpetrators of the atrocities at any time that they occurred, and that the accused did not then and does not now condone, excuse or justify any atrocities or violation of the laws of war.
>
> On the matter of control we shall elaborate upon a number of facts that have already been suggested to the Commission in our cross-examination of the Prosecution's witnesses:
>
> 1. That widespread, devastating guerilla activities created an atmosphere in which control of troops by high ranking officers became difficult or impossible.
> 2. That guerilla activities and American air and combat activities disrupted communications and in many areas

> destroyed them altogether, making control by the accused a meaningless concept.
>
> 3. That in many of the atrocities alleged in the Bill of Particulars there was not even paper control; the chain of command did not channel through the accused at all. . . .
>
> You will see the picture of a General working under terrific pressure and difficulty, subject to last-minute changes in tactical plans ordered from higher headquarters, and a man who when he arrived in Luzon actually had command over less than half of the ground troops in the Island. * * *

Defence Counsel attacked the evidence of the Prosecution concerning some few of the alleged offences, but in general the Defence did not deny that the atrocities alleged by the Prosecution had actually taken place, and the principal aim of Counsel was to show that the accused was not legally responsible for these offences.

Great stress was placed on the difficulties which had faced the accused on his taking command of the 14th Army Group on 9th October, 1944. It was claimed that:

> The 14th Army Group was subordinate to the Supreme Southern Command under Count Terauchi, whose headquarters was in Manila. The navy was under a separate and distinct command, subordinate only to the naval command in Tokyo. * * * Therefore, out of approximately 300,000 troops in Luzon, only 120,000 were under General Yamashita's command. An acute shortage of food existed, and the Japanese army was exceedingly short in both motor transport and gasoline. The accused found that the general state of affairs in the 14th Army Group was very unsatisfactory. * * * The 14th Army Group was of insufficient strength to carry out the accused's mission, inasmuch as it was, in his opinion, about five divisions short of what would be required. His troops were of poor calibre and not physically up to standard requirements. The morale of his men was poor. In addition, a strong anti-Japanese feeling existed among the Filipino population. Preparations for defence were practically non-existent. * * * After the American victory on Leyte, the Japanese situation on Luzon became extremely precarious. The American blockade became more and more effective; the shortage of food became critical. The American air force continually strafed and bombed the Japanese transportation facilities and military positions. General Yamashita, charged specifically with the duty of defending the Philippines, a task that called for the best in men and equipment, of which he had neither, continued to resist our army from 9th October to 2nd September of this year, at which time he surrendered on orders from Tokyo.

The Defence maintained that the Manila atrocities were committed by the naval troops, and that these troops were not under General Yamashita's command. How, it was asked, could he be held accountable for the actions of troops which had passed into his command only one month before, at a time when he was 150 miles away—troops whom he had never seen, trained or inspected, whose commanding officers he could not change or designate, and over whose actions he had only the most nominal control?

In the submission of the Defence no kind of plan was discernible in the Manila atrocities: "We see only wild, unaccountable looting, murder and rape. If there be an explanation of the Manila story, we believe it lies in this: Trapped in the doomed city, knowing that they had only a few days at best to live, the Japanese went berserk, unloosed their pent-up fears and passions in one last orgy of abandon."

It was pointed out that General Yamashita arrived in Manila on 9th October and left on 26th December. Until 17th November, General Yamashita was not even the highest commander in the City of Manila since his immediate superior, Count Terauchi, was there and in charge. It was Count Terauchi and not General Yamashita who was handling affairs concerning the civilian population, relations with the civil government and the discouragement and suppression of anti-Japanese activities. The crucial period, therefore, was from 17th November to 26th December, a matter of a mere five weeks, during which General Yamashita was in Manila and in charge of civilian affairs. Could it be seriously contended that a commander who was beset and harassed by the enemy and was staggering under a successful enemy invasion to the south and expecting at any moment another invasion in the north could in such a short period gather in all the strings of administration? Even so, the accused took some steps in an attempt to curb the activities of the Japanese military police who were terrorising the civilian population. * * *

The Defence anticipated that the Prosecution would claim that there were so many of these atrocities, that they covered so large a territory, that General Yamashita must have known about them. The reply of the Defence was that, in the first place, a man was not convicted on the basis of what someone thought he must have known but on what he has been proved beyond reasonable doubt to have known; and in the second place, General Yamashita did not know and could not have known about any of these atrocities. Practically all of the atrocities took place at times when and in areas where the communication of news of such matters was practically impossible. Further, the accused's orders were clear: to attack armed [Filipino] guerrillas and to befriend and win the co-operation of other civilians. When atrocities occurred, they were committed in violation of General Yamashita's orders, and it was quite natural that those who violated these orders would not inform him of their acts. * * *

The Prosecution * * *

The evidence had shown that the accused became for all intents and purposes after the 17th November, 1944, the military governor of the Philippine Islands. He was the highest military commander in this area. It was his duty, in addition to his duty as a military commander, to protect the civilian population. Whereas Defence Counsel had referred to the atrocities as having been committed by "battle-crazed men under the stress and strain of battle," there was in fact evidence that in many instances those acts were committed under the leadership of commissioned officers. That is quite a far cry from the sudden breaking of bounds of restraint by individuals on their own initiative. The submission of the Prosecution was that the evidence showed that these atrocities were carefully planned and carefully supervised; they were in fact commanded.

The Prosecution recalled that the accused had asserted that he had no knowledge of these acts, and that if he had had knowledge or any reason to foresee these acts he would have taken affirmative steps to prevent them. In explanation of his claim that he had no knowledge he had asserted that his communications were faulty. The Prosecution submitted however that there was nothing in the record to the effect that the accused did [not] have adequate communications. For instance, the accused had acknowledged that reports from Batangas concerning guerrilla activity were received from time to time. Even if it were accepted that the accused did not know of what was going on in Batangas, the fact remained that he did not make an adequate effort to find out. It was his duty to know what was being done by his troops under his orders. The accused had pleaded that he was too hard pressed by the enemy to find out what was the state of discipline among his troops. The Prosecution claimed however that the performance of the responsibility of the commanding officer toward the civilian populations is as heavy a responsibility as the combating of the enemy. And if he chose to ignore one and devote all of his attention to the other he did so at his own risk. * * *

Yamashita had claimed that the naval troops in Manila were only under his tactical command, but General Muto [Yamashita's Chief of Staff] had acknowledged that any officer having command of troops of another branch under him did have the authority and duty of restraining those men from committing wrongful acts. The atrocities committed by these naval troops were not the acts of irresponsible individuals, acting according to a whim or while in a drunken orgy; nor were they usually committed in the heat of battle. They were acting under officers, sometimes in concert with officers. Obviously, their acts constituted a deliberate, planned enterprise. * * * The Prosecution regarded the present case to be a clear case, in the international field, of criminal negligence. * * *

The Prosecution concluded that if Yamashita could not control his troops, it was his duty to mankind, to say nothing of his duty to his country to inform his superiors of that fact so that they might have taken steps to relieve him. There was no evidence that he did that.

The Verdict and Sentence

The findings of the Commission were delivered on 7th December, 1945. The President of the Commission, after repeating the charge and summarising the offences contained in the Bills of Particulars, pointed out that it was "noteworthy that the accused made no attempt to deny that the crimes were committed, although some deaths were attributed by Defence Counsel to legal execution of armed guerrillas, hazards of battle and action of guerrilla troops favourable to Japan." * * *

The Judgment of the Commission was delivered by the President in the following words:

> This accused is an officer of long years of experience, broad in its scope, who has had extensive command and staff duty in the Imperial Japanese Army in peace as well as war in Asia, Malaya, Europe, and the Japanese Home Islands. Clearly, assignment to command military troops is accompanied by broad authority and heavy responsibility. This has been true in all armies throughout recorded history. It is absurd, however, to consider a commander a murderer or rapist because one of his soldiers commits a murder or a rape. Nevertheless, where murder and rape and vicious, revengeful actions are widespread offences, and there is no effective attempt by a commander to discover and control the criminal acts, such a commander may be held responsible, even criminally liable, for the lawless acts of his troops, depending upon their nature and the circumstances surrounding them. Should a commander issue orders which lead directly to lawless acts, the criminal responsibility is definite and has always been so understood. The *Rules of Land Warfare*, Field Manual 27–10, United States Army, are clear on these points. It is for the purpose of maintaining discipline and control, among other reasons, that military commanders are given broad powers of administering military justice. The tactical situation, the character, training and capacity of staff officers and subordinate commanders as well as the traits of character, and training of his troops are other important factors in such cases. These matters have been the principal considerations of the Commission during its deliberations.
>
> General Yamashita: The Commission concludes: (1) That a series of atrocities and other high crimes have been committed by members of the Japanese armed forces under your command against people of the United States, their allies and dependencies throughout the Philippine Islands; that they were

not sporadic in nature but in many cases were methodically supervised by Japanese officers and non-commissioned officers; (2) That during the period in question you failed to provide effective control of your troops as was required by the circumstances. Accordingly upon secret written ballot, two-thirds or more of the members concurring, the Commission finds you guilty as charged and sentences you to death by hanging.

NOTES & QUESTIONS

1. Case Outcome

Several days before the Commission announced its verdict, an informal poll of journalists covering the trial unanimously concluded that they would not hang General Yamashita on the basis of the evidence produced. George F. Guy, *The Defense of Yamashita*, 4 WYO. L. J. 153, 171 (1994). (Guy was Yamashita's defense counsel.) The prediction proved wrong. An appeal for clemency to President Truman was declined, and General MacArthur—named as the sole reviewing authority—confirmed the sentence of the Commission. General Yamashita was executed by hanging on February 23, 1946.

2. Defense Counsel

The Staff Judge Advocate to Lt. General Wilhelm D. Styer, the Commanding General of the American Forces Western Pacific (AFWESPAC), appointed General Yamashita's defense counsel. In addition, General Yamashita asked for his Chief of Staff, Akiro Motu, and his Assistant Chief of Staff, General U. Utunomiya, to serve as defense counsel, notwithstanding that the former would also be called as a witness. In his testimony, General Motu stressed the difficulties faced by General Yamashita in unifying and executing his command and indicated that at no time had the defendant issued an illegal order. General Motu was subsequently tried by the Tokyo Tribunal and was also executed.

3. General Douglas MacArthur

General MacArthur had a long history in the Philippines. His father helped defeat the Spanish in the Philippines during the 1898 Spanish-American War and was at one time Governor General of the Philippines when it was a U.S. possession. General MacArthur himself served on the islands in several capacities, and during WWII, he was appointed Allied Commander of the Philippines. However, he did not have the resources to build a force capable of resisting Japanese expansionism at the outset. Within weeks after Pearl Harbor, the Japanese military destroyed the United States forces, and General MacArthur was forced to retreat to the Bataan peninsula and then to Australia. He vowed to return, but it was not until October 1944 that he waded ashore at Leyte and, from there, eventually liberated the rest of the Philippines. On September 2, 1945, he presided over the Japanese surrender on board the U.S.S. Missouri, bringing WWII to an end.

Upon winning full control of the Philippines, General MacArthur created a War Crimes Board to investigate allegations of military misconduct during the Japanese occupation of the Philippines. General Yamashita was the first defendant tried. It has been argued that the proceedings against General Yamashita were in many respects a personal vendetta of General MacArthur in retaliation for his forces having been routed by the Japanese and for the destruction of Manila, General MacArthur's adopted home and the former "pearl of the Orient." Others have argued that the Commission was susceptible to "command influence" given MacArthur's dual role as commanding officer and reviewing authority. President Truman later appointed General MacArthur to the U.S. military mission charged with preparing the islands for full independence in 1946 and head of the Allied occupation of Japan, where he took responsibility for organizing the Tokyo Tribunal.

4. The Law of Land Warfare Army Field Manual 27–10

The excerpt of the judgment against Yamashita makes mention of Army Field Manual 27–10, which was originally published in 1940 and then substantially updated in 1956 when the United States ratified the four Geneva Conventions of 1949. Field manuals provide authoritative guidance to military personnel on the customary and treaty law applicable to the conduct of war, often in response to humanitarian law treaties requiring the dissemination of treaty norms. Manuals usually contain excerpts from relevant treaties and official interpretations thereof. What weight should be given to such national military manuals in elucidating the content of international criminal law? Although the Manual is binding upon members of the U.S. Army:

> those provisions of the Manual which are neither statutes nor the text of treaties to which the United States is a party should not be considered binding upon courts and tribunals applying the law of war. However, such provisions are of evidentiary value insofar as they bear upon questions of custom and practice.

Department of the Army, *Army Field Manual*, No. 27–10, § 1 (1956).

In terms of superior responsibility, FM 27–10 states:

> 501. Responsibility for Acts of Subordinates. In some cases, military commanders may be responsible for war crimes committed by subordinate members of the armed forces, or other persons subject to their control. Thus, for instance, when troops commit massacres and atrocities against the civilian population of occupied territory or against prisoners of war, the responsibility may rest not only with the actual perpetrators but also with the commander. Such a responsibility arises directly when the acts in question have been committed in pursuance of an order of the commander concerned. The commander is also responsible if he has actual knowledge, or should have knowledge, through reports received by him or through other means, that troops or other persons subject to his control are about to commit or have committed a war crime

and he fails to take the necessary and reasonable steps to insure compliance with the law of war or to punish violators thereof.

For years, the Department of Defense engaged in a process of modernizing these rules with an eye towards creating a new and updated Joint Services Law of War Manual. In 2012, the principal author of the new manual, W. Hays Parks, complained that the effort had been stymied by the inter-agency clearance process and might be abandoned. *See* W. Hays Parks, *Update on the DOD Law of War Manual*, ABA 22ND ANNUAL REVIEW OF THE FIELD OF NATIONAL SECURITY LAW (Nov. 12, 2012). In the end, the new Manual indicates that it "is an institutional publication and reflects the views of the Department of Defense," and that, although it "has benefited significantly from the participation of experts from the Department of State, Office of the Legal Adviser, and the Department of Justice, Office of Legal Counsel, * * * the views in this manual do not necessarily reflect the views of those Departments or the U.S. Government as a whole." Department of Defense, LAW OF WAR MANUAL, v–vi (Dec. 2016). It was originally published in June 2015 (consuming over 1,000 pages and almost 7,000 footnotes) and was then reissued with amendments in December 2016 following significant feedback—much of it critical—from academics, the media, elements of the public, and other stakeholders. *See* David Glazier et al., *Failing our Troops: A Critical Assessment of the Department of Defense Law of War Manual*, 42 YALE J. INT'L L. 215 (2017); Charlie Dunlop, *The DoD Law of War Manual and its Critics: Some Observations*, 92 INT'L L. STUD. 85 (2016).

5. *Habeas Corpus*

While the Commission was still in session, General Yamashita's defense counsel sought a writ of *habeas corpus* and a writ of prohibition before the Supreme Court of the Philippines—the highest court of a land only recently liberated from a brutal Japanese occupation. General Styer, the respondent, did not appear, although the Commission allowed a Filipino law firm to appear as an *amicus*. Yamashita's defense counsel raised the same points that they would later raise before the United States Supreme Court: that the military commission was improperly constituted and as such was without jurisdiction, that the charge did not set forth a violation of the laws of war, and that the commission proceedings had denied the defendant due process of law. The Philippines Supreme Court denied the petition on December 4, 1945, the day before the conclusion of the final argument before the military commission. In a move apparently orchestrated by General MacArthur, the military commission announced its verdict on December 7, 1945—the 4th anniversary of the attack on Pearl Harbor.

This same day, defense counsel filed parallel petitions in the U.S. Supreme Court for writs of *habeas corpus,* prohibition, and *certiorari* from the Philippines proceedings. On *certiorari*, the Supreme Court denied the writs over two vigorous dissents by Justices Rutledge and Murphy. In so doing, the Court did not consider the factual guilt or innocence of the accused, but only the authority of the commission to try him on the alleged charge. The dissent by Justice Murphy, who had also coincidently served as Governor General to the Philippines, appears below:

In re Yamashita

327 U.S. 1 (1946).

In the Supreme Court of the United States.

■ MR. JUSTICE MURPHY, dissenting.

The significance of the issue facing the Court today cannot be overemphasized. An American military commission has been established to try a fallen military commander of a conquered nation for an alleged war crime. The authority for such action grows out of the exercise of the power conferred upon Congress by Article I, § 8, Cl. 10 of the Constitution to "define and punish . . . Offences against the Law of Nations . . ." The grave issue raised by this case is whether a military commission so established and so authorized may disregard the procedural rights of an accused person as guaranteed by the Constitution, especially by the due process clause of the Fifth Amendment.

The answer is plain. The Fifth Amendment guarantee of due process of law applies to "any person" who is accused of a crime by the Federal Government or any of its agencies. No exception is made as to those who are accused of war crimes or as to those who possess the status of an enemy belligerent. Indeed, such an exception would be contrary to the whole philosophy of human rights which makes the Constitution the great living document that it is. The immutable rights of the individual, including those secured by the due process clause of the Fifth Amendment, belong not alone to the members of those nations that excel on the battlefield or that subscribe to the democratic ideology. They belong to every person in the world, victor or vanquished, whatever may be his race, color or beliefs. They rise above any status of belligerency or outlawry. They survive any popular passion or frenzy of the moment. No court or legislature or executive, not even the mightiest army in the world, can ever destroy them. Such is the universal and indestructible nature of the rights which the due process clause of the Fifth Amendment recognizes and protects when life or liberty is threatened by virtue of the authority of the United States.

The existence of these rights, unfortunately, is not always respected. They are often trampled under by those who are motivated by hatred, aggression or fear. But in this nation individual rights are recognized and protected, at least in regard to governmental action. They cannot be ignored by any branch of the Government, even the military, except under the most extreme and urgent circumstances.

The failure of the military commission to obey the dictates of the due process requirements of the Fifth Amendment is apparent in this case. The petitioner was the commander of an army totally destroyed by the superior power of this nation. While under heavy and destructive attack by our forces, his troops committed many brutal atrocities and other high crimes. Hostilities ceased and he voluntarily surrendered. At that point he was entitled, as an individual protected by the due process clause of the Fifth Amendment, to be treated fairly and justly according to the accepted rules of law and procedure. He was also entitled to a fair trial as to any alleged crimes and to be free from charges of legally unrecognized crimes that would serve only to permit his accusers to satisfy their desires for revenge.

A military commission was appointed to try the petitioner for an alleged war crime. The trial was ordered to be held in territory over which the United States has complete sovereignty. No military necessity or other emergency demanded the suspension of the safeguards of due process. Yet petitioner was rushed to trial under an improper charge, given insufficient time to prepare an adequate defense, deprived of the benefits of some of the most elementary rules of evidence and summarily sentenced to be hanged. In all this needless and unseemly haste there was no serious attempt to charge or to prove that he committed a recognized violation of the laws of war. He was not charged with personally participating in the acts of atrocity or with ordering or condoning their commission. Not even knowledge of these crimes was attributed to him. It was simply alleged that he unlawfully disregarded and failed to discharge his duty as commander to control the operations of the members of his command, permitting them to commit the acts of atrocity. The recorded annals of warfare and the established principles of international law afford not the slightest precedent for such a charge. This indictment in effect permitted the military commission to make the crime whatever it willed, dependent upon its biased view as to petitioner's duties and his disregard thereof, a practice reminiscent of that pursued in certain less respected nations in recent years.

In my opinion, such a procedure is unworthy of the traditions of our people or of the immense sacrifices that they have made to advance the common ideals of mankind. The high feelings of the moment doubtless will be satisfied. But in the sober afterglow will come the realization of the boundless and dangerous implications of the procedure sanctioned today. No one in a position of command in an army, from sergeant to general, can escape those implications. Indeed, the fate of some future President of the United States and his chiefs of staff and military advisers may well have been sealed by this decision. But even more significant will be the hatred and ill-will growing out of the application of this unprecedented procedure. That has been the inevitable effect of every method of punishment disregarding the element of personal culpability. The effect in this instance, unfortunately, will be magnified infinitely, for here we are dealing with the rights of man on an international level. To subject an enemy belligerent to an unfair trial, to charge him with an unrecognized crime, or to vent on him our retributive emotions only antagonizes the enemy nation and hinders the reconciliation necessary to a peaceful world. * * *

War breeds atrocities. From the earliest conflicts of recorded history to the global struggles of modern times, inhumanities, lust and pillage have been the inevitable by-products of man's resort to force and arms. Unfortunately, such despicable acts have a dangerous tendency to call forth primitive impulses of vengeance and retaliation among the victimized peoples. The satisfaction of such impulses in turn breeds resentment and fresh tension. Thus does the spiral of cruelty and hatred grow.

If we are ever to develop an orderly international community based upon a recognition of human dignity it is of the utmost importance that the necessary punishment of those guilty of atrocities be as free as possible from the ugly stigma of revenge and vindictiveness. Justice must be tempered by compassion rather than by vengeance. In this, the first case involving this momentous problem ever to reach this Court, our responsibility is both lofty and difficult. We must insist, within the confines of our proper jurisdiction, that the highest standards of justice be applied in this trial of an enemy commander conducted under the authority of the United States. Otherwise stark retribution will be free to masquerade in a cloak of false legalism. And the hatred and cynicism engendered by that retribution will supplant the great ideals to which this nation is dedicated.

This Court fortunately has taken the first and most important step toward insuring the supremacy of law and justice in the treatment of an enemy belligerent accused of violating the laws of war. Jurisdiction properly has been asserted to inquire "into the cause of restraint of liberty" of such a person. 28 U.S.C. § 452. Thus the obnoxious doctrine asserted by the Government in this case, to the effect that restraints of liberty resulting from military trials of war criminals are political matters completely outside the arena of judicial review, has been rejected fully and unquestionably. This does not mean, of course, that the foreign affairs and policies of the nation are proper subjects of judicial inquiry. But when the liberty of any person is restrained by reason of the authority of the United States the writ of *habeas corpus* is available to test the legality of that restraint, even though direct court review of the restraint is prohibited. The conclusive presumption must be made, in this country at least, that illegal restraints are unauthorized and unjustified by any foreign policy of the Government and that commonly accepted juridical standards are to be recognized and enforced. On that basis judicial inquiry into these matters may proceed within its proper sphere. * * *

The Court, in my judgment, demonstrates conclusively that the military commission was lawfully created in this instance and that petitioner could not object to its power to try him for a recognized war crime. [H]owever, I find it impossible to agree that the charge against the petitioner stated a recognized violation of the laws of war. * * *

The findings of the military commission bear out the absence of any direct personal charge against the petitioner. The commission merely found that atrocities and other high crimes "have been committed by members of the Japanese armed forces under your command . . . that they were not sporadic in nature but in many cases were methodically supervised by Japanese officers and noncommissioned officers; . . . That during the period in question you failed to provide effective control of your troops as was required by the circumstances."

In other words, read against the background of military events in the Philippines subsequent to October 9, 1944, these charges amount to this: "We, the victorious American forces, have done everything possible to destroy and disorganize your lines of communication, your effective control of your personnel, your ability to wage war. In those respects we have succeeded. We have defeated and crushed your forces. And now we charge and condemn you for having been inefficient in maintaining control of your troops during the period when we were so effectively besieging and eliminating your forces and blocking your ability to maintain effective control. Many terrible atrocities were committed by your disorganized troops. Because these atrocities were so widespread we will not bother to charge or prove that you committed, ordered or condoned any of them. We will assume that they must have resulted from your inefficiency and negligence as a commander. In short, we charge you with the crime of inefficiency in controlling your troops. We will judge the discharge of your duties by the disorganization which we ourselves created in large part. Our standards of judgment are whatever we wish to make them."

Nothing in all history or in international law, at least as far as I am aware, justifies such a charge against a fallen commander of a defeated force. To use the very inefficiency and disorganization created by the victorious forces as the primary basis for condemning officers of the defeated armies bears no resemblance to justice or to military reality.

International law makes no attempt to define the duties of a commander of an army under constant and overwhelming assault; nor does it impose liability under such circumstances for failure to meet the ordinary responsibilities of command. The omission is understandable. Duties, as well as ability to control troops, vary according to the nature and intensity of the particular battle. To find an unlawful deviation from duty under battle conditions requires difficult and speculative calculations. Such calculations become highly untrustworthy when they are made by the victor in relation to the actions of a vanquished commander. Objective and realistic norms of conduct are then extremely unlikely to be used in forming a judgment as to deviations from duty. The probability that vengeance will form the major part of the victor's judgment is an unfortunate but inescapable fact. So great is that probability that international law refuses to recognize such a judgment as a basis for a war crime, however fair the judgment may be in a particular instance. It is this consideration that undermines the charge against the petitioner in this case. The indictment permits, indeed compels, the military commission of a victorious nation to sit in judgment upon the military strategy and actions of the defeated enemy and to use its conclusions to determine the criminal liability of an enemy commander. Life and liberty are made to depend upon the biased will of the victor rather than upon objective standards of conduct. * * *

There are numerous instances, especially with reference to the Philippine Insurrection in 1900 and 1901, where commanding officers were found to have violated the laws of war by specifically ordering members of their command to commit atrocities and other war crimes. And in other cases officers have been held liable where they knew that a crime was to be committed, had the power to prevent it and failed to exercise that power. In no recorded instance, however, has the mere inability to control troops under fire or attack by superior forces been made the basis of a charge of violating the laws of war. * * *

No one denies that inaction or negligence may give rise to liability, civil or criminal. But it is quite another thing to say that the inability to control troops under highly competitive and disastrous battle conditions renders one guilty of a war crime in the absence of personal culpability. Had there been some element of knowledge or direct connection with the atrocities the problem would be entirely different. Moreover, it must be remembered that we are not dealing here with an ordinary tort or criminal action; precedents in those fields are of little if any value. Rather we are concerned with a proceeding involving an international crime, the treatment of which may have untold effects upon the future peace of the world. That fact must be kept uppermost in our search for precedent. * * *

At a time like this when emotions are understandably high it is difficult to adopt a dispassionate attitude toward a case of this nature. Yet now is precisely the time when that attitude is most essential. While peoples in other lands may not share our beliefs as to due process and the dignity of the individual, we are not free to give effect to our emotions in reckless disregard of the rights of others. We live under the Constitution, which is the embodiment of all the high hopes and aspirations of the new world. And it is applicable in both war and peace. We must act accordingly. Indeed, an uncurbed spirit of revenge and retribution, masked in formal legal procedure for purposes of dealing with a fallen enemy commander, can do more lasting harm than all of the atrocities giving rise to that spirit. The people's faith in the fairness and objectiveness of the law can be seriously undercut by that spirit. The fires of nationalism can be further kindled. And the hearts of all mankind can be embittered and filled with hatred, leaving forlorn and impoverished the noble ideal of malice toward none and charity to all. These are the reasons that lead me to dissent in these terms.

NOTES & QUESTIONS

1. Superior Responsibility Generally

Did the Commission—as reported above and described in Justice Murphy's dissent—adequately identify the constitutive elements of the doctrine of superior responsibility? Were there facts in the record that established each of these elements? How compelling was General Yamashita's defense? Which elements of the doctrine did General Yamashita attempt to defeat? What evidence did the two parties marshal in support of their respective positions? Is this even a superior responsibility case at all or did the military commission assume that General Yamashita had ordered the offenses because they were "not sporadic" and involved Japanese commissioned and non-commissioned officers?

2. *Mens Rea*

What was the *mens rea* standard applied by the military commission, if any? Did the commission treat the doctrine as one of strict liability by dispensing with the need to prove *mens rea*? In the alternative, is the doctrine essentially one of negligence—i.e., the inadvertent failure to know of abuses? Recall that the Model Penal Code defines the mental state of negligence as follows:

> A person acts negligently with respect to a material element of an offense when he should be aware of a substantial and unjustifiable risk that the material element exists or will result from his conduct. The risk must be of such a nature and degree that the actor's failure to perceive it, considering the nature and purpose of his conduct and the circumstances known to him, involves a gross deviation from the standard of care that a reasonable person would observe in the actor's situation.

Model Penal Code § 2.02(d). Alternatively, is the superior responsibility doctrine based more upon a notion of recklessness, which exists when a person:

> consciously disregards a substantial and unjustifiable risk that the material element exists or will result from his conduct. The risk must be of such a nature and degree that, considering the nature and purpose of the actor's conduct and the circumstances known to him, its disregard involves a gross deviation from the standard of conduct that a law-abiding person would observe in the actor's situation.

Model Penal Code § 2.02(c). In continental systems, this mental state is closest to the concept of "*dolus eventualis*," meaning that the actor is reconciled with the fact that a crime will occur. As compared with negligence, recklessness focuses more acutely on the actor's subjective state of mind, and a choice to disregard a known risk, rather than on an "objective" deviation from the operative standard of care and a failure to perceive a risk.

3. Admiral Toyoda

Would it be possible for two commanders in separate chains of command to be criminally responsible for the same acts of the same subordinates? The

Allied Powers prosecuted additional Japanese defendants in military commissions separate and apart from the Tokyo Tribunal. For example, Soemu Toyoda, an Admiral in the Imperial Japanese Army, was charged under the doctrine of superior responsibility with "willfully and unlawfully disregarding and failing to discharge his duties as an officer by ordering, directing, inciting, causing, permitting, ratifying and failing to prevent" various abuses committed by Japanese naval personnel under his "command, control and supervision." *U.S.A. v. Soemu Toyoda*, Official Transcript of Trial (1948). The alleged unlawful acts were many of the same acts committed during the "Rape of Manila" that provided the basis for charges against General Yamashita, in part because the Commission that tried General Yamashita found that the naval forces were under Yamashita's command. Admiral Toyoda's defense counsel argued that the military commission should take judicial notice of the *Yamashita* judgment and refrain from trying Admiral Toyoda for the same criminal acts:

> The very question involved—of command responsibility for the commission of those atrocities—has been judicially determined, in a prosecution initiated by the same representative of the United States Government as this Tribunal, then as now acting as the Supreme Commander of the United States forces in the Pacific area, on charges and specifications signed and sworn by the same accuser who swore to the identical incidents here charged—or to put it in legal language, the question is *res judicata*.

Ann Marie Prévost, *Race and War Crimes: The 1945 War Crimes Trial of General Tomoyuki Yamashita*, 14 HUM. RTS. Q. 303, 333 (1992). Admiral Toyoda was acquitted on all counts—the only Japanese defendant to be completely exonerated—on the grounds that he could not have known of the alleged atrocities and that matters concerning prisoners of war did not pass through his operational chain of command. As a result, the tribunal concluded that Admiral Toyoda had no knowledge, and no means of gaining knowledge, about the abuses that were the subject of the indictment against him:

> [T]his tribunal cannot but conclude that this defendant did not in fact know of such things. It has not been shown that machinery existed for reports or that persons reported such to him. This may be in part credited to the magnitude of the task which devolved upon him in these days of the high point and already apparent down-grade of Japanese military fortune. He had under his command the great share of the nation's homeland naval supporting activities, numbering 190 separate units and some 600,000 personnel, scattered over a vast area, and he had the duty of seeing that they produced at peak capacity.

Toyoda at 5019. In his remarks after the reading of the judgment of acquittal, Admiral Toyoda stated:

> Had my ability and character been more superior and stronger it might well have been that some or all of these crimes could have been prevented or stopped; and for this failure I feel a deep sense

> of repentance and a strong sense of guilt of moral responsibility. In this regard I take this occasion as a member and on behalf of the former Japanese Navy to express and offer my deepest apology to the Allied Powers.

Toyoda at 5020–21. Toyoda's testimony at trial revealed that General Yamashita was not in fact fully in command of the naval forces that committed many of the atrocities for which General Yamashita was hanged. There was evidence in the record that while General Yamashita had been given partial command over naval forces, those forces retained a veto power over the exercise of that command and had in fact disregarded General Yamashita's orders. How can the outcomes of the *Yamashita* and *Toyoda* proceedings be reconciled? Can they be attributed to the fact that at the time the *Toyoda* commission rendered its judgment, United States foreign policy was geared toward the rehabilitation of Japan as an ally? Is this the "dominance of politics over law"? Kenneth Armstrong & Jo Shaw, *Integrating Law: An Introduction*, 36 J. COMMON MARKET STUD. 147, 148 (1988).

4. Kōki Hirota and Civilian Superiors

The Tokyo Tribunal indicted Kōki Hirota on Count 55, reproduced above, as well as under Count 1 (participating in a common plan or conspiracy to wage aggressive war) and Count 27 (waging war in China). He was acquitted of other aggression counts (involving wars against Western powers) and of war crimes (Count 54).

Hirota, a diplomat and politician, had been Foreign Minister of Japan from 1933–38, interrupted by a brief stint as Prime Minister in 1936. Hirota is on record as having opposed the escalation of the Second Sino-Japanese war. Nonetheless, during Hirota's second term as Foreign Minister, Japan's Army invaded China and committed atrocities over a seven-week period in and around the city of Nanking, then China's capital, in what has been called the "Rape of Nanking."

According to the Tokyo Tribunal transcripts, the evidence showed that Prime Minister Hirota helped to establish an embassy in Nanking when the Japanese Army took control in 1937. Embassy officials were aware that the Army intended to destroy Nanking and insisted that they would intervene. Despite these assurances, the Japanese Army committed numerous acts of violence against the predominantly civilian population. Japanese soldiers, among other things, committed acts of rape, looting, arson, and the execution of prisoners of war and civilians. In total, it is estimated that over 300,000 Chinese were killed and 20,000 women were raped during the seven-week period. Many of the atrocities occurred around the University of Nanking, located close to the Japanese Embassy.

The evidence showed that Hirota received reports about the conduct of the Army. In his capacity as Foreign Minister, however, he had no power or authority to issue orders to troops, although the evidence showed that he complained about abuses to the War Ministry. The evidence suggested that Hirota accepted assurances from the Ministry that the problem would be resolved despite continuing reports.

The Tokyo Tribunal held that Hirota's behavior constituted a dereliction of duty:

> Hirota was derelict in his duty in not insisting before the Cabinet that immediate action be taken to put an end to the atrocities, failing any other action open to him to bring about the same result. He was content to rely on assurances which he knew were not being implemented while hundreds of murders, violations of women and other atrocities were being committed daily. His inaction amounted to criminal negligence.

The Record of Proceedings of the International Military Tribunal for the Far East (1946–1949), *reprinted in* 103 THE TOKYO MAJOR WAR CRIMES TRIAL 49,791 (R. John Pritchard et al. eds., 1981). Judge Röling (the Netherlands), in dissent, argued that Hirota should have been acquitted on the grounds that "a Tribunal should be very careful in holding civil government officials responsible for the behaviour of the army in the field." Hirota was also found guilty of conspiracy to commit aggression and waging a war of aggression against China. He was sentenced to death for these crimes—the only civilian to be hanged following the Tokyo proceedings.

As you read the materials below on the liability of civilian superiors, ask yourself if Hirota would have been convicted for the crimes of members of the Japanese Army under a superior responsibility theory of liability based upon the reasoning adopted below in the *Bagilishema* case before the ICTR? What about under the ICC standard for non-military superiors, found in Article 28(2)(b) of the ICC Statute?

5. Subsequent Proceedings

The doctrine of superior responsibility received a more detailed treatment in other post-WWII cases, especially those brought under Control Council Law No. 10 (CCL 10). Most notably, the so-called High Command Case involved the trial of senior German officers for the execution of civilians and prisoners of war. There, the tribunal rejected the notion—advanced by the prosecution—that the command responsibility doctrine provided for the *per se* liability of a commander within a chain of command when it stated that "criminality does not attach to every individual in this chain of command from that fact alone." Rather, the tribunal established the principle that to be held liable, the commander must have had knowledge of abuses by subordinates and must have committed a personal dereliction by failing to act in the face of such knowledge. A personal dereliction occurs when "the act is directly traceable to him or where his failure to properly supervise his subordinates constitutes criminal negligence on his part. In the latter case, it must be a personal neglect amounting to a wanton, immoral disregard of the action of his subordinates amounting to acquiescence." 11 TRIALS OF WAR CRIMINALS BEFORE THE NUREMBERG MILITARY TRIBUNALS UNDER CONTROL COUNCIL LAW NO. 10, 543–44 (1951).

In another CCL 10 case, defendants argued that reports did not come to their attention. The tribunal responded:

> An army commander will not ordinarily be permitted to deny knowledge of reports received at his headquarters, they being sent

> there for his special benefit. Neither will he ordinarily be permitted to deny knowledge of happenings within the area of his command while he is present therein. It would strain the credulity of the Tribunal to believe that a high ranking military commander would permit himself to get out of touch with current happenings in the area of his command during wartime.

The Hostage Case, 11 TRIALS OF WAR CRIMINALS BEFORE THE NUREMBERG MILITARY TRIBUNALS UNDER CONTROL COUNCIL NO. 10, 757, 1260 (1950) (convicting top German officers for war crimes in occupied territories, including the unlawful taking and killing of hostages). Did the CCL 10 military commissions apply the same doctrine of superior responsibility as the *Yamashita* military commission?

6. My Lai

The case against Captain Ernst Medina was the only command responsibility case brought against a U.S. officer during the Vietnam War. Capt. Medina was the commanding officer of platoon leader Lt. William L. Calley Jr., who had been convicted by a court martial of ordering the 1968 massacre of Vietnamese citizens at My Lai. *United States v. Calley*, 22 U.S.C.M.A. 534 (1973). Lt. Calley was sentenced to dismissal and confinement to hard labor for 20 years. Captain Medina was charged under the Uniform Code of Military Justice with murder. For conviction, the military judge required the jury to find that Capt. Medina had "actual knowledge" that his troops were improperly killing non-combatants and did not attempt to intervene to prevent abuses. The military judge gave the following instruction:

> [M]ere presence at the scene without knowledge will not suffice. That is, the commander-subordinate relationship alone will not allow an inference of knowledge. While it is not necessary that a commander actually see an atrocity being committed, it is essential that he know that his subordinates are in the process of committing atrocities or about to commit atrocities.

Medina v. Resor, 43 C.M.R. 243 (1971), *quoted in* Kenneth A. Howard, *Command Responsibility for War Crimes*, 21 J. PUB. L. 7, 11 (1972). Capt. Medina was acquitted.

Lt. Calley raised the defense of superior orders in his proceedings by testifying that Capt. Medina had ordered his platoon by radio to "waste" the civilians they encountered when they entered the My Lai hamlet—an order Capt. Medina denied making. In the end, fourteen officers were charged with covering up or failing to investigate the massacre, but only one (Col. Oran Henderson, former commanding officer of the 11th Infantry Brigade) was brought to trial, and he was acquitted. The division commander, General Samuel W. Koster, was among the fourteen officers charged, but not prosecuted, in connection with the massacre. *Koster v. United States*, 685 F.2d 407 (1982) (affirming administrative sanctions where defendant received reports of My Lai but conducted an inadequate investigation into the matter).

One commentator has opined that the "actual knowledge test, in a context like My Lai, is an invitation to the commander to see and hear no evil. It is not consistent with a serious effort to make the command structure responsive to the humanitarian goals involved." Roger S. Clark, *Medina: An Essay on the Principles of Criminal Liability for Homicide*, 5 RUTGERS-CAM. L. J. 59, 78 (1973–4). Does a military justice system lose credibility when it prosecutes only low-level personnel while leaving higher-ups untouched? Does such a practice risk being branded as "scapegoating?" For further reading on My Lai, *see* Joseph Goldstein, et al., THE MY LAI MASSACRE AND ITS COVER UP: BEYOND THE REACH OF LAW? (1976); Note, *Command Responsibility for War Crimes*, 82 YALE L. J. 1274 (1973). The rampant sexual violence committed at My Lai prior to the massacre—exemplified by the so-called Black Blouse Girl—was downplayed in all accounts of the event. *See* Valerie Wieskamp, *My Lai, Sexual Assault and the Black Blouse Girl: Forty-Five Years Later, One of America's Most Iconic Photos Hides Truth in Plain Sight*, READING THE PICTURES (Oct. 29, 2013).

How does the Army Field Manual standard reproduced above compare to the command responsibility instruction given in the My Lai proceedings? Why would the Field Manual standard not govern the My Lai proceedings? For a history of the Field Manual and the changes made following the ratification of the Geneva Conventions, *see* William F. Fratcher, *The New Law of Land Warfare,* 22 MO. L. REV. 143 (1957).

7. Enforcing the Doctrine of Superior Responsibility

There is no express doctrine of superior responsibility in the Uniform Code of Military Justice (UCMJ), adopted in 1951, even though it appeared in the contemporaneous Army Field Manual 27–10, as discussed above. Instead, prosecutors must use complicity doctrines (e.g., under Articles 77 or 78 of the UCMJ)—although these provisions require proof that the defendant shared the criminal intent of the primary perpetrator—or the concept of dereliction of duty (Article 92) to prosecute superiors whose subordinates commit prosecutable crimes. *See* Victor Hansen, *What's Good for the Goose is Good for the Gander: Lessons from Abu Ghraib: Time for the United States to Adopt a Standard of Command Responsibility Toward its Own*, 42 GONZ. L. REV. 335 (2007).

Under United States military law, it is the potential defendant's commanding officer who is normally the convening authority for any court martial. Is this placement of prosecutorial discretion suitable for the doctrine of superior responsibility? Instead, should prosecutorial discretion lie outside the command structure in some independent body? Is this system likely to reach either officers at the apex of the military hierarchy or non-military superiors, such as cabinet members, members of the Department of Defense, members of the intelligence services (e.g. the U.S. Central Intelligence Agency), or members of the investigative agencies (e.g. the U.S. Federal Bureau of Investigations)? On unlawful command influence, *see* Luther C. West, *A History of Command Influence in the Military Justice System*, 18 UCLA L. REV. 1 (1970); William C. Peters, *Article 37 of the UCMJ and Command responsibility for War Crimes—Unlawful Command Influence as (Rogue) Elephant in the Room*, 5 ELON L. REV. 329 (2013).

8. Modern Day Military Commissions

The Military Commissions Act of 2009 at § 950q states that:

> Any person punishable under this chapter who . . . (3) is a superior commander who, with regard to acts punishable by this chapter, knew, had reason to know, or should have known, that a subordinate was about to commit such acts or had done so and who failed to take the necessary and reasonable measures to prevent such acts or to punish the perpetrators thereof, is a principal.

The U.S. Department of Defense draft instructions for guidance to military commissions states: "A person is criminally liable for a completed substantive offense if that person commits the offense, aids or abets the commission of the offense, solicits commission of the offense, or is otherwise responsible due to command responsibility," and provides the following elements:

- The accused had command and control, or effective authority and control, over one or more subordinates;
- One or more of the accused's subordinates committed, attempted to commit, conspired to commit, solicited to commit, or aided or abetted the commission of one or more substantive offenses triable by military commission;
- The accused either knew or should have known that the subordinate or subordinates were committing, attempting to commit, conspiring to commit, soliciting, or aiding and abetting such offense or offenses; [and]
- The accused failed to take all necessary and reasonable measures within his or her power to prevent or repress the commission of the offense or offenses.

This provision can only be invoked before military commissions; there is no general superior responsibility doctrine in the federal penal code (Title 18). Why might this be the case? How is this articulation of the doctrine the same or different from that employed in the *Yamashita* case?

9. Abu Ghraib

In his dissent in the *Yamashita* case, Justice Murphy warns that a U.S. President might be at risk of prosecution under the superior responsibility standard established by that case. Under what circumstances could a U.S. President, or members of his or her cabinet, be found liable for the acts of U.S. troops under the doctrine of superior responsibility? Could former Secretary of Defense Donald Rumsfeld or President George W. Bush incur superior responsibility for abusive acts by military personnel, or private contractors retained by the military, implicated in the abuse of detainees at the Abu Ghraib prison or elsewhere? One of the investigative reports commissioned after the Abu Ghraib revelations charged that "commanding officers and their staffs at various levels failed in their duties" and that "such failures contributed directly or indirectly to detainee abuse." James R. Schlesinger, et al., THE INDEPENDENT PANEL TO REVIEW DOD DETENTION OPERATIONS 43 (Aug. 24, 2004). Several other reports described tangled command relationships between the military police, military intelligence units, CIA operatives, and private contractors that complicate a finding of effective command. Might pursuing individuals higher in the chain of command escape these difficulties?

The American Civil Liberties Union filed several civil suits under the Alien Tort Statute against Secretary Rumsfeld and others on a superior responsibility theory. Secretary Rumsfeld and his co-defendants moved to dismiss the case against them, arguing that they are immune from suit. The district court agreed in 2007. *See Ali et al. v. Rumsfeld*, 479 F. Supp. 2d 85 (D.D.C.2007). Additionally, the Center for Constitutional Rights filed a criminal suit against Secretary Rumsfeld in Germany. The German court dismissed that case on the ground that the United States was in the process of investigating abuses at Abu Ghraib and elsewhere. Upon the resignation of Secretary Rumsfeld, the suit was refiled, and plaintiffs argued that only low-level perpetrators have been investigated to date. The complaint also names law professors John Yoo (Berkeley Law) and Jay Bybee (formerly on the faculty on the University of Nevada, Las Vegas, and now a judge on the Ninth Circuit Court of Appeals), who as Justice Department lawyers helped draft legal guidelines for the mistreatment of detainees. The German court again dismissed the case, reasoning that it had insufficient links to Germany. For the application of the doctrine of superior responsibility with respect to the Abu Ghraib abuses, *see* Allison Marston Danner & Jenny S. Martinez, *Guilty Associations: Joint Criminal Enterprise, Command Responsibility, and the Development of International Criminal Law,* 93 CALIF. L. REV. 75, 130 (2005); James W. Smith III, *A Few Good Scapegoats: The Abu Ghraib Courts-Martial and the Failure of the Military Justice System,* 27 WHITTIER L. REV. 671 (2006).

10. For Further Reading

For additional commentary on the *Yamashita* case, *see* Charles Fairman, *The Supreme Court on Military Jurisdiction: Martial Rule in Hawaii and the Yamashita Case*, 59 HARV. L. REV. 833 (1946); R. L. Lael, THE YAMASHITA PRECEDENT: WAR CRIMES AND COMMAND RESPONSIBILITY (1982); Bruce D. Landrum, *The Yamashita War Crimes Trial: Command Responsibility Then and Now,* 149 MIL. L. REV. 293 (1995). For accounts of the proceeding by General Yamashita's U.S. defense counsel, *see* George F. Guy, *The Defense of Yamashita*, 4 WYO. L. J. 153 (1949) and Frank A. Reel, THE CASE OF GENERAL YAMASHITA (1949). For a fictionalized account of the proceedings, *see* James Webb, THE EMPEROR'S GENERAL (1999).

B. CODIFICATION OF THE SUPERIOR RESPONSIBILITY DOCTRINE

Despite this fertile WWII precedent, the four Geneva Conventions, promulgated at the close of World War II, did not codify the doctrine of superior responsibility. Drafters optimistically assumed that domestic proceedings under the penal provisions of the Conventions would apply domestic military or criminal law liability doctrines. Thus, it was not until 1977 that the drafters of Protocol I to the Conventions included at

Article 86 and 87 a rendition of the three-part superior responsibility standard employed in the postwar cases:

Article 86: Failure to Act

1. The High Contracting Parties and the Parties to the conflict shall repress grave breaches, and take measures necessary to suppress all other breaches, of the Conventions or of this Protocol which result from a failure to act when under a duty to do so.
2. The fact that a breach of the Conventions or of this Protocol was committed by a subordinate does not absolve his superiors from penal or disciplinary responsibility, as the case may be, if they knew, or had information which should have enabled them to conclude in the circumstances at the time, that he was committing or was going to commit such a breach and if they did not take all feasible measures within their power to prevent or repress the breach.

Article 87: Duty of Commanders

1. The High Contracting Parties and the Parties to the conflict shall require military commanders, with respect to members of the armed forces under their command and other persons under their control, to prevent and, where necessary, to suppress and to report to competent authorities breaches of the Conventions and of this Protocol.
2. In order to prevent and suppress breaches, High Contracting Parties and Parties to the conflict shall require that, commensurate with their level of responsibility, commanders ensure that members of the armed forces under their command are aware of their obligations under the Conventions and this Protocol.
3. The High Contracting Parties and Parties to the conflict shall require any commander who is aware that subordinates or other persons under his control are going to commit or have committed a breach of the Conventions or of this Protocol, to initiate such steps as are necessary to prevent such violations of the Conventions or this Protocol, and, where appropriate, to initiate disciplinary or penal action against violators thereof.

Protocol Additional to the Geneva Conventions of 12 August 1949, and Relating to the Protection of Victims of International Armed Conflicts (Protocol I), June 8, 1977, 1125 U.N.T.S. 3. (Protocol I extends the protections of the Geneva Conventions to situations of armed conflicts "in which peoples are fighting against colonial domination and alien occupation and against racist régimes in the exercise of their right of self-determination.") What is the relationship between Articles 86 and 87? No such provision appears in the contemporaneous Protocol II governing non-international armed conflicts (NIACs). A proposal to require all parties to take measures to ensure observance of Protocol II by their military and civilian agents and persons subject to their authority was ultimately not adopted. The Commentary noted:

> In order that the authorities of the parties to the conflict, particularly those in command of the armed forces or of armed groups, may discharge their obligations under the present article, their military or civilian subordinates must be organized and subject to adequate discipline.

International Committee of the Red Cross, DRAFT ADDITIONAL PROTOCOLS TO THE GENEVA CONVENTIONS OF AUGUST 23, 1949: COMMENTARY 169 (Geneva, October 1973).

The U.N. Security Council in drafting the Statutes of the ICTY and ICTR adopted a slightly different formulation of superior responsibility. For example, according to 6(3) of the ICTR Statute:

> The fact that any of the acts [criminalized in] the present Statute was committed by a subordinate does not relieve his or her superior of criminal responsibility if he or she knew or had reason to know that the subordinate was about to commit such acts or had done so and the superior failed to take the necessary and reasonable measures to prevent such acts or to punish the perpetrators thereof.

The doctrine of superior responsibility was also codified in the ICC Statute, again slightly differently, as follows:

> Article 28: Responsibility of Commanders and Other Superiors
>
> In addition to other grounds of criminal responsibility under this Statute for crimes within the jurisdiction of the Court;
>
> (a) A military commander or person effectively acting as a military commander shall be criminally responsible for crimes within the jurisdiction of the Court committed by forces under his or her effective command and control, or effective authority and control as the case may be, as a result of his or her failure to exercise control properly over such forces, where:
>
> (i) That military commander or person either knew or, owing to the circumstances at the time, should have known that the forces were committing or about to commit such crimes; and
>
> (ii) That military commander or person failed to take all necessary and reasonable measures within his or her power to prevent or repress their commission or to submit the matter to the competent authorities for investigation and prosecution.

(b) With respect to superior and subordinate relationships not described in paragraph (a), a superior shall be criminally responsible for crimes within the jurisdiction of the Court committed by subordinates under his or her effective authority and control, as a result of his or her failure to exercise control properly over such subordinates, where:

(i) The superior either knew, or consciously disregarded information which clearly indicated, that the subordinates were committing or about to commit such crimes;

(ii) The crimes concerned activities that were within the effective responsibility and control of the superior; and

(iii) The superior failed to take all necessary and reasonable measures within his or her power to prevent or repress their commission or to submit the matter to the competent authorities for investigation and prosecution.

Separate and apart from these treaty formulations, the International Committee of the Red Cross (ICRC) considers the doctrine to be part of customary international law. Rule 153 in the organization's comprehensive study of the customary law of armed conflict provides:

> Commanders and other superiors are criminally responsible for war crimes committed by their subordinates if they knew, or had reason to know, that the subordinates were about to commit or were committing such crimes and did not take all necessary and reasonable measures in their power to prevent their commission, or if such crimes had been committed, to punish the persons responsible.

NOTES & QUESTIONS

1. Protocol I and *Mens Rea*

How does the Protocol I superior responsibility standard differ from the one employed in the *Yamashita* case or contained within the ICTY, ICTR, and ICC Statutes? What is the *mens rea* contained in the treaty—is it negligence or does Protocol I employ an elevated standard? What type of information would enable superiors "to conclude in the circumstances at the time, that [a subordinate] was committing or was going to commit such a breach?" How would a prosecutor acquire such evidence? May knowledge be presumed where abuses by a defendant's subordinates were widespread and notorious?

Of all the standards above, which is the easiest *mens rea* standard to meet from the perspective of the prosecution? Why would these different *mens rea* standards develop under the law? Imagine that you serve on a domestic court and must research the customary international law of superior responsibility—what is the operative *mens rea* standard? Must you apply the standard that is most favorable to an accused?

2. Military and Non-Military Superiors

The ICTY/ICTR Statutes do not make a distinction between military and civilian superiors. Why would the drafters of the ICC Statute distinguish between military commanders (Article 28(a)) and other "superior and subordinate relationships" (Article 28(b))? How does the prosecution's burden of proof differ under the two standards? What is the significance of sub-section 28(b)(ii) in the ICC Statute? Is this a fourth element of the doctrine or a sub-element of the subordination prong? How will defense counsel likely employ this provision? As you read the cases that follow, especially *Delalić* and *Bagilishema*, *infra*, consider whether the two *ad hoc* tribunals have developed a distinction between the duties of military and civilian superiors through their jurisprudence.

3. Non-International Armed Conflicts

As discussed more fully in Chapter 6 on the Legal Regulation of Armed Conflict, the primary rules applicable to non-international armed conflicts (NIACs) are found in Protocol II to the 1949 Geneva Conventions, completed in 1977, and common Article 3 of the 1949 Geneva Conventions. Neither Protocol II nor common Article 3 contains penal provisions defining substantive crimes or any forms of responsibility, no less superior responsibility. Why might this be so? Nonetheless, the ICTY has ruled that the doctrine of superior responsibility applies equally in NIACs. *See Prosecutor v. Hadžihasanović*, Case No. IT–01–47–AR72, Decision on Interlocutory Appeal Challenging Jurisdiction in Relation to Command Responsibility (July 16, 2003). How might the parties have argued this issue and on what grounds might the Tribunal have ruled?

Will the doctrine apply differently with respect to armed non-state actors, irregular armed militia, insurrectionists, or terrorist groups? The doctrine of superior responsibility is premised on the existence of a pre-existing legal duty to act. From where does this duty emanate in these non-state groups and what is its substantive content? Are such groups sufficiently organized to exercise command and control over subordinates? Does it matter if such groups are not structured in a classic pyramidal hierarchy but are rather more decentralized, flat in structure, or only loosely networked? Indeed, might a "franchise" structure be adaptive, allowing subgroups a greater degree of autonomy in terms of target selection and tactics, flexibility to exploit targets of opportunity, and a heightened ability to thwart detection, infiltration, and defection? What would be an appropriate internal disciplinary system for such a group in the absence of national courts or a formal system of military justice? For a discussion, *see* Sandesh Sivakumaran, *Command Responsibility in Irregular Groups*, 10 J. INT'L CRIM. JUST. 1129 (2012); Jelena Pejic, *The Protective Scope of Common Article 3: More than Meets the Eye*, 93 INT'L REV. RED CROSS 1, 9–10 (2011) (discussing the power of non-state actors to establish courts to prosecute law-of-war violations).

4. Superior Responsibility and the Khmer Rouge

The Khmer Rouge held power in Cambodia from 1975–1979. Two former members of the Khmer Rouge leadership—Ieng Thirith (former Minister of Social Affairs) and her husband Ieng Sary (former Foreign Minister)—invoked the doctrine of *nullum crimen since lege* ("no crime without law") to challenge the superior responsibility charges brought against them in the Extraordinary Chambers in the Courts of Cambodia (ECCC). They argued that customary international law did not recognize superior responsibility as a basis of liability during the Khmer Rouge era, particularly for civilian superiors. Therefore, they could not be held criminally responsible for their subordinates' actions.

The Pre-Trial Chamber found that during 1975–1979, superior responsibility had crystallized into a norm of customary international law that was sufficiently specific and accessible so as to make it foreseeable to the accused that criminal sanctions could be imposed on them for their failures of command. *See Prosecutor v. Ieng Sary*, Case No. 002/19–09–2007–ECCC/OCIJ (PTC75), Decision on Ieng Sary's Appeal Against the Closing Order (Apr. 11, 2011). (In the ECCC, a Closing Order is similar to an indictment in that it contains notional charges against the accused as identified by the Co-Investigating Judges). For a discussion and a critique of the ECCC's reasoning, *see* Rehan Abeyratne, *Superior Responsibility And The Principle Of Legality At The ECCC*, 44 GEO. WASH. INT'L L. REV. 39 (2012).

If you represented the accused, how would you argue this motion? How would you address the fact that Protocols I and II were finalized in 1977, halfway through the Khmer Rouge's reign, particularly since Protocol II is silent as to command responsibility? Could the defendants reasonably have believed that their conduct was lawful at the time? Neither case went to judgment, by the way. Ieng Sary died of heart failure mid-trial in March 2013, and his wife, Ieng Thirith, was declared incompetent to stand trial in November 2011.

C. THE ELEMENTS OF THE MODERN DOCTRINE OF SUPERIOR RESPONSIBILITY

1. SUBORDINATION

The superior responsibility doctrine is premised on a relationship of subordination between the defendant and the direct perpetrators of international crimes. Thus, the subordination prong operates as a threshold element to ensure the applicability of the doctrine. If subordination is not present, then the defendant may only be found liable for the acts of another through other principles of direct or derivative liability, such as complicity, co-perpetration, or conspiracy. Determining the existence of a relationship of subordination in the military context may seem a simple exercise; either the perpetrator is, or is not, in the defendant's chain of command. As the cases that follow reveal, however, subordination is a more nuanced concept, with *de jure* and *de facto* dimensions.

Consider the next case, arising out of acts of abuse perpetrated in a detention camp in the village of Čelebići, located in central Bosnia-Herzegovina, during 1992. (See the Appendix for a map of Yugoslavia.) The region in question was of strategic importance as the former Yugoslavia began breaking up, because it was a hub for communications and transportation lines from Sarajevo to other parts of Bosnia and also housed several important military facilities, such as barracks and munitions factories of the former Yugoslavia. At this time in the war, Bosnian Muslim and Bosnian Croat forces were working in tandem to defeat Bosnian Serb forces after Bosnian Serbs declared their intention to create a distinct Serbian entity within Bosnia-Herzegovina. Joint Muslim and Croat forces staffed Čelebići camp, which confined Bosnian Serb civilians and fighters who had been expelled from their homes or captured during the hostilities.

The *Čelebići* case was the first ICTY case to involve Bosnian Serb victims. The accused included Hazim Delić and Zdravko Mucić, who were alleged to have acted in the capacity of camp commanders. The Prosecution alleged that Zejnil Delalić exercised authority over the Čelebići prison camp by virtue of being a commander of joint, and later Bosnian, forces in the area. Esad Landžo was a guard in the camp. The Indictment charged the four accused with grave breaches of the Geneva Conventions of 1949, under Article 2 of the ICTY Statute, and with violations of the laws or customs of war, under Article 3 of the ICTY Statute. The Indictment primarily charged Defendants Mucić and Delalić pursuant to Article 7(3) of the ICTY Statute for crimes committed by their subordinates, including those alleged to have been committed by co-accused Landžo and Delić.

The Trial Chamber found that defendants Mucić, Delić and Landžo killed, tortured, sexually assaulted, and mistreated Čelebići detainees. Defendant Delalić was acquitted on the grounds that he did not exercise sufficient command and control over the Čelebići camp or the guards who worked there to give rise to criminal responsibility for their actions. Defendant Mucić appealed the Trial Chamber's determination of his command responsibility, among other things. The Prosecution appealed certain legal findings of the Trial Chamber with respect to the doctrine that led to the acquittal of defendant Delalić. The Appeals Chamber decision on these points follows:

The Prosecutor v. Delalić et al., Case No. IT–96–21–A, Judgement (Feb. 20, 2001)

In the Appeals Chamber

IV. Grounds of Appeal Concerning Command Responsibility

182. In the present appeal, Mucić and the Prosecution have filed grounds of appeal which relate to the principles of command responsibility. * * *

183. The ninth ground of Mucić's appeal alleges both a legal and factual error on the part of the Trial Chamber in finding that Mucić had, at the time when the crimes concerned in this case were being committed, the *de facto* authority of a commander in the Čelebići camp. Most of the arguments presented by Mucić are concerned with the Trial Chamber's factual findings. * * *

186. In his brief, Mucić appeared to contest the issue of whether a *de facto* status is sufficient for the purpose of ascribing criminal responsibility under Article 7(3) of the Statute. It is submitted that *de facto* status must be equivalent to *de jure* status in order for a superior to be held responsible for the acts of subordinates. He submits that a person in a position of *de facto* authority must be shown to wield the same kind of control over subordinates as *de jure* superiors. In the appellant's view, the approach taken by the Trial Chamber that the absence of formal legal authority, in relation to civilian and military structures, does not preclude a finding of superior responsibility, "comes too close to the concept of strict responsibility." Further, Mucić interprets Article 28 of the ICC Statute as limiting the application of the doctrine of command responsibility to "commanders or those effectively acting as commanders." He submits that "the law relating to *de jure/de facto* command responsibility is far from certain" and that the Appeals Chamber should address the issue. * * *

188. The Trial Chamber found:

> [. . .] a *position of command is indeed a necessary precondition* for the imposition of command responsibility. However, this statement must be qualified by the recognition that the existence of such a position *cannot be determined by reference to formal status alone*. Instead, the factor that determines liability for this type of criminal responsibility is the *actual possession, or non-possession, of powers of control over the actions of subordinates*. Accordingly, formal designation as a commander should not be considered to be a necessary prerequisite for command responsibility to attach, as such responsibility may be imposed by virtue of a person's *de facto*, as well as *de jure*, position as a commander. * * *

190. The *Blaškić* Judgement, referring to the Trial Judgement and to Additional Protocol I, construed control in terms of the material ability of a commander to punish:

> What counts is his material ability, which instead of issuing orders or taking disciplinary action may entail, for instance, submitting reports to the competent authorities in order for proper measures to be taken.[246]

191. In respect of the meaning of a commander or superior as laid down in Article 7(3) of the Statute, the Appeals Chamber held in *Aleksovski*:

> Article 7(3) provides the legal criteria for command responsibility, thus giving the word "commander" a juridical meaning, in that the provision becomes applicable only where a superior with the required mental element failed to exercise his powers to prevent subordinates from committing offences or to punish them afterwards. This necessarily implies that a superior must have such powers prior to his failure to exercise them. If the facts of a case meet the criteria for the authority of a superior as laid down in Article 7(3), the legal finding would be that an accused is a superior within the meaning of that provision.[247] * * *

193. The power or authority to prevent or to punish does not solely arise from *de jure* authority conferred through official appointment. In many contemporary conflicts, there may be only *de facto*, self-proclaimed governments and therefore *de facto* armies and paramilitary groups subordinate thereto. Command structure, organised hastily, may well be in disorder and primitive. To enforce the law in these circumstances requires a determination of accountability not only of individual offenders but of their commanders or other superiors who were, based on evidence, in control of them without, however, a formal commission or appointment. A tribunal could find itself powerless to enforce humanitarian law against *de facto* superiors if it only accepted as proof of command authority a formal letter of authority, despite the fact that the superiors acted at the relevant time with all the powers that would attach to an officially appointed superior or commander. * * *

195. The Trial Chamber had already considered the origin and meaning of *de facto* authority with reference to existing practice. Based on an analysis of World War II jurisprudence, the Trial Chamber also concluded that the principle of superior responsibility reflected in Article 7(3) of the Statute encompasses political leaders and other civilian superiors in positions of authority. The Appeals Chamber finds no reason to disagree with the Trial Chamber's analysis of this jurisprudence. The principle that military and other superiors may be held criminally

---

[246] *Blaškić* Judgement, para. 302.

[247] *Aleksovski* Appeal Judgement, para. 76.

responsible for the acts of their subordinates is well-established in conventional and customary law. The standard of control reflected in Article 87(3) of Additional Protocol I may be considered as customary in nature. In relying upon the wording of Articles 86 and 87 of Additional Protocol I to conclude that "it is clear that the term 'superior' is sufficiently broad to encompass a position of authority based on the existence of *de facto* powers of control," the Trial Chamber properly considered the issue in finding the applicable law.

196. "Command," a term which does not seem to present particular controversy in interpretation, normally means powers that attach to a military superior, whilst the term "control," which has a wider meaning, may encompass powers wielded by civilian leaders. In this respect, the Appeals Chamber does not consider that the rule is controversial that civilian leaders may incur responsibility in relation to acts committed by their subordinates or other persons under their effective control. Effective control has been accepted, including in the jurisprudence of the Tribunal, as a standard for the purposes of determining superior responsibility. The showing of effective control is required in cases involving both *de jure* and *de facto* superiors. This standard has more recently been reaffirmed in the ICC Statute, Article 28 * * *.[255]

197. In determining questions of responsibility it is necessary to look to effective exercise of power or control and not to formal titles. This would equally apply in the context of criminal responsibility. In general, the possession of *de jure* power in itself may not suffice for the finding of command responsibility if it does not manifest in effective control, although a court may presume that possession of such power *prima facie* results in effective control unless proof to the contrary is produced. The Appeals Chamber considers that the ability to exercise effective control is necessary for the establishment of *de facto* command or superior responsibility and thus agrees with the Trial Chamber that the absence of formal appointment is not fatal to a finding of criminal responsibility, provided certain conditions are met. Mucić's argument that *de facto* status must be equivalent to *de jure* status for the purposes of superior responsibility is misplaced. Although the degree of control wielded by a *de jure* or *de facto* superior may take different forms, a *de facto* superior must be found to wield substantially similar powers of control over subordinates to be held criminally responsible for their acts. The Appeals Chamber therefore agrees with the Trial Chamber's conclusion:

> While it is, therefore, the Trial Chamber's conclusion that a superior, whether military or civilian, may be held liable under the principle of superior responsibility on the basis of his *de facto* position of authority, the fundamental considerations

---

[255] *Tadić* Appeal Judgement, para. 223, which states that the text of the ICC Statute may be taken to express the legal position *i.e.*, *opinio juris* of those States that adopted the Statute, at the time it was adopted. Mucić's reliance on the ICC Statute in support of his arguments is thus not helpful in relation to the determination of the law as it stood at the time of the offences alleged in the Indictment.

underlying the imposition of such responsibility must be borne in mind. *The doctrine of command responsibility is ultimately predicated upon the power of the superior to control the acts of his subordinates.* A duty is placed upon the superior to exercise this power so as to prevent and repress the crimes committed by his subordinates, and a failure by him to do so in a diligent manner is sanctioned by the imposition of individual criminal responsibility in accordance with the doctrine. *It follows that there is a threshold at which persons cease to possess the necessary powers of control over the actual perpetrators of offences and, accordingly, cannot properly be considered their "superiors" within the meaning of Article 7(3) of the Statute.* While the Trial Chamber must at all times be alive to the realities of any given situation and be prepared to pierce such veils of formalism that may shield those individuals carrying the greatest responsibility for heinous acts, *great care must be taken lest an injustice be committed in holding individuals responsible for the acts of others in situations where the link of control is absent or too remote.*

Accordingly, it is the Trial Chamber's view that, in order for the principle of superior responsibility to be applicable, *it is necessary that the superior have effective control over the persons committing the underlying violations of international humanitarian law, in the sense of having the material ability to prevent and punish the commission of these offences.* With the caveat that such authority can have a *de facto* as well as a *de jure* character, the Trial Chamber accordingly shares the view expressed by the International Law Commission that the doctrine of superior responsibility extends to civilian superiors only to the extent that they exercise a degree of control over their subordinates which is similar to that of military commanders.

198. As long as a superior has effective control over subordinates, to the extent that he can prevent them from committing crimes or punish them after they committed the crimes, he would be held responsible for the commission of the crimes if he failed to exercise such abilities of control.

199. The remainder of Mucić's ground of appeal concerns the sufficiency of the evidence regarding the existence of his *de facto* authority. This poses a question of fact, which the Appeals Chamber will now consider.

200. At the appeal hearing, Mucić argued that the Trial Chamber's reliance on the evidence cited in the Trial Judgement in support of the finding that he exercised superior authority was unreasonable. He made a number of arguments which were ultimately directed to his central contention that the evidence was insufficient to support a conclusion that

he was a *de facto* commander for the entire period of time set forth in the Indictment. His submissions particularly emphasised that he had no authority in the camp during the months of May, June, or July of 1992. * * *

204. In paragraphs 737–767 of the Trial Judgement, a thorough analysis of evidence led the Trial Chamber to conclude that Mucić "had all the powers of a commander" in the camp. The conclusion was also based on Mucić's own admission that he had "necessary disciplinary powers." Mucić, who disputes this conclusion on appeal, must persuade the Appeals Chamber that the conclusion is one which could not have reasonably been made by a reasonable tribunal of fact, so that a miscarriage of justice has occurred. * * *

206. Having concluded that "the actual exercise of authority in the absence of a formal appointment is sufficient for the purpose of incurring criminal responsibility" provided that the *de facto* superior exercises actual powers of control, the Trial Chamber considered the argument of Mucić that he had no "formal authority." It looked at the following factors to establish that Mucić had *de facto* authority: Mucić's acknowledgement of his having authority over the Čelebići camp since 27 July 1992, the submission in the defence closing brief that Mucić used his "limited" authority to prevent crimes and to order that the detainees not be mistreated and that the offenders tried to conceal offences from him, the defence statement that when Mucić was at the camp, there was "far greater" discipline than when he was absent, the evidence that co-defendant Delić told the detainees that Mucić was commander, the evidence that he arranged for the transfer of detainees, his classifying of detainees for the purpose of continued detention or release, his control of guards, and the evidence that he had the authority to release prisoners. At trial, the Trial Chamber accepted this body of evidence. The Appeals Chamber considers that it has not been shown that the Trial Chamber erred in accepting the evidence which led to the finding that Mucić was commander of the camp and as such exercised command responsibility. * * *

214. For the foregoing reasons, the Appeals Chamber dismisses this ground of appeal and upholds the finding of the Trial Chamber that Mucić was the *de facto* commander of the Čelebići camp during the relevant period indicated in the Indictment. * * *

Whether Delalić Exercised Superior Responsibility

242. The Prosecution's second ground of appeal alleges an error of law in the Trial Chamber's interpretation of the nature of the superior-subordinate relationship which must be established to prove liability under Article 7(3) of the Statute. The Prosecution contends that the Trial Chamber wrongly "held that the doctrine of superior responsibility requires the perpetrator to be part of a subordinate unit in a direct chain of command under the superior." This legal error, it is said, led to the erroneous finding that Delalić did not exercise superior responsibility

over the Čelebići camp and thus was not responsible for the offences of the camp staff. * * *

253. However, the argument of the Prosecution goes further than challenging the perceived requirement of *direct* subordination. The key focus of the Prosecution argument appears to be the Trial Chamber's rejection of the Prosecution theory that persons who can exert "substantial influence" over a perpetrator who is not necessarily a subordinate may, by virtue of that influence, be held responsible under the principles of command responsibility. The Prosecution does not argue that *anyone* of influence may be held responsible in the context of superior responsibility, but that a superior encompasses someone who "may exercise a substantial degree of influence over the perpetrator or over the entity to which the perpetrator belongs."

254. The Trial Chamber understood the Prosecution at trial to be seeking "to extend the concept of the exercise of superior authority to persons over whom the accused can exert substantial influence in a given situation, who are clearly not subordinates," which is essentially the approach taken by the Prosecution on appeal. The Trial Chamber also rejected the idea, which it apparently regarded as being implicit in the Prosecution view, that a superior-subordinate relationship could exist in the absence of a subordinate:

> The view of the Prosecution that a person may, in the absence of a subordinate unit through which authority is exercised, incur responsibility for the exercise of a superior authority seems to the Trial Chamber a novel proposition clearly at variance with the principle of command responsibility. The law does not know of a universal superior without a corresponding subordinate. The doctrine of command responsibility is clearly articulated and anchored on the relationship between superior and subordinate, and the responsibility of the commander for actions of members of his troops. It is a species of vicarious responsibility through which military discipline is regulated and ensured. This is why a subordinate unit of the superior or commander is a *sine qua non* for superior responsibility.

The Trial Chamber thus unambiguously required that the perpetrator be subordinated to the superior. While it referred to hierarchy and chain of command, it was clear that it took a wide view of these concepts:

> The requirement of the existence of a "superior-subordinate relationship" which, in the words of the Commentary to Additional Protocol I, should be seen "in terms of a hierarchy encompassing the concept of control," is particularly problematic in situations such as that of the former Yugoslavia during the period relevant to the present case—situations where previously existing formal structures have broken down and where, during an interim period, the new, possibly

> improvised, control and command structures may be ambiguous and ill-defined. It is the Trial Chamber's conclusion . . . that persons effectively in command of such more informal structures, with power to prevent and punish the crimes of persons who are in fact under their control, may under certain circumstances be held responsible for their failure to do so.

The Trial Chamber's references to concepts of subordination, hierarchy and chains of command must be read in this context, which makes it apparent that they need not be established in the sense of formal organisational structures so long as the fundamental requirement of an effective power to control the subordinate, in the sense of preventing or punishing criminal conduct, is satisfied. * * *

258. The Prosecution relied at trial and on appeal on the *Hostage case* in support of its position that the perpetrators of the crimes for which the superior is to be held responsible need not be subordinates, and that substantial influence is a sufficient degree of control. The Appeals Chamber concurs with the view of the Trial Chamber that the *Hostage case* is based on a distinction in international law between the duties of a commander for occupied territory and commanders in general. That case was concerned with a commander in occupied territory. The authority of such a commander is to a large extent territorial, and the duties applying in occupied territory are more onerous and far-reaching than those applying to commanders generally. Article 42 of the Regulations Respecting the Laws and Customs of War on Land, annexed to the Hague Convention (IV) Respecting the Laws and Customs of War on Land 1907, provides:

> Territory is considered occupied when it is actually placed under the authority of the hostile army. The occupation extends only to the territory where such authority has been established and can be exercised.

Article 43 provides:

> The authority of the legitimate power having in fact passed into the hands of the occupant, the latter shall take all the measures in his power to restore, and ensure, as far as possible, public order and safety, while respecting, unless absolutely prevented, the laws in force in the country.

This clearly does not apply to commanders in general. It was not then alleged, nor could it now be, that Delalić was a commander in occupied territory, and the Trial Chamber found expressly that he was not. * * *

266. The Appeals Chamber considers, therefore, that customary law has specified a standard of *effective* control, although it does not define precisely the means by which the control must be exercised. It is clear, however, that substantial influence as a means of control in any sense which falls short of the possession of effective control over subordinates, which requires the possession of material abilities to prevent subordinate

offences or to punish subordinate offenders, lacks sufficient support in State practice and judicial decisions. Nothing relied on by the Prosecution indicates that there is sufficient evidence of State practice or judicial authority to support a theory that substantial influence as a means of exercising command responsibility has the standing of a rule of customary law, particularly a rule by which criminal liability would be imposed.

267. The Appeals Chamber therefore finds that the Trial Chamber has applied the correct legal test in the case of Delalić. There is, therefore, no basis for any further application of that test to the Trial Chamber's findings, whether by the Appeals Chamber or by a reconstituted Trial Chamber.

NOTES & QUESTIONS

1. "The Forgotten Case"

The *Čelebići* case generated six years of litigation, bouncing between the Trial Chamber and the Appeals Chamber several times. As one of the first contested cases to go to final judgment, and the first to involve multiple defendants, the ICTY issued a number of important interlocutory rulings on issues of first impression concerning the form of the indictment, the availability of provisional release during trial, the assignment of defense counsel, the management of joint trials, and the presentation of evidence. The case also involved the first conviction on superior responsibility issued from an international tribunal since the WWII period. (The *Akayesu* case before the ICTR was the first international case to consider the doctrine, although the accused was acquitted of the superior responsibility charges brought against him, apparently because the doctrine was improperly alleged in the Indictment.) The *Čelebići* Appeals Chamber confirmed sentences of up to 18 years for the convicted defendants to be served in Finland. The Appeals Chamber recommended that defendant Mucić's sentence be increased from seven to nine years to take into account his dual role as individual perpetrator and responsible commander. Mucić was released early on July 18, 2003 since he had been in custody since March 18, 1996. For a discussion of the sentences, and an argument that they are too lenient given the superior responsibility of the accused, *see* Christine Bishai, *Superior Responsibility, Inferior Sentencing: Sentencing Practice at the International Criminal Tribunals*, 11 NW. J. INT'L HUM. RTS. 83 (2013).

2. Effective Control and Substantial Influence

What is the difference between command and control? How is that distinction relevant to prosecutions of military versus non-military superiors? How does the Tribunal define "effective control"? Does the doctrine of superior responsibility offer incentives to defendants to relinquish their powers of command and control, or to allow subordinates to operate autonomously, in order to avoid the risk of responsibility? Has the ICTY made it too difficult to convict superiors with its formulation of the subordination element of the doctrine of superior responsibility?

The Appeals Chamber in the principal case rejects the Prosecution's argument that evidence of a defendant's "substantial influence" over the direct perpetrators should be sufficient to hold the former liable for the criminal acts of the latter. Does the Tribunal take too limited a view of the power individuals may have over others outside of any formal command relationship? Should it be enough that a defendant has such a degree of influence over the direct perpetrator that the defendant would have had the actual ability to encourage the perpetrator to commit a crime or to intervene to prevent the crime?

3. Superior Responsibility During Occupation

The principal case highlights a distinction between the responsibilities of a commander on the battlefield versus in a situation of occupation. Occupation occurs when territory is placed under the control of a hostile army. Sovereignty does not technically pass to the occupying state. Rather, it is held "in trust" by the occupying state until the cessation of hostilities and the re-establishment of the local government. Articles 42 and 43 of the Regulations annexed to the Fourth Hague Convention of 1907 address the responsibilities of a foreign military occupying the territory of a hostile state. These responsibilities are elaborated upon in Section III of the Fourth Geneva Convention.

How and why does the doctrine of superior responsibility differ in battlefield versus occupation scenarios? How far does superior responsibility extend in occupation scenarios? Could a commander be liable for all criminal acts within the area of occupation, including crimes committed by the local civilian populace, by virtue of his executive power? In the Hostages Case, the tribunal held that a commander of occupied territory

> is charged with notice of occurrences taking place within that territory. * * * If he fails to require and obtain complete information, the dereliction of duty rests upon him and he is in no position to plead his own dereliction as a defense.

The Hostages Case, 11 TRIALS OF WAR CRIMINALS BEFORE THE NUREMBERG MILITARY TRIBUNALS UNDER CONTROL COUNCIL NO. 10, 764, 1271 (1950). Major William H. Parks surmises that General Yamashita was held to a higher duty because he was also military governor of the Philippines. "As military governor, all trust, care, and confidence of the population were reposed in him. This was in addition to his duties and responsibilities as a military commander." Maj. William H. Parks, *Command Responsibility for War Crimes*, 62 MIL. L. REV. 1, 38 (1973).

4. National Reconciliation

The *Čelebići* case was also important because it highlighted abuses against Serbian victims by Muslim perpetrators. (Defendants Delalić, Delić, and Landžo are Bosnian Muslims; defendant Mucić is a Bosnian Croat). Upon its inception, the Tribunal was scorned as "anti-Serb" by some Serbian observers, in part because most of the original indictments were issued against defendants of Serbian ethnicity. Is the *Čelebići* case likely to convince Serbian observers that the Tribunal is dealing out more than victor's justice? How is this case likely to impact claims of Bosnian Muslim victimhood in the

Balkan wars? For a new study of the impact of the ICTY on ethnic relations in the former Yugoslavia, see Diane Orentlicher, SOME KIND OF JUSTICE: THE ICTY'S IMPACT IN BOSNIA & SERBIA (2019).

Note that a similar dilemma exists in Rwanda, where Hutu victims unsuccessfully called for the ICTR to indict perpetrators from the Rwandan Patriotic Front (RPF), the Tutsi rebel group that eventually ousted the Hutu majority government responsible for the genocide. In situations of ethnic conflict, should an international prosecutor aim to issue indictments that are proportional to the ethnic makeup of the population or the suffering of the various groups involved in the conflict? Or, should the prosecutor be unconcerned with the allocation of indictments along ethnic lines? Which approach is more likely to be perceived of as legitimate by the parties involved or by the international community? Which approach is more likely to achieve national or ethnic reconciliation? Should the reconciliation of warring groups be a concern of tribunals adjudicating international criminal law in the wake of armed conflict? Note that Security Council Resolution 955 establishing the ICTR asserts that the Tribunal was designed to "contribute to the process of the national reconciliation and to the restoration and maintenance of peace." S.C. Res. 955, U.N. SCOR, 49th Sess., 3453rd mtg., U.N. Doc. S/Res/955 (1994).

5. *De Jure* v. *De Facto* Superiors

How did the Tribunal adapt the principle of superior responsibility to the unique context of the war in the former Yugoslavia, which featured informal militia and paramilitaries operating outside of any formal command structure and small unit commando raids organized by individuals with a high degree of delegated authority? Will the doctrine of superior responsibility apply where such militias are created to provide deniability on the part of the central authorities for abuses, as has been alleged in the Sudan with respect to the *janjaweed*? What about where militias are genuinely independent of the national or centralized authorities, as is the case in Colombia? What about in the context of insurgencies, characterized by negligible command structures, high degrees of autonomy, and spontaneous warfare "more resembling heavily armed anarchy than organized warfare?" J.P. Mackley, *The Balkan Quagmire Myth: Taking on the Serbs would be Much More Grenada than Vietnam*, WASH. POST (Mar. 7, 1993).

What is the difference between *de jure* and *de facto* command and control? Which is easier to prove? Is it necessary to demonstrate effective control for both *de jure* and *de facto* superiors? If not, should it be? Should the fact that a defendant occupied a *de jure* position of command be sufficient to satisfy the subordination prong of the doctrine? The Tribunal at para. 197 above intimates that a showing of *de jure* command gives rise to a rebuttable presumption that the defendant commander exercised effective control. What is the effect of this presumption? Does it shift the burden of production or of persuasion or both? Is such a presumption appropriate in the criminal law setting? How would a *de jure* commander of troops rebut this presumption? Might a superior's *de facto* command or control exceed her *de jure* command or control and vice versa? How would a prosecutor demonstrate this through the presentation of evidence?

6. The Chain of Command

Although organizational structures vary across national systems, a formal armed force is typically organized with the following structure: A team contains 4–5 people; two teams, plus a non-commissioned officer as squad leader, make up a squad. A platoon, containing 2–4 squads and 25–40 troops, is typically the smallest military unit led by a commissioned officer (a lieutenant)—an individual empowered by a sovereign to exercise command. A company (or battery with respect to artillery units) is commanded by a captain and contains 2–8 platoons or 60–250 troops. A battalion (or squadron) is composed of 2–6 companies of 300–1000 troops and is commanded by a lieutenant colonel. A battalion is generally the smallest military unit capable of independent operations (i.e. not attached to a higher command). A battalion may be homogeneous with respect to type (e.g. an infantry battalion or a tank battalion). A regiment (or brigade) usually contains 3–4 battalions of 2–5,000 troops and is commanded by a colonel. A division usually contains 2–5 brigades or regiments (plus an aviation brigade and headquarters brigade) and is commanded by a major general. A corps, commanded by a lieutenant general, consists of more than one division, plus support brigades. An army contains 50,000 plus soldiers, combining two or more corps. An army is commanded by a lieutenant general or higher. *See* Department of the Army, Organization of the United States Army, DA Pamphlet 10–1.

Consider this description of the distinction between operational and tactical command in the military context:

> Senior military officers [with operational command] do not issue orders directly to troops, but instead order and direct the commanders of smaller groupings. At the end of the scale, tactical commanders, who are most commonly officers in the field, exercise direct command over troops. Tactical command is limited subject to the directions of operational and strategic command. At this level, virtually any person of whatever rank may become a tactical commander, since even a private can assume tactical command of a unit whose other superiors have been incapacitated from battle.

Ilias Bantekas, PRINCIPLES OF DIRECT AND SUPERIOR RESPONSIBILITY IN INTERNATIONAL HUMANITARIAN LAW 75–6 (2002). *See also* Ilias Bantekas, *The Contemporary Law of Superior Responsibility*, 93 AM. J. INT'L L. 573, 584 (1999) ("While operational command supposes vested authority over units linked to the operational superior through the leader of each unit, tactical command refers to a state of actual control over a defined number of subordinates."). How does this distinction play out in the context of the doctrine of superior responsibility? Do such concepts translate to the civilian context?

7. The Defense

How does a defendant commander defend against a charge of command responsibility? Does the doctrine of superior responsibility place defendants in an evidentiary bind? If they want to defeat the first prong of the doctrine (the effective command and control), they must show that they did not have the material ability to issue orders that would be obeyed by subordinates. If they want to defeat the third prong of the doctrine, however, they have to show that they issued orders in an effort to prevent abuses. Consider how defendant Mucić, and others in this chapter, navigated the intersection of these two elements. What is a commander to do to avoid criminal liability if they have lost effective control over their troops, as General Yamashita argued had happened to him? Mutiny? Surrender their unit? Resign? What about a commander of an unprofessional army that has been hastily formed in a civil war scenario? Or a commander whose *de jure* troops may have ethnic or other prior allegiances to other individuals? Or a commander who is preoccupied with implementing offensive tactics or countermanding an enemy assault? Should the law recognize a defense of "impossibility of performance"? Consider these questions as you undertake the next problem, the facts of which are drawn from a case before the ICTY.

PROBLEM

When the civil war broke out in the former Yugoslavia, what was later to become the Army of Bosnia-Herzegovina ("ABiH") initially consisted of more or less organised units alongside spontaneously created militia that were not part of any military structure. Bosnian authorities slowly transformed the various units into a functioning and organised army. The result was the Territorial Defence ("TO"), which was formally established on April 8, 1992, and which turned into the ABiH on April 12, 1992. In the beginning of its existence, including during the Indictment period, the ABiH was multi-ethnic in character. During this time, the ABiH was inadequately funded and was not a fully-functioning army. A system of ranks was only introduced in late 1993 or 1994. A number of persons commanded units who did not have any formal military training. Authorities attempted to appoint as commanders those who had military training or a background in the Yugoslav National Army ("JNA"). The evidence showed that there was distrust and even animosity between the commanders with a military background and those who lacked such a background.

Defendant was born in Serbia on January 6, 1952. After his military education he became an officer in the JNA. Once the war began, he was appointed by the Presidency of the Republic of Bosnia and Herzegovina ("RBiH") as Commander of the TO on May 25, 1992. Defendant was thus Supreme Commander, with the title "Chief," of the Main Staff of the ABiH.

On August 18, 1992 the Presidency formed five corps of the ABiH with Defendant as Chief of the Supreme Command Staff/Chief of the Main Staff. The 1st Corps was established on September 1, 1992 and was headquartered in Sarajevo. In 1993, the 1st Corps consisted of approximately 75,000 soldiers and was commanded by Vahid Karavelić. Subordinated to the 1st Corps were a number of units, including the 9th Motorised Brigade, the 10th Mountain Brigade, and the 2nd Independent Battalion.

The 9th Brigade was created by merging the 3rd Mountain Brigade, which was under the command of Ramiz Delalić, and the 7th Mountain Brigade. Vahid Karavelić testified at trial that the Presidency of Bosnia-Herzegovina decided to merge the brigades for two reasons: first, there were complaints that the 3rd Mountain Brigade did not carry out orders consistently and merging the brigades would therefore make it easier for the 1st Corps commander to exercise command and control, and secondly, in order to remove Ramiz Delalić from the post of brigade commander, which is why he was made Deputy Commander of the new 9th Brigade. Vahid Karavelić was doubtful, however, of how effective this removal of Ramiz Delalić was and testified that the soldiers who came from the previous 3rd Mountain Brigade probably respected Ramiz Delalić more than the new commander Sulejman Imsirović, a former JNA colonel. Zlatan Okić, an agent with the Ministry of the Interior State Security Service, testified to this as well, saying that although Ramiz Delalić "was not the commander any longer [. . .] he was still in charge."

The new 9th Brigade consisted of around 5,000 soldiers and was headquartered in central Sarajevo. The 9th Brigade had four combat battalions, one logistics battalion, a military police company, an artillery company, and an engineering company. In addition, each combat battalion had a sabotage platoon of 30 soldiers. The 9th Brigade's main operative task was the defence of a part of Sarajevo. The brigade was one of the stronger brigades of the 1st Corps in terms of composition, manpower, and equipment. Unlike the situation in many other ABiH brigades where only 25 to 30 percent of the soldiers were armed, in the 9th Brigade approximately 65 to 70 percent of the soldiers were armed. The 10th Brigade was a slightly smaller unit (three battalions and one 100-man strong assault company) than the 9th Brigade and was commanded by Musan Topalović.

The evidence as to the reputation of the 9th Brigade and the 10th Brigade varied significantly at trial. Vahid Karavelić, the 1st Corps commander and thus the brigades' superior commanding officer, testified that "not a single member of these units was ever described as a criminal in any way." Jusuf Jašarević, the Chief of the Main Staff, gave a more nuanced opinion and testified that:

> most of the members of these brigades were honest people. A very small number of people were involved in breaches of discipline, and at that time we were dealing with the problem of this lack of discipline, which escalated gradually and contained elements of serious crimes.

However, Jusuf Jašarević also testified that "even outside the 1st Corps there were units where there was talk of indiscipline or insubordination." According to Devad Tirak, the 6th Corps chief of staff, not all members of these units caused incidents or mistreated the general population. He testified that instead it was the two brigade commanders and people around them who caused trouble. Nevertheless, in his opinion these two brigades had the worst reputation in terms of discipline and frequent incidents. Zlatan Okić testified that:

> both in the 9th and the 10th Brigades there were 95 per cent of patriots and perhaps only 5 per cent of people who were high-ranking people, but they had a pretty bad reputation. Those commanders surrounded themselves by groups of—well, I don't know whether I should call them common criminals or semi-criminals, but they were there.

Vehbija Karić, a senior officer in the Main Staff, stated that a number of soldiers within the two brigades had a criminal background and acted unpredictably and were undisciplined.

Defendant held the position of Supreme Commander of the ABiH until June 8, 1993, when the new position of "Commander of the Main Staff" of the ABiH was established (the "June 8 decision"). The June 8 decision, issued by the President of the RBiH Alija Izetbegović, appointed Rasim Delić to the position of ABiH Commander and provided that Defendant would retain the position of "Chief of the Main Staff" of the ABiH. In addition, the decision established two Deputy Commander positions to which Stjepan Šiber and Jovan Divjak were appointed. This retention of the post of Chief of the Main Staff, while establishing the post of Commander, appears to be at odds with the fundamental principle of single authority in command, which was applied in the ABiH. This principle ensures that there can only be one commander at any given level of the military hierarchy and one individual making decisions regarding subordinates for which he is solely responsible. Salko Gušić, the Commander of the 6th Corps, testified that "control" is more akin to direction or management than command. "Control" does not imply issuing orders. "Command," on the other hand, means the issuing of tasks to subordinate units.

Approximately six weeks after the June 8 meeting, on July 18, 1993, President Alija Izetbegović issued a decision further restructuring the ABiH ("July 18 decision"). The July 18 decision made the Chief of the Main Staff a Deputy Commander, thus increasing the number of Deputy Commanders to three, and specified that one Deputy Commander would be "Croat," one "Muslim," and one "Serb." According to the decision, the Deputy Commanders would "assume the duties of the Chief of the Main Staff on rotational basis." It appears, therefore, that this decision in practice removed Defendant from the post of Chief of the Main Staff and, thus, that he was the subject of a demotion. However, the evidence also shows that after the July 18 decision Defendant continued to sign documents as Chief of the Main Staff of the ABiH.

Ambiguity in the record existed concerning Defendant's position within the structure of the Main Staff following the June 8 and July 18 decisions. This ambiguity was in part as a consequence of the ABiH not being a fully-functional army. Witnesses referred to Defendant's position as being one of "chief of staff." Military witnesses testified that the "chief of staff" usually participates in coordination and planning. However, solely by virtue of his position, a chief of staff does not have the authority to issue combat orders but can only do so if his commander authorises him. In situations when the commander authorises his deputy commander to command, orders by the deputy are signed on behalf of the commander. In other words, a chief of staff was not "structurally speaking" in the line of command. The chief of staff would have a duty or even an obligation to explain and clarify to subordinate units the meaning of orders issued by the commander to whom the chief of staff was subordinated. Importantly, a chief of staff could not directly punish soldiers or units for violations of military discipline or law; he could, however, suggest to the commander to take disciplinary measures.

However, neither the June 8 decision nor the July 18 decision mentioned a separate "staff" component of the Main Staff or a position of "chief of staff." The evidence showed that a Main Staff chief of staff would have been directly in charge of, for instance, the Intelligence Administration. However, the July 18 decision plainly put this administration directly under the Commander of the Main Staff, Rasim Delić. The evidence was thus unclear as to what Defendant's position, *de jure* or *de facto*, was within the Supreme Command of the ABiH, the Main Staff.

The events in question concern the ABiH operation (called "Neretva-93") to counter a blockade by Bosnian Croat forces ("HVO") of Mostar, a city in Central Bosnia. (See the Appendix for a map of Yugoslavia.) The aim of the blockade was to isolate the city in order to enable a military occupation, eliminate Bosnian Muslims from the town, and eventually incorporate Mostar and surrounding areas into the Croat political entity, Herzeg-Bosna. The Prosecution alleged that Neretva-93 was planned at a meeting held in Zenica from August 21–22, 1993, and attended by most of the senior commanders of the ABiH including its Commander Rasim Delić. It is alleged attendees discussed an "Operational Plan," prepared and tabled by Defendant. It was agreed that an "Inspection Team," headed by Defendant, would go to Bosnia-Herzegovina "to command and co-ordinate the Operation." According to the Prosecution, "Defendant was the commander of the Operation and as such the troops, involved in the 'Neretva-93' Operation were under his command and control."

There was evidence that the 9th and 10th Brigades and the 2nd Independent Battalion were sent to Bosnia-Herzegovina following an order of Defendant dated September 2. However, there was also evidence that the Commander of the 1st Corps, Vahid Karavelić, did not carry out the order of Defendant as issued. Instead, there was evidence that only after confirming Defendant's order with the Commander of the Main Staff, Rasim Delić, Karavelić postponed the departure of the troops until September 6. Vahid Karavelić testified that at the time he had not seen Defendant's order. There was also testimony from the Deputy Commander of the 9th Brigade, Ramiz Delalić, that "[w]e were not able to leave because the superior command of the corps and the Supreme Staff could not agree amongst themselves." Thus, it appears that the 9th Brigade did not leave Sarajevo until September 7. There was evidence that Vahid Karavelić ordered the 9th Brigade to return to Sarajevo seven days later and that he had issued similar orders to the 2nd Independent Battalion. No combat order signed by Defendant was entered into evidence. There was, however, a combat order issued by Zulfikar Alipago, as commander of one axis of attack involving the 9th Motorised Brigade, the 10th Mountain Brigade, and the 2nd Independent Battalion. There was testimony in the record that Zulfikar Alipago, upon receiving an order from the Inspection Team concerning combat operations, tore up the order and wrote his own.

Evidence in the record indicated that on September 8, 1993, the 9th Brigade and a part of the 10th Brigade were billeted in the village of Grabovica. At this point in time, the 2nd Independent Battalion was already billeted there. Soldiers of the 9th Brigade had problems securing accommodation with the local Bosnian Croat civilian population in Grabovica. On September 8 and 9, 1993, thirty-three Bosnian Croat civilians were killed in Grabovica. It was established that seven of the killings in Grabovica were carried out by members of the 9th Brigade. For six of the killings, the evidence was not clear which units of the ABiH were involved. There was little evidence as to the perpetrators of the remainder of the killings. The Indictment further alleged that Defendant was notified during the night of September 8 about the killing of civilians and that once "notified and having knowledge of the criminal reputation of the 9th and 10th Brigades, Defendant was duty bound to act urgently."

In relation to the investigations of the crimes in Grabovica, there was evidence that Defendant, in the evening of September 9, instructed the Inspection Team to work together with the Ministry of the Interior and to keep "the Sarajevo command," rather than himself, informed. The evidence shows that at this point in time investigations were already under way. The evidence does not show that Defendant initiated the investigations or that the investigations were in any way carried forward through his actions. The evidence further shows that the 6th Corps Military Security Services, the Military Police Battalion of the 6th Corps, and the Military Police of the 44th Brigade were involved in the investigation into the events in Grabovica and that the Chief of the Main Staff Security Administration, Jusuf Jašarević, was kept informed of the results of their investigations. There was evidence that Rasim Delić ordered Defendant on September 12, 1993, "to re-consider the scope of the 'Neretva-93' Operation, to isolate the perpetrators of the incident, to take active measures and to immediately report on the measures he had taken." The Prosecution alleged that Defendant failed to implement the order of Rasim Delić resulting in a failure to punish the perpetrators of the crime, who were in the area until September 19, 1993.

In the Indictment, the Prosecution alleged that Defendant, "by virtue of his position and authority as Commander of the Operation," had effective control over the units subordinated to him, including the 9th Brigade, the 10th Brigade, and the 2nd Independent Battalion. It is alleged that Defendant, knowing of the 9th and the 10th Brigades' "notorious reputations for being criminal and uncontrolled in behaviour," ordered the deployment of units of these Brigades to Bosnia-Herzegovina. In view of the above, Defendant was charged with murder, punishable under Article 3 of the Statute as recognised by Common Article 3(1)(a) of the Geneva Conventions. The Indictment alleges that Defendant incurs criminal responsibility under Article 7(3) of the Statute since "notwithstanding his duties as a commander [. . .] Defendant did not take effective measures to prevent the killings of civilians in Grabovica" and "did not take steps to carry out a proper investigation to identify the perpetrators of the killings in Grabovica and as commander of the Operation to punish them accordingly."

Imagine that you are a member of the Trial Chamber hearing this case. How do you rule on defendant's liability under Article 7(3) for the deaths in the village of Grabovica? Which elements of the doctrine of superior responsibility are satisfied? By what evidence? Are there elements of the doctrine that are not satisfied? What type of evidence would you need to have in the record in order to be satisfied beyond a reasonable doubt that liability had been established?

2. CIVILIAN SUPERIORS

Precedent stemming from the World War II period confirms that the doctrine of superior responsibility applies to civilian—in addition to military—superiors. Tribunals in the World War II era held cabinet officials, government agents, and even non-state actors, such as German industrialists, liable for the acts of their subordinates.

The modern criminal tribunals have been somewhat more hesitant in extending the doctrine of superior responsibility beyond the military context. In *Čelebići*, defendant Mucić was a civilian warden of a prison-camp without formal appointment or military rank. Did this status impact the way in which the Tribunal applied the doctrine of superior responsibility? Should it have? How might the liability of civilian superiors differ from those of military superiors? Do different duties apply to non-military superiors? Is effective control exercised differently?

The full reach of the doctrine in the civilian context remains in flux. For example, Ignace Bagilishema was *bourgmestre* of Mabanza Commune in Kibuye Prefecture in Rwanda. The Indictment against him alleged that during the period of the genocide in Rwanda, thousands of Tutsi individuals sought refuge in Mabanza, including in the communal office and local stadium, from attacks that had occurred elsewhere in Kibuye. Once there, Tutsi citizens were allegedly attacked by members of the *Gendarmerie Nationale*, communal staff, police officers, *interahamwe* militiamen, and armed residents using guns, grenades, machetes, spears, and other makeshift weapons under the direction of Bagilishema and others. The Indictment also alleged that the defendant encouraged the *interahamwe* to set up roadblocks at strategic locations to screen individuals coming and going from the commune. For his involvement in these events in his commune, the Prosecutor charged Bagilishema with genocide, crimes against humanity, and war crimes under Article 6(3), the superior responsibility provision in the ICTR Statute.

The Trial Chamber determined that only some of the groups of perpetrators were subordinates in the sense that the defendant possessed the power of command and control over them. The Trial Chamber noted:

> 41. The first guilty verdict by an International Tribunal under the doctrine of command responsibility was entered in the ICTY's *Čelebići* case. Mucić, a civilian warden of a prison-camp, was held responsible for the ill-treatment of prisoners by camp guards.

Although the accused held his post without a formal appointment, he manifested, according to the Trial Chamber, all the powers and functions of a formal appointment as commander. Since the *Čelebići* judgement, the ICTY has found another civilian prison-camp warden guilty on the grounds of superior responsibility [Aleksovski], and the ICTR has found two civilians, a *préfet* [Kayishema] and a tea factory director [Musema], responsible as commanders for atrocities committed in Rwanda.

42. While there can be no doubt, therefore, that the doctrine of command responsibility extends beyond the responsibility of military commanders to encompass civilian superiors in positions of authority, the Chamber agrees with the approach articulated by the International Law Commission, and, more recently, in *Čelebići*, namely that the doctrine of command responsibility "extends to civilian superiors only to the extent that they exercise a degree of control over their subordinates which is similar to that of military commanders."

43. According to the Trial Chamber in *Čelebići*, for a civilian superior's degree of control to be "similar to" that of a military commander, the control over subordinates must be "effective," and the superior must have the "material ability" to prevent and punish any offences. Furthermore, the exercise of *de facto* authority must be accompanied by "the trappings of the exercise of *de jure* authority." The present Chamber concurs. The Chamber is of the view that these trappings of authority include, for example, awareness of a chain of command, the practice of issuing and obeying orders, and the expectation that insubordination may lead to disciplinary action. It is by these trappings that the law distinguishes civilian superiors from mere rabble-rousers or other persons of influence. * * *

152. In what follows, the Chamber will consider the character of the *de jure* or *de jure*-like relationships between the Accused and groups of persons which the Prosecution has alleged were at various times "subordinate" to him, in the sense of Article 6(3) of the Statute. The discovery of *de jure* aspects is only the first step towards satisfying the formal condition of subordination; for the character of a civilian's *de jure* authority (whether real or contrived) must be comparable to that exercised in a military context. If the relationship of the Accused to a particular group had no *de jure* aspects, and if moreover it lacked even the trappings of *de jure* command, then by definition no member of that group can be considered a subordinate of the Accused. The relationship will have been too dissimilar to that enjoyed by a *de jure* commander. * * *

165. [T]he Chamber is unable to conclude from the evidence before it that the employees of Mabanza *commune* were, vis-à-vis the Accused, in a *de jure*-like relationship, whether pre-existing or contrived, that bore the marks of a military-style command. The Prosecution has not adduced sufficient proof on this point, even

> though its charges of command responsibility presuppose such evidence. The Chamber therefore finds that no administrative communal employees were subordinates of the Accused in the sense required by Article 6(3) of the Statute. * * *

Prosecutor v. Bagilishema, Case No. ICTR–95–1A–T, Judgement (June 7, 2001). Bagilishema was the first defendant acquitted by the ICTR. He now lives in France with his family. The Tribunal also acquitted Bagilishema's assistant bourgmestre, Laurent Semanza, for the counts brought under Article 6(3) on the ground that a "simple showing of an accused's general influence in the community is insufficient to establish a superior-subordinate relationship." *Prosecutor v. Semanza*, Case No. 97–20–T, Judgement, para. 415 (May 15, 2003).

NOTES & QUESTIONS

1. Other Civilian Contexts

How might the doctrine of superior responsibility apply in the context of a civilian peacetime government, a political party, a church hierarchy, a police precinct, or a corporation? Revisit the Hirota case discussed *supra*. In *Prosecutor v. Musema*, Case No. ICTR–96–13, the Trial Chamber invoked the doctrine of superior responsibility in the industrial context against the director of a tea factory in Rwanda. In *Prosecutor v. Nahimana*, Case No. ICTR–99–52–T, an ICTR Trial Chamber convicted under Article 6(3) one of the founders and top executives of a media outlet involved in inciting genocide. The other founder (Barayagwiza), who had not been indicted under Article 6(3), was convicted on the basis of Article 6(1). The Trial Chamber reasoned:

> 970. The Chamber has considered the individual criminal responsibility of [defendants] Ferdinand Nahimana and Jean-Bosco Barayagwiza for RTLM [*Radio Télévision Libres des Mille Collines*] broadcasts, by virtue of their respective roles in the creation and control of RTLM. * * * Nahimana and Barayagwiza were, respectively, "number one" and "number two" in the top management of the radio. They represented the radio at the highest level in meetings with the Ministry of Information; they controlled the finances of the company; and they were both members of the Steering Committee, which functioned in effect as a board of directors for RTLM. Nahimana chaired the Program Committee of this board, and Barayagwiza chaired its Legal Committee. While the Chamber recognizes that Nahimana and Barayagwiza did not make decisions in the first instance with regard to each particular broadcast of RTLM, these decisions reflected an editorial policy for which they were responsible. [A]ll the RTLM broadcasters down the chain of command were ultimately accountable to the Steering Committee * * *. Nahimana's contention that the board did not intervene directly at the level of journalists has no legal relevance to his and Barayagwiza's exercise of authority at the highest

decision-making level. They intervened at a higher managerial level.

971. The broadcasts collectively conveyed a message of ethnic hatred and a call for violence against the Tutsi population. This message was heard around the world. "Stop that radio" was the cry Alison Des Forges [an expert witness from Human Rights Watch] heard from Rwanda during the killings, and it was the cry conveyed to the United Nations by Reporters Without Borders in May 1994. As board members responsible for RTLM, including its programming, Nahimana and Barayagwiza were responsible for this message and knew it was causing concern, even before 6 April 1994 and as early as October 1993 when they received a letter from the Rwandan Minister of Information. Their supervisory role in RTLM was acknowledged and exercised by them in their defence of the radio at meetings in 1993 and 1994 with the Minister. In the face of his concern, both Barayagwiza and Nahimana knew that RTLM programming was generating concern [and] defended the programming in their meetings with him. To the extent that they acknowledged there was a problem and tried to address it, they demonstrated their own sense of responsibility for RTLM programming. Ultimately, the concern was not addressed and RTLM programming followed its trajectory, steadily increasing in vehemence and reaching a pitched frenzy after 6 April [when the genocide began].

972. After 6 April 1994, although the evidence does not establish the same level of active support, it is nevertheless clear that Nahimana and Barayagwiza knew what was happening at RTLM and failed to exercise the authority vested in them as office-holding members of the governing body of RTLM, to prevent the genocidal harm that was caused by RTLM programming. That they had the *de facto* authority to prevent this harm is evidenced by the one documented and successful intervention of Nahimana to stop RTLM attacks on UNAMIR [U.N. Assistance Mission for Rwanda] and General Dallaire [the UNAMIR Force Commander]. * * *

973. For these reasons, the Chamber finds that Nahimana and Barayagwiza had superior responsibility for the broadcasts of RTLM. The Chamber notes that Nahimana has not been charged for genocide pursuant to Article 6(3) of its Statute. Only Barayagwiza is so charged. For his active engagement in the management of RTLM prior to 6 April, and his failure to take necessary and reasonable measures to prevent the killing of Tutsi civilians instigated by RTLM, the Chamber finds Jean-Bosco Barayagwiza guilty of genocide pursuant to Article 6(3) of its Statute.

On appeal, Barayagwiza successfully argued that he did not exercise effective control over RTLM after April 6, 1994. Thus the Appeals Chamber concluded that Barayagwiza could not be held liable under a theory of superior responsibility for the broadcasts after April 6, 1994, that were found to have instigated the genocide. *Prosecutor v. Nahimana*, Case No. ICTR–99–52–A, Judgement, paras. 621–636 (Nov. 28, 2007). Defendants also had ultimate authority over banking, corporate management, public relations, hiring and firing of employees, and broadcast content of the RTLM; however, they were not as involved in the day-to-day running of the station as Musema was in the tea factory. Nor were defendants present when the crimes were occurring; indeed, they were out of the country during the genocide. How do the elements of superior responsibility apply under these facts? Consider this theory:

> The Tribunal's judgment seems to turn more on a "Deistic" approach to superior responsibility: i.e., the defendants established RTLM, financed it, controlled its initial programming and tone, continued their stewardship even after intense censure regarding message of hate, and then left it to run its horrific course during the genocide.

Gregory S. Gordon, *"A War of Media, Words, Newspapers, and Radio Stations:" The ICTR Media Trial Verdict and a New Chapter in the International Law of Hate Speech*, 45 VA. J. INT'L L. 139, 190 (2004). Deism is a theological theory that posits that God created the universe but then has been hand's off ever since. *Id.* at n.283. Is this approach to the doctrine of superior responsibility consistent with the way in which the doctrine has been applied in the military context?

Barayagwiza was convicted under Article 6(3) in his capacity as the head of a political party for criminal acts of members of his party:

> 976. * * * The Chamber has considered the extent to which [defendant] Barayagwiza, as leader of the CDR, a political party, can be held responsible pursuant to Article 6(3) of its Statute for acts committed by CDR party members and *Impuzamugambi* ["those who have the same goal"—a militia group]. The Chamber recognizes that a political party and its leadership cannot be held accountable for all acts committed by party members or others affiliated to the party. A political party is unlike a government, military or corporate structure in that its members are not bound through professional affiliation or in an employment capacity to be governed by the decision-making body of the party. Nevertheless, the Chamber considers that to the extent that members of a political party act in accordance with the dictates of that party, or otherwise under its instruction, those issuing such dictates or instruction can and should be held accountable for their implementation. In this case, CDR party members and *Impuzamugambi* were following the lead of the party, and of Barayagwiza himself, who was at meetings, at demonstrations, and at roadblocks, where CDR members and *Impuzamugambi* were marshaled into action by party officials, including Barayagwiza or under his authority as leader of the party. In these circumstances, the Chamber holds that Barayagwiza was responsible for the activities of CDR members and *Impuzamugambi*, to the extent that

> such activities were initiated by or undertaken in accordance with his direction as leader of the CDR party.
>
> 977. The Chamber finds that Barayagwiza had superior responsibility over members of the CDR and its militia, the *Impuzamugambi*, as President of CDR at Gisenyi Prefecture and from February 1994 as President of CDR at the national level. He promoted the policy of CDR for the extermination of the Tutsi population and supervised his subordinates, the CDR members and *Impuzamugambi* militia, in carrying out the killings and other violent acts. For his active engagement in CDR, and his failure to take necessary and reasonable measures to prevent the killing of Tutsi civilians by CDR members and *Impuzamugambi*, the Chamber finds Barayagwiza guilty of genocide pursuant to Article 6(3) of its Statute.

Is the Tribunal's reasoning with respect to the liability of the head of a political party convincing? For a discussion of how the doctrine of superior responsibility might play out in the context of clergy sex abuse and the Vatican, *see* Paul Moses, *Putting Church Above Children*, COMMONWEAL (July 22, 2019).

2. Head of State Liability

Slobodan Milošević, the former President of Yugoslavia, became the first head of state to be prosecuted under a superior responsibility theory. The Japanese Emperor Hirohito escaped prosecution before the Tokyo Tribunal in part because the allies were concerned that his indictment would destabilize Japan. The former Rwandan head of state, Jean Kambanda, tendered a guilty plea. *See Prosecutor v. Jean Kambanda*, Case No. ICTR–97–23, Judgement, para. 3 (Sept. 4, 1998). President Milošević was alleged to be responsible for the crimes committed by Yugoslav troops in the region of Kosovo. He was also indicted under a superior responsibility theory for crimes committed by troops of Serbian ethnicity operating within the territories of the newly independent Croatia and Bosnia-Herzegovina, even though these troops were not in his formal chain of command. Milošević died in 2006 during the presentation of his defense. How would the ICTY Prosecutor have proved that ethnic Serbian militia acting in Bosnia-Herzegovina and Croatia were under Milošević's effective control?

The ICC OTP has attempted to prosecute two current heads of state with international crimes, but neither has been charged pursuant to a superior responsibility theory of responsibility. Instead, they have been charged with "indirect co-perpetration," considered more closely in Chapter 15, which consists of the following elements:

> (i) the suspect must be part of a common plan or an agreement with one or more persons; (ii) the suspect and the other co-perpetrator(s) must carry out essential contributions in a coordinated manner which result in the fulfillment of the material elements of the crime; (iii) the suspect must have control over the organization; (iv) the organization must consist of an organized and hierarchal apparatus of power; (v) the execution of the crimes must

> be secured by almost automatic compliance with the orders issued by the suspect; (vi) the suspect must satisfy the subjective elements of the crimes; (vii) the suspect and the other co-perpetrators must be mutually aware and accept that implementing the common plan will result in the fulfillment of the material elements of the crimes; and (viii) the suspect must be aware of the factual circumstances enabling him to exercise joint control over the commission of the crime through another person(s).

Prosecutor v. Kenyatta, Case No. ICC–01/09–02/11, Decision on the Confirmation of Charges Pursuant to Article 61(7)(a) and (b) of the Rome Statute, para. 297 (Jan. 23, 2012).

In issuing an arrest warrant against the head of Sudan, Omar Al Bashir, ICC Pre-Trial Chamber I concluded that there are reasonable grounds to believe that:

- Sudanese forces, including the Sudanese Armed Forces and their allied *Janjaweed* Militia, the Sudanese Police Force committed international crimes.
- Omar Al Bashir is the *de jure* and *de facto* President of the State of Sudan and Commander-in-Chief of the Sudanese Armed Forces who "played an essential role in coordinating, with other high-ranking Sudanese political and military leaders, the design and implementation of the abovementioned [Government of Sudan] counter-insurgency campaign."
- The role of Al Bashir went beyond coordinating the design and implementation of the common plan; he was in full control of all branches of the "apparatus" of the State of Sudan, including the Sudanese Armed Forces and their allied *Janjaweed* Militia, the Sudanese Police Force, the National Intelligence and Security Service; and he used such control to secure the implementation of the common plan.
- Al Bashir is criminally responsible as an indirect perpetrator, or as an indirect co-perpetrator, under article 25(3)(a) of the Statute.

Why would the Prosecutor not have sought to indict Al Bashir or Kenyatta under a superior responsibility theory pursuant to Article 28?

3. For Further Reading

For a discussion of the doctrine of superior responsibility in the civilian context, *see* Avi Singh, *Criminal Responsibility for Non-State Civilian Superiors Lacking De Jure Authority: A Comparative Review of the Doctrine of Superior Responsibility and Parallel Doctrines in National Criminal Laws,* 28 HASTINGS INT'L COMP. L. REV. 267 (2005); Greg R. Vetter, *Command Responsibility of Non-Military Superiors in the International Criminal Court (ICC)*, 25 YALE J. INT'L L. 89 (2000).

3. MENS REA

The *mens rea* standard associated with the superior responsibility doctrine has been the subject of great debate. Each codification formulates this element somewhat differently. Indeed, even the English and French language versions in Protocol I to the 1949 Geneva Conventions are not identical. This doctrinal variation has led to considerable confusion as to the precise mental state required to hold a superior liable for the acts of his subordinates. Consider how the ICTY established a working standard in the case set forth below.

General Blaškić was convicted by the Trial Chamber on the basis of Article 7(1) of the Statute for ordering the crimes at issue. The Trial Chamber also stated in the disposition of the judgment that "[i]n any event, as a commander, he failed to take the necessary and reasonable measures which would have allowed these crimes to be prevented or the perpetrators thereof to be punished." Therefore, the Trial Chamber also convicted him under Article 7(3) of the Statute under the doctrine of superior responsibility. The Trial Chamber said the following about the *mens rea* standard:

> 307. Knowledge may not be presumed. However, the Trial Chamber agrees that "knowledge" may be proved through either direct or circumstantial evidence. With regard to circumstantial evidence, the Trial Chamber concurs with the view expressed by the Trial Chamber in the *Čelebići* case and holds that in determining whether in fact a superior must have had the requisite knowledge it may consider *inter alia* the following indicia enumerated by the Commission of Experts in its Final Report: the number, type and scope of the illegal acts; the time during which the illegal acts occurred; the number and type of troops involved; the logistics involved, if any; the geographical location of the acts; the widespread occurrence of the acts; the speed of the operations; the *modus operandi* of similar illegal acts; the officers and staff involved; and the location of the commander at the time.
>
> 308. These indicia must be considered in light of the accused's position of command, if established. Indeed, as was held by the *Aleksovski* Trial Chamber, an individual's command position *per se* is a significant indicium that he knew about the crimes committed by his subordinates.

The Trial Chamber imposed a single sentence of 45 years' imprisonment.

Blaškić appealed this decision. The Appeals Chamber reversed most of the Trial Chamber's convictions under Article 7(1) and 7(3) as set forth below.

Prosecutor v. Blaškić, Case No. IT–95–14–A, Judgement (July 29, 2004)

In the Appeals Chamber

Command Responsibility Under Article 7(3) of the Statute * * *

54. The Appellant claims that the *mens rea* under Article 7(3) of the Statute is actual knowledge or "information which, if at hand, would oblige the commander to conduct further inquiry." Regarding actual knowledge, the Appellant submits that it requires more than proof of a person's rank as a military commander, and that the Trial Chamber failed to look beyond the Appellant's status to establish his knowledge, thus relying "almost exclusively" on the Appellant's rank and status. This, the Appellant contends, is an unacceptable form of strict liability which in effect shifts the burden of proof. * * *

56. The Appeals Chamber notes that the Appellant has not taken issue with the requirements set out by the Trial Chamber with regard to the circumstantial evidence to be used in support of the finding of a superior's actual knowledge. Rather, he challenges the statement of the Trial Chamber in paragraph 308 of the Trial Judgement that:

> [t]hese indicia must be considered in light of the accused's position of command, if established. Indeed, as was held by the *Aleksovski* Trial Chamber, an individual's command position *per se* is a significant indicium that he knew about the crimes committed by his subordinates.

The Appellant contends that this statement applies the standard of strict liability by founding his actual knowledge on the basis of his position of command.

57. The Appeals Chamber disagrees with this interpretation of the Trial Judgement. The Trial Chamber referred to the Appellant's position of command in addition to the indicia it set out in paragraph 307 of the Trial Judgement, and regarded the position of command not as the criterion for, but as indicia of the accused's knowledge. Given that paragraph 308 appears in the section of the Trial Judgement discussing Article 7(3) of the Statute, and given the fact that the Trial Chamber recognised, at the beginning of its discussion of Article 7(3), that to establish responsibility under that article, proof was required of, among other things, the accused's knowledge, there is no merit in the Appellant's allegation of the application of strict liability by the Trial Chamber to his case. This aspect of the appeal is dismissed.

58. The Appellant next submits that the "had reason to know" standard is not a mere negligence standard and does not imply a general duty to know on the part of the commander. He argues that the Trial Chamber's view that the Appellant's negligence in informing himself may serve as a basis for establishing his liability under Article 7(3) of the Statute is contrary to the role, function, and interpretation of that

provision and creates in effect a form of strict liability which infringes upon the presumption of innocence of the Appellant by focusing exclusively on his position. He submits that even if it were admitted that command responsibility is a form of liability based on negligence, all of the underlying offences with which the Appellant was charged require more than negligence as the *mens rea*, and that offences such as "negligent murder" or "negligent persecutions" simply do not exist under international law. He concludes that what the Trial Judgement does by allegedly lowering the *mens rea* standard of command responsibility is to create new criminal offences such as "negligent murder," thereby violating the principle of *nullum crimen sine lege*. * * *

62. The Appeals Chamber considers that the *Čelebići* Appeal Judgement has settled the issue of the interpretation of the standard of "had reason to know." In that judgement, the Appeals Chamber stated that "a superior will be criminally responsible through the principles of superior responsibility *only if information was available to him* which would have put him on notice of offences committed by subordinates." Further, the Appeals Chamber stated that "[n]eglect of a duty to acquire such knowledge, however, does not feature in the provision (Article 7(3)) as a separate offence, and a superior is not therefore liable under the provision for such failures but only for failing to take necessary and reasonable measures to prevent or to punish." There is no reason for the Appeals Chamber to depart from that position. The Trial Judgement's interpretation of the standard is not consistent with the jurisprudence of the Appeals Chamber in this regard and must be corrected accordingly.

63. As to the argument of the Appellant that the Trial Chamber based command responsibility on a theory of negligence, the Appeals Chamber recalls that the ICTR Appeals Chamber has on a previous occasion rejected criminal negligence as a basis of liability in the context of command responsibility, and that it stated that "it would be both unnecessary and unfair to hold an accused responsible under a head of responsibility which has not clearly been defined in international criminal law." It expressed that "[r]eferences to 'negligence' in the context of superior responsibility are likely to lead to confusion of thought. . . ." The Appeals Chamber expressly endorses this view.

The appeal in this respect is allowed, and the authoritative interpretation of the standard of "had reason to know" shall remain the one given in the *Čelebići* Appeal Judgement, as referred to above. * * *

401. The Trial Chamber held that:

> since [the Appellant] had reason to know that crimes had been, or were, about to be, committed, as the hierarchical superior of the forces in question, the accused was bound to take reasonable measures to forestall or prevent them. [. . .] [T]he Trial Chamber considers that the accused knew that crimes had been or were about to be committed and took no action as a consequence.

402. The Trial Chamber did not believe the Appellant's argument that he was unaware—until 22 April 1993—of the crimes that had been committed against civilians as he was trapped in the basement of the Hotel Vitez. The Trial Chamber relied on witnesses who testified that they tried to see the Appellant on 16 April 1993 and were told that no one was there, the fact that at least two of the Appellant's colleagues were able to leave the Hotel Vitez, and evidence that the HVO [Croatian Defence Council] repeatedly tried to keep foreigners from visiting the village.

403. The Trial Chamber noted that members of the ECMM [European Community Monitoring Mission] witnessed signs of fighting coming from the direction of the village, and expressed disbelief that ABiH forces were located in Ahmići. The Trial Chamber concluded that the sounds of gunfire and smoke arising from the area of Ahmići must have alerted the Appellant to the crimes being committed.

404. The Appellant argued that even if he had noticed the sounds of gunfire and smoke arising from the direction of Ahmići, he would have had no reason to believe they were evidence of anything but lawful military combat. The Appeals Chamber notes that [the] additional evidence supports the conclusion that there was a Muslim military presence in Ahmići, and that the Appellant had reason to believe that the ABiH intended to launch an attack along the Ahmići-Šantići-Dubravica axis. * * *

406. In this regard, the Appeals Chamber considers that the mental element "had reason to know" as articulated in the Statute, does not automatically imply a duty to obtain information. The Appeals Chamber emphasizes that responsibility can be imposed for *deliberately* refraining from finding out but not for negligently failing to find out.

407. The analysis of the evidence underlying the Trial Chamber's finding that the Appellant knew that crimes had been or were about to be committed, reveals no evidence that the Appellant *had information* which put him on notice that crimes had been committed by his subordinates in the Ahmići area on 16 April 1993.

408. Further, the additional evidence admitted on appeal lends support to the Appellant's argument that he had no reason to believe that crimes had been committed in light of the military conflict taking place at that time between the HVO and the ABiH.

409. Exhibit 2 to the Second Rule 115 Motion, an [ABiH] 3rd Corps Security Report dated 16 April 1993, issued by the 7th Muslim Brigade and addressed to the 3rd Corps Security Sector, shows that all units of the 7th Muslim Brigade were in a state of readiness. The report recounts that fierce fighting was taking place in Ahmići.

410. Exhibit 12 to the Fourth Rule 115 Motion, an Order issued by the ABiH 3rd Corps Commander, Enver Hadžihasanović, addressed to the Lašva Operative Group and the 325th Mountain Brigade on 16 April

1993, shows that there were ABiH troops deployed in Ahmići on that date. The order states that the 1st Battalion of the 303rd Mountain Brigade and the 7th Muslim Mountain Brigade had been tasked with assisting ABiH forces present in Ahmići.[815]

411. Witness BA3 testified that the ABiH 3rd Corps received information about a major crime being committed in Ahmići only 10 to 15 days after 16 April 1993, and stated that during a meeting held in Zenica on 21 April 1993, attended by the Appellant and the ABiH 3rd Corps chiefs of staff, the chiefs of staff still did not know about the crimes committed in Ahmići.

412. The Trial Judgement further addresses the attempts made by the Appellant to carry out an investigation of the crimes, noting that even when he was appointed HVO Deputy Chief of Staff in 1994, he did not manage to recover the SIS report [drafted by the Croatian Intelligence Service (*Hrvatska Izvestajna Sluzba*)] on Ahmići. Yet, the Trial Chamber found as follows:

> . . . In any event, it is clear that he never took any reasonable measure to prevent the crimes being committed or to punish those responsible for them.

413. The Trial Chamber had concluded that it is a commander's material ability that determines which are the reasonable measures required, either to prevent a crime or to punish a perpetrator, and held that, a commander may discharge his obligation to (prevent or) punish by reporting the crimes to the competent authorities.

414. The Appellant thus was not obliged to issue orders concerning further investigations or able to take disciplinary measures himself. However, the Trial Chamber also noted that no one was ever punished by the HVO for crimes committed in Ahmići, Šantići, Pirići, and Nadioci. The Appeals Chamber finds some guidance in paragraph 488 of the Trial Judgement regarding those "reasonable measures" not taken by the Appellant.[823]

---

[815] *See* relevant parts which read as follows:

In accordance with the unfolding events and in connection with the attack by HVO [Croatian Defence Council] units on units of the BH Army in the zone of responsibility of the 325th bbr and the newly arisen situation, the Corps Command is taking measures with the aim of assisting our forces and tying down the HVO forces. In the spirit of the Commander's decision, the following orders have been issued:

> . . . the 1st Battalion of the 303rd Mountain Brigade has been sent to Kuber . . . with the task to organize the defence . . . and be in readiness to assist our forces in the villages of Putis, Jelinak, Lonari, Nadioci and Ahmići.

The document also recounts that 7th Muslim Mountain Brigade:

> . . . has been sent to the Ahmići village sector with the task to organize and carry out a march and arrive in the Ahmići village sector, where it is to assist our forces in the defence and organize the defence and be in readiness to carry out an infantry attack on the Ahmići-Šantići-Dubravica axis.

[823] The Trial Chamber emphasizes that the Appellant failed to contact the commander of the Military Police, Paško Ljubišcić; he did not take any measures to seal off the area and ensure that evidence was preserved; he did not order an autopsy on any body before it was buried; and

415. The Trial Chamber rejected the Appellant's claim that he sought the help of international organizations such as the ECMM and UNPROFOR to carry out the investigations regarding Ahmići. It appears that in reaching that conclusion, it relied heavily upon the testimony of Colonel Duncan from the BRITBAT [the British Battalion contingent of UNPROFOR], who testified that during a meeting, the Appellant explained to him that:

> . . . the crimes committed at Ahmići had been carried out either by Muslims wearing HVO uniforms or by Muslim extremists who were out of control, or even by Serbs who could have infiltrated the HVO controlled zone.

416. During the hearing on appeal, the Prosecution referred to this statement allegedly made by the Appellant. In reply, the Appellant stated that Duncan had misidentified the Appellant. Witness Stewart, who was also present at the meeting, testified that the Appellant would have never made such a statement, and confirmed that it was another individual who made that claim.

417. The Appeals Chamber considers that even though a determination of the necessary and reasonable measures that a commander is required to take in order to prevent or punish the commission of crimes, is dependent on the circumstances surrounding each particular situation, it generally concurs with the *Čelebići* Trial Chamber which held:

> [i]t must, however, be recognised that international law cannot oblige a superior to perform the impossible. Hence, a superior may only be held criminally responsible for failing to take such measures that are within his powers. The question then arises of what actions are to be considered to be within the superior's powers in this sense. As the corollary to the standard adopted by the Trial Chamber with respect to the concept of superior, we conclude that a superior should be held responsible for failing to take such measures that are within his material possibility.

418. Evidence admitted on appeal supports the conclusion that the Appellant requested that an investigation into the crimes committed in Ahmići be carried out, and that the investigation was taken over by the SIS Mostar. For instance, Exhibit 1 to the Second Rule 115 Motion (SIS report), states that the Appellant asked Slišković to carry out an investigation of the events which occurred in Ahmići so that he could send a report to Mostar. This document states that Slišković allegedly conducted the investigation inefficiently, and obstructed it.

419. The Appeals Chamber has admitted as additional evidence on appeal documents that contain information on those allegedly responsible for the crimes committed in the Ahmići area; this evidence

---

he did not attempt to interview any survivors although they were detained at the school in Dubravica.

supports the conclusion that the Appellant was not informed of the results of the investigation, and that the names of the perpetrators were not disclosed to him. For instance, Exhibit 4 to the First Rule 115 Motion, an HIS Report dated 17 February 1994, addressed to Franjo Tudjman (then President of the Republic of Croatia), signed and stamped on 18 February 1994 by Miroslav Tudjman, Head of the Croatian Information Service, states that others were responsible for the crimes in Ahmići, the poor organization of production in the Vitez Slobodan Princip Seljo plant, and the destruction of invaluable documents.[831]

420. The Appeals Chamber considers that the trial evidence assessed together with the additional evidence admitted on appeal shows that the Appellant took the measures that were reasonable within his material ability to denounce the crimes committed, and supports the conclusion that the Appellant requested that an investigation into the crimes committed in Ahmići be carried out, that the investigation was taken over by the SIS Mostar, that he was not informed of the results of the investigation, and that the names of the perpetrators were not disclosed to him.

421. For the foregoing reasons, and having examined the legal requirements for responsibility under Article 7(3) of the Statute, the Appeals Chamber concludes that the Appellant lacked effective control over the military units responsible for the commission of crimes in the Ahmići area on 16 April 1993, in the sense of a material ability to prevent or punish criminal conduct, and therefore the constituent elements of command responsibility have not been satisfied.

422. In light of the foregoing, the Appeals Chamber is not satisfied that the trial evidence, assessed together with the additional evidence admitted on appeal, proves beyond reasonable doubt that the Appellant is responsible under Article 7(3) of the Statute for having failed to prevent the commission of crimes in Ahmići, Šantići, Pirići, and Nadioci on 16 April 1993 or to punish the perpetrators.

NOTES & QUESTIONS

1. Case Outcome

The Appeals Chamber affirmed convictions on three counts for detention-related crimes and the use of protected persons for the construction of defensive military installations. General Blaškić's sentence was reduced from 45 years to 9 years, minus time served in detention since his voluntary surrender on April 1, 1996. The President of the Appeals Chamber granted General Blaškić early release four days after the Appeals Chamber's opinion issued. The Appeals Chamber dismissed the Prosecutor's request for a review of the Appeals Judgment. Did the Appeals Chamber

[831] * * * Ex. 1 to the First Rule 115 Motion, which informs that the attack on Ahmići was carried out by the *Jokers* under the command of Vlado Ćosić and the commander of the regional Military Police Paško Ljubišcić, and also by an attached squad of criminals who had been released from the Kaonik prison and included in combat operations.

reverse the Trial Chamber on factual or legal grounds? Was the new evidence submitted by General Blaškić important to the reversal?

The Tribunal later convicted a regional politician, Dario Kordić, for planning and instigating the attacks. Although a civilian, Kordić exercised considerable power over the military activities of the Croatian Defence Council (the HVO), including negotiating cease-fire agreements, issuing orders that were directly or indirectly of a military nature, representing himself as an HVO Colonel, dressing in an HVO uniform, having a military operations room in his office, and negotiating the passage of relief convoys or United Nations vehicles through check-points in Central Bosnia. *See Prosecutor v. Kordić*, Case No. IT–95–14/2, Judgement (Feb. 26, 2001). The Appeals Chamber affirmed his twenty-five year sentence, and he is serving his sentence in Austria.

2. *Mens Rea*

All formulations of the doctrine of superior responsibility provide that some level of constructive knowledge will suffice to satisfy the *mens rea* element. However, the precise standard for this constructive knowledge remains elusive. Has the ICTY adopted a standard of negligence, gross negligence, or recklessness? Is there a general duty to acquire knowledge of subordinates' activities? Or, must it be shown that a defendant willfully failed to acquire knowledge? Consider this summary of ICTY jurisprudence provided by the Appeals Chamber decision in *Prosecutor v. Strugar*, Case No. IT–01–42–A, Judgement (July 17, 2008):

> 297. Pursuant to Article 7(3) of the Statute, the knowledge required to trigger a superior's duty to prevent is established when the superior "knew or had reason to know that [his] subordinate was about to commit [crimes]". The Trial Chamber in *Čelebići* interpreted this requirement in light of the language used in Article 86(2) of Additional Protocol I and held that, under the "had reason to know" standard, it is required to establish that the superior had "information of a nature, which at the least, would put him on notice of the risk of [. . .] offences by indicating the need for additional investigation in order to ascertain whether such crimes were committed or were about to be committed by his subordinates". As a clarification, the Trial Chamber added that "[i]t is sufficient that the superior was put on further inquiry by the information, or, in other words, that it indicated the need for additional investigation in order to ascertain whether offences were being committed or about to be committed by his subordinates".
>
> 298. The Appeals Chamber in *Čelebići* endorsed this interpretation and held that the rationale behind the standard set forth in Article 86(2) of Additional Protocol I is plain: "failure to conclude, or conduct additional inquiry, in spite of alarming information constitutes knowledge of subordinate offences". It noted that this information may be general in nature and does not need to contain specific details on the unlawful acts which have been or are about to be committed. It follows that, in order to

demonstrate that a superior had the *mens rea* required under Article 7(3) of the Statute, it must be established whether, in the circumstances of the case, he possessed information sufficiently alarming to justify further inquiry.

299. In *Krnojelac*, the Trial Chamber found that "[t]he fact that the Accused witnessed the beating of [a detainee, inflicted by one of his subordinates], ostensibly for the prohibited purpose of punishing him for his failed escape, is not sufficient, in itself, to conclude that the Accused knew or [. . .] had reason to know that, other than in that particular instance, beatings were inflicted for any of the prohibited purposes". The Appeals Chamber rejected this finding and held that "while this fact is indeed insufficient, in itself, to conclude that Krnojelac knew that acts of torture were being inflicted on the detainees, as indicated by the Trial Chamber, it may nevertheless constitute sufficiently alarming information such as to alert him to the risk of other acts of torture being committed, meaning that Krnojelac had reason to know that his subordinates were committing or were about to commit acts of torture". The Appeals Chamber also reiterated that "an assessment of the mental element required by Article 7(3) of the Statute should, in any event, be conducted in the specific circumstances of each case, taking into account the specific situation of the superior concerned at the time in question".

300. In *Hadžihasanović and Kubura*, the Trial Chamber found that "the Accused Kubura, owing to his knowledge of the plunder committed by his subordinates in June 1993 and his failure to take punitive measures, could not [ignore] that the members of the 7th Brigade were likely to repeat such acts". The Appeals Chamber in that case found that the Trial Chamber had erred in making this finding as it implied "that the Trial Chamber considered Kubura's knowledge of and past failure to punish his subordinates' acts of plunder in the Ovnak area as automatically entailing that he had reason to know of their future acts of plunder in Vareš." The Appeals Chamber thus applied the correct legal standard to the evidence on the trial record: "While Kubura's knowledge of his subordinates' past plunder in Ovnak and his failure to punish them did not, in itself, amount to actual knowledge of the acts of plunder in Vareš, the Appeals Chamber concurs with the Trial Chamber that the orders he received on 4 November 1993 constituted, at the very least, sufficiently alarming information justifying further inquiry."

301. As such, while a superior's knowledge of and failure to punish his subordinates' past offences is insufficient, in itself, to conclude that the superior knew that similar future offences would be committed by the same group of subordinates, this may, depending on the circumstances of the case, nevertheless constitute sufficiently alarming information to justify further inquiry under the "had reason to know" standard. In making such an assessment,

> a Trial Chamber may take into account the failure by a superior to punish the crime in question. Such failure is indeed relevant to the determination of whether, in the circumstances of a case, a superior possessed information that was sufficiently alarming to put him on notice of the risk that similar crimes might subsequently be carried out by subordinates and justify further inquiry. In this regard, the Appeals Chamber stresses that a superior's failure to punish a crime of which he has actual knowledge is likely to be understood by his subordinates at least as acceptance, if not encouragement, of such conduct with the effect of increasing the risk of new crimes being committed.

Does this summary clarify, or confuse, the *mens rea* required for superior responsibility? Suppose abuses are a matter of public knowledge, are numerous, occur over a large area, or occur over a prolonged period of time. Is such notoriety, without more, sufficient to trigger superior liability? What exactly must a defendant "know" to trigger the duty to act? Must the defendant know that specific subordinates are committing, or are going to commit, specific crimes (particularized by time, place, and manner) to be held liable for those crimes? Or, may a superior be held liable for any crimes when there is evidence that the defendant knew that subordinates generally were committing abuses?

Suppose that a superior has actual knowledge that some of his subordinates are pillaging villages. Can he then be held liable for the physical abuse of civilians in those villages even if he did not have actual knowledge of those violations? Is there a duty to make reasonable inferences from facts that would suggest that subordinates are committing abuses? Is there a duty to anticipate that troops might commit abuses when, for example, such troops are poorly trained, when a chain of command is weak, when there have been disciplinary problems in the past, when morale is low, when a particularly aggressive strategy is used, when the armed conflict has ethnic dimensions, or when a communications network has been severed in battle? Might there be different standards on these points for superiors who are close in rank and geographic location to the actual perpetrators as compared with higher-level commanders?

3. Superior Responsibility for Genocide

Protocol I of the Geneva Conventions provides expressly for superior responsibility over grave breaches of the Protocol and the four Geneva Conventions. In contrast, the Genocide Convention at Article 3 lists only the following culpable forms of liability: direct liability, complicity, conspiracy, incitement, and attempt. Why would the Genocide Convention not specifically mention superior responsibility? Does the specific intent element of genocide complicate a finding of superior responsibility for genocide? Must the superior possess the genocidal *mens rea* (the intent to destroy a protected group in whole or in part) herself? Or, is it the subordinate's intent that matters, such that the only *mens rea* to be proven in the prosecution of a superior is the superior's actual or constructive knowledge that subordinates were committing, or had committed, genocide? Would a conviction for genocide without genocidal *mens rea* be appropriate or fair to a defendant superior given the great stigma attached to the crime? How should a tribunal determine the *mens rea* of a superior's subordinates when those subordinates are not before the court?

4. For Further Reading

For more on the *mens rea* of the doctrine of superior responsibility, *see* Arthur Thomas O'Reilly, *Command Responsibility: A Call to Realign Doctrine with Principles,* 20 AM. U. INT'L L. REV. 71 (2004); Michael Stryszak, *Command Responsibility: How Much Should a Commander be Expected to Know?*, 11 USAFA J. LEG. STUD. 27, 44 (2000); Jenny S. Martinez, *Understanding* Mens Rea *in Command Responsibility: From* Yamashita *to* Blaškić *and Beyond*, 5 J. INT'L CRIM. JUST. 638 (2007). For a discussion of the *mens rea* of superior responsibility in the context of the crime of genocide, *see* Paul Mysliwiec, *Accomplice to Genocide Liability: The Case for a Purpose* Mens Rea *Standard*, 10 CHI. J. INT'L L. 389 (2009).

4. *ACTUS REUS*: OMISSION

The superior responsibility doctrine premises liability on an omission by a defendant: the failure to prevent or punish known abuses by subordinates. Omissions as culpable conduct are less common in penal law than liability for affirmative conduct. Where omissions give rise to criminal liability, it may be because there are statutory duties to act (e.g., a statute requiring the payment of taxes). Alternatively, there may be a duty to act as a result of a special relationship between parties (e.g., the duties parents owe their children). What is the basis for allowing omissions to serve as the foundation for criminal liability in the superior responsibility context?

Consider this as you review the next opinion. On May 24, 2008, Senator Jean-Pierre Bemba Gombo of the Democratic Republic of the Congo (DRC) was arrested based on a warrant that accused him of "effectively acting as a military commander" over the commission of crimes against humanity and war crimes—including murder, rape, and pillaging—that were allegedly committed in the Central African Republic (CAR) between October 2002 and March 2003. (See the Appendix for a map of the Central African Republic.) At that time, Bemba was the President of a political party, the *Mouvement de Libération du Congo* (MLC), as well as the Commander-in-Chief of the MLC's military branch, the *Armée de Libération du Congo* (ALC). The ICC Trial Chamber found that Bemba established the MLC in the city of Gbadolite in 1998 to overthrow the government in Kinshasa, but the movement "gradually transformed from a rebel movement into a political party." A Statute adopted by the MLC in 1999 declared that the organization's goal was "to establish a democratic state in the DRC based on free and transparent elections and respect for individual human rights and liberties." Bemba acted as the "primary authority" over both the political and military spheres of the MLC, and was the "ultimate authority over the decision-making." He had "authority over strategic military decisions," such as commencing and commanding military operations, but he generally "did not direct operations at the tactical level or issue orders regarding the specific manoeuvres of the various units in the field."

The ALC consisted of 20,000 soldiers and was structured like a national military force. Most ALC soldiers received rapid military training that varied in its substance. The ALC's Code of Conduct included "murder of a civilian or of some other person" and "abduction and rape" as "*infractions*" that "may be punishable by death," but failed to clarify terms and made no mention of pillaging as an offense. Although political commissioners were tasked with popularizing the Code of Conduct with MLC soldiers, the Code of Conduct was only written in French, and commanders often had to translate it orally into Lingala (a commonly spoken language in the DRC) for lower-ranked soldiers.

Bemba's alleged crimes arose in response to a series of attacks conducted by a rebel faction of the Central African Armed Forces, or *Forces Armées Centrafricaines* (FACA). Led by former FACA chief of staff General François Bozizé, the rebel faction began an advance across the Chadian border and into the CAR in October 2002, precipitating a bombing campaign by FACA and CAR forces. On October 25, 2002, when "General Bozizé's rebels" entered the capital city of Bangui, CAR president Ange-Félix Patassé of CAR called upon Bemba and the ALC to help defend his government. Bemba subsequently deployed three ALC battalions, totaling about 1,500 soldiers. These remained in the CAR until their withdrawal to the DRC on March 15, 2003. They continued to occupy the capital, Bangui, despite the fact that General Bozizé's rebels had abandoned the city by the end of October. Throughout this deployment, crimes of murder, rape, and pillaging against the civilian population were committed by people identified by the alleged victims as "Banyamulengués," "Bemba's men," or "MLC soldiers." Bemba himself admonished his troops for their "misbehavior," "stealing," and "brutalis[ing]" of the civilian population in a November 2002 speech, but the Trial Chamber found no evidence that he took any concrete measures in response to allegations of crimes by MLC soldiers or followed up on or enforced general warnings he publicly made to his troops against abuse of the civilian population.

Pursuant to Article 74(2) of the Statute, the Pre-Trial Chamber established in June 2009 that Bemba was responsible for the crimes committed as a person effectively acting as a military commander within the meaning of Article 28(a). The Trial Chamber found Bemba guilty of (a) murder as a crime against humanity under Article 7(1)(a) of the Statute; (b) murder as a war crime under Article 8(2)(c)(i) of the Statute; (c) rape as a crime against humanity under Article 7(1)(g) of the Statute; (d) rape as a war crime under Article 8(2)(e)(vi) of the Statute; and (e) pillaging as a war crime under Article 8(2)(e)(v) of the Statute. Using the elements of Article 28(a)—which states that a military commander "shall be criminally responsible for crimes within the jurisdiction of the Court committed by forces under his or her effective command and control"—the Trial Chamber analyzed Bemba's command responsibility liability:

> 59. The Pre-Trial Chamber found sufficient evidence to establish substantial grounds to believe that (i) Mr. Bemba was a person effectively acting as military commander ("first element"); (ii) forces under his effective command and control committed crimes within the jurisdiction of the Court ("second element"); (iii) crimes were committed as a result of his failure to exercise control properly over such forces ("third element); (iv) he knew the forces were committing or about to commit such crimes ("fourth element"); and (v) he failed to take all necessary and reasonable measures within his power to prevent or repress their commission or to submit the matter to the competent authorities for investigation and prosecution ("fifth element"). * * *
>
> 61. * * * The Pre-Trial Chamber relied on five factors in confirming that the Accused had effective authority and control: (i) Mr. Bemba's official position within the MLC structure; (ii) Mr. Bemba's power to issue orders, which were complied with; (iii) Mr. Bemba's power to appoint, promote, demote, and dismiss, as well as arrest, detain, and release MLC commanders; (iv) Mr. Bemba's power to prevent and repress the commission of crimes; and (v) Mr. Bemba's retention of effective authority and control over the MLC troops.

The Trial Chamber also examined Bemba's functioning as a military commander:

> 177. Article 28(a) not only provides for the liability of military commanders, but also extends to "person[s] effectively acting as military commander[s]"—the latter being, in the submission of the Prosecution, the appropriate characterisation of Mr. Bemba's position in the case. These individuals are not formally or legally appointed as military commanders, but they will effectively act as commanders over the forces that committed the crimes. In addition, the phrase "military commander or person effectively acting as a military commander" includes individuals who do not perform exclusively military functions. * * *
>
> 201. Under Article 28(a)(ii), three distinct duties are imposed upon commanders: (i) preventing the commission of crimes; (ii) repressing the commission of crimes; or (iii) submitting the matter to the competent authorities for investigation and prosecution. Although the Statute uses alternative language ("or") it is clear that failure to discharge any of these duties may attract criminal liability. For example, a failure to prevent the crimes, when the commander was under

a duty to do so, cannot be remedied by subsequently punishing the perpetrators.

The Trial Chamber further found that, "on the basis of corroborated, credible, and reliable evidence . . . Mr. Bemba held primary disciplinary authority over the MLC contingent in the CAR." It further wrote:

> 693. In the Confirmation Decision, the Pre-Trial Chamber found that there was sufficient evidence to establish substantial grounds to believe that, from on or about 26 October 2002 to 15 March 2003, (i) MLC forces committed crimes within the jurisdiction of the Court; (ii) Mr. Bemba effectively acted as a military commander and had effective authority and control over the MLC troops in the CAR; (iii) Mr. Bemba knew that MLC troops were committing or about to commit the crimes against humanity of murder and rape and the war crimes of murder, rape, and pillaging in the CAR; (iv) Mr. Bemba failed to take all necessary and reasonable measures within his power to prevent or repress the commission of the crimes by MLC troops in the CAR; and (v) Mr. Bemba's failure to fulfil his duties to prevent crimes increased the risk of their commission by the MLC troops in the CAR. * * *
>
> 700. From the entirety of the evidentiary record, the Chamber is satisfied that Mr. Bemba exercised effective control over the MLC contingent in the CAR at all relevant times of the 2002–2003 CAR Operation. Mr. Bemba ordered the initial deployment of the MLC troops to the CAR, including, in consultation with the General Staff, selecting the units and commanders to be deployed. Following deployment, Mr. Bemba maintained regular, direct contact with senior commanders in the field on the state of operations, and additionally received numerous detailed operations and intelligence reports. Further, the MLC hierarchy in the DRC, controlled by Mr. Bemba, continued to provide logistical support and equipment to the MLC troops in the CAR. The Chamber recalls in this regard its factual findings regarding the MLC contingent in the CAR, including that the MLC troops, with the small number of CAR troops frequently accompanying them, mainly operated independently of other armed forces in the field and that throughout the 2002–2003 CAR Operation command remained with the MLC hierarchy. Whether or not Mr. Bemba issued direct operational orders to the MLC forces in the CAR is not determinative, but the Chamber nonetheless notes its finding that Mr. Bemba did issue such orders, which were relayed and implemented by Colonel Moustapha. * * *
>
> 704. Finally, the Chamber recalls that, as evidenced both by Mr. Bemba's discussions with General Cissé in November 2002 and in the final withdrawal in March 2003, Mr. Bemba

retained the power and authority to order the withdrawal of the MLC troops from the CAR. Once Mr. Bemba actually ordered the withdrawal of the troops, that decision was complied with. * * *

731. In light of the wide range of available measures at his disposal, the Chamber finds that the measures Mr. Bemba did take patently fell short of "all necessary and reasonable measures" to prevent and repress the commission of crimes within his material ability.

The Trial Chamber thus concluded "beyond reasonable doubt that Mr. Bemba is criminally responsible under Article 28(a) for the crimes against humanity of murder and rape, and the war crimes of murder, rape, and pillaging committed by his forces in the course of the 2002–2003 CAR Operation." He was sentenced to 18 years' imprisonment. *Prosecutor v. Bemba*, Case No. ICC–01/05–01/08, Judgment Pursuant to Article 74 of the Rome Statute, para. 742 (March 21, 2016). The Appeals Chamber opinion and a dissent follow.

Prosecutor v. Jean-Pierre Bemba Gombo, Case No. ICC–01/05–01/08 A, Judgment (June 8, 2018)

Third Ground of Appeal: Command Responsibility: Mr. Bemba took all Necessary and Reasonable Measures * * *

121. The Trial Chamber found that what constitutes "all necessary and reasonable measures" is to be established on a "case-by-case basis," focusing on the "material power" of the commander.

122. The Trial Chamber found that Mr. Bemba took "a few measures" in response to allegations of crimes committed by MLC troops in the CAR which included the following. First, the Mondonga Inquiry, established in the "initial days of the 2002–2003 CAR Operation," which led to Colonel Mondonga, on 27 November 2002, forwarding the case file containing information on the proceedings against Lieutenant Willy Bomengo and other soldiers of the 28th Battalion arrested in Bangui on 30 October 2002 on charges of pillaging ("Bomengo case file"), to the MLC Chief of Staff, copying Mr. Bemba. Second, the visit to the CAR "on or around 2 November 2002," during which Mr. Bemba met with the UN representative in the CAR (General Cissé) and President Patassé. Third, a speech Mr. Bemba gave at PK12 "sometime" in November 2002. Fourth, the trial of Lieutenant Bomengo and others at the Gbadolite court-martial which commenced on 5 December 2002 with the report of conviction transmitted to Mr. Bemba on 12 December 2002. Fifth, the Zongo Commission which, between 25 and 28 December 2002, questioned witnesses in Zongo, with the head of the commission sending a report on 17 January 2003 to the MLC Secretary General, copied to Mr. Bemba. Sixth, a letter written by Mr. Bemba to General Cissé dated 4 January 2003. Seventh, correspondence in response to the FIDH Report, namely

Mr. Bemba's letter to the President of the FIDH of 20 February 2003 and the latter's reply on 26 February 2003. Eighth, the establishment of the Sibut Mission at the "end of February" 2003.

123. The Trial Chamber concluded that these measures were all "limited in mandate, execution, and/or results." * * *

131. The Trial Chamber, having found that the measures taken by Mr. Bemba were inadequate in the circumstances, noted that their inadequacy was "aggravated" by indications that they were not "genuine." The Trial Chamber noted "corroborated evidence" that the "measures were primarily motivated by Mr. Bemba's desire to counter public allegations and rehabilitate the public image of the MLC." It found that the "minimal and inadequate measures," when taken with evidence as to his motives for ordering such measures, "illustrate[d] that a key intention behind the measures Mr. Bemba took was to protect the image of the MLC," concluding that "[h]is primary intention was not to genuinely take all necessary and reasonable measures within his material ability to prevent or repress the commission of crimes, as was his duty."

132. In relation to the motives behind specific measures taken, the Trial Chamber noted that the Mondonga Inquiry was "allegedly" established to: (i) counter media allegations by showing that only minor items had been looted from the CAR; (ii) demonstrate that action was taken to address allegations of crimes; (iii) vindicate the MLC leadership of responsibility for alleged acts of violence; and (iv) generally rehabilitate the MLC's image. It noted further that the letter that Mr. Bemba sent to General Cissé, the U.N. Representative in the CAR, was, according to witness testimony, intended to "demonstrate good faith and maintain the image of the MLC, particularly, against a backdrop of negotiations in the DRC as to, inter alia, the role of the MLC in the transitional institutions." With respect to the withdrawal from the CAR, the Trial Chamber noted that this action was motivated, *inter alia*, by "pressure from the international community," "directly related to the negotiation of the Sun City agreements."

133. The Trial Chamber noted that "[i]n addition to or instead of the insufficient measures" that Mr. Bemba took and "in light of his extensive material ability to prevent and repress the crimes, he "could have, inter alia" taken the following measures:

> (i) ensured that the MLC troops in the CAR were properly trained in the rules of international humanitarian law, and adequately supervised during the 2002–2003 CAR Operation; (ii) initiated genuine and full investigations into the commission of crimes, and properly tried and punished any soldiers alleged of having committed crimes; (iii) issued further and clear orders to the commanders of the troops in the CAR to prevent the commission of crimes; (iv) altered the deployment of troops, for example, to minimise contact with civilian populations; (v)

> removed, replaced, or dismissed officers and soldiers found to have committed or condoned any crimes in the CAR; and/or (vi) shared relevant information with the CAR authorities or others and supported them in any efforts to investigate criminal allegations.

134. The Trial Chamber further emphasised that whilst "one key measure at Mr. Bemba's disposal was withdrawal of the MLC troops from the CAR," that measure was executed for political reasons and only in March 2003 whereas it found that Mr. Bemba had first contemplated withdrawing in November 2002. * * *

136. The Trial Chamber ultimately found that Mr. Bemba failed to take "all necessary and reasonable measures within his power to prevent or repress the commission of crimes by his subordinates during the 2002–2003 CAR Operation, or to submit the matter to the competent authorities." The Appeals Chamber notes that the Trial Chamber did not link Mr. Bemba's putative failure to take adequate measures to any of the specific criminal acts * * * which he was ultimately convicted of. * * *

166. * * * Mr. Bemba raises several arguments against the Trial Chamber's finding that he "failed to take all necessary and reasonable measures within his power to prevent or repress the commission of crimes by his subordinates during the 2002–2003 CAR Operation, or to submit the matter to the competent authorities." His overall contention is that no reasonable trial chamber could have reached this conclusion. For the reasons that follow, the Appeals Chamber finds, by majority, Judge Monageng and Judge Hofmański dissenting, that the Trial Chamber's finding was indeed unreasonable because it was tainted by serious errors. * * *

169. * * * [I]t is not the case that a commander must take each and every possible measure at his or her disposal. Despite the link between the material ability of a commander to take measures (which is directly connected to his or her level of authority) and what he or she might reasonably have been expected to do, it is not the case that a commander is required to employ every single conceivable measure within his or her arsenal, irrespective of considerations of proportionality and feasibility. Article 28 only requires commanders to do what is necessary and reasonable under the circumstances.

170. In assessing reasonableness, the Court is required to consider other parameters, such as the operational realities on the ground at the time faced by the commander. Article 28 of the Statute is not a form of strict liability. Commanders are allowed to make a cost/benefit analysis when deciding which measures to take, bearing in mind their overall responsibility to prevent and repress crimes committed by their subordinates. This means that a commander may take into consideration the impact of measures to prevent or repress criminal behaviour on ongoing or planned operations and may choose the least disruptive

measure as long as it can reasonably be expected that this measure will prevent or repress the crimes. * * *

171. Turning to the case at hand, Mr. Bemba submits that the Trial Chamber did not take into account what was feasible and possible for him in the circumstances, given the "unique conditions of this case." In other parts of his appeal he argues that his case was one of non-linear command, for which there is one sole precedent in the jurisprudence of the ad hoc tribunals. The Appeals Chamber notes that the Trial Chamber had some regard to Mr. Bemba's submissions as to the difficulties he faced in implementing relevant investigatory measures, but found these reasons to be unpersuasive. * * * In finding that Mr. Bemba did not adopt all "necessary and reasonable measures" it arrived at this conclusion "in light of his extensive material ability to prevent and repress the crimes." Nevertheless, while the Trial Chamber's finding in this respect has to be read alongside its earlier findings as to the extensiveness of Mr. Bemba's control over the MLC forces in the CAR, the Trial Chamber paid insufficient attention to the fact that the MLC troops were operating in a foreign country with the attendant difficulties on Mr. Bemba's ability, as a remote commander, to take measures. * * *

173. Thus, although the limitations alluded to by Mr. Bemba did not completely curtail his ability to investigate crimes committed by MLC troops in the CAR, the Trial Chamber did not conduct a proper assessment as to whether, in the particular circumstances that existed at the time, the range of measures taken by Mr. Bemba could be regarded as the extent of the necessary and reasonable measures that he could have taken, given the limitations upon his material abilities. The Trial Chamber accepted that the MLC contingent had cooperated with the CAR authorities throughout the 2002–2003 CAR Operation and that such cooperation was both "logical in a situation where a contingent of foreign forces is unfamiliar with the terrain and enemy" and a "regular feature of the operations." However, in the assessment of the measures that Mr. Bemba took, this aspect was disregarded, resulting in an unrealistic assessment of the "wide range of available measures at his disposal." The Trial Chamber even acknowledged that, in so far as the evidence of witnesses supported the proposition that the CAR authorities had retained "some, but not primary or exclusive," disciplinary or investigative authority over the MLC forces, this was not "inconsistent with the corroborated and reliable evidence that Mr. Bemba and the MLC had ultimate disciplinary authority" over the MLC contingent in the CAR. Moreover, even if Mr. Bemba had ultimate disciplinary authority in the CAR, this does not mean that this disciplinary authority was not in any way subject to limitations or impeded to a degree—a reality which the Trial Chamber ought to have given weight in its assessment of the measures that Mr. Bemba took. * * *

176. The Appeals Chamber also considers that the Trial Chamber inappropriately took Mr. Bemba's motives into consideration when

determining whether the measures he had taken were necessary and reasonable. While the Appeals Chamber rejects Mr. Bemba's submission that the motives of an accused commander are always irrelevant to the assessment of "necessary and reasonable measures" because a commander is required to act in good faith in adopting such measures and must show that he "genuinely" tried to prevent or repress the crimes in question or submit the matter to the competent authorities, it finds that the Trial Chamber took an unreasonably strict approach.

177. The Trial Chamber found that the measures Mr. Bemba took "were primarily motivated by Mr. Bemba's desire to counter public allegations and rehabilitate the public image of the MLC." It further found "that a key intention behind the measures Mr. Bemba took was to protect the image of the MLC." The Appeals Chamber accepts Mr. Bemba's submission that measures taken by a commander motivated by preserving the reputation of his or her troops do not intrinsically render them any less necessary or reasonable in preventing or repressing the commission of crimes, and ensuring their prosecution after proper investigation.

178. The Appeals Chamber notes that the Trial Chamber's preoccupation with Mr. Bemba's motivations appears to have coloured its entire assessment of the measures that he took. * * *

179. Moreover, the motivations that the Trial Chamber found established, namely, the broad desire to maintain the image of the MLC and counter public allegations are not in fact intrinsically "negative" motivations, as the Trial Chamber appears to have considered them. Nor do they necessarily conflict with the taking of genuine and effective measures. There may be multiple motives behind the measures taken by a commander. In this respect it is conceivable that a commander may discharge his duty to take "necessary and reasonable measures" and in doing so accomplish multiple, additional or extraneous purposes, such as protecting the public image of his forces. Therefore, in considering Mr. Bemba's motivation to protect the image of the MLC, the Trial Chamber erred because it took into consideration an irrelevant factor. In any event, the Trial Chamber failed to make an assessment as to how *in concreto* such alleged motive ultimately affected the necessity or reasonableness of the measures taken by Mr. Bemba.

180. Turning to the remainder of Mr. Bemba's arguments, the Appeals Chamber recalls that the Trial Chamber faulted the measures Mr. Bemba took because they were limited in "mandate, execution, and/or results." The Trial Chamber appears to have lost sight of the fact that the measures taken by a commander cannot be faulted merely because of shortfalls in their execution. When a commander establishes an independent commission, inquiry or judicial process—of which he or she is not part—it must be left to freely fulfill its mandate. Whilst limitations in the results of an inquiry might be attributable to the manner of its establishment (for example, through deliberate exclusion

or limitation of mandate), this is not necessarily so. It is important to establish, in this regard: (i) that the shortcomings of the inquiry were sufficiently serious; (ii) that the commander was aware of the shortcomings; (iii) that it was materially possible to correct the shortcomings; and (iv) that the shortcomings fell within his or her authority to remedy. The Trial Chamber did not make this assessment in the present case. * * *

191. The Appeals Chamber finds that the errors that it has identified have a material impact on the Trial Chamber's finding that Mr. Bemba failed to take all necessary and reasonable measures. In particular, it is apparent that the Trial Chamber's error in considering Mr. Bemba's motivation had a material impact on the entirety of its findings on necessary and reasonable measures because it permeated the Trial Chamber's assessment of the measures that Mr. Bemba had taken. Furthermore, the Trial Chamber's failure to fully appreciate the limitations that Mr. Bemba would have faced in investigating and prosecuting crimes as a remote commander sending troops to a foreign country had an important impact on the overall assessment of the measures taken by Mr. Bemba.

192. Indeed, in faulting the results of measures taken by Mr. Bemba, the Trial Chamber failed to appreciate that, as a remote commander, Mr. Bemba was not part of the investigations and was not responsible for the results generated. Had it done so, the Trial Chamber's assessment of the measures Mr. Bemba had taken would have been necessarily different. It must also be noted that the 2002–2003 CAR Operation was conducted within the short space of a few months, which notwithstanding, Mr. Bemba took numerous measures in response to crimes committed by MLC troops. In this regard, the Appeals Chamber recalls that the Trial Chamber failed to properly establish how many crimes had been committed.

193. Had the Trial Chamber properly assessed the measures that Mr. Bemba took and had the Trial Chamber properly considered the list of measures that it stated that Mr. Bemba could have taken in light of the limitations that he faced in the specific circumstances in which he was operating, it would not have been open to it to reach the same conclusion. The errors the Trial Chamber made resulted in an unreasonable assessment of whether Mr. Bemba failed to take all necessary and reasonable measures in the circumstances existing at the time.

194. In light of the foregoing, the Appeals Chamber finds, by majority, Judge Monageng and Judge Hofmański dissenting, that the Trial Chamber's conclusion that Mr. Bemba failed to take all necessary and reasonable measures in response to MLC crimes in the CAR, was materially affected by the errors identified above. Thus, one of the elements of command responsibility under article 28 (a) of the Statute was not properly established and Mr. Bemba cannot be held criminally

liable under that provision for the crimes committed by MLC troops during the 2002–2003 CAR Operation. * * *

197. In these circumstances, the Appeals Chamber considers it appropriate to reverse the conviction of Mr. Bemba * * *.

Prosecutor v. Jean-Pierre Bemba Gombo, Case No. ICC–01/05–01/08 A, Dissenting Opinion of Judges Sanji Mmasenono Monageng & Judge Piotr Hofmański (June 8, 2018)

43. As explained in detail below, we have reviewed the Trial Chamber's findings in light of the arguments raised by Mr. Bemba on appeal and we are unable to identify any error in the Trial Chamber's findings or any unreasonableness in the overall conclusions. We would therefore have rejected Mr. Bemba's arguments and confirmed the findings and conclusions of the Trial Chamber.

44. The Majority reaches an alternative conclusion based on an analysis that we are unable to accept and find to be deeply flawed. Regarding the measures actually taken by Mr. Bemba, the Majority finds that the Trial Chamber: (i) paid insufficient attention to the fact that the MLC troops were operating in a foreign country with the attendant difficulties on Mr. Bemba's ability to take measures; (ii) treated Mr. Bemba's motivations as determinative of the adequacy or otherwise of the measures; and (iii) failed to establish that Mr. Bemba purposively limited the mandates of the commissions and inquiries.

45. In our view, the first error identified is based on an erroneous assessment of a limited part of the evidentiary record and the uncritical acceptance of Mr. Bemba's unsubstantiated argument, which does not point to any attempts to investigate that were in fact made and proved impossible. The second error identified is not argued by Mr. Bemba and appears to reflect the Majority's subjective view of the Trial Chamber's reasoning, which has no basis in the Conviction Decision, as will be further explained below. Regarding the third error identified, we consider the Majority's position to misconstrue the nature of criminal liability under article 28 of the Statute. Notably, in faulting the Trial Chamber for failing to make findings as to whether the shortcomings in the measures that Mr. Bemba took could be attributed to him and whether he purposively limited the mandates of the commissions and inquiries that he set up, the Majority seems to lose sight of the focus of article 28 of the Statute, namely holding a commander responsible for his failures and not for his actions. * * *

52. To the extent that the Majority suggests that the Trial Chamber failed to conduct such an assessment [as to whether Bemba had taken necessary and reasonable measures], we consider such criticism to be unfounded. A proper reading of the Conviction Decision shows that the

Trial Chamber in fact conducted such an assessment based on the wealth of evidence on the available measures considered necessary and reasonable in the circumstances prevailing at the time. The list of measures set out by the Trial Chamber is a reflection of its findings on effective control, which were challenged by Mr. Bemba during trial and on appeal. Therefore, and contrary to the Majority's position, it was not difficult for Mr. Bemba to attempt to "disprove" them. The Trial Chamber went on to assess what the impact would have been had Mr. Bemba taken the available measures and found that, under the circumstances, he was obligated to take these measures. Therefore, having found that the measures that Mr. Bemba took were insufficient, the Trial Chamber clearly identified *in concreto* what other measures Mr. Bemba should have taken to prevent, repress or punish the commission of crimes by his subordinates.

53. Finally, it is striking that, having determined how the assessment of necessary and reasonable measures should be carried out and having apparently found that the Trial Chamber failed to satisfy this requirement, the Majority does not itself carry out the assessment it deems necessary. This may be a result of the application of the standard of "serious doubts," which the Majority advocates and which apparently exempts it from the obligation to either enter its own factual findings, or remit the matter to the Trial Chamber. In our view, it is incompatible with the interests of justice that issues material to the assessment of guilt should be left unresolved in this manner at the conclusion of the appeals proceedings. * * *

59. Mr. Bemba has made no effort to substantiate his argument that the evidentiary analysis and conclusions of the Trial Chamber were flawed. Mr. Bemba argues that the idea that MLC soldiers were able to "insert themselves into a warzone" in a third state to conduct an investigation is unreasonable, especially as victims are unlikely to voluntarily submit to an interview with foreign armed soldiers, in addition to other logistical difficulties. He submits that "the MLC's ability to take measures within CAR territory was limited, and dependent on cooperation with the CAR authorities." However, Mr. Bemba does not specify how actual measures that he took or attempted to take to investigate MLC crimes on the CAR territory during the height of the CAR conflict were affected by the limitations to which he alludes. To this extent, Mr. Bemba's submissions that his ability to order investigations into crimes in the CAR was limited are speculative.

60. In our view, therefore, the Trial Chamber reasonably assessed the evidence on this question and Mr. Bemba has not identified any error in the reasoning or conclusions of the Trial Chamber such that would establish a misappreciation of the limitations on the MLC's jurisdiction and competence to investigate crimes in the CAR or Mr. Bemba's disciplinary authority over his troops. * * *

262. The next component of the ground of appeal concerning command responsibility concerns the required mental element on the part of Mr. Bemba (as a military commander or person effectively acting as such) as to knowledge of the crimes committed by forces under his effective control in accordance with article 28 (a) (i) of the Statute. * * *

265. We recall that in order to be held liable pursuant to article 28 (a) of the Statute, it must be established that the accused commander had the requisite mental element, as set out in sub-paragraph (i) of the above mentioned article, namely, that the accused commander either "knew, or owing to the circumstances at the time, should have known" that forces under his or her effective command and control or effective authority and control were committing or about to commit crimes within the jurisdiction of the Court. Article 28 (a) (i) of the Statute thus distinguishes, on its face, between two standards of knowledge; where the accused, on the one hand, knew (actual knowledge) and, on the other hand, where the accused should have known owing to the circumstances at the time, that the forces were committing or about to commit the crimes in question. Mr. Bemba asserts that the Trial Chamber misdirected itself as to the law and considered the facts against the wrong mental element: whereas it had purported to carry out an assessment of whether Mr. Bemba "knew" of the crimes of MLC troops, it had, in fact, carried out an assessment of whether Mr. Bemba "should have known." We are not persuaded by Mr. Bemba's argument. Liability under article 28(a) of the Statute is triggered irrespective of which of the two standards is satisfied. * * *

268. To the extent that Mr. Bemba could be understood as arguing that a commander's knowledge may not be inferred and thus appears to take issue with the Trial Chamber's determination that knowledge may be founded on circumstantial evidence, we reject the argument. We recall that the Trial Chamber found that actual knowledge may be established through direct or circumstantial evidence, but could not be presumed. In reaching its conclusion, the Trial Chamber cited the Confirmation Decision and jurisprudence of the ICTY and ICTR. We do not consider this issue controversial. The jurisprudence of the ICTY and the ICTR on superior responsibility has long established that actual knowledge cannot be presumed on the existence of certain facts. * * *

309. We concur with the Trial Chamber that article 28 of the Statute neither requires that a commander knew the identities of the specific individuals who committed the crimes, nor that he mastered every detail of each crime committed. Nevertheless, whilst the commander need not to have known specific details, in line with the jurisprudence of the ICTY, it must be shown that the commander knew or, owing to the circumstances at the time, should have known that "offences such as those charged" were being committed or about to be committed by his or her subordinates. It is insufficient that the accused was aware of general criminal behaviour. * * *

318. Having rejected Mr. Bemba's argument with respect to the Trial Chamber's conclusions on the mental element of article 28 (a) (i) of the Statute, we find that it was not unreasonable for the Trial Chamber to conclude that Mr. Bemba knew that MLC troops were committing or about to commit acts of murder, rape and pillage. * * *

328. [In terms of the issue of "causation," the] question of whether superior responsibility under article 28 (a) of the Statute requires that the superior's omission caused the subordinates' crimes turns on the interpretation of the "result of"-element in the *chapeau* of the provision, which reads, in relevant part, as follows:

> A military commander [. . .] shall be criminally responsible for crimes within the jurisdiction of the Court committed by forces under his or her effective command and control [. . .], as a result of his or her failure to exercise control properly over such forces, where:
>
> (i) That military commander [. . .] either knew or, owing to the circumstances at the time, should have known that the forces were committing or about to commit such crimes; and
>
> (ii) That military commander [. . .] failed to take all necessary and reasonable measures within his or her power to prevent or repress their commission or to submit the matter to the competent authorities for investigation and prosecution.

329. As noted above, the Trial Chamber found that the term "result of" in the *chapeau* of article 28(a) of the Statute linked the failure to exercise control properly with the phrase "crimes within the jurisdiction of the Court committed by forces under [the superior's] effective control," thus requiring that it be established that the crimes in question were committed as a result of the failure to exercise proper control. The Prosecutor proposes an alternative interpretation of the "result of"-element, according to which the element merely explains why the superior is held criminally responsible for the crimes committed by his or her subordinates—namely because of his or her failure to exercise control properly over his subordinates. Based on such interpretation, the "result of"-element would not suggest the need to establish that the superior's failure to control his or her subordinates properly caused the commission of crimes by them.

330. In our view, the relevant passage of the *chapeau* of article 28(a) of the Statute is indeed open to two readings. The correct interpretation of this provision is to be identified by applying the principles of interpretation set out in Articles 31 et seq. of the Vienna Convention on the Law of Treaties. Accordingly, the starting point for any interpretation must be the ordinary meaning of the terms of the treaty "in their context and in the light of its object and purpose."

331. We note that the text of article 28(a) of the Statute—at least in its English version—strongly suggests that it has to be established that the superior's failure to exercise control properly caused the commission of crimes by his or her subordinates. Moreover, we observe that, unlike other provisions in the Statute, article 28 of the Statute explicitly stipulates a nexus requirement by stating that the crimes of the subordinates be committed "as a result of" the commander's failure to exercise control properly. * * *

332. As to the argument that requiring causation is not compelling given that not only failure to take necessary and reasonable measures to prevent crimes leads to criminal responsibility under article 28, but also failure to repress and to punish crimes, in relation to which causation cannot be required as a matter of logic, the Pre-Trial Chamber explained:

> [A]rticle 28(a)(ii) of the Statute refers to three different duties: the duty to prevent crimes, repress crimes, or submit the matter to the competent authorities for investigation and prosecution. The Chamber considers that a failure to comply with the duties to repress or submit the matter to the competent authorities arises during or after the commission of crimes. Thus, it is illogical to conclude that a failure relating to those two duties can retroactively cause the crimes to be committed. Accordingly, the Chamber is of the view that the element of causality only relates to the commander's duty to prevent the commission of future crimes. Nonetheless, the Chamber notes that the failure of a superior to fulfil his duties during and after the crimes can have a causal impact on the commission of further crimes. As punishment is an inherent part of prevention of future crimes, a commander's past failure to punish crimes is likely to increase the risk that further crimes will be committed in the future.

333. To overcome this [retroactivity] problem, the Pre-Trial Chamber considered that, as far as the duties to repress and to punish are concerned, causation needs to be demonstrated in respect of subsequent crimes that were committed because of the failure to punish earlier crimes. This is indeed a convincing approach. * * *

334. In keeping with this principle, holding a commander "criminally responsible for crimes within the jurisdiction of the Court" committed by subordinates is only justified and indeed justifiable if there is a personal nexus between the crime and the superior—it would be irreconcilable with basic tenets of criminal law if a superior were to be held responsible for crimes to which he or she has no connection. * * *

336. In sum, we find that the Trial Chamber was correct in finding that the "result of" element requires a showing that the superior's failure to exercise control properly caused the commission of crimes by his or her subordinates. We shall now turn to the question of what exactly this requirement entails. We recall that in the Conviction Decision itself, the Trial Chamber did not specifically define the requisite standard of

causation, while noting that the "nexus requirement would clearly be satisfied when it is established that the crimes would not have been committed, in the circumstances in which they were, had the commander exercised control properly, or the commander exercising control properly would have prevented the crimes." The Trial Chamber found, however, that "such a standard is [. . .] higher than required by law." * * *

341. We have found that the causation requirement in article 28 of the Statute is satisfied where it is established that, had the commander exercised control properly, there is a high probability that the crimes would have been prevented [in keeping with the test in Judge Steiner's separate opinion]. We note that, in the context of an omission, causation is necessarily an assessment that entails consideration of what would or might have happened, had the commander taken the measures that could have been expected of him. The element of causation is thus intrinsically and inextricably linked to the Trial Chamber's assessment of the adequacy of the measures taken by the commander and the feasibility and efficacy of the measures the commander failed to take. For that reason, we see no error in the Trial Chamber's use of a comparative list of measures to illustrate that the crimes would have been prevented, had Mr. Bemba taken these measures. Thus the argument that the Trial Chamber erroneously conflated the "measures" and "causation" elements of article 28 of the Statute should have been rejected. * * *

348. * * * In light of the circumstances and behaviour of the MLC troops described by the Trial Chamber, we consider that it was not unreasonable to find that the risk that the soldiers would pillage or rape for self-compensation, and murder those who resisted, would have been reduced, if not eliminated, had they received adequate payment and rations. * * *

360. Moreover, we find that the statement regarding inadequacy on the part of Mr. Bemba in terms of supervision is sufficiently rooted in the overall factual findings made by the Trial Chamber. For example, the Trial Chamber notes that there was no evidence that Mr. Bemba took any measures in response to information transmitted internally within the MLC of crimes committed by MLC soldiers from, for example, the MLC intelligence services, and that his reactions were limited to general, public warnings to his troops not to mistreat the civilian population. * * *

371. It is recalled that in its assessment as to who had effective control of the MLC troops in the CAR, the Trial Chamber noted that Mr. Bemba retained the "power and authority" to withdraw the MLC troops and ultimately gave the order to withdraw from the CAR (which was complied with) in March 2003. * * *

373. The Trial Chamber stated that "Mr. Bemba ultimately ended the commission of crimes by MLC soldiers by withdrawing them from the CAR in March 2003." It observed that had Mr. Bemba withdrawn his troops earlier, a possibility it found that Mr. Bemba had acknowledged as early as November 2002, "crimes would have been prevented." * * *

376. Whilst it may be conceivable that, in appropriate circumstances, the failure to withdraw, in and of itself, could give rise to criminal responsibility on the part of a commander, we note that this was not the approach adopted by the Trial Chamber in the instant case, which found that Mr. Bemba's failure to take a range of measures, of which withdrawal formed part, was causally related to the commission of crimes by his troops in the CAR. The Trial Chamber also found that Mr. Bemba could have redesigned his military operations (falling short of outright withdrawal) so as to avoid primarily civilian areas or otherwise limited contact with them, thereby minimising the opportunity for the commission of crimes. Far from holding Mr. Bemba responsible for his failure in one particular respect (that is, timely withdrawal), as averred, the Trial Chamber arrived at its conclusion based upon an assessment of multiple failures in Mr. Bemba's exercise of his duties and an assessment as to the causal link thereto.

377. As to the pertinence of withdrawal in the Trial Chamber's analysis, if a commander had the power to deploy his troops and in doing so endangered a civilian population, then it is also relevant to the necessary and reasonable measures and causation assessment whether and to what extent such commander exercised the power available to him to redeploy his troops (either wholly or partially) so as to remove this source of endangerment. Whilst the duty to take necessary and reasonable measures is a case-specific assessment, we note that this line of reasoning is supported by the jurisprudence of the ICTY in *Strugar*, where it was held that the failure of the commander to ensure the timely withdrawal of his troops from the vicinity of a protected object contributed to the finding that he did not take all necessary and reasonable measures to prevent the subsequent shelling of such object. In sum, we find no fault in the Trial Chamber's conclusions as to the relevance of Mr. Bemba's ability to withdraw the troops, either wholly or partially, in its assessment of the necessary and reasonable measures open to a commander.

NOTES & QUESTIONS

1. Case Outcome

Despite the acquittal, Bemba initially remained in detention because he was also prosecuted under Article 70 of the ICC Statute for interfering in the administration of justice through witness tampering. That judgment was upheld on appeal. The Article 70 conviction likely quashes his aspirations to run for president in the DRC given a provision in Congolese law that excludes those convicted of corruption from running for office.

2. The Reaction of Commentators and Victims

Many Court-watchers were stunned by the reversal. *See* UCLA ICC Forum, *What Does the Bemba Appeal Judgment Say about Superior Responsibility under Article 28 of the Rome Statute?* (June 8, 2018). Many have suggested that the Appeals Chamber effectively gutted the doctrine of superior liability while also undermining the very legitimacy of the Court. Do you agree? Does the majority's discussion of a commander's cost/benefit analysis find expression elsewhere in this jurisprudence? Does the opinion introduce a new legal rule on the question of the commander's motive? The Appeals Chamber decision turns in part on Bemba's remoteness from the events in question. Does blameworthiness turn on the relative remoteness of an accomplice? Or does the opinion encourage commanders to remain far from their troops in order to prepare their defense in the event that their subordinates commit international crimes? How would you compare Bemba's relationship to the acts at issue with that of Yamashita? Return to this when you consider the *Perišić* case later in Chapter 15.

The decision rocked the region. *See* International Crisis Group, *DR Congo: The Bemba Earthquake*, (Briefing no. 140. June 15, 2018). Many victims and victims' advocates in the CAR were left "confused, discouraged, and disillusioned." Nadia Carine, *A Belief Shattered: The International Criminal Court's Bemba Acquittal*, JUST SECURITY (June 25, 2018). This may have been exacerbated by the following observation in one of the separate concurring opinions suggesting that the dissenters, and presumably the Trial Chamber, were swayed by their empathy for the victims:

> Today's Judgment is thus neither a victory, nor a failure. It is the conclusion that a dispassionate application of the Statute compels us to accept. This does not mean that emotionally we do not empathise with the pain and loss of the victims. However, even if Aristotle's dictum that law should be reason, free from passion, may strike us in the 21st century as somewhat inhuman, it remains true more than two thousand years later that, as humans, we can only hope to establish the rule of law if we discipline ourselves to be guided by rationality and resist the urge to allow emotions to determine judicial decisions.

Prosecutor v. Bemba, Case No. ICC–01/05–01/08 A, Separate Opinion of Judges Van den Wyngaert and Morrison, para. 79 (June 8, 2018).

The ICC's Trust Fund for Victims announced that it would accelerate its assistance program for victims notwithstanding the acquittal. The response among Congolese observers was mixed, with many assuming that Bemba's prosecution was an effort by foreign powers to bolster Joseph Kabila, then the President of the DRC and Bemba's rival, and that his acquittal also served Western interests once Kabila lost Western favor. Ambassador (ret.) Herman Cohen (formerly U.S. Undersecretary of State for African Affairs), for example, wrote a letter to the ICC in his then-personal capacity calling for Bemba's release so that Bemba could "assume his political leadership" once Kabila stepped down. *See* Olivia Bueno, *Impact of Bemba Acquittal Already Seen in the Democratic Republic of Congo*, INT'L JUST. MONITOR (Aug. 2, 2018).

3. Omissions and Causality

The *Bemba* prosecution garnered numerous concurring and dissenting opinions. In a separate opinion accompanying the Trial Chamber Judgment, Judge Sylvia Steiner of Brazil focused heavily on the fact that "a link between the commander's failure to exercise control properly and the crimes committed by the subordinates is required." *Prosecutor v. Bemba*, Case No. ICC–01/05–01/08, Separate Opinion of Judge Steiner, para. 4 (March 21, 2016). Judge Steiner reasoned that "a connection is required between the omission and the crimes, and not between the crimes and the responsibility of the commander," as "[a]ll forms of accessory liability require a connection between conduct and an unlawful result." *Id.* at para. 7. She also agreed with the Pre-Trial Chamber that "it is only necessary to prove that the commander's omission increased the risk of the commission of the crimes charged in order to hold him criminally responsible under article 28(a) of the Statute," when the risk creates a "high probability" of crimes occurring. *Id.* at paras. 23–24.

Similarly, Judge Kuniko Ozaki (Japan) wrote "the Chamber has found that Article 28 provides for a mode of liability for the crimes committed, as opposed to an independent crime of omission. As noted in the Judgment, it is a core principle of criminal law that individual criminal responsibility should only attach to an accused where there is some form of personal nexus to the crime." *Prosecutor v. Bemba*, Case No. ICC–01/05–01/08, Separate Opinion of Judge Ozaki, para. 9 (March 21, 2016).

Is an increased risk of criminal behavior the correct standard to apply in cases of command responsibility? Consider this excerpt from another separate opinion:

> The failure to take measures is a failure to reduce an existing risk that something will happen. If the superior does nothing, the risk that subordinates will commit a crime stays the same, his failure to act does not increase that risk. The responsibility of the commander is precisely to decrease the risk that his/her subordinates will commit crimes. Failing to reduce a risk can hardly be seen as causing the manifestation of said risk.

Prosecutor v. Bemba, Separate Opinion of Judges Van den Wyngaert and Morrison, at para. 55. Should omissions be subject to a different measure of causality than commissions, such as Bemba's failure to prevent his soldiers from committing war crimes and crimes against humanity? Does such an omission create a strong enough "personal nexus to the crime" if the criminal behavior of a commander's inferiors was not inevitable in light of the omission?

4. Standard of Review

The opinion was controversial not only on substance, but also when it comes to the standard of review employed by the majority in the Appeals Chamber. The majority, whose opinion is quite brief in proportion to its impact, did not undertake a thorough analysis of the evidence but rather indicated that they had reasonable doubts about the Trial Chamber's factual findings; the dissenters—who hail from Botswana and Poland—painstakingly reviewed the Trial Chamber record in crafting their opinion in support of affirming the judgment below.

Notwithstanding their own thorough canvassing of the lower court opinion, the dissenters argued that the Appeals Chamber should have accorded more deference to the finders of fact below. Citing the *Lubanga* Appeals decision, they identify the correct standard of review as "whether a reasonable Trial Chamber could have been satisfied beyond reasonable doubt as to the finding in question. The Appeals Chamber will not assess the evidence *de novo* with a view to determining whether it would have reached the same factual finding." *Prosecutor v. Lubanga*, Case No. ICC–01/04–01/06, Judgment, para. 27 (Dec. 1, 2014). The Appeals Chamber majority appeared to reject this precedent when they announced that the "Appeals Chamber must be satisfied that factual findings that are made beyond reasonable doubt are clear and unassailable, both in terms of evidence and rationale. Accordingly, when the Appeals Chamber is able to identify findings that can reasonably be called into doubt, it must overturn them." Bemba Appeal, *supra*, at para. 3, and it "may interfere with the factual findings of the first-instance chamber whenever the failure to interfere may occasion a miscarriage of justice." *Id.* at para. 40. To support this standard the judges in the majority cited two provisions of the ICC Statute: Article 83 (1), which grants the Appeals Chamber "all the powers of the Trial Chamber," and Article 74(5), which obliges the Trial Chamber to render a decision containing "a full and reasoned statement of the Trial Chamber's findings on the evidence and conclusions."

The Rome Statute does not indicate what the standard of review should be on appeal. How should Appeals Chambers approach the question of deference? If the Appeals Chamber had doubts about the record, should it have ordered a new trial rather than substituting its judgment, as was preferred by Judge Chile Eboe-Osuji of Nigeria (now President of the Court)? Does the fact that Bemba had already served 10 years in pre-trial detention alter your views? If you count judges on the Pre-Trial Chamber, 8 of the 11 judges who looked at this case found at least some evidence of Bemba's guilt. For a discussion, *see* Alex Whiting, *Appeals Judges Turn the ICC on its Head with Bemba Decision*, JUST SECURITY (June 14, 2018).

5. Prevent or Punish

Under the doctrine of command responsibility a superior is held liable for failing to respond to abuses in the face of a duty to act. As these opinions teach, the doctrine is formulated in the disjunctive: liability will be found where the defendant failed to prevent *or* to punish abuses by subordinates. Indeed, in Bemba, the Pre-Trial Chamber interpreted the ICC Statute to encompass three distinct duties:

> 435. In order to find the suspect responsible under command responsibility, once the mental element is satisfied, it is necessary to prove that he or she failed at least to fulfil one of the three duties listed under article 28(a)(ii) of the Statute: the duty to prevent crimes, the duty to repress crimes or the duty to submit the matter to the competent authorities for investigation and prosecution.
>
> 436. The Chamber first wishes to underline that the three duties under article 28(a)(ii) of the Statute arise at three different stages in the commission of crimes: before, during and after. Thus, a failure to fulfil one of these duties is itself a separate crime under

> article 28(a) of the Statute. A military commander or a military-like commander can therefore be held criminally responsible for one or more breaches of duty under article 28(a) of the Statute in relation to the same underlying crimes.

Prosecutor v. Jean-Pierre Bemba Gombo, Case No. ICC–01/05–01/08, Decision Pursuant to Article 61(7)(a) and (b) of the Rome Statute on the Charges of the Prosecutor against Jean-Pierre Bemba Gombo (June 15, 2009).

Should a defendant be able to absolve herself of responsibility for failing to prevent abuses by punishing subordinates after the fact? The ICTY said no: "the obligation to 'prevent or punish' does not provide the accused with two alternative and equally satisfying options. Obviously, where the accused knew or had reason to know that subordinates were about to commit crimes and failed to prevent them, he cannot make up for the failure to act by punishing the subordinates afterwards." *Prosecutor v. Blaškić*, Case No. IT–95–14–T, Judgement, para. 336 (March 3, 2000).

Article 7(3) of the ICTY Statute speaks of the duty of the superior to take "necessary and reasonable measures." "Necessary" measures are understood to mean those measures that are required to discharge the defendant's obligation to prevent and punish criminal behavior under the prevailing circumstances. "Reasonable" measures are those measures that the defendant was in a position to take under those circumstances. How are tribunals to determine what measures were "necessary and reasonable" under the circumstances, especially given that international judges rarely have military, or even military justice, experience? In *Bagilishema*, the ICTR made clear that

> A superior may be held responsible for failing to take only such measures that were within his or her powers. Indeed, it is the commander's degree of effective control—his or her material ability to control subordinates—which will guide the Chamber in determining whether he or she took reasonable measures to prevent, stop, or punish the subordinates' crimes.

Prosecutor v. Bagilishema, Case No. ICTR–95–1A–T, Judgement, para. 48 (June 7, 2001).

Does this element of the doctrine require the prosecution to prove a negative, namely that the defendant did not exercise powers he possessed? Should the burden shift to the defendant to show that he did all that was required of him under international law? How should such "Monday morning adjudications" account for the proverbial fog of war? Should judges construct a legal fiction of a "reasonable commander" as a counterpart to the domestic law "reasonable person"? How many preventative measures must a defendant superior implement in order to avoid liability for abuses by subordinates? Must a defendant undertake a reasonable effort to prevent and punish abuses or must he exert maximum effort?

What is the basis for holding a commander liable for failing to punish the acts of a subordinate? Is the assumption that the commander has ratified the conduct? Is this species of superior responsibility the equivalent of being an "accessory after-the-fact" or of engaging in misprision (failing to report criminal conduct)? An accessory after-the-fact is one who, knowing that a crime has been committed, assists the principal in escaping detection or apprehension. At common law, the accessory after-the-fact was treated as a party to the underlying crime. Under modern law, most systems usually treat such accessories under the rubric of "obstruction of justice," which is often a different and less serious offense than the underlying substantive crime. On accessory-after-the-fact liability, *see* Michael J. Yeager, *Survey of Criminal Law*, 52 MD. L. REV. 605 (1993); E. L. Matthews, *Extent of Criminal Responsibility of an Accessory in Roman-Dutch Law*, 7 J. COMP. LEG. & INT'L L. 179 (1925) (presenting a comparative view of the doctrine).

Can a commander be exonerated for a failure to punish when crimes are committed in the midst of battle requiring complete attention to mission accomplishment? When should a commander be held liable for a malfunctioning military justice system? Is a commander absolved of command responsibility once she refers a matter to a court-martial process? What if the direct perpetrator is acquitted or receives only a light sentence? Is there a continuing duty on the commander to utilize non-judicial punishment under these circumstances?

6. Dereliction of Duty

What is the nature of the command responsibility doctrine: Is the defendant convicted for the substantive offense committed by the subordinates? Or is the defendant convicted of his own dereliction of duty? A noted law-of-war scholar has argued: "It must be accentuated that command responsibility is all about dereliction of duty. The commander is held accountable for his own act (of omission), rather than incurring 'vicarious liability' for the acts (of commission) of the subordinates." Yoram Dinstein, THE CONDUCT OF HOSTILITIES UNDER THE LAW OF ARMED CONFLICT 238 (2004). Which is the better approach? Which approach better allows a criminal court to calibrate punishment and the stigma that inevitably accompanies a finding of liability under international criminal law? For an argument that the commander who fails to punish is an accomplice with respect to the underlying act, *see* Amy J. Sepinwall, *Failures to Punish: Command Responsibility in Domestic and International Law*, 30 MICH. J. INT'L L. 251 (2009). For an argument that superior responsibility should be treated as both a mode of liability and also a separate offense, *see* Elies van Sliedregt, *Article 28 of the ICC Statute: Mode of Liability and/or Separate Offense*, 12 NEW CRIM. L. REV. 420 (2009).

7. Sentencing

If the defendant is convicted of the substantive offense committed by the subordinate, should he receive an equivalent sentence to that of the subordinate? Is the superior's conduct sufficiently blameworthy to justify such equal treatment, or should any penalty be mitigated by the fact that the defendant was not the direct perpetrator? Alternatively, should the penalty be aggravated by the fact that the defendant was in a position of superiority over the direct perpetrators and was under a duty to control his subordinates?

8. Causation

The Bemba opinion engages the question of what role causation places in the doctrine. The concept of *actus reus* is usually defined as a criminal act that causes harm. Joshua Dressler, UNDERSTANDING CRIMINAL LAW § 9.01 (3rd ed. 2001). Is causation an element of the doctrine of superior responsibility? In other words, is it necessary for the prosecution to demonstrate that the failure of the defendant to undertake the necessary and reasonable preventative measures caused the criminal conduct by the subordinate? Is it fair to hold someone liable for conduct that she has in no way caused? How would a causation element work in the context of the defendant superior's failure to punish criminal conduct by subordinates?

In *Delalić*, the ICTY ruled that causation was not an element of the doctrine:

> Notwithstanding the central place assumed by the principle of causation in criminal law, causation has not traditionally been postulated as a *conditio sine qua non* ["a condition without which it could not be"] for the imposition of criminal liability on superiors for their failure to prevent or punish offences committed by their subordinates. * * * This is not to say that, conceptually, the principle of causality is without application to the doctrine of command responsibility insofar as it relates to the responsibility of superiors for their failure to prevent the crimes of their subordinates. In fact, a recognition of a necessary causal nexus may be considered to be inherent in the requirement of crimes committed by subordinates and the superior's failure to take the measures within his powers to prevent them. In this situation, the superior may be considered to be causally linked to the offences, in that, but for his failure to fulfill his duty to act, the acts of his subordinates would not have been committed.

Prosecutor v. Delalić, Case No. IT–96–21–T, Judgement, paras. 398–99 (Nov. 16, 1998). What does the Tribunal mean when it speaks of "a necessary causal nexus" being "inherent in the requirement of crimes committed by subordinates and the superior's failure to take the measures within his powers to prevent them"? A U.S. District Court in *Ford v. Garcia*—a case brought under the Alien Tort Statute and Torture Victim Protection Act—gave the following proximate cause instruction to the jury that acquitted the defendants in that case:

> The plaintiffs may recover only those damages arising from those omissions that can be attributed to the defendant. Each plaintiff must therefore prove that the compensation he/she seeks relates to damages that naturally flow from the injuries proved. In other words, there must be a sufficient causal connection between an omission of the defendant and any damage sustained by a plaintiff. This requirement is referred to as "proximate cause." As I have told you, international law and the law of the United States impose an affirmative duty on military commanders to take appropriate measures within their power to control troops under their

> command to prevent torture and extrajudicial killing. If you find that one or more of the plaintiffs have established all of the elements of the doctrine of command responsibility, as defined in these instructions, then you must determine whether the plaintiffs have also established by a preponderance of the evidence that the churchwomen's injuries were a direct or a reasonably foreseeable consequence of one or both defendants' failure to fulfill their obligations under the doctrine of command responsibility. Keep in mind that a legal cause need not always be the nearest cause either in time or in space. In addition, in a case such as this, there may be more than one cause of an injury or damages. Many factors or the conduct of two or more people may operate at the same time, either independently or together, to cause an injury.

Ford v. Garcia, 289 F.3d 1283, 1287 n.4 (11th Cir. 2002). On appeal, the 11th Circuit found that the inclusion of the instruction constituted unreviewable invited error, because Plaintiffs-Appellants had participated in the drafting of the instruction. *Id.* at 1294.

In her concurrence, Judge Rosemary Barkett suggested that the 11th Circuit should consider adopting the approach from other Circuits whereby the invited error doctrine gives way in "exceptional circumstances" when it is "necessary to preserve the integrity of the judicial process or prevent a miscarriage of justice." She reasoned that the proximate cause instruction was erroneous because:

> the concept of proximate cause is not relevant to the assignment of liability under the command responsibility doctrine. The doctrine does not require a direct causal link between a plaintiff victim's injuries and the acts or omissions of a commander. Once a plaintiff establishes a *prima facie* case by proving the doctrine's three prongs, the command responsibility doctrine requires no further showing to assign liability unless the commander presents a defense. * * * Indeed, a proximate cause requirement practically eviscerates the command responsibility doctrine's theory of liability.

Id. at 1299. She further argued that causation must

> be demonstrated between the victims' injuries and the armed forces that committed the crimes. Causation, therefore, was undisputedly established in this case: the troops raped and murdered the nuns. Upon proof of its three prongs, the command responsibility doctrine assigns responsibility for those crimes to the commander of the troops, absent any defense.

Id.

9. Causation and the ICC

Review Article 28 of the ICC Statute. Is causation an element of superior responsibility in that formulation? In the decision confirming charges against Jean Pierre Bemba, a Pre-Trial Chamber held:

> 423. * * * The Chamber therefore considers that the *chapeau* of article 28(a) of the Statute includes an element of causality between a superior's dereliction of duty and the underlying crimes. This interpretation is consistent with the principle of strict construction mirrored in article 22(2) of the Statute which, as a part of the principle *nullum crimen sine lege*, compels the Chamber to interpret this provision strictly.
>
> 424. * * * [However because] a failure to comply with the duties to repress or submit the matter to the competent authorities arise during or after the commission of crimes * * * the element of causality only relates to the commander's duty to prevent the commission of future crimes. * * *
>
> 425. * * * [A] possible way to determine the level of causality would be to apply a "but for test," in the sense that, but for the superior's failure to fulfil his duty to take reasonable and necessary measures to prevent crimes, those crimes would not have been committed by his forces. However, contrary to the visible and material effect of a positive act, the effect of an omission cannot be empirically determined with certainty. In other words, it would not be practical to predict exactly what would have happened if a commander had fulfilled his obligation to prevent crimes. There is no direct causal link that needs to be established between the superior's omission and the crime committed by his subordinates. Therefore, the Chamber considers that it is only necessary to prove that the commander's omission increased the risk of the commission of the crimes charged in order to hold him criminally responsible under article 28(a) of the Statute.

The Chamber acknowledged that this conclusion marks a departure from the jurisprudence of the *ad hoc* tribunals. *Prosecutor v. Jean-Pierre Bemba Gombo*, Case No. ICC–01/05–01/08, Decision Pursuant to Article 61(7)(a) and (b) of the Rome Statute on the Charges of the Prosecutor against Jean-Pierre Bemba Gombo (June 15, 2009). How did this issue get resolved on appeal in the above decision?

10. An Assessment

One commentator has argued that the superior responsibility doctrine "persists as a utilitarian tool of victor's justice favoring deterrence of crimes and the punishment of superiors over the principle of individualized fault." Arthur Thomas O'Reilly, *Command Responsibility: A Call to Realign Doctrine with Principles*, 20 AM. U. INT'L L. REV. 71, 72 (2004). Do you agree? Does the doctrine stray too far from the culpability principle of criminal law, which provides that criminal liability should depend on some fault of the defendant? Is O'Reilly overly optimistic in assuming that the doctrine will serve utilitarian goals of deterrence? Or, is the doctrine still too inexact and inconsistent to influence military conduct? Are "good" men and women likely to be deterred from serving in positions of command given the confused state of the doctrine? As an alternative, will abuses be better prevented by focusing international law enforcement on states through state liability?

11. For Further Reading

For more on the history of superior responsibility, *see* Matthew Lippman, *Humanitarian Law: The Uncertain Contours of Command Responsibility*, 9 TULSA J. COMP. & INT'L L. 1 (2001); Andrew D. Mitchell, *Failure to Halt, Prevent or Punish: The Doctrine of Command Responsibility for War Crimes*, 22 SYDNEY L. REV. 381 (2000); Maj. W.H. Parks, *Command Responsibility for War Crimes*, 62 MIL. L. REV. 1 (1973); Maj. Michael L. Smidt, Yamashita, Medina *and Beyond: Command Responsibility in Contemporary Military Operations*, 164 MIL. L. REV. 155 (2000). For the application of superior responsibility in the case law preceding the ICTY, *see* L.C. Green, *Command Responsibility in International Humanitarian Law*, 5 TRANSNAT'L L & CONTEMP. PROBLEMS 319 (1995). For discussion of superior responsibility before the ICTY and ICTR, *see* Beatrice I. Bonafé, *Finding a Proper Role for Command Responsibility,* 5 J. INT'L CRIM. JUST. 599 (2007). For analogs to domestic doctrines of criminal law, *see* Amy J. Sepinwall, *Failures to Punish: Command Responsibility in Domestic and International Law*, 30 MICH. J. INT'L L. 251 (2009); Timothy Wu & Yong-Sung (Johnathan) Kang, *Criminal Liability for the Actions of Subordinates—the Doctrine of Command Responsibility and its Analogues in United States Law*, 38 HARV. INT'L L. J. 272 (1997).

PROBLEMS

1. *Yamashita* Redux

Assuming all of the evidence against General Yamashita were true, would he have been convicted and executed under the contemporary formulation of the superior responsibility doctrine? Consider, in particular, questions of whether he exercised effective command and control over the responsible subordinates and whether the evidence presented would have satisfied the modern understanding of the *mens rea* of command responsibility beyond a reasonable doubt.

2. The Liability of Latecomers

Defendant is a former professional military officer of the Yugoslav National Army ("JNA"). In 1992, Defendant left the JNA with the rank of Captain and joined the nascent Army of Bosnia-Herzegovina ("ABiH"). He was posted as Assistant Chief of Staff and then Chief of Staff for Operations and Instruction Matters of the ABiH 3rd Corps, 7th Muslim Mountain Brigade. From April 1, 1993 to July 20, 1993, Defendant served as ABiH 3rd Corps 7th Muslim Mountain Brigade Commander.

Although Defendant took up his position as acting commander of the 3rd Corps, 7th Muslim Mountain Brigade on 1 April 1993, the Prosecution charged him with being criminally responsible in relation to those crimes that were committed by troops of the ABiH 3rd Corps, 7th Muslim Mountain Brigade prior to his assignment. In particular, Defendant was charged with responsibility for the cruel treatment and killing of civilians in January 1993—offences committed or started more than two months before he became the commander of the troops on April 1, 1993. The Indictment alleged that Defendant "knew or had reason to know about these crimes.

After he assumed command, he was under the duty to punish the perpetrators."

Defendant has filed a motion to dismiss the Indictment against him on grounds of lack of jurisdiction for crimes committed by individuals who were not his subordinates at the time they committed the abuses in question. How would you argue Defendant's case? How would the Prosecution oppose the motion? How should the Tribunal rule?

CHAPTER 15

DIRECT AND INDIRECT RESPONSIBILITY

I. INTRODUCTION

The principal to a crime is the party who "with the relevant *mens rea* does distinct acts which together constitute a sufficient act for the *actus reus* of an offence." Card, Cross & Jones, CRIMINAL LAW, Sec. 23.1 (1992). While identifying the principal offender is usually relatively straightforward, the determination of who else should be criminally responsible for an offence by virtue of his or her involvement therein can be more difficult. This chapter discusses several doctrines that may be employed to address the criminal responsibility of individuals who associate themselves with criminal activity. These are: collective responsibility, complicity, joint criminal enterprise, and co-perpetration. (The inchoate offenses of conspiracy and incitement have their own chapter). Before beginning, consider Article 25(3) of the ICC Statute, which sets out forms of responsibility—other than superior responsibility which is addressed in Article 28—that are prosecutable before the ICC:

> 3. In accordance with this Statute, a person shall be criminally responsible and liable for punishment for a crime within the jurisdiction of the Court if that person:
>
> (a) Commits such a crime, whether as an individual, jointly with another or through another person, regardless of whether that other person is criminally responsible;
>
> (b) Orders, solicits or induces the commission of such a crime which in fact occurs or is attempted;
>
> (c) For the purpose of facilitating the commission of such a crime, aids, abets or otherwise assists in its commission or its attempted commission, including providing the means for its commission;
>
> (d) In any other way contributes to the commission or attempted commission of such a crime by a group of persons acting with a common purpose. Such contribution shall be intentional and shall either:
>
> (i) Be made with the aim of furthering the criminal activity or criminal purpose of the group, where such activity or purpose involves the commission of a crime within the jurisdiction of the Court; or

(ii) Be made in the knowledge of the intention of the group to commit the crime;

(e) In respect of the crime of genocide, directly and publicly incites others to commit genocide;

(f) Attempts to commit such a crime by taking action that commences its execution by means of a substantial step, but the crime does not occur because of circumstances independent of the person's intentions. However, a person who abandons the effort to commit the crime or otherwise prevents the completion of the crime shall not be liable for punishment under this Statute for the attempt to commit that crime if that person completely and voluntarily gave up the criminal purpose.

As you review the materials that follow, consider the degree to which Article 25 covers the field in terms of prosecutable conduct, particularly in light of the jurisprudence from the other international tribunals.

II. THE WORLD WAR II EXPERIMENT IN COLLECTIVE RESPONSIBILITY

The crimes committed by Nazi Germany were distinctive in world history in that they were perpetrated on a massive and systematic scale and required the coordination of the state, military, and party bureaucracy as well as private industry. At the close of World War II, the Allies were thus faced with the prospect of bringing to justice potentially thousands of war criminals. To respond to these unprecedented events, the American negotiators to the Nuremberg drafting conference introduced two controversial innovations into international criminal law: the law of conspiracy and the concept of the unlawful criminal organization.

Colonel Murray C. Bernays, a lawyer from the U.S. Department of War, first conceived of a two-part plan to ensure that responsibility for the crimes of the Third Reich would not be placed solely on the shoulders of the top leaders who would be prosecuted by the Nuremberg Tribunal, but would also reflect the willing participation of the German rank-and-file. Under phase one of his proposal, the Prosecution would indict implicated organizations—such as the *Sturmabteilungen* (SA), or the so-called stormtroopers; the *Schutzstaffel* (SS), an elite paramilitary unit; and the Gestapo, the SS secret police—and then seek a declaration from the Nuremberg Tribunal on the illegality of each. In phase two, members of those organizations would be subject to arrest and prosecution before national courts based solely upon their membership in a convicted organization. The Tribunal's declaratory judgment would be *res judicata* in individual proceedings against organization members. The burden would then shift to the defendants to prove either that membership in the organization was involuntary or that they did not know the organization's criminal object and purpose. As Col. Bernays envisioned it, once the organizational criminality was established, "[p]roof of membership, without more, would establish guilt of participation in the . . . conspiracy." *See* Bradley F. Smith, THE AMERICAN ROAD TO NUREMBERG, THE DOCUMENTARY RECORD 1944–1945, Document 16 (1982).

Although the U.S. allies expressed considerable resistance to the idea of group criminality, pragmatism eventually prevailed in light of concerns that organization members would go free in the absence of specific evidence of personal wrongdoing. A French memorandum in support of the plan argued that the extraordinary nature of mass criminality required a novel penal response. The Nuremberg Charter thus contained many features of the original United States proposal, albeit in somewhat compromised form:

> Article 9. At the trial of any individual member of any group or organization the Tribunal may declare (in connection with any act of which the individual may be convicted) that the group or organization of which the individual was a member was a criminal organization. After the receipt of the Indictment the Tribunal shall give such notice as it thinks fit that the Prosecution intends to ask the Tribunal to make such declaration and any member of the organization will be entitled to apply to the Tribunal for leave to be heard by the Tribunal upon the question of the criminal character of the organization. The Tribunal shall have power to allow or reject the application. If the application is allowed, the Tribunal may direct in what manner the applicants shall be represented and heard.
>
> Article 10. In cases where a group or organization is declared criminal by the Tribunal, the competent national authority of any Signatory shall have the right to bring individuals to trial for membership therein before national, military, or occupation courts. In any such case the criminal nature of the group or organization is considered proved and shall not be questioned.

The United States took the lead on presenting the case against the six organizations indicted for crimes against the peace, crimes against humanity, war crimes, and criminal conspiracy: the Reich Cabinet, the Leadership Corps of the Nazi Party, the General Staff and High Command of the German Armed Forces, the SS, the Gestapo, and the SA.

Pursuant to Article 9, the Tribunal gave public notice through the media and in POW camps of the intention to prosecute organizations and the right of members to be heard. Thousands of requests to give evidence were submitted, most by individual members claiming conscription, lack of knowledge, or that the group was actually multiple groups, some of which were wholly innocent in their activities. The Tribunal appointed counsel to represent each organization. During the proceedings, defense counsel challenged the project at its core, arguing that the law on criminal organizations was contrary to fundamental tenets of justice, was improper retroactive legislation, and would unfairly impose liability on millions of unrepresented and absent German citizens. Defense counsel presented testimony from numerous group members on whether membership in the indicted groups was voluntary and whether their purposes were notorious or secret. The senior U.S. judge, Francis Biddle, twice argued in deliberations that all the charges against the organizations should be thrown out even though as Attorney General under President Franklin D. Roosevelt, he had supported Col. Bernays's proposal.

Ultimately, the Tribunal declared only three of the indicted organizations to be criminal: the SS, the Gestapo, and the Leadership Corps of the Nazi Party. The Reich Cabinet was acquitted for largely the same reasons as the General Staff/High Command—the Tribunal determined that it was an instrumentality of the state rather than a membership organization. The Tribunal acquitted the SA (the largest of the groups) because its criminal actions predated the invasion of Poland and by 1939 it was composed largely of "ruffians and bullies" unconnected to the Nazi plans to engage in aggressive war. Although there was some authority in the Charter of the International Military Tribunal for the Far East to criminalize organizations, the prosecutor, Joseph B. Keenan of the United States, did not indict any organizations to which the Japanese defendants belonged.

On the authority of Article II(1)(d) of Control Council Law No. 10 (CCL 10), which served as the basis for prosecutions of lesser defendants in occupation courts throughout Germany and penalized "membership in * * * a criminal group or organization declared criminal by the International Military Tribunal," hundreds of trials went forward in occupation courts against members of the groups declared criminal at Nuremberg. In these trials, a point of contention emerged surrounding the placement of the burden of proof. Although Col. Bernays's original intentions were clear that knowledge and voluntariness would be presumed but rebuttable, the Nuremberg Tribunal was more vague about how this should operate in the subsequent proceedings. Compare these two approaches adopted by occupation tribunals in the U.S. zone of occupation:

> **"The I.G. Farben Trial," Trial of Karl Krauch and Twenty-Two Others, X LAW REPORTS OF TRIALS OF WAR CRIMINALS 1, 59 (U.S. Mil. Trib. 1948):** In its Preliminary Brief the Prosecution says that "it seems totally unnecessary to anticipate any contention that intelligent Germans, and in particular persons who were S.S. members for a long period of years, did not know that the S.S. was being used for the commission of acts 'amounting to war crimes and crimes against humanity.' " This

> assumption is not, in our judgment, a sound basis for shifting the burden of proof to a defendant or for relieving the Prosecution from the obligation of establishing all of the essential ingredients of the crime. Proof of the requisite knowledge need not, of course, be direct, but may be inferred from the circumstances duly established.
>
> **"The Justice Trial," Trial of Josef Altstötter and Others, VI LAW REPORTS OF TRIALS OF WAR CRIMINALS 1, 69–72 (U.S. Mil. Trib. 1947):** The evidence in this case clearly established that the defendant joined and retained his membership in the SS on a voluntary basis. The remaining fact to be determined is whether he had knowledge of the criminal activities of the SS as defined in the London Charter. * * * In this regard the Tribunal is of the opinion that the activities of the SS and the crimes which it committed as pointed out by the Judgment of the International Military Tribunal * * * are of so wide a scope that no person of the defendant's intelligence, and one who had achieved the rank of *Oberführer* in the SS, could have been unaware of its illegal activities, particularly a member of the organization from 1937 until the surrender. * * * Surely, whether or not he took a part in such activities [organizing pogroms and the provision of concentration camp security] or approved of them, he must have known of that part which was played by an organization of which he was an officer.

In general, most subsequent proceedings identified voluntariness and knowledge of the group's criminal purposes as elements that had to be proved by the prosecution. This, of course, largely nullified the goal of a streamlined process for the subsequent trials. Under the circumstances, should the presumption of innocence have trumped the compelling considerations of expediency?

NOTES & QUESTIONS

1. Lustration After World War II

Col. Bernays's two-phase plan to criminalize organizations and mere membership envisioned de-Nazification through judicial means. The Allies also pursued de-Nazification through administrative means by barring members of the Nazi party from certain key posts in postwar Germany. Indeed, de-Nazification was a central pillar of the Potsdam Agreement governing the occupation and reconstruction of postwar Germany. Article II(A)(6) provided:

> All members of the Nazi Party who have been more than nominal participants in its activities and all other persons hostile to Allied purposes shall be removed from public and semi-public office, and from positions of responsibility in important private undertakings. Such persons shall be replaced by persons who, by their political

> and moral qualities, are deemed capable of assisting in developing genuine democratic institutions in Germany.

Protocol of Proceedings Approved at Berlin (Potsdam), § II(A)(6), Aug. 2, 1945, 3 Bevans 1207 (1945). Why would de-Nazification be implemented with respect to the private sector in addition to the public sector? In the U.S. zone of occupation, the United States put in place an elaborate bureaucratic mechanism to screen individuals for past support of Nazi policies. Individuals were categorized according to the level and strength of their involvement and were accordingly subject to various punishments and exclusions. The Soviets took the most radical approach by killing or interning Nazi Party members without any right to process. As the Cold War set in, a strong Germany began to be seen in the West as an important bulwark against Communism, and the de-Nazification programs were disbanded even though proceedings were far from complete. *See* John H. Herz, *Denazification and Related Policies*, *in* FROM DICTATORSHIP TO DEMOCRACY: COPING WITH THE LEGACIES OF AUTHORITARIANISM AND TOTALITARIANISM (John H. Herz ed., 1982).

A less robust lustration policy was implemented in occupied Japan. Much of the prewar imperial bureaucracy was allowed to remain in place, and many high-ranking wartime Japanese officials either retained power or soon returned to power. The "purge," as it was called, expired in 1952 when Japan regained its independence. Class B and C war criminals who were serving their sentences around the region were gradually repatriated, and Article 11 of the 1952 San Francisco Peace Treaty gave the right to grant clemency or parole to the prosecuting power. So, in 1952, President Harry S. Truman issued Executive Order 10393, which established a Clemency and Parole Board for War Criminals to address mounting demands in Japan that convicted war criminals be paroled. By 1958, all convicted individuals had been released from prison. One of the individuals originally designated as among the Class A war criminals (Nobusuke Kishi), who had been accused of using Chinese forced labor, was never tried and was later elected prime minister. For a discussion, *see* Sandra Wilson, *After the Trials: Class B and C Japanese War Criminals and the Post-War World*, 31(2) JAPANESE STUDIES 141 (Sept. 7, 2011). How would you explain these two different approaches?

2. Concentration Camps as Illegal Organizations

When Poland joined the London Agreement establishing the Nuremberg Tribunal, it brought its municipal law into line with the then prevailing international criminal law on criminal organizations. Under the new legislation, Polish courts declared the criminality of, among others, the concentration camp staff at Auschwitz and the officials administrating the Lodz ghetto, an area of the city that was sealed off for the city's 230,000 Jewish residents. Were such prosecutions contrary to the Nuremberg Tribunal's reasoning with respect to the General Staff/High Command: that such entities were not membership organizations? Concentration camp inmates who assisted in the running of the camps were excluded from prosecution under this provision on the grounds that they worked under compulsion and were not part of the group as a result of a common aim or ideological tie. Prosecutors did prosecute these "*kapos*" (*Kameraden Polizei*) for their own international crimes. *See Trial of Obersturmbannführer Rudolf Franz Ferdinand Hoess* (Supreme National Tribunal of Poland 1947), VII LAW REPORTS OF TRIALS OF WAR CRIMINALS 11, 20–21 (discussing cases).

3. Domestic Laws on Criminal Organizations

Some national codes recognize the concept of a criminal organization. In the United States, the still extant Smith Act of 1940 (a.k.a. the Alien Registration Act) enables the prosecution of anyone who "organizes or helps or attempts to organize any society, group, or assembly of persons who teach, advocate, or encourage the overthrow or destruction of any such government by force or violence; or becomes or is a member of, or affiliates with, any such society, group, or assembly of persons." 18 U.S.C. § 2385 (2000). The now-repealed 1950 Suppression of Communism Act and the 1960 Unlawful Organizations Act in South Africa were used to prosecute communists, black nationalists, and liberals during apartheid. The law of the former Yugoslavia once assigned liability to individuals who established criminal organizations. Such individuals were accountable for all crimes that flowed from the criminal scheme undertaken by organizations they established. *See* Article 26 of the 1976 Yugoslav Criminal Code:

> Anybody creating or making use of an organization, gang, cabal, group or any other association for the purpose of committing criminal acts is criminally responsible for all criminal acts resulting from the criminal design of these associations and shall be punished as if he himself has committed them, irrespective of whether and in what manner he himself directly participated in the commission of any of those acts.

This code section was heavily criticized for being used as an instrument to combat political opposition. The successor states of the former Yugoslavia dropped this form of organizational liability from their criminal law.

4. Providing Material Support for Terrorism

The United States has criminalized the provision of material support to terrorists and designated terrorist groups in two related facilitation statutes:

> 18 U.S.C. § 2339A. Providing material support to terrorists
>
> (a) Offense.—Whoever provides material support or resources or conceals or disguises the nature, location, source, or ownership of material support or resources, knowing or intending that they are to be used in preparation for, or in carrying out, a violation of [multiple code sections relating to violent acts and terrorism crimes] or in preparation for, or in carrying out, the concealment of an escape from the commission of any such violation, or attempts or conspires to do such an act, shall be fined under this title, imprisoned not more than 15 years, or both, and, if the death of any person results, shall be imprisoned for any term of years or for life.
> * * *
>
> (b) Definitions.—As used in this section—
>
> (1) the term "material support or resources" means any property, tangible or intangible, or service, including

currency or monetary instruments or financial securities, financial services, lodging, training, expert advice or assistance, safe houses, false documentation or identification, communications equipment, facilities, weapons, lethal substances, explosives, personnel (1 or more individuals who may be or include oneself), and transportation, except medicine or religious materials. * * *

18 U.S.C. § 2339B. Providing material support or resources to designated foreign terrorist organizations

(a) Prohibited activities.—

(1) Unlawful conduct.—Whoever knowingly provides material support or resources to a foreign terrorist organization, or attempts or conspires to do so, shall be fined under this title or imprisoned not more than 20 years, or both, and, if the death of any person results, shall be imprisoned for any term of years or for life. To violate this paragraph, a person must have knowledge that the organization is a designated terrorist organization, that the organization has engaged or engages in terrorist activity * * *, or that the organization has engaged or engages in terrorism. * * *

(d) Extraterritorial jurisdiction.

(1) In general. There is jurisdiction over an offense under subsection (a) if—

(A) an offender is a national of the United States * * *;

(C) after the conduct required for the offense occurs an offender is brought into or found in the United States, even if the conduct required for the offense occurs outside the United States;

(D) the offense occurs in whole or in part within the United States;

(E) the offense occurs in or affects interstate or foreign commerce; or

(F) an offender aids or abets any person over whom jurisdiction exists under this paragraph in committing an offense under subsection (a) or conspires with any person over whom jurisdiction exists under this paragraph to commit an offense under subsection (a). * * *

(h) Provision of personnel. No person may be prosecuted under this section in connection with the term "personnel" unless that person has knowingly provided, attempted to provide, or conspired to provide a foreign terrorist organization with 1 or more individuals (who may be or include himself) to work under that terrorist organization's direction or control or to organize, manage,

> supervise, or otherwise direct the operation of that organization. Individuals who act entirely independently of the foreign terrorist organization to advance its goals or objectives shall not be considered to be working under the foreign terrorist organization's direction and control.

This latter provision provided the basis for one of the charges brought against the "American Taliban," John Walker Lindh. *U.S. v. Lindh*, 212 F. Supp. 2d 541 (E.D. Va. 2002). Why would one provision apply extraterritorially and not the other?

5. Designated Organizations

The U.S. State Department's Office of Counterterrorism utilizes the following criteria in designating terrorist organizations:

1) The organization must be a foreign organization.
2) The organization must engage in terrorist activity or terrorism or retain the capability and intent to engage in terrorist activity or terrorism (as defined in U.S. law).
3) The organization's terrorist activity or terrorism must threaten the security of U.S. nationals or the national security (national defense, foreign relations, *or* the economic interests) of the United States.

See 8 U.S.C. § 1189. Do these provisions herald a return to notions of group criminality? Some organizations listed as terrorist organizations, or organizations seeking to work with, or support, listed organizations, have attacked—in some cases successfully—these provisions on vagueness, overbreadth, First Amendment, and due process grounds. In response to these challenges, Congress has repeatedly tinkered with the formulation of 18 U.S.C. § 2339B by, for example, adding the qualifier "knowingly" in (a)(1) and clarifying the definition of "personnel" in (h). *See, e.g., Holder v. Humanitarian Law Project*, 561 U.S. 1 (2010). In *Humanitarian Law Project*, the U.S. Supreme Court ruled that Congress intended to prevent even aid organizations like the plaintiff from offering various forms of training and assistance to designated groups such as the Kurdistan Workers' Party (PKK) and the Liberation Tigers of Tamil Eelam (LTTE), even for the purpose of facilitating the nonviolent pursuits of those organizations.

6. For Further Reading

On the law of criminal organizations, *see generally* Stanisaw Pomorski, *Conspiracy and Criminal Organization*, *in* THE NUREMBERG TRIAL AND INTERNATIONAL LAW 213 (George Ginsburgs & V.N. Kudriavtsev eds., 1990); Harold Levanthal, et al., *The Nuernberg Verdict*, 60 HARV. L. REV. 857, 887–902 (1946–47); T. Taylor, ANATOMY OF THE NUREMBERG TRIALS: A PERSONAL MEMOIR 583–87 (1992). For a defense of the law of criminal organizations by the U.S. Chief Prosecutor at Nuremberg, *see* Robert H. Jackson, *The Law Under Which Nazi Organizations Are Accused of Being Criminal*, 19 TEMP. L. Q. 371 (1945–1946). For an account by the defense counsel of the High Command and the General Staff, *see* H. Laternser, *Looking Back at the Nuremberg Trials With Special Consideration of the Processes Against*

Military Leaders, 8 WHITTIER L. REV. 557 (1986). For an argument on reviving the notion of the criminal organization in Rwanda, *see* Nina H.B. Jørgensen, *A Reappraisal of the Abandoned Nuremberg Concept of Criminal Organisations in the Context of Justice in Rwanda*, 12 CRIM. L. FOR. 371 (2001).

III. COMPLICITY

The law of complicity is a doctrine of criminal imputation that governs the circumstances in which one person (who will be called the secondary actor or accessory) is held liable for the criminal act of another (referred to as the primary actor, principal, or perpetrator). Complicity liability thus involves at least two individuals: the principal, who with the requisite *mens rea* commits the predicate offense, and the accomplice, who with the requisite *mens rea* assists the principal. Accomplice liability is derivative in nature, which is to say that the criminal responsibility of the accomplice derives from the criminal act of another. As a general proposition, there is no standalone crime of complicity. Different legal systems assign the terms "principal" and "accomplice" to different types of participatory conduct. (For U.S. law, which contains an inclusive definition of "principal," *see* 18 U.S.C. § 2). Acts of complicity can thus exist along a continuum that includes situations in which the accomplice serves as the moving force behind the criminal operation (as is the case of "causing crime by an innocent") to situations in which she merely facilitates or encourages the principal. Assisting can encompass many forms of conduct, such as aiding, abetting, encouraging, soliciting, condoning, etc. This assistance can be by physical conduct, psychological influence, or a failure to act.

The Nuremberg Charter mentioned complicity liability only obliquely where it stated that "[l]eaders, organizers, instigators and accomplices participating in the formulation or execution of a common plan or conspiracy to commit any of the foregoing crimes [crimes against the peace, war crimes, and crimes against humanity] are responsible for all acts performed by any persons in execution of such plan." With respect to many of the Third Reich's criminal acts, the convicted defendants were perhaps more properly considered superiors or accomplices, because the actual perpetrators of the crimes were not before the Tribunal. The modern international tribunals have all included provisions setting forth various forms of complicity liability. *See, e.g.*, Article 7(1) of the ICTY Statute ("A person who planned, instigated, ordered, committed or otherwise aided and abetted in the planning, preparation or execution of a crime referred to in articles 2 to 5 of the present Statute, shall be individually responsible for the crime.").

Consider the case that follows. Anto Furundžija was the local commander of the Jokers, a special unit within the armed forces of the Croatian Defense Council (HVO). Members of the multinational Stabilization Force in Bosnia (SFOR) arrested him pursuant to a sealed Indictment. As set forth in the Indictment excerpts below, Furundžija was accused of being present while Witness A, a Muslim woman, was raped during an interrogation by a fellow member of the Jokers:

> 25. On or about 15 May 1993, at the Jokers Headquarters in Nadioci (the "Bungalow"), Anto Furundžija the local commander of the Jokers, [REDACTED] and another soldier interrogated Witness A. While being questioned by Furundžija, [REDACTED] rubbed his knife against Witness A's inner thigh and lower stomach and threatened to put his knife inside Witness A's vagina should she not tell the truth.
>
> 26. Then Witness A and Victim B, a Bosnian Croat who had previously assisted Witness A's family, were taken to another room in the "Bungalow." Victim B had been badly beaten prior to this time. While Furundžija continued to interrogate Witness A and Victim B, [REDACTED] beat Witness A and Victim B on the feet with a baton. Then [REDACTED] forced Witness A to have oral and vaginal sexual intercourse with him. Furundžija was present during this entire incident and did nothing to stop or curtail [REDACTED] actions.

The Indictment against Furundžija charged him with violations of the laws and customs of war, specifically torture (Count 13) and outrages upon personal dignity, including rape (Count 14). The Prosecution initially redacted portions of the Indictment identifying Furundžija's co-accused, who turned out to be his deputy Miroslav Bralo. In his defense at trial, Furundžija argued that he was not present during the assault and that Witness A's testimony was unreliable. The Trial Chamber's discussion of the law of complicity follows.

Prosecutor v. Anto Furundžija, Case No. IT–95–17/1–T, Judgement (December 10, 1998)

In the Trial Chamber

Aiding and Abetting

190. The accused is charged with torture and outrages upon personal dignity, including rape. For the purposes of the present case however, it is necessary to define "aiding and abetting" as used in Article 7(1) of the Statute.

191. Since no treaty law on the subject exists, the Trial Chamber must examine customary international law in order to establish the content of this head of criminal responsibility. In particular, it must establish both whether the accused's alleged presence in the locations where Witness A was assaulted would be sufficient to constitute the *actus reus* of aiding and abetting, and also the relevant *mens rea* required to accompany this action for responsibility to ensue.

Actus Reus

192. With regard to the *actus reus*, the Trial Chamber must examine whether the assistance given by the aider and abettor need be tangible in nature or may consist only of encouragement or moral support. The Trial Chamber must also examine the proximity required between the assistance provided and the commission of the criminal act. In particular, it will have to consider whether the actions of the aider and abettor need to have a causal effect, so that without his contribution the offence would not be committed, or whether the acts of the aider and abettor need simply facilitate the commission of the offence in some way.

193. Little light is shed on the definition of aiding and abetting by the international instruments providing for major war trials: the London Agreement, the Charter of the International Military Tribunal for the Far East, establishing the Tokyo Tribunal, and Control Council Law No. 10. It therefore becomes necessary to examine the case law. * * *

195. First of all, there are the [WWII] cases stemming from U.S. military commissions or, in territory occupied by U.S. forces, by courts and tribunals set up by the military government. While the military commissions operated under different directives within each theatre of U.S. military operations, each applied a provision identical to that of the London Agreement with relation to complicity. In occupied territories, the courts and tribunals operated under the terms of Control Council Law No. 10.

196. The Trial Chamber will also rely on [WWII] case law from the British military courts for the trials of war criminals, whose jurisdiction was based on the Royal Warrant of 14 June 1945, which provided that the rules of procedure to be applied were those of domestic military courts, unless otherwise specified. In fact, unless otherwise provided, the law applied was domestic, thus rendering the pronouncements of the British courts less helpful in establishing rules of international law on this issue. However, there is sufficient similarity between the law applied in the British cases and under Control Council Law No. 10 for these cases to merit consideration. The British cases deal with forms of complicity analogous to that alleged in the present case. The term used to describe those liable as accomplices (in killing) is that they were "concerned in the killing." * * *

Nature of Assistance

199. The Trial Chamber will first examine the nature of the assistance required to establish *actus reus*. The cases which follow indicate that in certain circumstances, aiding and abetting need not be tangible, but may consist of moral support or encouragement of the principals in their commission of the crime.

200. In the British case of *Schonfeld*, four of the ten accused were found guilty of being "concerned in the killing of" three Allied airmen, who had been found hiding in the home of a member of the Dutch

resistance. All four claimed that their purpose in visiting the scene had been the investigation and arrest of the Allied airmen. One admitted to shooting the three airmen but claimed it was in self-defence; he was found guilty and sentenced to death. The roles of the three others were less direct. One drove a car to the scene and was the first to enter the house. Another had obtained the original information, searched a different house for the airmen earlier and claimed to have stood guard at the back entrance to the house along with the fourth convicted person. All except one denied having fired any shots themselves.

201. The court did not make clear the grounds on which it found these three to have been "concerned in the killing."[223] However, the Advocate General, citing the position in English law, outlined the role of an accessory who is not present at the scene but procures, counsels, commands or abets another to commit the offence, and that of an aider and abettor, either of which could have formed the basis of the court's decision. In doing so he gave an example of how an individual may participate without giving tangible assistance:

> if he watched for his companions in order to prevent surprise, or remained at a convenient distance in order to favour their escape, if necessary, or was in such a situation as to be able readily to come to their assistance, the knowledge of which was calculated to give additional confidence to his companions, he was, in contemplation of law, present, aiding and abetting.

202. Again, in giving "additional confidence to his companions" the defendant facilitates the commission of the crime, and it is this which constitutes the *actus reus* of the offence.

203. In the British case of *Rohde* six persons were found guilty of being "concerned in the killing" of four British women prisoners in German hands. The women were executed by lethal injection and their bodies disposed of in the prison camp crematorium. In defining the term "concerned in the killing," the Judge Advocate explained that actual presence at the crime scene was not necessary to be "concerned in the killing." He gave the example of a lookout, who would be "concerned in the killing" by providing a service to the commission of the crime in the knowledge that the crime was going to be committed.

204. In the case of one of the accused, assistance *ex post facto* was found to be sufficient for criminal responsibility. As this was not the position under English law, the inference is warranted that the court

[223] The prosecutor referred to Regulation 8 (ii) of the Royal Warrant concerning units or groups of men discussed above, and this may have been taken into consideration by the court. In his reference to English substantive law on complicity, the Advocate General included the doctrine of "common design," whereby if a group sets out to commit a crime, all are equally guilty of the act committed by one of them in the pursuance of that criminal goal whether or not they *materially* contribute to the execution of the crime.

applied a different law to these international crimes.[227] The service provided by the cremator may be analogous to that of the lookout, in that the knowledge that the bodies will be disposed of, in the same way that the knowledge that they will be warned of impending discovery in the lookout scenario, reassures the killers and facilitates their commission of the crime in some significant way.

205. Guidance can also be derived from the following cases, which were heard under the terms of Control Council Law No. 10. In the *Synagogue* case, decided by the German Supreme Court in the British Occupied Zone, one of the accused was found guilty of a crime against humanity (the devastation of a synagogue) although he had not physically taken part in it, nor planned or ordered it. His intermittent presence on the crime-scene, combined with his status as an "*alter Kämpfer*" (long-time militant of the Nazi party) and his knowledge of the criminal enterprise, were deemed sufficient to convict him. * * *

207. It may be inferred from this case that an approving spectator who is held in such respect by the other perpetrators that his presence encourages them in their conduct, may be guilty of complicity in a crime against humanity.

208. The *Synagogue* case may be contrasted with the *Pig-cart parade* case, also from the German Supreme Court in the British Occupied Zone. The accused, P had attended, as a spectator in civilian dress, a SA (*Stürmabteilung*) "parade" in which two political opponents of the NSDAP (*Nationalsozialistische Deutsche Arbeiterpartei*—the Nazi Party) were exposed to public humiliation. P had followed the "parade" without taking any active part. The court found that P,

> followed the parade only as a spectator in civilian clothes, although he was following a service order by the SA for a purpose yet unknown ... His conduct cannot even with certainty be evaluated as objective or subjective approval. Furthermore, silent approval that does not contribute to causing the offence in no way meets the requirements for criminal liability.

P was found not guilty. He may have lacked the necessary *mens rea*. But in any event, his insignificant status brought the effect of his "silent approval" below the threshold necessary for the *actus reus*.

209. It appears from the *Synagogue* and *Pig-cart parade* cases that presence, when combined with authority, can constitute assistance in the form of moral support, that is, the *actus reus* of the offence. The supporter must be of a certain status for this to be sufficient for criminal responsibility. * * * Furthermore, it can be inferred that assistance need not be tangible. In addition, assistance need not constitute an

[227] In English law, the law relating to accessories after-the-fact has generally been a separate statutory offence of "assisting an offender" rather than a form of aiding and abetting (*see* section 4(1) of the Criminal Law Act 1967).

indispensable element, that is, a *conditio sine qua non* for the acts of the principal. * * *

Effect of Assistance on the Act of the Principal

217. [I]n the *Einsatzgruppen* case, heard by a U.S. Military Tribunal sitting at Nuremberg, all of the accused except for one (Graf) were officers charged with war crimes and crimes against humanity pursuant to Control Council Law No. 10. The Tribunal held that the acts of the accomplices had to have a substantial effect on those of the principals to constitute the *actus reus* of the war crimes and crimes against humanity charged. This conclusion is illustrated by the cases of four of the accused: Klingelhoefer, Fendler, Ruehl and Graf. Klingelhoefer held a variety of positions, the least important of which was that of interpreter. The court said that even if this were his only function,

> it would not exonerate him from guilt because in locating, evaluating and turning over lists of Communist party functionaries to the executive of his organisation he was aware that the people listed would be executed when found.

218. Fendler served in one of the *Kommandos* of the *Einsatzgruppen* for a period of seven months. The prosecution case against him was not that he himself conducted an execution but rather "that he was part of an organisation committed to an extermination programme." The Court noted that:

> The defendant knew that executions were taking place. He admitted that the procedure which determined the so-called guilt of a person which resulted in him being condemned to death was "too summary." But, there is no evidence that he ever did anything about it. As the second highest ranking officer in the *Kommando*, his views could have been heard in complaint or protest against what he now says was a too summary procedure, but he chose to let the injustice go uncorrected.

Both of these defendants [Fendler and Klingelhoefer] were found guilty.

219. The cases of Ruehl and Graf provide a contrast which helps delineate the *actus reus* of the offence. The Tribunal held that both had the requisite knowledge of the criminal activities of the organisations of which they were a part. Ruehl's position, however, was not such as to "control, prevent, or modify" those activities. His low rank failed to "place him automatically into a position where his lack of objection in any way contributed to the success of any executive operation." He was found not guilty.

220. Graf was a non-commissioned officer. The court held that:

> Since there is no evidence in the record that Graf was at any time in a position to protest against the illegal actions of the others, he cannot be found guilty as an accessory under counts

one and two [war crimes and crimes against humanity] of the indictment.

221. It is clear, then, that knowledge of the criminal activities of the organization combined with a role in that organisation was not sufficient for complicity in this case and that the defendants' acts in carrying out their duties had to have a substantial effect on the commission of the offence for responsibility to ensue. This might be because their failure to protest made some difference to the course of events, or, in the case of Klingelhoefer, that his transmission of the lists of names led directly to the execution of the members of those lists.

222. In the British case of *Zyklon B*, the three accused were charged with supplying poison gas used for the extermination of allied nationals interned in concentration camps, in the knowledge that the gas was to be so used. The owner and second-in-command of the firm were found guilty; Drosihn, the firm's first gassing technician, was acquitted. The Judge Advocate set out the issue of Drosihn's complicity as turning on

> whether there was any evidence that he was in a position either to influence the transfer of gas to Auschwitz or to prevent it. If he were not in such a position, no knowledge of the use to which the gas was put could make him guilty.

223. This clearly requires that the act of the accomplice has at least a substantial effect on the principal act—the use of the gas to murder internees at Auschwitz—in order to constitute the *actus reus*. The functions performed by Drosihn in his employment as a gassing technician were an integral part of the supply and use of the poison gas, but this alone could not render him liable for its criminal use even if he was aware that his functions played such an important role in the transfer of gas. Without influence over this supply, he was not guilty. In other words, *mens rea* alone is insufficient to ground a criminal conviction.

224. In *S. et al.*, hereafter "*Hechingen Deportation*," heard by a German court in the French occupied zone, five accused were charged with complicity in the mass deportation of Jews in 1941 and 1942 as a crime against humanity under Control Council Law No. 10. The accused, S, was the local administrative authority responsible for organising the execution of Gestapo orders. He had complied with a Gestapo decree concerning the deportations. The court of first instance found S guilty of aiding and abetting the Gestapo in its criminal activity. His objection that his conduct in no way contributed to the crimes, because others would have taken his place if he had refused to comply with the Gestapo decree, was dismissed. The court pointed out that the culpability of an aider and abettor is not negated by the fact that his assistance could easily have been obtained from another. * * *

227. The two international instruments useful for these purposes are the 1996 Draft Code of Crimes Against the Peace and Security of

Mankind adopted by the International Law Commission, and the Rome Statute. Neither instrument is legally binding internationally. The Draft Code was adopted in 1996 by the United Nations International Law Commission, a body consisting of outstanding experts in international law, including governmental legal advisers, elected by the United Nations General Assembly. The Draft Code was taken into account by the General Assembly: in its resolution 51 (160) of 30 January 1997 it expressed its "appreciation" for the completion of the Draft Code and among other things drew the attention of the States participating in the Preparatory Committee on the Establishment of an International Criminal Court to the relevance of the Draft Code to their work. In the light of the above the Trial Chamber considers that the Draft Code is an authoritative international instrument which, depending upon the specific question at issue, may (i) constitute evidence of customary law, or (ii) shed light on customary rules which are of uncertain contents or are in the process of formation, or, at the very least, (iii) be indicative of the legal views of eminently qualified publicists representing the major legal systems of the world. As for the Rome Statute, at present it is still a non-binding international treaty (it has not yet entered into force). It was adopted by an overwhelming majority of the States attending the Rome Diplomatic Conference and was substantially endorsed by the General Assembly's Sixth Committee on 26 November 1998. In many areas the Statute may be regarded as indicative of the legal views, i.e. *opinio juris* of a great number of States. Notwithstanding article 10 of the Statute, the purpose of which is to ensure that existing or developing law is not "limited" or "prejudiced" by the Statute's provisions, resort may be had *cum grano salis* ["with a grain of salt"] to these provisions to help elucidate customary international law. Depending on the matter at issue, the Rome Statute may be taken to restate, reflect or clarify customary rules or crystallise them, whereas in some areas it creates new law or modifies existing law. At any event, the Rome Statute by and large may be taken as constituting an authoritative expression of the legal views of a great number of States.

228. The Code of Crimes against the Peace and Security of Mankind deals with aiding and abetting in article 2(3)(d), which would impose criminal responsibility upon an individual who "knowingly aids, abets or otherwise assists, directly and substantially, in the commission of such a crime, including providing the means for its commission."

229. In the absence of specification, it appears that assistance can be either physical or in the form of moral support. Encouragement given to the perpetrators may be punishable, even if the abettor did not take any tangible action, provided it "directly and substantially" assists in the commission of a crime. This proposition is also supported by a passage from the International Law Commission's Commentary concerning *ex post facto* assistance:

> The Commission concluded that complicity could include aiding, abetting or assisting *ex post facto*, if this assistance had been agreed upon by the perpetrator and the accomplice prior to the perpetration of the crime.

230. This conclusion implies that action which decisively encourages the perpetrator is sufficient to amount to assistance: the knowledge that he will receive assistance during or after the event encourages the perpetrator in the commission of the crime. From this perspective, willingness to provide assistance, when made known to the perpetrator, would also suffice, if the offer of help in fact encouraged or facilitated the commission of the crime by the main perpetrator.

231. The International Law Commission's Commentary also states that "participation of an accomplice must entail assistance which *facilitates* the commission of a crime *in some significant way*." The word "facilitates" suggests that it is not necessary for the conduct of the aider and abettor to cause the commission of the crime; it need not be a *conditio sine qua non* of the crime. The "directly and substantially" requirement in article 2, and the word "significant" used in the International Law Commission Commentary, however, clearly exclude any marginal participation. Article 25(3), in particular paragraphs (c) and (d), of the Rome Statute deals with aiding and abetting:

> 3. In accordance with this Statute, a person shall be criminally responsible and liable for punishment for a crime within the jurisdiction of the Court if that person: . . .
>
> (c) For the purpose of facilitating the commission of such a crime, aids, abets or otherwise assists in its commission or its attempted commission, including providing the means for its commission;
>
> (d) In any other way contributes to the commission or attempted commission of such a crime by a group of persons acting with a common purpose. Such contribution shall be intentional and shall either:
>
> (i) Be made with the aim of furthering criminal activity or criminal purpose of the group, where such activity or purpose involves the commission of a crime within the jurisdiction of the Court; or
>
> (ii) Be made in the knowledge of the intention of the group to commit the crime.

This wording is less restrictive than the Draft Code, which limits aiding and abetting to assistance which "facilitate[s] in some significant way," or "directly and substantially" assists the perpetrator. Article 25 of the Rome Statute, like the Draft Code, also clearly contemplates assistance in either a physical form or in the form of moral support. Indeed, the word "abet" includes mere exhortation or encouragement. * * *

234. The position under customary international law seems therefore to be best reflected in the proposition that the assistance must have a substantial effect on the commission of the crime. This is the position adopted by the Trial Chamber.

235. In sum, the Trial Chamber holds that the *actus reus* of aiding and abetting in international criminal law requires practical assistance, encouragement, or moral support which has a substantial effect on the perpetration of the crime.

Mens Rea

236. With regard to *mens rea*, the Trial Chamber must determine whether it is necessary for the accomplice to share the *mens rea* of the principal or whether mere knowledge that his actions assist the perpetrator in the commission of the crime is sufficient to constitute *mens rea* in aiding and abetting the crime. The case law indicates that the latter will suffice.

237. For example in the *Einsatzgruppen* case, knowledge, rather than intent, was held to be the requisite mental element.

238. The same position was taken in *Zyklon B* where the prosecution did not attempt to prove that the accused acted with the intention of assisting the killing of the internees. It was accepted that their purpose was to sell insecticide to the SS (for profit, that is, a lawful goal pursued by lawful means). The charge as accepted by the court was that they knew what the buyer in fact intended to do with the product they were supplying.

239. Two of the not guilty verdicts in *Schonfeld* also provide an indication of the *mens rea* necessary to amount to being "concerned in the killing." Both concerned drivers who claimed to have followed instructions without knowing the purpose of the mission, and were therefore found not guilty. Despite having made a physical contribution to the commission of the offence, they had no knowledge that they were doing so.

240. In the *Hechingen Deportation* case, the court of first instance considered the *mens rea* required for aiding and abetting and concluded that this mental element encompassed both the knowledge of the crime being committed by the principals and the awareness of supporting, by aiding and abetting, the criminal conduct of the principals. As mentioned above, the subsequent acquittal of the accused Ho., K., and B. on appeal was based on a different legal standard concerning the *mens rea* of those accused, requiring the aider and abettor to have acted out of the same cast of mind as the principal.[262] * * *

---

262 The relevant part of the judgement reads as follows: "Under Article II, 2(a) to (c), Control Council Law No. 10 treats all thinkable forms of perpetration and of complicity as equal. It does not distinguish between being a perpetrator and being an accomplice [as opposed to German law]. The aider and abettor of a crime against humanity 'is deemed to have committed a crime against humanity without regard to the capacity in which he acted.' As a consequence

245. The above analysis leads the Trial Chamber to the conclusion that it is not necessary for the accomplice to share the *mens rea* of the perpetrator, in the sense of positive intention to commit the crime. Instead, the clear requirement in the vast majority of the cases is for the accomplice to have knowledge that his actions will assist the perpetrator in the commission of the crime. This is particularly apparent from all the cases in which persons were convicted for having driven victims and perpetrators to the site of an execution. In those cases the prosecution did not prove that the driver drove for the purpose of assisting in the killing, that is, with an intention to kill. It was the knowledge of the criminal purpose of the executioners that rendered the driver liable as an aider and abettor. Consequently, if it were not proven that a driver would reasonably have known that the purpose of the trip was an unlawful execution, he would be acquitted.

246. Moreover, it is not necessary that the aider and abettor should know the precise crime that was intended and which in the event was committed. If he is aware that one of a number of crimes will probably be committed, and one of those crimes is in fact committed, he has intended to facilitate the commission of that crime, and is guilty as an aider and abettor. * * *

249. In sum, the Trial Chamber holds the legal ingredients of aiding and abetting in international criminal law to be the following: the *actus reus* consists of practical assistance, encouragement, or moral support which has a substantial effect on the perpetration of the crime. The *mens rea* required is the knowledge that these acts assist the commission of the offence. This notion of aiding and abetting is to be distinguished from the notion of common design, where the *actus reus* consists of participation in a joint criminal enterprise and the *mens rea* required is intent to participate. * * *

273. The position of the accused has already been discussed. He did not personally rape Witness A, nor can he be considered, under the circumstances of this case, to be a co-perpetrator. The accused's presence and continued interrogation of Witness A encouraged Accused B and substantially contributed to the criminal acts committed by him.

274. On the evidence on record, the Trial Chamber is satisfied that the Prosecution has proved its case against the accused beyond reasonable doubt. In accordance with Article 7(1) and the findings of the Trial Chamber that the *actus reus* of aiding and abetting consists of assistance, encouragement, or moral support which has a substantial effect on the perpetration of the crime and that the *mens rea* required is the knowledge that these acts assist the commission of the offence, the Trial Chamber holds that the presence of the accused and his continued interrogation aided and abetted the crimes committed by Accused B. He

---

of this complete equality between perpetrator and aider and abettor, *the aider and abettor has to have acted out of the same cast of mind as the principal, i.e. out of an inhuman cast of mind, or, in the case of persecutions, motivated by a political, racist or religious ideology.*" * * *

is individually responsible for outrages upon personal dignity including rape, a violation of the laws or customs of war under Article 3 of the Statute.

275. The Trial Chamber therefore finds the accused, for aiding and abetting, guilty of a Violation of the Laws or Customs of War (outrages upon personal dignity including rape) on Count 14.

NOTES & QUESTIONS

1. Case Outcome

Based on the Trial Chamber's finding that the defendant was present during, and did participate in, the interrogation of Witness A, it convicted him of torture as a co-perpetrator. The Trial Chamber sentenced Furundžija to ten years under Count 13 (torture) and eight years under Count 14 (rape) (with sentences to be served concurrently). On appeal, the defendant argued that the Prosecutor did not prove beyond reasonable doubt "that the Appellant gave Accused B assistance, encouragement, or moral support that had a substantial effect on the perpetration of the rape or that he knew that his acts assisted Accused B in the commission of the rape." In reply, the Prosecutor argued that "knowing presence" that "has a substantial effect on the commission of an offence is sufficient for a finding of participation and attendant liability." The Appeals Chamber held:

> 126. The Trial Chamber found that the Appellant's "presence and continued interrogation of Witness A encouraged Accused B and substantially contributed to the criminal acts committed by him." As the Trial Chamber found that the Appellant was not only present in the Pantry, but that he acted and continued to interrogate Witness A therein, it is not necessary to consider the issue of whether mere or knowing presence constitutes aiding and abetting. Although the Appellant disputed Witness A's testimony in this regard, the Trial Chamber was in the best position to assess the demeanour of the witness and the weight to be attached to that testimony. This Chamber can find no reason to disturb this finding.

Prosecutor v. Furundžija, Case No. IT–95–17/1–A, Judgement, paras. 124–127 (July 21, 2000). The Appeals Chamber affirmed the judgment and sentence.

Furundžija served his sentence in Finland. In 2004, the Government of Finland requested early release after Furundžija had served approximately seven years of his sentence pre- and post-conviction. The President of the Tribunal granted the request. Furundžija's co-accused, Miroslav Bralo, voluntarily surrendered to the Tribunal and pled not guilty to the charges against him, including the torture and rape of Witness A. The Prosecution subsequently filed a proposed "streamlined" amended Indictment on July 19, 2005, with reduced charges. On the same date, the Prosecution filed a Plea Agreement pursuant to Rule 62*ter* of the Rules of Procedure and Evidence, in which the Accused agreed to plead guilty to all eight counts of the amended Indictment. The Trial Chamber sentenced Bralo to twenty years' imprisonment. Furundžija was the local commander of the Jokers; why would the Prosecution not pursue a superior responsibility theory of liability here? As you review the following material on Conspiracy, Co-Perpetration, and Joint Criminal Enterprise, consider whether Furundžija could have been prosecuted under any of these theories of liability as well.

2. Principals and Accessories

Although it was once the case at common law, under modern law the conviction of the principal is not necessary to convict the accessory. *Standefer v. United States*, 447 U.S. 10, 25 (1980) (convicting accessory notwithstanding principal's acquittal and noting that "[w]hile symmetry of results may be intellectually satisfying, it is not required."). As such, the secondary actor's liability derives not from the primary actor's *liability*, but from her *wrongful act*, or from the liability of the principal at the time she acted, even though such liability can no longer be imputed to her. Sanford Kadish, *Complicity, Cause and Blame: A Study in the Interpretation of the Doctrine*, 73 CAL. L. REV. 323, 340–1 (1985). Proof of the commission of the underlying crime, however, remains necessary to convict the accomplice.

3. The Elements of Complicity

What are the elements of complicity—in terms of *actus reus* and *mens rea*—as identified by the Trial Chamber and the post-WWII jurisprudence? Are the cases cited by the Trial Chamber consistent in their articulation of the doctrine? How much assistance must be provided in order to invoke accomplice liability? Most domestic systems provide that any aid—no matter how insignificant—triggers complicity liability. This seems to be the approach adopted in the mere presence cases cited above, such as *Synagogue* and *Einsatzgruppen* (especially with respect to defendant Fendler). In contrast, other cases suggest that an individual must make a more substantial contribution to the crime. At the same time, there are cases in which an individual makes a significant contribution to a crime but is otherwise acquitted. For example, in the *Zyklon B* case, the technician who managed the gas chambers was acquitted. How can these cases be reconciled? Which is the approach adopted by the Trial Chamber above? Which is the better approach? Did the Trial Chamber set too high or too low a bar to find complicity liability? Would the Trial Chamber have acquitted the gas technician, for example, in the *Zyklon B* case?

4. *Mens Rea*

What is the *mens rea* of accomplice liability with respect to conduct? Note that complicity liability involves two mental states: first, the accessory's mental state vis-à-vis his act of assistance; and second, the accessory's mental state vis-à-vis the substantive crime. With respect to the accessory's culpability as to her own contribution to the crime, the law of complicity generally requires that the secondary actor act intentionally. In other words, if the accessory was duped, asleep, innocently clumsy, or insane when he acted in such a way that provided the assistance to the perpetrator, he will not be considered an accessory. *See* Paul H. Robinson, *Imputed Criminal Liability*, 93 YALE L. J. 609, 637 n.100 (1984).

With respect to the second level *mens rea* vis-à-vis the predicate crime, the cases cited by the Trial Chamber—and national systems—suggest two approaches. Under one approach, the prosecution must demonstrate that the accused accomplice shared the *mens rea* of the predicate crime (*Hechingen Deportation*). Under the second approach, the prosecution need only show that the accused acted with knowledge that her acts would provide assistance (*Zyklon B & Halberstam v. Welch*, 705 F.2d 472 (D.C. Cir. 1983)). The Trial Chamber adopted this second approach, which has been the general approach of most international criminal tribunals, illustrated most recently in a 2013 opinion of the appeals chamber of the Special Court for Sierra Leone upholding the conviction of Charles Taylor for aiding and abetting war crimes. *Prosecutor v. Charles Ghankay Taylor*, Case No. SCSL-03-01-A, Judgement (Sept. 26, 2013) (discussed further below in the Notes after the *Perišić* case excerpt). The exception is the ICC, which in Article 25(3) limits aiding and abetting liability to cases in which the suspect acts "for the purpose of facilitating the commission of such a crime," indicating that more than mere knowledge is require. Which is the better approach for international criminal law? If a knowledge standard is adopted, is it necessary to show that the accomplice knew that a particular crime would be committed, or should it be enough to show that the accomplice knew that defendant would undertake one of a range of criminal acts?

The language in Article 25(3) has garnered a good deal of confusion and scholarly debate about how, or even whether, the ICC has departed from the more traditional knowledge requirement. James Stewart has persuasively argued in a lengthy blog post that the ICC standard is much closer to the traditional knowledge standard adopted by other international criminal tribunals. James G. Stewart, *An Important New Orthodoxy on Complicity in the ICC Statute*, JAMESSTEWART.COM (January 21, 2015). Review Articles 25(3) and 30 of the ICC Statute. Can you construct an argument that the ICC standard is close to the traditional knowledge standard?

5. Causality

National systems vary on whether causation must be shown in convicting an individual for complicity. Some require a causal link between the accomplice's act and the crime ultimately committed; others do not. See, for example, the Model Penal Code provision cited above, which imputes liability for attempts to aid a crime. In systems that do not require causality to be proven, the theory is that proof that the principal caused the social harm satisfies the requirement of causation for the accomplice. Which rule should prevail in international criminal law? In *Tadić*, the ICTY held that the accomplice's act must make a "direct and substantial" contribution to the crime. *Prosecutor v. Tadić*, Case No. IT–94–1–T, Judgement, paras. 674, 688–692 (May 7, 1997). Is this the equivalent of a causation requirement? Should non-causal accomplices be punished less severely than causal accomplices in keeping with retributive principles of "just deserts?"

6. Complicity in Genocide

The accomplice's liability depends upon a showing that the predicate crime was committed. What is the *mens rea* that must be proven to prosecute an accomplice to a specific intent crime, such as genocide? Should the accomplice be liable for genocide where he does not possess genocidal intent but only knowingly assisted the principal in the commission of genocide? If so, how would a prosecutor prove that the principal acted with genocidal intent? Consider this argument:

> The specific intent requirement of genocide should apply not only to the basic crime of genocide, but also to the various forms of participation. Accomplice, conspirator, planner and abettor must all share the intent to destroy, in whole or in part, the national, racial, ethnic or religious group, as such. [To provide otherwise] is illogical, precisely because the accomplice or the conspirator may be as guilty or even more guilty than the principal offender who technically commits the crime.

William A. Schabas, GENOCIDE IN INTERNATIONAL LAW 259 (2000). This question will be considered more closely in Section IV on Joint Criminal Enterprise, below.

7. Mere Presence

Under what circumstances will mere presence at the scene of a crime constitute complicity? In *Prosecutor v. Akayesu*, the ICTR Trial Chamber found that the defendant (a local political leader) was present while civilians were raped and abused. The Trial Chamber ruled that the Prosecution had proven that "by his presence, his attitude and his utterances, Akayesu encouraged such acts, one particular witness testifying that Akayesu addressed the *Interahamwe* who were committing the rapes and said 'never ask me again what a Tutsi woman tastes like.'" In the opinion of the Chamber, this constituted "tacit encouragement to the rapes that were being committed." It thus found Akayesu criminally responsible "for having abetted in the preparation or execution of the killings of members of the Tutsi group and the infliction of serious bodily or mental harm" by his presence. *Prosecutor v. Akayesu*, Case No. ICTR–96–4–T, Judgement, paras. 706–7 (Sept. 2, 1998). *See also Prosecutor v. Aleksovski*, Case No. IT–95–14/1, Judgement, para. 87 (June 25, 1999) (convicting defendant of aiding and abetting prisoner abuse: "[b]y being present during the mistreatment, and yet not objecting to it notwithstanding its systematic nature and the authority he had over its perpetrators, the accused was necessarily aware that such tacit approval would be construed as a sign of his support and encouragement. He thus contributed substantially to the mistreatment."). Was *Furundžija* a mere presence case or was his contribution to the crimes more substantial? Under the Tribunal's reasoning in *Furundžija*, are there situations in which mere presence would be insufficient to ascribe liability? Should the law require some form of tangible assistance in order to satisfy the *actus reus* of complicity liability?

8. Accessory After-the-Fact

Under what circumstances does international criminal law recognize the notion of accessory after-the-fact—a person who gives aid to a perpetrator after the commission of the crime? Most jurisdictions no longer consider accessories after-the-fact to be accomplices in the true sense by virtue of their involvement in a crime *ex post* and their lack of any involvement in the commission of the crime itself. *See* Stephen A. Saltzburg et al., CRIMINAL LAW 671 (1994). Instead, they are treated as an obstructer of justice and are subject to different and lesser penalties. (See more below on accessory after-the-fact in the Notes after the *Tadić* case.)

9. Bystanders

In general, a bystander can observe the commission of a crime with impunity, even if the bystander is sympathetic to what the principal is trying to accomplish. However, a bystander can be converted to an accomplice if the bystander communicates his support or his willingness to assist if necessary. *Johnson v. United States*, 195 F.2d 673 (8th Cir. 1952). Moreover, where a bystander has a duty to intervene, a failure to act can give rise to accomplice liability. For a perspective on the role of bystanders in enabling mass crimes, *see* Laurel E. Fletcher, *From Indifference to Engagement: Bystanders and International Criminal Justice*, 26 MICH. J. INT'L L. 1013 (2005). Fletcher writes:

> The protagonists of international criminal trials are the accused and victims. Punishment and justice acknowledge the relationship of perpetrators and victims to the processes that lead to mass violence. Yet in the case of mass violence, there is another category implicated in the events, even if it is not an explicit focus of proceedings: bystanders. Mass violence relies on a social apparatus to execute its bloody aims. Political leaders count on a measure of popular support to achieve power (and even military dictatorships depend on a degree of cooperation from segments of civil society). Once mass killing starts, one scholar reviewing the literature on bystanders has concluded, "the majority will either willingly join the violence, or they will comply, submit, and remain passive when faced with brutality."[35] In other words, those who orchestrate mass violence are aided by the failure of spectators to intervene. In this context, "doing nothing" is "doing something"—bystanders are thus an integral part of the killing apparatus. * * *
>
> International criminal trials constrict the subject of the law's focus such as to render bystanders virtually invisible. The absence of bystanders as legal subjects has particular consequences for the impact of trials. One consequence is that trials create a paradox: trials of individuals are justified as debunking popular calls for collective accountability. Yet the absence of bystanders in the jurisprudence may mean that individuals identify with the member of their national group who is a legal subject of the court—either victim or perpetrator. Where that person is the convicted wrongdoer, bystanders may understand perpetrators as the symbolic placeholder for "their" member group. Thus, trials may inadvertently promote group thinking rather than reduce it. If one aim of social reconstruction is to encourage bystanders to acknowledge their relationship to mass violence, how do trials help or hurt this process? * * *

---

[35] Steven James Bartlett, THE PATHOLOGY OF MAN: A STUDY OF HUMAN EVIL 177 (2005).

> [I]nternational criminal law adjudications are not able to parse out the variety of roles and relationships that bystanders may have to the atrocities, and therefore judgments condemning perpetrators are unlikely to change the opinion of the unreconciled or complicit bystanders—those who continue supporting the political project for which the perpetrator committed the atrocities. Second, international criminal convictions single out and stigmatize the accused, normalizing the behavior of bystanders and potentially creating a false moral innocence for the unindicted and their bystander supporters. Finally, international criminal law constrains the doctrinal ability of international justice mechanisms to address more directly the role of bystanders in atrocities. The principles of fundamental fairness and due process which strengthen the credibility of these institutions also limit their ability to promote role acknowledgment among bystanders. * * *

Id. at 1026, 1029, 1075–6. *See also* Zachary D. Kaufman, *Protectors or Predators or Prey: Bystanders and Upstanders Amid Sexual Crimes*, 92 S. CAL. L. REV. ___ (forthcoming 2019) (arguing for a "more holistic, aggressive approach to prompt involvement by third parties who are aware of specific instances of sexual crimes in the United States").

10. Duties of Disclosure

The *Furundžija* case was marred by allegations that the Prosecution had failed to adhere to its disclosure obligations vis-à-vis the Defense. After closing arguments, the Prosecution disclosed that Witness A had received psychological counseling at Medica Women's Therapy Center in Bosnia-Herzegovina and may be suffering from Post-Traumatic Stress Disorder (PTSD). At the Defense's request, the Trial Chamber issued a *subpoena duces tecum* to Medica, which produced a number of documents that were ultimately revealed to the parties and subjected to expert testimony. The Defense successfully moved to reopen the proceedings in connection with the treatment received by Witness A. The Trial Chamber issued a separate decision on the Prosecution's misconduct and lodged a complaint to the Prosecutor, who opened an investigation into the conduct of her office. The Trial Chamber held:

> 108. * * * Witness A's memory regarding material aspects of the events was not affected by any disorder which she may have had. The Trial Chamber accepts her evidence that she has sufficiently recollected these material aspects of the events. There is no evidence of any form of brain damage or that her memory is in any way contaminated by any treatment which she may have had. * * *
>
> 109. The Trial Chamber bears in mind that even when a person is suffering from PTSD, this does not mean that he or she is necessarily inaccurate in the evidence given. There is no reason why a person with PTSD cannot be a perfectly reliable witness.

Prosecutor v. Furundžija, Case No. IT–95–17/1–A, Judgement, paras. 108–109 (Dec. 10, 1998).

11. Rape in International Humanitarian Law

The revelation that soldiers were committing rape in the former Yugoslavia on mass and systemic grounds galvanized global public opinion and the international women's movement and helped lead to the establishment of the ICTY to try offenders. The Statute of the ICTY lists rape as a crime against humanity; however, the war crimes articles are silent as to the prosecutability of rape since rape is not listed as a grave breach of the Geneva Conventions (although it is prohibited in Article 27 of the Fourth Convention). This is in contradistinction to the ICTR Statute at Article 4, which incorporates breaches of Protocol II to the Geneva Conventions operative in internal armed conflicts. Article 4(2)(e) of Additional Protocol II prohibits "outrages upon personal dignity, in particular humiliating and degrading treatment, rape, enforced prostitution and any form of indecent assault." As discussed *infra* in Chapter 7 on War Crimes, the ICTY interpreted Article 3 of its Statute to incorporate Protocol II, thus enabling the charge of rape as a war crime against Furundžija.

For other cases involving rape charges, *see Prosecutor v. Bosco Ntaganda,* Case No. ICC–01/04–02/06 (discussed *infra*); *Prosecutor v. Karemera,* Case No. ICTR–98–44–I; *Prosecutor v. Muhimana,* Case No. ICTR–95–1B–T; *Prosecutor v. Kvočka,* Case No. IT–98–30/1–T; *Prosecutor v. Krstić,* Case No. IT–98–33–T. For further reading, *see* Hilary Charlesworth & Christine Chinkin, THE BOUNDARIES OF INTERNATIONAL LAW: A FEMINIST ANALYSIS (2002); Janet Halley et al., *From the International to the Local in Feminist Legal Responses to Prostitution/Sex Work and Sex Trafficking,* 29 HARV. J. L. & GENDER 335 (2006); Rebecca L. Haffajee, Note, *Prosecuting Crimes of Rape and Sexual Violence at the ICTR,* 29 HARV. J. L. & GENDER 201 (2006).

12. The Punishment of an Accomplice

In many common law systems, the accomplice is punished as if she were a perpetrator. The distinction between perpetrators and accomplices may thus have little practical effect at sentencing. Other systems, primarily in civil law countries (e.g., Germany, the Netherlands, and Russia), punish accessories with lesser penalties. For example, under Dutch law, principals include "[t]hose who commit a criminal offense, either personally or jointly with another or others, or who cause an innocent person to commit a criminal offense." Pen. Code. § 47(1.1) (Neth). Accessories are those "who intentionally assist during the commission of the serious offense." *Id.* § 48. Punishment for accessories is one-third that of principals, *id.* § 49.1, and in no case shall exceed 15 years. *Id.* § 49.2. Consider the distinction between complicity and co-perpetration when you read the materials in the next Section.

13. Corporate Complicity

Plaintiffs in Alien Tort Statute (ATS) cases have deployed theories of complicity drawn from international criminal law to sue corporations engaged in joint ventures with repressive states. Under what circumstances should a private entity doing business abroad be held liable for crimes committed by a host government? What body of law should apply to answer this question? In 1996, Burmese villagers brought a class action suit under the ATS against Unocal Corp., Total S.A., Myanmar Oil, the Myanmar (Burma) Military, Unocal's President, and Unocal's CEO alleging that Defendants' conduct in connection with a joint venture gas production project had caused the death of family members, assault, rape, torture, forced labor, and the loss of their homes and property. *Doe v. Unocal Corp.*, 963 F.Supp. 880, 883 (C.D. Cal. 1997). The District Court dismissed the claims against the Myanmar Military and Myanmar Oil on the grounds that these defendants were entitled to immunity pursuant to the Foreign Sovereign Immunities Act. In 2000, the District Court granted Unocal's consolidated motions for summary judgment on all of Plaintiffs' remaining federal claims on the ground that Plaintiff could not show that Unocal controlled the Myanmar military. Thus, the court found that the company could not be held liable for the human rights violations committed by the Burmese government or its instrumentalities. *Doe v. Unocal Corp.*, 110 F. Supp. 2d 1294 (C.D. Cal. 2000). The Ninth Circuit reversed and grappled with the choice of law question on appeal. Over a dissent by Judge Stephen Reinhardt, who argued that domestic complicity precepts should apply, the Ninth Circuit looked to the ICTY and ICTR jurisprudence (including *Furundžija*) and ruled:

> We hold that the standard for aiding and abetting under the ATS is * * * knowing practical assistance or encouragement that has a substantial effect on the perpetration of the crime.

Doe v. Unocal, 395 F.3d 932, 947 (9th Cir. 2002). After the Circuit Court granted *en banc* review, the case settled for an undisclosed amount, allegedly in the range of $30 million. A number of similar cases were brought against other corporations for similar abuses in other countries.

The Supreme Court recently imposed some additional limitations on these and other cases, holding that cases brought under the ATS must involve conduct that "touches and concerns" the territory of the United States "with sufficient force to displace the presumption against extraterritorial application." *Kiobel v. Royal Dutch Petroleum Co.*, 569 U.S. 108, 125 (2013). In addition, it is increasingly difficult to bring cases against foreign corporations. *Jesner v. Arab Bank*, 584 U.S. ___, 138 S.Ct. 1386 (2018).

14. Foreign Assistance to Armed Groups

To what extent could the *Furundžija* precedent be employed to hold principals within one national army responsible for the crimes of a co-belligerent? What about situations in which one nation provides weapons or other materiel to another national army, or rebel group, which then commits international crimes? Consider the next case, which was brought against Momčilo Perišić, who was the highest-ranking Yugoslav official before the ICTY at the time of his indictment. Perišić was accused of providing material assistance to the Bosnian Serb forces operating in neighboring Bosnia-Herzegovina. The Trial Chamber convicted Perišić on a complicity theory of liability. The Appeals Chamber opinion is below.

Prosecutor v. Momčilo Perišić, Case No. IT–04–81–A, Judgement (February 28, 2013)

In the Appeals Chamber

I. Introduction

2. The underlying events giving rise to this case took place in the territory of Bosnia and Herzegovina ("BiH" or "Bosnia") and the Republic of Croatia ("Croatia") in the period between August 1993 and November 1995. Starting on 26 August 1993 and through the rest of this period, Perišić served as Chief of the Yugoslav Army ("VJ") General Staff, a position that made him the VJ's most senior officer.

3. Perišić was charged with aiding and abetting crimes in the Bosnian towns of Sarajevo and Srebrenica for his role in facilitating the provision of military and logistical assistance from the VJ to the Army of the Republika Srpska ("VRS") [the Serbian army operating in Bosnia]. In this regard, the Indictment alleged that Perišić was responsible for the crimes of murder, extermination, inhumane acts, attacks on civilians, and persecution as crimes against humanity and/or violations of the laws or customs of war. The Indictment further alleged that Perišić had superior responsibility for crimes committed in Sarajevo, Srebrenica, and the Croatian town of Zagreb. * * *

4. The Trial Chamber, Judge Moloto dissenting, found Perišić guilty, as an aider and abettor, of the following crimes that took place in Sarajevo and Srebrenica: murder, inhumane acts (injuring and wounding civilians, inflicting serious injuries, wounding, forcible transfer), and persecutions as crimes against humanity; and murder and attacks on civilians as violations of the laws or customs of war. The Trial Chamber, Judge Moloto dissenting, also found Perišić guilty as a superior for failing to punish the following crimes related to events in Zagreb: murder and inhumane acts (injuring and wounding civilians) as crimes against humanity; and murder and attacks on civilians as violations of the laws or customs of war. The Trial Chamber sentenced Perišić to a single term of 27 years of imprisonment.

5. Perišić submits seventeen grounds of appeal challenging his convictions and sentence. He requests that the Appeals Chamber overturn all of his convictions or, in the alternative, that his sentence be reduced. The Prosecution responds that Perišić's appeal should be dismissed in its entirety. * * *

II. Standard Of Review * * *

9. Where the Appeals Chamber finds an error of law in the trial judgement arising from the application of an incorrect legal standard, the Appeals Chamber will articulate the correct legal standard and review the relevant factual findings of the trial chamber accordingly. In so doing, the Appeals Chamber not only corrects the legal error, but, when necessary, also applies the correct legal standard to the evidence

contained in the trial record and determines whether it is itself convinced beyond reasonable doubt as to the factual finding challenged by the appellant before that finding is confirmed on appeal. * * *

III. Aiding And Abetting (Grounds 1–12) * * *

14. The Trial Chamber considered a broad range of evidence in assessing whether Perišić aided and abetted the VRS crimes in Sarajevo and Srebrenica. This evidence included, *inter alia*, the war strategy of the VRS leadership. The Trial Chamber, specifically making reference to VRS objectives involving Sarajevo and Srebrenica, found that this strategy encompassed the systematic perpetration of crimes against civilians as a military objective. The Trial Chamber also reviewed evidence regarding Perišić's role in implementing the Federal Republic of Yugoslavia's ("FRY") policy of having the VJ provide logistical assistance to the VRS, including the supply of weapons, ammunition, fuel, and various other types of support. Finally, the Trial Chamber considered Perišić's role in facilitating the secondment of VJ personnel to the VRS, including the payment of salaries to and provision of benefits for these soldiers, some of whom served as high-ranking VRS officers.

15. The Trial Chamber further found, *inter alia*, that Perišić was informed about "acts of violence against Bosnian Muslims perpetrated in the BiH theatre of war [that] made Perišić aware of the VRS's propensity to commit crimes"; was aware of the essential elements of the VRS crimes in Sarajevo and Srebrenica; and was aware that his actions provided practical assistance to these crimes.

16. Perišić contends that the Trial Chamber erred by holding that acts of an aider and abettor need not be specifically directed towards assisting crimes of principal perpetrators. * * *

Specific Direction

17. The Trial Chamber, Judge Moloto dissenting, concluded that the *actus reus* of aiding and abetting was proved based on the finding that VJ assistance "had a substantial effect on the crimes perpetrated by the VRS in Sarajevo and Srebrenica." In assessing Perišić's liability as an aider and abettor, the Trial Chamber stated that " 'specific direction' is not a requisite element of the *actus reus* of aiding and abetting," citing the *Mrkšić and Šljivančanin* Appeal Judgement.[37] Relying on that appeal judgement, the majority of the Trial Chamber did not consider whether aid from the VJ to the VRS was specifically directed to the commission of crimes.

18. Perišić asserts, *inter alia*, that the Trial Chamber erred in law by convicting him for aiding and abetting without requiring proof that his acts were specifically directed towards assisting the crimes of principal perpetrators. In particular, Perišić avers that the Trial

---

[37] *Prosecutor v. Mile Mrkšić & Veselin Šljivančanin*, Case No. IT–95–13/1–A, Judgement (May 5, 2009).

Chamber relied on the *Mrkšić and Šljivančanin* Appeal Judgement to support its finding that specific direction was not an element of aiding and abetting liability. However, he submits that the *Mrkšić and Šljivančanin* Appeal Judgement erroneously interpreted the *Blagojević and Jokić* Appeal Judgement in holding that a conviction for aiding and abetting did not require proof of specific direction. Perišić contends that specific direction was included as an element of the *actus reus* of aiding and abetting in the *Tadić* Appeal Judgement, and that this element distinguishes aiding and abetting from liability for participation in a Joint Criminal Enterprise ("JCE"), a mode of liability that does not require specific direction. He also maintains that the specific direction element of aiding and abetting liability is distinct from the "substantial effect" element. * * *

19. * * * Perišić maintains that the Trial Chamber's approach effectively "amounts to a form of strict liability" where "to in any way assist the VRS in their conduct of hostilities was to aid and abet their criminal acts." * * *

21. The Prosecution responds, *inter alia*, that the Trial Chamber did not err in setting out the parameters of Perišić's liability and that it correctly found that specific direction was not a required element of aiding and abetting. In particular, the Prosecution asserts that conduct is directed towards a crime if it facilitates or causes this crime. In this context, the Prosecution contends that specific direction has no independent meaning and is part of the substantial effect requirement. * * *

24. The Prosecution underscores the extensive nature of assistance provided by the VJ to the VRS in this case, suggesting that the scale of this aid alone gives rise to aiding and abetting liability. In this regard, the Prosecution asserts that Perišić knew of VRS crimes but nonetheless "voluntarily provided indispensable, massive, and consistent personnel and logistical assistance" to the VRS, interacted regularly with "VRS perpetrators" of crimes, "visited the war zone several times," and "continuously and actively lobbied the FRY Supreme Defence Council ("SDC") to ensure that the VRS's ability to wage war in Bosnia was sustained." The Prosecution further asserts that attacks against civilians, including those in Sarajevo and Srebrenica, were so central to the VRS's overall military strategy that it "was not possible" for Perišić to direct military assistance only towards the VRS's legitimate war efforts. Finally, the Prosecution contends that Perišić's personal motives with respect to VRS crimes are irrelevant to a determination of his criminal liability in this regard, as he knew that the assistance provided to the VRS would probably facilitate the commission of crimes.

Specific Direction as a Component of Aiding and Abetting Liability * * *

26. The Appeals Chamber recalls that the first appeal judgement setting out the parameters of aiding and abetting liability was the *Tadić*

Appeal Judgement, rendered in 1999, which described the *actus reus* of criminal liability for aiding and abetting as follows:

> The aider and abettor carries out acts specifically directed to assist, encourage or lend moral support to the perpetration of a certain specific crime (murder, extermination, rape, torture, wanton destruction of civilian property, etc.), and this support has a substantial effect upon the perpetration of the crime. * * *

29. The Appeals Chamber notes that, while certain appeal judgements rendered after the *Tadić* Appeal Judgement made no explicit reference to specific direction, several of these employed alternative but equivalent formulations. In particular, the *Simić* Appeal Judgement defined the *actus reus* of aiding and abetting as "acts directed to assist, encourage or lend moral support to the perpetration of a certain specific crime." Similarly, the *Orić* Appeal Judgement, discussing aiding and abetting in the context of omission liability, explained that the "omission must be directed to assist, encourage or lend moral support to the perpetration of a crime and have a substantial effect upon the perpetration of the crime." The ICTR's *Ntawukulilyayo and Rukundo* Appeal Judgements referred to acts that are "specifically aimed" towards relevant crimes. Finally, the ICTR's *Karera* Appeal Judgement stated that the "*actus reus* of aiding and abetting is constituted by acts or omissions that assist, further, or lend moral support to the perpetration of a specific crime." The Appeals Chamber considers that these judgements effectively included specific direction as an element of the *actus reus* of aiding and abetting. * * *

32. Mindful of the foregoing, the Appeals Chamber now turns to the 2009 *Mrkšić and Šljivančanin* Appeal Judgement, and Perišić's contention that this judgement erroneously departed from settled jurisprudence by stating that specific direction is not an element of the *actus reus* of aiding and abetting. In discussing the *mens rea* of aiding and abetting, the *Mrkšić and Šljivančanin* Appeal Judgement stated, in passing, that "the Appeals Chamber has confirmed that 'specific direction' is not an essential ingredient of the *actus reus* of aiding and abetting." This statement may be read to suggest that specific direction is not an element of the *actus reus* of aiding and abetting. However, the Appeals Chamber, Judge Liu dissenting, is not persuaded that the *Mrkšić and Šljivančanin* Appeal Judgement reflected an intention to depart from the settled precedent established by the *Tadić* Appeal Judgement.

33. At the outset, the Appeals Chamber observes that the *Mrkšić and Šljivančanin* Appeal Judgement's reference to specific direction not being an "essential ingredient" is found in a section of the judgement analysing the *mens rea* rather than *actus reus* of aiding and abetting. In the context of rejecting Šljivančanin's assertion that aiding and abetting by omission requires a heightened *mens rea*, the Appeals Chamber explained that Šljivančanin's reference to specific direction as part of "the

mens rea standard applicable to aiding and abetting" was erroneous because specific direction "forms part of the *actus reus* not the *mens rea* of aiding and abetting." The Appeals Chamber then stated that specific direction was "not an essential ingredient" of the *actus reus* of aiding and abetting. The only authority cited to support this latter conclusion was the *Blagojević and Jokić* Appeal Judgement's holding that specific direction is a requisite element of aiding and abetting liability, albeit one that may at times be satisfied by an implicit analysis of substantial contribution. * * *

34. The Appeals Chamber recalls its settled practice to only "depart from a previous decision after the most careful consideration has been given to it, both as to the law, including the authorities cited, and the facts." The *Mrkšić and Šljivančanin* Appeal Judgement's passing reference to specific direction does not amount to such "careful consideration". Had the Appeals Chamber found cogent reasons to depart from its relevant precedent, and intended to do so, it would have performed a clear, detailed analysis of the issue, discussing both past jurisprudence and the authorities supporting an alternative approach. Instead, the relevant reference to specific direction: was made in a section and paragraph dealing with *mens rea* rather than *actus reus*; was limited to a single sentence not relevant to the Appeals Chamber's holding; did not explicitly acknowledge a departure from prior precedent; and, most tellingly, cited to only one previous appeal judgement, which in fact confirmed that specific direction does constitute an element of aiding and abetting liability. These indicia suggest that the formula "not an essential ingredient" was an attempt to summarise, in passing, the *Blagojević and Jokić* Appeal Judgement's holding that specific direction can often be demonstrated implicitly through analysis of substantial contribution, rather than abjure previous jurisprudence establishing that specific direction is an element of aiding and abetting liability. * * *

36. Accordingly, despite the ambiguity of the *Mrkšić and Šljivančanin* Appeal Judgement, the Appeals Chamber, Judge Liu dissenting, considers that specific direction remains an element of the *actus reus* of aiding and abetting liability. The Appeals Chamber, Judge Liu dissenting, thus reaffirms that no conviction for aiding and abetting may be entered if the element of specific direction is not established beyond reasonable doubt, either explicitly or implicitly.

Circumstances in Which Specific Direction Must Be Explicitly Considered

37. At the outset, the Appeals Chamber, Judge Liu dissenting, recalls that the element of specific direction establishes a culpable link between assistance provided by an accused individual and the crimes of principal perpetrators. In many cases, evidence relating to other elements of aiding and abetting liability may be sufficient to demonstrate specific direction and thus the requisite culpable link.

38. In this respect, the Appeals Chamber notes that previous appeal judgements have not conducted extensive analyses of specific direction. The lack of such discussion may be explained by the fact that prior convictions for aiding and abetting entered or affirmed by the Appeals Chamber involved relevant acts geographically or otherwise proximate to, and thus not remote from, the crimes of principal perpetrators. Where such proximity is present, specific direction may be demonstrated implicitly through discussion of other elements of aiding and abetting liability, such as substantial contribution. For example, an individual accused of aiding and abetting may have been physically present during the preparation or commission of crimes committed by principal perpetrators and made a concurrent substantial contribution. In such a case, the existence of specific direction, which demonstrates the culpable link between the accused aider and abettor's assistance and the crimes of principal perpetrators, will be self-evident.

39. However, not all cases of aiding and abetting will involve proximity of an accused individual's relevant acts to crimes committed by principal perpetrators. Where an accused aider and abettor is remote from relevant crimes, evidence proving other elements of aiding and abetting may not be sufficient to prove specific direction. In such circumstances, the Appeals Chamber, Judge Liu dissenting, holds that explicit consideration of specific direction is required.

40. The factors indicating that acts of an accused aider and abettor are remote from the crimes of principal perpetrators will depend on the individual circumstances of each case. However, some guidance on this issue is provided by the Appeals Chamber's jurisprudence. In particular, the Appeals Chamber has previously concluded, in discussing aiding and abetting liability, that significant temporal distance between the actions of an accused individual and the crime he or she allegedly assisted decreases the likelihood of a connection between that crime and the accused individual's actions. The same rationale applies, by analogy, to other factors separating the acts of an individual accused of aiding and abetting from the crimes he or she is alleged to have facilitated. Such factors may include, but are not limited to, geographic distance.

The Trial Chamber's Analysis of Aiding and Abetting in this Case

* * *

42. The Appeals Chamber observes that Perišić's assistance to the VRS was remote from the relevant crimes of principal perpetrators. In particular, the Trial Chamber found that the VRS was independent from the VJ, and that the two armies were based in separate geographic regions. In addition, the Trial Chamber did not refer to any evidence that Perišić was physically present when relevant criminal acts were planned or committed. In these circumstances, the Appeals Chamber, Judge Liu dissenting, further considers that an explicit analysis of specific direction would have been required in order to establish the necessary link

between the aid Perišić provided and the crimes committed by principal perpetrators.

43. * * * Accordingly, the Appeals Chamber will proceed to assess the evidence relating to Perišić's convictions for aiding and abetting *de novo* under the correct legal standard, considering whether Perišić's actions were specifically directed to aid and abet the VRS crimes in Sarajevo and Srebrenica.

44. The Appeals Chamber notes that previous judgements have not provided extensive analysis of what evidence may prove specific direction. However, the Appeals Chamber recalls again that the *Tadić* Appeal Judgement indicated that specific direction involves finding a closer link between acts of an accused aider and abettor and crimes committed by principal perpetrators than is necessary to support convictions under JCE. The types of evidence required to establish such a link will depend on the facts of a given case. Nonetheless, the Appeals Chamber observes that in most cases, the provision of general assistance which could be used for both lawful and unlawful activities will not be sufficient, alone, to prove that this aid was specifically directed to crimes of principal perpetrators. In such circumstances, in order to enter a conviction for aiding and abetting, evidence establishing a direct link between the aid provided by an accused individual and the relevant crimes committed by principal perpetrators is necessary.

The Extent to Which Perišić Specifically Directed Assistance to VRS Crimes * * *

46. As a preliminary matter, the Appeals Chamber recalls that the Trial Chamber did not find the VRS *de jure* or *de facto* subordinated to the VJ. In particular, the Trial Chamber found that the VRS had a separate command structure: the President of the Republika Srpska served as Commander-in-Chief of the VRS, with a Commander of the VRS Main Staff assuming delegated authorities. Broader questions of VRS military strategy were addressed by the Republika Srpska's Supreme Command, composed of the Republika Srpska's President, Vice President, Speaker of the Assembly, and Ministers of Defence and Interior. While the Trial Chamber noted that the VRS received support from the VJ, the Trial Chamber also identified sources of support other than the FRY. In addition, the Trial Chamber found that Perišić was not proved beyond reasonable doubt to have exercised effective control over VJ troops seconded to the VRS. Finally, the Trial Chamber observed that Ratko Mladić, the Commander of the VRS Main Staff, refused to accept peace plans urged by the VJ and FRY leadership. The Appeals Chamber, having considered this evidence in its totality, agrees with the Trial Chamber's determination that the evidence on the record suggests that "the VRS and the VJ [were] separate and independent military entities."

47. Having reaffirmed the Trial Chamber's conclusion that the VRS was independent of the VJ, the Appeals Chamber will now consider whether VJ assistance to the VRS, which Perišić acknowledged having

facilitated, was specifically directed towards VRS crimes. In particular, the Appeals Chamber will assess: (i) Perišić's role in shaping and implementing the FRY policy of supporting the VRS; (ii) whether the FRY policy of supporting the VRS was specifically directed towards the commission of crimes by the VRS; and (iii) whether Perišić either implemented the SDC policy of assisting the VRS in a way that specifically directed aid to the VRS crimes in Sarajevo and Srebrenica, or took action to provide such aid outside the context of SDC-approved assistance. The Appeals Chamber considers that the relevant evidence in this case is circumstantial and thus can only support a finding of specific direction if this is the sole reasonable interpretation of the record.

48. The Appeals Chamber underscores that the parameters of its inquiry are limited and focus solely on factors related to Perišić's individual criminal liability for the VRS crimes in Sarajevo and Srebrenica, not the potential liability of States or other entities over which the Tribunal has no pertinent jurisdiction. The Appeals Chamber also underscores that its analysis of specific direction will exclusively address *actus reus*. In this regard, the Appeals Chamber acknowledges that specific direction may involve considerations that are closely related to questions of *mens rea*. Indeed, as discussed below, evidence regarding an individual's state of mind may serve as circumstantial evidence that assistance he or she facilitated was specifically directed towards charged crimes. However, the Appeals Chamber recalls again that the *mens rea* required to support a conviction for aiding and abetting is knowledge that assistance aids the commission of criminal acts, along with awareness of the essential elements of these crimes. By contrast, as set out above, the long-standing jurisprudence of the Tribunal affirms that specific direction is an analytically distinct element of *actus reus*.

The SDC Policy of Providing Support to the VRS

52. The Appeals Chamber considers that two inquiries are relevant to assessing whether SDC assistance to the VRS was specifically directed to facilitate the latter's criminal activities. The first inquiry assesses whether the VRS was an organisation whose sole and exclusive purpose was the commission of crimes. Such a finding would suggest that assistance by the VJ to the VRS was specifically directed towards VRS crimes, including the VRS crimes in Sarajevo and Srebrenica. The second inquiry assesses whether the SDC endorsed a policy of assisting VRS crimes; such a finding would again suggest that the assistance from the VJ to the VRS was specifically directed towards, *inter alia*, the VRS crimes in Sarajevo and Srebrenica.

53. With respect to the first inquiry, the Appeals Chamber recalls that the Trial Chamber did not characterise the VRS as a criminal organisation; indeed, it stated that "Perišić is not charged with helping the VRS wage war *per se*, which is not a crime under the Statute." Having reviewed the evidence on the record, the Appeals Chamber agrees with the Trial Chamber that the VRS was not an organisation whose actions

were criminal *per se*; instead, it was an army fighting a war. The Appeals Chamber notes the Trial Chamber's finding that the VRS's strategy was "inextricably linked to" crimes against civilians. However, the Trial Chamber did not find that all VRS activities in Sarajevo or Srebrenica were criminal in nature. The Trial Chamber limited its findings to characterising as criminal only certain actions of the VRS in the context of the operations in Sarajevo and Srebrenica. In these circumstances, the Appeals Chamber considers that a policy of providing assistance to the VRS's general war effort does not, in itself, demonstrate that assistance facilitated by Perišić was specifically directed to aid the VRS crimes in Sarajevo and Srebrenica.

54. Turning to the second inquiry, the Appeals Chamber first observes that the Trial Chamber discussed evidence indicating SDC approval of measures to secure financing for the VJ's assistance to the VRS and to increase the effectiveness of this assistance by systematising the secondment of VJ personnel and the transfer of equipment and supplies. The Trial Chamber determined that this evidence "conclusively demonstrate[s] that the SDC licensed military assistance to the VRS." However, the Trial Chamber did not identify any evidence that the SDC policy directed aid towards VRS criminal activities in particular.

55. The Appeals Chamber's *de novo* review of the evidentiary record also reveals no basis for concluding that it was SDC policy to specifically direct aid towards VRS crimes. Instead, the SDC focused on monitoring and modulating aid to the general VRS war effort. For example, SDC discussions addressed difficulties in providing particular levels of assistance requested by the VRS; salaries of VJ personnel seconded to the VRS; and instances where members of the VJ provided supplies to the VRS without official approval.

56. The Appeals Chamber notes the Prosecution's suggestion that the magnitude of VJ aid provided to the VRS is sufficient to prove Perišić's *actus reus* with respect to the VRS crimes in Sarajevo and Srebrenica. However, the Appeals Chamber observes that while the Trial Chamber considered evidence regarding volume of assistance in making findings on substantial contribution, this analysis does not necessarily demonstrate specific direction, and thus such evidence does not automatically establish a sufficient link between aid provided by an accused aider and abettor and the commission of crimes by principal perpetrators. In the circumstances of this case, indicia demonstrating the magnitude of VJ aid to the VRS serve as circumstantial evidence of specific direction; however, a finding of specific direction must be the sole reasonable inference after a review of the evidentiary record as a whole.

57. The Appeals Chamber underscores that the VRS was participating in lawful combat activities and was not a purely criminal organisation. In addition, as explained above, other evidence on the record does not suggest that SDC policy provided that aid be specifically directed towards VRS crimes. In this context, the Appeals Chamber,

Judge Liu dissenting, considers that a reasonable interpretation of the evidence on the record is that the SDC directed large-scale military assistance to the general VRS war effort, not to the commission of VRS crimes. Accordingly, specific direction of VJ aid towards VRS crimes is not the sole reasonable inference that can be drawn from the totality of the evidence on the record, even considering the magnitude of the VJ's assistance.

58. In view of the foregoing, the Appeals Chamber, Judge Liu dissenting, concludes that the SDC policy of assisting the VRS was not proved to involve specific direction of VJ aid towards VRS crimes, as opposed to the general VRS war effort. In these circumstances, insofar as Perišić faithfully executed the SDC policy of supporting the VRS, the aid Perišić facilitated was not proved to be specifically directed towards the VRS's criminal activities. * * *

60. The Appeals Chamber notes that the Trial Chamber found that Perišić supported continuing the SDC policy of assisting the VRS. During meetings of the SDC, Perišić argued both for sustaining aid to the VRS and for adopting related legal and financial measures that facilitated such aid. However, the Trial Chamber did not identify evidence demonstrating that Perišić urged the provision of VJ assistance to the VRS in furtherance of specific criminal activities. Rather, the Trial Chamber's analysis of Perišić's role in the SDC deliberations indicates that Perišić only supported the continuation of assistance to the general VRS war effort. * * *

62. The Appeals Chamber recalls that indicia demonstrating the nature and distribution of VJ aid could also serve as circumstantial evidence of specific direction. The Appeals Chamber notes in this regard that the Trial Chamber classified the assistance provided by the VJ to the VRS in two broad categories: first, secondment of personnel, and, second, provision of military equipment, logistical support, and military training.

63. With respect to the secondment of VJ soldiers to the VRS, the Appeals Chamber recalls that the Trial Chamber found that Perišić persuaded the SDC to create the 30th PC, a unit of the VJ that served as the administrative home of VJ soldiers and officers seconded to the VRS and which was used to increase and institutionalise the support already provided to seconded VJ soldiers and officers. The Trial Chamber also found that the establishment of the 30th PC constituted practical assistance to the VRS, as the 30th PC helped sustain soldiers already seconded to the VRS and facilitated the secondment of additional personnel. However, the record contains no evidence suggesting that the benefits provided to seconded soldiers and officers—including VJ-level salaries, housing, and educational and medical benefits—were tailored to facilitate the commission of crimes. Rather, evidence on the record indicates that such benefits were structured to mirror those offered by the VJ and thus provide seconded soldiers and officers with the same

level of support as they received prior to secondment. In addition, the evidence on the record does not suggest that VJ soldiers and officers were seconded in order to specifically assist VRS criminal acts. In the Appeals Chamber's view, the fact that VJ soldiers seconded to the VRS may have been involved in criminal acts after secondment does not, alone, prove that their secondments were specifically directed to supporting these criminal acts. * * *

64. With respect to the second category of assistance provided by the VJ to the VRS, the Appeals Chamber recalls the Trial Chamber's finding that the VJ supplied the VRS with "comprehensive" logistical aid, often not requiring payment for this assistance. In particular, the Trial Chamber concluded that the VJ provided the VRS with military equipment and supplies on a large scale, including semi-automatic rifles, machine guns, pieces for machine-gun barrels, cannons, bullets, grenades, rocket launchers, mortar ammunition, mines, rockets, anti-aircraft ammunition, and mortar shells. The Trial Chamber further concluded that the VJ offered military training to VRS troops and assisted with military communications. The Appeals Chamber's review of evidence on the record also demonstrates that, pursuant to the overall policy of the FRY, as expressed in decisions of the SDC, Perišić administered and facilitated the provision of large-scale military assistance to the VRS.

65. The Appeals Chamber considers that the types of aid provided by the VJ to the VRS do not appear incompatible with lawful military operations. * * *

66. The manner in which Perišić distributed VJ aid to the VRS also does not demonstrate specific direction. The Trial Chamber determined that part of this assistance was sent to certain VRS units involved in committing crimes. However, the Appeals Chamber, Judge Liu dissenting, considers that neither the Trial Chamber's analysis nor the Appeals Chamber's *de novo* review identified evidence that aid was provided to the VRS in a manner directed at supporting its criminal activities. Evidence on the record instead suggests that Perišić considered the VRS's requests as a whole and that VJ assistance was delivered to multiple areas within BiH to aid the general VRS war effort. * * *

68. Finally, the Appeals Chamber notes that the Trial Chamber considered extensive evidence suggesting that Perišić knew of crimes being committed by the VRS, especially with respect to Sarajevo. However, the Appeals Chamber, Judge Liu dissenting, recalls that evidence regarding knowledge of crimes, alone, does not establish specific direction, which is a distinct element of *actus reus*, separate from *mens rea*. Indicia demonstrating that Perišić knew of the VRS crimes in Sarajevo and Srebrenica may serve as circumstantial evidence of specific direction; however, a finding of specific direction must be the sole

reasonable inference after a review of the evidentiary record as a whole.
* * *

Conclusions from *De Novo* Review of Evidence on the Record

70. The Appeals Chamber, Judge Liu dissenting, has clarified that, in view of the remoteness of Perišić's actions from the crimes of the VRS, an explicit analysis of specific direction was required. As detailed above, the Appeals Chamber's review of the Trial Chamber's general evidentiary findings and *de novo* assessment of evidence on the record do not demonstrate that SDC policy provided for directing VJ aid towards VRS crimes. Similarly, the Trial Chamber's conclusions and evidence on the record do not suggest that Perišić's implementation of SDC policy specifically directed aid towards VRS crimes, or that Perišić took other actions to that effect.

71. The Appeals Chamber has already noted that the Trial Chamber identified evidence of the large scale of VJ assistance to the VRS, as well as evidence that Perišić knew of VRS crimes. However, having considered these Trial Chamber findings alongside its *de novo* analysis of the record, the Appeals Chamber, Judge Liu dissenting, is not convinced that the only reasonable interpretation of the totality of this circumstantial evidence is that Perišić specifically directed aid towards VRS crimes. Instead, a reasonable interpretation of the record is that VJ aid facilitated by Perišić was directed towards the VRS's general war effort rather than VRS crimes. Accordingly, the Appeals Chamber, Judge Liu dissenting, is not convinced that the VJ aid which Perišić facilitated was proved to be specifically directed towards the VRS crimes in Sarajevo and Srebrenica.

72. As demonstrated above, the Appeals Chamber considers that assistance from one army to another army's war efforts is insufficient, in itself, to trigger individual criminal liability for individual aid providers absent proof that the relevant assistance was specifically directed towards criminal activities. The Appeals Chamber underscores, however, that this conclusion should in no way be interpreted as enabling military leaders to deflect criminal liability by subcontracting the commission of criminal acts. If an ostensibly independent military group is proved to be under the control of officers in another military group, the latter can still be held responsible for crimes committed by their puppet forces. Similarly, aid from one military force specifically directed towards crimes committed by another force can also trigger aiding and abetting liability. However, as explained above, a sufficient link between the acts of an individual accused of aiding and abetting a crime and the crime he or she is charged with assisting must be established for the accused individual to incur criminal liability. Neither the findings of the Trial Chamber nor the evidence on the record in this case prove such a link with respect to Perišić's actions.

73. The Appeals Chamber, Judge Liu dissenting, recalls that specific direction is an element of the *actus reus* of aiding and abetting

liability, and that in cases like this one, where an accused individual's assistance is remote from the actions of principal perpetrators, specific direction must be explicitly established. After carefully reviewing the evidence on the record, the Appeals Chamber, Judge Liu dissenting, concludes that it has not been established beyond reasonable doubt that Perišić carried out "acts specifically directed to assist, encourage or lend moral support to the perpetration of [the] certain specific crime[s]" committed by the VRS. Accordingly, Perišić's convictions for aiding and abetting must be reversed on the ground that not all the elements of aiding and abetting liability have been proved beyond reasonable doubt.

Prosecutor v. Momčilo Perišić, Case No. IT–04–81–A, Partially Dissenting Opinion of Judge Liu (Feb. 28, 2013)

2. While I recognise that the specific direction requirement has been mentioned in the relevant jurisprudence, I note that it has not been applied consistently. Indeed, the cases cited by the Majority as evidence of an established specific direction requirement merely make mention of "acts directed at specific crimes" as an element of the *actus reus* of aiding and abetting liability. In the majority of these cases the Appeals Chamber simply restates language from the *Tadić* Appeal Judgement without expressly applying the specific direction requirement to the facts of the case before it. Moreover, the jurisprudence of the Tribunal demonstrates that aiding and abetting liability may be established without requiring that the acts of the accused were specifically directed to a crime. In these circumstances, I am not persuaded that specific direction is an essential element of the *actus reus* of aiding and abetting liability—or that it is necessary to explicitly consider specific direction in cases where the aider and abettor is remote from the relevant crimes.

3. Given that specific direction has not been applied in past cases with any rigor, to insist on such a requirement now effectively raises the threshold for aiding and abetting liability. This shift risks undermining the very purpose of aiding and abetting liability by allowing those responsible for knowingly facilitating the most grievous crimes to evade responsibility for their acts. The present appeal is a case in point.

4. The Trial Chamber held Perišić responsible for facilitating the criminal acts of the VRS in Sarajevo and Srebrenica. Although the Trial Chamber did not characterise the VRS as a wholly criminal organisation, it nonetheless found that the crimes committed by the VRS were "inextricably linked to the war strategy and objectives of the VRS leadership." It further found that the VRS "wag[ed] a war that encompassed systematic criminal actions against Bosnian Muslim civilians as a military strategy and objective." In this regard, the Trial Chamber found that the siege of Sarajevo was instrumental to the implementation of a VRS objective and that the "systematic and

widespread sniping and shelling of civilians in Sarajevo by the VRS over a period of three years demonstrate[d] that the VRS's leading officers relied on criminal acts to further the siege." With regard to Srebrenica, the Trial Chamber found that the VRS pursued a strategic objective "aimed at establishing a corridor in the Drina River valley and eliminating the Drina River as a border between the Serbian states." It concluded that "this goal was implemented through the plan of 'plunging the Bosnian Muslim population into a humanitarian crisis and ultimately eliminating the enclave'." * * *

6. The Trial Chamber found that Perišić presided over "a system providing comprehensive military assistance to the VRS." It noted that this assistance included "considerable quantities of weaponry comprising a very large part of the VRS's munitions requirements" and the transfer of a number of VJ officers and key personnel to the VRS. The Trial Chamber carefully assessed the magnitude of the logistical aid Perišić directed towards the VRS and found that "[w]ithout the regular supply of considerable quantities of ammunition and other weaponry, as well as fuel, technical expertise, repair services and personnel training, the VRS would have been hampered in conducting its operations in Sarajevo and Srebrenica." Significantly, the Trial Chamber established that "important logistical and technical support was provided to the units involved in perpetrating the charged crimes" in Sarajevo and Srebrenica. * * *

8. The Trial Chamber also reviewed extensive evidence in finding that Perišić was aware of the VRS's propensity to commit criminal acts. It found that, from the early stages of the war, "Perišić was provided with information, from a variety of sources, of the VRS's criminal behaviour and discriminatory intent. This information related to acts of violence against Bosnian Muslims perpetrated in the BiH theatre of war and made Perišić aware of the VRS's propensity to commit crimes." The Trial Chamber concluded that Perišić knew "of the VRS criminal intent in the implementation of its war strategy" and nonetheless provided assistance to the VRS war effort in the Sarajevo campaign. It further found that Perišić "knew that individual crimes committed by the VRS before the attack on Srebrenica would probably be followed by more crimes committed by the VRS after the take-over of the enclave in July 1995" and that "Perišić had contemporaneous knowledge of allegations that the VRS was committing crimes in Srebrenica." * * *

10. In these circumstances, I would have upheld Perišić's convictions for aiding and abetting the crimes committed by the VRS in Sarajevo and Srebrenica.

NOTES & QUESTIONS

1. Specific Direction

Is the opinion above consistent with the prior ICTY precedent, as insisted by the majority, or is it a major departure, as argued by Judge Liu Daqun (China) in dissent? Which is the better approach? Would the Appeals Chamber have reached a different conclusion if the Tribunal had determined the VRS to be a criminal organization at base? What sort of evidence would have led the Tribunal to this conclusion?

Judge Theodor Meron, the Presiding Judge on the 2013 *Perišić* appeal, was also presiding on the panel (along with Judge Liu) that decided the 2009 Appeal in the *Mrkšić and Šljivančanin* case. There, the Appeals Chamber held:

> 134. The Appeals Chamber recalls that while individual criminal responsibility generally requires the commission of a positive act, this is not an absolute requirement. In particular, the Appeals Chamber has previously found that "the omission to act where there is a legal duty to act can lead to individual criminal responsibility under Article 7(1) of the Statute." Moreover, the Appeals Chamber has consistently found that, in the circumstances of a given case, the *actus reus* of aiding and abetting may be perpetrated through an omission. * * *
>
> 146. The *mens rea* and *actus reus* requirements for aiding and abetting by omission are the same as for aiding and abetting by a positive act. The critical issue to be determined is whether, on the particular facts of a given case, it is established that the failure to discharge a legal duty assisted, encouraged or lent moral support to the perpetration of the crime, and had a substantial effect on it. In particular, the question as to whether an omission constitutes "substantial assistance" to the perpetration of a crime requires a fact based enquiry. * * *
>
> 159. * * * The fact that an "omission must be directed to assist, encourage or lend moral support to the perpetration of a crime" forms part of the *actus reus* not the *mens rea* of aiding and abetting. In addition, the Appeals Chamber has confirmed that "specific direction" is not an essential ingredient of the *actus reus* of aiding and abetting. It reiterates its finding that the required *mens rea* for aiding and abetting by omission is that: (1) the aider and abettor must know that his omission assists in the commission of the crime of the principal perpetrator; and (2) he must be aware of the essential elements of the crime which was ultimately committed by the principal. * * * The Appeals Chamber further recalls that it has previously rejected an elevated *mens rea* requirement for aiding and abetting, namely, the proposition that the aider and abettor needs to have intended to provide assistance, or as a minimum, accepted that such assistance would be a possible and foreseeable consequence of his conduct.

Is Judge Meron's reasoning consistent between these two opinions? Why might he have changed course?

In a subsequent appeal in the *Nikola Sainović* case, the ICTY Prosecutor invited a differently-constituted Appeals Chamber—now presided over by none other than Judge Liu—to reject the reasoning in *Perišić*. The Appeals Chamber conducted an exhaustive analysis of prior case law dating back to the World War II period, treaties, and national penal codes and jurisprudence, and came to the "compelling conclusion that 'specific direction' is not an element of aiding and abetting liability under customary international law [and] unequivocally rejects the approach adopted in the *Perišić* Appeal Judgement." *Prosecutor v. Nikola Šainović et al.*, Case No. IT–05–87–A, Judgement, paras. 1649–50 (Jan. 23, 2014). A year later the rejection of the specific direction doctrine was affirmed, though with little analysis or reasoning and with dissents that argued it should not be so rejected in two subsequent cases. *See Prosecutor v. Popović*, Case No. IT–05–88–A, Judgement, para. 1758 (Jan. 30, 2015); *Prosecutor v. Stanišić and Simatović,* Case No. IT–03–69–A, Judgement (Dec. 9, 2015). How would you have argued this appeal, particularly given the principle of *stare decisis*? What does the short lifespan of specific direction say about the rigor of international criminal law reasoning?

This outcome is consistent with an empirical study conducted by Professor James Stewart, who also concluded that "specific direction" finds little mention in the jurisprudence, has no basis in customary international law, and is not addressed in the scholarship on accomplice liability. Professor Stewart's database is available on the University of British Columbia's webpage. The specific direction doctrine has also been summarily rejected by the Extraordinary Chambers in the Courts of Cambodia (ECCC) (*see* Case No. 002/19-09-2007/ECCC/TC, Judgment, para. 707–710 (Aug. 7, 2014)) and, as discussed below, by the Special Court for Sierra Leone (SCSL) in the *Taylor* decision. For further discussion, *see* Manuel J. Ventura, *Farewell 'Specific Direction': Aiding and Abetting War Crimes and Crimes Against Humanity in Perišić, Taylor, Sainović et al., and U.S. Alien Torture Jurisprudence, in* THE WAR REPORT: ARMED CONFLICT IN 2013 (S. Casey-Maslen ed., 2014).

2. *Mens Rea* or *Actus Reus?*

Do you agree that the issue of "specific direction," such as it is, should be addressed within the context of the *actus reus* of complicity or is it rather a function of a defendant's *mens rea*? In a separate opinion in the *Perišić* appeal, President Meron and Judge Carmel Agius (Malta) expressed some ambivalence in this regard:

> 4. [W]ere we setting out the elements of aiding and abetting outside the context of the Tribunal's past jurisprudence, we would consider categorising specific direction as an element of *mens rea*. However, we are satisfied that specific direction can also, as the Appeal Judgement's analysis demonstrates, be reasonably assessed in the context of *actus reus*. The critical issue raised by the requirement of specific direction, regardless of whether it is

considered in the context of *actus reus* or *mens rea*, is whether the link between assistance of an accused individual and actions of principal perpetrators is sufficient to justify holding the accused aider and abettor criminally responsible for relevant crimes. In these circumstances, we do not believe that cogent reasons justify departure from the Tribunal's precedent of considering specific direction in the context of *actus reus*.

3. Paragraph 72

Review paragraph 72, above. During closing arguments at trial, Judge Bakone Justice Moloto (South Africa)—who dissented to the judgment convicting Perišić—posed a question to Senior Trial Attorney Mark Harmon (United States), who also served as Co-Investigating Judge at the ECCC, concerning the potential complicity liability of co-belligerents in armed conflicts. This colloquy ensued:

> Judge Moloto: [M]y question is what is the authority for the proposition that: if an army assists another army in war and crimes are committed of the nature that are charged in this indictment, the assisting army, or commander of the assisting army, is guilty of aiding and abetting those crimes?
>
> Mr. Harmon: Your Honour, General Perišić provided assistance knowing that that assistance was going to assist the VRS and it was likely that that assistance would be used in the commission of crimes.
>
> Judge Moloto: Okay. Let me paint you an analogous scenario and get your comment on it. A war began in Afghanistan in 2001, and it is generally known that there are allegations of crimes having been committed at least since 2002. Does that make the commanders of the various NATO armies that are jointly participating in that war guilty of the crimes that are alleged to have been committed, and are still being committed, like detentions in Guantánamo, in Bagram, in Kabul, and all these places?
>
> Mr. Harmon: Your Honour, you are asking me obviously, an explosive political question.
>
> Judge Moloto: No, no. It's a legal question.
>
> Mr. Harmon: I would like to answer your question. The objectives, as I understand, of the NATO forces isn't to ethnically cleanse parts of Afghanistan. It is to be engaged in a military campaign against the Taliban. * * * Where I make my distinction is the purpose or objectives. The objectives of Bosnian Serbs, strategic objective number one, was to ethnically cleanse—if you will, that is a much broader term—it was to separate the Serbs from the non-Serbs. That act gave rise to conduct, long-standing conduct, of the VRS taking populations of Muslims and Croats and removing them from their homes by force. That was no mystery. General Perišić was aware, as we say in our brief, was fully aware of the conduct of the Bosnian Serbs, and with the knowledge of that conduct, he provided them with assistance that enabled them to

continue to conduct the war, continue to commit crimes, and the assistance that he provided had a substantial effect on the commission of those crimes. So, I make a distinction between the Afghan war, where there is not the stated purpose which is to remove and ethnically cleanse. I also make one other observation about the Afghan war. In the Afghan war, and I'll take the United States as an example, because I'm familiar with the United States' participation in part in that. When there were crimes that were committed by American soldiers, those crimes were prosecuted in the United States and people are serving life prison sentences as a result of those crimes committed against Afghan civilians. In this situation, there were no prosecutions whatsoever, either in the VRS or in the Federal Republic of the Yugoslavia for war crimes.

Judge Moloto: You see, unfortunately, we don't seem to be on the same wavelength. * * * [T]he point I'm asking simply is because the armies, the commanders of the remaining NATO countries that are participating in Afghanistan are aware of the fact that crimes have been committed, crimes against humanity have been committed, and yet those commanders are still continuing to participate in that war, are they then guilty of those crimes that are being committed? * * * If anybody is guilty of those crimes, then they are equally guilty, because they are aware of those crimes being committed and yet they are continuing to participate in that war.

Mr. Harmon: I draw a distinction, Your Honours, between continuing to participate in the war. The position we assert here is identical to the situation in your hypothetical situation.

Judge Moloto: And, therefore, if it is identical, then you are saying, yes, they ought to be guilty if anybody else is guilty.

Mr. Harmon: Your Honour, I don't want to go that far. I'm saying that the situation is identical in terms of the framework of our case.

Judge Moloto: I won't force you to go any further than that.

How would you have answered Judge Moloto's questions?

Apparently Harmon's answers did not alleviate Judge Moloto's concerns, and he dissented at trial. The crux of his argument is as follows:

3. In my view, providing assistance to the VRS to wage war cannot and should not be equated with aiding and abetting the crimes committed during such war. The provision of assistance by Perišić to the VRS is too remote from the crimes committed during the war to qualify as aiding and abetting such crimes. To conclude otherwise, as the Majority has done, is to criminalise the waging of war, which is not a crime according to the Statute of the Tribunal. In addition, it raises the question: where is the cut-off line? For instance, would a manufacturer of weapons who supplies an army with weapons which are then used to commit crimes during a war also be criminally responsible?

Do you agree? Is prosecuting one party for the provision of assistance to an armed group known to commit international crimes the equivalent of the penalization of war? Review the definition of the crime of aggression discussed in Chapter 8 in formulating your answer.

4. Charles Taylor

The former President of Liberia, Charles Taylor, was prosecuted by the SCSL. The *Taylor* case is notable in that Taylor is not a Sierra Leonean national and appears not to have set foot in Sierra Leone during the indictment period, and yet he was prosecuted for his contributions from Liberia to crimes committed in neighboring Sierra Leone. Liberia was not a party to the SCSL Agreement between Sierra Leone and the United Nations, although it did not object to the prosecution. Indeed, newly-elected President Johnson Sirleaf appealed to Nigeria, where Taylor had taken refuge after stepping down from the presidency, to surrender him to the SCSL.

Taylor was indicted for aiding and abetting the crimes of militia groups active in the armed conflict in Sierra Leone. He was accused of providing a whole range of forms of support even while geographically distant. The Appeals Chamber of the SCSL held that the *actus reus* of aiding and abetting liability consists of the provision of assistance (even so-called neutral assistance in contradistinction to assistance that is inherently criminal) that has a "substantial effect" on the commission of crimes, although this assistance need not rise to the level of a "but for" contribution. Strict causation is thus not an element of aiding and abetting. Forms of moral support and encouragement are actionable in addition to more practical or tangible forms of assistance. In addition, such assistance may be provided at all stages of the crime, including planning, preparation, and execution. It is of no moment that an aider or abettor acts at a time and place removed from the actual crime if the substantial effect of his or her conduct is proven.

Most importantly, the SCSL Appeals Chamber also rejected *Perišić* and held that to gain a conviction, customary international law (CIL) does not require the prosecution to prove that the defendant provided "specific direction" aimed at the commission of particular crimes or to the direct perpetrators. The SCSL distinguished *Perišić* by reasoning that the ICTY did not undertake an empirical CIL analysis, but rather identified "specific direction" as a factor unique to "internally binding" ICTY precedent that was raised primarily in a discussion about the difference between liability as an accomplice and as a participant in a joint criminal enterprise. As such, the Special Court determined that there were no compelling reasons to follow the ruling in the *Perišić* case. Unlike in *Bemba*, it was of no moment that Taylor was "remote" from the events in question. *See Prosecutor v. Charles Ghankay Taylor*, Case No. SCSL–03–01–A, Judgement, para. 452 et seq. (Sept. 26, 2013). The *Taylor* judgment marked the end of the SCSL's activities, although legacy issues continue to be dealt with by the Residual Special Court for Sierra Leone (RSCSL).

The *Taylor* case is also unique in that it involves the prosecution of a former head of state, and the concomitant abrogation of any head-of-state immunity. (Taylor became President of Liberia in 1997; upon his indictment in 2003, he went into exile in Nigeria, where he was arrested in 2006). The judgment is thus the first contested conviction by an international court for war crimes and crimes against humanity of a former head of state since Nuremberg.

5. Foreign Assistance to Armed Groups, Redux

The issue of foreign assistance to armed groups was squarely presented in the *Taylor* proceedings. Taylor's counsel argued that states have the right to supply materiel to parties to an armed conflict even if there is evidence that those parties are engaged in the regular commission of crimes. The Prosecution countered that states do not "assert a prerogative to aid and abet armed groups knowing that the group uses an operational strategy of terror against the civilian population, to aid and abet atrocities and to assist the commission of crimes against humanity and war crimes." The *Taylor* Appeals Chamber sided with the Prosecution in rejecting the defendant's claim that states may provide assistance to an armed group knowing that the group is committing war crimes. In so ruling, the Chamber cited the United States' Leahy Law (which actually appears in different incarnations in the Foreign Assistance Act of 1961 and the annual Department of Defense Appropriations Act when directed at the Departments of State and Defense, respectively) as an example of an effort to prevent such assistance from going to rights abusers. Quoting from the original text of the Foreign Assistance Act, the Chamber noted that the U.S.:

> prohibits funding to governments and foreign military units if they are "engaged in a consistent pattern of gross violations of internationally recognised human rights" or have "committed a gross violation of human rights," unless all necessary corrective steps have been taken.

Some exceptions apply, for example if "such country is taking effective steps to bring the responsible members of the security forces unit to justice" or if the Secretary of Defense waives the restrictions in the face of "extraordinary circumstances."

Likewise, the Appeals Chamber cited the recently-adopted Arms Trade Treaty (ATT), as evidence of emerging *opinio juris* and state practice. The ATT provides at Article 6(3) that:

> A State Party shall not authorize any transfer of conventional arms covered under Article 2(1) or of items covered under Article 3 or Article 4, if it has knowledge at the time of authorization that the arms or items would be used in the commission of genocide, crimes against humanity, grave breaches of the Geneva Conventions of 1949, attacks directed against civilian objects or civilians protected as such, or other war crimes as defined by international agreements to which it is a Party.

The Appeals Chamber noted that assistance to armed groups who commit isolated criminal acts can be distinguished from assistance to armed groups engaged in a campaign of abuses against a civilian population:

> Where the crime is an isolated act, the very fungibility of the means may establish that the accused is not sufficiently connected to the

> commission of the crime. Similarly, on the facts of a case, an accused's contribution to the causal stream leading to the commission of the crime may be insignificant or insubstantial, precluding a finding that his acts and conduct had a substantial effect on the crimes. In terms of the effect of an accused's acts and conduct on the commission of the crime through his assistance to a group or organisation, there is a readily apparent difference between an isolated crime and a crime committed in furtherance of a widespread and systematic attack on the civilian population. The jurisprudence provides further guidance, but it is the differences between the facts of given cases that are decisive.

Do states interested in assisting one or more sides in an armed conflict have anything to fear from the *Taylor* ruling? What limiting principles might be employed? Notwithstanding the fungibility of aid, might the type of aid matter as the donor state moves along the continuum from humanitarian aid to dual-use equipment to lethal aid to illicit forms of assistance (such as the ingredients to create chemical weapons)?

6. For Further Reading

For more on complicity liability, *see* Michael S. Moore, *Causing, Aiding, and the Superfluity of Accomplice Liability,* 156 U. PA. L. REV. 395 (2007); Joshua Dressler, *Reassessing the Theoretical Underpinnings of Accomplice Liability*, 37 HASTINGS L. J. 91 (1985); Sanford Kadish, *Complicity, Cause and Blame: A Study in the Interpretation of the Doctrine*, 73 CAL. L. REV. 323 (1985); Grace E. Mueller, Note, *The* Mens Rea *of Accomplice Liability*, S. CAL. L. REV. 2169 (1988); Gary R. Ostos-Irwin, *Wisconsin's Party to a Crime Statute: The* Mens Rea *Element Under the Aiding and Abetting Subsection, and Aiding and Abetting-Choate Conspiracy Distinction*, 1984 WIS. L. REV. 769; Paul H. Robinson, *Imputed Criminal Liability*, 93 YALE L. J. 609 (1984). For a discussion of complicity under international law, *see* Markus D. Dubber, *Criminalizing Complicity: A Comparative Analysis*, 5 J. INT'L CRIM. JUST. 977 (2007); Anita Ramasastry, *Corporate Complicity: From Nuremberg to Rangoon; An Examination of Forced Labor Cases and Their Impact on the Liability of Multinational Corporations*, 20 BERKELEY J. INT'L L. 91 (2002).

IV. JOINT CRIMINAL ENTERPRISE

The joint criminal enterprise doctrine (also at times called the common purpose doctrine) finds early expression in international criminal law cases from the post-WWII period involving concentration camps and other institutions. For example, in the *Hadamar* case, individuals employed by a hospital as administrators, physicians, and nurses were jointly prosecuted for their role in killing ill Polish and Russian nationals who had been employed as forced laborers. The Prosecution argued the application of the common purpose doctrine as follows:

> At this Hadamar mill there was operated a production line of death. Not a single one of these accused could do all the things that were necessary in order to have the entire scheme of things

> in operation. For instance, the accused Klein, the administrative head, could not make the initial arrangements, receive those people, attend to undressing them, make arrangements for their death chamber, and at the same time go up there and use the needles that did the dirty work, and then also turn around and haul the bodies out and bury them, and falsify the records and the death sentences. No, when you do business on a wholesale production basis as they did at the Hadamar Institution, that murder factory, it means that you have to have several people doing different things of that illegal operation in order to produce the results, and you cannot draw a distinction between the man who may have initially conceived the idea of killing them and those who participated in the commission of those offenses. Now, there is no question but that any person who participated in that matter, no matter to what extent, technically is guilty of the charge that has been brought . . . every single one of the accused has overtly and affirmatively participated in this entire network that brought about the illegal result.

"The Hadamar Trial," The Trial of Alfons Klein and Six Others, I LAW REPORTS OF TRIALS OF WAR CRIMINALS 46 (U.S. Mil. Trib. 1948). Klein and two nurses were sentenced to death; other defendants received lesser sentences.

In the case below, the notion of the common purpose doctrine was revived after an ICTY Trial Chamber acquitted defendant Duško Tadić of his involvement in the killing of five people from the village of Jaskići after the group to which he belonged passed through the Prijedor municipality in an ethnic cleansing mission. Tadić had been indicted as follows:

> 12. About 14 June 1992, armed Serbs, including Duško TADIĆ, entered the area of Jaskići and Sivci in *opština* Prijedor and went from house to house calling out residents and separating men from the women and children. The armed Serbs killed Sakib Elkasević, Osme Elkasević, Alija Javor, Abaz Jaskić and Nijaz Jaskić in front of their homes. They also beat Meho Kenjar, Adam Jakupović, Salko Jaskić, Ismet Jaskić, Beido Balić, Sefik Balić, Nijas Elkasević and Ilijas Elkasević and then took them from the area to an unknown location. By his participation in these acts, Duško Tadić committed: [the grave breaches of wilful killing and wilfully causing great suffering or serious injury to body or health, and the war crime and crime against humanity of murder.]

The Prosecution appealed, arguing that the Trial Chamber had erred when it decided that it could not, on the evidence before it, be satisfied beyond reasonable doubt that the accused had played any part in the killing of the five men from the village of Jaskići. The Appeals Chamber reversed the acquittal as follows.

Prosecutor v. Tadić, Case No. IT–94–1–A, Judgement (July 15, 1999)

In the Appeals Chamber

The Armed Group to Which the Appellant Belonged Committed the Killings

178. The Trial Chamber found, amongst other facts, that on 14 June 1992, the Appellant, with other armed men, participated in the removal of men, who had been separated from women and children, from the village of Sivci to the Keraterm camp, and also participated in the calling-out of residents, the separation of men from women and children, and the beating and taking away of men in the village of Jaskići. It also found that five men were killed in the latter village. * * *

181. * * * [F]our of them were shot in the head. Nothing else as to who might have killed them or in what circumstances was known. The Trial Chamber referred, however, to the large force of Serb soldiers, of which the Appellant was a member, that invaded the nearby village of Sivci on the same day, without any villager there being killed. It then stated that the:

> possibility that the deaths of the Jaskići villagers were the result of encountering a part of that large force [of Serb soldiers that invaded Sivci] would be enough, in the state of the evidence, or rather, the lack of it, relating to their deaths, to prevent satisfaction beyond reasonable doubt that the accused was involved in those deaths.

182. The Trial Chamber did not allude to any witness suggesting that another group of armed men might have been responsible for the killing of the five men. In fact, none of the witnesses suggested anything to that effect.

183. In the light of the facts found by the Trial Chamber, the Appeals Chamber holds that, in relation to the possibility that another armed group killed the five men, the Trial Chamber misapplied the test of proof beyond reasonable doubt. On the facts found, the only reasonable conclusion the Trial Chamber could have drawn is that the armed group to which the Appellant belonged killed the five men in Jaskići. * * *

The Individual Criminal Responsibility of the Appellant for the Killings

185. The question therefore arises whether under international criminal law the Appellant can be held criminally responsible for the killing of the five men from Jaskići even though there is no evidence that he personally killed any of them. The two central issues are:

(i) whether the acts of one person can give rise to the criminal culpability of another where both participate in the execution of a common criminal plan; and

(ii) what degree of *mens rea* is required in such a case.

186. The basic assumption must be that in international law as much as in national systems, the foundation of criminal responsibility is the principle of personal culpability: nobody may be held criminally responsible for acts or transactions in which he has not personally engaged or in some other way participated (*nulla poena sine culpa*) ["no punishment without fault"]. In national legal systems this principle is laid down in Constitutions, in laws, or in judicial decisions. In international criminal law the principle is laid down, *inter alia,* in Article 7(1) of the Statute of the International Tribunal which states that:

> A person who planned, instigated, ordered, committed or otherwise aided and abetted in the planning, preparation or execution of a crime referred to in Articles 2 to 5 of the present Statute, shall be *individually responsible* for the crime. (Emphasis added). * * *

Article 7(1) sets out the parameters of personal criminal responsibility under the Statute. Any act falling under one of the five categories contained in the provision may entail the criminal responsibility of the perpetrator or whoever has participated in the crime in one of the ways specified in the same provision of the Statute.

187. Bearing in mind the preceding general propositions, it must be ascertained whether criminal responsibility for participating in a common criminal purpose falls within the ambit of Article 7(1) of the Statute. * * *

189. An interpretation of the Statute based on its object and purpose leads to the conclusion that the Statute intends to extend the jurisdiction of the International Tribunal to *all* those "responsible for serious violations of international humanitarian law" committed in the former Yugoslavia (Article 1). As is apparent from the wording of both Article 7(1) and the provisions setting forth the crimes over which the International Tribunal has jurisdiction (Articles 2 to 5), such responsibility for serious violations of international humanitarian law is not limited merely to those who actually carry out the *actus reus* of the enumerated crimes but appears to extend also to other offenders (see in particular Article 2, which refers to committing or ordering to be committed grave breaches of the Geneva Conventions and Article 4 which sets forth various types of offences in relation to genocide, including conspiracy, incitement, attempt and complicity). * * *

190. * * * Thus, all those who have engaged in serious violations of international humanitarian law, whatever the manner in which they may have perpetrated, or participated in the perpetration of those violations, must be brought to justice. If this is so, it is fair to conclude

that the Statute does not confine itself to providing for jurisdiction over those persons who plan, instigate, order, physically perpetrate a crime or otherwise aid and abet in its planning, preparation or execution. The Statute does not stop there. It does not exclude those modes of participating in the commission of crimes which occur where several persons having a common purpose embark on criminal activity that is then carried out either jointly or by some members of this plurality of persons. Whoever contributes to the commission of crimes by the group of persons or some members of the group, in execution of a common criminal purpose, may be held to be criminally liable, subject to certain conditions, which are specified below.

191. The above interpretation is not only dictated by the object and purpose of the Statute but is also warranted by the very nature of many international crimes which are committed most commonly in wartime situations. Most of the time these crimes do not result from the criminal propensity of single individuals but constitute manifestations of collective criminality: the crimes are often carried out by groups of individuals acting in pursuance of a common criminal design. Although only some members of the group may physically perpetrate the criminal act (murder, extermination, wanton destruction of cities, towns or villages, etc.), the participation and contribution of the other members of the group is often vital in facilitating the commission of the offence in question. It follows that the moral gravity of such participation is often no less—or indeed no different—from that of those actually carrying out the acts in question.

192. Under these circumstances, to hold criminally liable as a perpetrator only the person who materially performs the criminal act would disregard the role as co-perpetrators of all those who in some way made it possible for the perpetrator physically to carry out that criminal act. At the same time, depending upon the circumstances, to hold the latter liable only as aiders and abettors might understate the degree of their criminal responsibility. * * *

194. However, the Tribunal's Statute does not specify (either expressly or by implication) the objective and subjective elements (*actus reus* and *mens rea*) of this category of collective criminality. To identify these elements one must turn to customary international law. Customary rules on this matter are discernible on the basis of various elements: chiefly case law and a few instances of international legislation.

195. Many post-World War II cases concerning war crimes proceed upon the principle that when two or more persons act together to further a common criminal purpose, offences perpetrated by any of them may entail the criminal liability of all the members of the group. Close scrutiny of the relevant case law shows that broadly speaking, the notion of common purpose encompasses three distinct categories of collective criminality.

196. The first such category is represented by cases where all co-defendants, acting pursuant to a common design, possess the same criminal intention; for instance, the formulation of a plan among the co-perpetrators to kill, where, in effecting this common design (and even if each co-perpetrator carries out a different role within it), they nevertheless all possess the intent to kill. The objective and subjective prerequisites for imputing criminal responsibility to a participant who did not, or cannot be proven to have, effected the killing are as follows: (i) the accused must voluntarily participate in one aspect of the common design (for instance, by inflicting non-fatal violence upon the victim, or by providing material assistance to or facilitating the activities of his co-perpetrators); and (ii) the accused, even if not personally effecting the killing, must nevertheless intend this result.

197. With regard to this category, reference can be made to the *Georg Otto Sandrock et al.* case (also known as the *Almelo Trial*). There a British court found that three Germans who had killed a British prisoner of war were guilty under the doctrine of "common enterprise." It was clear that they all had had the intention of killing the British soldier, although each of them played a different role. They therefore were all co-perpetrators of the crime of murder.[234] * * *

199. It can be noted that some cases appear broadly to link the notion of common purpose to that of causation. In this regard, the *Ponzano* case, which concerned the killing of four British prisoners of war in violation of the rules of warfare, can be mentioned. Here, the Judge Advocate adopted the approach suggested by the Prosecutor, and stressed:

> the requirement that an accused, before he can be found guilty, must have been concerned in the offence. [T]o be concerned in the commission of a criminal offence [. . .] does not only mean that you are the person who in fact inflicted the fatal injury and directly caused death, be it by shooting or by any other violent means; it also means an indirect degree of participation [. . .]. [I]n other words, he must be the cog in the wheel of events

---

[234] The accused were German non-commissioned officers who had executed a British prisoner of war and a Dutch civilian in the house of whom the British airman was hiding. On the occasion of each execution one of the Germans had fired the lethal shot, another had given the order and a third had remained by the car used to go to a wood on the outskirts of the Dutch town of Almelo, to prevent people from coming near while the shooting took place. The Prosecutor stated that "the analogy which seemed to him most fitting in this case was that of a gangster crime, every member of the gang being equally responsible with the man who fired the actual shot." In his summing up the Judge Advocate pointed out that:

> There is no dispute, as I understand it, that all three [Germans] knew what they were doing and had gone there for the very purpose of having this officer killed; and, as you know, if people are all present together at the same time taking part in a common enterprise which is unlawful, each one in their (*sic*) own way assisting the common purpose of all, they are all equally guilty in point of law.

All the accused were found guilty, but those who had ordered the shooting or carried out the shooting were sentenced to death, whereas the others were sentenced to fifteen years imprisonment.

> leading up to the result which in fact occurred. He can further that object not only by giving orders for a criminal offence to be committed, but he can further that object by a variety of other means. [. . .]

Further on, the Judge Advocate submitted that while the defendant's involvement in the criminal acts must form a link in the chain of causation, it was not necessary that his participation be a *sine qua non,* or that the offence would not have occurred but for his participation.[242] Consonant with the twin requirements of criminal responsibility under this category, however, the Judge Advocate stressed the necessity of knowledge on the part of the accused as to the intended purpose of the criminal enterprise. * * *

202. The second distinct category of cases is in many respects similar to that set forth above, and embraces the so-called "concentration camp" cases. The notion of common purpose was applied to instances where the offences charged were alleged to have been committed by members of military or administrative units such as those running concentration camps; i.e., by groups of persons acting pursuant to a concerted plan. Cases illustrative of this category are *Dachau Concentration Camp,* decided by a United States court sitting in Germany and *Belsen* decided by a British military court sitting in Germany. In these cases the accused held some position of authority within the hierarchy of the concentration camps. Generally speaking, the charges against them were that they had acted in pursuance of a common design to kill or mistreat prisoners and hence to commit war crimes.[250] In his summing up in the *Belsen* case, the Judge Advocate adopted the three requirements identified by the Prosecution as necessary to establish guilt in each case: (i) the existence of an organised system to ill-treat the detainees and commit the various crimes alleged; (ii) the accused's awareness of the nature of the system; and (iii) the fact that the accused in some way actively participated in enforcing the system, i.e., encouraged, aided and abetted or in any case participated in the realisation of the common criminal design. The convictions of several of the accused appear to have been explicitly based upon these criteria.

---

242 In this regard, the Judge Advocate noted that: "[o]f course, it is quite possible that [the criminal offence] might have taken place in the absence of all these accused here, but that does not mean the same thing as saying [. . .] that [the accused] could not be a chain in the link of causation [. . .]."

250 *See Dachau Concentration Camp* case, UNWCC, vol. XI, p. 14:

> It seems, therefore, that what runs throughout the whole of this case, like a thread, is this: that there was in the camp a general system of cruelties and murders of the inmates (most of whom were allied nationals) and that this system was practiced with the knowledge of the accused, who were members of the staff, and with their active participation. Such a course of conduct, then, was held by the court in this case to constitute "acting in pursuance of a common design to violate the laws and usages of war." Everybody who took any part in such common design was held guilty of a war crime, though the nature and extent of the participation may vary.

203. This category of cases (which obviously is not applicable to the facts of the present case) is really a variant of the first category, considered above. The accused, when they were found guilty, were regarded as co-perpetrators of the crimes of ill-treatment, because of their objective "position of authority" within the concentration camp system and because they had "the power to look after the inmates and make their life satisfactory" but failed to do so. It would seem that in these cases the required *actus reus* was the active participation in the enforcement of a system of repression, as it could be inferred from the position of authority and the specific functions held by each accused. The *mens rea* element comprised: (i) knowledge of the nature of the system and (ii) the intent to further the common concerted design to ill-treat inmates. It is important to note that, in these cases, the requisite intent could also be inferred from the position of authority held by the camp personnel. Indeed, it was scarcely necessary to prove intent where the individual's high rank or authority would have, in and of itself, indicated an awareness of the common design and an intent to participate therein. All those convicted were found guilty of the war crime of ill-treatment, although of course the penalty varied according to the degree of participation of each accused in the commission of the war crime.

204. The third category concerns cases involving a common design to pursue one course of conduct where one of the perpetrators commits an act which, while outside the common design, was nevertheless a natural and foreseeable consequence of the effecting of that common purpose. An example of this would be a common, shared intention on the part of a group to forcibly remove members of one ethnicity from their town, village or region (to effect "ethnic cleansing") with the consequence that, in the course of doing so, one or more of the victims is shot and killed. While murder may not have been explicitly acknowledged to be part of the common design, it was nevertheless foreseeable that the forcible removal of civilians at gunpoint might well result in the deaths of one or more of those civilians. Criminal responsibility may be imputed to all participants within the common enterprise where the risk of death occurring was both a predictable consequence of the execution of the common design and the accused was either reckless or indifferent to that risk. Another example is that of a common plan to forcibly evict civilians belonging to a particular ethnic group by burning their houses; if some of the participants in the plan, in carrying out this plan, kill civilians by setting their houses on fire, all the other participants in the plan are criminally responsible for the killing if these deaths were predictable.

205. The case-law in this category has concerned first of all cases of mob violence, that is, situations of disorder where multiple offenders act out a common purpose, where each of them commit offences against the victim, but where it is unknown or impossible to ascertain exactly which acts were carried out by which perpetrator, or when the causal link

between each act and the eventual harm caused to the victims is similarly indeterminate. * * *

206. As is set forth in more detail below, the requirements which are established by these authorities are two-fold: that of a criminal intention to participate in a common criminal design and the foreseeability that criminal acts other than those envisaged in the common criminal design are likely to be committed by other participants in the common design. * * *

220. In sum, the Appeals Chamber holds the view that the notion of common design as a form of accomplice liability is firmly established in customary international law and in addition is upheld, albeit implicitly, in the Statute of the International Tribunal. As for the objective and subjective elements of the crime, the case law shows that the notion has been applied to three distinct categories of cases. First, in cases of co-perpetration, where all participants in the common design possess the same criminal intent to commit a crime (and one or more of them actually perpetrate the crime, with intent). Secondly, in the so-called "concentration camp" cases, where the requisite *mens rea* comprises knowledge of the nature of the system of ill-treatment and intent to further the common design of ill-treatment. Such intent may be proved either directly or as a matter of inference from the nature of the accused's authority within the camp or organisational hierarchy. With regard to the third category of cases, it is appropriate to apply the notion of "common purpose" only where the following requirements concerning *mens rea* are fulfilled: (i) the intention to take part in a joint criminal enterprise and to further—individually and jointly—the criminal purposes of that enterprise; and (ii) the foreseeability of the possible commission by other members of the group of offences that do not constitute the object of the common criminal purpose. Hence, the participants must have had in mind the intent, for instance, to ill-treat prisoners of war (even if such a plan arose extemporaneously) and one or some members of the group must have actually killed them. In order for responsibility for the deaths to be imputable to the others, however, everyone in the group must have been able to *predict* this result. It should be noted that more than negligence is required. What is required is a state of mind in which a person, although he did not intend to bring about a certain result, was aware that the actions of the group were most likely to lead to that result but nevertheless willingly took that risk. In other words, the so-called *dolus eventualis* is required (also called "advertent recklessness" in some national legal systems).

221. In addition to the aforementioned case law, the notion of common plan has been upheld in at least two international treaties. The first of these is the International Convention for the Suppression of Terrorist Bombing, adopted by consensus by the United Nations General Assembly through resolution 52/164 of 15 December 1997 and opened for signature on 9 January 1998. Pursuant to Article 2(3)(c) of the

Convention, offences envisaged in the Convention may be committed by any person who:

> [i]n any other way [other than participating as an accomplice, or organising or directing others to commit an offence] contributes to the commission of one or more offences as set forth in paragraphs 1 or 2 of the present article by a group of persons acting with a common purpose; such contribution shall be intentional and either be made with the aim of furthering the general criminal activity or purpose of the group or be made in the knowledge of the intention of the group to commit the offence or offences concerned.

The negotiating process does not shed any light on the reasons behind the adoption of this text. This Convention would seem to be significant because it upholds the notion of a "common criminal purpose" as distinct from that of aiding and abetting (couched in the terms of "participating as an accomplice [in] an offence"). Although the Convention is not yet in force, one should not underestimate the fact that it was adopted by consensus by all the members of the General Assembly. It may therefore be taken to constitute significant evidence of the legal views of a large number of States.

222. A substantially similar notion was subsequently laid down in Article 25 of the Statute of the International Criminal Court, adopted by a Diplomatic Conference in Rome on 17 July 1998 ("Rome Statute"). At paragraph 3(d), this provision upholds the doctrine under discussion as follows:

> [In accordance with this Statute, a person shall be criminally responsible and liable for punishment for a crime within the jurisdiction of the Court if that person . . .]
>
> (d) In any other way [other than aiding and abetting or otherwise assisting in the commission or attempted commission of a crime] contributes to the commission or attempted commission of such a crime by a group of persons acting with a common purpose. Such contribution shall be intentional and shall either:
>
> i. Be made with the aim of furthering the criminal activity or criminal purpose of the group, where such activity or purpose involves the commission of a crime within the jurisdiction of the Court; or
>
> ii. Be made in the knowledge of the intention of the group to commit the crime.

223. The legal weight to be currently attributed to the provisions of the Rome Statute has been correctly set out by Trial Chamber II in *Furundžija*. There the Trial Chamber pointed out that the Statute is still a non-binding international treaty, for it has not yet entered into force. Nevertheless, it already possesses significant legal value. The Statute

was adopted by an overwhelming majority of the States attending the Rome Diplomatic Conference and was substantially endorsed by the Sixth Committee of the United Nations General Assembly. This shows that that text is supported by a great number of States and may be taken to express the legal position i.e. *opinio juris* of those States. This is consistent with the view that the mode of accomplice liability under discussion is well-established in international law and is distinct from aiding and abetting.[282] * * *

226. The Appeals Chamber considers that the consistency and cogency of the case law and the treaties referred to above, as well as their consonance with the general principles on criminal responsibility laid down both in the Statute and general international criminal law and in national legislation, warrant the conclusion that case law reflects customary rules of international criminal law.

227. In sum, the objective elements (*actus reus*) of this mode of participation in one of the crimes provided for in the Statute (with regard to each of the three categories of cases) are as follows:

i. *A plurality of persons.* They need not be organised in a military, political or administrative structure, as is clearly shown by the *Essen Lynching* and the *Kurt Goebell* cases.

ii. *The existence of a common plan, design or purpose which amounts to or involves the commission of a crime provided for in the Statute.* There is no necessity for this plan, design or purpose to have been previously arranged or formulated. The common plan or purpose may materialise extemporaneously and be inferred from the fact that a plurality of persons acts in unison to put into effect a joint criminal enterprise.

iii. *Participation of the accused in the common design* involving the perpetration of one of the crimes provided for in the Statute. This participation need not involve commission of a specific crime under one of those provisions (for example, murder, extermination, torture, rape, etc.), but may take the form of assistance in, or contribution to, the execution of the common plan or purpose.

228. By contrast, the *mens rea* element differs according to the category of common design under consideration. With regard to the first category, what is required is the intent to perpetrate a certain crime (this

282 Even should it be argued that the objective and subjective elements of the crime, laid down in Article 25(3) of the Rome Statute differ to some extent from those required by the case law cited above, the consequences of this departure may only be appreciable in the long run, once the Court is established. This is due to the inapplicability to Article 25(3) of Article 10 of the Statute, which provides that "[n]othing in this Part shall be interpreted as limiting or prejudicing in any way existing or developing rules of international law for purposes other than this Statute." This provision does not embrace Article 25, as this Article appears in Part 2 of the Statute, whereas Article 25 is included in Part 3.

being the shared intent on the part of all co-perpetrators). With regard to the second category (which, as noted above, is really a variant of the first), personal knowledge of the system of ill-treatment is required (whether proved by express testimony or a matter of reasonable inference from the accused's position of authority), as well as the intent to further this common concerted system of ill-treatment. With regard to the third category, what is required is the *intention* to participate in and further the criminal activity or the criminal purpose of a group and to contribute to the joint criminal enterprise or in any event to the commission of a crime by the group. In addition, responsibility for a crime other than the one agreed upon in the common plan arises only if, under the circumstances of the case, (i) it was *foreseeable* that such a crime might be perpetrated by one or other members of the group and (ii) the accused *willingly took that risk.*

229. In light of the preceding propositions it is now appropriate to distinguish between acting in pursuance of a common purpose or design to commit a crime, and aiding and abetting.

(i) The aider and abettor is always an accessory to a crime perpetrated by another person, the principal.

(ii) In the case of aiding and abetting no proof is required of the existence of a common concerted plan, let alone of the pre-existence of such a plan. No plan or agreement is required: indeed, the principal may not even know about the accomplice's contribution.

(iii) The aider and abettor carries out acts specifically directed to assist, encourage or lend moral support to the perpetration of a certain specific crime (murder, extermination, rape, torture, wanton destruction of civilian property, etc.), and this support has a substantial effect upon the perpetration of the crime. By contrast, in the case of acting in pursuance of a common purpose or design, it is sufficient for the participant to perform acts that in some way are directed to the furthering of the common plan or purpose.

(iv) In the case of aiding and abetting, the requisite mental element is knowledge that the acts performed by the aider and abettor assist the commission of a specific crime by the principal. By contrast, in the case of common purpose or design more is required (i.e., either intent to perpetrate the crime or intent to pursue the common criminal design plus foresight that those crimes outside the criminal common purpose were likely to be committed), as stated above.

The Culpability of the Appellant in the Present Case

230. In the present case, the Trial Chamber found that the Appellant participated in the armed conflict taking place between May

and December 1992 in the Prijedor region. An aspect of this conflict was a policy to commit inhumane acts against the non-Serb civilian population of the territory in the attempt to achieve the creation of a Greater Serbia. It was also found that, in furtherance of this policy, inhumane acts were committed against numerous victims and "pursuant to a recognisable plan." The attacks on Sivci and Jaskići on 14 June 1992 formed part of this armed conflict raging in the Prijedor region.

231. The Appellant actively took part in the common criminal purpose to rid the Prijedor region of the non-Serb population, by committing inhumane acts. The common criminal purpose was not to kill all non-Serb men; from the evidence adduced and accepted, it is clear that killings frequently occurred in the effort to rid the Prijedor region of the non-Serb population. That the Appellant had been aware of the killings accompanying the commission of inhumane acts against the non-Serb population is beyond doubt. That is the context in which the attack on Jaskići and his participation therein, as found by the Trial Chamber as well as the Appeals Chamber above, should be seen. That nobody was killed in the attack on Sivci on the same day does not represent a change of the common criminal purpose.

232. The Appellant was an armed member of an armed group that, in the context of the conflict in the Prijedor region, attacked Jaskići on 14 June 1992. The Trial Chamber found the following:

> Of the killing of the five men in Jaskići, the witnesses * * * saw their five dead bodies lying in the village when the women were able to leave their houses after the armed men had gone; Senija Elkasović saw that four of them had been shot in the head. She had heard shooting after the men from her house were taken away.

The Appellant actively took part in this attack, rounding up and severely beating some of the men from Jaskići. * * * Accordingly, the only possible inference to be drawn is that the Appellant had the intention to further the criminal purpose to rid the Prijedor region of the non-Serb population, by committing inhumane acts against them. That non-Serbs might be killed in the effecting of this common aim was, in the circumstances of the present case, foreseeable. The Appellant was aware that the actions of the group of which he was a member were likely to lead to such killings, but he nevertheless willingly took that risk.

233. The Trial Chamber erred in holding that it could not, on the evidence before it, be satisfied beyond reasonable doubt that the Appellant had any part in the killing of the five men from the village of Jaskići. The Appeals Chamber finds that the Appellant participated in the killings of the five men in Jaskići, which were committed during an armed conflict as part of a widespread or systematic attack on a civilian population. The Appeals Chamber therefore holds that under the provisions of Article 7(1) of the Statute, the Trial Chamber should have found the Appellant guilty.

NOTES & QUESTIONS

1. The Common Purpose Doctrine and Article 7(1)

Examine Article 7(1) of the ICTY Statute. How can the Appeals Chamber convict Tadić under a common purpose theory of liability when that form of responsibility is not enumerated in Article 7(1)? As is clear from the Indictment excerpt above, the Prosecution had not charged Tadić with participating in a common purpose or joint criminal enterprise; rather, this argument was raised on appeal. Did the Appeals Chamber in effect amend Tadić's Indictment, or the ICTY Statute for that matter? If the ICTY Statute is broad enough to encompass all three forms of the joint criminal enterprise liability, is it broad enough to encompass conspiracy to commit war crimes and crimes against humanity as well? Is joint criminal enterprise liability truly a form of commission or complicity liability, or is it merely conspiracy liability by another name? Can you imagine a case in which an individual would be acquitted on a conspiracy theory, but convicted on the basis of the joint criminal enterprise doctrine or vice versa?

2. *Pinkerton* Liability

The extended or "Type 3" form of the doctrine provides that individuals may be held liable for all crimes that are a natural and foreseeable consequence of acting according to the common purpose. In this way, the ICTY adopted the so-called *Pinkerton* doctrine from United States conspiracy law. In *Pinkerton v. United States*, 328 U.S. 640 (1946), the U.S. Supreme Court ratified the principle that co-conspirators are essentially accomplices to any crimes actually committed by other persons involved in the conspiracy in furtherance of the common purpose of the agreement. No additional proof of aiding or abetting is required.

In *Pinkerton*, two brothers were prosecuted for tax evasion. Brother 1 was imprisoned for a different prior offense at the time that brother 2 acted. Nonetheless, brother 1's conviction for crimes committed by brother 2 in the execution of the conspiracy between them was upheld. *Id.* at 645–647. In dissent, Justice Rutledge, who also dissented in the *Yamashita* case discussed *supra* in Chapter 14, argued that the principle announced "either convicts one man for another's crime or punishes the man convicted twice for the same offense." *Id.* at 649 (Rutledge, J. dissenting). He reasoned:

> The looseness with which the charge may be proved, the almost unlimited scope of vicarious responsibility for others' acts which follows once agreement is shown, the psychological advantages of such trials for securing convictions by attributing to one proof against another, these and other inducements require that the broad limits of discretion allowed to prosecuting officers in relation to such charges and trials be not expanded into new, wider and more dubious areas of choice.

Id. at 650. Three years later, Justice Jackson, having returned to the Supreme Court from his service in Nuremberg, objected strongly to the *Pinkerton* doctrine for sustaining "a conviction of a substantive crime where there was no proof of participation in or knowledge of it, upon the novel and dubious theory that conspiracy is equivalent in law to aiding and abetting."

Krulewitch v. United States, 336 U.S. 440, 451 (1949) (Jackson, J., concurring).

The full application of *Pinkerton* has been criticized, even within common law systems, as an overly expansive application of liability. Alternatively, some jurisdictions apply a "natural and probable consequences" rule, which allows for the imposition of liability only when the co-conspirator should have known that particular acts were to be committed in furtherance of the objectives of the conspiracy. In other words, liability is limited to offenses that are reasonably foreseeable consequences of executing the criminal agreement. The natural and probable consequences rule generally requires the prosecution to demonstrate that the crimes were committed in furtherance of the objectives of the conspiracy and the crimes were a natural and probable consequence of the conspiracy (i.e. foreseeable). The drafters of the U.S. Model Penal Code, for example, diverged from common law doctrine and rejected the *Pinkerton* doctrine, noting that "the law would lose all sense of just proportion if simply because of the conspiracy itself each [co-conspirator] were accountable for thousands of additional offenses of which he was completely unaware and which he did not influence at all." § 2.06, Comment at 307 (1985).

If ethnic cleansing is the object of a joint criminal enterprise, what other international crimes are "natural and foreseeable?" Presumably, deportation and/or forcible transfer directed at a civilian population would be within the object of the enterprise. What about unlawful detention or torture? Is the commission of genocide natural and foreseeable? Where torture is practiced, is summary execution natural and foreseeable? Where civilian objects are deliberately targeted, are crimes against humanity natural and foreseeable? Does the requirement of foreseeability have any limiting power? Or, in a situation of mass violence or armed conflict, are all international crimes foreseeable?

3. *Mens Rea*

The required state of mind of the accused differs according to whether the crime charged was within the object of the joint criminal enterprise or whether it went beyond the object of that enterprise. In the opinion above, the Appeals Chamber formulates the *mens rea* standard of a Type 3 joint criminal enterprise in at least three different ways:

> Para. 204: "Criminal responsibility may be imputed to all participants within the common enterprise where the risk of death occurring was both a predictable consequence of the execution of the common design and the accused was either reckless or indifferent to that risk."
>
> Para. 220: "What is required is a state of mind in which a person, although he did not intend to bring about a certain result, was aware that the actions of the group were most likely to lead to that result but nevertheless willingly took that risk. In other words, the so-called *dolus eventualis* is required (also called 'advertent recklessness' in some national legal systems)."

> Para. 228: "[W]hat is required is the *intention* to participate in and further the criminal activity or the criminal purpose of a group and to contribute to the joint criminal enterprise or in any event to the commission of a crime by the group. In addition, responsibility for a crime other than the one agreed upon in the common plan arises only if, under the circumstances of the case, (i) it was *foreseeable* that such a crime might be perpetrated by one or other members of the group and (ii) the accused *willingly took that risk*."

Are these formulations identical or do they contain material differences? Each formulation contains a subjective and an objective component. In terms of a defendant's subjective intent, is there a distinction between a perception that an event is possible and a perception that an event is likely or probable? Which formulation places a greater burden on the prosecution? In terms of an objective *mens rea* component, is the fact that an event is predictable the equivalent to an event that is foreseeable? In a subsequent case, a Trial Chamber chose the following formulation:

> [I]n the case of a participant in the joint criminal enterprise who is charged with a crime committed by another participant which goes beyond the agreed object of that enterprise, the Trial Chamber interprets the *Tadić* Conviction Appeal Judgment as requiring the prosecution to establish:
>
> (i) that the crime was a natural and foreseeable consequence of the execution of that enterprise, and
>
> (ii) that the accused was aware that such a crime was a possible consequence of the execution of that enterprise, and that, with that awareness, he participated in that enterprise.
>
> The first is an *objective* element of the crime, and does not depend upon the state of mind on the part of the accused. The second is the *subjective* state of mind on the part of the accused which the prosecution must establish. None of the various formulations in [the] *Tadić* Conviction Appeal Judgement require the prosecution in such a case to establish that the accused intended such further crime to be committed, or that he shared with that other participant the state of mind required for that further crime.

Prosecutor v. Brđanin & Talic, Case No. IT–99–36–T, Decision on Form of Further Amended Indictment and Prosecution Application to Amend, para. 30 (June 26, 2001). Might the lesser *mens rea* standard associated with a "Type 3" joint criminal enterprise actually render a conviction easier to obtain than a conviction for a "Type 1" or "Type 2" joint criminal enterprise?

How does the *mens rea* of the doctrine of joint criminal enterprise interact with the *mens rea* element of specific intent crimes? In a genocide prosecution, for example, must all members of the joint criminal enterprise possess the intent to commit genocide? Or, may they be prosecuted where some other perpetrator acted with genocidal intent? Must this actor be a member of the original enterprise? The late Antonio Cassese, a prominent Italian jurist who was the first President of the ICTY, argued that Type 3 JCE should not apply to specific intent crimes like genocide. Antonio

Cassese, *The Proper Limits of Individual Responsibility under the Doctrine of Joint Criminal Enterprise*, 5 J. INT'L CRIM. JUST. 109 (2007). The ICTY declined to require a different *mens rea* for specific intent crimes under Type 3 JCE. *See Prosecutor v. Karadžić,* Case No. IT–95–5/18–T, para. 570 (Mar. 24, 2016).

4. The Reach of Type 3 Liability

Are there any limits to the doctrine of joint criminal enterprise or is it a "silver bullet" for the prosecution? Is a *de minimis* contribution to the enterprise sufficient to convict the defendant of all criminal results of the enterprise? Is it reasonable to allege that an entire rebel army, such as the army of the Republika Srpska (the VRS), is itself a joint criminal enterprise? (Recall that the Trial Chamber in *Perišić* declined to reach this conclusion). What about all inhabitants of a secessionist region, such as Republika Srpska? How would the doctrine apply in the Rwandan context? Could ICTR prosecutors allege that the elimination of the Tutsi population along with moderate Hutus constituted a national joint criminal enterprise and thus hold every perpetrator liable for every act of violence undertaken in furtherance of that goal? In contrast, should the prosecution confine its vision of a joint criminal enterprise to a discrete institution (such as a concentration camp), organization, or operation (such as the murders at Jaskići addressed in *Tadić*)? How would you narrow the charge doctrinally if warranted?

5. The Breadth of the JCE

In the *Brđanin* case, the prosecution alleged a broad joint criminal enterprise involving everyone from the President of Republika Srpska to members of the VRS and Serb paramilitary members. Both defendants challenged on multiple occasions the form of the Indictment, arguing that the Prosecution had not clearly pled the criminal object of the joint criminal enterprise or which crimes were within the object of the enterprise and which were beyond that object. During this process, the Prosecutor amended the Indictment against Brđanin six times and that against his co-defendant Talić four times. At one point, the Trial Chamber observed:

> 44. The Trial Chamber accepts that, where there could be a number of different criminal objects of a joint criminal enterprise, it is not necessary for the prosecution to prove that *every* participant agreed to every one of those crimes being committed. But it *is* necessary for the prosecution to prove that, between the person who personally perpetrated the further crime charged and the person charged with that crime, there was an agreement (or a common purpose) to commit at least *a* particular crime, so that it can then be determined whether the further crime charged was a natural and foreseeable consequence of executing *that* agreed crime. Without such proof, it cannot be held that the accused was a member of a joint criminal enterprise together with the person who committed that further crime charged. The real difficulty which the prosecution faces in identifying the agreed criminal object of the enterprise in which *these* accused were members together with the

persons who committed the crimes charged may lie in the extraordinarily wide nature of the case which it seeks to make in the present prosecution.

45. Although joint criminal enterprise cases *can* be applicable in relation to ethnic cleansing, as the *Tadić* Conviction Appeal Judgement recognises, it is obvious that the Appeals Chamber had in mind a somewhat smaller enterprise than that which is invoked in the present case.[146] If, in the course of an armed conflict and a widespread or systematic attack directed against a civilian population, the commander of a small group of soldiers directs those soldiers to collect all the inhabitants of a particular ethnicity within a particular town and to remove them forcibly out of the region, he becomes a participant in an enterprise to commit deportation and forcible transfer (as crimes against humanity), and there could be little doubt, having regard to previous episodes of ethnic cleansing in the former Yugoslavia, that, for example, murder (as another crime against humanity) and wanton destruction of the town (as a violation of the laws and customs of war) were natural and foreseeable consequences of the execution of that enterprise. There would be no difficulty in determining what crimes fell within the agreed criminal object of the enterprise and whether any further crimes charged were natural and foreseeable consequences in the execution of *that* enterprise. It is only when the prosecution seeks to include within that joint criminal enterprise persons as remote from the commission of the crimes charged as are the two accused in the present case that a difficulty arises in identifying the agreed criminal object of that enterprise. That difficulty is of the prosecution's own making, as it is a difficulty necessarily arising out of the case it seeks to make. That very difficulty *may*, of course, indicate that a case based upon a joint criminal enterprise is inappropriate in the circumstances of the present prosecution. That is a matter which will have to be determined at the trial. But the prosecution cannot avoid its difficulty simply by seeking to avoid pleading properly the joint criminal enterprise upon which it relies. It is sufficient at this stage for the Trial Chamber to say merely that, if the prosecution does plead that *all* of the crimes charged went *beyond* the object of the joint criminal enterprise, it must identify in the indictment the agreed criminal object of the enterprise upon which it relies.

Prosecutor v. Brđanin & Talić, Case No. IT–99–36–T, Decision on Form of Further Amended Indictment and Prosecution Application to Amend (June 26, 2001).

---

146 The example given in para. 204 [of *Tadić*] is of "a common, shared intention on the part of a group to forcibly remove members of one ethnicity from *their* town, village or region (to effect 'ethnic cleansing') with the consequence that, in the course of doing so, *one or more* of the victims is shot and killed."

6. Charging Preferences

According to one study, 64% of indictments confirmed by the ICTY since the emergence of the doctrine and prior to 2004 expressly included joint criminal enterprise allegations. Other indictments alleging that the defendant "acted in concert" have been interpreted to invoke the joint criminal enterprise doctrine, thus raising the percentage of indictments implicating the joint criminal enterprise doctrine to 81%. Allison Marston Danner & Jenny S. Martinez, *Guilty Associations: Joint Criminal Enterprise, Command Responsibility, and the Development of International Criminal Law*, 93 CALIF. L. REV. 75, 107 (2005). What explains this trend? Does JCE threaten to eclipse the doctrine of superior responsibility? Should it?

Some indictments craft the alleged joint criminal enterprise quite narrowly. For example, the indictment against Miroslav Deronjić, a President of several Serbian Crisis Staffs, accuses the defendant of participating in a joint criminal enterprise to bring about "the permanent removal, by force or other means, of Bosnian Muslim inhabitants from the village of Glogova." *Prosecutor v. Deronjić*, Case No. IT–02–62, ICTY Second Amended Indictment, para. 3 (Sept. 29, 2004). In comparison, the Indictment against Milan Martić, the self-proclaimed president of the Serb Krajina, accuses the defendant of participating in a joint criminal enterprise aimed at "the forcible removal of a majority of the Croat, Muslim and other non-Serb population from approximately one-third of the territory of the Republic of Croatia * * * and large parts of the Republic of Bosnia and Herzegovina." *Prosecutor v. Martić*, Case No. IT–95–11, Third Amended Indictment, para. 4 (July 14, 2003). Indeed, it is striking to compare the first Indictment confirmed against Martić with the final one. The first Indictment alleged a single count of war crimes involving the unlawful shelling of the city of Zagreb. *Prosecutor v. Martić*, Indictment, Case No. IT–95–11 (July 25, 1995). The opinion addressing the whole panoply of crimes is presented in Chapter 7 on War Crimes.

7. JCE and Other Forms of Liability

How does joint criminal enterprise liability compare with superior responsibility liability, complicity liability, the co-perpetration doctrine, and conspiracy liability? As between the various doctrines, which is easier to prove from the perspective of the prosecution? Which of the doctrines is easiest to defend against from the perspective of the defense? Some have quipped that JCE stands for "Just Convict Everyone"—do you agree? Does the joint criminal enterprise theory of responsibility have the potential to overlook different degrees of power, participation, and responsibility? By classifying everyone as co-participants, do tribunals risk overlooking the role that leaders play in instigating violence? Does the joint criminal enterprise doctrine reach criminal conduct that a straight complicity charge would not?

8. The ICC

The bulk of the ICTY joint criminal enterprise jurisprudence postdated the drafting of the ICC Statute. Yet, the ICC Statute does enumerate a version of the common purpose doctrine as a form of responsibility at Article 25. *See Tadić*, *supra*, at para. 222. As noted above, *Tadić* para. 221, Article

25's language is borrowed from Article 2(3) of the International Convention for the Suppression of Terrorist Bombings, UN GAOR, 52d Sess., Annex, Agenda Item 152, U.N. Doc. A/RES/52/164 (1998). While this language was employed to facilitate prosecutions, it also provided a compromise between delegations from civil law and common law systems who differed over the propriety of including a general conspiracy provision. *See* Per Saland, *International Criminal Law Principles*, *in* THE INTERNATIONAL CRIMINAL COURT: THE MAKING OF THE ROME STATUTE 189, 199–200 (Roy S. Lee ed., 1999). How should the ICC interpret this concerted ambiguity? Is the common purpose doctrine as contained in Article 25 the equivalent of the JCE doctrine as articulated by the ICTY? Would it reach Type 3 JCEs? Is JCE an inchoate offense, like common law conspiracy, that may be prosecuted even in the absence of a substantive crime or is it a form of responsibility only?

V. CO-PERPETRATION

Article 25(3)(a) of the ICC Statute provides that a person may be found guilty if she commits "a crime, whether as an individual, jointly with another or through another person, regardless of whether that other person is criminally responsible." Drawing upon this language as well as German penal law concepts of *Organisationsherrschaft* ("control over an organization"), the ICC has developed theories of perpetration (the direct commission of a crime), co-perpetration (the commission of a crime jointly with another person), and indirect perpetration (the commission of a crime through another person, regardless of whether that other person is criminally responsible). When collective criminality involving a plurality of persons is at issue, German law distinguishes between principals and accessories based on the perpetrators' control over the crime or ability to exercise "hegemony over the act" (*tatherrschaft*). Those who are in control of the crime in terms of ensuring its realization or cessation (as direct perpetrators or the power behind an organization) are considered principals; all other participants are considered accessories. The ICC's Office of the Prosecutor has focused on the concept of co-perpetration in preliminary indictments rather than advancing theories of joint criminal enterprise, straight complicity, or superior responsibility as employed in the *ad hoc* tribunals. As you review the materials that follow, consider why this might be so. For a discussion of this variation in charging patterns, *see* Harmen G. van der Wilt, *The Continuous Quest for Proper Modes of Criminal Responsibility*, 7 J. INT'L CRIM. JUST. 307 (2009); Florian Jessberger & Julia Geneuss, *On The Application Of A Theory Of Indirect Perpetration In Al Bashir: German Doctrine At The Hague?*, 6 J. INT'L CRIM. JUST. 853 (2008).

The judgment that follows concerns Thomas Lubanga Dyilo ("Lubanga"), the first individual to be arrested and tried by the ICC. Lubanga founded the *Union des Patriots Congolais* (UPC) (later renamed *Union des Patriotes Congolais/Réconcilation et Paix*—Union of Congolese Patriots/Reconciliation and Peace (UPC/RP)), which included an armed military wing, the *Forces Patriotiques pour la Libération du Congo* (FPLC). The Prosecution sought to indict Lubanga—commander-in-chief of the FPLC—under Article 8(2)(e)(vii) of the ICC Statute for the war crime of conscripting and enlisting children under the age of fifteen years into the FPLC and using them to participate actively in hostilities. The classification of this conflict was discussed in Chapter 6. Lubanga's trial opened in January 2009. (See the Appendix for a map of the DRC.)

Prosecutor v. Lubanga, Case No. ICC–01/04–01/06, Judgment Pursuant to Article 74 of the Statute (March 14, 2012)

Trial Chamber 1

917. The prosecution charged Thomas Lubanga as a co-perpetrator under Article 25(3)(a) of the Statute, and the Pre-Trial Chamber confirmed the charges on this basis.[2595] * * *

Analysis

The Objective Requirements

976. In the view of the Majority, both the Romano Germanic and the Common Law legal systems have developed principles about modes of liability. However, at their inception, neither of these systems was intended to deal with the crimes under the jurisdiction of this Court, i.e. the most serious crimes of concern to the international community as a whole. The Statute sets out the modes of liability in Articles 25 and 28 and they should be interpreted in a way that allows properly expressing and addressing the responsibility for these crimes.

977. Articles 25(3)(a) to (d) establish the modes of individual criminal responsibility under the Statute, other than the "[r]esponsibility of commanders and other superiors," which is addressed in Article 28. Under Article 25(3)(a), an individual can be convicted of committing a crime: (i) individually; (ii) jointly with another; or (iii) through another person. Under Articles 25(3)(b) to (d), an individual can be convicted of: (i) ordering, soliciting or inducing a crime; (ii) acting as an accessory to a crime; or (iii) contributing to a crime committed by a group acting with a common purpose.

978. The Pre-Trial Chamber decided, pursuant to Article 61(7) of the Statute, there was sufficient evidence to establish substantial grounds to believe that Mr. Lubanga committed the crimes charged, under Article 25(3)(a), as a direct co-perpetrator. The Chamber will limit its analysis of Mr. Lubanga's responsibility to this mode of liability.

979. In considering the scope of liability under Article 25(3)(a) of the Rome Statute, the Chamber notes, as set out above, that the Appeals

---

[2595] *Prosecutor v. Lubanga*, Case No. ICC–01/04–01/06, Decision on the Confirmation of Charges, para.410 (Jan. 29, 2007).

Chamber has stated that the provisions of the Statute are to be interpreted in conformity with Article 31(1) of the Vienna Convention on the Law of Treaties. Hence, the relevant elements of Article 25(3)(a) of the Statute, that the individual "commits such a crime [. . .] jointly with another [. . .] person," must be interpreted in good faith in accordance with the ordinary meaning to be given to the language of the Statute, bearing in mind the relevant context and in light of its object and purpose.

The Common Plan or Agreement

980. Article 25(3)(a) stipulates that a crime can be committed not only by an individual acting by himself or through another person, but also by an individual who acts jointly with another. To establish liability as a co-perpetrator under Article 25(3)(a), it is necessary there are at least two individuals involved in the commission of the crime. This is evident from the use of terms "jointly with another" in Article 25(3)(a).

981. As the Pre-Trial Chamber concluded, co-perpetration requires the existence of an agreement or common plan between the co-perpetrators. This provides for a sufficient connection between the individuals who together commit the crime and it allows responsibility to be established on a "joint" basis.

982. As set out above, the Pre-Trial Chamber decided that the plan "must include 'an element of criminality,' although it does not need to be specifically directed at the commission of a crime." In the Confirmation Decision, it was held to be sufficient: (i) that the co-perpetrators have agreed: (a) to start the implementation of the common plan to achieve a non-criminal goal, and (b) to only commit the crime if certain conditions are met; or (ii) that the co-perpetrators (a) are aware of the risk that implementing the common plan (which is specifically directed at the achievement of a noncriminal goal) will result in the commission of the crime, and (b) accept such outcome.

983. While the prosecution supports this interpretation, the defence argues that in order to establish criminal liability on the basis of co-perpetration, the common plan must be intrinsically criminal. It is argued that participation in a plan which "in itself is not criminal but merely capable of creating conditions conducive to the commission of criminal acts cannot be regarded as characterising the *actus reus* of criminal co-perpetration." Therefore, it is suggested "mere knowledge 'of the risk that implementing the common plan will result in the commission of the crime' is insufficient to engage criminal responsibility by way of co-perpetration."

984. In the view of the Majority of the Chamber, the prosecution is not required to prove that the plan was specifically directed at committing the crime in question (the conscription, enlistment or use of children), nor does the plan need to have been intrinsically criminal as suggested by the defence. However, it is necessary, as a minimum, for

the prosecution to establish the common plan included a critical element of criminality, namely that, its implementation embodied a sufficient risk that, if events follow the ordinary course, a crime will be committed.

985. In order to establish the statutory scope of this first objective requirement, the Majority of the Chamber finds guidance in the manner that the plan is mirrored in the mental element. A combined reading of Articles 25(3)(a) and 30 leads to the conclusion that committing the crime in question does not need to be the overarching goal of the co-perpetrators.

986. The conscription, enlistment and use of children under the age of 15 and using them to participate actively in hostilities is said by the prosecution to have been the result of the implementation of the common plan. Under Article 30(2)(b), intent is established if the person is aware that a consequence will occur in the ordinary course of events. Similarly, Article 30(3) provides that "knowledge" of a consequence means awareness that it (the consequence) "will occur in the ordinary course of events." Hence, in the view of the Majority, the mental requirement that the common plan included the commission of a crime will be satisfied if the co-perpetrators knew that, in the ordinary course of events, implementing the plan will lead to that result. "Knowledge," defined as awareness by the co-perpetrators that a consequence will occur (in the future), necessarily means that the co-perpetrators are aware of the risk that the consequence, prospectively, will occur. This interpretation is discussed in greater detail below in the section dealing with the mental element.

987. The Majority of the Chamber concludes that as to the objective part of this requirement, this means that the agreement on a common plan leads to co-perpetration if its implementation embodies a sufficient risk that, in the ordinary course of events, a crime will be committed.

988. Furthermore, co-perpetration does not require that the agreement or the common plan is explicit in order for the individual conduct of each co-perpetrator to be connected. Finally, although direct evidence of the plan is likely to assist in demonstrating its existence, this is not a legal requirement. The agreement can be inferred from circumstantial evidence.

The Essential Contribution

989. The Pre-Trial Chamber concluded that the contribution of the alleged co-perpetrator must be "essential." It stated its conclusion as follows:

> In the view of the Chamber, when the objective elements of an offence are carried out by a plurality of persons acting within the framework of a common plan, only those to whom essential tasks have been assigned—and who, consequently, have the power to frustrate the commission of the crime by not

> performing their tasks—can be said to have joint control over the crime.

990. The prosecution submits that co-perpetration requires that the accused has "functional control" over the crime:

> This means that, when conceiving the common plan, the Accused must have been assigned a role that was central to the implementation of the common plan, in the sense that the common plan would not have been carried out in the manner agreed upon without that role being performed. This concept has been labelled as "functional control."

991. However, the prosecution qualifies this suggested requirement by submitting that as long as the accused was assigned a central role in the implementation of the plan, it will suffice if in retrospect it appears his or her contribution was substantial, rather than essential. A "substantial" contribution is said to be established when "the crime might still have occurred absent the contribution of the Accused, but not without great difficulty."

992. The defence contends that a "substantial" contribution is insufficient. It argues the contribution should be *conditio sine qua non* of the crime and this requirement must be assessed in light of the facts as they actually occurred, rather than assessed on the basis of the "role" assigned to the accused within the framework of a pre-agreed plan.

993. An analysis of the accused's contribution gives rise to two interrelated questions. The first question is whether it is necessary for the prosecution to establish a connection between the accused's contribution, taken in isolation, and the crimes that were committed. The second question relates to the nature of the contribution that gives rise to joint responsibility: should it be described as either "more than *de minimis*," "substantial" or "essential"?

994. In the view of the Majority of the Chamber, the wording of Article 25(3)(a), namely that the individual "commits such a crime [. . .] jointly with another," requires that the offence be the result of the combined and coordinated contributions of those involved, or at least two of them. None of the participants exercises, individually, control over the crime as a whole but, instead, the control over the crime falls in the hands of a collective as such. Therefore, the prosecution does not need to demonstrate that the contribution of the accused, taken alone, caused the crime; rather, the responsibility of the co-perpetrators for the crimes resulting from the execution of the common plan arises from mutual attribution, based on the joint agreement or common plan. * * *

996. Both Articles 25(3)(a) and (d) address the situation in which a number of people are involved in a crime. In the judgment of the Majority, the critical distinction between these provisions is that under Article 25(3)(a) the co-perpetrator "commits" the crime, whilst under Article 25(3)(d) the individual "contributes in any other way to the commission"

of a crime by a group of individuals acting with a common purpose. The Majority's view is that a systematic reading of these provisions leads to the conclusion that the contribution of the co-perpetrator who "commits" a crime is necessarily of greater significance than that of an individual who "contributes in any other way to the commission" of a crime.

997. Article 25(3)(c) establishes the liability of accessories—those who aid, abet or otherwise assist in the commission or attempted commission of the crime. In the view of the Majority, principal liability "objectively" requires a greater contribution than accessory liability. If accessories must have had "a substantial effect on the commission of the crime" to be held liable, then co-perpetrators must have had, pursuant to a systematic reading of this provision, more than a substantial effect.

998. The conclusion that principal liability must require more than accessory liability is supported, in the view of the Majority, by the statutory provision on attempt liability (Article 25(3)(f) of the Statute). Only those individuals who attempt "to commit" a crime, as opposed to those who participate in a crime committed by someone else, can be held liable under that provision. The same conclusion is supported by the plain language of Articles 25(3)(b) and (c), which require for secondary liability that the perpetrator at least attempt to commit the crime. As such, secondary liability is dependent on whether the perpetrator acts. Conversely, principal liability, which is closer to the violation of the legal interests protected by the norm, is not the subject of such dependence. Hence, the Majority concludes that this confirms the predominance of principal over secondary liability, which, in turn, supports a notion of principal liability that requires a greater contribution than accessory liability.

999. The Majority is of the view that the contribution of the co-perpetrator must be essential, as has been consistently and invariably established in this Court's jurisprudence. The Statute differentiates between the responsibility and liability of those persons who commit a crime (at Article 25(3)(a)) and those who are accessories to it (at Articles 25(3)(b) to (d)). It would be possible to expand the concept of principal liability (or "commission" or "perpetration"), to make it more widely applicable, by lowering the threshold that the accused's contribution be essential. However, lowering that threshold would deprive the notion of principal liability of its capacity to express the blameworthiness of those persons who are the most responsible for the most serious crimes of international concern. Instead, a notion of co-perpetration that requires an essential contribution allows for the different degrees of responsibility to be properly expressed and addressed.

1000. The determination as to whether the particular contribution of the accused results in liability as a co-perpetrator is to be based on an analysis of the common plan and the role that was assigned to, or was assumed by the co-perpetrator, according to the division of tasks. In the view of the Majority what is decisive is whether the co-perpetrator performs an essential role in accordance with the common plan, and it is in this sense that his contribution, as it relates to the exercise of the role and functions assigned to him, must be essential. * * *

1002. The defence submits that co-perpetration requires "personal and direct participation in the crime itself," and that the responsibility of those who do not participate directly in the execution of a crime is reflected in Article 25(3)(b) rather than Article 25(3)(a). It contends that Article 25(3)(a) requires direct participation in the crime.

1003. However, the Chamber agrees with the conclusions, firstly, of the Pre-Trial Chamber that criminal liability in this context is "not limited to those who physically carry out the objective elements of the offence, but also include(s) those who, in spite of being removed from the scene of the crime, control or mastermind its commission because they decide whether and how the offence will be committed." Secondly, the Chamber agrees with the prosecution that "[i]t is not necessary that the accused physically perpetrated any of the elements of the crimes or that he was present at the crime scene."

1004. Those who commit a crime jointly include, *inter alia*, those who assist in formulating the relevant strategy or plan, become involved in directing or controlling other participants or determine the roles of those involved in the offence. This conclusion makes it unnecessary for the prosecution to establish a direct or physical link between the accused's contribution and the commission of the crimes.

1005. Hence, the Chamber is of the view that the accused does not need to be present at the scene of the crime, so long as he exercised, jointly with others, control over the crime.

1006. The Majority therefore concludes that the commission of a crime jointly with another person involves two objective requirements: (i) the existence of an agreement or common plan between two or more persons that, if implemented, will result in the commission of a crime; and (ii) that the accused provided an essential contribution to the common plan that resulted in the commission of the relevant crime. These two requirements must be assessed on the basis of all the evidence related to the alleged crime.

The Mental Element

1007. Article 30 defines the requirement of "intent" by reference to three particular factors: conduct, consequence and circumstance. First, pursuant to Article 30(2)(a), a person has intent if he or she "means to engage in the conduct." Second, under Article 30(2)(b) and in relation to a consequence, it is necessary that the individual "means to cause that consequence or is aware that it will occur in the ordinary course of events." Third, by Article 30(3) "knowledge" "means awareness that a circumstance exists or a consequence will occur in the ordinary course of events."

1008. As noted earlier, the Pre-Trial Chamber decided that the subjective elements that the suspect must fulfil are the following: (i) "[t]he suspect and the other co-perpetrators [. . .] must all be mutually aware of the risk that implementing their common plan may result in the realisation of the objective elements of the crime, and [. . .] must all mutually accept such a result by reconciling themselves with it or consenting to it"; and (ii) "the awareness by the suspect of the factual circumstances enabling him or her to jointly control the crime."

1009. The Pre-Trial Chamber decided that the "cumulative" reference to "intent" and "knowledge" in Article 30 means there must be a "volitional element" on the part of the accused. This encompasses not only situations in which the suspect: i) knows that his or her actions or omissions will bring about the objective elements of the crime, and ii) undertakes such actions or omissions with the concrete intent to bring about the objective elements of the crime (also known as *dolus directus* of the first degree) but also the "other forms of the concept of *dolus*." The Pre-Trial Chamber was of the view that these include: i) situations in which the suspect, without having the concrete intent to bring about the objective elements of the crime, is aware that such elements will be the necessary outcome of his or her actions or omissions (also known as *dolus directus* of the second degree); and ii) situations in which the suspect (a) is aware of the risk that the objective elements of the crime may result from his or her actions or omissions, and (b) accepts such an outcome by reconciling himself or herself with it or consenting to it (also known as *dolus eventualis*).

1010. The Pre-Trial Chamber considered that within *dolus eventualis* "two kinds of scenarios are distinguishable." First, if the co-perpetrator was aware of a substantial risk that his conduct will bring about "the objective elements of the crime," his intent can be inferred from the fact that he acted in the manner agreed in spite of this level of awareness. Second, if there was a low risk of bringing about "the objective elements of the crime," "the suspect must have clearly or expressly accepted the idea that such objective elements may result from his or her actions or omissions."

1011. The conscription or enlistment of children under the age of 15 or using them to participate actively in hostilities is said by the prosecution to have been the result of the implementation of a common plan. The drafting history of the Statute suggests that the notion of *dolus eventualis*, along with the concept of recklessness, was deliberately excluded from the framework of the Statute (*e.g.* see the use of the words "unless otherwise provided" in the first sentence of Article 30). The plain language of the Statute, and most particularly the use of the words "will occur" in Article 30(2)(b) as opposed to "may occur," excludes the concept of *dolus eventualis*. The Chamber accepts the approach of Pre-Trial Chamber II on this issue.

1012. In the view of the Majority of the Chamber, the "awareness that a consequence will occur in the ordinary course of events" means that the participants anticipate, based on their knowledge of how events ordinarily develop, that the consequence will occur in the future. This prognosis involves consideration of the concepts of "possibility" and "probability," which are inherent to the notions of "risk" and "danger." Risk is defined as "danger, (exposure to) the possibility of loss, injury or other adverse circumstance." The co-perpetrators only "know" the consequences of their conduct once they have occurred. At the time the co-perpetrators agree on a common plan and throughout its implementation, they must know the existence of a risk that the consequence will occur. As to the degree of risk, and pursuant to the wording of Article 30, it must be no less than awareness on the part of the co-perpetrator that the consequence "will occur in the ordinary course of events." A low risk will not be sufficient.

1013. The Chamber is of the view that the prosecution must establish, as regards the mental element, that: (i) the accused and at least one other perpetrator meant to conscript, enlist or use children under the age of 15 to participate actively in hostilities or they were aware that in implementing their common plan this consequence "will occur in the ordinary course of events"; and (ii) the accused was aware that he provided an essential contribution to the implementation of the common plan.

1014. As already highlighted, the general mental element contained in Article 30(1) ("intent" and "knowledge") applies to all crimes under the jurisdiction of the Court "[u]nless otherwise provided." Article 8(2)(e)(vii), which gives the Court jurisdiction over the war crime of "conscripting and enlisting children under the age of 15 years into armed forces or groups or using them to participate actively in hostilities" does not derogate from this principle. However, under Article 8(2)(e)(vii) of the Elements of Crimes the following requirement is set out: "3. The perpetrator knew or should have known that such a person or persons were under the age of 15 years."

1015. This lesser mental element raises a number of issues, including: (i) whether it is possible, under the framework of the Rome Statute, for the Elements of Crimes to alter any of the material elements of the crimes established in the Statute; and (ii) the scope and interpretation of this "should have known" requirement. However, as set out above, the prosecution does not invite a conviction of the accused on the basis "he should have known" that the individuals who were conscripted or enlisted, or who were used, were under the age of 15 years. It submits the Chamber should convict the accused only if it finds he knew there were children under 15 years. The Majority of the Chamber considers it is unnecessary to approach the case on any other basis, and it would be inappropriate to rule on these substantive issues in the abstract. * * *

Conclusions of the Chamber

1018. For the reasons set out above, the prosecution must prove in relation to each charge that: (i) there was an agreement or common plan between the accused and at least one other co-perpetrator that, once implemented, will result in the commission of the relevant crime in the ordinary course of events; (ii) the accused provided an essential contribution to the common plan that resulted in the commission of the relevant crime; (iii) the accused meant to conscript, enlist or use children under the age of 15 to participate actively in hostilities or he was aware that by implementing the common plan these consequences "will occur in the ordinary course of events"; (iv) the accused was aware that he provided an essential contribution to the implementation of the common plan; and (v) the accused was aware of the factual circumstances that established the existence of an armed conflict and the link between these circumstances and his conduct.

The Facts

1019. The prosecution submits Thomas Lubanga, Floribert Kisembo, Bosco Ntaganda, Chief Kahwa Panga Mandro, Rafiki Saba Aimable, and other senior FPLC commanders, including commanders Tchaligonza, Bagonza and Kasangaki—the alleged co-perpetrators in this case—agreed upon a plan and acted together in order to build an army that included young people and to create a political movement. Furthermore, it is said they used political and military means to take control of Bunia and to exercise authority throughout Ituri. The accused is alleged to have coordinated and to have had the "final say" as to the group's activities. As a result, children under the age of 15 were allegedly conscripted and enlisted, and used to participate actively in hostilities. * * *

1023. In determining whether Thomas Lubanga is criminally responsible for the crimes charged, the Chamber has considered, first, whether a common plan existed between the accused and his alleged co-perpetrators, and, second, whether the contribution of the accused amounted to an essential contribution. The Chamber has examined the context of the creation of the UPC; the objectives of that organisation; the events leading up to the takeover of Bunia; the creation and the structures of the FPLC (the armed wing of the UPC); and the roles of Thomas Lubanga and the alleged co-perpetrators, before and during the timeframe of the charges. Thereafter, the Chamber has examined whether the prosecution has proved the required mental element on the part of the accused. * * *

[The Chamber then goes on to discuss at length the relationship between the alleged co-perpetrators and the various roles played by the defendant in effectuating the goals of the UPC and in particular in recruiting, training, and deploying child soldiers. Photos and videos were introduced into evidence showing the defendant in the vicinity of obviously under-aged soldiers. Witnesses included an individual who works with a non-governmental organization dedicated to the demobilization and rehabilitation of child soldiers.]

1045. Viewed overall, the evidence rehearsed above provides strong support for the suggestion that during the period prior to the confirmation of the charges—specifically in the summer of 2000—the accused and some of his principal alleged co-perpetrators, including Floribert Kisembo, Bosco Ntaganda, Chief Kahwa and commanders Kisangaki, Tchaligonza, and Bagonza, were jointly involved in organising the training of Hema youths in the context of the mutiny. Mr. Lubanga, *inter alia*, visited the children, liaised with individuals in Uganda to prevent attacks against the mutineers and was involved in the reintegration of the children following their training. * * *

1219. Military leaders dealing with forces on this scale will not be involved in all aspects of the decision-making process. The evidence demonstrates that there was a hierarchy within the army and a functioning structure that would have enabled an appropriate degree of delegation, certainly as regards routine operational decisions. This conclusion does not diminish the extent to which the accused was aware of what was happening within the armed forces or his overall responsibility for, or involvement in, their activities. Instead, it is an inevitable result of his position as the overall commander. The Chamber is persuaded beyond reasonable doubt that the evidence demonstrates that Thomas Lubanga was the ultimate authority within the organisation and he was informed, on a substantive basis, as to the operations carried out by the FPLC officials, including his co-perpetrators Floribert Kisembo and Bosco Ntaganda. As mentioned above, the period of conflict between 6 March and June 2003, when the UPDF was in Bunia, and the defections of some of the commanders may have had an adverse effect on the structures within the UPC, but the Chamber is not persuaded that they led to a breakdown of the chain of command or significantly undermined the authority of the accused as the head of the organisation. According to P-0041, after the return of the UPC to Bunia in around May 2003, the accused held meetings and issued decrees, thus acting as President and Commander-in-Chief of the UPC/FPLC in exactly the same way as prior to the takeover of Bunia by the UPDF in March 2003.

1221. Thomas Lubanga has not been charged on the basis of acts undertaken by his subordinates solely on account of his position within the UPC/FPLC. It is necessary for the Chamber to address the questions as to whether, *inter alia*, he led the UPC/FPLC and whether he had knowledge of the crimes in determining whether his role under the common plan was essential.

1222. The evidence discussed above demonstrates, beyond reasonable doubt, that the accused's function within the hierarchy of the UPC/FPLC, along with his involvement in planning military operations and his key role in providing logistical support—including weapons, ammunition, food, uniforms, military rations and supplies for the FPLC troops—resulted in his role being essential within the UPC/FPLC. * * *

1270. The Chamber concludes beyond reasonable doubt that the accused, by virtue of his position as President and Commander-in-Chief from September 2002 onwards, was able to shape the policies of the UPC/FPLC and to direct the activities of his alleged co-perpetrators. The established reporting structures; the lines of communication within the UPC/FPLC; and the meetings and close contact between the accused and at least some of the alleged co-perpetrators, support the conclusion that he was kept fully informed throughout the relevant period and he issued instructions relating to the implementation of the common plan. Thomas Lubanga personally assisted in the military affairs of the UPC/FPLC in a variety of ways. He was involved in planning military operations and he exercised a key role in providing logistical support, by ensuring weapons, ammunition, food, uniforms and military rations and other supplies were available for the troops. The fact that other alleged co-perpetrators, such as Floribert Kisembo and Bosco Ntaganda, were more involved with the day-to-day recruitment and training of soldiers, including those under the age of 15, does not undermine the conclusion that Mr. Lubanga's role was essential to the implementation of the common plan. In addition, the accused and other commanders were protected by guards, some of whom were below 15. As set out above, the use of children as bodyguards for the commanders amounts to their use to participate actively in hostilities. The role of the accused within the UPC/FPLC and the hierarchical relationship with the other co-perpetrators, viewed in combination with the activities he carried out personally in support of the common plan, as demonstrated by the rallies and visits to recruits and troops, lead to the conclusion that the implementation of the common plan would not have been possible without his contribution.

1271. Viewed in its entirety, the evidence demonstrates that the accused and his alleged co-perpetrators, including particularly Floribert Kisembo, Chief Kahwa and Bosco Ntaganda, worked together and each of them made an essential contribution to the common plan that resulted in the enlistment, conscription and use of children under the age of 15 to participate actively in hostilities.

1272. In light of the evidence above, the Chamber is persuaded beyond reasonable doubt that the accused made an essential contribution to the common plan for the purposes of Article 25(3)(a).

Mental Element

Intent and knowledge

1273. Pursuant to Article 30, the prosecution has the obligation of establishing that Thomas Lubanga committed the crimes of conscripting, enlisting and using children below the age of 15 to participate actively in hostilities, with the necessary intent and knowledge.

1274. It is necessary, therefore, for the prosecution to establish that Thomas Lubanga intended to participate in implementing the common plan, and, additionally, that he was aware that the conscription, enlistment or use of children below the age of 15 "will occur in the ordinary course of events" as a result of the implementation of the common plan. The Chamber needs to be satisfied the accused knew that the children were under the age of 15 years and, additionally, he was aware that he was providing an essential contribution to the implementation of the common plan. * * *

1276. The defence argues the alleged crimes were not a virtually certain consequence of creating the armed force and thereafter using it in the armed conflict. Equally, the defence suggests the prosecution has not established that voluntary enlistment in the FPLC by children under the age of 15 was the virtually certain consequence of the various recruitment activities. It is argued that although it was difficult to verify the ages of recruits, a policy requiring age verification was in place and was implemented, thereby considerably reducing the risk that children under the age of 15 would be enlisted. Any deliberate enlistment of children under the age of 15 by the military authorities was, therefore, in violation of this prohibition. The defence further argues the prosecution has not established how the essential contribution ascribed to the accused inevitably resulted in the conscription or use of children under the age of 15 to participate actively in hostilities. The defence contends there is no evidence to suggest that the accused was personally involved, or had knowledge of, any forcible recruitment of children under the age of 15 into the FPLC or their use to participate actively in hostilities. Finally, the Chamber is reminded the accused has not been prosecuted on the basis of superior responsibility, and it is suggested it has not been established that he condoned or participated in the crimes with which he is charged. * * *

1278. The accused visited UPC/FPLC training camps, and specifically at the Rwampara camp he gave a morale-boosting speech to recruits who included young children below the age of 15. The Chamber is of the view that the video footage of this event provides compelling evidence on Thomas Lubanga's level of knowledge, which is directly relevant to the mental element of the charges. * * * Irrespective of whether or not there was a policy of verifying the ages of the recruits, it has been established that the accused was aware that the FPLC was recruiting and using child soldiers who were clearly below the age of 15 and he condoned, and he took steps to implement, this policy, along with his co-perpetrators.

1279. The Chamber is persuaded the evidence discussed in the sections above demonstrates that the accused had intent and knowledge with respect to the crimes with which he is charged.

1280. The prosecution suggests that the demobilisation orders issued by the accused were a "sham" and that during the period when the accused was supposedly demobilising children under the age of 18, he failed to question their use as bodyguards or soldiers on the occasions when he saw them. It is argued the evidence has demonstrated that he condoned the continued recruiting and using child soldiers. The prosecution alleges the demobilisation orders were issued by the accused in response to pressure from the media and the international community.

1281. This is challenged by the defence, and it argues the accused was opposed to the recruitment of minors throughout the relevant period, and he took appropriate steps to end this practice and to ensure that children were demobilised. The defence submits that this undermines the suggested mental element. * * * [The Chamber discussed evidence that the members of the UPC had refused to work with, and had in fact threatened, humanitarian aid agencies dedicated to demobilizing child soldiers.]

1290. On the basis of the evidence discussed above, the Chamber is persuaded that by May 2003 at the latest Thomas Lubanga was fully aware of the prohibition on child recruitment and was aware of the concerns of outside bodies as to the recruitment and use of child soldiers, and that this issue was repeatedly raised regardless of the precise nature or context of their meetings. Moreover, the evidence demonstrates the UPC/FPLC attempted to impede the work of the organisations which were involved with helping child soldiers during the period of the charges. On the basis of the testimony of D-0019, D-0037 and D-0011, the Chamber is satisfied that complaints about the use of child soldiers were levelled at the UPC/FPLC by late 2002 and early 2003, and it accepts D-0019's evidence that these complaints were discussed at meetings. * * *

1346. On the basis of the evidence discussed above, the Chamber is persuaded that whether or not the demobilisation orders were implemented for some of the children under the age of 15, others were simultaneously recruited, re-recruited and used by the FPLC throughout the timeframe of the charges. The demobilisation orders additionally prove that Mr. Lubanga knew that the recruitment of children was prohibited and that children remained amongst the ranks of the UPC/FPLC in spite of the prohibition.

1347. Focusing on the mental element of the charges, the Chamber is of the view that Thomas Lubanga was fully aware that children under the age of 15 had been, and continued to be, enlisted and conscripted by the UPC/FPLC and used to participate actively in hostilities during the timeframe of the charges. This occurred, in the ordinary course of events, as a result of the implementation of the common plan—to ensure that the UPC/FPLC had an army strong enough to achieve its political and military aims.

1348. Within a functioning military hierarchy, it is necessary that orders are complied with. The defence has been imprecise as to whether the demobilisation order of 21 October 2002 and the decree of 1 June 2003 lead to the conclusion that the resulting crimes did not occur in the ordinary course of events, or whether it is only suggesting that the accused did not have the "intention" to commit the crimes. However, the lack of cooperation on the part of the UPC/FPLC with the NGOs working within the field of demobilisation and the threats directed at human rights workers who were involved with children's rights tend to undermine the suggestion that demobilisation, as ordered by the President, was meant to be implemented. Instead, Thomas Lubanga used child soldiers below the age of 15 as his bodyguards within the PPU3646 and he gave speeches and attended rallies where conscripted and enlisted children below the age of 15 were present. Mr. Lubanga was aware that children under the age of 15 were within the personal escorts of other commanders. Moreover, the accused visited UPC/FPLC camps, and particularly at the Rwampara camp he gave a morale-boosting speech to recruits who included young children who were clearly below the age of 15. As already set out, the Chamber concludes that this video, filmed on 12 February 2003, contains compelling evidence as to Thomas Lubanga's awareness of, and his attitude towards, the enduring presence of children under the age of 15 in the UPC. * * *

1355. The Chamber is satisfied beyond reasonable doubt that as a result of the implementation of the common plan to build an army for the purpose of establishing and maintaining political and military control over Ituri, boys and girls under the age of 15 were conscripted and enlisted into the UPC/FPLC between 1 September 2002 and 13 August 2003. Similarly, the Chamber is satisfied beyond reasonable doubt that the UPC/FPLC used children under the age of 15 to participate actively in hostilities, including during battles. They were also used, during the relevant period, as soldiers and as bodyguards for senior officials, including the accused.

1356. Thomas Lubanga was the President of the UPC/FPLC, and the evidence demonstrates that he was simultaneously the Commander-in-Chief of the army and its political leader. He exercised an overall coordinating role over the activities of the UPC/FPLC. He was informed, on a substantive and continuous basis, of the operations of the FPLC. He was involved in planning military operations, and he played a critical role in providing logistical support, including as regards weapons, ammunition, food, uniforms, military rations and other general supplies for the FPLC troops. He was closely involved in making decisions on recruitment policy and he actively supported recruitment initiatives, for instance by giving speeches to the local population and the recruits. In his speech at the Rwampara camp, he encouraged children, including those under the age of 15 years, to join the army and to provide security for the populace once deployed in the field following their military training. Furthermore, he personally used children below the age of 15 amongst his bodyguards and he regularly saw guards of other UPC/FPLC members of staff who were below the age of 15. The Chamber has concluded that these contributions by Thomas Lubanga, taken together, were essential to a common plan that resulted in the conscription and enlistment of girls and boys below the age of 15 into the UPC/FPLC and their use to actively participate in hostilities.

1357. The Chamber is satisfied beyond reasonable doubt, as set out above, that Thomas Lubanga acted with the intent and knowledge necessary to establish the charges (the mental element required by Article 30). He was aware of the factual circumstances that established the existence of the armed conflict. Furthermore, he was aware of the nexus between those circumstances and his own conduct, which resulted in the enlistment, conscription and use of children below the age of 15 to participate actively in hostilities.

Prosecutor v. Lubanga, Case No. ICC–01/04–01/06, Separate Opinion of Judge Adrian Fulford (March 14, 2012)

6. As set out above, the Pre-Trial Chamber's adoption of the control of the crime theory was founded, in the first place, on the perceived necessity to establish a clear dividing line between the various forms of liability under Article 25(3)(a)–(d) of the Statute and, in particular, to distinguish between the liability of "accessories" under Article 25(3)(b) and that of "principals" under Article 25(3)(a) of the Statute. I respectfully disagree with this view.

7. In my judgment, the plain text of Article 25(3) defeats the argument that subsections (a)–(d) of Article 25(3) must be interpreted so as to avoid creating an overlap between them. Article 25(3)(a) establishes the concept of committing a crime through another, whilst Article 25(3)(b) focuses on ordering, soliciting and inducing the commission of the offence. These concepts, which appear in separate subsections, will often be indistinguishable in their application vis-à-vis a particular situation, and by creating a clear degree of crossover between the various modes of liability, Article 25(3) covers all eventualities. Put otherwise, in my judgment the plain language of Article 25(3) demonstrates that the possible modes of commission under Article 25(3)(a)–(d) of the Statute were not intended to be mutually exclusive.

8. Some have suggested that Article 25(3) establishes a hierarchy of seriousness as regards the various forms of participation in a crime, with Article 25(3)(a) constituting the gravest example and Article 25(3)(d) the least serious. I am unable to adopt this approach. In my judgment, there is no proper basis for concluding that ordering, soliciting or inducing a crime (Article 25(3)(b)) is a less serious form of commission than committing it "through another person" (Article 25(3)(a)), and these two concepts self-evidently overlap. Similarly, I am unable to accept that the criminality of accessories (Article 25(3)(c)) is greater than those who participate within a group (Article 25(3)(d)), particularly since many of

history's most serious crimes occurred as the result of the coordinated action of groups of individuals, who jointly pursued a common goal.

9. I am also unpersuaded that it will assist the work of the Court to establish a hierarchy of seriousness that is dependent on creating rigorous distinctions between the modes of liability within Article 25(3) of the Statute. Whilst it might have been of assistance to "rank" the various modes of liability if, for instance, sentencing was strictly determined by the specific provision on which an individual's conviction is based, considerations of this kind do not apply at the ICC. Article 78 of the Statute and Rule 145 of the Rules of Procedure and Evidence, which govern the sentences that are to be imposed, provide that an individual's sentence is to be decided on the basis of "all the relevant factors," "including the gravity of the crime and the individual circumstances of the convicted person." Although the "degree of participation" is one of the factors listed in Rule 145(1)(c) of the Rules, these provisions overall do not narrowly determine the sentencing range by reference to the mode of liability under which the accused is convicted, and instead this is simply one of a number of relevant factors.

10. The control of the crime theory has its origins in the post-war German legal system, where particular domestic considerations—which do not exist at the ICC—have made it appropriate to apply this principle. In adopting this theory, the Pre-Trial Chamber focused substantially on a minority view from the *ad hoc* tribunals. * * * In these two instances, the judges relied heavily on the scholarship of the German academic Claus Roxin as the primary authority for the control theory of co-perpetration, and in the result, this approach was imported directly from the German legal system. While Article 21(1)(c) of the Statute permits the Court to draw upon "general principles of law" derived from national legal systems, in my view before taking this step, a Chamber should undertake a careful assessment as to whether the policy considerations underlying the domestic legal doctrine are applicable at this Court, and it should investigate the doctrine's compatibility with the Rome Statute framework. This applies regardless of whether the domestic and the ICC provisions mirror each other in their formulation. It would be dangerous to apply a national statutory interpretation simply because of similarities of language, given the overall context is likely to be significantly different.

11. This case demonstrates why a detailed assessment of this kind is necessary. Under the German legal system, the sentencing range is determined by the mode of liability under which an individual is convicted, and it is therefore necessary to draw clear distinctions between principals on the one hand and accessories on the other. As set out above, these considerations do not apply at the ICC, where sentencing is not restricted in this way, and this example of the differences that exist is of significance in this context.

12. The second justification advanced by the Pre-Trial Chamber for adopting the control of the offence theory was to establish "principal" liability for individuals who, "in spite of being removed from the scene of the crime, control or mastermind its commission because they decide whether and how the offence will be committed." However, as developed below, in my judgment a plain reading of Article 25(3)(a) establishes the criminal liability of co-perpetrators who contribute to the commission of the crime notwithstanding their absence from the scene, and it is unnecessary to invoke the control of the crime theory in order to secure this result. * * *

16. [A] plain text reading of Article 25(3)(a) establishes the following elements for co-perpetration:

a. The involvement of at least two individuals.

b. Coordination between those who commit the offence, which may take the form of an agreement, common plan or joint understanding, express or implied, to commit a crime or to undertake action that, in the ordinary course of events, will lead to the commission of the crime.

c. A contribution to the crime, which may be direct or indirect, provided either way there is a causal link between the individual's contribution and the crime.

d. Intent and knowledge, as defined in Article 30 of the Statute, or as "otherwise provided" elsewhere in the Court's legal framework.

17. Not only is the above approach supported by the plain text of the Statute, it also provides a realistic basis for the Court to conduct its work. It avoids a hypothetical investigation as to how events might have unfolded without the accused's involvement (which is necessary under the "essential contribution" formulation) and it places appropriate emphasis on the accused's state of mind, once it is established that he or she contributed to the offence. It seems to me to be important to stress that an *ex post facto* assessment as to whether an individual made an essential contribution to war crimes, crimes against humanity or genocide will often be unrealistic and artificial. These crimes frequently involve a large number of perpetrators, including those who have controlling roles. It will largely be a matter of guesswork as to the real consequence for the particular crime if the accused is (hypothetically) removed from the equation, and most particularly it will not be easy to determine whether the offence would have been committed in any event.

NOTES & QUESTIONS

1. Case Update

Lubanga was sentenced on July 10, 2012, to a total of fourteen years imprisonment. The verdict and sentence were confirmed by the Appeals Chamber on December 1, 2014. On December 19, 2015, Lubanga was transferred to a prison facility in the DRC to serve his sentence. On December 15, 2017, the Trial Chamber held that Lubanga was liable for U.S. $10 million in reparations with respect to 425 identified victims and "any other victims who may be identified." Both Lubanga and a group of victims appealed the decision. The Appeals Chamber mostly confirmed the Trial Chamber's decision on July 18, 2019, but added a requirement that victims who were found ineligible to receive reparations, and who consider that their failure to sufficiently substantiate their allegations resulted from insufficient notice of the requirements for eligibility, may seek a new assessment of their eligibility. For further discussion of Lubanga's sentence and reparations order, see Chapter 18.

2. Co-Perpetration

What are the elements of the co-perpetration doctrine as you can identify them from the opinion? Is this doctrine the functional equivalent of the joint criminal enterprise doctrine as you understand it? If not, where does it differ? Given the facts as you know them, what other forms of responsibility might the Prosecution have charged under the circumstances? Why might the Prosecution have focused on the co-perpetration doctrine, which is little known in international criminal law as yet, rather than charge (or even cumulatively charge) under more established doctrines such as joint criminal enterprise, complicity, or superior responsibility? The title of the doctrine suggests that the defendant in this case is being tried as a principal, rather than an accomplice. What are the implications of this? Do you agree with Judge Adrian Fulford (United Kingdom) that the Trial Chamber has unnecessarily complicated the doctrine?

3. *Mens Rea*

Is the opinion clear as to the *mens rea* requirement of the co-perpetration doctrine? How does the *mens rea* requirement of the doctrine mesh with the *mens rea* requirement of the substantive offense (the enlistment etc. of child soldiers)? The opinion above discusses several forms of *mens rea*, including *dolus directus* (when a person intends to achieve the prohibited result or commit the prohibited act), *dolus indirectus* (when the person realizes that if he wants to achieve the primary goal, the prohibited result or act will be necessary), *dolus eventualis* (where the person foresees that there is a possibility that the prohibited result or act may occur, and is reconciled to that outcome even though he may not desire it), recklessness (where the person disregards a known risk that the prohibited result or act may happen), and negligence (where the person is unaware that the prohibited result or act may occur). Which mental state should be actionable?

4. Co-Perpetration and the *Ad Hoc* Tribunals

In *Stakić*, a Trial Chamber of the ICTY convicted the defendant under the doctrine of co-perpetration, even though this was not alleged in the indictment. *See Prosecutor v. Stakić*, Case No. IT–97–24–T, Judgement, paras. 440–442, 468–498, 741 (July 31, 2003) (identifying the accused as a co-perpetrator where he was the perpetrator behind the direct perpetrator). The Appeals Chamber of the ICTY ruled that the ICTY Prosecutor cannot indict on the basis of the doctrine of co-perpetration on the ground that the doctrine is not within the Statute and does not constitute part of customary international law. *Prosecutor v. Stakić*, Case No. IT–97–24–A, Judgement, paras. 58–63 (Mar. 22, 2006) (reversing the Trial Chamber by noting that co-perpetratorship "does not have support in customary international law or in the settled jurisprudence of this Tribunal, which is binding on the Trial Chambers" in contradistinction to the joint criminal enterprise doctrine, which is well established and which was alleged in the indictment). The Appeals Chamber reviewed the evidence and the findings to conclude that the defendant should have been convicted under a theory of joint criminal enterprise. *Id.* at paras. 85, 98. Why would the ICTY Trial Chamber go beyond the allegations in the indictment to convict the defendant under an uncharged doctrine without precedent? Why might the ICTY find the doctrine of joint criminal enterprise to be part of customary international law, but not co-perpetratorship?

5. *Katanga & Chui*

In a challenge to the co-perpetration doctrine before the ICC, the Pre-Trial Chamber of the ICC rejected the ICTY Appeals Chamber's reasoning in *Stakić* on the basis that Article 21 of the ICC Statute directs the Court to consider its own Statute, first and foremost, as a source of law, so that whether or not the contested mode of liability forms part of customary international law is of no moment. *Prosecutor v. Katanga & Chui*, Case No. ICC–01/04–01/07–717, Decision on the Confirmation of Charges, para. 508 (Sept. 30, 2008). The Pre-Trial Chamber of the ICC noted, "[t]his is a good example of the need not to transfer the *ad hoc* tribunals' case law mechanically to the system of the Court." *Id.* In its confirmation decision, the Pre-Trial Chamber treated this form of liability as an alternative to the doctrine of superior responsibility:

> through a combination of individual responsibility for committing crimes through other persons together with the mutual attribution among the co-perpetrators at the senior level, a mode of liability arises which allows the Court to assess the blameworthiness of 'senior leaders' adequately.

Id. at para. 492. It also analogized the idea of committing a crime through another with the domestic law concept of "perpetrator-by-means," whereby the defendant (the "perpetrator behind the perpetrator") uses the direct perpetrator as a tool or instrument for the commission of the crime. *Id.* at para. 495. This doctrine is also useful in situations in which the defendant controls an organization or "organized apparatus of power" that has been used to commit crimes. *Id.* at para. 511. Under these circumstances, a Pre-Trial Chamber of the ICC noted that the organization in question

> must be based on hierarchical relations between superiors and subordinates. The organisation must also be composed of sufficient subordinates to guarantee that superiors' orders will be carried out, if not by one subordinate, then by another. These criteria ensure that orders given by the recognised leadership will generally be complied with by their subordinates.

Katanga & Chui, supra, at para. 512. Indeed, "[t]he main attribute of this kind of organisation is a mechanism that enables its highest authorities to ensure automatic compliance with their orders." *Id.* at para. 517. The Pre-Trial Chamber noted that such organizations are often formed by virtue of subjecting their members to intensive and violent training regimens. *Id.* at para. 518.

6. Other Offenses

In addition to using child soldiers, the *Union des Patriots Congolais* has been accused of committing other war crimes and crimes against humanity, including ethnic massacres, torture, sexual violence, and mutilation. A coalition of human rights groups urged the ICC Prosecutor to seek to amend the original indictment to charge additional crimes. They reasoned:

> We are disappointed that two years of investigation by your office in the DRC has not yielded a broader range of charges against Mr. Lubanga. Charging those most responsible for the more serious crimes committed in Ituri * * * with representative crimes for which there is a strong evidentiary basis is crucial for the victims of these crimes and for ending the culture of impunity in the DRC and in the Great Lakes region. We believe that the failure to include additional charges in the case against Mr. Lubanga could undercut the credibility of the ICC in the DRC. Moreover, the narrow scope of the current charges may result in severely limiting victims' participation in the first proceedings before the ICC. This could negatively impact on the right of victims to reparations.

Letter to Luis Moreno-Ocampo from Avocats Sans Frontières, et al. (July 31, 2006). In May 2009, lawyers for victims argued that under-aged female recruits in the militia were used as sex slaves and that the charges against Lubanga should be amended to reflect this. On July 14, 2009, the ICC Trial Chamber ruled that pursuant to Regulation 55 (entitled "authority of the Chamber to modify the legal characterisation of facts"), it was possible to add new charges (sexual slavery as a war crime and crime against humanity and cruel and inhumane treatment as a war crime) so long as they were based on existing evidence. *Prosecutor v. Lubanga*, Case No. ICC–01/04–01/06–2049, Decision Giving Notice to the Parties and Participants that the Legal Characterization of the Facts may be Subject to Change in accordance with Regulation 55(2) of the Regulations of the Court (July 14, 2009).

Judge Fulford again dissented, arguing that only the Pre-Trial Chamber can frame and alter the charges and that once the trial has begun, the Trial Chamber cannot alter the legal characterization of the charges. *Prosecutor v. Lubanga*, Case No. ICC–01/04–01/06, Minority Opinion on the "Decision Giving Notice to the Parties and Participants that the Legal Characterisation of Facts may be Subject to Change in accordance with Regulation 55(2) of the Regulations of the Court" (July 17, 2009). Both the Prosecution and Defense appealed this decision. The Appeals Chamber reversed the Trial Chamber, concluding that Regulation 55 could not be used to "exceed the facts and circumstances described in the charges or any amendment thereto." *Prosecutor v. Lubanga*, Case No. ICC–01/04–01/06 OA

15 OA 16, Judgment on the Appeals of Mr. Lubanga Dyilo and the Prosecutor against the Decision of Trial Chamber I of 14 July 2009 entitled "Decision Giving Notice to the Parties and Participants that the Legal Characterisation of the Facts may be Subject to Change in accordance with Regulation 55(2) of the Regulations of the Court" (December 8, 2009). In particular, the Appeals Chamber disagreed with the Trial Chamber's assertion that it could consider additional facts introduced into trial through a change of their legal characterization under Regulation 55, as this would be in conflict with Article 74(2) of the Statute which provides that "The decision [of the Trial Chamber at the end of the trial] shall not exceed the facts and circumstances described in the charges and any amendments to the charges." For more on Regulation 55 see Chapter 13 on Charging International Crimes.

7. Girl Soldiers

Several of the witnesses who testified against Lubanga at trial were young women. When should girls who are integrated into a fighting force be considered "child soldiers"? While the phenomenon of child soldiery has received considerable international attention, it is often portrayed as a male phenomenon in ways that may overlook the experiences of girls who form part of armed groups. The operational contributions of girls during armed conflicts are often ignored or devalued, even though such contributions may be crucial to the girls' particular fighting force. In addition, NGOs and governments may exclude girls from disarmament, demobilization, and reintegration (DDR) processes in the post-conflict period, which include the provision of benefits such as tools, education, and job training. (For a discussion of the crime of recruiting, enlisting and using child soldiers, see Chapter 17 on Defenses Under International Criminal Law).

In this regard, see the clarifications in the ICC's Elements of Crimes with respect to the crime of conscripting or enlisting child soldiers or using them in combat:

> The words 'using' and 'participate' have been adopted in order to cover both direct participation in combat and also active participation in military activities linked to combat such as scouting, spying, sabotage and the use of children as decoys, couriers or at military checkpoints. It would not cover activities clearly unrelated to the hostilities such as food deliveries to an airbase or the use of domestic staff in an officer's married accommodation. However, use of children in a direct support function such as acting as bearers to take supplies to the front line, or activities at the front line itself, would be included in the terminology.

In the U.S. legislation criminalizing the use of child soldiers, the term "participate actively in hostilities" means taking part in—"(A) combat or military activities related to combat, including sabotage and serving as a decoy, a courier, or at a military checkpoint; or (B) direct support functions related to combat, including transporting supplies or providing other services." 18 U.S.C. § 2442(d)(1). The statute supports expansive jurisdiction over the offense. For more on girl soldiers, *see* Myriam Denov, GIRLS IN FIGHTING FORCES: MOVING BEYOND VICTIMHOOD (2007). What are the implications for characterizing girls within fighting forces as soldiers from the perspective of IHL, for example with respect to targeting doctrines or POW treatment?

8. *Brady* Obligations Under International Criminal Law

In *Brady v. Maryland*, 373 U.S. 83, 87 (1963), the U.S. Supreme Court held that "the suppression by the prosecution of evidence favorable to an accused upon request violates due process where the evidence is material either to guilt or to punishment, irrespective of the good faith or bad faith of the prosecution." On June 13, 2008, Trial Chamber I rendered a decision staying *sine die* (indefinitely) the proceedings against Lubanga on the ground that a fair trial was impossible in light of the revelation that the Prosecutor had withheld potentially exculpatory information from the accused. The Prosecutor argued that he had withheld the information because he had promised to ensure its confidentiality pursuant to Article 54(3)(e) of the ICC Statute, which allows the Prosecutor to receive information on the condition of confidentiality so long as such information will not be used at trial and will be used only for the purpose of generating new evidence. Article 67(2) sets forth the Prosecutor's disclosure duties:

> In addition to any other disclosure provided for in this Statute, the prosecutor shall, as soon as practicable, disclose to the defence evidence in the Prosecutor's possession or control which he or she believes shows or tends to show the innocence of the accused, or to mitigate the guilt of the accused, or which may affect the credibility of prosecution evidence. In case of doubt as to the application of this paragraph, the Court shall decide.

The information in question apparently came from the United Nations itself as well as from various NGOs.

Several weeks after staying the proceedings, the Trial Chamber ordered Lubanga's release, reasoning that this was "the logical—indeed the inevitable—consequence" of the stay. *Prosecutor v. Lubanga*, Case No. ICC–01/04–01/06–1401, Decision on the Consequences of Non-disclosure of Exculpatory Materials Covered by Article 54(3)(e) Agreements and the Application to Stay the Prosecution of the Accused, together with Certain Other Issues Raised at the Status Conference on 10 June 2008 (June 13, 2008). The Chamber explained that none of the reasons for pre-trial detention remained valid since the trial was indefinitely suspended. In so ruling, the Trial Chamber rejected arguments by the victims that Lubanga's release may send a dangerous message to, and ignite tensions in, Ituri and place victims at risk. The Appeals Chamber subsequently ordered the release to be suspended pending the Prosecutor's appeal. In the meantime, the Prosecutor began working with information providers to put agreements and procedures in place (such as *in camera* review, *ex parte* proceedings, redactions, the use of summaries, the oral presentation or recitation of evidence, *et cetera*) to reach the necessary balance between disclosure and confidentiality. Eventually, the Trial Chamber was satisfied that the

port, Hodeidah. This penetration into the Arabian peninsula by its ancient foe provoked the Saudis, who sought to prevent the Houthi-Saleh rebellion from further consolidating power across the country and to bolster the Hadi government, much of which is living in exile in Riyadh. The Saudis organized a coalition of Gulf states—including the United Arab Emirates, Bahrain, Kuwait, and Jordan—against the Houthis and their backers. United States and European support for the coalition has been essential: the Royal Saudi Air Force is equipped almost entirely with U.S. and British planes. It is dropping U.S. and British munitions daily. Indeed, in addition to supplying planes, bombs, and other *materiel*, the United States is also servicing the jets, coordinating air-to-air refueling, upgrading software, and training pilots. Media recount that U.S. intelligence officers are in the flight rooms in Riyadh guiding Saudi commanders on their targeting decisions and compiling "no-strike" lists of critical infrastructure. The war, coupled with an air and naval blockade, has created one of the worst humanitarian catastrophes in the world. Millions of Yemenis are dying, or at risk of dying, of starvation and disease, including cholera.

In 2016, hundreds of mourners had gathered for the funeral of a prominent Yemeni, the patriarch of his family. Suddenly, the building collapsed and was enveloped in fire. The airstrike killed more than 100 people and injured another 600. Saudi Arabia eventually expressed regret for the bombing, suggesting that shortcomings in intelligence and targeting were to blame. This botched attack joins dozens more on hospitals, schools, markets, and other elements of the civilian infrastructure. Notwithstanding these targeting tragedies, the United States has dickered on halting its weapons sales given that the Saudis are spending upwards of $200 million per day on the war, so billions of U.S. dollars are at stake for U.S. weapons manufacturers.

Might United States or British officials be liable under any of the forms of responsibility discussed above for the attack on the funeral hall or other harm to the civilian populations occasioned by the war in Yemen? What about U.S. weapons manufacturers, such as Raytheon? How would you formulate a theory of responsibility? How would you defend against these theories? What additional evidence would bolster a prosecutor's case?

CHAPTER 16

Inchoate Crimes: Conspiracy & Incitement

I. Introduction

In general, the criminal law does not punish criminal thoughts alone; rather, for liability to attach, there must be a punishable act or conduct that has resulted in undesirable consequences. The inchoate offenses (*infractions formelles*)—e.g., unsuccessful attempt, some forms of incitement, possession, and conspiracy—provide exceptions to this general rule. These offenses are committed prior to and in preparation for what may be a more serious offense, and yet they are complete offenses in and of themselves, even if the principal offense is never committed or would, in fact, be impossible to commit. (Indeed, many commentators do not consider these to be offenses at all, but rather ways in which actors may be punished even in the absence of a completed criminal offense in light of their proven propensity to commit crimes). As such, these offenses are punishable as such and not as a consequence of their commission.

The inchoate crimes have not been as fully integrated into international criminal law as they are in domestic criminal law. Indeed, international law recognizes only certain inchoate crimes (e.g., conspiracy and incitement to commit genocide, and conspiracy to engage in counterfeiting, drug trafficking, and slavery) and not others. There is no established tradition of prosecuting conspiracy to commit torture or war crimes, for example. In addition, the law of attempt remains rudimentary in international law. As you review the materials in this chapter, consider why this might be the case.

II. Conspiracy in International Criminal Law

Conspiracy law has been described as "the darling of the modern prosecutor's nursery." *Harrison v. United States*, 7 F.2d 259, 263 (2d Cir. 1925). As you review the materials in this chapter, consider if this holds true in international criminal law. Conspiracies play two roles in the criminal law: first, as a substantive inchoate offense that may be charged even when the crimes that are the object of the conspiracy have not been executed, and second, as a form of collective liability that requires proof of the commission of some crime that was the object of the conspiracy. In the latter sense, in some systems (notably the United States), the law allows the state to hold all members of the conspiracy liable not only for the commission of crimes that were the object of the conspiracy, but also for the commission of crimes that were the foreseeable result of executing the conspiracy.

The rationales for criminalizing conspiracies are twofold: first, to recognize the special dangers of group criminality and second, to provide a preventative mechanism by empowering law enforcement during the preparatory stages of crime. As the Model Penal Code commentary explains:

> In the course of preparation to commit a crime, the act of combining with another is significant both psychologically and practically, the former because it crosses a clear threshold in arousing expectations, the latter because it increases the likelihood that the offense will be committed. Sharing lends the fortitude to purpose. The actor knows, moreover, that the future is no longer governed by his will alone; others may complete what he has had a hand in starting, even if he has had a change in heart.

§ 5.03 cmt. a. An alternative approach that addresses the first rationale is to consider collective criminality an aggravating circumstance at sentencing. *See* Wienczyslaw J. Wagner, *Conspiracy in Civil Law Countries*, 42 J. CRIM. L., CRIMINOLOGY & POLICE SCI. 171 (1951). This chapter invites you to consider the way in which conspiracy operates in international criminal law, particularly given attempts to prosecute conspiracy as a war crime in military commissions in the United States.

The postwar trials before the International Military Tribunals at Nuremberg and Tokyo represent the first prosecutions for conspiracy at the international level. As such, these efforts present a starting point for any consideration of conspiracy liability under international criminal law. During the deliberations around the creation of the Nuremberg Tribunal and its proceedings, conspiracy liability emerged as another contentious issue among the Allies. As mentioned briefly in the prior chapter, in addition to proposing the concept of the criminal organization, the innovative Col. Bernays also developed the idea that the Nuremberg defendants could be charged with participating in a criminal conspiracy as a substantive offense along with the commission of crimes against the peace, war crimes, and crimes against humanity.

At first, the United States' Allies resisted the notion of the crime of conspiracy:

> during much of the discussion, the Russians and French seemed unable to grasp all the implications of the concept; when they finally did grasp it, they were genuinely shocked. The French viewed it entirely as a barbarous legal mechanism unworthy of modern law, while the Soviets seemed to have shaken their head in wonderment—a reaction, some cynics may believe, prompted by envy.

Bradley F. Smith, REACHING JUDGMENT AT NUREMBERG 51 (1977). Even then-U.S. Attorney General Herbert Weschler expressed concern about designating the crime of conspiracy as a substantive crime over and above a form of responsibility on the ground that "the common-law conception of the criminality of an unexecuted plan is not universally accepted in the civilized world." *Id.* at 86. Nonetheless, the Americans prevailed, and the Nuremberg Charter provided:

> Article 6. The following acts, or any of them, are crimes coming within the jurisdiction of the Tribunal for which there shall be individual responsibility:
>
> (a) CRIMES AGAINST PEACE: namely, planning, preparation, initiation or waging of a war of aggression, or a war in violation of international treaties, agreements or assurances, or participation in a common plan or conspiracy for the accomplishment of any of the foregoing;
>
> (b) WAR CRIMES * * *;
>
> (c) CRIMES AGAINST HUMANITY * * *.
>
> Leaders, organizers, instigators and accomplices participating in the formulation or execution of a common plan or conspiracy to commit any of the foregoing crimes are responsible for all acts performed by any persons in execution of such plan.

Thus, the notion of conspiracy seemed to appear in two forms in the Charter: as a substantive crime in 6(a) (conspiracy to commit crimes against the peace) and as a form of responsibility for all the crimes set forth in the Charter. The Allies assigned the presentation of the conspiracy count to the United States. Accordingly, Count One of the Nuremberg Indictment charged the defendants with conspiracy to commit all three substantive crimes.

The Nuremberg Tribunal, however, rejected this interpretation of the Charter and ruled that it had no jurisdiction to try persons participating in a common plan to commit war crimes or crimes against humanity:

> Count One charges not only the conspiracy to commit aggressive war, but also to commit war crimes and crimes against humanity. But [Article 6 of] the Charter does not define as a separate crime any conspiracy except the one to commit acts of aggressive war. * * * In the opinion of the Tribunal these words do not add a new and separate crime to those already listed. The words are designed to establish the responsibility of persons participating in a common plan [to commit crimes against the peace]. The Tribunal will therefore disregard the charges in Count One that the defendants conspired to commit war crimes and crimes against humanity, and will consider only the common plan to prepare, initiate and wage aggressive war.

Nuremberg Opinion and Judgment, *reprinted in* 41 AM. J. INT'L L. 172 (1947). Thus, by this interpretation, the only conspiracy recognized by the Nuremberg Tribunal was one to commit acts of aggressive war. The Tokyo Tribunal followed suit, holding that "the Charter does not confer any jurisdiction in respect of a conspiracy to commit any crime other than a crime against peace." International Military Tribunal, Judgment, *in* INTERNATIONAL MILITARY TRIBUNAL FOR THE FAR EAST 48,413, 48,449–51 (1948). Although the Prosecution indicted all twenty-two German defendants under Count One, the Nuremberg Tribunal only convicted eight defendants of conspiracy. In reaching this result, the Tribunal rejected arguments that there can be no conspiracy in a dictatorship. For example, defendant Raeder had argued that "A dictator enters into no conspiracy, or agreement; he dictates." Tr. 12970 (July 4th). The Tribunal ruled:

> The argument that such common planning cannot exist where there is complete dictatorship is unsound. A plan in the execution of which a number of persons participate is still a plan, even though conceived by only one of them; and those who execute the plan do not avoid responsibility by showing that they acted under the direction of the man who conceived it. Hitler could not make aggressive war by himself. He had to have the co-operation of statesmen, military leaders, diplomats, and businessmen. When they, with knowledge of his aims, gave him their co-operation, they made themselves parties to the plan he had initiated. They are not to be deemed innocent because Hitler made use of them, if they knew what they were doing. That they were assigned to their tasks by a dictator does not absolve them from responsibility for their acts. The relation of leader and follower does not preclude responsibility here any more than it does in the comparable tyranny of organised domestic crime.

Given the novelty of the crimes against the peace charge, especially as compared to the well-established prohibitions against war crimes, why would the Nuremberg judges compound problems of legality by rendering conspiracy applicable to crimes against the peace only?

Conspiracy under international criminal law, like the concept of the criminal organization, faded in significance at the close of the Nuremberg proceedings. Why do you think these concepts did not exhibit more traction in international criminal law?

III. CONSPIRACY IN MODERN INTERNATIONAL CRIMINAL LAW

From this start, conspiracy law has occupied an uncertain status in international criminal law. Many international criminal law treaties do not include conspiracy to commit the offense as a punishable act. Exceptions include the United Nations Convention Against Illicit Traffic in Narcotic Drugs and Psychotropic Substances, Dec. 19, 1998, art. 3(1)(c)(iv), 28 I.L.M. 493 (1989) (including conspiracy to commit drug trafficking as an offense); the Council of Europe Convention on Laundering, Search, Seizure and Confiscation of the Proceeds from Crime, Nov. 8, 1990, art. 6(1)(d), E.T.S. No. 141, 3 (requiring parties to adopt legislation establishing conspiracy to commit laundering offenses as an offense under domestic law); the International Convention on the Suppression and Punishment of the Crime of *Apartheid*, 1015 U.N.T.S. 243 (1973) (providing for responsibility for those who "[c]ommit, participate in, directly incite or conspire in the commission of the acts [of apartheid]"); and the Supplementary Convention on the Abolition of Slavery, the Slave Trade, and Institutions and Practices Similar to Slavery, Sept. 7, 1956, art. 6(1), T.I.A.S. 6418, 266 U.N.T.S. 3, 43 (making conspiracy to engage in the slave trade a punishable act).

Most importantly for modern international criminal law jurisprudence is the inclusion of conspiracy to commit genocide in the Genocide Convention as a punishable act. Thus, Article 3 of the Genocide Convention prohibits the following:

(a) Genocide;

(b) Conspiracy to commit genocide;

(c) Direct and public incitement to commit genocide;

(d) Attempt to commit genocide;

(e) Complicity in genocide.

Convention on the Prevention and Punishment of the Crime of Genocide, art. 3, Dec. 11, 1948, 78 U.N.T.S 277. During the drafting of the Genocide Convention, states wrestled with how to translate the common law concept of conspiracy into civil law legal terminology and even into the French language. The latter debate turned on whether the term "*complot*" or "*entente*" should be used. The former usually indicates an agreement to commit a crime that is reflected in material acts. The final French text ultimately employed "*entente*," suggesting that it is not necessary to prove any overt acts in support of the conspiracy. The Swedish delegate stated that

> the French and English expressions here in question—incitement, conspiracy, attempt, complicity, etc.—are subject to certain variations in many systems of criminal law represented here. When those expressions have to be translated in order to introduce the text of the Convention into our different criminal codes in other languages, it will no doubt be necessary to resign ourselves to the fact that certain differences in meaning are inevitable. It would therefore be advisable to indicate in the Committee's report that article [III] . . . of the Convention does not bind signatory States to punish the various types of acts to a greater extent than the corresponding acts aimed at the most

> serious crimes, as, for example, murder and high treason, already recognized under national laws.

Nicodème Ruhashyankiko, *Study of the Question of the Prevention and Punishment of the Crime of Genocide*, U.N. Doc. E/CN.4/Sub.2/416, p. 28 (July 4, 1978).

The Statutes of the ICTY/R criminalized inchoate conspiracy only to commit genocide; other forms of responsibility (planning, instigating, ordering, aiding and abetting) could be charged with respect to the other international crimes. In *Prosecutor v. Musema*, who as director of the Gisovu Tea Factory was charged with conspiracy to commit genocide, the ICTR noted that:

> The "*Travaux Préparatoires*" [drafting history] of the Genocide Convention suggest that the rationale for including such an offence was to ensure, in view of the serious nature of the crime of genocide, that the mere agreement to commit genocide should be punishable even if no preparatory act has taken place. Indeed, during the debate preceding the adoption of the Convention, the Secretariat advised that, in order to comply with General Assembly resolution 96 (I), the Convention would have to take into account the imperatives of the prevention of the crime of genocide:
>
> > This prevention may involve making certain acts punishable which do not themselves constitute genocide, for example, certain material acts preparatory to genocide, an agreement or a conspiracy with a view to committing genocide, or systematic propaganda inciting to hatred and thus likely to lead to genocide.

Prosecutor v. Musema, Case No. ICTR-96-13-A, Judgement and Sentence, para. 185 (Jan. 27, 2000). The Tribunal defined the offense quite straightforwardly as "an agreement between two or more persons to commit the crime of genocide." *Id.* at para. 191. With respect to the *mens rea* of the crime, the Trial Chamber held that it turns on

> the concerted intent to commit genocide, that is to destroy, in whole or in part, a national, ethnic, racial or religious group, as such. Thus, it is the view of the Chamber that the requisite intent for the crime of conspiracy to commit genocide is, *ipso facto,* the intent required for the crime of genocide, that is the *dolus specialis* [special intent] of genocide.

Id. at para. 192.

Although the conspiracy charge can be a useful one, it can be hard to prove, especially in the absence of—but even with—a completed crime. In the case against Callixte Nzabonimana, the former Minister of Youth of Rwanda, the ICTR noted:

> The *actus reus* of conspiracy to commit genocide may be proven by evidence of meetings to plan genocide. The agreement may also be inferred from other evidence, such as the conduct of the conspirators. Specifically, the concerted or coordinated action of a group of individuals may constitute evidence of an agreement. When the Prosecution seeks to prove the existence of an agreement on the basis of circumstantial evidence, the existence of a conspiracy to commit genocide must be the only reasonable inference based on the totality of the evidence.

Prosecutor v. Nzabonimana, Case No. ICTR–98–44D–T, Judgement and Sentence, para. 1739 (May 31, 2012). The conspiracy in question was with members of the Interim Government, including selected Ministers and *bourgmestres*. For his involvement in a conspiracy to commit genocide and his incitement to commit genocide, Nzabonimana was sentenced to life imprisonment.

The agreement to commit genocide is thus the lynchpin of the offense. A conspiracy can be prosecuted once the agreement is made. Conspiracies are often, by nature, clandestinely formed. Nonetheless, the existence of the agreement must still be proven, and a mere coincidence of aims between individuals is insufficient to establish a conspiracy. The *Musema* Trial Chamber, for example, acquitted the defendant of conspiracy to commit genocide on the lack of evidence of the predicate agreement, attesting to the central importance of that element of the doctrine. The ICTR has ruled that although the court may infer the existence of an agreement, the law requires that "the existence of the conspiracy * * * be the only reasonable inference from the evidence." *Prosecutor v. Zigiranyirazo*, Case No. ICTR–01–73–T, Judgement, para. 394 (Dec. 18, 2008). That said, the nature of the proof required to establish the existence of a conspiratorial agreement is less rigid than the "meeting of the minds" necessary to establish contract formation.

The ICTR offered several theories for how the finder of fact may infer the existence of an agreement from circumstantial evidence. This may include an interdependency of parties or clear cooperation on the part of the conspirators over a period of time demonstrating that they were aware of the purpose and existence of the conspiracy and agreed to participate in it. In *Nzabonimana*, for example, the ICTR Trial Chamber concluded:

> Considering the concerted and coordinated actions of Nzabonimana and the Ministers of the Interim Government, the Chamber is convinced beyond a reasonable doubt that the only reasonable inference based on the totality of the evidence is that an agreement with the specific intent to destroy Rwanda's Tutsi population in whole or in part materialised on 18 April 1994. The Chamber considers that the conduct of Nzabonimana and Kambanda after the 18 April 1994 meeting reinforces the conclusion that Nzabonimana, other Ministers and the Prime

> Minister of the Interim Government entered into an agreement to encourage the destruction of the Tutsi population, as such in Gitarama *préfecture.*

Nzabonimana, supra, at para. 1747. The agreement need not be express; there need not be direct contact between parties; parties may tacitly agree to their shared purposes; and individuals can enter into an agreement without being aware of each other's existence.

Whereas political leaders such as Nzabonimana have been convicted of joining an agreement to commit genocide, the ICTR controversially acquitted the defendants in the so-called *Military I* case of conspiracy to commit genocide, even though they were high-level officials in the Rwandan Military under Prime Minister Kambanda, who pled guilty to the offense. *See Prosecutor v. Kambanda,* Case No. ICTR–97–23–S, Judgement and Sentence (Sept. 4, 1998) (plea agreement containing accepted facts). The primary defendant in *Military I,* Théoneste Bagosora, held the position of *directeur du cabinet* in Rwanda's Ministry of Defense and was widely believed to have been a major architect of the genocide in Rwanda. He and three other military commanders were prosecuted together for genocide, conspiracy and complicity to commit genocide, crimes against humanity, and war crimes. Alleged crimes included the murder of the Rwandan Prime Minister (Agathe Uwilingiyimana) and ten Belgian peacekeepers assigned for her protection. Bagosora was convicted of genocide, crimes against humanity, and war crimes, including the killing of the Prime Minister and the Belgian peacekeepers. Bagosora and two of his co-accused were sentenced to life imprisonment.

In *Military I,* the Trial Chamber ruled as follows on the conspiracy counts:

> 2097. Turning now to the elements underpinning the allegation of planning and conspiracy, the Prosecution acknowledges that its case is principally circumstantial. There are only a few alleged meetings which could be characterised as planning genocide. The allegations instead refer, among other things, to statements made by the Accused, their affiliation with certain clandestine organisations, general warnings, of which some were circulated publicly, that the *Interahamwe* or groups with the military were plotting assassinations and mass killings, and their role in the preparation of lists as well as the arming and training of civilians. * * *
>
> 2109. [T]here was a campaign to secretly arm and train civilian militiamen and efforts to put in place a "civil defence" system made up of "resistance" groups. The Chamber found that Bagosora, Nsengiyumva and Kabiligi [the defendants] were involved in some of these efforts in varying degrees. In particular, the outlines of the core of the proposed civil defence system were recorded as notes in Bagosora's agenda, during

meetings at the Ministry of Defence in early 1993, after the [rebel Rwandan Patriotic Front (RPF)] resumed hostilities and advanced towards Kigali. Furthermore, lists primarily aimed at identifying suspected accomplices of the RPF and opponents of the Habyarimana regime or [a Hutu political party] were prepared and maintained by the army. However, in the context of the ongoing war with the RPF, this evidence does not invariably show that the purpose of arming and training these civilians or the preparation of lists was to kill Tutsi civilians.

2110. After the death of President Habyarimana, these tools were clearly put to use to facilitate killings. When viewed against the backdrop of the targeted killings and massive slaughter perpetrated by civilian and military assailants between April and July 1994 as well as earlier cycles of violence, it is understandable why for many this evidence takes on new meaning and shows a prior conspiracy to commit genocide. Indeed, these preparations are completely consistent with a plan to commit genocide. However, they are also consistent with preparations for a political or military power struggle. The Chamber recalls that, when confronted with circumstantial evidence, it may only convict where it is the only reasonable inference. It cannot be excluded that the extended campaign of violence directed against Tutsis, as such, became an added or an altered component of these preparations. * * *

2112. Other or newly discovered information, subsequent trials or history may demonstrate a conspiracy involving the Accused prior to 6 April to commit genocide. This Chamber's task, however, is narrowed by exacting standards of proof and procedure, the specific evidence on the record before it and its primary focus on the actions of the four Accused in this trial. In reaching its finding on conspiracy, the Chamber has considered the totality of the evidence, but a firm foundation cannot be constructed from fractured bricks.

Prosecutor v. Bagosora, Case No. ICTR–98–41–T, Judgement (Dec. 18, 2008). On appeal, the defendants' sentences were dramatically reduced from life sentences to 15- and 35-year sentences. *Prosecutor v Bagosora*, Case No. ICTR–98–41–A, Judgement (Dec. 14, 2011).

Likewise, the Appeals Chamber in the companion *Military II* case overturned the convictions of two senior military commanders and reduced the sentence of a third. *Prosecutor v. Ndindiliyimana et al.*, Case No. ICTR–00–56–A, Judgement (Feb. 11, 2014). The Trial Chamber had ruled that the killing of Prime Minister Uwilingiyimana and the Belgian peacekeepers by one of the defendants was insufficient evidence to support a conclusion that the defendants had joined a conspiracy to commit genocide. *Prosecutor v. Ndindiliyimana*, Case No. ICTR–00–56–T, Judgement and Sentence, paras. 513–517 (May 17, 2011). The

Prosecutor's theory was that the Prime Minister and her security detail were killed in order to diminish resistance to the implementation of a conspiracy to commit genocide. *Id.* at paras. 508, 512. When a genocide occurs alongside an armed conflict, will it ever be the case that a conspiracy to commit genocide is the only reasonable inference that can be drawn in the absence of direct evidence of an express agreement to commit genocide?

As mentioned in Chapter 7 on War Crimes, the Presiding Judge of the Appeals Chamber of the ICTY and ICTR, Theodore Meron—who joined a number of high-profile acquittals, including *Military I* and *Military II*—has been personally criticized for these outcomes. Documents released by WikiLeaks imply that Meron has an inappropriately close relationship with the United States government; others have accused him of acting at the behest of foreign militaries that might be nervous about expansive doctrines of vicarious liability. Although there have been a number of conspiracy to commit genocide convictions, some defendants have been acquitted of this charge, such as Musema. And yet, almost all ICTR defendants have been convicted of genocide proper. Why might it be easier to prove genocide rather than conspiracy to commit genocide? Are these results consistent with the intentions of the drafters of the Genocide Convention? There have been few conspiracy to commit genocide cases before the ICTY.

Early versions of the International Law Commission's Draft Code of Offenses Against the Peace and Security of Mankind, a precursor to the Rome Statute, listed conspiracy as a punishable form of responsibility but not as a standalone offense. Early versions of the ICC Statute also at one point contained a conspiracy provision that read:

> 1. A person is criminally responsible and is liable for punishment for conspiracy if that person, [with the intent to commit a specific crime] agrees with one or more persons to perpetrate that crime [or that a common intention to commit a crime will be carried out] and an overt act is committed by that person [or by another party to the agreement] [for the purpose of furthering the agreement] [that manifests the intent].*
>
> 2. A person is guilty of conspiracy even if the object of the conspiracy is impossible or is prevented by a fortuitous event.
>
> 3. A person shall only be criminally responsible for conspiracy in respect of a crime where so provided in this Statute.
>
> 4. A person who is criminally responsible for conspiracy is liable for the same punishment as the person who committed or would have committed the crime as a principal.

Report of the Preparatory Committee on the Establishment of an International Criminal Court, U.N. GAOR, 51st Sess., Supp. No. 22A, at

* Text in brackets remained contentious or preliminary at the time they were circulated.

94–95, U.N. Doc. A/51/22 (1996), *reprinted in* M. Cherif Bassiouni, THE STATUTE OF THE INTERNATIONAL CRIMINAL COURT: A DOCUMENTARY HISTORY 489 (1998). Accounts of the proceedings report strongly divergent views with respect to this provision, and it was eventually dropped. Nonetheless, one pair of commentators suggests that the ICC judges could read conspiracy liability back in to the Statute:

> One may interpret these events by attributing to the drafters a pragmatic judgment made necessary by the many uncertainties and disagreements surrounding the ICC's development. In light of these difficulties, the drafters may have chosen to sacrifice clear authorization for conspiracy prosecutions in the interest of completing the enterprise. In other words, by avoiding the word conspiracy, the drafters increased the likelihood that the ICC would become a reality, yet left open the possibility that prosecutors may pursue conspiracy convictions under the more oblique version of co-perpetration liability that currently appears in the statute. Consistent with this theory, one could argue that judges interpreting the ICC statute may appropriately read conspiracy into the statute. The ICTY's expansive reading of co-perpetrator liability and articulation of the contours of the joint criminal enterprise theory provides precedent for such an approach.

Richard P. Barrett & Laura E. Little, *Lessons of Yugoslav Rape Trials: A Role for Conspiracy Law in International Tribunals*, 88 MINN. L. REV. 30, 82 (2003).

Drafts of the ICC Statute also reproduced Article III of the Genocide Convention, suggesting that conspiracy to commit genocide might constitute a standalone crime. By the conclusion of the Rome Conference, however, all references to conspiracy had been eliminated from the Treaty. Why would the drafters of the ICC reject conspiracy liability for all crimes, even conspiracy to commit genocide, which has a clear treaty basis? One commentator suggests that "the discrepancy between the Genocide Convention and the Rome Statute was probably an oversight of exhausted drafters." William A. Schabas, GENOCIDE IN INTERNATIONAL LAW: THE CRIME OF CRIMES 264 (2000). Might there have been something more substantive going on?

NOTES & QUESTIONS

1. Conspiracy in Comparative Law

As the principal case discusses, conspiracy originated as, and largely remains, a common law concept. Although a comparatively broad doctrine of conspiratorial liability has not emerged in other systems, civil law countries do criminalize conspiracies formed for the purpose of carrying out certain particularly serious offenses that threaten the very survival of the state. This disparity between civil and common law systems has led one noted commentator to opine that "in international law no customary rule has evolved on conspiracy on account of the lack of support from civil law countries for this category of crime." Antonio Cassese, INTERNATIONAL CRIMINAL LAW 197 (2003).

United States federal law recognizes a generic inchoate crime of conspiracy to commit offenses against the United States (i.e., any federal offense).

> 18 U.S.C. 371: Conspiracy to Commit Offense or to Defraud United States. If two or more persons conspire either to commit any offense against the United States, or to defraud the United States, or any agency thereof in any manner or for any purpose, and one or more of such persons do any act to effect the object of the conspiracy, each shall be fined under this title or imprisoned not more than five years, or both.

In addition, certain substantive offenses also contain conspiracy provisions that provide for more serious penalties. *See* 21 U.S.C. § 846 (conspiracy to manufacture, dispense, etc. a controlled substance) and § 963 (conspiracy to import, etc. a controlled substance). Not all of these specialized statutes require an overt act. Studies suggest that upwards of 25% of federal criminal prosecutions in the U.S. now involve conspiracy charges. *See* Raphael Prober & Jill Randall, *Federal Criminal Conspiracy*, 39 AM. CRIM. L. REV. 571, 572 n.9 (2002). The Model Penal Code treats conspiracy as a form of responsibility at § 5.03(1):

> A person is guilty of conspiracy with another person or persons to commit a crime if with the purpose of promoting or facilitating its commission he: (a) agrees with such other person or persons that they or one or more of them will engage in conduct that constitutes such crime or attempt or solicitation to commit such crime; or (b) agrees to aid such other person or persons in the planning or commission of such crime or of an attempt or solicitation to commit such crime.

An overt act is required except with respect to conspiracies to commit a felony. *Id.* at § 5.01(5).

2. Merger of Conspiracy and Substantive Offense

At early common law, the conspiracy (which was a misdemeanor) was said to merge into the substantive offense (the object of the conspiracy) if the latter was committed. This precluded conviction and punishment for both the conspiracy and the completed offense (just as modern law precludes the punishment of both the attempt and the completed offense). This approach reflects the original purpose of the conspiracy doctrine, which was to deter preparatory criminal activity (a purpose no longer served once the substantive crime has been committed).

National legal systems have adopted different approaches to the question of merger. Some systems continue to treat conspiracy like other anticipatory offenses (such as attempt) that is punishable only if the criminal objective is not realized. In these systems, a conspiracy charge provides for alternative, rather than cumulative, punishment under the theory that a defendant should not be punished twice for the same bad act. The contemporary common law approach holds that "the conspiracy and the crime which was its object are separate and distinct offenses" such that it is possible for a defendant to be convicted and punished for both. LaFave & Scott, HANDBOOK ON CRIMINAL LAW 567 (1972). This approach reflects a concern that conspiracy should be criminalized to prevent not only the danger of the specific object of the conspiracy, but also the diffused and heightened danger associated with group criminality. In addition, allowing both crimes to be prosecuted adds to the deterrent effect of the law by raising the cost of joining a conspiracy, particularly where the individual may be liable for all crimes committed in furtherance of the conspiracy beyond the subject crime, as discussed below.

IV. CONSPIRACY AS A WAR CRIME

In a November 13, 2001, Executive Order governing the "Detention, Treatment and Trial of Certain Non-Citizens in the War Against Terrorism," U.S. President George W. Bush provided that individual members of al Qaeda engaged in violent acts against the United States would be tried by military commission. The Uniform Code of Military Justice establishes the jurisdiction of military commissions over "offenders or offenses that by statute or by the law of war may be tried by military commissions." 10 U.S.C. § 821. Prior to this point, Congress had statutorily established that military commissions could prosecute individuals for two codified violations of the laws of war: aiding the enemy (10 U.S.C. § 904) and spying (10 U.S.C. § 906). All other offenses triable by military commission would derive from the "law of war."

In 2006, Congress passed the Military Commission Act of 2006 (subsequently updated in 2009). The MCA contains a list of war crimes (for the text, see Chapter 7 on War Crimes) that includes several more controversial crimes, including conspiracy, terrorism, murder by an unprivileged belligerent, and providing material support for terrorism. In 2012, the Department of Defense issued a revised Manual for Military Commissions (M.C.M.), which sets forth the procedural and evidentiary rules and the elements of crimes applicable to U.S. military commissions. The definition of the crime and the elements of a conspiracy charge are set forth below.

Manual for Military Commissions: Crimes triable by military commission

The following offenses shall be triable by military commission under chapter 47A of title 10, United States Code, at any time. * * *

(29) CONSPIRACY.

a. *Text.* "Any person subject to this chapter who conspires to commit one or more substantive offenses triable by military commission under this chapter, and who knowingly does any overt act to effect the object of the conspiracy, shall be punished, if death results to one or more of the victims, by death or such other punishment as a military commission under this chapter may direct, and, if death does not result to any of the victims, by such punishment, other than death, as a military commission under this chapter may direct."

b. *Elements.*

(1) The accused entered into an agreement with one or more persons to commit one or more substantive offenses triable by military commission or otherwise joined an enterprise of persons who shared a common criminal purpose that involved, at least in part, the commission or intended commission of one or more substantive offenses triable by military commission;

(2) The accused knew the unlawful purpose of the agreement or the common criminal purpose of the enterprise and joined willfully, that is, with the intent to further the unlawful purpose; and

(3) The accused knowingly committed an overt act in order to accomplish some objective or purpose of the agreement or enterprise.

c. *Comment.*

(1) Two or more persons are required in order to have a conspiracy. Knowledge of the identity of co-conspirators and their particular connection with the agreement or enterprise need not be established. A person may be guilty of conspiracy although incapable of committing the intended offense. The joining of another conspirator after the conspiracy has been established does not create a new conspiracy or affect the status of the other conspirators. The agreement or common criminal purpose in a conspiracy need not be in any particular form or manifested in any formal words.

(2) The agreement or enterprise must, at least in part, involve the commission or intended commission of one or more substantive offenses triable by military commission. A single conspiracy may embrace multiple criminal objectives. The agreement need not include knowledge that any relevant offense is in fact "triable by military commission." Although the accused must be subject to the MCA, other co-conspirators need not be.

(3) The overt act must be done by the accused, and it must be done to effectuate the object of the conspiracy or in furtherance of the common criminal purpose. The accused need not have entered the agreement or criminal enterprise at the time of the overt act.

(4) The overt act need not be in itself criminal, but it must advance the purpose of the conspiracy. Although committing the intended offense may constitute the overt act, it is not essential

that the object offense be committed. It is not essential that any substantive offense, including the object offense, be committed.

(5) Each conspirator is liable for all offenses committed pursuant to or in furtherance of the conspiracy by any of the co-conspirators, after such conspirator has joined the conspiracy and while the conspiracy continues and such conspirator remains a party to it.

(6) A party to the conspiracy who withdraws from or abandons the agreement or enterprise before the commission of an overt act by any conspirator is not guilty of conspiracy. An effective withdrawal or abandonment must consist of affirmative conduct that is wholly inconsistent with adherence to the unlawful agreement or common criminal purpose and that shows that the party has severed all connection with the conspiracy. A conspirator who effectively withdraws from or abandons the conspiracy after the performance of an overt act by one of the conspirators remains guilty of conspiracy and of any offenses committed pursuant to the conspiracy up to the time of the withdrawal or abandonment. The withdrawal of a conspirator from the conspiracy does not affect the status of the remaining members.

(7) That the object of the conspiracy was impossible to effect is not a defense to this offense.

(8) Conspiracy to commit an offense is a separate and distinct offense from any offense committed pursuant to or in furtherance of the conspiracy, and both the conspiracy and any related offense may be charged, tried, and punished separately. Conspiracy should be charged separately from the related substantive offense. It is not a lesser-included offense of the substantive offense.

d. *Maximum punishment.* Death, if the death of any person occurs as a result of the conspiracy or joint enterprise. Otherwise, confinement for life.

So far, the U.S. military commissions' Convening Authority—who refers charges to trial—and the Chief Prosecutor—who prepares charges and represents the United States at trial—have charged conspiracy in its two forms: as a standalone offense (*see, e.g.*, the case against propagandist Ali Hamza Ahmad Suliman al-Bahlul, below) and as a form of responsibility for completed offenses (*see, e.g.*, the case against Abd Al Hadi Al-Iraqi, who was charged with denying quarter, attacking protected property, using treachery or perfidy, and conspiracy). A key case that also raises important issues under the U.S. Constitution involved Salim Ahmed Hamdan, allegedly Osama bin Laden's bodyguard and driver, who was captured by militia forces in Afghanistan in November 2001. About two years later, he became the first individual to be tried by military commission on charges that included one count of conspiracy, alleging that he "willfully and knowingly joined an enterprise of persons who shared a common criminal purpose and conspired and agreed with [named members of al Qaeda] to commit the following offenses triable by military commission: attacking civilians; attacking civilian objects; murder by an unprivileged belligerent; and terrorism." The charging document alleged that Hamdan committed certain overt acts in furtherance of the conspiracy, including transporting weapons used by al Qaeda members and receiving weapons training at an al Qaeda training camp. One of Hamdan's arguments was that the conspiracy charge was not triable by military commission per the laws of war or the Uniform Code of Military Justice. He also challenged the legitimacy of the military commission system, an issue taken up by the U.S. Supreme Court. Only a plurality of Justices—Justices Stevens, Souter, Ginsburg, and Breyer—reached the conspiracy issue, and so the charge went to trial. *Hamdan v. Rumsfeld*, 548 U.S. 557 (2006).

The military jury convicted Hamdan of providing material support to terrorism during the years 1996–2001, but acquitted him on the conspiracy count. They sentenced Hamdan to 66 months' imprisonment, with credit for time served. In November 2008, Hamdan was released to his home state of Yemen, a month before he completed his sentence and almost seven years to the day after his capture in Afghanistan. Notwithstanding his release, he continued to press his appeals. (A defendant's direct appeal of a conviction is not mooted by the individual's release from custody). A D.C. Circuit panel reversed his conviction for material support for terrorism, on the ground that material support for terrorism was not a war crime under the international law of war at the time he acted. *Hamdan v. United States*, 696 F.3d 1238 (D.C. Cir. 2012) ("*Hamdan II*").

Meanwhile, Ali Hamza Ahmad al Bahlul, a fellow Yemeni citizen accused of being al Qaeda's public relations director, was convicted of conspiracy, soliciting the murder of protected persons, and providing material support to terrorism; he was sentenced to life in prison. Although he refused to participate in his own defense at trial, Bahlul appealed his conviction to the D.C. Circuit, arguing that *Hamdan II* required his conspiracy conviction be reversed because conspiracy is not a law-of-war offense under international law. Surprisingly, the U.S. government conceded this point under the *Hamdan II* rationale, but argued that *Hamdan II* was wrongly decided. Instead, the government argued that the relevant reference point was the *domestic* law of war, rather than the *international* law of war. A D.C. Circuit panel disagreed and reversed Bahlul's conviction. *Al Bahlul v. United States*, 2013 WL 297726 (D.C. Cir. Jan. 25, 2013). The D.C. Circuit then considered the case *en banc* at the Government's request. That opinion appears below.

Ali Hamza Ahmad Suliman Al Bahlul v. United States of America

767 F.3d 1 (D.C. Cir. 2014) (D.C. Cir. 2014).

When Bahlul committed the crimes of which he was convicted, section 821 granted—and still grants—military commissions jurisdiction "with respect to offenders or offenses that by statute or by the law of war may be tried by military commissions." 10 U.S.C. § 821. Section 821 and its predecessor statute have been on the books for nearly a century. * * * We must therefore ascertain whether conspiracy to commit war crimes was a "law of war" offense triable by military commission under section 821 when Bahlul's conduct occurred because, if so, Bahlul's *ex post facto* argument fails.

In answering this question, we do not write on a clean slate. In *Hamdan*, seven justices of the Supreme Court debated the question at length. Four justices concluded that conspiracy is not triable by military commission under section 821. *Hamden*, 548 U.S. at 603–13 (plurality opinion of Stevens, J.). Three justices opined that it is. *Id.* at 697–704 (Thomas, J., dissenting). Both opinions scoured relevant international and domestic authorities but neither position garnered a majority. The case was resolved on other grounds and the eighth vote—one justice was recused—left the conspiracy question for another day, noting that the Congress may "provide further guidance in this area." *See id.* at 655 (Kennedy, J., concurring). In light of the uncertainty left by the split, it was not "plain" error to try Bahlul for conspiracy by military commission pursuant to section 821. * * *

The reason for the uncertainty is not only the divided result in *Hamdan* but also the High Court's failure to clearly resolve a subsidiary question: What body of law is encompassed by section 821's reference to the "law of war"? That dispute takes center stage here. Bahlul contends that "law of war" means the *international* law of war, full stop. The Government contends that we must look not only to international precedent but also "the common law of war developed in U.S. military tribunals." E.B. Br. of United States 28; *see also* Oral Arg. Tr. 15 ("[W]e believe the law of war is the international law of war as supplemented by the experience and practice of our wars and our wartime tribunals."). The answer is critical because the Government asserts that conspiracy is *not* an international law-of-war offense.

In *Hamdan II*, the Court said that "law of war" as used in section 821 is a term of art that refers to the international law of war. 696 F.3d at 1248; *see also id.* at 1252 (noting that "U.S. precedents may inform the content of international law"). Language in several Supreme Court opinions supports that proposition. *See, e.g., Ex parte Quirin*, 317 U.S. 1, 27–28 (1942) ("[T]his Court has recognized and applied the law of war as including that part of the law of nations which prescribes, for the conduct of war, the status, rights and duties of enemy nations as well as of enemy individuals."); *id.* at 29 (describing law of war as "branch of international law"); *see also Hamdan*, 548 U.S. at 603 (plurality) (citing *Quirin* and describing offense alleged therein as being "recognized as an offense against the law of war" both "in this country and internationally"); *id.* at 610–11 (analyzing international law sources); *id.* at 641 (Kennedy, J., concurring) ("[T]he law of war . . . is the body of international law governing armed conflict." * * * *In re Yamashita*, 327 U.S. 1, 12–16 (1946) (analyzing international precedent in determining whether offense was violation of law of war). * * *

Ultimately, we need not resolve *de novo* whether section 821 is limited to the international law of war. It is sufficient for our purpose to say that, at the time of this appeal, the answer to that question is not "obvious." * * * As seven justices did in *Hamdan*, we look to domestic wartime precedent to determine whether conspiracy has been traditionally triable by military commission. That precedent [including the assassination of Abraham Lincoln, which was prosecuted by a military commission and the trial of Nazi saboteurs] provides sufficient historical pedigree to sustain Bahlul's conviction on plain-error review.

NOTES & QUESTIONS

1. The Impact of *Bahlul*

The other convictions of the military commission all involve charges of material support and/or conspiracy, so all are in jeopardy. Indeed, three judgments involve only these charges: Australian David Hicks (who pleaded guilty to providing material support); Ibrahim Ahmed Mahmoud al-Qosi (who pleaded guilty to one count of each); and Noor Uthman Mohammed (same). The latter two defendants have been transferred to their native Sudan, and David Hicks is back in Australia. The sentences of other convicted enemy combatants may also be appealed. For example, Majid Khan—who pleaded guilty to conspiracy, murder, attempted murder, providing material support for terrorism and spying—was to serve 19 years in exchange for his cooperation in subsequent trials (and potentially 25 years if he fails to cooperate). The appeal probably does not materially impact the September 11th charges against Khalid Sheikh Mohammad and his three co-defendants, although they too were charged with inchoate conspiracy. The *Ex Post Facto* issue—deemed waived by Bahlul—could also scuttle a number of Guantánamo cases; all but one individual has been charged for pre-MCA conduct. For scholarship on the case that predates the *en banc* ruling, *see* Peter Margulies, *Defining, Punishing, and Membership in the Community of Nations: Material Support and Conspiracy Charges in Military Commissions*, 36 FORDHAM INT'L L. J. 1 (2013); Steve Vladeck, *The Laws of War as a Constitutional Limit on Military Jurisdiction*, 4 J. NAT'L SEC. L. & POL'Y 295 (2010). Does the opinion address the legality of conspiracy charges for conduct that post-dates the 2006 MCA?

2. The Role of Defense Counsel

Bahlul's counsel, David Frakt, is a Lieutenant Colonel in the U.S. Air Force JAG Corps Reserve and a former lead defense counsel with the Office of Military Commissions. Frakt was instructed by Bahlul not to mount a defense. What would you have done under the circumstances?

Frakt also represented Mohammed Jawad, who along with Omar Khadr were prosecuted for acts they allegedly committed while juveniles. Jawad apparently travelled from his native Pakistan to Afghanistan to take a job clearing mines. In 2002, when he was somewhere between 12 and 16 years old, Jawad was captured fleeing the scene of a grenade attack. He was accused of tossing a grenade into the window of a jeep carrying two U.S. soldiers, Sergeants First Class Michael Lyons and Christopher Martin, and their interpreter, Assadullah Khan Omerk; the three were wounded in the attack. Upon capture, Jawad was first taken to Bagram Air Base in Afghanistan and then to the Naval Base at Guantánamo. A victim of the so-called frequent flier program—a sleep deprivation technique that involved waking detainees up every couple of hours to change cells—Jawad was moved 112 times in a two-week period. Jawad apparently tried to kill himself while in detention by slamming his head repeatedly against a wall. (The then-Prosecutor, Lieutenant Colonel Darrel Vandeveld, a U.S. Army Reserve JAG, voluntarily turned over the records of Jawad's treatment; Vandeveld eventually resigned from his post and issued a scathing critique of the military commission system). Frakt sought to have the charges against Jawad dismissed on grounds of torture and "outrageous government conduct." He eventually prevailed; District Court Judge Ellen Segan Huvelle granted Jawad's *habeas corpus* petition, and Jawad was transferred to his native Afghanistan.

3. For Further Reading

For more on the law of conspiracy, *see Developments in the Law—Criminal Conspiracy*, 72 HARV. L. REV. 920 (1959); P. MacKinnon, *Developments in the Law of Criminal Conspiracy*, 59 CAN. BAR REV. 301 (1981); Richard P. Barrett & Laura E. Little, *Lessons Of Yugoslav Rape Trials: A Role Of Conspiracy Law In International Tribunals*, 88 MINN. L. REV. 30 (2003); George P. Fletcher, *The Hamdan Case and Conspiracy as a War Crime: A New Beginning for International Law in the U.S.*, 4 J. INT'L CRIM. JUST. 442 (2006); Jens Meierhenrich, *Conspiracy in International Law*, 2 ANNUAL REV. L. & SOC. SCIENCE 341 (2006).

PROBLEM

Imagine a multi-ethnic state wracked by years of escalating violence between two main ethnic groups competing for political and economic ascendancy. For some time, the country had a vibrant free press. As the society became more polarized along ethnic lines, however, a number of publications and media outlets targeted to specific readership groups emerged. In addition, political parties began to form along ethnic lines.

A full-scale civil war eventually erupted, pitting ethnically-based militia against the state military forces, which were populated and controlled by the majority ethnic group. The civil war unleashed community-level violence during which time members of the majority ethnic group committed several massacres against members of the minority group. The media were essential in facilitating these acts of genocide by disseminating incendiary and persecutory tracts and commentary urging the extermination of rival group members.

The civil war finally came to a close, and a fragile power-sharing regime was put in place. As part of a transitional justice process that included a truth commission and reparations scheme, the State Prosecutor launched genocide prosecutions against the alleged architects of the genocide pursuant to a local law that implements Articles II and III of the Genocide Convention (defining genocide and punishable acts, including conspiracy). In particular, the Prosecutor jointly indicted three individuals associated with ethnically-based media companies and political parties with conspiracy to commit genocide and incitement to genocide. The defendants are "A," the founder and Chairman of the Steering Committee of the media company (which controlled a radio and television station) and a member of one ethnically-oriented political party; "B," the founder of another ethnically-oriented political party and a member of the same Steering Committee, and "C," a magazine publisher and founding member of first political party.

At trial, the Prosecutor put on the following evidence: A & B were the most active members of the Steering Committee and had the power to sign checks on behalf of the company. Another member of the Steering Committee was on the editorial board of the magazine. The magazine was a shareholder in the media company. All other shareholders were members of one of the two political parties. Together, all three defendants attended political rallies and demonstrations; meetings of the two political parties; and meetings at the Ministry of Information, at which they represented their respective organizations. There was evidence in the record that the three had conversations about the role that the stations, magazine, and political parties could play in the struggle between the two ethnic groups. All three media outlets published similar stories calling for ethnic solidarity, preaching hate against the rival victim ethnic group, and urging the majority populace to rise up and fight for dominance. The magazine favorably featured the establishment of the media company, and the television station promoted the magazine to its viewers. The radio station and the magazine engaged in a joint promotion to teach the populace the "real facts" about inter-ethnic relations that portrayed the victim group as ambitious and combative. The radio station used the magazine to poll its listeners about the content of radio broadcasts. All three media outlets welcomed the creation of the two political parties. The magazine urged its readers to join one of the political parties.

In her Closing Argument, the Prosecutor argued that the three defendants regularly interacted and collaborated with each other, using the institutions they controlled to promote a joint agenda and common media front in order to bring about the destruction of the victim group in whole or in part. The Prosecutor argued that the totality of the evidence showed the existence of a conspiracy among the group to commit genocide. Imagine that you are representing the defendants in this case; how would you rebut the Prosecutor's arguments? Assume that the court found all the above facts had been proven beyond a reasonable doubt and that other evidence existed that proved each defendant possessed genocidal intent. How should the court rule on the conspiracy counts?

V. INCITEMENT IN INTERNATIONAL CRIMINAL LAW

Incitement involves convincing, encouraging, or persuading another to commit a crime. In domestic criminal law, incitement is treated alternatively as an inchoate offense that may be prosecuted even if the crime is not ultimately committed (the situation prevailing in most common law jurisdictions) or as a form of complicity, which requires proof that the incitement was successful (as is the case in most civil law jurisdictions). In international criminal law treaties, incitement is penalized only with respect to the crime of genocide and only when the incitement is both direct and public. However, the statutes of the *ad hoc* tribunals and the ICC recognize related forms of responsibility—such as instigation, solicitation, inducement, and abetting—as punishable forms of participation with respect to all crimes within their jurisdiction.

Like so much in this field, incitement entered international criminal law at Nuremberg, specifically with the prosecutions of Julius Streicher and Han Fritzsche. Streicher was the editor of *Der Stürmer* ("The Storm"). In considering the evidence against Streicher, the International Military Tribunal held that "he infected the German mind with the virus of anti-Semitism and incited the German people to active persecution." It continued:

> Twenty-three different articles of "Der Stürmer" between 1938 and 1941 were produced in evidence, in which the extermination "root and branch" was preached. Typical of his teachings was a leading article in September 1938, which termed the Jew a germ and a pest, not a human being, but "a parasite, an enemy, an evil-doer, a disseminator of diseases who must be destroyed in the interest of mankind." Other articles urged that only when world Jewry had been annihilated would the Jewish problem have been solved, and predicted that fifty years hence the Jewish graves "will proclaim that this people of murderers and criminals has after all met its deserved fate." * * * Such was the poison Streicher injected into the minds of thousands of Germans which caused them to follow the National Socialist policy of Jewish persecution and extermination.

Although Streicher denied any knowledge of mass executions of Jews, the evidence made clear that he received regular information on the progress of the "final solution," including from Jewish newspapers that were reporting on casualties. Although acquitted of crimes against the peace, Streicher was convicted of the crime against humanity of persecution on political and racial grounds and sentenced to death.

Fritzsche was a radio commentator and head of the Home Press Division of the Reich Ministry of Popular Enlightenment and Propaganda. Although the Tribunal concluded that he was a devoted anti-Semite, the evidence suggested that his position was not sufficiently important to "infer that he took part in originating or formulating propaganda campaigns." Moreover, his "speeches did not urge persecution or extermination of Jews." And, there "was no evidence that he was aware of their extermination in the East." In acquitting him, the Tribunal noted:

> It appears that Fritzsche sometimes made strong statements of a propagandistic nature in his broadcasts. But the Tribunal is not prepared to hold that they were intended to incite the German people to commit atrocities on conquered peoples, and he cannot be held to have been a participant in the crimes charged. His aim was rather to arouse popular sentiment in support of Hitler and the German war effort.

The Soviet judge, Major-General Iona Timofeevich Nikitchenko, dissented from this "unfounded acquittal." He argued:

> For the correct definition of the role of defendant Hans Fritzsche it is necessary, firstly, to keep clearly in mind the importance attached by Hitler and his closest associates (as Goering, for example) to propaganda in general and to radio propaganda in particular. This was considered one of the most important and essential factors in the success of conducting an aggressive war. [In] the Germany of Hitler, propaganda was invariably a factor in preparing and conducting acts of aggression and in training the German populace to accept obediently the criminal enterprises of German fascism. * * * The dissemination of provocative lies and the systematic deception of public opinion were as necessary to the Hitlerites for the realization of their plans as were the production of armaments and the drafting of military plans. Without propaganda, founded on the total eclipse of the freedom of press and of speech, it would not have been possible for German Fascism to realize its aggressive intentions, to lay the groundwork and then to put to practice the war crimes and the crimes against humanity.

Following these proceedings, the international community drafted the Convention on the Prevention and Punishment of Genocide. The Genocide Convention lists "direct and public incitement" as a punishable form of responsibility in Article III along with conspiracy, complicity, and attempt. By including incitement as a punishable offense, treaty drafters expressly sought to enable the *prevention* of genocide by criminalizing acts that precede actual genocide. Indeed, the Soviet delegate considered incitement to be indispensable to genocide, arguing that it "was impossible that hundreds of thousands of people should commit so many crimes unless they had been incited to do so and unless the crimes had been premeditated and carefully organized." The Soviet Union also sought to have hate crimes and racist propaganda treated as preparation for genocide. By contrast, the U.S. delegate to the drafting proceedings resisted the inclusion of incitement to genocide in the treaty unless the crime was qualified by language requiring a showing that genocide might reasonably result from the defendant's statements. He later sought to exclude reference to incitement altogether. For more on the drafting history, *see* William A. Schabas, GENOCIDE IN INTERNATIONAL LAW 266–271 (2000).

An early version of the Genocide Convention included the phrase "whether such incitement be successful or not" in Article III (c), but these words were deleted in a subsequent draft pursuant to an amendment proposed by the representative from Belgium. The delegate explained that his amendment was meant to offer a compromise to enable ratification by those states that did not recognize incitement as an inchoate crime. Some states, such as Germany, treat incitement as a form of complicity that is punishable only upon the commission of the principal crime. *See* German Criminal Code, Section 111 (providing for the prosecution of incitement only if it results in the commission or at least attempt of an offense). Incitement that does not lead to the commission of the principal offense is subject to a lesser punishment. In comparison, at common law, it is an offense to incite a person to commit an offense, regardless of whether the offense is actually committed. Thus, incitement is not ancillary to the commission of the principal offense in common law systems as it is in continental systems.

The inclusion of incitement within the Convention was identified as one of the reasons the United States did not ratify the treaty until 1986. As they grew closer to finally supporting ratification, members of the Senate Foreign Relations Committee struggled with the notion of incitement to commit genocide. In particular, there was concern that the Convention was unclear about how probable genocide would have to be in order to prosecute mere incitement as an inchoate crime. *See* S. Exec. Rept. No. 2, 99th Cong. (1st Sess. 1985), *reprinted in* 28 I.L.M. 754, 764–5 (1989). The legislation penalizing genocide defines "incite" to mean urging "another to engage imminently in conduct in circumstances under which there is a substantial likelihood of imminently causing such conduct." 18 U.S.C. § 1093(3).

VI. THE MODERN LAW OF INCITEMENT

The use of the media to incite violence was a defining aspect of the 1994 genocide in Rwanda. (See the Appendix for a map of Rwanda.) Accordingly, ICTR prosecutors indicted several high-level media personalities and executives, including Ferdinand Nahimana, a founding member of *Radio Télévision Libres des Mille Collines* (RTLM); Hassan Ngeze, the owner and editor of the Hutu extremist newspaper *Kangura*; and Jean-Bosco Barayagwiza, another founder of RTLM and the

Coalition pour la Défense de la République (CDR), a Hutu power political party. Barayagwiza was also public affairs director in Rwanda's Foreign Affairs Ministry. The Trial Chamber convicted all three defendants. The Appeals Chamber substantially affirmed the convictions and sentences of the three defendants, but modified and clarified some of the legal conclusions of the Trial Chamber in the opinion below.

Prosecutor v. Ferdinand Nahimana, Jean-Bosco Barayagwiza & Hassan Ngeze, Case No. ICTR–99–52–A, Judgement (Nov. 28, 2007)

In the Appeals Chamber

Crime of Direct and Public Incitement to Commit Genocide

677. A person may be found guilty of the crime specified in Article 2(3)(c) of the Statute if he or she directly and publicly incited the commission of genocide (the material element or *actus reus*) and had the intent directly and publicly to incite others to commit genocide (the intentional element or *mens rea*). Such intent in itself presupposes a genocidal intent.

678. The Appeals Chamber considers that a distinction must be made between instigation under Article 6(1) of the Statute and public and direct incitement to commit genocide under Article 2(3)(c) of the Statute. In the first place, instigation under Article 6(1) of the Statutes is a mode of responsibility; an accused will incur criminal responsibility only if the instigation in fact substantially contributed to the commission of one of the crimes under Articles 2 to 4 of the Statute. By contrast, direct and public incitement to commit genocide under Article 2(3)(c) is itself a crime, and it is not necessary to demonstrate that it in fact substantially contributed to the commission of acts of genocide. In other words, the crime of direct and public incitement to commit genocide is an inchoate offence, punishable even if no act of genocide has resulted therefrom. This is confirmed by the *travaux préparatoires* to the Genocide Convention, from which it can be concluded that the drafters of the Convention intended to punish direct and public incitement to commit genocide, even if no act of genocide was committed, the aim being to forestall the occurrence of such acts. The Appeals Chamber further observes—even if this is not decisive for the determination of the state of customary international law in 1994—that the Statute of the International Criminal Court also appears to provide that an accused incurs criminal responsibility for direct and public incitement to commit genocide, even if this is not followed by acts of genocide.

679. The second difference is that Article 2(3)(c) of the Statute requires that the incitement to commit genocide must have been direct and public, while Article 6(1) does not so require. * * *

Hate Speech and Direct Incitement to Commit Genocide

692. The Appeals Chamber considers that there is a difference between hate speech in general (or inciting discrimination or violence) and direct and public incitement to commit genocide. Direct incitement to commit genocide assumes that the speech is a direct appeal to commit an act referred to in Article 2(2) of the Statute; it has to be more than a mere vague or indirect suggestion. In most cases, direct and public incitement to commit genocide can be preceded or accompanied by hate speech, but only direct and public incitement to commit genocide is prohibited under Article 2(3)(c) of the Statute. This conclusion is corroborated by the *travaux préparatoires* to the Genocide Convention.

693. The Appeals Chamber therefore concludes that when a defendant is indicted pursuant to Article 2(3)(c) of the Statute, he cannot be held accountable for hate speech that does not directly call for the commission of genocide. The Appeals Chamber is also of the opinion that, to the extent that not all hate speeches constitute direct incitement to commit genocide, the jurisprudence on incitement to hatred, discrimination and violence is not directly applicable in determining what constitutes direct incitement to commit genocide. * * *

694. After recalling the jurisprudence of the Nuremberg Tribunal, the United Nations Human Rights Committee and the European Court of Human Rights, the Trial Chamber held that:

- Editors and publishers have generally been held responsible for the media they control;
- It is necessary to review whether the aim of the discourse is a lawful one, having regard, for example, to the language used and to the content of the text (in particular, whether it is intended to establish a critical distance from the words of others);
- The speech must be considered in its context when reviewing its potential impact;
- It is not necessary to prove that the speech at issue produced a direct effect. * * *

696. Furthermore, the Appeals Chamber notes that several extracts from the Judgement demonstrate that the Trial Chamber drew a distinction between hate speech and direct and public incitement to commit genocide, for example:

- The Trial Chamber held that one RTLM broadcast constituted hate speech, but that "this broadcast, which does not call on listeners to take action of any kind, does not constitute direct incitement;"
- After holding that the RTLM broadcasts as a whole denigrated the Tutsi, the Trial Chamber cited a broadcast

which, in its view, did constitute public and direct incitement to commit genocide;

– The Trial Chamber concluded that "[m]any of the writings published in *Kangura* combined ethnic hatred and fear-mongering with a call to violence to be directed against the Tutsi population, who were characterized as the enemy or enemy accomplices." It then noted that "not all of the writings published in *Kangura* and highlighted by the Prosecutor constitute direct incitement," citing the example of an article "brimming with ethnic hatred but [that] did not call on readers to take action against the Tutsi population."

697. The Appeals Chamber will now turn to the Appellants' submissions that the Trial Chamber erred (1) in considering that a speech in ambiguous terms, open to a variety of interpretations, can constitute direct incitement to commit genocide, and (2) in relying on the presumed intent of the author of the speech, on its potential dangers, and on the author's political and community affiliation, in order to determine whether it was of a criminal nature. The Appellants' position is in effect that incitement to commit genocide is direct only when it is explicit and that under no circumstances can the Chamber consider contextual elements in determining whether a speech constitutes direct incitement to commit genocide. For the reasons given below, the Appeals Chamber considers this approach overly restrictive.

Speeches That Are Open to Several Interpretations

698. In conformity with the *Akayesu* Trial Judgement, the Trial Chamber considered that it was necessary to take account of Rwanda's culture and language in determining whether a speech constituted direct incitement to commit genocide. In this respect, the Trial Chamber quotes the following excerpts from the *Akayesu* Trial Judgement:

> However, the Chamber is of the opinion that the direct element of incitement should be viewed in the light of its cultural and linguistic content. Indeed, a particular speech may be perceived as "direct" in one country, and not so in another, depending on the audience. The Chamber further recalls that incitement may be direct, and nonetheless implicit. [. . .]
>
> The Chamber will therefore consider on a case-by-case basis whether, in light of the culture of Rwanda and the specific circumstances of the instant case, acts of incitement can be viewed as direct or not, by focusing mainly on the issue of whether the persons for whom the message was intended immediately grasped the implication thereof.

699. The Appeals Chamber notes that this approach has been adopted in several other judgements and by the Supreme Court of Canada in *Mugesera*.

700. The Appeals Chamber agrees that the culture, including the nuances of the Kinyarwanda language, should be considered in determining what constitutes direct and public incitement to commit genocide in Rwanda. For this reason, it may be helpful to examine how a speech was understood by its intended audience in order to determine its true message.[1674]

701. The principal consideration is thus the meaning of the words used in the specific context: it does not matter that the message may appear ambiguous to another audience or in another context. On the other hand, if the discourse is still ambiguous even when considered in its context, it cannot be found beyond reasonable doubt to constitute direct and public incitement to commit genocide.

702. The Appeals Chamber is not persuaded that the *Streicher* and *Fritzsche* cases demonstrate that only discourse explicitly calling for extermination, or discourse that is entirely unambiguous for all types of audiences, can justify a conviction for direct and public incitement to commit genocide. First, it should be recalled that Streicher and Fritzsche were not charged with direct and public incitement to commit genocide, as there was no such crime under international law at the time. Second, it should be noted that the reason Fritzsche was acquitted is not because his pronouncements were not explicit enough, but rather because they did not implicitly or explicitly, "[intend] to incite the German people to commit atrocities on conquered peoples."

703. The Appeals Chamber therefore concludes that it was open to the Trial Chamber to hold that a speech containing no explicit appeal to commit genocide, or which appeared ambiguous, still constituted direct incitement to commit genocide in a particular context. The Appeals Chamber will examine below if it was reasonable to conclude that the speeches in the present case constituted direct and public incitement to commit genocide of the Tutsi.

Reliance on the Intent of the Speech's Author, Its Potential Dangers and the Author's Political and Community Affiliation

704. * * * Appellants Nahimana and Ngeze contend that the Trial Chamber erred in holding that speech containing no direct appeal to extermination could nevertheless constitute the *actus reus* of the crime of incitement simply because its author had a criminal intent. * * *

706. It is apparent * * * that the Trial Chamber employed the term "intent" with reference to the purpose of the speech, as evidenced, *inter alia*, by the language used, and not to the intent of its author. The Appeals Chamber is of the opinion that the purpose of the speech is indisputably a factor in determining whether there is direct and public incitement to commit genocide, and it can see no error in this respect on

---

1674 In this respect, while it is not necessary to prove that the pronouncements in question had actual effects, the fact that they did have such effects can be an indication that the receivers of the message understood them as direct incitement to commit genocide.

the part of the Trial Chamber. It is plain that the Trial Chamber did not find that a speech constitutes direct and public incitement to commit genocide simply because its author had criminal intent.

707. Appellants Barayagwiza and Ngeze further submit that the Trial Chamber erred in finding * * * that the media's intention to cause genocide was evidenced in part by the fact that genocide did occur. The Prosecutor responds that the Trial Chamber committed no error and submits that the fact that genocide was perpetrated can be one of many indices of *mens rea*. * * *

709. The Appeals Chamber is not persuaded that the mere fact that genocide occurred demonstrates that the journalists and individuals in control of the media intended to incite the commission of genocide. It is, of course, possible that these individuals had the intent to incite others to commit genocide and that their encouragement contributed significantly to the occurrence of genocide (as found by the Trial Chamber), but it would be wrong to hold that, since genocide took place, these individuals necessarily had the intent to incite genocide, as the genocide could have been the result of other factors. However, the Appeals Chamber notes that * * * the Judgement concludes that the fact that "the media intended to [cause genocide] is evidenced *in part* by the fact that it did have this effect." The Appeals Chamber cannot conclude that this reasoning was erroneous: in some circumstances, the fact that a speech leads to acts of genocide could be an indication that in that particular context the speech was understood to be an incitement to commit genocide and that this was indeed the intent of the author of the speech. The Appeals Chamber, notes, however, that this cannot be the only evidence adduced to conclude that the purpose of the speech (and of its author) was to incite the commission of genocide. * * *

712. Appellant Nahimana submits that the Trial Chamber erred in evaluating the criminal character of a speech on the basis of the political or community affiliation of its author. He bases his submission on paragraphs 1008 and 1009 of the Judgement:

> 1008. The Chamber notes that international standards restricting hate speech and the protection of freedom of expression have evolved largely in the context of national initiatives to control the danger and harm represented by various forms of prejudiced communication. The protection of free expression of political views has historically been balanced in the jurisprudence against the interest in national security. The dangers of censorship have often been associated in particular with the suppression of political or other minorities, or opposition to the government. The special protections developed by the jurisprudence for speech of this kind, in international law and more particularly in the American legal tradition of free speech, recognize the power dynamic inherent in the circumstances that make minority groups and political

opposition vulnerable to the exercise of power by the majority or by the government. These circumstances do not arise in the present case, where at issue is the speech of the so-called "majority population," in support of the government. The special protections for this kind of speech should accordingly be adapted, in the Chamber's view, so that ethnically specific expression would be more rather than less carefully scrutinized to ensure that minorities without equal means of defense are not endangered.

1009. Similarly, the Chamber considers that the "wider margin of appreciation" given in European Court [of Human Rights] cases to government discretion in its restriction of expression that constitutes incitement to violence should be adapted to the circumstance of this case. At issue is not a challenged restriction of expression but the expression itself. Moreover, the expression charged as incitement to violence was situated, in fact and at the time by its speakers, not as a threat to national security but rather in defence of national security, aligning it with state power rather than in opposition to it. Thus there is justification for adaptation of the application of international standards, which have evolved to protect the right of the government to defend itself from incitement to violence by others against it, rather than incitement to violence on its behalf against others, particularly as in this case when the others are members of a minority group.

713. The Appeals Chamber has a certain difficulty with these paragraphs. It notes, on the one hand, that the relevant issue is not whether the author of the speech is from the majority ethnic group or supports the government's agenda (and by implication, whether it is necessary to apply a stricter standard), but rather whether the speech in question constitutes direct incitement to commit genocide. On the other hand, it recognises that the political or community affiliation of the author of a speech may be regarded as a contextual element which can assist in its interpretation.

714. In the final analysis, the Appeals Chamber is not persuaded that the Trial Chamber was in effect more inclined to conclude that certain speeches constituted direct incitement to commit genocide because they were made by Hutu or by individuals speaking in support of the Government at the time. In this respect, the Appeals Chamber notes that, in its analysis of the charges against the Appellants, the Trial Chamber made no reference to their political or community affiliation. The Appeals Chamber concludes that no error has been shown. * * *

Application of the Legal Principles to the Facts of the Case * * *

737. The Appeals Chamber will begin by considering Appellant Nahimana's submission that the historical and political context shows that the broadcasts prior to 6 April 1994 did not call for the extermination

of the Tutsi population but rather denounced the [Tutsi Rwandan Patriotic Front's] actions and intentions. * * *

739. The Appeals Chamber would begin by pointing out that the broadcasts must be considered as a whole and placed in their particular context. Thus, even though the terms *Inyenzi* and *Inkotanyi** may have various meanings in various contexts (as with many words in every language), the Appeals Chamber is of the opinion that it was reasonable for the Trial Chamber to conclude that these expressions could in certain cases be taken to refer to the Tutsi population as a whole. The Appeals Chamber further considers that it was reasonable to conclude that certain RTLM broadcasts had directly equated the Tutsi with the enemy. * * *

741. * * * The Trial Chamber found that [the RTLM's 1 January 1994] broadcast "heated up heads." The Appeals Chamber agrees with the Trial Chamber: the broadcast of 1 January 1994 encouraged ethnic hatred. The Appeals Chamber notes that the broadcast also wanted to "warn" the Hutu majority against an impending "threat." The implicit message was perhaps that the Hutu had to take action to counter that "threat." However, in the absence of other evidence to show that the message was actually a call to commit acts of genocide against the Tutsi, the Appeals Chamber cannot conclude beyond reasonable doubt that the broadcast was a direct and public incitement to commit genocide.

742. * * * The Trial Chamber found that the broadcast [of 5 January 1994] was an "example of inflammatory speech," that the journalist's obvious intention "was to mobilize anger against the Tutsis" and to make fun of them. However, the broadcast contains no direct and public incitement to commit genocide against the Tutsi. * * *

744. * * * The broadcast [of 14 March 1994] named a person said to be a [Tutsi Rwandan Patriotic Front (RPF)] member and his family members. The broadcast did not directly call on anyone to kill the children, although it was perhaps an implicit call to do so. However, in the absence of other evidence to that effect, the Appeals Chamber cannot conclude beyond reasonable doubt that the broadcast directly and publicly incited the commission of genocide. * * *

746. * * * The Trial Chamber, after initially finding that there was nothing to support the view that the term *Inkotanyi* as cited in the broadcast [of 16 March 1994] referred to the Tutsi as a whole, even though that might be the case in other broadcasts, later stated the following:

> Although some of the broadcasts referred to the *Inkotanyi* or *Inyenzi* as distinct from the Tutsi, the repeated identification of the enemy as being the Tutsi was effectively conveyed to

* Eds.: Inyenzi means "cockroach." The *Inkotanyi* were a militia of a 19th century Tutsi feudal king who dominated the majority Hutus. The term was used to link the Tutsi-led RPF with memories of past Tutsi oppressors in the minds of Hutu listeners.

> listeners, as is evidenced by the testimony of witnesses. Against this backdrop, calls to the public to take up arms against the *Inkotanyi* or *Inyenzi* were interpreted as calls to take up arms against the Tutsi. Even before 6 April 1994, such calls were made on the air, not only in general terms, such as the broadcast by Valerie Bemeriki on 16 March 1994, saying "we shall take up any weapon, spears, bows" [. . .]

At first sight, the Trial Chamber's findings may appear contradictory. However, the Appeals Chamber understands that what the Trial Chamber meant was that, if the broadcast of 16 March 1994 were to be taken in isolation, it could not be concluded that the term *Inkotanyi* referred to the Tutsi as a whole; when other broadcasts were taken into account as contextual background (those naming the enemy as the Tutsi or equating the *Inkotanyi* and *Inyenzi* with the Tutsi population), the broadcast of 16 March 1994 could in fact be understood as a call to take up arms against the Tutsi. However, the Appeals Chamber is not satisfied that this was the only reasonable interpretation of the broadcast: it is possible the journalist was calling for arms to be taken up only against the RPF. The Appeals Chamber cannot therefore conclude beyond reasonable doubt that the broadcast represented a direct and public incitement to commit genocide. * * *

748. * * * The Trial Chamber found that the broadcast [of 1 April 1994] falsely accused certain doctors (one of whom was clearly a Tutsi) of the murder of a Hutu called Katumba and added that it "note[d] the request that if rumours of Dr. Ngirabanyiginya's support for the *Inkotanyi* were true, 'let his neighbours telephone us again and tell us that the doctor and his family are no longer in his house', a request, in the Chamber's view, that action be taken against the doctor and his family." In the Appeals Chamber's view, the Trial Chamber failed to show the evidence on which it based its assessment, and its findings thus appear speculative. In the absence of other evidence that this broadcast was indeed an incitement to kill designated individuals principally because they were of Tutsi ethnicity, the Appeals Chamber cannot conclude beyond reasonable doubt that this broadcast was a direct and public incitement to commit genocide.

749. * * * It is possible that the persons accused in the broadcast [made between 1 and 3 April 1994] of being *Inkotanyi* accomplices were so accused simply because of their Tutsi ethnicity and that the broadcast's real message was to call for their murder (which would amount to direct and public incitement to commit genocide). However, in the absence of evidence that these individuals had been falsely accused, and that the real reason for their being singled out was their ethnicity, the Appeals Chamber cannot conclude beyond reasonable doubt that this broadcast was a direct and public incitement to commit genocide. * * *

751. * * * Even if [the broadcast of 3 April 1994] was calculated to cause fear among the population by predicting an imminent attack by the

RPF, the Appeals Chamber cannot conclude beyond reasonable doubt that it was a direct and public incitement to commit genocide. * * *

754. The Appeals Chamber * * * finds that, although it is clear that RTLM broadcasts between I January and 6 April 1994 incited ethnic hatred, it has not been established that they directly and publicly incited the commission of genocide. * * *

756. * * * [T]he Trial Chamber * * * considered that other broadcasts made after 6 April 1994 explicitly called for the extermination of the Tutsi:

> Many of the RTLM broadcasts explicitly called for extermination. In the 13 May 1994 RTLM broadcast, Kantano Habimana spoke of exterminating the *Inkotanyi* so as "to wipe them from human memory," and exterminating the Tutsi "from the surface of the earth . . . to make them disappear for good." In the 4 June 1994 RTLM broadcast, Habimana again talked of exterminating the *Inkotanyi*, adding "the reason we will exterminate them is that they belong to one ethnic group." In the 5 June 1994 RTLM broadcast, Ananie Nkurunziza acknowledged that this extermination was underway and expressed the hope that "we continue exterminating them at the same pace." On the basis of all the programming he listened to after 6 April 1994, Witness GO testified that RTLM was constantly asking people to kill other people, that no distinction was made between the *Inyenzi* and the Tutsi, and that listeners were encouraged to continue killing them so that future generations would have to ask what *Inyenzi* or Tutsi looked like.

These broadcasts constitute, as such, direct and public incitement to commit genocide. Appellant Barayagwiza does not raise any argument relating to them.

757. Regarding the assertion by Appellant Barayagwiza that "the country was under attack, and it could therefore be expected that the virulence of the broadcasts would increase in response to fear of what the consequences would be if the RPF invasion were successful," this has no impact on the finding that the RTLM broadcasts in fact targeted the Tutsi population. As the Trial Chamber noted, RTLM broadcasts exploited "the fear of armed insurrection, to mobilize the population, whipping them into a frenzy of hatred and violence that was directed largely against the Tutsi ethnic group."

758. The Appeals Chamber finds that it has not been demonstrated that the Trial Chamber erred in considering that some of the RTLM broadcasts after 6 April 1994 called for the extermination of Tutsi and amounted to direct and public incitement to commit genocide. * * *

763. Appellant Ngeze submits that it was the exceptional events of 1994 which led to the genocide; that the genocide would still have occurred even if the articles published in *Kangura* had never existed, and

that it has thus not been proved that these articles incited genocide; moreover, at the time when the genocide was being committed *Kangura* was not being published. * * *

766. The Appeals Chamber summarily dismisses Appellant Ngeze's argument that the genocide would have occurred even if the *Kangura* articles had never existed, because it is not necessary to show that direct and public incitement to commit genocide was followed by actual consequences. Regarding the argument that *Kangura* was not being published at the time of the genocide, this is not relevant in deciding whether the *Kangura* publications constituted direct and public incitement to commit genocide. * * *

771. In an article headed the "Last Lie," which appeared in No. 54 of *Kangura* (January 1994), Appellant Ngeze wrote:

> Let's hope the *Inyenzi* will have the courage to understand what is going to happen and realize that if they make a small mistake, they will be exterminated; if they make the mistake of attacking again, there will be none of them left in Rwanda, not even a single accomplice. All the Hutus are united . . .

The Appeals Chamber agrees with the Trial Chamber that the term "accomplice" refers to the Tutsi in general, in light of the sentence which immediately follows this reference and which was written by the Appellant: "All the Hutus are united. . . ." The Appeals Chamber considers that this article called on the Hutu to stand united in order to exterminate the Tutsi if the RPF were to attack again. In the view of the Appeals Chamber, the fact that this call was conditional on there being an attack by RPF does nothing to lessen its impact as a direct call to commit genocide if the condition should be fulfilled; the Appeals Chamber finds that this article constituted direct and public incitement to commit genocide.

772. An article headed "Who Will Survive the War of March?," which appeared in issue No. 55 (January 1994) and was signed *Kangura*, included the following passage:

> If the *Inkotanyi* have decided to massacre us, the killing should be mutually done. This boil must be burst. The present situation warrants that we should be vigilant because they are difficult. The presence of U.N. forces will not prevent the *Inkotanyi* to start the war (. . .). These happening are possible in Rwanda, too. When the *Inkotanyi* must have surrounded the capital of Kigali, they will appeal to those of Mulindi and their accomplices within the country, and the rest will follow. It will be necessary for the majority people and its army to defend itself . . . On that day, blood will be spilled. On that day, much blood must have been spilled.

The Appeals Chamber notes that this article contains an appeal to "the majority people" to kill the *Inkotanyi* and their "accomplices within the country" (meaning the Tutsi) in case of an attack by the RPF. Accordingly, the Appeals chamber finds that this article constituted direct and public incitement to commit genocide.

773. An editorial signed by Appellant Ngeze and published in issue No. 56 of *Kangura* (February 1994) stated that, after the departure of the United Nations troops, "[a]ll the Tutsis and cowardly Hutus will be exterminated." The Trial Chamber found that this editorial was both a prediction and a threat. In the opinion of the Appeals Chamber, this article goes even further: it implicitly calls on its readers to exterminate Tutsi (and "cowardly Hutus") after the departure of the United Nations troops. The Appeals Chamber finds that this article constituted direct and public incitement to commit genocide against the Tutsi.

774. Paragraphs 227 to 229 of the Judgement also refers to an extract from an article headed "One Would Say That Tutsis Do Not Bleed, That Their Blood Does Not Flow," published in issue No. 56 of *Kangura* (February 1994). This article does not appear to threaten all Tutsi, but only the Tutsi who acclaimed Tito Rutaremara and who, in doing so, demonstrated their support for an armed insurrection. In the absence of any element demonstrating that all the Tutsi were actually targeted by this article, or that some Tutsi were targeted on the sole basis of their ethnicity, the Appeals Chamber cannot find that this article constituted direct incitement to commit genocide. * * *

Crimes Against Humanity: Persecution

970. The Trial Chamber found the Appellants guilty of persecution on the following grounds:

- Appellant Nahimana: for RTLM broadcasts in 1994 advocating ethnic hatred or inciting violence against the Tutsi population, guilty of persecution under Articles 3(h), 6(1) and 6(3) of the Statute;
- Appellant Barayagwiza: for RTLM broadcasts in 1994 advocating ethnic hatred or inciting violence against the Tutsi population [and for the activities of CDR that advocated ethnic hatred or invited violence], guilty of persecution under Articles 3(h) and 6(3) of the Statute; * * *
- Appellant Ngeze: for *Kangura* publications advocating ethnic hatred or inciting violence against the Tutsi population, as well as for his own acts that advocated ethnic hatred or incited violence against the Tutsi population, guilty of persecution under Articles 3(h) and 6(1) of the Statute.

971. The Appellants allege that the Trial Chamber erred in law and in fact in finding them guilty of persecution as a crime against humanity. * * *

983. The Trial Chamber defined the crime of persecution as "'a gross or blatant denial of a fundamental right reaching the same level of gravity' as the other acts enumerated as crimes against humanity under the Statute." The Chamber then stated:

> It is evident that hate speech targeting a population on the basis of ethnicity, or other discriminatory grounds, reaches this level of gravity and constitutes persecution under Article 3(h) of its Statute. In *Ruggiu*, the Tribunal so held, finding that the radio broadcasts of RTLM, in singling out and attacking the Tutsi ethnic minority, constituted a deprivation of "the fundamental rights to life, liberty and basic humanity enjoyed by members of the wider society." Hate speech is a discriminatory form of aggression that destroys the dignity of those in the group under attack. It creates a lesser status not only in the eyes of the group members themselves but also in the eyes of others who perceive and treat them as less than human. The denigration of persons on the basis of their ethnic identity or other group membership in and of itself, as well as in its other consequences, can be an irreversible harm.

984. The Trial Chamber explained that the speech itself constituted the persecution and that there was therefore no need for the speech to contain a call to action, or for there to be a link between persecution and acts of violence. It recalled that customary international law prohibits discrimination and that hate speech expressing ethnic and other forms of discrimination violates this prohibition. It found that the expressions of ethnic hatred in the RTLM broadcasts, *Kangura* publications and the activities of the CDR constituted persecution under Article 3(h) of the Statute.

985. The Appeals Chamber reiterates that "the crime of persecution consists of an act or omission which discriminates in fact and which: denies or infringes upon a fundamental right laid down in international customary or treaty law (the *actus reus*); and was carried out deliberately with the intention to discriminate on one of the listed grounds, specifically race, religion or politics (the *mens rea*)." However, not every act of discrimination will constitute the crime of persecution: the underlying acts of persecution, whether considered in isolation or in conjunction with other acts, must be of a gravity equal to the crimes listed under Article 3 of the Statute. Furthermore, it is not necessary that these underlying acts of persecution amount to crimes in international law. Accordingly, there is no need to review here the Appellants' arguments that mere hate speech does not constitute a crime in international criminal law.

986. The Appeals Chamber considers that hate speech targeting a population on the basis of ethnicity, or any other discriminatory ground, violates the right to respect for the dignity of the members of the targeted group as human beings, and therefore constitutes "actual

discrimination". In addition, the Appeals Chamber is of the view that speech inciting to violence against a population on the basis of ethnicity, or any other discriminatory ground, violates the right to security of the members of the targeted group and therefore constitutes "actual discrimination". However, the Appeals Chamber is not satisfied that hate speech alone can amount to a violation of the rights to life, freedom and physical integrity of the human being. Thus other persons need to intervene before such violations can occur; a speech cannot, in itself, directly kill members of a group, imprison or physically injure them.

987. The second question is whether the violation of fundamental rights (right to respect for human dignity, right to security) is as serious as in the case of the other crimes against humanity enumerated in Article 3 of the Statute. The Appeals Chamber is of the view that it is not necessary to decide here whether, in themselves, mere hate speeches not inciting violence against the members of a group are of a level of gravity equivalent to that for other crimes against humanity. As explained above, it is not necessary that every individual act underlying the crime of persecution should be of a gravity corresponding to other crimes against humanity: underlying acts of persecution can be considered together. It is the cumulative effect of all the underlying acts of the crime of persecution which must reach a level of gravity equivalent to that for other crimes against humanity. Furthermore, the context in which these underlying acts take place is particularly important for the purpose of assessing their gravity.

988. In the present case, the hate speeches made after 6 April 1994 were accompanied by calls for genocide against the Tutsi group and all these speeches took place in the context of a massive campaign of persecution directed at the Tutsi population of Rwanda, this campaign being also characterized by acts of violence (killings, torture and ill-treatment, rapes . . .) and of destruction of property. In particular, the speeches broadcast by RTLM—all of them by subordinates of Appellant Nahimana—considered as a whole and in their context, were, in the view of the Appeals Chamber, of a gravity equivalent to other crimes against humanity. The Appeals Chamber accordingly finds that the hate speeches and calls for violence against the Tutsi made after 6 April 1994 (thus after the beginning of a systematic and widespread attack against the Tutsi) themselves constituted underlying acts of persecution. In addition, as explained below, some speeches made after 6 April 1994 did in practice substantially contribute to the commission of other acts of persecution against the Tutsi; these speeches thus also instigated the commission of acts of persecution against the Tutsi.

NOTES & QUESTIONS

1. Case Outcome

The Trial Chamber convicted the Accused of incitement to commit genocide, genocide, conspiracy to commit genocide, and crimes against humanity (extermination and persecution). Ferdinand Nahimana, founder and board member of RTLM, and Hassan Ngeze, former editor of *Kangura* newspaper, both received the maximum sentence of life imprisonment. Nahimana and Barayagwiza were found directly responsible under Article 6(1) of the ICTR Statute as well as responsible as superiors under Article 6(3). The Trial Chamber convicted Ngeze under Article 6(1) only. The tribunal said that, in principle, life imprisonment would also have been the appropriate punishment for Jean-Bosco Barayagwiza, an RTLM board member and former leader of the CDR. The Chamber ruled, however, that it was bound by a previous ruling that Barayagwiza's sentence should be reduced if he were convicted, because his rights had been violated while in detention; in particular, Cameroon had held the accused in constructive custody without charges or access to a judge for three months before he was brought before the Tribunal. The Chamber, therefore, reduced Barayagwiza's sentence to thirty-two years, eight of which he had already served in detention. Barayagwiza's convictions for incitement of genocide, genocide, persecution, and extermination were reversed, mostly because he was found to no longer be in control of the RTLM after the start of the genocide. His conviction for speech acts he committed outside of the media was upheld. He died in 2010 of Hepatitis C, with his family claiming he had not received adequate treatment while in detention.

The Appeals Chamber affirmed Ngeze's conviction for incitement of genocide, but reversed his convictions on genocide and persecution, in part because most of the statements used to support those convictions occurred prior to 1994. His sentence was reduced to thirty-five years. Nahimana's convictions for incitement of genocide, persecution, and instigation of persecution were upheld, but his convictions for instigating genocide and for extermination were reversed. His sentence was reduced from life to thirty years.

2. A Theory of Criminal Speech

The renowned feminist scholar Catharine MacKinnon criticized the Appeals Chamber Judgment as lacking any coherent theory of when speech constitutes incitement:

> Where the trial chamber, with close factual analysis, presented penetrating insights on the role of expression in this genocide with incisive justifications at each step, the appeals chamber has no guiding theory in view. Even terms referring to the consequences of media—the subject at hand—are few, "the incendiary discourse" of *Kangura* or "the extermination discourse of the CDR" (Trial Judgment, paras. 519, 521) mentioned rarely and in passing. The appeals chamber's sense of direction must be inferred through a blizzard of outcomes, as timing substitutes for compass. In hundreds of single-spaced pages, one finds no theory on the relation between speech and action, no animating concept except two dates, and no air of reality to breathe.
>
> Context is the first casualty, accountability the last. With the vast corpus of relevant media evidence excised, the

> decontextualized inquiry that is left misses the forest for the trees—especially inapt in a genocide, which is all about forest. Eliminating pre-1994 material on the real, but not unbridgeable, jurisdictional date, as well as much evidence from before April 6, imposes a staggeringly short attention span. The court repeatedly refers to material published "years" before. The most distant is four years, much is within three months. It is as if the genocide sprang full blown on the day physical hostilities broke out.

Catharine A. MacKinnon, *International Decision: Prosecutor v. Nahimana, Barayagwiza, & Ngeze*, 103 AM. J. INT'L L. 97 (2009). In this piece, MacKinnon states a clear preference for the Trial Chamber opinion over the Appeals Chamber opinion, concluding that the Trial Chamber decision is "profound and lucid," "foundational," and "even visionary." In her seminal work, ONLY WORDS (1993), MacKinnon argues that hate speech, along with pornography and sexual harassment, constitute speech acts that promote subordination and discrimination.

3. Elements of Incitement

What are the elements of incitement as identified by the Appeals Chamber in terms of *mens rea*, *actus reus*, causation, and any circumstantial elements? Must the prosecution lead evidence that the defendant possessed genocidal intent, or is it enough that the individuals who are incited by the speech possessed this degree of specific intent? When does an intent to provoke ethnic animosity or resentment rise to the level of an intent to provoke others to commit genocide? The Appeals Chamber suggests that the context in which the words are spoken matters in whether the defendant can be convicted of incitement. Does the Tribunal provide enough guidance for applying this test outside of the context of an ongoing genocide? Is it proper for the intent to commit an inchoate offense (incitement) to be demonstrated by the occurrence of a non-inchoate offense (genocide)? Should incitement to genocide include an imminence requirement, or is this unworkable in the context of the crime?

Is the Appeals Chamber sufficiently clear about which statements are incitement to genocide and which might be aimed at encouraging listeners to join the war effort against the RPF, mobilizing a preemptive strike against a possible invasion by the RPF, or just raising "ethnic consciousness"? If statements did not constitute incitement, did they possess some other relevance to the case? Does the tribunal provide adequate guidance for determining when hate speech rises to the level of incitement? Would a statement praising and congratulating "valiant combatants" who successfully engaged in "battle" against the Tutsis be considered incitement under the *Nahimana* rationale? What about statements calling upon listeners to rejoice because the "*Inkotanyi*" have been exterminated?

4. The Genocide Convention

The Genocide Convention criminalizes only "direct and public" incitement. What do these modifiers require the prosecution to prove? In *Prosecutor v. Akayesu*, the ICTR adjudicated the first modern case under international criminal law involving incitement to genocide. *Prosecutor v.*

Akayesu, Case No. ICTR–96–4–T, Judgement (Sept. 2, 1998). The defendant was convicted of incitement to genocide for making a speech in a volatile environment that called upon his listeners to kill Tutsi individuals, "the real and the only enemy of the Hutu." *Id.* at para. 334. The Trial Chamber held that the public element of incitement involves an inquiry into several factors: "the place where the incitement occurred and whether or not assistance was selective or limited." *Id.* at para. 556. In addition, "[t]he direct element of incitement should be viewed in the light of its cultural and linguistic content." *Id.* at para. 557. The Trial Chamber determined that it would "consider on a case-by-case basis whether, in light of the culture of Rwanda and the specific circumstances of the instant case, acts of incitement can be viewed as direct or not, by focusing mainly on the issue of whether the persons for whom the message was intended immediately grasped the implications thereof." *Id.* at para. 558. In *Akayesu*, the Tribunal relied on expert and factual witness testimony to decode Akayesu's speech. For example, this testimony explained that when Akayesu called upon his listeners to kill the "*Inkotanyi*," he meant members of the Tutsi group.

5. Incitement and Instigation

Genocide is the only crime that may be prosecuted under an incitement theory of liability according to treaty law, the statutes of the two *ad hoc* tribunals, and the ICC Statute—why might this be so? By contrast, prosecutors in these tribunals can charge instigation or abetting for all three core crimes. Articles 7(1) (ICTY) and 6(1) (ICTR) thus provide that "[a] person who planned, instigated, ordered, committed or otherwise aided and abetted in the planning, preparation or execution of a crime . . . shall be individually responsible for the crime." What is the difference between incitement and instigation or abetting? The Appeals Chamber in *Nahimana* defined instigation as follows:

> 480. The *actus reus* of "instigating" implies prompting another person to commit an offence. It is not necessary to prove that the crime would not have been perpetrated without the involvement of the accused; it is sufficient to demonstrate that the instigation was a factor substantially contributing to the conduct of another person committing the crime. The *mens rea* for this mode of responsibility is the intent to instigate another person to commit a crime or at a minimum the awareness of the substantial likelihood that a crime will be committed in the execution of the act or omission instigated.

In examining the evidence linking the broadcasts to particular deaths, the Appeals Chamber found:

> 513. In the opinion of the Appeals Chamber, evidence of a link between the broadcasts aired on RTLM before 6 April 1994 and the acts of genocide committed against the individuals so named seems, at the very least, tenuous, especially when the date of the broadcast in question is not provided or when the period between the broadcast denouncing a person and the killing of that person is relatively long. * * * Thus the longer the lapse of time between a broadcast and the killing of a person, the greater the possibility

> that other events might be the real cause of such killing and that the broadcast might not have substantially contributed to it. Moreover, even though RTLM was widely listened to in Rwanda, there is no evidence that the unidentified persons responsible for killing Charles Shamukiga and Daniel Kabaka heard the RTLM broadcasts denouncing them. The Appeals Chamber is therefore of the opinion that it has not been sufficiently demonstrated that RTLM broadcasts before 6 April 1994 substantially contributed to the killing of these individuals.

Could someone be convicted of inciting the deaths of these individuals, but not instigating the crimes? If statements contribute to a climate of ethnic animosity and violence, are they punishable as either incitement or instigation? Does classifying someone as an instigator or inciter lessen their responsibility for the crime by suggesting that the direct perpetrators are more responsible? In the alternative, does placing blame on the inciter tend to deflect attention from the direct perpetrators, implying that they are of diminished responsibility because they were "incited" to act?

6. Incitement and Persecution

What is the relationship between incitement and persecution? Should speech that expresses ethnic hatred, but without a call to action, be penalized? The Trial Chamber ruled at para. 1073 that the crime of persecution "is not a provocation to cause harm" but "is itself the harm" such that "there need not be a call to action in communications that constitute persecution." As part of the appeal, the Open Society Justice Initiative filed an *amicus curiae* brief in the case on behalf of a number of human rights organizations interested in free speech and the protection of journalists. Amici argued that the Trial Chamber had blurred the distinction between hate speech, which states are entitled to penalize but that does not rise to the level of an international crime, and acts of incitement, which are criminalized under international law.

In *Prosecutor v. Kordić and Čerkez,* Case No. IT–94–14/2–T, Judgement, para. 209 (Feb. 26, 2001), an ICTY Trial Chamber concluded that promoting hatred, by itself, did not constitute an international crime on the theory that hate speech alone "does not rise to the same level of gravity as the other acts enumerated" the ICTY's provision defining crimes against humanity. It also held that "the criminal prohibition of this act has not attained the status of customary international law. Thus, to convict the accused for such an act as is alleged as persecution would violate the principle of legality." Which is the better approach?

7. Incitement via Social Media

In *Akayesu*, the Trial Chamber adopted the position set forth in Article 91 of the Rwandan Penal Code that incitement may be committed "through speeches, shouting or threats uttered in public places or at public gatherings, or through the sale or dissemination, offer for sale or display of written material or printed matter in public places or at public gatherings, or through the public display of placards or posters, or through any other means of audiovisual communication." *Prosecutor v. Akayesu*, Case No. ICTR–96–

4–T, Judgement, paras. 553, 559 (Sept. 2, 1998). Is it true that "[w]ritten materials can be utilized in a similarly insidious fashion to promote and incite genocide? Periodicals can trigger the same mass effects that radio propaganda can activate"? Joshua Wallenstein, *Punishing Words: An Analysis of the Necessity of the Element of Causation in Prosecutions for Incitement to Genocide*, 54 STAN. L. REV. 351, 391 (2001). Is incitement by text less "public" or "direct" than incitement through verbal speech? What about incitement via social media platforms, such as Twitter, Facebook, or Instagram? Organizations such as Ushahidi, a non-profit tech company formed after the post-election violence in Kenya, have created tools to track dangerous speech (including hate speech and incitement) over the internet and via mobile technologies.

8. Jurisdiction *Ratione Temporis*

Article 1 of the ICTR Statute provides:

> The International Tribunal for Rwanda shall have the power to prosecute persons responsible for serious violations of international humanitarian law committed in the territory of Rwanda and Rwandan citizens responsible for such violations committed in the territory of neighbouring States between 1 January 1994 and 31 December 1994, in accordance with the provisions of the present Statute.

Article 7 reaffirms that the "temporal jurisdiction of the International Tribunal for Rwanda shall extend to a period beginning on 1 January 1994 and ending on 31 December 1994." Yet, many of the statements cited in the case were made prior to January 1994. Indeed, Ngeze had stopped publishing *Kangura* by the time the genocide began on April 6, 1994. The Appeals Chamber drew a strong distinction between those speech acts committed prior to January 1, 1994 and those after, allowing the former into evidence only to provide context, but not as acts that themselves are within the jurisdiction of the Tribunal:

> 723. The Appeals Chamber is of the opinion that the Trial Chamber erred in considering that incitement to commit genocide continues in time "until the completion of the acts contemplated." The Appeals Chamber considers that the crime of direct and public incitement to commit genocide is completed as soon as the discourse in question is uttered or published, even though the effects of incitement may extend in time. The Appeals Chamber accordingly holds that the Trial Chamber could not have jurisdiction over acts of incitement having occurred before 1994 on the grounds that such incitement continued in time until the commission of the genocide in 1994.

Judge Shahabuddeen in dissent disagreed with the strict temporal approach of the majority, arguing that incitement is a continuous crime, and thus statements made in the past may still have direct effects in the future. Do you agree with the majority's approach? When is an act of incitement committed—at the time the words are uttered or when the incited criminal act is committed? One of the reasons that the Rwandan representative to the

Security Council voted against the establishment of the ICTR Statute was that the Tribunal's temporal jurisdiction would not encompass the genocide's planning and preparatory acts but did include its aftermath. *See* U.N. SCOR, 49th Sess., 3453rd mtg., at para. 14 U.N. Doc. S/PV.3453 (1994).

Is incitement a continuing crime? BLACK'S LAW DICTIONARY defines continuing crime as follows

1. A crime that continues after an initial illegal act has been consummated; a crime that involves ongoing elements * * *
2. A crime (such as driving a stolen vehicle) that continues over an extended period.

In some states, the statute of limitation for incitement starts with the completion of the criminal offense, rather than with the utterance of the inciting words. If statements outside of the temporary jurisdiction of the particular tribunal cannot be considered acts of incitement *per se*, what other purpose might such evidence serve in a criminal prosecution? Should they be admitted into evidence or are they likely to be prejudicial to the accused? Some states will punish incitement more harshly if it is effective. French incitement law is in accord. *See* Code Pénal, Art. 211–2 (Fra.).

9. The Free Speech International Standard

In addition to the two Nuremberg era cases (*Streicher* & *Fritzsche*) in which criminal incitement was directly at issue, the Trial and Appeals Chamber also cite a number of cases emanating from the Human Rights Committee and the European Court of Human Rights to identify the "international standard" of free speech. Under certain conditions, these bodies accept petitions from individuals claiming to be victims of violations of the International Covenant on Civil and Political Rights (ICCPR) or the European Convention on Human Rights, respectively. These bodies have balanced free speech rights against the right to be free from discrimination in considering the circumstances in which states can restrict, or even criminalize, speech.

For example, in the case of *Robert Faurisson v. France*, the petitioner had published his views doubting the existence of gas chambers used to exterminate detainees at Nazi concentration camps. France prosecuted Faurisson for inciting his readers to anti-Semitic behavior. Faurisson challenged his conviction for incitement before the Human Rights Committee on the ground that it violated his free speech rights. The Committee ruled that France was entitled to place limits on free speech rights where the exercise of those rights would constitute incitement to discrimination. *Faurisson v. France*, U.N.Doc. CCPR/C/58/550/1993 (1996). Neither of these bodies exercises criminal jurisdiction over individuals. How might an international criminal tribunal use rulings from these bodies? How relevant are these rulings to the question presented in *Nahimana*?

10. Georges Ruggiu

Georges Ruggiu, a former RTLM journalist, pled guilty to direct and public incitement to commit genocide and crimes against humanity (persecution). As part of the ICTR's first persecution judgment, the Trial

Chamber sentenced him to 12 years' imprisonment in 2000. He testified against the three Media Case defendants that "[t]he editorial policy of RTLM was to diabolize the RPF and pro-RPF personalities and to prove that U.N. peacekeepers deployed in the country were biased in favor of the RPF." *Id.* at para. 44. He also testified that RTLM received information from Hutu *Interahamwe* militia about operations they planned and "search" notices for people or cars, which was then broadcast on the radio to enable apprehension and elimination. Ruggiu helped to decode some of the cryptic references in the articles and broadcasts. For example, he testified that calls to "go to work" meant start killing Tutsis. *Prosecutor v. Georges Ruggiu*, Case No. ICTR 97–32–I, Judgement and Sentence (June 1, 2000). Ruggiu, a Belgian national, was the only European to be prosecuted by the ICTR. In *Ruggiu*, the ICTR held that hate speech targeting a population on the basis of ethnicity constituted persecution under Article 3(h) of the ICTR Statute. *Id.* at paras. 22–23. Would such statements have been protected viewpoint speech under United States law? Many European states, such as Denmark, France, the Netherlands, and the United Kingdom, have criminalized hate speech as a function of public order and to protect human dignity.

11. Prevention

Where violence is being propagated through the public media, should the international community "jam" broadcasts? Before and during the Rwandan genocide, NGOs and some members of Congress unsuccessfully called upon the United States to jam the airwaves and prevent RTLM from broadcasting. Consider this account of the United States' historic reticence to engage in jamming:

> From a policy perspective, there are perhaps four major reasons why the United States has consistently opposed any form of nonmilitary radio jamming in the postwar world. First, American officials legitimately believed that fostering the free and unimpeded flow of information would promote freedom of expression across the globe. Second, as a net exporter of information, the United States stood to gain more from a free-flow standard than from a standard with exceptions. Third, by maintaining a pure standard, Washington was able to take the moral high ground when it condemned Soviet bloc states for illegal jamming. Fourth, making exceptions for certain types of interference, the Americans may well have feared, would have set a dangerous precedent for interference with satellites, television broadcasts and, most recently, the Internet. * * *

This same commentator favors the use of jamming:

> While permitting the limited use of offensive radio jamming in defense of human rights may play only a small role in preventing genocide and other mass abuses, jamming can be a potentially effective and relatively low-risk tool for keeping tensions in check, or at least countering one important means of delivering dangerous messages inciting people to violence. As one of a larger set of intermediate actions between international neglect and

> humanitarian intervention, it can increase the armory of responsive tools available to address such violations. As has been discussed, stripped of its Cold War overtones, the international law regarding radio jamming is not nearly as uniform and absolute as it may once have seemed, even if the strong presumption toward the free flow of information and against jamming continues to fulfill a valuable international role.

Jamie Frederic Metzl, *Rwandan Genocide And The International Law Of Radio Jamming*, 91 AM. J. INT'L. L. 628, 644–50 (1997). *See also* Samantha Power, A PROBLEM FROM HELL: AMERICA AND THE AGE OF GENOCIDE 371–2 (2002) (recounting U.S. deliberations); William A. Schabas, *Hate Speech in Rwanda: The Road to Genocide*, 46 MCGILL L. J. 141, 148 (2000).

12. A Threat to Free Speech and Democracy?

Does the *Nahimana* opinion risk undermining the establishment of democracy in Rwanda? Consider this view:

> Possibly the most central premise of democracy is that a self-governing people must have virtually complete freedom in presenting and hearing ideas and proposals, no matter how venal, offensive, unwise, or inhumane the idea or proposal—otherwise people's capacity to be self-governing would be denied. Moreover, in the real world of passionate advocacy of ideas and proposals, the offensive nature of the presentation cannot be a justification for suppression. On the other hand, this same premise of respect for individual decision-making autonomy that requires expressive freedom also means that people can and should be held responsible for their acts. The premise of respect for people's capacity to be self-governing means that a person should seldom be permitted to deflect responsibility for what she does on to another person, for example, because the other person suggested the act in which she subsequently engaged. The distinction between speech—which offers itself for acceptance, rejection, or discussion—and action is fundamental if people are to be treated as free and responsible. * * *
>
> Thus, a central requirement for democratic society is that the law recognizes, and that people learn, that actions do not follow automatically, and should not be understood to follow automatically, from expression. Action requires the independent decision by the listener to accept the speaker's counsel and then to act on the basis of that counsel. Self-governing individuals must learn to take responsibility for what they do, while democracy must operate on the premise that advocacy of any action, no matter how heinous, merely presents one view for people to consider. * * * The world's—and the law's—responsibility is not to prevent evil ideas from being expressed but rather is, in the first instance, to prevent them from being acted upon and, eventually, to engage in more speech and teaching that convinces people that these ideas are unpersuasive. In a world filled with unrepentant racial antagonism

> and beliefs of ethnic superiority, peace and toleration almost surely will not be produced by attempted suppression or by prohibiting the advocacy of such ideas. Rather, as Justice Holmes implies, the only responsible basis for a long term hope of peace and reconciliation is that people—and media and countries—learn to answer other people's objectionable advocacy. Hope lies in learning to effectively present more persuasive, more appealing, views and alternatives.

C. Edwin Baker, *Genocide, Press Freedom, and the Case of Hassan Ngeze* (U. of Penn. Law School, Public Law Working Paper No. 46) (available on SSRN). Does this position hold true in a situation of an imperfectly consolidated democracy?

13. Protection of Journalists

Is there a risk that authoritarian governments will justify the repression of critical media by invoking a supposed duty under international criminal law to suppress hate speech or incitement? Imagine a situation in which journalistic reporting on government shortcomings fuels a political protest. The government labels the reporting as incitement to rebellion, or incitement to hatred, and either summarily shuts down the offending media outlet or takes legal action against the journalist. Might the government invoke *Nahimana* to justify its actions, arguing that it had a legal obligation to take measures against the media outlets because of its capacity to fuel large-scale ethnic violence? The Committee to Protect Journalists documented nearly 50 such cases in such countries as Burundi, Central African Republic, Togo, Gabon, Zimbabwe, and Rwanda. *See* Joel Simon, *Of Hate and Genocide: In Africa, Exploiting the Past*, COLUM. JOURNALISM REV. (Jan./Feb. 2002). In Rwanda, for example, public incitement to divisionism is a crime punishable by up to five years in prison, heavy fines, or both. Art. 8, Law 47/2001 of 18/12/2001 (15 Feb. 2002). The Tutsi-led government, which consolidated power in 2003, has increasingly used allegations of ethnic divisionism to silence critics. Such allegations have been levied against Rwanda's only independent newspaper, *Umuseso*. Should the Trial Chamber have anticipated the potential "misuse" of its incitement doctrine?

14. For Further Reading

For another critical view of the Appeals Chamber opinion *see* George William Mugwanya, *Recent Trends in International Criminal Law: Perspectives from the UN International Criminal Tribunal for Rwanda*, 6 NW. U. J. HUM. RTS. 415 (2008). For a more sympathetic take, *see* William A. Schabas, *International Criminal Tribunals: A Review of 2007*, 6 NW. U. J. INT'L HUM. RTS. 382 (2008). For a critique of the Trial Chamber opinion *see* Diane F. Orentlicher, *Criminalizing Hate Speech in the Crucible of Trial:* Prosecutor v. Nahimana, 21 AM. U. INT'L L. REV. 557 (2006). In support of the Trial Chamber opinion, *see* Susan Benesch, *Inciting Genocide, Pleading Free Speech*, 21 WORLD POLICY J. 62 (2004); Gregory S. Gordon, *"A War of Media, Words, Newspapers, and Radio Stations": The ICTR Media Trial Verdict and a New Chapter in the International Law of Hate Speech*, 45 VA. J. INT'L L. 139 (2004); Recent Case: *U.N. Tribunal Finds that Mass Media*

Hate Speech Constitutes Genocide, Incitement to Genocide, and Crimes Against Humanity, 117 HARV. L. REV. 2769 (2004).

PROBLEM

Consider the speech below, which was delivered in 1993, prior to the official start of the Rwandan genocide. Would it constitute incitement under the standard set forth in the *Media Case*? To the naked ear, is the meaning of the speech always clear? Are courts, especially international courts or courts far from the events in question, qualified to understand culturally-specific coded language?

> Long life to our movement. Long life to President Habyarimana. Long life to ourselves, the militants of the movement at this meeting. Militants of our movement, as we are all met here, I think you will understand the meaning of the word I will say to you. The first point I have decided to discuss with you is that you should not let yourselves be invaded. Tell me, if you as a man, a mother or father, who are here, if someone comes one day to move into your yard and defecate there, will you really allow him to come again? It is out of the question. In any case, you understand yourselves, the priests have taught us good things: our movement is also a movement for peace. However, we have to know that, for our peace, there is no way to have it but to defend ourselves. Some have quoted the following saying: "Those who seek peace always make ready for war." Thus, in our prefecture, this is the fourth or fifth time I am speaking about it, there are those who have acted first. It says in the Gospel that if someone strikes you on one cheek, you should turn the other cheek. I tell you that the Gospel has changed in our movement: if someone strikes you on one cheek, you hit them twice on one cheek and they collapse on the ground and will never be able to recover! So here, never again will what they call their flag, even what they call their militant, come to our soil to speak: I mean throughout this prefecture, from one end to the other!
>
> A proverb says: "Hyenas eat others, but when you go to eat them they are bitter"! They should know that one man is as good as another, our party will not let itself be invaded either. There is no question of allowing ourselves to be invaded, let me tell you. There is also something else I would like to talk to you about, concerning "not being invaded," and which you must reject, as these are dreadful things. Tell me, dear parents gathered here, have you ever seen, I do not know if she is still a mother, have you ever seen this woman who heads the Ministry of Education,* come herself to find out if your children have left the house to go and study or go back to school? Have you not heard that she said that from now on no one will go back to school? And now she is attacking teachers!

---

* Eds.: This is probably a reference to Agathe Uwilingiyimana, who as Minister of Education in 1992 ended ethnic quotas in schools in favor of a merit system. She later became Prime Minister of Rwanda and was killed in the early days of the genocide.

You have also heard on the radio that nowadays she is even insulting our President! Have you ever heard a mother insulting people in public? So what I would like to tell you here, and this is the truth, there is no doubt, to say it would be this or that, there might be among them people who have behaved flippantly. Frankly, will you allow them to invade us to take the party away from us and to take our men?

I am asking you to take two very important actions. The first is to write to this shameless woman who is issuing insults publicly and on the airwaves of our radio to all. I want you to write her to tell her that these teachers, who are ours, are irreproachable in their conduct and standards, and that they are looking after our children with care; these teachers must continue to educate our children and she must mend her ways. Then, you would all sign together: paper will not be wanting. Let everyone whom she has appointed be there, let them go to her town to look after the education of her children. As for ours, they will continue to be educated by our own people. This is another important point on which we must take decisions: we cannot let ourselves be invaded: this is forbidden!

Something else which may be called "not allowing ourselves to be invaded" in the country, you know people they call "*Inyenzis*" (cockroaches), no longer call them "*Inkotanyi*" (tough fighters), as they are actually "*Inyenzis*." These people called *Inyenzis* are now on their way to attack us.

You know what it is, dear friends, "not letting ourselves be invaded," or you know it. You know there are "*Inyenzis*" in the country who have taken the opportunity of sending their children to the front, to go and help the "*Inkotanyis*." That is something you intend to speak about yourselves. Everywhere people told me of the number of young people who had gone. They said to me "Where they are going, and who is taking them . . . why are they are not arrested as well as their families?" So I will tell you now, it is written in the law, in the book of the Penal Code: "Every person who recruits soldiers by seeking them in the population, seeking young persons everywhere whom they will give to the foreign armed forces attacking the Republic, shall be liable to death." It is in writing.

Why do they not arrest these parents who have sent away their children and why do they not exterminate them? Why do they not arrest the people taking them away and why do they not exterminate all of them? Are we really waiting till they come to exterminate us?

I should like to tell you that we are now asking that these people be placed on a list and be taken to court to be tried in our presence. If the judges refuse, it is written in the Constitution that "justice is rendered in the people's name." If justice therefore is no longer serving the people, as written in our Constitution which we voted for ourselves, this means that at that point we who also make up the population whom it is supposed to serve, we must do something ourselves to exterminate this rabble. I tell you in all truth, as it says in the Gospel, "When you allow a serpent biting you to remain attached to you with your agreement, you are the one who will suffer."

I have to tell you that a day and a night ago, a small group of men armed with pistols entered a cabaret and demanded that cards be shown. They separated the party people. When a party member showed his card, he was immediately shot; I am not lying to you, they even tell you on the radio; they shot this man and disappeared into the Kigali marshes to escape, after saying they were "*Inkotanyis*." So tell me, these young people who acquire our identity cards, then they come back armed with guns on behalf of the "*Inyenzis*" or their accomplices to shoot us! I do not think we are going to allow them to shoot us! The representatives of those parties who collaborate with the "*Inyenzis*," those who represent them—I am telling you, and I am not lying—they only want to exterminate us. They only want to exterminate us: they have no other aim. The time has come when we will also be defending ourselves, so that we will never agree to die because the law refuses to act! I should like to tell you that they have begun killing. That is actually what is happening! They attack homes and kill people.

There is another important point I would like to talk to you about so that we do not go on allowing ourselves to be invaded: you will hear mention of the Arusha Peace Accords. What I will tell you is that the delegates you will hear are in Arusha do not represent Rwanda. They do not represent all of Rwanda, I tell you that as a fact. The delegates from Rwanda, who are said to be from Rwanda, are led by an "*Inyenzi*," who is there to discuss with "*Inyenzis*." As for what they call "discussions," we are not against discussions. I have to tell you that they do not come from Rwanda: they are "*Inyenzis*" who conduct discussions with "*Inyenzis*," and you must know that once and for all! In any case, we will never accept these things which come from there!

So in order to conclude, I would remind you of all the important things I have just spoken to you about: the most essential is that we should not allow ourselves to be invaded, lest the very persons who are collapsing take away some of you. Do not be afraid, know that anyone whose neck you do not cut is the one who will cut your neck. Let me tell you, these people should begin leaving while there is still time and go and live with their people, or even go to the "*Inyenzis*," instead of living among us and keeping their guns, so that when we are asleep they can shoot us. Let them pack their bags, let them get going, so that no one will return here to talk and no one will bring scraps claiming to be flags!

Thank you for listening to me and I also thank you for your courage, in your arms and in your hearts. I know you are men, you are young women, fathers and mothers of families, who will not allow yourselves to be invaded. May your lives be long! Long life to President Habyarimana! Long life and prosperity to you!

The text above has been adapted from a speech made by Leon Mugesera, a Hutu government official in Rwanda. The speech was given in 1992, a year and a half before the official start of the Rwandan genocide. In 1993, Mugesera successfully applied for permanent residence in Canada. Mugesera was later identified by Rwandan ex-patriots and brought to the attention of the Ministry of Citizenship and Immigration. In 1995, Canadian immigration authorities commenced deportation proceedings against him, on the basis of a provision allowing the deportation of a permanent resident if it is determined that the individual committed criminal acts or offenses. Canadian Criminal Code, R.S.C., c.C-46, s.464 (1985). In this case, the Minister of Citizenship and Immigration determined that Mugesera, by his speech, had incited murder, genocide and hatred, and had committed a crime against humanity. An adjudicator concluded that the allegations were valid and issued a deportation order.

The Immigration and Refugee Board (Appeal Division) ("IAD") upheld the decision. A federal court, however, dismissed the application for judicial review on the allegations of incitement to commit murder, genocide or hatred, but allowed it on the allegation of crimes against humanity. The Federal Court of Appeal ("FCA") reversed several findings of fact made by the IAD, found the Minister's allegations against Mugesera to be unfounded, and set aside the deportation order on the grounds that Mugesera did not mean to tell his audience to kill Tutsi, and could not have foreseen that they would understand him that way if they did in fact subsequently attack Tutsi individuals. The FCA ruled: "there is nothing in the evidence to indicate that Mr. Mugesera, even under the cover of anecdotes or imagery, deliberately incited murder, hatred or genocide."

The Supreme Court disagreed and held that the deportation order was valid and should be restored. *Mugesera v. Canada*, [2005] S.C.R. 100 (Can.). The full speech was translated from Kinyarwanda by Prof. Thomas Kamanzi, Linguist Director of the Centre Études Rwandaises at the Institut de Recherche Scientifique et Technologique, and is an appendix to the Canadian Supreme Court opinion. Mugesera apparently requested that rather than be deported, he be tried in Canada, under the Crimes Against Humanity and War Crimes Act (S.C., 2000, c. 24), enacted to implement Canada's obligations under the ICC Statute. He was deported on January 23, 2012.

The proceedings against Mugesera are administrative in nature and operate under a "balance of the probabilities" standard as opposed to the criminal law standard of "beyond a reasonable doubt." Would the speech attributed to him be sufficient to convict him criminally under the incitement standard adopted by the ICTR in *Nahimana*? So far, one Rwandan (Désiré Munyaneza) has been convicted under the Canadian statute; a second (Jacques Mungwarere) was acquitted.

CHAPTER 17

DEFENSES UNDER INTERNATIONAL CRIMINAL LAW

I. INTRODUCTION

Even if sufficient evidence exists that an individual was connected to a crime, a defendant may be exonerated if they have a valid factual or legal defense or if their conduct is justified or excused. "[T]o say that an action is justified is to say * * * that though the action is of a type that is usually wrong, in these circumstances it was not wrong. To say that an action is excused, by contrast, is to say that it was indeed wrong (and the agent did commit the act we are saying was wrong), but the agent is not blameworthy." Marcia Baron, *Justifications and Excuses*, 2 OHIO ST. J. CRIM. L. 387, 389–390 (2005). This chapter will explore some of the defenses available to individuals accused of violations of international criminal law. Most of the defenses found in domestic legal systems—such as mistake of law, mistake of fact, incapacity, consent, and self-defense—are also found in the jurisprudence of international criminal law. We focus here on those defenses that are most commonly raised in international criminal law proceedings or that present special issues when raised at the international level: *nullum crimen sine lege*, superior orders, duress, *tu quoque*, reprisals, necessity, combat immunity, head of state immunity, and amnesties.

II. *NULLUM CRIMEN SINE LEGE*

The defense of *nullum crimen sine lege* ("no crime without law") is the international criminal law manifestation of the prohibition against retroactive legislation. It states that an individual cannot be convicted of acts that were not criminal at the moment they were committed. The term originated in the works of German legal scholar Paul Johann Anselm Ritter von Feuerbach (1775–1833) in reaction to Hobbesian notions of sovereign omnipotence in juridical matters. The charge of *nullum crimen sine lege* was central to the defendants' defense at Nuremberg, particularly with respect to the crimes against the peace and against humanity charges. However, the Tribunal addressed itself only to the legality of the crimes against the peace charge, stating that:

> The Charter makes the planning or waging of a war of aggression or a war in violation of international treaties a crime; and it is therefore not strictly necessary to consider whether and to what extent aggressive war was a crime before the execution

> of the London Agreement. * * * It was urged on behalf of the defendants that a fundamental principle of all law—international and domestic—is that there can be no punishment of crime without a pre-existing law. "*Nullum crimen sine lege, nulla poena sine lege.*" It was submitted that *ex post facto* punishment is abhorrent to the law of all civilized nations, that no sovereign power had made aggressive war a crime at the time that the alleged criminal acts were committed, that no statute had defined aggressive war, that no penalty had been fixed for its commission, and no court had been created to try and punish offenders.
>
> In the first place, it is to be observed that the maxim *nullum crimen sine lege* is not a limitation of sovereignty, but is in general a principle of justice. To assert that it is unjust to punish those who in defiance of treaties and assurances have attacked neighboring states without warning is obviously untrue, for in such circumstances the attacker must know that he is doing wrong, and so far from it being unjust to punish him, it would be unjust if his wrong were allowed to go unpunished. * * * On this view of the case alone, it would appear that the maxim has no application to the present facts.

Judicial Decision, International Military Tribunal (Nuremberg), Judgment and Sentences, October 1, 1946, *reprinted in* 41 AM. J. INT'L L. 172, 217 (1947). The Tribunal went on to rebut the defense's arguments by pointing out that extant treaties outlawed aggressive war, such as the Kellogg-Briand Pact and the Treaty of Versailles. These treaties are discussed more fully in Chapter 8 on Aggression. There was little precedent, by contrast, to support the crimes against humanity charges.

Likewise, Justice Röling, in his dissent in the Tokyo proceedings, noted that the principle is

> valid only if expressly adopted, so as to protect citizens against arbitrariness of courts . . . as well as arbitrariness of legislators. . . . [T]he prohibition of *ex post facto* law is an expression of political wisdom, not necessarily applicable in present international relations. This maxim of liberty may, if circumstances necessitate it, be disregarded even by powers victorious in a war fought for freedom.

Bernard V.A. Röling, *Opinion*, *in* THE TOKYO JUDGMENT: THE INTERNATIONAL MILITARY TRIBUNAL FOR THE FAR EAST (IMTFE) 29 April 1946–12 November 1948 (B.V.A. Röling and C. F. Rüter eds., 1977). In other words, at the time, "the *nullum crimen sine lege* principle could be regarded as a moral maxim destined to yield to superior exigencies whenever it would have been contrary to justice not to hold persons accountable for appalling atrocities. The strict legal prohibition of *ex post facto* law had not yet found expression in international law." Antonio Cassese, INTERNATIONAL CRIMINAL LAW 72 (2003).

Although international criminal law is significantly more codified today than it was at the time of Nuremberg, the defense of *nullum crimen sine lege* is still raised with respect to novel situations and charges. Consider the next decision rendered by the Special Court for Sierra Leone (SCSL). (See the Appendix for a map of Sierra Leone.) As has been discussed, the Special Court was a hybrid tribunal established by the United Nations and the Government of Sierra Leone to try those who "bear the greatest responsibility" for serious violations of international humanitarian law committed during the country's civil war, which began in March 1991 when guerrillas calling themselves the Revolutionary United Front (RUF) invaded the country from neighboring Liberia, with assistance from Liberian President Charles Taylor who was eventually prosecuted by the SCSL. *See Report of the Secretary-General on the Establishment of a Special Court for Sierra Leone,* 55th Sess., at 5, U.N. Doc. S/2000/915 (2000). The Special Court had jurisdiction for crimes committed after November 1996.

The defendant in question was Sam Hinga Norman, the former leader of the Civil Defence Forces (CDF), a pro-government militia group that formed primarily of Kamajors (traditional hunters from the Mende ethnic group who believed they could be rendered invincible) to repel the RUF. The Indictment against Norman and others accused him of systematically utilizing small boys in armed combat (so-called "small boy units"), a defining feature of the decade-long Sierra Leonean civil war in which more than 10,000 children served as child soldiers in the country's three major armed forces: the RUF, the Armed Forces Revolutionary Council, and the CDF. In the majority opinion by Judge Renate Winter (of Austria) below, the Special Court considers Norman's motion to dismiss Count 8 of the Indictment, which charged him with recruiting children into the armed forces or using them to participate actively in hostilities in violation of Article 4(c) of the Statute of the Special Court. In his motion, Norman argued that although humanitarian law may have prohibited the enlistment of child soldiers at an earlier point, such conduct did not become an international crime until the ICC Statute entered into force in 2002.

Prosecutor v. Sam Hinga Norman, Case No. SCSL–2004–14–AR72(E), Decision on Preliminary Motion Based on Lack of Jurisdiction (May 31, 2004)

9. To answer the question before this Court, the first two sources of international law under Article 38(1) of the Statute of the International Court of Justice ("ICJ") have to be scrutinized:

1) international conventions, whether general or particular, establishing rules especially recognized by the contesting states

2) international custom, as evidence of a general practice accepted as law * * *

International Conventions

10. Given that the Defence does not dispute the fact that international humanitarian law is violated by the recruitment of children, it is not necessary to elaborate on this point in great detail. Nevertheless, the key words of the relevant international documents will be highlighted in order to set the stage for the analysis required by the issues raised in the Preliminary Motion. It should, in particular, be noted that Sierra Leone was already a State Party to the 1949 Geneva Conventions and the two Additional Protocols of 1977 prior to 1996. * * *

12. Both Additional Protocols were ratified by Sierra Leone in 1986. Attention should be drawn to the following provisions of Additional Protocol I:

Article 77. Protection of children

2. The Parties to the conflict shall take all feasible measures in order that children who have not attained the age of fifteen years do not take a direct part in hostilities and, in particular, they shall refrain from recruiting them into their armed forces. In recruiting among those persons who have attained the age of fifteen years but who have not attained the age of eighteen years, the Parties to the conflict shall endeavour to give priority to those who are oldest.

3. If, in exceptional cases, despite the provisions of paragraph 2, children who have not attained the age of fifteen years take a direct part in hostilities and fall into the power of an adverse Party, they shall continue to benefit from the special protection accorded by this Article, whether or not they are prisoners of war. * * *

13. 137 States were parties to Additional Protocol II as of 30 November 1996. Sierra Leone ratified Additional Protocol II on 21 October 1986. The key provision is Article 4 entitled "fundamental guarantees" which provides in relevant part:

Article 4. Fundamental guarantees

3. Children shall be provided with the care and aid they require, and in particular:

(c) Children who have not attained the age of fifteen years shall neither be recruited in the armed forces or groups nor allowed to take part in hostilities

14. The Convention on the Rights of the Child of 1989 ("CRC") entered into force on 2 September 1990 and was on the same day ratified by the Government of Sierra Leone. In 1996, all but six states existing at the time had ratified the Convention. The CRC recognizes the protection of children in international humanitarian law and also requires States

Parties to ensure respect for these rules by taking appropriate and feasible measures.

15. On feasible measures:

> Article 38
>
> 1. States Parties undertake to respect and to ensure respect for rules of international humanitarian law applicable to them in armed conflicts which are relevant to the child.
>
> 2. States Parties shall take all feasible measures to ensure that persons who have not attained the age of fifteen years do not take a direct part in hostilities.
>
> 3. States Parties shall refrain from recruiting any person who has not attained the age of fifteen years into their armed forces. In recruiting among those persons who have attained the age of fifteen years but who have not attained the age of eighteen years, States Parties shall endeavour to give priority to those who are oldest. * * *

Customary International Law

17. Prior to November 1996, the prohibition on child recruitment had * * * crystallized as customary international law. The formation of custom requires both state practice and a sense of pre-existing obligation (*opinio iuris*). "An articulated sense of obligation, without implementing usage, is nothing more than rhetoric. Conversely, state practice, without *opinio iuris*, is just habit."[23]

18. As regards state practice, the list of states having legislation concerning recruitment or voluntary enlistment clearly shows that almost all states prohibit (and have done so for a long time) the recruitment of children under the age of 15. Since 185 states, including Sierra Leone, were parties to the Geneva Conventions prior to 1996, it follows that the provisions of those conventions were widely recognized as customary international law. Similarly, 133 states, including Sierra Leone, ratified Additional Protocol II before 1995. Due to the high number of States Parties one can conclude that many of the provisions of Additional Protocol II, including the fundamental guarantees, were widely accepted as customary international law by 1996. Even though Additional Protocol II addresses internal conflicts, the ICTY Appeals Chamber held in *Prosecutor v. Tadić* that "it does not matter whether the 'serious violation' has occurred within the context of an international or an internal armed conflict." This means that children are protected by the fundamental guarantees, regardless of whether there is an international or internal conflict taking place.

19. Furthermore, as already mentioned, all but six states had ratified the Convention on the Rights of the Child by 1996. This huge acceptance, the highest acceptance of all international conventions,

[23] Edward T. Swaine, *Rational Custom*, 52 DUKE L. J. 559, 567–68 (December 2002).

clearly shows that the provisions of the CRC became international customary law almost at the time of the entry into force of the Convention.

20. The widespread recognition and acceptance of the norm prohibiting child recruitment in Additional Protocol II and the CRC provides compelling evidence that the conventional norm entered customary international law well before 1996. * * *

21. The African Charter on the Rights and Welfare of the Child, adopted the same year as the CRC came into force, reiterates with almost the same wording the prohibition of child recruitment:

> Article 22(2): Armed Conflicts
>
> States Parties to the present Charter shall take all necessary measures to ensure that no child shall take a direct part in hostilities and refrain, in particular, from recruiting any child.
>
> * * *

24. The central question which must now be considered is whether the prohibition on child recruitment also entailed individual criminal responsibility at the time of the crimes alleged in the indictments. * * *

Nullum Crimen Sine Lege, Nullum Crimen Sine Poena

25. It is the duty of this Chamber to ensure that the principle of non-retroactivity is not breached. As essential elements of all legal systems, the fundamental principle *nullum crimen sine lege* and the ancient principle *nullum crimen sine poena*, need to be considered. In the ICTY case of *Prosecutor v. Hadžihasanović*, it was observed that "In interpreting the principle *nullum crimen sine lege*, it is critical to determine whether the underlying conduct at the time of its commission was punishable. The emphasis on conduct, rather than on the specific description of the offence in substantive criminal law, is of primary relevance." In other words it must be "foreseeable and accessible to a possible perpetrator that his concrete conduct was punishable." As has been shown in the previous sections, child recruitment was a violation of conventional and customary international humanitarian law by 1996. But can it also be stated that the prohibited act was criminalized and punishable under international or national law to an extent which would show customary practice?

26. In the ICTY case of *Prosecutor v. Tadić*, the test for determining whether a violation of humanitarian law is subject to prosecution and punishment is set out thus:

> The following requirements must be met for an offence to be subject to prosecution before the International Tribunal under Article 3 [of the ICTY Statute]:
>
> (i) the violation must constitute an infringement of a rule of international humanitarian law;

(ii) the rule must be customary in nature or, if it belongs to treaty law, the required conditions must be met;

(iii) the violation must be "serious," that is to say, it must constitute a breach of a rule protecting important values, and the breach must involve grave consequences for the victim [. . .];

(iv) the violation of the rule must entail, under customary or conventional law, the individual criminal responsibility of the person breaching the rule. * * *

30. Regarding point iv, the Defence refers to the Secretary-General's statement that "while the prohibition on child recruitment has by now acquired a customary international law status, it is far less clear whether it is customarily recognized as a war crime entailing the individual criminal responsibility of the accused." The ICTY Appeals Chamber upheld the legality of prosecuting violations of the laws and customs of war, including violations of Common Article 3 and the Additional Protocols in the Tadić case in 1995. In creating the ICTR Statute, the Security Council explicitly recognized for the first time that serious violations of fundamental guarantees lead to individual criminal liability and this was confirmed later on by decisions and judgments of the ICTR. In its Judgment in the *Akayesu* case, the ICTR Trial Chamber, relying on the *Tadić* test, confirmed that a breach of a rule protecting important values was a "serious violation" entailing criminal responsibility.[44] The Trial Chamber noted that Article 4 of the ICTR Statute was derived from Common Article 3 (containing fundamental prohibitions as a humanitarian minimum of protection for war victims) and Additional Protocol II, "which equally outlines 'Fundamental Guarantees.'" The Chamber concluded that "it is clear that the authors of such egregious violations must incur individual criminal responsibility for their deeds." Similarly, under the ICTY Statute adopted in 1993, a person acting in breach of Additional Protocol I to the Geneva Conventions may face criminal sanctions, and this has been confirmed in ICTY jurisprudence.

31. The Committee on the Rights of the Child, the international monitoring body for the implementation of the CRC, showed exactly this understanding [that child recruitment violates customary international law] while issuing its recommendations to Uganda in 1997. The Committee recommended that: "awareness of the duty to fully respect the rules of international humanitarian law, in the spirit of article 38 of the Convention, *inter alia* with regard to children, should be made known to the parties to the armed conflict in the northern part of the State Party's territory, and that violations of the rules of international

[44] *Prosecutor v. Akayesu*, Case No. ICTR–96–4–T, Judgement, 2 September 1998, paras. 616–17.

humanitarian law entail responsibility being attributed to the perpetrators."

32. In 1998, the Rome Statute for the International Criminal Court was adopted. It entered into force on 1 July 2002. Article 8 includes the crime of child recruitment in international armed conflict and internal armed conflict, the elements of which are elaborated in the Elements of Crimes adopted in 2000. * * *

33. The Defence argues that the Rome Statute created new legislation. This argument fails for the following reasons: first, the first draft of the Rome Statute was produced as early as 1994 referring generally to war crimes; second, in the first session of the Preparatory Committee it was proposed that the ICC should have the power to prosecute serious violations of Common Article 3 and Additional Protocol II; third, discussion continued during 1996 and 1997 when Germany proposed the inclusion of child recruitment under the age of fifteen as a crime "within the established framework of international law;" and finally, it was the German proposal to include "conscripting or enlisting children under the age of fifteen years [. . .]" that was accepted in the final draft of the Statute. With regard to the United States, an authoritative report of the proceedings of the Rome Conference states "the United States in particular took the view that [the prohibition against child recruitment] did not reflect international customary law, and was more a human rights provision than a criminal law provision. However, the majority felt strongly that the inclusion was justified by the near-universal acceptance of the norm, the violation of which warranted the most fundamental disapprobation." The question whether or not the United States could be said to have persistently objected to the formation of the customary norm is irrelevant to its status as such a norm. The discussion during the preparation of the Rome Statute focused on the codification and effective implementation of the existing customary norm rather than the formation of a new one. * * *

38. A norm need not be expressly stated in an international convention for it to crystallize as a crime under customary international law. What, indeed, would be the meaning of a customary rule if it only became applicable upon its incorporation into an international instrument such as the Rome Treaty? * * *

42. In the instant case, further support for the finding that the *nullum crimen* principle has not been breached is found in the national legislation of states, which includes criminal sanctions as a measure of enforcement.

43. The Defence submitted during the oral hearing that there is not a single country in the world that has criminalized the practice of recruiting child soldiers and that child recruitment was not only not a war crime but it was doubtful whether the provisions of the CRC protected child soldiers. A simple reading of Article 38 of the CRC disposes of the latter argument. Concerning the former argument, it is

clearly wrong. An abundance of states criminalized child recruitment in the aftermath of the Rome Statute, as for example Australia. In response to its [2002] ratification of the Rome Statute, Australia passed the International Criminal Court (Consequential Amendments) Act. Its purpose was to make the offences in the Rome Statute offences under Commonwealth law. Section 268.68(1) creates the offence of using, conscripting and enlisting children in the course of an international armed conflict and sets out the elements of the crime and the applicable terms of imprisonment. Section 268.88 contains similar provisions relating to conflict that is not an international armed conflict.

44. By 2001, and in most cases prior to the Rome Statute, 108 states explicitly prohibited child recruitment, one example dating back to 1902, and a further 15 states that do not have specific legislation did not show any indication of using child soldiers. The list of states in the 2001 Child Soldiers Global Report clearly shows that states with quite different legal systems—civil law, common law, Islamic law—share the same view on the topic. * * *

46. More specifically in relation to the principle *nullum crimen sine poena*, before 1996 three different approaches by states to the issue of punishment of child recruitment under national law can be distinguished.

47. First, as already described, certain states from various legal systems have criminalized the recruitment of children under 15 in their national legislation. Second, the vast majority of states lay down the prohibition of child recruitment in military law. However, sanctions can be found in the provisions of criminal law as for example in Austria and Germany or in administrative legislation, criminalizing any breaches of law by civil servants. Examples of the latter include Afghanistan and Turkey. Legislation of the third group of states simply makes it impossible for an individual to recruit children, as the military administration imposes strict controls through an obligatory cadet schooling, as for example in England, Mauritania and Switzerland. In these states, provisions for punishment are unnecessary as it is impossible for the crime to be committed. * * *

49. When considering the formation of customary international law, "the number of states taking part in a practice is a more important criterion [. . .] than the duration of the practice."[88] It should further be noted that "the number of states needed to create a rule of customary law varies according to the amount of practice which conflicts with the rule and that [even] a practice followed by a very small number of states can create a rule of customary law if there is no practice which conflicts with the rule."[89]

---

[88] Michael Akehurst, *Custom As a Source of International Law*, BRIT. Y.B. INT'L L. 16 (1974–1975).

[89] *Ibid.*, p. 18.

50. Customary law, as its name indicates, derives from custom. Custom takes time to develop. It is thus impossible and even contrary to the concept of customary law to determine a given event, day or date upon which it can be stated with certainty that a norm has crystallized. One can nevertheless say that during a certain period the conscience of leaders and populations started to note a given problem. In the case of recruiting child soldiers this happened during the mid-1980s. One can further determine a period where customary law begins to develop, which in the current case began with the acceptance of key international instruments between 1990 and 1994. Finally, one can determine the period during which the majority of states criminalized the prohibited behaviour, which in this case, as demonstrated, was the period between 1994 and 1996. It took a further six years for the recruitment of children between the ages of 15 and 18 to be included in treaty law as individually punishable behavior. The development process concerning the recruitment of child soldiers, taking into account the definition of children as persons under the age of 18, culminated in the codification of the matter in the [2002] CRC Optional Protocol II [establishing a minimum age for participating in hostilities].

51. The overwhelming majority of states, as shown above, did not practice recruitment of children under 15 according to their national laws and many had, whether through criminal or administrative law, criminalized such behavior prior to 1996. The fact that child recruitment still occurs and is thus illegally practiced does not detract from the validity of the customary norm. It cannot be said that there is a contrary practice with a corresponding *opinio iuris* as states clearly consider themselves to be under a legal obligation not to practice child recruitment.

52. The rejection of the use of child soldiers by the international community was widespread by 1994. * * * Specifically concerning Sierra Leone, the Government acknowledged in its 1996 Report to the Committee on the Rights of the Child that there was no minimum age for conscripting into armed forces "except the provision in the Geneva Convention that children below the age of 15 years should not be conscripted into the army." This shows that the Government of Sierra Leone was well aware already in 1996 that children below the age of 15 should not be recruited. Citizens of Sierra Leone, and even less, persons in leadership roles, cannot possibly argue that they did not know that recruiting children was a criminal act in violation of international humanitarian law. * * *

54. For all the above-mentioned reasons the Preliminary Motion is dismissed.

Prosecutor v. Sam Hinga Norman, Case No. SCSL–2004–14–AR72(E), Dissenting Opinion of Justice Geoffrey Robertson (May 31, 2004)

2. The crime of "enlisting children under the age of fifteen years into armed forces or groups," which I shall call for short "child enlistment," has never been prosecuted before in an international court nor, so far as I am aware, has it been the subject of prosecution under municipal law, although many states now have legislation which would permit such a charge. The Applicant argues that "child enlistment" is not a war crime; alternatively, that it became such only on the entry into force in mid-2002 of two important treaties—the Rome Statute which established the International Criminal Court ("ICC") and the Optional Protocol to the Convention on the Rights of Child. The Prosecution declines to pinpoint a date on which the offence crystallized in international criminal law: it argues that such point was in all events prior to 30th November 1996, and upon the correctness of that contention the fate of this application turns. * * *

4. The first point to note is that Article 4(c) [of the statute of the Special Court] as eventually adopted by the Security Council is not the Article 4(c) offence proposed by the Secretary-General. His original draft, in his Report presented to the Security Council in October 2000, would have endowed the court with jurisdiction over:

> c. Abduction and forced recruitment of children under the age of fifteen years into armed forces or groups for the purpose of using them to participate actively in hostilities.

This is a much more precise and certain definition of a narrower offence. It made the *actus reus* turn on the use of physical force or threats in order to recruit children and the *mens rea* element required an intention to involve them in potentially lethal operations. This was in my view a war crime by November 1996: indeed, it would have amounted to a most serious breach of Common Article 3 of the Geneva Convention. Why did the Secretary-General prefer this formulation to the wider definition in the Rome Statute? For the very good reason that he was unsure as to whether the Rome Statute formulation reflected the definition of a war crime either by 1996 or even by the time of his Report (October 2000). As that Report explains,

> 17. [In] 1998 the Statute of the International Criminal Court criminalized the prohibition and qualified it as a war crime. But while the prohibition on child recruitment has by now acquired a customary international law status, it is far less clear whether it is customarily recognised as a war crime entailing the individual responsibility of the accused.
>
> 18. Owing to the doubtful customary nature of the ICC's statutory crime which criminalizes the conscription or

enlistment of children under the age of fifteen, whether forced or "voluntary," the crime which is included in Article 4(c) of the Statute of the Special Court is not the equivalent of the ICC provision.

5. The Secretary-General's Report accurately identifies the conduct which, by November 1996, had become the war crime of forcibly recruiting children under fifteen for use in combat. But notwithstanding the Secretary-General's reasoned position, the offence defined in 4(c) was quite crucially changed, to the different crime of conscripting or enlisting children, or using them in hostilities. This crime of child recruitment, as it was finally formulated in 4(c) of the Statute, may be committed in three quite different ways:

a. by conscripting children (which implies compulsion, albeit in some cases through force of law),

b. by enlisting them (which merely means accepting and enrolling them when they volunteer), or

c. by using them to participate actively in hostilities (i.e. taking the more serious step, having conscripted or enlisted them, of putting their lives directly at risk in combat).

These are, in effect, three different crimes, and are treated as such by some states which have implemented the Rome Treaty in their domestic law. * * *

6. It might strike some as odd that the state of international law in 1996 in respect to criminalization of child enlistment was doubtful to the U.N. Secretary-General in October 2000 but was very clear to the President of the Security Council only two months later. If it was not clear to the Secretary-General and his legal advisers that international law had by 1996 criminalized the enlistment of child soldiers, could it really have been any clearer to Chief Hinga Norman or any other defendant at that time, embattled in Sierra Leone? If international criminal law shares the basic principle of common law crime, namely that punishment must not be inflicted for conduct that was not clearly criminal at the time it was committed, then the Prosecution has an obvious difficulty in proceeding with an "enlistment" charge that does not specifically allege the use of some kind of force or pressure. If international criminal law adopts the common law principle that in cases of real doubt as to the existence or definition of a criminal offence, the benefit of that doubt must be given to the defendant, then this would appear to be such a case. * * *

10. So when did child enlistment—as distinct from forcible recruitment of children or subsequently using them in combat—become a war crime? That depends, as we shall see, first on identifying a stage—or at least a process—by which prohibition of child enlistment became a rule of international law binding only on states (i.e. on their governments) and with which they were meant to comply (although

nothing could be done if they declined). Then, at the second stage, on further identifying a subsequent turning point at which that rule—a so-called "norm" of international law—metamorphosed into a criminal law for the breach of which individuals might be punished, if convicted by international courts. Before identifying and applying the appropriate tests—and the second stage test is contentious—let me explain why this second-stage process is necessary, even—indeed, especially—in relation to conduct which is generally viewed as abhorrent. * * *

12. It must be acknowledged that like most absolute principles, *nullum crimen* can be highly inconvenient—especially in relation to conduct which is abhorrent or grotesque, but which parliament has not thought to legislate against. Every law student can point to cases where judges have been tempted to circumvent the *nullum crimen* principle to criminalize conduct which they regard as seriously anti-social or immoral, but which had not been outlawed by legislation or by established categories of common-law crimes. This temptation must be firmly resisted by international law judges, with no legislature to correct or improve upon them and with a subject—international criminal law—which came into effective operation as recently as the judgement at Nuremberg in 1946. Here, the Prosecution asserts with some insouciance that

> the principle of *nullum crimen sine lege* is not in any case applied rigidly, particularly where the acts in question are universally regarded as abhorrent and deeply shock the conscience of humanity.

On the contrary, it is precisely when the acts are abhorrent and deeply shocking that the principle of legality must be most stringently applied, to ensure that a defendant is not convicted out of disgust rather than evidence, or of a non-existent crime. *Nullum crimen* may not be a household phrase, but it serves as some protection against the lynch mob.

13. The principle of legality, sometimes expressed as the rule against retroactivity, requires that the defendant must at the time of committing the acts alleged to amount to a crime have been in a position to know, or at least readily to establish, that those acts may entail penal consequences. Ignorance of the law is no defence, so long as that law is capable of reasonable ascertainment. The fact that his conduct would shock or even appall decent people is not enough to make it unlawful in the absence of a prohibition. The requisite clarity will not necessarily be found in there having been previous successful prosecutions in respect of similar conduct, since there has to be a first prosecution for every crime and we are in the early stages of international criminal law enforcement. Nor is it necessary, at the time of commission, for there to be in existence an international court with the power to punish it, or any foresight that such a court will necessarily be established. In every case, the question is whether the defendant, at the time of conduct which was not clearly outlawed by national law in the place of its commission, could have

ascertained through competent legal advice that it was contrary to international criminal law. That could certainly be said on 1 July 2002, the date of ratification of the ICC Statute, which in terms makes it an offence to commit acts of "conscripting or enlisting children under the age of fifteen years into armed forces or groups or using them to participate actively in hostilities." That is too late for any indictment in this court, and the applicant puts the Prosecution to proof that the offence thus defined came into existence in or by 1996 * * *.

17. * * * In this context, for an international court to recognize the creation of a new criminal offence without infringing the *nullum crimen* principle, I would formulate the test as follows:

> i. The elements of the offence must be clear and in accordance with fundamental principles of criminal liability;
>
> ii. That the conduct could amount to an offence in international criminal law must have been capable of reasonable ascertainment at the time of commission;
>
> iii. There must be evidence (or at least inference) of general agreement by the international community that breach of the customary law rule would or would now, entail international criminal liability for individual perpetrators, in addition to the normative obligation on States to prohibit the conduct in question under their domestic law. * * *

20. * * * In order to become a criminal prohibition, enforceable in that sphere of international law which is served by international criminal courts, the "norm" must satisfy the further, second-stage test, identified at paragraph 17 above. It must have the requisite qualities for a serious criminal prohibition: the elements of the offence must be tolerably clear and must include the mental element of a guilty intention. Its existence, as an international law crime, must be capable of reasonable ascertainment, which means (as an alternative formulation) that prosecution for the conduct must have been foreseeable as a realistic possibility. Most significantly, it must be clear that the overwhelming preponderance of states, courts, conventions, jurists and so forth relied upon to crystallize the international law "norm" intended—or now intend—this rule to have penal consequences for individuals brought before international courts, whether or not such a court presently exists with jurisdiction over them. In this case we must be satisfied, after an examination of the sources claimed for the customary norm prohibiting child enlistment, that by 1996 it was intended by the international community to be a criminal law prohibition for the breach of which individuals should be arrested and punished.

33. * * * In 1996, ironically, the Government of Sierra Leone acknowledged in its report to the Committee on the Rights of the Child that there was no minimum age for recruitment of persons into the armed forces "except provision in the Geneva Convention that children below

the age of fifteen years should not be conscripted into the army." The Committee did not get around to answering Sierra Leone until five years later, when it suggested that the country should pass and enforce a law to prohibit the recruitment of children. This rather makes the point that, so far as local legislation was concerned, the applicant could not, back in 1996, have understood there to be any criminal law against enlisting children who volunteered to serve in militias. That is because Articles 24 and 51 of the Geneva Convention did not prohibit child enlistment other than by an "occupying power" and Additional Protocol II called upon States "to take all feasible measures" to stop child recruitment. * * *

36. For a specific offence—here, the non-forcible enlistment for military service of under fifteen volunteers—to be exhibited in the chamber of horrors that displays international law crimes, there must be proof of general agreement among states to impose individual responsibility, at least for those bearing the greatest responsibility for such recruitment. There must * * * be general agreement to a formulation of the offence which satisfies the basic standards for any serious crime, namely a clear statement of the conduct which is prohibited and a satisfactory requirement for the proof of *mens rea*—i.e. a guilty intent to commit the crime. The existence of the crime must be a fact that is reasonably accessible. I do not find these conditions satisfied, as at November 1996, in the source material provided by the Prosecutor or the amici. Geneva Convention IV, the 1977 Protocols, the Convention on the Rights of the Child and the African Charter are, even when taken together, insufficient. What they demonstrate is a growing predisposition in the international community to support a new offence of non-forcible recruitment of children, at least for front-line fighting. What they do not prove is that there was a universal or at least general consensus that individual responsibility had already been imposed in international law. It follows that the Secretary-General was correct to doubt whether a crime of "conscripting or enlisting" child soldiers had come into existence by 30th November 1996.

38. The first point at which that can be said to have [crystallized in international criminal law] was 17th July 1998, the conclusion of the five-week diplomatic conference in Rome which established the Statute of the International Criminal Court. * * * I do not think, for all the above reasons, that it is possible to fix the crystallization point of the crime of child enlistment at any earlier stage, although I do recognize the force of the argument that July 1998 was the beginning and not the end of this process, which concluded four years later when sufficient ratifications (that of sixty states) were received to bring the Rome Treaty into force. Nonetheless, state practice immediately after July 1998 demonstrates that the Rome Treaty was accepted by states as a turning point in the criminalization of child recruitment. * * *

50. I differ with diffidence from my colleagues, but I have no doubt that the crime of non-forcible enlistment did not enter international

criminal law until the Rome Treaty in July 1998. That it exists for all present and future conflicts is declared for the first time by the judgments in this Court today. * * * By the judgments today, we declare that international criminal law can deal with these abhorrent actions. But so far as this applicant is concerned, I would grant a declaration to the effect that he must not be prosecuted for an offence of enlistment, under Article 4(c) of the Statute, that is alleged to have been committed before the end of July 1998.

NOTES & QUESTIONS

1. Case Outcome

Sam Hinga Norman died of natural causes weeks before the Judgment was issued. (For more on the circumstances surrounding his death, *see* the Note after the excerpt from the *Norman* case in Chapter 4 on Hybrid Tribunals). A Trial Chamber of the SCSL found Norman's co-accused Allieu Kondewa guilty of "enlisting children under the age of 15 into an armed force or group and/or using them to participate actively in hostilities" by virtue of his role initiating child soldiers for battle. *Prosecutor v. Fofana*, Case No. SCSL–04–14–T, Judgement, paras. 968–970 (Aug. 2, 2007). On appeal, Kondewa argued that *initiation* should not have been considered the equivalent of *enlistment*. The Appeals Chamber noted that enlistment means " 'accepting and enrolling individuals when they volunteer to join an armed force or group,' " that there must be a nexus between the act of the accused and a child joining an armed force or group, and that "enlistment" should not be narrowly defined as a formal process. *Prosecutor v. Fofana*, Case No. SCSL–04–14–A, Judgement, paras. 139, 144 (May 28, 2008).

Reviewing the facts in the record, the Appeals Chamber concluded that the child soldier in question had already been forcibly enlisted when he was captured by the Civil Defense Forces (CDF) and put to work—all of which happened prior to his initiation by Kondewa. Accordingly, the Appeals Chamber reversed the conviction on the count of enlisting child soldiers. The acquittal of Kondewa's co-accused, Moinina Fofana, was upheld on appeal on the ground that his mere presence at meetings in which child soldiers were referenced or present was insufficient to render Fofana personally responsible for such crimes. Judge Winter, who penned the principal opinion above, dissented in this case, arguing that Fofana's presence at meetings "constituted tacit approval, encouragement and moral support to the commanders and Kamajors to continue to enlist and use children under the age of 15 to participate actively in hostilities." *Prosecutor v. Fofana*, Case No. SCSL–04–14–A, Partially Dissenting Opinion of Honourable Justice Renate Winter, para. 37 (May 28, 2008). The crime of recruiting child soldiers is now firmly entrenched in the war crimes canon. Liberia's former President Charles Taylor became the first former President to be convicted of the crime of recruiting and using child soldiers. *See Prosecutor v. Charles Ghankay Taylor*, Case No. SCSL–03–01–T, Judgement (May 18, 2012).

Several ICC indictments feature the crime of using child soldiers. *See, e.g., Prosecutor v. Lubanga*, Case No. ICC–01/04–01/06, Decision on the

Confirmation of Charges (Jan. 29, 2007); *Prosecutor v. Katanga & Chui*, Case No. ICC–01/4–01/07, Decision on the Confirmation of Charges (Sept. 30, 2008); *Prosecutor v. Ntaganda*, Case No. ICC–01/04–02/06, Decision Pursuant to Article 61(7)(a) and (b) of the Rome Statute on the Charges of the Prosecutor Against Bosco Ntaganda (June 9, 2014); *Prosecutor v. Ongwen*, Case No ICC–02/04–01/15, Decision on the Confirmation of Charges against Dominic Ongwen (Mar. 23, 2016). The child soldiers aspect of the *Lubanga* case is addressed in Chapter 15 on Direct and Indirect Responsibility. The *Lubanga* case is also the first case that has resulted in ICC-ordered reparations. The reparations plan includes benefits for child soldiers. The reparations aspect of the case is discussed in Chapter 18 on Sentencing and Reparations. The child solders aspect of the *Ntaganda* case is addressed in Chapter 7 on War Crimes.

2. Sources of Law

This case exemplifies the challenge of identifying proper sources of public international law. In addition to custom and treaties, the ICJ Statute identifies additional sources of law: (c) the general principles of law recognized by civilized nations and (d) subject to the provisions of Article 59, [i.e. that only the parties are bound by a decision in any particular case] judicial decisions and the teachings of the most highly qualified publicists of the various nations, as subsidiary means for the determination of rules of law.

The Prosecutor indicted the defendant Norman under a provision of the Statute of the Special Court that expressly criminalizes the recruitment of child soldiers. However, outside of the Statute of the ICC, this provision was *sui generis* in international criminal law and was drafted and promulgated, like the ICC Statute, well after the events underlying the Indictment. Thus, the question presented by this case is whether the prosecution under this count can go forward without offending the principle of *nullum crimen sine lege*. On what sources of law did the Special Court in *Norman* rely? How were the various authorities characterized as state practice or *opinio juris*? The *Norman* majority does not analyze this question according to general principles of law, another recognized source of international law. Why do you think they did not examine this source of law? Who has the better argument, the majority or the dissent penned by Judge Robertson, a British human rights lawyer?

Incidentally, counsel for the RUF defendants challenged Judge Robertson on the basis of disparaging comments he had made about the RUF in a book on Sierra Leone that he published prior to his appointment to the SCSL. The Appeals Chamber determined that the comments did give an appearance of bias and so ruled that while Robertson could remain on the Appeals Chamber, he would not sit on any cases involving the RUF defendants.

3. Customary International Law

The majority in the *Norman* case concludes that the recruitment and use of child soldiers was criminally prohibited under customary international law prior to its codification in the ICC Statute and/or the

Statute of the Special Court. Although one may agree with the result reached on normative grounds, are you convinced that there is sufficient state practice and *opinio juris* regarding the criminality of such conduct in the general treaty rules or in the domestic legislation cited to find a rule of customary international law? Or should Justice Winter have confined herself to declaring, in *dicta*, that the offense now exists under international law, but it did not so exist at the time the defendant acted? How useful is the "test" set forth in *Tadić* to answering the case before the Special Court? Given the sources cited by the parties and the Special Court, which prongs of that test do you think have been satisfied?

4. State Practice

In terms of state practice, the majority notes that almost all states prohibit the recruitment of children under the age of fifteen for use in armed conflict. Of these, only some states specifically criminalized the practice at the time (e.g., Ireland and Norway). Is it significant that there appeared to be minimal state practice in terms of actual prosecutions? Most states as a matter of policy do not recruit children under the age of fifteen. Is there any indication that these states have adopted the provisions and practices in response to a sense of legal obligation (*opinio juris*)? What other reasons might states have for adopting such a practice? The United States, which does not condone child conscription but allows youths aged seventeen and above to enlist with parental consent, took the position that the Rome Statute created new law on this point. What weight should be given to such statements?

In 2008, the United States enacted a statute providing for extraterritorial jurisdiction over the recruitment, enlistment, or conscription of children below the age of fifteen. 18 U.S.C. § 2442. The United States has also ratified the U.N. Convention of the Rights of the Child's Optional Protocol on the Involvement of Children in Armed Conflict (CRC OPAC), although not the parent treaty, which establishes eighteen years as the minimum age for compulsory recruitment into the armed forces and requires that governments ensure that recruitment of younger individuals is genuinely voluntary and undertaken with the informed consent of the child's parents. In addition, members of the armed forces under the age of eighteen may not take a direct part in hostilities.

5. The Relativity of International Criminal Law

Is it significant that, to the extent that there is legislation prohibiting the recruitment of children, it appears in well-developed states and not weak states wracked by civil wars where child recruitment is likely to be practiced as a feature of "total war" and where the passions for one's cause might compel the recruitment of entire populations into the armed forces? Indeed, could it be argued that a form of regional or local custom has developed in West Africa supporting the use of child soldiers, or at least rejecting any customary international prohibition of the process? The International Court of Justice recognized the possibility of a regional custom in the *Asylum Case (Colom. v. Peru)*, 1950 I.C.J. Reports 266, though in that specific case the

Court held there was insufficient evidence that a regional customary rule had developed.

6. Notice to Defendants

Are defendants on notice that a particular type of conduct might be criminal when that practice is universally viewed as abhorrent? Is this functional notice rationale the only value served by the *nullum crimen sine lege* principle? Notwithstanding Judge Cassese's observation that the *nullum crimen sine lege* principle was not immediately applicable at the birth of international criminal law, is the principle perhaps most relevant while a penal regime is in its formative years? In dissent, Judge Robertson distinguished conscription from enlistment. Is the majority's approach more defensible with respect to conscription—compulsory military service—than voluntary enlistment?

7. Common Law Crimes

The early criminal law in England was primarily found in the common law. Wayne LeFave has noted:

> Thus by the 1600's the judges, not the legislature, had created and defined the felonies of murder, suicide, manslaughter, burglary, arson, robbery, larceny, rape, sodomy and mayhem; and such misdemeanors as assault, battery, false imprisonment, libel, perjury, and intimidation of jurors. During the period from 1660 (the Restoration of the monarchy of Charles II after Cromwell) to 1860 the process continued, with the judges creating new crimes when the need arose and punishing those who committed them: blasphemy (1676), conspiracy (1664), sedition (18th century), forgery (1727), attempt (1784), solicitation (1801). From time to time the judges, when creating new misdemeanors, spoke of the court's power to declare criminal any conduct tending to "outrage decency" or "corrupt public morals," or to punish conduct *contra bonos mores* [against good morals]; thus they found running naked in the streets, publishing an obscene book, and grave-snatching to be common law crimes.

1 SUBST. CRIM. L. § 2.1 (2nd Ed. 2007). Today, criminal law in England is primarily statutory. While the nascent United States initially imported the English practice of common law crimes, the criminal law in the United States today is also largely statutory with a few exceptions. U.S. states that retain common law crimes usually limit them to those recognized as common law crimes in England before either 1607 (when the first colony, Jamestown, was established), or 1775 (when the colonies broke with England). Consider the following discussion of the pros and cons of a system of common law crimes:

> [T]here is the question whether it is wiser to retain or wiser to abolish common law crimes. The advantage of retaining such crimes is that there are no gaps. So the argument goes, if something ought to be a crime, but the legislature forgot to declare it a crime, the courts can step in and make it a crime. It is useful to have a reservoir of substantive criminal law to plug loopholes left by the legislative branch. "It is impossible to find precedents for all

offences. The malicious ingenuity of mankind is constantly producing new inventions in the art of disturbing their neighbors. To this invention must be opposed general principles, calculated to meet and punish them."

The principal argument against common law crimes is expressed in the maxim *nullum crimen sine lege,* the basis of which is that the criminal law ought to be certain, so that people can know in advance whether the conduct on which they are about to embark is criminal or not. * * * To require one who intends to tread close to the line of criminality (yet remaining on the side of legality) to study the criminal statutes (and the cases construing those statutes) may be fair enough; but to make him read the English and American cases on common law crimes and speculate on their scope is worse; and it is even more unfair (so the argument runs) to make him guess at his peril as to what a court will hold in a new situation never before encountered by the courts. * * * The fact that Nazi Germany and Soviet Russia once adhered to the policy of punishing as criminal activity which no statute expressly covered tends to make Americans wonder about the democratic basis of common law crimes. * * *

To a great extent, a decision on whether it is better to retain or to abolish common law crimes depends upon one's view of the theories of punishment. If punishment is imposed primarily for revenge or retribution, common law crimes punishing anti-social conduct of novel sorts are justified. Likewise, if the primary purpose is to jail and therefore disable for a time persons dangerous to society, or to reform those with anti-social tendencies, it makes greater sense to recognize common law crimes. But if the primary purpose is to deter future offenders through fear of punishment, it has been suggested that new kinds of bad conduct should not be punished, "for if the first wrongdoer had no certain foresight that he would be punished, the threat of punishment could not deter him, and the punishment would be useless." It could be argued, however, that certainty of punishment is not necessary to the deterrent theory (as, indeed, one must recognize from the fact that although many who commit statutory crimes escape punishment for one reason or another, many of us are deterred), and that a substantial chance that punishment will be inflicted for new forms of bad conduct will still deter.

It was only natural that judges should create crimes from general principles in medieval England, because such legislature as there was sat only infrequently and legislation was scanty. Today in the United States, as in modern England, the various legislatures meet regularly. The principal original reason for common law crimes has therefore disappeared. And thus it is not surprising that as more and more states have enacted comprehensive new criminal codes in place of the miscellaneous collection of uncoordinated statutes, they have generally abolished

> common law crimes. [Furthermore, whenever a loophole is discovered, the modern legislature can and usually does act quickly to plug it.]

1 SUBST. CRIM. L. § 2.1 (f) (2nd ed. 2007). The above excerpt concerns the wisdom of adopting common law crimes within a domestic legal system. How well do the arguments advanced by the author apply to a discussion about the creation of international criminal law by customary international law? Professor Alicia Gil Gil of Spain argues that customary international law crimes should not be invoked in the Spanish courts, as invoking such law would violate the requirements under Spanish law for specificity and certainty for criminal law. *See* Alicia Gil Gil, *The Flaws of the Scilingo Judgment*, 3 J. INT'L CRIM. JUST. 1082 (2005).

8. Treaties as Sources of Law

Does joining a treaty constitute a form of state practice or an expression of *opinio juris*? Where states do not comply with, or implement, the treaties to which they are a party, is ratification in itself sufficient to show state practice or *opinio juris*? What role do the treaties cited by the parties play in the two opinions? Even the majority must concede that no applicable treaty specifically criminalizes the recruitment or use of child soldiers. The Geneva Conventions (1949) create special protections for children in a time of war, but nowhere criminalize their use in combat or even, for that matter, specifically prohibit the practice. Common Article 3 to the Geneva Conventions broadly prohibits inhumane treatment in non-international armed conflicts, but it does not specifically mention child recruitment. Protocol II to the Geneva Conventions (1977), also addressed to internal armed conflict, similarly creates special protections for children and prohibits the recruitment of children under fifteen as a "fundamental guarantee" (Art. 4). It also urges states to refrain from recruiting children between the ages of fifteen and eighteen. However, the Protocol does not treat such conduct as a grave breach subject to individual criminal responsibility. Indeed, the Protocol contains no penal regime.

9. Human Rights Treaties

The Convention on the Rights of the Child (CRC) mirrors Protocol II by specifically prohibiting the use of children under 15 in combat, but it too seems to concede that children between the ages of 15 and 18 may, under certain circumstances, be employed in armed conflict. This is one of the most widely ratified treaties (as of September 2019 all states but the United States are parties), so its impact on customary international law is not to be understated. Yet it fails to direct state parties to criminalize the practice of child conscription or recruitment. The Defense made note of a statement by the United States that the prohibition against child recruitment is "more of a human rights provision than a criminal law provision"—what does this mean? Are human rights treaties relevant to an international criminal law prosecution? Should tribunals adjudicating these norms endeavor to align international criminal law with international human rights norms?

10. The ICC Statute's Criminalization of Child Recruitment

Imagine a timeline of legal developments; when did the recruitment and use of child soldiers become an international crime? The ICC Statute (which was drafted in 1998 and entered into force in 2002) criminalized child recruitment for the first time on the international level. Germany first proposed the inclusion of a provision on child recruitment in 1997, but there was no consensus on this point at that time. What is the relevance of the date of the initial *proposal* for such a rule? Can one use a proposed rule as evidence in support of a rule of customary international law? Against such a rule? Does it matter if the proposed rule was later adopted into the treaty? The law was clearly evolving at the time the defendants' acted. When do you think the penal norm crystallized?

11. The Principle of Specificity

Even if some general prohibition against child recruitment could be cobbled together from these disparate domestic and international examples condemning—and at times criminalizing—child recruitment, would it remain too vague to satisfy the principle of specificity, a corollary to the *nullum crimen sine lege* principle? When Justice Winter announced and read out the opinion, she stated that "the principle of legality and the principle of specificity are both upheld" by the majority opinion. And yet, there is no meaningful discussion about the principle of specificity in the full written opinion. *See Prosecutor v. Norman,* Case No. SCSL–2004–14–AR72(E), Decision on Preliminary Motion Based on Lack of Jurisdiction (Summary), para. 6 (May 31, 2004). Why would the Court mention specificity in its oral recitation and yet neglect to mention it in the written opinion?

The ICTY tackled the issue of specificity when confronted with the catch-all crime against humanity of "other inhumane acts." The Tribunal noted that "[t]here is concern that this category lacks precision and is too general to provide a safe yardstick for the work of the Tribunal and hence, that it is contrary to the principle of the 'specificity' of criminal law. It is thus imperative to establish what is included within this category." *Prosecutor v. Kupreškić, et al.,* Case No. IT–95–14, Judgement, para. 563 (Jan. 14, 2000). Would you consider the prohibition against child recruitment to be as vague as that against "other inhumane acts?" Are there instances in which it is desirable to leave the definition of a crime ambiguous? On the issue of the obligation to provide "humane treatment" under common Article 3 of the Geneva Conventions, the International Committee for the Red Cross has commented:

> [I]t is always dangerous to try to go into too much detail [defining "humane treatment"]—especially in this domain. However great the care taken in drawing up a list of all the various forms of infliction, it would never be possible to catch up with the imagination of future torturers who wished to satisfy their bestial instincts; and the more specific and complete a list tries to be, the more restrictive it becomes. The form of wording adopted is flexible and, at the same time, precise.

ICRC COMMENTARY ON THE IVTH GENEVA CONVENTION RELATIVE TO THE PROTECTION OF CIVILIAN PERSONS IN TIME OF WAR (1958, repr. 1994), p. 39. Do you agree with this reasoning? Would the same reasoning apply to the issue of child recruitment?

12. *Lubanga*: A Reprise

During the ICC proceedings confirming the charges against Thomas Lubanga Dyilo of the Democratic Republic of Congo (DRC), the defendant argued that he could not have been expected to know of the prohibition against the use of child soldiers in 2002, because the governments of Uganda and the DRC had failed to make known to the population that they had ratified the ICC Statute. *Prosecutor v. Lubanga*, Case No. ICC–01/04–01/06, Decision on the Confirmation of Charges, paras. 294–296 (Jan. 29, 2007). The Pre-Trial Chamber characterized Lubanga's argument as one of mistake of law, which is not generally recognized as a defense before the ICC pursuant to Article 32(2) ("A mistake of law as to whether a particular type of conduct is a crime within the jurisdiction of the Court shall not be a ground for excluding criminal responsibility"). The Chamber ruled that (1) it was sufficient that the ICC Statute was in force at the time of the alleged offenses, (2) the formulation of the crime in the Statute covers the alleged conduct, (3) in any case, the prohibition was part of international law prior to the entry into force of the ICC Statute (citing the Additional Protocol I to the Geneva Conventions and the *Norman* decision excerpted above), and (4) the defendant had actual knowledge of the prohibition given his position as putative head of state. *Id.* at paras. 303–314.

How were other embattled belligerents to know that they were suddenly subject to criminal prosecution for using child soldiers? Is this notion of notice a defensible fiction? In a dramatic moment, the first witness against Lubanga at trial—an eleven-year-old former child soldier who appeared anonymously and goes by the name Dieumerci—testified that he had been recruited by Lubanga's subordinates to serve in the defendant's militia. After a break, however, the witness recanted his testimony and stated that an NGO had told him what to say at trial. Two weeks later, after several hearings about witness safety, Dieumerci returned to the stand and elaborated upon his original testimony about serving as a child soldier in Lubanga's army.

III. SUPERIOR ORDERS

The defense of superior orders is frequently asserted in war crimes trials and highlights tension between the imperatives of military discipline and criminal accountability. For example, in a Civil War-era case in the United States, the Tennessee Supreme Court upheld as a correct reflection of the law the following jury instruction:

> A soldier in the service of the United States is bound to obey all lawful orders of his superior officers, or officers over him, and all he may do in obeying such lawful orders, constitutes no offense as to him. But an order illegal in itself, and not justified by the rules and usages of war, or in its substance being clearly

> illegal, so that a man of ordinary sense and understanding would know, as soon as he heard the order read or given, that such order was illegal, would afford a private no protection for a crime committed under such order, provided the act with which he may be charged, has all the ingredients in it which may be necessary to constitute the same crime in law. Any order given by an officer to his private, which does not expressly and clearly show on its face, or in the body thereof, its own illegality, the soldier would be bound to obey, and such order would be a protection to him. No person in the military service, has any right to commit a crime in law, contrary to the rules and usages of war, and outside of the purposes thereof; and the officers are all amenable for all crimes thus committed, and the privates likewise are answerable to the law for crimes committed in obeying all orders illegal on their face and in their substance, when such illegality appears at once to a common mind, on hearing them read or given.

Riggs v. State, 43 Tenn. 85 (1866).

Almost a century later, the following rule was applied by the International Military Tribunal at Nuremberg:

> The fact that a Defendant acted pursuant to order of his Government or of a superior shall not free him from responsibility, but may be considered in mitigation of punishment if the Tribunal determines that justice so requires.

Charter of the International Military Tribunal of Aug. 8, 1945, art. 8, *annexed to* Agreement for the Prosecution and Punishment of the Major War Criminals of the European Axis, Aug. 8, 1945, 59 Stat. 1544. In a post-Nuremberg judgment, a military commission noted

> The obedience of a soldier is not the obedience of an automaton. A soldier is a reasoning agent. He does not respond, and is not expected to respond, like a piece of machinery. It is a fallacy of widespread consumption that a soldier is required to do everything his superior officer orders him to do. . . .

The Einsatzgruppen Case, 4 TRIALS OF WAR CRIMINALS BEFORE THE NUERNBURG MILITARY TRIBUNALS UNDER CONTROL COUNCIL LAW NO. 10, 470 (1946–1949). The judge presiding over one of the My Lai massacre cases borrowed this automaton metaphor in his instructions to the panel. *See United States v. Calley*, 46 C.M.R. 1131, 1183 (1973), aff'd 22 U.S.C. M.A. 534 (1973).

Despite this early precedent, the status and acceptance of the doctrine of superior orders as a defense in international law is hardly settled. Because of the difficulty in reaching an agreement, several of the major multilateral treaties are silent on the issue. The absence is perhaps most notable in the Hague and Geneva Conventions, including the 1977 Protocols. The Genocide Convention drafters were unable to agree upon a provision. An abandoned draft Article 5 would have provided that "command of law or superior orders shall not justify genocide." Most multilateral treaties that do address the issue categorically preclude superior orders as a defense. *See, e.g.,* Convention against Torture and Other Cruel, Inhuman or Degrading Treatment or Punishment art 2(3), June 26, 1987, 1465 U.N.T.S. 85 ("An order from a superior officer or a public authority may not be invoked as a justification of torture."); Inter-American Convention on the Forced Disappearance of Persons, § 5, art. VIII, June 9, 1994 (establishing that "the defense of due obedience to superior orders or instructions that stipulate, authorize, or encourage forced disappearance shall not be admitted"). By contrast, the language of the ICTY and ICTR Statutes are nearly identical to the Nuremburg Charter provision in allowing evidence of superior orders for mitigation. *See* Statute of the International Tribunal for the Former Yugoslavia (ICTY), art. 7(4); Statute of the International Tribunal for Rwanda, art. 6(4).

The ICC Statute recognizes the defense of superior orders in Article 33:

> Article 33: Superior Orders and Prescription of Law
>
> 1. The fact that a crime within the jurisdiction of the Court has been committed by a person pursuant to an order of a Government or of a superior, whether military or civilian, shall not relieve that person of criminal responsibility unless:
>
> (a) The person was under a legal obligation to obey orders of the Government or the superior in question;
>
> (b) The person did not know that the order was unlawful; and
>
> (c) The order was not manifestly unlawful.
>
> 2. For the purposes of this article, orders to commit genocide or crimes against humanity are manifestly unlawful.

This provision emerged as a compromise between three negotiating positions: that subordinates cannot be expected to verify the legality of orders they receive, that only lawful orders create obligations to obey, and that the existence of an order from a superior may operate as a mitigating circumstance. Article 31(d) also articulates the defense of duress:

> The conduct which is alleged to constitute a crime within the jurisdiction of the Court has been caused by duress resulting from a threat of imminent death or of continuing or imminent serious bodily harm against that person or another person, and the person acts necessarily and reasonably to avoid this threat, provided that the person does not intend to cause a greater harm than the one sought to be avoided. Such a threat may either be:
>
> (i) Made by other persons; or

(ii) Constituted by other circumstances beyond that person's control.

NOTES & QUESTIONS

1. The ICC Formulation

Why would the drafters of the ICC Statute choose the above formulation for the defense of superior orders? How does it reflect and balance the three negotiating positions discussed above? For a discussion, *see* Paola Gaeta, *The Defence of Superior Orders: The Statute of the International Criminal Court versus Customary International Law*, 10 EUROP. J. INT'L L. 172 (1999).

2. Superior Orders

What is the theory by which a defendant acting under orders might be exonerated from criminal liability? What arguments would support allowing such a complete defense? What argues against such a defense? How would such a defense affect the deterrent function of international criminal law? How would it affect the justice function of international criminal law? The framers of the Model Penal Code justified the defense of duress as follows:

> [L]aw is ineffective in the deepest sense, indeed * * * it is hypocritical, if it imposes on the actor who has the misfortune to confront a dilemmatic choice, a standard that his judges are not prepared to affirm that they should and could comply with if their turn to face the problem should arise. Condemnation in such a case is bound to be an ineffective threat; what is, however, more significant is that it is divorced from any moral base and is unjust.

MODEL PENAL CODE COMMENTARIES, § 2.09, at 374–375. Do these same rationales apply to the defense of superior orders?

3. Superior Orders and Duress

Under the formulation of Article 33, how is a soldier in the service of an armed force to know the legality or illegality of an order from a superior or recognize a manifestly unlawful order? Is the defense based on an objective or a subjective standard? How are subordinates to confirm the legality of the orders they receive given that the "fog of war" often results in incomplete information and given the indeterminacy of many of the rules of warfare? To what degree may they rely upon the presumptive legality of orders from their superiors?

The excerpt below reveals some conceptual overlap between the defenses of superior orders and duress. In *Prosecutor v. Erdemović*, the defendant stood accused of participating in a firing squad that resulted in the death of at least 1200 Muslim men. Erdemović pleaded guilty to one count of committing crimes against humanity, but at the time of his plea he claimed he was acting under duress because he was under orders to kill the victims. In this regard, he testified as follows:

> Your Honour, I had to do this. If I had refused, I would have been killed together with the victims. When I refused, they told me: "If you're sorry for them, stand up, line up with them and we will kill you too." I am not sorry for myself but for my family, my wife and

son who then had nine months, and I could not refuse because then they would have killed me.

Prosecutor v. Erdemović, Case No. IT–96–22–T, Sentencing Judgement, para. 10 (Nov. 29, 1996). He also testified that he believed he had personally killed about seventy people in connection with the massacre. Erdemović challenged his initial sentence of ten years as inappropriate given the evidence that he had acted under duress. In the context of his appeal, the Appeals Chamber considered whether his plea was valid, which required a showing that it was voluntary, unequivocal, and informed. A majority determined that the plea was invalid, although the judges differed in their methodology and rationale for reaching this conclusion. *See Prosecutor v. Erdemović*, Case No. IT–96–22–A, Judgement (Oct. 7, 1997). In the concurring and dissenting opinions that follow, consider how the judges of the Appeals Chamber utilized the sources doctrine to determine the validity of Erdemović's guilty plea.

Prosecutor v. Erdemović, Case No. IT–96–22–A, Joint Separate Opinion of Judge McDonald and Judge Vohrah (Oct. 7, 1997)

In the Appeals Chamber

Can Duress Be A Complete Defence in International Law to the Killing of Innocents?

32. [T]hree factors bear upon this general statement of the issue. Firstly, the particular war crime or crime against humanity committed by the Appellant involved the killing of innocent human beings. Secondly, as will be shown in the ensuing discussion, there is a clear dichotomy in the practice of the main legal systems of the world between those systems which would allow duress to operate as a complete defence to crimes involving the taking of innocent life, and those systems which would not. Thirdly, the Appellant in this case was a soldier of the Bosnian Serb army conducting combat operations in the Republic of Bosnia and Herzegovina at the material time. As such, the issue may be stated more specifically as follows: In law, may duress afford a complete defence to a soldier charged with crimes against humanity or war crimes where the soldier has killed innocent persons? * * *

49. Although some [domestic jurisprudence] may clearly represent the positions of national jurisdictions regarding the availability of duress as a complete defence to the killing of innocent persons, neither they nor the principles on this issue found in decisions of the post-World War Two military tribunals are, in our view, entitled to be given the status of customary international law. For a rule to pass into customary international law, the International Court of Justice has authoritatively restated in the *North Sea Continental Shelf* cases that there must exist extensive and uniform state practice underpinned by *opinio juris sive necessitatis*. To the extent that the domestic decisions and national laws

of States relating to the issue of duress as a defence to murder may be regarded as state practice, it is quite plain that this practice is not at all consistent. The defence in its Notice of Appeal surveys the criminal codes and legislation of 14 civil law jurisdictions in which necessity or duress is prescribed as a general exculpatory principle applying to all crimes. The surveyed jurisdictions comprise those of Austria, Belgium, Brazil, Greece, Italy, Finland, the Netherlands, France, Germany, Peru, Spain, Switzerland, Sweden and the former Yugoslavia. Indeed, the war crimes decisions cited in the Separate Opinion of Judge Cassese are based upon the acceptance of duress as a general defence to all crimes in the criminal codes of France, Italy, Germany, the Netherlands and Belgium. In stark contrast to this acceptance of duress as a defence to the killing of innocents is the clear position of the various countries throughout the world applying the common law. These common law systems categorically reject duress as a defence to murder. The sole exception is the United States where a few states have accepted Section 2.09 of the United States Model Penal Code which currently provides that duress is a general defence to all crimes. Indeed, the rejection of duress as a defence to the killing of innocent human beings in [a series of World War II-era cases before national military tribunals] reflects in essence the common law approach.

50. Not only is State practice on the question as to whether duress is a defence to murder far from consistent, this practice of States is not, in our view, underpinned by *opinio juris*. Again to the extent that state practice on the question of duress as a defence to murder may be evidenced by the opinions on this question in decisions of national military tribunals and national laws, we find quite unacceptable any proposition that States adopt this practice because they "feel that they are conforming to what amounts to a legal obligation" at an international level. * * *

55. [I]t is our considered view that no rule may be found in customary international law regarding the availability or the non-availability of duress as a defence to a charge of killing innocent human beings. The post-World War Two military tribunals did not establish such a rule. We do not think that the decisions of these tribunals or those of other national courts and military tribunals constitute consistent and uniform state practice underpinned by *opinio juris sive necessitatis*. * * *

56. It is appropriate now to inquire whether the "general principles of law recognised by civilised nations," established as a source of international law in Article 38(1)(c) of the ICJ Statute, may shed some light upon this intricate issue of duress. * * *

57. A number of considerations bear upon our analysis of the application of "general principles of law recognised by civilised nations" as a source of international law. First, although general principles of law are to be derived from existing legal systems, in particular, national systems of law, it is generally accepted that the distillation of a "general

principle of law recognised by civilised nations" does not require the comprehensive survey of all legal systems of the world as this would involve a practical impossibility and has never been the practice of the International Court of Justice or other international tribunals which have had recourse to Article 38(1)(c) of the ICJ Statute. Second, it is the view of eminent jurists * * * that one purpose of this article is to avoid a situation of *non-liquet*, that is, where an international tribunal is stranded by an absence of applicable legal rules. Third, a "general principle" must not be confused with concrete manifestations of that principle in specific rules. * * * In light of these considerations, our approach will necessarily not involve a direct comparison of the specific rules of each of the world's legal systems, but will instead involve a survey of those jurisdictions whose jurisprudence is, as a practical matter, accessible to us in an effort to discern a general trend, policy or principle underlying the concrete rules of that jurisdiction which comports with the object and purpose of the establishment of the International Tribunal. * * *

59. The penal codes of civil law systems, with some exceptions, consistently recognise duress as a complete defence to all crimes. The criminal codes of civil law nations provide that an accused acting under duress "commits no crime" or "is not criminally responsible" or "shall not be punished." We would note that some civil law systems distinguish between the notion of necessity and that of duress. Necessity is taken to refer to situations of emergency arising from natural forces. Duress, however, is taken to refer to compulsion by threats of another human being. Where a civil law system makes this distinction, only the provision relating to duress will be referred to. * * * [The Appeals Chamber then surveyed the penal codes of France, Belgium, the Netherlands, Spain, Germany, Italy, Norway, Sweden, Finland, Venezuela, Nicaragua, Chile, Panama, and Mexico, all of which adopt a similar position].

The Penal Code of the Socialist Federal Republic of Yugoslavia defined the general principles of criminal law, including the elements of criminal responsibility, and was applied by the constituent Republics and Autonomous Provinces of the former Yugoslavia which supplemented the federal code with their own specific penal legislation. In the 1990 amendment of the code, Article 10 provides for the defence of extreme necessity. Article 10 reads:

(1) An act committed in extreme necessity is not a criminal offence.

(2) An act is committed in extreme necessity if it is performed in order that the perpetrator avert from himself or from another an immediate danger which is not due to the perpetrator's fault and which could not have been averted in any other way, provided that the evil created thereby does not exceed the one which was threatening.

(3) If the perpetrator himself has negligently created the danger, or if he has exceeded the limits of extreme necessity, the court may impose a reduced punishment on him, and if he exceeded the limits under particularly mitigating circumstances it may also remit the punishment.

(4) There is no extreme necessity where the perpetrator was under an obligation to expose himself to the danger. * * *

60. In England, duress is a complete defence to all crimes except murder, attempted murder and, it would appear, treason. Although there is no direct authority on whether duress is available in respect of attempted murder, the prevailing view is that there is no reason in logic, morality or law in granting the defence to a charge of attempted murder whilst withholding it in respect of a charge of murder.

The English position that duress operates as a complete defence in respect of crimes generally is followed in the United States and Australia with variations in the federal state jurisdictions as to the precise definition of the defence and the range of offences for which the defence is not available. * * * [The Appeals Chamber surveys the law of Canada, South Africa, India, Malaysia, and Nigeria, which echo this approach]. * * *

63. In numerous national jurisdictions, certain offences are excepted from the application of the defence of duress. Traditional common law rejects the defence of duress in respect of murder and treason. Legislatures in many common law jurisdictions, however, often prescribe a longer list of excepted offences.

64. Despite these offences being excluded from the operation of duress as a defence, the practice of courts in these jurisdictions is nevertheless to mitigate the punishment of persons committing excepted offences unless there is a mandatory penalty of death or life imprisonment prescribed for the offence. In the United Kingdom, section 3(3)(a) of the Criminal Justice Act 1991 provides that a court "shall take into account all such information about the circumstances of the offence. * * *

In the United States, duress constitutes a specific category for mitigation of sentences under the Federal Sentencing Guidelines and Policy Statements issued pursuant to Section 994(a) of Title 28, United States Code, which took effect on 1 November 1987. Policy Statement 5K2.12, "Coercion and Duress" provides:

> If the defendant committed the offence because of serious coercion, blackmail or duress, under circumstances not amounting to a complete defence, the court may decrease the sentence below the applicable guideline range. The extent of the decrease ordinarily should depend on the reasonableness of the defendant's actions and on the extent to which the conduct

would have been harmful under the circumstances as the defendant believed them to be. Ordinarily coercion will be sufficiently serious to warrant departure only when it involves a threat of physical injury, substantial damage to property or similar injury resulting from the unlawful action of a third party or from a natural emergency. * * *

65. Courts in civil law jurisdictions may also mitigate an offender's punishment on the ground of duress where the defence fails. In some systems, the power to mitigate punishment on the ground of duress is expressly stated in the provisions addressing duress. In other jurisdictions in which the criminal law is embodied in a penal code, the power to mitigate may be found in general provisions regarding mitigation of sentence.

66. Having regard to the above survey relating to the treatment of duress in the various legal systems, it is, in our view, a general principle of law recognised by civilised nations that an accused person is less blameworthy and less deserving of the full punishment when he performs a certain prohibited act under duress. * * * This alleviation of blameworthiness is manifest in the different rules with differing content in the principal legal systems of the world as the above survey reveals. On the one hand, a large number of jurisdictions recognise duress as a complete defence absolving the accused from all criminal responsibility. On the other hand, in other jurisdictions, duress does not afford a complete defence to offences generally but serves merely as a factor which would mitigate the punishment to be imposed on a convicted person. Mitigation is also relevant in two other respects. Firstly, punishment may be mitigated in respect of offences which have been specifically excepted from the operation of the defence of duress by the legislatures of some jurisdictions. Secondly, courts have the power to mitigate sentences where the strict elements of a defence of duress are not made out on the facts. * * *

72. It is clear from the differing positions of the principal legal systems of the world that there is no consistent concrete rule which answers the question whether or not duress is a defence to the killing of innocent persons. It is not possible to reconcile the opposing positions and, indeed, we do not believe that the issue should be reduced to a contest between common law and civil law. We would therefore approach this problem bearing in mind the specific context in which the International Tribunal was established, the types of crimes over which it has jurisdiction, and the fact that the International Tribunal's mandate is expressed in the Statute as being in relation to "serious violations of international humanitarian law." * * *

75. The resounding point from these eloquent passages is that the law should not be the product or slave of logic or intellectual hair-splitting, but must serve broader normative purposes in light of its social, political and economic role. It is noteworthy that the authorities we have

just cited issued their cautionary words in respect of domestic society and in respect of a range of ordinary crimes including kidnapping, assault, robbery and murder. Whilst reserving our comments on the appropriate rule for domestic national contexts, we cannot but stress that we are not, in the International Tribunal, concerned with ordinary domestic crimes. The purview of the International Tribunal relates to war crimes and crimes against humanity committed in armed conflicts of extreme violence with egregious dimensions. We are not concerned with the actions of domestic terrorists, gang-leaders and kidnappers. We are concerned that, in relation to the most heinous crimes known to humankind, the principles of law to which we give credence have the appropriate normative effect upon soldiers bearing weapons of destruction and upon the commanders who control them in armed conflict situations. The facts of this particular case, for example, involved the cold-blooded slaughter of 1200 men and boys by soldiers using automatic weapons. We must bear in mind that we are operating in the realm of international humanitarian law which has, as one of its prime objectives, the protection of the weak and vulnerable in such a situation where their lives and security are endangered. Concerns about the harm which could arise from admitting duress as a defence to murder were sufficient to persuade a majority of the House of Lords and the Privy Council to categorically deny the defence in the national context to prevent the growth of domestic crime and the impunity of miscreants. Are they now insufficient to persuade us to similarly reject duress as a complete defence in our application of laws designed to take account of humanitarian concerns in the arena of brutal war, to punish perpetrators of crimes against humanity and war crimes, and to deter the commission of such crimes in the future? If national law denies recognition of duress as a defence in respect of the killing of innocent persons, international criminal law can do no less than match that policy since it deals with murders often of far greater magnitude. If national law denies duress as a defence even in a case in which a single innocent life is extinguished due to action under duress, international law, in our view, cannot admit duress in cases which involve the slaughter of innocent human beings on a large scale. It must be our concern to facilitate the development and effectiveness of international humanitarian law and to promote its aims and application by recognising the normative effect which criminal law should have upon those subject to them. Indeed, Security Council resolution 827 (1993) established the International Tribunal expressly as a measure to "halt and effectively redress" the widespread and flagrant violations of international humanitarian law occurring in the territory of the former Yugoslavia and to contribute thereby to the restoration and maintenance of peace. * * *

78. We do not think our reference to considerations of policy are improper. It would be naïve to believe that international law operates and develops wholly divorced from considerations of social and economic policy. There is the view that international law should distance itself

from social policy and this view has been articulated by the International Court of Justice in the *South West Africa* Cases,[165] where it is stated that "[l]aw exists, it is said, to serve a social need; but precisely for that reason it can do so only through and within the limits of its own discipline." We are of the opinion that this separation of law from social policy is inapposite in relation to the application of international humanitarian law to crimes occurring during times of war. It is clear to us that whatever is the distinction between the international legal order and municipal legal orders in general, the distinction is imperfect in respect of the criminal law which, both at the international and the municipal level, is directed towards consistent aims. At the municipal level, criminal law and criminal policy are closely intertwined. There is no reason why this should be any different in international criminal law. We subscribe to the views of Professor Rosalyn Higgins (as she then was) when she argued:

> Reference to the 'correct legal view' or 'rules' can never avoid the element of choice (though it can seek to disguise it), nor can it provide guidance to the preferable decision. In making this choice one must inevitably have consideration for the humanitarian, moral, and social purposes of the law. . . . Where there is ambiguity or uncertainty, the policy-directed choice can properly be made.[166]

It appears that the essence of this thesis is not that policy concerns dominate the law but rather, where appropriate, are given due consideration in the determination of a case. This is precisely the approach we have taken to the question of duress as a defence to the killing of innocent persons in international law. Even if policy concerns are entirely ignored, the law will nevertheless fail in its ambition of neutrality "for even such a refusal [to acknowledge political and social factors] is not without political and social consequences. There is no avoiding the essential relationship between law and politics."[167] * * *

88. After the above survey of authorities in the different systems of law and exploration of the various policy considerations which we must bear in mind, we take the view that duress cannot afford a complete defence to a soldier charged with crimes against humanity or war crimes in international law involving the taking of innocent lives. We do so having regard to our mandated obligation under the Statute to ensure that international humanitarian law, which is concerned with the protection of humankind, is not in any way undermined.

---

[165] *South West Africa Cases,* I.C.J. Reports (1966) 6 at para. 49.

[166] Rosalyn Higgins, PROBLEMS AND PROCESS: INTERNATIONAL LAW AND HOW WE USE IT (Clarendon Press, Oxford, 1994), pp. 5–7.

[167] Rosalyn Higgins, *Integrations of Authority and Control* at p. 85, *referred to in* Higgins, PROBLEMS AND PROCESS: INTERNATIONAL LAW AND HOW WE USE IT (Clarendon Press, Oxford, 1994), p. 5.

89. In the result, we do not consider the plea of the Appellant was equivocal as duress does not afford a complete defence in international law to a charge of a crime against humanity or a war crime which involves the killing of innocent human beings.

Prosecutor v. Erdemović, Case No. IT–96–22–A, Joint Separate Opinion of Judge Cassese (Oct. 7, 1997)

11. I * * * respectfully disagree with the conclusions of the majority of the Appeals Chamber concerning duress, as set out in the Joint Separate Opinion of their Honours Judge McDonald and Judge Vohrah and on the following grounds:

(i) After finding that no specific international rule has evolved on the question of whether duress affords a complete defence to the killing of innocent persons, the majority should have drawn the only conclusion imposed by law and logic, namely that the general rule on duress should apply—subject, of course, to the necessary requirements. In logic, if no exception to a general rule be proved, then the general rule prevails. Likewise in law, if one looks for a special rule governing a specific aspect of a matter and concludes that no such rule has taken shape, the only inference to be drawn is that the specific aspect is regulated by the rule governing the general matter;

(ii) Instead of this simple conclusion, the majority of the Appeals Chamber has embarked upon a detailed investigation of "practical policy considerations" and has concluded by upholding "policy considerations" substantially based on English law. I submit that this examination is extraneous to the task of our Tribunal. This International Tribunal is called upon to apply international law, in particular our Statute and principles and rules of international humanitarian law and international criminal law. Our International Tribunal is a court of law; it is bound only by international law. It should therefore refrain from engaging in meta-legal analyses. In addition, it should refrain from relying exclusively on notions, policy considerations or the philosophical underpinnings of common-law countries, while disregarding those of civil-law countries or other systems of law. What is even more important, a policy-oriented approach in the area of criminal law runs contrary to the fundamental customary principle *nullum crimen sine lege.* On the strength of international principles and rules my conclusions on duress differ widely from those of the majority of the Appeals Chamber. I shall set out below the legal reasons which I believe support my dissent.

12. In short, I consider that: (1) under international criminal law duress may be generally urged as a defence, provided certain strict requirements are met; when it cannot be admitted as a defence, duress may nevertheless be acted upon as a mitigating circumstance; (2) with regard to war crimes or crimes against humanity whose underlying

offence is murder or more generally the taking of human life, no special rule of customary international law has evolved on the matter; consequently, even with respect to these offences the general rule on duress applies; it follows that duress may amount to a defence provided that its stringent requirements are met. For offences involving killing, it is true, however, that one of the requirements * * * —proportionality—would usually not be fulfilled. Nevertheless, in exceptional circumstances this requirement might be met, for example, when the killing would be in any case perpetrated by persons other than the one acting under duress (since then it is not a question of saving your own life by killing another person, but of simply saving your own life when the other person will inevitably die, which may not be 'disproportionate' as a remedy); (3) the Appeals Chamber should therefore remit the case to a Trial Chamber on the issue of duress (as well as on the issue that the plea was not informed), directing the Trial Chamber to enter a not-guilty plea on behalf of Dražen Erdemović * * * and then to satisfy itself, in trial proceedings, whether or not the Appellant acted under duress and consequently, whether or not he is excused. * * *

In sum, the customary rule of international law on duress, as evolved on the basis of case-law and the military regulations of some States, does not exclude the applicability of duress to war crimes and crimes against humanity whose underlying offence is murder or unlawful killing. However, as the right to life is the most fundamental human right, the rule demands that the general requirements for duress be applied particularly strictly in the case of killing of innocent persons. * * *

49. * * * It should therefore be no surprise that I do not share the views of the majority of the Appeals Chamber, according to which, since international criminal law is ambiguous or uncertain on this matter, it is warranted to make a policy-directed choice and thus rely on "considerations of social and economic policy." I disagree not only because, as I have already repeatedly stated, in my view international law is not ambiguous or uncertain, but also because to uphold in this area of criminal law the concept of recourse to a policy-directed choice is tantamount to running afoul of the customary principle *nullum crimen sine lege.* An international court must apply *lex lata,* that is to say, the existing rules of international law as they are created through the sources of the international legal system. If it has instead recourse to policy considerations or moral principles, it acts *ultra vires.*

In any event, even assuming that no clear legal regulation of the matter were available in international law, arguably the Appeals Chamber majority should have drawn upon the law applicable in the former Yugoslavia. In the former Yugoslavia and in the present States of the area the relevant criminal law provides that duress (called "extreme necessity") may amount to a total defence for any crime, whether or not implying the killing of persons. A national of one of the States of that region fighting in an armed conflict was required to know those national criminal provisions and base his expectations on their contents. Were *ex hypothesi* international criminal law really ambiguous on duress or were it even to contain a gap, it would therefore be appropriate and judicious to have recourse—as a last resort—to the national legislation of the accused, rather than to moral considerations or policy-oriented principles. In the specific instance under discussion, where the State at stake is one of the former Yugoslavia, this approach would also be supported by the general maxim *in dubio pro reo* (which in this case should be *in dubio pro accusato)* [the principle that any ambiguity must accrue to the defendant's advantage].

NOTES & QUESTIONS

1. Case Outcome

Upon remand, the Trial Chamber reduced the sentence to five years. *Prosecutor v. Erdemović*, Case No. IT–96–22–T, Sentencing Judgement (March 5, 1998). Erdemović has testified in a number of trials at the ICTY, most recently that of the former Bosnian Serb leader Radovan Karadžić.

2. A Clash of Titans

What methodology did Judges Gabrielle Kirk McDonald (United States) and Lal Chand Vohrah (Malaysia) utilize to determine if there was an international rule on the question of duress as a general principle of law? Upon determining that there was no consistent rule, how did they avoid a finding of *non liquet* ("it is not clear")? Does the statute of the ICTY empower them to undertake the methodology that they did or were they indeed acting *ultra vires*, as charged by the late Judge Antonio Cassese (Italy) in dissent? How, in their estimation, is the result reached the best one for the system of international criminal justice?

Do you agree that international criminal law cannot be divorced from social policy—the humanitarian, moral, and social purposes of the law? Judges McDonald and Vohrah cite then-Professor Rosalyn Higgins, who later became a judge on the International Court of Justice, for the proposition that "[w]here there is ambiguity, the policy-directed choice can be made." Might this claim hold less force in the international criminal law realm than the public international law realm? What are the risks of an international criminal tribunal relying upon such meta-legal analysis? Are "activist judges" more acceptable in the international law realm than in the domestic context? Or is Judge Cassese correct in stating that the policy-oriented methodology adopted by the majority threatens the legitimacy of the tribunal? Are the majority's policy-oriented considerations based upon international law, or are they simply the common law's underlying policy considerations repackaged as international law? Consider the following criticism of judicial activism in international criminal law by a member of the U.S. delegation to the Rome Conference dedicated to drafting the ICC Statute:

> Equally important * * * are concerns that ICC judges * * * might apply their varied and not always pertinent experiences to shape the law in unforeseen ways. Such judicial activism is improper for anybody not directly accountable to the people, and it is especially inappropriate for a criminal court. An institution that purports to enforce the law must itself be bound by it.

William K. Lietzau, *International Criminal Law After Rome: Concerns From a U.S. Military Perspective,* 64 LAW & CONTEMP. PROBS. 119, 123 (Winter 2001).

3. Civil Law v. Common Law Approaches

Consider the divergent approaches taken by common law and civil law systems to the question of duress. Why might these two positions develop along such different trajectories? At what stage does the fact of duress operate in the two systems: at the time of determining the culpability of the accused or as a mitigating factor in sentencing? What does this say about the role of the judiciary and the prosecutor (or investigating judge) in the two systems? In international criminal law, where should the discretion lie where situations of duress are at issue: with international prosecutors deciding whom to indict or with international judges meting out mitigated sentences? Which approach, that of Judges McDonald and Vohrah or that of Judge Cassese, is more flexible and under which approach is justice most likely to be served? Is the disagreement between the two opinions simply one of a common law majority against a civil law minority? Where the ICTY Statute was silent, should the tribunal have simply applied the law of the former Yugoslavia, reproduced above after para. 59 and as argued by Judge Cassese, since this was the legal system with which the accused would have been familiar? Would the principle of *in dubio pro reo* [when in doubt, rule in favor of the defendant] dictate this result?

4. For Further Reading

See Jeanne L. Bakker, *Defense of Obedience to Superior Orders: The Mens Rea Requirement*, 17 AM. J. CRIM. L. 55 (1989–90); Yoram Dinstein, THE DEFENSE OF "OBEDIENCE TO SUPERIOR ORDERS" IN INTERNATIONAL LAW (1965); James B. Insco, *Defense of Superior Orders Before Military Commissions*, 13 DUKE J. COMP. & INT'L. L. 389 (2003); Mark J. Osiel, OBEYING ORDERS: ATROCITY, MILITARY DISCIPLINE & THE LAW OF WAR 41 (1999). A thorough history of the defense can be found in Matthew R. Lippman, *Humanitarian Law: The Development and the Scope of the Superior Orders Defense*, 20 PENN ST. INT'L L. REV. 153 (2001).

PROBLEM

Consider how Article 33 of the ICC Statute might apply in a prosecution of the subordinates described in the following hypothetical scenarios:

1. In an urban combat situation, a superior commander orders his subordinate to fire on a building clearly designated as a school on the ground that militants have commandeered it to store and distribute weapons. The subordinate questions the order to fire on the school. The superior threatens

disciplinary action if his order is not complied with. The attack goes forward. The building turns out to genuinely be a school, and three children are killed.

2. In an ethnic civil war situation, a superior commander orders her subordinates to capture, detain, and interrogate all military-aged men of a rival ethnic group on the ground that they are all either militants or potential militants. Over the course of the conflict, the subordinates detain hundreds of men in concentration-camp conditions, but due to resource constraints, they are held without adequate food, water, or shelter. Many individuals in custody die on account of the conditions of life.

3. In an international armed conflict involving an active air campaign, a superior commander orders his subordinates to launch an air strike with laser-guided missiles against a factory that produces munitions in addition to other products. The commander further orders the attack to take place at night when no civilians will likely be present. The order is carried out, and dozens of civilian employees building tractors on the night shift are killed.

4. In an international armed conflict, a superior commander orders her subordinates to drop multiple unguided cluster munitions on the runway of an air base used exclusively for military traffic. The base is located next to a civilian village. Weeks later, when the front has shifted, several children die or are injured when they play with unexploded ordinance (UXO).

5. In an international armed conflict, a superior in the air force orders his subordinates to use one-ton bombs to destroy surface-to-air defense capabilities of the opponent that have been located in the immediate vicinity of an historic mosque. The subordinates are ordered to fly at 50,000 feet in order to avoid the air defense system. One of the dropped bombs damages part of the mosque.

6. In a civil war launched by a minority group attempting to unseat the current regime, the Minister of Defense gives a speech telling the populace to rise up against the rebels to defend the homeland. A civil defense force forms and attacks a nearby village populated by members of the minority group, killing everyone in sight.

IV. NECESSITY

Necessity has been described as "the mother of all justifications." Markus D. Dubber, CRIMINAL LAW: MODEL PENAL CODE 194 (2002). The U.S. Model Penal Code (MPC), for example, describes the "choice of evils" defense at § 3.02(1) as follows:

> Conduct that the actor believes to be necessary to avoid a harm or evil to himself or to another is justifiable, provided that . . . the harm or evil sought to be avoided by such conduct is greater than that sought to be prevented by the law defining the offense charged.

The defense is premised on principles of rationality and justice and the understanding that

> the law ought to promote the achievement of higher values at the expense of lesser values, and sometimes the greater good for society will be accomplished by violating the literal language of the criminal law.

1 LaFave & Scott, HANDBOOK ON CRIMINAL LAW 5.4(a), at 629 (1986).

As formulated in the MPC, the defense is premised on the subjective beliefs of the actor—rather than an objective, *ex post* evaluation of the situation—subject to the recognition that the actor may be negligent or reckless in appraising the necessity of her conduct. That said, the actor's weighing of the "choice of evils" is evaluated according to an objective standard: the evil sought to be avoided must objectively be worse than the evil committed. Some formulations of the defense also require proof that the actor did not cause the situation of necessity in the first place, that the harm to be avoided was imminent, that the greater evil comes from physical forces beyond the actor's control, or that the actions by the accused were the only possible means by which the actor could avoid the more serious harm.

Compare the MPC's formulation to the way in which the defense is discussed in the opinion below from the Israeli Supreme Court. (See the Appendix for a map of Israel.) In this matter, the Court was asked to determine the legality of certain security measures—including shaking, the use of stress positions, the "*Shabach*" method, and sleep deprivation—in the absence of authorizing legislation. The *Shabach* method was described by the Supreme Court as a technique involving "a number of cumulative components: the cuffing of the suspect, seating him on a low chair, covering his head with an opaque sack and playing powerfully loud music in the area." Both the U.N. Committee Against Torture and U.N. Special Rapporteur on Torture and Other Cruel, Inhuman and Degrading Treatment had already concluded that the techniques were impermissible. The Israeli Supreme Court agreed that each of these techniques lacked legal authorization under existing law, although it did not call them "torture." As part of its defense of these techniques, the Israeli Government invoked the defense of necessity, which is discussed in the excerpt below.

Judgment Concerning the Legality of the General Security Service's Interrogation Methods, 38 I.L.M 1471, 1474–84 (1999)

■ PRESIDENT A. BARAK:

The facts presented before this Court reveal that one hundred and twenty one people died in terrorist attacks between [January 1, 1996 and May 14, 1998]. Seven hundred and seven people were injured. A large number of those killed and injured were victims of harrowing suicide bombings in the heart of Israel's cities. Many attacks—including suicide bombings, attempts to detonate car bombs, kidnappings of citizens and soldiers, attempts to highjack buses, murders, the placing of explosives, etc.—were prevented due to the measures taken by the authorities responsible for fighting the above-described hostile terrorist activities on a daily basis. The main body responsible for fighting terrorism is the General Security Service (GSS).

In order to fulfill this function, the GSS also investigates those suspected of hostile terrorist activities. The purpose of these interrogations is, among others, to gather information regarding terrorists and their organizing methods for the purpose of thwarting and preventing them from carrying out these terrorist attacks. In the context of these interrogations, GSS investigators also make use of physical means. The legality of these practices is being examined before this Court in these applications. * * *

8. The physical means employed by the GSS investigators were presented before this Court by the GSS investigators. The State's attorneys were prepared to present them for us behind closed doors (*in camera*). The applicants' attorneys were opposed to this proposal. Thus, the information at the Court's disposal was provided by the applicants and was not tested in each individual application. This having been said, the State's position, which failed to deny the use of these interrogation methods, and even offered these and other explanations regarding the rationale justifying the use of [one] interrogation method or another, provided the Court with a picture of the GSS's interrogation practices. * * *

22. An interrogation, by its very nature, places the suspect in a difficult position. "The criminal's interrogation," wrote Justice Vitkon over twenty years ago, "is not a negotiation process between two open and fair vendors, conducting their business on the basis of maximum mutual trust." An interrogation is a "competition of minds," in which the investigator attempts to penetrate the suspect's thoughts and elicit from him the information the investigator seeks to obtain. Quite accurately, it was noted that:

> Any interrogation, be it the fairest and most reasonable of all, inevitably places the suspect in embarrassing situations, burdens him, intrudes his conscience, penetrates the deepest crevices of his soul, while creating serious emotional pressure.

Y. Kedmi, ON EVIDENCE, Part A, at 25 (1991). Indeed, the authority to conduct interrogations, like any administrative power, is designed for a specific purpose, which constitutes its foundation, and must be in conformity with the basic principles of the [democratic] regime. In crystallizing the interrogation rules, two values or interests clash. On the one hand, lies the desire to uncover the truth, thereby fulfilling the public interest in exposing crime and preventing it. On the other hand, is the wish to protect the dignity and liberty of the individual being interrogated. This having been said, these interests and values are not absolute. A democratic, freedom-loving society does not accept that investigators use any means for the purpose of uncovering the truth. * * *

23. [A] number of general principles are * * * worth noting: First, a reasonable investigation is necessarily one free of torture, free of cruel, inhuman treatment of the subject and free of any degrading handling whatsoever. There is a prohibition on the use of "brutal or inhuman means" in the course of an investigation. Human dignity also includes the dignity of the suspect being interrogated. This conclusion is in perfect accord with (various) international law treaties—to which Israel is a signatory—which prohibit the use of torture, "cruel, inhuman treatment" and "degrading treatment." These prohibitions are "absolute." There are no exceptions to them and there is no room for balancing. Indeed, violence directed at a suspect's body or spirit does not constitute a reasonable investigation practice. The use of violence during investigations can potentially lead to the investigator being held criminally liable.

Second, a reasonable investigation is likely to cause discomfort: it may result in insufficient sleep; the conditions under which it is conducted risk being unpleasant. Indeed, it is possible to conduct an effective investigation without resorting to violence. Within the confines of the law, it is permitted to resort to various machinations and specific sophisticated activities which serve investigators today (both for Police and GSS); similar investigations—accepted in the most progressive of societies—can be effective in achiev[ing] their goals. In the end result, the legality of an investigation is deduced from the propriety of its purpose and from its methods. Thus, for instance, sleep deprivation for a prolonged period, or sleep deprivation at night when this is not necessary to the investigation time wise may be deemed a use of an investigation method which surpasses the least restrictive means. * * *

Physical Means and the "Necessity" Defense

33. [A]n explicit authorization permitting GSS to employ physical means is not to be found in our law. An authorization of this nature can, in the State's opinion, be obtained in specific cases by virtue of the criminal law defense of "necessity," prescribed in the Penal Law. The language of the statute is as follows (Article 34(1)):

> A person will not bear criminal liability for committing any act immediately necessary for the purpose of saving the life, liberty, body or property, of either himself or his fellow person, from substantial danger of serious harm, imminent from the particular state of things [circumstances], at the requisite timing, and absent alternative means for avoiding the harm.

The State's position is that by virtue of this "defense" to criminal liability, GSS investigators are also authorized to apply physical means, such as shaking, in the appropriate circumstances, in order to prevent serious harm to human life or body, in the absence of other alternatives. The State maintains that an act committed under conditions of "necessity" does not constitute a crime. Instead, it is deemed an act worth committing in such circumstances in order to prevent serious harm to a human life or body. We are therefore speaking of a deed that society has an interest in encouraging, as it is deemed proper in the circumstances. It is choosing the lesser evil. Not only is it legitimately permitted to engage in the fighting of terrorism, it is our moral duty to employ the necessary means for this purpose. This duty is particularly incumbent on the state authorities—and for our purposes, on the GSS investigators—who carry the burden of safeguarding the public peace. As this is the case, there is no obstacle preventing the investigators' superiors from instructing and guiding them with regard to when the conditions of the "necessity" defence are fulfilled and the proper boundaries in those circumstances. From this flows the legality of the directives with respect to the use of physical means in GSS interrogations. In the course of their argument, the State's attorneys submitted the "ticking time bomb" argument. A given suspect is arrested by the GSS. He holds information respecting the location of a bomb that was set and will imminently explode. There is no way to diffuse the bomb without this information. If the information is obtained, however, the bomb may be diffused. If the bomb is not diffused, scores will be killed and maimed. Is a GSS investigator authorized to employ physical means in order to elicit information regarding the location of the bomb in such instances? The State's attorneys answered in the affirmative. The use of physical means shall not constitute a criminal offence, and their use is sanctioned, to the State's contention, by virtue of the "necessity" defence.

34. We are prepared to assume that—although this matter is open to debate—the "necessity" defence is open to all, particularly an investigator, acting in an organizational capacity of the State in interrogations of that nature. Likewise, we are prepared to accept—although this matter is equally contentious—that the "necessity" exception is likely to arise in instances of "ticking time bombs," and that the immediate need ("necessary in an immediate manner" for the preservation of human life) refers to the imminent nature of the act rather than that of the danger. Hence, the imminence criteria is satisfied even if the bomb is set to explode in a few days, or perhaps even after a few weeks, provided the danger is certain to materialize and there is no alternative means of preventing its materialization. In other words, there exists a concrete level of imminent danger of the explosion's occurrence.

35. Indeed, we are prepared to accept that in the appropriate circumstances, GSS investigators may avail themselves of the "necessity" defence, if criminally indicted. This, however, is not the issue before this Court. We are not dealing with the potential criminal liability of a GSS investigator who employed physical interrogation methods in circumstances of "necessity." Moreover, we are not addressing the issue of admissibility or probative value of evidence obtained as a result of a GSS investigator's application of physical means against a suspect. We

are dealing with a different question. The question before us is whether it is possible to infer the authority to, in advance, establish permanent directives setting out the physical interrogation means that may be used under conditions of "necessity." Moreover, we are asking whether the "necessity" defence constitutes a basis for the GSS investigator's authority to investigate, in the performance of his duty. According to the State, it is possible to imply from the "necessity" defence, available (*post factum* [after the fact]) to an investigator indicted of a criminal offence, an advance legal authorization endowing the investigator with the capacity to use physical interrogation methods. Is this position correct?

36. In the Court's opinion, a general authority to establish directives respecting the use of physical means during the course of a GSS interrogation cannot be implied from the "necessity" defence. The "necessity" defence does not constitute a source of authority, allowing GSS investigators to make use [of] physical means during the course of interrogations. The reasoning underlying our position is anchored in the nature of the "necessity" defence. This defence deals with deciding those cases involving an individual reacting to a given set of facts; it is an *ad hoc* endeavour, in reaction to an event. It is the result of an improvisation given the unpredictable character of the events. Thus, the very nature of the defence does not allow it to serve as the source of a general administrative power. The administrative power is based on establishing general, forward looking criteria, as noted by Professor Enker:

> Necessity is an after-the-fact judgment based on a narrow set of considerations in which we are concerned with the immediate consequences, not far-reaching and long-range consequences, on the basis of a clearly established order of priorities of both means and ultimate values. . . . The defence of necessity does not define a code of primary normative behaviour. Necessity is certainly not a basis for establishing a broad detailed code of behaviour such as how one should go about conducting intelligence interrogations in security matters, when one may or may not use force, how much force may be used and the like.

In a similar vein, Kremnitzer and Segev note:

> [t]he basic rationale underlying the necessity defence is the absence of the possibility to establish accurate rules of behaviour in advance, appropriate in concrete emergency situations, whose circumstances are varied and unexpected. From this it follows that the necessity defence is not well suited for regulating a general situation, the circumstances of which are known and (often) repeat themselves. In similar cases, there is no reason for not setting the rules of behaviour in advance, in order that their content be determined in a thought out and well-planned manner, in advance, permitting them to apply in a uniform manner to all.

Moreover, the "necessity" defence has the effect of allowing one who acts under the circumstances of "necessity" to escape criminal liability. The "necessity" defence does not possess any additional normative value. In addition, it does not authorize the use of physical means for the purposes of allowing investigators to execute their duties in circumstances of necessity. The very fact that a particular act does not constitute a criminal act (due to the "necessity" defence) does not in itself authorize the administration to carry out this deed, and in doing so infringe upon human rights. The Rule of Law (both as a formal and substantive principle) requires that an infringement on a human right be prescribed by statute, authorizing the administration to this effect. The lifting of criminal responsibility does not imply authorization to infringe upon a human right.

37. In other words, general directives governing the use of physical means during interrogations must be rooted in an authorization prescribed by law and not from defences to criminal liability. The principle of "necessity" cannot serve as a basis of authority. If the State wishes to enable GSS investigators to utilize physical means in interrogations, they must seek the enactment of legislation for this purpose. This authorization would also free the investigator applying the physical means from criminal liability. This release would flow not from the "necessity" defence but from the "justification" defense which states:

> A person shall not bear criminal liability for an act committed in one of the following cases: (1) He was obliged or authorized by law to commit it.

(Article 34(13) of the Penal Law).

The defence to criminal liability by virtue of the "justification" is rooted in an area outside of the criminal law. This "external" law serves as a defence to criminal liability. This defence does not rest upon the "necessity," which is "internal" to the Penal Law itself. Thus, for instance, where the question of when an officer is authorized to apply deadly force in the course of detention arises, the authority is found in a provision of the Law of Detention, external to the Penal Law. If a man is killed as a result of the application of force, the provision is likely to give rise to a defence, by virtue of the "justification." The "necessity" defence cannot constitute the basis for the determination of rules respecting the needs of an interrogation. It cannot constitute a source of authority on which the individual investigator can rely for the purpose of applying physical means in an investigation that he is conducting. The power to enact rules and to act according to them requires legislative authorization, by legislation whose object is the power to conduct interrogations. Within the boundaries of this legislation, the Legislator, if he so desires, may express his views on the social, ethical and political problems connected to authorizing the use of physical means in an interrogation. These considerations did not, from the nature of things, arise before the Legislature at the time when the "necessity" defence was enacted. The "necessity" defence is not the appropriate place for laying out these considerations. Endowing GSS investigators with the authority to apply physical force during the interrogation of suspects suspected of involvement in hostile terrorist activities, thereby harming the latters' dignity and liberty, raise basic questions of law and society, of ethics and policy, and of the rule of law and security. These questions and the corresponding answers must be determined by the Legislative branch. This is required by the principle of the separation of powers and the rule of law, under our very understanding of democracy.

38. Our conclusion is therefore the following: According to the existing state of the law, neither the government nor the heads of security services possess the authority to establish directives and bestow authorization regarding the use of liberty-infringing physical means during the interrogation of suspects suspected of hostile terrorist activities, beyond the general directives which can be inferred from the very concept of an interrogation. Similarly, the individual GSS investigator—like any police officer—does not possess the authority to employ physical means which infringe upon a suspect's liberty during the interrogation, unless these means are inherently accessory to the very essence of an interrogation and are both fair and reasonable.

An investigator who insists on employing these methods, or does so routinely, is exceeding his authority. His responsibility shall be fixed according to law. His potential criminal liability shall be examined in the context of the "necessity" defence, and according to our assumptions, the investigator may find refuge under the "necessity" defence's wings (so to speak), provided this defence's conditions are met by the circumstances of the case. Just as the existence of the "necessity" defence does not bestow authority, so too the lack of authority does not negate the applicability of the necessity defense or that of other defences from criminal liability. The Attorney General can instruct himself regarding the circumstances in which investigators shall not stand trial, if they claim to have acted from a feeling of "necessity." Clearly, a legal statutory provision is necessary for the purpose of authorizing the government to instruct in the use of physical means during the course of an interrogation, beyond what is permitted by the ordinary "law of investigation," and in order to provide the individual GSS investigator with the authority to employ these methods. The "necessity" defence cannot serve as a basis for this authority.

39. This decision opens with a description of the difficult reality in which Israel finds herself security wise. We shall conclude this judgment by re-addressing that harsh reality. We are aware that this decision does not ease dealing with that reality. This is the destiny of democracy, as not all means are acceptable to it, and not all practices employed by its enemies are open before it. Although a democracy must often fight with one hand tied behind its back, it nonetheless has the upper hand. Preserving the rule of law and recognition of an individual's liberty

constitutes an important component in its understanding of security. At the end of the day, they strengthen its spirit and its strength and allow it to overcome its difficulties. This having been said, there are those who argue that Israel's security problems are too numerous, thereby requiring the authorization to use physical means. If it will nonetheless be decided that it is appropriate for Israel, in light of its security difficulties to sanction physical means in interrogations (and the scope of these means which deviate from the ordinary investigation rules), this is an issue that must be decided by the legislative branch which represents the people. We do not take any stand on this matter at this time. It is there that various considerations must be weighed. The pointed debate must occur there. It is there that the required legislation may be passed, provided, of course, that a law infringing upon a suspect's liberty "befitting the values of the State of Israel," is enacted for a proper purpose, and to an extent no greater than is required. (Article 8 to the Basic Law: Human Dignity and Liberty).

40. Deciding these applications weighed heavy on this Court. True, from the legal perspective, the road before us is smooth. We are, however, part of Israeli society. Its problems are known to us and we live its history. We are not isolated in an ivory tower. We live the life of this country. We are aware of the harsh reality of terrorism in which we are, at times, immersed. Our apprehension that this decision will hamper the ability to properly deal with terrorists and terrorism disturbs us. We are, however, judges. Our brethren require us to act according to the law. This is equally the standard that we set for ourselves. When we sit to judge, we are being judged. Therefore, we must act according to our purest conscience when we decide the law.

NOTES & QUESTIONS

1. Necessity Defense

As the above excerpt reveals, the necessity defense is commonly raised in connection with debates about the legality, morality, and efficacy of torture and other harsh interrogation tactics. The necessity defense also appears in war crimes cases, especially where questions of military necessity are at issue. *See, e.g.*, Article 8(2)(iv), ICC Statute (penalizing extensive destruction of property "not justified by military necessity"). Would the defense ever be applicable in a prosecution for crimes against humanity or genocide?

2. Ticking Time Bombs

Some have argued that extraordinary circumstances might justify the use of torture, notwithstanding that the Torture Convention rejects this argument explicitly in Article 2(2), which states "[n]o exceptional circumstances whatsoever . . . may be invoked as a justification of torture." (Note that the same admonition does not, however, apply to acts of cruel, inhuman and degrading treatment or punishment). In this regard, the ticking time bomb scenario is often raised to argue that torture should be allowed in some extreme circumstances. Consider the following:

> Necessity as a justification derives from consequential moral theories, according to which wrongful actions may be morally deemed by the goodness of their consequences. It justifies the sacrifice of legitimate interests to protect other interests of substantially higher value. It does not grant the individual "a license to determine social utility." It is rather limited to emergency cases in which there is an imminent and concrete danger to an interest recognized by the legal system. In the context of this discussion, such an emergency exists in the "ticking bomb" situation, in which a bomb has been set to explode imminently and innocent people are likely to be killed. The only hope for saving their lives is to get information about the location of the bomb in order to defuse it. Should necessity justify the use of force in an attempt to coerce the person under interrogation to reveal such information?
>
> The justification of necessity rests on the balance between interests of innocent persons. The sacrifice of an innocent person's interests is justified when necessary to save those of another, when that other person's interests have a higher value. Therefore, if necessity is to apply to ticking bomb situations it will justify the use of interrogational force against the *innocent*. Taken to extreme, necessity might *prima facie* justify the use of force against a terrorist's child in order to force the terrorist to reveal the information about the location of a bomb he has planted. Even to consequentialists the use of force against the child might seem morally repugnant. No one should torture innocent children—even when done to produce a sizeable gain in aggregate welfare.

Miriam Gur-Arye, *Can the War Against Terror Justify the Use of Force in Interrogation? Reflections in Light of the Israeli Experience*, *in* TORTURE: A COLLECTION 191 (Sanford Levinson ed., 2004).

If necessity should be a defense, what test would you devise for such a situation? Does it matter if, as a result of the torture, the individual discloses the location of the bomb and it is defused? What if the suspect discloses the location, but there is not enough time to stop its detonation? What if the individual does not disclose the location of the bomb, and the bomb is detonated? What if it turns out there was no bomb? How does the scenario impact rhetorically the way in which the legality and efficacy of torture is debated? *See also* Michael Levin, *Torture and Other Extreme Measures Taken for the General Good: Further Reflections on a Philosophical Problem*, *in* PSYCHOLOGY AND TORTURE 89 (Peter Suedfeld ed., 1990) (arguing that torture is permissible in emergencies, such as when used to force a terrorist to disclose the location of a bomb). For a critique of the use of the necessity defense in connection with the Argentinean "dirty war," *see* Carlos S. Nino, RADICAL EVIL ON TRIAL 170–173 (1996) (arguing that the defense of necessity should not be available to torturers). For a discussion of the ticking time bomb scenario, *see* Association for the Prevention of Torture, DEFUSING THE

TICKING TIME BOMB SCENARIO—WHY WE MUST SAY NO TO TORTURE, ALWAYS (2007).

3. Necessity and U.S. Interrogation Practices

The defense of necessity featured prominently in at least one of the so-called Torture Memos discussed in Chapter 11. The memo argued "under current circumstances, necessity or self-defense may justify interrogation methods that violate" the criminal prohibition on torture. U.S. Dept. of Justice, Office of Legal Counsel, Memorandum for Alberto R. Gonzales, Counsel to the President *Standards of Conduct for Interrogation under 18 U.S.C. §§ 2340–2340A* (Aug. 1, 2002). The authors continued:

> It appears to us that under the current circumstances the necessity defense could be successfully maintained in response to an allegation of a 18 U.S.C. § 2340A violation [penalizing torture]. On September 11, 2001, al Qaeda launched a surprise covert attack on civilian targets in the United States that led to the deaths of thousands and losses in the billions of dollars. According to public and governmental reports, al Qaeda has other sleeper cells within the United States that may be planning similar attacks. Indeed, al Qaeda plans apparently include efforts to develop and deploy chemical, biological and nuclear weapons of mass destruction.
>
> Under these circumstances, a detainee may possess information that could enable the United States to prevent attacks that potentially could equal or surpass the September 11 attacks in their magnitude. Clearly, any harm that might occur during an interrogation would pale to insignificance compared to the harm avoided by preventing such an attack, which could take hundreds or thousands of lives. Under this calculus, two factors will help indicate when the necessity defense could appropriately be invoked.
>
> First, the more certain that government officials are that a particular individual has information needed to prevent an attack, the more necessary interrogation will be. Second, the more likely it appears to be that a terrorist attack is likely to occur, and the greater the amount of damage expected from such an attack, the more that an interrogation to get information would become necessary.
>
> Of course, the strength of the necessity defense depends on the circumstances that prevail, and the knowledge of the government actors involved, when the interrogation is conducted. While every interrogation that might violate Section 2340A does not trigger a necessity defense, we can say that certain circumstances could support such a defense.

Do you agree? The authors go on to suggest that self-defense might also arise as a potential defense. Under what theory might this be the case? Imagine that you represent an interrogator charged by court martial with mistreating a detainee. How would you argue the applicability of either defense? Note that the Department of Justice released a new memorandum in 2004 that superseded this memo. The 2004 memo does not discuss defenses. *See* U.S. Dept. of Justice, Memorandum for James B. Comey, Deputy Attorney General, *Legal Standards Applicable Under 18 U.S.C. §§ 2340–2340A* (Dec. 30, 2004).

4. Professional Responsibility

The drafters of this memo opined that "[a]lthough there is no federal statute that generally establishes necessity or other justifications as defenses to federal criminal laws, the Supreme Court has recognized the defense." *See United States v. Bailey*, 444 U.S. 394, 410 (1980) (relying on Model Penal Code definition of necessity defense, among others). In so arguing, the authors neglected to cite a more recent Supreme Court case, *United States v. Oakland Cannabis Buyers' Co-op.*, 532 U.S. 483, 490–1 (2001) (finding only one express statutory exception to liability, not relevant to the instant case). The *Oakland* case calls into question whether federal criminal law contains a free-standing common-law necessity defense absent a specific statutory provision. Should the Office of Legal Counsel have brought this case to the Attorney General's attention in the memorandum? Is the failure to do so a violation of professional ethics?

5. The ICC and Necessity

The ICC expressly allows for the defense of necessity in Article 31(1)(d):

> 1. In addition to other grounds for excluding criminal responsibility provided for in this Statute, a person shall not be criminally responsible if, at the time of that person's conduct: * * *
>
> (d) The conduct which is alleged to constitute a crime within the jurisdiction of the Court has been caused by duress resulting from a threat of imminent death or of continuing or imminent serious bodily harm against that person or another person, and the person acts necessarily and reasonably to avoid this threat, provided that the person does not intend to cause a greater harm than the one sought to be avoided. Such a threat may either be:
>
> (i) Made by other persons; or
>
> (ii) Constituted by other circumstances beyond that person's control.

The ICC Statute combines the defense of duress and necessity into one section. Why do you think this is done? What is the difference between duress and necessity? For a critical treatment of Article 31's combination of duress and necessity, *see* Benjamin J. Risacher, *No Excuse: The Failure of the ICC's Article 31 "Duress" Definition*, 89 NOTRE DAME L. REV. 1403 (2014).

V. COMBAT IMMUNITY

As discussed *supra* in Chapter 7 on War Crimes, privileged belligerents are entitled to combat immunity from criminal prosecution for lawful acts of war, including proportional collateral damage. (They can, however, be prosecuted for war crimes or violations of domestic law).

The theory is that such combatants commit no wrong when they engage in combat operations at the behest of their sovereign. That said, combat immunity is not available to everyone who takes up arms in a conflict, as discussed in the next opinion.

United States v. John Phillip Walker Lindh

212 F. Supp. 2d 541 (E.D. Va. 2002).

■ ELLIS, DISTRICT JUDGE.

John Phillip Walker Lindh ("Lindh") is an American citizen who, according to the ten-count Indictment filed against him in February 2002, joined certain foreign terrorist organizations in Afghanistan and served these organizations there in combat against Northern Alliance and American forces until his capture in November 2001. In seven threshold motions, Lindh sought dismissal of certain counts of the Indictment on a variety of grounds, including lawful combatant immunity and selective prosecution. * * *

The Indictment's allegations may be succinctly summarized. In mid-2001, Lindh attended a military training camp in Pakistan run by Harakat ul-Mujahideen ("HUM"), a terrorist group dedicated to an extremist view of Islam. After receiving several weeks of training, Lindh informed HUM officials that "he wished to fight with the Taliban in Afghanistan." Thus, in May or June 2001, he traveled from Pakistan into Afghanistan "for the purpose of taking up arms with the Taliban," eventually arriving at a Taliban recruiting center in Kabul, Afghanistan—the Dar ul-Anan Headquarters of the Mujahedeen. On his arrival, Lindh presented a letter of introduction from HUM and advised Taliban personnel "that he was an American and that he wanted to go to the front lines to fight."

While at the Dar ul-Anan Headquarters, Lindh agreed to receive additional and extensive military training at an al Qaeda training camp. He made this decision "knowing that America and its citizens were the enemies of Bin Laden and al Qaeda and that a principal purpose of al Qaeda was to fight and kill Americans." In late May or June 2001, Lindh traveled to a bin Laden guest house in Kandahar, Afghanistan, where he stayed for several days, and then traveled to the al Farooq training camp, "an al Qaeda facility located several hours west of Kandahar." He reported to the camp with approximately twenty other trainees, mostly Saudis, and remained there throughout June and July. During this period, he participated fully in the camp's training activities, despite being told early in his stay that "Bin Laden had sent forth some fifty people to carry out twenty suicide terrorist operations against the United States and Israel." As part of his al Qaeda training, Lindh participated in "terrorist training courses in, among other things, weapons, orientating, navigation, explosives and battlefield combat." This training included the use of "shoulder weapons, pistols, and rocket-propelled grenades, and the construction of Molotov cocktails." During his stay at al Farooq, Lindh met personally with bin Laden, "who thanked him and other trainees for taking part in jihad." He also met with a senior al Qaeda official, Abu Mohammad Al-Masri, who inquired whether Lindh was interested in traveling outside Afghanistan to conduct operations against the United States and Israel. Lindh declined Al-Masri's offer in favor of going to the front lines to fight. It is specifically alleged that Lindh swore allegiance to jihad in June or July 2001.

When Lindh completed his training at al Farooq in July or August 2001, he traveled to Kabul, Afghanistan, where he was issued an AKM rifle "with a barrel suitable for long range shooting." Armed with this rifle, Lindh, together with approximately 150 non-Afghani fighters, traveled from Kabul to the front line at Takhar, located in Northeastern Afghanistan, where the entire unit was placed under the command of an Iraqi named Abdul Hady. Lindh's group was eventually divided into smaller groups that fought in shifts against Northern Alliance troops in the Takhar trenches, rotating every one to two weeks. During this period, Lindh "carried various weapons with him, including the AKM rifle, an RPK rifle he was issued after the AKM rifle malfunctioned, and at least two grenades." He remained with his fighting group following the September 11, 2001 terrorist attacks, "despite having been told that Bin Laden had ordered the [September 11] attacks, that additional terrorist attacks were planned, and that additional al Qaeda personnel were being sent from the front lines to protect Bin Laden and defend against an anticipated military response from the United States." Indeed, it is specifically alleged that Lindh remained with his fighting group from October to December 2001, "after learning that United States military forces and United States nationals had become directly engaged in support of the Northern Alliance in its military conflict with Taliban and al Qaeda forces."

In November 2001, Lindh and his fighting group retreated from Takhar to the area of Kunduz, Afghanistan, where they ultimately surrendered to Northern Alliance troops. On November 24, 2001, he and the other captured Taliban fighters were transported to Mazar-e-Sharif, and then to the nearby Qala-i-Janghi (QIJ) prison compound. The following day, November 25, Lindh was interviewed by two Americans—Agent Johnny Michael Spann from the Central Intelligence Agency (CIA) and another government employee. Later that day, it is alleged that Taliban detainees in the QIJ compound attacked Spann and the other employee, overpowered the guards, and armed themselves. Spann was shot and killed in the course of the uprising and Lindh, after being wounded, retreated with other detainees to a basement area of the QIJ compound. The uprising at QIJ was eventually suppressed on December 1, 2001, at which time Lindh and other Taliban and al Qaeda fighters were taken into custody by Northern Alliance and American forces.

Following his capture, Lindh was interrogated, transported to the United States, and ultimately charged in this district with the following offenses in a ten-count Indictment:

(i) conspiracy to murder nationals of the United States, including American military personnel and other governmental employees serving in Afghanistan following the September 11, 2001 terrorist attacks, in violation of 18 U.S.C. § 2332(b)(2) (Count One);

(ii) conspiracy to provide material support and resources to HUM, a foreign terrorist organization, in violation of 18 U.S.C. § 2339B (Count Two);

(iii) providing material support and resources to HUM, in violation of 18 U.S.C. § 2339B and 2 (Count Three); * * *

(x) using and carrying firearms and destructive devices during crimes of violence, in violation of 18 U.S.C. §§ 924(c)(1)(A), 924(c)(1)(B)(ii) and 2 (Count Ten). * * *

Lindh claims that Count One of the Indictment should be dismissed because, as a Taliban soldier, he was a lawful combatant entitled to the affirmative defense of lawful combatant immunity.[16]

Also worth noting is that the government has not argued here that the Taliban's role in providing a home, a headquarters, and support to al Qaeda and its international terrorist activities serve to transform the Taliban from a legitimate state government into a terrorist institution whose soldiers are not entitled to lawful combatant immunity status. Put another way, the government has not argued that al Qaeda controlled the Taliban for its own purposes and that so-called Taliban soldiers were accordingly merely agents of al Qaeda, not lawful combatants.

Lawful combatant immunity, a doctrine rooted in the customary international law of war, forbids prosecution of soldiers for their lawful belligerent acts committed during the course of armed conflicts against legitimate military targets. Belligerent acts committed in armed conflict by enemy members of the armed forces may be punished as crimes under a belligerent's municipal law only to the extent that they violate international humanitarian law or are unrelated to the armed conflict. This doctrine has a long history, which is reflected in part in various early international conventions, statutes and documents. But more pertinent, indeed controlling, here is that the doctrine also finds expression in the Geneva Convention Relative to the Treatment of Prisoners of War, Aug. 12, 1949, 6 U.S.T. 3316, 75 U.N.T.S. 135 ("GPW"), to which the United

[16] Lindh makes no claim of lawful combatant immunity with respect to the Indictment's allegations that he was a member or soldier of al Qaeda. Instead, Lindh focuses his lawful combatant immunity argument solely on the Indictment's allegations that he was a Taliban member. This focus is understandable as there is no plausible claim of lawful combatant immunity in connection with al Qaeda membership. Thus, it appears that Lindh's goal is to win lawful combatant immunity with respect to the Taliban allegations and then to dispute factually the Indictment's allegations that he was a member of al Qaeda.

States is a signatory. Significantly, Article 87 of the GPW admonishes that combatants "may not be sentenced . . . to any penalties except those provided for in respect of members of the armed forces of the said Power who have committed the same acts." Similarly, Article 99 provides that "no prisoner of war may be tried or sentenced for an act which is not forbidden by the law of the Detaining Power or by international law, in force at the time the said act was committed." These Articles, when read together, make clear that a belligerent in a war cannot prosecute the soldiers of its foes for the soldiers' lawful acts of war.

The inclusion of the lawful combatant immunity doctrine as a part of the GPW is particularly important here given that the GPW, insofar as it is pertinent here, is a self-executing treaty[20] to which the United States is a signatory. It follows from this that the GPW provisions in issue here are a part of American law and thus binding in federal courts under the Supremacy Clause. This point, which finds support in the cases,[22] is essentially conceded by the government. Moreover, the government does not dispute that this immunity may, under appropriate circumstances, serve as a defense to criminal prosecution of a lawful combatant.

Importantly, this lawful combatant immunity is not automatically available to anyone who takes up arms in a conflict. Rather, it is generally accepted that this immunity can be invoked only by members of regular or irregular armed forces who fight on behalf of a state and comply with the requirements for lawful combatants.[24] Thus, it is well-established that

> the law of war draws a distinction between the armed forces and the peaceful populations of belligerent nations and also between those who are lawful and unlawful combatants. Lawful combatants are subject to capture and detention as prisoners of war by opposing military forces. Unlawful combatants are likewise subject to capture and detention, but in addition they are subject to trial and punishment by military tribunals for acts which render their belligerency unlawful.

---

[20] Treaties are typically classified as self-executing or executory. Executory treaties are addressed to the Congress and require congressional action before becoming effective in domestic courts, whereas a self-executing treaty "is one that operates of itself without the aid of legislation." 74 AM. JUR. 2D TREATIES § 3. The portions of the GPW relevant here neither invite nor require congressional action and hence fall properly into the self-executing category. *See* C. Vasquez, *The Four Doctrines of Self-Executing Treaties,* 89 AM. J. INT'L L. 695 (1995).

[22] *See United States v. Noriega,* 808 F. Supp. 791, 799 (S.D. Fla. 1990) ("It is inconsistent with both the language and spirit of the [GPW] and with our professed support of its purpose to find that the rights established therein cannot be enforced by individual POWs in a court of law.").

[24] *See, e.g.,* Howard S. Levie, *Prisoners of War in International Armed Conflict,* 59 NAVAL WAR COLLEGE INT'L L. STUD. 53 n.192 (1977). Neither presented nor decided here is the question whether lawful combatant immunity is available to one who takes up arms in combat against his own country, as the Indictment alleges Lindh did in this case. At least one commentator suggests that principles of international law permit a nation to prosecute any of its citizens who take up arms against it for treason, even if the citizen does so as part of a lawful armed force. *See* Allan Rosas, THE LEGAL STATUS OF PRISONERS OF WAR 383 (1976).

Ex Parte Quirin, 317 U.S. 1, 30–31 (1942) (footnote omitted). The GPW also reflects this distinction between lawful and unlawful combatants, with only the former eligible for immunity from prosecution. *See* GPW, art. 87, 99. Thus, the question presented here is whether Lindh is a lawful combatant entitled to immunity under the GPW.

The starting point in the analysis of Lindh's immunity claim is recognition that the President has unequivocally determined that Lindh, as a member of the Taliban, is an unlawful combatant and, as such, may not invoke lawful combatant immunity. On February 7, 2002, the White House announced the President's decision, as Commander-in-Chief, that the Taliban militia were unlawful combatants pursuant to GPW and general principles of international law, and, therefore, they were not entitled to POW status under the Geneva Conventions. This presidential determination, according to the government, is significant, indeed decisive, because the President, as the "Commander in Chief of the Army and Navy of the United States," has broad constitutional power to issue such a determination. Moreover, in the current conflict, he has also been "authorized" by Congress "to use all necessary and appropriate force against those nations, organizations, or persons he determines planned, authorized, committed, or aided the terrorist attacks that occurred on September 11, 2001, or harbored such organizations or persons." Authorization for Use of Military Force, Pub. L. No. 107–40, § 2, 115 Stat. 224 (2001). Thus, the government argues, the decision of the President to use force against the Taliban and al Qaeda, as endorsed by Congress, represents the exercise of the full extent of his constitutional presidential authority. It follows, the government contends, that the President's determination that Taliban members are unlawful combatants was made pursuant to his constitutional Commander-in-Chief and foreign affairs powers and is therefore not subject to judicial review or second guessing because it involves a quintessentially non-justiciable political question.

This argument, while not without appeal, is ultimately unpersuasive. Because the consequence of accepting a political question argument is so significant—judicial review is completely foreclosed—courts must subject such arguments to searching scrutiny, for it is central to the rule of law in our constitutional system that federal courts must, in appropriate circumstances, review or second guess, and indeed sometimes even trump, the actions of the other governmental branches. At a minimum, this scrutiny requires careful consideration of whether the circumstances that trigger the application of the political question doctrine are present here. Thus, it is difficult to see, except at the highest level of abstraction, a textually demonstrable constitutional commitment regarding this issue. Moreover, it is difficult to see why the application of the GPW's lawful combatant immunity doctrine to Lindh's case involves a lack of judicially discoverable and manageable standards. Indeed, the contrary appears to be true. The presence of any remaining factors is also doubtful. To sum up briefly then, while it may be argued that some of the triggering circumstances for a political question are present to some degree here, others plainly are not and thus the government's political question argument is ultimately unpersuasive. Understandably and appropriately, therefore, courts have recognized that treaty interpretation does not implicate the political question doctrine and is not a subject beyond judicial review.

This, however, does not end the analysis, for it remains important to determine the precise nature of judicial review that is appropriate here, including, in particular, what, if any, respect or effect should be afforded the President's determination that Lindh and the Taliban are not lawful combatants entitled to lawful combatant immunity. The answer to this question may be found both in settled caselaw and in sound principle. Thus, courts have long held that treaty interpretations made by the Executive Branch are entitled to some degree of deference. This result also finds support in the principles underlying the *Chevron* doctrine, which holds that deference to an agency's reasonable interpretation of an ambiguous statute is appropriate where the agency has been charged with administering the statute. The rationale of *Chevron* is that a statutory ambiguity is essentially a delegation of authority by Congress to the responsible agency to resolve the ambiguity. By analogy, treaty interpretation and application warrants similar *Chevron* deference to the President's interpretation of a treaty, as American treaty-makers may be seen as having delegated this function to the President in light of his constitutional responsibility for the conduct of foreign affairs and overseas military operations.

It is important to recognize that the deference here is appropriately accorded not only to the President's interpretation of any ambiguity in the treaty, but also to the President's application of the treaty to the facts in issue. Again, this is warranted given the President's special competency in, and constitutional responsibility for, foreign affairs and the conduct of overseas military operations. It is also crucial to be precise regarding the nature of the deference warranted. Conclusive deference, which amounts to judicial abstention, is plainly inappropriate. Rather, the appropriate deference is to accord substantial or great weight to the President's decision regarding the interpretation and application of the GPW to Lindh, provided the interpretation and application of the treaty to Lindh may be said to be reasonable and not contradicted by the terms of the treaty or the facts. It is this proviso that is the focus of the judicial review here of the President's determination that Lindh is an unlawful combatant under the GPW.

The GPW sets forth four criteria an organization must meet for its members to qualify for lawful combatant status:

i. the organization must be commanded by a person responsible for his subordinates;

ii. the organization's members must have a fixed distinctive emblem or uniform recognizable at a distance;

iii. the organization's members must carry arms openly; and

iv. the organization's members must conduct their operations in accordance with the laws and customs of war.

See GPW, art. 4(A)(2). Nor are these four criteria unique to the GPW; they are also established under customary international law and were also included in the Hague Regulations of 1907. *See* Hague Convention Respecting the Laws and Customs of War on Land, Oct. 18, 1907, 36 Stat. 2277, T.S. No. 539 (Hague Regulations).[35]

In the application of these criteria to the case at bar, it is Lindh who bears the burden of establishing the affirmative defense that he is entitled to lawful combatant immunity, *i.e.,* that the Taliban satisfies the four criteria required for lawful combatant status outlined by the GPW. On this point, Lindh has not carried his burden; indeed, he has made no persuasive showing at all on this point. For this reason alone, it follows that the President's decision denying Lindh lawful combatant immunity is correct. In any event, a review of the available record information leads to the same conclusion. Thus, it appears that the Taliban lacked the command structure necessary to fulfill the first criterion, as it is manifest that the Taliban had no internal system of military command or discipline. As one observer noted, "there is no clear military structure with a hierarchy of officers and commanders while unit commanders are constantly being shifted around," and the Taliban's "haphazard style of enlistment . . . does not allow for a regular or disciplined army." Kamal Matinuddin, THE TALIBAN PHENOMENON: AFGHANISTAN 1994–97 59 (1999). Thus, Lindh has not carried his burden to show that the Taliban had the requisite hierarchical military structure.

Similarly, it appears the Taliban typically wore no distinctive sign that could be recognized by opposing combatants; they wore no uniforms or insignia and were effectively indistinguishable from the rest of the population. The requirement of such a sign is critical to ensure that combatants may be distinguished from the non-combatant, civilian population. Accordingly, Lindh cannot establish the second criterion.

Next, although it appears that Lindh and his cohorts carried arms openly in satisfaction of the third criterion for lawful combatant status,

---

[35] Lindh asserts that the Taliban is a "regular armed force," under the GPW, and because he is a member, he need not meet the four conditions of the Hague Regulations because only Article 4(A)(2), which addresses irregular armed forces, explicitly mentions the four criteria. This argument is unpersuasive; it ignores long-established practice under the GPW and, if accepted, leads to an absurd result. First, the four criteria have long been understood under customary international law to be the defining characteristics of any lawful armed force. Thus, all armed forces or militias, regular and irregular, must meet the four criteria if their members are to receive combatant immunity. Were this not so, the anomalous result that would follow is that members of an armed force that met none of the criteria could still claim lawful combatant immunity merely on the basis that the organization calls itself a "regular armed force." It would indeed be absurd for members of a so-called "regular armed force" to enjoy lawful combatant immunity even though the force had no established command structure and its members wore no recognizable symbol or insignia, concealed their weapons, and did not abide by the customary laws of war. Simply put, the label "regular armed force" cannot be used to mask unlawful combatant status.

it is equally apparent that members of the Taliban failed to observe the laws and customs of war. *See* GPW, art. 4(A)(2). Thus, because record evidence supports the conclusion that the Taliban regularly targeted civilian populations in clear contravention of the laws and customs of war, Lindh cannot meet his burden concerning the fourth criterion.[39]

In sum, the President's determination that Lindh is an unlawful combatant and thus ineligible for immunity is controlling here (i) because that determination is entitled to deference as a reasonable interpretation and application of the GPW to Lindh as a Taliban; (ii) because Lindh has failed to carry his burden of demonstrating the contrary; and (iii) because even absent deference, the Taliban falls far short when measured against the four GPW criteria for determining entitlement to lawful combatant immunity.

NOTES & QUESTIONS

1. Lindh's Confession

Lindh "confessed" to the majority of the allegations in his indictment to journalist and adventurist Robert Young Pelton (working, at the time, for CNN) and later to his U.S. captors. The confessions were made after he was released from the makeshift Qala-i-Janghi (QiJ) prison, where he and other captive Taliban fighters had been trapped underground for a week while being shot at, burned, starved, and almost drowned when Northern Alliance forces diverted freezing water from an irrigation stream into the underground cells. As noted in the opinion, an uprising at this prison had resulted in the death of U.S. CIA agent Michael Spann. Photos later emerged of Lindh being held by U.S. forces. Lindh was naked, bound with duct tape to a stretcher, and wearing an obscenity-covered blindfold. While interrogated, he was denied a lawyer despite several requests and despite the fact that his father had hired lawyers in California to represent him.* A document produced by the U.S. government in connection with the case revealed that a bullet Lindh had received while trapped in QiJ was not immediately removed in order to keep him "uncomfortable" during interrogations. Although Lindh's lawyers filed a suppression motion to restrict the use of any statements made by Lindh under these circumstances, the motion was never ruled upon because Lindh was offered, and accepted, a plea bargain.

2. The Plea

Lindh ultimately pled guilty to two charges—providing services to the Taliban army in violation of U.S. sanctions and a weapons enhancement charge (18 U.S.C. § 844(c) prohibiting the use or possession of a weapon to commit any felony). The plea included a "gag order" preventing him from making any public statements about his pre-trial detention for the duration of his twenty-year sentence and a pledge not to pursue any claims that he

39 What matters for determination of lawful combatant status is not whether Lindh personally violated the laws and customs of war, but whether the Taliban did so. *See* GPW, art. 4.

* Professor van Schaack was a member of Lindh's legal defense team.

may have been mistreated or tortured by U.S. military personnel in Afghanistan and aboard two military ships during December 2001 and January 2002. He served most of a 20-year sentence (with some good behavior reduction). He was in a medium-security prison in Victorville, northeast of Los Angeles, but he was later transferred to a medium security prison in Indiana after being attacked in prison. He was released in 2019.

3. Combat Immunity

The questions of Lindh's status as a combatant and entitlement to combat immunity arose in the context of a motion to dismiss a count of the Indictment against him alleging that he provided material support to the Taliban. Should Lindh's counsel have made a formal petition for POW status? How would they have done this within the context of the federal criminal justice system? What sort of immunity does the defense of combat immunity provide? Why did Lindh's defense of combat immunity fail? Did the U.S. District Court apply the Geneva Conventions correctly? What is the import of the court's ruling that the Conventions are "self-executing?"

4. Duress or Necessity

The opinion made much of the fact that Lindh remained with the Taliban Forces after September 11, 2001. These allegations supported the charge that Lindh entered into a conspiracy to kill Americans in violation of 18 U.S.C. § 2332. Days after that attack, the United States launched a major offensive against the Taliban Forces that included providing significant tactical and military support to the Northern Alliance Forces operating in Takhar province in north-eastern Afghanistan. At the time, Lindh was billeted with the Taliban in Takhar fighting the Northern Alliance. Was it realistic to expect Lindh to extricate himself from the Taliban forces under these circumstances? Might the defense of duress or necessity have been available to him?

Consider the case of *In re Territo*, 156 F.2d 142 (9th Cir. 1946). Territo, who was born in the United States, moved with his father to Italy as a young boy. He admitted that he did not know he was a U.S. citizen until 1939, when he was 24 years old. By then, he had already served six months in the Italian Army. In 1940, Territo was again called to serve in the Italian Army. He claims that he told authorities that he was an American citizen at that time, but was too afraid to press the issue. He served as a private in army engineers corps, doing manual labor while the United States and Italy were at war. In 1943, he was captured by American Forces in Sicily. Held as a prisoner of war, Territo petitioned the federal courts for his release. Territo argued that he should not be held as a POW because he was impressed against his will into the Italian army. The Ninth Circuit Court of Appeals found that "the status of volunteer or that of draftee, as a prisoner of war who is captured upon the field of battle, is not different." How are the situations of Territo and Lindh similar? Different? Should a court find duress or necessity in either circumstance? What would constitute duress or necessity in combat?

5. Prisoners of War and Citizenship

Would Lindh's status as a U.S. citizen impact his ability to apply for POW status? In *In re Territo, supra*, the Ninth Circuit suggested that a U.S. citizen could receive POW status even if he were fighting for an enemy force. While not faced with the issue directly, the U.S. Supreme Court stated in 1942:

> Citizenship in the United States of an enemy belligerent does not relieve him of the consequences of a belligerency which is unlawful because in violation of the law of war. Citizens who associate themselves with the military arm of the enemy government, and with its aid, guidance and direction enter this country bent on hostile acts, are enemy belligerents within the meaning of the Hague Convention and the law of war.

Ex Parte Quirin, 317 U.S. 1, 38–39 (1942). Is this decision applicable to the *Lindh* case? In order to bolster its argument, the court in *In re Territo* analogized that situation to that of Irishmen who took an oath of allegiance to the South African Republic during the Boer War. The Irish were treated as POWs notwithstanding the fact that they were subjects of Great Britain. Is this analogous to Territo's situation? To Lindh's? For a discussion *see* Melysa H. Sperber, Note *John Walker Lindh and Yaser Esam Hamdi: Closing the Loophole in International Humanitarian Law for American Nationals Captured Abroad While Fighting with Enemy Forces*, 40 AM. CRIM. L. REV. 159 (2003).

6. Treason

The opinion states at note 24 that Lindh could have been prosecuted for treason. Why would the government not pursue such a charge? Under United States law, someone is guilty of treason if, "owing allegiance to the United States, [s/he] levies war against them or adheres to their enemies, giving them aid and comfort within the United States and elsewhere." 18 U.S.C. § 2381. This statute is derived from Article III, Section 3, clause 1 of the U.S. Constitution. The Constitution further provides that: "No person shall be convicted of Treason unless on the Testimony of two Witnesses to the same overt Act, or on Confession in open Court." Another procedural component applicable to the crime of treason is that "[t]he defendant shall be allowed, in his defense to make any proof that he can produce by lawful witnesses, and shall have the like process of the court to compel his witnesses to appear at his trial, as is usually granted to compel witnesses to appear on behalf of the prosecution." 18 U.S.C.S. § 3005. How would these provisions have affected a potential charge of treason against Lindh? Note that a person found guilty of treason may lose her U.S. citizenship.

7. Sedition

Compare the *Lindh* case with *United States v. Rahman*, 189 F.3d 88 (2d Cir. 1999). This case involved ten defendants who were convicted of crimes associated with "a wide-ranging plot to conduct a campaign of urban terrorism. Among the activities of some or all of the defendants were rendering assistance to those who bombed the World Trade Center in 1993, planning to bomb bridges and tunnels in New York City, murdering Rabbi

Meir Kahane, and planning to murder the President of Egypt." Faced with evidence that several defendants aided in the World Trade Center bombing (as well as other hostile acts against the United States), the prosecutor chose to charge the defendants with "seditious conspiracy" rather than treason. The seditious conspiracy statute provides:

> If two or more persons in any State or Territory, or in any place subject to the jurisdiction of the United States, conspire to overthrow, put down or to destroy by force the Government of the United States, or to levy war against them, or to oppose by force . . . they shall be fined . . . or imprisoned . . . or both.

18 U.S.C. § 2384. On appeal, the defendants argued that the seditious conspiracy statute was illegal as it punishes conspiracy to "levy war" without conforming to the two-witness requirement of the crime of treason. In upholding the convictions, the court found that the U.S. Constitution's Treason Clause does not apply because the crime differs from treason not only in name but also in its elements and punishment. Can you identify other essential differences between the crimes? Why would there be jurisdictional restrictions on the seditious conspiracy statute? While noting that whether any of the defendants in fact owed allegiance to the United States was immaterial, the court went on to say that "treason imports a betraying. . . . [It] is a breach of allegiance, and can be committed by him only who owes allegiance." *Rahman*, 189 F.3d at 114. Perhaps this is why the original punishment of treason in the United States was exceptionally cruel: "the traitor was hanged by the neck, then cut down alive, that his entrails are then taken out, and burned, while he is yet alive, that his head is cut off, and that his body is then divided into four parts." *Rahman*, 189 F.3d at 112. Considering this punishment, the court figured that "the Framers may have intended to limit the applicability of the most severe penalties . . . to instances of levying war against, or adhering to enemies of, the United States." *Id.*

8. Defense Strategy

Would Lindh have been better off being treated as a criminal defendant or as a POW or as a wartime detainee on Guantánamo? Recall that at the time the case was to go to trial, almost exactly a year after the attacks of September 11, 2001, in a courtroom several miles from the Pentagon, there were over a thousand individuals detained in Guantánamo Bay without access to counsel and several more in various offshore brigs and detention centers. Lindh had been indicted in the Northern District of Virginia, a district referred to as the "rocket docket" for the speed at which it completes cases; defense counsel's opening statement would have proceeded on or about the first anniversary of the September 11th attacks. Recall also that in September 2004, Yaser Hamdi, another American citizen held as an enemy combatant at the same time as Lindh, was released from captivity without charges and allowed to return to his home in Saudi Arabia. In exchange, Hamdi gave up his U.S. citizenship and was barred from visiting Afghanistan, Iraq, Israel, Pakistan, Syria, the West Bank, and Gaza. How can these two disparate outcomes be explained? Which individual got the better deal? Would you have recommended that your client accept the 20-

year plea deal? At a minimum, does the disparate treatment of Lindh and Hamdi suggest Lindh should have been eligible for an executive pardon? His lawyers have so argued, and petitioned President George W. Bush to pardon or reduce his sentence. In January 2009, in one of his last acts before leaving office, President Bush denied the petition. Should President Obama have granted it?

9. For Further Reading

For more on combatant immunity, *see* Nathaniel Berman, *Privileging Combat? Contemporary Conflict and the Legal Construction of War*, 43 COLUM. J. TRANSNAT'L L. 1 (2004).

VI. *TU QUOQUE* & REPRISALS

One of the arguments sometimes raised in defense against a charge of an international humanitarian law violation is that the "other side" is equally guilty of such conduct. This *tu quoque* ["you also"] argument suggests that if one side to a conflict is in breach of the law, then the other side is no longer obligated to follow the same rules. In fact, some would argue, in such a circumstance, complying with the law might result in a strategic disadvantage to the initially conforming party, and thus would make it more likely that the non-complying party might win the battle, or the war. The *tu quoque* defense is related to the doctrine of reprisals. This doctrine—once a staple enforcement mechanism of international law—allows a state to engage in otherwise illegal action in response to a breach by another party. Both doctrines rely upon the lack of compliance of one party to justify the lack of compliance by another.

The following case before the ICTY addresses the legitimacy of the *tu quoque* argument and of the use of reprisals. (See the Appendix for a map of Yugoslavia.) Zoran Kupreškić, a member of the Croatian Defense Council (HVO), was indicted for his involvement in the attack of the Bosnian village of Ahmići-Šantići on April 16, 1993 (as discussed in Chapter 10 on Crimes against Humanity). The villages were shelled from a distance and then groups of HVO soldiers went house-to-house attacking Bosnian Muslim civilians and burning their houses, barns, and livestock. Kupreškić raised in defense the doctrines of *tu quoque* and reprisal. He also argued that many of the inhabitants of the village were combatants and not civilians as the Prosecution alleged, thus making the village a legitimate military target. The Tribunal, in a part of the opinion not reproduced here, rejected the latter argument.

Prosecutor v. Zoran Kupreškić, Case No. IT–96–12–T, Judgement (Jan. 14, 2000)

In the Trial Chamber

The *Tu Quoque* Principle Is Fallacious and Inapplicable: The Absolute Character of Obligations Imposed by Fundamental Rules of International Humanitarian Law

515. Defence counsel have indirectly or implicitly relied upon the *tu quoque* principle, i.e. the argument whereby the fact that the adversary has also committed similar crimes offers a valid defence to the individuals accused.[767] This is an argument resting on the allegedly reciprocal nature of obligations created by the humanitarian law of armed conflict. This argument may amount to saying that breaches of international humanitarian law, being committed by the enemy, justify similar breaches by a belligerent. Or it may amount to saying that such breaches, having been perpetrated by the adversary, legitimise similar breaches by a belligerent in response to, or in retaliation for, such violations by the enemy. Clearly, this second approach to a large extent coincides with the doctrine of reprisals, and is accordingly assessed below. Here the Trial Chamber will confine itself to briefly discussing the first meaning of the principle at issue.

516. It should first of all be pointed out that although *tu quoque* was raised as a defence in war crimes trials following the Second World War, it was universally rejected. The U.S. Military Tribunal in the *High Command* trial, for instance, categorically stated that under general principles of law, an accused does not exculpate himself from a crime by showing that another has committed a similar crime, either before or after the commission of the crime by the accused. Indeed, there is in fact no support either in State practice or in the opinions of publicists for the validity of such a defence.

517. Secondly, the *tu quoque* argument is flawed in principle. It envisages humanitarian law as based upon a narrow bilateral exchange of rights and obligations. Instead, the bulk of this body of law lays down absolute obligations, namely obligations that are unconditional or in other words not based on reciprocity. This concept is already encapsulated in Common Article 1 of the 1949 Geneva Conventions, which provides that "The High Contracting Parties undertake to respect [. . .] the present Convention *in all circumstances*" (emphasis added). Furthermore, attention must be drawn to a common provision (respectively Articles 51, 52, 131 and 148 [of Geneva Conventions I-IV]) which provides that "No High Contracting party shall be allowed to absolve itself or any other High Contracting Party of any liability

---

[767] See for instance the cross-examination of Witness Y, where defence counsel Ms. Glumac gave a list of Croatian villages from which Croats were allegedly expelled and their houses burnt, supporting the inference that the Croats justified the massacres in Ahmići in terms of revenge (T. 3344–46).

incurred by itself or by another High Contracting Party in respect of breaches referred to in the preceding Article (i.e. grave breaches)." Admittedly, this provision only refers to State responsibility for grave breaches committed by State agents or *de facto* State agents, or at any rate for grave breaches generating State responsibility (e.g. for an omission by the State to prevent or punish such breaches). Nevertheless, the general notion underpinning those provisions is that liability for grave breaches is absolute and may in no case be set aside by resort to any legal means such as derogating treaties or agreements. *A fortiori* such liability and, more generally individual criminal responsibility for serious violations of international humanitarian law, may not be thwarted by recourse to arguments such as reciprocity.

518. The absolute nature of most obligations imposed by rules of international humanitarian law reflects the progressive trend towards the so-called "humanization" of international legal obligations, which refers to the general erosion of the role of reciprocity in the application of humanitarian law over the last century. After the First World War, the application of the laws of war moved away from a reliance on reciprocity between belligerents, with the consequence that, in general, rules came to be increasingly applied by each belligerent despite their possible disregard by the enemy. The underpinning of this shift was that it became clear to States that norms of international humanitarian law were not intended to protect State interests; they were primarily designed to benefit individuals *qua* human beings. Unlike other international norms, such as those of commercial treaties which can legitimately be based on the protection of reciprocal interests of States, compliance with humanitarian rules could not be made dependent on a reciprocal or corresponding performance of these obligations by other States. This trend marks the translation into legal norms of the "categorical imperative" formulated by Kant in the field of morals: one ought to fulfil an obligation regardless of whether others comply with it or disregard it.

519. As a consequence of their absolute character, these norms of international humanitarian law do not pose synallagmatic obligations, i.e. obligations of a State *vis-à-vis* another State. Rather—as was stated by the International Court of Justice in the *Barcelona Traction* case (which specifically referred to obligations concerning fundamental human rights)—they lay down obligations towards the international community as a whole, with the consequence that each and every member of the international community has a "legal interest" in their observance and consequently a legal entitlement to demand respect for such obligations.

520. Furthermore, most norms of international humanitarian law, in particular those prohibiting war crimes, crimes against humanity and genocide, are also peremptory norms of international law or *jus cogens*, i.e. of a non-derogable and overriding character. One illustration of the

consequences which follow from this classification is that if the norms in question are contained in treaties, contrary to the general rule set out in Article 60 of the Vienna Convention on the Law of Treaties, a material breach of that treaty obligation by one of the parties would not entitle the other to invoke that breach in order to terminate or suspend the operation of the treaty. Article 60(5) provides that such reciprocity or in other words the principle *inadimplenti non est adimplendum* ["One has no need to respect his obligation if the counter-party has not respected his own"] does not apply to provisions relating to the protection of the human person contained in treaties of a humanitarian character, in particular the provisions prohibiting any form of reprisals against persons protected by such treaties.

The Prohibition of Attacks on Civilian Populations

521. The protection of civilians in time of armed conflict, whether international or internal, is the bedrock of modern humanitarian law. * * *

522. The protection of civilians and civilian objects provided by modern international law may cease entirely or be reduced or suspended in three exceptional circumstances: (i) when civilians abuse their rights; (ii) when, although the object of a military attack is comprised of military objectives, belligerents cannot avoid causing so-called collateral damage to civilians; and (iii) at least according to some authorities, when civilians may legitimately be the object of reprisals. * * *

527. As for reprisals against civilians, under customary international law they are prohibited as long as civilians find themselves in the hands of the adversary. With regard to civilians in combat zones, reprisals against them are prohibited by Article 51(6) of the First Additional Protocol of 1977, whereas reprisals against civilian objects are outlawed by Article 52(1) of the same instrument. The question nevertheless arises as to whether these provisions, assuming that they were not declaratory of customary international law, have subsequently been transformed into general rules of international law. In other words, are those States which have not ratified the First Protocol (which include such countries as the U.S., France, India, Indonesia, Israel, Japan, Pakistan and Turkey), nevertheless bound by general rules having the same purport as those two provisions? Admittedly, there does not seem to have emerged recently a body of State practice consistently supporting the proposition that one of the elements of custom, namely *usus* or *diuturnitas* ["long duration"] has taken shape. This is however an area where *opinio iuris sive necessitatis* may play a much greater role than *usus*, as a result of the aforementioned Martens Clause.* In the light of

* Eds.: The Martens clause provides: "Until a more complete code of the laws of war is issued, * * * populations and belligerents remain under the protection and empire of the principles of international law, as they result from the usages established between civilized nations, from the laws of humanity and the requirements of the public conscience." For more on the Martens clause, see *supra* Chapter 7 on War Crimes.

the way States and courts have implemented it, this Clause clearly shows that principles of international humanitarian law may emerge through a customary process under the pressure of the demands of humanity or the dictates of public conscience, even where State practice is scant or inconsistent. The other element, in the form of *opinio necessitates* ["moral obligation"], crystallising as a result of the imperatives of humanity or public conscience, may turn out to be the decisive element heralding the emergence of a general rule or principle of humanitarian law.

528. The question of reprisals against civilians is a case in point. It cannot be denied that reprisals against civilians are inherently a barbarous means of seeking compliance with international law. The most blatant reason for the universal revulsion that usually accompanies reprisals is that they may not only be arbitrary but are also not directed specifically at the individual authors of the initial violation. Reprisals typically are taken in situations where the individuals personally responsible for the breach are either unknown or out of reach. These retaliatory measures are aimed instead at other more vulnerable individuals or groups. They are individuals or groups who may not even have any degree of solidarity with the presumed authors of the initial violation; they may share with them only the links of nationality and allegiance to the same rulers.

529. In addition, the reprisal killing of innocent persons, more or less chosen at random, without any requirement of guilt or any form of trial, can safely be characterized as a blatant infringement of the most fundamental principles of human rights. It is difficult to deny that a slow but profound transformation of humanitarian law under the pervasive influence of human rights has occurred. As a result, belligerent reprisals against civilians and fundamental rights of human beings are absolutely inconsistent legal concepts. * * *

530. It should be added that while reprisals could have had a modicum of justification in the past, when they constituted practically the only effective means of compelling the enemy to abandon unlawful acts of warfare and to comply in future with international law, at present they can no longer be justified in this manner. A means of inducing compliance with international law is at present more widely available and, more importantly, is beginning to prove fairly efficacious: the prosecution and punishment of war crimes and crimes against humanity by national or international courts. This means serves the purpose of bringing to justice those who are responsible for any such crime, as well as, albeit to a limited extent, the purpose of deterring at least the most blatant violations of international humanitarian law. * * *

535. It should also be pointed out that at any rate, even when considered lawful, reprisals are restricted by: (a) the principle whereby they must be a last resort in attempts to impose compliance by the adversary with legal standards (which entails, amongst other things, that they may be exercised only after a prior warning has been given

which has failed to bring about the discontinuance of the adversary's crimes); (b) the obligation to take special precautions before implementing them (they may be taken only after a decision to this effect has been made at the highest political or military level; in other words they may not be decided by local commanders); (c) the principle of proportionality (which entails not only that the reprisals must not be excessive compared to the precedent unlawful act of warfare, but also that they must stop as soon as that unlawful act has been discontinued); and (d) "elementary considerations of humanity."

536. Finally, it must be noted, with specific regard to the case at issue, that whatever the content of the customary rules on reprisals, the treaty provisions prohibiting them were in any event applicable in the case in dispute. In 1993, both Croatia and Bosnia and Herzegovina had ratified Additional Protocol I and II, in addition to the four Geneva Conventions of 1949. Hence, whether or not the armed conflict of which the attack on Ahmići formed part is regarded as internal, indisputably the parties to the conflict were bound by the relevant treaty provisions prohibiting reprisals.

NOTES & QUESTIONS

1. Case Outcome

Zoran Kupreškić was found guilty of persecution as a crime against humanity and sentenced to ten years. He was acquitted of the charge of murder as a crime against humanity. The Appeals Chamber reversed Kupreškić's conviction, holding that the original Indictment was too vague to adequately inform the defendant of the material facts of the charges against him. While the Appeals Chamber noted that such a defect does not automatically result in acquittal but may result in a retrial, acquittal was appropriate here given that the defendant raised a number of objections to the factual findings of the Trial Chamber that undermined the evidentiary basis of his conviction. *See Prosecutor v. Kupreškić*, Case No. IT–95–16–A, Judgement (Oct. 23, 2001).

2. *Tu Quoque*

Tu quoque is an argument that responds to criticism of an action by pointing to the commission of the same act by the accuser. As a matter of logic, it is a fallacy: whether the accuser is guilty of the same wrong is irrelevant to the accuracy of the original charge. However, as a rhetorical device in the context of war, it is a frequent and often effective tactic, since the accuser is put on the defensive and frequently feels compelled to defend against the accusation. *See* S. Morris Engel, WITH GOOD REASON: AN INTRODUCTION TO INFORMAL FALLACIES 204–06 (5th ed.1994).

3. The Doctrine of Reprisals

A reprisal is an otherwise unlawful act taken as a self-help measure in response to a breach of law by an adversary designed as an effort to compel compliance from the adversary. The ICRC has identified five conditions that must be met in order for a reprisal to be lawful: 1) it must only be taken in reaction to a prior serious violation of international humanitarian law, and only for the purpose of inducing compliance with the law; 2) it must be a measure of last resort; 3) it must be proportional to the violation it aims to stop; 4) the decision to resort to reprisals must be taken at the highest levels of government; and 5) the reprisal must cease as soon as the adversary complies with the law. Jean-Marie Henckaerts & Louise Doswald-Beck, 1 CUSTOMARY INTERNATIONAL HUMANITARIAN LAW (2005) (hereinafter "CUSTOMARY IHL"), Rule 145.

As the excerpt above reveals, reprisals do not necessarily follow the *lex talionis*—"an eye for an eye." Rather, they are also subject to "elemental principles of humanity." *See* Frits Kalshoven, BELLIGERENT REPRISALS (1971). Additional Protocol I went far beyond prior humanitarian law in prohibiting most (but not all) reprisals; these provisions have been cited as one reason the U.S. has not joined that treaty. *See* George H. Aldrich, *Prospects for United States Ratification of Additional Protocol I to the 1949 Geneva Conventions*, 85 AM. J. INT'L L. 1, 15–17 (1991) (noting that the U.S. wanted to reserve the right to engage in certain reprisals). The U.S. Department of the Army, THE LAW OF LAND WARFARE, Field Manual 27–10 (1956), stated at para. 497(b): "Even when appeal to the enemy for redress has failed, it may be a matter of policy to consider, before resorting to reprisals, whether the opposing forces are not more likely to be influenced by a steady adherence to the law of war on the part of their adversary." Why and when might this be the case?

4. Reprisals and Protected Persons and Objects

Are civilians treated differently than combatants with respect to their legitimacy as a target of reprisal under the law? Should they be? The First Geneva Convention also prohibits reprisals against the wounded and the sick at Article 46; the same is true vis-à-vis prisoners of war in Article 13 of the Third Geneva Convention. The ICRC has concluded that no reprisals may be directed against any of the following protected persons as a matter of customary international law: the wounded, sick and shipwrecked, medical and religious personnel, captured combatants, civilians in occupied territory, and other categories of civilians in the power of the adverse party to the conflict. CUSTOMARY IHL STUDY, Rule 146. In addition, the ICRC asserts that as a matter of customary international law reprisals are prohibited against certain objects, including the property of protected persons, medical objects and facilities, and cultural property.

Given the five guiding principles identified by the ICRC and the restrictions on legitimate targets of reprisals, what is left of the doctrine of reprisals under modern IHL? Could, for example, a party to a conflict utilize a prohibited weapon (such as a blinding laser weapon) against an adversary who had used such a weapon on its soldiers or who had otherwise breached IHL? What about a situation in which one party used disproportionate force against a lawful military objective? Why might the resort to reprisals be increasingly circumscribed in modern times? The ICRC's study of customary IHL states somewhat controversially that "Parties to non-international armed conflicts do not have the right to resort to belligerent reprisals. Other countermeasures against persons who do not or who have ceased to take a direct part in hostilities are prohibited." CUSTOMARY IHL, Rule 148. How might the authors have identified this as a customary rule? Does this rule make sense?

5. Reciprocity in IHL

What are the rationales underlying the irrelevancy of reciprocity in international humanitarian law? Is it realistic in the context of armed conflict to ask one party to adhere to the laws of war in the face of another party's breach, especially where they may believe the survival of their state or community is at issue? Does such a rule make IHL a "suicide pact"? Does a rule against reprisals tend to benefit or hinder well-developed states with professional armies? Is current doctrine likely to be effective in today's armed conflicts?

6. *Dicta* and the Development of International Criminal Law

The Tribunal notes at paragraph 536 that all of the relevant states were bound by the prohibitions against reprisals by treaty. Why then does the Tribunal go to such lengths to establish an applicable rule of customary international law? Does the existence of applicable treaty provisions make the discussion of customary international law *dictum*? It is a common practice of domestic courts to only reach issues that are necessary for the resolution of the dispute before them. Why might international courts eschew such a practice of abstention? Should a court that is applying international law be more or less willing to opine on issues not necessary for the resolution of the dispute before it?

VII. HEAD OF STATE IMMUNITY

Government officials under both domestic and international law may claim immunity from accountability for acts they commit while in office. Heads of state have enjoyed such immunity for centuries, due in large part to the conflation of the head of state with the state itself. Thus, head of state immunity was grounded in the more general notion of sovereign immunity. Sovereign and head of state immunity developed as doctrines rooted in the comity that one state owed another. In other words, it was accepted that except in limited and exceptional circumstances, a state would not assert its judicial power over another state.

Such deference began to break down in domestic jurisprudence, first with the development of a doctrine of limited sovereign immunity, and second with the recognition that certain acts performed by state actors, including heads of state, should not benefit from immunity from accountability. Limited sovereign immunity distinguishes between those acts that are considered official and proper for a government, and those that are personal or exceed appropriate sovereign prerogatives. For international criminal law, the dilemma is how to categorize war crimes, acts of torture, or genocide ostensibly committed on behalf of a state: as legitimate and official acts of a state; as improper, though official, acts of a state; as unlawful acts of a state; or as personal acts of an official? In addition, it is not clear how the comity-based arguments supporting sovereign and head of state immunity—that one state will not sit in judgment on the official acts of another state—apply when the court before which an official is brought is an international one.

In a seminal opinion, the U.K. House of Lords—the upper house of Parliament and at that time the highest court of appeals—addressed a claim of head of state immunity by General Augusto Pinochet of Chile. General Pinochet came to power in Chile in 1973 in a U.S.-supported coup that overthrew the democratically-elected government of President Salvador Allende. During Pinochet's reign, thousands of people were tortured, disappeared, killed, and detained. As part of *Operación Cóndor*, General Pinochet's government coordinated with other South American countries to track down, repress, and in some cases disappear dissidents from Chile and other countries. After 17 years in power, General Pinochet stepped down and was replaced by a democratically-elected President, Patricio Aylwin. To ensure his continued immunity from prosecution, General Pinochet insisted on being named "Senator for Life," a title that included immunity from prosecution.

In 1998, while visiting the United Kingdom, General Pinochet was arrested pursuant to a warrant issued by the Spanish judge, Baltasar Garzón, for torture, murder, illegal detention, and the disappearances of both Chilean and Spanish citizens. In proceedings in the United Kingdom, General Pinochet challenged the right of the United Kingdom to extradite him and the authority of the Spanish courts to prosecute him. One of the issues before the British authorities was whether General Pinochet was entitled to immunity for acts committed while he was head of state. The legal proceedings in Britain lasted for seventeen months and culminated in a decision by the House of Lords finding that General Pinochet could be held accountable (and thus extradited) for acts of torture that had occurred after 1988, which was when the United Kingdom passed legislation making torture committed outside the territory of the United Kingdom a crime under British law.

The opinion by Lord Browne-Wilkinson held that a former head of state continues to enjoy immunity *ratione materiae,* but loses immunity *ratione personae*, on ceasing to be head of state. Lord Browne-Wilkinson presented the question for decision as:

> whether the alleged organisation of state torture by Senator Pinochet (if proved) would constitute an act committed by Senator Pinochet as part of his official functions as head of state. It is not enough to say that it cannot be part of the functions of the head of state to commit a crime. Actions which are criminal under the local law can still have been done officially and therefore give rise to immunity *ratione materiae.*

Lord Browne-Wilkinson concluded, after canvassing both national and international authority, that torture as defined in the Convention

Against Torture cannot, by definition, qualify as a state function, and is thus not covered by immunity *ratione materiae*. Lord Browne-Wilkinson anchored his opinion on the United Kingdom's ratification of the Convention Against Torture, stating that he had "doubts whether, before the coming into force of the Torture Convention, the existence of the international crime of torture as *jus cogens* was enough to justify the conclusion that the organisation of state torture could not rank for immunity purposes as performance of an official function."

The House of Lords held, by a vote of 6–1, that General Pinochet could be extradited to Spain to be tried for acts of torture committed after December 8, 1988, the date on which the United Kingdom made torture committed outside of its territory a crime. Two of the Lords concluded that, as a matter of customary international law, former heads of state could not claim immunity for acts of torture (Lords Millett and Philipps). Three of the Lords joined Browne-Wilkinson and held that it was the ratification of the Torture Convention that stripped former heads of state from immunity and not customary international law (Lords Hope, Hutton, and Saville). The effect of the decision was that the Law Lords empowered the Home Secretary to extradite General Pinochet to Spain on the condition that he be tried only for his responsibility for acts of torture that occurred after 1988. The decision to extradite was a discretionary one, and the Home Secretary ultimately declined to send General Pinochet to Spain, citing the General's fragile health (a contested point). General Pinochet returned to Chile on March 2, 2000.

After his return to Chile, General Pinochet became the subject of a number of domestic prosecutions and civil suits. The Supreme Court of Chile voted to remove General Pinochet's immunity, and he was placed under house arrest in December 2004. For the next two years until his death, General Pinochet moved in and out of house arrest in connection with numerous criminal investigations and prosecutions related to human rights violations, corruption, and other abuses committed during his reign of power. He died on December 10, 2006. For more on the Pinochet case, *see* THE PINOCHET PAPERS: THE CASE OF AUGUSTO PINOCHET IN SPAIN AND BRITAIN (Reed Brody & Michael Ratner eds., 2000); Naomi Roht-Arriaza, THE PINOCHET EFFECT: TRANSITIONAL JUSTICE IN THE AGE OF HUMAN RIGHTS (2006).

While the House of Lords decision in the *Pinochet* case was important in the development of the international law of head of state immunity, it only addressed the contours of immunity enjoyed by a *former* head of state. The case below concerning the immunity of President Omar Al Bashir of the Sudan is significant because it addresses the immunity enjoyed under international law by a *sitting* head of state. It is also a momentous decision in the developing jurisprudence of the ICC on an issue that continues to provoke significant debate among international criminal law scholars and practitioners, and is one of the issues cited by some members of the African Union in their criticism of the ICC.

In 2009 and 2010, the ICC issued two arrest warrants against President Al Bashir for genocide, crimes against humanity, and war crimes. (For a brief background of the events leading up to the indictment of Al Bashir see Chapter 9 on Genocide. See the Appendix for a map of the Sudan.) The Government of the Sudan refused to cooperate with the ICC arguing, *inter alia*, that Al Bashir enjoyed absolute immunity given his position of head of state and the fact that the Sudan was a not a party to the Rome Treaty. The Pre-Trial Chamber rejected this argument in its decision issuing an arrest warrant against Al Bashir, though without much analysis. *Prosecutor v. Al Bashir*, Case No. ICC–02/05–01/09, Decision on the Prosecution's Application for a Warrant of Arrest against Omar Hassan Ahmad Al Bashir (Mar. 4, 2009).

Notwithstanding the warrants against him, and the Registrar of the Court sending (at the request of the Pre-Trial Chamber) a formal reminder to all member states highlighting their obligation to cooperate with the Court and thus to implement the arrest warrants against him, Al Bashir visited a range of countries, many of which are ICC members states. After Al Bashir traveled to Malawi in 2011, the Registrar reminded Malawi through a *Note Verbale* of its obligation to cooperate under the Rome Statute, and invited Malawi to consult with the Court if there was "any difficulty" in effectuating the arrest warrant against Al Bashir. The Registrar then filed a report on Al Bashir's visit to Malawi before the Pre-Trial Chamber. Malawi responded that because Al Bashir was a head of state, he was immune from arrest and prosecution while in office, and that Article 27 of the Rome Statute did not apply as the Sudan was not a party to the Rome Statute. Further, Malawi argued that Article 98 prevented it from surrendering Al Bashir to the Court because to do so would breach obligations it owed to the Sudan. The Pre-Trial Chamber rejected Malawi's arguments. *Prosecutor v. Al Bashir,* Case No. ICC–02/05–01/09, Corrigendum to the Decision Pursuant to Article 87(7) of the Rome Statute on the Failure by the Republic of Malawi to Comply with the Cooperation Requests Issued by the Court with Respect to the Arrest and Surrender of Omar Hassan Ahmad Al Bashir (Dec. 13, 2011).

Al Bashir's visit to Chad on August 7–8, 2011, to attend the inauguration of Chad's head of state, Idriss Déby, resulted in a similar decision issued the same day by the Pre-Trial Chamber. *Prosecutor v. Al Bashir*, Case No. ICC–02/05–01/09, Decision Pursuant to Article 87(7) of the Rome Statute on the Refusal of the Republic of Chad to Comply with the Cooperation Requests Issued by the Court with Respect to the Arrest and Surrender of Omar Hassan Ahmad Al Bashir (Dec. 13, 2011). Additional opinions were issued concerning visits by Al Bashir to the DRC, *Prosecutor v. Al Bashir*, Case No. ICC–02/05–01/09, Decision on the Cooperation of the Democratic Republic of the Congo Regarding Omar Al Bashir's Arrest and Surrender to the Court (April 9, 2014), and South

Africa, *Prosecutor v. Al Bashir*, Case No. ICC–02/05–01/09, Decision under article 87(7) of the Rome Statute on the non-compliance by South Africa with the request by the Court for the arrest and surrender of Omar Al-Bashir (July 6, 2017).

In March 2017 Al Bashir attended the 28th Summit of the Arab League in Amman, Jordan. Jordan did not arrest and surrender Al Bashir to the ICC. The Pre-Trial Chamber found that Jordan had failed to comply with its obligations under the Rome Statute to arrest Al Bashir, and—like the previous decisions—rejected the claim that Al Bashir was immune from arrest because of his status as a head of state. The Pre-Trial Chamber also decided that Jordan's non-compliance should be referred to the Assembly of State Parties and to the U.N. Security Council. Jordan appealed the decision. The African Union, the League of Arab States, and sixteen individuals (including prominent international criminal law advocates and scholars) submitted arguments before the Chamber as *amici curiae*. The Appeals Chamber's decision follows.

Prosecutor v. Omar Hassan Ahmad Al Bashir, Case No. ICC–02/05–01/09 OA2, Judgment in the Jordan Referral re Al Bashir Appeal (May 6, 2019)

In the Appeals Chamber

1. The 'Decision under article 87(7) of the Rome Statute on the non-compliance by Jordan with the request by the Court for the arrest and surrender o[f] Omar Al-Bashir' is unanimously confirmed to the extent that Pre-Trial Chamber II found that the Hashemite Kingdom of Jordan had failed to comply with its obligations under the Statute by not executing the Court's request for the arrest of Mr. Omar Hassan Ahmad Al-Bashir and his surrender to the Court while he was on Jordanian territory on 29 March 2017.

2. The Appeals Chamber unanimously finds that Jordan's failure to comply with the Court's request prevented the Court from exercising an important function and power. However, the Appeals Chamber finds (Judge Ibáñez and Judge Bossa dissenting) that in the particular circumstances of this case, Pre-Trial Chamber II erroneously exercised its discretion to refer Jordan to the Assembly of States Parties and to the Security Council of the United Nations. To that extent, the decision of Pre-Trial Chamber II is reversed (Judge Ibáñez and Judge Bossa dissenting). * * *

17. * * * On 21 February 2018, the Pre-Trial Chamber granted Jordan's request on the following three issues:

(i) The Chamber erred with respect to matters of law in its conclusions regarding the effects of the Rome Statute upon the immunity of President Al-Bashir, including its conclusions that Article 27(2) of the Rome Statute excludes the application of

Article 98; that Article 98 establishes no rights for States Parties; that Article 98(2) does not apply to the 1953 Convention [on the Privileges and Immunities of the Arab League]; and that even if Article 98 applied it would provide no basis for Jordan not to comply with the Court's request;

(ii) The Chamber erred with respect to matters of law in concluding that U.N. Security council resolution 1593 (2005) affected Jordan's obligations under customary and conventional international law to accord immunity to President Omar Hassan Ahmad Al-Bashir; and

(iii) Even if the Chamber's Decision with respect to non-compliance was correct (*quod non*), the Chamber abused its discretion in deciding to refer such non-compliance to the Assembly of States Parties and the U.N. Security Council. * * *

Applicable Legal Framework

36. Articles 13, 27 and 87(7), 97 and 98 of the Statute, as well as articles 25 and 103 of the Charter of the United Nations and Resolution 1593 are relevant for the present appeal. * * *

40. Article 98 deals with the cooperation with respect to waiver of immunity and consent to surrender and stipulates that

1. The Court may not proceed with a request for surrender or assistance which would require the requested State to act inconsistently with its obligations under international law with respect to the State or diplomatic immunity of a person or property of a third State, unless the Court can first obtain the cooperation of that third State for the waiver of the immunity.
2. The Court may not proceed with a request for surrender which would require the requested State to act inconsistently with its obligations under international agreements pursuant to which the consent of a sending State is required to surrender a person of that State to the Court, unless the Court can first obtain the cooperation of the sending State for the giving of consent for the surrender.

41. Article 97 pertains to the consultations and provides as follows:

Where a State Party receives a request under this Part in relation to which it identifies problems which may impede or prevent the execution of the request, that State shall consult with the Court without delay in order to resolve the matter. Such problems may include, *inter alia*: * * * (c) The fact that execution of the request in its current form would require the requested State to breach a pre-existing treaty obligation undertaken with respect to another State.

42. Article 25 of the Charter of the United Nations provides:

The Members of the United Nations agree to accept and carry out the decisions of the Security Council in accordance with the present Charter.

43. Article 103 of the Charter of the United Nations provides:

In the event of a conflict between the obligations of the Members of the United Nations under the present Charter and their obligations under any other international agreement, their obligations under the present Charter shall prevail.

44. Resolution 1593 provides:

The Security Council, * * *

1. *Decides* to refer the situation in Darfur since 1 July 2002 to the Prosecutor of the International Criminal Court;

2. *Decides* that the Government of Sudan and all other parties to the conflict in Darfur, shall cooperate fully with and provide any necessary assistance to the Court and the Prosecutor pursuant to this resolution and, while recognizing that States not party to the Rome Statute have no obligation under the Statute, urges all States and concerned regional and other international organizations to cooperate fully. * * *

96. [A]t issue under the first two grounds of appeal is primarily the question of whether Head of State immunity finds application in a situation where the Court requests a State Party of the Rome Statute to arrest and surrender the Head of State of another State (in this instance, Sudan), which, while not being party to the Rome Statute, is the subject of a referral to the Court by the UN Security Council and, in terms of Resolution 1593, obliged to fully cooperate with the Court.

97. The central issue in this appeal is whether Mr. Bashir, in his capacity as Head of State of Sudan, enjoyed immunity before this Court which Jordan was obligated to respect in the absence of a waiver from Sudan. * * * [T]he Appeals Chamber is satisfied that the issues in this appeal ultimately rest on a proper construction of the provisions of the Rome Statute, in particular articles 27(2), 86, 89 and 98 of the Statute. It will address the impact of article 27(2) of the Statute on requests for cooperation relating to Heads of State of States Parties [below, section (b)]. It will then address the legal situation of Sudan in light of the UN Security Council referral of the Darfur situation [below, section (c)].

98. In the context of construing the provisions of the Statute, the Appeals Chamber considers it convenient to address whether customary international law actually provides for immunity of a Head of State if arrest and surrender are sought by the Court [below, section (a)], especially given the importance generated by that question in the context of this appeal. * * *

(a) Article 27(2) of the Statute and Customary International Law

101. The Appeals Chamber notes that Head of State immunity, which has been asserted in the case at hand, is a manner of immunity that is, as such, accepted under customary international law. That immunity prevents one State from exercising its criminal jurisdiction over the Head of State of another State. It is important to stress that immunity of that kind operates in the context of relations between States.

102. The most direct effect of article 27(2) of the Statute is that a Head of State cannot claim Head of State immunity when he or she appears before the ICC for prosecution in accordance with the provisions on the exercise of jurisdiction under articles 12 *et seq.* of the Statute. Nor does Head of State immunity present a bar to the Court opening an investigation in relation to or issuing a warrant of arrest against a Head of State. This was specifically recognised by the ICJ in the *Arrest Warrant Case.**

103. It is of note that article 27(2) of the Statute is a clear provision in conventional law; but it also reflects the status of customary international law. [The Chambers goes on to cite to the following as evidence of lack of head of state immunity for international crimes under customary international law: the Nuremberg Charter; U.N. General Assembly resolutions; the International Law Commission; the Convention against Genocide; the Statutes of the ICTY, ICTR, and SCSL; and the SCSL indictment of Charles Taylor.] * * *

110. Turning to the jurisprudence of the ICC, the Appeals Chamber recalls that Pre-Trial Chamber I, in the 'Corrigendum to the Decision Pursuant to Article 87(7) of the Rome Statute on the Failure by the Republic of Malawi to Comply with the Cooperation Requests Issued by the Court with Respect to the Arrest and Surrender of Omar Hassan Ahmad Al Bashir' [the '*Malawi* Decision'], reached the same conclusion in a situation that was identical to the case at hand: a State Party to the Rome Statute having failed to execute a request for the arrest and surrender of Mr. Al-Bashir. Pre-Trial Chamber I, having recalled the irrelevance of Head of State immunity in respect of international courts since the end of the First World War, distinguished the case before it from that decided by the ICJ in the *Arrest Warrant Case*, noting that the latter was 'concerned solely with immunity across national jurisdictions' and therefore 'distinct from the present circumstances, as here an *international court* is seeking arrest for international crimes'. Pre-Trial Chamber I also recalled the passage of the judgment in the *Arrest Warrant Case* that recognises that Head of State immunity does not find application before international courts.

* Eds.: See Chapter 3 and Note 7 below for discussion of the *Arrest Warrant Case.*

111. Pre-Trial Chamber I found that:

> [T]he principle in international law is that immunity of either former or sitting Heads of State cannot be invoked to oppose a prosecution by an international court. This is equally applicable to former or sitting Heads of States not Parties to the Statute whenever the Court may exercise jurisdiction. In this particular case, the Chamber notes that it is exercising jurisdiction following a referral by the United Nations Security Council made under Chapter VII of the United Nations Charter, in accordance with article 13(b) of the Statute.

112. Pre-Trial Chamber I considered that 'Malawi, and by extension the African Union, are not entitled to rely on article 98(1) of the Statute to justify refusing to comply with the Cooperation Requests', noting, *inter alia*, 'an increase in Head of State prosecutions by international courts in the last decade', which shows 'that initiating international prosecutions against Heads of State have gained widespread recognition as accepted practice'. It also noted the number of States Parties to the Rome Statute and the fact that States not parties to the Statute allowed twice for situations to be referred to the Court by the UN Security Council. Pre-Trial Chamber I concluded that the 'international community's commitment to rejecting immunity in circumstances where international courts seek arrest for international crimes has reached a critical mass' and that '[t]here is no conflict between Malawi's obligations towards the Court and its obligations under customary international law; therefore, article 98(1) of the Statute does not apply'.

113. The Appeals Chamber fully agrees with Pre-Trial Chamber I's conclusions in the *Malawi* Decision as well as that of the SCSL's Appeals Chamber in the *Taylor* case and notes that there is neither State practice nor *opinio juris* that would support the existence of Head of State immunity under customary international law *vis-à-vis* an international court. To the contrary, * * * such immunity has never been recognised in international law as a bar to the jurisdiction of an international court. To be noted in that regard is the role of judicial pronouncements in confirming whether or not a rule of customary international law has as such 'crystallized.' The Appeals Chamber is satisfied that the pronouncements of both the Pre-Trial Chamber in the *Malawi* Decision and of the Appeals Chamber of the Special Court for Sierra Leone have adequately and correctly confirmed the absence of a rule of customary international law recognising Head of State immunity before international courts in the exercise of jurisdiction. The Appeals Chamber accordingly rejects any contrary suggestion of the Pre-Trial Chamber in that regard, in both this case and in the case concerning South Africa.

114. The absence of a rule of customary international law recognising Head of State immunity *vis-à-vis* international courts is relevant not only to the question of whether an international court may issue a warrant for the arrest of a Head of State and conduct proceedings

against him or her, but also for the horizontal relationship between States when a State is requested by an international court to arrest and surrender the Head of State of another State. * * * [N]o immunities under customary international law operate in such a situation to bar an international court in its exercise of its own jurisdiction.

115. The Appeals Chamber considers that the absence of a rule of customary international law recognising Head of State immunity *vis-à-vis* an international court is also explained by the different character of international courts when compared with domestic jurisdictions. While the latter are essentially an expression of a State's sovereign power, which is necessarily limited by the sovereign power of the other States, the former, when adjudicating international crimes, do not act on behalf of a particular State or States. Rather, international courts act on behalf of the international community as a whole. Accordingly, the principle of *par in parem non habet imperium* ["an equal has no power over an equal"], which is based on the sovereign equality of States, finds no application in relation to an international court such as the International Criminal Court.

116. The Appeals Chamber notes further that, given the fundamentally different nature of an international court as opposed to a domestic court exercising jurisdiction over a Head of State, it would be wrong to assume that an exception to the customary international law rule on Head of State immunity applicable in the relationship between States has to be established; rather, the *onus* is on those who claim that there is such immunity in relation to international courts to establish sufficient State practice and *opinio juris*. * * * [T]here is no such practice or *opinio juris*.

117. In sum, the Appeals Chamber finds that there was no rule of customary international law that would have given Mr. Al-Bashir immunity from arrest and surrender by Jordan on the basis of the request for arrest and surrender issued by the Court. It follows that there was no ground for Jordan not to execute the request for arrest and surrender and that therefore it did not comply with its obligation to cooperate with the Court pursuant to articles 86 *et seq.* of the Statute. * * *

(b) Articles 27(2) and 98 of the Statute and their impact on obligations between State Parties

120. The Pre-Trial Chamber found that the effect of article 27(2) of the Statute on States Parties of the Rome Statute is two-fold: it prevents them from invoking any immunity belonging to them under international law (i) 'as a ground for refusing arrest and surrender of a person sought by the Court (vertical effect)'; and (ii) 'when cooperation in the arrest and surrender of a person to the Court is provided by another State Party (horizontal effect)'. * * *

(i) Article 27(2) of the Statute and its 'vertical effect' in relation to cooperation by States Parties

121. The Appeals Chamber recalls that, pursuant to article 86 of the Statute, States Parties to the Rome Statute are under an obligation to cooperate fully with the Court, in accordance with the Statute; pursuant to article 89 of the Statute, the Court may request the arrest and surrender of a person against whom a warrant of arrest has been issued. The extent of the obligation of States Parties to cooperate fully must be understood in the context of the Statute as a whole and bearing in mind its object and purpose. The Court was set up to exercise jurisdiction 'over persons for the most serious crimes of international concern' and its States Parties expressed their determination to 'put an end to impunity for the perpetrators of these crimes'. On that basis, the Appeals Chamber considers it to be clear, that, if a warrant of arrest were to be issued against the Head of State of a State Party to the Rome Statute and the Court requests that State Party to arrest and surrender the person who is the subject of the warrant, the requested State Party could not refuse to comply with the request on the ground that its Head of State enjoys immunity, be it under international or domestic law. This is a direct consequence of article 27(2) of the Statute, to which all States Parties to the Rome Statute have consented by virtue of their ratification of, or accession to, the Statute.

122. The Appeals Chamber is unpersuaded by Jordan's argument that article 27(2), which is situated in Part 3 of the Statute, only addresses the Court's ability to exercise jurisdiction, and not the arrest and surrender of persons to the Court, which is regulated in Part 9. While articles 27 and 86 *et seq*. are located in different parts of the Statute, they must be read together and any possible tension between them must be reconciled. In the view of the Appeals Chamber, this is best achieved by reading article 27(2), both as a matter of conventional law and as reflecting customary international law, as also excluding reliance on immunity in relation to a Head of State's arrest and surrender. This follows from a number of considerations. First, it is clear that the purpose of article 27(2) is to ensure that immunities do not stand in the way of the exercise of the Court's jurisdiction; the Court's jurisdiction must be effective. This purpose would be all but defeated if a State Party, which is obliged to cooperate fully with the Court, were allowed to invoke immunity as a ground to refuse the arrest and surrender of its Head of State to the Court, given that the Court depends on State cooperation to execute warrants of arrest. The result would be that, in effect, the Court would be barred from exercising its jurisdiction because of the existence of immunities, which would be contrary to the letter and spirit of article 27(2). If such an interpretation of article 27(2) were to be adopted, an important provision of the Statute would become potentially meaningless.

123. The Appeals Chamber notes in this regard that the obligation of States Parties to cooperate with the Court when exercising its jurisdiction over crimes listed in article 5 of the Statute (the crime of genocide, crimes against humanity, war crimes and the crime of aggression) relates to breaches of fundamental norms of international law that have, such as the prohibition of genocide, the character and force of *jus cogens*. The obligation to cooperate with the Court reinforces the obligation *erga omnes* to prevent, investigate and punish crimes that shock the conscience of humanity, including in particular those under the jurisdiction of the Court and it is this *erga omnes* character that makes the obligation of States Parties to cooperate with the Court so fundamental. These considerations are reflected in the possibility, pursuant to article 87(7) of the Statute, of referring non-compliance with these obligations to the Assembly of States Parties and, in case the situation to which the cooperation request relates was referred to the Court by the UN Security Council, to the UN Security Council. The resulting importance of the duty to cooperate lends further weight to the argument that the duty to cooperate under articles 86 *et seq*. of the Statute must be interpreted in light of article 27(2) of the Statute.

124. As stated by Pre-Trial Chamber II in the *South Africa* Decision, if States Parties to the Statute were allowed to rely on immunities or special procedural rules to deny cooperation with the Court, this would create a situation which would 'clearly be incompatible with the object and purpose of article 27(2) of the Statute'. Indeed, as noted by Pre-Trial Chamber II 'the Court's jurisdiction with respect to persons enjoying official capacity would be reduced to a purely theoretical concept if States Parties could refuse cooperation with the Court by invoking immunities based on official capacity'. If article 27(2) were to be read narrowly only to encompass proceedings before the Court (i.e. the Court's adjudicatory jurisdiction), it would be unclear, as noted by the Prosecutor, whether any Head of State—even of a State Party—could ever be effectively arrested and surrendered, absent an express waiver by the State concerned. To read the Statute in this way would be contrary to the principle of effectiveness.

125. Furthermore, the reference in article 27(2) to immunities 'under national law' suggests that the provision also applies to the relationship between the Court and States Parties because national law could in any event not be invoked before the Court; the reference to 'national law' would be meaningless if article 27(2) were considered to be unrelated to Part 9 of the Statute. Therefore, contrary to the submissions of Jordan and some of the *amici curiae*, article 27(2) is relevant not only to the adjudicatory jurisdiction of the Court, but also to the Court's 'enforcement jurisdiction' *vis-à-vis* States Parties to the Rome Statute.

126. In light of the above, the term 'cooperate fully' in article 86 must be understood and interpreted in the context of article 27(2). A State Party would not be cooperating fully with the Court if, when faced

with a request for the arrest and surrender of its Head of State, it refused to comply with this request, relying on Head of State immunity. The Pre-Trial Chamber's finding in this regard was therefore correct in law.

(ii) Article 27(2) of the Statute and its 'horizontal effect'

127. Jordan argues that, if at all, article 27(2) is relevant only in respect of the relationship between the Court and States Parties *vis-à-vis* their own Heads of State. According to this argument, article 27(2) has no impact on the continuing existence of Head of State immunity in the horizontal relationship between States Parties. The Appeals Chamber is unpersuaded by this argument. States Parties to the Rome Statute, have, by virtue of ratifying the Statute, accepted that Head of State immunity cannot prevent the Court from exercising jurisdiction—which is in line with customary international law. There is no reason why article 27(2) should be interpreted in a way that would allow a State Party to invoke Head of State immunity in the horizontal relationship if the Court were to ask for the arrest and surrender of the Head of State by making a request to that effect to another State Party. The law does not readily condone to be done through the back door something it forbids to be done through the front door. It must be noted that, in such situations, the requested State Party is not proceeding to arrest the Head of State in order to prosecute him of her before the courts of the requested State Party: it is only lending assistance to the Court in its exercise of proper jurisdiction.

128. The Appeals Chamber recognises the relevance of article 98 of the Statute in this context and the apparent tension with article 27(2). In this regard, it is recalled that Jordan, the African Union and the League of Arab States argue that article 98 preserves the immunity of officials of both States Parties and States not parties to the Statute from foreign criminal jurisdiction, whether under customary international law or conventional international law, and that the Court must obtain a waiver of such immunity before making a request for arrest and surrender.

129. The Appeals Chamber recalls that, pursuant to article 98(1) of the Statute, the Court shall not make a request for surrender or assistance to a State Party which would require the State Party to act inconsistently with its obligations under international law with respect to the State or diplomatic immunity of a person or property of a 'third State'. In other words, the Court may not, without first obtaining a waiver of immunity, request a State Party to arrest and surrender the Head of State of another State if that would require the requested State Party to act inconsistently with its obligations under international law.

130. It must be underlined, however, that article 98(1) of the Statute does not itself stipulate, recognise or preserve any immunities. It is a *procedural* rule that determines how the Court is to proceed where any immunity exists such that it could stand in the way of a request for cooperation. Accordingly, the existence of immunities must be

established on the basis of the Court's sources of law, pursuant to article 21(1) of the Statute. As noted above, article 27(2) of the Statute prevents any reliance on Head of State immunity both vertically in the State Parties' relationship with the Court and horizontally in the relationship between States Parties when cooperation is sought by the Court. As a result, in the absence of Head of State immunity, article 98(1) of the Statute is not in its own right a fountain of immunity. In those circumstances, no waiver is required as there is no immunity to be waived.

131. The above reading does not deprive article 98(1) of meaning. Article 98(1) of the Statute is indeed, as stated by Jordan, a 'conflict-avoidance rule', ensuring that States Parties are not placed in a situation where their cooperation obligations require them to breach an obligation owed to a third State. Article 98(1) remains an important procedural safeguard as it requires the Court to consider whether a requested State owes an obligation to a 'third State' before proceeding with a request for arrest and surrender (or any other request for cooperation). Nevertheless, article 98(1) provides no basis for the presumption that immunity exists; it merely imposes a procedural requirement for the Court to consider whether any international law obligation exists and applies with regard to the requested State in a particular situation. In this case, the Pre-Trial Chamber correctly found that no such obligation applied.

132. In sum, the Appeals Chamber finds that, by ratifying or acceding to the Statute, States Parties have consented to the inapplicability of Head of State immunity for the purpose of proceedings before the Court. As a result, both in the State Parties' vertical relationship with the Court and in the horizontal relationship between States Parties there is no Head of State immunity if the Court is asking for the arrest and surrender of a person. Therefore, the Pre-Trial Chamber correctly found that a State Party cannot refuse to arrest and surrender the Head of State of another State Party on the ground of Head of State immunity.

(c) Resolution 1593 and the applicability of article 27(2) of the Statute to Sudan

133. The Appeals Chamber will now turn to the next question, namely the effect of Resolution 1593 on the issue of whether Sudan can invoke Head of State immunity in relation to warrants of arrest issued by the Court for alleged crimes arising from the situation in Darfur, Sudan. In this regard, the Pre-Trial Chamber found that, as a result of Resolution 1593 triggering the jurisdiction of the Court under article 13(b) of the Statute, 'the legal framework of the Statute applies, in its entirety, with respect to the situation referred', and that 'article 27(2) of the Statute applies equally with respect to Sudan, rendering inapplicable any immunity on the ground of official capacity belonging to Sudan that would otherwise exist under international law'. Accordingly, in the Pre-

Trial Chamber's view, Sudan cannot invoke Head of State immunity *vis-à-vis* the Court, or *vis-à-vis* States Parties that are executing requests by the Court for Mr. Al-Bashir's arrest and surrender.

134. On appeal, Jordan argues that Sudan cannot be regarded to be a State Party of the Statute, even after the referral, and that the referral only affects the vertical relationship between Sudan and the Court, and does not remove immunity *vis-à-vis* other States. The Appeals Chamber finds these arguments unpersuasive, for the following reasons.

135. As mentioned above, in accordance with article 13(b) of the Statute, the exercise of the Court's jurisdiction can be triggered by a referral by the UN Security Council, acting under Chapter VII of the UN Charter. Article 13(b) puts the ICC at the disposal of the UN Security Council as a tool to maintain or restore international peace and security, thus obviating the need for the UN Security Council to create new *ad hoc* tribunals for this purpose. This is what occurred in relation to the situation in Darfur, Sudan, which was referred to the Prosecutor of the Court by virtue of Resolution 1593. The *chapeau* of article 13 stipulates that, regardless of how the Court's jurisdiction is triggered, it must be exercised 'in accordance with [the] Statute'. This means that, also in case of a referral by the UN Security Council, the Court is bound by the provisions of the Statute. This includes the cooperation regime, which is regulated by Part 9 of the Statute.

136. The Appeals Chamber notes that, leaving aside any cooperation obligations that States may have as a result of resolutions of the UN Security Council, the cooperation regime, as set out in Part 9 of the Statute, makes a distinction between the obligations of States Parties to the Rome Statute on one hand, and cooperation by States not parties to the Statute on the other hand. As concerns the former, article 86 of the Statute stipulates the general obligation of States Parties to cooperate fully with the Court; the more specific obligations are set out in the subsequent articles. Cooperation of States not parties to the Statute is addressed in article 87(5), which provides, in its sub-paragraph (a), that the Court may 'invite any State not party to [the] Statute to provide assistance under [Part 9 of the Statute] on the basis of an ad hoc arrangement, an agreement with such State or any other appropriate basis'. Sub-paragraph (b) provides for the possibility of bringing cases of non-compliance under certain conditions before the Assembly of States Parties or the UN Security Council.

137. While the UN Security Council may obligate States not parties to the Statute to cooperate with the Court, it is of note that the Statute does not provide for a third regime of cooperation specific to UN Security Council referrals. Thus, given that the Court must exercise its jurisdiction 'in accordance with [the] Statute', cooperation by a State following a referral by the UN Security Council must either follow the rules provided for States Parties (articles 86 *et seq.* of the Statute) or the more limited regime for States not parties to the Statute (article 87(5) of

the Statute). That is to say, in the absence of a comprehensive regime of cooperation spelt out in a Security Council resolution, with the clear intention of replacing the two cooperation regimes provided for in the Rome Statute, cooperation must be governed by either of the two regimes provided for under the Rome Statute. The question that then arises is under which of the two regimes cooperation by Sudan in respect of the situation in Darfur falls, given that Resolution 1593 does not provide any comprehensive regime of cooperation that would guide the Darfur referral.

138. On its face, it would appear that the answer is straightforward: Sudan is not party to the Statute and any cooperation would therefore seem to fall under article 87(5) of the Statute. This would mean that it is open to Sudan to enter into *ad hoc* arrangements or agreements with the Court regarding cooperation, but that it is not required to do so, and that, in the absence of such an arrangement or agreement, there is simply no obligation for Sudan to cooperate with the Court. In the view of the Appeals Chamber, however, such an approach would be overly simplistic and disregard Sudan's legally binding obligations under Resolution 1593.

139. In this regard, it is important to stress that Resolution 1593 is a specific jurisdictional trigger contemplated by article 13(b) of the Rome Statute. * * * As such, Resolution 1593 is a decision of the UN Security Council which has a binding force upon all UN Members States according to the applicable provisions of the UN Charter.

140. Resolution 1593 stipulates that 'the Government of Sudan [. . .] shall cooperate fully with and provide any necessary assistance to the Court and the Prosecutor [. . .]'. The formulation of the resolution suggests that the obligation imposed on Sudan is stronger than the one addressed to States not parties to the Statute, which are 'urge[d]' to cooperate fully. Under article 25 of the UN Charter, Sudan—a Member State of the United Nations—is obliged to accept and carry out decisions of the UN Security Council. Resolution 1593 therefore creates an obligation to 'fully cooperate' that is legally binding on Sudan. It is of significance for the question at hand that the language used with respect to Sudan's obligation to cooperate reflects that of article 86 of the Statute, which provides that 'States Parties shall, in accordance with the provisions of this Statute, cooperate fully with the Court'.

141. In the view of the Appeals Chamber, the fact that Sudan is obliged to fully cooperate with the Court, as per Resolution 1593, means that the cooperation regime for States Parties to the Rome Statute is applicable to Sudan's cooperation with the Court, and not article 87(5) of the Statute. This is because the latter regime is clearly inappropriate for a State that actually has a legally binding duty to cooperate with the Court. Therefore, exercise of jurisdiction by the Court 'in accordance with [the] Statute' means, in relation to cooperation by Sudan, cooperation on the basis of the regime established for States Parties to the Statute.

142. In this regard, the Appeals Chamber notes Jordan's argument that '[i]f the Statute applied in its entirety simply by virtue of a referral under article 13(b), paragraph 2 of resolution 1593 (2005) would not have been needed'. This argument is unpersuasive. Had the UN Security Council not included an obligation on Sudan to cooperate fully with the Court, the cooperation regime under article 87(5) of the Statute would have been applicable, while the effect of paragraph 2 of Resolution 1593 is to bring Sudan into the cooperation regime applicable to States Parties. The Appeals Chamber underlines that this does not make Sudan a State Party to the Rome Statute, with all the attendant obligations and powers. It simply means that the applicable cooperation regime is that for States Parties, as the one for States not parties to the Rome Statute is clearly inappropriate and a 'third regime' does not exist.

143. As noted above, the cooperation regime for States Parties—including article 98(1) of the Statute—must be understood and interpreted in light of article 27(2) of the Statute. A State Party cannot invoke Head of State immunity if another State Party proceeds to arrest and surrender the former State's Head of State on the basis of a request for cooperation by the Court. There is no reason to assume that article 27(2) would not be applicable to cooperation by Sudan. In the view of the Appeals Chamber, 'full cooperation' in accordance with the Statute encompasses all those obligations that States Parties owe to the Court and that are necessary for the effective exercise of jurisdiction by the Court. Article 27(2) applies in the sense that immunities that Sudan may otherwise enjoy under international law, as a matter of its relations with another State, cannot bar the Court's exercise of jurisdiction. There would simply be no 'full cooperation' if Sudan could invoke immunities *vis-à-vis* the Court that may otherwise exist under national or international law, as a matter of its relations with another State. If that were the case, the Court's ability to punish crimes that may have been committed in the Darfur situation would be limited from the start, and the Court's exercise of jurisdiction would not be effective.

144. Given that Sudan was therefore not in a position to rely on Head of State immunity of Mr. Al-Bashir, the Appeals Chamber considers that there was no need for the Court to obtain a waiver from Sudan before it could proceed with a request to Jordan for Mr. Al-Bashir's arrest and surrender, in accordance with article 98(1) of the Statute. As noted above, article 98(1) does not itself generate or preserve any immunity. As Sudan could not invoke Head of State immunity *vis-à-vis* a request by the Court for the arrest and surrender of Mr. Al-Bashir, there was nothing that could have been waived. The legal obligation under Resolution 1593, which imposed upon Sudan the same obligation of cooperation that the Rome Statute imposes upon States Parties, including with regard to the applicability of article 27(2) of the Statute, prevailed as *lex specialis* over any immunity that would otherwise exist between Sudan and Jordan.

145. For that reason, there were also no 'irreconcilable legal obligations' that Jordan was facing when being asked to arrest and surrender Mr. Al-Bashir to the Court. Nor was this a situation where customary or conventional international law existing in the relationship between Sudan and Jordan was modified by the Statute without Sudan becoming a party to the Statute—the modification was effected by Resolution 1593, which imposed legally binding obligations on Sudan. * * *

149. In sum, Resolution 1593 gives the Court power to exercise its jurisdiction over the situation in Darfur, Sudan, which it must exercise 'in accordance with [the] Statute'. This includes article 27(2), which provides that immunities are not a bar to the exercise of jurisdiction. As Sudan is obliged to 'cooperate fully' with the Court, the effect of article 27(2) arises also in the horizontal relationship—Sudan cannot invoke Head of State immunity if a State Party is requested to arrest and surrender Mr. Al-Bashir. Therefore, there was no Head of State immunity that Sudan could invoke in relation to Jordan, had the latter arrested Mr. Al-Bashir on the basis of an arrest warrant issued by the Court. Accordingly, there was also no immunity that Jordan would have been required to 'disregard' by executing the Court's arrest warrant. And there was no need for a waiver by Sudan of Head of State immunity. The Appeals Chamber therefore concludes that the Pre-Trial Chamber did not err when it found that, as a result of Resolution 1593, Sudan could not invoke Head of State immunity. * * *

NOTES & QUESTIONS

1. Al Bashir Overthrown

On April 11, 2019, Al Bashir was overthrown and arrested by the Sudanese Armed Forces following escalating protests prompted by the deteriorating Sudanese economy. In July 2019, the Transitional Military Council and a group of protesters represented by the Forces of Freedom and Change agreed to a power-sharing agreement that would lead to a transition to civilian leadership through elections to be held in 2022. Despite calls to have Al Bashir handed over to the ICC, the Sudanese military has kept him in detention. On June 16, 2019, the Public Prosecutor announced that Al Bashir would be prosecuted for corruption and other related financial crimes. There is also some indication that he may be prosecuted domestically for the killing of protesters during the events that led up to his overthrow. There is no suggestion so far that the local prosecution will include the crimes that are the subject of the ICC arrest warrants.

The ICC Prosecutor has publicly called for the Sudanese authorities to hand Al Bashir and four other suspects wanted for atrocities in Darfur over to the ICC. She stated, "Sudan remains under a legal obligation to transfer these suspects to the ICC to stand trial unless it can demonstrate to the judges of the ICC that it is willing and able to genuinely prosecute them for the same cases." Should the Sudanese government hand Al Bashir over to the ICC? What arguments would you make on behalf of the Sudanese government not to hand him over? What arguments would you make on behalf of the ICC Prosecutor that he should be handed over to the Court? If you were a lawyer within the government of Sudan, how would you convince your "client" to transfer him to the Court?

2. Customary International Law v. Security Council Referral

The majority opinion relies upon customary international law to find that Al Bashir enjoys no immunity *vis-à-vis* the Court or *vis-à-vis* States Parties. Could the Court have relied upon the Security Council referral resolution instead? How would that argument go? Which argument is stronger from a legal perspective? How does the Court conceptualize the basis for its jurisdiction in this opinion?

3. Other Relevant Treaties

Jordan also argued that the Pre-Trial Chamber erred when it found that Article 98(2) of the Statute did not apply to the League of Arab States' 1953 Convention on Privileges and Immunities. Early in the litigation, it was not clear whether Sudan had actually ratified the treaty. That was confirmed by the time the Appeals Chamber ruled. Jordan argued that the Pre-Trial Chamber had disregarded Article 11 of the 1953 Convention, which—in its estimation—"squarely addresses the situation of the representatives of a Member State 'journeying' to and from conferences convened by the Arab League, and their immunity from person arrest or detention in 'the place of the meeting.'" Jordan also noted that article 14 of the 1953 Convention "expressly addresses the circumstances under which the Member State might consent to the arrest or surrender of its representative." Although the Appeals Chamber found that while the treaty provisions were relevant to Article 98(1) of the Statute, the effect of Sudan's duty under Resolution 1593 to cooperate fully with the Court is that Sudan could not invoke such immunities if the Court seeks the arrest of a person otherwise entitled to such immunity.

In addition, the Court noted:

> 161. * * * that both Jordan and Sudan are parties to the Convention against Genocide. Article I of the Convention against Genocide provides that the contracting parties 'undertake to prevent and punish' the crime of genocide. The Appeals Chamber notes that Mr. Al-Bashir is alleged to be responsible for the crime of genocide. Thus, Jordan was under an obligation to cooperate in the arrest and surrender of Mr. Al-Bashir at the request of the Court not only as a State Party to the Rome Statute, but also by virtue of its being party to the Convention against Genocide.

Are these arguments compelling? Would the members of the League of Arab States not be entitled to assume that the 1953 Convention would bar members from arresting each other's officials? Has that treaty been effectively abrogated by the Court? Some African states have made similar arguments concerning their obligations under the treaty creating the African Union which, they claim, takes precedence over the Rome Statute. *See* Note 8 below for more on efforts to create an African regional criminal regime.

4. Domestic Jurisprudence on Efforts to Arrest Al Bashir

Parallel to the efforts before the ICC to put pressure on member states to arrest Al Bashir and hand him over to the Court, justice advocates in Kenya and South Africa went to court and successfully argued that their respective governments were obligated to effectuate the ICC's arrest warrants against Al Bashir. In August 2010, Al Bashir visited Kenya to attend the formal ceremony to adopt the new Kenyan Constitution. Al Bashir was allowed by the Kenyan government to freely enter the country, attend the ceremony, and then depart. In response to the failure to arrest Al Bashir, the Kenya chapter of the International Commission of Jurists went to court and, a year later, secured a High Court judgment that the government was obligated under the Rome Statute to arrest Al Bashir if he were again to be present on Kenyan territory. Al Bashir never returned to Kenya after that judgment. *See Kenya Section of the International Commission of Jurists v. Attorney General*, [2011] Misc. Criminal Application 685 of 2010 (Nov. 28, 2011).

In June 2015, Al Bashir attended a summit of the African Union in South Africa. The South African Litigation Centre brought an urgent action before the High Court to force the government to arrest Al Bashir pursuant to the ICC arrest warrant. The High Court issued an interim order barring Al Bashir from leaving the country until it addressed the merits of the claim. Notwithstanding the High Court order, Al Bashir was permitted to surreptitiously leave South Africa from a South African military base. The South African High Court later ruled that the government had been obligated to detain Al Bashir. *See South African Litigation Centre v. Minister of Justice and Constitutional Development & Others*, 2015 (5) SA 1 (GP) (June 24, 2015).

5. Referral to the Assembly of State Parties and the U.N. Security Council

In a part of the opinion not reproduced above, the Appeals Chamber reversed the decision of the Pre-Trial Chamber holding that the failure of Jordan to cooperate with the Court should be referred to the Assembly of State Parties and the U.N. Security Council for the determination of what, if any, enforcement mechanism should be utilized against Jordan. As noted in the opinion above, Judges Luz del Carmen Ibáñez Carranza (Peru) and Solomy Balungi Bossa (Uganda) dissented on the finding that the Pre-Trial Chamber abused its discretion by referring Jordan to the Assembly of State Parties and the Security Council. The dissenters argued that there were sufficient legal and factual bases for the Pre-Trial Chamber to make such referrals. The majority and dissent differed on how to interpret various communications that Jordan made to the Court in the lead up to Al Bashir's visit, with the Pre-Trial Chamber and dissent finding that the actions did not amount to statutory "consultations" to clarify the legal status of Al Bashir's immunities as required by the Rome Statute. By contrast, the majority found that, while Jordan could have acted more clearly and decisively, the actions they did undertake were committed in good faith and thus do not warrant a referral. What value is there in finding that Jordan violated its obligation to cooperate with the Court without seeking any enforcement action?

6. Personal v. Functional Immunities

Historically, international law makes a distinction between immunity *ratione personae* (personal immunity) and immunity *ratione materiae* (functional immunity). These doctrines apply in both civil and criminal proceedings, although they operate somewhat differently in these two contexts. While the doctrine governing immunities *ratione personae* is relatively stable, the scope of common law immunities *ratione materiae* is still being litigated.

Personal or status-based immunities are strong: they prohibit the exercise of jurisdiction not only over actions taken in an official capacity, but also over private acts committed while the individual is in office. (Certain forms of special mission immunity that apply in the host state, however, do not apply to state officials abroad on a private visit). While the individual remains in office, personal immunities also apply to actions taken prior to the assumption of office. This form of immunity is generally imparted for the benefit of the state; as such, it dissipates once the head of state or diplomat leaves office and can be waived by the state.

Status-based immunities were historically considered necessary to ensure the smooth conduct of international relations; they also reflect considerations of comity and the notion of "symbolic sovereignty" since such high-ranking officials are deemed to personify the state. Foreign officials who do not qualify for immunity *ratione personae* may be entitled to functional immunity for official acts taken on behalf of the state. This immunity is conduct-based rather than status-based. Because the immunity attaches to the official act, rather than to the actor in question, it does not apply to acts taken before an official assumed office and may continue to offer protection from prosecution for such officials after they step down for conduct committed while in office. Former heads of state and diplomats may thus enjoy some degree of foreign official immunity for official acts undertaken while they were in office. In these ways, immunity *ratione materiae* is both broader and narrower than doctrines of immunity *ratione personae*.

Many national courts confronted with the potential criminal or civil liability of sitting heads of state will bar the suit from going forward. For example, in January 2004, an English District Judge rejected an application for the arrest and extradition of President Robert Mugabe of Zimbabwe to stand trial for torture on grounds of immunity. A U.S. district court had earlier reached a similar conclusion in a civil suit brought by victims of the Mugabe regime (*Tachiona v. Mugabe*, 169 F.Supp.2d 259 (S.D.N.Y. 2001)). Likewise, a French appeals court determined that the lower court could not prosecute Colonel Muammar Gaddafi of Libya for the 1989 bombing of a French airliner over Niger; a Spanish court reached a similar result with respect to Fidel Castro in 1998 and Paul Kagame of Rwanda in 2008.

A notable exception to the seemingly absolute nature of head-of-state immunity before domestic courts is apparent in the prosecution of General Manuel Antonio Noriega who was forcibly brought into the United States to stand trial for narcotics-related charges. *United States v. Noriega*, 117 F.3d 1206 (11th Cir. 1997). The United States, however, never recognized Noriega as the legitimate President of Panama since he had assumed power after the Panamanian Parliament deposed the then-President, Eric Arturo Delvalle, and subsequent elections were disputed. In particular, the U.S. court ruled that by pursuing Noriega's capture and prosecution, the U.S. Executive Branch "manifested its clear sentiment that Noriega should be denied head-of-state immunity." In addition, the court noted that Panama did not seek immunity for Noriega and the charged acts were committed for his personal enrichment. In 2010, and after Noriega had served more than 20 years in prison, the United States extradited him to France to stand trial for money laundering. Following his conviction there, he was again extradited to Panama to serve time for prior convictions for murder and corruption.

Even functional immunities may be eroding. The cyber-spying indictments issued against top Chinese officials suggest a willingness to disregard functional foreign official immunities in the United States.

7. Heads of State in the Dock

Technically, the first head of state to face an international tribunal was Karl Dönitz, whom Hitler named as his successor in his last will and testament during the final days of the war. Dönitz served as head of state of Germany for a mere 23 days. The Nuremberg Tribunal convicted him of crimes against the peace and humanity in his capacity as Germany's chief naval officer. He served ten years in prison and died in 1980 in Germany.

Since the *Pinochet* case, a number of current and former heads of state have been brought before international tribunals to stand trial for violations of international criminal law. Slobodan Milošević was indicted by the ICTY on May 24, 1999, while he was the President of Yugoslavia, for ethnic cleansing against Albanians in the Yugoslav province of Kosovo. Milošević was arrested in April 2001, and transferred to The Hague for trial in June 2001. Milošević died on March 14, 2006, before his trial was completed. For a brief discussion of head of state immunity in connection with the Milošević prosecution, *see Prosecutor v. Milošević,* Case No. IT–02–54, Decision on Preliminary Motions (Nov. 8, 2001). Prime Minister Jean Kambanda pled guilty to genocide before the ICTR.

Charles Taylor, the former President of Liberia, was tried and convicted by the Special Court for Sierra Leone (sitting in The Hague) for war crimes, crimes against humanity, and other serious violations of international humanitarian law. Both Taylor and the Prosecutor appealed his conviction and sentence, but the Judgment and 50-year sentence were affirmed. Taylor was indicted in March 2003, and an arrest warrant was issued against him in June 2003, while he was still head of state of Liberia. Before he stepped down in August 2003, Taylor moved to have the Indictment dismissed on the grounds that he enjoyed immunity for all of the acts he committed while he was sitting head of state. The Appeals Chamber of the Special Court upheld the Indictment, ruling that Taylor did not enjoy immunity even though the acts for which he was being prosecuted were committed while he was a sitting head of state. The Appeals Chamber reached this decision based upon the Special Court's Statute, which states that the official position of an accused person, including Head of State, shall not relieve that person of criminal responsibility, and the fact that the Special Court was an international tribunal and thus any head of state or other immunity that might apply before a domestic court was not applicable. *Prosecutor v. Charles Ghankay Taylor*, Case No. SCSL–2003–01–I, Decision on Immunity from Jurisdiction (May 31, 2004). The current President and Deputy President of Kenya, Uhuru Kenyatta and William Ruto respectively, were being tried before the ICC for acts they allegedly committed prior to their election. (For more on the Kenya cases see Chapter 5 on the ICC.)

Closer to the domestic front, Hissène Habré, the former dictator of Chad, stood trial in Senegal for abuses committed during his regime. A Senegalese court first held that Habré was immune from prosecution, citing to the ICJ's *Yerodia* opinion (discussed below). In response to criticism of this opinion, Senegal referred the matter to the African Union, which recommended that Habré stand trial in Senegal. In February 2013, Senegal—with assistance from the African Union—created the Extraordinary African Chambers within its court system, and in July charged Habré with crimes against humanity, torture, and war crimes. He is serving a life sentence. Both the *Habré* and *Yerodia* cases are discussed further in Chapter 3 on Domestic Jurisdiction.

8. The African Union and Immunity for Government Officials

On June 27, 2014, the African Union voted in favor of a protocol ("the Malabo Protocol") to the statute of the yet to be launched African Court of Justice and Human Rights that would provide broad immunity to senior government officials. The protocol would add an Article 46A*bis* that reads:

> No charges shall be commenced or continued before the Court against any serving African Union Head of State or Government, or anybody acting or entitled to act in such capacity, or other senior state officials based on their functions, during their tenure of office.

The African Court of Justice and Human and Rights will merge the regional African human rights court—the African Court on Human and People's Right—with the nascent Court of Justice of the African Union. In addition, a chamber of the newly formed court would be given penal jurisdiction over violations of international criminal law. The expansion of jurisdiction to include international crimes was in part a reaction to universal jurisdiction cases in Europe involving African defendants and the ICC charges brought against Sudanese President Al Bashir and President Kenyatta and Deputy President Ruto of Kenya. Elements within the African Union have called on member states not to cooperate with the ICC with respect to the Al Bashir case.

Once created, the chamber would be the first regional criminal court and, given the above amendment, would be the first international criminal tribunal to expressly provide immunity to senior government officials. Every other international criminal tribunal to date has express language making clear that the official status of an accused, including that of Head of State or Head of Government, does not affect the criminal responsibility of any individual. Why do you think the African Union is moving in this direction? Do you think the creation of a regional international criminal tribunal will increase or decrease the prospects for international criminal justice?

While fifteen African states have signed the Malabo Protocol, none has ratified it. Given the discussion of the League of Arab States treaty in the Al Bashir opinion above, how would you predict the ICC would address a claimed conflict between the Malabo Protocol (assuming it comes into effect) and the ICC?

9. Yerodia

As discussed in connection with the principle of Universal Jurisdiction in Chapter 2, the Democratic Republic of the Congo (DRC) brought a case against Belgium before the International Court of Justice (ICJ) challenging a Belgian arrest warrant that had been issued against Mr. Abdulaye Yerodia Ndombasi of the DRC. The warrant was issued in connection with a suit brought against Mr. Yerodia under Belgium's universal jurisdiction statute for war crimes and crimes against humanity. At the time the warrant was issued, Mr. Yerodia was the Foreign Minister of the DRC, although he was in a non-ministerial post at the time of the acts alleged in the Indictment. The ICJ held, by a vote of 15 to 1, that under customary international law, sitting foreign ministers enjoy full immunity from criminal jurisdiction of another state, and the very issuance and circulation of the arrest warrant against an incumbent breached Yerodia's immunity.

The Court did note in *dicta* that such immunity did not necessarily equate with impunity, as there were three ways that a Foreign Minister could be held accountable for violations of international criminal law while still in office. First, the home state of the Foreign Minister could prosecute him. Second, the state could waive the immunity, thus allowing another state to prosecute him. Third, the immunity was not valid against a prosecution undertaken by an international tribunal. *See Case Concerning the Arrest Warrant of 11 April 2000 (Congo v. Belg.)*, 2002 I.C.J. Reports 3 (Feb. 14). Why would such immunity apply to a prosecution by another state, but not to a prosecution before an international tribunal? What impact does such immunity have on the deterrent effect of international criminal law? The *Yerodia* case only concerned the immunity of a Foreign Minister, but would likely apply *a fortiori* to heads of state or government—the so-called *troika* of plenipotentiaries capable of binding the state in treaty negotiations. Should the same degrees of immunity apply to other government ministers? A Minister of Education, for example? Note that Ministers of Defense are not generally considered to be part of the *troika*.

10. Diplomatic Immunity

Head of state immunity is a more specialized form of both sovereign immunity and diplomatic immunity. Diplomats have long been entitled to immunity from legal process in a foreign country while they hold diplomatic office, and after they leave office for official acts performed while in office. The two major treaties governing diplomatic immunity are the Vienna Convention on Diplomatic Relations of 1961, 500 U.N.T.S. 95, and the Vienna Convention on Consular Relations of 1963, 596 U.N.T.S. 261. The

1969 U.N. Convention on Special Missions, 1400 U.N.T.S. 231, may also be applicable. These treaties provide a hierarchy of protection from criminal and civil suit in a foreign country, reserving the highest level of protection to diplomats and their immediate families, and lesser protections to administrative and technical staff. Since the immunity is justified as a concession to encourage relations among states, a state may waive the immunity of its diplomat. For more on immunity defenses generally, *see* Micæla Frulli, *The ICJ Judgement on the Belgium v. Congo Case (14 February 2002): A Cautious Stand on Immunity from Prosecution for International Crimes*, 3 GERMAN L. J. 1 (2002). For a good discussion of immunities before international tribunals, *see* Dapo Akande, *International Law Immunities and the International Criminal Court,* 98 AM. J. INT'L L. 407 (2004). *See also* Michael B. McDonough, *Privileged Outlaws: Diplomats, Crime and Immunity*, 20 SUFFOLK TRANSNAT'L L. REV. 475 (1997); and Rosalyn Higgins, *The Abuse of Diplomatic Privileges and Immunities: Recent United Kingdom Experience,* 79 AM. J. INT'L L. 641 (1985).

11. State Immunity

While international criminal law focuses on immunities that may attach to persons, the entity of the state is also entitled to immunity from legal process in certain situations. In a case brought before the International Court of Justice, Germany asserted sovereign immunity as a defense against judgments entered against it in Italian and Greek courts arising from atrocities committed by the Nazi government during World War II. The Italian courts had held that there was a human rights exception to the traditional doctrine of sovereign immunity. Twelve of the fifteen judges found in favor of Germany, holding that sovereign immunity from civil suits rested firmly on the concept of the sovereign equality of states, and that military operations such as those at issue in the Italian and Greek cases are at the core of this sovereign character, and thus should be punished by the international system and not by national courts through tort liability. *Jurisdictional Immunities of the State (Germany v. Italy: Greece Intervening)*, Judgment, 2012 I.C.J. Reports 99 (Feb. 3).

In the United States, civil claims against states are governed by the Foreign Sovereign Immunities Act, 28 U.S.C. §§ 1330 et seq. The FSIA does not address claims against individuals, however, which are adjudicated under common law principles of immunity. *Samantar v. Yousef*, 560 U.S. 305 (2010). *Samantar* involved human rights claims under the Alien Tort Statute against an individual who held the posts of Vice President, Minister of Defense, and Prime Minister of Somalia in the 1980s. He was ultimately found liable. The family of intrepid war corresdpondent Marie Colvin won a $300 million judgment against the state of Syria in 2019 under the "state sponsor of terrorism" exception to sovereign immunity. *Colvin v. Syrian Arab Republic*, 363 F. Supp. 3d 141 (2019). Colvin was assassinated in Syria in 2012.

12. Immunities Under International and Domestic Law

The opinion and materials above suggest that immunities operate differently before international and domestic courts. Can you map the way in which the various forms of immunity apply in domestic and international proceedings? Why might the systems be dissimilar? For a discussion of cases in domestic courts, *see* International Law Commission, *Immunity of State Officials from Foreign Criminal Jurisdiction: Memorandum Prepared by the Secretariat*, U.N. Doc. A/CN.4/596 (March 31, 2008). Given what you know about hybrid tribunals, such as the Special Court for Sierra Leone, what elements render such a court sufficiently international to trigger the rule applicable to international courts? Charles Taylor, for example, unsuccessfully argued that the SCSL was a domestic court and so should respect his head-of-state immunity. *Prosecutor v. Taylor*, Case No. SCSL–2003–01–I, Decision on Immunity from Jurisdiction (May 31, 2004). If the prohibitions against international crimes constitute *jus cogens* norms, would they not trump immunities in any normative hierarchy? For further reading, *see* R. Van Alebeek, THE IMMUNITY OF STATES AND THEIR OFFICIALS IN INTERNATIONAL CRIMINAL LAW AND INTERNATIONAL HUMAN RIGHTS LAW (2008).

VIII. AMNESTY

One of the most common responses of governments to abuses by their own officials has been the granting of an amnesty, or immunity from legal accountability. General Pinochet's government, for example, enacted an amnesty in 1978 for any acts committed by government agents. Amnesties usually protect an individual from both criminal and civil liability. Human rights organizations generally oppose the use of amnesties in any circumstances, arguing that they further impunity and undercut domestic and international efforts to deter future gross violations of human rights. Many domestic courts that have reviewed their own amnesties have upheld their legality. Exceptions to this general trend are in Chile, whose courts ultimately rejected General Pinochet's defense of amnesty in proceedings brought against him after he was returned from the United Kingdom in 2000, and El Salvador, which invalidated its longstanding amnesty in 2016. All international tribunals that have evaluated the legality of amnesties have found them to violate fundamental principles of justice, including the right of victims to have their claims adjudicated by a court of law.

The Special Court for Sierra Leone was presented with the question of whether to recognize an amnesty. (See the Appendix for a map of Sierra Leone.) Beginning in 1991 when the Revolutionary United Front (RUF) invaded Sierra Leone from Liberia, an armed conflict existed in Sierra Leone. The conflict was a particularly brutal one, and the RUF became known for its practice of amputating the hands, arms, legs, and other body parts of civilians, including young children. In 1999, a peace agreement, the "Lomé Agreement," was reached among the parties to the conflict under the auspices of the United Nations. Part of that agreement included an amnesty that would protect members of the RUF from accountability for the atrocities they had committed against the civilian population. That peace agreement did not hold, though the amnesty provision was still treated as valid. For more background on the Sierra Leone conflict and the creation of the Special Court, *see* the discussion in Chapter 4. Two of the defendants before the Special Court, Morris Kallon and Brima Bazzy Kamara, raised as a defense the amnesty contained within the Lomé Peace Agreement. Two other interested defendants, Augustine Gbao and Moinina Fofana, intervened in the case.

Prosecutor v. Kallon, Case No. SCSL–2004–15–R72(E), Decision on Challenge to Jurisdiction: Lomé Accord Amnesty (Mar. 13, 2004)

1. In summary, the grounds of the two applications, in so far as they are relevant to this Decision, are that the Government of Sierra Leone is bound to observe the amnesty granted under Article IX of the Peace Agreement between the Government of Sierra Leone and the Revolutionary United Front of Sierra Leone ("Lomé Agreement"); the Special Court should not assert jurisdiction over crimes committed prior to July 1999 when an amnesty was granted by virtue of the Lomé Agreement and it would be an abuse of process to allow the prosecution of any of the alleged crimes pre-dating the Lomé Agreement.

2. The Prosecution puts its opposition to the Preliminary Motions in several ways. The Prosecution argues that the Special Court is bound by Article 10 of its Statute and that the Lomé Agreement, being an agreement between two national bodies, is limited in effect to domestic law and was, in any event, not intended to cover crimes mentioned in Articles 2 to 4 of the Statute of the Special Court ("Statute"). Furthermore, it is contended that given the gravity of the crimes charged, discretion should not be exercised to grant a stay of proceedings on the basis that there has been an abuse of process of the Court.

Historical Background

3. It is commonly said, though no such factual finding is made and can be made at this stage, that on 23 March 1991 forces of the Revolutionary United Front (RUF) entered Sierra Leone from Liberia and launched a rebellion to overthrow the one-party rule of the All People's Congress (APC). That was believed to be the beginning of the armed conflict in Sierra Leone which lasted until 7 July 1999 when the parties to the conflict signed the Lomé Agreement. There was an earlier peace agreement between the Government of Sierra Leone and RUF signed in Abidjan on 30 November 1996 ("Abidjan Peace Agreement") but that collapsed soon after it was signed.

4. On 7 July 1999, the Lomé Agreement was signed between the Government of Sierra Leone and the RUF, the parties to the Agreement having met in Lomé, Togo from 25 May 1999 to 7 July 1999 under the auspices of the Chairman of the [Economic Community Of West African States (ECOWAS)] at the time, President Gnassingbe Eyadema.

5. Among other things, the parties to the Lomé Agreement stated that they were moved "by the imperative need to meet the desire of the people of Sierra Leone for a definitive settlement of the fratricidal war in their country and for genuine national unity and reconciliation."

6. Article 34 of the Lomé Agreement shows that the Government of the Togolese Republic, the United Nations, the [Organization of African Unity (OAU)], ECOWAS and the Commonwealth of Nations stood as moral guarantors of the implementation of the Lomé Agreement with integrity and in good faith by both parties.

Article 9 of the Lomé Agreement

7. At the center of these proceedings is Article 9 of the Lomé Agreement which provides as follows:

> Article IX Pardon and Amnesty
>
> 1. In order to bring lasting peace to Sierra Leone, the Government of Sierra Leone shall take appropriate legal steps to grant Corporal Foday Sankoh absolute and free pardon.
>
> 2. After the signing of the present Agreement, the Government of Sierra Leone shall also grant absolute and free pardon and reprieve to all combatants and collaborators in respect of anything done by them in pursuit of their objectives, up to the time of the signing of the present Agreement.
>
> 3. To consolidate the peace and promote the cause of national reconciliation, the Government of Sierra Leone shall ensure that no official or judicial action is taken against any member of the RUF/SL, ex-AFRC, ex-SLA or CDF [various militia groups] in respect of anything done by them in pursuit of their objectives as members of those organizations since March 1991, up to the signing of the present Agreement. In addition, legislative and other measures necessary to guarantee immunity to former combatants, exiles and other persons, currently outside the country for reasons related to the armed conflict shall be adopted ensuring the full exercise of their civil and political rights, with a view to their reintegration within a framework of full legality.

8. By a letter dated 12 June 2000 written to the President of the Security Council by the President of Sierra Leone on behalf of the Government and people of Sierra Leone, the President of Sierra Leone requested the President of the Security Council to initiate a process whereby the United Nations would resolve on the setting up of a Special Court for Sierra Leone. * * *

Prosecutorial Choice of Sierra Leone

20. Whether to prosecute the perpetrators of rebellion for their act of rebellion and challenge to the constituted authority of the State as a matter of internal law is for the state authority to decide. There is no rule

against rebellion in international law. The State concerned may decide to prosecute the rebels. It may decide to pardon them, generally or partially, conditionally or unconditionally. It is where, and in this case because, the conduct of the participants in the armed conflict is alleged to amount to international crime that the question arises whether in such a situation a State has the same choice to dispense with the prosecution of the alleged offenders. Furthermore, if it claims to have such choice and exercises it to grant amnesty to alleged offenders, does this conclusively bar prosecution for the alleged commission of grave crimes against humanity in an international tribunal or, for that matter, by another state claiming universal jurisdiction to prosecute?

21. The preliminary Motions with which this ruling is concerned arose because the Government of Sierra Leone included in the Lomé Agreement Article IX which contained Pardon and Amnesty provisions in terms already stated above, whereby, among other things, it undertook to "grant absolute and free pardon and reprieve to all combatants and collaborators" and undertook also to "ensure that no official or judicial action is taken against any member of the RUF/SL, ex-AFRC, ex-SLA or CDF in respect of anything done by them in pursuit of their objectives as members of those organizations." The Motions argue, in effect, that the amnesty granted by the Lomé Agreement in Article IX amounts to an unconditional pardon and that, as such, it was a choice validly made by the Sierra Leone Government that conclusively precluded the prosecution of the accused Kallon and Kamara for any crime whatsoever allegedly committed before the date of the Lomé Agreement by this Court. * * *

The Status of the Lomé Agreement

36. In view of the submissions made and in order to put the issues in proper perspective, the starting point is to determine the character of the Lomé Agreement. The Defence argues that it is an international agreement having the character of a treaty. The Prosecution, the *amici curiae* agreeing, argue that it is an agreement within municipal law between two bodies within the state.

37. In regard to the nature of a negotiated settlement of an internal armed conflict it is easy to assume and to argue with some degree of plausibility, as Defence counsel for the defendants seem to have done, that the mere fact that in addition to the parties to the conflict, the document formalizing the settlement is signed by foreign heads of state or their representatives and representatives of international organizations, means the agreement of the parties is internationalized so as to create obligations in international law. * * *

40. Almost every conflict resolution will involve the parties to the conflict and the mediator or facilitator of the settlement, or persons or bodies under whose auspices the settlement took place but who are not at all parties to the conflict, are not contracting parties and who do not

claim any obligation from the contracting parties or incur any obligation from the settlement.

41. In this case, the parties to the conflict are the lawful authority of the State and the RUF which has no status of statehood and is to all intents and purposes a faction within the state. The non-contracting signatories of the Lomé Agreement were moral guarantors of the principle that, in the terms of Article XXXIV of the Agreement, "this peace agreement is implemented with integrity and in good faith by both parties." The moral guarantors assumed no legal obligation. It is recalled that the U.N. by its representative appended, presumably for avoidance of doubt, an understanding of the extent of the agreement to be implemented as not including certain international crimes.

42. An international agreement in the nature of a treaty must create rights and obligations regulated by international law so that a breach of its terms will be a breach determined under international law which will also provide principle means of enforcement. The Lomé Agreement created neither rights nor obligations capable of being regulated by international law. An Agreement such as the Lomé Agreement which brings to an end an internal armed conflict no doubt creates a factual situation of restoration of peace that the international community acting through the Security Council may take note of. That, however, will not convert it to an international agreement which creates an obligation enforceable in international, as distinguished from municipal, law. A breach of the terms of such a peace agreement resulting in resumption of internal armed conflict or creating a threat to peace in the determination of the Security Council may indicate a reversal of the factual situation of peace to be visited with possible legal consequences arising from the new situation of conflict created. Such consequences such as action by the Security Council pursuant to Chapter VII arise from the situation and not from the agreement, nor from the obligation imposed by it. Such action cannot be regarded as a remedy for the breach. A peace agreement which settles an internal armed conflict cannot be ascribed the same status as one which settles an international armed conflict which, essentially, must be between two or more warring States. The Lomé Agreement cannot be characterized as an international instrument. That it does not have that character does not, however, answer the further question whether, as far as grave crimes such as are stated in Article 2 to 4 of the Statute of the Court are concerned, it offers any promise that is permissible or enforceable in international law. * * *

Legal Consequences of Article 10 of the Statute

51. In these proceedings the validity of the constitutive instruments of the Special Court is not in issue. They are the documents that define the competence and jurisdiction of the Court and the provisions with which this Court is bound to comply. * * *

53. Article I(1) of the Statute of the Special Court spells out the temporal jurisdiction of the Court while Article 10 expressly provides:

An amnesty granted to any person falling within the jurisdiction of the Special Court in respect of crimes referred to in Articles 2 to 4 of the present Statute shall not be a bar to prosecution.

54. Counsel for Kallon submitted that notwithstanding Article 10, this Court should exercise discretion to stay the proceedings as being an abuse of process of the Court. The amnesty is thus not pleaded only as a legal bar to prosecution.

55. Counsel for Kallon put his submissions, summarized, thus: The claim by the Prosecution and Redress Trust [an NGO] that Article 10 closes the door on any consideration of the applicability of the Lomé Accord to proceedings before the Special Court should not be accepted. The Special Court of Sierra Leone is a "hybrid" court, established pursuant to an agreement between the U.N. and the Government of Sierra Leone. Thus, it could not have been established without the consent and agreement of the Government of Sierra Leone. If the Special Court were a truly international tribunal, established by Security Council Resolution (as in the case of the International Criminal Tribunals for Rwanda and the Former Yugoslavia), it is accepted that the actions of the Government of Sierra Leone and the amnesty would be of no relevance. This was confirmed by the Trial Chamber of the International Criminal Tribunal for the Former Yugoslavia (ICTY) in *Prosecutor v. Furundžija* in which it was held that a domestic amnesty law would not prevent prosecution for torture before the ICTY or indeed in any other foreign jurisdiction. *Furundžija* did not consider, and is silent on, the circumstances in which it could be an abuse of process to prosecute torture in a domestic court after an undertaking that no criminal prosecution would ensue. In *Furundžija* the Trial Chamber set out the jurisdictions in which an individual could be prosecuted for torture following an amnesty: (i) international tribunal, (ii) foreign State, or (iii) in their own State under a subsequent regime.

56. Counsel for Kallon went on to argue that in the Lomé Accord, the Government of Sierra Leone clearly undertook to "ensure that no official or judicial action is taken against any member of the RUF/SL." The Defence submitted that this would include acceding to an extradition request which would require "judicial action" and, moreover, that there can be no doubt that the establishment of a Special Court to prosecute alleged crimes committed in Sierra Leone since 30 November 1996 amounts to both "official" and "judicial" action. Thus, according to the Defence, in engaging in negotiations with the U.N. and then ultimately concluding an agreement with them for the establishment of the Special Court, the Government of Sierra Leone clearly reneged on its undertaking in the Lomé Accord. * * *

58. It was further argued that there was an inconsistent approach to amnesty in that the temporal jurisdiction of the Special Court, pursuant to Article 1(1) of the Statute commenced on 30 November 1996, selected to coincide with the conclusion of the Abidjan Peace Agreement,

whereas Article 14 of the Abidjan Agreement granted an amnesty to all members of the RUF from any official or judicial action being taken against them. It was, therefore, contended that it was both arbitrary and illogical of both the U.N. and Government of Sierra Leone to appear to honour the terms of one agreement and respect the amnesty granted, but not another. * * *

The Limits of Amnesty

66. Black's Law Dictionary defines "amnesty" in the following terms:

> A sovereign act of oblivion for past acts, granted by a government to all persons (or to certain persons) who have been guilty of crime or delict, generally political offences—treason, sedition, rebellion—and often conditioned upon their return to obedience and duty within a prescribed time.

It is also stated that:

> Amnesty is the abolition and forgetfulness of the offence; pardon is forgiveness. (*Knote v. U.S.* 95 U.S. 149, 152.) The first is usually addressed to crimes against the sovereignty of the nation, to political offences, the second condones infractions of the peace of the nation. (*Burdick v. United States*, 236 U.S. 79 (1915)).

67. The grant of amnesty or pardon is undoubtedly an exercise of sovereign power which, essentially, is closely linked, as far as crime is concerned, to the criminal jurisdiction of the State exercising such sovereign power. Where jurisdiction is universal, a State cannot deprive another State of its jurisdiction to prosecute the offender by the grant of amnesty. It is for this reason unrealistic to regard as universally effective the grant of amnesty by a State in regard to grave international crimes in which there exists universal jurisdiction. A State cannot bring into oblivion and forgetfulness a crime, such as a crime against international law, which other States are entitled to keep alive and remember. * * *

69. The question is whether the crimes within the competence of the Court are crimes susceptible to universal jurisdiction. The crimes mentioned in Articles 2–4 of the Statute are international crimes and crimes against humanity. Indeed, no suggestion to the contrary has been made by counsel. The crimes under Sierra Leonean law mentioned in Article 5 do not fall into the category of such crimes and are not mentioned in Article 10.

70. One consequence of the nature of grave international crimes against humanity is that States can, under international law, exercise universal jurisdiction over such crimes. In *Attorney General of the Government of Israel v. Eichmann* the Supreme Court of Israel declared:

> The abhorrent crimes defined in this Law are not crimes under Israeli law alone. These crimes which struck at the whole of

> mankind and shocked the conscience of nations are grave offences against the law of nations itself (*delicta juris gentium*). Therefore, so far from international law negating or limiting the jurisdiction of countries with respect to such crimes, international law is, in the absence of an International Court, in need of the judicial and legislative organs of every country to give effect to its criminal interdictions and to bring the criminals to trial. The jurisdiction to try crimes under international law is universal.

Also, in *Congo v. Belgium* it was held by the International Court of Justice that certain international tribunals have jurisdiction over crimes under international law. This viewpoint was similarly held by the ICTY in *Furundžija*.

71. After reviewing international practice in regard to the effectiveness or otherwise of amnesty granted by a State and the inconsistencies in state practice as regards the prohibition of amnesty for crimes against humanity, Cassese conceptualized the status of international practice thus:

> There is not yet any general obligation for States to refrain from amnesty laws on these crimes. Consequently, if a State passes any such law, it does not breach a customary rule. Nonetheless if a court of another State having in custody persons accused of international crimes decide to prosecute them although in their national State they would benefit from an amnesty law, such court would not thereby act contrary to general international law, in particular to the principle of respect for the sovereignty of other States.[59]

The opinion stated above is gratefully adopted. It is, therefore, not difficult to agree with the submission made on behalf of Redress that the amnesty granted by Sierra Leone cannot cover crimes under international law that are the subject of universal jurisdiction. In the first place, it stands to reason that a state cannot sweep such crimes into oblivion and forgetfulness which other states have jurisdiction to prosecute by reason of the fact that the obligation to protect human dignity is a preemptory norm and has assumed the nature of obligation *erga omnes*.

72. In view of the conclusions that have been arrived at in paragraph 69, it is clear that the question whether amnesty is unlawful under international law becomes relevant only in considering the question whether Article IX of the Lomé Agreement can constitute a legal bar to prosecution of the defendants by another State or by an international tribunal. There being no such bar, the remaining question is whether the undertaking contained in Article IX is good ground for

[59] A. Cassese, INTERNATIONAL CRIMINAL LAW (Oxford, 2003), 315.

holding that the prosecution of the defendants is an abuse of process of the Court.

73. It is not difficult to agree with the submissions made by the *amici curiae,* Professor Orentlicher and Redress that, given the existence of a treaty obligation to prosecute or extradite an offender, the grant of amnesty in respect of such crimes as are specified in Articles 2 to 4 of the Statute of the Court is not only incompatible with, but is in breach of an obligation of a State towards the international community as a whole. Nothing in the submissions made by the Defence and the interveners detracts from that conclusion. The case of *Azapo v. President of the Republic of South Africa*[62] is purely one dealt with under the domestic laws of South Africa. It was not a case in which the jurisdiction of another State or of an international court to prosecute the offenders is denied. The decisive issues which have arisen in the case before us did not arise in that case.

74. It may well be noted that the President of Sierra Leone did acknowledge that "there are gaps in Sierra Leonean law as it does not encompass such heinous crimes as those against humanity and some of the gross human rights abuses committed" and also that the intention of the amnesty granted was to put prosecution of such offences outside the jurisdiction of national courts.

NOTES & QUESTIONS

1. Peace Agreements

Why does the Court spend so much time on the question of whether the Lomé Agreement is a treaty or not? What difference does it make if the Agreement is a treaty? Christine Bell, in a thoughtful discussion of peace agreements, notes that some may qualify as treaties, and others may not. The legal categorization of a peace agreement, Bell argues, is a crucial element in the probability of a party's compliance. Consider her discussion of the *Kallon* opinion:

> The positive legal status of peace agreements also remains important to compliance because it carries weight in legal forums: courts and tribunals use it as a starting point in determining their own jurisdiction. Here, positivist law categories hold sway, no matter how unfashionable, because they provide a rational basis for clear decision making. This can be illustrated by the *Kallon* case of the appeals chamber of the Special Court for Sierra Leone * * *. The appeals chamber found itself considering the legal status of the agreement signed by the government and the RUF, so as to determine the validity of the amnesty. With respect to the status of the RUF and the Lomé Agreement, the chamber distinguished between being bound under common Article 3 of the Geneva Conventions (which it accepted as applicable), and the RUF's

62 *Azapo v. President of the Republic of South Africa* (4) SA 653 (1996) [upholding the amnesty law as valid under international law and mandated by the South African Constitution].

treaty-making ability, stating that "[i]nternational law does not seem to have vested [the RUF] with such capacity." * * * The need to overrule the amnesty of the Lomé Agreement might appear to demonstrate why states should not concede that peace agreements signed with nonstate actors are binding on the international level. However, rejection of Lomé as a binding agreement let the RUF off the hook as regards compliance, while leaving the state subject to arguments that it was still bound to comply by virtue of its interstate commitments and its national legislation. Moreover, rejection of the international legal status of Lomé was not necessary in order to invalidate its amnesty provision. The *Kallon* result could have been reached by applying notions of treaty breach (the RUF having continued fighting in violation of the cease-fire commitments); or by deeming the amnesty provision invalid to the extent that it covered certain crimes against humanity, serious war crimes, torture, and other gross violations of human rights; or even by finding that the amnesty section applied only to future domestic law proceedings (for which a tenuous basis can be discerned in the wording).

Kallon does not stand alone: a range of international tribunals may be called upon to adjudicate on the compatibility of peace agreements with international law for a variety of reasons. Domestic courts, too, often end up examining the political and legal questions at the heart of the agreement, through constitutional or legislative adjudication that must determine the extent to which the peace agreement is a foundational interpretive document, or indeed a treaty, and where it is a political document to be deferred to as dealing with political questions only. To be sure, in many situations the role of courts and tribunals will be marginal to an agreement's success or failure: courts and tribunals are likely to be ineffective in sustaining an agreement in the face of fundamental and violent dissent. However, marginal relevance is not the same as irrelevance. Courts and tribunals have the capacity to extend and develop the agreement's meaning where they find it to be part of the legal framework. More negatively, they have the capacity to terminate the operation of an agreement even in the face of political chances to sustain it. The positive law status of peace agreements therefore remains important to their implementation. This importance, in turn, begins to explain innovations in legal form, which enable parties to frame obligations so that they fall within recognizable traditional legal categories.

Christine Bell, *Peace Agreements: Their Nature and Legal Status*, 100 AM. J. INT'L L. 373, 387–389 (2006). Do you agree with Bell's analysis of the *Kallon* decision? Could the Court have determined the applicability of the amnesty without addressing the legal form of the Peace Agreement under international law?

2. South Africa and Amnesty

The defendants in the principle case raised the situation in South Africa in their defense. South Africa enacted a unique amnesty—largely praised by the international community—to be administered by a Truth and Reconciliation Commission. While most amnesties have provided automatic and blanket protection to their beneficiaries, the South African amnesty was not automatic. In order to receive amnesty, an individual had to apply to the amnesty committee of the Truth and Reconciliation Commission. In cases involving acts of violence, applicants were required to participate in a public hearing where they were to present their case for amnesty, and where they were subject to examination by the committee members, by an evidence leader, and by victims or their representatives. In order to receive amnesty, the individual had to convince the committee that (1) he had made full disclosure concerning the relevant facts of the incidents for which he was seeking amnesty, and (2) the act for which he was seeking amnesty was an "act associated with a political objective." An act was associated with a political objective if it was committed pursuant to an order by, or consistent with the policy of, an established and publicly known organization, such as the state or an opposition party or military organization. 2,548 applicants out of 7,116 applications were subject to the public hearing requirement. 362 of those subject to a public hearing were refused amnesty. A total of 1,312 were granted amnesty. *See* Martin Coetzee, *An Overview of the TRC Amnesty Process, in* THE PROVOCATIONS OF AMNESTY: MEMORY, JUSTICE, AND IMPUNITY 181, 193 (Charles Villa-Vicencio and Erik Doxtader eds., 2003).

In one of its first opinions, the new post-apartheid Constitutional Court rejected a challenge to the TRC amnesty provisions as violating both the South African Constitution as well as international law. *See Azapo v. South Africa*, 1996 (4) SALR 671 (CC). For a critical discussion of the South African amnesty, *see* Lorna McGregor, *Individual Accountability in South Africa: Cultural Optimum or Political Façade?*, 95 AM. J. INT'L L. 32 (2001); LOOKING BACK, REACHING FORWARD: REFLECTIONS ON THE TRUTH AND RECONCILIATION COMMISSION OF SOUTH AFRICA (Charles Villa-Vicencio and Wilhelm Verwoerd eds., 2000); and THE PROVOCATIONS OF AMNESTY: MEMORY, JUSTICE, AND IMPUNITY (Charles Villa-Vicencio and Erik Doxtader eds., 2003).

3. Inter-American Human Rights System and Amnesties

The most well-developed jurisprudence on amnesties at the international level has issued from the Inter-American human rights system. Amnesties from Argentina, Chile, El Salvador, Peru, and Uruguay have been the subject of opinions of either the Inter-American Commission or Court of Human Rights. An illustrative case from 2006 involved Chile. *Almonacid Arellano and Others v. Chile*, Inter-Am. Ct. H.R., Ser. C, No. 154 (Sept. 26, 2006). The following summary was prepared by Karen Keck from the Inter-American Court:

> In *Almonacid Arellano and Others v. Chile*, the Inter-American Court of Human Rights was asked to determine whether: a) Chile complied with its obligations under articles 1.1 and 2 of the

American Convention on Human Rights (the "American Convention") by maintaining Decreto Ley No. 2.191 (the "Amnesty Law") in force after Chile ratified the American Convention in 1990; and b) whether the post-ratification application of the Amnesty Law to the 1973 extrajudicial killing of Mr. Almonacid Arellano was a violation of articles 1.1, 8 and 25 of the American Convention.

To answer these issues, the Inter-American Court conducted a five-fold analysis. First, based upon a historical review of international law, it found that there was ample evidence to conclude that in 1973 the commission of crimes against humanity, including a murder executed within the context of a generalized and systematic attack against sectors of the civilian population, violated customary international law.

Next, the Inter-American Court held that the extra-judicial murder of Mr. Almonacid Arellano took place during the time when Chile was governed by a military dictator that, under a State policy aimed at causing fear, launched a massive and systemic attack against sectors of the civilian population considered to be opponents of the regime. In view of this, the Inter-American Court found that there was sufficient evidence to support the conclusion that the 1973 extrajudicial killing by state agents of Mr. Almonacid Arellano was part of a crime against humanity.

The judgment then indicates that the obligation under international law to prosecute and punish the perpetrators of crimes against humanity is found in article 1.1 of the American Convention. Article 1.1 obligates states parties to prevent, investigate and punish violations of the American Convention, including crimes against humanity, because such crimes violate a series of non-derogable rights recognized by the American Convention. Amnesty laws therefore may not be applied to crimes against humanity because they prevent state parties from fulfilling the aforementioned obligations. Consequently, amnesty could not be granted for the extra-judicial killing of Mr. Almonacid Arellano based on the finding that it was a crime against humanity.

The Inter-American Court then goes on to review the Amnesty Law in light of article 2 of the American Convention. The Amnesty Law granted amnesty to anyone responsible for committing, *inter alia*, crimes against humanity that were committed from September 11, 1973 to March 10, 1978. As such laws leave victims defenseless and perpetuate impunity for crimes against humanity, they are manifestly incompatible with the letter and spirit of the American Convention and undoubtedly affect the rights set forth therein. Under article 2 of the American Convention, states parties are obligated to legislatively abolish all laws that violate the American Convention and implement necessary practices to observe the guarantees thereof. The Inter-American Court therefore concludes that Chile violated article 2 of the American

> Convention by permitting the Amnesty Law to remain in force for 16 years after Chile ratified said instrument.
>
> Finally, the Inter-American Court looks at the obligations of Chile under articles 8 and 25. It states that when the legislative branch of government fails to suppress laws that are contrary to the American Convention, the judiciary remains obligated to guarantee the rights therein and must abstain from applying any law that is contrary thereto. As such, the Inter-American Court found that Chile violated articles 8 and 25 when the judiciary applied the Amnesty Law, as this action resulted in the immediate cessation of the investigations and the closure of the file related to the death of Mr. Almonacid Arellano, leaving those responsible for the death of Mr. Almonacid Arellano in impunity.

In an earlier decision the Inter-American Court also held that a Peruvian amnesty law violated the Inter-American Convention. *Barrios Altos Case*, Inter-Am. Ct. H.R., Ser. C, No. 75 (Mar. 14, 2001), *reprinted at* 41 I.L.M. 93 (2002). The *Barrios Altos* case involved the government-sponsored killing of fifteen individuals in Peru in 1991. The government passed an amnesty law protecting individuals involved in any human rights abuses from 1980 to 1995. Faced with a challenge to the amnesty law before the Inter-American Commission on Human Rights, Peru unsuccessfully tried to withdraw from the Inter-American human rights system. On the merits, the Inter-American Court found the Peruvian amnesty law violated numerous provisions of the American Convention on Human Rights, and opined that all amnesty laws were incompatible with the human rights obligations of states in the American system as such laws precluded investigation of human rights violations and the punishment of those responsible. The Argentinean Supreme Court cited the decision in the *Barrios Altos* case to strike down two laws—known as the "Full Stop" and "Due Obedience" laws—that had prevented investigation and punishment for human rights abuses committed by the military government during that country's "Dirty War" from 1976 to 1983. *See* Corte Suprema de Justicia [CSJN], 6/14/2005, *"Simon, Julio Hector y otros s/ privacion ilegitima de la libertad, etc.,"* S. 1767 (XXXVIII) (Arg.).

The most recent decision by the Inter-American Court of Human Rights concerning an amnesty law was issued against El Salvador, holding that the country's amnesty law cannot be used to prevent investigations into gross violations of human rights committed during that country's civil war. The case focused on the 1981 massacre of El Mozote, believed to be the largest massacre in modern Latin American history. It resulted in the killing of approximately a thousand people spread over at least six villages. *Case of the Massacres of El Mozote and Neighboring Locations*, Merits Judgment, Series C No. 252 (Oct. 25, 2012). Significantly, the President of the Inter-American Court, Diego Garcia Sayan, along with four of the six other judges of the Court, issued a concurring opinion that argued that amnesties enacted as part of a negotiation to end a civil war should be distinguished from amnesties enacted after a dictatorship, and that in the former circumstances the right to peace should be taken into account and balanced against victims' rights to truth, justice, reparations, and guarantees of non-repetition. A local court in El Salvador is now prosecuting individuals accused of masterminding and committing the El Mozote massacre. Do you think a distinction should be made, as the concurring opinion above suggests, between amnesties at the end of a civil war and amnesties at the end of a dictatorship? What arguments can you make that such leniency at the end of a civil war may be justified, but not so after a dictatorship?

4. Amnesty in Cambodia

The ECCC was faced with a claim of amnesty by one of its defendants, Ieng Sary. (See the Appendix for a map of Cambodia.) Sary also raised in his defense his 1979 conviction *in absentia* for genocide by a Vietnamese-backed court for the crimes of the Khmer Rouge. (As a result of that conviction, both Ieng Sary and Pol Pot were sentenced to death.) The issue arose in the context of a challenge by Ieng Sary of his detention before trial. The Co-Investigating Judges first found that the amnesty, promulgated in 1994, did not provide a bar to prosecution before the ECCC. The Pre-Trial Chamber rejected the applicability of the amnesty and the prior conviction. We reproduce below that portion of the opinion rejecting the amnesty argument:

Case of Ieng Sary, Case No. 002/19–09–2007–ECCC/OCIJ (PTC03), Decision on Appeal against Provisional Detention Order of Ieng Sary, Pre-Trial Chamber (October 17, 2008)

26. On 7 July 1994, the National Assembly of the Kingdom of Cambodia in Phnom Penh approved the "Law on the Outlawing of the 'Democratic Kampuchea' Group" ("1994 Law"). This 1994 Law reads, in relevant part:

> The National Assembly of the Kingdom of Cambodia [. . .] Seeing that throughout the period since the election in 1993 to the present the "Democratic Kampuchea" group [a.k.a. the Khmer Rouge] has continually committed criminal, terrorist and genocidal acts which has been a characteristic of the group since it captured power in April 1975 [. . .]
>
> Realizing that the leadership of the "Democratic Kampuchea" group cannot take the Paris Peace Agreement as a legal shield to conceal and escape from their responsibility of committing criminal, terrorist and genocidal acts since the time that the Pol Pot regime took power in 1975–78. The crime of genocide has no statute of limitations. [. . .]
>
> [H]ereby approves the following law: [. . .]
>
> Article 3: Members of the political organization or the military forces of the "Democratic Kampuchea" group or any persons who commit crimes of murder, rape, robbery of people's

property, the destruction of public and private property, etc. shall be sentenced according to existing criminal law.

Article 4: Members of the political organization or the military forces of the "Democratic Kampuchea" group or any persons who commit

- seccession [sic],
- destruction against the Royal Government,
- destruction against organs of public authority, or
- incitement or forcing the taking up of arms against public authority

shall be charged as criminals against the internal security of the country and sentenced to jail for 20 to 30 years or for life.

Article 5: This Law shall grant a stay of six months after coming into effect to permit people who are members of the political organization of military forces of the "Democratic Kampuchea" group to return to live under the control of the Royal Government in the Kingdom of Cambodia without facing punishment for crimes which they have committed.

Article 6: For leaders of the "Democratic Kampuchea" group the stay describe above does not apply.

Article 7: The King shall have the right to give partial or complete amnesty or pardon as stated in Article 27 of the Constitution. [. . .]

Article 9: Any persons who use this law to violate the rights of the people by incorrectly threatening, charging, arresting, detaining, jailing, torturing or violating their homes shall be punished and be jailed from two to five years. Any persons who give false information, false witness, or false evidence in order to serve his or her interests by using this law to violate the rights of people shall be punished and jailed from two to five years. Victims of injustice have the right to appeal for damages arising from the above-mentioned violations.

27. On 14 September 1996, Royal Decree No. NS/RKT/0996/72 was proclaimed, which states:

We, Preah Bat Norodom Sihanouk Varma, King of Cambodia [. . .] hereby proclaim

Article 1: An amnesty to Mr. Ieng Sary, former Deputy Minister in charge of Foreign Affairs in the Government of Democratic Kampuchea, for the sentence of death and confiscation of all his property imposed by order of the People's Revolutionary Tribunal of Phnom Penh, dated 19 August 1979; and an amnesty for prosecution under the Law to Outlaw the Democratic Kampuchea Group; * * *

28. On 6 June 2003, an agreement was signed between the United Nations and the Royal Government of Cambodia concerning the prosecution under Cambodian law of crimes committed during the period of Democratic Kampuchea ("Agreement"). This Agreement provides in Article 11(2):

> This provision is based upon a declaration by the Royal Government of Cambodia that until now, with regard to matters covered in the law, there has been only one case, dated 14 September 1996, when a pardon was granted to only one person with regard to a 1979 conviction on the charge of genocide. The United Nations and the Royal Government of Cambodia agree that the scope of this pardon is a matter to be decided by the Extraordinary Chambers.

29. On 27 October 2004, the Law on the Establishment of Extraordinary Chambers in the Courts of Cambodia for the prosecution of crimes committed during the period of Democratic Kampuchea ("ECCC Law") was promulgated, which provides in Article 40 new:

> [. . .] The scope of any amnesty or pardon that may have been granted prior to the enactment of this Law is a matter to be decided by the Extraordinary Chambers. * * *

57. The Pre-Trial Chamber finds that the meaning of the word "amnesty" cannot necessarily be found by applying a grammatical interpretation. In this respect, the Pre-Trial Chamber notes that the use of the Khmer word for amnesty is used inconsistently. The word "amnesty" in the first sentence of Article 1 is used as "amnesty from a sentence" while in the second part of the article it is used as "amnesty from prosecution." Both amnesties mentioned in the Royal Decree are inconsistent with the provision on amnesty in Article 27 of the Constitution of Cambodia of 1993. The Pre-Trial Chamber further notes that at the time the Royal Decree was proclaimed, the death penalty had already been abolished in Cambodia by Article 32 of the Constitution.

58. In the light of these issues surrounding the amnesty for the sentence related to the conviction for genocide, the Pre-Trial Chamber considers that the validity of the amnesty is uncertain. The Pre-Trial Chamber finds that it is therefore not manifest or evident that this part of the Royal Decree will prevent a conviction for genocide before the ECCC.

59. In the context of the inconsistent use of the word "amnesty," the Pre-Trial Chamber finds that the second "amnesty" in the Royal Decree can be interpreted as meaning that the Charged Person "will not be proceeded against" in respect of the sentence given or breaches of Reach Kram No. 1, NS 94, dated 15 July 1994. * * *

61. The scope of this part of the amnesty is limited to the prosecution under the Law to Outlaw the Democratic Kampuchea Group, promulgated by Reach Kram No 1, NS 94, dated 14 July 1994. The

offences mentioned in this Law are not within the jurisdiction of the ECCC. The Pre-Trial Chamber finds therefore that this part of the amnesty in the Decree cannot be seen as having the possible effect of preventing a conviction by the ECCC. It is therefore not manifest or evident that it prevents a conviction by the ECCC.

NOTES & QUESTIONS

1. Case Update

Ieng Sary was a co-founder of the Khmer Rouge with his brother-in-law Pol Pot. He served as both foreign minister and deputy prime minister in the Khmer Rouge government that ruled Cambodia from 1975 to 1979. In 2007, Ieng Sary was arrested, and his trial before the ECCC began in 2011. Before a verdict could be reached, Ieng Sary died at the age of 87 on March 14, 2013.

2. Amnesties Before the ICC

During the negotiations for the treaty establishing the International Criminal Court, delegates considered but rejected a proposal that would have required the ICC to defer to an arrangement like the South African Truth & Reconciliation Commission, and thus not prosecute individuals in receipt of such a conditional amnesty. Recall the provisions of the ICC Statute concerning admissibility (Art. 17). Could an amnesty like the South African one provide a viable defense for a defendant arguing against admissibility? Might there be situations in which the Prosecutor might appropriately exercise prosecutorial discretion not to prosecute individuals covered by a domestic amnesty? Article 53 presumably governs such situations, and states:

> The Prosecutor shall, having evaluated the information made available to him or her, initiate an investigation unless he or she determines that there is no reasonable basis to proceed under this Statute. In deciding whether to initiate an investigation, the Prosecutor shall consider whether: * * * (c) Taking into account the gravity of the crime and the interests of victims, there are nonetheless substantial reasons to believe that an investigation would not serve the interests of justice.

Under what conditions should a prosecutor defer to a domestic amnesty regime? Are some amnesties more legitimate than others?

3. Amnesties in International Humanitarian Law

If amnesties are so disfavored in international law, why would Article 6 of Additional Protocol II include the following language?

> Article 6: Penal Prosecutions
>
> 1. This Article applies to the prosecution and punishment of criminal offences related to the armed conflict. * * *
>
> 5. At the end of hostilities, the authorities in power shall endeavour to grant the broadest possible amnesty to persons who have participated in the armed conflict, or those deprived of their

liberty for reasons related to the armed conflict, whether they are interned or detained.

For that matter, how do we explain the name of Amnesty International? Are the amnesties contemplated in these sources different from the blanket amnesty countries have imposed following a period of armed conflict or repression?

4. For Further Reading

For a thorough and empirical study of amnesties, *see* Louise Mallinder, AMNESTY, HUMAN RIGHTS, AND POLITICAL TRANSITIONS: BRIDGING THE PEACE AND JUSTICE DIVIDE (2008). For another comprehensive analysis of amnesties, *see also* Mark Freeman, NECESSARY EVILS: AMNESTIES AND THE SEARCH FOR JUSTICE (2009). For more on the legality of amnesty laws, *see* Ronald C. Slye, *The Legitimacy of Amnesties under International Law and General Principles of Anglo-American Law: Is a Legitimate Amnesty Possible?*, 43 VA. J. INT'L L. 173 (2002); Andrew S. Brown, Note, *Adios Amnesty: Prosecutorial Discretion and Military Trials in Argentina*, 37 TEX. INT'L L. J. 203 (2002); Darryl Robinson, *Serving the Interests of Justice: Amnesties, Truth Commissions and the International Criminal Court*, 14 EUR. J. INT'L L. 481 (2003). For a discussion of amnesty and the ICC, *see* Carsten Stahn, *Complementarity, Amnesties and Alternative Forms of Justice: Some Interpretative Guidelines for the International Criminal Court*, 3 J. INT'L CRIM. JUST. 695 (2005). For a discussion of the Sierra Leone amnesty by one of the members of the Sierra Leone Truth and Reconciliation Commission, *see* William A. Schabas, *Amnesty, the Sierra Leone Truth and Reconciliation Commission, and the Special Court for Sierra Leone,* 11 U.C. DAVIS J. INT'L L. AND POL'Y 145 (2004).

CHAPTER 18

SENTENCING & REPARATIONS

I. INTRODUCTION

While most students of international criminal law tend to focus on the jurisprudential developments of the various domestic, hybrid, and international tribunals, less attention is paid to the consequences of these trials. For the victims, however, the punishment inflicted upon the defendant and any reparations are often as important as the judicial process and a finding of guilt. Civil forfeiture may also be available. In many legal systems, the remedy available to a victim is limited to serving as a witness in a public trial, in which the defendant is required to defend or explain her actions, and the sentence. The drafters of the International Criminal Court (ICC) were determined to provide a more robust role for victims. They created a system that gives victims an enhanced status within the entire adjudicative process and established a Trust Fund for Victims that is designed to provide reparations and other benefits. The Extraordinary Chambers in the Courts of Cambodia (ECCC) are also empowered to take victim impact testimony and award reparations. For example, in its conviction of Khieu Samphan and Nuon Chea, the ECCC granted moral and collective reparations in the form of memorialization, therapy and other psychological assistance to victims, documentation, and educational opportunities. In Chapter 1, we touched upon truth commissions and other alternative modes of accountability. The appeal of many of these transitional justice mechanisms is their victim-centeredness and the perception that they are better designed to address the multifaceted needs and concerns of victims and the communities in which they live.

Notwithstanding these alternative responses to international crimes, criminal trials remain central in international criminal law and will produce a sentence if the defendant is convicted. In general, the judges enjoy wide discretion in awarding the term of years given that there are no formal sentencing guidelines. As you review the materials in this chapter on some of the issues raised by sentencing at the *ad hoc* international tribunals and the ICC, consider whether sentencing guidelines might improve the process. You might also reflect upon how well the tribunals have balanced the at times competing imperatives of retribution, fairness to all parties, deterrence, and rehabilitation. Consider also how well the sentences awarded by the various tribunals advance the multiple goals of the criminal law and where tensions exist within sentencing practice, doctrine, and theory. Relevant considerations explored by the materials below include the theoretical hierarchy of international crimes under international criminal law, plea bargaining, and the identification of mitigating and aggravating circumstances in the context of armed conflict and mass violence.

II. A HIERARCHY OF CRIMES?

Is there a hierarchy of international crimes and is this relevant to sentencing? Dražen Erdemović was the first individual to surrender himself to the International Criminal Tribunal for the Former Yugoslavia (ICTY). (See the Appendix for a map of Yugoslavia.) Erdemović had been indicted on May 22, 1996, on one count alleging his commission of a crime against humanity and on an alternative count alleging his commission of a violation of the laws or customs of war in connection with his involvement in a firing squad of the Bosnian Serb Army that resulted in the deaths of hundreds of Bosnian Muslim male civilians. At his initial appearance, he pled guilty to the crime against humanity count. The Trial Chamber accepted his guilty plea and dismissed the alternative war crimes count. The Trial Chamber sentenced Erdemović on November 29, 1996, to ten years' imprisonment. In December 1996, he lodged an appeal against the Sentencing Judgment, arguing that the sentence was too high in light of the fact that he had acted under duress. The Appeals Chamber remanded the case to a new Trial Chamber, holding, *inter alia*, that Erdemović's plea of guilty was not informed and that while duress does not afford a complete defense to a soldier charged with the killing of innocent human beings, it is admissible in mitigation. In particular, the Appeals Chamber reasoned that Erdemović had not been fully informed of the distinction between the two crimes and the fact that crimes against humanity were more serious than war crimes. The Appeals Chamber ordered that Erdemović be allowed to replead with full knowledge of the nature of the charges against him. On January 14, 1998, Erdemović then pled guilty to the war crimes count and the alternative crimes against humanity count was dropped.

In his separate and dissenting opinion, Judge Li (China) rejected the argument of his fellow judges that there is a meaningful distinction between pleading guilty to war crimes versus crimes against humanity.

Prosecutor v. Erdemović, Case No. IT–96–22–A, Separate and Dissenting Opinion of Judge Li (Oct. 7, 1997)

18. [I]t is said that an act classified as a crime against humanity will be punished more severely than when it is classified as a war crime, because a crime against humanity is said to be a crime not only against the persons who are killed, but also "against humanity as a whole." It is argued that from an interpretation of Article 5 of the Statute of this International Tribunal, the same conclusion can be drawn. As the Appellant pleaded guilty to the more serious crime, it is probable that he

had not been informed of the difference between these two crimes and had thus been placed in a disadvantageous position. So it is necessary to send the case back to the Trial Chamber.

19. With respect to these arguments, I submit, in the first place, that the gravity of a criminal act, and consequently the seriousness of its punishment, are determined by the intrinsic nature of the act itself and not by its classification under one category or another. Take the present case: the Appellant killed seventy to one hundred innocent Muslim civilians. Whether his criminal act is classified under crimes against humanity or war crimes, the harm done to individuals and society is exactly the same, neither an iota more nor less. Then, why should he be punished more severely if his criminal act is subsumed under crimes against humanity and not war crimes?

20. Second, it is groundless to assert that a crime against humanity is necessarily more serious than a war crime. Let us compare the crime against humanity of the Appellant with a war crime of another person who is charged under Article 3(c) of the Statute of this International Tribunal for bombardment of an undefended town, causing the death of one million civilians. Can we say that the crime against humanity committed by the Appellant is more serious than this war crime?

This is because all the war crimes listed in Article 3 of the Statute of this International Tribunal are not lesser offences, but are particularly grave offences against the laws of war. Indeed, Dinstein has pointed out the popular fallacy misconceiving that every violation of the laws of war is necessarily a war crime. And owing to their particularly grave nature, obviously they cannot be less serious offences than crimes against humanity. Of course, crimes against humanity have the characteristics of being committed systematically or on a large scale. However, war crimes can also be committed in such a manner. For instance, prisoners of war may be killed systematically or on a large scale, as they were habitually and atrociously executed by the Nazi regime in the Second World War.

21. Third, the crime against humanity has its origin in the Charter of the International Military Tribunal of Nürnberg annexed to the London Agreement of 8 August 1945 * * *. As is well known, Article 6(a), (b) and (c) provides for crimes against peace, war crimes and crimes against humanity for the jurisdiction of the International Military Tribunal.

Prior to the Second World War, there were in international law only war crimes and no crimes against humanity. War crimes must be committed during war and principally against the combatants and prisoners of war of the other belligerent nation and the civilians in occupied territory. But, before and during that war, the Nazi regime and its agents, besides committing massive and monstrous traditional war crimes, also committed many horrendous atrocities against its own nationals, particularly German Jews and anti-Nazi German politicians and intelligentsia. These atrocities, according to the international law before that war, were not war crimes and therefore could not be within the jurisdiction of the International Military Tribunal at Nürnberg. However, they were so shocking to the conscience of mankind that the Allied Governments were determined to punish the offenders. This is the sole reason why the Charter, in addition to war crimes, provides for a further category of crimes against humanity and confers on the International Military Tribunal the jurisdiction over these crimes. * * *

Nevertheless, it must be pointed out that the Charter, in providing for crimes against humanity, does not create a crime more serious than a war crime, for the same acts of "extermination, enslavement, deportation, and other inhumane acts against any civilian population," which constitute crimes against humanity according to Article 6(c) of the Charter, if committed during war by the belligerent forces of one state against the nationals of another state, constitute war crimes. Likewise, the same "persecutions on political, racial or religious grounds." which constitute crimes against humanity according to the same provision of the Charter as above-mentioned, if committed during war against the civilian population of enemy country, also constitute war crimes. These war crimes can be found in the 1863 Lieber Code, the 1899 and 1907 Hague Conventions and the 1864 and 1929 Geneva Conventions long before the adoption of the Charter. It must be emphasised that as the criminal acts pertaining to these two crimes were exactly the same in the Charter, their seriousness cannot but be exactly the same.

Therefore, the Judgement of the International Military Tribunal at Nürnberg on the one hand declared emphatically that "to initiate a war of aggression . . . is not only an international crime, it is the supreme international crime, differing only from other war crimes in that it contains within itself the accumulated evil of the whole," while on the other hand uttered not a single word asserting that crimes against humanity were more serious in nature than war crimes, although many accused were convicted of both crimes. This shows that the International Military Tribunal at Nürnberg treated both crimes on the same level.

22. Fourth, soon after the London Charter, Article II(c) of Control Council Law No. 10, of 20 December 1945, provides that war crimes, crimes against peace and crimes against humanity can be punished by death. Once again it shows that war crimes are not less serious than crimes against humanity. Furthermore, in the practical application of this provision by the United States Military Tribunal at Nürnberg, the 24 accused condemned to death were all found guilty of war crimes as well as, in certain cases, crimes against peace, and crimes against humanity. But no accused was condemned to death for committing crimes against humanity without being found guilty of war crimes. In the *Justice Trial* decided by the United States Military Tribunal, the accused Oswald Rothaug was found guilty of crimes against humanity, and despite the fact that the Military Tribunal found no mitigating

circumstances, was sentenced to life imprisonment rather than death. This constitutes irrefutable proof that the Military Tribunal considered that the crimes against humanity committed by the accused were even less serious than war crimes.

23. Fifth, recently, the United States War Crimes Act of 1996, which provides that the offender of a grave breach of the Geneva Conventions of 1949 causing the death of the victim shall be subject to the penalty of death, also shows that a war crime is not less serious than a crime against humanity.

24. Sixth, the Convention on the Non-Applicability of Statutory Limitations to War Crimes and Crimes against Humanity, adopted by the General Assembly of the United Nations on 26 November 1968 and entering into force on 11 November 1970, does not consider crimes against humanity more serious than war crimes.

The Preamble to this Convention emphasises, *inter alia,* that "war crimes and crimes against humanity are among the gravest crimes in international law," and that "the effective punishment of war crimes and crimes against humanity is an important element in the prevention of such crimes, the protection of human rights and fundamental freedoms, the encouragement of confidence, the furtherance of co-operation among people and the promotion of international peace and security." * * *

25. Seventh, that the seriousness of crimes against humanity is equal to that of war crimes is further shown by the Yugoslav Criminal Law. According to the provisions of Articles 141–143 of the said law concerning the crime of genocide, and war crimes against the civilian population and the wounded and the sick, the penalties for these crimes are the same: from five to twenty years of imprisonment.

26. Eighth, it is not true to say that a crime against humanity is one against the whole of mankind. This has been explained very convincingly by Schwelb in the following terms:

> The word "humanity" (*l'humanité*) has at least two different meanings, the one connoting the human race or mankind as a whole, and the other, humaneness, i.e., a certain quality of behaviour. It is submitted that in the Charter, and in the other basic documents which will be discussed in this article, the word "humanity" is used in the latter sense. It is, therefore, not necessary, for a certain act, in order to come within the notion of crimes against humanity, to affect mankind as a whole. A crime against humanity is an offence against certain general principles of law which, in certain circumstances, become the concern of the international community, namely, if it has repercussions reaching across international frontiers, or if it passes in magnitude or savagery any limits of what is tolerable by modern civilisations.

27. From what is said above my final conclusion on this question is: the Appellant's plea of guilty is unambiguous and valid.

NOTES & QUESTIONS

1. A Hierarchy of Crimes

Do the different elements of war crimes and crimes against humanity suggest that one crime is worse than the other? If not, should we continue to distinguish between the two types of crimes? Why? Professor Allison Marston Danner has a thoughtful analysis of sentencing before the international tribunals. She argues that a hierarchy can be discerned from the *chapeau* elements of each crime.* Consider the following:

> The idea that there is a hierarchy of crimes in international humanitarian law has been the subject of debate since the ICTY handed down its first sentence. * * * The ICTR, by contrast, has had little trouble endorsing the notion of a hierarchy of crimes under international law. The ICTR has frequently referred to genocide as the "crime of crimes." It has also stated that war crimes "are considered as lesser crimes than genocide or crimes against humanity." As one of the ICTY Trial Chambers noted, "a hierarchy of crimes seems to emerge from the case-law of the ICTR," but "the ICTY has not yet transposed this hierarchy of crimes to the sentencing phase." * * *
>
> The *chapeau* elements allow for grading the categories of offenses within the Tribunals' jurisdictions because they provide information about the harms caused by a perpetrator's crime beyond those directly associated with a perpetrator's commission of an enumerated act.[285] In addition to these considerations, however, the *chapeau* elements should be considered at sentencing for two reasons. They are the essence of what makes a crime international, and they reflect a hierarchy of evolving norms about the relative gravity of each category of crimes. * * *
>
> Expressive conceptions of punishment * * * support a hierarchy of crimes in international law. Assuming that the international community believes some categories of crimes are more dangerous or more offensive than others, longer sentences for those categories realize these beliefs in concrete terms. Given the widespread acknowledgement of genocide as the "crime of crimes,"

---

* Recall that the *chapeau* elements of an offence are those elements—such as *mens rea*, motive, or circumstantial elements—that apply to all of the enumerated acts that constitute an international crime. Thus for genocide, the *mens rea* of specific intent to destroy a group in whole or in part is required to transform a murder or other act into an act of genocide.

[285] This Article's argument for a hierarchy of crimes rests not just on the outcome of any particular offense but on the predicted consequences of an act falling within a specific category of crime. Thus, a crime against humanity—because of its elements of collective perpetration and collective victimization—will generally, although not always, be more serious than a war crime. Therefore, the hierarchy of crimes is important, not just because it allows for a full examination of the harms caused by an individual perpetrator's commission of a specific category of crime, but also because it makes a prediction about the likely differences in the harms associated with each category of crime in the abstract.

> its location at the apex of the normative pyramid is unlikely to elicit controversy. * * *
>
> Admittedly, there is a certain amount of artificiality to the distinction [I make] between war crimes and crimes against humanity. * * * Does it really matter, to either the victim or to the perpetrator, whether the latter commits rape as a war crime or rape as a crime against humanity? [I maintain] that it may matter and that the distinction is important enough to be reflected at sentencing.
>
> Certainly, the Muslim rape victims in *Kunarac* (the "Foča case") likely cared deeply that they were victimized because of their ethnicity, as part of a larger attack on the Muslims of Foča. The perpetrators of such crimes also very likely took encouragement, comfort, and resolve from the violent context in which they acted. Thus, the *chapeau* elements of a crime against humanity have significance in practice as well as in theory. Whether a perpetrator commits a war crime, a crime against humanity, or genocide should matter to the international community, and the expressive function of punishment supports taking this factor into account at sentencing.

Allison Marston Danner, *Constructing a Hierarchy of Crimes in International Criminal Law Sentencing*, 87 VA. L. REV. 415, 467–95 (2001).

Imagine two defendants. Each issued an order that resulted in the death of 20 people. The first deaths occurred within the context of an internal armed conflict when a rebel commander ordered his subordinates to kill all civilians found in an enclave loyal to the government. The second occurred when the head of a criminal gang ordered the murder of people living in territory associated with a rival gang. The latter was one of several such massacres in a region of the country wracked by the drug trade. The first defendant is charged with war crimes and the second with crimes against humanity. Should their sentences be identical if their personal circumstances (age, etc.) are similar?

2. Plea Bargaining in Comparative Perspective

The *Erdemović* case was the first modern ICL case to end with a plea bargain. Plea bargaining, which may include both charge bargaining and sentence bargaining, is a common practice in the U.S. and other adversarial systems. It is a less familiar concept in civil-law inquisitorial systems, although some such systems have incorporated versions of the practice. Why would plea bargaining be more suited to an adversarial system? Consider the following:

> [In adversarial systems] the guilty plea, which enables the defendant to end the determination of guilt or innocence, has provided the defense with a bargaining tool in its negotiations with the prosecution. In addition, the fact that the judge, as a passive decision-maker, usually accepts the agreement reached by the parties (the real owners of the process) also provides an incentive for the development of such practices. Given the usual deference of

the judge toward the requests of the parties, the defendant can be relatively certain that the bargain struck with the prosecutor will be fulfilled, even in those situations in which the judge may not be limited by the requests of the parties, as with certain sentencing bargains. In addition, because the prosecutor has the power to drop charges or lessen a charge, the broad prosecutorial discretion found in the model of the dispute provides the prosecutor with powerful and flexible tools to negotiate with the defense toward a guilty plea.

Conversely, there are few practices that are more incompatible with the inquisitorial system and the model of the official investigation than plea bargaining. First, the very concept of the guilty plea does not exist in the inquisitorial system. Second, there are no two parties who negotiate and bargain, as in the adversarial system, and who could reach a compromise not only about their respective claims but also about the facts of the case. In the model of the official investigation, the prosecutor is not a party to the case but rather another official, who, like the judge, has to determine what has happened. In this model, the "real" truth has to be determined by the prosecutor; it cannot be negotiated and compromised. In any case, the judge has the final word on the investigation's conclusions. Furthermore, the very act of negotiating with the defendant has traditionally been considered improper conduct by these officials. In negotiations and bargains, the parties have to recognize each other as equals, at least on a certain level. But in the model of the official investigation, the prosecutor, the judge, and the defendant are not equals because the latter has an interest at stake in the process that the former do not.

Moreover, most of the conditions required for the potential development of plea bargaining do not exist in the inquisitorial system. Not only does the concept of the guilty plea not exist in that system, but the prosecutor also has more limited discretion to decide what cases and charges she wants to move forward, as symbolized and regulated by the rule of compulsory prosecution. Furthermore, judges do not usually feel constrained by requests the parties may make regarding sentencing.

Nevertheless, despite this apparent incompatibility between plea bargaining and the model of the official investigation, a substantial number of civil law countries have recently shown an interest in translating this mechanism into their procedures. The reasons vary from jurisdiction to jurisdiction, but one common reason has been increasing crime rates in most of these countries in recent years. This situation has produced an increasing burden on their criminal procedures, requiring them to handle more criminal cases in less time than before. Obtaining a defendant's consent, therefore, through negotiations or the offering of benefits, could render unnecessary, or provide a justification to simplify or directly avoid, the regular inquisitorial criminal proceedings. Understood within this context, the introduction of consensual

> negotiating mechanisms has been seen as a way of making the rigid inquisitorial systems more flexible.

Maximo Langer, *From Legal Transplants to Legal Translations: The Globalization of Plea Bargaining and the Americanization Thesis in Criminal Procedure*, 45 HARV. INT'L L. J. 1, 36–38 (2004).

3. Plea Bargaining in International Criminal Law

How do the arguments justifying or limiting plea bargaining translate to the international criminal level? Are there special concerns with allowing plea bargaining at the international level that are not present at the domestic level? Plea bargaining can perhaps be reconciled with the classical goals of the criminal law (deterrence, retribution, and rehabilitation); might the practice contribute to, or undermine, the more ambitious goals of international criminal law (peace, security, and reconciliation)? Are there reasons to encourage plea bargains in international criminal justice beyond their practical utility?

At their inception, the ICTY and ICTR rejected the practice of plea bargaining as inconsistent with their unique function and the gravity of the crimes within the purview. *See* Statement of the President [Antonio Cassese] Made at a Briefing to Members of Diplomatic Missions, U.N. Doc. IT/29 (Feb. 11, 1994), *reprinted in* Virginia Morris & Michael P. Scharf, 1 AN INSIDER'S GUIDE TO THE INTERNATIONAL CRIMINAL TRIBUNAL FOR THE FORMER YUGOSLAVIA 112 (1995). Later, however, the judges reconsidered this stance. (Incidentally, this shift coincided with the assumption of the Presidency of Gabrielle Kirk McDonald, a former U.S. district court judge from Texas). One of the most controversial plea bargains—which included dropped charges in addition to suggestions of sentencing leniency—occurred in the case of Biljana Plavšić, whose Sentencing Judgment appears in the next section. Plea bargaining was finally specifically mentioned in the twelfth revision of the ICTY Rules. *See* ICTY Rules of Procedure and Evidence, Rule 62*bis*, IT/32/Rev. 12 (Nov. 12, 1997).

4. Kambanda

Should a defendant be guaranteed leniency if he undertakes a plea bargain even in connection with charges of genocide? Consider the following:

> When Jean Kambanda, former prime minister of Rwanda, pled guilty to genocide and crimes against humanity for his role in the mass violence that engulfed his country in 1994, he expected leniency in return. Brought before the International Criminal Tribunal for Rwanda, the seemingly repentant Kambanda not only expressed his intention to plead guilty immediately, he also provided the prosecution with nearly ninety hours of recorded testimony for use in subsequent trials of senior political and military leaders and promised to testify for the prosecution in those trials. For these efforts, Kambanda got nothing. The ICTR Trial Chamber acknowledged that guilty pleas are generally considered mitigating circumstances in the domestic courts of most countries but nonetheless followed the prosecution's recommendation and sentenced Kambanda to the most severe penalty that the ICTR can

> impose: life imprisonment. Outraged, Kambanda immediately stopped cooperating with the prosecution, and he sought to revoke his guilty plea and proceed to trial. On appeal, Kambanda claimed, among other things, that the Trial Chamber had failed to consider the general principle of law that a guilty plea warrants a sentence reduction. The Appeals Chamber rejected Kambanda's appeal, but it did not call into question his assertion that guilty pleas are normally compensated, as it were, by sentence reductions. Indeed, Kambanda is correct: The countries that use guilty pleas—primarily Anglo-American countries—usually secure those pleas by means of the controversial practice of plea bargaining.

Nancy Amoury Combs, *Copping a Plea to Genocide: The Plea Bargaining of International Crimes*, 151 U. PA. L. REV. 1, 3–4 (2002). Is this a good outcome? Why might Kambanda have been denied leniency? *See Prosecutor v. Kambanda*, Case No. ICTR–97–23–S, Judgement and Sentence (Sept. 4, 1998); *Kambanda v. Prosecutor*, Case No. ICTR–97–23–A, Judgement (Oct. 19, 2000).

5. Plea Bargaining at the ICC

The ICC Statute at Article 65 explicitly allows plea bargaining. Professor Roger Clark has noted that during the negotiations for the ICC Statute, a proposal to allow plea bargaining resulted in "puzzled comments from civil and Islamic lawyers." Roger S. Clark, *The Proposed International Criminal Court: Its Establishment and Its Relationship with the United Nations*, 8 CRIM. L. F. 411, 430 n.64 (1997). For more on plea bargaining in an adversarial system generally, *see* William J. Stunz, *Plea Bargaining and Criminal Law's Disappearing Shadow*, 117 HARV. L. REV. 2548 (2004). *See also* Geoffrey R. Watson, *The Changing Jurisprudence of the International Criminal Tribunal for the Former Yugoslavia (ICTY)*, 37 NEW ENG. L. REV. 871 (2003) and Diane Marie Amann, *Harmonic Convergence? Constitutional Criminal Procedure in an International Context*, 75 IND. L. J. 809 (2000).

6. The Death Penalty

The excerpt above mentions that the U.S. War Crimes legislation, 18 U.S.C. § 2441(a), allows for the death penalty in the event of a conviction for war crimes if death resulted to the victim. Both the Nuremberg and Tokyo Tribunals sentenced certain defendants to death. Reflecting a global trend in national law and human rights principles opposed to the death penalty, none of the modern international or hybrid ICL tribunals imposes the death penalty. The Iraqi High Tribunal, which was basically a domestic court applying Iraqi law to international crimes with the involvement of some international experts, was empowered to sentence an accused to death, as occurred in the first case against Saddam Hussein.

The debate over the death penalty during the drafting of the ICC Statute was intense, with several blocs of states insisting that the tribunal be allowed to impose this ultimate sentence given the gravity of crimes within the jurisdiction of the ICC. A group of Caribbean and Islamic nations led the debate in favor of allowing the death penalty. They expressed concern that the exclusion of the death penalty within the ICC would contribute to arguments that the penalty is prohibited by international law. As a compromise in the waning days of negotiations, delegates agreed to Article 80 of the Statute, which states: "Nothing in this part [penalties] affects the application by States of penalties prescribed by their national law, nor by the law of States which do not provide for penalties prescribed in this part." In addition, a statement to this effect was read into the record during the final negotiating session. As a result of this compromise, the Court can impose terms of imprisonment of up to 30 years or life imprisonment when justified by the gravity of the case. In addition, the Court may order fines and the forfeiture of proceeds, property, or assets derived from the crime. For a discussion of these debates, *see* William A. Schabas, THE ABOLITION OF THE DEATH PENALTY IN INTERNATIONAL LAW 251–258 (3d. ed. 2002); William A. Schabas, *Life, Death and the Crime of Crimes: Supreme Penalties and the ICC Statute*, 2 PUNISHMENT & SOCIETY 263 (2000).

III. THE TERM OF INCARCERATION

How does a tribunal determine the length of a proper sentence, or punishment, for a convicted defendant? None of the substantive international criminal law treaties includes provisions on sentencing. The Nuremberg Charter also provided little guidance, stating only that "[t]he Tribunal shall have the right to impose upon a Defendant, on conviction, death or such other punishment as shall be determined by it to be just." Charter of the International Military Tribunal, Aug. 8, 1945, art. 27, 59 Stat. 1544, 1552, 82 U.N.T.S. 284, 300. The ICTY and ICTR Statutes made minimal reference to sentencing. They both provided that "the penalty imposed by the Trial Chamber shall be limited to imprisonment." They also indicated that they are to take into account the sentencing practices of the former Yugoslavia and Rwanda respectively and "such factors as the gravity of the offence and the individual circumstances of the convicted person." ICTY Statute at Art. 24; ICTR Statute at Art. 23. The Rules of the ICTY included the following additional guidance:

> (A) A convicted person may be sentenced to imprisonment for a term up to and including the remainder of the convicted person's life.
>
> (B) In determining the sentence, the Trial Chamber shall take into account the factors mentioned in Article 24, paragraph 2 of the Statute, as well as such factors as:
>
> (i) any aggravating circumstances;
>
> (ii) any mitigating circumstances including the substantial cooperation with the Prosecutor by the convicted person before or after conviction;
>
> (iii) the general practice regarding prison sentences in the courts of the former Yugoslavia;

(iv) the extent to which any penalty imposed by a court of any State on the convicted person for the same act has already been served, as referred to in Article 10, paragraph 3 of the Statute.

(C) Credit shall be given to the convicted person for the period, if any, during which the convicted person was detained in custody pending surrender to the Tribunal or pending trial or appeal.

ICTY Rules of Procedure and Evidence, Rule 101. The ICTR adopted a similar rule on sentencing. ICTR Rules of Procedure and Evidence, Rule 101.

Theoretical justifications for punishment can be divided into consequentialist, deontological, and expressive approaches. Consequentialists argue that the proper sentence is one that furthers the public welfare. Such an approach requires a weighing of the benefits of a particular sentence (specific and general deterrence, rehabilitation) with the costs (financial cost of incarceration, harm to the defendant). Alternatively, one might justify a particular sentence from a moral, or deontological, point of view separate and apart from any apparent utility. Retribution, or the idea that punishment is justified based upon the moral character of the act or actor and is indifferent to the costs and benefits to society, is one of the most common deontological justifications for punishment. Expressive justifications for punishment focus on the communicative function of a sentence. The punishment accorded to an individual convicted of a crime serves as a public statement of intolerance of the underlying act, as well as a reaffirmation of the values violated by the wrongful act.

Which approach should the international criminal justice system adopt? Can and should a balanced approach drawing upon all three justifications be developed? As you read through the following two case excerpts, ask yourself which approaches and values are guiding the Tribunal's decisions. The first two decisions arise out of guilty pleas. How does a guilty plea affect your analysis of sentencing under the three schools of thought? How did a guilty plea affect the two decisions below? We conclude this chapter with the first reparations judgment from the ICC.

Prosecutor v. Erdemović, Case No. IT–96–22–T, Sentencing Judgement (March 5, 1998)

In the Trial Chamber

1. The accused, Dražen Erdemović, came into the custody of the International Tribunal for the Prosecution of Persons Responsible for Serious Violations of International Humanitarian Law Committed in the Territory of the former Yugoslavia since 1991, hereinafter referred to as

the "International Tribunal," on 30 March 1996, further to an order for his transfer to the custody of the International Tribunal made by Judge Fouad Riad on 28 March 1996. * * *

3. Since his transfer to the International Tribunal, the accused has been cooperating with the investigators of the Office of the Prosecutor, hereinafter referred to as the "OTP," with respect to events surrounding the fall of Srebrenica. In July 1996, he testified at a hearing pursuant to Rule 61 of the Rules of Procedure and Evidence of the International Tribunal in the case of *Prosecutor v. Radovan Karadžić and Ratko Mladić*. * * *

13. * * * The parties were agreed on the facts. In particular, the accused agreed that the events alleged in the indictment were true, and the Prosecutor agreed that the accused's claim to have committed the acts in question pursuant to superior orders and under threat of death was correct. In these circumstances, the Trial Chamber accepts as fact the version of events which the parties have submitted, that is that the facts alleged in the indictment and the version of events described by the accused in his previous testimonies are statements of fact. * * *

14. However, the Trial Chamber also accepts that the accused committed the offence in question under threat of death. * * * Before Trial Chamber I dealing with the Rule 61 proceedings against Radovan Karadžić and Ratko Mladić on 5 July 1996:

Q. What happened to those civilians?

A. We were given orders to fire at those civilians, that is, to execute them.

Q. Did you follow that order?

A. Yes, but at first I resisted and Brano Gojkovic told me if I was sorry for those people that I should line up with them; and I knew that this was not just a mere threat but that it could happen, because in our unit the situation had become such that the Commander of the group has the right to execute on the spot any individual if he threatens the security of the group or if in any other way he opposes the Commander of the group appointed by the Commander Milorad Pelemis. * * *

Application of the Law to the Facts

15. Aggravating factors: The Trial Chamber accepts that hundreds of Bosnian Muslim civilian men between the ages of 17 and 60 were murdered by the execution squad of which the accused was part. The Prosecution has estimated that the accused alone, who says that he fired individual shots using a Kalashnikov automatic rifle, might have killed up to a hundred (100) people. This approximately matches his own estimate of seventy (70) persons. No matter how reluctant his initial decision to participate was, he continued to kill for most of that day. The Trial Chamber considers that the magnitude of the crime and the scale of the accused's role in it are aggravating circumstances to be taken into

account in accordance with Article 24(2) of the Statute of the International Tribunal.

16. Mitigating factors: * * * At the time of the killings at the Pilica collective farm, the accused was 23 years old. He is now 26 years old and evidence has been provided that he is "not a dangerous person for his environment." The Trial Chamber believes that his circumstances and character (see below) indicate that he is reformable and should be given a second chance to start his life afresh upon release, whilst still young enough to do so.

The accused has a wife, who is of different ethnic origin, and the couple have a young child who was born on 21 October 1994. Defence Counsel has submitted that the accused's family has fallen on hard times and will suffer hardship due to his serving a prison sentence.

The accused is a locksmith by training and was drawn into the maelstrom of violence that engulfed the former Yugoslavia. He has professed pacifist beliefs and claims to have been against the war and nationalism. He claims that he had to join the [Bosnian Serb Army (BSA)] in order to feed his family. In July 1995, he was a private in the 10th Sabotage Detachment where he was not in a position of command. He was, apart from a two month period as a sergeant in that unit, a mere foot soldier whose lack of commitment to any ethnic group in the conflict is demonstrated by the fact that he was by turns a reluctant participant in the Army of the Republic of Bosnia-Herzegovina, hereinafter referred to as the "ABH," the Croatian Defence Council, hereinafter referred to as the "HVO," and the BSA. The possibility of his being a soldier of fortune has not been suggested by any of the parties.

The 10th Sabotage Detachment was involved with reconnaissance in enemy territory and placing explosives in the artillery of the areas controlled by the ABH. According to the accused, he chose this unit because "it did not involve the loss of human lives. It involved artillery, old iron." In addition, he chose it as there were other non-Serb soldiers in it and it did not have a reputation for brutality at the material time. * * *

Witness X, who had been in the HVO Military Police with the accused, testified before Trial Chamber I that the accused had saved his life on Mount Majevica. The accused was with some other soldiers of the BSA when they came across Witness X, and he prevented his fellow soldiers from killing his former colleague. It was upon the insistence of the accused that Witness X was finally released unharmed.

Witness Y, who also testified before Trial Chamber I, met the accused in 1993 and they were part of a group of multi-ethnic friends. According to this witness, the accused was not a nationalist. He was a popular, vivacious and outgoing person who was non-confrontational. Witness Y was certain that the accused hated the war and the army but believed that he simply had to do all of it; he was not the sort of person to kill of his own free-will.

According to the evidence of the accused before Trial Chamber I, admitted by this Trial Chamber, he had helped a family of Serb civilians, mainly women and children, to escape from the Tuzla area to Republika Srpska, which led to his being assaulted by soldiers from the HVO. He also appears to have been imprisoned as a result. The accused has told the International Tribunal that during the killings at the Pilica collective farm, he tried to save a man, but was not able to do so because his commander, Brano Gojkovic, said that he did not want to have any witnesses to that crime.

Admission of Guilt

The Trial Chamber notes the submission of Defence Counsel that the accused's statements as to guilt should "above all, be taken as his moral attitude towards the truth on the one hand and as a plea for understanding of how far the limits of the abuse of man in this region were stretched, not only in his local environment but also in the wider scope." An admission of guilt demonstrates honesty and it is important for the International Tribunal to encourage people to come forth, whether already indicted or as unknown perpetrators. Furthermore, this voluntary admission of guilt which has saved the International Tribunal the time and effort of a lengthy investigation and trial is to be commended.

Remorse

The accused told Trial Chamber I that:

> I only wish to say that I feel sorry for all the victims, not only for the ones who were killed then at that farm. I feel sorry for all the victims in the former [sic] Bosnia and Herzegovina regardless of their nationality.

On 24 June 1996, the Commission of Medical Experts noted that the accused had an ambivalent feeling about his guilt. "He knew he killed innocent civilians, but he had no choice himself. There were other people who ordered him to shoot people. In a legal sense he doesn't feel guilty of the crimes he is accused of." The post-traumatic stress which the accused suffered from in the aftermath of the Srebrenica atrocities demonstrates how he himself has suffered from being forced to commit the killings against his will.

The Trial Chamber also takes note of the testimony of Mr. Jean-René Ruez [an ICTY investigator]. Having been able to study the accused closely in the course of the OTP's investigations, Mr. Ruez has told the Trial Chamber that he had no doubt that the accused's feelings of sorrow and remorse were genuine and real, and that he really was going through an emotional process. * * *

Cooperation with the OTP

"The collaboration of Dražen Erdemović has been absolutely excellent." These are words rarely spoken by the Prosecution of an accused. The Trial Chamber, remembering its obligation to consider such cooperation under Rule 101 of the Rules of Procedure and Evidence of the International Tribunal, takes note accordingly. It also notes the submission of the Prosecution, supported by the testimony of Mr. Ruez, that the accused cooperated without asking for anything in return and that the extent and value of his cooperation has been such as to justify considerable mitigation.

Whilst the OTP knew in general terms of the killings committed in Srebrenica, the testimony of the accused was particularly valuable for providing them with details of four incidents of which they did not previously know: the killings at the Pilica collective farm, those at the Pilica cultural hall, the killing of an unidentified civilian male of military age in Srebrenica as the accused entered the town, and a killing in Vlasenica on 13 July 1996 after he returned to Bijeljina, by soldiers who, under orders, cut the throat of a prisoner. Prior to the testimony of the accused, the OTP had no knowledge of these incidents.

The accused provided substantial details in connection with the aforementioned incidents such as the identification of his commanders and fellow executioners, as well as information on the Drina Corps, the structure of the BSA and the units that were involved in the takeover of Srebrenica such as the 10th Sabotage Detachment and the Bratunac Brigade.

On 5 July 1996, the accused gave evidence in the Rule 61 hearing of the case brought against Radovan Karadžić and Ratko Mladić. His testimony was significant in two respects: it contributed to the decision of the Rule 61 Chamber to issue international arrest warrants for the two, and secondly, his testimony, that of an insider in the BSA, is evidence of what happened in Srebrenica.

Duress

The Trial Chamber has applied the ruling of the Appeals Chamber that "duress does not afford a complete defence to a soldier charged with a crime against humanity and/or a war crime involving the killing of innocent human beings." It may be taken into account only by way of mitigation.

It has been accepted by the parties and the Trial Chamber that there was duress in this case. The earlier testimony of the accused has been cited above. Mr. Ruez has testified of the circumstances of a very vicious and cruelly fought war, the brutal nature of the battle for Srebrenica, the attendant environment of soldiers killing pursuant to superior orders, the accused's vulnerable position as a Bosnian Croat in the BSA and his history of disagreements with his commander, Milorad Pelemis, and subsequent demotion. He feels that had the accused refused to shoot, "most certainly, he would get into very deep trouble. . . ."

The accused displays a tendency to feel the helpless victim; there are several references in his testimonies to his having no choice in a variety of situations. He speaks of his having to become a soldier, that he had no choice in leaving the Republic of Croatia for Republika Srpska, that he had to join the BSA "to feed my family," that he "simply had to" go to the military barracks and leave behind his bedridden wife and sick child, that he had no choice in taking part in the Srebrenica operation, and that he "had to shoot those people" murdered in the Pilica collective farm massacre. On the other hand, he has provided testimony of incidents when he broke out of this chain of helplessness and took positive action; such as when he saved some Serbs in Tuzla, when he saved Witness X, when he refused to comply with the orders of Lieutenant Milorad Pelemis, when he tried to refuse to kill at the collective farm and when he refused to kill at the hall in Pilica. Thus, he was capable of taking positive action, once he had weighed up his options. The risks that he took appear to have been calculated and considered.

The evidence reveals the extremity of the situation faced by the accused. The Trial Chamber finds that there was a real risk that the accused would have been killed had he disobeyed the order. He voiced his feelings, but realised that he had no choice in the matter: he had to kill or be killed.

Plea Bargain Agreement

18. On 8 January 1998, both sides filed with the Registry a "Joint Motion for Consideration of Plea Agreement between Dražen Erdemović and the Office of the Prosecutor." Attached thereto was a plea agreement between the parties, the purpose of which was expressed to be to clarify the understanding of the parties as to the nature and consequences of the accused's plea of guilty, and to assist the parties and the Trial Chamber in ensuring that the plea entered into by the accused was valid, according to the rules of the International Tribunal. The essential elements of the plea agreement were that:

(a) The accused would plead guilty to count 2, a violation of the laws or customs of war, in full understanding of the distinction between that charge and the alternative charge of a crime against humanity, and the consequences of his plea.

(b) The accused's plea was based on his guilt and his acknowledgement of full responsibility for the actions with which he is charged.

(c) The parties agreed on the factual basis of the allegations against the accused, and in particular the fact that there was duress.

(d) The parties, in full appreciation of the sole competence of the Trial Chamber to determine the sentence, recommended that seven years' imprisonment would be an appropriate sentence in this case, considering the mitigating circumstances.

(e) In view of the accused's agreement to enter a plea of guilty to count 2, the Prosecutor agreed not to proceed with the alternative count of a crime against humanity.

19. Plea bargain agreements are common in certain jurisdictions of the world. There is no provision for such agreements in the Statute and Rules of Procedure and Evidence of the International Tribunal. This is the first time that such a document has been presented to the International Tribunal. The plea agreement in this case is simply an agreement between the parties, reached on their own initiative without the contribution or encouragement of the Trial Chamber. Upon being questioned by the Presiding Judge of the Trial Chamber, the accused confirmed his agreement to and understanding of the matters contained therein. The parties themselves acknowledge that the plea agreement has no binding effect on this Chamber, although submissions recommending it were made by both the Prosecutor and Defence Counsel at the hearing on 14 January 1998, in addition to the recommendations in the joint motion. Whilst in no way bound by this agreement, the Trial Chamber has taken it into careful consideration in determining the sentence to be imposed upon the accused.

Sentencing Policy of the Chamber

20. In addition to the aggravating and mitigating circumstances already discussed, the sentence determined by the Trial Chamber has taken into account the circumstances of the killings, looking in particular at the degree of suffering to which the victims of the massacre were subjected before and during the killings, the means used by the accused to kill and his attitude at the time. The atmosphere of terror and violence has been well-illustrated to the Trial Chamber by the accused and Mr. Ruez; the victims were, in particular after the arrival on the scene of members of the Bratunac Brigade, subjected to physical assault, humiliation and verbal abuse. For the victims who arrived after the first set of killings, there was the certain knowledge of death, as they will have seen the bodies of those already murdered and heard the gunshots fired by the accused and his fellow executioners. The degree of suffering of these people cannot be overlooked. But the accused's reluctance to participate and his reaction to having to perform this gruesome task have already been discussed elsewhere in this Judgement. It is clear that he took no perverse pleasure from what he did.

21. It is in the interests of international criminal justice and the purposes of the International Tribunal to give appropriate weight to the cooperative attitude of the accused. He truthfully confessed his involvement in the massacre at a time when no authority was seeking to prosecute him in connection therewith, knowing that he would most probably face prosecution as a result. Understanding of the situation of those who surrender to the jurisdiction of the International Tribunal and who confess their guilt is important for encouraging other suspects or unknown perpetrators to come forward. The International Tribunal, in

addition to its mandate to investigate, prosecute and punish serious violations of international humanitarian law, has a duty, through its judicial functions, to contribute to the settlement of the wider issues of accountability, reconciliation and establishing the truth behind the evils perpetrated in the former Yugoslavia. Discovering the truth is a cornerstone of the rule of law and a fundamental step on the way to reconciliation: for it is the truth that cleanses the ethnic and religious hatreds and begins the healing process. The International Tribunal must demonstrate that those who have the honesty to confess are treated fairly as part of a process underpinned by principles of justice, fair trial and protection of the fundamental rights of the individual. On the other hand, the International Tribunal is a vehicle through which the international community expresses its outrage at the atrocities committed in the former Yugoslavia. Upholding values of international human rights means that whilst protecting the rights of the accused, the International Tribunal must not lose sight of the tragedy of the victims and the sufferings of their families.

Credit for Time Served

22. Under Rule 101(E) of the Rules of Procedure and Evidence of the International Tribunal, the Trial Chamber is required to give credit to the convicted person for the period, if any, during which he was detained in custody pending his surrender to the International Tribunal, or pending trial or appeal. Time spent in custody in respect of domestic prosecutions is not given credit for, until a formal request for deferral to the jurisdiction of the International Tribunal is made. In the instant case, an "Order for Transfer to the Custody of the International Tribunal" was made by Judge Fouad Riad on 28 March 1996. The relevant period of time spent in custody will therefore run from that date.

Penalty

23. For the foregoing reasons, having considered all of the evidence and the arguments of the parties and the jurisprudence of the International Tribunal, the Trial Chamber, in accordance with the Statute and Rules of Procedure and Evidence, imposes on Dražen Erdemović the sentence of five (5) years' imprisonment for the violation of the laws or customs of war to which he pleaded guilty on 14 January 1998, with credit to be given for his time in detention since 28 March 1996.

Prosecutor v. Plavšić, Case No. IT–00–39 & 40/1–T, Sentencing Judgement (Feb. 27, 2003)

In the Trial Chamber

1. The accused, Biljana Plavšić, surrendered voluntarily to the International Criminal Tribunal for the Former Yugoslavia (ICTY) ("International Tribunal") on 10 January 2001. * * *

2. * * * An amended consolidated indictment * * * contained counts against the accused alleging genocide, complicity in genocide, and the following crimes against humanity: persecutions, extermination and killing, deportation and inhumane acts.

3. At her initial appearance before Trial Chamber III on the 11 January 2001 the accused pleaded not guilty to all counts and was remanded to the United Nations Detention Unit ("UNDU"). * * *

5. At a hearing on the 2 October 2002 the accused pleaded guilty to Count 3, persecutions, a crime against humanity. The Trial Chamber, being satisfied that the plea was voluntary, informed and unequivocal, and that there was a sufficient factual basis for the crime and the accused's participation in it, then entered a finding of guilt. The accused's plea was entered pursuant to a Plea Agreement made between the parties dated 30 September 2002. In the Agreement, paragraphs 3 and 9(a), the Prosecutor agreed to move to dismiss the remaining counts of the Indictment following the accused's plea of guilty and they were dismissed by a Decision by the Trial Chamber on 20 December 2002.

The Facts

8. Count 3, to which the accused has pleaded guilty, alleges that between 1 July 1991 and 30 December 1992 the accused, acting individually and in concert with others in a joint criminal enterprise, planned, instigated, ordered and aided and abetted persecutions of the Bosnian Muslim, Bosnian Croat and other non-Serb populations of 37 municipalities in Bosnia and Herzegovina ("BH"). The Count, together with accompanying Schedules, sets out the persecutions, and is annexed to this Judgement.

9. A written Factual Basis for the crime described above and for the participation of the accused was filed with the Plea Agreement. The Factual Basis was agreed by the accused and forms the basis upon which the Trial Chamber now passes sentence. It is summarised in the following paragraphs.

10. The Factual Basis first deals with the career of the accused. Mrs. Plavšić is now aged 72 years, having been born on 7 July 1930 in Tuzla, Bosnia and Herzegovina. She had a distinguished academic career as a Professor of Natural Sciences and Dean of Faculty in the University of Sarajevo. She was not involved in politics until she joined the Serbian Democratic Party ("SDS") in July 1990. However, she very soon rose to become a prominent member of the party and to occupy a position of leadership with the Serb Republic of BH. She was elected as a Serbian Representative to the Presidency of the Socialist Republic of Bosnia and Herzegovina on 11 November 1990 until December 1992. The accused was active in the Presidency of the Republic of BH, and in that of the Serbian Republic of BH: from 28 February to 12 May 1992 she was acting co-President, and from May until December 1992 she was a member of the collective and expanded Presidencies of Republika Srpska. * * *

13. In commenting on the individual roles of the participants, the Factual Basis states that numerous individuals participated in devising and executing the above objective. There were differences both as to their knowledge of the details and their participation in the execution of the objective. For her part, Mrs. Plavšić

> embraced and supported the objective [. . .] and contributed to achieving it. She did not participate with Miloševic, Karadžić, Krajišnik and others in its conception and planning and had a lesser role in its execution than Karadžić, Krajišnik and others.

14. * * * The Main Staff of the VRS [army of the Serbian Republic] was responsible to the Presidency, which in May-June 1992 was composed of Radovan Karadžić, Nikola Koljevic and Mrs. Plavšić. Thereafter, the collective Presidency was expanded to include Momcilo Krajišnik and Branko Djeric. The Presidency also had authority over the Bosnian Serb police, [territorial defense] and civilian authorities. * * *

17. The Factual Basis also deals with the reaction of the Bosnian Serb leadership, including the accused, to [the crimes alleged in the indictment]. It sets out that

> Mrs. Plavšić participated in the cover up of these crimes by making public statements of denial for which she had no support. When she subsequently had reason to know that these denials were in fact untrue, she did not recant or correct them.

18. The Bosnian Serb leadership, including Mrs. Plavšić, ignored the allegations of crimes committed by their forces: Mrs. Plavšić disregarded reports of widespread ethnic cleansing and publicly rationalised and justified it. She was aware that the key leaders of the Serbian Republic of BH ignored these crimes despite the power to prevent and punish them. As the objective of ethnic separation by force continued to be achieved through the crimes mentioned above, Mrs. Plavšić continued to support the regime through her presence within the leadership structure, through her public praise and defence of Bosnian Serb forces and through the denial of Bosnian Serb crimes. * * *

21. Thus in determining sentence the Trial Chamber must take account of the following factors:

- the gravity of the crime;
- any aggravating circumstances;
- any mitigating circumstances;
- the general practice regarding prison sentences in the courts of the former Yugoslavia.

22. The Appeals Chamber of the International Tribunal has held that retribution and deterrence are the main principles in sentencing for international crimes. These purposive considerations should form the context within which an individual accused's sentence must be determined.

23. As set out in detail in the *Todorović* Sentencing Judgement, the principle of retribution must be understood as reflecting a fair and balanced approach to the exaction of punishment for wrongdoing. This means that the penalty must be proportionate to the wrongdoing; in other words, the punishment must fit the crime. This principle is reflected in the requirement in the Statute that the Trial Chambers, in imposing sentences, must take into account the gravity of the offence.

24. The Appeals Chamber has held that deterrence "is a consideration that may legitimately be considered in sentencing" and has further recognised the "general importance of deterrence as a consideration in sentencing for international crimes." Again, as noted in the *Todorović* Sentencing Judgement, the Trial Chamber understands this to mean that deterrence is one of the principles underlying the determination of sentences, in that the penalties imposed by the International Tribunal must, in general, have sufficient deterrent value to ensure that those who would consider committing similar crimes will be dissuaded from doing so.

25. The cardinal feature in sentencing is the gravity of the crime. The Appeals Chamber has described this as the "primary consideration" and stated that the "sentences to be imposed must reflect the inherent gravity of the criminal conduct of the accused."[28]

Sentencing Factors

26. The Trial Chamber will, therefore, begin its consideration of the various factors by first considering the gravity of the offence, bearing in mind, as the Appeals Chamber said, that this requires a consideration of the particular circumstances of the case, as well as the form and the degree of the participation of the accused in the crime. * * * [The opinion next describes the organized and systematic campaign of persecution conducted by the Bosnian Serb forces throughout Bosnia-Herzegovina including forced expulsion and transfer, widespread killings, destruction of property and religious buildings, and cruel or inhumane treatment in detention facilities.]

Gravity of the Crime

27. The Prosecution submits that the distinctive feature of the crime of persecution, namely a discriminatory intent and the incorporation of other crimes, means that a more severe penalty is justified. The Prosecution further submits that the scale of the campaign, in which the accused participated, was massive and over a vast area, with hundreds and thousands expelled and many killed: the campaign was conducted with particular brutality and cruelty including torture and sexual violence.

---

[28] *Čelebići* Appeal Judgement, para. 731, citing *Prosecutor v. Kupreškić* et al., Case No. IT–95–16–T, Trial Judgement, para. 852 (Jan. 14, 2000); and *Aleksovski* Appeal Judgement, para. 182.

28. The Defence acknowledges that Bosnian Serb forces conducted a campaign of persecution which was organised, systematic and widespread. The Defence accepts that the gravity of the offence and the form and participation of Mrs. Plavšić in it are detailed in Count 3 of the Indictment and in the Factual Basis.

29. The Prosecution also attached, in Annex II to its Brief, extracts from the testimony of witnesses in other cases before the International Tribunal to demonstrate the impact of the crimes upon them. * * *

49. Many of those persons who were forcibly transferred or expelled remain traumatised by their experiences, ten years after the events. * * *

51. Mrs. Plavšić also made a statement to the Trial Chamber where she admitted her role in the victimisation and persecution of countless innocent people. Mrs. Plavšić stated that

> although I was repeatedly informed of allegations of cruel and inhuman conduct against non-Serbs, I refused to accept them or even to investigate. In fact, I immersed myself in addressing the suffering of the war's innocent Serb victims. This daily work confirmed in my mind that we were in a struggle for our very survival and that in this struggle, the international community was our enemy, and so I simply denied these charges, making no effort to investigate. I remained secure in my belief that Serbs were not capable of such acts. In this obsession of ours to never again become victims, we had allowed ourselves to become victimisers.

Aggravating Circumstances

53. The Prosecution identifies three aggravating factors:

(i) the leadership position of the accused;

(ii) the vulnerability of the victims; and

(iii) the depravity of the crimes to which the victims were subjected.

54. In relation to the first factor, the Prosecution notes that the International Tribunal has consistently viewed the leadership position of an accused as an aggravating factor. The Prosecution cites the trial judgement in Krstić in contending that the consequences are necessarily more serious if individuals who occupy top military or political positions use those positions to commit crimes. The Prosecution also draws the attention of the Trial Chamber to cases where leadership positions lower than that occupied by Mrs. Plavšić have been found to be aggravating circumstances. The Prosecution moreover observes that in the *Kambanda* case at the International Criminal Tribunal for Rwanda ("ICTR") the Chamber emphasised the aggravating impact of Kambanda's leadership position when assessing the weight of aggravating factors. Jean Kambanda was the Prime Minister of Rwanda at the time of the commission of the crimes in question. * * *

56. The Defence accepts that the scope of the crimes outlined in Count 3 of the Indictment and the manner in which they were committed may be taken into account as an aggravating factor. The Defence also accepts that such aggravating factors may include the scale and planning of the offence, the number of victims, the length of time over which the crimes were committed, the violence associated with the crimes and the repeated and systematic nature of the crimes. However, the Defence submits that a high rank in the political field should not, in itself, result in a harsher sentence for an accused, but accepts that an individual who wrongly exercises or abuses power deserves a harsher sentence than a person acting on his or her own. Further, it notes that while the direct participation of a high level superior in a crime under Article 7(1) of the Statute is an aggravating circumstance, the extent of such aggravation depends on the level of authority and the form of participation of the accused.

57. The Trial Chamber accepts that the superior position of the accused is an aggravating factor in the case. The accused was not in the very first rank of the leadership: others occupied that position. She did not conceive the plan which led to this crime and had a lesser role in its execution than others. Nonetheless, Mrs. Plavšić was in the Presidency, the highest civilian body, during the campaign and encouraged and supported it by her participation in the Presidency and her pronouncements. * * *

60. The Trial Chamber, therefore, has to determine an appropriate sentence for an accused who was in the high leadership position described and was involved in crimes of the utmost gravity. The Trial Chamber is unable to accept the submission of the Prosecution that the severest sentence, i.e. imprisonment for the rest of her life, which this International Tribunal is capable of passing would be appropriate in the absence of a plea of guilty. On the other hand, the Trial Chamber does accept that misplaced leniency would not be fitting and that a substantial sentence of imprisonment is called for.

Mitigating Circumstances

61. There is in this case substantial mitigation, covering a number of relevant factors which may conveniently be set out from the Prosecution's Brief. Indeed, the Prosecution acknowledges that Mrs. Plavšić has undertaken unprecedented steps to mitigate the crime against humanity for which she is responsible. The Prosecution submits that the relevant mitigating circumstances include:

- entry of a guilty plea and acceptance of responsibility;
- remorse;
- voluntary surrender;
- post-conflict conduct;

- previous good character; and
- age.

62. It has not been disputed that the above together with reconciliation are the relevant mitigating circumstances for the Trial Chamber to consider. Before considering them, it is necessary to consider the law as it applies to mitigating circumstances.

63. An accused's "substantial" co-operation with the Prosecutor is the only mitigating circumstance that is expressly mentioned in the Rules. As noted in the *Todorović* and *Sikirica* sentencing judgements, this Trial Chamber holds that the determination as to whether an accused's co-operation has been substantial depends on the extent and quality of the information he or she provides. However, in the present case the Prosecution asserts that there has been no such co-operation. On the other hand, the Defence submits that the accused has provided substantial co-operation by her plea of guilty.

64. As noted, co-operation with the Prosecutor is a mitigating circumstance, but it does not follow that failure to do so is an aggravating circumstance. Therefore, the accused's unwillingness to give evidence is not a factor to be taken into account in determining sentence.

65. A Trial Chamber has the discretion to consider any other factors which it considers to be of a mitigating nature. These factors will vary with the circumstances of each case. In addition to substantial co-operation with the Prosecutor, Chambers of the International Tribunal have found the following factors relevant to this case to be mitigating: voluntary surrender; a guilty plea; expression of remorse; good character with no prior criminal conviction; and the post-conflict conduct of the accused. These matters will now be discussed.

Guilty Plea Including Remorse and Reconciliation

66. The Prosecution points out that the accused entered a guilty plea before the commencement of trial, and that this is to be regarded as a circumstance in mitigation of sentence for the following two reasons. First, a guilty plea before the beginning of the trial obviates the need for victims and witnesses to give evidence and may save considerable time, effort and resources. Second, the Prosecution cites dicta from the *Todorović* Sentencing Judgement that a guilty plea "is always important for the purpose of establishing the truth in relation to that crime" and from the *Erdemović* Sentencing Judgement that the discovery of truth is "a fundamental step on the way to reconciliation." * * *

68. The Defence submits that in the jurisprudence of the International Tribunal a guilty plea has given rise to a reduction in the sentence which the accused would otherwise have received for the following reasons: a) it demonstrates honesty; b) it contributes to the fundamental mission of the International Tribunal to establish the truth in relation to crimes within its jurisdiction; c) it provides a unique and unquestionable fact-finding tool that greatly contributes to peace-

building and reconciliation among the affected communities: individual accountability leads to the return of the rule of law, reconciliation and the restoration of peace across the territory of the former Yugoslavia; d) it contributes to public advantage and the work of the International Tribunal by saving considerable resources for investigation, counsel fees and trial costs; and e) it may relieve some victim witnesses from the stress of giving evidence. Further, the Defence submits that an accused who pleads guilty prior to the commencement of trial will usually receive "full credit" for that plea.

69. The significance of the plea of guilty in this case was highlighted in the evidence of Professor Elie Wiesel. He said that whereas others similarly accused deny the truth about their crimes and thereby assist those who want to falsify history, Mrs. Plavšić, who once moved in the highest circles of power, has made an example by freely and wholly admitting her role in the crime. * * *

70. Two matters related to a plea of guilt concern expression of remorse and steps toward reconciliation. In this regard, the Prosecution notes that the accused has expressed her remorse "fully and unconditionally" and the hope that her guilty plea will assist her people to reconcile with their neighbours. The Prosecution states that this expression of remorse is noteworthy since it is offered from a person who formerly held a leadership position, and that it "merits judicial consideration." * * *

72. In her statement at the Sentencing Hearing Mrs. Plavšić said that she had "now come to the belief and accept the fact that many thousands of innocent people were the victims of an organised, systematic effort to remove Muslims and Croats from the territory claimed by Serbs." She added that at the time she convinced herself that it was a matter of survival and self-defence. However, the fact was that the Bosnian Serb leadership, of which she was "a necessary part, led an effort which victimised countless innocent people." She continued by saying that in their fear, especially those for whom the Second World War was more than a memory, the leadership violated the basic duty to restrain itself and to respect the human dignity of others: "the knowledge that I am responsible for such human suffering and for soiling the character of my people will always be with me."

73. The Trial Chamber accepts this, together with expressions in her earlier statement in support of the motion to change her plea, as an expression of remorse to be considered as part of the mitigating circumstances connected with a guilty plea. Indeed, it may be argued that by her guilty plea, Mrs. Plavšić had already demonstrated remorse. This, together with the substantial saving of international time and resources as a result of a plea of guilty before trial, entitle the accused to a discount in the sentence which would otherwise have been appropriate. However, there is a further and significant circumstance to be considered, namely the role of the guilty plea of the accused in establishing the truth in

relation to the crimes and furthering reconciliation in the former Yugoslavia.

74. This theme was first sounded in Mrs. Plavšić's statement in support of her change of plea in which she referred to the need for acknowledgement of the crimes committed during the war in BH as a necessary step towards peace and reconciliation and her hope that her acceptance of responsibility would enable her people to reconcile with their neighbours. She concluded the statement:

> To achieve any reconciliation or lasting peace in BH, serious violations of humanitarian law during the war must be acknowledged by those who bear responsibility—regardless of their ethnic group. This acknowledgement is an essential first step. * * *

79. With regard to reconciliation generally, the Trial Chamber reiterates the words of Security Council Resolution 827 in which the establishment of the International Tribunal and the bringing to justice of persons responsible for serious violations of international humanitarian law was said to "contribute to the restoration and maintenance of peace" in the former Yugoslavia. Further, in a 1999 General Assembly Resolution concerning the situation in BH, the General Assembly stressed "the importance and urgency of the work of the International Tribunal as an element of the process of reconciliation and as a factor contributing to the maintenance of international peace and security" in BH and in the region as a whole. The Trial Chamber must attach importance to these statements.

80. The Trial Chamber accepts that acknowledgement and full disclosure of serious crimes are very important when establishing the truth in relation to such crimes. This, together with acceptance of responsibility for the committed wrongs, will promote reconciliation. In this respect, the Trial Chamber concludes that the guilty plea of Mrs. Plavšić and her acknowledgement of responsibility, particularly in the light of her former position as President of Republika Srpska, should promote reconciliation in Bosnia and Herzegovina and the region as a whole.

81. The Trial Chamber will accordingly give significant weight to the plea of guilty by the accused, as well as her accompanying expressed remorse and positive impact on the reconciliatory process, as a mitigating factor.

Voluntary Surrender

83. The [Prosecutor and] Defence also submits that a voluntary surrender to the International Tribunal is a mitigating factor. * * *

Post-Conflict Conduct

85. The Prosecution accepts that Mrs. Biljana Plavšić, as President of Republika Srpska, demonstrated considerable support for the 1995

General Framework Agreement for Peace in Bosnia and Herzegovina ("Dayton Agreement") after the cessation of hostilities in Bosnia and Herzegovina. It also accepts that in that position, the accused also attempted to remove obstructive officials from office, and contributed significantly to the advancement of the Dayton peace process under difficult circumstances in which she manifested courage.

86. The Defence also submits that the accused's post-conflict conduct should be considered in mitigation of sentence. It states that the accused made extraordinary contributions to the post war process in Bosnia and Herzegovina: beginning in 1996, as President of Republika Srpska, the accused broke with the leadership of the SDS of BH and became instrumental in the implementation of the Dayton Agreement. In June 1997, she was in a power struggle with the Pale-based leadership of the SDS, and over the next months, she removed obstructive officials from office, dissolved the hard-line dominated National Assembly and transferred government offices from Pale to Banja Luka. The accused left the SDS and created the Serbian People's Alliance, which formed part of the government after the elections in November 1997. She presided over the creation of a multi-ethnic coalition that effectively took control of political life in Republika Srpska, which in turn significantly advanced the implementation of the Dayton Agreement. In August 1998 the accused remained committed to the Dayton Agreement, which resulted in her loss of the Presidency of the Republika Srpska to a hard-line, nationalist candidate. However, the accused remained a voice in favour of it as a member of the National Assembly. * * *

89. In the spring of 1997 there was further confrontation between Mrs. Plavšić, as President of Republika Srpska, who was based in Banja Luka, and the Bosnian Serb powers in Pale, and she came increasingly under threat. According to Carl Bildt there were three or four cases which were judged as "serious, direct, also physical threats against her as part of attempts by Pale to get rid of her, because [. . .] they judged that [. . .] full Dayton implementation was a threat to them."

94. * * * The Trial Chamber is satisfied that Mrs. Plavšić was instrumental in ensuring that the Dayton Agreement was accepted and implemented in Republika Srpska. As such, she made a considerable contribution to peace in the region and is entitled to pray it in aid in mitigation of sentence. The Trial Chamber gives it significant weight. * * *

Age

104. First, the Trial Chamber rejects the Defence's contention that any sentence in excess of 8.2 years is tantamount to life imprisonment and would constitute inhumane or degrading punishment. Neither in the Statute nor in international human rights law is there any prohibition against the imposition of a sentence (including a life sentence) on an offender of advanced age. The ECHR has held that in certain circumstances the detention of an elderly person over a lengthy period

may raise the issue of the prohibition against inhumane and degrading treatment. Any such treatment must attain a minimum level of severity to fall within the scope of Article 3 of the European Convention on Human Rights. However, regard is to be had to the particular circumstances of each specific case. In the instant case, the Trial Chamber can find no such relevant circumstances: the medical report submitted by the accused does not indicate that she is suffering from any condition which would prevent the imposition of a prison sentence.

105. Second, the Trial Chamber is not persuaded by the Defence submission that a calculation of the accused's life expectancy is a crucial factor in determining sentence. However, the Trial Chamber considers that it should take account of the age of the accused and does so for two reasons: First, physical deterioration associated with advanced years makes serving the same sentence harder for an older than a younger accused. Second, as the New South Wales Court of Appeal observed in *Holyoak*, an offender of advanced years may have little worthwhile life left upon release.

106. Thus, the Trial Chamber prefers * * * to determine an appropriate sentence corresponding to the gravity of the offence, taking into account the age and the circumstances of the accused. For the above reasons, the Trial Chamber considers as a mitigating factor the advanced age of the accused and in doing so, it takes into account the medical report filed on her behalf. * * *

Determination of Sentence

126. * * * [T]he Trial Chamber also has in mind that these crimes did not happen to a nameless group but to individual men, women and children who were mistreated, raped, tortured and killed. This consideration and the fact that this appalling conduct was repeated so frequently, calls for a substantial sentence of imprisonment. The Trial Chamber has already found this to be a crime of the utmost gravity. That is the starting point for determination of sentence.

127. Furthermore, the seriousness of the offence is aggravated, as the Trial Chamber finds, by the senior leadership position of the accused. Instead of generally preventing or mitigating the crimes, she encouraged and supported those responsible. Any sentence must reflect this factor.

128. In its Sentencing Brief the Prosecution, having acknowledged the mitigating factors, in particular the acknowledgement of crimes, acceptance of responsibility and expression of remorse from a former leader, points out, correctly, that these factors must be appropriately balanced against the gravity of the crime and the factors in aggravation: the Prosecution submits that an appropriate sentence in this case is a term of imprisonment of not less than 15 years and not more than 25 years. This submission was reiterated by the Prosecution at the Sentencing Hearing. * * *

131. The Defence, on the other hand, has made no recommendation as to an appropriate sentence, submitting that since the life expectancy of the accused is eight years any sentence beyond that would amount to life imprisonment and would be inappropriate. The Trial Chamber has already held that the reference to life expectancy is irrelevant. It also considers that a sentence of eight years imprisonment would fail to meet the gravity of this offence.

132. The Trial Chamber has to pass sentence on a 72-year-old former President for her participation in a crime of the utmost gravity. On the other hand, as the Trial Chamber has found, there are very significant mitigating circumstances, in particular the guilty plea and the post-conflict conduct. Nonetheless, undue leniency would be misplaced. No sentence which the Trial Chamber passes can fully reflect the horror of what occurred or the terrible impact on thousands of victims. Giving due weight to the various factors set out above, the Trial Chamber has come to the conclusion that a sentence of eleven years' imprisonment is appropriate in this case.

NOTES & QUESTIONS

1. Case Outcomes

Erdemović served his time in a Norwegian prison and appeared as a witness for the prosecution in the *Krstić* case where he testified about General Krstić's role in the Srebrenica massacre. *Prosecutor v. Krstić,* Case No. IT–98–33, Judgement (April 19, 2004). This case was excerpted in Chapter 9 on Genocide. What would you say to a journalist who asked you whether you thought the sentence imposed on Erdemović for the killing of 70–100 people was appropriate? For more on the *Erdemović* case, *see* L.C. Green, *Dražen Erdemović: The International Criminal Tribunal for the Former Yugoslavia in Action,* 10 LEIDEN J. INT'L L. 363 (1997); Robert Cryer, *One Appeal, Two Philosophies, Four Opinions and a Remittal: The* Erdemović *Case at the ICTY Appeals Chamber*, 2 J. ARMED CONFLICT L. 193 (1997); David Turns, *The International Criminal Tribunal for the Former Yugoslavia (ICTY): The* Erdemović *Case*, 47 INT'L & COMP. L. Q. 461 (1998).

Plavšić is serving her sentence in Sweden. A request for pardon in 2007 was denied. In 2009, she was granted early release for "good behavior" and "substantial evidence of rehabilitation."

2. Principles of Sentencing and Sources of Law

Where does the Tribunal look for legal principles to apply to its sentencing decisions? What principles do you think should be emphasized? Consider this summary of the jurisprudence of the ICTY:

> Early judgments identified deterrence and retribution as the two primary purposes of sentencing in international criminal justice. Some trial chambers added two more principles to create "four parameters" for international sentencing: retribution, deterrence, rehabilitation, and protection of society. However, it is fair to say that rehabilitation was never highly significant and did not act as

> a meaningful "parameter" to limit the sentence, as made apparent in the Trial Chamber's judgment of General Blaškić. Despite acknowledging "rehabilitation" as one of the parameters guiding its determination of Blaškić's sentence and despite its own factual findings strongly indicating the possibility of rehabilitation in his individual case, the Trial Chamber nevertheless decided to not give these factors any weight and certainly its 45 year sentence leaves little trace of rehabilitation considerations, especially since Blaškić was 40 years old when he was sentenced. Such a sentence suggests that the Tribunal, early on, was eager to send a strong signal of deterrence and that this predominated in its sentencing considerations, even to the extent, some would argue, of trial chambers distributing exemplary sentences or exemplary justice and placing that foremost in their considerations.

Shahram Dana, *Genocide, Reconciliation and Sentencing Jurisprudence in the ICTY*, *in* THE CRIMINAL LAW OF GENOCIDE 259 (Ralph Henham & Paul Behrens eds., 2007). Incidentally, as discussed in Chapter 14 on Superior Responsibility, the Appeals Chamber ultimately reduced Blaškić's sentence. Do the excerpts above illustrate an overly retributive or restorative jurisprudence? Or is there no clear principle that one can derive from the jurisprudence? For an attempt to articulate a global set of principles for sentencing, *see* Olaoluwa Olusanya, SENTENCING WAR CRIMES AND CRIMES AGAINST HUMANITY UNDER THE INTERNATIONAL CRIMINAL TRIBUNAL FOR THE FORMER YUGOSLAVIA (2005). As the tribunals develop sentencing practices, how helpful would domestic sentencing practices likely be? Are the principles governing international justice so different from those governing domestic justice that the utility of the latter is minimal to the former?

3. The Interests of the Victims

How important are the interests of victims to the Tribunal in imposing an appropriate sentence? How important should they be? The *Erdemović* Judgment primarily focuses on characteristics of the accused, and not the impact on the victims. The *Plavšić* decision, by contrast, discusses the impact of her actions on victims, including testimony by the Nobel Prize winner, Elie Wiesel. What explains this difference in emphasis? Is it justified?

4. Hierarchy and Sentencing

Should the level of an individual within a military or government hierarchy be taken into account in sentencing? Should the direct participants be sentenced more severely than their superiors, on the theory that the latter were more "active" participants in the crime? One ICTY Trial Chamber considered, but rejected, this reasoning:

> The fact that the accused did not directly participate may be taken as a mitigating circumstance when the accused holds a junior position within the civilian or military command structure. However, the Trial Chamber considers the fact that commanders, such as. . . [Blaškić] at the time of the crimes, played no direct part cannot act in mitigation of the sentence when found guilty.

Prosecutor v. Tihomir Blaškić, Case No. IT–95–14–T, para. 768 (Mar. 3, 2000). Do you agree? How did a consideration of rank influence the sentences imposed on Erdemović and Plavšić? For a discussion of how the ICC should take into account the *mens rea* of superiors in their sentencing, *see* Volker Nerlich, *Superior Responsibility Under Article 28 ICC Statute: For What Exactly is the Superior Held Responsible?*, 5 J. INT'L CRIM. JUST. 665 (2007). Empirically, the superior responsibility sentences of the ICTR have been higher than those at the ICTY. Why might this be so? Should the fact that most of the ICTR defendants were civilian, rather than military, leaders be relevant? For a discussion of superior responsibility and sentencing generally, *see* Amy Sepinwall, *Failures to Punish: Command Responsibility in Domestic and International Law*, 30 MICH. J. INT'L L. 251 (2009).

5. Reconciliation and Justice

The *Plavšić* Tribunal heard testimony from the late Dr. Alex Boraine, the former Deputy Chair of the South African Truth and Reconciliation Commission, concerning the importance of acknowledgment on the process of reconciliation. Is reconciliation an appropriate subject of sentencing? Is it unjust to impose a sentence that exacerbates tensions between parties to a conflict? Or are reconciliation and justice better dealt with separately? For a discussion of the relationship between justice and reconciliation drawing upon the South African context, *see* Alex Boraine, A COUNTRY UNMASKED: INSIDE SOUTH AFRICA'S TRUTH AND RECONCILIATION COMMISSION (2001); Desmond Tutu, NO FUTURE WITHOUT FORGIVENESS (2000) and TRUTH V. JUSTICE (Robert I. Rotberg & Dennis Thompson eds., 2000). Should Plavšić's post-conflict conduct have been considered a mitigating factor? Although she did admit her responsibility for the deaths of many individuals and a recitation of stipulated facts underlying the charge of persecution that was appended to her plea, she otherwise did not offer much cooperation and refused to testify in the trial of Slobodan Milošević.

6. Deterrence and Incentives

Do these sentencing judgments create a sufficient incentive for officials to work against their government's involvement in violations of international criminal law? Kōki Hirota, the Japanese foreign minister during World War II, was convicted before the Tokyo Tribunal for waging aggressive war even though he was on record as having been opposed to Japanese expansionism and forced out of government for his stance. Justice Röling in his dissent in that case noted that Hirota had assumed office with the intention of preventing, rather than advancing, war. As he later noted, "The rules as applied by the Tokyo Tribunal condemn acceptance of a responsible post, even if this is done with the design to acquit an advantageous position to promote peace." *See* Bert V.A. Röling, *Crimes Against Peace*, *in* THE CURRENT LEGAL REGULATION OF THE USE OF FORCE (Antonio Cassese ed., 1986). Would taking into account at the sentencing stage the motivations of the individual in taking an official position adequately address Justice Röling's concerns?

7. Critiques and Further Reading

For a critique of the sentencing practices of the ICTY and ICTR, *see* Steven Glickman, *Victims' Justice: Legitimizing the Sentencing Regime of the*

International Criminal Court, 43 COLUM. J. TRANSNAT'L L. 229 (2004) (contending that war criminals have been under-penalized by the international criminal tribunals); Andrew N. Keller, *Punishment for Violations of International Criminal Law: An Analysis of Sentencing at the ICTY and ICTR*, 12 IND. INT'L & COMP. L. REV. 53 (2001) (arguing that the light sentences imposed do not serve the penological goals of retribution and deterrence); M. Cherif Bassiouni & Peter Manikas, THE LAW OF THE INTERNATIONAL CRIMINAL TRIBUNAL FOR THE FORMER YUGOSLAVIA (ICTY) 701–2 (1996) (proposing a twenty-year maximum on all sentences, and arguing that verdicts exceeding that limit may violate principles of legality and prohibition against *ex post facto* laws); and Nancy Amoury Combs, *Copping a Plea to Genocide: The Plea Bargaining of International Criminal Crimes*, 151 U. PA. L. REV. 1 (2002) (asserting that the sentences of those who have pled guilty are too harsh, and will deter others from coming forth with guilty pleas in the future). For a critique of the sentencing practices of the ICC, *see* Ashley Joy Stein, *Reforming the Sentencing Regime for the Most Serious Crimes of Concern: The International Criminal Court through the Lens of the Lubanga Trial,* 39 BROOK. J. INT'L L. 521 (2014) (arguing that the ICC has failed to consider penal theories and to set forth an appropriate penalty framework). For an argument that augmented sentencing by the ICC is warranted for perpetrators of sex crimes against children, *see* Rachel F. Braden, *Innocence Lost: Instituting Harsher International Criminal Court Sentences for Perpetrators of Sex Crimes against Children*, 26 FLA. J. INT'L L. 25 (2014).

Additionally, *see* Robert Sloane, *The Evolving Common Law of Sentencing at the ICTR*, 5 J. INT'L CRIM. JUST. 713 (2007); Mark Drumbl, *Collective Violence and Individual Punishment: The Criminality of Mass Atrocity*, 99 NW. U. L. REV. 539 (2005); William Schabas, *Sentencing by International Tribunals: A Human Rights Approach*, 7 DUKE COMP. & INT'L L. 461 (1997); Margaret M. DeGuzman, *Proportionate Sentencing at the International Criminal Court, in* THE LAW AND PRACTICE OF THE INTERNATIONAL CRIMINAL COURT (Carsten Stahn ed., 2014); Christine Bishai, *Superior Responsibility, Inferior Sentencing: Sentencing Practice at the International Criminal Tribunals,* 11 NW. J. INT'L HUM. RTS. 83 (2013).

IV. REPARATIONS

The prosecution and conviction of Thomas Lubanga Dyilo for crimes committed in the DRC provided the ICC with the opportunity to issue not only its first sentencing judgment, but also its first reparations judgment. (For more on the background of Lubanga and the case against him, see Chapter 6 on the Legal Regulation of Armed Conflict and Chapter 15 on Direct and Indirect Responsibility.) The trial of Lubanga was fraught with allegations of prosecutorial misconduct and claims that the rights of the defendant to a fair trial were violated. First, the Court found that then-Prosecutor Luis Moreno-Ocampo improperly withheld exculpatory evidence from the defense and the judges. The Prosecutor had argued that he had received the information from several sources, including the United Nations, on the condition that he keep the information confidential. The Trial

Chamber ordered Lubanga to be released because of this alleged misconduct by the Prosecutor. That order was stayed, and eventually reversed when an accommodation was made between the sources and the judges allowing the latter to have access to the documents. Second, after the trial commenced, the Trial Chamber issued another order to release Lubanga, asserting that a fair trial was no longer possible given the Prosecutor's failure to comply with an order to reveal to the defense the names and other necessary identifying information of an anonymous intermediary who was a part of the proceedings, and the undue delay in the prosecution of the case. The Appeals Chamber reversed this decision too. Finally, as discussed in the excerpt below, the Prosecutor was criticized by the Trial Chamber for not including a set of broader claims against Lubanga, including claims of sexual and gender-based violence.

Prosecutor v. Thomas Lubanga Dyilo, Case No. ICC–01/04–01/06, Decision on Sentence Pursuant to Article 76 of the Statute (July 10, 2012)

In the Trial Chamber

Sexual Violence

60. The Chamber strongly deprecates the attitude of the former Prosecutor in relation to the issue of sexual violence. He advanced extensive submissions as regards sexual violence in his opening and closing submissions at trial, and in his arguments on sentence he contended that sexual violence is an aggravating factor that should be reflected by the Chamber. However, not only did the former Prosecutor fail to apply to include sexual violence or sexual slavery at any stage during these proceedings, including in the original charges, but he actively opposed taking this step during the trial when he submitted that it would cause unfairness to the accused if he was convicted on this basis. Notwithstanding this stance on his part throughout these proceedings, he suggested that sexual violence ought to be considered for the purposes of sentencing. * * *

61. The prosecution suggests that although the Chamber did not base its Article 74(2) decision on evidence relating to sexual violence and rape, the evidence of the witnesses on this issue was credible and reliable and it may "assist as regards sentence." On this basis, the prosecution submits that the sexual violence and rape to which some girl soldiers were subjected demonstrates that the crimes of conscription, enlistment and use of children were committed with marked cruelty, and they were directed at victims who were particularly defenceless, within the meaning of Rule 145(2)(b)(iii) of the Rules.

67. The prosecution's failure to charge Mr. Lubanga with rape and other forms of sexual violence as separate crimes within the jurisdiction of the Court is not determinative of the question of whether that activity is a relevant factor in the determination of the sentence. The Chamber is

entitled to consider sexual violence under Rule 145(1)(c) of the Rules as part of: (i) the harm suffered by the victims; (ii) the nature of the unlawful behaviour; and (iii) the circumstances of manner in which the crime was committed; additionally, this can be considered under Rule 145(2)(b)(iv) as showing the crime was committed with particular cruelty.

68. For the reasons set out above in the section establishing the procedure to be adopted at this stage, the Chamber is entitled to consider sexual violence in determining the sentence that is to be passed, notwithstanding the fact that it did not form part of the Confirmation Decision. Given the procedural safeguards, there will be no consequential unfairness if the Chamber decides that sexual violence is a relevant factor.

69. However, that said, it remains necessary for the Chamber to be satisfied beyond reasonable doubt that: (i) child soldiers under 15 were subjected to sexual violence; and (ii) this can be attributed to Mr. Lubanga in a manner that reflects his culpability, pursuant to Rule 145(1)(a) of the Rules. * * * [The Chamber here recounts the testimony of a number of witnesses concerning rape and sexual violence committed against girls and women in the camps].

74. On the basis of the totality of the evidence introduced during the trial on this issue, the Majority is unable to conclude that sexual violence against the children who were recruited was sufficiently widespread that it could be characterised as occurring in the ordinary course of the implementation of the common plan for which Mr. Lubanga is responsible. Moreover, nothing suggests that Mr. Lubanga ordered or encouraged sexual violence, that he was aware of it or that it could otherwise be attributed to him in a way that reflects his culpability.

75. Although the former Prosecutor was entitled to introduce evidence on this issue during the sentencing hearing, he failed to take this step or to refer to any relevant evidence that had been given during the trial. As a result, in the view of the Majority, the link between Mr. Lubanga and sexual violence, in the context of the charges, has not been established beyond reasonable doubt. Therefore, this factor cannot properly form part of the assessment of his culpability for the purposes of sentence.

76. In a separate Decision, the Chamber will assess whether this factor is relevant to the issue of reparations.

NOTES & QUESTIONS

1. Lubanga's Sentence and Imprisonment

The Prosecutor asked for a sentence of thirty years, the maximum sentence allowed under the Rome Statute. The Trial Chamber above imposed terms of imprisonment for three separate crimes: thirteen years for conscripting children under the age of fifteen; twelve years for enlisting children under the age of fifteen; and fourteen years for using children under the age of fifteen to participate actively in hostilities. The Trial Chamber determined that each of these sentences were to be served concurrently, so Lubanga was sentenced to fourteen years' imprisonment. Lubanga entered the ICC detention facilities on March 16, 2006, and with credit for time already served in detention his fourteen-year sentence will be completed on or about March 16, 2020.

2. Dissent

Judge Elizabeth Odio Benito (Costa Rica) issued a strongly-worded dissent from the sentencing decision that began, "I strongly disagree with the Majority of the Chamber that disregards the damage caused to the victims and their families, particularly as a result of the harsh punishments and sexual violence suffered by the victims of these crimes." Do you agree that the Majority did not adequately take into account the harms suffered by the child victims? For a discussion of the verdict and sentence, *see* Diane Marie Amann, *Children and the First Verdict of the International Criminal Court*, 12 WASH. U. GLOB. STUD. L. REV. 411 (2013).

The Majority notes that a number of individuals were convicted of violations related to child soldiers before the Special Court for Sierra Leone (SCSL), and that sentences of thirty-five and fifty years were imposed for the recruitment and use of child soldiers. What explains the discrepancy between those sentences and the one imposed here? Notwithstanding her dissent, Judge Benito would have sentenced Lubanga to fifteen years, rather than the fourteen years of the Majority. For a discussion of sentencing at the SCSL, *see* Shahram Dana, *The Sentencing Legacy of the Special Court for Sierra Leone*, 42 GA. J. INT'L & COMP. L. 615 (2014).

3. Sexual Violence Charges

As noted in the excerpt above, the Prosecutor did not include sexual violence charges in his original indictment and argued against amending the charges to include such violations. The failure to include a charge concerning sexual violence in the *Lubanga* case—particularly given the widespread use of such violence against child soldiers—has generated numerous criticisms of the Prosecutor's approach to this case. Given the failure to include such a charge, is it appropriate for the Chamber to address the issue at the sentencing phase? Does the sentencing phase provide a "second bite at the apple" for the Prosecutor with respect to these and other charges? Does this infringe on the rights of the accused?

4. Child Soldiers

Are child soldiers victims, perpetrators, or both? Should the fact that some of them have committed atrocities affect whether they should receive reparations, or in other ways affect how we treat them? By treating all child soldiers as victims, lacking agency and choice, do we ignore the reality of some young people, especially teens, who voluntarily join a fighting force to defend their families and communities, earn their keep, seek a better life, or contribute to an ideological or political project? Do we disempower them from contributing to post-conflict reconstruction and reconciliation? For a detailed and nuanced discussion of child soldiers that tackles these and other issues, *see* Mark A. Drumbl, REIMAGINING CHILD SOLDIERS IN INTERNATIONAL LAW AND POLICY (2012).

5. The Lubanga Reparations Decisions

As noted in the excerpt above, the Trial Chamber subsequently issued a decision setting forth the principles and procedures to be applied to reparations in the case. *Prosecutor v. Lubanga,* Case No. ICC–01/04–01/06, Decision Establishing the Principles and Procedures to be Applied to Reparations (Aug. 7, 2012). In this initial decision, the Trial Chamber drew upon submissions by the Prosecutor, defense counsel, the ICC Registry, the ICC Office of the Public Counsel for Victims, two teams of victims' lawyers, UNICEF, and non-governmental organizations including the Women's Initiative for Gender Justice. In fact the Women's Initiative for Gender Justice was invited to join the other parties in appearing before the Chamber during the hearings convened for determining reparations. Professor Amann summarizes the Trial Chamber opinion:

> According to the chamber, reparations help ensure that perpetrators are held to account and "repair the harm they caused to the victims" Acknowledging the indigence of the defendant, the chamber noted that he could make a voluntary apology, yet stressed repeatedly that he could not be compelled to apologize. It called for a "broad and flexible," "gender-inclusive," and "community-based" approach that would include both monetary and nonmonetary remedies. Given the large number of persons affected and the "very limited financial resources available in this case," collective reparations primarily were envisaged; however, the chamber also contemplated individual awards in special circumstances, as well as "affirmative action" measures for sexual violence victims, HIV patients, and other acutely vulnerable persons. The chamber declined to limit reparations to the eighty-five applications previously filed; it made clear that "victims were to be treated fairly and equally" without regard to whether "they participated in the trial proceedings". Those included would be not only "direct victims" of the conscription, enlistment, and use of child soldiers, but also ""indirect victims" like family members and persons harmed while trying to help direct victims. Human beings and entities such as schools, hospitals, and nonprofit organizations were to be considered. The chamber wrote that entitlement to reparations required "a 'but/for' relationship between the crime and the harm"; that is, proof by a balance of probabilities that "the crimes for which Mr. Lubanga was convicted were the "proximate cause' of the harm for which reparations are sought".
>
> Having outlined the contours, the chamber delegated implementation steps to the Trust Fund for Victims. It tasked the fund, which according to its website has 1 million euros available for reparations, to raise money for the eventual award. The fund was also instructed to embark on an evaluation process: first, to pinpoint the Ituri localities due reparations; next, to work with experts in consulting with persons in those localities, assessing

harm and identifying victims and beneficiaries; and finally, to present a reparations plan for the chamber's approval.

Diane Marie Amann, *Prosecutor v. Lubanga. Case No. ICC–01/04–01/06. Judgment, Decision on Sentence, Decision on Reparations*, 106 AM. J. INT'L L. 809 (2012).

After a series of decisions by both the Trial and Appeals Chambers, the Trial Chamber granted an award of $10 million for 425 victims. *Prosecutor v. Lubanga*, Case No. ICC–01/04–01/06, Corrected Version of the "Decision Setting the Size of the Reparations Award for Which Thomas Lubanga Dyilo is Liable (Dec. 12, 2017). Both Lubanga and some of the victims appealed the decision, challenging both the amount awarded and the methodology employed to reach that amount. The Appeals Chamber judgment follows.

Prosecutor v. Thomas Lubanga Dyilo, Case No. ICC–01/04–01/06, Judgment on the Appeals against Trial Chamber II's 'Decision Setting the Size of the Reparations Award for which Thomas Lubanga Dyilo is Liable' (July 18, 2019) (Public Redacted)

In the Appeals Chamber

36. The Appeals Chamber recalls that the reparations ordered in this case include restitution, compensation and rehabilitation. The Appeals Chamber would particularly note the principle of *restitutio in integrum* and the fact that the Appeals Chamber stated that '[r]estitution should, as far as possible, restore the victim to his or her circumstances before the crime was committed'. The TFV [Trust Fund for Victims] and the Trial Chamber, in the implementation process, and in formulating particular reparations programmes, should be guided by the principle of *restitutio in integrum* bearing in mind the particular circumstances of the case and the type of reparations ordered.

37. The Appeals Chamber recalls that the reparations proceedings in this case concern harm caused to children under the age of fifteen years who were conscripted or enlisted into the FPLC, or used to participate actively in hostilities, as well as to indirect victims—including family members of those children. The situation of such children is particular and requires measures to be taken which properly address those particularities. The Appeals Chamber recognised the situation of such children in its amended reparations order in 2015. It stated, *inter alia*, that

> [r]eparation orders and programmes in favour of child soldiers, should guarantee the development of the victims' personalities, talents and abilities to the fullest possible extent and, more broadly, they should ensure the development of respect for human rights and fundamental freedoms. For each child, the measures should aim at developing respect for their parents,

> cultural identity and language. Former child soldiers should be helped to live responsibly in a free society, recognising the need for a spirit of understanding, peace and tolerance, showing respect for equality between the sexes and valuing friendship between all peoples and groups.

38. Also, and as pointed to by the OPCV [Office of the Public Counsel for Victims], the Appeals Chamber stresses the need to recognise and address, as one type of harm, in the projects being implemented, the damage to a life plan/the project of life, which these children may have suffered. Again, the Appeals Chamber recalled this concept in the Lubanga Amended Reparations Order, noting that 'the concept of "damage to a life plan", adopted in the context of State responsibility at the [Inter-American Court of Human Rights], may be relevant to reparations at the Court'. In identifying the harm to direct victims of, specifically, Mr. Lubanga's crimes, the Appeals Chamber included '[i]nterruption and loss of schooling' and '[t]he non-development of "civilian life skills" resulting in the victim being at a disadvantage, particularly as regards employment'. The Appeals Chamber emphasises that it is crucial, in the reparations provided, that the specific situation of the children at issue in this case is recognised and that their harm is appropriately remedied through the particular reparations provided.

39. Similarly, the situation of indirect victims in this case must be addressed in an appropriate manner, again appreciating the difference in needs that such victims have, as they most likely require reparations that differ from those required for direct victims. * * *

40. Although the reparations ordered in this case are collective in nature, the Appeals Chamber finds it important to recall that, as it has previously stated, '[i]ndividual and collective reparations are not mutually exclusive, and they may be awarded concurrently'. Future chambers should have this in mind when reaching determinations as to the appropriateness of particular reparations in the cases before them. Also, although it would not attempt to set out, in an exhaustive manner, how the concept of 'collective' reparations should be understood—bearing in mind the many permutations possible, which will also be dependent on the facts of particular cases—the Appeals Chamber would, nevertheless, also stress now that, in awarding collective reparations to victims, this can include reparations which are individualised; in this respect, collective reparations can include the payment of sums of money to individuals to repair harm suffered and the possibility for individuals to participate in particular programmes that address the specific harm that those individuals have suffered. The Appeals Chamber recalls that it has held that, '[w]hen collective reparations are awarded, these should address the harm the victims suffered on an individual and collective basis'. Finally, it would also recall that '[r]eparations are entirely voluntary and the informed consent of the recipient is necessary prior to

any award of reparations, including participation in any reparations programme'. * * *

76. Mr. Lubanga argues on appeal that the Trial Chamber erred by making an award for reparations 'on its own motion' to, or in respect of, the unidentified victims who had not made a request for reparations, without having established that there were 'exceptional circumstances' and without following the procedure set out in rule 95 of the Rules. Mr. Lubanga also makes a more general argument that, although in collective reparations the trial chamber does not need to rule on the quantum of the individual harm to the victims who have applied for reparations, it may not 'consider the situation of unidentified possible victims who have made no application to the Court'. The Appeals Chamber is not persuaded by Mr. Lubanga's arguments for the reasons that follow.

77. The central provision regulating reparations before the Court is article 75 of the Statute, which stipulates in the first sentence of its paragraph 1 that the Court 'shall establish principles relating to reparations to, or in respect of, victims, including restitution, compensation and rehabilitation'. The second sentence of article 75(1) concerns, *inter alia*, the trigger for reparations proceedings: upon conviction of a person by the Court, the trial chamber will enter into the reparations phase of proceedings (i) if it has received requests for reparations by individuals identifying themselves as victims, or (ii) on its own motion, if exceptional circumstances exist. In the interpretation proposed by Mr. Lubanga, the manner in which reparations proceedings are initiated (either upon request or on the Court's own motion) also limits the scope of the ultimate award for reparations. The Appeals Chamber, however, notes that the applicable provisions of the law do not provide for such limitation.

78. Article 75(2) of the Statute provides that the Court may make an order for 'appropriate reparations' directly against the convicted person, or through the TFV. A trial chamber's role is, therefore, to determine what reparations are 'appropriate'. In making this determination, a trial chamber must consider, *inter alia,* the 'scope and extent of any damage, loss and injury to, or in respect of victims' (article 75(1), second sentence). As to what this means, the Appeals Chamber recalls that it has found that

> article 75 (1) of the Statute requires a trial chamber to "determine the scope and extent of any damage, loss and injury to, or in respect of victims". The Appeals Chamber considers that, in doing so, a trial chamber should, generally speaking, establish the types or categories of harm caused by the crimes for which the convicted person was convicted, *based on all relevant information before it*, including the decision on conviction, sentencing decision, submissions by the parties or

amici curiae, expert reports and the applications by the victims for reparations.

79. It is, for example, conceivable that the conviction decision contains findings as to the number of victims of the crimes for which the conviction was entered, the type of harm they suffered, etc. Such findings are likely to be relevant for determining the appropriateness of reparations and there is no reason why a trial chamber should be forced to ignore them only because not all of the victims have filed a request for reparations with the Court. If the trial chamber were limited to determining the scope of the harm based only on the requests for reparations it had received—as Mr. Lubanga contends—the resulting finding would almost inevitably be incomplete and reflect only part of the harm actually caused by the crimes for which the person was convicted.

80. Furthermore, the Appeals Chamber notes rule 98(2) of the Rules and regulations 60–65 of the Regulations of the TFV. These provisions specifically provide for verification by the TFV, in the case of individual awards, of whether persons are members of the beneficiary group in cases where the trial chamber has not identified the beneficiaries in its reparations order. As stipulated in rule 98(2) of the Rules, this may occur where 'it is impossible or impracticable to make individual awards directly to each victim'. This possibility presupposes that the reparations order is, at least in part, based on information other than that contained in requests for reparations filed before the Chamber. It would run contrary to this logic if, at the same time, the scope of the convicted person's liability for reparations could be determined only in respect of victims who have filed requests for reparations.

81. Requiring that, barring exceptional circumstances, the reparations order may only be based on requests for reparations already received would also have a negative impact on the efficiency of the reparations process. This would mean that, for example in cases where there are large numbers of victims, in order to avoid prejudice to those victims, and in order to provide them with a sufficient opportunity to submit requests for reparations, the trial chamber would need to set generous time limits for their submissions. The implementation process, however, could not begin until the reparations order was actually issued and the trial chamber had determined the status of all of those who had at that point applied for reparations. The result would be that valuable time would be lost during which victims would have to wait for reparations—even though they may have already submitted their requests for reparations early on during the trial proceedings.

82. The Appeals Chamber also notes that collective reparations, referred to in rule 98(3) of the Rules, may take forms that do not necessarily require identifying individual victims at any stage of the reparations process—for instance in cases where memorials are erected as reparations measures or other symbolic reparations imposed. Limiting

the reparations process in such circumstances to those who have applied for reparations would serve no apparent purpose.

83. Finally, the Appeals Chamber recalls its finding, made previously in this case, that a requirement that collective reparations may only be awarded on the basis of individual requests for reparations would contravene the principle that reparations 'oblige those responsible for serious crimes to repair the harm they caused to the victims and they enable the Chamber to ensure that offenders account for their acts'.

84. It is for these reasons that the Appeals Chamber is unable to accept the argument that the requirement set out in article 75(1) of the Statute, that the Court proceed 'upon request or on its own motion', limits the trial chamber's determination of the scope of damage to the information contained in requests for reparations, save for exceptional circumstances where it acts on its own motion. As indicated earlier and in view of the foregoing, this part of the provision only regulates how the reparations proceedings are triggered. * * *

90. In deciding what reparations are 'appropriate', a trial chamber must take into account the rights of the convicted person. The reparations order must not go beyond the crimes for which he or she was convicted. The convicted person must be given a sufficient opportunity to make submissions on the scope of reparations, the scope of victimhood to be repaired, the type of reparations, etc., so as to comply with the requirements of fairness. To that end, the trial chamber must give notice to the parties of the manner in which it intends to conduct the reparations proceedings before it, especially where it does not intend to make individual determinations with respect to each victim who has filed a request. In this regard, it must ensure that the convicted person is adequately on notice as to the information on which it will rely in making its order, so that he or she has a meaningful opportunity to make representations thereon, and it must give notice as to the manner in which it intends to assess that information—e.g. does it intend to assess each request individually? The Trial Chamber must also ensure that the parties are on notice as to the standard of proof that will be applied in the proceedings so that they are aware of the manner in which the information will be assessed. * * * If the trial chamber resorts to estimates as to the number of victims, such estimates must be based on a sufficiently strong evidential basis; any uncertainties must be resolved in favour of the convicted person (for instance, by assuming a lower number of victims, or by discounting the amount of liability). Furthermore, awarding reparations beyond those who have filed a request under rule 94 of the Rules may not be appropriate in all cases. * * *

108. The amount of the convicted person's liability should be fixed taking into account the cost of reparations considered to be appropriate and that are intended to be put in place (which can include reparations programmes) and the different harms suffered by the different victims,

both individual victims (direct and indirect) in addition to, in particular circumstances, the collective of victims. In setting the amount, the trial chamber must also ensure that it takes into account the convicted person's rights and interests. The goal is to set an amount that is fair and properly reflects the rights of the victims, bearing in mind the rights of the convicted person. If the information and evidence upon which the trial chamber relies does not enable it to set the amount of liability with precision, for example, because it cannot obtain precise information as to the costing of specific reparations programmes, then it may, with caution, consider whether to rely on estimates. In this regard, depending on the type of reparations contemplated, and the information it has managed to obtain, the trial chamber may have to rely on estimates as to the cost of reparations programmes. In doing so, it should, however, make every effort to obtain estimates that are as accurate as possible in the circumstances of the case. It is also important, and in the interests of both the victims and the convicted person, that the trial chamber conducts the reparations proceedings as expeditiously as possible. It may, therefore, need to weigh the need for accuracy of estimates against the goal of awarding reparations without delay. * * *

172. Victims V01 submit that, while some previously participating victims were excluded from reparations, 'after judicial proceedings in which the Defence was afforded notice and the opportunity to be heard, and against the advice of the Trust Fund', the eligibility of the victims who come forward in the future will be determined by the TFV 'after a purely administrative procedure'.

173. The Appeals Chamber notes that the Impugned Decision does not set out a detailed procedure for the future assessment of potential victims' eligibility, the Trial Chamber indicating that screening would be carried out by the TFV but providing no further details as to what the procedure would entail. The Appeals Chamber notes that the Trial Chamber directed the TFV to follow the method of screening of the victims for eligibility, which it devised in the Impugned Decision, and that this was aimed at ensuring that the same method would apply to all victims. The Appeals Chamber further recalls that, in the *Lubanga* Amended Reparations Order, it stated that the Trial Chamber should 'monitor and oversee the implementation stage of the [amended reparations] order, including having the authority to approve the draft implementation plan submitted by the Trust Fund'. In the context of this case, and bearing in mind the procedure put in place by the Trial Chamber prior to the Impugned Decision, in particular its approach to the assessment of the eligibility for reparations of the applicants who had submitted requests for reparations—as considered under Victims V01's first ground of appeal—the Appeals Chamber understands that such monitoring and oversight should, in this case, include the Trial Chamber's approval of the TFV's findings as to victims' eligibility for reparations. This would ensure that both the victims who have already

been assessed, and those who will come forward, all have the benefit of judicial approval. In taking this matter forward, the TFV and the Trial Chamber should ensure that they follow the guidance set out in this judgment, in addition to that contained in its 2015 judgment and that contained in the Impugned Decision.

174. In finding in this way, the Appeals Chamber notes that the goal of Victims V01 was presumably to ensure only administrative review by the TFV, without involvement by the Trial Chamber, and that the Appeals Chamber's conclusion here results in future victims and, as seen below, the victims in, *inter alia*, the Victims V01 group, who have been found ineligible, being subjected to both administrative and judicial review. However, the Appeals Chamber finds that this result simply follows on from the Trial Chamber's approach in this case and the need to ensure equal treatment for the potential victims in this case. In addition, and for the reasons that follow, the Appeals Chamber considers that the victims in the Victims V01 group, who raised this argument, are not prejudiced as such, as they will have a second opportunity to convince the TFV and the Trial Chamber of their eligibility for reparations, based on the findings in the Impugned Decision and this judgment.

175. In this regard, the Appeals Chamber notes that the approach taken by the Trial Chamber, to have two phases in which potential victims may seek reparations, results in future victims, coming forward during the second phase, potentially having an advantage, vis-à-vis the victims already assessed by the Trial Chamber, in knowing in detail the factors which the Trial Chamber found relevant in its assessment and the Trial Chamber's reasons for concluding that some victims were ineligible for reparations. It is only in the Impugned Decision that most of these specific criteria were clearly set out, as were shortcomings in the dossiers, which led to their rejection. * * * The Trial Chamber, therefore, was presumably aware that it was providing guidance in the Impugned Decision for the benefit of future victims and those victims being assessed by it in the Impugned Decision could, consequently, not have been fully on notice as to what the Trial Chamber would take into account in reaching its decisions; on the contrary, potential victims who will come forward in future will be able to benefit from this detailed indication of what is required. The Appeals Chamber considers that this brings about a risk of discrimination. * * *

179. As a result of all of the above, the Appeals Chamber finds that the Trial Chamber's overall procedure for the eligibility assessment failed to ensure equal conditions for all victims and amounts to an error. This error materially affects the Impugned Decision, as some of the victims concerned may have been found eligible had they known more fully what was expected of them in submitting their dossiers, and the Trial Chamber could have given them an additional opportunity to supplement their dossiers or clarify their accounts.

180. * * * The Appeals Chamber therefore amends the Impugned Decision to the extent that the Trial Chamber finds that 48 persons had not proven, to the requisite standard, that they qualify as victims for reparations in this case. The Impugned Decision is amended such that the victims whom the Trial Chamber found ineligible to receive reparations, and who consider that their failure to sufficiently substantiate their allegations, including by supporting documentation resulted from insufficient notice of the requirements for eligibility, may seek a new assessment of their eligibility by the TFV, together with other victims who may come forward in the course of the implementation stage and as envisaged by the Trial Chamber in the Impugned Decision any recommendations as to eligibility made by the TFV shall be subject to the approval of the Trial Chamber, as set out above.

181. The Appeals Chamber notes that this amendment may result in some or all of the above-mentioned 48 persons being found eligible for reparations. However, they will be considered along with any other potential victims who may come forward, as referred to above, during the implementation process and therefore this amendment does not affect the overall monetary award made in this case; the procedure adopted in this case, which has not been overturned on appeal, was such that the monetary award was fixed in the Impugned Decision, while a second phase allows for additional victims to come forward; the 48 victims may take part in the latter phase. * * *

Assessment of the Individual Applications

[The Chamber here first summarizes the relevant portions of the Trial Chamber opinion].

183. Mr. Lubanga asserts that the Trial Chamber misapplied the standard of proof of a 'balance of probabilities', which it had stated should apply. He argues that most of the victims deemed eligible for reparations did not provide any supporting documentation. * * *

190. In addressing '[t]he concept of victim: conditions and standards applicable to the reparations phase', the Trial Chamber first recalled that in order for a natural person to qualify as a victim for the purposes of reparations under rule 85(a) of the Rules, he or she must provide identification and sufficient proof of the harm suffered and of the causal nexus between the crime and the harm. Harm may be material, physical or psychological. The Trial Chamber also underlined that the harm to the victim need not be direct but must have been personally suffered. It stated that, in determining the eligibility of an indirect victim, 'it is a prerequisite that there was a close personal relationship between the direct victim and the indirect victim, such as that binding a child soldier and his or her parents'.

191. The Trial Chamber explained that the standard of causation requires that the crimes of which the person was convicted were the 'proximate cause' of the harm for which reparations are sought, and

consists of a 'but-for' relationship between the harm and the crime. Lastly, it noted that the standard of proof as to whether a victim qualifies for an award is a balance of probabilities. * * *

195. The Trial Chamber further stated that, in this case, 'the crimes of which Mr. Lubanga was convicted entail as a precondition to qualify for reparations as a victim direct or indirect—that the enlistment, conscription or active participation in hostilities of a child under the age of 15 years in the UPC/FLPC's armed forces in a non-international armed conflict between 1 September 2002 and 13 August 2003 ("child-soldier status") be established on a balance of probabilities'. The Trial Chamber then set out the criteria for eligibility as follows:

> So, in the case of a potentially eligible direct victim, the Chamber verifies (1) identity and looks at (2) the direct victim's child-soldier status. In the case of a potentially eligible indirect victim whose identity it has verified, the Chamber looks at (3) the child-soldier status of the direct victim and whether there was a close personal relationship between the direct and the indirect victim. Where the direct victim's child-soldier status is established and, in the case of an application from an indirect victim, where the close personal relationship with the direct victim is established, the Chamber then considers (4) whether the potentially eligible direct or indirect victim has established on a balance of probabilities the existence of the harm alleged and (5) the causal nexus between the harm alleged and the crimes of which Mr. Lubanga was convicted. * * *

Determination by the Appeals Chamber

207. The Appeals Chamber notes at the outset that Mr. Lubanga does not assert that the standard of 'a balance of probabilities', which the Trial Chamber set out to apply to its assessment of eligibility in the Impugned Decision, should not have been employed, or that some other standard should apply in the circumstances. Therefore, the Appeals Chamber will not address whether that standard was appropriate. However, Mr. Lubanga does allege that the methods relied on by the Trial Chamber fell short of the requirements of that standard. He argues that the Trial Chamber found a number of victims eligible whose uncorroborated accounts it considered 'coherent and credible', although 'the standard of proof based on the "coherent and credible" nature of the applicants' statements is lower than the standard of a balance of probabilities'. As such, he argues that the Trial Chamber erred.

208. The Appeals Chamber finds this argument to be based upon an incorrect premise because it is apparent that the Trial Chamber did indeed set out to apply the standard advocated by Mr. Lubanga. That is, the Trial Chamber clearly stated that 'the standard of proof as to whether a victim qualifies for an award is a balance of probabilities' and it proceeded to analyse the evidence and information available to it and relevant to each of the requisite elements for victim status to see whether

the elements were proven to that standard. The Trial Chamber determined that a 'precondition to qualify for reparations' was that the victim status was 'established on a balance of probabilities'. And, following its analysis, the Trial Chamber found that 425 applicants had 'shown on a balance of probabilities' that they were victims entitled to reparations. Therefore, the Appeals Chamber finds that the Trial Chamber did in principle assess victim status for the purpose of reparations on the standard of a balance of probabilities. * * *

211. Mr. Lubanga's principal argument, in relation to the submission of uncorroborated statements, appears to be that the Trial Chamber erred in law by finding that the applicants' claims, albeit 'coherent and credible', were established on a balance of probabilities where they were not accompanied by corroborating evidence. Mr. Lubanga presents jurisprudence of the ECCC, Supreme Court Chamber, to support the principle that 'statements of civil parties uncorroborated by any other evidence are not sufficient'. The Appeals Chamber notes, at the outset, that these arguments relate to the evidence supporting requests for reparations. Although the Trial Chamber did not make specific findings on the merits of requests for individual reparations, it did examine them in order to assess the eligibility of victims from the sample for collective reparations and to make a finding as to Mr. Lubanga's monetary liability. Therefore, in its determination of the issues raised under the present ground of appeal, the Appeals Chamber will be guided by relevant aspects of rule 94 of the Rules.

212. The Appeals Chamber observes that rule 94(1)(g) of the Rules states that, in conjunction with a written description of the victim's allegations, a request for reparations must contain '[t]o the extent possible, any relevant supporting documentation, including names and addresses of witnesses' The Appeals Chamber considers that the requirement to provide, to the extent possible, supporting documents and information under rule 94(1)(g) of the Rules, both serves to assist a trial chamber in its assessment of a claim while also providing the convicted person with an opportunity to challenge the requests submitted. However, the rule also allows for the possibility that a request that is not supported by relevant documentation may nevertheless be filed. In this regard, and as correctly noted by the Trial Chamber, rule 94(1)(g) of the Rules acknowledges that victims are not always in a position to provide supporting documentation. Consequently, the Appeals Chamber considers that the fact that potential victims generally did not submit documents in support of their written allegations does not lead inexorably to the conclusion that the Trial Chamber was prevented from finding that their victimhood was established to a balance of probabilities.

213. In reparations proceedings, the Appeals Chamber has stated that 'what is [. . .] "sufficient" for purposes of an applicant meeting the burden of proof will depend upon the circumstances of the specific case'.

The Appeals Chamber considers that the trial chamber enjoys a certain amount of flexibility in the assessment of claims that have been submitted. In this regard, an assessment of the 'sufficiency' of the evidence is not limited to the evidence submitted by the victim in question. Rather, corroboration may come from extrinsic evidence, including the testimonial and documentary evidence entered into the record and the statements of other victims in their requests. In the exercise of its discretion, a trial chamber may consider that a victim's account has sufficient probative value in light of the totality of the evidence so as to find that the allegations therein satisfy the burden of proof, even in the absence of supporting documents. A trial chamber may also consider the significance of the allegation sought to be proven. In this respect, some allegations are critical to the overall assessment of the person's eligibility and, unless they are otherwise corroborated, the trial chamber may decline to find the person eligible without documentation supporting those allegations.

214. Mr. Lubanga argues that '[t]here are no cogent grounds to reasonably explain the lack of corroborating evidence', including witness statements and civil status documents. The argument appears to be that, if a request for reparations is not supported by documentation, cogent grounds must exist to explain the absence of such documentation. The Appeals Chamber notes that, as just discussed, a trial chamber may find a person eligible for reparations, even where he or she has not supplied any documentation. It also recalls that the difficulty victims may face in obtaining supporting documentation can be taken into consideration when determining the appropriate standard of proof in reparations proceedings. The Appeals Chamber considers that a trial chamber is also not prevented from finding a person eligible for reparations in circumstances where he or she did not give reasons for his or her inability to provide supporting documentation. However, to allow the trial chamber to properly reach a conclusion, it is in the interest of the person who is unable to supply any documentation to explain his or her reasons for this inability. At any rate, the trial chamber's enquiry is whether the relevant facts have been established to the applicable standard of proof. Such was the Trial Chamber's enquiry in the present case. The Appeals Chamber also notes the Trial Chamber's finding that, 'in most cases the potentially eligible victims were not in a position to submit supporting documentation to prove their allegations', and its reference to 'the circumstances in the DRC and the many years that have elapsed since the material events'.

215. The Appeals Chamber therefore rejects the argument that, without more, the absence of 'cogent grounds' for victims' inability to provide documentation should have prevented the Trial Chamber from finding those victims eligible.

216. In view of the foregoing, the Appeals Chamber finds that Mr. Lubanga has not demonstrated an error in the Trial Chamber's approach to corroboration. * * *

298. Mr. Lubanga submits that the Trial Chamber, in fixing his liability for reparations, erred in how it took into account his level of responsibility for the crimes of which he was found guilty, the level of responsibility of others, and in how it took into account several other factors. He submits that the Trial Chamber erred in holding him liable in full for the victims' harm regardless of the existence of other co-perpetrators who contributed to such harm and that it failed to take into account the degree of his participation in the commission of the crimes, including his alleged efforts to demobilise children. He avers that, despite his indirect criminal intent, he was not indifferent to the fate of minors deployed in hostilities and on various occasions attempted to remedy this situation. In his view, the Trial Chamber did not make these considerations in determining his liability for reparations.

299. Mr. Lubanga also argues that the Trial Chamber failed to consider his personal efforts to promote peace. He submits that fairness demands that his purported efforts to promote peace and reconciliation be considered in the determination of his liability for reparations. Mr. Lubanga also submits that the Trial Chamber did not consider his arguments regarding the specific circumstances of the case. He argues that, 'in the light of the conduct of the national and international authorities who had a responsibility to protect the civilian population, fairness demands fair apportionment of the burden of the reparations', and that the Trial Chamber made an error of law or misappreciated the facts. * * *

312. As to the law, the Appeals Chamber recalls that, in its *Lubanga* Appeal Judgment on Reparations, it observed that,

> the scope of a convicted person's liability for reparations may differ depending on, for example, the mode of individual criminal responsibility established with respect to that person and on the specific elements of that responsibility. Accordingly, the Appeals Chamber finds it necessary to be guided by [the] principle [. . .] that: A convicted person's liability for reparations must be proportionate to the harm caused and, *inter alia*, his or her participation in the commission of the crimes for which he or she was found guilty, in the specific circumstances of the case. * * *

314. The Appeals Chamber noted [in previous decisions] that,

> [. . .] in principle, the question of whether other individuals may also have contributed to the harm resulting from the crimes for which the person has been convicted is irrelevant to the convicted person's liability to repair that harm. While a reparations order must not exceed the overall cost to repair the

harm caused, it is not, *per se*, inappropriate to hold the person liable for the full amount necessary to repair the harm.

. . . [I]n some cases it may be appropriate for a trial chamber to take into account the role of the convicted person *vis-à-vis* others in the commission of the crimes when deciding on a reparations order against that person. For example, if more than one person is convicted by the Court for the same crimes at the same time, it may be appropriate to apportion liability for the costs to repair. Nevertheless, the focus in all cases should be the extent of the harm and cost to repair such harm, rather than the role of the convicted person. * * *

316. The Trial Chamber * * * referred to the gravity of the crimes of which Mr. Lubanga was convicted, as well as their large-scale and widespread nature. It addressed his participation in the crimes, noting that he was convicted as a co-perpetrator. In considering Mr. Lubanga's participation, the Trial Chamber recalled relevant findings from the *Lubanga* Appeal Judgment on Conviction. First, it recalled that Mr. Lubanga 'and his co-perpetrators agreed to, and participated in, a common plan to build an army for the purpose of establishing and maintaining political and military control over Ituri', which resulted 'in the conscription and enlistment of boys and girls under the age of 15, and their use to participate actively in hostilities'. Second, it recalled that during times relevant to Mr. Lubanga's charges, 'a significant number of high-ranking members of the UPC/FPLC and other personnel conducted a large-scale recruitment exercise directed at young people, including children under the age of 15, whether voluntarily or by coercion'. Third, it recalled that Mr. Lubanga 'was the President of the UPC/FPLC, and [. . .] the Commander-in-Chief of the army and its political leader', and that he 'exercised an overall coordinating role over the activities of the UPC/FPLC'. The Trial Chamber also recalled the finding of Trial Chamber I that '[the] contributions by Thomas Lubanga, taken together, were essential to a common plan that resulted in the conscription and enlistment of girls and boys below the age of 15 into the UPC/FPLC and their use to actively participate in hostilities'. * * *

320. Mr. Lubanga further argues that he made efforts to demobilise children, and that the evidence at trial showed that, 'far from being indifferent to the fate of the minors involved in the hostilities, on numerous occasions [he] made the situation his concern and attempted to remedy it'. * * *

321. The Appeals Chamber considers that, in awarding reparations, a trial chamber must remain within the confines of the conviction and sentencing decisions. The efforts that Mr. Lubanga referred to could only be relevant at this stage of the proceedings, in which the focus is on repairing the harm, if Mr. Lubanga had been able to show that, for example, in relation to a considerable number of victims, especially those assessed as samples by the Trial Chamber, he had helped to demobilise

them and that these efforts reduced the level of harm suffered by those victims. If this was the case, this could arguably be relevant to the Trial Chamber's assessment of the overall harm suffered. However, Mr. Lubanga has not pointed to any arguments made before the Trial Chamber, during the reparations proceedings, showing how his alleged demobilisation efforts mitigated or reduced the harm.

322. While the Appeals Chamber notes that Mr. Lubanga submitted before the Trial Chamber as well that he was concerned and attempted to remedy the situation, he has not demonstrated how such alleged concerns or attempts had any impact on the harm the victims suffered. * * * The Appeals Chamber therefore rejects these arguments by Mr. Lubanga.

NOTES & QUESTIONS

1. Lubanga's Liability for Reparations

Lubanga apparently has no known assets that can be used to provide reparations or other assistance to his victims. This means that any reparations that might be provided will most likely come from the Trust Fund for Victims (TVF). The TFV, however, has only collected from State Parties a little over €5 million for all of its reparations-related activities in all of the situations before the Court.

Given these limited resources, how useful do you think the reparative functions of the Court will be? Should the Prosecutor take reparations into account in determining whom to charge? Should she aim to charge those individuals who are known to have large assets that could be used to pay an appropriate fine if convicted?

2. The ICC and Reparations

While the Lubanga case was the first to result in an order for reparations, the ICC has issued orders for reparations in two other cases. With respect to the situation in Mali, the Court has ordered reparations in the *Al Mahdi* case. Ahmad Al Faqi Al Mahdi was sentenced on September 27, 2016, to nine years' imprisonment as a co-perpetrator of the war crime of intentionally directing attacks against historical monuments and buildings dedicated to religion, including nine mausoleums and one mosque, in Timbuktu. On August 17, 2016, the Trial Chamber found that Al Mahdi was liable for €2.7 million in both individual and collective reparations for the community of Timbuktu. Noting that Al Madhi is indigent, the Chamber encouraged the TFV to complement the reparations award and to develop an implementation plan to provide such reparations. *Prosecutor v. Al Mahdi*, Case No. ICC–01/12–01/15, Reparations Order (Aug. 17, 2016). The Reparations Order was mostly affirmed on appeal. *Prosecutor v. Al Mahdi*, Case No. ICC–01/12–01/15 A, Judgment on the Appeal of the Victims against the 'Reparations Order" (Mar. 8, 2018).

With respect to the situation in the DRC, a reparations order was issued in the *Katanga* case. Germain Katanga was sentenced to twelve years as an accessory for crimes against humanity and war crimes, including murder, attacking a civilian population, and destruction of property. The Trial Chamber awarded 297 victims with a symbolic compensation of $250 per victim, and collective reparations in the form of support for housing, income-generative activities, education, and psychological treatment. As with the other reparations cases, Katanga is also indigent, thus leaving it to the TFV to develop a plan to provide reparations to the victims. In May 2017, the TFV decided to provide $1 million for reparations to the victims in the *Katanga* case. The Government of the Netherlands made a voluntary contribution of €200,000 to cover the cost of individual awards.

3. The ICC Trust Fund for Victims

The ICC is empowered to issue reparations to victims through the TFV. The TFV was "established by decision of the Assembly of States Parties (ASP), which is composed of all members of the International Criminal Court (ICC) for the benefit of victims of crimes within the jurisdiction of the Court, and of the families of such victims." The TFV provides its assistance under two mandates. First, pursuant to Rule 98(2)–(4), it provides assistance to victims through reparations that are ordered by the Court (so-called "victims in the case"). Second, it provides a range of rehabilitative and restorative assistance to victims in ICC situation countries through voluntary donations from organizations, countries, individuals, and corporations (so-called "victims in the situation"). The United Kingdom, for example, pledged £500,000 in connection with its Preventing Sexual Violence Initiative, a priority of its G-8 presidency. In addition, upon the acquittal of Jean-Pierre Bemba, the TFV expedited this elements of its mandate in the Central African Republic. These latter forms of support are provided independent of any judgment against a particular individual.

Oversight of the TFV is provided by a five-member *pro bono* Board of Directors elected by the ASP to serve for a duration of three years. The Board's members are drawn from ASP members and have regional representation (currently Uruguay, Mali, United Kingdom, and Georgia have representatives on the Board). As designed and as structured, the TFV is an entirely separate institution from the ICC, although it is linked to the Court by virtue of its common provenance in the Rome Statute and its ability to dispense reparations following a Court judgment.

In conducting its work to date, the TFV has operated primarily under its second mandate—providing reparations to individuals and communities in ICC situation countries pre-judgment. In this capacity, it has disbursed over $5 million with a concentration on three forms of assistance:

- physical rehabilitation (including reconstructive surgery, post-operative care, bomb fragment removal, and prosthetic devices);
- psychological rehabilitation (including individual and group counseling, public service announcements, mobile museums, reconciliation programs, and art projects); and
- material support (including shelters, day care centers for the children of former child soldiers, vocational training, re-

integration kits, micro-credit support, education grants, and literacy classes).

At the moment, the TFV has projects in the Central African Republic, the Democratic Republic of the Congo (DRC), Kenya, and Northern Uganda. In the DRC, the TFV operates in the Ituri, North Kivu, and the South Kivu districts; in fact, it was working in the Kivus two years before the Office of the Prosecutor initiated its first case against Lubanga. In Uganda, it operates in the Northern, Acholi, Lango, Teso, West Nile areas. All told, it is reaching an estimated 81,500 direct beneficiaries and over 180,000 indirect beneficiaries in the two situations. The recipients of assistance from the TFV need not be participating as formal witnesses in any case; it is the ICC's own Victim and Witness Unit that provides assistance to witnesses appearing in criminal trials under an entirely separate mandate.

4. Types of Reparations

Reparations can come in many forms. The opinion above makes a reference to collective as well as individual reparations. Reparations can also be monetary, in-kind, or symbolic. Collective reparations can be both substantive and symbolic. Substantive collective reparations can take the form of providing services to a community that was displaced or otherwise lost land, or that suffered from the destruction of important infrastructure, such as schools, clinics, electricity, water, etc. Symbolic collective reparations can take the form of institutional apologies, memorials that acknowledge past violations and pay tribute to victims, the renaming of towns and streets, etc. As the opinion above illustrates, determining individual reparations can be complex and difficult. Does this lead you to think that collective reparations are more appropriate than individual reparations for the types of mass atrocities heard by the ICC?

5. Gender and Reparations: Girl Soldiers

As noted above, the history of the *Lubanga* case with respect to sexual crimes committed against women and girls by Lubanga is problematic. While Lubanga was not convicted of such crimes (because as noted above the Prosecutor did charge him for these crimes), the reparations order does apply to such victims. The decision setting forth the principles and procedures to be applied to reparations said in relevant part:

> 202. A gender-inclusive approach should guide the design of the principles and procedures to be applied to reparations, ensuring that they are accessible to all victims in their implementation. Accordingly, gender parity in all aspects of reparations is an important goal of the Court.
>
> 203. The victims of the crimes, together with their families and communities should be able to participate throughout the reparations process and they should receive adequate support in order to make their participation substantive and effective. * * *
>
> 207. The Court should formulate and implement reparations awards that are appropriate for the victims of sexual and gender-based violence. The Court must reflect the fact that the consequences of these crimes are complicated and they operate on

a number of levels; their impact can extend over a long period of time; they affect women and girls, men and boys, together with their families and communities; and they require a specialist, integrated and multidisciplinary approach.

208. The Court shall implement gender-sensitive measures to meet the obstacles faced by women and girls when seeking to access justice in this context, and accordingly it is necessary that the Court takes steps to ensure they are able to participate, in a full sense, in the reparations programmes.

209. Therefore, the approach taken by the Court should enable women and girls in the affected communities to participate in a significant and equal way in the design and implementation of any reparations orders.

Prosecutor v. Lubanga, Case No. ICC–01/04–01/06, Decision Establishing the Principles and Procedures to be Applied to Reparations (Aug. 7, 2012).

6. Inter-American System and Reparations

As noted in the opinion above, the Inter-American Human Rights system has developed a sophisticated jurisprudence on reparations. For a general introduction to the system, including the reparations jurisprudence, *see* Thomas Antkowiak & Alejandra Gonza, THE AMERICAN CONVENTION ON HUMAN RIGHTS: ESSENTIAL RIGHTS (2017). For a critical treatment of the American system's reparations jurisprudence, *see* David L. Attansio, *Extraordinary Reparations, Legitimacy, and the Inter-American Court*, 37 U. PA. J. INT'L L. 813 (2016).

7. Reparations Before the ECCC

The ECCC's Internal Rules also allow it to issue reparations to victims. Originally, it was envisaged that the convicted person would satisfy any reparations award. However, the standard for such individualized reparations awards is quite high and difficult to meet (there must be a clear specification of the nature of the relief, its link to the harm caused by the accused, and the amount due to give effect to the remedy), particularly when an accused pleads indigence. Case 001 did not generate any meaningful reparations for victims in part because the defendant was deemed indigent and in part because the requests were considered to be outside of the ECCC framework. Moreover, the ECCC itself cannot enforce a reparations order; rather, victims would have to pursue relief through the ordinary Cambodian court system.

Given the bitter disappointment among victims following Case 001, the Rules were amended in 2010 to allow for an additional option: reparations funded by external resources (e.g., from donor countries, private entities, etc.). These reparations are to be implemented through the ECCC's Victims Support Section (VSS) with assistance from the Civil Party lawyers in cooperation with relevant governments and non-governmental organizations. (The victims' are separately represented before the ECCC as they are before the ICC.) Case 002/01 addresses the forced evacuation of Phnom Penh as well as executions at Tuol Po Chrey of members of the former regime and was brought against the surviving regime leaders (whose plea of indigence went (remarkably) unchallenged). The VSS and the Civil Party lawyers were able to secure funding commitments from various states (e.g., Australia, Germany, and Switzerland) in order to enable the ECCC to make a more meaningful reparations order. Instrumental to this outcome was Professor David Scheffer of Northwestern Law School, the U.N. Secretary General's Special Expert on the ECCC, who worked tirelessly to secure funding for the projects and the ECCC itself. The Australian government, for example, funded a therapy program administered by the Transcultural Psychosocial Organization (TPO).

Per Internal Rule 23*quinquies*(1), the ECCC may award only "collective and moral" reparations to Civil Parties, who appear at trial in a quasi-representative capacity on behalf of other victims not present. These reparations are meant to acknowledge the harm suffered by Civil Parties and provide some benefits to address that harm by way of rehabilitation, reintegration, and restoration of dignity. In other words, the ECCC will not order individual cash payments to particular victims. In this way, the ECCC differs from human rights courts, which exercise jurisdiction over states and which can order responsible states to make reparations to victims of human rights violations because it cannot impose obligations on the Cambodian state or parties not before it.

Almost 4,000 civil party applications were deemed admissible in Case 002 following an appeal, and 31 Civil Parties gave oral testimony (written accounts were also submitted into the record). Per Internal Rule 23*quinquies*(2), the Civil Parties must submit a single claim for reparations through the Lead Co-Lawyers containing reasoned arguments for how the awards sought will address the harm suffered as well as a mode of implementation. In a pre-verdict ruling, the ECCC made clear that it could only endorse reparations measures upon a showing that they were fully funded and would enjoy the consent and cooperation of any necessary third party.

The Co-Lead Lawyers proposed 13 discrete reparations to the Trial Chamber, of which 11 were endorsed by the Trial Chamber:

- A National Remembrance Day (May 20). This had the assent of the Royal Government of Cambodia, and no funding was deemed required. The Trial Chamber agreed that "an official national holiday amounts to a nationwide and official acknowledgement of the harm suffered by the victims. Public memorials may further assist to restore the dignity of victims, provide public acknowledgement of the crimes committed and harm suffered, and assist in healing the wounds of all victims by diffusing their effects far beyond the individuals who were admitted as Civil Parties."
- A Public Memorials Initiative to establish five public, accessible, educational, and sustainable memorial sites throughout Cambodia. Although this project enjoyed the support of the government and the NGOs that would implement it, no funding had been secured at the time of the

judgment. Nor had details been provided as to the proposed locations or other supplementary information. Accordingly, the Trial Chamber did not endorse it.

- A memorial within Phnom Penh to acknowledge the victims of forced evacuation. The French Embassy and other French entities had pledged to fund this project. The Trial Chamber endorsed this project as well.
- Construction of a memorial to Cambodian victims living in France, a project that had the support of the City Hall of Paris and several French NGOs. Because fundraising was still ongoing, the Chamber did not endorse this project.
- Testimonial Therapy, i.e., the recording of testimonies of traumatic experiences by mental health workers and their distribution during ceremonies throughout Cambodia. The Trial Chamber found that this project, as well as the next one, constitute an appropriate form of reparation.
- The facilitation of Self-Help Groups to provide therapy developed by the TPO. Funding for training of personnel and other costs in connection with the implementation of these two projects in Phnom Penh was secured from the Australian, German, and Swiss governments. Additional funding is being sought to extend these two projects outside of the capital. In endorsing these two projects, the Trial Chamber noted that it is "likely to promote public awareness of the harm suffered by the victims of Khmer Rouge era crimes and thereby may contribute to national reconciliation."
- A Permanent Exhibition with German funding in five provinces regarding the ECCC proceedings and the participation of the Civil Parties.
- A Mobile Exhibition and Education Project on Transitional Justice, with German funding. The Trial Chamber noted that these Documentation and Education projects are collective and moral in nature and will advance the goals of acknowledgement, remembrance, and awareness.
- Adaptations to the school curriculum to discuss forced population movements and executions in the teaching manual produced by the Documentation Center of Cambodia (DC-Cam). The Chamber endorsed this project with the understanding that it would indicate that certain facts had not be fully adjudicated since the judgment is open to appeal.

Which of these are likely to be most meaningful to victims?

APPENDIX: MAPS

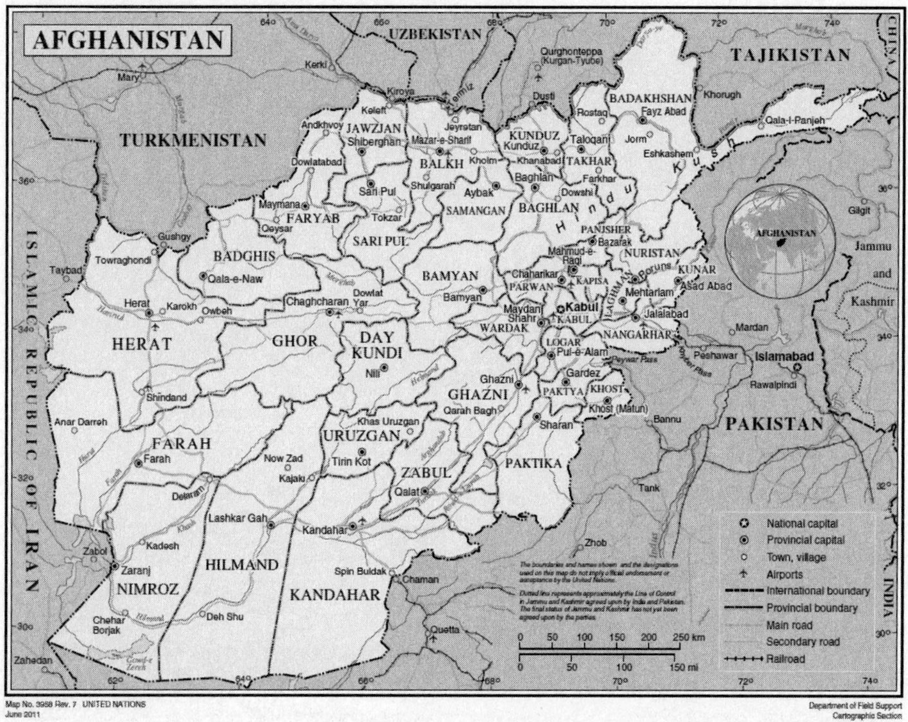

Map No. 3958 Rev. 7, July 2011, United Nations, reprinted with permission.

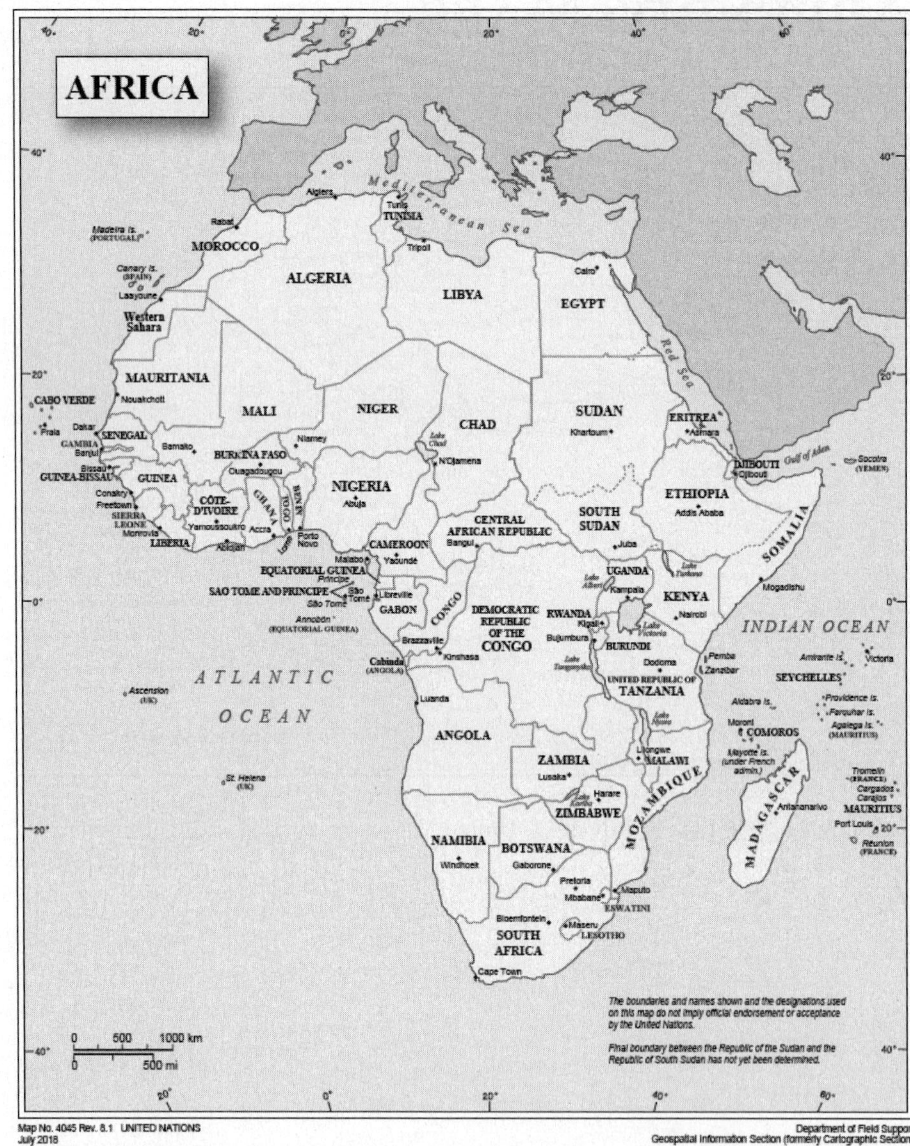

Map No. 4045 Rev. 8.1, July 2018, United Nations, reprinted with permission.

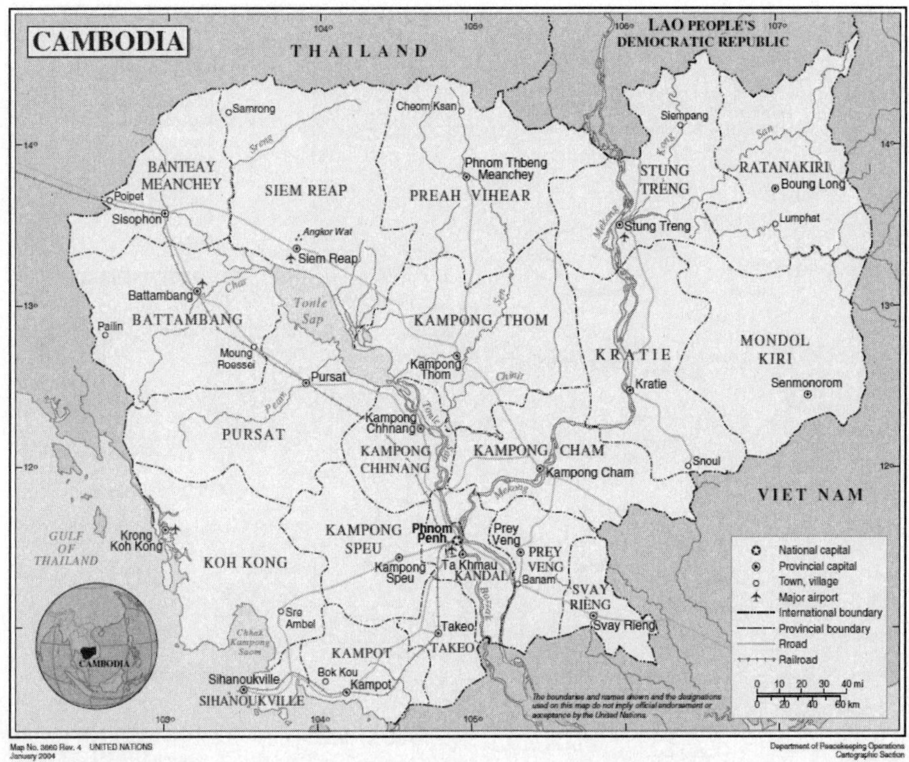

Map No. 3860 Rev. 4, Jan. 2004, United Nations, reprinted with permission.

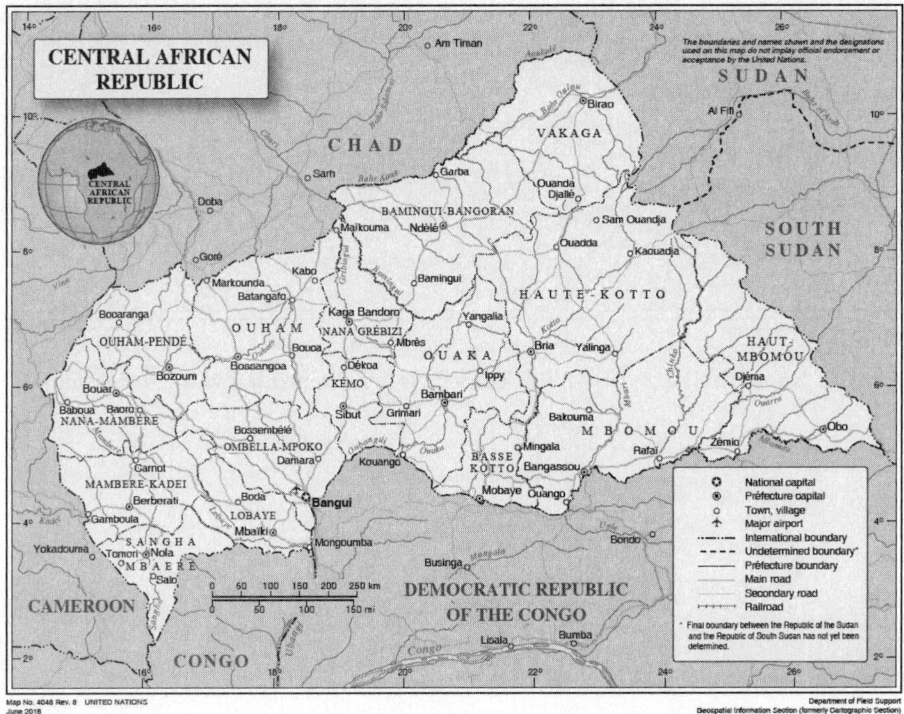

Map No. 4048 Rev. 8, June 2016, United Nations, reprinted with permission.

Map No. 4312 Rev. 3, Dec. 2011, United Nations, reprinted with permission.

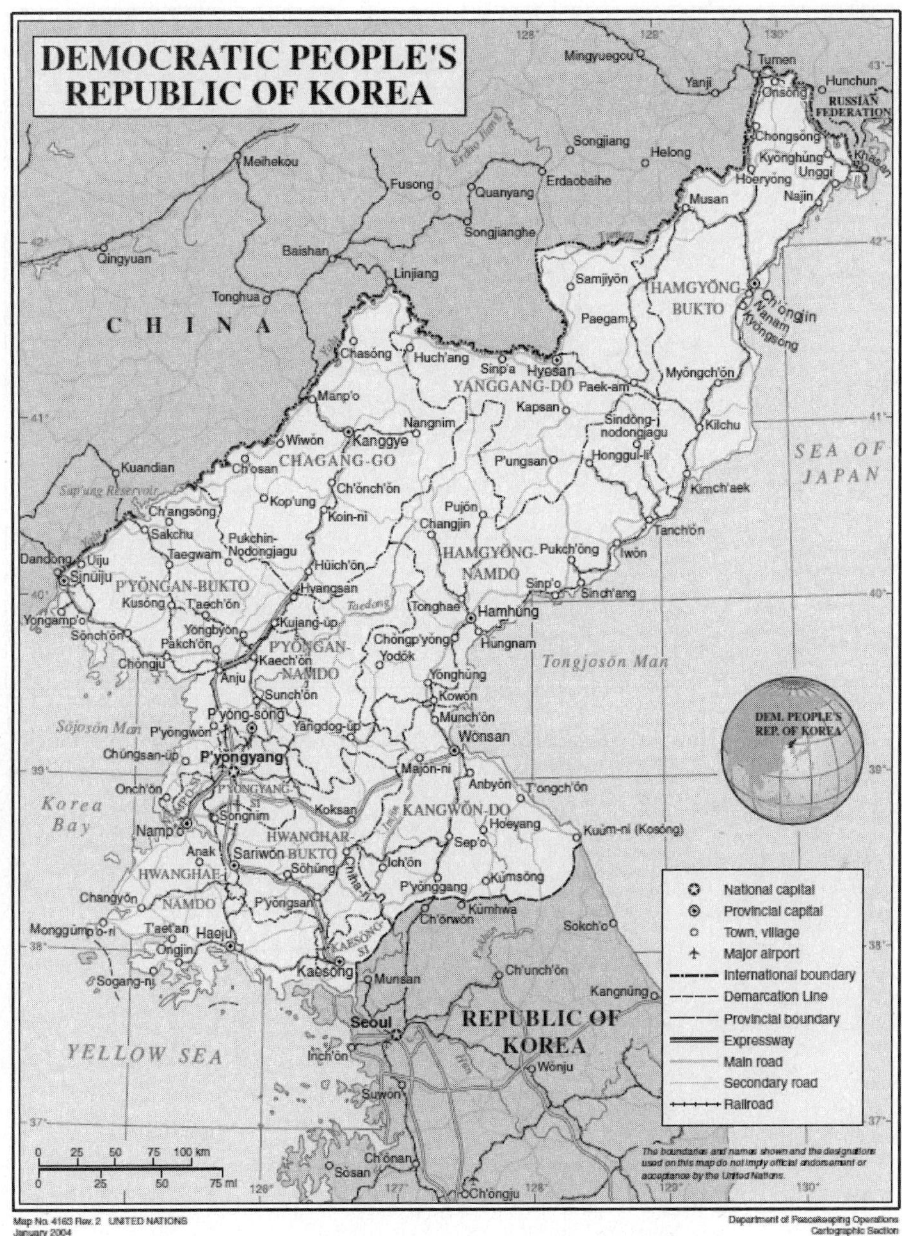

Map No. 4163 Rev. 2, Jan. 2004, United Nations, reprinted with permission.

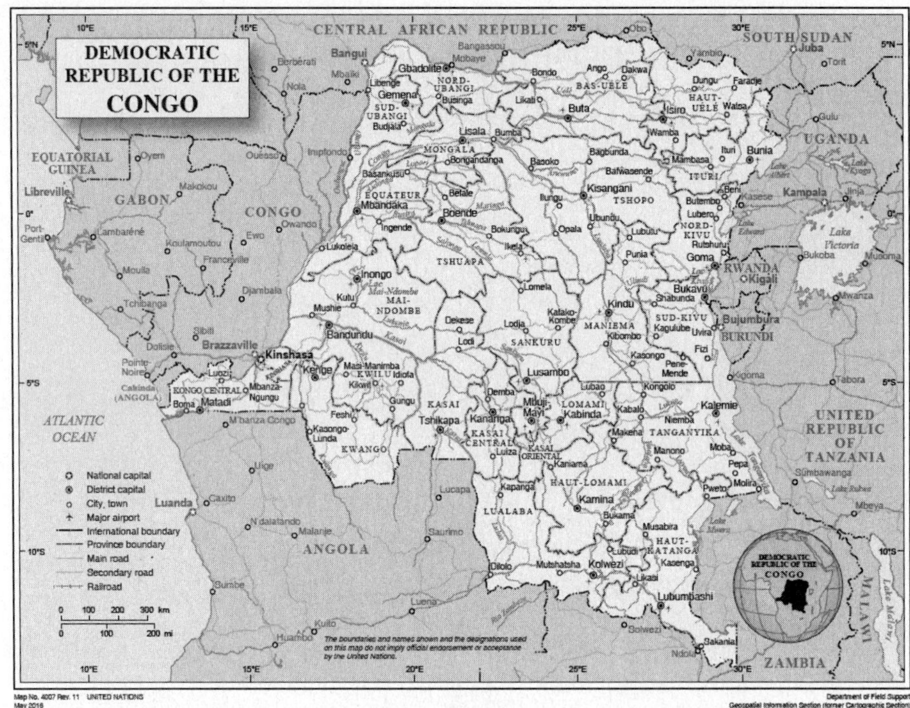

Map No. 4007 Rev. 11, May 2016, United Nations, reprinted with permission.

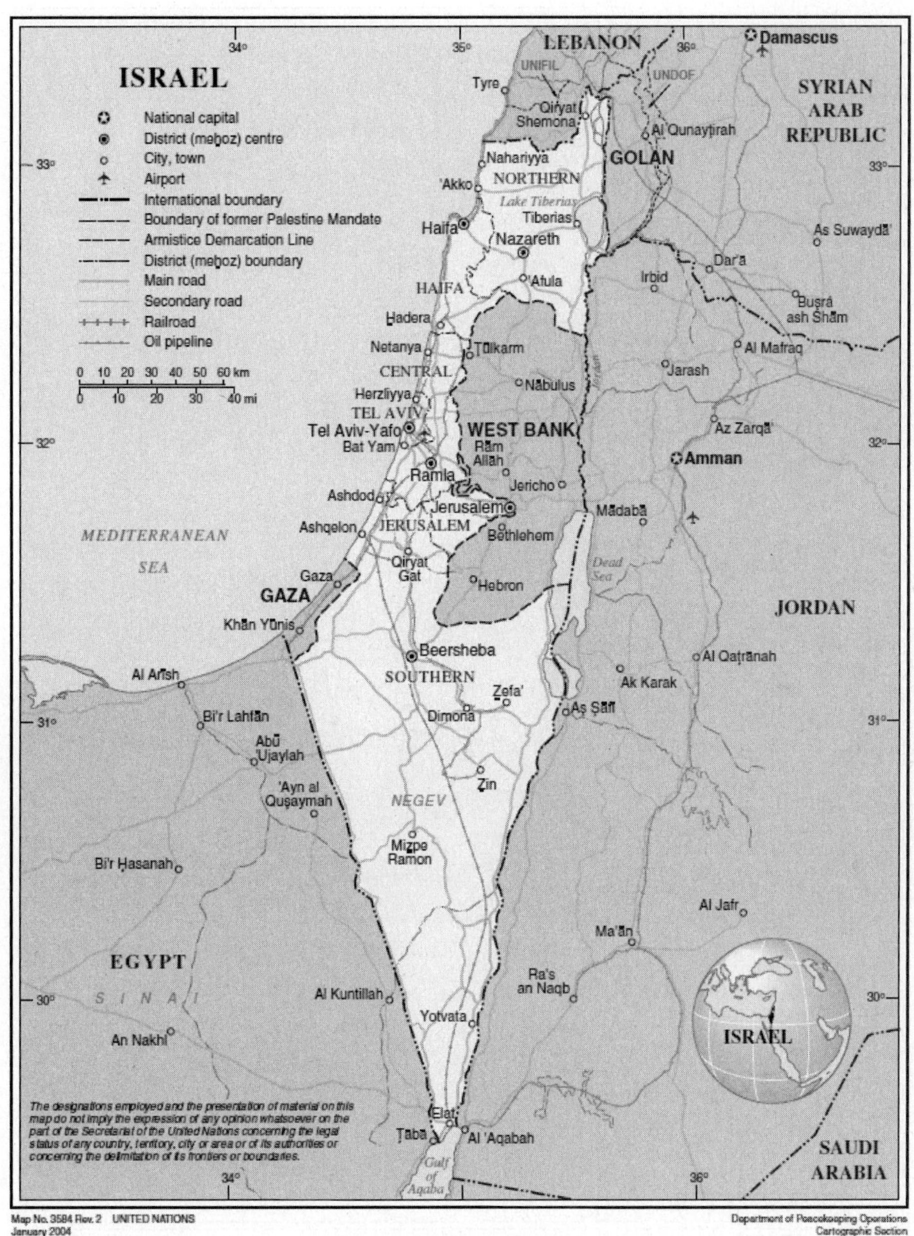

Map No. 3584 Rev. 2, Jan. 2004, United Nations, reprinted with permission.

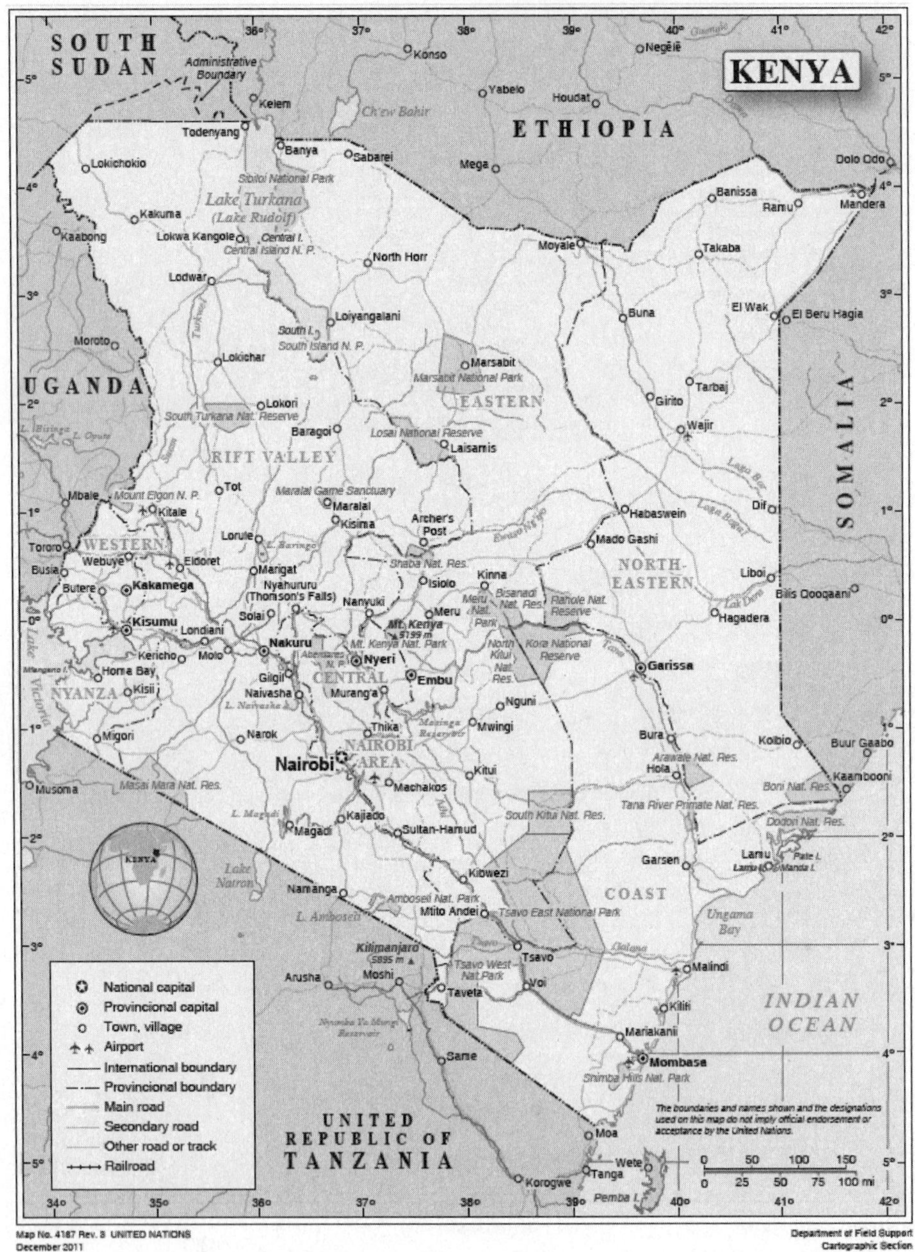

Map No. 4187 Rev. 3, Dec. 2011, United Nations, reprinted with permission.

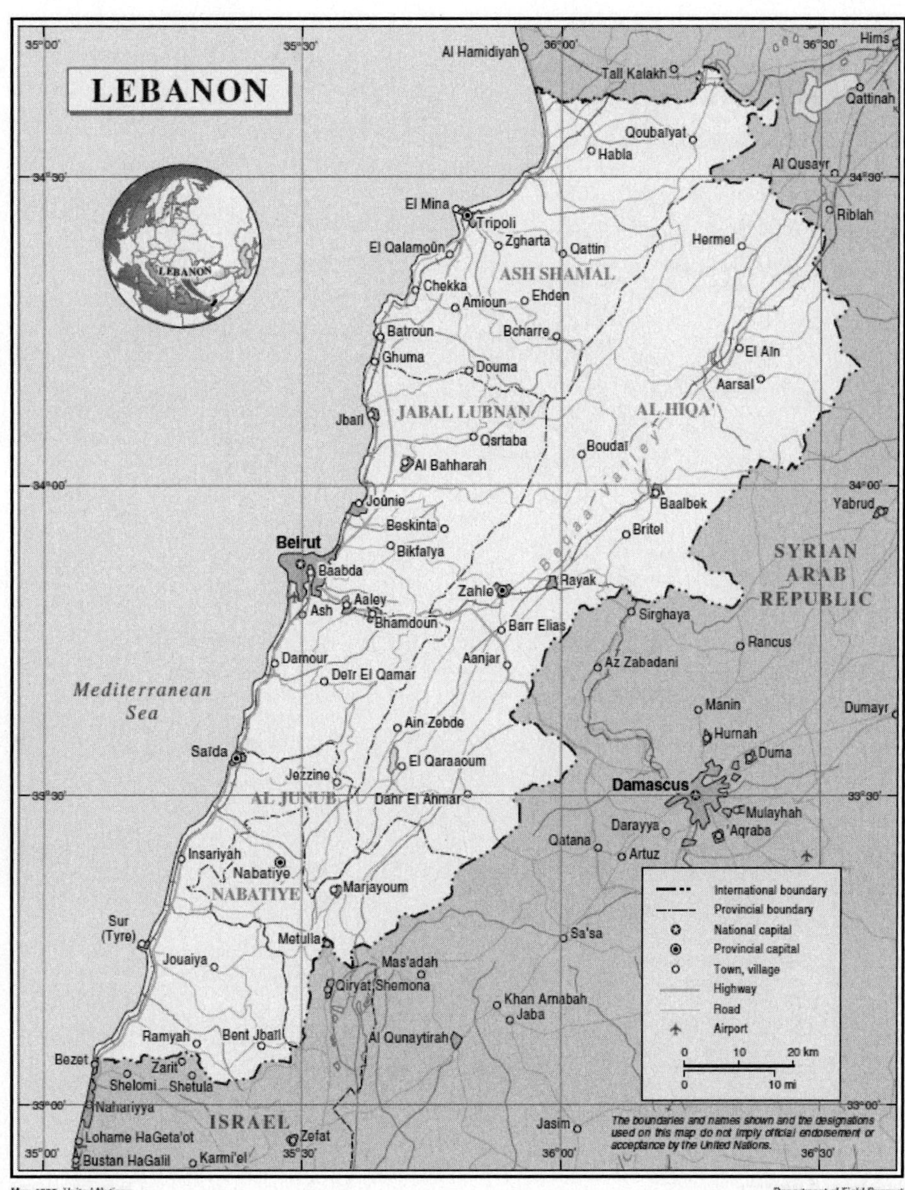

Map No. 4282, Jan. 2010, United Nations, reprinted with permission.

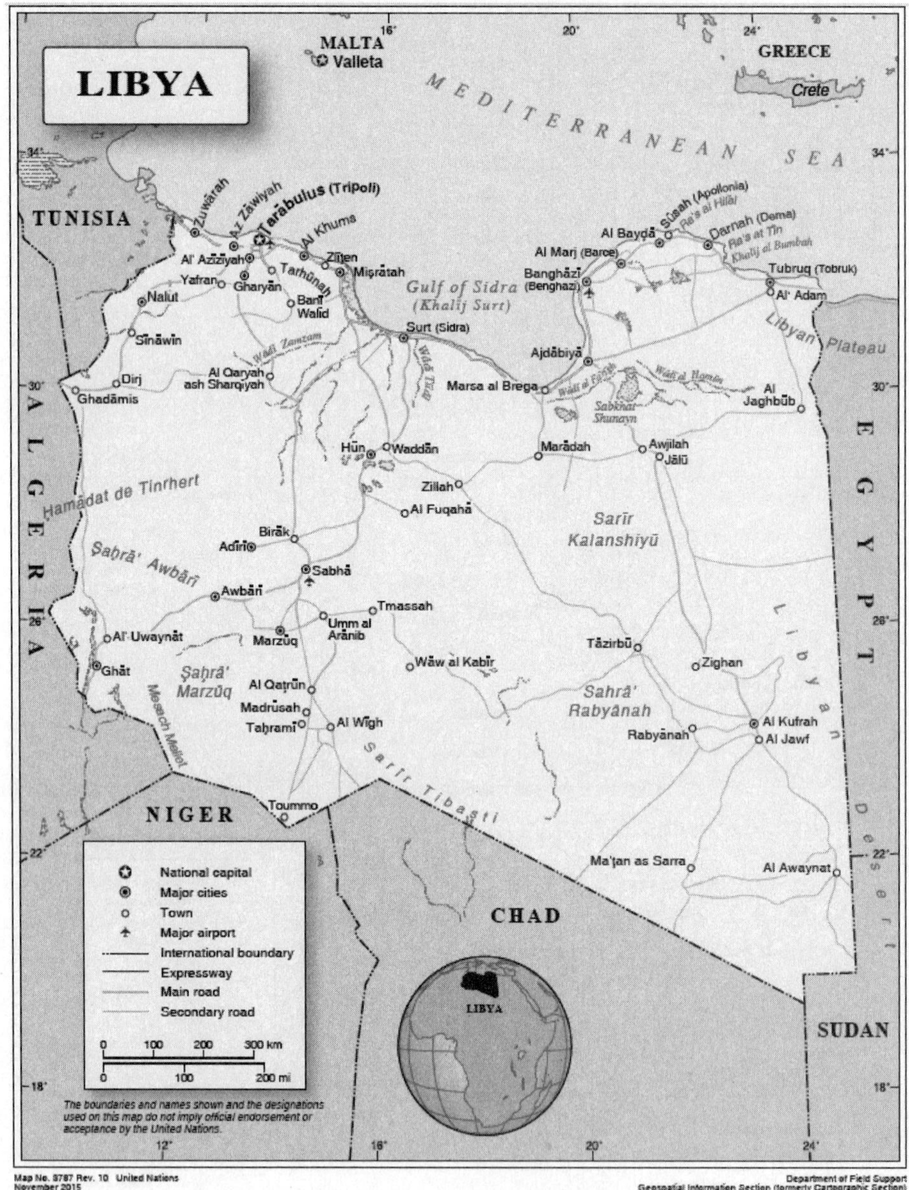

Map No. 3787 Rev. 10, November 2015, United Nations, reprinted with permission.

Map No. 4168 Rev. 3, June 2012, United Nations, reprinted with permission.

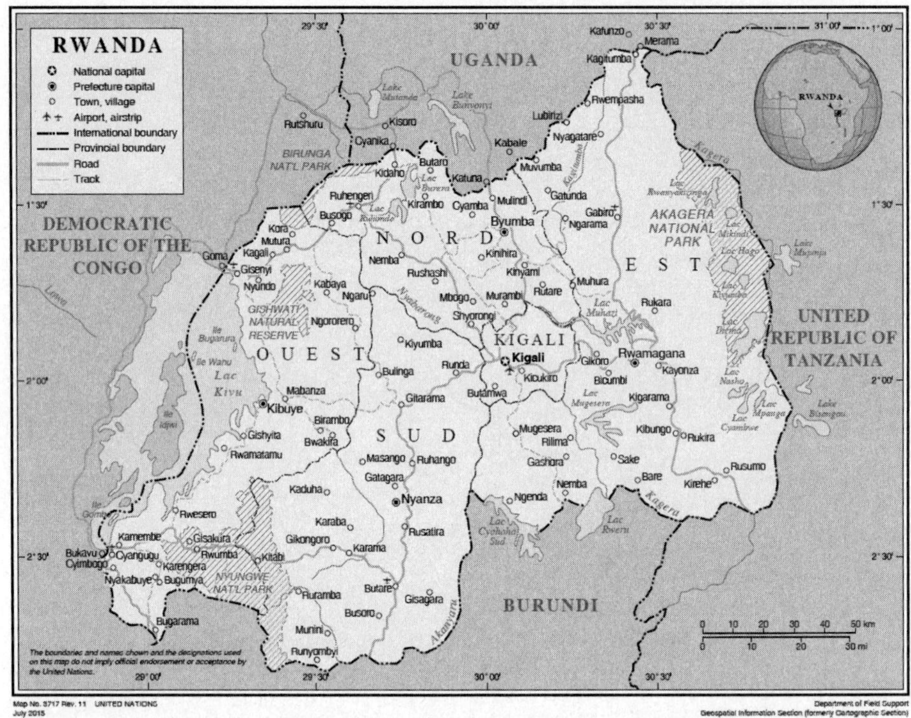

Map No. 3717 Rev. 11, July 2015, United Nations, reproduced with permission.

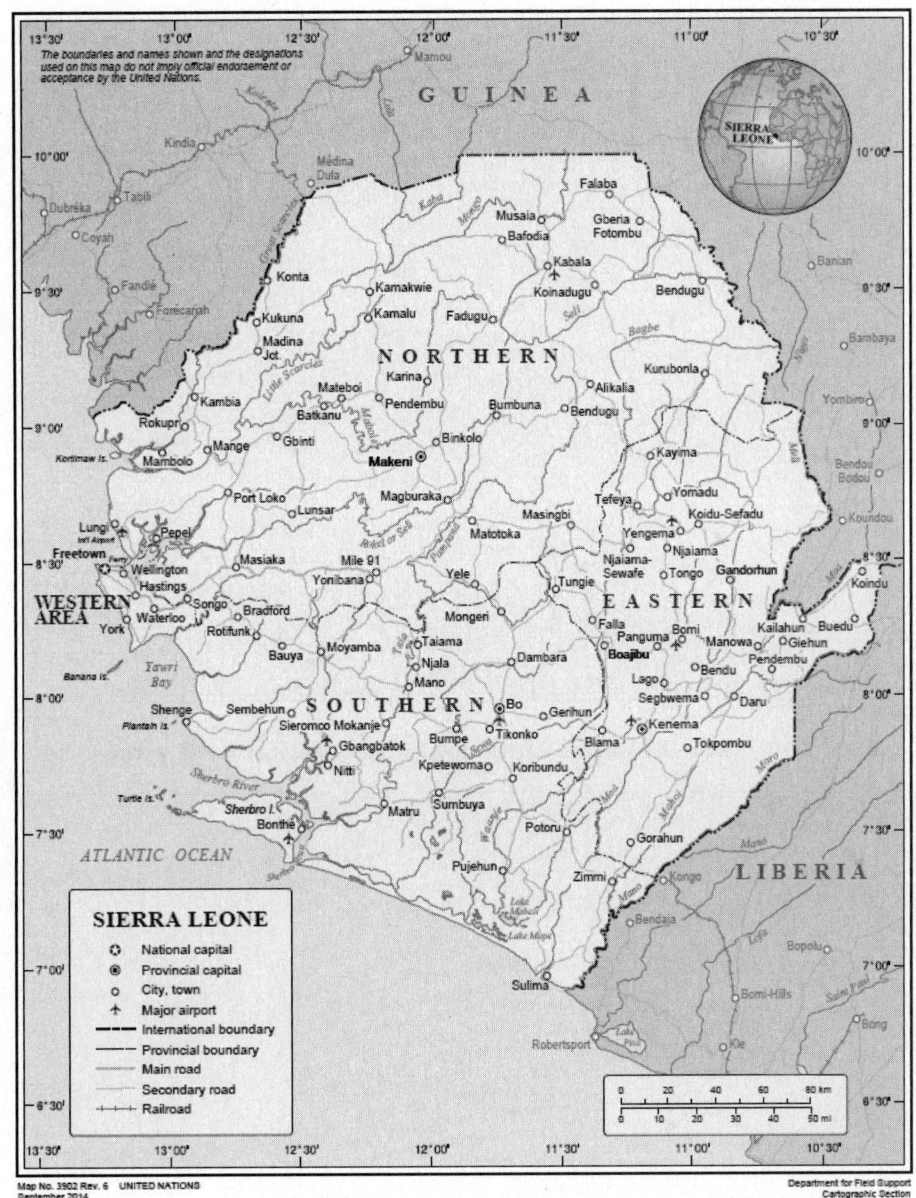

Map No. 3902 Rev. 6, Sept. 2014, United Nations, reprinted with permission.

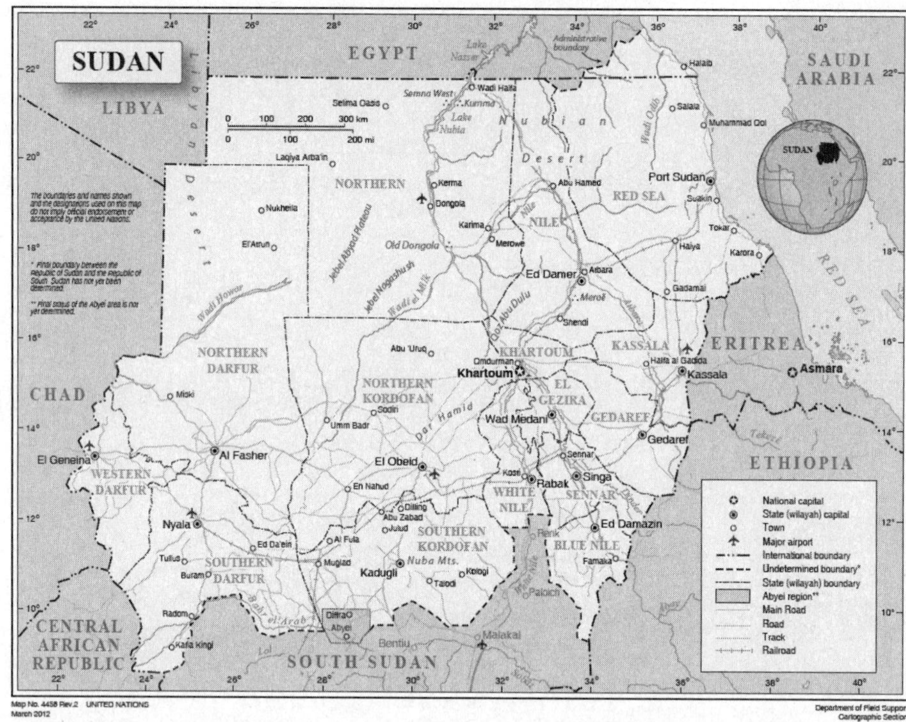

Map No. 4458 Rev. 2, March 2012, United Nations, reprinted with permission.

Map No. 3689 Rev. 12, June 2007, United Nations, reproduced with permission.

INDEX

References are to Pages